*Persona*
A Biography of Yukio Mishima

# *Persona*
## A Biography of Yukio Mishima

Naoki Inose
with Hiroaki Sato

Stone Bridge Press • *Berkeley, California*

*Published by*
Stone Bridge Press
P. O. Box 8208, Berkeley, CA 94707
510-524-8732 • sbp@stonebridge.com • www.stonebridge.com

Front jacket design by Noda Masaaki and Noda Emi. Back jacket photograph © Museum of Modern Japanese Literature, Tokyo. Used by permission.

Text © 2012 Naoki Inose and Hiroaki Sato.

This is an expanded adaptation in English of *Persona: Mishima Yukio den*, published in 1995 by Bungei Shunjū (Tokyo, Japan).

First English edition published in 2012. First paperback on-demand edition published in 2020.

All rights reserved.

No part of this book may be reproduced in any form without permission from the publisher.

Printed in the United States of America.

LIBRARY OF CONGRESS CATALOGING-IN-PUBLICATION DATA
Inose, Naoki.
 [Perusona. English]
 Persona: a biography of Yukio Mishima / Naoki Inose; with Hiroaki Sato.
    p. cm.
 Includes bibliographical references and index.
 ISBN 978-1-61172-064-8 (pbk); ISBN 978-1-61172-524-7 (ebk).
 1. Mishima, Yukio, 1925–1970. 2. Authors, Japanese—20th century—Biography. I. Sato, Hiroaki, 1942–. II. Title.
PL833.I7Z63713 2012
895.6'35—dc23
[B]
                            2012030595

*For Ron Bayes and Rand Castile*

*The range, variety, and publicness of the career sound ominously familiar to me....*

*I only regret we never met, for friends found him a good companion, a fine drinking partner, and fun to cruise with.*

GORE VIDAL

*Mishima definitely lived. He was a true genius in living.*

NOSAKA AKIYUKI

# Contents

*Preface   ix*

*Prologue   3*

| | |
|---|---|
| CHAPTER ONE | Peasant Ancestors and Grandfather   *8* |
| CHAPTER TWO | Samurai Ancestors and Grandmother   *32* |
| CHAPTER THREE | "The Boy Who Writes Poems"   *57* |
| CHAPTER FOUR | Literary Correspondents   *77* |
| CHAPTER FIVE | First Love   *99* |
| CHAPTER SIX | The War and Its Aftermath   *126* |
| CHAPTER SEVEN | To Be a Bureaucrat or a Writer   *147* |
| CHAPTER EIGHT | Confessions   *168* |
| CHAPTER NINE | Boyfriends, Girlfriends   *192* |
| CHAPTER TEN | Going Overseas   *219* |
| CHAPTER ELEVEN | The Girlfriend   *241* |
| CHAPTER TWELVE | The Kinkakuji   *265* |
| CHAPTER THIRTEEN | Overseas Again   *288* |
| CHAPTER FOURTEEN | Marriage   *311* |

| | |
|---|---|
| CHAPTER FIFTEEN | *Kyōko's House*  333 |
| CHAPTER SIXTEEN | The 2.26 Incident, *Yūkoku*  358 |
| CHAPTER SEVENTEEN | Assassinations  381 |
| CHAPTER EIGHTEEN | Contretemps  409 |
| CHAPTER NINETEEN | The Nobel Prize  435 |
| CHAPTER TWENTY | Shinpūren, Men of the Divine Wind  459 |
| CHAPTER TWENTY-ONE | "The Way of the Warrior is to die"  482 |
| CHAPTER TWENTY-TWO | Death in India  509 |
| CHAPTER TWENTY-THREE | The Anti–Vietnam War Movement  533 |
| CHAPTER TWENTY-FOUR | *Sun and Steel*  557 |
| CHAPTER TWENTY-FIVE | The Shield Society, Counterrevolution  580 |
| CHAPTER TWENTY-SIX | The Yakuza  605 |
| CHAPTER TWENTY-SEVEN | Wang Yangming: "To know is to act"  627 |
| CHAPTER TWENTY-EIGHT | The Constitution  651 |
| CHAPTER TWENTY-NINE | Hailstones, Ghouls, Golden Death  673 |
| CHAPTER THIRTY | Toward Ichigaya  689 |
| CHAPTER THIRTY-ONE: | The Seppuku  713 |
| | *Epilogue*  730 |
| | *Notes*  739 |
| | *Bibliography*  803 |
| | *Index*  819 |

# Preface

This is an expanded adaptation in English of Inose Naoki's biography *Persona: Mishima Yukio den* (Bungei Shunjū, 1995). Inose's *Persona* is a unique depiction of the bureaucratic and political aspects of Japanese history since the late nineteenth century as they relate to Mishima. This English adaptation greatly augments Mishima's literary, theatrical, and ideological theories and activities, not to mention his pursuit of various sports, to suggest how he brought them all together into one focus: death.

Since Inose wrote *Persona*, partly based on interviews conducted in 1994, a number of things have changed—notably, Japan's bureaucratic structures and positions in consequence of administrative reforms in the past dozen years. But such things are left as they were up to the mid-1990s so far as they do not affect this account of Mishima's life.

In this book, all Japanese names are given the Japanese way, family name first (except on the cover). Following Japanese custom, Japanese people are sometimes referred to by their personal name, rather than by their surname. Among the prominent writers since the late nineteenth century this occurs most notably with Natsume Sōseki, who is usually called Sōseki, and Mori Ōgai, Ōgai. Mishima Yukio was the penname of Hiraoka Kimitake. His teachers and school friends most often addressed him by his surname with or without a post-nominal compellation: -sama, -san, -kun. His family members or close friends usually called him by his personal name, often by his pet name, Kimi-chan or Kō-chan, the second one because the sinified pronunciation of Kimitake is Kōi.

The macron is used to indicate a long vowel in Japanese except where common use makes it needlessly conspicuous (as in Tōkyō for Tokyo) and where the theaters and other establishments have their own roman spellings (as in Nissay for Nissei in the theater name).

The word *tennō*, usually *translated* as "emperor," is retained in this book, except when used as a title, as in the Emperor Meiji, and in a few other circumstances. This is because the Japanese word, along with the English word "emperor," has created a host of misconceptions, both in Japan (intentionally) and abroad (willfully) after the country tried to join the imperialist powers in the second half of the nineteenth century. More important, the *tennō* institution had a special meaning in Mishima's thinking all his life, but particularly when it came to the fore in his argument on Japanese history and Constitutions.

Unless noted, translations from the Japanese are all mine.

---

Many people have helped to make this this expanded English adaptation possible, starting with Inose Naoki. He sent me books, including many of his own, answered questions, and provided me with some of the interview transcripts. The unreferenced quotations in this book come from the interviews he conducted.

Hirata Shigeru, Ishii Tatsuhiko, Takagaki Chihiro, and Kakizaki Shōko helped to collect books for this biography. Among them, Shōko-san is hardest to thank. She went out of her way to find and buy many books for me.

Kyoko Selden helped me with a range of things with her erudition; she also found for me part of a text of *Le Martyre de Saint Sébastien* at Cornell University Library. Ishii Tatsuhiko acquired a number of articles related to Mishima and helped me with his extensive knowledge of theater. Jeffrey Angles made many magazine articles in English available to me online. Alexander Truskinovsky acquired for me Melvin J. Lasky's *A Letter from Salzburg*, a lively account of the selection process of the fourth Formentor Literary Prize, in 1961. Ken Aoki at The Institute for Medieval Japanese Studies, Columbia University, copied for me Kihira Teiko's *Mishima Yukio no tegami*, an account of her association with Mishima in the early postwar years that was serialized in eighteen installments in the weekly *Asahi*, from December 13, 1974 to April 11, 1975.

Lili Selden sent me the English translations of Akutagawa Ryūnosuke's story, *Butōkai*, and Pierre Loti's story, *Un Bal a Yeddo*.

Col. Jaxon Teck and his wife, Arlene, helped me with US military terms; Arlene also edited one chapter. Ueda Akira and Takii Mitsuo got in touch with the Japan Self-Defense Forces (SDF) to clarify certain matters. Akira-san also gave me information on Tokyo that I, a New York City resident, could not readily acquire, such as distances and the state of certain institutions. Noguchi Nobuya helped me with the Japanese judiciary. Carlin Barton straightened me out on certain Latin and Greek names and terms; in doing so she determined that the name of one figure assumed to be from classical Greece in *Confessions of a Mask* cannot be clarified with certainty. Doris Bargen and Guido Keller helped me with some German terms and expressions.

Gail Malmgreen and Peter Filardo, of Tamiment Library/Robert F. Wagner Labor Archives, New York University, found information on Pearl Kluger at the American Committee for Cultural Freedom, Mishima's guide in New York when he visited the United States for the first time, in 1952. Peggy McElveen, Director of Equestrian Programs at Saint Andrews Presbyterian College, answered my equestrian questions. Sakai Tatemi clarified the use of agents in Japan. Takagaki Chihiro enlightened me on certain films. Liza Dalby and Nagasaka Junko imparted some of their deep knowledge on kimono.

Nagasaka Toshihisa went to the Film Center, of the National Museum of Modern Art, Tokyo, to see and acquire details on what is left of the 1945 Japanese movie *Ware ni tsuzuku o shinzu*, one of the films the US Occupation confiscated and did not return to Japan until 1967.

Donald Richie gave me details on Meredith Weatherby, the translator of *Confessions of a Mask* and *The Sound of Waves*, and matters related to Mishima in New York, in 1952.

Ron Bayes and Rand Castile told me about their meetings with Mishima. Mr. Bayes, a North Carolina poet laureate, opened for me a path to Mishima Yukio by asking me to translate one of his plays, *My Friend Hitler*, for *St. Andrews Magazine* more than three decades ago. He followed it with a request to translate *The Terrace of the Leper King*—the "leper king" being the appellation of Jayavarman VII, the builder of Angkor Tom. These translations led J. Thomas Rimer to commission me, for the Pacific Basin Institute, to translate the Mishima novel *Silk and Insight* (M. E. Sharpe, 1998). The same translations also led to *My*

*Friend Hitler and Other Plays of Yukio Mishima* (Columbia University Press, 2002).

I thank Luke Bouvier for finding and translating *Refrains*, a poem by Guy-Charles Cros; Forrest Gander for translating a stanza of García Lorca's poem, *Llanto por Ignacio Sánchez Mejías;* Guido Keller for translating a stanza from Friedrich Hölderlin's *Heimkunft*; Michael O'Brien for translating passages from Baudelaire and stanzas from Gabriele d'Annunzio's *Le Martyre de Saint Sébastien;* and Alexander Truskinovsky for translating a paragraph from Dostoevsky's *The Brothers Karamazov.*

I thank Susan Lyn McCombs for her invaluable editorial assistance in correcting and clarifying a number of words, phrases, and paragraphs.

Finally, as always, I thank my wife Nancy for reading countless revisions of the manuscript with patience and care, over a period of ten years.

HIROAKI SATO
*New York City*

*Persona*

## Hiraoka Kimitake (Mishima Yukio) Family Tree

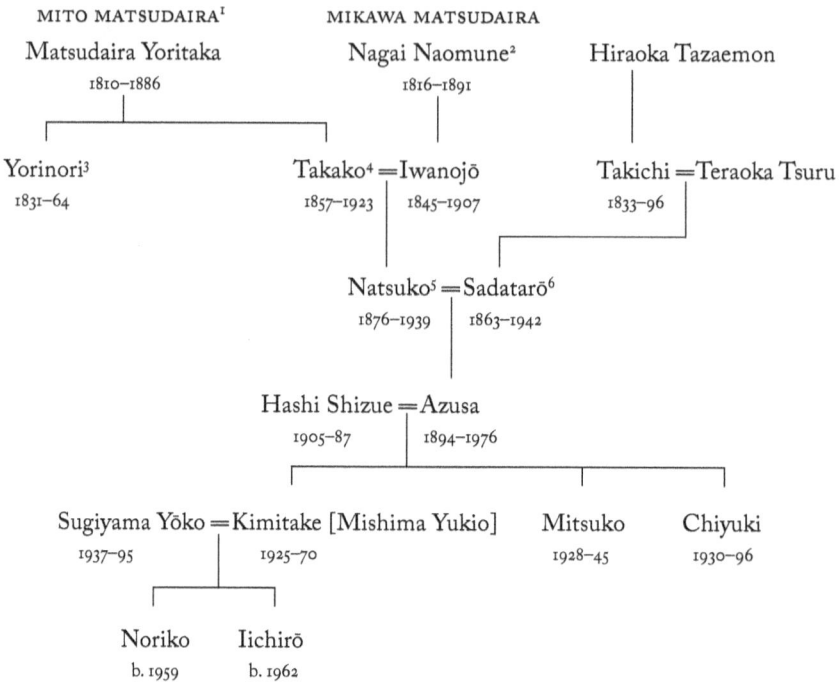

1. The Matsudaira was the family that produced the founder of the Tokugawa shogunate (1603–1867), Ieyasu (1543–1616). The family necessarily spawned a number of branches but continued to represent the most prestigious samurai lineage under Tokugawa rule—second only to the Tokugawa.
2. Naomune was a descendent of the Matsudaira, but was adopted by the Nagai family. The Chinese characters for his name are also read Naoyuki, Naotoshi, Naotada.
3. Yoritaka's first son, who was forced to disembowel himself because of political contretemps. His second son, Yoriyasu (1854–1940), became the subject of Mishima's short stories. His third son, Yorihira (1858–?), became a swords judge for the Imperial Household.
4. Yoritaka's third daughter; she had four other sisters.
5. Iwanojō's first daughter and one of his twelve children (six girls and six boys). Of the twelve children, the boys, except for one who died of Spanish flu when in higher school, all attained distinguished positions: naval commander, economist, banker, and corporate president (two). All six girls, including Natsuko, married men who attained high positions.
6. Takichi's second son; he had one older and one younger brother and a sister. Sadatarō's older brother, Manjirō (1860–1923), became a distinguished lawyer.

# Prologue

The Tokyo Shōken Kaikan is located in Kayaba-chō, Nihonbashi. Despite its name, Tokyo Securities Hall, it is an office building that has no direct involvement with securities trade. But among its tenants are the Japan Securities Dealers Association and the Association of Tokyo Stock Exchange Regular Members. After all, just two buildings to the west the place name changes to Kabuto-chō, which is Japan's Wall Street, where the buildings for the Tokyo Stock Exchange and prominent brokerage houses stand shoulder to shoulder. The Bank of Japan is less than half a mile from the Tokyo Stock Exchange, in Hongoku-chō. Near the central bank is the namesake of the Nihonbashi District, the Japan Bridge, though the view of the concrete bridge is largely blocked by the superhighway that runs by the bank. All distances in Japan are measured from its midpoint.

The Association of Tokyo Stock Exchange Regular Members occupies the third floor of the Tokyo Shōken Kaikan. When interviewed, Nagaoka Minoru had just become its advisor. He was short, somewhat on the plump side, and seventy years old. In a dark-brown suit made of English fabric and a Mila Shön tie of a similar color, he had a youthful complexion, with few wrinkles, and maintained a gentle smile on his face. He smoked, three packs daily of the domestic brand Miné (Peak), though by then antismoking had become the rage. He charmed you, moving the topic of conversation with sophisticated ease from the writings of the magical manipulator of traditional Japanese Izumi Kyōka, the *kiyomoto* recitation, haiku, to the baseball team Yomiuri Giants—although, even as he made it clear he'd be prepared to respond to any question you might think of, his eyes occasionally showed a cold, forbidding glint.

The position of advisor to the Association of Tokyo Stock Exchange Regular Members is a nebulous one. It would not be widely off the mark to describe it as a kind of medal for someone with an illustrious career who recently completed his five-year stint as chairman of the Tokyo Stock Exchange. One sign of his status was the spaciousness of his office. Add the reception area, and it was more than one thousand square feet. The office had been refurbished for him, with new armchairs and rugs, color-coordinated to match a Marie Laurencin painting hanging on a wall.

Nagaoka was also one of the five members of the National Public Safety Commission. Chaired by the Minister of Home Affairs, the commission met every Thursday morning in a special room at the Ministry of Home Affairs, in Kasumigaseki. It had the authority to appoint and dismiss the commissioner of the National Police Agency, the superintendent of the Tokyo Metropolitan Police Department, and the heads of all prefectural police agencies. In some ways the commission membership was honorary. But in government ranking, its members were one notch above the administrative vice minister, the highest position Japanese bureaucrats could attain. Each ministry had two vice ministers, parliamentary and administrative, but their boss, the minister, and the parliamentary vice minister were members of the Diet and were thus political appointees. The administrative vice minister actually ran the place. That was the rank Nagaoka had attained, and he had done so at the Ministry of Finance, which traditionally scooped up, as a matter of entitlement, the cream of the crop from the annual higher civil-service examination takers, the elite of the elite of Japanese society.

Nagaoka, in fact, had enjoyed all the plums attendant to those who achieved highest bureaucratic ranks. In 1980, upon retiring from the ministry as administrative vice minister, he "descended from heaven" to become chairman of the Japan Tobacco Monopoly. He spearheaded its privatization, one fad of the day, and, when the work was done, became president of the privatized entity, Japan Tobacco, Inc. He then became chairman of the Tokyo Stock Exchange. The advisorship to the association mentioned earlier and other positions and powers followed. His had been a model career or, as the Japanese put it, one "drawn for a pictorial illustration" of an illustrious man.

Nagaoka was called The Don of Finance. A man sitting on top of the old-boy network of the Ministry of Finance, he most recently had helped place two of his former colleagues in prestigious positions amid the rising calls for taking such powers away from bureaucrats to give them to politicians: Yamaguchi Hidemitsu as chairman of the Tokyo Stock Exchange and Matsushita Yasuo as chairman of the Bank of Japan.

Imagine: Mishima Yukio could have been this man.

---

On December 24, 1947, Wednesday, twenty-six future bureaucrats reported to work on their first day with the Ministry of Finance. It was two years and four months after Japan's calamitous defeat in the Second World War. US Occupation forces had absolute sway, things American were swamping the land, and it was Christmas Eve. But there was nothing festive about the day. The Finance Ministry building in Kasumigaseki having been requisitioned by the Occupation, the agency was housed in an elementary school in Yotsuya. The rickety doors squeaked. The smoke from coal-burning stoves filled the rooms. Petitioners packed the corridors. The general atmosphere was dark, dirty, and dismal.[1]

Each of the twenty-six men was handed two papers: one announcing his appointment to the ministry and the other his assigned post. The monthly base salary was ¥1,350, a sum less than what a carpenter working full-time would make. Nagaoka Minoru was assigned to the budget bureau. Among the remaining twenty-five was Hiraoka Kimitake 平岡公威, who was assigned to the banking bureau. Nagaoka recognized him. He had seen him twice before: once, when they happened to be seated side by side while waiting for their employment interviews; the other, just about a week before that, when he went to a dance hall named, in English, The Esquire. Social dance had recently come into style. The most popular were American types such as fox trot, jitterbug, and rumba, but the Continental tango also had a solid following.

Nagaoka hadn't really thought of going to the dance hall. Even though his father, who when a bureaucrat was once stationed in France, loved to dance with his wife, Nagaoka was a product of the period when university students were drafted into war. He looked askance at the postwar craze for Western, American dance, regarding the dancing youth, though in truth not much younger than himself, as frivolous or worse.

But his father's acquaintance, Megata Tsunayoshi, who was famed for bringing social dance from France as a young baron, told him to give it a try; he did, and liked it. So, when a *dance party* was announced at The Esquire, he went along with his family. It was there that he spotted a man his age, skinny, pale, the shaven parts of his face looking bluish. He thought the man was a fop. Even so, when he found himself seated next to him at the Finance Ministry, he began by saying, "Didn't I see you somewhere recently?"

As it turned out, the two men's backgrounds were strikingly similar. Their families lived not far apart, in Shibuya, in rented houses. Hiraoka went to the Gakushūin—hereafter to be called by its English name, the Peers School—from grammar school on to higher school, but his sister, Mitsuko, who was three years younger, went to the same grammar school as Nagaoka and was in the same class as Nagaoka's younger brother. Hiraoka's brother, Chiyuki, who was five years younger, also went to the same grammar school and was in the same class as Nagaoka's youngest brother. Both Nagaoka and Hiraoka were prone to be ill as schoolboys and suffered from the same illness, hilar tuberculous adenitis.

More to the point, their fathers were career bureaucrats. Both had followed the standard elite course for public service, from the First Higher School to the Faculty of Law of the Imperial University of Tokyo. Nagaoka's father, Nobukatsu, retired as director-general of postal policy at the Ministry of Communications. Hiraoka's father, Azusa, retired as director-general of fisheries at the Ministry of Agriculture and Forestry.

As to the two men themselves, Nagaoka had followed the course his father had, from the First Higher School to the Law Faculty (English Law) of the Imperial University of Tokyo. Hiraoka had followed a somewhat different one, from the Higher School Division of the Peers School to the Law Faculty (German Law) of the Imperial University of Tokyo.

But in bureaucratic lineage, you could say Hiraoka was a step above Nagaoka; his grandfather, Sadatarō, was also a ranking bureaucrat. After graduating from the Law Faculty of the Imperial University (the name did not include "Tokyo" at the time because it was the only one of its kind until 1897), Sadatarō joined the Home Ministry, in a way the most powerful administrative organ of the government: it had under its jurisdiction the equivalents of today's National Police Agency and the ministerial functions of internal affairs, construction, labor, and health and welfare. In addition, it had the power to appoint prefectural governors from among its ranks. Sadatarō rose to the position of administrator of the Karafuto (Sakhalin) Agency.

These things are worth noting because, in modern Japan, bureaucrats have played the leading role in shaping the country and because for both Nagaoka Minoru and Hiraoka Kimitake to become a bureaucrat was, in a sense, destiny. However, whereas Nagaoka, like many of the other twenty-four, fulfilled his career as a bureaucrat, Hiraoka resigned from the Finance Ministry in just nine months and set to work two months later, with resolve, on a novel titled *Confessions of a Mask* (*Kamen no kokuhaku*), the work that would establish the reputation of the author known as Mishima Yukio 三島由紀夫.

CHAPTER ONE

# Peasant Ancestors and Grandfather

*Long Live the Emperor!*
—Mishima's will upon receipt of induction order

"The earth around here is quite solid," Funae Fujio said. One of the many who wrote down what they remembered about Mishima after his sensational death, Funae was asked about the characteristics of the Kako River Basin, in the Banshū (Harima) Plain, northwest of Kobe. "So much so that when there was talk of moving the capital in the aftermath of the Great Kantō Earthquake, this area suddenly attracted a great deal of attention."

Funae was right. The calamity that struck on the first day of September 1923 and claimed more than one hundred thousand dead or missing, prompted some to consider moving the seat of government out of Tokyo, even though the government itself announced the capital would stay where it was. In particular, the army, which had long feared the indefensibility of Tokyo in case of war because of its closeness to the Pacific Ocean, conducted a top-secret study led by Maj. Imamura Hitoshi, on the General Staff. Imamura, one of the few honorable and admired generals to come out of the war two decades later, finally came up with three candidates: Ryūzan (today's Yongsan, Korea; Japan had annexed the country in 1910); Hachiōji, west of Tokyo; and the Kako River Basin.[1]

But the government stuck to its promise not to move. And the army's fears would prove correct. The US air raids on the night of March 9, 1945, alone would incinerate one hundred thousand people—although, of course, by then the long-range aircraft developed in the meantime had rendered the distance from the Pacific Ocean or any ocean pointless.

## Taking Draft Physicals

In May 1944, the nineteen-year-old Hiraoka Kimitake—he had been given the penname Mishima Yukio two years earlier, but we will use his real name for the time being—left Tokyo to go to the town of Shikata to take physicals for those of draft age. After Kobe, his train chugged along across the Banshū Plain until it crossed a large bridge shortly after Kakogawa and arrived at Hōden Station. Hōden, "treasure palace," is somewhat unusual as a place name. The novelist Shiba Ryōtarō has a description of it in a long, drawn-out, fictionalized account of one of the region's more famous characters, the Christian warrior-commander Kuroda Yoshitaka, commonly known as Kuroda Kanbē (1546–1604).

"The Banshū Plain, probably because the foreign-born Hata family originally developed the area, retains some of the things that the Japanese sensibility nurtured after the Nara Period finds hard to fathom," wrote the exceedingly popular and prolific writer of historical yarns and travel reports. "What is called the Stone Treasure Palace, located east of Himeji, is one of them. It is a box shape carved out of a huge granite rock. The stone itself is as large as some kind of building structure, but apparently the work was abandoned midway, and you can't tell what they were trying to make."

Shiba assumed that the Hata family came from the Korean Peninsula, bringing their own deity, which became the prototype of the various deities of the region.[2]

The Ōshiko Shrine that deifies this giant rock is placed behind the innermost building and is on the Inland Sea side of Hōden Station. Hiraoka, then a senior at the Higher School Division of the Peers School, walked out of the other side of the station. Rice paddies spread before him. There weren't many houses. A road two yards wide stretched straight north. The area was dotted with irrigation ponds and a number of low hills. He took the bus for the about two and a half miles from the station to the center of Shikata—at the time part of Innami County, now merged with Kakogawa City, of Hyōgo Prefecture. Only this section of the town had businesses: a sake store, a timepiece store, a drugstore, a stationery shop, a tobacco shop, a rice shop.

Hiraoka turned right at the crossroads and came upon an imposing, dignified, old house with a latticed front. It had roof tiles and, on its second floor, hole-like windows that suggested a storehouse. It was the residence of the wealthy Kōta family his grandfather knew well. He stayed there that night. The Hiraoka family's "domicile" or legal permanent residence was located only several hundred yards east of the center of town, but he did not visit it. The next morning, provided with a guide, he went to the Shikata Elementary School to attend the orientation that the local veterans association held for the physicals scheduled two days later in the Town Hall, in Kakogawa City.

The men who had to take draft physicals that year, 1944, were those born in 1924 and 1925. Normally, only those born in a single year had to have them as they reached the conscription age. But by then the war that had started with a series of spectacular victories had reaped one stupendous defeat after another, creating enormous casualties, and that had forced the military to come up with replacements fast.

Shikata was small enough to need just one elementary school, and most of the young men who gathered, about a hundred, recognized one another. But Funae Fujio did not know Hiraoka. In fact, it was because he was a stranger among the familiar locals that Funae remembered to write about him after his death.

Before the orientation started, the young men stood around in small groups chatting, having fun with one another—in the playground, in the roofed corridor connecting buildings, and so forth. Funae was a third-year student at the Tomioka Higher Commercial School. But only a handful went from grammar school to junior high school and even fewer from junior high to higher school. Most started to work for their family businesses as soon as they were done with grammar school or junior high school. The area was mainly agricultural, though many households were in the thriving knitting industry that had started at the end of the preceding century. Most of the youths gathered there were deeply tanned, with well-developed muscles, obviously farmers.

Funae, in any case, spotted a man standing apart, all alone, at the entrance of the auditorium. What struck him first was his pale face.

Then, he thought the man's dark-blue jacket that resembled that of the navy officer's uniform was incongruous with the gaiters that covered the lower halves of his legs. The moment he noted the incongruity, Funae had a whiff of Tokyo. He had never been to the capital.

While casting a furtive glance at the stranger, Funae overheard a schoolteacher saying to him, "I've never seen you before. Where are you from?" In the ensuing exchange, he heard the pale-face man say, "Gakushūin" (Peers School) and "Hiraoka." He quickly grasped the situation. The name Hiraoka, mentioned along with the school that immediately conjured up the image of Tokyo, could only mean that he was a relative of the greatest man the region had produced in recent memory: Hiraoka Sadatarō,[3] who became administrator of the Karafuto Agency.

The recipient of glances of rude curiosity directed to an outsider, the student looked defenseless. Funae decided he had to be protective of him. When the gathered youths went into the auditorium, he casually took a seat behind him. The instructions members of the veterans association gave weren't of much importance, such as "Put on clean underwear" and "Do some setting-up exercises beforehand." The young man from the Peers School sat ramrod straight and nodded at each instruction.

The physicals were held two days later at Kakogawa Town Hall, a solid, surprisingly modern four-story structure with its front window adorned with stained glass reminiscent of a Christian church. It has since been renovated to serve as the city's public library, but Funae said its appearance had changed little since it was built in 1935. On one side of the building grew a single pine tree leaning to one side. The spread of its branches also had changed little over the years. Lined up in front of the pine tree, the young men were tested for their strength. The aim was to lift a farmer's rice bag. It had sand instead of rice in it, and that made it weigh forty kilograms or ninety-seven pounds. Taking their jackets off, many of the young men readily raised the bag above their head, with a shout. Funae managed to do that, too.

It was Hiraoka's turn. He took his jacket off. His skinny chest made his ribcage prominent. Probably never exposed to sunlight, it was white and looked unhealthy. Again, Funae found something incongruous: ample black hair on his chest. Not many Japanese males have body hair. Chest hair is rarer.

The eyes of all the hundred or so men were turned to Hiraoka.

He tried to lift the bag with his thin arms. The bag wouldn't leave the ground. His face reddened with exertion. He struggled with the bag for a while and gave up. He would describe this experience in the book that would bring him fame only five years later, *Confessions of a Mask*: "Farm youths lifted the rice bag as many as ten times as if it were something light, but I couldn't pull it up even to my chest and merely won a sneer from the examiner." Funae distinctly remembered the scene that day. No one "sneered" at Hiraoka. Funae himself watched him, worried. "'Not even pulling it up to my chest' was an overstatement. The rice bag wouldn't budge," Funae said. "As if glued to the ground, it wouldn't rise an inch."

Next day they gave a simple written test and a vision test. Then the announcement was made orally: "Funae Fujio passes in Class A!" There were three passing grades: Class A, First Class B and, far below them, Second Class B. During the Taishō Era (1912–26), though Japan was involved in the First World War, passing draft physicals in the Class A category did not mean induction, which was often determined by lottery. There was a surplus of soldiers, especially following the Washington Naval Treaty of 1922 that forced not just the navy but also the army to cut troop strength sharply.

Now, in 1944, Japan was getting closer to defeat in a total war. Even those who would be regarded as physically unfit in other times "passed," in the Second Class B category. Only those who were myopic or handicapped or suffered from tuberculosis were dropped on the spot. Though he was "fairly myopic,"[4] Hiraoka Kimitake passed as Second Class B, which meant, as he wrote in *Confessions*, he'd "some day receive an induction order, in the end getting inducted into a crude countryside army unit."

About this turn of events, there obviously was a miscalculation on the part of Hiraoka's father, Azusa. *Confessions* says: "Because feeble-bodied men like me weren't rare in cities, father came up with this shrewd notion that my feebleness would be more pronounced if I were examined by an army unit in a rural area—and our domicile was in such an area—and I would therefore be more likely to be rejected. In consequence, I was undergoing examinations in H Prefecture, in the Kinki Region, where our domicile was."

As a rule, anyone who received a draft notice took the physicals in the place of his domicile. But you could change the place to the municipality of your actual residence by taking certain steps. Instead of taking those steps, however, Azusa sent his son, Kimitake, more than four hundred miles west of Tokyo in the midst of war—thirteen hours from Tokyo to Kobe, one hour from Kobe to Kakogawa by train, and another hour by a different train from Kakogawa to Hōden—hoping for a greater possibility of his son's rejection among brawny, robust farm boys.

Even while waiting for his turn in the rice-bag-lifting test of strength, Hiraoka had stayed apart from the rest of the young men. After some hesitation, Funae walked up to him. It was partly because he thought the man might need someone to talk to, but partly because he wanted to talk to someone from Tokyo where he might be going soon. Hiraoka was reading something that looked like a newspaper under a tree as if what was taking place not far from him was of no concern. Approaching him, Funae saw he was reading the *Nihon Dokusho Shinbun*. So he's brought a book-review monthly to the draft physicals! Funae marveled. He started to open his mouth but couldn't think of anything pertinent to say.

"Sir, you are a grandson of Mr. Hiraoka Sadatarō, former administrator of the Karafuto Agency, aren't you?" He found himself blurting out. "And you are from the Peers School." Hiraoka seemed to hesitate. Funae asked, "That means you are studying with Princess Teru, doesn't it?"

That was an odd question to ask, Funae admitted. Princess Teru was the first child born to the then ruling monarch, Hirohito, and his wife, Nagako. She was followed by three girls, then by a boy, Akihito. But because she was the first child, Funae, who was born on October 13, 1924, had even remembered the date of her birth: December 6, 1925. And because she was only about a year younger than himself, Funae had simply assumed that Hiraoka, who was from the Peers School, might have seen her up close.

Princess Teru, whose personal name was Shigeko, had married Morihiro, the first son of Prince Higashikuni Naruhiko, a year earlier, and would have three sons and two daughters but die prematurely, in 1961, at age thirty-five. As it would develop, her father-in-law would play a notable historical role.

A French-trained general who was commander-in-chief of air defense at the time, Prince Naruhiko would become prime minister following Japan's defeat. He thus would become the only imperial prince to assume prime ministership—an ironic fate for a man who had been considered for that position in an attempt to avert the war but set aside so as not to involve someone in close imperial lineage in such a momentous role.[5] Assuming office two days after defeat nonetheless, he would send imperial emissaries to various lands to forestall any military unit from resisting surrender, and carry out the total disarmament as demanded by the victors.

To Funae's question, Hiraoka responded politely, "Yes, I know her." He apparently wasn't eager to pursue the conversation further. But Funae persisted, "That's the *Nihon Dokusho Shinbun* you're reading, isn't it?" Hiraoka said, "Yes, it is," with a courteous smile. Finally, Funae found what he thought would be a common topic, which was also a pressing one. "I'm a third-year student at the Takaoka Higher Commercial School. Last month I applied for 'short duty.' You have, too, haven't you?"

The "short duty" was the navy's Short-term Active Duty Program that was created in the mid-1930s as the arms race set in, to make up for the extraordinary shortage of officers as a result of the 1922 Washington Naval Treaty that reduced armament. The navy's Accounting School administered the program in its Tsukiji branch, in Tokyo. If accepted, you trained for two years and were commissioned as an ensign. If you were then assigned to the navy's budget section, you were relatively "safe."

"No, I haven't. I plan to move on to the Imperial University in the fall," Hiraoka replied. By "the Imperial University," he meant the Imperial University of Tokyo. It was the most prestigious institution of higher education in Japan, and the graduates of the Higher School Division of the Peers School were expected to move on to it.

Still, Hiraoka's reply surprised Funae. At that juncture, the life-or-death question for any student in higher school was: In which way to take part in the war? Student mobilization had started in the previous year, in October 1943, and the choices were stark. You could apply for "short duty" or the officer-candidate course or else you waited to be drafted as a regular soldier. Evidently, Hiraoka had decided not to pursue the officer-candidate route, either.

There was a vast difference between going to war as an officer and doing so as a regular soldier summoned by an *akagami*, "red paper," as the draft card was called. The difference was as between heaven and earth—in food and all other matters. True, in some ways, in the Japanese military at the time, the officers' chances of getting killed in battle were greater than those of regular soldiers in proportion to their numbers. But making it through as a private second class, which was what you would be if drafted by an *akagami*, was another matter. It required greater stamina, a greater ability to put up with all the abuses that the draftees were subjected to. By simply looking at Hiraoka, Funae could tell he'd never make it as a private second class. Either way, there was no way of avoiding the military machine unless you were found ill.

---

His application accepted, Funae went to Tokyo in September 1944—September, because, though the normal school year in Japan starts in April and ends in March, the war had shortened the higher-school term by six months. The Tsukiji branch of the Navy Accounting School was near the Kachidoki Bridge that spanned the Sumida River. His class had nine-hundred students. These were divided evenly into ten units. Each unit was given a large room where double-bunk beds were built like silkworm shelves. A bunk near his was occupied by a man who had come from the Imperial University of Tokyo. He was small, quick, and aggressive. If Funae were to carry an indelible impression of Hiraoka at the draft screening in Shikata for the rest of his life, he was destined to do likewise with this man.

"In physical education, the navy focused on sumo wrestling and boat rowing," Funae explained. "As you know, in sumo *utchari*"—throwing your opponent sidewise—"is a legitimate technique, but not in the navy. If you did that, you lost. They wanted to emphasize the aggressive spirit, so they encouraged you to concentrate on pushing and shoving, not *sophisticated* techniques." The man occupying a bunk near Funae's took this navy approach to heart. In sumo, he simply dashed into his opponent with amazing ferocity. Funae remembered him as having firm muscles and a healthy, lustrous skin. His name was Nagaoka Minoru—the one who would go on to be called The Don of Finance.

Nagaoka excelled academically. He had finished the five-year middle school of those days in four, enabling him to go to higher school, then to university, one year earlier than his fellow students. That was why he was a freshman at the Imperial University of Tokyo when Hiraoka, of the same age, was still a third-year student in the Higher School Division of the Peers School. By the time Hiraoka got into the Imperial University of Tokyo, in October 1944, Nagaoka was in the Navy Accounting School. He graduated from the university the same year Hiraoka did simply because his demobilization was delayed.

## *The Will He Left*

On February 4, 1945, Sunday, Hiraoka Kimitake came home expecting to spend a few days with his family. In the previous month, as part of the student labor mobilization program, he had been assigned to the Koizumi plant of the Nakajima Aircraft Manufacturing Company in Gunma. It was, as he put it in *Confessions*, "a mysterious factory": "Modern scientific techniques, modern management methods, the precise, rational cogitations of many a superior brain—all these were together devoted to just one thing: to wit, 'death.' This giant factory geared to the production of Zero fighters for 'special attacks' itself felt like a dark religion, which rumbled, groaned, wept and shrieked, and roared."

Around ten in the evening that day, Hiraoka received a telegram: an *akagami* ordering him to enlist at once at the place of his family domicile. On the sixth, he wrote to his classmate Mitani Makoto, who had become his weekly correspondent since the latter's induction into the officer-candidate course in the preceding fall: "The induction notice that I had eagerly awaited came on the fourth."[6] This was an addendum to one of the letters that the two called "Saturday communications," and he may well have been truthful in that sentiment. He had expected the notice by January and had, somehow, even learned that he'd be assigned to the infantry, but January had come and gone.

Having received the induction order, Hiraoka wrote a will in ink with a brush, cut his nails and some hair, and put them in an envelope, according to custom. The will read in its entirety:

> **Will**
> Hiraoka Kimitake (seal)
> Item: Father
> Mother
> Professor Shimizu and

other teachers
who gave me such kindly tutelage
while I was at the Peers School and at the Imperial University of Tokyo
I hereby express my gratitude to your large-hearted generosity.
Item: My classmates and seniors at the Peers School
I shall be hard put to forget your friendships
May your futures be full of glory!
Item: Younger sister Mitsuko, and Younger brother Chiyuki,
do your utmost on your older brother's behalf in serving
Father and Mother in filial duty
Chiyuki in particular: Follow his older brother to become
as soon as possible
a panther in the Imperial Army
so he may return a smidgen of the Imperial Favor
Long Live the Emperor!

The will may appear formal and formulaic to a fault, though written by someone highly educated. Not many ordinary persons would have been able to use classical Chinese words so freely, even words such as the one translated here as "panther" (*hikyū*; *pixiu* in Chinese), although official pronouncements from government and the military in those days were laden with such ancient Chinese vocabulary. The word *hikyū* comes from Sima Qian's history, and refers to the legendary ferocious animal deployed to fight human soldiers in battle. Later it became a metaphor for a strong army.

Two decades later, when the monthly *Bungei Shunjū* asked him for something unpublished, Hiraoka—by then few would have recognized Mishima Yukio's real name, so here we will begin using the penname where appropriate—pulled this out and offered it as part of an essay reflecting on what could have prompted a twenty-year-old youth to compose such a will. New draftees were expected to go to the military with a will like that, and it may be, Mishima thought, that he did not want to incur unnecessary ire by writing something out of line, should the will fall into the hands of the military censor. There may also have been a touch of *dandyism* in this "impeccable impersonality."

"At the same time, you can't really explain the whole thing by resorting to worldly considerations or dandyism," he continued. There must have been something, "a separate, large hand," that made a young man—even one who had already published a novel, as he had—come up with a composition like this with ease. It was "neither the nation's iron hand nor militarism, but something that had seeped into my heart, was it not, and that something made another heart of a different dimension live *even* in me"?

Reflecting further on the matter, Mishima wondered if something akin to the Catholic Church may not have been at work in Japan during the war. There must be "*another heart*"—emphasis his—"that represents us that works as our agent and our surrogate. Only the Protestant-style conscience helped form the modern self and severely narrowed our heart, our conscience, did it not?"[7] The induction order, in any event, was to report to the designated base on February 15. So, on the tenth, Mishima headed back to Shikata, Hyōgo, this time accompanied by his father, Azusa. His mother, Shizue, took it hard.

"When I left home, because she did not think I'd come home right away, mother kept standing at the gate as she saw me off, her hair wild, weeping," Mishima said, recalling years later his mother's appearance that day "with extraordinary clarity" on a TV program, *Talking about Mother*. Shizue was suffering from a cold. "If I had gone off as a soldier [and never returned], I think the impression that I was just a lovely son would have remained with her." Chiyuki, Mishima's younger brother, remembered her as looking "so thoroughly beaten that she did not appear to be a person of this world."[8]

It was not an exaggerated reaction on Shizue's part. B-29s had begun bombing Tokyo itself the previous November. "The 20th Year of Shōwa opened with air raids," Mishima noted in his brief New Year greetings to Mitani, adding, "This is a felicitous year that I, too, join the military."[9] The situations for Japanese soldiers in combat zones overseas had become so bleak that some committed suicide upon receipt of the induction notice. Even as the government called for the readiness of the entire populace to die—*ichioku gyokusai*, "the 100 million to shatter like a jewel"—the military tried to be circumspect in certain cases. It would notify a university of an impending induction telegram so the student might be with his family when the telegram arrived. In Mishima's case, the Imperial University of Tokyo made up an errand for him to run. That explains why he was home when the *akagami* came.[10]

Mishima himself had a slight fever when he left Tokyo, having gotten it, he thought, from a fellow at the factory. By the time he and his father reached Shikata, his fever had become pretty bad and he could hardly stand on his feet. The Kōta family, the same people with whom he had stayed nine months earlier, took very good care of him, but the fever would not subside until, finally, on the morning of physicals, the febrifuge he had taken showed some effect and Mishima felt more or less all right. The regiment to which he was to be inducted was in Kasai County, north of Innami County where Shikata was located. A dilapidated wooden structure—Mishima called it "a real *barrack*," using the English word,[11] a point to be noted here because English was an "enemy language" and frowned upon—stood on a barren hill covered with withered pampas grass.

In *Confessions* Mishima condensed what happened the previous May and that February, so the reader not paying close attention may fail to distinguish the two, but here's what happened in the barrack: "While we wandered about, stripped naked like animals for the induction checkup, I *sneezed* a number of times. Not only did the callow army doctor mistake the rustling sound in my bronchi for *Rasselgeräusch*"— crackles, crepitations; German medical terms were routinely used at the time—"but he confirmed his misdiagnosis from my own illness report and went on to have my blood precipitation measured." The upshot: the doctor diagnosed it as "amyloidal infiltration of the lungs" and ordered Mishima home right away. "Once out of the gate of the military compound, I started to run. A bleak wintry road descended toward the village."

Mishima wrote as if he was alone, but Azusa was with him, and he described this run in far greater detail. "The moment we stepped out of the gate I grabbed my son by the hand and we started to run blindly," Azuza recalled, with obvious pleasure. "We were so fast, so fast, we truly ran. I no longer remember what the distance was, but it was considerable. And all the way we kept turning back to look. We were mortally, yes mortally, afraid that a soldier might run after us and bark, 'That was a mistake, your rejection was canceled, you passed fine, congratulations!'" Azusa even compared themselves to jailbreakers seen on TV, a term that didn't exist in Japan in 1945. When the two finally got on the train, "Gradually, joy brimmed up in me, and I didn't know what to do with it."

For Azusa, the army's rejection of his son as unfit for service was something he, like every member of his or any family, had hoped for but had scarcely expected to come true. The letter of joy and relief that Shizue's mother, Tomiko, then a seventy-year-old widow living in Kanazawa where she'd been evacuated, wrote Mishima on receiving his card bringing the news that he wasn't inducted after all, attests, endearingly, to how ordinary citizens felt about losing any of their kin to the military service.

When she first heard he was finally going to the front, she accepted the fact, Tomiko wrote, though she also wished he'd get sick on the military food and come home quickly, as she spent several days "agitated as my heart was in a thousand ways." Then she received the card. She at once prostrated herself and offered prayers of gratitude to it. So she composed two "clumsy tanka" (*koshiore*) and appended them "for laughs," she said. The first of the two poems uses traditional puns (*kakekotoba*) and related words (*engo*) and, in the guise of describing the bamboo branches outside the window sagging under the snow, was congratulatory, in essence saying: "May you live for a long, long time." The second one was consolatory, saying simply this: "There are ways of serving His Majesty as innumerable as grains of sand that are in the end inexhaustible."[12]

But what about Mishima himself? He explained his shifting feelings in *Confessions*. When the order actually came, he didn't really feel sanguine about joining the army. On the other hand, he had "some expectations for a spirited way of dying." But once he was let go the same day, he ran "toward something that was not 'death' in any case, something that was not 'death' whatever it might be."

It was not black and white. Azusa, though he remembered all the outpourings of relief and joy when they returned to Tokyo, found he had no memory of his son's reactions. Much later he would be surprised to learn from Shizue what he had told her: "I wish I had passed the checkup, been sent to the front, and made to join the special attack corps."[13]

Mrs. Kōta remembered seeing a disheartened young man return from the barracks. Only some hours earlier, well past midnight, the Kōtas had summoned a doctor for him. As a result, Hiraoka appeared to feel better toward morning. And he, with his father, had gone off to the enlistment checkup, but came back and said it didn't work after all. "We were surprised. We didn't know how to console him." Was the young Mishima acting?

"Still, when they went back to Tokyo, we gave them rice, miso, and vegetables," Mrs. Kōta recalled. Rural areas had enough to eat even as cities were suffering from severe food shortages. "I think Kimi-chan carried them on his back. I still remember they looked heavy on him as they left our house."[14]

## *Hiraoka Sadatarō and His Ancestors*

The question is: Why did Mishima not visit with his grandfather's relatives—or why did Azusa not arrange for that? Mishima went to Sadatarō's hometown only twice in his life, once for the physicals for draftees, once for induction, to take advantage of the Hiraoka domicile. He says in *Confessions* that there was not a piece of property left there after his grandfather went bankrupt, but that was not entirely true. The Hiraoka domicile was not far from the Kōta house, and relatives still lived there, in Kamitomiki Yokoyama.

The question is worth asking. Evidently proud of his paternal grandmother Natsuko's lineage, Mishima explored it and wrote about some of the people on that line, including Natsuko, but he seldom, if ever, talked about his paternal grandfather Sadatarō or his ancestors. This is odd. If Natsuko's forebears, the Nagais and Matsudairas, included men who played notable roles during the upheaval as Japan was forced, with the 1853 visit of Commodore Matthew C. Perry, of the US Navy, to discard the isolationist policy that had lasted for more than two centuries, Sadatarō's forebears, the Hiraokas, employed wit and talent to deal with the sweeping social change inevitable as the new era arrived.

The simple explanation of the discrepancy may well be that, whereas his grandmother came from illustrious samurai families, his grandfather was of peasant/merchant stock. Even so, the disparity has puzzled many and put some off. It has even provoked the suggestion that the Hiraokas may have been from the untouchable class and that Mishima did not want to be reminded of it.

One story told in that regard is what Azusa called "the Akamon (Red Gate) Incident." When Azusa's great grandfather Tazaemon learned that one of the wealthiest daimyo, the Maeda, built an extravagant red gate at the entrance of his Edo mansion to welcome a bride from the shogunate, Tazaemon built a similar gate for the family temple, Shinpuku-ji. But apparently the temple itself has no record of such a gift from a parishioner.[15]

A variant of this story has it that Tazaemon was punished because his son Takichi killed a crane or secretly hunted pheasants when the hunting of either bird was the prerogative of the lord-president of the fiefdom. Either act was judged to be *lèse majesté*, and he was subjected to the penalty known as *tokorobarai*, a ban on living in the area of one's residence. The penalty was tantamount to class downgrading. Tazaemon in any event was deprived of whatever holdings he may have had and had to start anew elsewhere.[16]

Mishima Yukio committed suicide on November 25, 1970. Shocked by his manner of death—by disembowelment (*seppuku*) and decapitation—Azusa decided to look into his own paternal genealogy. He asked his cousin, Ono Shigeru, to do the work. Ono was a son of Sadatarō's younger sister, Mume. He at once went to Shikata and examined the death registers at the Shinpuku Temple. He also collected information on local history and put together a report in February of the following year. He made a copy of the handwritten report for himself and sent the original to Azusa. To paraphrase somewhat, Ono said the following in his report:

> Genealogical research going far back in history is difficult when the family temple is of the Zen sect. At Zen temples resident monks are not hereditary, so each time a new monk is appointed some documents tend to be lost. There is also the fact that during the Edo Period most commoners did not have surnames. But some of the prosperous class adopted 'store names' in lieu of surnames to indicate their higher social status. In the case of the Hiraoka family, the store name *Shioya* [Salt Dealer] begins to appear in the death register with Magozaemon during the Genroku Era. It appears that this area prospered in salt production, its reputation second only to that of Akō.[17]

The Genroku Era (1688–1704) was one of the cultural high points of the Edo Period. It was toward the end of that era that Akō, about twenty-five miles west of Shikata, suddenly attracted national attention as the fiefdom that produced the spectacular vendetta carried out by forty-seven samurai. As Ono noted, it was also well known for its salt farms. But this knowledge may have led him to misread the store name or, rather, the type of business the person engaged in, which may have been *shiomonoya*, "dealer of salted foods." If Magozaemon was a "salt dealer," he probably started out on a small scale and would have needed to do other things to make a living, unless he was a "salt headman" managing a sizable salt farm as the owner of the land. If he were a "dealer of salted foods," he definitely would have needed to do other things to survive.[18]

What prompted Azusa to look closely into his paternal genealogy was the thought that his father might—just might—have a samurai ancestor. He probably was certain that was not the case; after all, he was the one who had cut off any links to his father's relatives in Shikata. But he urged Ono to track down the death register as far back as he could because during the Edo Period, samurai were obliged to become farmers often enough for a variety of reasons. He also knew that Uchida Ryōhei, a prominent figure in Japan's rightwing patriotic movement, was related to another nationalist leader, Hiraoka Kōtarō, and that Hiraoka came from a notable samurai family in Fukuoka, Kyūshū. That was why, when done with his investigation in Shikata and headed back to Tokyo, Ono asked the resident monk of the Shinpuku Temple to find out if the Hiraoka in Shikata was connected in any way to the Hiraoka clan in Fukuoka. The monk's letter that followed in due course confirmed what Azusa had expected: There appeared to be no such linkage.[19]

Azusa's motive in a genealogical search aside, what Ono found clearly showed how a peasant family dealt with changing circumstances from one generation to another. "Hiraoka Takichi"—Azusa's grandfather—"was a prosperous landowner-cum-farmer," Ono reported. "He was also a rural intellectual with a poetic bent who always carried with him a case of writing implements and verse sheets. (That was symbolic of the master class in those days.) He sent two of his sons, Manjirō and Sadatarō, to the private school that Hashimoto Kansetsu's father-in-law ran in Akashi for them to learn Chinese classics and calligraphy; he then sent them off to the Eastern Capital [Tokyo] to study." "Takichi's wife, Tsuru," Ono did not forget to mention, "was known in the area as an exceptionally wise spouse."

It was Takichi's father, Tazaemon, who provided impetus for the Hiraoka family to improve upon a regular peasant's life. After the banishment he moved to a neighboring village, cultivated new lands, grew indigo plants, made charcoal, and raised fish. Takichi expanded on his father's approach with the help of his "exceptionally wise spouse" and eventually acquired land ten times the size of what an ordinary peasant owned in those days. He was born in 1833 and was thirty-five when the Tokugawa rule ended and a new regime came into being, in 1868. It was a time of wrenching change. Takichi had talent and an ability to cope with it, though local stories say that he expanded his holdings mainly through money-lending that was at times unsavory.

Takichi and Tsuru had three sons and a daughter. They were doing well enough by the local standards but weren't rich enough to support their first and second sons, Manjirō and Sadatarō, in Tokyo. But Takichi had created a network of intellectuals to work with before the 250-year Tokugawa rule ended. As the general view of the Tokugawa regime has it, it was a feudalistic period of rigid class immobilization. The truth was different. It tolerated a fair degree of interclass fluidity, especially as it became destabilized and faced collapse. In 1872, the new government abolished the existing four classes—which in social order were samurai, peasants, artisans, and merchants—and reclassified them into three—nobility (*kazoku*), gentry (*shizoku*), and commoners (*heimin*). This new class system was more lax, the notion that was promoted being *ikkun banmin*, "All men are equal under one monarch."

One thing that did not change for quite some time was a loose system of mutual help that members of each locality maintained when they went to live in a large city like Tokyo. The Tokugawa government was noted for the *sankin kōtai* arrangement that required each daimyo to spend every other year in Edo. This in effect created for each fief a liaison office in the largest city of Japan. Shikata was closest to the Himeji fiefdom, so it was to a former samurai of Himeji that Manjirō and Sadatarō turned when they went to Tokyo. He was Furuichi Kimitake, whom Takichi knew. Furuichi enrolled in Kaisei School,[20] the forerunner of the Imperial University of Tokyo, in 1870, when he was fifteen. In 1875 he went to France to study, with the financial support of Himeji. After returning to Japan, he joined the Civil Engineering Bureau of the Home Ministry and eventually rose to the rank of director-general. After leaving the ministry, he became a professor emeritus at the

Imperial University of Tokyo. For some years after arriving in Tokyo, Manjirō and Sadatarō stayed with him as *shosei*, "live-in students."

Manjirō, born in 1860, graduated from Senshū School, the predecessor of today's Senshū University, which Megata Tanetarō founded with his friends, in 1880, as the first private institution to teach economics and law. He became a lawyer, a new profession. Sadatarō, born in 1863, financially depended on his brother while attending Tokyo Senmon School, the predecessor of today's Waseda University, which Ōkuma Shigenobu founded, in 1882, to teach government and law. Both Megata and Ōkuma were illustrious representatives of the Meiji Era (1868–1912): Megata became, among other things, ambassador to the League of Nations, and Ōkuma became prime minister twice. But in the case of Senmon School, it was Ōkuma's right-hand man, Ono Azusa, who actually managed the school and helped Sadatarō both materially and spiritually. That was why Sadatarō named his son Azusa and, later, when asked to serve as godfather for his first grandson, named the boy Kimitake, the name of his first sponsor in Tokyo.

Sadatarō graduated from the Imperial University in 1892 when he was twenty-nine. Manjirō had urged him to attend it after he finished Tokyo Senmon School. Having chosen to be a lawyer, Manjirō had become keenly aware that one had to be part of the power center, the government bureaucracy, to play any significant role in the new age the Meiji Restoration had ushered in and the best way to accomplish that was to graduate from the Imperial University and work for the Home Ministry, the most powerful bureaucracy with the authority to appoint prefectural governors from among its own ranks.

Sadatarō followed Manjirō's advice, although graduating from the private Tokyo Senmon School and then going to the national Imperial University in effect meant having a college education twice. He did not do so solely for the personal gain he could expect by becoming a bureaucrat, however. Many who opted for public service during that period carried a sense of mission. "The university student's greatest ambition was to become a civil servant, one of the bureaucracy, which has raised Japan to its present place," an American observer more than half a century later put it, describing the youthful days of Vice Adm. Shimizu Fumio, who designed the eighteen-inch gun barrels aboard the battleship *Yamato*. "His motive was not the security that drove so many European students later to prize the life of the *petit functionnaire*.

It was an active desire to participate in the growing family life of the country."[21]

The Meiji government had started out without even an adequate legal system—not one based on Western principles at any rate. One way of remedying this situation was to send bright young men abroad to study in advanced countries and transplant to Japan whatever they learned about American and European law. Another was to invite foreign scholars and experts to Japan so the Japanese might learn from them to work out legal codes appropriate for local Japanese conditions. The Imperial University was established primarily for that purpose and had a number of *oyatoi gaikokujin*, "foreigners in government employ."

Japan at the time needed a great many bright minds, and fast. There was not much time for class considerations. Every capable person had to be put to use at once. And Sadatarō was a bright man. Four months before he graduated from the Faculty of Law (English Law), of the Imperial University, in July 1892, he had published, with his classmate Fukuhara Ryōjirō, *International Private Law* (*Kokusai shihō*). The five-hundred-page book came with an English preface by Alexander Tison, a Harvard graduate and a "foreigner in government employ." Tison commended the book by noting that there had been no book in Japanese on international private law and that the two authors tried to remedy this.

The book's timing was right. One of Meiji Japan's pressing concerns was the elimination of unequal treaties foisted on it by Western powers. The two essential features of unequal treaties were extraterritoriality and the loss of tariff autonomy. The Western powers' one excuse for extraterritoriality, if they ever needed one, was lack of internationally applicable laws, including private law. In 1889 Japan had promulgated its first modern Constitution, the basic framework for launching Japan as a nation of laws. But the country still did not have an array of legal codes to deal with international issues, nor did it have authorities on international law. As it happened, the proposed revisions of unequal treaties that Foreign Minister Ōkuma Shigenobu prepared in the same year had provisions that would allow foreigners to live, travel, run a business, and own land in any part of Japan to make up for the elimination of extraterritoriality. However, the rules and regulations needed to implement these provisions were weak or nonexistent.

The book Sadatarō and his friend wrote explained a range of civil law issues that would arise when foreigners were allowed to live in Japan, such as citizenship, marriage, ownership, inheritance, and lawsuits. It appeared two years before Japan and Britain initialed the Anglo-Japanese Commercial Treaty of 1894—the first important step to eliminate extraterritoriality and gain tariff autonomy. Thus Sadatarō, along with Fukuhara, had become the authority in the field just in time.

As planned, Sadatarō entered the Home Ministry upon graduation. Toward the end of the following year he, who was thirty, married Nagai Natsuko, who was seventeen. His local postings began in October 1894, as counselor to Tokushima Prefecture, then as chief of police of Tochigi Prefecture, in 1896. The following year he returned to Tokyo to serve as secretary to the House of Representatives, then as councilor to the Ministry of Home Affairs as well. During the two years before his next local posting—this time as director of home affairs of Hiroshima—he wrote and published two books: one on international public law (1898) and one on statute of limitation law (1899). Following Japan's victory in the Sino-Japanese War, in 1895, negotiations for treaty revisions were quickening their pace. Sadatarō's reputation as a legal expert continued to grow.

His government postings went on smoothly, along with his substantial accomplishments. As governor of Fukushima, from 1906 to 1908, for example, he built nursery schools, kindergartens, agricultural schools, and women's schools in his prefecture. He pushed for public works, building parks, railroads, and dams. And in every local post, he was treated as a dignitary, as he indeed was; every man of any local importance wished to gain and maintain influence with officials of the central government, and Sadatarō was a very important person. Expensive gifts flowed, and ladies from the pleasure quarters were made readily available as was done to any man of importance from Tokyo.

In 1908 Sadatarō became administrator of Karafuto. While in that post he paid a triumphant visit to his hometown—a "homecoming in brocade," as the saying goes. Hōden Station had not been built yet, so the long line of jinrikisha rolled out of Kako River Station, with people lining the streets, reminding some of the pomp and glory of a great daimyo procession of days not long past. But, as with a daimyo procession, Sadatarō's authoritarian behavior on that occasion, such as taking land from some people to make a road for his jinrikisha, also bred some resentment among the residents.[22]

A history of notable figures of Hyōgo Prefecture, published in 1911, has this to say about Sadatarō: "Early on he went to Tokyo to study and graduated from the College of Law, of the Imperial University, in the twenty-fifth year of Meiji [1892]. He did so well as a student that some strongly urged him to stay on and become an academic scholar. But he had a hegemonic temperament and could not imagine himself confined in a small corner of academia and spending his whole life as a walking dictionary. As a result, he entered the Home Ministry."

The editor of this history visited Sadatarō while he was in Tokyo with the Diet in session and found the man to be "someone rare in Banshū": "warmhearted by nature, easygoing, while at the same time refreshing," "talking to the visitor as if he were someone long-acquainted," and yet "stern in temperament."[23]

All that while Natsuko stayed in Tokyo. She would not get used to "rural life," she proclaimed. Kabuki and jōruri (puppet theater) were indispensable pleasures of life for her, and they weren't common outside Tokyo. She took it for granted that she could stay in Tokyo while her husband was posted in some other city. As long as his fat salaries and expensive gifts came her way, without interruption, his absence did not matter. As his rank and pay rose, the number of domestics in her household increased.

But in June 1914 the elite bureaucrat Sadatarō's career came to an abrupt end. He was trapped in the difficulties of managing a newly acquired territory and in the shifting fortunes of the two major political parties of the day.

## *The Scandal*

In 1908, when Sadatarō became its administrator, Karafuto was brand-new to governance. The southern half of Sakhalin had become Japanese territory only a few years earlier, with the Portsmouth Treaty engineered by President Theodore Roosevelt following the Russo-Japanese War, from 1904 to 1905, and it was called Karafuto, Japan's name for the entire salmon-shaped island. One result was that Sadatarō had to write a number of laws for Karafuto himself: criminal law, criminal enforcement law, prison law, tariff law, tariff-rate law, tobacco monopoly law, revenue-stamp crime punishment law, and so forth.

The territory was poor, with a resident population of a mere twenty thousand—thirty thousand with migrant workers added—practically all of them subsistence fishermen, and these fishermen were in dire conflict with capital-backed fishing companies that focused on salmon, herring, and trout. Sadatarō's well-meaning attempt to help the poor fishermen backfired. Almost all the mining and other development ventures he pushed for increasing revenues failed. Desperate, he devised discounts for the volume sales of postal and revenue stamps, and that led to a political problem.[24]

The political problem may well have been touched off by the slander of his classmate at the Imperial University, Nakagawa Kojūrō. As another classmate, the novelist Natsume Sōseki, suggested, in 1912, when he was asked for a preface to his former student Takahara Misao's account of trekking through Karafuto, *Kyokuhoku Nippon* (Northernmost Japan), Nakagawa was an ambitious, overtly confident man.

"I wasn't that close to Mr. Hiraoka but had a particularly close relationship with Mr. Nakagawa," Sōseki recalled. Takahara had written how Administrator Hiraoka explained his plans for Karafuto to him, while First Director Nakagawa looked after his needs. "As I remember it, it was when we graduated from the school and several of us acquaintances got together for some reason. It was the same Mr. Nakagawa that looked around those seated and wondered aloud, Who among us will be the first to ride in a horse carriage? Before anyone responded, it was the same Mr. Nakagawa who said, Well, I think I'll be the one." Riding in a horse carriage meant attaining a high social stratum. "I of course do not know, because I haven't checked into the matter, whether any of the several graduates who were there then is riding in a horse carriage now, but at least Mr. Nakagawa must be riding a sled as he crisscrosses Karafuto."[25]

Nakagawa was an able man. He accomplished a great deal, not just in government but in business as well, and promoted worthy causes such as women's education and the expansion of higher education as a whole. Yet because of political alignments, Sadatarō went ahead of Nakagawa in bureaucratic advancement. When he became Administrator of Karafuto, Nakagawa followed him as his deputy, and that bred resentment, which, in turn, led to the revelation of Sadatarō's scheme to increase revenues to the Karafuto Agency. After his forced resignation, Sadatarō was found to have created a deficit of one hundred thousand yen, today's equivalent of one billion yen. National newspapers treated the discovery as a big scandal, although Karafuto's local daily strongly defended Sadatarō, pointing out the difficulties of colonial finances.[26]

After nearly two years of investigation, Sadatarō was acquitted, with both the prosecutor and the preliminary judge recognizing "the embezzlement" for what it was: a casualty of a political conflict at the central government. Sadatarō's lawyer Hanai Takuzō's fabled eloquence and able defense, pointing to "partisan slander," helped. Also, by the time the investigation was underway, Sadatarō had paid for the "deficit" with his own money, by borrowing large sums.

In the year Sadatarō was thrust into the scandal, his brother Manjirō won considerable fame choosing to defend those accused in the Siemens Scandal, the German concern's bribery of high Japanese government officials.[27] He had become a member of the House of Representatives, in 1898, and later headed the Tokyo Bar Association, but he had no financial wherewithal to help Sadatarō.

---

Having sent his first two sons off to Tokyo, Takichi had one son left to inherit his estate, Hisatarō, who indeed took over. Hisatarō had two sons, Yoshio and Yoshikazu. Yoshio started a brewery near the new road. Though his sister, Mume, was married to a thriving brewer not far away, Tanaka Toyozō, Yoshio himself apparently had no business sense. He kept piling up debts, until he went bankrupt. He lost all his father's land that he had used as collateral. Not long afterward he left his hometown and disappeared.

Yoshikazu was said to be an eccentric. Sometimes he was seen walking up and down the main street, stripped naked except for his loincloth. He was married, but he spent more time in his storehouse than in the main house, sometimes cooping himself up there all day. If neighborhood children came by and looked in, he would show them the pictures he'd painted—of men and women copulating—with no indication of an awareness that he was showing something lewd to children. They were as colorful as *ukiyo-e* prints. No one bought his erotic paintings. Nor, apparently, did he have any intention of selling them. He painted them for his own pleasure.

So Hiraoka Takichi, the "rural intellectual with a poetic bent," left two strands of descendants. One was urban and elitist. It started with

Sadatarō and led to Azusa, then to Kimitake or Mishima Yukio. The other was rural and far from elitist. It started with Hisatarō and led to Yoshio, who went bankrupt, and Yoshikazu, who was an eccentric ne'er-do-well. When Azusa made the arrangement for his son's visit to his father's hometown, he evidently did not want to bring him face to face with his cousin, who was, in his eyes, a failed rustic. And Mishima Yukio apparently tried to avoid as best he could anything associated with Shikata. There is a telling episode.

In the spring of 1951, Mishima, by now a writer of considerable repute with the burst of fame his *Confessions* had earned him, was visiting Fuji Masaharu in his home in Ibaraki City, Osaka. Fuji, whose life as a writer was jolted forward by his reading of Virginia Woolf's *Orlando*, had helped Mishima publish his first book and a collection of five stories, *The Forest in Full Bloom* (*Hanazakari no mori*), during the war, in 1944.

When the two of them were chatting, a young man came to visit. As soon as Fuji introduced him to Mishima as "someone from your hometown," Mishima frowned as if he had seen something distasteful, quickly rose to his feet, and, without saying a word, left.

Looking back on the incident more than forty years later, Matsumoto Mitsuaki, who was the young visitor, could still not hide his incredulity. "It was as though he regarded my presence itself as odious," he said. An aspiring writer at the time, he later concentrated on the knitwear factory he inherited in Shikata.

CHAPTER TWO

# Samurai Ancestors and Grandmother

*In me flows the blood of a distant samurai, and the steely blood of a Mito man at that, though only a little.*
            —Letter to Hayashi Fusao, November 4, 1947

Nagai Naomune,[1] the paternal grandfather of Natsuko, the seventeen-year-old whom Hiraoka Sadatarō married, in 1893, was a son of a distinguished Matsudaira family who was adopted by the Tokugawa *hatamoto* Nagai Naonori. The Matsudairas were prestigious because it was the family into which the founder of the Tokugawa government, Ieyasu, was born. It necessarily produced a number of branches over the years, but its status remained special in the hereditary samurai system.

The *hatamoto*, "bannerman" or shogunate aide-de-camp, on the other hand, was not that special. The samurai under that nomenclature were the Tokugawa shogun's direct vassals whose annual income, measured in rice, was above five hundred *koku* but less than ten thousand. (One *koku* is about five bushels.) Someone with the assessed income of ten thousand *koku* and above was a daimyo. There were eighty thousand *hatamoto*.[2] Still, despite his relatively low rank, Naomune was chosen to serve a round of important posts during the last tumultuous phase of the Tokugawa government because of his brilliance and would be later counted among "the three outstanding Tokugawa vassals" of the period.[3]

With mounting foreign pressure, the government had to decide what to do with its isolationist policy that had been instituted in the mid-seventeenth century. The policy was partial, in that trade with Korea, China, and Holland had continued, but one important aspect of it was a total ban on the construction of ocean-going ships. The ruling class, the samurai, was martial, but Japan had no navy as a result. So, Naomune, while visiting Nagasaki as inspector-at-large in the mid-1850s, set up a college to study naval matters and train in handling large ships with the Dutch and started a shipyard with Dutch material and equipment that later developed into Mitsubishi Shipyard.[4] In 1858, he was appointed magistrate for foreign affairs, thus Japan's first foreign minister—although, to be exact, to put it that way misleads: Naomune assumed that position with another brilliant samurai, Iwase Tadanari. As Britain's first Consul General to Japan, Rutherford Alcock caustically observed, "the whole administrative machinery [of the Tokugawa shogunate] is in duplicate";[5] two or more men were put in the same position simultaneously.

In that capacity, in any case, Naomune dealt with some of the foreign diplomats as the country started to abandon its isolationist policy and open, negotiating with Iwase a treaty of amity and commerce with the first US Consul General Townsend Harris, in 1858. The two were duly chosen to head Japan's first embassy to the United States to exchange the ratified treaties. That opportunity never came, however, in part because of the same treaty.

In 1859, Naomune was appointed to another newly created position of magistrate for warships, this time alone, in effect becoming Japan's first navy minister.[6] The Great Ansei Persecution—the consequence of the clash between those who opened the country without the Tennō's consent and those who thought that was wrong *and* the shogunate succession schism that came to the fore about the same time—found Nagai and Iwase under house arrest. Then in 1860, while the embassy was visiting the United States, sans the two men, Grand Administrator Ii Naosuke, who instigated the persecution and forcefully carried it out, was assassinated.[7] In 1862 Naomune regained the shogunate's good graces and became magistrate of Kyoto. In that position he associated with Kondō Isami, who led a shogunate guard unit, a group of swordsmen licensed to kill those who might bring danger to the shogunate. Naomune also negotiated with anti-Tokugawa groups that included Sakamoto Ryōma, who gained extraordinary fame as a farsighted man following his assassination.

In 1866 when Yoshinobu became the fifteenth and last Tokugawa shogun, he appointed Naomune first inspector-general, then deputy-administrator. These were the kinds of promotion that were difficult to achieve in a shogunate that stressed status and precedent, as the shogun himself later recollected.[8] After Tokugawa forces were badly beaten in the Toba-Fushimi Battle, in January 1868, that touched off the sixteen-month-long civil war, Naomune joined the Tokugawa fleet commanded by one of his students, Enomoto Takeaki, and escaped aboard a Dutch-built warship named *Kaiyō* (*Voorlichter*) to Hakodate, in Hokkaidō.[9] With Enomoto's defeat imminent, Naomune surrendered and was jailed. But in 1872 he was recalled to serve the new Meiji government. First, he was appointed secretary to the commissioner of Hokkaidō colonization. He later became acting secretary for the Council of Elders, comparable to the US Senate.

An adopted son, Naomune himself adopted a descendent of another Nagai branch who would become Natsuko's father, Iwanojō. Iwanojō fought by his adoptive father's side during the Battle of Hakodate, in May 1869. He later chose law for his career, in the end serving as associate justice of the Supreme Court. One of Iwanojō's six sons, Ōya Atsushi, recalled his father when he was asked to contribute to the famous "My Resumé" series of the *Japan Economic Journal* (The Nikkei).

"My father was sternness itself, with no flexibility whatsoever," wrote Mishima's granduncle who, among his many industrial posts, became president of Sumitomo Chemical Industries and served the Bank of Japan as governor of policy. "He would not touch on any aspect of his children's education, but his everyday demeanor was that of an ancient samurai. I never saw him sitting informally, legs crossed—not even once. In those days judges' salaries were paltry in comparison with those for government administrators." Ōya, himself adopted out, added: "He nevertheless had to take care of his twelve children. Naturally, the family was downright poor."

## *Yakuza Ancestor and Great-granduncle's Seppuku*

The woman who became Iwanojō's wife, that is, Natsuko's mother, Taka, was born to a secondary wife of Matsudaira Yoritaka, lord-president of the Shishido fiefdom. Secondary wives and concubines of fief lords routinely came from the commoner class. Taka's mother was a niece of the commoner Shinmon Tatsugorō, the legendary head of a firefighting group in Edo, hence a yakuza boss. The "beloved concubine" of the last shogun, Yoshinobu, was one of Tatsugorō's daughters. Katsu Kaishū, another low-ranking *hatamoto* who played a crucial role in the transition from the Tokugawa government to the new, Meiji regime, counted Tatsugorō among the lawless men he admired. He described Tatsugorō as someone who "would not be intimidated by money or authority but dealt with you only on the gut level."[10] Katsu captained the Dutch-built warship *Kanrin Maru* that escorted the USS *Powhatan*—Perry's flagship when he visited Japan seven years earlier—that carried Japan's first embassy to the United States, in 1860.[11]

Ōya was proud that he had Tatsugorō's blood in him, beside the fact that his grandmother, whom he had met, was "very beautiful."[12] So probably was Mishima Yukio proud. Though he does not seem to have left any word on Tatsugorō in his writings, Mishima was a great fan of yakuza; he loved to dress like one and had a couple among his friends.

Shishido, the fief with the minimum annual rice income for the daimyo category of ten thousand *koku* and, like most other 260 fiefs, insolvent, was a subsidiary of the Mito, one of the Three Tokugawa Houses set up to buttress the shogunate.[13] The second and most influential head of the Mito House was Mitsukuni (1628–1701). Mitsukuni embarked on an extensive scholarly enterprise of compiling a history of Japan on the subversive premise that Japan's sovereign was the Tennō and the shogun was nothing more than his "head flag bearer."[14] That culminated in the ninth, fiery head of the house, Nariaki (1800–1860)—the father of the last shogun, Yoshinobu—advocating *sonnō jōi*, "Revere the Tennō, Expel the Barbarians." This was the slogan that, in the end, helped to bring down the Tokugawa or samurai rule in the turmoil created by foreign threats.[15]

Mitsukuni's enterprise also led, in its last phase, to a strong emphasis on the Wang Yangming ideal of "to know is to act" and the credo that a proper samurai must be accomplished in both literary (*bun*) and martial (*bu*) arts (*bunbu ryōdō*). The two would profoundly affect Mishima.[16] But, long before then, the slogan *sonnō jōi* changed the fate of Matsudaira Yoritaka's children.

His first son, Yorinori, was forced to disembowel himself, along with fifty (or seventy) of his vassals, in 1864, precisely because of the argument of the Tennō-as-legitimate-sovereign. The foreign menace had become a pressing issue since the Opium War or the Anglo-Chinese War, from 1839 to 1842, but especially since Perry forced Japan to open in 1854. The rapid developments following Perry's deed intensified the political schism between the two factions that had come into being under Nariaki after he became lord-president of the Mito fiefdom, in 1829.

In March 1864, the more radical of the two groups that advocated an absolute expulsion of the foreigners revolted against the more moderate "reform" group that had taken over the Mito government, and set up camp on Mt. Tsukuba, southwest of Mito. Yorinori was asked to be the emissary to allay the internecine conflict, but the reform group would not allow him into the Mito Castle. In the end, Yorinori was entrapped into armed skirmishes and, judged to have moved against the Tokugawa government, was condemned to death. That was in August. The rebels themselves, who marched toward Kyoto in order to appeal to the Tennō directly, finally surrendered toward the end of the year, in Tsuruga, northeast of Kyoto. The Tokugawa government was pitiless and executed almost four hundred of them. Worse, all that while and for some years afterward the reform group carried out reprisals against the families and relatives in Mito. The number of people who were killed, put to death, or died in prison is estimated to have totaled two thousand.

With Yorinori's disembowelment—his farewell-to-the-world poem read: "Had I ever expected to end up a paddy-field scarecrow that perishes without a shot from his bamboo bow?"—the Shishido fiefdom was abolished,[17] and his family members were put in "house prison," which meant a life of poverty. With the Meiji Restoration, Yoritaka's house was rehabilitated because it was judged Yorinori had died for the imperial cause and, as the new government created five peerage ranks of prince (duke), marquis, count (earl), viscount, and baron, Yoritaka was awarded the rank of viscount.

But the rehabilitation did not help the family much financially. The main Tokugawa house—what was left of it after the Meiji Restoration—took pity and arranged to have Yorinori's younger and Taka's older brother Yoriyasu appointed chief priest of the Tōshō Shrine in Kan'ei-ji, the main temple of the Tokugawa shogunate, in Ueno. In that position, however, Yoriyasu squandered so much money—to finance his womanizing and things such as his hobby of photography to create pornography (with a camera of the latest model from America)—that he was banished to a small villa, with a small stipend, where he died.

## *The Shrine-Officiator, Lecher, and Monster*

This genealogy on his paternal grandmother's side fascinated young Mishima. On Nagai Naomune, he evidently wrote a biography as a class composition, though it appears to have been lost. On Matsudaira Yoriyasu, Natsuko's uncle, whom Mishima actually met a number of times, he prepared substantial notes as well as wrote a school composition, two short stories, and one incomplete story.[18] The notes included a sentence (struck out) saying that the man who started the line of Matsudaira was Tokugawa Ieyasu's favorite son.

The class composition, titled "The Shrine Officiator" (*Shinkan*), describes Yoriyasu and Natsuko visiting each other.[19] It is as impressive a piece of writing as his review of Leni Riefenstahl's film *Olympia* that he is thought to have written about the same time.[20] Appropriately for a class composition, it is a tame affair, but his notes on Yoriyasu suggest that Mishima may well have been saturated with talk of sadism and sexual misconduct within his household in his early teens or even earlier. A decade later he fully realized the man's lechery in "The Lecher" (*Kōshoku*) and his sadism in "The Monster" (*Kaibutsu*).

Of the two, "The Lecher" is a story in which Mishima used real names, as he seldom did, including his own: "In this story the author is determined to rely solely on what Kimitake heard and never to turn to his own imagination, no matter how trivial the episode may be," Mishima states. It is a hilarious yet loving portrait of an oddball with a nose like that of Cyrano de Bergerac. But one aim Mishima had in describing Yoriyasu in this story was to describe his great-grandmother, whom he brings in deftly as a "digression": "Princess Taka, Yoriyasu's younger sister, was a beautiful, tough-minded woman. From photographs late in her life, you can sense that the high-spirited, refreshing feeling around her eyebrows, her prominent nose, and her small, modest, shapely mouth display a delicate, graceful harmony. There you can see the somewhat cruel beauty filled with stoic clarity that was unique to the women of the feudal age."

Taka spent her girlhood in extreme poverty—for six years, from seven to thirteen, according to Mishima's notes—and then married a "downright poor" judicial officer. She bore a dozen children—six girls and six boys and had to deal with them.[21] She entrusted her first daughter, Natsuko, to "serve" in the household of Imperial Prince Arisugawa Taruhito, in 1888, when the girl was twelve. Entrusting girls to wealthy families to serve with them for a period of time to learn etiquette and manners was as routine as putting up children, male or female, for adoption with people you knew. The ostensible reason in Natsuko's case was no different though she was a particularly difficult girl. But her service was also simply to reduce the number of mouths to feed.

The Arisugawa was one of the four collateral Imperial Houses, and Prince Taruhito was accorded a round of high-ranking positions. Commander-in-chief of imperial forces against the Tokugawa shogunate at the start of the Meiji regime and later army chief of staff, chief of the General Staff, and president of the Council of Elders, he lived in a manner befitting his exalted status. His neo-classical Victorian-style mansion on twelve acres in Kasumigaseki, Tokyo, took four years to build and was completed in 1884. A history of the Arisugawa family compiled in 1940, described it: "Its interior decorations, to go with the beauty of the radically new and grand design, were breathtaking in opulence."[22]

For the seventeen-year-old Natsuko, marrying the thirty-year-old Hiraoka Sadatarō was a letdown, particularly as it occurred soon after living in a mansion of such status, elegance, and grandeur. At the time the academic degree of bachelor of arts carried the kind of prestige unimaginable today and Sadatarō was a graduate of the most prestigious one, the Imperial University. He was handsome and dignified, but no matter. There was the class chasm: She was a descendant of shogunate families, Sadatarō of peasantry.[23] Her fiery temper and irritability, hauteur, and the extreme neurosis she would later develop went on to magnify her discontent with her husband. "My father was truly a man of heroic temperament. He liked to drink, he liked to womanize," Sadatarō's son Azusa said.[24] And that, too, did not help.

---

Not that the luxuries Sadatarō brought with his considerable and rising salaries were anything to be embarrassed about. The luxuries obviously did not match what Natsuko had seen in the Arisugawa mansion, but they were first class. The house he built on a 0.6-acre plot in Hongō, Tokyo, by bringing carpenters and craftsmen from Kyoto—and that was in his fifth year as administrator of Karafuto—stood out even in the residential area noted for its elegant houses. Behind the imposing stone gate rose pines and two large cherry trees. The front garden was adorned with a Western-style lawn. On the other side of the house was a stand of giant zelkova trees. Enter the impressive entrance and you walked into a spacious hall. The house had five guestrooms and elegant quarters for Natsuko. It had a large detached room connected with a corridor over a pond and a separate building for servants.[25]

With the collapse of Sadatarō's bureaucratic career, the family may have "started sliding down a slope at the easygoing speed of someone humming a song," as Mishima put it in *Confessions*, but Natsuko was able to keep up her vanity for a number of years. Most of the private enterprises Sadatarō pursued subsequently failed. But compared with the size of the debt, the expenses needed to keep up Natsuko's sense of entitlements were not large. The failure of his initial business venture, Japan's first zinc manufacturing plant that went bankrupt with the onset of recession as the Great War ended, saddled Sadatarō with seven hundred thousand yen—at a time when the prime minister's annual pay was twelve thousand yen and the prefectural governor's thirty-six hundred yen.[26]

It was some time after the Hiraoka family moved to a less grand house, in 1919, that the uncontrollable aspects of Natsuko's nature and behavior began to surface.

"It was none other than my father who brazenly gave my mother fierce, ferocious *hits*," Azusa wrote, using an odd baseball metaphor. "Mother's sisters gave birth to numerous children, one after another, but she had only one, me. It didn't take long for her dark speculations to reach the thought that Father must have been afflicted with *Tripper*"—German for gonorrhea—"in view of his routine behavior. Not just that, she herself came down with ferocious sciatic gout, which tormented her for the rest of her life. I remember hearing her whisper to her doctor that Father was to blame for that one, too."[27]

One outlet Natsuko found for her frustrations was her uncle Yoriyasu while he was alive. "I suffer so much because of Hiraoka, I think of this, think of that, sleep less all night, and you don't mean to make fun of me on that, do you?" she would tearfully remonstrate with him. "I'm not suffering like this because I like it. Who'd like to do anything like this ...?" That's how Mishima recreated Natsuko's words in "The Lecher."

"Her status as the oldest daughter in a large family, her excessive pride in family lineage, my father's transcendental conduct, her sciatic gout—with all these combined, her spiritual and physical pains drove her to terrible hysterics," Azusa adds after speaking of Sadatarō imparting gonorrhea to Natsuko. Or, as Mishima wrote in *Confessions*: "She was stubborn, indomitable, a maddening sort of poetic soul. A chronic brain neuralgia ate into her nerves in a roundabout, steady manner. At the same time, it added useless clarity to her intellect. Who knew that these paroxysms of insanity that continued until her death were the memento of my grandfather's sins in his prime?"

"This large-scale typhoon" that was Natsuko "blew into every corner of our house, creating a disaster whose damage you could only imagine," Azusa recalled. "Well, it was in such family circumstances that my son grew up. You could say that was my son's destiny." It was odd for him to talk about his son as if he had no part in his growth, but he was right. The one affected the most by Natsuko's conditions was the young Mishima Yukio.

## *The Birth of Kimitake, Mishima Yukio*

In April 1924 Azusa married Hashi Shizue. The bride's father, Kenzō, was the principal of the Kaisei Middle School. Born to a samurai of the Kaga (Maeda) fiefdom, he was adopted by Hashi Kendō, a professor of Chinese classics at the Kaga fief school Sōyūkan set up in 1853 to teach Western military tactics, English, and Chinese classics. Kendō's father, Ippa, was a Chinese scholar and calligrapher who was permitted to take a surname and carry swords; he was, in other words, given samurai status.[28] Shizue was a quiet woman who loved to read.

The marriage was arranged. But the go-between naturally did not tell Shizue and her family about the turmoil and difficulties of the Hiraoka household. After the marriage, her mother-in-law's behavior in particular would come to the nineteen-year-old woman as a great shock.

At nine on the evening of January 14, 1925, a small boy weighing less than 5.3 pounds was born and named Kimitake. It was the fourteenth year of the Taishō Era, but on December 25 of the following year the Tennō, Yoshihito, died. Crown Prince Hirohito ascended the throne, and the era name was changed to Shōwa. As a result, even though the first year of Shōwa lasted only for seven days, Mishima would feel, and say, that his life began with the new era. (The era name Taishō, "broad justice," comes from a passage in *The Book of Changes*: "In proceeding broadly, take up justice as a means for doing so. That is the way of the subcelestial realms," and Shōwa, "bright harmony," from a passage in *The Book of Documents*: "All people illuminated, cooperation and harmony for all countries." As has been pointed out by many, the Shōwa Era would utterly fail to live up to what those who selected the name meant it to be.)

"On the seventh night, my grandfather, before the assembled family, wrote my name on votive paper, put the paper on a dedicatory tray, and placed the tray in the alcove," Mishima wrote in *Confessions*. The house "had many dark rooms and there were six maids. Along with grandfather, grandmother, father, and mother, a total of ten people walked about and slept in this house, which creaked like an old cabinet." Mishima could have added that four of the six maids were dedicated to Natsuko.[29] Sadatarō and Natsuko took up the first floor, Azusa and Shizue the second.

It was an old, rented two-story house in Yotsuya—in those days one of the thirty-five "wards" (*ku*) of Tokyo, later subsumed into Shinjuku Ward. To leap a decade forward, on May 21, 1935, the man-of-letters Nagai Kafū, Natsuko's distant relative who lived not very far away, had some errand to run and walked through the Yochō-machi street where Shizue and her son would take a walk from time to time. Kafū had lived in Kalamazoo, New York, Lyon, and Paris, from 1904 to 1908, and despised everything Japanese for a few years after his return to his country, as was the wont of many Japanese with similar experiences. Then he made an about-face and became an extoller of Japanese traditions, professing dislike for anything Western.

That day in Yochō-machi, he saw that his former residence, which he had moved out of, back in 1918, and had subsequently become the residence of the late novelist and Shakespearean translator Dr. Tsubouchi Shōyō, was still standing after the great earthquake of 1923. "The road remains as it was in the past," he wrote in his diary. But the area had totally declined in the preceding two decades.

Automobiles cannot go back and forth. It's so narrow you must make way each time a bicycle comes by. The filth of the shops that continue on. There are a couple of dubious bars. I look at shopping women; some in dubious western clothes with both legs exposed; some in lined kimono with Tang wrinkle finish with a sloppy narrow sash, hair unkempt, only white powder painted thick on their faces. The town looks somehow obscene, and couples who come and go all strike me as illicitly married.[30]

Kafū noted it was near where Ichigaya Prison used to be. He might have added that the street was lined with cheap inns where male prostitutes plied their trade. Mishima would take it to go to school until his parents moved.

On the forty-ninth day after the child was born, Natsuko took him away from Shizue "with the pretext that it was dangerous to raise a baby on the second floor." The period of forty-nine days after death is Buddhist postmortem limbo in which the dead soul's fate remains undecided. Whether this had anything to do with Natsuko's action is not clear, but with that act began Mishima's days of incarceration as a child. "In grandmother's sickroom that was always closed up, suffocating with illness and the odor of old age," Mishima wrote, "I was raised with my bed laid next to her sickbed."

Grandmothers taking care of their grandchildren were common, but Natsuko was different because of her illness, hysteria, and willfulness. In his school composition "The Shrine Officiator," Mishima noted that those around her accepted this last trait.[31] There probably was no other choice as regards the other manifestations of her being. In "The Forest in Full Bloom," the sophisticated tale of dreams and ancestral longings he began at age fifteen and completed a year later and that became the title story of Mishima's debut collection, Mishima described Natsuko's disease.

Grandmother suffered neuralgia and had spasms constantly. As if she were possessed, her unavoidable spasms would start. As her low moans began, invisible waves of spasms would fill the space above the small pieces of equipage of the sickroom such as the tobacco tray, the medicine cabinet, and the incense burner. Then, a brief moment, the whole room would be enclosed by a tension as if paralyzed, and as it swiftly receded like a mountain mist, the whole room—the incense burner, the small box, the medicine bottle—was uniformly filled with the low, painful, monotonous groans. Such moans and groans, as if they were the room's own, must be something someone else could never imagine. But as the spasms continued a whole day or, in some cases, for many nights in a row, a more obvious sign would appear. That is, The Disease had spread throughout the whole house as if he owned it.

In an autobiography he wrote in classical language when he was nineteen, Mishima hinted that Natsuko decided to make her physical problems more pronounced as she took him away from his mother. "The neuralgia that would become her chronic illness just surfaced about that time and, unable to do anything as she pleased, began to take to bed."[32] Whether she feigned her illness to some degree or not, there is no question Natsuko behaved in a manner so tyrannically willful as to be comical were it not for the fact that it entailed an unweaned baby—until the child grew to be an adolescent—and a defenseless young mother. And neither her husband, Sadatarō, nor her son, Azusa, would intervene.

The situation was made worse by her refusal to allow the child to be exposed to sun and air.

"My mother-in-law wouldn't let Kimitake stay far from her pillow," Shizue wrote in what may be called her joint remembrances of Mishima with her husband. "She always carried a pocket watch with her and every four hours, punctually, would come to the second floor and ring the bell. Breastfeeding Kimitake had to be done every four hours, and the time for it was also set. As the hour grew close, my breasts would become full and painful. At such times, I would worry that Kimitake must be very hungry, and I wept many a time, anxious to hold him in my arms and allow him to drink his fill."

Natsuko would come up to Shizue's room on the second floor with a maid carrying the baby in her arms. While Shizue nursed him, she timed it, watch in hand, standing over the mother and child. And as soon as the time was up, she would snatch the baby from her and take him to her room downstairs.

When Mishima grew old enough to play with other children, the rule Natsuko laid down was "no boys."

"It was dangerous to have boys for his playmates, mother said, and she would call together in her room three older girls she handpicked," Shizue continues. "As a result, the games were naturally limited to playing at housekeeping, origami, and wood blocks. Any other games that boys might like were out of the question." Shizue sometimes even tried to "steal" her own baby. "When it was bright outside but dark and damp in the house, I would quietly try to take him out for some air and to expose him to some sunlight. Mother would suddenly wake and forbid me to move outside, forcing me back to the dark, gloomy room, its sliding doors closed up, where her sickbed lay."[33]

It was a trying period for Shizue, to state the obvious. "If Kimitake said he wanted me to do something for him or indicated that he did, mother would harshly scold him and me. If for any reason he put 'Mother,' which is the way he addressed me, before 'Grandmother,' which is the way he addressed my mother, that would immediately put her in a foul mood. This was because, it seemed to me, she thought she was the central figure in everything in the household and everyone had to obey her orders."

---

Natsuko's irascible, pettifogging, sickly demands that extended to the kinds of food that should be fed to the infant Mishima, not to mention the enforced female companionship, girls and maids, took their toll. By his own assessment at age nineteen, Mishima, born prematurely and feeble, "suffered from autointoxication just about twenty times," from the time he was four or five to eleven and twelve. "Once I barely escaped death after an asphyxia that lasted for one and a half hours." That happened when he was five, and everyone expected him to die.[34] The upshot: "I ended up acquiring an odd personality: working myself into a fury at the drop of a hat or into uncontrollable excitement at the most trivially happy thing."

Natsuko also instilled into the prepubescent Mishima not just the sense that he was from distinguished samurai families, but perchance something more, which, along with her contempt for her husband, may well have been the very source of Mishima's overt disregard of Sadatarō.

In "The Forest in Full Bloom," the narrator says, almost insouciantly: "It's a rare thing, but I have both samurai and aristocratic families among my ancestors." Historically, marriages between members of samurai and aristocratic families were not rare. But because there apparently was no aristocratic blood in Mishima's genealogy, this narrative aside led Nosaka Akiyuki to speculate, in his book on Mishima, that Natsuko may well have fallen in love with Arisugawa Taruhito's adopted, unusually good-looking son, Takehito, while serving with the princely family. It was an affair that had to end tragically, Natsuko knew, and it did, but she nonetheless intimated to Mishima that he had *that* blood in him, Nosaka imagined.[35]

## *Natsuko's Influence*

Still, it may not do to simply dismiss Natsuko as a monstrosity, a psychologically warped product whose sense of class was damaged by a marriage to one of the peasant class, aggravated by the gonorrhea she suspected her husband had given her and the financial ruin he had brought to the family. After all, it was Natsuko who without any fuss—utterly ignoring the usual considerations of whether this or that is appropriate for a child of this age or that age—took Mishima deeply into the world of literature and theater. And it was Shizue who had a sympathetic understanding of her mother-in-law, however overbearing and petty her conduct, for all the pain and anxiety she had to go through for a dozen years.

It was obvious to Shizue that Natsuko wanted to instill in her grandson as much as she could the upperclass elegance she believed she had inherited and acquired. Many of her son's social virtues came straight from Natsuko, Shizue judged: his "speech, etiquette, and courtesy, his habit of returning obligations and favors, his insistence on being punctual, and his punctiliousness." The words the child Mishima used for "mother" and "grandmother" in Shizue's account above, for example, are *o-kā-sama* and *o-bā-sama*, both formal and courteous. Such politesse in speech would create some awkward situations for Mishima after he became part of the more plebian world at large.[36] It would also win awe and admiration from some of those with whom he associated.

There is no question that Mishima favored Natsuko over Sadatarō.

Take a short essay he wrote for the *Asahi Shinbun* in 1962, when he was thirty-seven. Entitled "Meiji and Bureaucrats—Meiji in the Middle of Tokyo," it's a gem by a writer who knows how to make a point in a limited space. He begins by noting that his father still pronounces certain words in the way Tokyo people used to during the Meiji Era. He then says: "My late grandmother"—Natsuko had died nearly a quarter century earlier—"as befits a daughter of a shogunate aide-de-camp was stern in training me on diction." As a matter of fact, "the trope of [my] plays greatly owes to the conversations that are mannerly, precise, and entertaining besides of the Meiji people that I have heard since infancy."

But in the concluding paragraph Mishima turns against his grandfather, the quintessential Meiji man, albeit indirectly. "The one thing I dislike about Meiji is that it was an era in which the 'bureaucrats' and the 'bureaucratic odor' came into being that have continued to this day," he writes. "Meiji bureaucrats thought so little of culture, in essence because they were rustics and could not comprehend cultural refinement. And the spirit that approves of that incomprehension casts its shadow even now."[37] Was Natsuko an embodiment of cultural refinement?

We may also ask: Is it possible that Sadatarō's imperturbable, quietly masculine presence like that of an "ancient samurai" (despite his ancestry)—once Natsuko in her fits slapped him on the cheek but he didn't even change his expression—is it possible that living with such a "strangely fascinating figure" left no imprint on Mishima? Mishima may have grown up as an unlikely, if not to say tragic, "grandmother kid" treated like a girl, a doll, but Sadatarō lived until Mishima was over seventeen—as a ubiquitous household presence until he was twelve. He was the kind of man whose admirers built a large statue for him while he was alive. Mishima attended the unveiling ceremony though he was only five years old.

As soon as he started to write about his notions of literature, Mishima put forward the coexistence of masculinity and femininity as the crucial feature of Japanese tradition. His peals of "strongman laughter" that everyone who spent any time with him would remember as distinctly Mishima's were, in fact, Sadatarō's.[38]

## The Bureaucrats Hiraoka Azusa and Kishi Nobusuke

What about Mishima's father, Azusa—he who wrote about the chaos of his household as if it were none of his business?

He said about himself, with a dose of sarcasm: "No one has to tell me that I am just an ordinary man with no talent whatsoever. So, as years pass, people will begin to bypass me in lineage and character, overlooking me, obliterating me, in the Hiraoka genealogy, and our posterity will assume that my son came directly from his grandfather, then wonder, This is odd, there's too much age difference between father and son. I think that's what may happen."[39]

His self-assessment may not be too far off the mark, especially as it relates to his reputation as a bureaucrat. Among those who entered the Ministry of Agriculture and Commerce with him in 1920, two years after the First World War, was Kishi Nobusuke, a future prime minister who would play, however indirectly, an important role in Mishima's life. Kishi had followed the same educational track as Azusa: from the First Higher School to the Imperial University of Tokyo. But, aside from the fact that Azusa was older by two years because he had flunked the entrance exams for the First Higher School for two years in a row, the two were a study in contrast. Azusa was amorphous and self-deprecating, though arbitrary and ruthless to his subordinate. Kishi was ambitious, aggressive, and supremely self-confident.

Kishi, in some ways, was more like Azusa's father, Sadatarō. His brilliance at the Imperial University of Tokyo was legendary; his academic performance was unprecedented. Along with his competitor in brilliance, Wagatsuma Sakae, later an authority on civil law, Kishi was expected to stay on to become an academic, but he did not. As Wagatsuma noted years later in a manner reminiscent of a description of Sadatarō, "his hegemonic ambition and talent did not allow him to stop at an ivory tower."

Why did such an ambitious, talented man choose the Ministry of Agriculture and Commerce? "In those days, the ministry to which the brightest flocked was the Ministry of Finance. The most glamorous for the bureaucrats, most appropriate for government officials, was the Home Ministry," Kishi recalled in a memoir of his youthful days.

But he decided to join Agriculture and Commerce after talking to an official there whose argument on stock trade was attracting both economists and businesspeople, and whose knowledge of the economic problems Europe was facing following the Great War impressed him.[40] He decided that "the substance of government in the future lay in the economy," he told one of his biographers.

In 1925, when the Ministry of Agriculture and Commerce was split into two, one for agriculture and forestry and one for commerce and industry, Kishi chose the latter, even as Azusa chose the former. He may have heard that Herbert Hoover had transformed his Commerce Department from a sleepy agency into a prominent one. The following year, he was sent off on a yearlong overseas tour. His first stop was the United States, where he saw the International Exposition to Celebrate the Sesquicentennial Anniversary of American Independence, in Philadelphia. The scale of America's industrial power, along with its waste, overwhelmed him, even generating "a kind of resentment." At the time Japan aimed to produce one million tons of iron and steel a year. The United States was producing more than five million tons of iron and steel *every month*!

"Everywhere I went, I saw heaps of old automobiles junked," he reminisced late in his life when interviewed for a history of the Ministry of International Trade and Industry, postwar successor of the Ministry of Commerce and Industry. "Now you can see such a spectacle in Japan, too, but Japan in those days had few automobiles. You repaired rickety-rackety cars and drove them. That was the norm." The US tour made Kishi "pessimistic" about the future of Japanese industry.

But he then went on to England and Germany, and the latter gave him hope. Then struggling to recover from the devastations of the Great War, the country "eliminated waste and was doing everything rationally. Compared with that, the American economy was all waste." "Germany, like Japan, lacked natural resources," Kishi said elsewhere, "but it was attempting economic development through advanced technologies and scientific management techniques. 'This is the way for Japan to go,' I was convinced."

The movement for industrial rationalization in Germany further impressed Kishi when he went to that country again in 1930. It reinforced his confidence in the great role bureaucrats could play in "enriching the nation and strengthening the military," the slogan of the Meiji government in which men from his prefecture, Yamaguchi (Chōshū), had an outsize presence.[41]

During the second half of the 1930s, Kishi became the leader of "reform bureaucrats," and he was the one who the Kwantung Army, a semi-autonomous unit of the Japanese Imperial Army set up in 1903 to protect Japanese interests in Northern China, chose as its man in Tokyo.

From 1936 to 1939 Kishi was counted among the five men who elected to "build" Manchukuo, the state Japan created in 1932. The four others were Lt. Gen. Tōjō Hideki, chief of the Kwantung Army's military police, then its chief of staff; Hoshino Naoki, who ran the day-to-day business of Manchukuo government as head of its General Affairs Agency (though the real power resided with Kishi); Matsuoka Yōsuke, president of the Southern Manchurian Railroad, who as Minister for Foreign Affairs had won some international notoriety; and Ayukawa Gisuke, head of Japan Industrial Corporation, a conglomerate, which had under it Nissan, Hitachi, Japan Mining, and Japan Chemicals. Because of their personal names, the five men were known as Two Ki's and Three Suke's.

Unlike Kishi, who would later be called a "monster," "ghoul," and "revolutionary,"[42] Hiraoka Azusa did not leave any imprint, either on the Japanese government or Japanese history—except in playing a part in wrecking an epochal farm bill, a matter that did not come to light until forty years later.

During the period before and after the era name changed from Taishō to Shōwa, tenant-farmer disputes increased alarmingly. In 1926 the number of disputes reached the prewar high of 2,713 cases, with more than 150,000 landless farmers taking part. To deal with the situation, the Ministry of Agriculture and Forestry prepared a bill that would give a piece of land to each tenant farmer, a landmark step. The plan, which by itself would have created a firestorm among landowners, called for the issuance of bonds amounting to ¥3 billion or today's equivalent of ¥30 trillion—a staggering sum. It was, therefore, kept tightly under wraps.

Kōno Ichirō, who after the war would serve as Minister of Agriculture and Minister of Construction, among other government posts, was a journalist at the time. Sensing something was afoot, he ferreted out the contents of the top-secret bill. The news made a huge headline in Kōno's newspaper, the *Asahi Shinbun*, on June 14, and the bill was buried even before it was submitted for Cabinet consideration.

The Tokyo Metropolitan Police Department was notified and tough internal investigations were made, but Kōno's source was never found. It was only in 1965 that Kōno disclosed in his autobiography that he obtained the information by snatching the relevant bill draft from "the writer Mishima Yukio's Papa, Hiraoka Azusa."[43]

## *Disjointed Memoirs*

Shizue's "joint remembrances" with Azusa were actually disjointed. Azusa sold the idea of writing about his famous son to a publisher soon after Mishima's death and started work. But early on he decided to allow his wife to have her own say. The man who would not raise a finger for his wife when she needed his help the most was oddly accommodating when it came to describing what their son was like. He freely let her interweave her observations into his own, often to contradict him. Early in their marriage Shizue had found her husband was not someone with whom she could have a proper "dialogue."[44]

John Nathan, who interviewed the couple for his biography of Mishima, tells of their open discord. When he went to see them at their house, Azusa came out and responded to Nathan's questions. Shizue, however, instead of joining them for the interview, positioned herself in the next room, just beyond the sliding doors, and would occasionally correct her husband, even upbraiding him at times. "My child cried because you threatened him," she said at one point. At another she said, "How can you tell? You weren't there. You were never close by when he needed you."

Nathan was discomfited by all this but managed to finish his interview. When he was done and was ready to step out of the foyer, Shizue suddenly emerged and declared with stern dignity, "Mr. Nathan, now you know what a sadist my husband is." Azusa, who was right there, did not even try to protest. Several days later, Shizue got in touch with Nathan and designated a place for him to ask her questions separately—a kimono store in Nihonbashi.[45]

If Shizue was somewhat unusual, Azusa, who flaunted what may be called amused detachment, was not much different. Before letting his wife step into his recollections, Azusa quotes her disparaging remark to him: "You are like a water buffalo, with no *delicacy*, only interested in action, an insensitive person, you can't possibly understand Kimitake's heart." The only caveat he makes about her is that the reader should ignore her if she started saying anything as wild as Mishima's testimony that he remembered being bathed right after birth, which opens *Confessions of a Mask*.

At any rate, when Shizue has given her account of Natsuko's bizarre conduct, writing for a dozen pages, Azusa butts in with "Let me interrupt a little . . . I couldn't stand watching my son growing up like a girl, glued to my mother, as always, and I don't know how many times I quarreled with her over that and forcibly took my son outside.

"One day, when I took him to Shinjuku"—by then Japan's main railway junction—"I happened to see a steam locomotive go by. At once we went near it. Between the plaza this side and the railroad was a fence made of charred piles. We were so close to the locomotive we could almost touch it just by stretching out our hands." The next train approached in no time, belching "great plumes of black smoke, barreling down upon us with roaring clatter." So: "I thought to myself, 'Wow, this is it! A once-in-a-lifetime chance to give him a Spartan education, fearless, unperturbed!'

"I picked him up and, protecting his face with my felt hat, got closer to the engine. I said to him, 'Scared? Don't worry. You cry, you're a weakling, I'll dump you in the ditch.' I watched his face. But, contrary to what I'd expected, he showed no reaction."

Azusa evidently was unaware of his own contradiction, but concluded that his son was "like a doggie not yet old enough to know what fear was or else he'd lost the ability to react to such a stirring, masculine phenomenon as a result of mother's girlie education." So he decided to take a different tack. "The next day I chose a quiet train and tried it on him once again, but it was no good. I thought he must burst into cheerful shouts, but he kept his nō-mask face. I gave up. I never could figure out the mystery."[46]

Azusa goes on to observe that Mishima in those days "was almost consistently expressionless, just as he was when he flunked the draftees' physicals and when we heard the Tennō's words at the end of the war in our relative's house in Akatsutsumi." On August 15, 1945, Hirohito for the first time spoke on the radio; it was to tell his subjects that Japan was conceding defeat and that the nation had to be prepared to "endure the unendurable." Azusa concludes that "the mystery" of his son's impassiveness "remained unsolved to the end."

This was no mystery to his wife. "I think my husband is wrong when he says, 'Until he began his loud laughter he was a man as expressionless as a nō mask,'" Shizue writes when her turn comes. After he became an established author, Mishima became known for startling bursts of laughter. "I think Kimitake assumed a nō mask to control perturbation as best he could whenever my husband said something unreasonable to him."

Perhaps because Azusa—and Shizue—told him this childhood story more than once, Mishima presented the same experience, but in a different light, when he had a chance to write about it in a story. In "The Forest in Full Bloom," there occurs this passage: "beyond the enclosure of black charred piles . . . in the mist, on the track, part of which was gleaming faintly white, [the child] saw a giant locomotive start to move, repeating spasms of asthmatic coughing."

The "steam train," in fantasy, is "cold-hearted," as it runs through a northern land "as it pleases, not turning its eyes to a village with sasanqua in early bloom, to a rundown factory town where smoke rarely rises, or even to sadness," loaded as it is with "many boxes of green apples and the salmon brought from more distant seas." But it is the narrator, "the child," who asks his father to leave him by the rail track: "Whenever his father took him to town, he let him stand by the fence next to the track for a while exactly as the child asked him to. Beyond the track, countless neon signs resembling the remnants of the red evening sun turned and turned like willful stars against a black backdrop."

Then comes this sentence: "Like a tropical man who wildly cheers each time an elephant rumbles by, each time an electric train sped by, the child jumped up in his father's arms, laughing, clapping wildly, recklessly."

Here, Mishima is projecting a child trying to "get into the cracks in his dreams as he sleeps alone." Also, a thundering steam locomotive becomes a smooth electric train. Still, we might as well not read too much into Azusa's observations. It was none other than Shizue who wrote in her diary, when her son was six years old, to marvel what a "cheerful" child he had turned out to be, always smiling, "for all the cruelties he suffers." She could not help thinking he had to be "a deity incarnate."[47]

In April 1931, Hiraoka Kimitake enrolled in the Elementary Division of Peers School, a school for sons and daughters of peerage. That was what Natsuko wanted, and for that she lined up Yoriyasu as sponsor. Yoriyasu had inherited the peerage rank of viscount from his father. The arrangement turned Azusa into the butt of dismissive, sneering jokes among his government colleagues. Mishima himself might have harbored some unease about the lack of a titled person among his immediate family members—a point his brother Chiyuki made and Shizue often complained about, although Muramatsu Takeshi, who asked some of Mishima's classmates, discounted this.[48]

In first grade, Kimitake wrote a composition titled "The Owl" in his Japanese class. It began, "Owl, you are the queen of the woods." He was one of the few pupils who were asked to read their writings in class that day. But what he read was clearly over the heads of most of the pupils, as well as his teacher. The pupils tittered nervously, and the teacher, apparently lost, mumbled, "Hiraoka is special, you know." He never asked Mishima to read his composition again, a classmate recalled years later. Confined to Natsuko's gloomy room much of the time, with his mother reading fairy tales to him every day, the child had created a world of fantasy.

He appeared sickly. He "looked uncomfortable with a dressing around his neck in his uniform with a stand-up collar," the same classmate remembered,[49] though the getup was largely because Natsuko demanded it. He readily took a day off, similarly at her behest. In second grade, asked to write a composition on the topic, "Things I Was Praised For," he wrote: "In first grade I took fifty days off. . . . In second grade so far I have not taken a single day off."[50]

In August 1933, when he was in third grade, the Hiraokas moved to a place near the Keiō University Hospital, in Shinano-chō, and the grandparents and the parents began to live in separate rented houses, both smaller than the previous house. Their move was the result of economic pressure. Three of their six maids were discharged. It was an opportunity for Shizue to take her son back from her mother-in-law's management. But she only won a small concession: she allowed Shizue to take him to school.

"We would go to the park in front of Yotsuya Station and together pick acorns and sing songs, the moment so happy I almost had tears," Shizue recalled. "Whenever I took him to a dentist, we would agree to a condition: he could have ice cream at Yotsuya Mitsuke, and I remember how happy he was. But once home, he had to have the three-o'clock meal mother-in-law had prepared; then, near her pillow, the hour for me to have him do his daily study would begin."[51] She thought the snack Natsuko prepared was too small. She would have fed him something more substantial.

But Natsuko, still fearful of the relapse of autointoxication, was convinced that she could give him only light food. Mishima describes how it was in *Confessions*: "When it came to fish, I knew only those with white flesh, such as flatfish and flounder; when it came to potatoes, I knew only the kind mashed then strained through cloth; when it came to cakes, those with bean paste inside were forbidden, with only light cookies and wafers given me. With fruits, I only knew thinly sliced apple and tiny portions of orange." The snack eaten, he was allowed to go to his parents' home. But he had to be back to his grandmother by suppertime.

Still, at school, the boy turned out to be no withdrawing, helpless weakling. His friends reported that in third grade, for example, he was counted among "the three pranksters." He was as vivacious as the next boy. Natsuko nicknamed him Shōko, "Little Tiger," although that may have contradictorily included her wish he'd be a samurai boy. He also was an irresistible laugher and cackler from childhood. Grownups said it was embarrassing to take him to a movie because he'd burst into laughter at the most unexpected spots. At school, some teachers avowed they could tell his presence because of his cheerful cackles. As an adult, a playwright friend once asked him to provide canned laughter, as it were, along with some other good laughers.[52]

---

There is a childhood recollection that Mishima wove into an early story that took Shizue by surprise when she read it. The story is "Sorrels" (*Sukanpō*), which Mishima wrote in 1938 when he was thirteen and would later count among his four "virgin works."

"Sorrels" concerns a boy and an escaped convict. The boy always wants to go to the hill nearby, which is overgrown with pink sorrel flowers, so he may fully relax and be free. But his mother forbids him to go near there. In one corner of the hill is a prison "filled with gray air";

besides, an escaped prisoner is abroad. Once, though, he ignores the warning and runs up to the hill. He throws a white ball high into the sky.

"The blue sky, following the ball, rose up high; then fell toward him with a terrifying speed. When he caught it, he was as happy as though he had made the blue sky his own." While he is absorbed in his play, darkness falls. He becomes lost in the woods. In front of the sobbing boy appears a man, an escaped convict.

Looking back on this story just before starting work on *Confessions*, Mishima wrote: "I symbolized in the sorrel flower the pure soul that a young boy's heart awakens in the dark heart of an escaped convict." John Nathan's judgment on this story was tough. Calling the story a "fantasy," he said: "the ecstatic identification with nature the boy achieves on the hill is sham, the earliest example of Mishima disguising his desire," adding, "The essential elements are a dark woods, a beautiful, weeping boy, and a murderer. Here is a model of the beauty that would compel and terrify Mishima all his life."[53]

Perhaps. "Sorrels" is a fantasy all right—a story complete with a meeting in the prison between the warden and the convict who has voluntarily returned after talking with the boy, the release of the reformed convict a year later and so forth. But Shizue saw something different in it. Prefacing her remarks with "When I was made to read 'Sorrels,' I was so startled I was speechless," she went on to recall: "When Kimitake was four or five years old, one fine autumn day, because his grandmother happened to be away, I was incited by my husband who insisted that we give him some sunbathing, and the three of us sauntered out with no particular place in mind. After we strolled awhile, suddenly houses became fewer, and we came out on a lonesome street that had a long, long wall on one side."

The three kept walking and reached a spot with a plaza-like space. Written on a plaque on the gate there was the name of the prison. It was Ichigaya Prison, which shut down in 1937. "Kimitake, who found himself in a somewhat menacing space that was just too bleak to me, seemed deeply shocked. He started to ask me what the building was, and he grew importunate. Not knowing how to respond properly, I finally said, 'Many bad people are put into here. We better go home and quick.' But he wouldn't budge.

"No, of course, there was nothing like sorrel flowers blooming anywhere," Shizue continued. "All over the place nothing but weeds grew; there was no one in the street nor inside or outside the gate. I can easily understand Kimitake, the child, perceived it to be an utterly strange landscape. The moment I read 'Sorrels,' I knew it described that outing of ours."[54]

Aside from the question of how the fantasy story portended Mishima's future, there was an orthographic dimension to its writing. Ten years after its initial publication, Mishima noted that at the time he wrote the story, he was reading the *Kōjirin*, then the dominant dictionary of the Japanese language, as his "No. 1 favorite book." He used "all the autumn flowers and spring flowers [he found in the dictionary] for the description of the field in the writing." The story is "comical," he wrote, "with the names of only the flowers unknown to me lined up."[55]

Lining up all the difficult Chinese characters for the names of common plants besides, he might have added. The wildflower named in the title, *sukanpō*, is familiar and plebian enough, and Mishima could have written it in simple Japanese syllabary, as is customary. But he chose for it a set of two difficult Chinese characters suggesting something like "acid mold." It was rather like calling a common wildflower by a Latin name. He did the same with all the other wildflowers he mentioned in the story.

CHAPTER THREE

# "The Boy Who Writes Poems"

*Mishima peeled himself one layer after another like an onion in order to find his true self, even as he covered himself up with one dress after another.*

—Nosaka Akiyuki

The year 1937, when Mishima advanced to the Middle Division of the Peers School, became a turning point in modern Japanese history. In early July, the Japanese Army clashed with the Chinese near the Marco Polo Bridge, southwest of Beijing. Toward the end of the month it started a general attack in North China—territory immediately south of Manchukuo, the state Japan had established just a few years earlier. In mid-August the army opened a front in Shanghai, landing its forces in the international city.

"In order to punish the Chinese Army for its immoral violence and thereby encourage the Nanjing government to mend its ways," Konoe Fumimaro, chosen for premiership with the expectation of reducing Japan's military presence in China, declaimed, on August 15, loading his statement with orotund classical Chinese words, "we now cannot help taking resolute measures." It was tantamount to a declaration of war, but the government decided to call this development an "incident." Calling it "war" could have led the United States and other nations to stop exporting war-related goods to Japan.[1] For that matter, neither China nor the United States, for each of its own reasons, called it war.[2]

But the situation was clear to Mishima. He at once sensed the coming of "the second Sino-Japanese War"—the first had occurred in 1894–95—"nay! the Second World War," he wrote in a brief essay, "Our Military in China." In impressive prose for a boy of twelve, he described an army fighting "its Holy War" near the Great Wall, then taking "the ferocious mountain battles" into Huairen. He imagined Japanese officers and soldiers drinking "muddy water" as they marched through "mountainous swamps," grappling with "120-degree burning, cruel heat." He thought of "the eagle's red eyes glowering beyond the Sea of Okhotsk," even as "the UNION JACK maintains a puzzling posture, darkly laughing." He ended the essay "praying for the health and military fortune" of the officers and their men.[3]

In December, the Japanese Army occupied the Chinese capital Nanjing and went on a rampage. The occupation was reported with fanfare. The Japanese back home took it to mean the termination of the war and held celebratory lantern parades all over Japan, but it merely expanded the war. The rampage part—called the Rape of Nanjing or Nanjing Massacre—was not known to most until after their country's defeat when "the Japanese newspapers carried, by order of the Occupation, full reports of the excesses and outrages committed by the Japanese Army and Navy" that were revealed during the proceedings of the International Tribunal for the Far East, as Elizabeth Gray Vining, Crown Prince Akihito's English tutor, put it.[4]

It was also that year, in the writer Tanabe Seiko's estimation in retrospect, that Japan's "modern culture" reached its zenith before "the war dumped water on it, made it shrivel, and wither." Among the writers Tanabe lists from the era, Kawabata Yasunari, whom Mishima would later choose as his mentor, published *Snow Country* (*Yukiguni*) that year.[5]

---

Earlier, in March, the government sent Azusa to tour Europe. How long his tour lasted or what the purpose was are not known, but Azusa brought back some art books, among other things.

As April, the month the new school year begins, approached, Sadatarō persuaded Natsuko to stop treating Mishima as her property separate from his two younger siblings whom she simply ignored: Mitsuko and Chiyuki. The boy was soon to be in junior high school—or the Middle Division as it was called at the Peers School—and was too old for that sort of thing, Sadatarō argued. Natsuko reluctantly agreed. Overjoyed, Shizue looked for a home for her family all over the city and finally found one in Ōyama-chō, in Shibuya: a two-story, outwardly Western-style house with a pointed, steep roof covered with red tiles, though all the rooms inside were covered with tatami flooring. The family moved in April, and would live in it for thirteen years, until the summer of 1950. Mishima was given a room on the second floor, which looked like an oversize gable, facing the street. The importance of having a room of his own, a new space, was immeasurable.

There was another significant event for the family that year: Azusa's removal from home in October. Promoted to director-general of forestry management in Osaka, he went to the assigned city alone, without his family. For a public servant or corporate employee to take up a distant post on assignment, domestic or foreign, without his family, was standard Japanese practice until the end of the twentieth century. This was a boon to Mishima—and to Shizue as well. As Shizue put it bluntly, "He's like my mother-in-law turned into a man exactly as she was, and I didn't like it at all." Both were nags; both were scolds.

There was a difference between the two, of course. If Natsuko treated Mishima like a fragile mechanical doll, though not doubting his intelligence for a moment, Azusa went in the opposite direction. "Resistance toughens a man," he averred with unshakable conviction. "That's why I treated him sternly." Mishima was terrified of Azusa. One day he was fiddling with the radio set with his brother, turning the tuner this way and that, removing the board at the back to peek into the mechanisms. The tuner stopped working properly. Angered, Azusa grabbed a wooden sword and threatened the two boys. Chiyuki quickly ran away. Mishima took a correct sitting position, knees bent, and apologized.

Azusa may have regretted that he had allowed his mother to bring up his son like a girl. To him, reading "literature" was an effeminate act when, to Mishima, it was the greatest salvation. Whenever Azusa caught his son reading a novel or anything of the sort, he would grab it, and toss it down on the floor. Liking cats was also "unmanly." Irritated that his son was fond of the cat the family kept, Azusa took it away someplace and abandoned it. When his son found another cat somewhere and brought him home, Azusa mixed iron powder in what the cat ate and boasted about it. His son would give up keeping a cat if one died, Azusa obviously reasoned. That, to Azusa, was "Spartan education."

## Twenty-Year-Old and Twelve-Year-Old

Not long after Azusa left for Osaka, the literary magazine of the Peers School, *Hojinkai Zasshi*, accepted five of Mishima's poems. One of them read:

### Autumn: Two Pieces[6]

*1*

When by my moonlit window crickets shirr,
when from the silvery seaside beach parasols disappear,
when the mountains and fields wearing a layer of green robe
change into golden lined clothes,
autumn's footfalls are heard.
Birds sensitive to cold, toward a land where oranges fruit,
those sensitive to heat, toward the Imperial Capital where
    heaters are longed for,
the sky reminiscent of an endless ocean
where small boats with red oars come and go,
the ripe persimmons are pecked at by the evil ones, the crows,
the shrikes screech their clumsy sopranos.
——Autumn at its prime.

*2*

From the vale
permeated with mysterious loneliness,
smoke from baking charcoal
comes up.
Columns of smoke,
unaware that they'll be buried
in small corners of the vast empty sky,
crawl up
longing for a painter's blue silk cloth.

A dog, one leg hurt, walks
away on the trail, limping.

The mouse a cat left unfinished
is on a mound of moist fallen leaves.

The rustle of dead leaves falling
on it
—is like a gray elegy.

A sign of a storm perhaps,
from between the mountains,
a black, giant-like cloud rises to its feet.

These poems prompted one senior student at the Peers School to seek Mishima out. He was Bōjō Toshitami, a third-year student at the Higher Division, which made him twenty years old. He had left the editorial board of the Literary Section a year earlier, but recommended publication of the poems in the *Hojinkai Zasshi*. Bōjō was not just Mishima's senior by eight years; he was an earl's son, with direct linkage to the blueblood Reizei and Irie families.

The Middle Division of the Peers School had periodic baseball games with the junior high school affiliated with a higher normal school nearby. As Bōjō recalled in the book he published a year after Mishima's death, he decided to look for Mishima in the midst of one of those games.

"It was very easy to spot the first-year students of the Middle Division in the cheerleaders' seats," Bōjō recalled. They were required to take part in those games as cheerleaders, who, with cheerleaders in higher grades, were grouped in one section. "Their school hats and badges were deliberately made to look soiled for an appearance of experience, but the freshness of the golden cherry blossoms in the collar insignias remained. Above all, with their high-pitched voices, they ceaselessly flitted about like birds. The first-year students weren't allowed to take leave from cheerleading."

He went to the section, tapped a first-year student on the shoulder, and asked, "Isn't there someone named Hiraoka Kōi?" Kōi was the sinified reading of the two Chinese characters for the name Kimitake, and Mishima's mother, among others, called him Kō-chan. The student spoken to turned round and snapped to attention. "Yes, sir, there is!" In Japan's school system in those days, the senior-junior order was as strict as the military ranks. As Bōjō noted, for the first-year students "the seniors were more intimidating than the teachers."

The student looked around. His eyes rested on the first row of benches where a group of students were making merry, snatching each other's hat. "There he is, sir. That pale fellow, sir."

"Would you mind fetching him for me?" Bōjō asked.

Mishima was obviously surprised that a senior not known to him had asked for him. "Through the throngs emerged a delicate boy, readjusting his hat. He had a thin neck, and his skin appeared snow-white," Bōjō recollected. "I am Hiraoka Kimitake, sir," the first-year student said.

Bōjō noticed Mishima's hat was a little too large for his head. Its bill came down close to his large eyes, which steadily looked at him.

"I am Bōjō, of the Literary Section," Bōjō introduced himself. Mishima apparently recognized his name. He appeared relieved, even happy. He looked so young that Bōjō did not use the masculine second person singular *kisama* that was standard at the Peers School, but the softer *kimi*. Bōjō took out a copy of *Sessen*, the magazine of the Literary Section.

"This one has my story in it. I'd be obliged if you read it. I have left my criticism of your poems in it, too."

Mishima shyly accepted the magazine and, when Bōjō nodded to signal dismissal, saluted, after a moment's hesitation. As he left, Bōjō imagined Mishima's classmates kidding him as the upperclassman's *chigo*, "lover boy." During the Edo Period and before, older men often indulged in having *chigo* around. At the Peers School at the time the *chigo* game was popular, not necessarily between older and younger boys, Bōjō wrote, making sure to add that the relationships so born were nothing like what you might imagine from the term "homosexual love."[7]

What prompted Bōjō to seek out Mishima was surely the extraordinary mastery of the Japanese language the twelve-year-old student showed in his poems. Sakai Hiroshi, one of the *Hojinkai* editors at the time and later a ranking official of the Bank of Japan, recalled the consternation and apprehension these and other submissions created among the editors, but especially in Toyokawa Noboru, the professor who nominally oversaw the magazine. A distinguished scholar of German philosophy and explicator of Kant and Rickert, among others, Toyokawa suspected they were plagiarisms and "set them aside"; they were too accomplished, some even too *steamy* for a first-year student of the Middle Division. So he told Sakai to look into the matter, and Sakai duly reported back that Mishima was in fact a first-year student, "all smiles and a little impish," and that there were no plagiarisms involved. Thereafter each *Hojinkai* issue carried Mishima's poems.[8]

Still, at least one such poem did not make it. A dozen years after the event, when the student newspaper of his alma mater asked him for an essay, Mishima wryly recollected how, when a student came to see him with the news of—he sensed at once—rejection, he suggested they print it using *fuseji*, that is, the number of characters of the offending word or phrase with an equal number of blank squares. With this practice, the reader so inclined could sometimes guess the original word or phrase. Censorship was routine at the time, and the prospect of seeing his poem in print, censored, excited him.

So he was let down when he learned the poem was rejected after all. It was an imitation of Jean Cocteau's short poem, Mishima wrote, and had a passage: "A port-town prostitute waits for her customers, her back against an electric pole. No customers come by. And the madame watching her from deep inside the store clucks her tongue."[9]

The following may well be the original, a poem in a collection with the English title, *Bad Poems*.

**Side Alley**[10]
Light-ink evening clouds
the sand of the striped sea
the lazy layer of the rough sea

power lines that skewer all landscapes,
under them, the nails of the woman bored of waiting
no light-pink but muddy amber

at the door behind her
the madame
glaring
clucks her tongue

"Poems came to him with utter ease, one after another, smoothly," Mishima wrote, when he was twenty-nine, in "The Boy Who Writes Poems" (*Shi o kaku shōnen*), an autobiographical story with the protagonist referred to as "the boy." "The thirty-page notebook with the name of the Peers School printed on it was immediately exhausted. Why do two or three poems a day come into being like this, the boy wondered. When he was laid up with illness for a week, he compiled an anthology called 'Collection of Poems for a Week.'" Mishima indeed left a collection with that title: poems written from May 12 to May 18, 1940, some days with three or more pieces, though it ends with one written on May 23, "Pastoral" (*Bokka*).[11]

"When he became ecstatic, a metaphorical world always materialized before his eyes," Mishima wrote, explaining how images overflowed.

> Caterpillars changed cherry leaves into laceworks, a thrown stone went over a bright oak to see the sea. A crane was messing up the wrinkled sheet, the sea, under a cloudy sky, looking for a drowned man under it. The peach a scarab approached wore light makeup, a running person had the disturbed, stagnant air clinging to him, like a flame on the back of a statue. The evening glow was an evil omen and had the color of thick iodine tincture. Winter trees had their artificial legs stretched into heaven. And the nude body of a girl by a fireplace looked like a burning rose but, when it walked up to the window, it was exposed to be an artificial flower, and her skin with goose pimples from the cold transformed itself into a petal of a flower made of shaggy velvet.

It is not just the ease with which poems formed in the mind of this teenager and the abundance of metaphors that came to it that astonish. The young man wrote more than five hundred poems, nearly two hundred haiku, and forty-five tanka, mostly in the four years from twelve until sixteen. These numbers alone would make anyone a respectable poet, but the poems are characterized by his early, ready mastery of syllabic patterns (comparable to metrical patterns in English versification)—a poem on a kitten he wrote when he was seven is made up of twelve lines, each line with seven syllables, the second six lines a variation of the first six, altogether a lovely lyric[12]—by his control and range in free verse, and, above all, by his command of language, classical and modern.

Among his early poems, in fact, there are many pieces he clearly wrote just to delight in knowing rarely used, difficult Chinese names (and characters) for ordinary plants, animals, birds, and such. He even wrote a four-stanza poem in English with the rhyme scheme of *aaaabbbbccccdddd*, a feat, certainly, if only because he wrote it in the second year after he started learning English. It comes with a Japanese version.[13] He translated Heine and Wilde. As with the case of Jean Cocteau, a great many of his poems were, it may be assumed, inspired by the wide range of readings that absorbed him. An academic investigator as well read as Mishima may have a heyday identifying the sources.

---

Mishima and Bōjō could meet at the school if they wanted to, and they sometimes did. Also, Bōjō occasionally invited Mishima to his spacious mansion, which was grand, as befit a noble house.[14] But the principal means of communication between them was letters. "The two of them exchanged long letters every day. The boy enjoyed the daily letter-writing task. Almost every morning R's apricot-colored Western-style envelope reached him," he writes in "The Boy." "R" is of course Bōjō. In this account the two correspondents are given as "a twenty-year-old youth and a fifteen-year-old boy." Mishima correctly decided that the actual age discrepancy of eight years would be too much even in a fictionalized account.

"No matter how thick a letter, its weight can't be much, but the lightness of the odd bulkiness of R's letters, the feeling that something light was packed into them, made the boy happy. At the end of their letters, they almost always wrote a recent poem, a piece just made that day, or, without either, an old poem.

"The content of their letters nonetheless was inconsequential," the boy continues to say. "They began with a criticism of the poem received in the previous letter, then moved on to endless chatter, as they wrote about the music they listened to, daily gossip about their families, the impressions of girls they thought beautiful, a report on a book read, the poetic experience in which a single word revealed the world of poetry, and detailed descriptions of last night's dreams."

Thus Mishima met someone to whom to convey his thoughts without worrying about anything else. Bōjō intended to be a writer and exchanged letters with a boy eight years younger because of his pride and confidence that he was the only one who recognized the boy's poetic talent. As Mishima wryly observes in "The Boy," the two became close because "R clearly regarded himself as a genius not treated as such and, despite the difference in age, recognized the boy as a genius, and geniuses had to become friends."

"The Boy" in the end has to do with a literary prodigy's awakening to the reality that "comic interventions always enter into such weighty matters as 'love' and 'life,' comic interventions without which you cannot live through 'life' and 'love.'" R confesses to the much younger man his sufferings as a consequence of his affair with a married woman, which his father, the earl, had discovered and put an end to. He talks about Goethe and *The Sorrows of Young Werther*, the affair between Prince Genji and his stepmother Empress Fujitsubo, Pelléas and Mélisande, Tristan and Iseult, la princesse de Clèves and le duc de Nemours, and such. But then, when he says his lover tells him his forehead is "very beautiful," the boy notices the forehead in question is too prominent to be beautiful and is struck by the dreadful but amusing thought that he himself may be living with similar illusions.

The autobiographical story was also an attempt, Mishima explained, to set down on paper how happy he was until he realized he was "a fake poet, or fake as a poet."[15] Or, as Bōjō put it with retrospective sophistication, at one point Mishima must have felt "embarrassed" because he could "excrete" any number of poems "effortlessly, naturally." At the Peers School in those days, Bōjō reflected years later, there often were "marvelous excretions that could not possibly be called creations. Mishima alone realized this."[16]

If that discovery was an embarrassment to Mishima, Bōjō had had his own a little earlier. Sometime in 1939 he visited Shiga Naoya, "the deity of fiction,"[17] to ask for a preface to a collection of short stories he and his fellow student Azuma Takashi had written—Azuma using his penname, Fumihiko, probably beginning with these stories—because his father's friend knew the famous author. Shiga declined, laconically noting, "Sentimental, I think."[18]

## *Kabuki Enters*

Four days after Mishima turned fourteen, on January 18, 1939, Natsuko died. She was sixty-four. He wrote a tanka:

> Over the wisteria trellis yellow jackets languorously fly criss-cross grandmother of high blood pressure having died[19]

The one great good Natsuko had done for Mishima before her death was to introduce him to kabuki. Natsuko was, Mishima said, "an old-fashioned daughter of a Tokugawa *hatamoto* and, even while liking American silent movies and kabuki actors, maintained feudalistic sentiments in daily life that are unthinkable today."[20] After agreeing to let him live with his parents, she perhaps thought she needed some explicit reason to treat him as she did. That may be why she decided to take him to kabuki, her favorite pastime. In a talk to a group of kabuki trainees at the National Theatre only a few months before his suicide, Mishima explained how kabuki-going came about in an endearing way.

"When I was a child, my parents and grandfather and grandmother were all strange people," Mishima told the aspiring kabuki actors with lively gestures, spiritedly. "Kabuki is no good for a child's education, don't see it, they said. It has obscene things in it, so don't see it. Movies are all right. Movies are healthy, so go right ahead and see them. I didn't know what was healthy about them, but thanks to all that, after I was a second or third grader in grammar school, I saw most of the Hollywood movies.... The Hollywood movies weren't as sensual as they are today, but they had kissing scenes, and those were far more direct than the lovemaking scenes of kabuki.

"When I was thirteen years old, they must have decided, Well now, now he's in junior high school, it should be all right to show him kabuki. So my grandmother took me, for the first time. And it turned out to be *Kanadehon chūshingura.*"[21] *Kanadehon chūshingura*, originally written for jōruri or puppet theater and then turned into a kabuki, is based on the famous vendetta of forty-seven samurai at the start of the eighteenth century, which, in a range of variations, went on to become the best-loved samurai narrative in Japan.

Once she started, Natsuko took Mishima to kabuki once every

month, though if his first visit to kabuki took place in October 1938, as it was supposed to, Natsuko managed to take him to kabuki only a couple of times before she died. Regardless, Mishima wasn't a reluctant companion. He loved every minute of what he saw. In fact, he would continue to see kabuki regularly, until he wrote *Confessions of a Mask*. Along the way he read all the major jōruri and kabuki plays, becoming a "kabuki maniac." He developed such a deep affinity with these theatrical genres that several of the more than seventy dramas he wrote were kabuki, including the last full-length one.

Mishima developed equal affinity with the other traditional theater, nō, as a result of, shall we say, familial competition. Shizue's mother, Tomiko, was a student of the Kanze school of nō chanting, and she started taking Mishima to nō when she saw that Natsuko was taking him to kabuki. The first nō play he thus saw was one of "the divine category," *Miwa*, which centers on the argument that the two sacred shrines Miwa and Ise are one and the same. The fact that the first kabuki he saw was the Grand Introduction (*daijo*) of *Chūshingura* and the first nō was *Miwa* led him to realize that "I was blessed with the special favors of Japan's deity of performing arts."[22]

---

With Natsuko's death, Mishima's love of his mother lost its single obstacle and became complete—even, to a third party, "incestuous." Yuasa Atsuko, who became a friend of his in his late twenties, recalled seeing him express unabashed concern if Shizue said something like "Kōi-san, Mommy's foot hurts," and lick the part of her foot where she indicated the hurt was—doing this in total disregard of other people who were there, including his father, Azusa.

What would startle anyone who was new to such a scene was Shizue's language as much as her son's behavior: she referred to herself as *o-kā-chama*, a child's sweet, polite word for mother.[23] Mishima's love for Shizue remained intense throughout his life. This came out most clearly, in the form of public statement, when he was interviewed on TBS for its series on various people talking about their mothers. "My grandmother brought me up, she took care of me for a long time," he said, "so I was a granny kid. Because of that, once I began living with my mother, I was ready to be spoiled by her."

"In my junior high school days I once wrote a composition called 'Hydrangea,' à la Izumi Kyōka, and was scolded by my teacher," he recalled. Kyōka wove stories about people retaining Edo mannerisms and attitudes in a sinuous, old-fashioned Japanese least affected by the Western syntax—a writer who "realized one of the supreme possibilities that lyrical and at the same time painterly Japanese prose can attain, in tone, in flavor, and in closeness."[24] Mishima read him from a very young age because Natsuko, who had urged him to "read classics and write a lot," was partial to his writings. Natsuko also had studied German and French with private tutors.

"My story was that a pretty woman with a Japanese hairdo steps out from behind the hydrangeas in the garden," Mishima explained. "At first I can't tell who she is, until I realize she's my mother." Dated about ten days before he turned fifteen, it is not just an improbably accomplished recreation of Kyōka's style. It elegantly evokes a languid childhood day. It is also another piece of writing in which Natsuko is described in some detail.[25]

"I'm her son and I shouldn't be saying something like this perhaps, but my mother was very pretty since her youth," Mishima added. "At school, if your mother is young and pretty, you tend to feel proud. So, comparing the mothers of any of my friends' with mine, I often thought, 'They deserve them.'"[26]

Shizue, who when young aspired to be a poet, was his secret conspirator in the matter of writing as well. Azusa ostentatiously despised literature, proclaiming it was no way to make a proper living. He would tear up his son's writings whenever he found them. Shizue, the only one to console him, would secretly supply him with new batches of paper.

Shizue also read everything he wrote. From junior high school onward, Mishima showed her all of his writings before publishing them, a routine he kept up to the very end, except for nonfiction writings, which he stopped showing her a few years before his death.[27]

---

How was Azusa doing in Osaka? He was indulging himself with women while remaining an oddball bureaucrat. Or, as author Nosaka Akiyuki has reported, Azusa, while in the post of director-general of forest management in Japan's second largest city, "squandered money on a Western-style dancer and had a woman with whom he was intimate at a small store in the Fukuhara Brothel Quarters in Kobe." Nosaka adds: "He also haunted teahouses in Soemon-chō, Hanakuma, and Ponto-chō, and behaved wantonly." The three places named here were the famous pleasure quarters in Osaka, Kobe, and Kyoto. Ponto-chō, in Kyoto, still is.

Nosaka debuted with *The Pornographers* (*Irogotoshi*), in 1963, which was translated into English at Mishima's recommendation and published by Alfred Knopf. Nosaka decided to trace the history of his own family to write about Mishima when someone claiming possession of Mishima's unpublished diaries approached him to sell them. The result, *The Brilliant Backlight* (*Kakuyaku-taru gyakkō*), is a unique attempt to illuminate Mishima and his family against the backdrop of Nosaka's own complicated life and family relations that included living with an adoptive grandmother.

"On his payday, [Azusa] would hand all the restaurant bills to his secretary and have them paid, leaving not a penny" of his salary, Nosaka tells us, although, typical of Japanese biographers, he does not specify where his various, vivid information came from. Government officials of Azusa's rank in those days were paid handsomely, and "he would declaim, My parents are rich, all this is just pocket money. A government official has to be *bourgeois* or his wife's family has to be terribly rich. Otherwise, you can't work for the government." In truth, by then Sadatarō and Natsuko were living on Sadatarō's government pension of two hundred yen a month and were far from rich. Shizue's parents were not rich, either.

Who, then, took care of the expenses of Azusa's family back in Tokyo? His cousins, Hiraoka Yoshiaki and Ono Shigeru.

Back in 1933, when he was director of rice, Azusa had helped Ono Shigeru—Mume's third son who had been adopted by another sake brewer and acquired the surname Ono—when the latter became independent in the warehousing business in Yokohama. He used his bureaucratic prerogatives to have him handle rice imported from Taiwan and Korea, both Japanese colonies, providing him with foundations for his own firm. When Shigeru made his older brother Yoshiaki the head of his Kobe branch, Azusa helped him as well.

In fact, while Azusa was stationed in Osaka, Yoshiaki was not just

Azusa's regular companion for nightly outings but he also took care of most of those pleasure expenses—and, with Shigeru, the expenses of Azusa's family. Azusa would often stay in his house talking until the wee hours of the morning—he was a good raconteur in his own way with a fancy vocabulary and witticisms—rather than in the hotel designated for men of his rank, called in English The Pine Crest, which he favored over his official residence. (After the war, Nosaka worked awhile at The Pine Crest that the Occupation requisitioned.)

Nosaka wrote that Azusa was "timid" but "of a so-called government official's temperament." He could be generous and helpful when he wanted to; but he could also be intolerably arrogant to those whom he regarded as beneath him. Azusa would bluntly tell Yoshiaki that he, a son of a sake brewer without much education, wasn't good enough to be in his company, even while shamelessly sponging on him. Yoshiaki went along because associating with a high-ranking bureaucrat gave him an air of prestige and economically benefited him.[28]

In his recollections of his son, Azusa quotes one of the letters he wrote during his Osaka days. Evidently, sometime earlier some writers had visited with the family and called Mishima "a genius," "precocious," "kind of creepy," and "weird," for Azusa begins by urging his son to "reflect on it," to wit, to change his ways. He explained his incongruous mixture of baby talk by saying he called his son *bōya*, "baby boy," in the letter because that was how he and his wife called him and he felt resistant to suddenly switching to Kōi, the name they used in referring to him as a third party.

> Mommy wrote Poppy, angry with me, repeating *many many* times how wrong was the way our baby boy was brought up. But there's no use bringing up the past at this late date. The only thing you can do is to think *hard* about the present and the future. Can't you decide to leave literature for a while and, because, fortunately, you have a good brain, to use that brain in the direction of physics, machinery, or chemistry? If you thrust your dedicated training *hard* in that direction, I think you can be someone considerable. Think fully. Our baby boy's present circumstances worry both Poppy and Mommy so we almost cry, though we don't show it.

Azusa then asks: "Can't you make up your mind about recanting? Don't you want to grow up a fine boy in Japan at this historic turning point?"[29]

The word "recant" (*tenkō*), which Azusa used apparently without irony, pointed to a phenomenon that had marked a crucial era in Japan's intellectual history in the first half of the twentieth century. In June 1933, Sano Manabu, chairman of the Japan Communist Party, and Nabeyama Sadachika, another Communist leader, both in jail, issued a joint statement addressed to their "defendant comrades" severely criticizing the JCP's "1932 Thesis" that faithfully adopted the slogans of the International Comintern. The two men did not use the word "recant," but the rejection of the official goals of USSR-led International Communism was tantamount to it, and the word "recant" soon became a popular word, with 133 out of 393 people in jail and 415 out of 1,370 people in detention following suit within a month.[30]

Behind the leaders' change of heart that touched off the collapse of the Communist movement in Japan was the savage persecution of Communists and their sympathizers under the Public Security Maintenance Law, enacted in 1925: repeated interrogation, detention, imprisonment, and torture. The writer Kobayashi Takiji, for one, died, in February that year, as a result of torture by the police.[31]

---

In citing the letter, Azusa doesn't give its date, but by the time he wrote it, his son certainly was doing far better than in the six-year Elementary Division of the Peers School where he had hovered in the middle of his class. There, what had stood out was that he was a weakling. His motor coordination was poor and he was a drag on his class in athletic exercises. Because he was skinny and pale, his classmates called him *Aojiro*, "Pale-blue"; *Aobyōtan*, "Pale Bottle Gourd"; *Shirakko*, "Albino Kid"[32]—although, as far as such things go, the oft-quoted story must be repeated: When a prankster once challenged him, "Hey, Pale-blue, your balls got to be pale-blue, too!" thereupon Mishima unbuttoned his pants and pulled out his stuff and pressed it on the boy, making him cringe. It was "unexpectedly large," a bystander reported.[33]

Mishima's writings, at any rate, were different. At the time of graduation, his teacher, noting his ability to write, suggested he become a "doctor of literature," but "not anything like a novelist." Hirohito, the Tennō, attended the graduation ceremony.

In the Middle Division, Mishima began to do even better in writing, although in the first year he was far below average in the class of eighty, barely squeaking through the grade. That year, however, the teacher of Japanese was Iwata Kurō, who would establish his reputation as an authority on Edo haikai after the war. He had his own haiku and tanka group called *Mokusei* (Fragrant Olive) and took his class on haiku excursions. At one tanka gathering, Mishima's pieces were singled out for praise.

In the third year, Shimizu Fumio, who would soon become Mishima's literary guide and mentor, had his students compose haiku and wrote out good pieces on the blackboard along with their writers' names. One of the haiku came with the name Blue-castle. The class guffawed. Even with a different set of Chinese characters, its reading was the same: *Aojiro*. Mishima had turned the nickname of mild ridicule to a romantic haiku penname. Haiku writers routinely adopt pennames. Still, overwhelmed by his classmates' reaction, he kept his head down during the class.[34]

Here are two of his haiku that appeared in the *Hojinkai Zasshi* with the tag of "Blue-castle."

In an autumn wind a sickly child points to the evening sun

In an autumn wind a man standing by the window does not move[35]

Through the Middle Division he gained self-confidence, even as his ranking fluctuated from year to year. In the third year he was seventh in the class of seventy; in the fourth year, sixteenth in the class of sixty-seven; in the fifth year, second in the class of sixty. His writing ability was impressive—and impressed his teachers. His paper assessing Itō Einosuke's *The Bush Warbler* (*Uguisu*) elicited from his teacher, most likely Iwata, this comment: "I have not read *The Bush Warbler* yet, but this paper makes me feel I am thoroughly familiar with the whole story. It is so thoughtfully detailed." Another paper assessing Tanizaki Jun'ichirō's *Yoshino Kudzu* (*Yoshino kuzu*) prompted Iwata to write, this time his name signed: "This gives the sense of having savored the master's skills with a perfect understanding and an artistic appreciation. It makes me feel in many ways that only this writer [i.e., Mishima] could manage this observation and expression."[36]

Mishima showed his growing confidence toward Bōjō. The tall senior of high-ranking aristocratic lineage may have been great to look up to when he approached him, but in time Mishima became keenly aware of his own worth and turned deliberately assertive where he was expected to be deferential.

"In truth," he wrote in "The Boy Who Writes Poems," "[the boy] did not even think much of R's talent. Among the seniors in the Literary Club"—responsible for the *Hojinkai Zasshi*—"R certainly had a conspicuous talent, but it wasn't as if his words had a special weight in the boy's mind. In the boy's mind there was a cold spot. If R had not used all sorts of words to praise his poetic talent, the boy probably would not have recognized R's talent."

"Even though people's praise pleased him, his arrogance saved him from getting drowned in it," Mishima said of his younger self. "For example, one of his quatrains that the seniors praised extravagantly was, he thought, lightheaded and embarrassing. The poem said, in sum, 'Because the cut section of transparent glass is so blue, your limpid eyes will be able to store many an affair of the heart.'"[37]

Such things were extending to matters of which he had little knowledge. Once, Bōjō showed Mishima a story he wrote, "Dance" (*Mai*), and asked him to critique it. It had to do with an illicit affair in which an Imperial University student has a series of assignations with a married woman in a villa in the resort town of Karuizawa. Bōjō, an earl's heir, intended the story to embody the world of *aware*—a heightened sensibility to the transience of things that was thought to represent the essence of the grand court romance *The Tale of Genji*—and set it against the backdrop of the increasingly militaristic, regimented Japan of the day. Japan at the time was transplanting Nazi Germany's notion of *Volk*, among others, renaming *shōgakkō*, "elementary school," to *kokumin gakkō*, perhaps in imitation of *Volksschule*. The word *kokumin*, though it had existed since ancient China, may well have added the sense of *Reichsbürger* in the late 1930s, and it began to be applied to other things as well, which, along with *kokubō*, "national defense," right-minded civilians were expected to adopt with patriotic zeal.

"Item: *kokumin* uniform, item: *kokubō* color. The battle hat. *Enthu-*

*siastic boy*," Bōjō wrote in "Dance." The original for *enthusiastic boy* is *harikiri boy*, a combination of Japanese and English words when the stress on patriotism driven by militarism was extending to a xenophobic preference for Japanese. "*Kokumin* ceremonials. All this series of horrible things were surely out to insult me, my literature, not to mention our ancestors, our country. And so I did not read newspapers. I simply did not want to look at such a society. I confined myself deep in my own shell, hoping to protect the world of *aware* single-mindedly. If I could, I thought I would fight such a society." Bōjō was certainly going against the current.

At any rate, as he read "Dance," Mishima would point out things such as "This kind of conversation can't happen" and "This kind of scenery can't happen"—observations that bewildered Bōjō. "You say these things can't happen," he protested. "Fact is, these things did happen. There is no way of gainsaying them. This is realism, pure and simple," he was driven to point out. "Dance" was a scarcely veiled autobiographical account. He had written the story with Mishima as reader in mind. Reflecting on the matter years later, Bōjō realized that in "The Boy" Mishima had omitted one crucial part of the point he had made. He had told Bōjō, "*In our literary world*"—that is, in the literary world you and I are creating—"this kind of conversation can't happen." Mishima stubbornly tried to persuade him to change the conversation.[38]

Bōjō, by then twenty-four or five, had sexual experience. Mishima, at fifteen or sixteen, still had nothing of the sort. As he pointed out in a series of candid talks on sex during his puberty he gave for the monthly *Myōjō* when he was thirty-two, there were, for one thing, at the Peers School two types of students: "stiffs" and "softies." Stiffs were stern moralists. Softies, mainly progenies of the upper crust of the aristocracy, were those who indulged in immoral or licentious conduct. Bōjō was a softie, though he was by no means an extreme type. Mishima, coming up far behind, barely knew what sex was. He was still in "a period of early boyhood when [the elements of] heterosexual and homosexual love [were] extremely mixed."

There was a good deal of knowing, blatant sex talk among his friends at the Middle Division—such as whether or not a photo of Deanna Durbin showed her sanitary belt under her shorts—but when it came to the real thing, Mishima was naïveté itself, however precocious he may have appeared in literary matters. For example, on the evening of the day when Mishima's family, along with relatives, went to Tokyo Station to see Azusa off to Osaka, he happened to find himself left alone with a very beautiful second cousin, sitting face to face with her in chairs, in the guest room of his house after everyone came home, "happy with the sense of liberation." Suddenly, the cousin, who was older by five or six years, cried, "Oh, I'm so tired," bent forward, and put her face on his lap. How "glad, fearful, and indescribably touched" he was, even though she did not keep her head on his knees for more than a minute!

So, "fragments of the sensation I received from the opposite sex may have come from my knees," he recalled. In those days, any self-respecting junior high school boy was supposed to have a "bus romance"—"'a girl you often see on a bus' was an image everyone must have." It was not difficult to spot an appropriate girl.

"I began to look forward to sitting next to a certain girl on a bus I took to school.... And if, by some accident, I sat next to her, the warmth of her knee that touched mine had an indescribably mysterious feeling and remained with me for a long time. And of course I didn't speak to her, didn't say hello to her, and we remained strangers to the end."[39]

Yet, without any experience of sex, without falling in love even once, "the boy" who wrote poems began to "increasingly handle love affairs as material for his poems." And "by some illogical conviction, he was able to believe that there was not one sentiment he had not experienced in this world," he wrote in the autobiographical story.

CHAPTER FOUR

# Literary Correspondents

*The writer of "The Forest in Full Bloom" is an utterly young man.*

—Hasuda Zenmei

In late 1940, Mishima received a letter that said: "To be honest, as someone whose works appear in the same magazine side by side with yours, you daunted me. Simply because I'm older by a few years doesn't mean I can behave like a big shot."[1] The writer was Azuma Takashi, the student who a year before had attempted to obtain a preface to a joint collection of stories with Bōjō from Shiga Naoya. The letter was dated November 30. *Hojinkai Zasshi* that month had carried Mishima's short story, "Tinted Glass" (*Damie garasu*), and Azuma wrote to praise the story, with some criticism.

"Tinted Glass" describes two couples, one middle-aged, the other young: Vice Admiral, Shipbuilding (Ret.),[2] Baron Munakata Teinosuke, who, while he acts young, is fearful of death in fact; his beautiful wife, Akiko; his nephew, Kennosuke, who comes to live with the couple (his father being stationed in Singapore); and the girl the nephew is in love with, Satomi Noriko, who, on her part, appears to be resentful of the fact that she is in love with the young man. The baron is aware that he is jealous of his nephew's youth.

The story, which attempts to superimpose the bygone youth of the older couple with the present youth of the younger couple through a garter belt (the era is that of flapper dresses), may not be entirely successful, but it surely and startlingly is so mature, so sophisticated, laden as it is with aphoristic observations, that it would have been a surprise had it not grabbed the attention of another aspiring but older writer. In reprinting it in the same *Hojinkai Zasshi* seven years later, Mishima himself wrote, "I doubt whether this writer has made any progress since."[3]

Azuma, who had graduated from the Middle Division top of his class, in 1938, was, like Bōjō, Mishima's senior, though in his case only by five years. Like Bōjō, he was an editor of the *Hojinkai Zasshi*, but by the time he wrote Mishima he was in an advanced state of laryngeal tuberculosis and had been bedridden for more than a year, forcing him to write, with his doctor's reluctant consent, while lying on his back. Mishima would correspond with him as eagerly as he did with Bōjō, but with Azuma that was practically the only means of communication. Indeed, Azuma's disease being highly infectious, few were allowed even to enter his room. Mishima was permitted to do so probably only once before Azuma's death on October 8, 1943, when, rushing to the Azuma house, he spent the night by his dying friend's side. He wrote two pieces on the event, one the following night, "Aggrieved over My Older Brother Azuma Takashi," and the other two nights later, in classical language, "A Funeral Tribute to Azuma Fumihiko."[4]

It was in his letters to Azuma that Mishima's literary precocity and his wide range of reading became evident. Indeed, the publication, in 1999, of these letters as Mishima's letters in his teens struck the literary world as a startling revelation.[5] The same must have been equally or even more evident in his letters to Bōjō, but Bōjō destroyed most of Mishima's letters from those years. When, in the spring of 1942, Azuma's father, concerned about his son's illness, suggested starting a members' magazine as a means of publishing his writings, Azuma invited Mishima, along with Tokugawa Yoshiyasu to join him,[6] but not Bōjō. The magazine was named *Akae*, the word meaning porcelain mainly tinted red.

For a glimpse of what Mishima read, we may examine a letter he wrote on January 21, 1941, a week after he told Azuma that he turned sixteen. It was apparently a response to Azuma's request to sum up his "literary life."

"During my Elementary Division days," he wrote, "I was infatuated with fairy tales by Bimei and Strindberg and loved to read collections of fairy tales from India." Ogawa Bimei, who began by writing gloomy novels under the influence of naturalism, opened a new frontier when he turned to children's stories, a genre being cultivated around 1920, by "starting to weave into daily life the world of fantasy," thereby "biting into you much more deeply," in fifteen-year-old Mishima's judgment.[7] The prolific Swedish author Johan Strindberg was known not only for his naturalistic plays and novels, but also for his children's stories.

Since he began writing poems "seriously" in sixth grade, Mishima went on to note, he had read, "in the order of absorption," Kitahara Hakushū, the most versatile among the prewar poets as far as poetic forms are concerned, who was accorded the title of "the national poet"; Oscar Wilde; French poets via Horiguchi Daigaku's translations assembled in *A Pack under the Moon* (*Gekka no ichigun*), a milestone in modern poetry translation, published in 1925; contemporary Japanese poets such as Maruyama Kaoru, a lyric poet in the Shiki (Four Seasons) School, and Kusano Shinpei, an anarchist poet in the proletarian movement. At the end of his letter, Mishima added Miyazawa Kenji, saying, "I deeply felt his greatness and thought of the clarity of Japan's Dadaism."

Miyazawa, whose second series of collected works, in seven volumes, was slowly coming out at the time, had published just one book of poems before his death, *Spring and Asura* (*Haru to shura*), though that single book had electrified those who read it. Here was someone, the poet Satō Sōnosuke wrote, who "wrote poems with meteorology, mineralogy, botany, and geology."[8]

In fiction, Mishima was "gradually absorbed by Wilde, read Tanizaki thoroughly, was moved by *Le bal du Comte d'Orgel*, and, before then, was infatuated with Akutagawa, came to know Morand," and now was "on friendly terms with *Swann's Way*," Mishima wrote. "At one time I was fascinated by the *setsuwa* style, and at the end of the year I became a freshman in the Middle Division, I started translating *Ōkagami* (*The Great Mirror*). That was enjoyable work. It continued on to 'Mansion' (*Yakata*)."

The term *setsuwa* style is amorphous, but Mishima evidently referred to "oral narrative" mode. Tanizaki refined a first-person narrative in which someone who (at times) is not highly literate describes his life in plebeian language. He had written a string of stories in that mode, beginning with Mishima's favorite at the time, *The Blind's Tale* (*Mōmoku monogatari*), published in 1932. It is told by a non-historical blind masseur of his devotion to a historical figure, O-Ichi-no-kata (1547?–83), a beautiful woman who became a pawn in her warlord brother Oda Nobunaga's strategic moves. Akutagawa based some of his stories on homiletic tales collected in the *Tales of Times Now Past* (*Konjaku monogatari*), of the twelfth century, and other ancient tales.

The eleventh-century court chronicle *The Great Mirror*, which covers the period from 850 to 1025, seems unlikely to be the sort of thing a boy in his early teens, however literarily precocious, would choose for translation, albeit into the modern version of his own language. But his was not an idle boast. Mishima was enchanted by the text his father had kept from a First Higher School course—despite his injunction against his son's literary endeavor, Azusa had been infatuated with literature when young, as Mishima noted in another letter[9]—and, though it was only skimpily annotated, he decided to translate it. When he was done with the first quarter or so, a fully annotated edition came out and he found his translation was riddled with errors. But there were at least two results of this endeavor: "Mansion," which he mentions, and "Retired Emperor Kazan" (*Kazan-in*), a school composition that he submitted about the time he wrote Azuma the letter we are looking at.

"Mansion," a novella the *Hojinkai Zasshi* had printed a year earlier, is made up of a court page's observations of his master, a marquis in some imagined Western land. The story does not really cohere, in part because it is left unfinished, and perhaps because its protagonist's sadistic behavior was too much for a fourteen-year-old boy to handle. Mishima himself called it "a pity, a failure." He did so in his letter referring to his father's infatuation with literature when young—"but now his favorite books are stuff like *Seven Mysteries of Europe* (*Sept mystères du destin de l'Europeis*) and *Tragedy in France* (*Tragédie en France*) and all he talks about is 'Nazis, Nazis, Nazis'!"[10]

"Retired Emperor Kazan," based on a passage in the chronicle *The Great Mirror*, shows Mishima's sure command of classical Japanese. His teacher, noting that it would be the last time he would check Mishima's compositions, gave it high marks, though with a warning that its content might no longer be appropriate in the time of rising militaristic fever. Mishima completed the manuscript on February 16, 1941.[11]

Mishima added: "I also enjoyed *The Pillow Book*. In spring last year, I wrote a fiction à la Radiguet's *Le Diable au corps* and was at once assaulted by self-loathing."[12] Raymond Radiguet had a special place in

Mishima's mind and would continue to do so in the years that followed. Most likely some months before he wrote this letter, he had written what might be called a scholarly assessment of the French writer on the basis of all the Japanese translations available at the time.[13]

The war with the West engulfed Japan soon and "because the genius Radiguet died at twenty and left such a masterpiece"—*Le bal du Comte d'Orgel*—"I put myself, who was bound to die at twenty in the war, into Radiguet's image and turned him into my rival by using the novel as a goal to catch up with," Mishima wrote years later.[14] Or, as he put it more innocuously: "How nice it would be if I could somehow write such a masterpiece before I turned twenty and die at twenty," although he noted that what had mesmerized him about the story was not so much the French writer's "psychologically penetrating eye" as "the uniquely dry *elegance*" of Horiguchi Daigaku's translation.[15] It was also through Horiguchi's translation of *Ouvert la nuit* that Mishima came to know Paul Morand. The French diplomat and Modernist's influence via Horiguchi is palpable in "Tinted Glass."[16]

Mishima's story imagining Radiguet's death, written in 1953 and called just that, takes the form of Jean Cocteau remembering the short-lived novelist's last days with him—the young man unable to focus on the proofs of *Le bal du Compte d'Orgel*, because of the typhus he contracted.

## *The World of Sexual Perversion*

Among Mishima's other remarks on his literary odyssey as a young man, one deserves special mention. In his letter to Azuma toward the end of the year, he brought up Inagaki Taruho. "Having read Inagaki Taruho's *Sanpūko*," Mishima wrote, "I can't help thinking, just the way you, sir, feel about Miyazawa Kenji and Makino Shin'ichi: Wow, if only I could write such dandy, madcap dreams!"

Born in 1900 and moonstruck by the advent of the aeroplane and cinema, Inagaki debuted, in the early 1920s, as a combination of "astronomer of fairy tales, aesthetist of celluloid, and spring-driven mechanical engineer," as Satō Haruo, the first to recognize the writer, aptly put it. He was an oddball artist who emerged in the maelstrom of the onrush into Japan of "Futurism, Cubism, Expressionism, Dadaism,

Suprematism, Constructivism, and Precisionism," which, among other things, prompted a group of writers, including Kawabata Yasunari and Yokomitsu Riichi, to speak of the creation of "a new sensibility." The group was later so labeled, the New Sensibility School.[17]

Partly as a result, Inagaki spelled his name, in Roman alphabet, as *Inaguaqui Taroupho* (here we will retain the standard spelling). Makino Shin'ichi, who had hanged himself, in 1936, was "rather close to Taruho," Mishima would write thirty years later, "in his fantasy of Western Europe transmuted to Japanese clime and land, his intellectual humor, his escape from the I-novel by way of a flight in his spiritual life."[18]

"Things Mr. Inagaki has been publishing in magazines of late have much dulled in color when compared with his old works (although they are so *unique* as to defy any comparison with the usual stories we find around us)," the sixteen-year-old literary assessor continued. "But he is someone who has failed to mature into a great writer, always badly treated as he was with foolish Confucian-style criticisms from the outset."

Mishima then quoted the critic Hisano Toyohiko as saying, "Mr. Inagaki Taruho's literature is not, to exaggerate somewhat, the sort of literature that can grow up in a literary world as boorish as that of Japan. How could his works be correctly understood by Japanese literary critics who are like brainless *sankaku*?"—the word, meaning triangle, here used in the sense of *fool*, rather like the English word *square*—"There is something that at first blush is terribly *kindlich* in his works. But that is an excessively superficial view. If his literature were nurtured in the literary world of France, for example, it would have managed an extraordinary development because of his genius."

Indeed, Inagaki's debut work, in 1922, *One Thousand and One-Second Stories* (*Issen ichibyō monogatari*), was a collection of "dandy, madcap dreams," short-shorts that are casual mixtures of the fantastic and the real. In contrast, the eight stories collected in *Sanpūko* are much more realistic as they are largely autobiographical. As a matter of fact, the word *sanpūko* is a *yijing* term referring to the time of year, Inagaki explained, when "worms germinate as the winds are pressed down at the base of mountains. In such an autumn, a man of honor determines to undertake a great reform and sees to it that he carries it out to the end." Reform aside, the title story depicts a disintegrating family with its narrator a perpetual, excessive drunkard.[19]

Mishima ended his comment on *Sanpūko* by noting that "the work such as 'Favorite'"—one of the stories in the selection, with the title given in English—"reminds me of *Les Enfants terribles*."[20] "Favorite" describes an adolescent boy's indirect and, shall we say, perverse sexual fascinations, including those of homosexual varieties. The opening paragraph typifies them.

> In the guest room hung a framed painting. It is a picture of a girl and her kid brother crossing a field in full bloom. She's got a briar thorn in her thigh. So she has tucked up her skirt and, revealing her snow-white part, is having her brother remove the thorn, her face expressing what appears to be painful, ticklish, and at any rate agreeable.... Watching the painting like that every day, the boy in time began to wish to savor the kind of feeling such as that within the girl of the picture. And, fearful of becoming sunburned, he would never go out; it was his wont to be absently looking out the window, with light makeup secretly put on. One such day, a sailor with a skinny belly, with a white hat perched askew on his head, passed by and, startled to notice the beautiful boy in the room, stopped, and beckoned him, smiling. The boy went to an inn with the sailor. It was the first time he became so embarrassed, but it was at the same time the first time he was so happy.

Inagaki's narrator tells the reader that what he has just said comes from a book and that the book also contains a description of a retired French sergeant who was found dead by hanging in his bachelor flat, his outlandish getup clearly indicating a botched attempt to satisfy his sadomasochistic impulses. He does not say what the book is but does say, parenthetically, that it often refers to Richard von Krafft-Ebing, the Austro-German sexologist and psychiatrist. Then, before moving on to describe his own experiences of varying sexual shade as a boy about to turn twelve, he confides: "Other than these stories, the several episodes he found in the same book, Tari"—the protagonist—"felt, offered the key to the problems entangled at the bottom of his heart."[21]

This stirred Mishima. In a letter a month and a half later, he reported to Azuma that he was reading Otto Weininger's *Sex and Character* and finding it "extremely interesting," adding that he regretted the volume covering the second half was missing.

That letter also gives another example of Mishima as a close, astute reader at age sixteen. Commenting on the two short stories Azuma sent with his letter, "Tree-searing Wind" (*Kogarashi*), which concerns a small group of young people at a riding arena, and "Winterscape" (*Fuyugeshiki*), which concerns a young man prone to fevers inadvertently put in a mental hospital, Mishima praised the former as "a fine wash drawing" and the latter as "an appropriate *dessin*"—the French word often used in the sense of *vignette* in Japan. Especially in "Winterscape," both form (description) and content (scenes described) perfectly "matched," he observed.

Still, if he were allowed to "wish for something better when you already have a good thing"—here he used an ancient Chinese idiom—what is missing might be "a poetic touch," the sixteen-year old told the writer, his senior by five years. Also, "The Bodhidharma suddenly started laughing," a simile for the "ugly smile" of an idiot girl in the hospital, might be unexpected, but not "eerie" enough, though that may be because of his "'House of Usher' fantasy," and so forth.[22]

Assuming that in his letter Mishima was quoting the Bodhidharma passage verbatim, Azuma took Mishima's comments on the Bodhidharma simile seriously, for in the final version of "Winterscape," which he noted he completed in November 1942, a year after Mishima's letter, the passage reads: "Besides, because [the idiot girl] had her face brimming with an ugly smile and had her red cape rolled up to her head, her figure had an unworldly eeriness as if Bodhidharma the Great Teacher in the picture had removed his jaw and suddenly started laughing."[23]

"Winterscape" was accepted by the *Mita Bungaku*, the magazine of Keiō University that had started in 1910, with Nagai Kafū as editor-in-chief, and saw print in its February 1943 issue. The magazine had accepted and printed another of Azuma's stories a year earlier.[24]

## *Hasuda Zenmei and National Learning*

Hiraoka Azusa returned from Osaka to Tokyo in October. By then Mishima's literary prowess had impressed people other than the editors of a school magazine. "The Forest in Full Bloom," which he had completed during the summer, had begun to be serialized in the September issue of *Bungei Bunka*, the magazine of his teacher Shimizu Fumio and his associates.

Shimizu, who had become an instructor of Japanese grammar and composition at the Peers School, in 1938, was soon afterward struck by a thirteen-year-old student's story, "Sorrels." The student was Hiraoka Kimitake. Four years later, in May 1941, the same student brought him a seventy-page manuscript. It was "The Forest in Full Bloom." "That night," Shimizu wrote, "after the dorm students went to sleep, I read it in one sitting. As I read, I savored the sensation of something asleep inside me being violently awakened."

At the time he was serving as one of the two superintendents of the school's Seiun (Constellation) Dormitory. Although Mishima never became a boarder at any of the dorms—his parents feared that he might acquire "the bad habit" if allowed to live with boys—it was while Shimizu was dorm superintendent there that Mishima developed what he called a "teacher-disciple" relationship with him. Recalling much later the days when Mishima used to visit him at the dorm, Shimizu wrote: "I often saw, through the window of my superintendent's room, the pale-faced, skinny figure of Mr. Hiraoka approach, holding a school bag by one hand, through the stand of zelkova trees between the drill hall and the gymnasium."[25]

Shimizu strongly recommended the novella for publication in *Bungei Bunka*, the group magazine of which he was one of the four founders. In a meeting held in July, the three others—Hasuda Zenmei, Ikeda Tsutomu, and Kuriyama Riichi—were equally impressed by Mishima's story. The four, all graduates of the Hiroshima University of Literature and Science, had started the magazine for "literary arts and culture," in 1938, to restore "the authority of tradition," illuminate "classics," and uphold "the Japanese spirit," as its statement of purpose announced. That may sound like inane bombast of narcissistic nationalists typical of the day; in fact, the group magazine was intended to counter the mindless chauvinism that was gaining the upper hand in politics and in other fields.

Early that year, on February 1, the government arrested a total of thirty-eight prominent scholars and leaders on suspicion of setting up the People's Front in Japan. That followed a mass arrest of four hundred and forty-six people in December. Their books were banned. In the Diet, nationalist politicians had a heyday accusing anyone they didn't like of contravening the notion of *kokutai*, "national polity."²⁶ Hasuda Zenmei, for one, fumed over these developments, noting in his diary that the rampant fear of "freedom" or "liberty"—as in liberalism; in Japanese, the word *jiyū* represent both "liberty" and "freedom"—as something akin to "a typhoid virus" would "endanger," rather than "defend," Japan.

Hasuda *was* an ardent nationalist himself and would become even "stubbornly" so in a few years, fixated on what he understood to be "the ancient" via the *kokugaku*, "national learning," that Moto'ori Norinaga (1730–1801) advocated, especially the ideal of devotion to the Tennō.²⁷ National Learning is a historico-literary movement that tried to eliminate Chinese, Confucian, and Buddhist influences in the Japanese language and literature and recover and establish what were thought to be things purely Japanese. As Norinaga put it in his introduction to *kokugaku*, "First, it is vital to wash away the Chinese mind and Confucian mind cleanly so you may firm up your Yamato spirit."²⁸

Linguistically, National Learning may have had some resemblance to the Anglo-Saxon revival that George Orwell, for one, desired. But like it, National Learning was a tall task.²⁹ It held sway over much of Japan's nationalist thinking nonetheless. In particular, the tanka in which Norinaga thought he expressed best the essence of the "Yamato spirit," *Yamato damashii*, or "Yamato heart," *Yamato gokoro*, became exceedingly popular among militarists during the 1930s and 1940s. It reads:

> *Shikishima no Yamato gokoro o hito towaba asahi ni niou yamazakurabana*

> If someone inquires of the Yamato heart, it is the wild cherry flowers abloom in the morning sun

Its popularity reached its crest when the devisers of the flying suicide missions, in the second half of the 1944, took advantage of the tradition that equates the scattering of cherry flowers with death after a fleeting glorious peak, and used some of the words in the tanka to name the initial units of "the special attack force."³⁰

Hasuda, among the four founders of *Bungei Bunka*, would leave an indelible imprint on Mishima in this and other ways, but with a caveat: Mishima's perspective and readings were much broader than Hasuda's.

Mishima, for example, surely knew that Ueda Akinari (1734–1809), another favorite writer of his, mocked his contemporary Moto'ori Norinaga's quest for nationalist purity. When Norinaga had his portrait with the poem quoted above written atop prepared and distributed to his disciples to celebrate his sixtieth year, Akinari condemned both that act and the notion of "Yamato spirit." He said that stuff like "Yamato spirit" is what constitutes the "odor," or the flaw, of each country, and that by sending his disciples a portrait with such a poem Norinaga turned himself into "the boss of self-aggrandizement." He also wrote a tanka dismissing Norinaga's composition and sent it to him.[31]

In the summer of 1943, Hasuda, who by then had created some disquiet among the literati for "roaring against" those he deemed not patriotic enough, would raise an unreasonable, incoherent fracas over Niwa Fumio's novel *Naval Battle* (*Kaisen*). Like a number of other writers, Niwa had been lined up and sent to the front to report on various battles. *Naval Battle* was his realistic account of the First Battle of the Solomon Sea, on August 8 and 9, 1942, aboard Vice Adm. Mikawa Gun'ichi's flagship, the heavy cruiser *Chōkai*. Niwa becomes unnerved and confounded when guns start blazing, but he struggles to record what he sees and hears, taking his writerly duty to heart. At the climax of the battle, *Chōkai* is hit by a salvo fired by the USS *Quincy* (or *Astoria*), itself heavily damaged and burning but dashing toward the Japanese cruiser, and Niwa is seriously wounded. He closely records that as well, to describe what war is like.

Yet, commenting on this novel, Hasuda condemned Niwa for not abandoning his pen in the midst of battle to help the crew by carrying shells, for example, as Niwa himself wrote that was what he should have done.

"It is a mistake to think that by carrying shells he would have interrupted battle observation or literature," Hasuda wrote indignantly. "By carrying shells he might have lost track of certain scenes, but had he carried shells, what he would have seen doing that would have been true war."

In truth, as his biographer, Odakane Jirō, guessed, Hasuda had probably been offended by what Niwa had written about his relationship to his pitiless mother as it was, not by *Naval Battle*. In short, his salvo against him was misdirected. Toward the end of 1967, that is, three years before his death, however, Mishima took up this matter to argue that literature cannot be a cog, a function in the division of labor, in a total war.[32]

By the time the four editors of *Bunka Bungei* met and decided to accept Mishima's story, Hasuda had served in the army and fought in central China, near Lake Dongting, as second lieutenant. Called up in 1938 at the age of thirty-four, two years later he returned home wounded, his right forearm shot through. In late 1943 he was called back to duty, this time as first lieutenant, and fought in various parts of Indonesia. But four days after Japan's surrender, in Johor Bahru, just north of Singapore, where three and a half years earlier Gen. Yamashita Tomoyuki had demanded and received surrender from Gen. Arthur Percival, he shot dead his regimental commander and then killed himself with the same gun.

This happened the day Maj. Gen. Prince Kan'in arrived in Saigon to convey the imperial message to regional regiments to accept Japan's surrender. The Japanese government, fearful that many of the military units overseas would not surrender but fight on, had dispatched the Tennō's relatives to tell them that the decision to surrender was His Majesty's. Prince Kan'in was one of them.

The reason for Hasuda's act, testimony of witnesses suggested, was that he was disturbed—deeply aggrieved—that the commander, Col. Nakajō Toyoma, had committed *lèse majesté* in his "farewell to the colors" speech two days earlier. He had spoken, Hasuda felt, in such a way as to "ascribe the responsibility for Japan's defeat to the Tennō, denigrate the future of the Imperial Army, and predict the collapse of the Japanese spirit." Nakajō, who had taken up the position of regimental commander just before Japan's defeat in a routine personnel transfer, gave the speech, it was said, because he sensed a revolt was afoot. A full complement of soldiers wanted to fight on and Hasuda was to be a battalion commander.[33]

Mishima would be deeply affected by Hasuda's violent action and death. In a gathering of friends for Hasuda in November 1946, Shimizu recalled Mishima writing in a memorial book for Hasuda's family, in classical Japanese: "You, who loved the clouds of ancient times, embodied the ancient times in yourself and hid yourself behind the clouds, whereas I, left in modern times, long in vain for the darkling clouds, myself about to be buried in bleak dusty earth."³⁴ Aside from his manner of death, however, Mishima had reason to remember Hasuda in a special way.

"The writer of 'The Forest in Full Bloom' is an utterly young man," Hasuda had written when the first installment of the story appeared, in the September 1941 issue of *Bungei Bunka*.

> What kind of person he is I'd like to keep in secrecy for the time being. This is because I believe that would be best. If someone were to truly want to know, I would simply reply that he is *a young version of ourselves*. That a young man like this is emerging in Japan is a joy I can hardly express in words, and would come as a surprise hardly believable to those with little confidence in Japanese literature. This young writer, however, is a God-send of Japan with its eternal history. This is the birth of someone who is far less than us in the number of years lived but already mature.³⁵

## *The Forest in Full Bloom*

As written by a sixteen-year-old boy, "The Forest" certainly has something about it that would impress anyone, but especially men like Shimizu and Hasuda who pursued what they believed to be the essences of classical Japanese literature and tradition. An overtly literary attempt to bring back some of the narrator's "many ancestors" that include, "as seldom happens, both samurai and aristocrats," the tale is imbued with an uncanny command of language.

The narrator, "a sleepless child," begins with his dreams or half-dreams with descriptions of immediate relatives, including his sickly grandmother, then moves on to the wife of a daimyo prone to illness. That "remote relative" was a Christian convert, of the sixteen or seventeenth century, who left a diary, from which the narrator quotes amply, though in modern Japanese. The story then moves on to an ancestor even more remote, a nobleman of the declining years of the Heian Court, although the subject has to do with a woman who was not from his "exalted" class and in fact "had no relation to my genealogy to the very end." Through the nobleman's nightly visits one summer, her passion for him flares up even as his interest cools. Her attention turns to a childhood friend, a Buddhist trainee who sends her passionate letters. She elopes with him, abandons him, then goes to a nunnery. There she writes a tale of her life and sends it to the nobleman.

The final part of the story describes "an aunt of my grandmother," a diplomat's daughter married to an earl who, after his death, married a rich merchant "of lowly birth" and lived for a while on an island in the South Seas. After divorcing him, she returned to Japan, built a purely Japanese-style house on her large estate and lived there for the rest of her life, occasionally talking about her past. "The Forest" ends with the aunt, now old, taking a visitor to an overlook in her spacious garden with a view of the sea.

> The visitor turned and gazed at the snow-white sky that gave a dazzling glimpse of itself as the upper part of an oak tree agitated in the wind swept away and receded. Pressed by an irritable anxiety he did not know the reason of, the visitor may have felt he was standing next to "death," right next to the stillness like that of a top spinning for life, a stillness resembling death, as it were.

Mishima told Azuma the title of the story came from a phrase in one of Guy-Charles Cros's poems, translated by Horiguchi Daigaku, explaining that he meant the title to "symbolize inner, supernatural *longings*."[36] The poem reads:

> **Refrains**
> The doctors were convinced they could save her,
> but the young girl died this year;
>
> she died just when all the woods are in bloom.
> Who knows if there are not greener branches, elsewhere?
>
> Yet those she left behind wept for the girl who was gone;
> as for me, I prefer to weep for girls full of life,
>
> those who will become women and bear children
> and so quickly forget about birds, flowers, songs....

The doctors were convinced they could save her,
but she must have better understood her true destiny.

She died just when all the woods are in bloom;
she knew other forests are greener, elsewhere.[37]

(Tr. Luke Bouvier)

Late in his life, Mishima said he no longer liked the story, because in this "Rilke-esque story, only the bad influence of Romanticism and the affectations like those of a prematurely old man stand out."[38] But he used it as the title story of his first book and, by the time of that judgment, in 1968, he had allowed it to be reprinted a number of times, including in the volume he wrote the afterword with the words just quoted.

There was one more important thing that Mishima carried forward from Hasuda Zenmei: a deep admiration for the deliberately anachronistic group of diehards known as the Shinpūren. Hasuda's father could have easily been in the forces that readily crushed the revolt of these men, in 1886, and Hasuda had a schoolteacher who was a son of one of them. He discussed the diehards via the teacher in *Bunka Bungei*.[39] Mishima surely read the article with great interest. We will look at the Shinpūren later.

## *How the Penname Came About*

The penname Mishima Yukio 三島由紀夫 was proposed during the editorial meeting of *Bungei Bunka* in July. The four men met in an inn near Shuzenji, on the Izu Peninsula, where the famous temple with that name is located. To go to Shuzenji from Tokyo, you first take the train on the Tōkaidō Line and go to Mishima 三島, where you switch to a local line south. So the names *Mishima* and *Yuki* ("to go" or "bound to") came naturally. *Yuki*, which also means "snow 雪," was appropriate as well in view of the permanent snow adorning the top of Mt. Fuji, which you saw soaring northwest from the train window. The "o" of Yukio is a common suffix to male names, so the name Mishima Yukio 三島ゆきお, came into being, with the personal part of the name left in the Japanese syllabary *hiragana*.

When Shimizu ventured to bring up the subject of a penname

with Mishima, the sixteen-year-old student asked, "Won't Hiraoka Kimitake do, sir?" Shimizu, the thirty-eight-year-old teacher, explained that it would be best to debut in an "outside" magazine with a penname. Also, Japanese writers and poets, following ancient Chinese custom, habitually adopted pennames. After thinking on the suggested name for a while, Mishima came up with the Chinese characters 由紀雄 for the personal part of the name. When Shimizu suggested that 雄 might be a bit heavy and offered 夫 instead, Mishima agreed.[40] With his father, who vowed not to allow his son to dabble in literature, back in the household, the adoption of the penname probably relieved Mishima of certain anxieties.[41]

## *The War*

Japan was rushing toward war with the United States, Great Britain, and the Netherlands. In September, Mishima wrote an essay simply to note that Japan is a special country because it has maintained the ways of ancient deities, which is what the phrase he chose for the title of the essay says: *Kamunagara no michi*. His command of language is impressive, and his argument cogent, except for one thing: like many who made such an argument, Mishima did not address the fact that both "the principal idea" that is the *raison d'être* of the Japanese Nation, "sincerity," *makoto* or *sei*, and the idea that forms "the patriotism unique to Japan," "loyalty," *chū*, came from Confucianism. What makes the essay Mishima-esque is that Mishima penned it after an elaborate treatise in exaltation of Raymond Radiguet.[42]

In October 1941, Kishi Nobusuke, who was promoting the idea of rebuilding Japan with "the defense industry at its core" since his return from Manchukuo, became Minister of Commerce and Industry in Tōjō's "war cabinet." In no time he issued an ordinance specifying "important industries," which included organization of a "control association" for each of the twelve sectors, such as iron and steel, coal, automobiles, and exports and imports. In Kishi's vision, a "total war" system had to be under the control of bureaucrats, not military officers. For that purpose, he ignored the bureaucratic protocol based on education and seniority and forced out key directors of his ministry to install hand-picked "reform bureaucrats."

On November 10, 1941, that is, four weeks before Japan's assault on Pearl Harbor, Mishima wrote to Azuma: "We appear to be going to war with America, but I think it's too late now. Germany will soon run out of gas, and may conclude a peace treaty with England. I think it unlikely that I'll be drafted as a soldier, but what will I do if I am? If anything, I wish there'd be an uproarious war, and it would end in about a year."[43]

The overall assessment of the day was that Japan had driven itself into a corner with the United States—or the United States had driven Japan into a corner. Germany's general offensive against Moscow that had started in October had stalled. The talk was that Russia's famed General Winter had stopped the Germans. About the time Japan attacked Pearl Harbor, on December 8 (Japan Time), the Soviet forces began to push back the German invaders from Moscow.

Mishima's wish that the war, were it to occur, would be "uproarious" and short, like a bunch of soldiers jumping out of their trenches and rushing to the enemy line shouting war cries, succinctly, uncannily, conveys the sense of the day. Japan had bogged down in China. There was an oppressive desire for some way out. Striking at the United States, the country that was tightening its screws on Japan, might be one way, though the escalation could be fatal.[44]

Japan, in any case, could not hope to win a protracted war with the country; the navy's strong opposition was no secret. Admiral Yamamoto Isoroku, who under duress planned the attack on the US naval base in Hawaii, is known to have observed that, if he had to wage war with the United States, he would be able to create havoc, but only for one year.[45]

―――

With his father reunited with the family, the situation changed again. Mishima wrote Azuma: "A joke maybe, but father calls me 'a national saboteur.' As he puts it, 'You only write this or that about Murasaki [Shikibu, the author of *The Tale of Genji*], *she* does this and that, things like that, you're pale-faced, you're absorbed only in trashy fiction,'" because doing such things was "inappropriate for the present situation."[46]

In March 1942, when the Japanese were drunk with the initial victories, Azusa "voluntarily" retired from the Ministry of Agriculture and Forestry as director-general of fisheries. (He had been expected to do so while in Osaka, before he attained director-generalship, but had managed to thwart the plan.) Then, "descending from heaven," he was given the presidency of Japan Charcoal-for-Gas Company, Inc., one of the government-sponsored enterprises for "national policy" that began to be set up during the Depression of the preceding decades.

The April 1942 issue of *Bunka Bungei* carried Mishima's poem "Imperial Declaration" (*Taishō*), which refers to the Shōwa Emperor's Declaration of War on December 8, 1941—the day of the Japanese Navy's assault on Pearl Harbor.[47] It is written in classical language, in the ancient "long song" form, with classical epithets.

> Our Sovereign Familiar with the Eight Corners,
> The day He declared His Imperial Declaration,
> All the birds ceased their sounds of crying;
> All the grasses lost their ability to waver.
> Heaven and earth, unable to damn their tears,
> Fell silent, voiceless.
> The Imperial Command, clear, melodious,
> Overflowed, indeed brimmed,
> In the Reed Plain, Fresh Rice-Stalk Country.
> Just then, in the South Sea, on the head of the querulous country,
> The tearful sword fell of the Country of High-Shining Sun's Child.
> Just then, a voice was released. From the sea the enemies had polluted,
> Ocean deities, raging, racing, smote down the enemy seafarers,
> Sank them off the seaweed-harvesting coast.
> The victorious shouts now resound,
> Our fortunes are ever more layered.
> But my heart, part of my innards, I cannot help it,
> Unable to raise a cry of joy, simply sheds tears.[48]

Odakane Jirō, who wrote a biography not just of Hasuda Zenmei but also a large one of the poet Itō Shizuo, thought that this piece was no more than Mishima's attempt to "imitate and learn from" Itō—"imitate and learn from" having been a centuries-old Asian tradition of "imitation is the best form of paying respect." One of the two Itō poems the biographer cited was "Imperial Declaration"—with the same title, dealing with the same subject as Mishima's poem, and with the last line more or less the same—and the other, "Spring Snow (*Haru no yuki*)," that describes light snow on the ancient Mimihara Imperial Mausoleum with no birds calling. Hasuda had praised the former extravagantly in the February issue of *Bungei Bunka* and printed the latter in its March issue. Itō's "Imperial Declaration" is short, and reads in full:

> December 8, Sixteenth Year of Shōwa
> What a day it was
> Driven by the refreshing thought
> We offered prayers toward the Imperial Palace in the distance
> And all of us
> —Who of us could have stopped our tears?[49]

There are indications that this "imitate-and-learn" form of flattery may not have particularly pleased the poet, as we will see in the next chapter.

On February 16, Mishima wrote Azuma and commented on the Fall of Singapore that had occurred the day before: "Singapore was a pointlessly fierce battle, I hear. To minimize the casualties on both sides, [Britain] should have raised a white flag earlier; it couldn't have been their heart's desire, even for Britain, to see many soldiers die every minute to save face for a single British general in the name of the honor of the entire British forces. A great many Japanese newspaper reporters also died; you can imagine what happened to the soldiers."[50]

---

On August 26, Sadatarō died, at age seventy-nine. Late that night Mishima wrote a threnody for him, in classical language. Describing his grandfather's "easeful sleep," he wrote: "Ah, even that easeful sleep must have been something / he was unable to get for years."

Fujiwara Ginjirō, chairman of Ōji Paper, presented the Hiraoka family with a "funeral gift" of ten thousand yen—an extravagant sum, as it was equal to Azusa's annual salary that itself was sumptuous as befits someone who had "descended from heaven." The reason for Fujiwara's largesse lay in his profound sense of indebtedness to Sadatarō. When

Sadatarō was administrator of the Karafuto Agency, he had helped Fujiwara build the first pulp factory in Japan. That led, in the end, to Fujiwara's status as King of Paper Manufacturing, especially after Ōji Paper became a virtual monopoly, in 1933, as a result of mergers promoted by the Ministry of Industry and Commerce. Three years earlier, in fact, he had built an outsize bronze statue of Sadatarō in the Karafuto Shrine, in Toyohara City (today's Yuzhno-Sakhalinsk) with the pretext of commemorating the twenty-fifth anniversary of Japan's possession of the southern half of Sakhalin and unveiled it on August 22. Mishima, then five, attended the ceremony with Sadatarō, Natsuko, and Shizue. In an interview on the occasion, Sadatarō said he had a two-pronged idea for the development of Karafuto: pulp and medicinal herbs.[51]

This family connection would come in handy when the idea of publishing *The Forest in Full Bloom* in book form arose in the last phase of the war when paper shortages, like that of many other things, had become an acute problem.

---

With Azuma as his intense literary correspondent, Mishima's relationship with Bōjō seems to have suffered. In early 1943, he gave Azuma a rather cool assessment of his other literary senior: "It appears Bōjō-san can never get out of Shiga [Naoya], Akutagawa [Ryūnosuke], [Villiers de] l'Isle-Adam."[52] Yet this did not mean Mishima had come to reject Bōjō as unworthy. In January 1944, he listed, as he at times did, his aphoristic judgments on some of the things he saw around him—apparently not for publication, because he wrote "I loathe the present age in which Nazism is triumphant"—and there he wrote: "Mr. Bōjō Toshitami's literature is still unknown to society and not accepted by people, but I do not doubt it will prove to be an astonishment when the eyes of those in the know with unfaked, true concern for the nation are liberated in postwar Japan."[53] The word he chose for "concern for the nation" was *yūkoku*.

And, a few years after the war, Mishima wrote that Bōjō "loved the dark, sensuous sorrow of French Symbolist poetry and was a passionate idolater of Comte de l'Isle-Adam" while at the same time "a devout convert to every formation of beauty of [Japan's] court period with *The Tale of Genji* as its symbol." He wrote this when asked for an afterword to Bōjō's collection of short stories, saying he was indebted to Bōjō for "the awakening of my initial artistic impulse."[54]

Then the relationship of the two faded and disappeared, until it revived unexpectedly toward the end of Mishima's life because of Bōjō's intimate knowledge of Japan's aristocratic society as it had existed before Japan's defeat in the war.

---

In July 1942, the first issue of *Akae* came out. The third member of the group, Tokugawa Yoshiyasu, was a recent graduate of the Peers School and now an art student at the Imperial University of Tokyo. As the name suggests, he was related, albeit through adoptions, to the founder of the Tokugawa dynasty, Ieyasu. He did the cover design and illustrations. He also designed the cover of Mishima's first book. It was in his letter to Tokugawa, in September 1943, that Mishima fulminated against the government's imposition of "a *kokumin* ceremonial" on the people.

"The other day I went to the New Japan Symphony Orchestra," he wrote. "All they had to do was simply to ask us to pray for the brave soldiers who have perished in battle, but through a loudspeaker they started mouthing homilies such as 'displaying the pledge of the 100 million as a single heart for the completion of the Holy War,' so I felt a bit of chill, when there was the command, 'Pray.' *At once* the orchestra performed 'When Seagoing.'"

"It was the same as a play riding the tides of the day at some playhouse in some alley in Asakusa or thereabouts," Mishima continued. Asakusa traditionally has been an area where "commoners," in the parlance of Mishima's days, or regular folks gather to enjoy themselves. In other words, what was done to the performance of a highbrow symphony orchestra was to bring it down to the vulgar level of commoners' taste. "It was awful in its sacrilege, and I was furious."[55]

The number "100 million" represented the round total of the Japanese, which at the time included peoples of Korea and Taiwan. "When Seagoing," *Umi yukaba*, is an ancient military vow incorporated into one of Ōtomo no Yakamochi's "long songs" in the *Man'yōshū*, the oldest extant anthology of Japanese poetry. It reads in its entirety:

> When seagoing, we might become watery corpses,
> mountain-going, corpses for grasses to grow from.
> Our wish is to die by our Sovereign's side
> with no looking back

Nobutoki Kiyoshi, a composer influenced by German Romanticism, composed the music in 1937. The song was soon adopted as a "semi-national anthem." In time it came to be broadcast before any announcement of an annihilative defeat of a Japanese military unit, *gyokusai*.

Tokugawa died a few years after the war, at age twenty-eight. Mishima did not think much of him as an artist or a writer, but a decade later he portrayed the young aristocrat in "The Nobility" *(Kiken)*. He wrote it à la Walter Pater's short stories such as "Sebastian Van Storck" and "Duke Carl Of Rosenmold," he explained.[56]

CHAPTER FIVE

# First Love

> *From there I could not see the shape of the Golden Pavilion. I could only see the swirling smoke and the fire soaring into heaven. An abundance of sparks flew among the trees, and the sky above the Golden Pavilion looked as though sprinkled with gold dust.*
>
> —*The Temple of the Golden Pavilion*

Why did Mishima *not* choose the officer-candidate course as his graduation from the Higher Division of the Peers School neared? Yamanashi Katsunoshin, President of the Peers School, sounded "accusatory" when he learned he had not taken the exam for officer candidates during the summer, Mishima wrote in *Confessions of a Mask*. They were in a car going to the Ministry for the Imperial Household, in September 1944. The top graduate in the school's department of literature that year, Mishima received a silver watch in the name of the Tennō and three German novels with the Nazi Hakenkreuz embossed on each from the German ambassador who attended the ceremony and books from the Peers Club. The trip was to express gratitude.[1]

As Japan prepared for war with the United States and others, the four-year college term was shortened by three months in late 1941, and the four-year higher-school term by six months the following year. In November 1943, the draft age was lowered from twenty to nineteen. It did not take a retired admiral, which Yamanashi was, to see that

Mishima would have a hard time as a soldier in private second class, which was what you became when drafted. Any sensible man with a higher education would have tried to be an officer candidate in one form or another.

Not that Mishima had not physically improved. "Until I was fifteen or sixteen I was terribly weak physically and was constantly bullied," he recalled some years after he started bodybuilding. Yet by the time he was eighteen, he was "strong and confident enough not to fall aside during a march."[2]

But that was his own assessment. His report card in his final year in the Higher Division shows that he got As in all subjects except for athletics, in which he got B+. The grade may seem good enough, but probably not to the army officer in charge.

Other than his draft physicals result of Second Class B, the reason Mishima did not opt for the officer-candidate course could have been simple. Each officer assigned for military training at schools reported to his regiment each student's physical aptitude.[3] The officer at the Peers School may not have recommended Mishima for that course. Though important, it was not as if everyone with his education opted for an officer candidate course even at that dire phase of the war. Of the twenty-four who graduated from the Peers School's liberal arts division that September, eight, including Mishima, chose not to.[4] Also, Mishima had not given up on an officer-candidate course, as he indicated in his letter to his parents in January 1945.[5]

In the event, Mitani was probably trying to put the best face on his friend when he later suggested that Mishima did not choose an officer-candidate course because he "wanted to fight the enemy through literature" for "his enmity was quite fierce," not because he might be lucky enough not to be drafted.[6]

## *Publishing His First Book*

Once the possibility arose of having his book out before being drafted, as it did, Mishima worked hard to see to it that this was done. It was Fuji Masaharu who came up openly with the idea first. In writing about Hayashi Fujima's poetry in the August 1943 issue of *Bunka Bungei*, Fuji suggested that "The Forest in Full Bloom," along with a few other stories, ought to be published as a book, adding that if no one published it, he would do it.

In his memoir, Fuji was vague about his role, saying it was the poet Itō Shizuo who urged him to publish such a book, even confessing he arranged the publication without reading the novella and other stories very well. He soon passed the matter on to the physician-poet Hayashi and wasn't really involved in the matter—all this because he was nonplussed by the young man's correct manners and polite language when he first met him; he was from a lower stratum of society and spoke the Osaka dialect, he explained.[7]

Behind it all was the effort of Shimizu and others of *Bunka Bungei* to have a book published for their extraordinarily talented young friend. Fuji wrote Hasuda on August 14: "Concerning Mr. Mishima's writings, I have made several soundings, and have now reached the point of needing the manuscript (a cutout from *Bunka Bungei* would do, too)." Hasuda, in turn, wrote Mishima on August 16, with Japan's postal system working fine despite the pressures of war. "My poet friend in Kyoto, Mr. Fuji Masaharu, has seriously thought about publishing a book of your fictional writings from a reputable publisher, and he says the chances are good," he said. "If you are agreeable, do accept his kind thoughts. Kindly put together a manuscript and send it to me. Also, consult Mr. Shimizu on this."

Overjoyed, Mishima told Azuma Fumihiko on September 4: "The idea of having a selection of my fictional writings out from a Kyoto publisher has suddenly come into being, so it appears that I can send my first book out to the world." He added: "Book-publishing these days takes an inordinate amount of time. Mr. Itō Shizuo's book of poems to be issued in mid-September (Kōbundō) has been under preparation since before February, Mr. Fuji says, and he says to me, Well, you better get used to the idea that it'll take a year [for my book to come out]."[8]

That fall when he met Mishima, Fuji told him that he planned to submit the "project application" after "the New Year"—January.[9] What is a "project application"?

In 1940 Kishi Nobusuke, along with other "reform bureaucrats," made a major effort to turn Japan into a "controlled economy," creating what would later be called the 1940 Regime. In August the government rearranged the publishing industry and in December set up an Association of Japanese Publishing Culture to "pursue and implement the mission of the publishing culture enterprise as it relates to the building of Japanese culture and the establishment of a national-defense nation and to devise a proper management of this industry, so that it may bear the fruit of patriotism in publishing." In short, the government added to the existing system of rationing of printing paper a requirement for permission on what could be published. The "project application" was part of the new censorship regime.

In February 1943, the association changed its name to the Association of Japanese Publishing (AJP) in compliance with the Publishing Enterprise Ordinance, which was issued on the basis of the National Mobilization Law of 1938 created in response to Japan's worsening war with China. The move was to put the publishing industry under tighter government control. In the process the total of 3,743 publishers that existed in Japan then were reduced to a mere 203 houses, forcing many to merge and many to go out of business.[10] It was "a great earthquake in the publishing world," as Mishima called it.[11]

"Because in those days paper needed for publishing was under control, and speech control was made during the procedure of applying for paper, I remember lining up for the item called 'purpose of publication' in the project application big bluffs that would pander to the trends of the day in various ways," Mishima recalled a dozen years later. "It seems that even in those days I wasn't a youth of excessive integrity."[12] The "trend of the day" was, of course, patriotism. So, Mishima said, among others, the publication of his stories would help "maintain and preserve the literary traditions of our Imperial Nation."[13]

Amid the paper shortage and rationing and the requirement for patriotic content, there was a loophole of sorts: a publisher could push for a publication if paper was made independently available. Mishima had a source for the needed paper, a great one.

At the time, because of the war, arranging an *ikōshū*—a posthumous collection of one's writings in book form—was common, not just by the surviving relatives and such but by writers themselves.[14] Shizue told Azusa that their son ought to have such a book out before he died. Azusa agreed, however reluctantly, and called Ōji Paper, knowing of course that Fujiwara Ginjirō did not just feel profoundly indebted to Mishima's grandfather, Sadatarō, but also revered him as the man who helped create the pulp industry in Japan.[15] Here's part of Mishima's "Journal for *The Forest in Full Bloom*." "Shichijō" is the publisher Shichijō Shoin.

February 4: phone Shichijō.
February 6, night: Mr. Okazaki [Kazuichi] comes to visit.
February 7: write a letter to Mr. Okazaki about the bookstore [Shichijō].
February 20: submit [a plan application] to the AJP.
February 24: go to Shichijō.
March 7: AJP gives informal approval.
March 8: send publication application to the bookstore.
[three items skipped]
April 14: Informal approval [for publication].
April 24: Formal approval [for publication] given.
[rest omitted][16]

Okazaki Kazuichi was the head of the secretariat at Ōji Paper, a position comparable to that of senior vice president in today's American corporation. Mishima probably called Shichijō Shoin on February 4 to ascertain that the publisher would expedite the publication of his book if paper were made available. Okazaki, in his visit with the Mishimas, probably promised to do his best to supply the needed paper.

At the time, Fujiwara Ginjirō himself was in an important government post. He was serving the Tōjō cabinet as "administrative inspector" with the portfolio of Minister of State. In November 1943, when Prime Minister and Minister of the Army Tōjō combined the Ministry of Commerce and Industry with the Planning Bureau to create the Ministry of Armament and assumed its ministership as well, he also created a new post of "administrative inspector" and gave it to Fujiwara.

A planned economy, whether controlled or centralized, inevitably creates unplanned surpluses and shortages, as is known from the Soviet Union's experience. One factory may have enough material for producing what it is supposed to, but not enough coal, let us say, that is needed to power the machines. Another factory may have enough coal but not enough material to use the coal. Such distortions worsened as general shortages became the norm in wartime Japan. The traditional rivalry between the two services, the army and the navy, did not help. The "administrative inspector" was tasked to assess and reduce such "inefficiencies." He was thus the overseer of wartime production.

This appointment in effect made Fujiwara Kishi Nobusuke's superior twice. In Admiral Yonai Mitsumasa's cabinet, which came into being in January 1940, Fujiwara was Minister of Commerce and Industry and Kishi its Vice Minister. In the new arrangement, Kishi was "demoted" from Minister of Commerce and Industry to Vice Minister of Armament, though he was also given the post of Minister of State without Portfolio. He had become Minister of Commerce and Industry under the Tōjō cabinet in October 1941 with the understanding that only *he* could manage the industrial production essential for a total war. Now, with Tōjō's cabinet restructuring, Kishi had two superiors: Tōjō, yes, and Fujiwara. This may have been one reason Kishi turned against Tōjō and led the way to his downfall.

## *Mishima and Poet Itō Shizuo*

As soon as he received the publication permission he had sought, on April 24, Mishima wrote Itō Shizuo to ask if he would write a preface to his book. Itō, a junior high school teacher in Osaka, was a lyric poet prominent in the Japan Romantic School. Devoted to German poets such as Rainer Maria Rilke, Erich Kästner, and especially Friedrich Hölderlin—while a student at the Imperial University of Kyoto he was reputed to own the largest collection of Hölderlin's poems and books about them in Japan[17]—Itō wrote poems of convoluted imagery and syntax and had a small but important coterie of admirers, among them Hagiwara Sakutarō.

Indeed, one aspect of Mishima's literary thinking was revealed in his letter to Shimizu mentioned above. Expressing his admiration for Hagiwara's poetry such as represented by the line "Spring flares out like smallpox"—his book in 1917, *Howling at the Moon* (*Tsuki ni hoeru*), with its neurosis and neurotic use of language, had ushered in modern poetry in Japan—Mishima asserted that "Japan would be in serious trouble" if it accepted unthinkingly the Asianist-Japanist theorist Ōkawa Shūmei's dismissal of Heian literature as "soft and feeble," adding that to think about the military crisis Japan faced was not the same as "applauding Tōjō-san's speeches."[18]

Ōkawa, who had studied Indian philosophy at the Imperial University of Tokyo and for a few decades had as wide an influence as the political theorist Kita Ikki, would become, following Japan's defeat, the only non-governmental civilian the International Military Tribunal for the Far East indicted for war crimes. But he was released during the trial because of his odd behavior. He famously kept slapping the head of Tōjō sitting in front of him, muttering nonsense, and was judged to be insane.

Itō, at any rate, contributed poems to *Bunka Bungei*, which published his second book of poems, in 1940, and the book, like his first, won a prize. His third, *Spring Hurries* (*Haru no isogi*), also won a prize. He sent a signed copy to Mishima when it came out, in the fall of 1943.

Itō's response to Mishima's request came soon enough, at the end of April. He declined. So Mishima decided to make the request face to face. As it happened, the following month he had to go to Kansai for the physicals for draftees. He left Tokyo one day earlier than necessary, and visited Itō on May 17. Itō wrote in his diary: "There was a telephone call at school; around two o'clock, Hiraoka Kimitake came. Before that Fuji Masaki [Masaharu's alternate name] had come to school; he said he'd taken a few days off and come home because he was finally being shipped off to the front on the Continent.... I went to visit him with Hiraoka; we were treated to supper."

On his way back to Tokyo after the physicals in Shikata, Mishima stopped in Osaka once more to see Itō. Itō's entry in his diary on the 22nd notes, "Hiraoka came to the school around three. Offered him supper. Philistine. Kanbori [Shinobu] came. Gave me apples. [Mishima] stayed until about nine-thirty. Walked him to the station."

"Philistine" is a strong word—so strong that Odakane Jirō, in his book on Hasuda and his death, suggested that Itō may have been the one who was a philistine, not Mishima. Kanbori, who went on to become a *Man'yōshū* scholar, was a student in Itō's class, and he had brought apples for Itō. In contrast, Mishima not only put himself in such a position as to require the poet to invite him to supper but also probably asked him for a foreword again. If Kanbori represented "deference," Mishima embodied "pride" approaching arrogance. Odakane even suggested Itō's inferiority complex deriving from class differences.[19]

But Odakane may have gone a little too far in making that argument. Itō was poor for most of his adult life, as he knew perfectly well, and out of his meager salary as a junior-high-school teacher he had to repay his father's large debt. Also, by the time Itō met Mishima, food shortages were so acute as to require most travelers to take their own food with them. And in this book, Odakane needed to emphasize

Hasuda's special relationship to Mishima and most likely planned to have Mishima's foreword, which he indeed asked for and got. Most tellingly, in his massive volume on Itō five years earlier, he almost skimped on the conflict, commenting only that Itō's reaction was quite like him.[20]

Mishima wrote to thank Itō as soon as he came home. That further put off the poet. Itō jotted in his diary on May 28: "Letter from Hiraoka; not amusing. Overreaching strained prose."[21]

Failing to have Itō's laudatory preface, Mishima chose to laud the poet in his afterword to his first book, an act he mocked himself, however lightly, when Itō died, in 1953.[22] The first proofs came on May 31 and there was no time for further maneuvering. He wrote:

> Mr. Itō Shizuo is a poet whom I have held dear and respected as a rare Romanticist since boyhood. When he, in his home not far from a mausoleum made in the ancient world, talked about Mr. Hagiwara Sakutarō, talked about the use of documents in National Learning, and talked about an *essential education* for a poet, his eyes, at once breezy and aflame, were beautiful.
>
> As he kindly walked me to the station along a dark cobbled road, he said, "I like things that are a bit warped and off, like someone who says something, then looks at you." Mysteriously, I still remember his words vividly. Then he talked about the goodness of an orderly who brings a meal for his superior officer and as he enters his room announces, "I'm coming in, sir!"

When Itō died, Mishima recalled to note that the citation of this story in his afterword showed how "to me in those days, military life was an *idée fixe* full of terror."[23]

Despite his private impressions of Mishima, Itō would remain courteous to the much younger man, at least outwardly, and Mishima a steadfast admirer of Itō's poetry: he would write half a dozen articles in praise of his poetry. In 1968, when asked, in one of those surveys of writers' opinions Japanese publishers routinely conduct, to name the verse he "loved to recite," Mishima quoted the opening lines of Itō's poem, "A Song of the Wilderness" (*Kōya no uta*): "For the beautiful day when I die, / fantasy of linked peaks! May you not erase / your white snow."[24]

The only thing left for Mishima to do was to wait for the appearance of the book, which was scheduled for October 15. The half-a-year waiting period was full of anxieties. The Allied Powers' large-scale bombings of Germany were adequately reported, and some in the military provided candid accounts of the coming catastrophes. In February 1944, for example, the ladies' monthly *Shufu no Tomo* carried an article by a Col. Katō Yoshihide, Staff Officer of the Central Antiaircraft Command, who wrote: "Judging from the way air raids are recently carried out in Europe, this is no longer something as lukewarm as a war of nerves. What they do is the so-called carpet bombings that make no distinction between day and night.... The enemies rain down incendiary bombs ... and the raids are conducted with one hundred bombers, two hundred bombers, and these they do repeatedly."

Mishima later wrote he had prayed there be no terrible air raids, lest the printer burn, until the book appeared, though in truth the bombing of Tokyo did not begin until after the book came out.

## *Kishi Nobusuke and Tōjō's Fall*

In June the US forces of 775 ships, with 15 aircraft carriers, began assaults on the Mariana Islands, Japan's mandate territory since 1919. On the 15th, they landed on Saipan, in the southern part of the island chain, just about eighty miles north-northeast of Guam. On July 7, the last remnants of the thirty thousand Japanese soldiers garrisoned on the island were annihilated, with only about one thousand of them captured alive.

As the details came out, though greatly distorted to Japan's advantage no doubt, Mishima wrote with sarcasm about "the sacrilege of the abuse of '*uchiteshi yamamu*'"—a phrase that occurs in the *Kojiki* and means "We won't stop until we've destroyed the enemy" that the military adopted as one of the war slogans.[25] Earlier in the same month, the operation to take Imphal, in eastern British India, had ended in an even greater disaster: thirty-two thousand soldiers dead (mostly from disease and starvation) and an additional forty thousand wounded or ill.[26]

Tōjō Hideki, who had insisted that Saipan was "hard to attack and impregnable," was shaken. By then the anti-Tōjō sentiments were widespread because of his power grab, which provoked cries of "constitutional violation," and his blatant use of the Kenpeitai. The political leadership was moving to end the war, and a separate political group was plotting to bring Tōjō down, with some contemplating his assassination.

In that milieu, Kishi refused to resign when Tōjō tried to reshuffle his cabinet. Earlier he had argued that with Saipan's fall, Japan would soon be within the US bombing range and that would make continued armament production difficult. After Saipan fell, he insisted that Tōjō had lost his ability to deal with the war situation and should go.[27]

The Tōjō cabinet collapsed, on July 18. On August 2, Tinian, an island three miles southwest of Saipan, fell. The Japanese archipelago was now indeed within the striking distance of B-29s; Tokyo lay fifteen hundred miles north. Tinian was more suited for an air base, and the United States set out to build what would then be the largest air base in the world and accommodate one thousand B-29s. Most of the heavy bombings of Japan were carried out from that base. It was from there, too, that the B-29s carrying "Little Boy" and "Fat Man" flew to Hiroshima and Nagasaki.

---

On August 1, Mishima finished the proofreading of his book on schedule. Facing graduation from the Higher Division, he did not take exams for any officer-candidate course, but his classmate Mitani Makoto, like many others, had, passed, and was waiting for induction. It was during that summer that Mishima fell in love. The woman with whom he fell in love was Mitani's younger sister, Kuniko.

In *Confessions of a Mask*, Mitani appears as Kusano and Kuniko as Sonoko. The Mitanis lived in a house built on an estate more than four times larger than the Mishimas'. It was a wooden, three-storied structure, elegantly designed. Makoto's father, Takanobu, was a diplomat, at the time of Mishima's encounter with Kuniko ambassador serving in Vichy France preparing to evacuate to Sigmaringen, in southern Germany, along with Marshal Pétain's government, as a result of the Allied invasion of France.

Mitani Takanobu was just two years older than Mishima's father and followed the same elite course of the First Higher School and the

Imperial University of Tokyo where he studied German Law. He first entered the Home Ministry. He recalled citing a variation of Frederick the Great's statement, "The prince is the first servant of his state," during the ministry's interview.

In two years, however, he was scouted into the Ministry for Foreign Affairs and, from the end of 1921 and early 1922, was a member of the Japanese delegation in the disarmament conference in Washington. Reviewing his diplomatic career, a great part of it spent in France, he would muse that the chain reactions caused by the decision by the United States and the United Kingdom to hem in Japan's power during the conference led to Japan's part in the disaster that was the Second World War.[28] After the war he went on to serve the Tennō as grand chamberlain for seventeen years, from 1948 to 1965.

While visiting Mitani Makoto, Mishima heard the sound of a piano. "Is that good? Seems to stumble from time to time," he asked, according to *Confessions*. Mitani replied, "She's my sister. Her teacher left just a while ago, and she's going over what she learned today." The piano was an expensive foreign instrument to own, but Takanobu, a Christian, was a well-traveled diplomat, and his wife, Rieko, née Nagao, was related to a prince. Though the Mitanis did not belong to the peerage by Meiji classification, the family was considered to be in the sphere where Europeans influences were taken for granted.

> We stopped our dialogue and again listened. Kusano's induction was coming up soon, and I guessed that what was ringing in his ears was not simply the sound of the piano in the next room, but the "dailiness" from which he would soon be pulled away, a kind of clumsy, frustrating beauty. The tone of the piano had the sort of familiarity of clumsy cookies someone made while looking at a [recipe] note.

Mitani had three younger sisters. Kuniko, who was playing the piano at that time, was the oldest of the three. She was eighteen, two years younger than Mitani. Mishima was sure he had seen the three girls before, but in Mitani's "Puritan" household, the girls hid themselves with bashful smiles as soon as they saw him.

The sound of the piano turned me into an awkward human

being toward his sister. After I listened to it, I somehow felt like someone who had heard about her secrets and no longer was able to look her in the eye or talk to her. When she happened to bring us tea, I saw only her agile legs that moved lightly in front of my eyes. Perhaps because the *monpe* and trousers were in fashion then and I wasn't used to seeing women's legs as they were, the beauty of her legs moved me.

The *monpe* is a baggy, pantaloon-like work garment used by farming women that was adopted by the government for women as a whole during the war for its alleged practicality and for a regimentation that favored drabness and little glamour.[29] Some in high society openly defied the regimentation as well as the drabness part of it. "In fashion" is Mishima's sarcasm.

Mishima spoke of the same encounter in *My Puberty* (*Waga shishunki*), an oral account serialized in *Myōjō*, in 1957. After recalling his flashily dressed and aggressive cousin who forced "frantic kissing" on him one night and how the experience stimulated him to "yearn for a more beautiful, innocent love affair," he goes on to say: His friend's sister "would never join us in the debate between my friend and me. But as I listened to her piano, I felt that she, for some reason, wanted us to listen to the sound of her piano.... In the savage air of wartime, I felt, in that sound of the piano, the warm, soft, and quiet world of women that I surely had forgotten."[30]

Years later when asked what she was playing at that fateful moment, Mitani Kuniko replied, "It was Chopin's 'Puppy Waltz.'"

---

On September 9, the Peers School held its commencement, half a year earlier than normal. On October 1, Mishima entered the Faculty of Law (German Law) of the Imperial University of Tokyo. That year the university did not hold its customary entrance examinations. Mishima was accepted on recommendation. He had wanted to go to the Faculty of Literature, but Azusa would not allow it. Ever a filial son, Mishima would later say that it was a good thing that he had studied law. "The art of writing a story and law have some odd linkage in the process." He liked "lawsuit procedures," in particular, which his father also had.

The complex "logic" required for building a lawsuit resembles that of constructing a story. "Studying literature wouldn't have worked, adding nothing to fiction writing."³¹ His avowed interest in lawsuit procedures evidently was true. He told his friend Mitani Makoto that he liked them because they reminded him of Scholasticism.³²

*The Forest in Full Bloom* came out on October 15; two days later he received a single advance copy. He took it to Ueno Station from which Mitani was to leave for Maebashi, Gunma, where the Army Reserve Officers School was located. He wanted to present it to his departing friend. For the occasion, he borrowed an Imperial University of Tokyo uniform, black with gold buttons, from an older student to be sent to the front soon. The understanding was that he would return the uniform to the student's family when *he* was sent to the front. Mitani's family, including Kuniko, came to the station.

There was a glitch, however. The note about the author Mishima Yukio had a typo: "The real name: Hiraoka Kimitake. Born in 1915. Still a student at the Higher Division of the Peers School." That made him twenty-nine, not nineteen! He asked the publisher to make the correction at once, but when six more copies arrived in early November, they still carried the typo. Shichijō Shoin promised to deliver at least twenty corrected copies Mishima wanted for the publication party which was set for November 10 and to which he had invited his teacher, Shimizu Fumio, among others. But the publisher could not deliver them—this time with the typo covered with a small piece of paper with a correct year of birth pasted on it—until one day after the party, on the 11th.

What saved the day was that Azusa, who had professed such hatred for literature, arranged a suitable place for the party: a famous restaurant at Ikenohata, Ueno, called Ugetsu-sō (Rain and Moon Mansion). His excuse was that his son was bound to be sent to the front and killed. Shizue remembered the occasion in her joint memoir with Azusa. "It was an astonishingly spacious banquet room that was almost dark, with black curtains tightly put up around it for the anti-air-raid blackout." The first fleet of B-29s based in Saipan would not appear in the sky of Tokyo and bomb the city until two weeks later, but the blackout had been in effect for some time by then. "The owner of the restaurant, though, had kindly scraped together a good deal of foodstuff to create an excellent banquet that belied the difficulties of the time. All of us were overjoyed."³³

Late in his life, when asked for an essay in praise of Ueno, Mishima chose to write about the evening in the innermost part of the Ugetsu-sō to say that "the memory of it was so beautiful all the publication parties since have seemed fake," and that was why he had firmly declined all the offers for gatherings for his books.[34]

*The Forest* contained the title story and four others. "A Moon on the Surface of the Water" (*Minomo no tsuki*) is a narrative woven from letters among three lovers, a woman and two men, in Heian Japan. "To Be Left for the Generations to Come" (*Yoyo ni nokosan*) is another love story with three lovers, two men and a woman, again set in the Heian Period, though here in its declining phase. A novella more than twice as long as "The Forest," it is inspired by the poetic autobiography left by Kenreimon'in Ukyō no Daibu (born 1157?), one woman who wrote about the effects of the five-year war waged by the two dominant military clans of the day, the Taira and Minamoto, from 1180 to 1185; she lost her lover, Taira no Sukemori, in the final battle of the war. These stories, along with "The Forest," again demonstrate Mishima's absorption in Heian literature and his mastery of classical style and themes.

"Otto and Maya" (*Ottō to Maya*), yet another love story but set in imagined Germany, is notable for its fanciful deployment of translatese—a style almost unavoidable to anyone attempting to transfer faithfully any of the European languages into Japanese.

"Prayer Diary" (*Inori no nikki*) is the only one in the group with no stylistic attempt to imitate classical Japanese or a translation from a Western language. Narrated by a young woman in her puberty in contemporary Japan, the "diary" has a psychological immediacy and persuasiveness that the other stories lack, especially "Otto and Maya," which may be, as Mishima admitted to Azuma, "foppish, giddy, and empty," though it fully shows Mishima's chameleon-like ability to switch from one style to another.[35]

## *The Nawate Incident*

When it comes to Mishima's writerly versatility, a short story he completed five days after *The Forest* came out cannot pass unmentioned: "The Nawate Incident" (*Nawate jiken*).

The story is based on an actual incident that occurred in Kyoto,

March 23, 1868 (the 29th of Second Month by the lunar calendar). Two samurai assaulted the British legation as it headed from their temporary abode, the Buddhist temple Chion'in, toward the Imperial Palace for an audience with the Mikado in a long procession appropriate for Great Britain's status as the dominant power of the day. Because the two assailants merely meant to kill foreigners, any foreigners, and did not target anyone in particular, they left unharmed Minister Sir Parkes and others on his staff, including Sir Ernest Satow, who would write a famous account of Japan during that period of great political transition, *A Diplomat in Japan*. But they did manage to wound nine British soldiers and three Japanese attendants before one of them was killed—by the two samurai accompanying the British, Gotō Shōjirō and Nakai Kōzō—and the other severely wounded and captured.

The story, which was discovered among Mishima's papers years after his death, makes a fine contrast to the stories in *The Forest*. It weaves a few vivid, gory details into what appears to be a matter-of-fact description in a series of staccato, masculine sentences. It concludes:

> Thus the incident more or less came to an end. The Minister [Parkes] and his entourage returned to the Chion'in. It was only after they walked in the main gate that they felt relieved enough to start talking to one another. Then there was another commotion at the main gate and a man soaked in blood ran in from there. Sir Harry, excited, rushed toward him, repeatedly calling out, "Nakai! Nakai!" But people restrained him; Nakai was carrying a head in his left hand. The head was placed in front of Sir Harry. A heathen joy revived among the people. The brain was visible in the triangular wound on the left side of the head. A wound was incised into the right jaw as well. Nakai had carried it by its hair so its facial features had become eerily lopsided. The neck was cut off straight so the head was suited to be placed as it was. Only the neck bone, muddy white, showed a somewhat uneven section. The head as a whole, because it was wet with blood plasma, seemed to soften its ghastly impression.
>
> Parkes' legs twitched as if he had a persistent fear even as he felt a childish satisfaction. That was because he was seeing a decapitated head for the first time.

Harry Parkes described the assault in his letter to his wife, and his secretary, A. M. Mitford (Lord Redesdale), wrote an article about it that saw print in *The London Times* on May 20.[36] Mishima evidently based his story on some account, but which account is not clear.

Equally unclear is why he did not have a chance to publish it—except perhaps that the idea of samurai guarding a British legation was not quite right while the war continued. One thing to be noted is that Mishima apparently thought that "Sir Harry" and Parkes were two different persons. He perhaps did not realize that the title "sir" normally was followed by a personal name, not by a family name.

In later writing about the publication of *The Forest*, Mishima noted several times that the book sold out quickly—all four thousand copies of the first printing. He explained that there weren't many first editions being issued at that time and that there was a strong appetite for new books. Apparently his book sold well, but some think not to the extent Mishima suggested. A few have even averred that Mishima took unsold copies to secondhand book dealers himself. Whatever the case, the confidence gained from having published a book, combined with the unusual access to paper, may have given Mishima an attitude that would rub at least one editor the wrong way.

## "*Circus*" (Zirkus)

With Kuriyama Riichi's recommendation, Noda Utarō, the editor of *Bungei*, by then the only literary magazine by a regular publishing house still standing, wrote Mishima toward the end of January to invite him to bring some fiction. In response, Mishima took "Circus" (*Sākasu*)[37] to Noda on February 22, 1945, the day Tokyo was struck by heavy snow in the continuing severely cold winter that was "dark, jittery, and oppressed" by constant US bombings.

Noda accepted and published one of Mishima's stories in the end, and he did a few other things for him, but he apparently did not get along with the young writer from the outset. Probably because he was used to dealing with established authors, he found Mishima to be too "impudent," too "self-confident," and too argumentative, to his taste, a youth more eager to get his stuff published than anything else; worse, he flaunted his access to paper. "Once he kindly asked if I needed paper,"

Noda recalled. "I declined the offer by saying, though I edit, I'm not a printer, so even if you gave me paper, I wouldn't know what to do with it." Another reason for his dislike of Mishima may well have been a preconception. Shiga Naoya, whom he had met a few weeks before Mishima showed up, had dismissed Mishima's fiction as all "fantasy" with little "sense of reality." (Shiga was another writer Mishima admired who did not reciprocate his sentiments.[38])

As he recalled, Noda took care to tell Mishima that Shiga's opinion itself did not mean much; Mishima could push his talent in a different direction. He believed that "Yisugei's Hunt" (*Esugai no kari*), the story he accepted, was a result of that suggestion. It describes a young Yisugei, Genghis Khan's father, robbing a bridegroom of his beautiful bride by murdering him. Evidently Mishima read a Japanese translation of *The Secret History of the Mongols* and turned a passage from it into a story.[39] It is another stylistic marvel, with short, image-packed sentences strung together.

In his memoir of his wartime work as editor, appropriately called *The Season of Ashes* (*Hai no kisetsu*), Noda wrote Mishima brought two stories that snowy day, suggesting that the other was "Yisugei's Hunt," which Mishima had yet to write. For that matter, he did not take "Circus," the story Mishima brought. He rather liked it, but "a single kissing scene" in it made it "totally unpublishable at the time." It is an innocuous story of a circus manager's masochistic fascination with a young couple in his troupe, a female tightrope artist and a male acrobatic horse rider. Stylistically, it showed Mishima's preference for paradoxes. It was a story to which Mishima would develop a great attachment. He revised it a number of times, included it in a number of selections, and even recorded it, himself reading it, in 1966, with the music composed for it.[40]

As to Mishima's writings as a whole, Noda detected "an influence of the stiff formalism of the Japan Romantic School"—the name that directly came from *Nihon Rōman-ha*, the magazine Yasuda Yojūrō founded in 1935. The magazine lasted for only three years, but its name became synonymous with a literary movement because of Yasuda's considerable influence as a Japanist for about a decade before Japan's defeat. Overall, Noda decided that Mishima, talented writer as he may be, was largely no more than a literary "*epigone*"—the English word is Noda's— which he thought he confirmed later when Mishima became famous. Like Fuji Masaharu, he was put off by Mishima, rather than drawn to him.[41]

A year earlier Mishima had asked Noda to introduce him to Kawabata Yasunari and Noda had passed Mishima's wishes to Kawabata. This time, perhaps with a copy of *The Forest* delivered via another writer, it worked quickly. Mishima received a letter from Kawabata, dated March 8, thanking him, saying that he had been interested in "your manner of writing since I read part of the story in *Bungei Bunka*." Thus the two started corresponding.⁴²

---

On March 3, 1945, in his "Saturday communication" to Mitani Makoto—the regular correspondence he had started with the officer candidate four months earlier—Mishima noted that there had been no air raids for five consecutive days, calling it "an eerie peace." By then air raids by B-29s had become routine. In fact, Mishima had written an unforgettable essay on one of them—the one on January 19 that threatened Ōta-chō, Gunma, where the Nakajima aircraft factory to which he was assigned for wartime labor since early January was located—though in the essay he depicted as more terrifying than the actual bombings the members of the militia. Ultra-rightwing thugs in reality, they were employed to goad the workers as they moved back and forth between factory and shelter by brandishing wooden swords.⁴³

Azusa himself reported to his son, with his disconcerting airiness, one air raid in Tokyo on January 27 that killed about one thousand people on the Ginza alone, with corpses piled up in Hibiya Park and people going there to see if they included missing family members.⁴⁴ In February, with air raids growing ever more frequent, the Metropolitan Police Department issued an order to kill all dogs to avoid "confusion" following bombings. Part of the reason was likely to prevent the spectacle of dogs eating corpses. Muramatsu Takeshi, later Mishima's literary associate who would write his literary biography, remembered his family following the ordinance and killing their dog, a Spitz, with an injection, on February 7, 1945.⁴⁵

For almost every "Saturday communication" Mishima used a postcard, packing it with a disproportionate volume of message written in small handwriting, which marveled Mitani. He used the rationed government-issue postcards evidently to avoid the trouble of censors opening his letters, but the recipient in the military school often wondered if he was going to be summoned for questioning.⁴⁶ It was at a time when English was condemned as an "enemy language" and reading European authors made you automatically suspect. Mishima's message on March 3, which is Girls' Day, managed to pack all of the following in the cramped space, beginning with the required seasonal observations:

> Monotonous everyday, days when I must irrigate my surroundings with water myself, stir ripples, plant waterweeds, and dream of a seascape more resplendent than the Mediterranean. I have grown somewhat used to such a life. Today is the fifth day we've had no air raids whatsoever. An eerier peace. Even in its midst the serene spring day has pushed itself close to my window. The remaining snow still feels hard to my feet stepping on it, but the young buds on the garden trees are growing with the kind of softness that makes me suspect they might melt more easily than the light snow. From now on I'll be able to do a lot of work. While wanting to embark on a full-length work, I am ducking the issue by writing an essay on Marcel Proust's "The Death of Baldassare Silvande." Speaking of such things, I'm tempted to write, with resolve, the essay on the *Chuci* that I once told you about, despite a shortage of material. For the moment, I am enjoying Nerval's novel, Valéry's essay on Mallarmé, plays of Yeats and Singe, and Karel Čapek's *Insect Play*. How long will this kind of carefree life of reading last? I don't know when the university is going to summon me back with "We don't care whether you have amyloid infiltration of the lungs or what, just show up." Whatever may happen will, then.
>
> From now on we must rigorously train the spirit of "supporting the tragedy," rather than "bearing the tragedy," I think. We don't have to seek our model in ancient Greece; the Genroku Era of Sōrinshi [Chikamatsu Monzaemon] that is close to us tells us in unadorned fashion what a renaissance is. The Yasuda Yojūrō–style optimistic theory of National Learning is remotest from me now.
>
> —I've talked only about myself. Please take good care of yourself.

Mishima did finish the essay on the first story in Proust's *Les Plaisirs et les Jours* and published it a year and a half later, which is to say, nine months after Japan's defeat. In it he wrote, "I dare say, with sneers fully expected, that in the excellent final chapter of 'La Mort de Baldassare' I have a whiff of the remaining fragrance of the *Orientalism* of decadent Romanticism," pointing to Alexis' "genuine curiosity, terror, and love concerning [his uncle's] death, as well as Baldassare's identification with the boy Alexis"⁴⁷—"a kindred feeling that, gradually spreading, turned into an immense stupefaction at the universal scandal of these existences, his own included, walking backward into death with their gaze still fixed on life."⁴⁸

The *Chuci* (*Soji* in Japanese) is an anthology of poems attributed to the Chu Dynasty statesman Qu Yuan (third to fourth centuries B.C.). Mishima had cited a few lines from it for Mitani in January in reporting his progress on "The Medieval Period" (*Chūsei*), saying that images in some of the poems bested those in "ancient poems of Ikhnaton, of Egypt." For that matter, he had told his parents, in a letter he wrote the same day, January 20: "Last night I borrowed the *Chuci* from a friend and read it; China is a great country. Something like 'Nine Songs' is several times superior to Song of Solomon in the Old Testament."⁴⁹

Had the military or civilian police censor been as well read as Mishima, he certainly would have confiscated this card or questioned its recipient Mitani—as he would have blocked the publication of *The Forest*. If the decadence and aestheticism of the stories in *The Forest* went totally against the militarism of the day,⁵⁰ Proust and "The Death of Baldassare Silvande" carried as much of the same qualities as the next writer Mishima mentioned, Karel Čapek, and *The Insect Play* carried Socialism.

Not just that the Czech writer's play, first produced in 1923, was an overtly socialist work, but the Čapek Brothers—Karel often worked with his brother Josef, as in the case of *The Insect Play*—were anti-Hitler to the core. Karel's last plays, before his death in 1938, were "written just before the entry of Hitler into Czechoslovakia, deal with the rise of dictatorship and the terrible consequences of war," whereas Josef was sent to a German concentration camp and would die in Belsen in April 1945.⁵¹ Even Mishima would not have dared to try to publish a list of aphoristic assertions he penned in January 1944 wherein he expressed his loathing of Nazism, predicting that "the various ideas of German Nazism [would be] the worst harm and poison for tomorrow's Japan."[52]

Mishima at times indulged in cultural chauvinism. In his missive in early January, he asked Mitani if he read Ōshima Masamitsu's *The Autumn at the Shūgakuin* (*Shūgakuin no aki*). The biologist, who had studied with David Starr Jordan at Stanford, had written about an American boy who had laughed at Shiobara Tasuke's horse but who nevertheless understood "the true import of Japan's sublime beauty," Mishima told Mitani, when he picked up a single maple leaf at the Shūgakuin Detached Palace. Mishima then wrote: "If Americans had made an effort to appreciate [Onoe Kikugorō] VI's 'Lion Dance'—or rather, if they had had a great people's flexibility, this war would not have happened."[53]

## *The Japan Romantic School*

One thing notable in the March 3 "communication" is that Mishima by the spring of 1945 was distancing himself from Yasuda Yojūrō, the founder of the Japan Romantic School, because Yasuda would go on to be invoked for Mishima, not just during his life but after his death. One recent American scholar, Alan Tansman, for example, has called Mishima "Yasuda's most famous epigone."[54] Somewhat earlier a Japanese scholar, Konishi Jin'ichi, had spoken of Yasuda's influence on Mishima before his "disappearance," as Yasuda was drafted into the army in 1945.[55] Perhaps more important, a few decades before Konishi, when Mishima's fame was spreading fast and wide, another Japanese scholar had described Yasuda in terms that eerily adumbrated what Mishima would be thought of: "Yasuda was something indefinable, one ultimate form of Japanese-style universalist from which you cannot escape." That scholar was the Asianist and student of Chinese literature Takeuchi Yoshimi.

"The philosophical role Yasuda played was to annihilate thought by destroying every categorization," Takeuchi wrote. "In this respect he was more advanced than the Kyoto School that subordinated the arbitrariness of concepts to categories." The Kyoto School refers to a group of scholars in the humanities at the Imperial University of Kyoto who were establishing their own views, theories, and philosophies on the basis of their knowledge of a range of developments in the rest of the world. The group included the prominent philosopher Nishida Kitarō who "synthesize[d] insights from the Japanese tradition with those of the European philosophical tradition," in the end founding his argument on "the logic of nothingness."[56]

Takeuchi continued: "[Yasuda] advocated total abnegation of Civilization and Enlightenment"—the slogan the Meiji government employed in urging the Japanese populace to catch up with the West—"but the Civilization and Enlightenment he meant was neither a trend, nor a fashion, nor a logic, but something that was at once a trend, a fashion, and a logic, that is, modern Japan in its entirety. Accordingly, it included himself as a matter of course. In him, it is to theticize himself." In other words, "his thought was 'a blank thought.'"[57] Takeuchi, Yasuda's high-school classmate, wrote these words as he became the first to reassess him following a round of his demonization after the war as "an ultranationalist, reactionary, and cultural fascist" and as "an extoller of a war of invasion."[58]

Yasuda, in any case, had a magnetic hold on young readers, Mishima among them. One question then is: How did such a swing occur in Yasuda's reputation before and after the war—from "a spiritual gem" (Takeuchi) to "a spiritual demon" (Tansman)? Yasuda went through three stages or layers of intellectual influence. In high school he was nicknamed a "Marx Boy." As a student of aesthetics at the Imperial University of Tokyo he absorbed German Romanticism and National Learning. After he won a prize for his aesthetic meditation titled *Japanese Bridges* (*Nihon no hashi*), he became a Japanist with his understanding of National Learning at the fore, albeit colored by a heavy dose of "irony" (*romantische Ironie*) and Nihilism. Given the times and circumstances, his aestheticism had the danger of being easily misconstrued because of its stress on Japanese tradition and "the Japanese spirit" (*Yamato damashii*) or "the Japanese heart" (*Yamato gokoro*).

A typical enunciation of Yasuda's may be one that appears in his 1943 essay, "The Great East Asia War and Japanese Literature." Citing a phrase from an ancient military vow that Ōtomo no Yakamochi (718?-85) incorporated in his poem in the *Man'yōshū*, Yasuda said:

> As far as arguments on the war in cultural and literary arts are concerned, everything ends in our resolve in going to the

battlefield. In addition, today's loyal and brave officers and men are living exactly what the ancients sang of, "Our wish is to die by our Sovereign's side." The ancients' desire, "Our wish is to die by our Sovereign's side," was simply that we want to die near our Sovereign. We think of nothing else. We don't talk about it. That was it. In the event, where is the cause of our having to discuss the meaning of dying on a battlefield (*uchijini*) with thoughts among Western barbarians (*Seijū*) such as world history and worldview?[59]

The phrase in question appears in the aforementioned *When Seagoing*. But Yasuda's use of encrusted, orotund words such as *uchijini* and *Seijū* makes it easy to overlook the fact that here he was taking on the day's grandiose talk of putting Japan on the world map through the Greater East Asian War and the challenge to European hegemony. There would be little wonder if the militarists, growing ever more sensitive as Japan began to lose one battle after another, found such atavistic thought subversive—or so thought Oketani Hideaki, a student of Japan's intellectual history, *Geistesgeschichte*. They placed Yasuda under surveillance of the Military Police, Kenpeitai, after July 1944, then suddenly drafted him, a man in his mid-thirties and ailing, in March 1945, and sent him directly to the front.[60]

Mishima's apparent rejection of Yasuda-style classicism at that juncture may seem abrupt. But Mitani was right in speculating—as he did in compiling Mishima's "Saturday communications" with commentaries after his death—that Mishima by then was beginning to find the Japanist's "dreamy" single-mindedness too simplistic. His deep interest in world literature obviously would not accommodate such a narrowing focus. But his skepticism of Yasuda also had to do with his disappointment with the man when he went to see him, in late 1943. He asked what he thought of the rhetorical style of nō plays. Yasuda's response was: "Well, it's been said since the old days to be like hand-woven brocade. You might say those sentences are like an encyclopedia of the day."

The verse sections of nō plays weave together parts of famous poems and well-known phrases through the punning devise called *kakekotoba*. So Yasuda most likely meant that those who composed the plays had to have an encyclopedic command of belles-lettres. Mishima, who half a year earlier had written an essay exalting the literary device, saying that *kakekotoba* are "the most beautiful bridges Mr. Yasuda has mentioned in *Japanese Bridges*,"⁶¹ had expected the avowed Romantic classicist to come up with some sort of witticism, not what was usually said. "The resplendent style of nō plays is an ultimate aesthetic resistance in language, with eschatological thoughts hidden behind it," Mishima thought. "A ready deployment of such an extremely artificial, gorgeous language must necessarily require an underpinning of a sense of despair."⁶²

## *The Greatest Air Raid*

The greatest air raid in Japan struck the night before the next "Saturday communication" was due. On the night of March 9, wave after wave of B-29s bombed Tokyo. In the end a total of three hundred "flying fortresses" dropped two thousand tons of incendiaries. By concentrating on one section of the city known as Shitamachi—in size, the equivalent of seven-tenths of Manhattan—the 2.2-hour bombings, which began a little after midnight, created the kind of firestorm seen in Dresden, "scorched and boiled and baked to death" more than eighty-nine thousand people, and deprived one million people of their homes. The catastrophe destroyed more lives than the atomic bombings of Hiroshima and Nagasaki five months later, according to the US Strategic Bombing Survey. But it was quickly laid aside because the atomic bomb was thought to have put "the continuity of life into question," as Mary McCarthy put it.⁶³

That night Mishima was in Maebashi, staying at an inn. Some days earlier Mitani's mother had telephoned to invite him to join the family going to see Mitani at his school. The officer candidates were occasionally allowed to see their families, and the next date for such meetings was set for the following Saturday, March 10. Kuniko was going, too, the mother said. Mishima agreed to go with them. Leaving Ueno on March 9, the group stayed in Maebashi overnight before visiting Mitani the next day.

On March 10, Army Day, Mitani's family, like many other visitors, had a picnic-style lunch on the wind-swept, withered lawns outside the soldier's quarters, which were halfway up Mt. Shiina. The day must have been cold. The night of the great Tokyo air raid is known to have been one of the coldest on record. Mitani pointed toward Tokyo and said,

"Last night it looked scarlet over there; it must have been horrible. You can't tell what may have happened to your house. During none of the air raids in the past did the sky above it look red like that." The previous night a friend of his who was up during the night to go to the latrine had seen columns of fire rising in Tokyo.[64] The metropolis is about sixty miles southeast of Maebashi.

On the way back to Tokyo, the Mitanis and Mishima ran into a tip of the terrifying consequences of the air raid. Ōmiya, Saitama's railway junction close to Tokyo, was overflowing with refugees from the devastated parts of Tokyo.

"Wrapped up in blankets, they revealed only unseeing, unthinking eyes or rather simply their eyeballs," Mishima wrote. "There was a mother who seemed to intend to rock her child on her lap eternally with the same width swing. A young woman lay collapsed against a long wicker chest, asleep, a half-scorched artificial flower in her hair." Mishima and the Mitanis were dressed up for a weekend visit, "bourgeois style." But here were people "who had seen all the various things that had defined their lives engulfed in the fire. They had seen human relations, love and hate, reason, assets engulfed in the fire before their own eyes."

"As our group passed through them, we weren't even rewarded with a reproachful glance. We were completely ignored. For the simple reason that we did not share their misfortune, our *raison d'être* was obliterated, and we were regarded as a shadowy existence."

Kuniko, terrified, clung to Mishima. Mishima for the first time held her, putting his arm over her shoulders, "not unnaturally."

B-29s continued to raid Tokyo and elsewhere, bombers and fighters to bomb and strafe, in the end laying 65 percent of all Japanese cities to waste.[65]

---

In April the Imperial University of Tokyo protested the treatment of its students at the Nakajima aircraft factory and withdrew them. Lectures at the Faculty of Law resumed, but in May, with too many professors unable to make their classes, these were abandoned again.

On the fifth of that month, Mishima's wartime assignment changed from an aircraft factory to a naval factory in Kōza, Kanagawa, where he worked as a librarian and a trench-digger. The letters between Mishima and Kuniko increased. They exchanged photographs. Kuniko even wrote, using a most courteously feminine locution in Japanese to say, "I long for you."

On May 24, there was another large-scale air raid by B-29s—the second largest, in fact, after the one on the night of March 9. This one destroyed Yamanote—an area where well-heeled families tended to live, including the Hiraokas. Mishima went home from the naval factory, walking half the way along the railroad on which the trains had stopped running. The ties were still smoldering.

Miraculously, the Hiraoka house along with those in its immediate neighborhood hadn't been hit or burnt. These houses stood out neatly, like an oasis in a desert. His family was unscathed, too. To celebrate their good fortune, they dug out canned sweet bean paste *yōkan* from the underground food storage buried for an emergency and ate it. Mishima's sister, then an acute and unreserved seventeen, asked him during the celebration.

"You are crazy about someone, aren't you?"
"Who told you something like that?"
"I can tell."
"Anything wrong about me liking someone?"
"Nope. When are you getting married?"

By then the Mitani family had evacuated to Karuizawa. It was an all-woman contingent: grandmother, mother, Kuniko, and her two sisters. (In *Confessions*, Kuniko's father is described as dead.) They sent an invitation to Mishima to visit them. Mishima did, in mid-June. Kuniko had come to meet him at Karuizawa Station. "I hadn't seen her, and had passed by her, when she poked me in the back, with 'Boo!' I turned round, and she turned red like a coquelicot. In such an act, her shyness, and a kind of innocent coquetry, there was something that made me clearly feel that we were lovers."

Both *Confessions* and *My Puberty* describe their first kiss—something Mishima wanted to do. However, there is a great difference between the two descriptions. The one in *Confessions* is loaded with Radiguet-like adolescent calculations. The one in *My Puberty* is simple.

Through her raincoat, I suddenly felt her fierce heartbeat coming to my chest. It was as though I were holding a large trembling bird. Then I saw right before my eyes the downy hair growing above her upper lip. She had her eyes closed tight. I pressed my lips on hers, which had no lipstick and were dry. She was quaking so hard that our teeth collided.

About a month after this incident, in late July, Mishima received from Mitani Makoto a letter, which the epistler said he was writing as "ambassador extraordinary": My family, Kuniko included, is taking her relationship with you seriously. My mother is even thinking of setting the wedding date. I don't know about the wedding, but I don't think it's too early for an engagement. But first we must know how you feel about it. We'd be of course delighted with YES, but we won't feel bad even if it's NO. Feel free to respond frankly.

The rapidity of the development alarmed Mishima. He came up with explanations as to why he couldn't marry Kuniko. In *Confessions*, the narrator explains to his mother the content of the letter he has just received and gives the reasons for declining the marriage so he may elicit her "stubborn objections": that "my father is neurotic and a scold and living with him in the same house is bound to make the person who is to be my wife suffer; that, on the other hand, I have no prospect for setting up a separate house for the time being; that my old-fashioned family and Sonoko's cheerful, easygoing family can't expect to get along with each other; that I myself don't want to have a wife so early and go through all the attendant problems...." The actual reasons he passed on to Mitani were probably more or less the same.

The familial explanations aside, it was a fact that Mishima was only twenty and still a student. Thus, the Mitani family's—or Kuniko's—urgency put a halt to Mishima's first love for the moment, at least in its overt form.

CHAPTER SIX

# The War and Its Aftermath

*I would like to contribute, to the best of my ability, ...
to a postwar renaissance in literature and arts, and the
ordering of them.*

—Letter to Mitani Makoto on August 22, 1945

On August 15, Japan surrendered.

To most assessors, Japan had no chance of winning the war with the United States, let alone the forces with England, and the Netherlands added to it. The Total War Research Institute the government set up in the spring of 1941 by assembling youthful men of keen intelligence and wide experience from a variety of fields made this abundantly clear.

Toward the end of August, the members of the institute formed a mock cabinet and in a two-day session presented to the actual cabinet, including Army Minister Tōjō Hideki, the conclusion that defeat was inescapable in the approaching war. In October, the political leadership chose Tōjō, the war advocate, as prime minister with the understanding that he would work to avert the war. The leadership thought he had the decisiveness to fire people who went against stated national policy. Tōjō took the job seriously enough but could not resolve the impasse he had helped to create himself.[1]

Besides the fact that Japan's military venture had bogged down in China, the basic reason for a projected surefire defeat in the event of war was simple: the vast economic discrepancy between Japan and the main enemy it was to take on, the United States. Lt. Gen. Ishihara Kanji put it perhaps most memorably: "It's a contest, isn't it," he is known to have kept telling anyone who would listen, "between Japan, which is going to buy ¥10,000 worth of things when it has only ¥1,000 in its wallet, and the United States, which is going to buy ¥10,000 worth of things when it has ¥1,000,000 in its wallet?" If you are Japan, "you might not notice it while buying this for ¥100 or that for ¥200, but after a while you quickly find you're ruined."[2]

Ishihara, a strategic thinker though also a religious fanatic, had predicted that the United States and Japan (Asia) would be the two last combatants in "the final world war"; the Manchurian Incident he had pulled off, in 1931, was part of his idea of unifying Asia for that eventuality. But he had also argued that Japan was far from ready, and insisted that Japan would lose even with its dazzling initial victories. In the fall of 1942, when the government was forced to withdraw from Guadalcanal and a meeting with Tōjō was arranged, Ishihara, ever blunt-spoken, told the man who had put him out of active duty in March 1941 and was now prime minister, to resign on the spot because Japan was sure to be defeated and destroyed as long as he ran the war. Tōjō responded by tightening the military and police surveillance of Ishihara.[3]

Ishihara survived under the Tōjō regime, but another fiery-tempered leader, Nakano Seigō, did not. The journalist-turned-politician who at one time advocated Hitler/Mussolini-style totalitarianism, Nakano became an outspoken critic of Tōjō as the latter accumulated dictatorial powers. On New Year's Day 1943 the *Asahi Shinbun* published his article titled "On Wartime Premiership" that cited Clemenceau, Lenin, and ancient Chinese leaders to suggest Tōjō lacked leadership qualities.[4] Although the article had passed pre-publication censorship, Tōjō banned that edition of the daily.

That fall the Kenpeitai arrested and interrogated Nakano—despite the fact he was an active member of the Diet—on the ground, as was revealed after the war, that he had accused the army and navy of interservice discord that had created the disaster earlier that year that was Guadalcanal. Upon release, Nakano committed suicide by disembowelment. His funeral is said to have drawn twenty thousand people when assembly was severely restricted.

In less than three years, Mishima would make friends with a young woman whom Nakano once wanted to adopt: his sister Mitsuko's best friend, Sassa Teiko.[5]

## *Uesugi Shinkichi and Japan's Mission*

Even as triumphant announcements of overwhelming losses inflicted upon the enemy in each major battle became ever more extravagant, a sense of doom spread. In his "Saturday communication" of April 14, 1945, Mishima was moved to invoke "the now deceased prominence in statist Constitutional studies at the Imperial University, Dr. Uesugi Shinkichi," Uesugi, he said, had written, in 1924, a "great tract" on the inevitability of a US-Japanese collision, arguing that even if "the Japanese race were to be annihilated," Japan would not be able to avoid fighting the United States because doing so would be "Japan's one great mission for the world."[6] Uesugi, who had died in 1929, had advocated Tennō absolutism in Constitutional interpretation on the ground that the Tennō possessed "divinity" and thus had been the adversary of Minobe Tatsukichi, another Constitutional scholar at the same university who argued that the Tennō was a "state organ." Of the controversy provoked by Minobe's theory, we will see more later.

Uesugi's dire fatalism, however "medieval" in its presentation,[7] reflected one major strain of the Zeitgeist of the 1920s, well into the 1930s. By that decade the inevitability of a clash between the United States and Japan had come to be widely accepted on both sides of the Pacific. Among the books predicting it on the US side were *Banzai!* by Parabellum (1908),[8] *The Valor of Ignorance* by Homer Lea (1909), and *The Great Pacific War* by Hector C. Bywater (1925). Nothing excites people's imagination more than the talk of war, and the Japanese fully reciprocated. Writers both serious and merely fantastic came up with accounts of the predicted war. Ishihara Kanji was different only because his prediction was based on his analysis of the history of war.

What provoked Mishima to invoke Uesugi was the unexpected courtesy the daily newspapers showed in reporting the death of President Franklin Delano Roosevelt, which Mishima guessed was a result of the influence of Gen. Anami Korechika. In the days when references to the United States and United Kingdom routinely came with the epithet "devil/beast," Anami's action was admirable, Mishima said. He remembered a story from two years earlier: the general had lamented the loss of whatever moral high ground Japan may have had when he saw a movie showing Japanese soldiers trampling upon the American flag as they marched. In early April, in what Mishima called a "coup," Ret. Adm. Suzuki Kantarō had formed a new cabinet and Anami was his choice for Minister of the Army. There was the instinctive feeling among the Japanese that Suzuki's task was to find some way of ending the war—a dread thought for the diehard core of the military. Anami himself continued to insist, to the very end, on fighting to the last man.

If Mishima citing Uesugi at that point surprises, his words on *tokkōtai* a week later, on April 21, may startle. *Tokkōtai*—an abbreviation of *tokubetsu kōgekitai*, "special attack force"—in this context refers to a squadron of warplanes tasked with crashing into enemy warships. A desperate measure that Vice Adm. Ōnishi Takijirō had formally introduced during the Battle of Leyte Gulf six months earlier, it was instantly given the epithet *kamikaze*, "the divine wind"—*kamikaze* being the Japanese reading of the Sinified word *shinpū*, the generic name officially devised for the force.[9] The naming came from the folkloric belief that it was "the divine wind," a typhoon in fact, that helped Japan repel two Mongolian invasions, in 1274 and 1281.[10] Respect for voluntary self-sacrifice in a hopeless situation was a traditional ideal and Mishima was writing at the height of the Battle of Okinawa in which the deployment of *tokkōtai* dominated. Still, the almost delirious tone of his April 21 letter makes us pause.

> ... the *tokkōtai* is not a resuscitation of the ancient era but an annihilation of the modern—that is, the "modern" that Japan's cultured class has tried for a long time to overcome but has been unable to—not overcoming but wounding and killing (this, one step higher, fiercer, and more beautiful than overcoming) of the "modern" that is vast, *monumental*, Kant's, Edison's, America's that we should never disdain. Through the *tokkōtai* has "modern man" for the first time been able to grasp the dawn light of "the present age" or, rather, of "our age" in its true sense; for the first time the intelligentsia, which was until now the illegitimate child of the modern, has become a historic heir.

Behind this apparent raving was a debate on "overcoming modernity" that had culminated in 1942. The question, which survives to this day, not just in Japan but elsewhere, was: Is modernization the same as Westernization? For Japan, which at the time seemed particularly successful among the latecomers in global self-assertion, it came with a nagging doubt: Is a modern Japan nothing more than an awkward imitation—"an illegitimate child," as Mishima put it—of the West? Was creating slogans such as "getting out of Asia to become part of the West," in the process, an embarrassment?

The matter came to a head when Japan went to war simultaneously with the United States, United Kingdom and the Netherlands and unexpectedly won a series of battles. In July 1942 the monthly *Bungakukai* convened a symposium on "overcoming modernity" with thirteen participants, among them a graduate of the Berlin National Music School and composer; a Catholic theologian; a historian of Medieval Europe; a physicist then engaged in atomic research; and a philosopher of science. (A month before the symposium the Japanese Navy had suffered a crushing defeat in the Battle of Midway, which the navy regarded as fatal and naturally kept top secret.[11])

These men were well aware that European thinkers had raised questions on the validity of modernity in their own context—that, for example, some focused on the scientific progress promoted in the nineteenth century, and others went back to the Renaissance, which necessarily led to the question of humanism. On that score, as Nakamura Mitsuo, one of the men-of-letters participating in the symposium, pointed out acidly, if the purpose of the symposium was simply to exalt Japan over the presumably declining West, it would be disgraceful to employ the term Europeans devised for themselves: "overcoming modernity."[12]

Still, the term became a catchword of sorts. For Mishima, then twenty, the advent of suicide air corps when Japan was on the brink was nothing as "lukewarm" as "a resuscitation of a myth," but the annihilation of modernity itself. It was "my own interpretation alone," he wrote Mitani, but he may well have been inspired to say this by Yokomitsu Riichi's essay simply titled *Tokkōtai* that had recently appeared in *Bungei*. In his essay, the writer who had turned from an admirer of things Western to a fervent nationalist wondered if "the *tokkō* spirit" is not "the most genuine world spirit that has been transmitted since the primeval time several thousand, tens of thousand years ago."[13]

Mishima went on to assert: "Herein lies the reason that all the cultured class of Japan, all the cultured people of the world, should genuflect before the *tokkōtai*." These strong words did not faze Mitani, at least as he assembled Mishima's letters forty years later. Instead, he wrote that these words showed his friend's true worth in this assessment of the *tokkōtai*.[14]

The idea that the suicide missions or the men who took part in them represented an inexorable yet worthy value would play an important role in Mishima's thinking later in his life. He determined that the *tokkōtai* was the ultimate form of "*decadence*," though a "paradoxical *decadence* (that cannot be so termed)" that he fully affirmed. That is how he put the matter in a testament he wrote four days after Japan's surrender "to commemorate August 1945."[15] But he knew the idea so stated was too outlandish for comprehension, so he quoted Satō Haruo restating his point before setting out to explain.

In the preceding decade, "Japan's literary fortune, long shriveled up, did not prosper. Romanticism that erupted at the start of the China Incident"—a clear reference to the advocacy of *Bunka Bungei*, the first issue of which appeared in July 1937—"fell apart showing no admirable blossoming and fruiting. It was an ominous sign. The level of Japan's modern literary arts never attained the level of the military, forced as they were either to follow the latter subserviently or to fall silent. In this imbalance lay one cause of Japan's defeat."

The need for a coequal existence of both martial and literary or intellectual sides of society was not something Mishima suddenly thought up. In his letter to his teacher Shimizu Fumio in June 1943, for example, he, lamenting the enfeeblement of literature at the Peers School in favor of things martial, had stressed his belief that "the literary way," that is, "poetry," had to "match the martial way" for it is "the only thing" a soldier "dashing through the battlefield" has to "count on."[16]

By late 1944, the war situation was such that "we," "the poets," were about to "head for grasping *decadence*," the result of much meditation on "the eschatological thought that flows straight through [Japan's] medieval literature," Mishima continued. "We may have prayed for the final progression of this malaise, but we no longer wanted its complete healing. We wanted our age to drive us to a furious death." By then, of course, militarists were loudly calling for the whole nation to fight to the last man, to "shatter like a jewel," as one military unit after another met that fate.

It was then that the first *tokkōtai* appeared, in the Philippines. "We saw a flood of modern predilections for tragic heroism in our towns or heard praises with optimistic mythological quotations in our streets." That was because what "we quickly intuited and prayed for" was to be with the pilots, to die. But then two things happened. For one, as suicide missions were repeated, "the old-fashioned puerile *humanism*"—Mishima used English just as he did for *decadence*—"from whose milk-smell we have long striven to escape" reared its head.

"Because it is nothing more than what provides man's instinctive sense of good or bad with a plausible excuse, *humanism* can be," Mishima wrote, "like the last descendant of ethics, meaningless, even harmful." But there must be something that "transcends all value judgments." War may be "a nation's supreme aim," Mishima suggested, but "when a contradiction is born between the supreme aim and humanity, the moral principle ceases to exist, the moral principle is lost." Still, "humanity" must be "maintained as powerfully and as persistently as the war effort so as to shed its outward 'weakness.'" Otherwise, a people "devoid of that good resolve" will be met with retribution.

For the other, the military planners deprived the *tokkōtai* pilots of their "divine seat" by calling their deployment "a tactic." It was in fact their advocacy for "victory" that revealed their "moral laxity" and that "moral laxity" was the reason for "the failure of defending Okinawa with death." Not that "the fall and loss of Okinawa" was no less awe-inspiring. "In the midst of the great air raids that made us think of the ultimate of the end of the world," Mishima mused, "we for the first time thought with immediacy and witnessed the two words, 'Divine Nation.'"

This argument may be as difficult to follow as the testament is abstruse, an attempt as it was to reconcile Mishima's by then indelible eschatology with two other strains of thought: his belief in what the authority on the Tennō institution Ben-Ami Shillony proposes to call "monarchial transcendence"[17] and his resolve to rebuild Japanese culture in general and Japanese literature in particular.

So it was that the Tennō stepped in to prevent further degradation and accepted surrender, Mishima averred. The imperial action was "the first ray of dawn" as it meant a return to the age of the Tennō's direct rule, that of Daigo, the sixtieth Tennō by tradition. And Mishima, who began the testament with a declaration that the war had intimated the onset of another Medieval Period, "the opening of a chaotic world," ended it by exhorting the youth of his generation to "build and recover" Japanese culture, to turn Japan into "the envy of a peaceful world." He had a specific prescription for literature: to "hone" its feminine aspect, *tawayameburi*, while for now subduing its masculine aspect, *masuraoburi*, because that is what "our everlasting history of literature continuously teaches us."

What did Mishima mean by the Medieval Period or "the chaotic world"? In his story "The Medieval Period," he designated the era not as the period so named in the standard historical divisions—that is, the period of four centuries that began in the mid-twelfth century as the samurai shunted aside the aristocracy as ruling class—but, rather, as the Age of Warring States that came into being as the decade-long Ōnin War was fading into the past, toward the end of the fifteenth century. The story, which again shows Mishima's absorption in classical language and literature, concerns Zen master Ryōkai's love of the young male dancer Kikuwaka, the eighth Ashikaga shogun Yoshimasa's love of the young vestal Ayaori, and, in the end, the love between Kikuwaka and Ayaori. Mishima later said it was one of the stories he wrote thinking "this may be my last work," expecting the entire Japanese population to be annihilated at any moment, "shattering like a jewel."[18]

What made him "intuit the opening of a chaotic world," as he put it at the outset of his testament, was a poem found in the manuscripts Lt. Wakabayashi left, Mishima wrote. Wakabayashi Tōichi was killed in January 1943, in the last phase of the Battle of Guadalcanal, yet another example of the Japanese military's strategic and logistical blunder that left fifteen thousand soldiers to die of wounds, illnesses, and starvation on the tropical island. But Wakabayashi's charisma was of the kind that would create instant legends. For example, his adjutant, who had been pulled back from the front, is reported to have said, when he heard about his commander's death, that he had no more reason to live and wandered off, with a grenade in hand, into the jungle where Wakabayashi was thought to have died, apparently to kill himself.[19]

In fact, his reputation was such that a movie was made about him, with the leading actor of the day, Hasegawa Kazuo, playing the lieutenant. It was exceptionally long, too. As the war wore on, the increasing power and material shortages had forced filmmakers to limit average movies to the length of one hour, but the movie, titled *Ato ni tsuzuku o shinzu*—based on what was reputed to be Wakabayashi's last words, *Ato ni tsuzuku mono o shinzu*, "I trust those who will follow me"—was ninety-two minutes. It was released in the spring of 1945.

The poem, which Mishima quotes in full, along with its title, "Holy Life," seems uncannily to adumbrate Mishima's thinking.

> Suffering layered upon suffering mornings and evenings,
> this day cannot *not* be another day of torment.
> Life begins and ends with suffering;
> the day of joy is the day of death—
> Who was it that took this view?
> Thus "Suffering being what I am,"
> I'll die to hurry to Nirvana, so saying,
> many a one has hastened to do that.
> Suicide is a kind of spasm,
> heretical in the view of life.
> If someone full of vigor and blood,
> full of spirit and life, is to say,
> I'd like to die, that's a falsity.
> If he says it is true,
> that's happiness-drunk falsehood.
> My life that is no accident,
> my only life that is holy,
> discard it for whose fame?
> Do not behave so intolerably.
> Our holy place to die,
> is holy, therefore beautiful.
> To train for the day to scatter and end,
> strive this moment, this very moment.[20]

Mishima wrote the testament on the war and surrender, he noted with a touch of self-conscious pomposity, "for future historical considerations." Perhaps luckily, it was not found and printed until almost a decade after he killed himself. But three days on he made his literary ambitions public, as it were. On August 22, he chose a good lined sheet of paper and wrote a rather formal letter to Mitani to tell him of his resolve in "the extraordinariness of this age." "I would hope to build, if only within my own self, a maximal, beautiful order. I would like to contribute, to the best of my ability, however slight it may be, to a postwar renaissance in literature and arts, and the ordering of them." The renaissance he had in mind was "William Butler Yeats' Irish Literary Revival," Mishima revealed to Noda Utarō ten days later.[21]

He would not be content to confine his design to Japan, Mishima went on to tell Mitani. Calling war "a phenomenon for cultural exchange," he declared he would do whatever he could "for the universalization of Japanese culture and its transfusion that goes beyond introduction."[22] Given that Japan had just been crushed in war, such ambition was daring. In addition, as he was starkly aware, Japan's efforts to disseminate its culture overseas was at a primitive stage (and would remain so for some time). Mitani guessed that his friend had made this resolution long before the day that might never come with himself alive: the end of the war. He probably was right.[23]

For example, in the early summer of 1944, when the government's war regimentation extended to the Peers School to force it to shut down its Literary Arts Society to replace it with something as "soul-stunting" as "daily-life society"—based perhaps on the authorities' idea that regular people, even the students at the Peers School, should mind dealing only with matters of daily living—Mishima wrote to Shimizu that he would continue to work toward "a daybreak," "the rise of the literary fortune." He disavowed "German-style culturalists'" judgment that "war retards culture by twenty, thirty years," encouraged as he was by "the last passage of Bashō's *Record of a Phantom Hut* (*Genjū-an no ki*)." That is where the haikai master vows to continue to pursue the path he has chosen, "devoid of ability and talent" as he is, ending the haibun with a hokku: "Not showing it is soon to die the cicada shrills."[24]

"There are only two roads for a great traditionalist nation: either extraordinarily feeble or militaristic," Mishima continued his thoughts on the calamitous war and its aftermath in mid-September, in a list of aphoristic statements he titled *Postwar Analects*. "A situation that is in itself healthy and uninterruptible does not exist. Tradition tells us of two things: barbarism and overripeness."

"*Shōshō hikkin* is a command for serious reflection," went another esoteric-sounding aphorism. "For the populace inflamed with a war fever to switch to a peace fever one morning, the casual escape from self-revolution should not be excused with these sacred words." The phrase he cited opens Article 3 of the Constitution attributed to Shōtoku Taishi (574–622): *Shōshō hikkin*, "When you receive an imperial edict, act in humility."[25] Lt. Gen. Kawabe Torashirō, "the last vice chief of staff," for one, had cited the phrase to tell the army to keep quiet, not to engage in any rebellious act, now that the Tennō accepted surrender. Mishima took it to be a warning, although in *The Decline and Fall of the Suzaku* (*Suzaku-ke no metsubō*), his play from three years before his death, he would use it as its theme, taking it in the sense Gen. Kawabe followed: "If the Tennō tells you not to do anything, do nothing." The result was self-destruction.[26]

He also took up "democracy" and "war responsibility." The Potsdam Declaration had said that there would be "stern justice" to "all war criminals," stating that the purpose of occupying Japan would be "the revival and strengthening of democratic tendencies among the Japanese people." Naturally, talk of democracy and debate on who were responsible for the war became rife in no time. "Blinded by the one word *democracy*, politicians are already busy in their sycophancy and ingratiation to the masses," Mishima observed with distaste.

> But the real war responsibility lies with the masses and their stupidity. Just as *The Tale of Genji* had the foundation of its being in the hordes of multitudinous unenlightened masses, so does the literature of our age owe for the most part to the *traditionally unenlightened masses* [Mishima's emphasis]. What precedes enlightenment is the hometown of literature. Enlightening these masses would be useful only in depriving Japan of the creativity of its great classical literature.—But that would never happen. I am at peace about this. Politicians will not indict the masses on war responsibility. They are afraid of them just as the Westerners are afraid of Asia. In this fear lies all our traditional sentiments. In this sense we have been democratic since ancient times.

Mishima followed all this with an assertion: "Only the conservation of Japanese-style nonrationality will contribute to world culture a hundred years from now."[27]

On the day of Japan's surrender, Azusa made a strange announcement to his son: "The world from now on is one for artists. You better become a novelist after all." This was part of what Mishima recalled in an essay, "Around August 15," in 1955, when the mass media wanted to mark the tenth anniversary of Japan's defeat.[28] Azusa's was, of course, no more than a blurt in a moment of chaos. The defeat had created a mass disorientation. The novelist Shiga Naoya, for example, proposed, with a straight face, that the Japanese abandon their own language in favor of French because, he reasoned, without their amorphous language the war would not have happened.[29] Azusa would soon regain his footing and resume urging Mishima to work toward employment at the Ministry of Finance—just as Shiga continued to write in Japanese.

But if Azusa's reversal was temporary, that of a more visible part of the Japanese populace in the face of a crushing defeat was not. Gen. Douglas MacArthur, Supreme Commander for the Allied Powers (SCAP), arrived in Atsugi Airfield on August 30. The route from Atsugi to Yokohama, where the Occupation Headquarters (GHQ) had been temporarily set up two days earlier, was guarded by Japanese troops lining both sides of it, guns ready but famously facing away from the caravan of Occupiers. The surrender ceremony was held on the battleship Missouri in Tokyo Bay, on September 2. On September 15, the GHQ was moved from Yokohama to the main building of the insurance company Daiichi Seimei, in Tokyo, that faced the Imperial Palace from the southeast corner, and the SCAP settled down in the former US Embassy, in Akasaka.

By early October, the about-face of the Japanese was complete. Writing to Mitani early that month, Mishima spoke of the "popularity . . . simply a bizarre popularity" of the Occupation troops he witnessed in the part of the Ginza where the Kabuki-za theater he frequented was located. Mitani, released from the officer-candidate course, had written about the great change that had descended on Karuizawa.

"I had a little errand to run and went to Owari-chō, where the fierce human traffic hasn't changed a bit since before the war," Mishima told his friend. "Still, there isn't a single store where the Japanese can buy things. The Occupation force popularity, shall we call it, it's simply a bizarre popularity; shabby dirty Japanese in khaki and *monpe* attire mill around." The ragged, beaten-dog appearance of his compatriots contrasted sharply with the vitality of the machinery Americans brought.

"On the streets jeeps and military trucks whiz back and forth incessantly, at wonderful speed." Mishima was witnessing what until a few months earlier used to amaze the Japanese soldiers exposed to US forces in battlefields: the sheer abundance of the mechanized part of the US military.

"Enchanted by shopping Occupation soldiers and women reporters, there are, I tell you, crowds upon crowds of people, mouths agape, listening gratefully to (though can't hope to understand) the responses in English. Nothing other than animal curiosity." Not only had Tokyo, once the vaunted "great city of the world," turned into "a dirty pockmarked map," Mishima observed, referring to the numerous bomb craters, but those who used to "put on airs as they sallied forth night after night in unaccustomed silk stockings and high heels or in ready-made jackets, heads oiled aglitter, have their true worth revealed." Now women were "in slovenly soiled *monpe*, men in worn-out khaki overalls that some workmen seem to have given up." And as they gawked at Americans and other foreigners, male and female, who have flooded the land, the Japanese "flaunted their real idiocy, grotesquery, ignorance profligately or, rather, as though they were enjoying it."

"There are some who frown on those begging for cigarettes from the Occupation troops and bemoan, 'The Japanese have fallen so low,'" Mishima concluded with sarcasm: "But this lament somewhat misses the point; their present ugly state neither adds anything to them nor subtracts anything from them. What a base, despicable, and yet loveable people the Japanese are!"[30]

In fact, the Japanese government had led the way in groveling to the victorious. Just three days after it announced surrender, the Police and Security Department of the Home Ministry, the central organ for censorship and for controlling overall civilian conduct, set up in Tokyo a Rest and Amusement Association—so named in English, but in a literal translation of the Japanese, "association for special comfort facilities" or, in plain language, brothels—for incoming foreign servicemen, and ordered municipalities to follow suit. This the Ministry did in the name of patriotism *and* weeks before the Occupation requisitioned a number of brothels for its own use. Less than ten days later, the first such brothel opened for business, in Ōmori, Ōta Ward, Tokyo. That was the day before the vanguard of the US force arrived in Atsugi Airport, on August 28.

By the time soldiers of the Allied Powers started arriving in earnest, the government-financed effort had lined up 1,360 women for them, even as women were evacuating from Yokohama and other areas for fear of "demons and beasts."[31] (Decades afterward, Japan would win notoriety for "comfort women.")

---

Later, Mishima would reflect on what Japan's defeat meant to him in a range of essays. "Japan's defeat, to me, was not an event to be sourly lamented," he recalled ten years later in "Starting out with an Eschatological Sense—A Self-Portrait in the 20th Year of Shōwa." Or, as he noted in "Around August 15," "At the end of the war, my sister, along with her friends, went to the Imperial Palace Plaza and wept, or so I heard, but tears were far from my state of mind at the time." This statement may not have been exactly true: the day after the surrender he had written Shimizu Fumio that he had shed tears when he heard the Tennō announce Japan's capitulation.[32]

Mishima did weep when his sister Mitsuko died, on October 23. A student at the College of the Sacred Heart, whose buildings were destroyed in an air raid, Mitsuko and her fellow students were mobilized after the war to help clear some of the ruins in Tokyo. After working in one such place she became ill—either because she drank well water or because she was infested by lice. Diagnosed as having a cold at first, she was rediagnosed as having typhus fever when her condition worsened. When she fell into coma, she was moved from Keiō Hospital to a quarantine hospital where Mishima stayed by her bedside. From time to time, he would suck up liquid food in a tube and move it to her mouth. The quarantine hospital was dilapidated. Azusa remembered his son shooing away swarms of insects flying in the window.

"Several hours before her death, though she was utterly unconscious, she said to me, 'My dear brother, thank you very much.' When I heard this, I wept aloud," Mishima wrote. The word she used to address him was *o-nii-chama*, a polite childhood form of addressing one's older brother. He had loved his vivacious sister with long glossy hair—kissing her on the cheeks, exclaiming, "You are so cute!" She was seventeen years old.[33]

Toward the end of the year, Mishima learned of Kuniko's engagement and half a year later of her marriage to a man twelve years older. "I was to be engaged to a woman I had made friends with during the war but, on account of my hesitations, she became another man's wife," he wrote. "These two incidents, my sister's death and this woman's marriage, became, it seems to me, the forces that drove my subsequent literary passion." What Kuniko did, in particular, almost drove Mishima to suicide or at least serious thought of it—if we are to assume that the first full-length novel he began a month or so afterward that would eventually become *The Bandit* (*Tōzoku*) is any indication. "Grief over the lost love and revenge on the one who betrayed him" would recur as a leitmotif in his stories for the next several years, Muramatsu Takeshi observed in his biography of his friend. Mishima mused, "The sense of barren blankness in my life in the several years after that scares me even now as I remember it."34

## *Theater Diary*

Not that Mishima fell into despondence. For one thing, he quickened his pace of theater-going. The notes on the kabuki and other plays he saw from January 1942 to the end of November 1947 and later assembled as a "theater diary" show that, of the one hundred times he went to theater during the six-year period, about half occurred in the first three and a half years, the other half in the two years and four months following Japan's defeat. One reason was worsening military censorship compounded by the growing shortages of all kinds under the bombings, including stage equipment. Mishima left no entry in the four months from May to August 1945 when Japan was disintegrating fast. With the Occupation came a different kind of censorship but that did not deter him.35

Mishima's postwar entries really begin on September 10. The entry that day noted the *Mainichi Shinbun* reporting the reopening of the Teikoku Theater with Onoe Kikugorō VI performing the following month. There was also news that the theater, which was right next to the Daiichi Seimei Building, now the GHQ, might be "offered" to the Occupation, but it was soon followed by the news that the Occupation rescinded the plan to use it. In early October, the head of the GHQ's "information dissemination" unit—which had been renamed the Civil Information and Education Service (CIE) by the time Mishima read the news—warned that Japanese theater had not eliminated "feudalistic" and "militaristic coloration" in contravention of the Potsdam Declaration, stressing the need to create new plays to encourage repatriated soldiers to engage in building a new Japan.[36]

In noting this, Mishima was moved to comment: "Ah, what would be left if feudalistic coloration and militarism were deducted from kabuki?" "Americans themselves should know the evils of propaganda drama." And: "I wish they would wait until knowledgeable people like Max Reinhardt come to Japan before interfering with theater inappropriately."[37] He was not aware that Reinhardt had died two years earlier.

But the CIE was tightening its censorship. In mid-November there was "the *Terakoya* Incident"; Japanese police, followed by US military police, stopped the "head-inspection" scene in *Terakoya*, the popular section of *Sugawara denju tenarai kagami*, in mid-performance, and banned the section altogether on November 20th.[38] (In kabuki many sections are staged independently.) On December 19, Mishima read that the GHQ would ban certain types of stories from kabuki and other plays. "With this the *maruhonmono*"—jōruri turned into kabuki—"are all out," he despaired. "Freedom of speech would be shocked to hear this." He then listed nine plays he predicted might be permitted.

The January 20, 1946 *Tokyo Shinbun* headline "Kabuki Disappears All At Once" drew an equally strong reaction from Mishima: "The last day for kabuki has finally come." The news report suggested that the main kabuki producer Shōchiku was dropping certain plays from its repertoire "voluntarily," though who was behind the move was unmistakable. Mishima copied the list of about eighty kabuki items the GHQ would permit.

Still, Mishima does not seem to have noted the long interview that appeared in the *Tokyo Shinbun* three days later, with the headline: "Regrettable Suicidal Step; Maj. Bowers Talks." Maj. Bowers is Faubion Bowers, then Gen. MacArthur's aide-de-camp and personal interpreter. Later called "the savior of kabuki," he had become a fan of this form of Japanese theater during his yearlong stay in Japan from early 1940 to early 1941. Indeed, arriving with Col. Charles Tench in the Atsugi Airfield on August 28 in the vanguard of the Occupation forces, he had famously amazed the gathered reporters with his first question, in Japanese, "Is Uzaemon doing well?" Virtually no Japanese expected a US military officer to speak Japanese, let alone to be a fan of kabuki. For that matter, it is likely that in the chaotic final months of the war, not many reporters knew that the glamorous kabuki actor Ichimura Uzaemon XV, whose father was the French-born American Gen. Joseph Émile Le Gendre, had died in May that year, in a quiet spa where he had evacuated. In any event, the interview with the *Tokyo Shinbun* on January 23 was Bowers's first salvo in his effort to counter the Occupation censors and remove restrictions on kabuki. In it he said the kind of things with which Mishima would have perfectly agreed.

"The United States is a democratic nation, but it keeps producing Shakespeare plays that use feudalistic monarchs as material," Bowers said. "Also, it still performs Wagner's operas even though the Nazi leaders insisted that their inspiration came from the myths and ideology.... Art is art. The greatness of kabuki lies far beyond political, feudalistic tendencies."[39]

The first fruit of Bowers's behind-the-scene effort may well have been the lifting of the ban on *Kanjinchō*, which Mishima duly noted in his entry of May 30 and went to see on June 7.[40]

## *Imperial Declaration of Humanity*

On New Year's Day in 1946, Hirohito—posthumously, the Shōwa Emperor—issued a rescript that would later be known as *ningen sengen*, "declaration of humanity" or "renunciation of divinity." As Mitani recollected, Mishima was "furious" at the news, but not so much at the declaration itself as at the fact that the Tennō appeared in subsequent newspaper photos in a Western suit, not in the formal Heian court attire *ikan sokutai*. He may have been merely sarcastic about the sartorial matter, but he was truly angry with the ensuing journalistic assault on the Tennō system, saying, "Society will not accept something like this in the end," Mitani wrote.[41]

That prediction would prove unfounded soon enough, but the "declaration" went against Mishima's view. "That which has reserved what is truly Oriental, the last line of Oriental mysticism, in the form of a modern constitutional state, is Japan's Tennō system," he stated in an undated piece but apparently written just about that time. "The Tennō system is the essence of all Oriental cultures of the past, the final conclusion of the sovereignty theory and the philosophy of life. When this is lost, Oriental culture's bridge to modern culture, the last bridge of its understanding, will also be lost."[42] This view of monarchical transcendence would play a pivotal role in the cultural argument Mishima would develop late in his life, so here we will examine what Hirohito actually did.

In the rescript all the major newspapers carried on the first of January, 1946,[43] the Tennō began by citing the Charter Oath, the proclamation in five simple, declarative clauses that the Meiji government issued at its birth, in 1868. The Oath urged that the people hold discussion throughout the land and subject everything to public debate; that the high and low endeavor to manage government with one mind; that all strive to fulfill their aspirations; that they break out of discredited customs and decide matters on the basis of just principles; and that they seek knowledge throughout the world to strengthen the Imperial foundations. The British historian G. B. Sansom called the oath "the first Constitution of modern Japan."[44]

The Tennō then stated that the wisdom manifested in the Charter Oath was self-evident and urged his people to adhere to pacifism so as to build a new Japan. He described the devastations and the sufferings brought about by the war, and urged his people to resolve to seek peace unwaveringly. Then, expressing grave concerns that the anxieties and disappointments caused by the war that had ended in defeat might lead to loss of moral principles and chaos, he went on to say:

> Nevertheless, the bonds between you, the people, and us [imperial we] are tied together from beginning to end by mutual trust, respect, and love, and are not something simply generated by myths and legends. They are not something based on the fantastical (*kakūnaru*) ideas that hold that the Tennō is an *akitsumikami*, that the Japanese are a race superior to others, and that, therefore, they possess the destiny to rule the world.

The Tennō ended by urging his people to strive mightily to contribute to mankind's welfare and improvement. What is notable is the proportion of the part about *akitsumikami*: it took up just one eighth of the whole at most. It is revealing, indeed, that, even as the foreign press such as the *New York Times* took the "renunciation of divinity" as the focal point of the rescript as the Occupation had intended, the headlines of the domestic dailies such as the *Asahi* and *Mainichi* made no mention of the "divinity" part of it. Apparently, most Japanese never believed the Tennō to be a god or deity—at least in the Western sense. They knew that the Tennō's role and position were "twisted by military chauvinists to support their propaganda" and that the "notions of national and especially Imperial superiority due to divine descent" were "false," as Harold G. Henderson, who became a conduit in delivering the Occupation's wishes to the Imperial household, put it. Shillony's observation was even more succinct. The "human" question "did not cause any sensation, because it stated the obvious."[45]

The question that remains is whether the Tennō wanted to renounce his being as *akitsumikami* as the term might have been understood as it came into being in ancient Japan. The usual translation, be it "deity incarnate" or "living god," is woefully inadequate. As Sansom observed, the word *kami* "carries the general sense of 'upper' or 'superior,' and a thing or person is called kami if it is felt to possess some superior quality or power. The same idea is expressed in Polynesian countries by the term *mana*. . . . The same or a similar idea appears in Roman beliefs, where the special quality is called *numen*." In other words, the Judeo-Christian concept of "god" or "deity" is misleading if applied to *kami*.[46]

As pertinent, if we are to accept the interpretation of the folklorist Orikuchi Shinobu, for the Tennō to renounce his being as *akitsumikami* would have meant to renounce his social and religious *raison d'être*. Orikuchi defined the original role of the Tennō as a medium and servant of the *amatsukami*, "kami of heaven," and his or her task as that of making sure that all the people of the land are adequately fed. In offering this explanation, Orikuchi added—at a time when chauvinistic and expansionist sentiments on the pretext of Japan's Tennō system were going out of control—that the Tennō "doesn't think of things like making a piece of land his own or expanding territory."[47]

Thirty-one years later, in 1977, in a rare news conference, a reporter asked His Majesty if it was true that, as various accounts had made clear by then, it was on his initiative that the Charter Oath was placed at the outset of "the declaration of humanity." In response, Hirohito said: "The primary purpose of that declaration" was to remind the Japanese people of the Charter Oath. "The divine status (*shinkaku*) and such were of a secondary question." He went on to explain: "At the time America and other foreign nations were so powerful that there was concern that they might overwhelm Japan." America's stated goal of occupying Japan was to bring democracy to Japan. But it was "Meiji the Great" who "adopted democracy," His Majesty said, and the Charter Oath embodied it. He thought "there was great need to show that democracy was not something imported."

In Japanese journalism, questions and answers are seldom printed verbatim as they are most often summaries, with inconvenient words and phrases dropped or changed. One can never be sure of what the quoted person said exactly. But, as far as the news conference as reported by the *Asahi Shinbun* on August 24, 1977, is concerned, the reporter did not ask what "the declaration of humanity" actually meant to Hirohito, and Hirohito did not say anything about that part of the rescript. However, in responding to a later question on how His and Her Majesties spent their leisure time, he clearly stated they were "human beings," suggesting that declaring himself to be human was utterly unnecessary.[48]

The matter, in truth, goes back at least to the aforementioned controversy over the Constitutional scholar Minobe Tatsukichi's "Tennō as a state organ" theory. In February 1935, the rightwing member of the House of Peers Lt. Gen. (retired) Kikuchi Takeo ferociously attacked Minobe, another member of the House, on his theory, calling him a "rebel," "traitor," and "warped scholar." Minobe's hour-long speech in rebuttal a week later was clear and detailed, and Kikuchi, who was no scholar, Constitutional or otherwise, is said to have been utterly impressed. Yet Kikuchi's original accusations inflamed the diehard elements of the rightwing.

During this controversy, it was the prosecutor of Hiraoka Sadatarō in his political scandal two decades earlier who tried to defend Minobe: Ohara Naoshi. Ohara, who became justice minister, in 1935, rode out the chauvinistic irrationality of the day by resisting the demand to indict Minobe on charges of *lèse majesté* because of his theory. Still, the enormous pressure forced Minobe to resign from the House of Peers. The following year he was shot by a rightwing thug and seriously wounded.

The irony in all this was that the Tennō, who had a firm grasp of the origins of the Meiji Constitution, completely agreed with Minobe's theory, though necessarily in private, pointing out that it was based on the Austrian legal philosopher Georg Jellinek's argument.[49]

As the Tennō recalled in his "monologue" recorded in the spring of 1946, but which did not come to light until 1990, he said he had explained the theory by comparing the national polity to the human body and also had his understanding conveyed to Inspector-General of Military Education Mazaki Jinzaburō. He was told that Mazaki "understood" His Majesty's stance on the matter. Nevertheless, just a year later Mazaki would emerge as the spiritual leader of the February 26 Incident. We will look at the incident in Chapter Sixteen, but it was largely based on the belief that the Tennō was not a mere "organ of the state."

As to his understanding of his kami status, the Tennō recalled in the same "monologue" that, once when his aide-de-camp suggested that he was a divine person, he told him: "I have the same body structure as an ordinary human being, so I am not a deity; such talk troubles me."[50] The word the Tennō cited—as perhaps coming from the then aide-de-camp Honjō Shigeru or Usami Okiie—was *arakami*, which is the same as *arahitogami* and *akitsumikami*. But no matter. He was after all a biologist by training and in accomplishment.

CHAPTER SEVEN

# To Be a Bureaucrat or a Writer

*"Minus 150 points."*
—Nakamura Mitsuo on Mishima's story

In early 1946 Mishima took several manuscripts, including "A Tale at the Cape" (*Misaki nite no monogatari*), to Chikuma Shobō. The publisher, which had absorbed Shichijō Shoin soon after the publication of *The Forest in Full Bloom*, had just launched a new literary magazine, *Tenbō*. Usui Yoshimi, the magazine's editor and a man of considerable literary repute, was impressed to read what Mishima brought. He thought Mishima was "a kind of genius" and, even though he found his writings not to his taste, thought of accepting one of the stories, "The Medieval Period."

Written in taut, condensed language at times suggestive of *kanbuntai*, a style created in imitation of a straightforward translation of classical Chinese, and with elaborate imagery, the story tells, in eight short chapters, of the aftermath of the premature death of the ninth Ashikaga shogun Yoshihisa (1465–89): the grief of his old father, the eighth shogun Yoshimasa, the man's dalliance with a young medium he summons to conjure his dead son, and an old Zen master's dalliance with a young male dancer, once Yoshihisa's lover. But, when asked for his opinion, Nakamura Mitsuo, one of the founders of *Tenbō* and Chikuma's advisor who had studied in France before the war at the French government's invitation, returned the story to Usui, with a curt note, "minus 150 points."

/ 147

This anecdote came out in a taidan, "dialogue,"[1] between Usui and Nakamura in 1952, and Mishima enjoyed recounting the episode later. But at the time, Nakamura's rejection came as another blow to the young man who, having survived the war in which he had expected to die one way or another, was under serious stress: He had to alter his way of thinking altogether or else.[2] He was forced to realize that all the accolades his admirers had given *The Forest in Full Bloom* had come to naught. As Usui pointed out years later, Nakamura went on to become the self-appointed "chairman of the PTA for Mishima," but in the years immediately following the war he did not see anything good in Mishima's writings.[3]

Mishima was under pressure. Unless he established himself as a credible writer soon, he would have no choice but to follow the route Azusa had prescribed for him: to take the higher civil service examination and live the rest of his life as a bureaucrat. (Within a few years, government reforms pushed by the Occupation would greatly reduce the salaries of elite bureaucrats, though not much of their power.) Yet the prospects for young men to make it in the literary world seemed almost insurmountable—even for someone like Mishima, a rising star at the end of the war. "At the time, new magazines sprouted one after another, but most were eager to seek manuscripts from established authors; the times weren't settled enough for them to actively look for new writers," Mishima recalled. "The works of great writers such as [Nagai] Kafū and [Masamune] Hakuchō were causing people to swoon with fresh charm as might"—and here a very Japanese analogy—"a fancy dinner with pure rice offered for the first time in a long while."[4]

The title Mishima thought up when, earlier, in January, a friend from the Peers School, Saitō Yoshirō, offered to arrange the publication of his poems in book form, may have reflected the state of his mind. "I've even come to think of giving this book of poetry the name *Hōjō no umi*, the name of the waterless sea in the bleak lunar world, the name that symbolizes the external surface of illusory luminance and the reality of total darkness, the brilliant illusion of life and the substance of death," Mishima responded.[5] The book was not published, but *Hōjō no umi*, "The Sea of Fertility," would become the title of Mishima's final work, the tetralogy he finished shortly before his death.

## *Meeting Kawabata Yasunari*

On January 27, Sunday, Mishima went to visit Kawabata, in Kamakura. At the time Kawabata lived in Nikaidō, northeast of the Kamakura (also, Ōtō or Daitō) Shrine, renting Kanbara Ariake's house, "cohabiting, as it were, with his landlord." Kanbara, a well-known poet who had stopped writing poetry in the early part of the century after establishing his reputation as a Symbolist, had been burnt out of his house in Tokyo during an air raid near the end of the war and was living in a room of his old house rented to Kawabata. Recalling the visit seventeen years later in his literary memoir, *My Pilgrimage Days* (*Watashi no henreki jidai*), serialized in the *Tokyo Shinbun*, Mishima wrote that, when he reached the house, "the guestroom was full of visitors" and these visitors provided someone who "had known only a monotonous school and family life" with the first opportunity to witness "the furious vitality of the postwar literary world."

"Publishers that had sprouted like bamboo shoots after rain had rushed to [Kawabata] to beg for permission to reprint his old works." Among the visitors were people he would later recognize as Kawasaki Chōtarō, Ishizuka Tomoji, and Kawakami Yasuko. "As I saw Mr. Kawasaki paddle away in his rubber boots, ignorant as I was of the literary world, I thought he was a real fishmonger." Kawasaki, noted for his writings about the women in the red-light district Makkō-chō, lived in poverty much of his life, at the time probably in a zinc-roofed shed. Kawabata "sat in their midst in silence, no different from what he looks today, in 1963, calm, neither amused nor funny."[6]

In truth, this was a case of memory prettifying what actually happened. Mishima no doubt met these people in his later, frequent visits with Kawabata; Kawabata was known for having constant visitors. But a description he jotted down evidently soon after his first encounter with a writer for whom he would maintain, at least outwardly, a respectful relationship to the end of his life tells a different story.

That particular day, Kawabata wasn't even up when Mishima arrived past eleven. Mishima had to wait in a *kotatsu* or foot warmer, a covered brazier under a low table draped with a quilt. The conversation after Kawabata showed up was desultory at best. He was, Mishima thought, utterly unlike Satō Haruo who would "lead a conversation by providing one topic after another." One of the few things Kawabata volunteered was the coming war between the United States and the USSR. Barely five months since the world war ended, it was on everyone's mind. The only topic on which he was "insistent" to any degree was the "habit" of staying up late to write. "If you write that way, you can put up with anything, be it democracy or socialism"—only to add, "but if you are like that, you are no good in a democracy, you are no good in the age of socialism even if it comes."

What left an indelible impression on Mishima was Kawabata's eyes. "His eyes were a go player's which, though they may appear restless at first glance, see the bull's eye." Mishima likely had read Kawabata's popular newspaper reportage on the grand go match between Hon'inbō Shūsai and Kitani Minoru that took six months to complete, in 1938, as well as his attempt, starting in 1942, to turn it into a somewhat fictionalized account that would eventually become *The Master* (*Meijin*).[7] (Unlike today, go matches were leisurely at the time, and for this grand match, each player was given forty hours to make his moves, as opposed to today's ten. Still, the match took nearly six months, from June 24 to December 4, in 1938, because the ailing master was too sick to play for three months.) Kawabata's eyes were "also a kendō master's," Mishima wrote, "the eyes that move with a moving sword. Theirs was not the dead sharpness of someone staring at you."

There was one thing Mishima said that "startled and troubled" Kawabata. That was when he made a "paradoxical" statement: "Hani Gorō"—a Marxist historian persecuted before and during the war—"is accusing the Tennō by citing the cruelties of [the twenty-first Tennō], but who would be happy to exalt anyone unless he is a descendant of a monarch who committed cruelties?" The account of Yūryaku, which appears in the *History of Japan* (*Nihon Shoki*), written originally in Chinese, in 720, presents him as a ruler of monstrous deeds of the kinds usually attributed to evil Chinese rulers.

Kawabata had a single visitor while Mishima was there that day: the poet and novelist Kawakami Kikuko who came to discuss a book. Her arrival made the conversation between the two men even more halting. Mishima says that when he left, the rain that had been occasional sprinkles when he reached Kawabata's house was steadily falling. Three days later he wrote Noda Utarō that he had stayed with Kawabata "until past three."[8]

## *Two Forms of Censorship*

Kawabata at the time was managing director of the Kamakura Bunko. It had started out, in May 1945, as a lending library that he and some of his fellow writers who did not evacuate out of the ancient city had set up by pooling their books and renting a toy store to supplement their incomes. Following Japan's defeat a mere three months later, a paper manufacturer offered to provide paper, and Kawabata quickly turned the library into a publishing house, with a monthly, *Ningen*, to go with it.[9] And he had chosen Kimura Tokuzō to edit the magazine by plucking him out of Kyoto.

Kimura, then thirty-four, had, as with most editors, experienced a severe form of censorship firsthand and would experience another form of censorship soon enough. The one he experienced was from the Japanese, and it was intended for outright suppression; the one he would soon experience was from the Americans, and it was for democracy, or so he was told.

Censorship in Japan, which became law in the early twentieth century, reached its brutal peak with the militarist takeover of governance. By the time Kimura was employed by Kaizōsha, in 1937, the days for the editors to be able to use *fuseji* were virtually over. The most infamous censorship action against his publisher would begin in early 1942. Later called the Yokohama Incident, it would see sixty people rounded up and tortured, leaving four dead.[10] Kaizōsha, during its heyday, had invited foreign luminaries such as the birth-control advocate Margaret Sanger for speaking tours in Japan.

Then came the Occupation. Its declared aim was to plant democracy in Japan. Freedom of speech was essential. But anything "undemocratic" must be eradicated. For that goal, every substantive tool of communication, be it film, theater, or print, had to be approved in advance. In other words, this freedom was conditional. Kimura filed, as required, the proofread galley of its inaugural issue of *Ningen* with the Occupation's Civil Information and Education Section. It included a translation of Thomas Mann's 1938 lectures in the United States, "The Coming Victory of Democracy." A few days later, he was summoned. The two Nisei officers who met him told him he could not publish two articles in the issue. Why?

One article, by Kon Hidemi, had the word *teki*, "enemy," as applied to the US forces. The article concerned Satomura Kinzō, who, along with Kon and others, had been sent to the Philippines by the military as a reporter at the end of 1944 and was killed a few months later during the Japanese retreat north from Manila.[11] The US military could not be referred to as "enemy," even though the war was over.

The reasons for the rejection of the other essay not only were indicative of the military mindset, Japanese or American, but also, as Kimura would find out, foretold the International Military Tribunals for the Far East that the Occupation would convene in half a year. The essay's writer, Komiya Toyotaka, was a feisty scholar of German literature and Japan's traditional arts, such as haiku. He had written several essays on the carpet bombings of Tokyo, mentioning the prospect of the landing of US forces in Japan. His focus was on the Japanese military that could not prevent such things from happening. The *Asahi Shinbun* had rejected all. The daily knew printing any such criticism of the military would be suicidal. The war was over, but the US military still did not want it to be known that there had been conjecture on its expected landing in Japan, Kimura was told. It was a "top military secret."

More important, the United States wanted no references to the air raids. That, as it would turn out, was no caprice on the part of individual censors. In planning military tribunals, for both Germany and Japan, the prosecuting nations had decided to pre-exonerate themselves of any war crimes, let alone the new categories of "crime against peace" and "crime against humanity."[12]

When the first issue of his magazine was ready and filed with the CIE, Kimura was summoned again. This time a middle-aged female officer with two Nisei aides met him. What was wrong? Kimura had left as blanks the several places in Kon's article where the word *teki* had appeared. As to Komiya's article, he had simply blacked it out. The officer's stern "guidance": No "traces of censorship" are allowed to show. She also objected to the drawing used for the cover. It was by the painter Suda Kunitarō and depicted a man and a woman, both nude, turning the other way. To Kimura the two figures looked like Adam and Eve as they were expelled from the Garden of Eden, and that was why he chose the drawing. But to the censor they looked liked "prisoners," suggesting that Japan was imprisoned by the Occupation.[13]

Nearly four decades later when he published a collection of his essays as editor in those days, Kimura used the same painting for the cover of his book.

## *Editorial Collaboration*

One day not long after *Ningen* started coming out, Kawabata passed two stories by Mishima to Kimura, "A Tale at the Cape" and "A Cigarette" (*Tabako*). The latter has to do with a boy who, forced to have the first taste of smoking that is forbidden at school, develops a yearning for the older, athletic boy who had pushed a cigarette on him. Kimura found both stories very good, but thought the former a bit "too stiff with Romantic nihilism and too contrived" and the latter straightforward and tightly constructed. Unable to make up his mind which to take, he told Kawabata so. Kawabata's response was: "You think that, too. Well then, print 'Cigarette' in *Ningen* when you have a chance. I'll return 'Cape' to him."

Kimura printed the story in the June 1946 issue of the magazine. Later, after he came to know Mishima, he reflected he would have taken "Cape" as more "Mishima-esque" had he known him at the time. Apart from that, he was impressed by the clean manuscripts, Mishima's handwriting more "appropriate for a brush," with few corrections, something all the editors who dealt with Mishima would note.

Kimura met Mishima in person soon enough. Kawabata said to him, "Mishima has brought me this fiction. He can apparently write something like this, too." It was "The Medieval Period." "I told him to come to see you." The Mishima Yukio who showed up at the Kamakura Bunko was "a young man neatly wearing his college uniform, with an oblong face of dull complexion, who you could tell at a glance was hypersensitive," Kimura recalled in his memoirs of men-of-letters with whom he associated. "He spoke courteously like the son of a good family in Yamanote, Tokyo, that he was, responding to my questions tidily, concisely. He listened and responded, without a smile, his eyes always on my face. I was impressed by the *monomaniacal* glint of his eyes more than anything else."

Kimura was straightforward with Mishima. He would suggest deleting several lines here, several lines there, pointing out that too much conversation would vulgarize a story. Mishima would react to each such editorial comment strongly, crossing out the offensive passage on the spot, or declaring he'd trash the whole story as he snatched up the manuscript to go home. The next time he came to visit he would thrust a revised version at Kimura triumphantly and, sure enough, the revisions had made the story much better.

"How many times did I repeat such a life-or-death fight with Mishima? Once a woman writer, whose manuscript I'd just rejected, happened to witness our ferocious exchange; she just stood there, glued to the spot, appalled. I never met a new writer like Mishima, before or after, whom I found it so worthwhile to advise."

Mishima later said of his early work published in *Ningen* that it would be "no exaggeration to say they were collaborations with Kimura." Comparing the relationship between new writer and literary editor to that of fresh boxer and experienced, wily trainer, he said he was fortunate to have Kimura as editor at that early stage. He added that for a while he was known as "the Mishima who's published fiction in *Ningen*," as though the accomplishment were part of his calling card.[14]

For all the intense, fruitful work with Kimura and the editor's obvious confidence in his talent—Kimura once told the writer, "I'd be happy to see a new story any time you finish one"—Mishima was far from satisfied. He was at a crucial point, and the need he felt to make his name as a writer was not being met fast enough. "Cigarette" was accepted in February but was not published until June. He pleaded with Kimura for an early publication. "Your kind decision to carry my clumsy 'Cigarette' was to me the largest of the 'rescuing hands,'" he wrote in a long letter to him in May. "Anyone would be shocked if someone, overjoyed by being rescued, shook the hand that he'd put out with no thought whatsoever. Worse, that person would surely be troubled if the wet, cold hand of someone who is drowning suddenly clung to it and blindly pulled it this way and that. I am afraid that this letter of mine, which is somewhat confessional, is giving you such a feeling."[15]

And when "Cigarette" finally appeared after keeping Mishima in a state of exasperation—he would check the newspaper ads of the magazine every month only to find his story not listed in its table of contents—it did not elicit any response. He decided to focus on the preparations for the higher civil service examination, which he would take in July 1947.

Kimura had occasion to observe Mishima as a serious student. One day they met in front of the library of the Imperial University of Tokyo. After talking about various matters for about an hour, Mishima excused himself for the next lecture he had to attend. Out of curiosity Kimura followed him into the building. "I peeked into Classroom No. 26 that Mishima had walked into. As many serious top students would, he appeared to have reserved his seat in advance. I saw him seat himself in the second row, right in front of the lectern. To me, indifferent as I was when a student, it was something unthinkable."[16]

## *The Great Listener Who Wanted a Kiss*

Mitani Kuniko was married on May 5, 1946. About a month later, Sassa Teiko came to see Mishima's sister Mitsuko. She did not know her best friend at the College of the Sacred Heart had died half a year earlier. Her father, Hiro'o, chief editorialist at the *Asahi Shinbun*, had evacuated her, along with her older brother, Katsuaki, first to Niigata after the great air raid in March 1945, then, upon learning that the city on the Japan Sea might be among those targeted for the "special bomb," to a village in inland Saitama. He had done so, explaining that warriors during Japan's Age of Warring States used to split their families, even arranging to have one group side with the potential enemy, lest their bloodline end. He descended from a famous warrior-commander who had to disembowel himself.[17] Teiko had come back to Tokyo well into September but in a struggle for survival in the devastated metropolis had not had time to be in touch with her friends.

Teiko's visit prompted Mishima to ask her to go out with him—to cafés, to dance, to take a walk, to movies. Teiko in time found there was a subtle difference between what Mishima sought in her and what she wanted in him. Mishima was a good listener who gave thoughtful answers to whatever questions she threw at him, and that was good for a young woman who had a variety of weighty, however youthful, topics she wanted to talk about: love, suffering, and such. He was always neatly dressed (at a time the majority were unable to do so), punctual, and, most important, gentlemanly, except for his enthusiasm for dancing—with a preference for cheek-to-cheek dancing. He was a clumsy dancer, Teiko thought, and she did not like body contact.

Whether to dance better with her or not, Mishima took lessons from the novelist Kunieda Shirō's widow toward the end of the year.[18] Western-style dancing, which, along with jazz, had been suppressed since the latter half of the 1930s, had revived in full force following Japan's defeat—just as dancing and jazz had become all the rage in Germany following *its* defeat.[19]

Dancing, as a matter of fact, would become Mishima's passion for much of his life, although most people who danced with him, as Sassa did, or saw him dance, would aver he could not dance. The Flamenco dancer-turned-writer Itasaka Gō was blunt. He observed that anyone unable to keep time with the simple music for "monkey dance," as Mishima was, had no right to want to study Flamenco, as Mishima fervently did at one time, though not with Itasaka but the famous dancer Katori Kiyoko.[20] Itasaka's book on Mishima, written a quarter century after his death, is built on the curious conjecture that Mishima's desire to learn Flamenco dance—the dance of the Gypsies—derived from his stark but suppressed knowledge of the humble background of one branch of his paternal ancestor.

Mishima was a good letter writer. It was in one of his many letters to Teiko that Mishima talked about Mitani Kuniko. "Miss K, now someone else's wife, was quite an ignorant, innocent, and passionate young lady, but she had no understanding whatsoever of what I would call an 'autonomous independent life,'" he wrote on July 5, 1947. "Her husband, a diplomat's son, already thirty-some years old, lives with his parents; as a result, she is constantly bullied by her frightening mother-in-law, but she isn't critical at all that her husband lives in the same house with his parents, depending on them."

Mishima's conclusion on what happened between Miss K and himself: "She was just simply too eager to marry someone, the sooner the better." In saying this, he thought of his own situation. "I at times think I am a fool, yearning for such a swallow-like autonomous independent life myself," he added.[21]

The friendship between the two effectively ended, at least for Teiko, on January 4, 1948, with "an incident." That day she was invited to Mishima's house for the New Year. She went dressed up, in kimono, and enjoyed chatting with Shizue. When the time for her to leave came and she stepped out of the house, Mishima, who had remained more or less silent while the two women chatted, came out and asked for a goodbye kiss; she refused. (In her memoir, she referred to what Mishima asked for as "a novelistic gesture of love," in the demure language of the day.)

Mishima then walked her to the station, and the two stayed in touch. But Sassa evidently felt whatever easygoing relationship she had with him was lost. So she was surprised to see him among those who came to her father's funeral that fall, properly dressed.[22]

Sassa Teiko would start working for the longtime advocate of women's rights, Ichikawa Fusae, in 1949, the year she married and assumed the family name Kihira. It is one of the many ironies of the Occupation that Ichikawa was "purged from public service"—in her case, because she did not get along with a woman lieutenant on the staff of the Supreme Commander for the Allied Powers.[23] Teiko became a member of the Diet herself late in her life, in 1989.

Whether Teiko was conscious of it or not, her father, Hiro'o, was Azusa's classmate at the Law Faculty of the Imperial University of Tokyo. So was Hiro'o's colleague on the editorial board of the *Asahi Shinbun*, Kaji Ryūichi, who would enable Mishima to make his first extended overseas trip beginning at the end of 1951. By then Teiko's older brother Katsuaki was a journalist with the *Asahi*. Many years later, her younger brother, "the fiercely patriotic boy" Atsuyuki,[24] would get involved with Mishima, however briefly, at the height of the student movement in 1968, as de facto field commander of the riot police. Both Katsuaki and Atsuyuki studied law at the University of Tokyo.

## *Reunion with Kuniko*

It was a delicate period for Mishima. Not just that he was studying law with the aim of gaining employment at the top bureaucracy of the Japanese government while trying to make a go of it as a writer. He was also entangled with Kuniko, now married.

On September 16, 1946, when Mishima was out in Azabu, someone called his name. It was Kuniko. Mishima's description of the encounter in *Confessions of a Mask* is different in detail from the diary-like description he left of it.

In the novel the unplanned reunion happens "one cloudy day during the rainy season," but the timing is off by two, three months. When Sonoko mentions Tanizaki's *Some Prefer Nettles* (*Tade kū mushi*) in response to his query on what kind of book she's been reading lately, Mishima asks if she also read a novel "in vogue." It was in fact his own short story "Cigarette" that had appeared in *Ningen*, and that was why she responded, "Of that naked woman?" referring to the drawing on the cover of the magazine. In real life, Mishima was startled and said, "What have you said? I haven't written anything of the sort!" To which Kuniko said, "No way.... I am talking about the picture on the cover."

The gist of the impression with which Mishima came away from the brief encounter may have been true to fact, however: he distinctly felt Kuniko was no longer "genuine and pure," that is, a virgin. Before the marriage, she would not have read anything like Tanizaki's "immodest" book or openly admitted she did, although in his diary-like entry he was careful to note that the unthinking way she mentioned it, she "may have barely read it." The 1930 novel has to do with a well-to-do man who has lost sexual interest in his wife and allows her to have a lover while he indulges in outside sex, including frequent visits to a foreign prostitute named Louise.[25]

One thing that a reader of the English translation of *Confessions* by Meredith Weatherby may overlook is the reference to *konnyaku*, which Sonoko and her old maid each is carrying in a bucket as they have just been to a rationing center. *Konnyaku* is made from a certain species of potato and has little dietary value. It is not despised as food but not something eaten in any quantity, either.[26] This is worth pointing out because Mishima seldom, if ever, emphasized food shortages and other economic difficulties of the time in his writings. He does suggest, in *Confessions*, that the large Mitani house (in real life) escaped requisition for Occupation use because of the family's powerful government connections. Many well-to-do families were not that lucky.

Learning that Kuniko would be visiting the Mitani family the following Saturday, September 21, Mishima went to visit with the pretext of meeting his friend, Makoto. (For some reason, on May 11, 1946, he started a detailed "accounting diary" mainly to note all the incomes and outgoes but also to note all the comings and goings of the day, and continued it until November 13, 1947. The encounter with Kuniko and the visit with Mitani Makoto are curtly noted in it.[27])

While chatting with Makoto, Mishima heard the sound of the piano. "It no longer had a childish tone, but had a sound that was ample, seemed to spurt, was full and brilliant," he wrote in *Confessions*. Sonoko finishes playing the piano and her brother fetches her. In the tête-à-tête conversation that follows, she says, "I have something I thought and thought of asking you but couldn't. I've been wondering why we couldn't get married. After receiving your response through my brother I no longer understood anything about the world. Every day I thought about it. Still I couldn't understand it. Even now, I don't understand why I couldn't marry you." This perturbs Mishima at once with joy and pain, and leads him to ask her to meet him again.

There was, in any event, one important thing Mishima completely left out of *Confessions*, as far as Kuniko was concerned: her husband, Nagai Kunio, and what happened to him. In the novel, the narrator and Sonoko continue to meet for a year until suddenly they are "awakened." Then comes the final parting. What happened in real life?

In May 1946, the month Kuniko was married, the International Military Tribunal for the Far East was convened for those charged with Class A crimes—"crimes against peace." Half a year after their marriage, Nagai Kunio, a bank employee, was arrested on accusations of POW abuse and sent to Hong Kong for detainment before trial. More than a year had passed since the war ended, but former Japanese soldiers as well as those involved with military-related activities continued to be indicted and tried on charges of various war crimes classed B ("crimes against humanity") and C ("conventional war crimes"), in the end a total of 5,700. Nagai Kunio was one of them. His arrest prompted Kuniko to send Mishima a telegram, on November 6.

Trials for the indicted were conducted locally, often outside Japan, in former colonies and occupied areas, and in the end a total of 920 of the accused were executed.[28] It was because of her husband's indeterminate detention overseas that Mishima and Kuniko could meet from time to time. He might be sentenced for life or executed. Or he might be cleared of charges and return to Japan, as he indeed was, and did, toward the end of 1947.

Mishima omitted this background in the novel. So the relationship between the narrator and Sonoko—"the friendship only of such a degree as to make me hesitate to call it a connection, not to mention a relationship," as the narrator circumspectly puts it—that had resumed after a chance encounter could only be half-hearted. "After a year passed, we were awakened," the narrator says. "We were not in a children's room but were inhabitants of an adults' room where the door that could open only halfway had to be repaired at once. The relationship between us, like a door that did not open beyond a certain point, had to be repaired sooner or later." What the "repair" was is left unexplained.

"I was Rimbaud's so-called 'child who never loves women,'" Mishima announced in "A Letter of Challenge to Those I Love," an aphoristic piece undated but probably written about the time Sassa Teiko decided to break with him. Presenting himself as a highly sensitive combination of a "genius" and a "clown," Mishima followed the Rimbaud reference with a *non sequitur*: "I learned that my women never get nearer to me beyond a certain demarcation point." The self-analysis, which is not really challenging anyone, male or female, ends with a statement: "A genius is a slaughterer of youth."[29]

## *The Encounter with Dazai*

In December 1946, what Mishima would later present as a dramatic literary encounter occurred. Or did it?

"My memory of the season of my visit with Mr. Dazai [Osamu] is also uncertain now, but if it was about the time his serialization of *The Setting Sun* (*Shayō*) ended, I would think it was in the autumn," he wrote in *My Pilgrimage Days*. "When it comes to my friends who took me [to the meeting], I think they were Mr. Yashiro Seiichi and his literary buddy who later died young, Mr. Harada [Ryūki] , but I am not certain about that either."

Dazai Osamu, born in 1909, was a novelist of considerable repute, a demigod among many a young reader in fact. But Mishima had developed an intense "physiological antipathy" toward the author after reading some of his works. The kind of "self-caricaturization" evident in such works as "The Wandering of Fiction" (*Kyokō no hōkō*) and "Das Gemeine," two of Dazai's works published under one cover in 1937, was what he "disliked the most," Mishima wrote, and "the consciousness of the literary establishment that flickered behind his works and the stuff like the rustic ambition of a boy who came up to Tokyo with a packing case on his back" what he "could not stand the most."

Dazai was, indeed, from Aomori, the northernmost prefecture of Japan's mainland, Honshū, and the country-boy-in-the-city theme was one undercurrent of modern Japanese literature well into the second half of the twentieth century. Dazai remained financially dependent on his well-to-do landowner-family back home for much of his life as a writer living in Tokyo. Then, the US Occupation's farmland reform had decimated his family's 620-acre land. *The Setting Sun*, the story Mishima mentioned, had to do with "the tragedy of the fallen class" or, as its author put it, "a Japanese version of *The Cherry Orchard*."[30] With this novella, "the Dazai fever has appeared to peak," Mishima had thought. But, again, it had put him off, from page one, this time because of Dazai's ignorance and mangling of the language of the aristocratic class Mishima had known from before the war.

Offered a chance to meet the famous author whose works he disliked, Mishima decked himself out in somewhat formal Japanese attire, "probably in an ikat kimono and hakama." He did not normally wear Japanese clothes, but he was dressed like that because he was "sufficiently conscious of Mr. Dazai. To exaggerate, I felt like a terrorist sallying forth with an assassin's knife hidden in his chest." The room he was taken to was appropriately foreboding.

> The place may have been the second floor of an eel restaurant; when I climbed the dark stairs and opened the *karakami* sliding door, I saw, in the guestroom of about twelve tatami, many people sitting under a dark electric lamp.
> 
> Or the electric lamp may have been pretty bright, but as I conjure up in my memory the air of "adoration of despair" of a certain period after the war, it absolutely has to have somewhat frazzled tatami and a dark electric lamp.

The gathering was no highbrow affair, as Yashiro Seiichi, who took Mishima to it, recalled. At the time Yashiro, Mishima's junior by two years, was already a man of the theater. One of his friends got hold of several bottles of sake on the black market and his group had invited Dazai, who flaunted his partiality to drinking and acting dissolutely. For some years after Japan's defeat only impure alcoholic drinks with swift but horrible effects were readily available. And Dazai had brought along Kamei Katsuichirō, a Marxist who, after jailing and interrogation, had turned away from Communism, in the end joining Yasuda Yojūrō in starting the *Nihon Rōman-ha* magazine.

Dazai and Kamei sat side by side in the space for the guests of honor, Mishima recalled, "and the young men sitting spread from there out to the four corners of the room." Introduced to those gathered, Mishima greeted them, was at once taken to the spot in front of Dazai, and offered a cup of sake. It is not clear whether Dazai emptied his cup and offered it to Mishima and filled it for him, as is the custom, or Mishima was simply given his own cup. Mishima was no drinker at the time, but he was known among his friends as "Mishima who has written for *Ningen*," as he explained himself.

> The atmosphere of the room, to me, felt like that which was somehow extremely indulgent, as between a priest and his followers who trusted each other, as if every one was moved by each pronouncement he made, shared the profundity among them, and at once waited for another revelation from him. ... [The indulgence] was one that was peculiar to that period, truly *pathetic*, even as it was filled with the confidence that they represented the malaise of the age, was crepuscular, lyrical, ... that is, too "Dazaiesque."
>
> I waited for the chance to say the one thing I had determined to say on my way there, no matter what. If I didn't say it, there'd be no meaning in my coming here, I'd lose sight of my literary life with it.
>
> But, shame on me, when I said it, I did so, I think, in a very tactless, sneery way. In other words, I said the following to the real Mr. Dazai who was right in front of me:
>
> "Mr. Dazai, I dislike your literature."[31]

Had Mishima truly been as brash and blatant to the famous author he met for the first time as he recalled he had? Surely, nine years after the meeting—and eight years before these recollections of his "pilgrimage days" appeared—Mishima had created a hubbub among literary critics by firing a giant salvo against him in a "diary" for publication that began thus:

> June 30 [1955], Thursday
> Somewhat hot. Cloudy. Met four or five guests.
> ○ We advise you not to despise Dazai Osamu but to read him in a kinder fashion.

> The disgust in which I hold Dazai Osamu's literature is in some way ferocious. First, I dislike his face. Second, I dislike his rustic preference for urban sophistication. Third, I dislike the fact that he played the roles that were not appropriate for him.[32]

Still, Mishima projecting an image of himself rudely and dramatically confronting Dazai seventeen years after the fact prompted at least two participants in the gathering to reconstruct the evening after Mishima's death: one is the aforementioned Yashiro Seiichi, the other Takahara Kiichi. And a dozen years later, the scholar Etsugu Tomoko looked into the case.

The first thing Yashiro found by checking his own diary was that the encounter occurred not in the fall of 1947, but in December 1946, a point confirmed by Mishima's own "accounting diary." To be exact, it occurred on December 14, 1946, Saturday. In the entry for that day, Mishima jotted down: "A sake party at Takahara's / Both Messrs Dazai and Kamei kindly came / Came home at twelve at night."[33] In other words, it had taken place a year before the serialization of *The Setting Sun* in *Shinchō* ended.

Had Mishima said to Dazai what he recalled he had? No one was sure. It was a gathering of twelve people—other than Dazai and Kamei there were ten college students, most of them admirers of Dazai—and it was not as if everyone was paying attention to what anyone else was saying.

But Yashiro, even as he admired Mishima for recreating the atmosphere of the gathering place more or less exactly and even as he recalled Mishima was intently listening to the aphorisms Dazai tossed off, thought whatever give-and-take may have occurred between the two probably never jibed. After all, Dazai was a thirty-seven-year-old who loved to drink and act like a man of the world, whereas Mishima was a deadly serious twenty-one-year-old who did not care to drink. The antipathy and aversion toward Dazai that Mishima flaunted later was, Yashiro thought, a result of the wounded feelings he had that night. He recalled how "triumphantly" Mishima pointed to Dazai's insufficient knowledge of the speech and daily customs of aristocratic society when *The Setting Sun* came out the next year.[34]

What wounded Mishima's feelings? Takahara Kiichi, who provided his boarding room for the gathering and procured food that night and later an editor of Dazai's complete works, remembered Mishima asking Dazai for his opinion of Mori Ōgai, one of the giant men of letters from the Meiji Era who was also a ranking officer in the Imperial Army. Dazai, he recalled, responded in his usual thuggish manner, "Listen, kid, Mori Ōgai was no novelist, I tell you. First of all, look at his photos in his complete works. He didn't mind having himself photographed in military uniform, did he? What can you say about someone like that?"

Dazai was of course joking, but Mishima took his response seriously and started questioning him and arguing to defend Ōgai. Naturally, Dazai refused to take him on. As another participant recalled, Mishima obviously did not understand Dazai's "clowning." And that visibly spoiled the mood of the party, if only for a while.[35]

What likely happened was that Mishima, recalling the encounter years later, retroactively applied to it Dazai's reputation and image that solidified with his two postwar novels, *The Setting Sun* and *No Longer Human* (*Ningen shikkaku*). If the title *The Setting Sun* alone provided "a metaphor" for Japan's calamitous defeat "after an era of marching under the sign of the rising sun," as an American biographer of Dazai put it, the title *No Longer Human* "domesticated that image to show the defeat of an individual removed from the large historical stage." The Dazai "malaise," then, was a clear reaction to "the poet of despair" that Dazai was.[36]

## *Meeting Hayashi Fusao*

In November 1947, Mishima graduated from the University of Tokyo ("imperial" was dropped two months earlier in education reform) and in December was employed by the Ministry of Finance. By then, he could easily have contented himself as a routinely published author. Kōdansha's monthly *Gunzō* carried "A Tale at the Cape" in November 1946, which was followed, in April 1947, by "Prince Karu and Princess Sotōri" (*Karu-no-miko to Sotōri-hime*), a love story featuring semi-mythological figures that ends in their suicide. *Ningen* published "The Medieval Period" in December 1946, "Preparations for the Night" (*Yoru no shitaku*) in August 1947, and "Haruko" in December. Several other magazines published his stories or solicited his contributions, some of which Mishima turned down.

Just about a week before his graduation, Sakurai Shoten published a small selection of Mishima's fiction in its "new writers" series. "A Tale at the Cape" was its title story and the volume included "The Medieval Period" and "Prince Karu and Princess Sotōri." Late that month, another publisher—this one in Kyoto—offered to publish another collection, again courtesy of Fujii Masaharu, although the company went bankrupt before fulfilling its offer.

Of these stories, "Preparations" was a barely disguised account of his experience with Kuniko, probably with some suggestive sexual elements added. In contrast, "Haruko" was a concoction—a story written in response to Kimura's request for a contribution for a special supplementary issue of *Ningen*. It describes a three-way relationship among the young narrator-protagonist, her aunt, and the aunt's sister-in-law. Including it in a 1970 selection, Mishima called "Haruko" "a postwar forerunner of fiction on lesbianism terribly fashionable now." For these two stories Mishima credited Kimura's exquisite and expert editing, saying they were almost "collaborative works" with him.[37]

"Preparations" drew favorable notices from some of the more established authors, among them Hayashi Fusao, and it was Hayashi whose reputation was at its nadir that Mishima chose to go visit, in November 1947. A writer who had started out in the 1920s in the vanguard of the Proletarian Movement, Hayashi fell victim to the Public Safety Preservation Law of 1925 created to suppress Communism. After repeated jailing, he recanted. He then wrote novels with nationalistic overtones that gained him fame and popularity. He even openly advocated expunging Marxism from literature altogether. When Japan was defeated in the war that he, like many others, had supported, Communists and other leftists who regained their voices denounced him as a turncoat or worse. So Hayashi was a man of infamy.

"Young fellows would have turned up their noses at a mere suggestion of association with him," but Mishima chose him for a visit because he wanted to "enjoy the thrill of a 'dangerous liaison,'" Mishima explained years later when he wrote an extended essay on the man.[38] More seriously, he had recoiled from the ideological about-face the majority had made.

"The newly acclaimed writer Mr. K looks upon me with a pitying smile because I have expressed indifference to political arguments," he wrote to Hayashi soon after his first visit, "but I'd rather respect someone who has been baptized by Communism."[39] Mishima would maintain a close interest in the older writer almost to the end of his life. Of Hayashi's stories, *The Youth* (*Seinen*), which he wrote soon after recanting, was the one Mishima particularly commended to the young men he would come to know. It dealt, in fictionalized form, with some of the Meiji leaders who reversed their outlook on the world after visiting the United States.

Mishima's own stories were being published, and the royalties he received, along with occasional lecture fees and such, were by no means negligible. For example, on October 27, 1947, he received a sum of ¥5,600 from his stories in *Ningen*, which, as he took care to note, came to ¥70 a manuscript page. But the *Ningen* payment was the largest sum he received during the eighteen-month period covered in the diary, and the total expenses for the period came to ¥13,366.50.[40] More important, the royalty income was not regular and, as yet, not enough to make an independent living.

As a result, Mishima's literary "successes" made Azusa all the more uneasy. After the war ended, Azuza's position became uncertain. The public company, from which he, as a former high-ranking bureaucrat, drew a salary close to that of the governor of Tokyo, stopped functioning. In October 1946 it changed its name. Although he went on to sit on several corporate boards[41] after the government shut down the public company, in January 1948, Azusa had reason to be concerned. He visited Kimura at the Kamakura Bunko.

"With a long oval face resembling Mishima's, and serious-looking, he palpably exuded bureaucratic airs," Kimura recalled. Azusa asked, "Is my son good enough to become an independent novelist whose work appears in the *Asahi Shinbun*?" Having a novel serialized in a national daily was the hallmark of writerly success, Azusa knew, and the *Asahi* was, as it remains today, among the top dailies.

Another question he asked was, "How much work will a novelist have to do before he can make a living?" Kimura was hardly in a position to respond to either question properly.[42] This pecuniary concern, which Mishima deeply understood, was practical, pressing, and enduring. To go beyond being content to be an author of a couple of books, Mishima wrote Kimura, one "must secure a living" outside writing or else "earn an adequate income to support a household by writing" and, to do the latter, "one must also write three-penny novels."[43]

That was exactly what Mishima did after he decided to become a writer. The same concern explains the reputation he gained early on for being strict on payments for his work. Henry Scott-Stokes, the British journalist who became friends with Mishima in the last part of his life, recalled two bank officers visiting him to demand payment for the article Mishima wrote, via Scott-Stokes, for a London newspaper. The paper had rejected the article.[44]

"He had to work very late at the government office," Azusa wrote of his son, "and did not come home until nine or ten." Elite bureaucrats were expected to work long hours then, as they are now. "He then would go into his study to prepare manuscripts. He would stay up half the night and have to get up early in the morning to go to work. He slept only three or four hours each day." He was in his office by eight-thirty every morning. The last day of August was a rainy day. Mishima on his way to work slipped on the platform at Shibuya Station and almost fell onto the track. When he walked home to change his muddied suit and saw his father at the front door, tears sprang to his eyes.

"You can do things only if you are alive, when the matter reached this point there was nothing left for me to do but to abandon my hundred-year strategy," Azusa later put it histrionically. "I told him, 'You can quit the government, now just be a writer and nothing else, my absolute condition is that you become Japan's Number One writer.'"

Or, as Shizue recalled, Azusa said, as dramatically: "We have reached a point where it's no longer a matter of theoretical argument. It's a matter of life [or death]. I surrender unconditionally. From today on, I will help you with all my might. I have trampled you, have beaten you down, but you still have broken out of it trying to become a writer. Perhaps you may become *something*."[45]

Azusa's permission to quit the government may have been part of the reason, but what truly prompted Mishima to resign from the Ministry of Finance was the request from the publisher Kawade Shobō in late August 1948, to write a novel for its new series. On September 2, he submitted to the Ministry a letter of resignation; three weeks later he received a formal letter of "dismissal by request." Mishima's life as an elite bureaucrat lasted only for nine months.

CHAPTER EIGHT

# Confessions

*Of all the kinds of masks, the mask called "a natural face" is the one I distrust the most.*

—Letter to Hayashi Fumio on November 4, 1947

*Mishima struggled hard to find a persona in which he felt comfortable—like a man in search of a perfect suit of clothes.*

—Donald Richie

Kawade Shobō's request would give birth to *Confessions of a Mask*. The first writer the publisher had chosen for its series was the popular author Shiina Rinzō, whose *Eternal Prelude* (*Eien naru joshō*) had come out in June. Kawade was taking some risk in choosing Mishima for the series. Though his first full-length novel, *The Bandit*, was scheduled to come out in November, with Kawabata's preface, Mishima was just beginning to be known.

When Kawade's editor Sakamoto Kazuki, along with a colleague of his, came to his office at the Finance Ministry to make the offer, on August 28, Mishima jumped at it, declaring he'd tender a letter of resignation at once to devote himself to writing. He and the two editors went out to lunch at a restaurant on the Ginza and ate hamburgers. It was just three years after Japan's defeat and hamburgers were pricey. At the time the Ministry was still in temporary digs, a former elementary school. For that matter, the envelope in which Kawabata sent his preface to *The Bandit*, in October 1948, reached Mishima with "Censored" stamped on it.[1]

Mishima spent two months deciding on what to write. On November 2 he told Sakamoto: "This next novel will be my first I-novel ever; of course, it won't be an I-novel of the Literary Establishment sort, but it will be an attempt to vivisect myself in which I will turn on myself the blade of psychological analysis that I have honed for the hypothetical figure so far. I will aim for as much scientific accuracy as I can; I will try to be Baudelaire's so-called 'victim and executioner.'"[2] "The hypothetical figure" obviously meant himself. Baudelaire's *L'Héautontimorouménos* says, in its penultimate stanza: "I am the wound and I am the knife! / I am the blow and I am the cheek! / I am the limbs and I am the wheel, / And the victim and the executioner!"[3]

The I-novel or *shishōsetsu*, one direct outgrowth of Naturalism and the Japanese adaptation of the *Ich-Roman*, is a mode of story-telling in which the protagonist, the thinly disguised (if at all) author, describes his or her own experience, preferably of a disreputable sort, presumably with unadorned honesty, even as the names, professions, and other details may be altered. What counts, in any case, is experience.

It was while struggling with *The Bandit* that Mishima, in a lengthy letter to Kawabata, in early March 1946, expounded on the importance of experience for writing fiction. He was showing each chapter to his mentor as soon as he finished it, but the direct impetus for his stress on experience in fiction writing was "The Weakness of Modern Japanese Fiction," an essay that *Ningen* carried in its February 1946 issue. Its author, Kuwabara Takeo, was a well-known professor of French literature at the Imperial University of Kyoto. During the war years he was absorbed by John Dewey's writings, in particular *Art as Experience*. What provoked Mishima was Kuwabara's statement: "Art is born of imitation." Calling it a "shallow conclusion" which cast the scholar's "sanity" into doubt, Mishima asked: "Isn't art born of experience after all?"

The experience he has in mind, he wrote, is "an experience one step higher than the experience in daily life, an experience turned into a symbol through a distilling effect." After restating this in a couple of sentences, he concluded: "in the formation of art, a supra-historical trigger is latent in the special experience of the first stage (a sort of languid inspiration), and a historical trigger is hidden in the involuntary distilling effect of the second stage. What appears to be imitation is no more than an excess of this historical trigger." It is not clear if this last sentence, in particular, made any sense to Mishima himself, but it is clear that he regarded experience as basic to his writing.[4]

In choosing the explicit I-novel format for *Confessions* to "vivisect" himself, Mishima may have decided to take head-on a writer who had created a sensation by committing double suicide in the middle of that year—the one he had met two years earlier. In mid-June Dazai Osamu threw himself into the Tamagawa Aqueduct with one of his latest mistresses, Yamazaki Tomie. Yamazaki, then working for two beauty parlors, one for the Occupation, was married at the end of 1944, but two weeks after the wedding, her husband, an employee of Mitsui & Co., was sent to Manila. As soon as he arrived there, the US forces landed in Luzon and he was lost in the Battle of Manila, in February. When Dazai met her, in March 1947, his wife, Michiko, had just had a second baby and he had just impregnated a third woman.

The Tamagawa Aqueduct was built to supply water from the Tamagawa River to the center of Edo in the mid-seventeenth century. Its use for that purpose was abandoned in 1901, but because of its swift current despite its narrow width it became "a great place for suicide." Up to the time Dazai and Yamazaki threw themselves into it that year, fifteen bodies had already been recovered, on top of thirty-three in the previous year, 1947. The day the bodies of the two were recovered, June 19, was the writer's thirty-ninth birthday, and his new novel, *No Longer Human*, was being serialized in *Tenbō*.

Dazai had gained enormous popularity the previous year with *The Setting Sun*, but his double suicide in the midst of the serialization of another work fanned the popular fascination with him. As soon as *No Longer Human* was published in book form, it became a runaway bestseller. Though it takes the form of a "madman's" notebooks that happened to have fallen into the narrator's hands, it closely chronicles, in a confessional mode, Dazai's life that was known to have been dissolute, aimless, and reckless. The number of "Dazai patients" skyrocketed.

However, if Dazai's success gave Mishima a hint in the selection of a confessional narrative mode, Mishima had no intention of following the writer in any other way. "I recognize his rare talent, but there are few writers who made me feel such a physiological antipathy from the start," Mishima recalled in *My Pilgrimage Days*, "probably because, following the law of love and hate, I was the type of writer who would deliberately expose those parts Dazai would have wanted the most to keep hidden. Accordingly, at the very point where many young writers found their own portraits in his writings, I may have hastily turned my face away."[5]

Indeed, what Mishima worked out may be said to have been "founded on the rejection of the 'logic of life'"—"the antinomy of life and art of the I-novelists" that Dazai most dazzlingly represented in postwar Japan, as the critic Aeba Takao put it.[6]

## *Sexual Confession*

Mishima told Sakamoto he would start work on *Confessions* on November 25. Methodical and punctual as he was, the date so specified more than three weeks ahead *and* after contemplating the matter for two months—the date he would choose for his own death by disembowelment and decapitation twenty-two years later—makes us wonder: Did it have some special meaning for him? Could it be, for example, that it was on that date three years earlier that Mishima learned of Mitani Kuniko's engagement?[7]

Sakamoto received the manuscript in two installments, the first 250 pages in late March 1949 and the remaining 90 pages a month later. Even before the manuscript was finished, he had urged Mishima to write ad copy for his own work. Mishima was happy to comply and wrote several, all professing his mental turmoil.

But first there is what he scribbled on the title page of his manuscript that was dropped when the story went into print.

Above and to the right of the title, *Kamen no Kokuhaku* written vertically, as Japanese is most of the time, he added, in German, twice: *das sonderbare Geschlechtsleben eines Mannes*, and below it, *das sonderbare*. Above the epigraph on the left side of the page, as Japanese progresses from right to left when written vertically, he scribbled *überspannte / sonderbare / seltsame / das exzentrische / ungewöhnliche Geschlechtsleben eines Mannes*.[8]

He would later replace the epigraph—in the manuscript a sentence from Baudelaire's *Le Spleen de Paris* in Japanese translation: "*Chacun* *d'eux portait sur son dos une énorme Chimère"*⁹—with most of the last paragraph of Book III, Chapter 3, of *The Brothers Karamazov*, "The Confession of a Passionate Heart—in Verse," where Dmitri exclaims to his brother Alyosha, "Sensuality is a tempest, is greater than a tempest!"—which Mishima omitted in quoting the passage—and goes on to say:

> I cannot bear that someone, even superior in the heart and with a high mind, begins with the ideal of the Madonna, but ends with the ideal of Sodom. Even more frightening, someone already with the ideal of Sodom in his soul does not repudiate the ideal of the Madonna either, and this ideal makes his heart burn, truly, truly burn, like it did in his youthful innocent years.
>
> (Tr. Alexander Truskinovsky)

In the Japanese translation of the Dostoevsky novel Mishima quoted, the word "confession" in the paragraph heading is given as the heavily religious *zange,* but he chose for the title of his story the more demotic *kokuhaku,* perhaps to make clear that his had nothing to do with religion.

Also, in the several pieces he wrote at Sakamoto's request, he tried to illuminate, as if for himself, what he intended to accomplish in the "novel." The self-advertisement published in the April 1949 issue of *Kindai Bungaku* was a piece he had written in January. In it he compares his work to two literary works, "Vita Sexualis" and *Armance.*

Of the two, "Vita Sexualis" is Mori Ōgai's account of his own sexual encounters since boyhood until his stay in Germany (Oct. 1884 to July 1888). When he published it, in 1909, Ōgai was surgeon general of the Imperial Army, and the army reprimanded him for it on the ground that the work was too unseemly for one of its top officers. *Armance* is Stendhal's early novel, which has one crucial mystery left unexplained to the very end: possibly, impotence. "Even though writing this work is an evident death of my existence," Mishima explained, "I feel that, while writing it, I am gradually recovering my life. What happened? My life before writing this work was the life of a corpse."

Why "confessions of a mask"? Mishima appended a note to his own ad copy: The "seemingly contradictory title derives from the paradox that to me the mask is one attached to the flesh and that there can be no *truer* confessions than those of a mask so attached to the flesh. A man can never make confessions, except that, though seldom, a mask deeply biting into the flesh can achieve them."[10]

Mishima's psychological turmoil may have been real, but his emphasis on sex was partly a response to the times. Open sexual expression was back in vogue. Previously, sex had blossomed as the subject of literature and entertainment during "the Taishō Democracy," from the 1910s to the 1920s, when *ero-guro nansensu*, things "erotic, grotesque, nonsensical," became popular. Academically, interest in sex was touched off by a translation in 1914 of Richard von Krafft-Ebing's *Psychopathia Sexualis*, which led to publication of a number of books dealing with "perverse sex," "perverse psychology," and the like.[11] In 1917, Kawabata Yasunari, for instance, noted in his diary that he was reading *On Perverse Lust* (*Hentai seiyoku-ron*) by Sawada Junjirō. Then a first-year student in The First Higher School, Kawabata had also bought the English books, *Sappho* and *Modern Man's Confession*. He was thinking of writing a story to be titled "Bestialism" (*Chikushōdō*).[12]

The open interest in sex began to be toned down, then suppressed, as Japan's war in China worsened in the 1930s, patriotism and such came to the fore, and constraints began to be placed on free, indulgent aspects of life such as luxury items. Sex became almost taboo during the Pacific War phase of the Second World War, except in ever more thriving brothels. With the revival of "democracy" following Japan's defeat, it made a comeback with vengeance. Popular books on various aspects of sex came out by the hundreds.

There was censorship, of course, and confusion. We have seen the Occupation's initial approach to it. To go somewhat ahead of *Confessions*, in January 1950 the police seized the Japanese translation of *The Naked and the Dead* claiming violation of obscenity laws; the translator had given *omanko* for Mailer's "pussy." The ban was lifted, however, when the American holder of the rights to the Japanese translation objected and the Occupation censors held the action of the Japanese police to be "undemocratic."

By then US censorship was easing. But the case of Itō Sei's translation of *Lady Chatterley's Lover*, the copies of which police confiscated in July of that year, must have posed a dilemma to the Occupiers. The reason the police gave for the action was that the D. H. Lawrence novel was banned in the United States. Itō and his publisher sued the state when the initial judgments went against them. It would go on to become a cause célèbre in relation to "freedom of speech" guaranteed by the new Constitution. The matter was not resolved until seven years later when the Supreme Court dismissed the case on the grounds of "public good," another item stressed by the new Constitution.

## *Kawabata and Youthful Homosexuality*

Mishima, in any event, chose to stress his youthful homosexual yearnings in *Confessions*. The question is: What made him do so? Here the answer may well have been simple: The diary-based story "The Boy" (*Shōnen*) that Kawabata was serializing since the May issue of *Ningen* of that year dealt directly with young "homosexual love," as the author put it plainly.

Kawabata based his stories on his diaries and recollections often enough, at times publishing early diaries only slightly edited, with comments and explanations. "The Boy" is one such story that includes part of a school composition done in epistolary form.

In 1916, Kawabata, then seventeen and a fifth grader in junior high school, became a "room chief" of the dormitory and fell in love with a pretty underclassman, Kiyono (real name: Ogasawara Yoshito). In "The Boy" he speaks of caressing—"your fingers, hands, arms, chest, cheeks, eyelids, tongue, teeth, legs"—though he, unlike some of his classmates, was too "timid" to take the next step that he called "soiling." Such lovemaking was common in single-sex dormitories and the teachers were not particularly abashed or disturbed by it, a point Kawabata makes clear.

Kawabata was acutely aware of himself as a young man. In the entry of January 21, 1917, for example, he wrote: "If each of my fantasies took some form and appeared, how long would I be able to stay unblushing? Can I even once look at a pretty boy or a pretty girl without thoughts of the flesh?" He reflected thus when he decided he was in no position to accuse a classmate of trying to take over as Kiyono's lover.

"I may have been sexually somewhat sickly because there was no feminine presence in my home, and I indulged in licentious fantasies from childhood," he wrote in a composition he submitted as a freshman at the First Higher School that he had left Osaka for Tokyo to attend. "And I may have felt a weird desire for a beautiful boy as well more than a normal person does. When I was preparing for tests, I was still more inclined to be tempted by a boy than by a girl, and even now I am thinking of dealing with such lust in my work. How many times did I wish acutely, If only you were a woman!" The composition was in the form of a letter to Kiyono.

The autobiographical story ends with the narrator, now twenty-one, visiting Kiyono in an isolated spot in Kyoto. By then an important member of the Shinto-inspired religious group Ōmoto, Kiyono was living an austere life with other converts. It was during the visit that Kawabata was disconcerted to discover that the youngest sibling of the erstwhile underclassman he so loved turned out to be a boy even though he looked and behaved like a girl.[13]

## *"Perverse Sex" Thwarted*

Expectations were that what purported to be a frank account of adolescent sex and how a young man failed in his first heterosexual act should sell. Perverse sex, assuming it was that, would be even better. It did not work out that way, at least initially. Perhaps the glut of books on sex had an opposite effect. The stress on sex ("the instinct of sex") and love ("the sexology of love"—a pun on *seiri*, which, despite what the inclusion of the character *sei*, "sex," suggests, actually means "destiny" or "principle," not "sexology") in Kawade Shobō's own ads, may have given the impression that *Confessions* was just another book in the genre. Few took notice of the book for months after it came out, on July 5, in 1949. Later, the view took hold that with this novel Mishima appeared on the literary scene like a meteor, but that was not the case. It took half a year for the book to begin to attract attention.

Mishima began to fret over his resignation from the Finance Ministry even as he continued to write and publish a stream of stories, essays, and plays. Shortly before the publication of the book, the Japanese economy started contracting quickly as a result of a US-imposed policy (as we will see soon), greatly affecting the publishing industry. But all four volumes in the Kawade series preceding *Confessions* had done well, especially the fourth, which had seen a second printing in two months, and that did not help . (The series would end with *Confessions*.) A selection of his short stories and plays Kawade published on the heels of *Confessions*, in August, sank into oblivion almost immediately. Mishima begged Kimura Tokuzō to carry a review in *Ningen*. Kimura agreed and asked Jinzai Kiyoshi to read the book.

Jinzai's review appeared in a two-page spread in the October issue of the magazine and it was exquisitely enticing. By first noting the words "Vita Sexualis" prominently printed on the book's band, Jinzai, a novelist and an outstanding translator of Russian literature, especially of Chekhov, suggested that if Ōgai's account was "paradoxical"—"Vita Sexualis" was a slap on the wrist of the Japanese Naturalists, "the acne worshippers"—Mishima's work is "even more paradoxical" because it is meant to be "a perfect confessional fiction." Of the four chapters that make up *Confessions*, the first two "consist of the most brilliant pages" of the entire volume. "In particular, the passage in Chapter 2 where 'I' describes the flesh of the martyr St. Sebastian that abruptly emerges and the first *ejaculation* he experiences as he faces its pictorial depiction struck me as a triumph in men's literature (or, to put it in extreme terms, I can say male literature) that is rare in world literature."

The picture in question is that of Guido Reni's painting *St. Sebastian* in the collection of the Palazzo Rosso, in Genoa, in an art book. The original passage reads:

> The moment I saw the painting my entire being was shaken by a certain heretical bliss. My blood rushed, my organ brimmed with the color of fury. This part of mine that had grown so gigantic as to tear apart any moment waited ferociously for my handling as it had never before, accusing me of ignorance, panting fiercely. Unbeknownst to myself, my hand started a movement no one had taught it. I had the sense that something dark and brilliant was coming up in quick steps from inside me to attack. In no time, it spurted out accompanied by a dizzying intoxication.

Jinzai denied he was exaggerating; anyone who doubted him could go to "the real thing." He even told the reader that this passage "almost" caused him to have an *ejaculation*, let alone *erectio*. Nonetheless, Jinzai did not forget to point to "some kind of indescribable chasm" he felt between the first and second halves of the story as the focus moves to "a Platonic (or rather stoic) love" for Sonoko, leaving the matter with a wonderment: Was the chasm "no more than an illusion" on the reviewer's part or "a shadow cast by what may be called a crisis that is actually assaulting the author"?[14]

Jinzai's review did not help much, however. Booksellers began returning unsold copies. The situation began to change only toward the end of the year and, once it did, it did so dramatically.

On December 26, 1949, the *Yomiuri Shinbun*, one of the top three national dailies, carried in the literary portion of its annual "The Year's Top Three" section the opinions of nine writers and critics, six of them naming *Confessions* among their choices. The six were Kawabata Yasunari; the literary critic and historian Hirano Ken; the Shakespearean translator and critic Fukuda Tsuneari; the student of European literature, novelist, and critic Itō Sei; the proletarian writer and critic Aono Suekichi; and the Buddhist monk-writer Niwa Fumio. This unusual outcome owed, to a large extent, to Hanada Kiyoteru's review titled "St. Sebastian's Face" in the January 1950 issue of *Bungei*—which, as is customary in magazine publishing, had gone on sale a month earlier, in early December 1949. Hanada had proclaimed: With this work, "in the literary realm, Japan's twentieth century begins, half a century late."

Hanada was impatient with his fellow writers who did not comprehend what Mishima had accomplished with the "I-Novel" form. One such story he mentioned was *Futon* by Tayama Katai, published in 1907. Called, in a 1930 commentary, "the forerunner [in Japan] of the *Ich-Roman*, the beginning of the description of one's self,"[15] the novella in Naturalist vein describes a married writer's impossible lust for a beautiful young woman whom he has accepted as a live-in "disciple." In the final scene, the protagonist, named Tokio, goes up to the woman's second-floor room after she was sent home and pulls out her futon and nightgown: "He put his face on the particularly soiled velvet collar of her nightgown and inhaled, to his heart's content, the smell of the woman he missed. / Sexual desire and pity and despair swiftly assaulted Tokio. He laid down the futon, spread the nightgown over it, and cried, face buried in the cold, soiled velvet collar." *Futon* kicked up a literary storm.

However, unlike Jinzai, who argued that Ōgai's "Vita Sexualis" was a criticism of Naturalists' writings such as *Futon*, Hanada asserted that Ōgai and Katai were on the same plane. "Both the mask with a wily expression that Ōgai consciously puts on in "Vita Sexualis" and the mask with a dumb expression that Katai consciously wears in *Futon* are, in Jungian terms, both 'extroversive,'" he wrote; "these masks, therefore, are functioning merely centrifugally." He then said what may have chagrined Mishima. "In contrast, the masks both Dazai and Mishima consciously use are equally 'introversive'; even though their expressions are markedly different, one blushing with embarrassment, the other showing off an arrogant mien, they are both constantly moving inwardly, functioning centripetally."

But there was one thing that crucially differentiated Mishima, not just from Ōgai and Katai but Dazai as well, Hanada continued. Whereas for those three, as well as their epigones, a mask became necessary because each had "a face—his own flesh"—and had to "hide it from the others' eyes or to stare at it himself, Mishima alone among them needs a mask to search his flesh that he lost completely." In this he is representative of Japan's "Lost Generation," born out of the Second World War, just as Radiguet was of a generation born out of the First. It isn't that "Mishima Yukio wears his mask because he is concerned in the least with what others might think. He wears an introversive mask called sexual perversion and searches his own body because he is dissatisfied with his own self that is rational, too rational, and is conducting a harsh self-criticism."

In the end, though, what prompted many writers to take note of *Confessions* may well have been not so much Hanada's psychological analysis as his harsh, contemptuous dismissal of the three writers who had discussed the work as a group in *Gunzō*—Hayashi Fusao, Nakano Yoshio, and Kitahara Takeo—as "those from the nineteenth century" and his flat assertion that neither "eighteenth-century-style emotionalists" nor "nineteenth-century-style intellectualists" could possibly understand what Mishima had done in the novel.[16]

## *Was Mishima Perverse?*

Was Mishima sexually perverse? Or, perhaps the question should be: What, aside from his desire to "vivisect himself" and become a successful author, impelled Mishima to insist on his own "sexual aberration"— that was what he said it was—in a confessional style? The question arises because there was in the first place what Jinzai Kiyoshi called "some kind of indescribable chasm" in the novel, a disconnect between the first half, Chapters One and Two, and the second, Chapters Three and Four. How could the narrator dispose of the principal character in the second half, Sonoko—Mitani Kuniko in real life—so abruptly? Was *Confessions* an attempt to cover up or rationalize his heartbreak in a standard or normal love affair?

The question, which remained strong for some time, was put to Mishima most acutely by a young woman poet in the early 1960s. Having heard Mishima denounce "the literary establishment," that "everyone who is part of it tells only lies," once too often, Shindō Ryōko, over a sizzling steak at a steakhouse he had invited her to, asked him, "You write a lie in *Confessions of a Mask*, don't you? When your first love became a bride, you were so sad you wanted to die, did you not?" At this unexpected sally from her, and this was long before biographical details became public, Mishima turned "painfully somber," Shindō recalled.[17]

The narrative gap in *Confessions*—between two very different narratives—is something any reader notices: the story of the narrator's growing fascination with members of his own sex, followed by that of an encounter with a young woman who attracts him. But the confessions end when the narrator is drawn to a young tough nearby even as he is with the woman. Mishima himself knew that the story was off balance.

In deciding to explore what he called his *Tendenz*, Mishima mined his considerable knowledge of world literature, including tracts on sexology. He also went to see at least one authority in the field. Kimura Tokuzō recalled Mishima visiting him a few months after he started to write what was to be "his representative work, *Confessions of a Mask*." Mishima was on his way back from a psychologist in Kimura's neighborhood. He excitedly talked about his "perverse tendencies" and his visit with the psychologist was to "elicit his opinions about them." He then talked at length about Wilde, Verlaine, and "homosexual literature ancient and modern, in the East and the West." This prompted Kimura to tell the young man that he expected to see from him a "'Vita Sexualis' as good as Ōgai's." "Mishima turned around and, with his *monomaniac* eyes glinting, said, 'So you can tell!'"[18]

"I think both in this country and in foreign countries there are few kinds of naked, confessional descriptions of *sexual inversion*," Mishima wrote to Shikiba Ryūzaburō when the psychiatrist who had written books on Aubrey Beardsley and Marquis de Sade acknowledged receipt of the copy of *Confessions*. "One of the few is Gide's *Si le grain ne meurt*, but it mainly stresses the aspect of spiritual history. I have seen the rare book called *Livre blanc* by Jean Cocteau, but it, too, is nothing more than a short story." He added, "In early summer last year I read *Sexual Inversion in Man* [sic] and *Love and Pain* [sic] by [Havelock] Ellis that deals with sexual psychology." Mishima explained that he had sent him the book in the hopes that his own account might be of some use to Shikiba's "research."[19]

In *Confessions*, it was neither Havelock Ellis nor Sigmund Freud but Magnus Hirschfeld that Mishima quoted at length for sexual self-analysis. It may well have been from the "psychologist," whom Kimura noted as Mishima having just been to see, that he learned the views of the German sexologist. That psychologist, Mochizuki Mamoru, had published articles on various aspects of sex in magazines before assembling them in *Sex and Life* (*Sei to seikatsu*), in March 1949. Mochizuki had also made his name the previous August by his pronouncement during the Tōhō labor strife, "Only warships didn't come." That was when the Occupation, which had encouraged a labor movement as part of Japan's democratization process, sent the Eighth US Army, including tanks and armored vehicles, to evict the strikers occupying the movie studio in opposition to a summary dismissal of twelve hundred workers.

When Mochizuki was writing, one theory divided homosexuals into two categories, "true" and "pseudo": that is, the hermaphrodites and those with no physical abnormalities but with marked tendencies toward sexual self-love. In the chapter on "self-centeredness of sexual love" in *Sex and Life*, Mochizuki termed the former abnormal, the latter perverse.

Although most boys have self-centered sexual desire and often fulfill it through masturbation, Mochizuki wrote, self-centeredness dissipates with most, persisting into adulthood only with a small minority. Those who remain self-centered tend to be shy, unable to play with other children, and to stay home when young. If a member of the same sex establishes contact with any of those, pseudo-homosexual love is born. If a member of the opposite sex manages to establish contact with him, he may be able to engage in what appears to be normal sex but remains the same at his core. In other words, "pseudo-perverts" do not have anything out of the ordinary in the way of sexual desire; it is simply that they are not constitutionally inclined to work with members of the other sex. This, Mochizuki wrote, is what Magnus Hirschfeld also recognizes.[20]

If this view appears somewhat deficient today, it may be well to remember that Mochizuki was writing just about the time Alfred Kinsey put together *Sexual Behavior in the Human Male* in which he rejected the view that "homosexuality is innate." In a commentary on the report, Lionel Trilling complained that Kinsey's treatment of homosexuality—"the sexual aberrancy which is, I suppose, the most complex and the most important in our cultural life"—was "oversimplified" and "confusing."[21]

Mochizuki noted Mishima's visit in his cryptic diary, and that he discussed with the young man, among other things, Brunswick, then a famous gay bar on the Ginza. He did not say he lent Hirschfeld's *Sexualpathologie* to Mishima, but in *Confessions* the narrator refers to Hirschfeld three times, the first time in relation to his first masturbatory ejaculation. He notes: "In my case, it is a very interesting coincidence that Hirschfeld should place the painting of St. Sebastian in first rank among the paintings and sculptures perverts favor." He then gives the life of Saint Sebastian: How, when his secret conversion to Christianity was exposed, he was shot dead with "countless arrows," but how, when he revived after a devout widow's care, he was bludgeoned to death with cudgels. The narrator concludes the section with "an unfinished prose poem" on Saint Sebastian he wrote years afterward.

The second reference occurs when the narrator describes how he gradually began to "transfer" his attention from "older young men" to boys younger than himself. His concern here is with the German sexologist's taxonomy. "Hirschfeld makes divisions among perverts," he reports, "calling *androphiles* those who are attracted only by the adults of the same sex and calling *ephebophiles* those who love only boys and those between boys and grown youths. I was beginning to understand *ephebophiles*." Or, as a summary of Hirschfeld's works in English puts it: "*Ephebophiles*, who are attracted to youths from puberty up to the early twenties; *androphiles*, who love persons between the early twenties and fifty."

The narrator of *Confessions* then gives the etymology of *ephebophiles*, noting that it "derives from Hebe, the daughter of Zeus and Hera and the wife of the immortal Hercules. The goddess Hebe was the cupbearer of the Olympian gods and was a symbol of youth." It may be added, if only because Mishima would later make clear his dislike for old men time and again, that Hirschfeld had another category: "*gerontophiles*, who love older men, up to senile old age."

The third reference occurs near the end of *Confessions*. The narrator describes his deliberate avoidance of women and his uncontrollable lust that at times drove him to indulge in "the bad habit as many as five times a day." In consequence, "Hirschfeld's theory that explains perversion as an utterly simple biological phenomenon disabused me of my ignorance."

Most notably perhaps, though Mishima makes no direct reference to it, *Sexualpathologie* includes a case study of a young homosexual presented through his letters. This young man bears a striking resemblance to Mishima, beginning with the fact that his father was a ranking government official and himself a law student.

Magnus Hirschfeld, who founded the Institute of Sexual Science in Berlin, in 1919, was among the greatest sexologists of the era who "ranked with Havelock Ellis and Sigmund Freud."[22] Because Paragraph 175 of the German Penal Code criminalized homosexuality, he was often called on to testify in courts, most notably during the Eulenberg Trial, in 1907, *Moltke v. Harden*, the biggest homosexual scandal of the period that engulfed the highest echelons of Kaiser Wilhelm's entourage.[23] But when the Nazis took over, in 1933, his open advocacy of sexual freedom, including the fact that he, a Jew, was an important member of the movement to abolish Paragraph 175, turned him into the Nazis' primary target, and his books, along with his vast collections at his institute, were destroyed in the Nazi Book Burning. He died an exile in Nice, in 1935.

## *Parallel Narratives Examined*

Was Mishima exaggerating or in some way faking his homosexual tendencies? Mitani Kuniko was convinced he was. Asked what she thought of *Confessions* when she read it, she said, "Mr. Mishima was a very sincere, serious person. He just feigned 'sexual perversion,' I thought."

Among those who have written about Mishima, Muramatsu Takeshi, for one, forcefully argued that Mishima decided to emphasize homosexual interests in *Confessions* because he had to give up on his love for Mitani Kuniko. Muramatsu, a student of French literature who observed the Eichmann Trial in Jerusalem, in 1961, and, in the following year, the Algerian War of Independence from the Algerian side, knew Mishima's family very well.

Muramatsu grew up not far from the residence of the Hashi family, and his mother knew Shizue since both were young. She would point out the Hashi house to him whenever the two passed by it, saying it was where the former principal of the Kaisei Middle School, that is, Shizue's father, lived. She also told him, in the early 1930s, that Shizue said she wanted a divorce from Azusa—the plaint she would repeat well into the mid-1960s when the two served as adjudicators in a family court.

Muramatsu knew there were some discrepancies between reality and fiction in Mishima. To start, Mishima wrote, in the novel, "After my sister's death, [Sonoko] was soon married. Shall I call it the feeling of a heavy burden taken off my shoulders? I made myself merry. I boasted to myself that it was the natural consequence of not her having abandoned me, but my having abandoned her." In truth, Mishima became hopelessly drunk on the night Kuniko married, on May 5. He, still a student, was not known to have had many opportunities to consume alcohol, but he became dead drunk "for the first time since he was born," Muramatsu recalled Shizue telling him.

As he saw it, all the homosexual talk in the first half of *Confessions* was fiction, although that would deny even a common adolescent fascination with members of the same sex. It was necessary for Mishima to "put a mask of homosexuality on the protagonist," Muramatsu judged, so as to "reverse the positions of man and woman in their mutual relationship." For him to feel "a heavy burden taken off his shoulders" at the news of the marriage of someone with whom he was in love, he *had* to have the knowledge that he had homosexual tendencies, even if that was not known to anyone else.[24]

Muramatsu—who reminded the *Times* (London) bureau chief in Tokyo, Henry Scott-Stokes, of "a bit of Action Française types, same combination of rightwing views and intelligence one saw in the Action Française in the 1930s" when the two met at Mishima's dinner party in 1968[25]—bases his rebuttal of the "homosexuality legend" pertaining to Mishima, along with the "rightwing legend," not just on his knowledge of a friend but also on his close, chronological reading of Mishima's writings.

Referring to the notes Mishima had taken in 1946 on kissing

Kuniko, for example, he points to a subtle but decisive role reversal Mishima managed in transferring the initial description into the novel. In the notes, it is "I" who was eager to kiss Kuniko, whereas she, unable to shake off the behavior expected of young women in those days, was "stiff like a doll" when kissed and embraced: "She was reluctant even to take her raincoat off. As though it were her underwear.... Not only that, she freely allowed me to kiss her lips but would not try to kiss mine. Also, she freely allowed me to hug her but would not try to hug me back. She was stiff like a doll." In the novel, Sonoko is "panting" in the narrator's arms, "her cheeks blushing crimson like fire," but "she still did not appeal to my desire."

Muramatsu does not overlook "A Tale at the Cape," the dreamy fragment of a romance Mishima wrote during the wrenching period astride Japan's surrender—that is, before he learned of Kuniko's engagement. By examining a contemporary translation, Muramatsu notes that the short story is based on Gabriele d'Annunzio's novel *Il trionfo della morte* that devotes its last two-thirds to "a tale at the cape."

Yet what stands out in light of Mishima's love for Kuniko is not the death of a young couple who appear airily in front of the eleven-year-old boy lost on the cape, which Mishima presents as an incident in *Märchenland*, Muramatsu suggests, so much as a description of the young woman. "The person who looked dazzlingly beautiful to my eyes," Mishima wrote, "surely had not passed twenty, and had a face very like that of someone whom I had drawn up in my mind for some time as what the bride who would visit me in the remote future would have to be like." In other words, Mishima, in writing the story, was envisaging Kuniko. That was three months before he learned of her betrothal.[26]

The change that occurred in Mishima upon Kuniko's engagement, then, is transforming, if you will, in the "long story" he embarked on "with the ambition of astonishing people," in January 1946. In what was finally titled *The Bandit*, Kuniko, now named Yoshiko, remains a beautiful young woman, "a person as beautiful as never seen before" (the Chinese characters Mishima chose for the name mean just that, "beautiful person"), but this time she emerges as a licentious woman.

After allowing the protagonist, a viscount's son named Akihide, to have a moment of dalliance with her, Yoshiko casually abandons him and goes on to misbehave openly. In recasting the same person as such a figure, Mishima perhaps merely brought to the fore d'Annunzio's nymphomaniac Ippolita, her sexual nature barely, if at all, hinted at in "Cape," but it was a vengeful act nonetheless. Similarly, in the novel Mishima stresses death that was barely glimpsed in the fairyland setting of the earlier story. When he realizes Yoshiko wasn't serious with him, Akihide decides to commit suicide, although, when he manages to do so, it is with another woman who has agreed to marry him, and he carries out the double suicide on the night of their wedding.

This contrived narrative, set in the mid-1930s, gave Mishima a great deal of trouble. He prepared detailed notes, character sketches, and drafts for the novel. In one memo he wrote for himself "because someone said the story reminded me of Radiguet," he took care to note: "The difference between me and Radiguet: Radiguet is a Romanticist who sees romance in the development of normal psychology itself; I am a Realist who tries to realistically embody a romantic psychology that is absolutely impossible."

Mishima wrote and rewrote the story, chapter by chapter, and at one point gave it up altogether. When he finally completed it, he characterized it as a piece in which all the literary influences he had received were "exposed, without any connecting links, randomly," adding, "The reader will be surprised by the odd blending of the two very opposite concepts of the French psychological novel and the German Romantic novel."

Kawabata, for one, sensed a deeply wounded young man behind what may be termed a series of obfuscating psychological interactions among the characters. In the preface he wrote, he spoke of "the flowering of Mishima's talent at so early an age" that he found "both dazzling and painful," suggesting that, even as some may see Mishima as someone "totally unwounded by his own work," others will see that his "work comes out of his many deep wounds."[27]

Mishima's love for Kuniko probably was as serious as any first love can be. Mishima said it was, on a number of occasions. Soon after writing *Confessions*, he wrote Ninagawa Chikayoshi, at the time on the editorial board of the Kamakura Bunko and another scholar of French literature who later became a professor at Waseda University: "I wouldn't have been able to live without writing about her. Even if the exaggerated expression of 'being unable to live' were not improper, I was overwhelmed by the being called Sonoko. . . . The woman called Sonoko is, [to use] the name of her real being, Kuniko. I have trouble conjuring the image of the real Kuniko, however I tried, as I kept writing the imagined name Sonoko in my work."

Mishima remained agitated even as he wrote about the novel he had finished. He certainly meant to write *tekitō*, "proper," not *futō*, "improper," and he certainly meant to say "had trouble," not "have trouble." Mishima was clear-headed enough to be aware of the discrepancy he thought he found between his literary creation and the real person, for he went on to say in his letter to Ninagawa: "The actual Kuniko did not have as much spirituality or sensitivity as 'Sonoko.'"[28]

The failure with Kuniko was a serious blow to Mishima. Japanese publishers routinely insert a "monthly report" called *geppō*, a kind of newsletter, in each new title. In his "notes" to *Confessions* in Kawade's monthly newsletter for July 1949, Mishima amplified the death-life part that he had described in the January précis: "This book is a testament of the realm of death that I have inhabited until now. To write this book has been for me suicide reversed. If you make a movie of someone leaping to death and run the film backward, the suicide jumps up from the bottom of the valley to the top of the cliff with a ferocious speed and returns to life. What I have attempted in writing this book is such an art of recovering life."

In his aforementioned letter to the psychiatrist Shikiba Ryūzaburō, Mishima wrote that his worry was "less about my inherent *Tendenz* than about my physical incompetence in the normal direction, so I thought confession would be the most effective as a mode of psychoanalysis." His concern about his "physical incompetence in the normal direction" would prove unfounded, if it had any foundations.

Muramatsu followed Mishima's writings with care and sympathy to show how the pain of the breakup with Mitani Kuniko never left Mishima till the end of his life. Toward the end of his life, indeed, there is, for example, Ayakura Satoko, a young woman from the blue-blood aristocracy who provides an undercurrent throughout Mishima's lifework, the tetralogy *The Sea of Fertility*.

Early on in the first of the four novels, *Spring Snow*, Satoko, in sudden turmoil, asks Matsugae Kiyoaki, the son of a low-ranking samurai accorded marquisate status as a result of his work for the Imperial Restoration: "Suppose I suddenly disappeared, Kiyo-sama, what would you do?" She already has a marriage offer and she wants to know if Kiyoaki, who feigns indifference, truly loves her. In describing the intimacy and the eventual breakup that ensue, Mishima surely was thinking of what might have happened to Kuniko and himself had not things happened as they did, Muramatsu suggests.[29]

Muramatsu also recounts what his sister, Eiko, observed when, just about a month before carrying out his planned death, Mishima had the theater troupe of his creation Rōman Gekijō (Romantic Theater) stage his 1958 play *The Rose and the Pirate (Bara to kaizoku)*. The play, which may well have been inspired by his unexpected encounter with Kuniko in New York, in December 1957, concerns a popular thirty-seven-year-old writer of fairy tales who, ever since marrying the man who raped her, has professed to disdain lust but falls in love with a handsome thirty-year-old idiot who visits her, convinced he is one of the boy characters she has created.

Muramatsu Eiko, the actress Mishima nurtured and who played the writer in the overtly fanciful drama, reported noticing Mishima cry at the end of Act Two during a rehearsal and, again, on opening day, October 22, when he was in the audience. Act Two is where the intimate, fairyland conversation between the two main characters ends with the idiot telling the writer: "I had told you just one lie. There was no such thing as a Kingdom." Muramatsu thinks this scene clearly indicates the "kingdom" that Mishima had imagined with Kuniko.[30]

Reading too much into such things can mislead, of course. In the case of *The Rose and the Pirate*, Mishima did not try to hide his crying. Many saw it, and some were alarmed. But asked about it, he laughed if off, "I was so deeply moved by the actors' wonderful performance." Azusa suggested that his son cried because he was distraught over the difficulties involving his private militia, The Shield Society.[31]

Muramatsu Eiko herself, whom Mishima expressly assigned to play the fairytale writer, was less struck by the tears he shed than by the realization later that the staging just before his death of this particular drama—which ends with the female writer declaring, at her wedding, "I have never had anything like a dream"—was part of his "last theatrical presentation" of himself. Before his death, he had scheduled production of another play of his, *Salome*, which, for all the shock and turmoil of his death, was staged as planned, in January 1971—at his wife Yōko's insistence.[32] Furthermore, he was known to be highly expressive as a theater viewer in the tradition of kabuki enjoyment.[33]

At any rate, Romano Vulpitta has suggested that Muramatsu

Takeshi may have gone too far in emphasizing the consequences of his friend's breakup with Mitani Kuniko on his psyche. Mishima's own "words and actions" are there, the Italian diplomat-turned-scholar of Japanese literature has pointed out, as "an obstacle to casually dismissing" the "homosexual legend," along with the "rightwing legend." Muramatsu was too eager in his attempt to remain "respectful" to Mishima Yukio.[34]

More to the point, there is, Muramatsu himself did not neglect to note, the problem you cannot really avoid in writing a biography: how "not to create personal trouble for those surrounding" the subject.[35] Among other things, Mishima's wife, Yōko, was alive when Muramatsu serialized the biography in *Shinchō*, from 1988 to 1990, and she was famous for working hard after her husband's death to tramp down any suggestion that he had had homosexual involvements. It is known that Muramatsu knew far more than he let on.

Indeed, Muramatsu would admit his friend's sexuality, albeit indirectly, long before taking on the difficult task of writing his biography. Shortly after Mishima's death, the University of Toronto asked him to give a series of lectures on Japanese views of life and death. Later he expanded and serialized them in *Shinchō*. He then revised them to turn them into a book, published in 1975.

The result was an unusual history of Japanese literature largely focused on death and, shall we say, love. In the section on "the aesthetic of double suicide," Muramatsu addressed homosexual love, pointing out that writings on male-male double suicide preceded those on female-male double suicide that Chikamatsu Monzaemon popularized in his plays, and added: "The average modern sensibility finds it hard to understand double-suicide by homosexuals."[36] After all, Chikamatsu's contemporary Ihara Saikaku (1642–93) could proclaim, in writing *Great History of Male Love* (*Nanshoku ōkagami*), that "no attempt [was] made to hide dislike of women" among the characters he chose to describe.

## *The Occupation Involvement*

In the fall of 1949, there was an unexpected turn of events: George Saito, of the Occupation's Public Opinion and Sociological Research Division, asked to meet Mishima, so the two met. Saito, later a scholar of

Japanese literature, told him that a Capt. Tufts, a composer, was looking for a Japanese who would write a libretto with a Japanese theme for a collaborative Japanese-American opera, and invited him to meet the composer and listen to some of his music.

Learning that Saito already knew Haniya Yutaka and was preparing to have his incomplete philosophical novel *Dead Souls (Shirei)* translated into English, Mishima asked Haniya to accompany him to the next meeting. Haniya, guessing that Mishima, like him, had "a phobia of being interviewed by a gaijin," came along. After Capt. Tufts played snatches of his composition on the piano, Haniya told the Americans that the composer would find "in Japan no one more appropriate than the young writer sitting next to me to write a libretto" for what he had in mind. He cannot forget, Haniya later wrote in his inimitably convoluted language, the way Mishima Yukio, at these words, "laughed as he looked down showing suddenly with his entire body the shyness that has tremulous innocence at its core."[37]

Mishima apparently told Saito and Tufts that his libretto would be based on "Prince Karu and Princess Sotōri" and their discussion went as far as revising the story to modify its tragic ending. According to a *Yomiuri Shinbun* interview in early December, Mishima expressed the hope to work out something with Capt. Tufts and see it staged "before the ratification of a peace treaty." But perhaps because of the Korean War that erupted half a year later the plan fizzled and nothing came of it.[38]

It may be, however, through this involvement with the CIE that Mishima came to know Herbert Passin, the progenitor of the Public Opinion and Sociological Research Division within the Occupation bureaucracy[39] who would help him two years later when the young writer decided to go to the United States for the first time.

## *And in the Meantime*

Also, in December, Mishima wrote Kimura Tokuzō: "I, right now, cannot forget, awake or asleep, the appearance of a boy at Brunswick, I sigh all the time, as if my adolescence has restarted. A loving heart is so pitiable, isn't it?" He then quoted parts of his own diary, saying "my confessional habit has raised its head again": "December 11—[The publisher] Sōjusha sent me three Zweig volumes. *Confusion of Feelings*—these are terrifying words. Each word, each phrase, penetrates my heart, penetrates into my organs and intestines. Heart confounded, I cannot work; the old professor protagonist's despair is the same as my state now. I shouldn't have read it. Terrifying. Terrifying. Now, writing a novel is a desperate desire for internal balance." Mishima also referred to Thomas Mann's *Death in Venice* and Marcel Proust's *Time Regained* as showing old age as a time when "despair" and "empty hope" can only get worse.[40]

That day, Mishima was in a mood to talk in a somewhat feverish vein. He penned another letter—this one to Dan Kazuo, a writer of the Japan Romantic School whose debut work *Flower Memento (Hanagatami)* had led him to write an elaborate appreciation five years earlier.[41] It was mainly to thank Dan for sending him his "novel," *Dazai Osamu*, which reminded him, Mishima said, of Eduard Friedrich Mörike's *Mozart on the Journey to Prague*. But he also talked about an outlandish dream he recently had about a gigantic peacock. He then stated, rather abruptly, that it was becoming clearer to him that "there cannot be any salvation in this world beyond writing sincerely, dedicatedly, a novel saying 'There can never, never, be any salvation in this world.'"

"Today a writer without a powerful idea dies or weakens just as a soldier without a powerful body dropped out during the war," Mishima insisted. "This is because in a mythical, monstrous, fabulous age such as the modern times, each person must act out a fierce drama, which he will not be able to bear if he tries to do it with his body alone."

"I am an affirmer of violence," he went on, "and I would like to act out, with spiritual violence, a very bloody evil deed. In fact, whenever I see a pretty boy, I want to splash oil all over him, light it, and burn him." His "ideal life" if he were to become rich enough would be to "keep a hungry lion" and, when the time for his own death approaches, to "throw all the boys I love into the lion cage and die, while watching the spectacle, by taking heroin," but not Philopon [Methamphetamine], nor Adolm [Cyclobarbital calcium], nor potassium cyanide—all closely associated with the war and its chaotic aftermath.[42]

What fascinates here, in retrospect, is Dan's summing-up of Dazai's life and literature in his foreword to his "novel"—in truth a memoir of the author's uncontrollably licentious days of "drinking and womanizing" with Dazai, from 1933 to 1941. "Dazai's death was what his life, which was in short his literary art, that was planned, hypothesized, and induced, over the length of forty years, finally lured him to," Dan observed. "The literary art Dazai had to pursue to the end devoured his body." And: "His hypothesized life was not completed unless he chose death."[43]

Did Mishima, later an avowed hater of Dazai, sometimes recall these words?

CHAPTER NINE

# Boyfriends, Girlfriends

*All human beings are bisexual.*

—Gore Vidal

*An innocent-looking scoundrel, a childlike adult, a man of common sense with talents of an artist, a conman who makes imitations.*

—Fukuda Tsuneari on Mishima

*Confessions* went into a second printing in early 1950. In June, when Shinchōsha published Mishima's next full-length novel, *Thirst for Love* (*Ai no kawaki*), the same imprint accepted *Confessions* in its paperback series (thereby undermining the sale of Kawade's hardcover edition and creating ill will). The publisher's blurb for the first edition of *Thirst for Love* was "An ambitious work by Mishima Yukio, the shining star of postwar literature!" In its second printing, the blurb was rewritten: "An ambitious work by Mishima Yukio that goes beyond *Confessions of a Mask!*"

Asked to write an afterword to the paperback edition of *Confessions*, Fukuda Tsuneari began by calling Mishima "a fertile barrenness" and ended it with the hope: "I look forward to watching him manipulate his mask at will."[1] Mishima did not disappoint the Shakespearean scholar and playwright. In the year 1950 alone, he published three novels dealing with three different themes. He followed *Thirst for Love*, in June, with *The Blue Age (Ao no jidai)* and *The Snow-White Night (Junpaku no yoru)*, both serialized before appearing in book form in December. This was in addition to two collected works, published in May and June: *The Lighthouse (Tōdai)*, which included three plays and eight stories, and *Monster*, which included one play and five stories.

The year also saw his first head-on involvement with theater. In February, he directed his own play, *The Lighthouse*, with the theater troupe Haiyū-za, "Actors Theater," that was founded in the midst of war, in 1944. Yashiro Seiichi arranged it, though he had already left the troupe by then. The one-act drama deals with a twenty-five-year-old repatriated soldier in love with his thirty-year-old stepmother. It had attracted enough attention at the end of the previous year to be staged by two different troupes, in Osaka and in Kyoto. When subjected to a group review earlier, the play had elicited a memorable comment from the novelist Nakayama Gishū: "What an astonishing talent. . . . No doubt about it, he's a genius. Maybe [another] Akutagawa Ryūnosuke. He's got no flesh but he's got brains."[2]

Mishima's directorial debut was a failure; he was more interested in the words he'd written than in how the actors performed them. Yashiro who came to see the rehearsal was blunt: "Mishima, directing is watching the actors' movements. If you like your script so much, take it home and read it"—or so Seki Hiroko recalled Yashiro telling Mishima. She was one of the actresses who appeared in the play[3] and, Yoshiro remembered, one of the women Mishima pursued at the time. But the experience put on firmer ground Mishima's association with actors, actresses, and directors. Then, in December, another, older troupe, Bungaku-za, founded in 1937, staged his play *Kantan* in its Atelier, the troupe's practice space.

(The name Bungaku-za was a straight translation of Littérature Théâtre. One of its three founding managers, Iwata Toyo'o decided on the name in order to stress the literary rather than political qualities of the plays to be presented at the theater. Along with another founder-manager Kishida Kunio, Iwata had studied drama in France after the First World War when anti-realism was in fashion. To the general reader he was better known as Shishi Bunroku, the writer of humorous stories; married to a Frenchwoman, he turned to the genre when he found he couldn't make a living in the theater. A third founder-manager was Kubota Mantarō, another important name in modern Japanese theater and also a haiku poet.)

*Kantan* is a twist on the nō drama with the same title that was based on a Chinese story from the Tang Dynasty. The original story is one of Buddhist enlightenment and tells of a man who suddenly becomes the ruler and enjoys all the attendant glories for fifty years—all while asleep on a magical pillow, only to find upon waking that everything had happened while millet was being cooked for him to eat. Mishima's play turns the homiletic tale upside down and tells of a man who spurns all seductive opportunities while asleep and finds upon waking that the world he had thought dead before falling asleep has revived. It would become the first of Mishima's "modern nō plays." Akutagawa Hiroshi, the first son of Ryūnosuke who committed suicide in 1927 at the age of thirty-five, directed it and played a role in it. He would go on to distinguish himself as a character actor.

Actually, Mishima's first play to be staged was *The House on Fire (Kataku)*, a one-act play about a loveless couple, and that had occurred a year before, in February–March 1949. Again, Yashiro was involved. Then still a member of the Haiyū-za and just twenty-two, he persuaded the group to stage the play and produced it. The troupe's founder, Senda Koreya, an outstanding actor who had studied theater in Germany in the 1920s and was often jailed after his return to Japan for promoting proletarian theater, played the lead role. In that regard, Mishima enjoyed "extraordinary luck and glory," as Yashiro put it. Mishima went to all the rehearsals and saw every performance of the play while it ran, from February 24 to March 2. It was, like his directorial debut a year later, a sobering experience. He was forced to realize how inadequate his grasp of his material was when actors asked him questions.[4]

Yashiro, incidentally, makes his appearance in *Confessions*, though unnamed. He is the one who takes the narrator to a red-light district where, faced with an ugly, lurid, and brazen prostitute, the narrator discovers or confirms his impotence with a member of the opposite sex. Most likely nothing of the sort happened, Yashiro wrote long after Mishima's death. As soon as tea was served, as is customary in any Japanese inn, Mishima paid the full amount and fled. How could Yashiro say that? Because that was exactly what he did. Two years younger than Mishima, he had pretended to be an experienced playboy, but he had never slept with a woman, a prostitute or otherwise. In fact, his "companion to be" that night was a healthy girl of seventeen or eighteen fresh from the countryside, and he was unable to forget her; as a result, he wrote a one-act play two decades later.

Yashiro, for that matter, even as he confessed he was unaware of Mishima's homosexual tendencies during the period these things happened, in 1947, recalled being introduced to a Peers School student in Mishima's house with whom he was on intimate terms. He did not make anything of it except to guess that Mishima was acting to amuse him—this partly because in Japan "intimacy" between young males is accepted. Yashiro does not say how the student looked. Kimura Tokuzō did. When Mishima died and the photo of the young man who died with him appeared, Kimura was startled to remember "the one young man who had attracted Mishima in his youthful days." The two looked so alike!⁵

## *Early Religious Interest*

The title of the play *The House on Fire* is a Buddhist metaphor for this work that comes from a well-known parable in *The Lotus Sutra*,⁶ and this may be a good place to note that Mishima's interest in religion had started early. This is clear just by looking at the nine plays he had written before *The House on Fire*, mostly in his early teens, although what is considered to be the first one, *Mamie*, had little to do with religion. As Mishima was meticulous to note, it was based on the tale *La Chèvre de M. Seguin* that Alphonse Daudet tells in one of his letters to the (fictitious) lyric poet Pierre Gringoire.

Among Mishima's eight other plays, however, *The Corpse and Treasure (Shibito to takara)*, "a verse drama in one act" with the subtitle *Bhalchandra*, has the format of a standard Buddhist tale. *The Route (Rotei)* is a drama of the Annunciation, with the citation of Luke 1:28, "And the angel came in unto her, and said, Hail, *thou that art* highly favoured, the Lord *is* with thee"), which, with a touch of *Macbeth*, refers to catacombs and Palestina (Act III, Scene 2). *The Wise Men from the East* (*Tōhō no hakase tachi*), based on Matthew 2:1-9 and again with a touch of *Macbeth*, describes the agitation of Herod on the night "the star" appears; it is an eerily accomplished play for a fourteen-year-old. Mishima also set out to write, but did not finish, a verse drama on the birth of Jesus Christ.⁷

As he wrote Azuma in a separate letter, because his father insisted that he read books on Nazism, he started reading those on Jewish issues, and he was also drawn to the Bible and commentaries on it for a while.[8]

*The House on Fire* became an impetus of sorts to Mishima as a professional playwright. In February *The Anxiety of Love (Ai no fuan)* saw print—a startling story of a young man and a young woman, both seventeen years old and in love with each other, who are shot dead by an adult who claims to be a four-month-old fetus she aborted, even as the couple start making love, apparently for the first time. In October two one-act plays came out. One was *Niobe*, which is about a woman who ends up losing all her five children she had with five different men while married to one, and the other, *A Saintly Woman (Seijo)*, was about a young man who forces his older sister to follow his every whim and eventually kills her, unhinged by her saintly willingness to do whatever she is told.

That same month Mishima published an essay, "A Fiction Writer Eager to Write Drama," in the theater magazine *Nihon Engeki*. "I understand all too well Hofmannsthal's yearning for Greek culture when he casually mentions 'the self-evident sense of form,'" he wrote. "My craving for dramatic literature is this, in the end.... Drama being by far an older genre than fiction, reconfirming 'the self-evident sense of form' which drama makes its natural requisite seems to be important work for me as a fiction writer." He added: "The plays that have moved me the most are, first, Racine's *Phèdre*, second, Porto-Riche's *Le Vieil Homme*, and, third, Mauriac's *Asmodée*."[9]

## Three Novels

Of the three novels that came out in December 1950, *Thirst for Love* concerns the young widow Etsuko's crazed love for a farm boy. Now the live-in mistress of her father-in-law, Etsuko loses heart at the climactic moment in her attempt to force sex on the boy—and ends up killing him. Mishima's epigraph is from Revelation, 17-4: "and I saw a woman sit upon a scarlet coloured beast," on whose forehead was written "the Mother of Harlots." To explain this story, Mishima wrote he was infatuated with novels of François Mauriac, adding "a comical confession" that he owed a great deal to Freud's *Studies of Hysteria*.

*The Snow-White Night* was turned into a movie the following year, thus becoming the first of Mishima's novels to be so treated. Serialized in *Fujin Kōron*, the monthly for educated women, from January to October, it was a drama of adultery. A beautiful young woman married to a bank official thirteen years older commits suicide the moment she discovers that the man she fell for wasn't serious about the affair or had, at best, simply taken advantage of the difficult situation she found herself in. The man, her husband's friend and customer as company president, is married and known to be a womanizer.

Mishima was not married, but this novel may be read as a revenge fantasy about Mitani Kuniko. Besides the overt similarities to real life, including the fact that the protagonist's name Ikuko as a Chinese character has a striking resemblance to the name Kuniko, Mishima lovingly describes her: "she had the air of someone who discounted a large portion of her innate beauty on her own. That beauty lay in lips as they naturally were. Nonetheless, she applied a US-made lipstick rather thickly to hide the madder red of their natural state. That beauty lay in svelte legs of someone who grew up in a Western-style house, not tortured by living on tatami. Nonetheless, she hid them with a longish skirt that had gradually come into fashion since the past summer but was still rare." And so forth.

The third novel, *The Blue Age*, was directly based on one of the sensational events of 1949. In November of that year, Yamazaki Akitsugu, "student president" of the Hikari (Light) Club, committed suicide by taking potassium cyanide. Yamazaki, a junior at the Faculty of Law at the University of Tokyo, set up an "American-style" investment-loan company in September 1948 with some of his fellow students. The company pledged investors a monthly return of 13 percent while charging borrowers a prepaid 21 to 30 percent interest. His business quickly expanded, and he moved his office to the Ginza the following January. But by the summer he was running into trouble. In July he was arrested on charges of illegal financing. He was released in September, but the credibility of the Hikari Club plummeted and he was unable to line up enough money to pay the creditors. He chose to kill himself.

Yamazaki's meteoric rise and fall had to do with Japan's defeat, the Occupation, and rapid US policy shifts. The Tokyo consumer price index, which was three times the level of 1935 in the year Japan was defeated, grew to be two hundred forty times that three years later. Meanwhile, the Communist takeover of China became certain and the United States's urgency to turn Japan into a bulwark against Communism in the Far East mounted. The Japanese economy had to be strengthened, and the Communist Party and activities associated with it, such as those of labor unions that the Occupation had legalized and encouraged, had to be curbed. What the Japanese called "course reversal" ensued.

In March 1949 the US government dispatched to Japan Joseph Dodge, the Chicago banker with an "antediluvian" view of the economy, to force the Japanese government to take extremely stringent economic measures for a "super-balanced budget," as Japanese officials called it, "without qualification or dissent." Dubbed "the Dodge Line," this policy aimed to "transform Japan into a low-cost, high-volume industrial exporter linked to its Asian neighbors," and was carried out by Ikeda Hayato who had just been installed as finance minister, even though it would have to overturn all the campaign promises the Democratic Liberal Party had made. Ikeda, later to serve as prime minister and implement the famous "income-doubling" plan, was an able former finance bureaucrat and had no choice but to meet Dodge's demands even as his government was thrown into an uproar. The effects were immediate: mass layoffs, bankruptcies, and deflation.[10]

The three incidents involving the Japanese National Railways in a span of six weeks, in July and August 1949, had to do with resultant social upheavals. Just after midnight on July 5, the body of the JNR president Shimoyama Sadanori was found on the rail tracks not far from the center of Tokyo, his head severed; late on the evening of July 15, railcars parked in a rolling-stock shelter in Mitaka, Tokyo, suddenly started to run and crashed into residences, killing six and injuring thirteen;[11] and in the early hours of August 17, in Matsukawa, Fukushima, north of Tokyo, a running train overturned on the spot where one rail was deliberately removed, killing three, including the engineers.

The Shimoyama and Mitaka incidents occurred following the first and second steps of the government-announced layoff of one hundred thousand JNR employees. After the incident in Mitaka, Prime Minister Yoshida wasted no time in accusing Communists and their sympathizers of creating those murderous acts, and the police arrested a sizable number of union members of a factory in Mitaka.

Then came the derailment in Matsukawa, which among the three incidents would create one of the most contentious court cases that would last for fourteen years. Instances of foul play continued to surface. The police were shown to have fabricated crucial evidence. The sole witness, who came forward to say he saw a dozen GIs remove the rail in question, was summoned to the Japanese police and the American Occupation's Counter Intelligence Corps and soon afterward found dead. It was nearly two decades later, in 1963, that the Supreme Court accepted the lower court's decision two years earlier and declared all the accused not guilty.

Other steps to curtail Communist influence were taken. In July 1949, an advisor to the Occupation's CIE gave a speech at Niigata University, urging that "Communist professors" be fired. In September the government discharged seventeen hundred schoolteachers. In June of the following year the Occupation purged twenty-four Communist Party members from public service and in July ordered removal of Communists and Communist sympathizers from newspapers and broadcasting. In September, the government happily complied with "the Red Purge" and forced more than ten thousand employees out of various sectors. Like victims of the McCarthyism then raging in the United States, those removed from work during this Red Purge would have a hard time finding employment in the many years that followed.

For all this social turbulence, Yamazaki's suicide was singular enough to mesmerize the mass media and the public in several respects. He was the top student at the elite faculty of the elite university and had hoped to become a professor and pursue "quantitative criminal law." He was from an illustrious family: his father and three older brothers were all physicians, besides the fact that the father served as mayor of Kisarazu, Chiba, when the town became a city, in 1942, as the navy decided to turn it into a base. He was mobilized as a student and was a second lieutenant in the army when Japan surrendered. Yamazaki used the prestige of his school for his business openly. He apparently had enough sexual drive to maintain a stable of eight mistresses.

Above all, Yamazaki displayed the kind of rational, detached, even amused cynicism that seemed to eminently symbolize the distortions of postwar chaos. He left a manuscript titled *I Am an Evil Faker*, which was posthumously published, and a testament, at least part of which he evidently wrote after he took poison. The first of the four items that made up the latter read:

> Caution. Do not touch the corpse before inquest. Because it is so set out in law, immediately notify Kyōbashi Police Station and subject the corpse to autopsy according to Postmortem Law. The cause of death is potassium cyanide (or so I was told when I obtained it; make certain that the one who handed it to me told the truth). Incinerate the corpse with those of marmots. Sell the ashes and bones to a farmhouse as fertilizer (Great if the tree that grows from it sprouts or sucks in money).

Item 2 consisted of a tanka: "So desiring, heart at peace, maple leaves scatter; there's the evidence of a rational life." The composition seemed to mock the custom of composing a farewell-to-this-world poem just before certain death. The memory of many military commanders writing such tanka before imminent self-immolation, especially toward the end of the war, was still fresh. The mass media called Yamazaki "a typical *après-guerre* youth," *après-guerre* being the French expression in vogue, and "a modern Faust."[12]

Kimura Tokuzō was among the many fascinated by Yamazaki. He thought of Julien Sorel and suggested a story idea to Mishima: Why not create out of the man Japan's postwar version of the protagonist of *Le Rouge et le Noir*? Mishima agreed that it was a great idea and said that he would start such a story "after giving it careful thought." Sometime afterward, however, he came back to Kimura and said that *Shinchō*, the magazine of Shinchōsha, proposed a similar idea to him, adding that the monthly offered to provide him with a special editor for the project and collect all the necessary material for the work. Would he, Kimura, mind if he worked on the idea for *Shinchō*?

"[Mishima's] wish to switch from *Ningen*, which was unstable in its existence, to *Shinchō*, which was of an old stable house, was not something unexpected; but in my heart I wasn't amused," Kimura wrote, recalling the incident years later. But he was philosophical. "Nevertheless, there was no contest between a writer who was the flower of the season and a magazine that was declining. Besides, I had to realize that my own idea, the wish that Mishima would create a Japanese Julien Sorel out of Yamazaki as basic material, was itself based on the recognition of the calculating approach common to the two men"—Julien and Mishima—"and I could only give myself a resigned smile."[13]

Not that *Ningen* treated its authors shabbily. For example, as noted earlier, the Kamakura Bunko that published it paid Mishima ¥5,600 in October 1947 for his contributions up to that time, when his starting monthly salary at the Ministry of Finance two months later was ¥1,350. (The inflation at the time is shown in the fact that Mishima received ¥8,925 for *The House on Fire* published by *Ningen* a year later or ¥255 a page; the earlier payment came to ¥70 a page.)

Still, the Kamakura Bunko had gone bankrupt before the end of 1949 and the magazine was sold to another publisher, Meguro Shoten. By luck, *Ningen* serialized a sensational story—a memoir of a life in Siberian concentration camps, "In the Shadow of Aurora" (*Aurora no kage ni*), by Takasugi Ichirō, the penname of Kimura's former boss, Ogawa Gorō—almost simultaneously as *Shinchō* serialized *The Blue Age*, but that did not help.

It was a sign of quickly changing times that Kimura, who had featured Thomas Mann's lectures, "The Coming Victory of Democracy," in its inaugural issue, felt it necessary to do a special on "agonizing democracy" in the first issue of *Ningen* under Meguro Shoten. Six months later, in June, the Korean War broke out.

## *The New Residence*

With *Confessions* and *Thirst for Love* selling well, the Hiraoka family moved to Midori-ga-Oka, in Meguro, in August 1950. It was their first move in thirteen years. Their house in Shibuya, built on a 280-square-yard site, was not small by the standard of later boom periods, but it was not large by the standards of self-respect the Hiraokas thought appropriate for themselves. Also, the house was rented. Both the size of the land and the rental status of the house were negative legacies, as it were, of the debt-ridden Sadatarō and the spendthrift Natsuko.

The new house was rented. In Midori-ga-Oka, the price of land did not change whether you rented or bought it. Most of the area belonged to two large landowners whose ancestors were district chiefs during the Edo Period. Unless you really wanted to buy the land, you rented it.[14] The site, at one thousand square yards, was more than three times as large as the one in Meguro, though in Midori-ga-Oka, the size was average. At the time, the house of a similar size probably cost ¥1–1.5 million, while the price tag for the one thousand square-yards of land probably did not exceed ¥600,000. But the house the Hiraokas chose was one in which someone had hanged himself. It hadn't had a taker for a long time as a result, and its asking price was half what it would have normally cost. The neighbors—mostly former high-ranking officers of the Imperial Navy and Army, now down on their luck—were more curious about the family moving into it than they would have been otherwise.

Mishima was able to make the move because his income suddenly increased. *Thirst for Love*, priced at ¥200, sold seventy thousand copies, bringing in royalties amounting to ¥1.4 million. Reflecting the stabilizing effect of the Dodge Line, it was priced the same as *Confessions* published a year earlier. Relative prices are notoriously hard to compare, but in 1950 the average daily pay for a carpenter was ¥180. Half a century later a carpenter would easily command a wage ten times the average price of a hardcover edition of a book for a day's work.[15] The paperback edition of *Confessions* was priced at ¥70 in June 1950; it had become ¥320 by 1984 when its eighty-first printing was issued. During the same period the carpenter's daily wage had become more than seventy times as large.

The move to Midori-ga-Oka seemed to cheer up the family. In the summer of 1950 Azusa was fifty-five, Shizue forty-five, and Mishima twenty-five. Shizue for the moment appeared to have given up the thought of divorcing Azusa. The three of them were at times seen walking down the road to Toritsu Daigaku Station, chatting and laughing among themselves. Azusa had a Japanese-style crew-cut known as *kakugari*—a hairstyle favored by carpenters and other artisans. Mishima sported a Regent: the hair on top made to rise, and the hair on the sides slicked back, with a generous dose of pomade.

Nosaka Akiyuki, who saw Mishima about that time, compared his face with that hairstyle to "a gourd growing at the tip of a vine, with the further impression of being deformed."[16] (The following year, when he had his hair cut short, his mother told him she'd no longer walk out with him, Mishima reported to Kawabata.[17]) Shizue was in her usual kimono. Chiyuki, who was then twenty and at the Faculty of Law of the University of Tokyo, was seldom, if ever, with them. He was occasionally seen dashing out in wooden clogs to buy roasted sweet potatoes from a passing vendor.

One of their neighbors was Sugai Takao, a medical student at

Keiō University. Later a physician with a thriving clinic, he was six feet tall, unusual for a Japanese in those days. From "an elegant family" and handsome as well, he loved to project himself as a playboy. Mishima got along with him. Once he asked the student, "Did you know mine is a house for pompom girls?" Sugai looked perplexed. During the Occupation years Japanese prostitutes who mainly went out with American soldiers were called *pompom girls*. How is Mishima's house a brothel?

"You know, the street address of my house is 2323"—pronounced *nii-san, nii-san*, "brother, brother," which is a vocative used when someone calls out to a stranger as when a prostitute wants to attract the attention of a potential customer—"you see, brother, brother, drop by for fun." It was a joke Mishima told many.[18]

Azusa, the one who had long railed against Mishima's desire to pursue writing as a career and pressured him to work for the ministry of finance, was now acting as if he were his son's business manager. One of his self-appointed tasks was to burn his botched manuscripts every day, except when it rained, in front of his house. One neighbor, who would go on to write a memoir about living in Midori-ga-Oka, was struck not just by the odd practice but also by the volume of manuscripts being burnt. One day she asked Azusa why he was doing what he was. His reply: "We don't want someone to collect them and sell them at high prices." His other task was to stamp the author's documentary stamp for each copy of his son's books. He was on several corporate boards and serving some others as advisor, as was the wont of former ranking bureaucrats.[19]

On August 2, the day after the family's move to the new house was completed, Mishima went to stay and work at the Green Hotel, in Karuizawa, a summer resort for the well-to-do. The hotel was famous— its design was attributed to Frank Lloyd Wright for a while—and there, one morning, he rode out with the wife of the professor of French literature at the University of Tokyo, Watanabe Kazuo. In an essay on the sojourn published the following year, he described the experience with some amusement: on that occasion it was Mrs. Watanabe, an easy, capable rider, who fell off her horse as it tried to follow Mishima's trotting away.[20]

Two years earlier, in October 1948, Mishima had taken up horse-riding at a club in Tokyo. One may wonder why. He was extremely clumsy with horses when horseback riding was part of military exercises at colleges and universities—"I am afraid of horses," as he simply admitted[21]—and now, following Japan's devastation of war, it was a hobby of a much diminished privileged class. Most likely he wanted to maintain the airs of being part of the upper crust of Japanese society precisely because it was utterly in ruins.

In fact, the short story he wrote out of that experience, "Distance-Riding Club" (*Tōnorikai*), is remarkable, even astonishing, in its total disregard of the social and economic realities of the day as it depicts the wife of the Grand Chamberlain who, while riding a horse with a group of club members, encounters a dignified general whose marriage offer she had spurned thirty years earlier when he was a captain. The general, as the story has it, had survived the war unscathed.

Mishima's essay on his Green Hotel stay has one notable point if only because of the description of Watanabe Kazuo. There he is identified as "Prof. Y" and is presented as someone whose erudite conversation was regaling, extending as it did to "the pagan passion of [Paul] Claudel." Yet Mishima had had a disheartening experience with the famous scholar.

In December 1946 he was deeply touched to read Watanabe's favorable comment on "A Tale at the Cape" in the *Tokyo Shinbun*. He had admired Watanabe's translation of Villiers de L'Isle-Adam. Also, Mrs. Watanabe was his mother's friend. So, in 1948, when Kōdansha decided to publish a collection of his stories, he asked Watanabe for a preface.

When he visited him to pick it up, however, the scholar endlessly complained about the economic hardships of the day in general, the difficulty of getting enough food in particular. It was during that period that a judge was reported to have died of malnutrition by sticking to the government-specified rations. But Mishima regarded Watanabe's behavior as unseemly. Even worse, though the scholar had complied with his request and written what was wanted, he had titled it a *gijo*, "counterfeit preface." This, and the fact that he found the man to be "so polite as to be insulting," had completely turned him off.[22]

Among the students Watanabe had about that time was the future-winner of the Nobel Prize, Ōe Kenzaburō.

At the Green Hotel, Mishima also ran into Nagai Kuniko.

## *Joining Groups*

That same month Mishima joined a "movement for the three-dimensionality of literature," Kumo no Kai, "Cloud Society," named after Aristophanes' comedy *The Clouds*. As befits the aspirations of a country emerging from a ruinous militarism and war, the group had a grand aim of uniting "literature, theater, art, music, film," and any other artistic endeavors, and it counted among its sixty-three members some of the more illustrious men and women of the day: Fukuda Tsuneari, Jinzai Kiyoshi, Kobayashi Hideo, Nakamura Mitsuo, Sugimura Haruko, Nagaoka Teruko, and Senda Koreya.[23] Its leader, Kishida Kunio, was the doyen of modern theater. He had been "purged" by the Occupation for having served, from 1940 to 1942, as director of culture of the government-sponsored national patriotic association Taisei Yokusan Kai. Regardless, he enjoyed great respect.

Upon the formation of the group, the *Asahi Shinbun* asked a few members, Mishima among them, for comment. Mishima sought as the group's antecedent André Gide and *La Nouvelle Revue Française* (NRF), observing that in the past, Japanese artists had confined themselves in their own narrow fields. That way they would never be able to appeal to the world. The idea for the new group might change it, he suggested.

However, when the Kumo no Kai had its first meeting the next month and staged for its inaugural presentation Strindberg's *Miss Julie*, with Senda, one of the group's executives, playing Jean, Mishima was disappointed. His main complaint was that the play showed how "boring" Naturalism could be. As a matter of fact, for all the excitement it generated among those concerned, especially among its members, the Kumo no Kai appears to have petered out after Kishida Kunio died four years later, in 1954.[24]

Mishima became the youngest member of the Hachi no Ki Kai, "Potted Tree Society," a small group that was definitely more informal in its setup and aim. Some of its members were also members of the Kumo no Kai: Jinzai Kiyoshi, Nakamura Mitsuo, Fukuda Tsuneari, the award-winning historian of European art Yoshikawa Itsuji, the scholar of English literature and the then prime minister's oldest son Yoshida Ken'ichi, and the student of Stendhal and novelist Ōoka Shōhei.

The name of the group *originally* came from the nō play *The Potted*

*Tree (Hachi no ki)* that describes a destitute samurai who burns his last and only possession, a potted tree, to warm an unexpected guest on a snowy day, although *directly* it came from a haiku Nakamura composed for Yoshikawa when the latter left for Europe that alluded to the play, or so Ōoka said in an entertaining essay he wrote a month before he left for the United States on a Rockefeller grant, in 1954. The group chose the name, in any case, because the members took turns inviting the others, along with their wives, to their homes and were expected to create a banquet by scraping together whatever food and drinks they might have for the evening.[25]

## *The Offer to Elope*

On October 23, the fifth anniversary of his sister Mitsuko's death, Mishima came home and found two young women chatting away with Shizue. When he learned that the visitors were Mitsuko's former school friends who had come to reminisce about her and told the name of one of them, Itaya Ryōko, he instantly recognized it: Mitsuko had often talked about her as one of her best friends. Itaya, then married and with the family name Moriwaki, had just moved near Toritsu Daigaku Station. From then on she would come to spend evenings with the Hiraokas often because her husband routinely stayed out late. This led to some entanglements.

Ryōko's husband ran the Japanese subsidiary of a Swedish trading company. As such his income was far above average and he showed it off. He drove foreign cars, a conspicuous "status symbol" at a time when domestic carmakers were far from establishing any kind of reputation. (The Imperial Household did not use domestic cars until 1967.)

Late one evening Ryōko was walking home along a dark street with Mishima as her escort—at Azusa's order—when a foreign car came from the opposite direction and stopped. It was her husband; he had come home earlier than usual because he had acquired a new car, a Chevrolet Prizm. He picked them up, took Mishima home. As soon as the two reached home, he bawled her out: What do you mean, walking hand in hand with "a threepenny writer" in the middle of the night?

Ryōko wasn't amused. Her father, Itaya Kōkichi, was one of the most successful corporate executives in prewar and wartime Japan, particularly famed for driving English tobacco out of China, and she, like her sisters, had grown up pampered, in a household with dozens of servants, with two foreign cars, a Chrysler and a Mercury.[26] She had a terrible fight with her husband that night, but he didn't leave the matter at that. The next morning he marched her, weeping, to the Hiraokas and demanded to know the truth. Mishima wasn't home. Azusa angrily told Ryōko's husband that his son might be fond of her, but there was nothing more to it than that.

Mishima felt bad about this development or else pitied Ryōko. Soon afterward, again while walking her back to her home, he said to her, rather abruptly, "From tomorrow I'll be *canned* in a hotel on Ōshima for a week or ten days. Make up your mind." Popular Japanese writers often sequester themselves—or publishers sequester them—in a hotel room to finish a story with a deadline, and for this act the word "can"—as in "canned food"—is used. Ōshima is a fairly large volcanic island off the east coast of Izu Peninsula, southwest of Tokyo. Mishima had visited it a couple of times before. He was inspired to write his play *The Lighthouse* during his visit to it in March of 1949 when he had one cup too many and was staring at the ceiling, unable to sleep.

"You mean I run away with you?" Ryōko remembered asking him.

"I'll take responsibility. Why don't you come with me?" Mishima said. Ryōko was momentarily tempted. But his next words put her off. "If we want to turn back, now's the time." Her retort: "If *you* want to turn back, do." Nothing came of the conversation. Still, she continued to visit the Hiraokas.

## *Forbidden Colors*

With the January 1951 issue of *Gunzō*, Mishima began to serialize what was to be his homosexual magnum opus, *Forbidden Colors (Kinjiki)*.[27] When ten installments (eighteen chapters) were finished, they were published in book form, in November. But even as the book came out, Mishima made clear his intention to carry his story forward. He wrote Part II, originally titled *The Secret Drug (Higyō)*, after he returned from his first overseas travels.

The long narrative deals with convoluted sexual vengeance. The old writer Hinoki Shunsuke has had only bitter experiences with women.

Among others, his third wife, a beautiful woman prone to blatant adultery, committed double suicide with a young lover. Three of the women who have treated him shabbily are still alive. When Shunsuke becomes acquainted with a handsome young man with a perfect physique named Minami Yūichi and learns that Yūichi, who should be irresistible to any woman conscious of her own sexual attraction, in fact is unable to love women, the old man plots to avenge himself on the three women through the young man. This is how Mishima describes the advent of the youth:

> At that moment, in the midst of the seawater, a single wake emerged, raising delicate splashes like white caps. The wake came headlong toward the beach. When it reached the shallows, the swimmer stood up in a wave about to collapse. For a moment his body was blotted out in a splash, then appeared again as if nothing had happened. His powerful legs kicking the seawater aside, he walked toward [where Shunsuke was sitting].
>
> He was an astonishingly beautiful youth. Not so much a statue in the classical period of Greece as an Apollo made by a bronze sculptor of the Peloponnesian School, his body, brimming with benign beauty of the kind that was frustrating in a way, had a nobly erect neck, sprawling shoulders, a slowly spreading chest, elegantly round arms, an abruptly narrow, chaste, solid stomach, and legs that were manly and taut like a pair of swords.

It was in May 1951, when the serialization of *Forbidden Colors* was in full swing, that another young man, this one a reader of the novel, made bold and sought out Mishima's house, clutching a sheet of paper with only this request written on it: "Where is the place called *Redon*, sir, that appears in your novel titled *Forbidden Colors*? I have come here hoping that you will tell me. As soon as you tell me, I will go away, so please." It was Fukushima Jirō, then a twenty-one-year-old college student who forty-seven years later would be subjected to a lawsuit by Mishima's children over his book describing his relationship to their father.

Fukushima, who had been deeply shaken by *Confessions* a year earlier—the shock was "as if a pill resembling a toxin, thrown into my body, had quickly spurted up blue bubbles, without melting, and spread throughout me"—felt exhilarated as he realized that the new novel, *Forbidden Colors*, was to deal with homosexuality head on. He thought he "heard a clarion trumpet at the launching of a snow-white, sleek new passenger ship with a pointed bow."

A maid came out, took and delivered Fukushima's note, came back, and invited him in to a small stylish room. It did not take much to impress Fukushima, a poor student from a complicated family in Kumamoto, but Mishima's house was in the kind of posh residential neighborhood he had never seen. In ten minutes or so, Mishima opened the fusuma door and came in: "his face lively, fresh-blue where he had just shaven, his slender body in a kimono with detailed indigo patterns against the white ground, which was swished up with a *heko* sash, creating about him the aura of the son of a good family who might appear in a Meiji or Taishō play."

While chitchatting, Mishima told Fukushima that the bar in question was in a labyrinthine place so he'd take him there himself one of these days. He then asked if Fukushima had time and, finding out that he did, said he was about to go out himself so they'd go together, and left the room. After a while, the maid came and said Mishima was ready and waiting. He indeed was, just outside the entrance door, but in a completely different garb though equally stylish: "in a light, indigo jacket and snow-white pants and shoes." After visiting Mishima's friend, apparently a man of means, for his large house was packed with antiques, Japanese and European, the two parted, Mishima handing him his card with the time and the name of the place where they were to meet written on it, in "somewhat blockish, manly letters"—a café named Redon on the Ginza. In the novel underway, Mishima had switched the locations of two gay bars, Redon and Brunswick.

Fukushima could not believe the famous author would be so casually friendly to him. After meeting in such fashion several times, Mishima finally invited him to a hotel. The result was not satisfactory to Fukushima. In time he would find that he derived pleasure only from a young boy.

Soon Fukushima became Mishima's factotum. Among the chores he ran—mostly chores that Mishima evidently devised so Fukushima might have something to do—was one that required him to take the unsold copies of his books from one bookstore to another. He also helped Azusa in gardening and other things. He observed how Mishima resembled Azusa in meticulousness and how close he was to Shizue.

That August, Mishima invited Fukushima to beautiful Imai Beach, on the southeast side of the Izu Peninsula. Mishima loved the sea, the ocean, but he couldn't swim, Fukushima found. (Mishima then went to Shizu'ura, south of Numazu, to "can" himself to write a story for Shinchōsha, and showed its editor, Sugawara Kunitaka, that he could swim about five yards. Watching this, Sugawara guffawed, called it *dog crawl*, and predicted that anyone who saw his desperate face while struggling in the water would be disillusioned, "even someone who has been in love with him for a hundred years." That's what he reported to Kawabata.[28])

Fukushima also learned that, even after getting pretty tipsy in the evening, and after having sex with him, he could, and would, work through much of the night, writing fluidly in his neat, clear, masculine handwriting in a manner that required little revision. He would sometimes show Fukushima the parts just written, telling him he was weaving him into some of the characters. Fukushima marveled to see the novel that had grabbed his imagination continue "live," right in front of him, now with parts of himself in it.

The problem for him was sex with Mishima. When he finally showed, despite himself, that he could not stand it, Mishima blanched. He cut short their stay at the luxury seaside inn. Back in Tokyo, Fukushima resumed visiting the Hiraoka household but the sudden, understandable aloofness of Mishima, and of Shizue, soon forced him to give up.

Later Fukushima suspected, though with the caveat that he could be aggrandizing himself in doing so, that three of Mishima's works might reflect what happened after the weeklong stay on the beach that ended in failure: the short story "Death in Midsummer" (*Manatsu no shi*) in which a woman loses two of her three children and her sister-in-law by drowning, all at once, while at a beach resort on Izu (the story comes with an epigraph, a sentence from Baudelaire's *Les Paradis artificiels*: "*La mort . . . nous affecte plus profondément sous le règne pompeux de l'été*");[29] a play; and the second part of *Forbidden Colors*. In this last, there appears a character named Fukujirō, the utterly unattractive petit-bourgeois uncle of Minoru, the high-school boy Minami Yūichi falls in love with.

Fukushima learned that there was a model for Yūichi and that he had jilted Mishima, plunging him into inconsolable grief. As the well-to-do antique collector whom Mishima had taken him to see the day he first visited him told him, Fukushima had shown up at the right time. As fate would have it, Fukushima would see the model himself twice, twenty years apart, both times someone pointing out the man as Yū-chan "in Mr. Mishima's novel."[30]

The English term "gay bar" became part of Japan's underground jargon as a result of the enormous presence of American soldiers and civilian employees that came with the Occupation. It would gain wider currency through *Forbidden Colors*.

## *The Party*

That same month, Mishima went to visit Kishida Kunio in northern Karuizawa where the playwright, somewhat impoverished, lived in a large estate. Itaya Ryōko was invited by her high-school friend Kanetaka Kaoru to come and stay in Karuizawa that summer because Kanetaka managed to rent a house, ramshackle but sizable. Ryōko, whose husband was to be away for two months in Europe, agreed. Soon she learned Mishima planned to be in Karuizawa about the same time, so they promised to meet up while he was there.

One evening Kanetaka decided to throw a big party. Ryōko phoned to invite Mishima. It fell on Mishima's last day in the resort town. He said he'd postpone his return to Tokyo by one day. Would she mind coming to pick him up because he didn't know what was where in Karuizawa? When Ryōko arrived by taxi, Mishima asked if he could bring a girl, Mr. Kishida's daughter, in fact, because he was supposed to take her back to Tokyo. This annoyed Ryōko, but she had no choice.

Kishida's daughter, Kyōko—who a dozen years on, in 1964, would be known worldwide appearing almost nude in the movie *Woman in the Dunes*, based on Abe Kōbō's novel—remembered the party night well, as Itaya Ryōko did. When she arrived at the place where Mishima was staying, she was surprised to see a taxi and a tall woman with striking features waiting. The woman looked at her with some animosity, an unexpected development for Kyōko. She hadn't thought Mishima had rounded up another woman for the night.

The three of them sat in the backseat, Mishima between the two women. As the taxi wound through a mist-shrouded mountain road, Kyōko was tense. She kept silently looking out the window. From time to time Ryōko would whisper into Mishima's ear, and he would laugh out loud. Years later Kyōko would learn she had some reason for her unease: some of the partiers had hatched a "show" in which one of the boys would make love to her so others might watch. Mishima had firmly said no and made them abandon the plan.

In time the car stopped by an ancient-looking building surrounded by larch trees. They got out of the car. An exotic beauty standing there in a black blouse and flared skirt smiled at them and said, "Welcome to you all." Kyōko did not think she had ever seen such a beautiful woman. Kanetaka, then twenty-three, had an Indian father. One step inside the house, Kyōko was struck by the casual urbanity of the young women and men gathered there, all obviously upper-class people. In a simple cotton dress, she felt like a country girl, out of place. The tables were loaded with liquor and wine, cheese, ham, and a variety of fruits—all luxury items at the time. Someone was playing the guitar. Some were dancing cheek to cheek. The room was full of cigarette smoke and body heat.

That night, when Kyōko had finally got into the mood of the thing and was enjoying dancing, she noticed Mishima wasn't there. She told Rose—Kanetaka's original given name—she was getting sleepy, and Rose promptly took her upstairs where there were futons already laid out.

When she was left alone, Kyōko heard some whispering in the next room. The rooms were divided by sliding doors. She opened the door and saw Mishima and Ryōko lying on a futon holding each other. She hastily closed the door. Feeling utterly lonesome, she started sobbing. Mishima opened the door, came into her room, and said to her gently but firmly, "Don't worry. I'll be here all night writing." When she woke to the chirping of birds in the morning, Mishima was still there, in her room, writing—or so Kyōko remembered. Ryōko remembered Mishima "shuttling" between Kyōko's room and her own for much of the night.

Mishima was known to stay up late to write even when he traveled with his classmates during college days. That night, he was likely to have been writing a couple of installments of a lighthearted novel

*Natsuko's Adventures* (*Natsuko no bōken*) that he had just begun serializing in the weekly *Asahi*, although he may also have been bringing to a close *Forbidden Colors*. Kyōko recalled how Mishima kept writing even as he chatted with her on the train back to Tokyo and how he handed the finished manuscript to the editor waiting at the station.

Kajima Mieko, one of several women to attract a good deal of Mishima's attention afterward, and perhaps as a result, also remembered well the exotic Kanetaka and what Mishima called a "*wild party*" in his letter to Kawabata.[31] Her father, Kajima Morinosuke, a diplomat, a historian, and, above all, president of Japan's largest general contractor, maintained a magnificent villa in the best area of Karuizawa, adjoining "Kajima Forest." Earlier that day, she saw a woman walk up to her villa straight through the large garden. When the woman saw her she stopped and, looking her in the eye, said clearly, "Miss Kajima, I'm having a party tonight. Would you care to come join us? You'd be most welcome."

It was unusually direct coming from a stranger, but something about the tone of her voice was irresistible, and Mieko said yes. Later in the decade, Kanetaka would start what would prove to be one of the most popular TV programs ever in Japan, TBS's "Travels through the World." It lasted for more than thirty years, until 1990.

## Gay Bars and the Girls

Over a period of several years that followed, Mishima pursued Mieko, overtly and not so overtly, until perhaps 1957 when she was married. He invited her to a variety of performances: ballet, kabuki, orchestra, or whatever he thought was appropriate for the daughter of one of the richest men in Japan. In his dealings with her, Mishima presented himself as a suave gentleman from the world of theater or film. He asked her to come in a black dress to the Comedie Française, in kimono to kabuki, and so forth. Mieko was rich enough to comply with each of his whimsical requests.

One day, and this could have been not long after they became acquainted with each other during Kanetaka's party in Karuizawa, he asked her to dress like a man. His invitation card said he would take her to a place she might never have thought existed. Mieko borrowed her older brother's jacket and Stetson. As usual, they met at Ketel on the Ginza, a restaurant established in 1930 by Hellmuth Ketel, a German POW during the First World War when Japan attacked Quindao, Germany's leased territory with a naval port, and took over.[32]

Mishima took Mieko across the tree-lined street, walked around Matsuzakaya to a place named Brunswick, which was behind the department store. As soon as they entered it, several young men spotted Mishima and surrounded him, crying, "Look, Mishima Sensei's here!" Mieko was miffed. Did Mishima bring her here just to show off his popularity among the people who were apparently queers? Besides, the first boy who deigned to talk to her, said, in feminine language, "You are a woman, I think." The world of gays was no surprise to her. She was more worldly than he had thought.

In the fall of 1951 Nosaka Akiyuki, a twenty-one-year-old student of literature at Waseda University, once came up close to Mishima during the ten days or so he worked at Brunswick. One day during his job search, he spotted a flyer glued to a utility pole. It said the bar Brunswick was recruiting bartender trainees and waiters. The daily pay was ¥750, more than double the day laborer's wage. When he got there, there were already two dozen men making a line.

"The owner-manager named Kelly, whose facial features had a Western touch, interviewed us though all he did was to chitchat," Nosaka recalled, "told us to seat ourselves, to wait in a place that looked more like a café than a bar, and in the end employed me and two others. When Kelly turned on the switch, the semi-dark interior snapped into another world: a large aquarium with tropical fish, hung on a wall were a bullfighting poster and a sombrero, behind the counter were lines of gorgeous liquor bottles, installed in one corner was a jukebox with doughnut disks casually stacked by it."[33]

As a bartender trainee, Nosaka's job was to make scotch with water, clean glasses, and wash the cleaning cloths. Brunswick was more or less a café during the day, though a fair number of customers began drinking liquor long before the sun set. Come evening, however, astonishingly pretty boys, who were primly dressed like virgin girls, would begin showing up and go straight to the second floor. With that, the drinking customers would also go upstairs. One particularly beautiful boy was Maruyama Akihiro. Then sixteen years old, he would become a singer and an actor and a close friend of Mishima's, appearing in two films based on Mishima's writings, one a play, *The Black Lizard (Kuro-tokage)*, and the other a novel, *Spring That Lasted Too Long (Nagasugita haru)*.

One day a group of three men seated themselves at the counter. Nosaka at once recognized one of them: Mishima. He had seen him several times before, the first time more than a year earlier. Enchanted by *Confessions of a Mask*, he read everything Mishima wrote that he could lay his hands on. The actual Mishima he had glimpsed in various places had not disappointed him. He was exactly what he had expected from his writings to be: a stylish punk. (Or in the assessment of some women who knew him, his attempt to be stylish was all embarrassingly wrong.) A little afterward, at the Kabuki-za, Nosaka even overheard some old men in the audience titter about the rumor that Mishima had just been jilted by a young *oyama*, an actor who exclusively plays a female role in kabuki.

That day Mishima took out a cigarette and tried to light it with a lighter without success. Nosaka quickly lit a match and offered it to him. Mishima said, "Thank you." His clear enunciation was memorable. The pretty boys hadn't arrived yet, but Kelly invited the men upstairs anyway. Thereupon Mishima said, changing an old ditty a bit for the occasion:

*Pass by the Ginza and you get an invite from upstairs,*
*Oh dear, deer-dappling on his sleeves beside!*

This was followed by a guffaw. Nosaka saw that Mishima was in a terrific mood, but he did not remember any other words Mishima uttered, because, he figured in retrospect, he was nervous being so close to the famous author. The day he decided to quit and informed Kelly, Kelly took him upstairs. It was an extravagantly appointed parlor. The box seats along the walls were already full, and on the floor at the center, apparently meant to be a dance floor, were pairs of customers and boys under bright lights, "lip on lip, holding each other, looking each other in the eye, totally unconscious of other people."[34]

Brunswick was not the only gay bar Mishima patronized. There were several others, among them one right in front of Shinjuku Station. The building had three floors: the first floor was a café specializing in sweets; the second was a beauty parlor doubling as a studio where you paid to take photos of nude women; the gay bar was on the third floor. There the walls were all covered with red velvet. The only brightly lit spot was the bar with a bartender. The rest of the spacious parlor was lit with only five tiny light-bulbs.

Called simply R, it was a favorite haunt of the famous detective story writer Edogawa Ranpo, the *nom de plume* that was a clever recreation in Japanese of Edgar Allan Poe, meaning "tottering along the Edo River." His real name couldn't be more mundane: Hirai Tarō. He was known as an authority on homosexuality.[35] Mishima's play mentioned above, *The Black Lizard*, was squarely based on Edogawa's novel with the same title—a story of a handsome private eye pursuing a gorgeous nude dancer who happens to be a criminal with extravagantly perverse tendencies.

As Mieko quickly learned, she was not the only woman Mishima took to Brunswick. The woman he chose as his frequent companion was none other than Ryōko's older sister, Atsuko. She was tall and good-looking enough to have easily been able to play a male role in the all-woman revue Takarazuka that had started out as a girls' operetta house in 1913.

Like her sister, Atsuko became a frequent visitor to Mishima's house. In her case, it came about because one of her "boyfriends," the tall, handsome medical student, Sugai Takao, took her to his "good friend's house," without telling her the friend was Mishima Yukio. As she recalled, the two fell in love with each other at first sight. How far that "love" went is not clear, but she would play some important roles for him, material, practical, and literary.

Told that Mishima wanted a refrigerator, a rare, expensive appliance at the time, she readily got one for him. She was married to Yuasa Shun—or Shun Yuasa, a Japanese-American and one of the great many Americans who poured into Japan with the Occupation forces. As such he had ready access to the PX. Further, a graduate of both the University of Washington and Gonzaga University, he was an elite mechanical engineer attached to the Occupation Headquarters. He then worked as a consultant to Tokyo Gas Company and helped promote the use of air-conditioners in Japan.

It was Atsuko's second marriage, her first being to a first lieutenant of the Imperial Navy and an accounting officer that had taken place toward the end of the war. She and her Nisei husband lived with her daughter from the naval officer, in a large house she inherited from her father. Shun allowed, and Atsuko took it as her birthright, an utterly free run of the household. A group of people from various fields, young and old, all of them Atsuko's friends, like Sugai and Mishima, came and went, doing whatever they pleased. She in effect ran a "salon," and it would provide the setting for Mishima's large novel several years later, *Kyōko's House (Kyōko no ie)*.

Atsuko would also help find a bride for Mishima, even as she knew several *gorgeous* or *graceful* women with good upbringing he pursued, among them Kajima Mieko and a Diet member's daughter Kobayashi Hidemi, whose mother was German. One means of his pursuit was letters—this she knew simply because she received many of them herself. At one point, she complained, "'*Shin* Yukio,' again?" Meaning "Your Subject Yukio," it was the epistolary valediction he routinely used—in his letters not just to her but also to other women.[36]

By the time Atsuko made this plaint, it must have been well into 1953 or beyond. On November 10, 1952, during the coming-of-age ceremony for Akihito in which he was formally designated Crown Prince, Yoshida Shigeru gave his congratulatory speech as prime minister, ending it with "*Shin* Shigeru" or "Your Subject Shigeru"—an old form of referring to oneself in a formal address to the sovereign. It was a custom seldom recalled even during the days when the Tennō had an outsize presence in Japanese consciousness.[37] In his speech Yoshida also used the word *kokutai*, so redolent of intractable Japanese politics until the country's defeat seven years earlier. The mass media made political hay out of these revelations, taunting Yoshida as being anachronistic, antidemocratic, or worse. Yoshida, after all, was, in postwar Japan, admired as a more enlightened politician: he was jailed for exploring ways of suing for peace toward the end of the war and was now working for democracy, the American dictate—although, in truth, he maintained an old-school reverence toward the Tennō throughout his life.[38] Mishima, in any event, delighted in taking up this form of imperial deference.

There may have been one woman Mishima pursued that Yuasa Atsuko was not aware of even as she regarded herself as his confidant in such matters: Kawabata Yasunari's adopted daughter, Masako. During the wake for Hayashi Fusao's wife, in June 1952, Mishima asked Mrs. Kawabata for the young woman's hand. "No, I haven't forgotten it. During the wake Mr. Mishima just so *unobtrusively* brought up the subject of marrying my daughter, and so I, too, just so *casually* but firmly turned it down," Mrs. Kawabata reminisced a dozen years after her husband's death, in 1972.

As his visits with Kawabata became regular, Mishima started to bring special gifts for Masako, a teenager, and to help her with her homework. With a touch of theatricality he once even declared: "I will bring her cakes and such until some handsome man begins to visit her with a large bouquet." Mrs. Kawabata did not explain why she rejected his proposal.

CHAPTER TEN

# Going Overseas

*The sun! The sun! The perfect sun!*

—*Apollo's Cup*

On September 11, 1951, soon after his time in Izu and Karuizawa, Mishima took a test at the Occupation's CIE. He had applied to participate in the American-sponsored International Conference of Young Artists to be held in the United States. As he had predicted in his letter to Kawabata the day before the exams, however, his English was judged inadequate, and he was rejected.[1] Thereupon he began to study English in earnest, buying for example a tape recorder, then brand new on the market and expensive, in order to practice English conversation.

As the Cold War worsened, the US was taking steps to promote cultural exchanges. The conference of young artists was one example. From the end of 1950 to early 1951, Wallace Earle Stegner, of Stanford University, whom Mishima mentions in his letter to Kawabata, had toured several Asian countries to collect short stories to be translated into English with a grant from the Rockefeller Foundation. In Japan, Stegner apparently asked Kawabata to take care of the Japanese contributors. Kawabata, in turn, asked some of the writers he thought well of to recommend their own stories. Mishima thought about it and said he would pick "Distance Riding Club."

In the year 1951 the economy was booming. The Korean War had created a "special demand." In January, with the Chinese Army resurgent in Korea, Gen. Douglas MacArthur, Supreme Commander for the Allied Powers, who in 1946 had given Japan the new Constitution with the contentious no-war clause, Article 9, re-emphasized the need for Japan's rearmament. In fact, with the outbreak of the Korean War in June of 1950, MacArthur had ordered the creation of a paramilitary force. When the Japanese government worked out a seventy-five thousand-man force two months later, it called the force Keisatsu Yobitai, "Police Reserve Force," insisting it was not a military, that the country was not "remilitarizing." This it was compelled to do to avoid the obvious conflict with the Constitution—Article 9 says the country shall never maintain "land, sea, and air forces [*riku-kai-kūgun*], as well as other war potential"—to accommodate the prevailing sentiments for peace.

The result was a monstrosity. Visiting the Police Reserve Force in September 1952 to spend a day with it, Hino Ashihei, who had garnered extraordinary fame and popularity as a "soldier writer" from the late 1930s to the early 1940s only to be accused of "war collaboration" on the heels of Japan's defeat,[2] found, in effect, a police force armed with "carbines, rifles, mortars, and bazookas"—and, yes, tanks and warplanes. Hino called it *nue*, "a chimera."[3]

The anomalous nature of the "non-military" military would dog the force after it changed its name to Hoantai, "security force," the following month, and to Jieitai, "self-defense forces," in July 1954. The palpable "sophistry," as the English professor-turned-social critic Nakano Yoshio later put it,[4] and the nebulous standing of the forces, would trouble Mishima as he involved himself with them in the last few years of his life.

On April 11, President Harry Truman fired MacArthur over differences with the general on the conduct and aim of the Korean War and replaced him with Gen. Matthew Ridgway.

Still, non-military matters were coming to the fore as well. On April 19, the Japanese runner Tanaka Shigeki won the Boston Marathon. In September, a Japanese delegation led by Prime Minister Yoshida went to San Francisco and signed a peace treaty with forty-eight nations and a mutual security treaty with the United States. Both treaties were initiated by the United States, with the peace treaty including a proviso requiring the existence of the security treaty. Both peace and security treaties had a sizable proportion of Japanese opposed to them, and the latter, the security treaty, would create the largest political upheaval toward the end of the decade. It would also go on to play an important role in Mishima's life a decade later.

Two days after the treaty was signed, on September 10, the news arrived that Kurosawa Akira's film, *Rashōmon*, had won the Grand Prix in Venice. A moral parable with four different accounts of a single event, the movie brought Japanese film to international attention for the first time and marked the beginning of Kurosawa's worldwide fame. (*The Snow-White Night*, the first movie based on a Mishima novel that came out at the end of August, was submitted to the Cannes Festival, but did not win any prize. Some of the more famous Japanese film stars of the day played the lead roles, and Mishima made a cameo appearance in a dancing scene.)

## Mishima in New York

Failing in his attempt to visit the United States on the pretext of taking part in the international conference, Mishima pulled some strings and finally succeeded. On December 25, 1951, Friday, he left Japan as a special overseas correspondent for the *Asahi Shinbun*. The director of the daily's bureau of publications, Kaji Ryūichi, was one of Azusa's classmates at the First Higher School. Kaji, himself a writer of historical bent, believed that one must know the world to be able to write.

The day before the departure for the United States, Mishima stayed up all night to finish a full-length play, *Nothing Is More Expensive Than Something Free* (*Tada yori takai mono wa nai*). A drama in three acts, it depicts the consequences of a couple's decision to employ a maid who offers to work for room and board only. The woman in truth was the husband's seductress twenty years earlier, not long after the couple's marriage. Back then a well-to-do German's mistress, she is now down and out, hence her offer.

The ship that awaited Mishima at Yokohama was America's top luxury liner, the SS *President Wilson*. Mishima's family, Sugai Takao, Atsuko and Ryōko, Nakamura Mitsuo, and some of the editors who worked with Mishima came to the pier to see him off. When he caught the clownish Takao's eye, he raised his arm to his face and moved it back and forth horizontally to indicate he was crying. Or he hastily put on dark sunglasses to hide his tears, according to one of the women Nakamura overheard tartly observe.[5]

The travels would last five and a half months, until May 10, 1952. Mishima went to Honolulu (a ten-hour stop), San Francisco, Los Angeles, New York, Miami, Puerto Rico (San Juan, one night), Rio de Janeiro, Sao Paolo, Lins, Geneva (a one-day stop because foul weather diverted his plane), Paris, London, Athens, and Rome. He wrote several accounts of these travels, the main one being *Apollo's Cup* (*Apollo no sakazuki*), many parts of which were published in various magazines.[6] Though he did not give any hint of it in any of the accounts, he continued to write literary work assiduously throughout his journey.

For the first three days aboard the *President Wilson* the sea was rough, the sun only occasionally appearing to cast gloomy light on the pitch-black waves. Mishima was picking up English fast. One day, at lunchtime, with the ship rolling, the cups and plates on his table started to slide. Trying to stop them, Mishima leaned forward, but his chair began to slide as well and continued to slide. The jolly old waiter, laughing, asked, "Where are you going?" Mishima didn't miss a beat: "To San Francisco." That, in any case, was the way he told the story.

On December 28 the sky was clear, the sea calm. The captain and the crew changed into white uniforms. Mishima stayed in a lounge chair out on deck until sunset. "The sun! The sun! The perfect sun!," he wrote, exulting in "the freedom to sunbathe all day, the freedom to stay in the sun for one whole day without being bothered with work and guests, the freedom to have your distinct shadow wait on you all day—staying on sundeck this one day, my face quickly became suntanned." Among the movies shown aboard the *President Wilson* were *Bambi*, *Cinderella*, and George Beck's *Behave Yourself*. Mishima loved them all.

He visited third-class cabins and found the "apocalyptic theory" he had heard appear to be true: that American liners did not take as good care of third-class passengers as Japanese liners had in prewar days, because Americans never went third-class. The third-class cabins he visited and saw were just like "silkworm shelves." Vomit was splattered everywhere, body odor and the smell of garlic filled the air. It was the veritable "Asiatic chaos." And the passengers were mostly young Asians—Japanese, Filipinos, Chinese—in stark contrast to first-class cabins which were mostly occupied by middle-aged Americans.

"They go to study America. They go from the Orient, which once exported their 'ancientness,' to import 'modernity,'" Mishima mused. "They are still far from importing enough of the latter. No matter how much import surplus they have, they can't stop importing." There may be differences between countries, however. "Only recently, for the second time since Meiji, have we experienced the age of civilization and enlightenment as a result of our defeat, but Japan with its weak stomach rapidly excretes what it can't digest, so it can't help becoming ever more greedy, taking in one new thing after another in rapid succession."

In comparison, "How gigantic and sturdy a stomach China the Middle Kingdom has! It will soon digest even Chinese Communism, erasing its form and substance completely. And then, not a single bruise sustained by 'modernity,' the Middle Kingdom will again wait for new imports, with its mouth agape, ready to swallow them all."[7] Mishima wrote this less than three years after Mao Zedong's Communist Party took over China.

As the *President Wilson* left Honolulu, Mishima spotted a "small, skinny woman near sixty" wistfully looking toward the receding city on the promenade deck, a Japanese. They struck up conversation. Forty years earlier she had emigrated from Sendai, a city in northern Japan, to California, and she was now on her way back to the United States from her fourth (and probably last) visit to her homeland. Her family ran a medium-size hotel in Los Angeles and was doing well, and her son and niece were US citizens, but, to her disbelief, the US government still had not allowed her to become its citizen. Every attempt she had made so far to naturalize had failed at the last minute.

Telling Mishima this reminded her of something else. She was one of the first to be arrested and thrown into jail following Japan's attack on Pearl Harbor—apparently weeks before the wholesale roundup of people of Japanese ancestry on the West Coast. Why she met that fate Mishima doesn't tell us, but from her account, she appears to have been one of the overtly pro-Japanese Japanese residents in the United States.

"In the prison there were nine women, including herself, and everyone regretted that the Japanese Navy only attacked distant Pearl Harbor and did not come to mount an assault on the US mainland," Mishima says the woman in a grayish-blue dress, with gold-rimmed glasses, and a lei around her neck recounted. "Just a glimpse of the spectacle of a Japanese landing operation on the US mainland would have made her so happy she'd gladly have seen herself sacrificed: she wouldn't have minded her body blown to smithereens by a Japanese artillery shell." It did not stop there. "The women were excited and prepared to die.... If they had to kill themselves, they'd hang themselves, they agreed. There was no rope in the prison, so they unraveled their socks and made thin ropes with the yarn."

In New York, Mishima had an organization-related caretaker. One of his American friends in Tokyo was Herbert Passin. He decided that the American PEN as it was then was too weak to be of much help to Mishima and turned to the American Committee for Cultural Freedom (ACCF), in particular its executive secretary and his friend, Pearl Kluger. The committee, which advocated anticommunist socialism, had only recently come into being as an affiliate of the (International) Congress for Cultural Freedom, itself established in 1950, and counted among its "correspondents," though not necessarily at the time Mishima arrived in New York, Arthur Miller, Robert Oppenheimer, David Reisman, John Kenneth Galbraith, and Irving Kristol. Passin must have told the organization "exaggerated stories about me," Mishima wrote. They welcomed and treated him in a manner that was "at once friendly and extremely courteous." Among them Mrs. Kluger's kindness was such that "your parent wouldn't be able to match it."

"Mrs. Kluger is a socialist," Mishima added, for the occasion copying with ease a certain American way of writing about such matters. "She is thirty-seven or -eight, and you can immediately tell she is bright and quick." Her German family name means just that. "She lives in an apartment with her husband and three children. A born New Yorker and a fast talker, she is truly efficient. Nonetheless, she is affected easily and, when her emotion runs high, she can abruptly turn into an ordinary woman—the type of woman who isn't really rare in Japan." Mishima's portrait of Pearl Kluger was probably a fond caricature of a vivacious, intelligent American working woman such as was commonly portrayed in Hollywood movies of the day.

> She goes to her office every day. She makes dozens of phone calls a day. Coming home, she cooks supper. She takes care of all domestic matters. Finally she goes to bed. Then, at midnight, her baby who has gone to bed early wakes up and begs her to play with him.... The day before a cocktail party, she splurges and buys a pair of suede shoes at a *chic* store. All that

night she forgets about socialism, drunk with the happiness of having bought the shoes. Sometimes she reflects on her married life and cries, wondering if she has not wasted twenty years of her life, having been a victim of her husband and children. She does this especially when she imagines that her husband must have a blonde mistress.

Mrs. Kluger herself is close to being blonde, and she sometimes feels jealous of redheads. She takes Mishima to the top of the Empire State Building and meekly confesses it's her first visit to the landmark, which reminds him that, having had monthly meetings near the Sengaku-ji for some months, he has never stepped inside the precincts of the famous temple where the forty-seven samurai are buried. She takes him to Radio City Music Hall and "demands" that he be impressed by the size of the theater. Having failed to elicit appropriate consternation, she makes the point of stopping an usher as the two leave the theater and asks him how many people it can accommodate. Getting the number she wanted, she exclaims, providing a model response: "Oh, my, *seven thousand* people!"

Not long after Mrs. Kluger looked after Mishima, Riesman and Galbraith resigned from the ACCF. Several years later, the committee announced its discovery that one of its funding entities was a CIA front organization, and said it would cut its relationship to it. The ACCF also changed its name. But in time the organization faded away. This may deserve mention partly because the Nihon Bunka Kaigi, Japan Cultural Congress, which Mishima and others would establish in 1968, was a vague offshoot of it and most likely affiliated with the CIA.

Everywhere he went, Mishima was asked, "What do you think of Mr. MacArthur?" Every questioner evidently expected a negative response. Quickly realizing that American intellectuals loathed the SCAP (Supreme Commander for the Allied Powers), now gone from the scene, "like a caterpillar," Mishima decided that MacArthur's "Supermanism" was what turned off the Americans, even though by then the general was "fading away" as he had predicted himself and his popular adulation was becoming a distant memory.

The day Mishima arrived in New York from Los Angeles, he was taken to the Metropolitan Opera House where he saw Richard Strauss's *Salome* and Puccini's *Gianni Schicchi*. The combination of two operas that evening was for a charity benefit and most in the audience were elaborately dressed. The interior of the opera house was "a copy of a European one, decorated as it was like a gilded Buddhist altar," but its halls and toilets were "as old and dirty as those of Japanese movie theaters." The opera house at the time was on Broadway and 39th Street.

Mishima left no words on *Gianni Schicchi* but many on *Salome*, an object of his "passionate love," ever since he read it at age eleven or twelve and was "thunderstruck" as it was "'a grownups' book where evil is let loose and sensuality and beauty liberated.'"[8]

"The stage set for *Salome* was operatic and conventional. It did not have a smidgen of the fin-de-siècle atmosphere Wilde intended, whose intent Strauss inherited," he wrote. "Strauss' music is nervous and rude music. In this single act, it insistently repeats the breathing of an emotion's terrifying exaggerations and reaches its apex as brutal lyricism develops following Iokanaan's beheading. Strauss is twentieth-century Wagner. He is direct heir to the scorpion Wagner that infuriated Nietzsche, a disciple of genuine decadence. For a long time I have loved extremely his symphonic poem 'Don Juan.' And I have fantasized letting him compose music for Thomas Mann's 'Death in Venice.'"

The stage set may have been conventional but Mishima liked it, on two counts: First, "the chorus was orderly and disciplined, intent on playing its role; second, the acting of the lead characters closely followed the music, in some parts close to kabuki, as exaggerated as possible."

He made these observations for "someone who might want to produce it in Japan," and described the way the opera proceeded, not forgetting to add that Ljuba Welitsch, who played Salome, was, in the Scene of the Seven Veils, too "optimistically fat to arouse interest." (That "someone" would prove to be himself. Eight years later, in directing *Salome*, he copied some actions that are not in Wilde, including the idea of "two pages lying on their backs around Herodias' feet bothering her with constant coquetry." Wilde's play has just one page.[9])

During his ten-day stay in the city he also saw the musicals *Call Me Madame* and *South Pacific*, the comedy *The Moon Is Blue*, the movies *Rashōmon* and *A Streetcar Named Desire*. The reputation of the Japanese film among the intelligentsia was "extraordinary," Mishima noted. Some years later, Mishima would make friends with Tennessee Williams, but at the time his English was inadequate and he did not understand the film based on his play very well.

One morning Meredith Weatherby, who had translated *Confessions of a Mask*, came to visit him in his hotel, and the two spent the entire day discussing the details of the translation. Weatherby had studied Japanese before the war and was working at a US consulate in Japan when the war broke out. While under house arrest in Kobe he translated nō plays and other pieces of Japanese literature. When Mishima came to New York, he was at Harvard University doing graduate work. He soon returned to Japan and would also translate another story of Mishima's, *The Sound of Waves* (*Shiosai*). Some years afterward he established the publishing house John Weatherhill, in Tokyo, and was much admired as a meticulous editor.

(In his letter to Kawabata in the previous September, Mishima had reported that Ivan Morris had written to question if Weatherby had finished his translation and had a good publisher for his translation. *Confessions* in fact would not be published until later in the decade. Was Morris' concern the novel's subject? Perhaps. *The City and the Pillar*, of Gore Vidal, published in 1948, had "shocked" those concerned, eliciting from reviewers such comments as "disgusting," "sterile," and "gauche," although it went on to become a bestseller. The novel sold thirty thousand copies in hardcover, earning the author "a vast $20,000," making him feel rich enough to go to Rome to stay in a hotel.)[10]

Weatherby then phoned Donald Richie, at Columbia, to ask him to take Mishima around the city. When the two met, Mishima told Richie what he wanted: "to visit every Saint Sebastian hanging in New York, to see the Strauss *Salome* at the Met, and to experience a real gay bar. He gave as reason for this last that he was halfway through his next novel, *Forbidden Colors*," Richie wrote in his diary. "There were several such in Greenwich Village, I had heard, and so we set out and eventually located one called Mary's. There we sat over our drinks and watched middle-aged men talk like women. This was something neither of us had expected and it was not very interesting. Nonetheless he gravely thanked me . . . he had the finest social manners of anyone I had ever met."

"With Mishima one became objective, saw oneself dispassionately," Richie continued. He would go on to know Mishima well. "It was he who created this heightened atmosphere because of an inner consistency upon which he insisted. To be with Mishima was to take part in a drama."[11]

Late one night Mishima was taken to a bar in Harlem and spent two and a half hours there—as he noted, from 12:30 to 3:00 in the morning. It was a boisterous joint packed with "prostitutes, pimps, sailors, gentlemen, actors, athletes, students, gigolos, and criminals rubbing shoulders as they drank." He saw a pair of black lesbians openly necking. There were only a few whites, including the Columbia student who took him there. Mishima identified him as "B" in his report on the trip. Richie guessed that "B" is "(probably) Holloway Brown, my roommate at Columbia, with whom Yukio got on very well indeed."[12]

A Mrs. Williams on the Occupation staff had asked the Department of State to help him in the United States, but he used only Herbert Passin's letters of introduction to avoid complicating appointments, Mishima explained to Kawabata in his letter from Brazil, in February. As it happened, Passin helped him in person as well, interpreting for him when necessary. He was back in New York because of a misfortune: his baby had died.

"Everyone in America was kind to me, but Miss Kluger, Mr. Passin's friend, took especially good care of me," Mishima wrote. "I was surprised that the Americans I met were all such nice people. But there is a bit of difference between a nice person and a nuanced person, and in being nuanced, nobody can match someone who has lived in Japan for a long time like Mr. Passin. Japan gives 'nuance' to a human being."[13] Abroad for the first time in his life and finding himself in a country where people seem almost instinctively nice, Mishima couldn't help being a bit of a cultural nationalist, though in a private letter.

## *Imperial Relative in Lins*

On January 27, as the Super Constellation carrying him reached the sky above Rio de Janeiro in the wee hours, he saw the lights along the coastline of Sugarloaf—"like a necklace left on a table made of black marble." Having written this, he added: "The impression of a fragile, pure beauty at a certain moment can only lend itself to a mediocre simile. Beauty tries hard to remain friendly with mediocrity lest its secret be known."

He went on: "But this first nightscape of Rio moved me. I called out the name, Rio. When the plane, preparing to land, tilted its wings, I felt I could happily crash into Rio's lights. I didn't know why I'd had such yearnings for Rio. There surely had to be something there. There had to be something that had ceaselessly pulled me from the other side of the earth."

Mishima's stay in Brazil was leisurely and lasted until Carnival was over at the end of February. Practicing for Carnival started early. In the first practice march he came across, he saw black boys dancing, arms on white girls' shoulders, arm in arm with white boys—"a spectacle never seen in the United States." The actual Carnival would turn out to be one of the high points of Mishima's travels. He turned his exhilarations into an operetta, *Bom Dia Señora*, with stage directions at one point suggesting using a record he, the playwright, brought back from Brazil. The opera house Shōchiku Kageki Dan, produced it in Kyoto, in September 1954.

On February 5 he went to Sao Paulo and, on the 11th, to Lins where, about ten miles outside the city, Tarama Toshihiko, formerly a member of the Imperial Higashikuni family and a grandson of Emperor Meiji, lived as owner of a coffee farm. Mishima knew him from his schooldays.

"Lins," Mishima wrote, "is the basis for Japanese immigrants" in Brazil, the second largest recipient of Japanese emigrants between the mid-nineteenth century and the outbreak of the Pacific War. Just outside the city there were "neither paved roads, electricity, gas, nor running water," showing "the cultural imbalances" within the country.

In Brazil, there is boundless undeveloped land, Mishima reported. Some among the richest Japanese immigrants with their own planes fly over undeveloped land and purchase large tracts by pointing to the land below, saying, "From that valley to that forest." There are extraordinary differences between those successful and those unsuccessful among the Japanese immigrants. Some successful ones own their own airport and several planes within their own coffee farm, as well as a church, a movie house, and a school for their employees. One of them is reputed to have built an additional airport to invite the President to his sukiyaki party.[14]

Mrs. Tarama, who adopted Higashikuni Toshihiko, was among the rich and she did so, obviously to "buy" a peerage rank, now abolished and useless. The abundance of nature Mishima observed in Lins reminded him of his childhood dream of becoming an entomologist. In one corner of his host's garden was a three-foot-tall termite mound, a veritable "old castle after the royalty has escaped the capital."

That, and the setting, inspired Mishima to write three years later a three-act play, *The Termite Mound* (*Shiroari no su*), which concerns love entanglements in the dispirited household of a former Japanese aristocrat, now the owner of a coffee farm in Lins. The aristocratic background of the protagonist, named Kariya Yoshirō, is barely concealed, and he is described as listless, indifferent, and mindless. Today the play might easily provoke a libel suit—unless, of course, the real former prince was an entirely different sort of man or else someone who could take such things in stride.

One night Mishima went out to watch, flashlight in hand, a large army of "market gardening ants" on a long, solemn march. These ants—he was told they were called *ha-kiri-ari*, "leaf-cutting ants," in Japanese—were mesmerizing enough for him to append a full description by Julian Huxley to his account of Lins.[15] This encounter also appears in *The Termite Mound*, which the Seinen-za produced, from October to November 1955.

## *Lack of Gay Life in Rio de Janeiro*

Carnival finally arrived on February 23. As Mishima reports it, it was initially an occasion for the rich to parade themselves, with the poor throwing confetti at them as spectators. Now their positions were reversed, with the rich as spectators, themselves having fun mainly in clubs and such. "I danced through three of the four nights, two of them at the night club, High Life, and the last one in a *baile à fantasia* at a yacht club," wrote Mishima. "The intoxication of Carnival has no value whatsoever in the eye of someone who just wants to watch it. As a result, I'd like to confess honestly that I was intoxicated."

At one point during the last night he danced out onto the street to join the wild crowds, shirt stripped off. That was one thing he had not been able to do until then.

One question some early biographers raised about Mishima's stay in Brazil is, in Saeki Shōichi's words, "If we are to compare Mishima to Gide, where on earth was Algeria for him—that is, the place where he had the first trigger for and practice of *homosexuality*?" After hedging quite a bit, for lack of evidence, Saeki concluded that it was Brazil.[16] (When Saeki was writing, the only thing to go on was the result of John Nathan's interview with Mishima's guide in Brazil, the *Asahi* correspondent Mogi Masa.) As it later came to light, Mishima himself had complained about a lack of *gay life* in a letter from Rio de Janeiro to one of his friends in Tokyo.

"I am in the salon of the Copacabana Palace," he wrote Kamogawa Tadashi, on February 3, 1952. "I am sorry to say, but here's no *gay life*. Already for a week or ten days, nothing has happened." *Gay life* is a term he used, in katakana. "Among the boys in the hotel salon, there is a cute one of sixteen or seventeen, but I have no language with which to make myself understood." According to Mogi, Mishima "regularly" brought to the hotel boys of "the sort who hung around in the parks." When asked how he managed it, he said that in "that world" there was no need for words.

"In America there were two *aventures* in ten days," Mishima went on, using a French word, but "Americans somehow do not stimulate my desire." He followed this with a revealing observation: "Further, I hate to be loved because it's claustrophobic."[17]

## *Cash Stolen in Paris*

Mishima stayed in Paris longer than in Brazil. Several days after his arrival on March 3, he was swindled of most of his cash—then a whopping sum of $1,350 in travelers checks—and he had to move out of the Grand Hotel to the only Japanese-run pension in Paris. He lived there, on practically nothing, for a month, until the money was recompensed. The relative economic status for most Japanese tourists and visitors overseas at the time may be discerned from the fact the film director Kinoshita Keisuke, who had received an award the previous year for his *Carmen Comes Home (Carmen kokyō ni keru)*, the first color film in Japan, was among those staying there. It was indeed through Kinoshita that Mishima found the cheap lodging.

Kinoshita introduced Mishima to Mayuzumi Toshirō, who lived nearby. Mayuzumi jotted down his first impression of Mishima in his diary: "Striking and weird-looking." Mishima was tanned and his large eyes under his prominent forehead seemed to glare. The first thing he asked Mayuzumi and Kinoshita to do was a surprise: to take him to a gay bar. They did—to one in Saint Germain called La Reine Blanche. The pretty boys all surrounded Mayuzumi and ignored Mishima.

Mayuzumi, later a well-known composer who, perhaps misconstruing the import of his good friend Mishima's death, went on to become the chairman of a large rightwing organization, was then a nattily dressed, French-speaking twenty-two-year-old with a born urbane air. Mishima didn't speak French. A week later, he announced he'd go there by himself, and he did.

Although he denied that losing his money tainted his view of Paris—according to his plan, Paris was merely a way station to Greece and Italy, he insisted—he titled a brief article published in the *Asahi Shinbun* shortly after his return to Japan "Not Falling in Love with Paris."[18]

"Because the Japanese newspapers I read in foreign countries persistently reported on the anti-American sentiments rapidly gaining momentum after the Peace Treaty took effect, I came back determined to become pro-American," he began his article, giving a characteristic twist on the matter, "but the fact that I didn't grow fond of France has nothing to do with this." The Japanese Diet had ratified the peace treaty, along with the security treaty with the United States, on April 28, 1952.

"Paris is a town where you go either intending to study painting for many years or else to have fun for several weeks, using money like hot bathwater every day, and promptly leave," he continued. "Paris is a city like an extremely sensitive, beautiful, haughty woman. If you can't spend years to seduce her, if you have just a brief while, the only thing you can do is to slap her on the face with a bundle of money." Then he made a specific point. "All Parisians have a Middle-Kingdom notion of themselves that regards all foreigners as country bumpkins, so even in a toilet a woman sits to beg for a tip."

Apparently Mishima did not have a chance to go to a hotel or restaurant with a similar arrangement during his time in America as he would five years later.

"Meanwhile, the yearning for Paris among young Japanese men and women is like their yearning for a novelist. No species of human being is as disappointing as the novelist when you see the real thing. Someone who goes to Paris out of yearning is just like a reader who, not content with the novel he has read, takes the trouble of going to see the novelist to adore him." Mishima then philosophizes à la Oscar Wilde. "The niggardliness of Paris is a hotbed for the birth of sublime art, and the baseness of Paris the reality of the nobility of art. I am not saying paradoxically that Paris is a hotbed of good art because it is born against Paris citizens' vulgarity. As Thomas Mann says, art is something extremely heinous. It is fated to have a structure like that of the Japanese house with the toilet right behind the alcove for art." The "alcove for art," *tokonoma*, is an especially built niche of a guestroom set aside for art objects, flowers, and offerings.[19]

After five days in London, from April 19 to 23, where he saw Benjamin Britten's opera *Billy Budd* and Shakespeare's play *Much Ado About Nothing*, Mishima arrived in Greece, "the place of my passionate love." As his plane crossed the Ionian Sea and reached the sky above the Gulf of Corinth at sunset, he called out the name, Greece.

"The name once led Lord Byron, who had bound himself into immobility with the comings and goings of women, to a battlefield, that nurtured the poetic thoughts of the Greek misanthrope Hölderlin, and that gave courage to Octave, the figure in Stendhal's novel *Armance*, in his last moments."

## *Asymmetry and Exteriority of Greece*

He accepted Greece—or, rather, the Greek ruins—as it might be presented in postcards. He was put up in an unclean third-class hotel because he had failed to make a reservation. Inflation was raging in the country at the time and a meal at a good restaurant cost seventy-five thousand drachma. He did not know a single Greek word so he could not tell what a shop sign said. But such things did not matter. He was ready.

What struck him first of all was the abundant, exquisite, almost "savage" blue of the sky that he determined was indispensable to the beauty of the ruins—the Acropolis, the Parthenon, the Olympia, and the Theater of Dionysus. If the sky were as stagnant and gloomy as that of Northern Europe, the effect would be reduced by half. Then there were the ruins. After giving it a good deal of thought, he deciphered the nature of their beauty: asymmetry. Having come away from France where "symmetry," along with "moderation," in art surfeited him, Mishima was startled by the beauty of asymmetry, not the least part of his surprise arising from the knowledge that Greece was the teacher of France in artistic matters.

As he knew, the asymmetry of the ruins was an effect brought about not by design, but accidentally by willful destruction. And, as he contemplated, the asymmetry of the ruins reminded him of the stone garden of the Ryōan-ji, the Rinzai Zen temple in Kyoto. Japanese artists in the past depended not on the "methodological consciousness" of the Western artists but on what might be called "persistent intuition." What they pursued was something *einmalig*—the German for "one of a kind"—in contrast to something universal. The beauty they created in the end and the beauty the Western artists created were the same in solidness, but for the Japanese each attempt was what counted. What was "mysterious" about the Greek ruins, Mishima concluded, was that their asymmetrical beauty, which was accidentally created, was the same as "the ultimate beauty the intuition explored and found."

In the midst of such musings, he interrupts himself to mention "a Greek boy of twelve or thirteen [who] has been following me, never wandering far away, for some time now, for some reason. Does he want money, does he want some of the English cigarettes I am smoking," he wonders, "or does he want to teach me the custom of boy-love of ancient Greece? If it's the last, I already know it." Then back to aesthetic speculations.

"The Greeks believed in the *exterior*. That was the great thought. Until Christianity invented the 'spirit,' human beings did not need anything like 'spirit' and lived proudly. The interior that Greeks thought of always maintained a bilaterality with the exterior. Greek drama has nothing like spirituality of the kind Christianity posited. It simply repeats, as it were, the lesson that excessive interior always suffers revenge. We should not think of the staging of any Greek drama separate from the Olympic games. Under this abundant, ferocious light I think of the pantheistic balance like the muscles of the contestants that incessantly sprang and stood still, incessantly tore and held themselves together again, and I am happy."

Mishima moved on to Rome on April 30. None of the ancient buildings, including the Colosseum, impressed him. But what he saw in the National Museum in Terme wiped away his first impressions of Rome. The Mother of Venus and the Daughter of Niobe, among others, tingled his spine, he wrote. At the Borghese Museum, Titian's *Sacred and Profane Love* and Veronese's *St. Anthony Preaching to the Fish* enchanted him. At the Palazzo dei Conservatori, he finally saw Saint

Sebastian—both, of course, Guido Reni's and, placed just a statue away, Ludovico Carracci's. In the end, his two weeks in Greece and Rome left him wondering: "Will this sense of continuity, of ceaseless rapture, visit me again in my life"?

The day before leaving Rome, on May 7, to go back to Japan, Mishima went to the Vatican, for the second time, to "say farewell to Antinous." The beauty of the famous bust of "Emperor Hadrian's favored boy and deified," had so mesmerized him two days earlier, he realized, that he hadn't noticed the statue right next to it. Mishima's guide here was Jacob Burckhardt's *Cicerone*, from which he quotes, at the end of his account, a passage on various images of Antinous.

Mishima's description given as a train of thought appears to contain one willful distortion, however. Standing in front of "the beautiful Antinous," he recalls Nietzsche and his "pessimism of strength," which in turn makes him think of "Greek pessimism." He then quotes the observation whose earliest attribution seems to be to the Greek gnomic poet Theognis: "Not to be born is, beyond all estimation, best; but when a man has seen the light of day, this is next best by far, that with utmost speed he should go back from where he came." Mishima concludes: "Antinous's melancholy is not his alone. He represents the pessimist of ancient Greece."

But Nietzsche, in *The Birth of Tragedy*, quoted those famous words—here, in reference to *Oedipus at Colonus*[20]—to condemn "the terrible wisdom of Silenus," the shaggy, old half-beast, half-man who mouths it to King Midas, thereby rejecting the philosophy of his teacher Schopenhauer that embraced it, according one interpretation.[21] Did Mishima deliberately ignore that part of Nietzsche's argument to confirm his own view?

## *La Ronde, Olympia, Les mal parties*

Upon his return from overseas travels, Mishima resumed writing on a range of subjects with knowledge and casual references.

In an essay for the nō house Kanze, for example, he gave a history of drama by way of complimenting Umewaka Manzaburō II on his performance of *Hanjo*. The essences of drama are in poetry and verse (dialogue), he argued, pointing out that while the verse drama started with the Greek tragedy in Attica, went through Racine and Shakespeare, and lives on in today's theater, Maurice Maeterlinck, the poets of the Irish Literary Revival, and Hugo Hofmannsthal, among others, questioned the validity of drama in that tradition. The dance drama, he explained, meanwhile developed as a compromise between verse drama and poetry, but its ultimate form, the ballet, is impure by its nature. From that perspective, it is in nō drama that a "superb poetic drama" is achieved as it harmonizes the two elements of drama and poetry.[22]

Speaking of the French film *La Ronde*, which he saw in London, Mishima noted that the movie version added a prologue and an epilogue to Arthur Schnitzler's original story and the unexpected playfulness of the raconteur played by Anton Walbrook, previously known as Adolf Wohlbrück (he added parenthetically), succeeds in recreating Europe's golden age of easy licentiousness in 1900. You cannot dismiss the film because of this subject, for it will be hard, will it not, he asked, to recreate the prevailing sentiment of everyday life in Japan around 1900 by making a film out of, let's say, *Takekurabe*? The story he brought up for comparison is by Higuchi Ichiyō, and it describes a spunky pubescent girl growing up in the red-light quarters who one day realizes what her life is going to be like.

The difference between the original *La Ronde* and its film version reminded Mishima of the bunraku *Ninokuchimura* that he saw recently and found far superior to its kabuki version in effecting pathos. Just as the pathos of love and its consequences is better conveyed through puppets and not by human actors, he noted, so is cynicism about lust; it may be conveyed unobtrusively in writing but not by human beings acting it out, hence the need for the raconteur. Among the actors and actresses in *La Ronde*, Daniel Gélin, who plays the young gentleman, is excellent, Mishima thought, though he didn't think much of him in *Le Plaisir* that combined three stories of Maupassant.[23]

Asked to review the translation of Jean Baptiste Rossi's novel *Les mal parties* for the *Mainichi Shinbun*, he couldn't help marveling, "France is an amazing country"—it has produced another precocious writer! Rossi at age sixteen described an affair between a fourteen-year-old boy and a twenty-eight-year-old nun.[24]

Among the other movies he reviewed from the fall of that year to early next year were *Olivia* and *Le diable au corps*. As to *Olivia*, the work of an all-female crew, the relationship between the headmistress of the finishing school, played by Edwige Feuillère, and the student, played by Marie-Claire Olivia, was like that of Delphine and Hippolyte in Baudelaire's *Femmes Damnées*, though Mishima had to sigh: "in reality there can't be such a beautiful pair of lesbians." The film also brought to mind the jōruri-turned-into-kabuki *Kagamiyama kokyō no nishikie*, which has to do with conflicts among women, with one of them, Onoe, committing suicide, just as the headmistress in *Olivia* attempts to.[25] About *Le diable au corps* he wrote twice; after all, the Radiguet story had captivated him so when he was young. In the first piece, he judged it to be "a well-made movie indeed ... but totally different from the original," and in the second, he explained what he meant after saying it's "not of good taste" to bring up the original in talking about a film.

"The original is a dry work and quite an ironic novel; the movie is a serious love story filled with 'wet oh so wet' love and emotion."[26] "Wet oh wet" is a phrase in Inpumon'in no Taifu's tanka in the *One Hundred Poems by One Hundred Poets (Hyakunin isshu)*.

## *Itō Shizuo and War Poems*

In March 1953 Itō Shizuo died of tuberculosis. In a memorial piece written for his "collected poems" published a few months later, Mishima said he'd heard Itō had wanted to delete from his work all the poems exalting the war, but his "war poems are not necessarily of low value." Although Itō wrote only a few poems that can be properly characterized as "war poems," the desire to remove all such pieces from one's writings was all too common in the chorus of "war crimes" and "collaboration" that arose following Japan's defeat. At any rate, they were, in Itō's case, "the inevitable results of his own youthful sufferings," Mishima wrote, and were "also half-despairing fantasies for recovering his youth."

Indeed, "the perfect, bright, poetic crystals" that are some of his war poems "suggest instead the premonitions of the laments of Hyperion betrayed by real Greece."[27] Hyperion here is the epistler-protagonist of Hölderlin's eponymous novel. Mishima, an admirer of the novel who had regretted he hadn't brought it with him as he stood on the hill of the Acropolis, would later mention the novel again to compare its description of nature with that of his in *The Sound of Waves*: if Hölderlin's attempt created a "mind-only," "idealistic" extreme, his own to create "my Arcadia" ended up making something as artificial as that of the Trianon Palace.[28]

In each piece Itō wrote, one can "clearly read the intellectuals' dark confusion before the Second World War, their youth spent there, the Romantic excitement at the outbreak of the war, the process in which it escaped toward a Classical equilibrium, and the premonitions of disillusionment," Mishima observed. The question then is: "Was this poet who constantly took the unhappy age as his inspiration, as his providence, an unhappy poet? Or was he a happy poet?"[29]

## *Safety Academy*

In July 1953 Mishima visited the Hoan Daigaku, "the security academy," one of the anomalous institutions set up in the process of creating a non-military military. As the government prepared to change the Police Reserve Force to the Security Force, it set up the security board and, along with it, what was meant to be a combination of the former Military and Naval Academies in an attempt to get rid of the unnecessary rivalries between the two officer candidate schools before Japan's defeat. The weekly *Asahi* had a series in which one writer would visit a school one whole day and write a report on it, and assigned Mishima to the newly created non-military military academy.

In each stage of devising and changing the names of non-military military institutions, the government studiously avoided anything suggestive of the armed services. But the military intent was clear to everyone else, and Mishima expected to find a military academy in the Hoan Daigaku as he was driven to the old Navy Communications School, in Yokohama, where it was located. What he found, superficially, was little different from a regular private college, except for the following: the uniform (resembling that of the old Japanese Naval Academy) and fatigues (US style), a group of US military "advisors" led by a lieutenant colonel permanently attached to the school, the fact that the drill instructors were mostly graduates of the Japanese Military and Naval Academies, and a strict curfew.

There was one thing that disappointed yet amused Mishima: the discovery of the English name given the institution: "safety academy."

If only the bureaucrats had had enough sense of humor to call it by its Japanese name, *anzen daigaku*, no one would have objected![30]

## *"Death-enchanted demon"*

Toward the end of the year, on December 22, the playwright Katō Michio hanged himself. He was a good friend and associate of Mishima but even more so, through Bungaku-za, of the playwright Yashiro Seiichi and the actor-translator Akutagawa Hiroshi. Katō was heavily influenced by Jean Giraudoux, so much so, in fact, that Yashiro, reading Giraudoux's *Tessa, la nymphe au cœur fidèle*—itself a free adaptation of Margaret Kennedy's stage version of her own novel, *The Constant Nymph*—was startled to find Katō had lifted, at times nearly verbatim, a sizable portion of it in his first play, *Nayotake*, which is set in medieval Japan. (Katō, in turn, was bemused to see the skinny, beautiful young American woman he used to see before the war—and yearn for—on her way to the American School in Tokyo appear, after the war, in the film *The Constant Nymph* as Joan Fontaine.)

Like Giraudoux, Katō was an absolute seeker of "purity," as Akutagawa put it, or, as Mishima put it, "I've associated with many artists since the war until now, but I've never seen someone as purity-pure as he was, such a gem-like personality."[31] And that, in the end, did him in.

Katō, who majored in English at Keiō University, was sent to New Guinea as an army interpreter in 1944 after finishing *Nayotake*. Coming down with malaria, he spent some delirious months during the rainy season of New Guinea, face to face with death in a field hospital, in truth no more than a collection of ramshackle huts built "in a gloomy, depressing jungle," where dozens of soldiers died every day. Returning from the war a year after it ended, he translated, among others, William Saroyan's play *The Time of Your Life* and Albert Camus' plays *Caligula* and *The Misunderstanding*.

"Mr. Katō, I think, is a poet who was killed by the war," Mishima wrote when Bungaku-za staged *Nayotake* two years after his death, in September 1955. "His death came in the eighth postwar year, but the dystrophy in New Guinea, the malaria he brought back from there, the poverty after the war, the pleurisy, the lung ailments—all these formed the causes that led him to death."

"His eight postwar years appeared to eventually move him toward happiness, but like leitmotifs in music, war and death resounded as undercurrents, until even the circumstances that might have shown a glimpse of light in a short while worked as tight presages that drove him to death."

Mishima called *Nayotake* Katō's "last work before he was sent to the front, the testament of youth, the material evidence of incorruptible health." It reminded him, he said, of Alain-Fournier's *Le Grand Meaulnes*, in that both were "the perfect testaments of youth."[32]

As Yashiro recalled, it was when friends gathered in a Ginza bar to mourn Katō a week or so after his death that Mishima slipped him a page from his memo book saying that he would henceforth change the combination of Chinese characters of his name to the one he had just written on it: 魅死魔幽鬼尾, "Death-enchanted-demon with a ghoulish tail."[33]

As it happened, it was the most complete or formal combination, if any such can be said to exist, of the varying sets of Chinese characters Mishima began to apply to his own name, in the early 1960s, in writing Donald Keene. Yashiro, of course, had no way of knowing his friend would start using those characters in his correspondence with the American scholar a decade or so later.

CHAPTER ELEVEN

# The Girlfriend

> Das Ewig-Weibliche / Zieht uns hinan.
> *[The eternally feminine draws us on.]*
> —Mishima quoting Goethe in a taidan with Nakamura Mitsuo

> Mr. Mishima was the greatest actor I ever knew.
> —Nakamura Utaemon VI, after Mishima's death

*The Sound of Waves*, the novel that came out in June 1954, begins: "Utajima is a small island with a population of fourteen hundred, with a circumference of less than 2.5 miles." Utajima, "Song Island," was closely modeled on what has for some time been called Kamishima, "Deity Island," though one of the island's older names was a variant of "Song Island."

In March of the previous year Mishima went to visit Kamishima, on Ise Bay, thirteen miles east off the coast of Shima Peninsula, in Mie Prefecture. Shima is where the Grand Shrine of Ise is located, and Kamishima is deeply linked to the shrine. He wanted to see an old fishing village on an isolated island for the next novel he planned to write. He consulted his father. Azusa called the bureau of fisheries at the Ministry of Agriculture and Forestry and asked for an island that would meet the conditions his writer-son set: one that is "not at all influenced by big cities, with beautiful scenery, and economically somewhat prospering," as Mishima wrote in a brief essay, "Remembering Kamishima."[1]

The ministry officials took the request made by a former director-general seriously and spent several days making long-distance telephone calls to various places, when such calls were expensive. They finally narrowed the selection to two: one in the north, one in the south. Mishima chose the latter for the name had ancient poetic associations. Azusa later described, happily and proudly, the officials' efforts as "excessive." He wrote: "The effect of the Tokyo authorities behind it all may have been too great," for his son enjoyed "the maximum welcome the locality could afford."

Indeed, with the letter of recommendation of the administrator of the agency for fisheries, Mishima was met by the head of the fishermen's association of the island who took him in. He stayed with him for a dozen days while he observed things. One surprise in the household with which he stayed was the bathtub. The family used an oil drum. It was a common substitute for the Japanese military on the battlefields.[2]

In August Mishima visited the island again—this time to see a stormy sea. He had left a request that he be informed when a typhoon was in the offing. He received a telegram and rushed to the place. By the time he reached Toba, at the tip of Shima Peninsula, the typhoon had passed by but the waves were still high. The ferryboat did not cancel its sailing but plunged right into the waves. Mishima, who was immune to seasickness, had the "thrill of riding up to the top of big waves that looked like mountain peaks, then plunging down to the bottom of the valley [that was] truly exhilarating."

From the island he telephoned Nagaoka Minoru, who he knew was then the head of management at the department of general affairs in the Mie Prefectural Government. Under the US Occupation's policy, the Japanese government had shed certain features of its centralized system, thereby losing its ability to appoint prefectural governors, for example. But it retained the power to assign career bureaucrats of its ministries to important positions in local governments.

Nagaoka was surprised. "What kind of business did you have on Kamishima?" The Mie prefectural government is in Tsu, and for many of the city's residents in those days, Kamishima felt as remote as Korea, although the island lies only thirty miles southeast as the crow flies.

"I'd like to write a story based on a Greek story before Christ, called

'Daphnis and Chloë,'" Nagaoka remembered Mishima saying. Though the story is Greek, Longus, the romancer of Daphnis and Chloë, is from the third or fourth century A.D. "The trouble was, it was difficult to find just the right place for the setting. In short, I looked for a place without a single pachinko parlor." The pachinko, which traces its origins to a pinball machine imported from the United States in 1920, became a craze after Japan's defeat, and by the early 1950s there was not a single town or village worth its name that didn't boast at least one gaudy, noisy pachinko parlor. Kamishima did not, in fact, have "a single pachinko parlor, nor a single drinking joint, nor a single barmaid," as Mishima wrote in the story.

In September, a month after completing the monthly serialization of Part II of *Forbidden Colors*, Mishima began to write *The Sound of Waves*. He wrote it in a non-serialization format known as *kakioroshi*, a piece of writing of substantial length published in one piece—the way novels and such usually are where serialization is no longer practiced.

It was indeed a Daphnis and Chloë story set in a fishing village in postwar Japan. The boy is Kubo Shinji, a poor youth whose father was killed while fishing by machine-gun strafing by the US Navy in the last phase of the war; the girl is Miyata Hatsue, the youngest daughter of the richest man on the island. They face the usual obstacles: A young man from a better house than Shinji's attempts to rape Hatsue, and Hatsue's father is an irascible curmudgeon. But Shinji and Hatsue remain chaste despite youthful temptations. After a show of bravery on Shinji's part on a stormy night, Hatsue's father allows the two to be betrothed.

How can anyone move from the complicated world of scheming gays to the simple world of a mythical romance with such ease? In 1959, when asked to write a "literary autobiography," he came up with the notion of *katagi*, "temperament" or "disposition," to explain the changes he had gone through in his principal writings up till then by first discounting the idea of "a writer's spiritual progress."

"I have been tormented by my temperament," he wrote, although in his boyhood he did not know any such torment, "being one with the temperament, happy to be vaguely floating with it. I was a fake poet, a [fake] writer of tales ("The Boy Who Wrote Poetry," 1954; "A Forest in Full Bloom," 1941; "Tinted Glass," 1940)." Then came "the state in which my awakening as a writer was opaquely entangled with my awakening in life," and it was in that state that "I began to write stories furiously."

The result was *The Bandit*, 1948, which is "filled with ambiguous expressions." In the end, "I had no choice but to recognize my temperament as my enemy and confront it. Unable any longer to put up with myself drawing out of my temperament only lyrical gains, a liar's gains, and the gains of novelistic technicality, I decided to settle everything and make a balance sheet." The result was *Confessions of a Mask*, 1949.

Having finished writing that "novel," he felt much better. So he tried to "reconcile" himself with his own temperament. *Thirst for Love*, 1950, was a "fully conscious" attempt to "merge temperament and novelistic techniques." Following that, "I tried to disengage from my temperament as best I could and disengage also from novelistic techniques with which I was endowed so far, in order to make an abstract drawing and failed (*The Blue Age*, 1950). My life started. I embraced a ballsy attempt to thoroughly fictionalize my temperament and bury my life in a story (*Forbidden Colors*: Part I, 1951; Part II, 1953). After such an attempt, I decided to make my opposite in every way and became captive of the idea of constructing, with language alone, thoughts and figures that could not possibly be ascribed to my responsibility (*The Sound of Waves*, 1954)."

And so went Mishima's candid self-explications, before moving on to later works.[3]

## *Movies Featuring Youth*

*The Sound of Waves* became an instant bestseller. It saw seventy printings in just three months. Mishima became a celebrity—if he hadn't already been one. The literary establishment did not make much of the story, at least initially, one commentator saying it had "pedestrian scenes typical of American movies"—scenes, that is, that readily appeal to the unsophisticated. Such a reaction may be ascribed to the fact that the novel fell in the romance category.

Regardless, the three major studios immediately competed for film rights to *The Sound of Waves*. Of the three, Shōchiku had turned two of Mishima's stories into films, *The Snow-White Night*, in August 1951, and *Natsuko's Adventures,* in January 1953, which was Japan's second color film, and Daiei, one, *Made-in-Japan* (*Nippon-sei*), in December 1953. This last was about a beautiful, Paris-trained fashion designer falling in love with a young practitioner of a very traditional Japanese sport: judo, thereby turning herself back into a "genuinely Japanese" woman after acquiring European airs. The film featured Yamamoto Fujiko, the winner of the first Miss Nippon contest, in 1950, reputedly the greatest beauty Japan ever produced.

Tōhō, which hadn't done any film based on a Mishima story, was the first to make an offer for *The Sound of Waves*. But Shōchiku and Daiei followed on its heels. In those days, as today, the use of agents was rare among Japanese authors. In consequence, the competition among the three turned into personal harassment. At home Mishima often feigned absence, and Azusa served as a watchdog. Once outside, Mishima was defenseless.

One day, when Mishima was shopping in a department store, a representative of one studio learning of his presence there turned to the store's public address system to request a meeting with him. Mishima finally asked Satō Yoshio, president of his principal publisher by then, Shinchōsha, to represent him, and Satō chose Tōhō, which offered to ask Nakamura Shin'ichirō to write the script. A student of French literature and one of the few poets who experimented with rhyming in Japanese, Nakamura at the time was at the height of his fame as a writer of radio dramas. Among those who commented on *The Sound of Waves*, he had praised it as "a sharp antidote to modern fiction."[4]

The studios were eager for film rights to this novel, as with his two earlier novels, but especially this one, because movies featuring young people had potential as great moneymakers. Tōhō's 1949 film, *The Blue Mountain Range* (*Aoi sanmyaku*), along with its title song, had become a runaway hit and created talk of "a newly born Japan." Based on a novel of the same title by the popular writer Ishizaka Yōjirō, the film portrays a young female teacher—played by Hara Setsuko—assigned to a rural high school who enlists her students to drive out the "feudalistic" forces of the locality. Feudalism, along with militarism and nationalism, was one of the elements of Japanese society the Occupation wanted to eradicate.

Ishizuka's story referred to the devastation and defeat of war and its causes, but it was free of angst and remained optimistic. The movie was directed by Imai Tadashi, who would go on to win fame for realistic themes with an emphasis on social justice. *The Sound of Waves*, if anything, was even better, though by then Occupation censors had decamped. It told a straightforward boy-meets-girl story. It was directed by Taniguchi Senkichi whose attempt, in the late 1940s, to make what was to be Japan's first film dealing with Korean "comfort women"—the script was by Kurosawa Akira—was totally mangled after more than a dozen demands for rewrite by the Occupation's CIE.[5]

Tōhō moved fast. It started the filming in mid-July, a month after the book came out. Mishima decided to see part of the shooting on location. He took the train late on the night of August 8—not from his house in Tokyo but from an inn in the hot-spring resort Atami where he was holed up to write. The trip was coordinated with the press. A group of eight journalists had boarded the train in Tokyo to cover the event. Mayuzumi Toshirō, who was to compose the music, was with them. When they arrived at the ferry, the boat had just left the pier but when they called out, it dutifully turned back to pick them up. "The ship here is not a machine," Mishima wrote in a piece on the trip, "but understands human sentiments." He learned the ferry's once-a-day round trip between Toba and Kamishima had been doubled during the shooting.

He stayed again with the head of the fishermen's association, this time with Mayuzumi. There was little choice. After the book was published, the number of tourists quickly increased and the island people were having difficulty devising ways of accommodating them, but now they suddenly had to cope with the influx of a film-making crew of sixty. As a result, they cancelled all the tourist reservations. Even so, they had to use the elementary school—luckily it was in summer recess—as well as the offices of the Yashiro Shrine and the rooms of ordinary people willing to rent them.

Mishima had to learn the hazards of modeling his characters on actual people once more. The college-age daughter of the lighthouse-keepers had taken offence at the way he described her. He had written that she, the character named Chiyoko, had "ceaselessly, stubbornly thought that she was not beautiful." Though he suggests otherwise—that some will "find attractive her cheerful face with the eyes and nose delineated in large strokes"—and in the end makes her act as an honorable, sensitive person, a normal young woman would likely find the overall treatment he accorded less than flattering. It was on this occasion, too, that he learned one of the lighthouse keepers and his family had been affected by "the death ashes" of the hydrogen bomb tests in the South Pacific.[6]

The film, with Mifune Toshirō playing the captain of a fishing boat, was shown nationwide on October 20 and created a sensation. It had a scene where Shinji and Hatsue hold each other nude—or almost. The Japanese movie industry had come very far in eight years. In 1946, Japanese actors and actresses were thrown into anguish when David Conde, the head of CIE's Motion Picture and Theater Division, demanded onscreen kissing be incorporated "for democracy."[7]

In December *The Sound of Waves* won Mishima his first literary prize, though it was a prize his publisher Shinchōsha had just set up. Following this, Mishima would win one prize after another.

## *The Young Woman in Kimono*

After watching the filming of *The Sound of Waves* on Kamishima for three days, Mishima was back in Tokyo, on August 11. He had to write a kabuki for Nakamura Utaemon VI, the beautiful *tate-oyama*, the lead female impersonator, of the Kabuki-za. Before succeeding to the illustrious name, in 1951, at the age of thirty-four, the actor had carried an equally illustrious name, Shikan. Enchanted by him early on, Mishima had written in 1949 an essay, "On Shikan," and in November 1953 adapted for him a short story by Akutagawa Ryūnosuke, "Infernal Transformation" (*Jigokuhen*).[8] The play was immediately staged, with Utaemon playing Kusatsuyu, a beautiful lady-in-waiting who is burned alive so her painter father Yoshihide may create the realistic picture of hell his lord commissioned.

"An actor of whom a frontal discussion as an actor is appropriate," Mishima had written of Shikan, displaying his fondness of paradoxes, "lacks the inherent condition for being a kabuki actor." He went on, "The beauty of Nakamura Shikan must lie in a kind of sense of crisis" he engenders, and he cited three female characters the actor played. One was Princess Yuki, of *The Temple of the Golden Pavilion* (*Kinkakuji*), which is the popular name for Act IV of the jōruri *Gion sairei shinkō ki*, first performed in 1757. As played by Shikan, the princess, whose name means "snow," "arches deeply backward, her hands tied behind her. She goes on to arch backward more deeply, with a thrilling slowness, until you worry her back may break. Cherry blossoms gloriously scatter onto her chest."[9]

The kabuki he wrote this time, *The Sardine Hawker & the Dragnet of Love* (*Iwashiuri koi no hikiami*), was based on a couple of children's stories from the Muromachi Period (1392–1573). It is a comedy. A sardine hawker disguises himself as a warlord to attract the attention of a courtesan whom he has no way of approaching otherwise. As it turns out, she, actually a princess, had fallen in love with him, the sardine hawker, and, having failed to approach him, had lost herself in the pleasure quarters. The play required a mastery of classical language as well as rhetorical and theatrical conventions of kabuki. In a brief essay he gives a glimpse of the difficulties involved, with his usual irony. As a devotee of kabuki since boyhood, he had hated kabuki composed in modern language or a half-digested "new kabuki language," he wrote. So he was happy when the Kabuki-za asked him to turn "Infernal Transformation" into a kabuki play.

> But once I started on it, it was difficult indeed to reproduce not just neoclassical language but also the jōruri style, which is in extreme bad taste and brims with grotesque, innocent humor. What may have been funny to me as audience or reader was far from funny once I put myself in the shoes of someone who writes it. After all, jōruri writers' heads were packed with what they had heard of ancient stories of Japan and China, but they did not have a single fragment of cultural education that might get in the way of writing jōruri. In contrast, we lead an irrational life of hearing Heifetz with the same ears with which we've just heard bunraku[10] and, on our way home, discussing Sartre in a bar. It would be too self-indulgent to propose to write a jōruri in such circumstances. This isn't to boast at all, but I almost suffered an attack of cerebral anemia when I finally completed the scenario, took it to the Kabuki-za, and started the reading.[11]

It was in Utaemon's greenroom, where he had become a frequent visitor, that Mishima met, toward the end of August, a young woman in kimono who, with her white skin, delicate arms, and large eyes tapering off toward the outer edges, looked like a bunraku doll. She was a nineteen-year-old daughter of a man who owned a famous Japanese-style restaurant in the high-end entertainment district, Akasaka. She would become Mishima's important companion for the next two and a half years. Her name was Toyoda Sadako.

A week after they met, they ran into each other on the Ginza. Mishima invited her to a café named Victoria. There he talked as if he had all the time in the world. It must have been a rare thing for him to do, especially with someone he was meeting only for the second time. He was constantly under pressure for work. Though few knew it, he had severe stomach cramps from time to time. This was something Mayuzumi discovered when he happened to hole up for work in a hotel room next to Mishima's. The walls of their hotel rooms must have been very thin; late one night he heard Mishima moaning. He rushed to the next room and found Mishima doubled up like a shrimp. To his surprise, Mishima had an injection syringe ready with him. The stomach pain didn't just occur that night. It happened often enough and he was prepared for it, though sometimes he had to call for a doctor.

Toyoda Sadako and Mishima agreed to meet several days later again, at the same café, and they did. After that, they made dates to see brand-new movies, Utaemon's performances, went to French restaurants on the Ginza, Japanese restaurants in Shinbashi, and so forth, until one day she agreed to go to an inn with him. It turned out to be an inconspicuous but elegant place in Shōtō, just outside the brothel district in Shibuya. It was formerly a mansion. Transformations of grand houses into restaurants and inns were common in the years that witnessed reversals in fortune as a result of the war, the abolishment of peerage, and the Occupation-led land reforms.

Following their time together at the Shōtō inn, the two started dating almost every day. Initially, they would first meet at a restaurant to eat and then go on to an inn to make love. Soon they reversed course: first make love, then eat. They then started going to night clubs after dinner. The mid-1950s was the golden age of night clubs. Mishima and Sadako tried all the well-known ones at the time: Golden Gate, in Iikura; Ginbasha (Silver Carriage), in Shinbashi; Cosmopolitan, in Nogizaka; Pearl and L'Ami, in Shibuya; Marunouchi Club, near Tokyo Station; and their favorite, Manuela, in Uchisaiwai-chō. Often they danced late into the night.

Sadako met Mishima each time in a different kimono. Wearing dressy kimono to go out came naturally to a young woman from the high, traditional end of the *mizu-shōbai*, "water trade," or, more elegantly, *karyūkai*, "the realm of flowers and willows"—a somewhat inclusive term for restaurants, bars, geisha houses, and at times brothels. It came with the territory.

Still, the kinds of kimono Sadako routinely wore for dating Mishima were costly, comparable to, let us say, dressing up each time in a different Chanel or Balenciaga suit. In the 1950s there were still many kimono craftsmen so an expensive kimono may have been comparable to a "designer dress" made to order, unlike the individual kimono made by a famous kimono maker today, which may cost up to one million yen. Also, during the days kimono was the standard garb, many of them were of as high quality as craft.[12]

The novel Mishima wrote next, *The Sunken Waterfall* (*Shizumeru taki*), clearly reflects his close association with Sadako. It has a female character who, aside from being exquisitely portrayed, is notable for her kimono and for the unmistakable intimacy Mishima brings to bear in describing it. Mishima was, of course, always meticulous in getting things right. He probably learned most of which fabric carried what specific name from his mother, who, after all, was routinely dressed in kimono, and from women friends, as well as kabuki people. But the kinds of kimono he describes in *The Sunken Waterfall* are different from what his kinsfolk ordinarily wore, both in material and make. So, for her first date with the male protagonist, Kidokoro Noboru, the woman, Kikuchi Akiko, shows up in a café, "a small cathedral," strikingly dressed.

> She was waiting in the innermost part, in a dimly lit corner. As he approached her, Noboru was surprised. She was dressed so gorgeously she looked out of place. Her kimono was of Hitokoshi silk crepe with large designs dyed into it—clusters of wisteria hanging down from her shoulders against the white ground and wild chrysanthemums growing up from the lower hem. Her obi was of handwoven brocade with large checkerboard design alternating gold and silver, her obi clasp made of scarlet and white votive paper cords. For all that, she looked neither suffocating nor boorish. It sat elegantly perfect on her slim body.
> 
> "I'm on my way home from a dance meeting," she said before he spoke, catching his surprised look. "I left midway."

"So you dance."
"I just watch."

As the story is set up, Noboru's surprise in this scene may be less than entirely convincing. The only grandson of a great industrialist and an inveterate playboy, he, at twenty-seven, has all the money he needs to pick an appropriate venue for any woman he chooses for the night, and his rule is to sleep with each just once. He keeps several rooms on hand at any time: "a luxurious hotel for a woman who likes everything to be luxurious, a neat little homey inn for a woman who likes a place like that, a stylish hotel for a woman who likes a stylish hotel," and so on. In the circumstances, he surely must have met any number of expensively attired women!

In any event, "Akiko was gorgeous and was in kimono. He telephoned a quiet Japanese inn in a residential area in Yamanote, which was said to have formerly been a daimyo's mansion."

Then comes this passage:

> To take a bath, Akiko changed clothes in the next room. Noboru vividly heard the sound of that gorgeous kimono with large designs slip down her round shoulders. The elegant silk, as if cutting the air sharply, fell to the floor of its own weight and made a faint rustle as it touched the tatami and collapsed.
>
> Lying in the guestroom part of the suite, Noboru heard it all. He asked himself: When was it that I began to like such elegant, soft things?

Later in the novel, during their second assignation, which happens many months later, Noboru and Akiko go to the same inn.

> Because Noboru asked her to leave her undergarments as they were, Akiko agreed with a smile, did as asked, and left for the bathroom.
>
> Noboru stood alone in front of her kimono of English flannel hung on a freestanding clothes-hanger and the undergarments laid down as she took them off. There was the scent of a woman's room that might linger a little while after its occupant left it.... The colors of the kimono of English flannel

were blurred like a rainbow, and on one edge of the tray for personal belongings were a pair of white lace gloves hanging with the lightness of feather. The dark-green obi hanging from the lower crosspiece of the clothes-hanger slowly waved downward as it slid to the middle of a tatami. At one end of the hanger dangled the rust-red obi clasp with its firm tuft neatly cut at one end, swinging. The white Western-style undergarments overflowed the tray, like froth left by a wave, as they faced these multicolored drifts.... Noboru put the undergarments up against his face....

Such things about Akiko are lovingly detailed. *The Sunken Waterfall* as a fiction, though, is an artificial and disjointed construct. If Noboru is a playboy who seeks a different woman each time, never sleeping with the same woman twice, Akiko is a married woman who is granted free rein in sexual liaisons by her husband, his sole stipulation being that she return home every day, however late.

Their first night together Noboru finds her frigid. Deciding as a result that he is a man incapable of spiritual love, she a woman incapable of physical love, he makes a proposal for the two of them: "Now that two persons who are unable to love have met, why not create a truth out of a lie, a fact out of an illusion, to see if they may synthesize love, like a mathematical formula that produces a positive number by multiplying a negative number by a negative number?" Akiko agrees. Thereupon Noboru removes himself to a remote dam construction site where he, along with some of his fellow workers, lives isolated during the long winter months. The isolation over, the two meet once again, but Noboru finds Akiko in love with him and is repelled. Confused, Akiko commits suicide.

In the fall Mishima had a taidan with Takamine Hideko, the lead actress in *Twenty-four Eyes* (*Nijūshi no hitomi*), Kinoshita Keisuke's latest film based on Tsuboi Sakae's story about a schoolteacher and the fate of the twelve children she taught on an island. The movie is reputed to have reduced the entire country to tears, as it indeed did the men in the audience when he saw it, belatedly, for the taidan, Mishima told Takamine. Asked if he cried, he replied he did not, citing "the English critic" John Symonds's observation to the effect that the simplest thing in art is to make a human being cry and feel prurient. Not that he is immune to such things, he added. Recently he reread Stendhal's *La Chartreuse de Parme* and was deeply touched.

Such high-flown talk did not faze Takamine. After all, she had debuted in film at age four and remained a star ever since. When the topic turned to kissing scenes in film, Takamine asked if he could direct one, and he said, no, he wouldn't be able to because he had never kissed himself. Thereupon, she said, "I'm sorry about that. Why don't you come to my place? I have plenty of bags of tricks."

When Takamine asked, "You still have girlfriends who stir your heart, don't you?," Mishima responded, "Yes, sure, some." "As I see it, though," judged the actress who had once fallen in love with Kurosawa Akira, "they are nothing more than research material, in your case."[13]

*Twenty-four Eyes* would win two prizes in Japan and become the first Japanese film to win the Golden Globe Award the following year.

## *Source of Literary Inspiration*

The dam sites Mishima visited to observe to write *The Sunken Waterfall*, in October 1954, were the ones at Naramata (later Sudagai), in northern Gunma, and, further north, at Okutadami, on the border of Niigata and Fukushima. The Naramata construction had begun two years earlier. Both dams were large-scale and on difficult mountainous terrain and were built with outsize American construction machinery and loans, as the Japanese economy began to recover from the war.

When the novel came out following serialization in the first four issues of *Chūō Kōron* in 1955, Mishima received a number of letters from construction workers faulting him on the descriptions of life during the winter isolation. He had based that aspect of the book—which takes up a bulk of the story—on information he received through scant correspondence with an employee of Tokyo Electric Power Company. The incident prompted him to resolve to stress basic background research in future works.[14]

In early November 1955, Mishima went to Kyoto to collect information for a new novel. His publisher had asked him to serialize one in its monthly, *Shinchō*, during 1956, and he chose the Kinkakuji, the Temple of the Golden Pavilion, for its subject.

The Kinkakuji, the popular name of the Rokuonji, the Deer Garden

Temple, has been so known because of its gilt pavilion, a reliquary for the Buddha's bones. The third Ashikaga shogun Yoshimitsu (1358–1408) built it, along with many halls and towers, toward the end of the fourteenth century, on a large estate for the Kitayama (North Mountain) Palace, once the aristocratic Saionji family's villa, in Kyoto. Following Yoshimitsu's will, the Kitayama Palace was renamed the Rokuonji after his death and turned into a Zen temple of the Rinzai school. Though most of the halls and such he built were moved or ruined in subsequent centuries, the Golden Pavilion remained more or less intact until July 2, 1950, when an acolyte and college student named Hayashi Shōken torched it. Shōken was his Buddhist name given at the temple; his real name, also Buddhist, was Yōken.

What stirred the literary imagination when that happened was not so much the burning down of a prominent national treasure itself as the confession of the arsonist, who was arrested in no time, that he did it to express his "antagonism to beauty," as phrased by Kobayashi Hideo, who just then was writing a series of critical essays for *Shinchō* and took up the incident at once. Hayashi himself had said in his police deposition that he "burnt it because of my thought of jealousy toward beauty." He had gone on to explain: "I once in a while had the thought that I was treated as a madman within the temple. It sometimes occurs to me that while I feel I am a negligible human being, I also think that I am a greater person than those who say they are heroes."[15]

These words fascinated Kobayashi. As Nakamura Mitsuo explained in writing an afterword to *The Golden Pavilion* a few years later, Kobayashi, who had "lived with a madman" in his youth—by "a madman" he apparently meant himself although his association with the poet Nakahara Chūya whose lover he stole was only too famous—couldn't regard Hayashi as "a stranger." The arsonist's words showed "a madman's speculation for the sake of speculation, reflection for the sake of reflection," Kobayashi wrote.

He also wrote that it was "an incident truly symbolic of our times." Recalling what he had observed when he visited the pavilion earlier that year, he suggested that madness had become commonplace since Japan was defeated in the war.

> Nothing had changed in the precincts, but a new attitude was evident among the viewers. A "gentleman" chased a woman,

trampling on the green moss as he did so, a woman climbed a red pine and struck a pose for a camera below, one man picked up a pebble and threw it to the pond as though practicing pitching. The guards of the Rokuonji roared themselves hoarse [as they tried to stop them], but there were too many of them to contend with. . . .

At the time, many Japanese professed to take "democracy," the Occupation gospel, to mean, seriously or otherwise, the freedom to behave as they pleased. For Kobayashi, the resultant unhinged behavior such as he witnessed the tourists exhibit around the Golden Pavilion was a form of madness, and he did not think it strange that a young man who worked at the temple should turn himself into an arsonist in such a milieu.[16]

Mishima, who had read Kobayashi's essay, decided to take up this "madman" who talked about "beauty," though in a brief essay much later, he wrote, "The Kinkaku that burnt down didn't have much attraction for me. . . . That the protagonist of my story thinks it's beautiful is enough for me; on that point I don't have much sympathy with him."

The direct impetus for Mishima, in fact, may have been the news in October 1955 of the completion of the rebuilt pavilion. Discussing "the aesthetic of Muromachi" in the same essay, Mishima said: "What I love is the freshly built, glittery gilt pavilion that people badmouth, likening it to a movie set," not the ancient or tired-looking one that had lost much of its luster over the centuries. "I think in that [glitter] lay the aesthetic of Muromachi, lay Shogun Yoshimitsu's bliss. Only with that glitter [the building] matches the design of the nō costumes."[17] What strikes many of those who see a nō drama staged for the first time is the incongruously resplendent costumes the actors wear in telling mostly somber stories ridden with anxiety and torment.

## *Competition*

But there may well have been an element of writerly competition in Mishima's choice of the burning of the Kinkakuji as his subject. "The Season of the Sun" (*Taiyō no kisetsu*), a novella by a university student named Ishihara Shintarō, created a sensation midyear. Printed in the

July 1955 issue of *Bungakukai* as the winner of that year's New Face Prize, the story depicted casual violence and sex among upper-class youths while focusing on a student boxer and his lover who dies of complications after an abortion.

Among the judges, Yoshida Ken'ichi said: "This is a work that has detailed to a revolting degree the speech and behavior of the pack of youths you often see around town these days whose bodies are well balanced but whose faces reveal a hopelessly idiotic state"; Takeda Taijun: "The offensiveness of this work became an issue. Except, its offensiveness is dry and not deliberate, and the work reads exceptionally well as fiction"; and Hirano Ken: "Before I had time to think of this and that, I was compelled to read it to the end. So the real *après-guerres* have taken root in Japan as well, I half-lamented, and I couldn't help thinking I don't have the ability to criticize this kind of world."

As the critic Okuno Takeo wrote two years later, citing these comments, Japan's "consumer culture was rapidly turning luxurious"—however inadequate it may seem a few decades later—"but the young had lost their dreams, oppressed as they were in their daily life as confining and boring as that before the war." As a result, "people were vaguely anticipating something shocking. "The Season of the Sun" appeared in that amply prepared soil as if readymade for it."[18]

Mishima's initial reaction to Ishihara's story was negative, even dismissive. When it appeared, he was writing a short book on criticism at Kōdansha's request, and he was carrying out this assignment in a diary format which, covering the period from June 24 to August 4, would be published in book form, late that year, as *A Novelist's Holiday* (*Shōsetsuka no kyūka*). By way of commenting on the story, he began with the Japanese notion of a connoisseur (*tsū*). That evening in July he ate a tempura dinner at the restaurant Ryokufūkaku, Green Wind Pavilion, in Atami, where he was staying, and the restaurant was famous for tempura.

To properly appreciate such things, you have to be a *tsū*. But connoisseurship is something even university students can attain to an astonishing degree, be it with nō drama, kabuki, tea ceremony, or flower arrangement, Mishima mused, and moved on to the not dissimilar idea of the Japanese notion of "the way of artistic skill" (*geidō*).

"Now, the novel is said to be a modern art, but our ready-made idea concerning the way of prose (*bunshō-dō*) has much that resembles Japan's way of artistic skill. There, too, is room for students to flaunt their connoisseurship, and we often encounter connoisseur-like prose ... and praise it as reserved, praise it as unscheming, or marvel how accomplished it is.

"Because I, too, used to write prose typical of a student versed in literature, I feel all the more embarrassed when I come in contact with such prose," Mishima went on. "The only hobby appropriate for a university student is probably sports. And the only prose appropriate for a university student must be an athletic one in its cleanliness. No matter how resplendent a costume it may wear, it must show a glimpse of healthy muscles underneath it."

Mishima then came to the point. "Incidentally, I recently read a story by a young man which was about a student boxer titled 'The Season of the Sun.' Whether it's good or bad, what was most regrettable to me was that this kind of material was written in a prose common to students versed in literature, a prose which was essentially the exact opposite [of what its subject requires]."[19] His was, in other words, a summary putdown of an upstart writer by someone with a chameleon-like mastery of style.

Yet "The Season of the Sun" went on to win the Akutagawa Prize toward the end of the year, making Ishihara the youngest to win the coveted prize. In February 1956, the weekly *Asahi* featured Ishihara, "the student writer who won the Akutagawa Prize." His first collection of stories, titled of course *The Season of the Sun*, sold three hundred thousand copies.

In March, Mishima apparently asked for a taidan with Ishihara and started the conversation by saying, with obvious ostentation, "Having written a variety of stories over the past decade, all the writers of postwar literature have attained field rank. I've been a perennial flag bearer, playing the role of regimental-flag bearer with no end in sight, but now I've found an appropriate person to whom I can hand over the regimental flag. Mr. Ishihara, I'd like to hand the tattered flag to you."[20]

Not that Mishima was completely taken with Ishihara. Asked to comment on the Ishihara phenomenon by the *Tokyo Shinbun* the following month, he began his essay: When his rival furiously trashes Ishihara, he, with an Edo-ite's compulsion to side with the loser or the maligned, ends up defending him; but should his rival praise the novella extravagantly, he would become a furious trasher. Ishihara's "originality" lay, Mishima suggested, in that he "offered to the literary establishment" the kind of "raw youth" one saw in the beach resort of Hayama, on the west coast of the Miura Peninsula, that provided the setting for Ishihara's story.[21]

"The Season of the Sun" was turned into a film, with Shintarō himself playing a bit role, and spawned three fad words: *taiyō-zoku*, "the sun tribe" (sullen youth loitering on a sun-bathed beach), *Shintarō-gari*, "the Shintarō cut" (a crewcut with a good deal of hair left on the top), and the adopted English word "*dry*" (casually, indifferently indulging in violence and sex). Mishima went on to engage in six more taidan with Ishihara, the last one in the fall of 1969.

---

*A Novelist's Holiday*, which came out in November, was characteristic of Mishima in its wide range of references, from Edward G. Robinson's film *Black Tuesday* (the title translated in Japanese as *Five Minutes before Execution*) to Terentius's observation, "I am a human being, so nothing human is strange to me." Mishima quoted the Roman writer to discuss the cultural chaos that Japan was thought to be going through at the time.

One entry in this "diary" may be peculiarly indicative of the time. On July 8, Mishima returned to Tokyo to attend a farewell party in the evening for a twenty-nine-year-old American. No doubt because it was only ten years after Japan's defeat, his departure to teach Japanese at Harvard University not just merited a farewell party but the party drew a dozen men of letters and theater.

"Mr. [V. H.] Viglielmo, this formidable master of the Japanese language, a lover of [Natsume] Sōseki, a mixture of lofty pride, and clumsy, youthful humility, a youth who, while being crushed by a dark impulse, straightforwardly believes in God and his own beautiful face," Mishima wrote. "He wished to die, like a Greek, while he remained youthful in appearance. And he would turn to me, older by a year or two, and say, You have missed a chance to die."

Among those who attended the party were: Akutagawa Hiroshi, the scholar of French literature Satō Saku, Yashiro Seiichi, Nakamura Shin'ichirō, and another French scholar and novelist Fukunaga Takehiko.[22]

Ever pressed for time for writing and suffering from lack of sleep for days on end as a result, Mishima took an unusual step for a writer at the time when he went to Kyoto to gather information for *The Temple of the Golden Pavilion*: he flew—from Haneda, in Tokyo, to Itami, in Osaka. The first successful jet-powered passenger aircraft, the Boeing 707, had started service in 1954, and the second, Douglas's DC-8, in June 1955. But the Japan Air Lines still used the propeller-driven DC-4s. As far as such things go, the ban on domestic aircraft manufacture in Japan instituted by the Occupation as part of the process of demilitarization was not lifted until the following year and Japan's first passenger aircraft would not be tested until 1962. The Itami Airport, when Mishima arrived there, had large weedy patches on its runways. He then hired a taxi to go to Kyoto.

The resident monk of the Kinkakuji firmly declined to cooperate and neither granted an interview nor allowed an examination of the personal quarters. His reason was simple: It was unthinkable to work with someone who was going to write a novel about the fire that destroyed his temple. All Mishima could do was to closely inspect all the nooks and corners of the temple compound that regular tourists were free to visit. He prepared a number of sketches and notes. He stayed at the Kamada Inn, an old lodge near the Nanzenji, the headquarters of Rinzai Zen.

He wrote Sadako: "Every day I go places to collect information and, back [in the inn], keep busy sorting things. I may not even have occasion to view the garden at the Gionji. Tomorrow I'll be going to East Maizuru to visit the hometown of the monk who set the Kinkakuji on fire. After that I will also stay at the Myōshinji."[23] The Gionji is also known as the Yasaka Shrine. The Myōshinji is another famous Rinzai Zen temple, though of a school different from that of the Rokuonji, which is not far from the Kinkakuji. This temple agreed to allow Mishima to stay one night, and Mishima closely observed the young monks training. He did not take part in zazen because that would have been too painful for his legs. One discovery he made there was that Zen temples served as mental clinics. He met a middle-aged man who was happy as he had recovered from a nervous breakdown he had suffered as a result of a divorce a month earlier.

Recalling the one-night stay at the temple a decade later, Mishima wrote: "Some may say it is an act fearless of heaven to write about life in a Zen temple after just a one-night stay, but I hear that Émile Zola had just one dinner with an actress at the Opera House in order to write *Nana*." And: "I still can't forget how delicious the rice was that was said to have been cooked on pine wood. I have never eaten a rice meal as tasteful as that since I was born."[24]

Maizuru is a port city in northern Kyoto. An important naval base until Japan's defeat, it became famous in the years that followed as an entry port for soldiers and other expatriates returning from the Soviet Union and other parts of the Asian Continent. Mishima was there during the war—from the end of June to early July 1944—to train in seafaring at the Maizuru Naval Engineering School, a few months before it became a branch of the Naval Academy. This is suggested in *Confessions of a Mask*.

East Maizuru is a town where Hayashi Shōken's father was born. The young man himself spent his middle-school years there, though he was born and grew up at Cape Nariu, a forlorn place north-northeast of East Maizuru, where his father had a temple. The cape juts into Wakasa Bay and faces the Japan Sea. Mishima visited the area this time with his father's friend in Kyoto as a guide. The fickle weather there in late fall impressed him. At the start of *The Temple of the Golden Pavilion*, he would write, with the protagonist narrating the story: "My father's hometown was land overflowing with sunlight. But in two months of the year, November and December, even on spectacularly fine days when you didn't seem to see a single cloud, a shower would pass four or five times a day. My variable mood may have been nurtured in that land."

Back at the Kamada Inn Mishima found the popular comedian Ban Junzaburō ("Banjun") staying there. Banjun saw him lifting a barbell on the verandah of his room and bantered about it. They went out to eat and became friends.[25]

## Bodybuilding

Mishima had taken up bodybuilding in September. That month he read an article in a weekly emphasizing how this new, postwar sport could transform the human body. Along with the spectator sport of professional wrestling, this American import focused on physical display, made famous by Charles Atlas, was becoming a vogue. Mishima at once sought an introduction to a man featured in the article, Tamari Hitoshi, captain of the Barbell Club at Waseda University. When they met, he hired him on the spot as his private coach. He arranged to have him visit him three times a week. When he had to go to Kyoto he asked him to have a lightweight barbell delivered to his inn.[26] He had decided to follow Tamari's instruction to do bodybuilding exercises every other day even while he traveled.

Years later Tamari, who remained Mishima's good friend and by then chairman of the Japan Bodybuilding Federation, recalled how Mishima explained to him the reason he took to bodybuilding with such dedication: "Why is it that so many of the Japanese writers are like Dazai Osamu and Akutagawa Ryūnosuke who either look neurotic or seem to have just recovered from TB? It's as though they can't write good stories unless they are sick and feeble and those around them approve of it. This is ridiculous. There ought to be a strict line between what you write and how you live. No matter how unquotidian or radical your writing may be, there is no reason for your daily life to be unhealthy or degenerate. Rather, it ought to be healthy."[27]

As Mishima himself noted, Dazai was well built and tall, though he willfully dissipated himself, mainly through drinking.[28] "Because I had found objectionable the tendency of the Japanese literary establishment to revere and value a work only because the writer wrote it laboring over it, losing weight, even getting ill," Mishima wrote, "I weighed myself before starting on *The Golden Pavilion* and, after finishing it and proving that I hadn't lost a single gram physically, shouted, 'Bravo!'"

That was Mishima's "literary" reason, if you will. The *real* reason was his "intense physical inferiority complex," as he freely admitted once his physique became more or less presentable, or so he thought. He took up bodybuilding because of the advent of Ishihara Shintarō.

Yuasa Atsuko, as a good friend, may have thought nothing of openly making fun of his miserable body (he was skinny, his legs looked fragile—the latter flaw he did not try to correct through bodybuilding),[29] but among his fellow writers, the critic Okuno Takeo noted, Mishima's "extraordinarily pale, unhealthy look, poor motor coordination, and clumsiness" was something of a taboo even to mention. But then there came along this young writer who grabbed Japan's imagination, and he was no ordinary young writer. He was "a sportsman capable of anything—sailing, soccer, and boxing—and who was not in the least embarrassed that he ... was a spoiled kid from a *bourgeois* household"—Okuno using the term *bourgeois* in the Japanese sense at the time of "the upper crust of the middle class." And the young man seemed to take it for granted as his birthright. Mishima was mortified.

Once he took up bodybuilding he never deviated from the path he chose. From September 1955 until his death he pursued physical improvement—not just through bodybuilding but also through boxing, kendō, *iai* (the art of cutting down an opponent from a sitting position), and karate—with "a superhuman effort that made you weep," in the end creating what Okuno has called "a modern miracle"—"a complete reformation [by a writer] of his own physique."[30]

Of these sports, however, boxing was where Mishima failed utterly. He took it up in September 1956, just a year after he started bodybuilding, with a well-known trainer Kojima Tomo'o. He did so because, with bodybuilding, his "physical self-confidence subjectively ballooned too much." Feeling "the iron wall that had separated me and sports having finally collapsed," he decided to take up "the toughest, the fiercest sport, the sport that would scare most men in their thirties," namely, boxing. But he had absolutely no aptitude for it. Ishihara Shintarō once came to visit him in his gym and filmed his sparring. Mishima made such a clumsy spectacle of himself that members of the Bungaku-za gathered in his house had a jolly time watching the film while playing recorded mambo music.[31]

Boxing lasted for just about a year for him, but he became a fan of the sport. He often went to see championship matches, wrote about them for newspapers, and from time to time had a taidan with a boxer.

## *The End of the Affair*

While still gathering information for *The Golden Pavilion* in Kyoto, Mishima wrote to Sadako: "I think I can come back earlier than planned, on the 17th, and will telephone you around noon on the 18th. Would you keep the afternoon of the 18th onward free for me? Kindly let me slip into the cracks of your extremely busy schedule. My desire is to take care of the arsonist monk as quickly as possible so I may see the beauty in

Tokyo the soonest." Mishima ended his missive with "To Imperial Princess Sadako. Your Subject Yukio."

The initial reaction to the serialization of *The Golden Pavilion* that began in the January 1956 issue of *Shinchō* was highly favorable. In March Mishima visited Kyoto again for further information. This time he took Sadako along. They put up in an elegant inn in Gion Hanami Kōji. There are in Japan restaurants and inns which, though not necessarily intended only for well-paying customers and guests, refuse to accept those the chef or the proprietor does not know directly or indirectly. The inn the two chose was one of those. Sadako arranged to stay there through her relative.

Mishima, for his part, had left word with his father that he'd be staying at the Miyako Hotel, the most prestigious Western-style lodging place in Kyoto. He knew Azusa would never accept his liaison with a restaurant owner's daughter, however high-class the establishment may be, let alone the fact that he'd stay in the same place with her. While in Tokyo Mishima did not need to tell his parents exactly where he was going to be, but he had to do so when away from the city.

It was three months later—in the wee hours of June 4—that Mishima telephoned Okuno, obviously drunk, and carried on and on, boasting how he'd finally been able to sexually satisfy a woman.[32] Okuno, only a year younger than Mishima and by then a good friend of his, had seen women attaching themselves to Mishima in bars and clubs but was still surprised by his cerebral friend's delirious manner.

Mishima was happy with Toyoda Sadako. Gradually, however, he sensed or decided that the affair would come to an end. And the two would indeed part from each other in May 1957. As Yuasa Atsuko saw it, the parting occurred largely because Sadako became uneasy as she realized Mishima was too far ahead of her, too knowledgeable and intelligent in everything, to catch up no matter how she might try. After resisting for quite a while, Mishima finally introduced Sadako to Atsuko, and the two women remained close friends thereafter.[33]

Mishima may well have foretold what was to come, and described what he thought of Sadako, in the short story "Boats for Feeding Hungry Ghosts" (*Segaki-bune*) that appeared in the October 1956 issue of *Gunzō*. Set in an inn in Atami known not so much as a lodging as for the food it serves, the story describes a meeting one summer evening between an old, famous writer named Tottori Yōichirō and his son

Fusatarō. Yōichiro's first, common-law wife, Katsue, has just died in an infirmary and newspapers have reported it in an indignant, accusing tone. Fusatarō, whose mother, Yōichiro's second wife, had died a few months after his birth, has asked to meet his father to find out the truth. Did he know Katsue was in an infirmary and, knowing that, did he do nothing for her? Unlike his own mother, who was rich and beautiful, Katsue was with Yōichirō when he was a poverty-ridden, struggling writer.

What is striking about this story is Yōichiro's description of Fusatarō's mother, who remains unnamed.

"Well, I must say, it was a happy life you would not be able to imagine. It was not just easeful, your mother was even dangerous. She wore a different kimono every day and changed her hairstyle in dizzying fashion," Yōichirō recalls for Fusatarō. "Since I was born, I had never been so close to something so human. I was gradually infected by it. I reconciled myself with everything human and accepted all the conventions of society. How nice and pleasant conventions were!"

When that "brief married life" ended, did he grieve? Fusatarō asks. Yes, he did, Yōichirō replies, he wept and continued to weep, until his friends who came to console him told him "he was like a sissy." "But," Yōichirō confesses, "it is hard to tell you this, your mother dying was a thoughtful gift for me."

This story was inspired by—was a thinly disguised account of—an evening Mishima spent with Sadako, as far as the setting is concerned. In mid-August he stayed in a hotel in Atami to finish the last installment of *The Golden Pavilion*, which he in fact did, on the sixteenth, the day after the O-bon Festival. Knowing he would complete his work as planned, always punctual in such matters as he was, he had invited Sadako for dinner with him at the aforementioned Ryokufūkaku, the restaurant famous for its tempura. It was atop a hill looking down upon Sagami Bay. From their room, as the night fell, Mishima and Sadako watched the Rite of Feeding the Hungry Ghosts—brightly lit boats, with prayers and drums, setting lanterns adrift on the dark water to soothe the souls of those who committed suicide by throwing themselves into the sea.

CHAPTER TWELVE

# The Kinkakuji

> .... *it is certain that it will turn to ashes.*
> —*The Temple of the Golden Pavilion*

*The Temple of the Golden Pavilion* received great reviews when it came out, and is still counted among Mishima's best works. Shortly after the novel's publication, the monthly *Bungei* set up a taidan for Kobayashi Hideo to discuss it with the author, and the taidan duly saw print. The redoubtable critic was altogether full of praise—equally of the novel and the novelist. "If there's anything that's terrifying in you, it's your talent," he said. Calling Mishima "the devil of talent," he said that the story is full of "inventions of images that bubble up," and that it "truly never bored me." *The Golden Pavilion* is "a lyric, rather than a novel," because "your Raskolnikov is protecting himself within the subjectivity called motive," Kobayashi said. It will become a novel if it deals with what happens after the protagonist burns down the pavilion.

One surprise comment Kobayashi had to offer was a question, "Why didn't you kill [the protagonist]?" Mishima responded somewhat disingenuously: "I was too bound to the actual records" to do otherwise.[1] On the face of it, he was correct. Hayashi Shōken, who set fire to the Golden Pavilion in the early hours of July 2, was found in the woods of a hill near the temple around four o'clock on the afternoon of the same day; he was arrested, sentenced to imprisonment in January of the following year, and lived until March 1956. But Mishima could have also "killed" him. Hayashi had attempted suicide.

After fleeing the scene of the crime, Hayashi stabbed himself in and near the heart with a pocketknife and took one hundred tablets of the sedative/sleep medication Calmotin—a drug a Japanese pharmaceutical company invented, so named, and put on the market during the war. It was while struggling with the self-inflicted wounds and the overdose of sleeping pills that he was discovered. As Mishima tells in his story, Hayashi had prepared both the knife and pills in advance, but Mishima obscures the reason and makes the man throw away the knife and pills after watching the pavilion burn to his heart's content. Moreover, Hayashi had died just about the time Mishima was preparing the fourth or fifth installment or chapter in his serialization of the novel. Earlier, in October 1955, when Mishima decided to take up the subject, Hayashi had been released from a hospital jail in Hachiōji, Tokyo, because of the tuberculosis he had contracted and the severe mental problems he had developed, and transferred to a hospital in Kyoto, via a brief stop in a nearby prison. That, too, could have provided Mishima with another rationale for letting his protagonist die.

Mishima did not allow the protagonist of the story, named Mizoguchi, to die at the end perhaps because he makes his own life run parallel to Mizoguchi's. Both Mishima and Mizoguchi lacked motor coordination and had youthful apprehensions about sex and botched sexual encounters. The "I" of *Confessions* comes upon a picture of Saint Sebastian while Mizoguchi witnesses in a temple an elegantly dressed young woman baring her breasts for a young army officer in uniform. Mishima apparently projects himself in Mizoguchi's imagining of the Golden Pavilion burning up in an air raid. He maintained a certain bravado and nonchalance in his letters written during the conflagrations, but he had witnessed fire-bombings, experienced the terror of being targeted for an air raid, and wandered in the immediate aftermath of citywide incinerations.

> The Golden Pavilion that summer [of 1944], feeding on the dark circumstances of war in which one disheartening news followed another, seemed to be shining in ever more lively manner. Already in June, the US forces had landed in Saipan and the Allied forces were dashing through Normandy. The

number of worshipers decreased markedly, and the Pavilion seemed to be enjoying the solitude, the quietude.

It was only natural that the turmoil of war and anxiety, countless corpses and overflowing blood, should enrich the beauty of the Golden Pavilion. After all, it was a building that anxieties had built.

Initially Mizoguchi, convinced that "the Golden Pavilion of Diamond Indestructibility and the scientific fire [of air raids] were alien to each other," does not even entertain the thought of the destruction of the Pavilion. But, as Saipan falls and talk of the inevitability of air raids on Japan proper becomes pervasive and the forced evacuation of parts of Kyoto starts, he begins to think of the possibility: "The Golden Pavilion may be burnt and destroyed by the fire of an air raid. If things go on in this fashion, *it is certain that it will turn to ashes*" [the emphasis in the original]. The possibility grows into delirious imaginings: "The thought that the fire that would burn and destroy me would also burn and destroy the Pavilion almost intoxicated me. In the destiny of the same calamity, of the same ominous fire, the Pavilion and the world I inhabited came to belong to the identical plane.... A fire engulfing the entire Kyoto City became my secret dream."

But the war ends with the Pavilion left intact. Sometime after the war, it was revealed that the US government had decided to spare the ancient cities of Nara and Kyoto from bombings, but no Japanese knew of any such decision while their cities were burning. On the day the Tennō announces Japan's surrender, Mizoguchi hurries from the factory to which he is assigned for wartime work back to his temple and finds his Pavilion deserted in the bright midsummer sun but appearing even more "transcendent of things like the shock of defeat and the grief of the race." And he has the revelation: "The *relationship* between the Golden Pavilion and me has been severed." Mizoguchi decides to do the burning himself. By burning it, he tells himself, "This rusted lock between my inner realm and outer realm would come undone wonderfully. There would be nothing to block the inner realm from the outer realm, and the wind would begin to blow through them back and forth, at will."

Once the main floor of the structure fully catches fire, Mizoguchi is suddenly struck with "the thought to die in the Kyūkyokuchō enveloped in this fire." The Kyūkyokuchō, the Ultimate Apex, makes up the third floor of the Pavilion. In contrast to the first two floors, the Hosui-in and the Chō'on-dō, which are spacious rooms adorned with statues and decorations, the Ultimate Apex is a small square room made in the manner of a Zen altar.

"Fleeing the fire, I ran up the narrow stairway.... I climbed further up the staircase and tried to open the door to the Kyūkyokuchō. The door would not open. The door on the third floor was firmly locked.... I pounded on the door.... What I dreamed of about the Kyūkyokuchō at that moment was surely a place of death for myself.... And, I dreamed at that moment with earnestness that verged on pain, that small room should have had gold foils all over the place." But suffocating with smoke, he is struck by the thought that he is "being refused." He does not hesitate but flees.

In real life, too, Hayashi seemed to have thought of dying in the top room—his own accounts in two police reports vary on this point—but was unable to go up to the second floor, let alone the Kyūkyokuchō, because the door to the second floor was "chain-locked." While he was hesitating, the fire caught up, and he fled.

In 1960, writing an afterword to the paperback edition of *The Golden Pavilion*, Nakamura Mitsuo compared Hayashi's "madness" as perceived by Kobayashi Hideo and Mishima and wrote that, though both saw in Hayashi Shōken's act "a 'symbol' of the madness of the period," Mishima "wished to recreate this 'symbol' through art in order to possess [sanity] firmly. For Mishima, there probably was no other way of maintaining sanity in modern times than trying to live artistically."[2]

Using the same word, "symbol," Saeki Shōichi saw something altogether different. "Firmly woven into the inner motive of the protagonist [of *The Golden Pavilion*] who is driven to the destruction of the building ... that may be the symbol of Japan's traditional beauty," wrote the student of American literature, "is Japan's defeat in the war as an indispensable, important link." And he suggested that the work showing the connection most directly is Mishima's play *Youths, Resurrect Yourselves! (Wakōdo yo yomigaere!)*.[3]

The play, published in the June 1954 issue of *Gunzō*, is in three acts, and it describes a group of law students assigned to a navy aircraft factory near the Atsugi Air Base (today the US Naval Air Facility) on three separate days in the summer of 1945. Act One covers August 7, the day after an atomic bomb was dropped on Hiroshima; Act Two, August 15, when Japan surrendered; and Act Three, August 26, when the Ministry for Armament and the Ministry for Greater East Asia were abolished. There are an array of characters with conflicting thoughts and remembrances, but the focus is on a young couple, the law student named Suzuki and a young woman he is in love with, Fusako. Once the war comes to an end, the two sharply differ on what it has done to their psyches.

Suzuki realizes that death, which during the final months of the war was the most abundant, cheapest "commodity" when everything else was in severe short supply, had distorted his thought and feelings. Fusako disagrees. At the end of Act Three, Suzuki tries to explain himself:

> Suzuki: ... Listen, don't you think this is what happened? That we, in the end, hadn't loved each other at all?
> Fusako: What?
> Suzuki: Yes, we had fallen into hallucination. We were caught in a fantasy. We thought we'd fallen in love, but that was an odd fantasy the war gave us. Air raids, dangers to our lives, things like that ganged up on us and made us think that we were in love. From the start we were not in love at all!
> Fusako: Why do you say, "from the start"? You just got tired, you just got tired of me.
> Suzuki: We must say "from the start." Unless we do that, we won't be liberated.
> Fusako: Liberated? (*She smiles coldly*) Here we go, another hallucination.
> Suzuki: We were drunk with the sound of sirens. We were drunk with the smell of death.
> Fusako: Stop saying "we." Say "I."
> Suzuki: It has to be "we."

In his afterword to the play, Mishima was uncharacteristically straightforward. Instead of trying to be ironic or casually erudite, he explained with earnestness how and why he wrote the play. He had never tried to turn his experience directly into some literary piece, but in this case, he made "an exception" for himself. He "became prisoner of a desire to recreate on stage my life during a certain period, to commemorate what I thought was a unique experience to me." He continued: "Not all the incidents written here correspond one by one to what I experienced at the time. But this play is different from my other works in that everything in it is based on facts." Because of this, he wrote, he urges his reader to "read this play as a historical drama."

"There were indeed, in our lives then, advocates of love for love's sake, innocent rightists, superstitious nihilists, and dreamy Communists such as described here. And, even though the wrinkles of complex emotions unique to youth were submerged under the pressure of the tense era and everyone looked idiotic not to a small extent, I never tried to draw a caricature in this work."[4]

The Haiyū-za staged the play with its founder Senda Koreya directing, in Tokyo, in November 1954. The play toured Osaka and Kyoto in the following January.

## *The Sea Did Not Split in Two*

Mishima wrote another work which was similarly important to him, though it showed the effect of the war indirectly. It is the short story "The Sea and the Evening Glow" (*Umi to yūyake*), his contribution to the January 1957 issue of *Gunzō*. To commemorate the one hundredth issue of the monthly, its editors lined up many of the prominent writers of the day. To Mishima's great disappointment, the story elicited little notice. He told a friend of his, Mushiake Aromu: "I wrote it to deal with what was to me a compelling question, so it was painful that it was utterly ignored when published. Had that piece been accurately understood when published, my life after that might have been different."[5]

"The Sea and the Evening Glow" has to do with an old sexton's reflection on the crucial turning point in his life that came in his youth. The narrative is as simple as the setting, which is one late summer evening of 1272 on a hill at the back of Kenchō-ji, in Kamakura. But the protagonist has a seemingly fantastic background. His name, Anri, is a direct transplant of the French name Henri.

When he was a boy shepherd in Cevenne, France, the Pope's call for the Fifth Crusade was issued and Henri saw Jesus Christ appear and heard the Lord tell him: "You are the one to take back Jerusalem, Henri. You boys take back Jerusalem from the infidels, the Turks. Gather together many comrades and go to Marseilles. The waters of the Mediterranean will split into two and guide you to Jerusalem."

Evidently Jesus told the same thing to children in many parts of France and Germany, for thousands of them, many tired and sick after long treks, gathered in Marseilles. But the sea did not split nor would it, however fervently the children prayed. In the event, a devout-looking owner of a ship appeared and offered to take them to the Holy Land, free. The children, who were troubled and lost, accepted the offer but were taken to Alexandria instead and sold in a slave market. Henri was bought by a Persian merchant. He then was sold to another man, who took him to India. There he met and was freed by the Chinese monk Dōryū (Daolong), who was in that land to study Buddhism. He followed when the monk returned to China and followed him further to Japan when the monk decided to come to this land.

The question that has haunted Henri all these years, long after he lost his faith, is "the mystery still unsolved ... hiding in the scarlet glitter of the sea" in the evening sun of Kamakura. "Probably in Anri's entire life, if the sea were to split into two, there could have been no other time than those moments"—in Marseilles when he and other children prayed. "The mystery was that even in those moments the sea spread itself silently as it burned in the evening glow."

When Mishima put together his favorite stories in one volume a few years before his death and included this one in it, he noted, "Any [reader of this story] will of course recall at once the most terrifying poetic despair of the Greater East Asian War, 'Why didn't the Divine Wind blow?'"[6] Mishima could assume this reaction on the part of the Japanese reader because the era he describes in the story was famous for the first of the two Mongolian invasions of Japan, in 1274 and 1281, which were both repelled by "the Divine Wind," a typhoon.

Daolong is a historical figure. Born in 1213, he arrived in Japan, in 1246, and, in 1253, at the request of the shogunate regent Hōjō Tokiyori (1227–63), founded the Zen temple Kenchō-ji. He died in 1278.

## Will Westerners Understand Japanese Fiction?

*The Golden Pavilion* came out in book form in October 1956 as the ten-installment serialization was completed. Priced at ¥280, it sold 123,000 copies by the end of the following year. Mishima also had a limited edition of two hundred copies printed, priced at ¥2,500. It was of a "*nouveau riche* taste and gilded," he wrote Kawabata in telling him he would be sending him a copy.⁷ The value of ¥2,500 at the time may be guessed from what Kawabata told Mishima in his letter of the same month. He had just received from Knopf a copy of *Snow Country* in Edward Seidensticker's translation. He was told it was a "low-priced" edition, at $1.25, but he was nonetheless surprised at "the high price"—in yen terms, that is. At the time, and until 1971, the exchange rate was pegged at ¥360 for a dollar, and a Japanese publisher could turn out a much-better-looking hardcover edition for an equivalent price of ¥450. The retail price of the regular edition of *The Golden Pavilion* came to seventy-eight cents.

Kawabata also told Mishima that he was "surprised" by the drawing of a geisha on the cover. Was it because the drawing was clumsy or because anything associated with Japan conjuring up the image of a geisha annoyed him? Kawabata did not say, but it was probably both: Mishima himself expressed appallment when he received Ivan Morris's English translation of *The Golden Pavilion* three years later and saw the "moldy sumi-e" illustrations—which, incidentally, have been retained in the paperback editions to this day. At the time he was serializing a diary-format account *The Nude and the Costume (Ratai to ishō)*.⁸ Kawabata went on to wonder about the worth of Japanese novels such as *Snow Country* and *Thousand Cranes* being translated "*into* the West"—a concern he had voiced to the Knopf editor and then principal promoter of Japanese literature, Harold Strauss, a year earlier.

"Mr. Seidensticker seems to be carrying forward his translation of *Snow Country*. It must be because of the good will of Mr. Kirpal and others of UNESCO HQ that such a work has been selected, but I am concerned how it may be received in America and Europe. It may not be appropriate for English translation. But once it leaves the author's hands, a work has its own destiny. In Japan," he added, "it was read by many during the war as well. It was a work that provoked homesickness especially among the soldiers who were in foreign lands." He was honest to a publisher of the country that had militarily overwhelmed his country just a decade earlier.⁹

Apprehensions among the Japanese about the Westerners' ability to understand their culture and literature were common in those days and for years to come. In 1959, Donald Keene, then in New York, indignantly reported to Mishima that all the Japanese who came to see him expressed the same misapprehensions.¹⁰ Not that there was no ground for such concern.

On November 10 the *Asahi Shinbun* carried a dispatch from New York. "Translations of Japanese novels are throwing their considerable weight around in the recent American publishing world," it said, and listed, among those already published, *The Sound of Waves*, Noma Hiroshi's *Zone of Emptiness* (*Shinkū chitai*), translated by Bernard Frechtman from French (1956), and Dazai Osamu's *The Setting Sun*, translated by Donald Keene (1956), and among those scheduled for publication *Snow Country* and Ōoka Shōhei's *Fire on the Plain (Nobi)*, translated by Ivan Morris (1957).

Of these, "*The Sound of Waves* has seen nearly ten thousand copies printed and for a time made a bestseller list, the publisher said," the dispatch reported. Mishima already knew that his book, which Knopf published in August, had made the *New York Times* bestseller list, for just one week. He also probably knew that *Time* magazine called him a "patriotic aesthete."

Japanese novels are, the correspondent went on, by no means as fashionable as "Japanese design" which has become highly popular in American architecture and interior decoration in the past several years. Still, American critics' reviews of Japanese novels of late are "more serious than you might expect" and their comments no longer strike the Japanese reader as "too odd."

This contrasts with the situation more than thirty years ago, the correspondent went on, in what most likely was his Tokyo editor's aside: In the November issue of *Chūō Kōron* Masamune Hakuchō recalls how an American commentator marveled, "So the Japanese, too, suffer," when he reviewed the English translation of Futabatei Shimei's story for the *New York Times*, "or something." Told this, Kuriyagawa Hakuson, an outstanding professor of English and thinker, could only grimace: "That's supremely insulting."[11] Futabatei was Japan's pioneer student of Russian literature.

The *Asahi* dispatch was a follow-up on the weekly *Asahi*'s earlier notice (September 18) on the "overseas" popularity of *The Sound of Waves*. But there obviously was a time lag between the dispatch and its publication or a gap in the information the correspondent had gathered.

For one thing, Kawabata had received his copy of *Snow Country* in the previous month. For another, even though the correspondent did not list it, among those already published was Osaragi Jirō's *Homecoming* (*Kikyō*), translated by Brewster Horwitz (1955), the first in a series of translations of Japanese novels put out under the aegis of Harold Strauss. In his letter to Strauss, Kawabata had expressed the hope that the publication of *Snow Country* would "not hurt the successes of *Homecoming* and *Some Prefer Nettles*." This last, Tanizaki Jun'ichirō's *Tade ku mushi*, also translated by Seidensticker, was not published until ten years later, however.

## Confessions

One arresting note in Mishima's letter to Kawabata that fall is what may be just a throwaway remark of a writer of rising fame and self-confidence: "I have cut all my ties with the translator Weatherby because he has made too much fuss over money. The next thing to do is to find a new translator."

Did Meredith Weatherby make a fuss about money? Perhaps. But if Mishima indeed cut him off as a translator, that did not affect their relationship. Mishima often went out with him, visited his famous residence in Roppongi, a large nineteenth-century farmhouse that was moved to the midst of Tokyo, and included him in a small group he invited to dinner a few weeks before his death.

It was in the garden of the Weatherby residence, indeed, that Mishima had Yatō Tamotsu take a series of photographs of him playing a naked samurai in the snow. Donald Richie watched the session from the window of what was once his room. "The photographer is bundled up with scarf and sweater, the author is naked except for a white loincloth. He also brandishes a sword and tries various poses. All these gestures illustrate some samurai extreme. Kneeling, sword in hand, he is expressing dedication. On his back in a drift, he is still valiantly defending himself...."[12]

On August 25, 1958, the day he received his first copy of *Confessions*, Mishima penned his appreciation of Weatherby as a translator in *The Nude and the Costume*. The tribute, here for public consumption, is worth quoting at length because it also speaks of the difficulties the book had encountered in finding a publisher in the United States for all the recommendations from various well-known authors.

> Came home and found the English version of *Confessions of a Mask* sent by Mr. Weatherby the translator. For the moment this is the only copy in Japan, and I must share this one copy with him until the two more sent by sea mail arrive.
>
> The jacket is tastefully done: a photograph of the face of a haniwa expanded [to fill the front cover] with *Confessions of a Mask* in black and the author's name in white against the khaki ground below. This is the first book I have out from New Directions, but the publisher having already issued two novels of Mr. Dazai Osamu, whom I hate, this is an unexpected case of "Wu and Yueh on the same boat." When I first met its editor-in-chief, Mr. [Robert] McGregor, in the United States, he asked me what I thought of Dazai. I said, "I hate him." He opened his eyes wide.

"Wu and Yueh in the same boat" is a Chinese idiom based on a statement in "The Nine Varieties of Ground" of *Sun Tzu*: "The peoples of Wu and Yueh hate each other, but if they meet a wind while making a crossing on the same boat, they will help each other as the right hand does with the left." The mention here of New Directions and Robert McGregor is chronologically a year ahead, but Mishima—at the time known to be the only Japanese writer who would welcome American or foreign writers, editors, and such with open arms when they came to Japan—had sent earlier, on June 3, some early Meiji "civilization and enlightenment" paintings to McGregor, as well as to James Merrill. In the spring of the following year, indeed, when McGregor came to Japan, he would go to welcome him at the Haneda Airport, take him to kabuki, invite him, along with Weatherby, to dinner, then on to a Rockabilly café Keyboard. McGregor would return the favor by inviting him to kabuki, then to dinner afterward at a restaurant called Hungary. When McGregor left Japan, on April 11, after a stay lasting longer than a month, Mishima saw him off at Haneda. But back to his tribute:

> Both Mr. Weatherby and I can only sigh in relief that the publication of this book has finally been realized. The original was published in July 1949. It was in the following year perhaps that Mr. Weatherby, who had fallen ill while staying in Korea, wrote me to ask for translation rights to the book, having almost finished translating it while laid up ill. At the time an Englishman had made the same request of me, but in the end I gave the rights to Mr. Weatherby.
>
> But for eight years after that it did not see the light of day. Neither Mr. Weatherby nor I wanted to have a sensational publisher put it out just for the sake of curiosity. So we asked our agent to find a first-class literary house for it, but all the publishers declined, fearful that both the house and the author would become a social scandal. This novel, though read in Japan with equanimity, was regarded as a terrifying book of moral turpitude in the United States.
>
> In time, though, the incomparable beauty of Mr. Weatherby's translation gradually attracted attention among those who read the manuscript. The first to recommend it enthusiastically was Mr. Donald Keene. He pushed it strongly to a couple of publishers, but, with no one accepting it, he carried excerpts from it under the title of "Omi" in *Modern Japanese Literature*, which he edited.[13] Some of the men-of-letters who came to Japan—Messrs. Angus Wilson, Christopher Isherwood, and James Merrill—all read the translation manuscript and regretted that it remained buried. Among them, Mr. Wilson, I heard, even said, I'll publish it in London at my own expense if no one in the United States does.
>
> Still, it continued to be shunned. Most of the rejection letters were similar: "We regret to inform you that we should not publish it, though we think it is a brilliant book." In fact, even at New Directions, its publication was thought difficult despite Mr. McGregor's enthusiasm.
>
> But in America all succor comes from a woman's hand.

The first female enthusiast of this book appeared: it was the wife of Mr. Laughlin, president of New Directions. Mr. Laughlin is one of the top steelmakers of the United States who manages this highbrow literary publishing house on the side. Mrs. Laughlin read the manuscript and, with her "crane's single call," the publication was soon decided. At the end of last year I signed the contract in New York and wrote Mr. Weatherby a letter of joy. Mr. Keene was very happy for me, too. But, though the publication has been decided, there still remains the danger of scandal.

James Laughlin, who established New Directions, in 1936, was heir to a steelmaker's fortune but never ran a steel company.

Mishima concluded: "I think it was the greatest of luck for my book to have a woman reader like Mrs. Laughlin who loved it. It is women who should wipe out prejudices to this kind of book."[14] Homosexuality was still taboo in America, even though or because Gore Vidal's *The City and the Pillar* had been published ten years earlier. Strauss, of Knopf, while gladly publishing *The Sound of Waves*, was among those who rejected *Confessions of a Mask*.

## The Rokumeikan

From November 27 to December 7 the Bungaku-za staged Mishima's four-act play, *The Rokumeikan*, a "melodrama," as he categorized it, with political intrigues and family complications set against a historical event: a government-sponsored grand ball held at the height of the initial phase of Japan's Westernization, in 1886.

Previewing it, Yamamoto Kenkichi, an erstwhile Marxist critic who went on to become a renowned explicator of haiku, said the play "realizes formal perfection in accordance with classical principles" such as had "never been written in Japan." Or, as the tanka poet and drama critic Ishii Tatsuhiko observed thirty years on, it is "a masterpiece that ought to be counted among the very best plays our generation has been able to have," notable for "its superb juxtaposition of artistry and plebeian quality."[15] The play was a great success. It won the Mainichi Drama Award while it was being staged in Tokyo, moved to Osaka and Kobe, and, from October 1957 to the fall of 1959, toured the country.

Mishima wrote *The Rokumeikan* at the Bungaku-za's request to commemorate its twentieth anniversary, with the role of Countess Asako specifically designed for the theater company's lead actress Sugimura Haruko. He admired Sugimura and had already written a one-act play for her, *The Puissance Wall* (*Daishōgai*), which had as its protagonist the mother of a college student who failed to clear the highest jumping hurdle in an equestrian contest and was killed. Mishima had a friend who met a similar fate, though we do not know if the friend's mother tried to seduce her dead son's classmate as the heroine of the play does.

The Rokumeikan, Deer Cry Hall, in the title of the play, was an actual building—a grand Italianate two-story hall the Japanese government built for an unconscionable amount of tax money in 1883 for the sole purpose of encouraging socialization between foreign dignitaries and members of the Japanese peerage. Foreign Minister Inoue Kaoru, the instigator of the enterprise, unabashedly proclaimed in his speech at the opening ceremony of the building, on November 28: "We have decided to make the Rokumeikan a place where from now on high officials and gentlemen in and outside Japan may meet and socialize, unaware that longitudes and latitudes ever existed, where they may form friendships and fellowships unlimited by national borders."

The building's name, *rokumei*, indeed, came from a poem in the Confucian *Odes*, which, in James Legge's fanciful translation, begins:

> With sounds of happiness the deer
>   Browse on the celery of the meads.
> A nobler feast is furnished here,
>   With guests renowned for noble deeds.[16]

In the notes he took to write the play, highly detailed for all his avowed "historical carelessness," Mishima quoted not just Inoue's speech in full but also a fairly lengthy article in the *Tokyo Nichinichi Shinbun* that fully described the giant ball on November 3, 1886, with sixteen hundred to seventeen hundred guests invited, that forms the climactic scene of the play.[17] As a boy, he had entertained nostalgic thoughts about the Rokumeikan and its glamorous Western atmosphere, although its glory days were long gone: the building, designed by the British architect Josiah Conder, then barely thirty years old, was "rented," in 1890, to the Peerage Society, which used it until the mid-1920s, then turned it over to commercial interests.[18] In 1940, when the building was taken apart, some newspapers ran mourning notices. That may have been one reason Mishima wrote these haiku the following year.

> Here's a stain of perfume on this old dance dress
>
> Airing clothes only the dance dress is elegant
>
> In distant thunder horse carriages gather for the ball
>
> Numerous fireflies released in the garden then the ball
>
> At the ball a souvenir from Russia a fan[19]

Not that Mishima was unaware of the obvious absurdity of the enterprise. In one program note to this play, he wrote: "The Age of the Rokumeikan, according to contemporary paintings and senryū, was truly ridiculous and *grotesque,* a kind of monkeys' theater for enlightenment," in which "bucktoothed midget Japanese men wearing ill-suited swallowtails bobbed their heads to foreigners and dwarflike women wearing dance dresses like wolves' clothes danced in the clutches of foreigners twice as tall." Here Mishima may well have been referring to the satiric cartoons the French painter Georges Bigot had a ball turning out. One report says there were perhaps not many more than three Japanese noblewomen who could dance Western-style dances, and the three were all educated in the United States.[20]

As to the ball of 1886, in which two murders, one a parricide, occur as the culmination of a political intrigue as his play has it, Mishima had this to say, deploying a paradox: "During the ball on the Emperor's Birthday, on November 3, of the nineteenth year of Meiji, nothing remotely resembling the incidents seen here happened. However, the flaw of history is that what is written is about things that happened, but not about things that did not. That's the crack through which novelists, playwrights, poets, and other frauds slip in."

*The Rokumeikan* was also Mishima's wry, amused reinterpretation of the French writer Pierre Loti's contemptuous description of the grand ball, which he, as a naval officer, had attended at the Japanese government's invitation. Partly on the basis of the description, *Un bal à Yeddo*, Akutagawa Ryūnosuke wrote, in 1919, a short story entitled "The Ball" (*Butōkai*), which presents the event as a dazzling evening in the memory of a Japanese woman who in her teens had attended the ball and danced with a courteous French officer—and who, even when she recalls the evening three decades later for a young man, does not realize that the officer who introduced himself to her as Julien Viaud was Loti. With *Madame Chrysanthème* and such, Loti by then had become well-known as a depicter of Japan, although, for some curious reason, not for his propensity to call the Japanese monkeys, apes, and crows or for his supercilious, albeit amused, attitude overall to a backward nation far from Europe.

*The Rokumeikan* had another literary layer: *Lucrèce Borgia*, Victor Hugo's play of "motherhood purifying moral deformity" that famously ends with Lucretia crying out, "Ah! You have killed me! Gennaro! I am your mother!"[21] Mishima, who admired and wanted to stage it himself, retained in this play only the mother-son relationship and homicide. In Hugo's drama, the son kills his mother—unknowingly.[22] In Mishima's, the son is killed by his father—knowingly.

In his program notes Mishima did not forget to mention the Age of the Rokumeikan as resembling the Occupation Period. There was, however, a difference: Following Japan's defeat, ladies of the former nobility "appeared to debase themselves partly because of the fall of the [peerage] class"—abolished by the Occupation. In contrast, the Japanese in the earlier times, "even as they offered flattery to foreigners," were "equipped both with the energy of a newly rising nation and the old feudal dignity."[23] That same "dignity" was, one might add, one thing Mishima maintained throughout his life.

Mishima played the walk-on role of the carpenter during the Tokyo production and wrote an essay about it and another on recent changes in acting. He began the latter, "A Small Scar on a Left Kneecap," this way: "During a rehearsal of *The Rokumeikan*, a question came up in the scene where Asako, played by Miss Sugimura Haruko, while talking to Hisao, the son whom she hadn't seen for twenty years, reveals their mother-son relationship by saying, 'I know . . . that you have a small, thin scar on your left kneecap. . . . One summer afternoon, after you fell asleep, I began to doze despite myself. But then you woke, crawled away, and stabbed your knee on a pair of scissors.'"

In this scene, Nakatani Noboru, playing Hisao, at first just listened intently to Asako's words, "without even turning his eyes toward his knee, let alone touching it with his hand." That was because, Mishima wrote, it was the mode of Shingeki acting. Nakamura Nobuo, watching this, offered: "The previous generation Ganjirō"—probably the kabuki actor Nakamura Ganjirō I—"would have made a big deal of this." Nakamura then showed what he meant: "Looking startled, he stiffened his body, put his hand on his knee, and exaggeratedly let it slide until it touched the floor."

The upshot was the consensus: Nakatani, playing Hisao, "did not have to go as far as putting his hand to the knee, but he could at least glance at it. Since then he has done so," Mishima added, "when absorbed in his role, even putting his hand on the knee without really meaning to."[24]

In the course of composing the play, Mishima also wrote, during the summer, a politico-economic tract, "Will the Tortoise Catch Up with the Hare?—Problems of the So-called Underdeveloped Countries." He considered "the dangerous distortions of our rapid modernization"[25] against Japan's recent history, with his focus on Mao-led Communist China and Nehru-led India that were on the rise.

## *"An Unpleasant Masterpiece"*

In the fall Mishima, who, along with Itō Sei and Takeda Taijun, had become a judge for an annual new writers contest that *Chūō Kōron* set up, recommended the novella *On the Narayama Song* (*Narayama-bushi kō*) by Fukazawa Shichirō for top prize. A stark retelling of a "poetic tale" in the tenth-century collection *Tales from Yamato* (*Yamato monogatari*), it describes, in a simple, realistic setting of a poor mountain village, and with artless language, the legendary practice of abandoning old people in remote places to save food. Though he had recommended it, Mishima found it to be "a *repellent* novel, one reading of which will give you gooseflesh," he wrote Kawabata, so much so that he was even afraid of touching the *Chūō Kōron* issue that carried it.[26] A dozen years later, in the last series of essays Mishima wrote, titled *What Is a Novel?*, for the magazine *Nami*, he remembered the time he read the novella as "the only time he felt a chill while reading a fresh manuscript."

> It was an unpleasant masterpiece. It was an unpleasant masterpiece which hides within it something that makes us feel as though our fundamental desire for beauty and order were mocked, a kind of consensus and agreement which we call "humanity" trampled upon, the sense of our intestines that normally lie unexposed to the outside air suddenly made to feel exposed to the air, the sublime and the trivial deliberately messed up, "tragedy" disdained, both the rational and the emotional rendered meaningless—makes us feel, after reading it, that there is nothing in this world that we can rely upon. My terror at Mr. Fukazawa's writings even to this day originates in the impression I had the first time I read *On the Narayama Song*.[27]

Early in the following year, on February 5, Mishima attended the publication party for the novella held well past midnight at Nichigeki Music Hall. Fukazawa played the guitar, guitar-strumming wanderer as he was, and there was a striptease show. Mishima's companions included not just Itō and Takeda but also Tanizaki Jun'ichirō and Masamune Hakuchō. A year on, the novella was turned into a film, with Kinoshita Keisuke directing.

On December 1, Mishima's dance drama *Orphée*, based on Jean Cocteau's film, was staged, Mishima directing. It featured an Edo courtesan dancing on a Parisian street.

In the same month another of Mishima's novels, *The Spring That Lasted Too Long (Nagasugita haru)*, which he serialized in a ladies' monthly at the same time as *The Golden Pavilion* but in twelve-installments, came out and it sold 150,000 copies in no time. In contrast to *The Golden Pavilion*, it was a lighthearted romantic comedy, written with the obvious expectations that it would be turned into a movie: A young couple become engaged, grow frustrated because of their inability to "do it" before the wedding, get entangled in embarrassing situations as a result, but manage to remain "chaste" to each other until their marriage. There are unlikely rescues by friends, narrow escapes, and an unconvincing denouement. Sure enough, it was turned into a film at once and shown in May of the following year.

On New Year's Day 1957 Mishima skipped his annual courtesy call to Kawabata, in Kamakura. Instead, he had an assignation with Toyoda Sadako at the Imperial Hotel, at three o'clock in the afternoon. (He went to see Kawabata the following day.) On January 29, he received the Yomiuri Literary Prize for *The Golden Pavilion*. In March, the April issue of *Gunzō* started to serialize his next novel, *Virtue Falters (Bitoku no yoromeki)*, ending it in the June issue. Mishima, who completed the three-installment novel as early as April 15, wrote it with focus and ease. It was his attempt to make his own version of Radiguet's *The Devil in the Flesh*, even though it is not narrated in the first person and its viewpoint is a woman's. It tells of a respectable married young woman's plunge into a yearlong affair with a bachelor the same age whom she once kissed, before the marriage, in a summer resort.

"I wonder about abruptly beginning with an immodest topic, but Mrs. Kurakoshi, though still twenty-eight years old, was truly blessed with the heavenly gift of sensuality," Mishima opens the story, in a manner that echoes, however obliquely, the opening of *The Devil in the Flesh*: "I am sure to incur a good deal of reproach. But what am I to do?" Mrs. Kurakoshi, or Setsuko, "grew up with very strict manners, in a house of aristocratic lineage." The description of Setsuko's family, the Fujiis, is reminiscent of passages in *Confessions* and the short story *Preparations for the Night*.

> ... members of the Fujii family were a graceful tribe without any sense of witticism. In a family where the head of the household, being very busy, is often absent and where women dominate, titters of laughter may constantly ripple, but witticism tends to grow thinner and thinner. This is all the more true with a graceful household. Setsuko, used to hypocrisy since childhood, would now be unable even to imagine that anything was wrong with it, but that was none of her fault.

For the reader who wants to see in the novel Mishima's backhanded revenge on Mitani Kuniko, what gives the game away may be the just one kiss Setsuko had with a man other than her husband before she was married. "The kiss, though you couldn't necessarily say it was playful, was of a very shabby sort, and all Setsuko remembered was the faint brush of the dry lips of a flustered, agitated man." Following marriage, her husband taught her "multifaceted" ways of kissing, though his sexual interest in her did not take long to wane. The reader can almost expect what comes next: "That the young man's kiss had happened only once, that it lasted just for a second, and that it was clumsy besides, increased its importance all the more in Setsuko's memory."

That may be what someone who botched any such first encounter would want to happen in the mind of the partner who has since gone out of reach and is unlikely to give him a second chance. But Mishima wasn't just happy to oblige his reader in that fantasy. Stoked by the memories of the kiss, Setsuko seeks to have an affair with the same man, succeeds, and, rather than be disappointed as often happens with such a "reunion," derives as much pleasure from the adventure as her partner does.

Further, when she realizes the affair is going nowhere, she quietly withdraws, without making any fuss that could be embarrassing, even though the extramarital affair forces her to have three abortions, the last almost killing her. She discovers from her father, who is part of the uppermost crust of social respectability, that the revelation of her affair would mean ruination for him. (The father is told nothing; the matter is discussed in reference to an unfortunate acquaintance's action.) She couldn't possibly allow that to happen. In short, she is an ideal partner for an affair. The novel is known to have been based partly on an affair Mishima actually had, though the amour did not last long.

The novel became a runaway bestseller upon publication in book form. And, like "the spring that lasted too long," the expression "virtue falters" and two ramifications thereof—*yoromeku*, "to commit adultery," and *yoromeki fujin*, "adulterous lady"—became popular words. When told of this, and that was soon after he returned from his second overseas trip, Mishima said he simply used someone's Japanese translation of the title of the Marquis de Sade's novel, *Les infortunes de la vertu*, adding that, as he did not know French, the translation may have been of *Justine ou les malheurs de la vertu*.[28]

## *Mishima the Playwright*

While writing these three novels—very different from one another—Mishima remained engaged in a range of activities. It was a period of his precipitously rising fame, but he perhaps attracted the greatest attention, if that was possible, in the genre of drama.

Other than the ones mentioned so far, he published *Collection of Modern Nō Plays* (*Kindai nōgaku shū*) in April 1956. In the fall he took on the task of preparing "a rhetorical rewrite" of Racine's *Britannicus* for the Bungaku-za. (In the previous year he had done a kabuki adaptation of the same playwright's *Phèdre*, which the Kabuki-za duly produced, with him directing.) When the Bungaku-za wanted to produce the play and its "supreme advisor," Iwata Toyo'o, demurred, saying the existing version was wanting, the troupe turned to Mishima, who was by then closely affiliated with them. So the translator Andō Shiny'a was lined up to prepare a "faithful word-for-word rendition"—in truth, a "word-for-word" translation from French into Japanese would make little sense—of the Racine drama so Mishima might touch it up rhetorically.

Still, when the work was done Mishima unstintingly praised the existing translation, by Naitō Arau, as "incomparably accurate" and "noble, elegant, and sensuous," although the translation was "deliberately not for stage use." As he mightily struggled with Andō's translation for rhetorical improvement, he would occasionally dip into Naitō's, only to find his Japanese to be "far superior" to his own and better as words to be enunciated on stage, so he stole from it "shamelessly and without permission."[29] When the play was published in book form, he gave four examples to show what he had done, each with the original, Andō's translation, his rhetorically changed version, and a comment, except for the last example, which was the last line of the play, where he added Naitō's translation to illustrate there was little to improve upon as it had the kind of dignity that was crucial to the conclusion of the play.[30]

*Britannicus* was staged at Daiichi Seimei Hall from March 5 to 23, with Yashiro Seiichi directing, Akutagawa Hiroshi playing Néron and Kishida Kyōko, Junie. On the last day Mishima appeared onstage among the armored guards. Then the play moved to Osaka, Kyoto, Kobe, Nagoya, and Yokohama.

April saw the Kabuki-za produce, for the second time, *Yuya*, Mishima's nagauta—a form of chanted narrative accompanied by kabuki dance—for nearly the entire month. From the 16th to the 25th, the Bungaku-za produced "a Mishima special," staging *The Puissance Wall* and the modern nō play *The Damask Drum*.

From the 5th to the 25th of May, the Shinpa produced *The Golden*

*Pavilion* at the theater Shinbashi Enbujō. Murayama Tomoyoshi, who adapted the novel for stage and directed it, was a versatile writer-artist. In 1921 he dropped out of the Imperial University of Tokyo and went to Germany where, fascinated by Constructivism, he once exhibited his artworks with the likes of Picasso and Braque. After his return to Japan he became a force in the modernist-proletarian movement, organizing an avant-garde art society MAVO and writing, directing, and designing plays. Though he recanted in the 1930s, he remained leftist. Beginning in 1960 he would write a famous series on ninja for the Communist daily *Akahata*, depicting them as accomplished but anonymous technicians fated to be ground down by larger forces. His prewar illustrations for children's stories, along with his calendar paintings, have continued to be reissued.

However, Mishima, who had doubts about dramatizing *The Golden Pavilion*, was lukewarm to Murayama's version of his novel. Although he said he was impressed that Murayama managed to tell the story meticulously, he quoted a statement of the German novelist and playwright Friedrich von Spielhagen to summarize his thoughts on the matter: "A roman cannot be rewritten into a drama but the material of a novella almost simultaneously becomes the material of a drama." *The Golden Pavilion*, of course, is a "roman" or a full-length novel, not a novella.[31]

Mishima took Toyoda Sadako to see the play, on May 15. That would become the last time the two saw each other.

Late that month the film *The Spring That Lasted Too Long* was released. On June 20 and 21 the Haiyū-za staged another of Mishima's modern nō plays, *Hanjo*. Partly exasperated that no theater troupe offered to stage it after it was published in the January 1955 issue of *Shinchō*, Mishima had had it staged two months earlier, on April 12, on the pretext of the appearance of Keene's English translation and the Knopf editor Harold Strauss' visit to Japan. He did so with three English people on hand, Helen McAlpine and Ivan Morris among them. He directed the play himself. In creating the new protagonist, Hanako, he had explained he had in mind "women in love" such as the Portuguese nun Marianna Alcoforado in Rilke's *Die Aufzeichnungen des Malte Laurids Brigge* or the Sappho as interpreted by him, who "at the height of her action ... mourned not for any man who had left her embrace empty, but for the one, no longer possible, who had grown equal to her love."[32]

On July 9 Mishima left for the United States. The second overseas trip would turn out to be much longer than he had planned. This time he went, he thought, as a well-known man. After all, he went to the United States at the invitation of Knopf to mark the publication of Keene's *Five Modern Nō Plays*. But America was different from Japan in the way it treated such people, and he would encounter the kind of difficulties he wouldn't have imagined as a celebrity writer in top form in his homeland.

On January 1958, in his first public appearance following his return from the trip, he stood on stage after the curtain of the last Tokyo production of *The Rokumeikan*. Among the remarks he made was that in New York he realized he was "a *spoiled child*"—he used English—of Japanese journalism. In New York he had once asked Keene what he should do to become famous. Keene drily replied, "No one would turn to look even if Hemingway and Faulkner walked arm in arm in Times Square." That was, in fact, exactly what he had observed. One day he saw Henry Fonda in FAO Schwarz. Fonda was soon to appear in a Broadway show, but none of the customers paid attention to him, overtly or covertly.[33]

CHAPTER THIRTEEN

# Overseas Again

*The producer Keith is the leader of a boy gang, . . . a fine Italian operetta troupe.*
    —Mishima on the group that tried to stage his play in New York

It was in July 1956, a year before Mishima left for the United States for the second time, that the Japanese government's annual "white paper" on the economy, titled *The Growth and Modernization of the Japanese Economy*, proclaimed: "We are no longer in the postwar era." Actually, the Economic Planning Agency had borrowed the expression from the title of the English professor-turned-social commentator Nakano Yoshio's essay that appeared in *Bungei Shunjū* earlier that year. In it Nakano had argued that it was about time the Japanese stopped being weighed down by the nation's defeat or being "simply emotional" and started, instead, looking forward to the future.

The economic agency meant that Japan had finally recovered from war devastations. This was welcome news to the Japanese who were going through an unrelieved series of domestic and international turmoil, political and economic. The statement, along with its variations, became a catchword of the day, although the economy was still feeble.

In industrial output, Japan had regained the 1935 level by 1950, but that was because, even as the nation's ability to produce was cut by half during 1945 as a result of intense bombing in the last phase of the war, its machinery and equipment was left remarkably untouched. What the ten-month bombing destroyed was much of the social stock—public structures such as railroads and waterworks, buildings, and houses—so much so that it took another five years for the country to regain the level of overall national wealth it had had in the mid-1930s, the standard "prewar" reference point. In other words, when the government announced the end of "the postwar era," the Japanese were finally living as they had two decades earlier—actually, still at a lower level when increases in population were taken into account.[1]

Having announced that the recovery period was over, the report spoke of the future, albeit cautiously; there remained a number of uncertainties. "To prevent the economy from slowing down," it said, Japan had to "reform its economic structure lest it fail to get onto the crest of global technological innovations," automation and nuclear power among them.

The mass media was catching on, talking about the coming age of "consumption revolution" to be led by "household electrification." The weekly *Asahi* revealed the true state of affairs when it wisecracked about the new trend by dividing Japanese households into "seven classes" by the home appliances owned (August 21, 1955): "Everyone probably has electric lamps. So let's say the households that have only lamps are seventh class. The ones that add a radio and an iron to them are sixth. An electric heater and a toaster make them fifth. An electric mixer, an electric fan, and a phone make them fourth. An electric washer makes them third. A refrigerator makes them second. A television and a vacuum cleaner make them first class."[2]

One telling photograph from about that time shows Mishima in a leather jacket, fashionable at the time among punks and hoods, sticking his head into what was then an oversize refrigerator for the Japanese household; the one, as noted, Yuasa Atsuko had acquired for him through her Nisei husband. He apparently thought it noteworthy enough to be photographed with it. It was still during a period when Mishima could simply assert, by citing Arnold Toynbee, that "a Zen temple with an electric washing machine is no longer a Zen temple."[3]

Internationally, Japan was beginning to compete, but mainly in light industries. In 1957, the year Mishima left for the United States, it led the world in shipbuilding, but its top exports were products such as staples and silk. The international balance of payments had turned so negative that Kishi Nobusuke, who became Prime Minister in February, had to term its reduction a national policy, just before leaving Japan to visit the United States, in June, and the Ministry of International Trade and Industry had to restrict the amount of money allocated for imports.

## *American Wealth*

The wonder is that Mishima, unlike most Japanese intellectuals who visited and stayed in America during that period—and, in fact, until some years later—was not cowed or discomfited by the great wealth of the country he saw or that, if he was, he did not show it. If anything, he made clear that the way people in American high society lived perfectly suited his taste, as when he was invited to Alfred A. Knopf, Sr.'s house in Purchase, New York, and, after cocktails, to dinner at the Century Country Club nearby.[4]

Mishima did marvel at the stark wealth discrepancy between Japan and America. On his earlier trip overseas he stayed only for about a month in the United States and appears to have had just one opportunity to spend some time with a wealthy American. During his second trip he was in New York for several months and came to know some well-to-do people and heard stories about the rich.

The one wealthy man he had met five year earlier was Julius Fleischmann—an heir of the Fleischmann Company that had started out as a yeast maker and grown into an empire. Julius, himself president of a whiskey brewery, was a supporter of the New York Public Library, Metropolitan Opera, the Ballet Russe de Monte Carlo, among other things, and a member of the American Committee for Cultural Freedom. He had literary aspirations and wrote plays. Probably at the committee's request, he invited Mishima to his "villa" in Naples, Florida, which he had been helping to establish as a resort town since the end of the Second World War.[5] The extent of the man's wealth on the bay was astonishing.

"On a moonlit night we took a walk along the endless beach of white sand that was his own personal property, during the day he took me to the botanical garden that was his personal property," Mishima recalled a dozen years later. Fleischmann took him to the yacht harbor that was also his personal property. One of his three boats could easily accommodate ten guests. It was on that boat the host took the young

Japanese offshore fishing one day. It had a skipper and an assistant. Mishima was the only guest. When the boat reached the fishing ground, it was naturally the biggest of all the boats that congregated there.

"One of his maids proudly showed me her wardrobe. The number of her clothes was such that it could easily match that of an upper-class lady's." Constantly astonished, Mishima once asked Fleischmann a "dumb question." "Sir, how many cars to do you have?" The answer he got was: "Well, son, I've never counted them and I don't know."[6]

That is a story Mishima tells in "The Rich in New York," one of the many essays he produced out of his second trip. He begins by observing: "I'm aware that the stories you hear about the rich in America are different by several orders of magnitude, but before you recover from one astonishing story, you hear another, which is far more astonishing, and it goes on and on like that."

One evening in December he was invited to Radio City Music Hall for a preview of a movie and was introduced to Mr. and Mrs. John D. Rockefeller, III. At the time the Rockefellers were at the apex of the pyramid of rich Americans. When they came out, it was unexpectedly pouring. At once Mishima conjured up a scene, right out of a film, of "a Rolls-Royce pulling up and a chauffer in uniform scrambling out to hold an umbrella over them and take them in." Instead, he saw the wealthy couple stand about lost, like everyone else, until someone caught a taxi for them. He later learned that the Rockefellers were popular because of that kind of "common touch."

Another time a friend of his pointed out for him a "personal taxi." The story was that the wife of a wealthy man who lived in a big house in the suburbs loved theater but was frustrated because she couldn't get a taxi as soon as she arrived at Grand Central. So she had her husband buy a Mercedes-Benz—"one of the most expensive cars," Mishima noted—and arranged to have it arrive at the station precisely when she got off the train. So the car became famous as "a taxi no one could use," he was told.

Visiting New York three years later, Mishima would find not just that this trick was still in force but also ride in one himself. The wealthy businessman husband of the sponsor of his play had his Mercedes-Benz painted yellow with the taxi fare of "25 cents & above" indicated outside, complete with a dedicated driver, and used it to run about town. It was explained to Mishima that the man did this because parking rules were much more lenient for taxis.[7] Apparently the use of limousines, as later became common, was unknown then.

"Americans love legends about the rich, and in time even true stories turn into snappy jokes. And even those jokes have a vastly different effect if they have real wealthy people in them," Mishima wrote, and went on to tell the one about Mrs. Vanderbilt ordering more ice cubes for her drink on the sinking *Titanic*. Once he was invited to a penthouse. While on the terrace, the host told him in the midst of a glorious nightscape of skyscrapers, "This fifty-story building where we live is mine. So is that sixty-story building rising right there." Mishima could only sigh: "I wish I could say something like that to my guest once in my lifetime even if I knew it was a lie."[8]

Apart from that, Mishima's celebrity status in Japan by then was such and traveling overseas still so limited that he was asked to leave a few parting words in the Bungaku-za's program. He will spend the first three days in Waikiki to "heal my soul fatigued by the troupe's torment," before going on to San Francisco, Los Angeles, then on to Detroit where he will give a speech at the University of Michigan, he wrote, adding, "It's a speech in English, mind you, gentlemen." Referring to his *Britannicus* work, he continued: "Forced as I was to work on something called 'rhetoric,' in Japan I've been unable to demonstrate fully the linguistic ability I'm equipped with, but now, finally, I will reveal my true worth. Make sure to observe the spirit of a Japanese male!"

The speech, "The Present State of Japan's Literary Establishment and its Relationship to Western Literatures," must have impressed his American audience—if his English were as good as advertised and if he managed to say most, if not all, of what he said in the Japanese version published in the September issue of *Shinchō*. Although the English version does not seem to remain nor does the University of Michigan have any record of the speech—one wonders who came to hear him in the midst of a summer recess—the Japanese version shows how well read he was in the works of his Japanese contemporaries and how solid his grasp was of the influences of Chinese, German, French, Russian, and American literatures on modern Japanese novelists and poets.[9] "Influences in Modern Japanese Literature," the English speech he gave at Tokyo Women's Club early the next year, may have been a simplified, recast version of the Michigan speech or at least the Japanese version thereof.[10]

"I will then go to New York and see *My Fair Lady*, the July 26 ticket for which I have already reserved," he wrote, adding, "I plan to come back around November."[11]

In inviting Mishima, Harold Strauss, of Knopf, or perhaps Alfred A. Knopf himself, apparently arranged for him meetings with some of the notable writers. That may have been how he met Christopher Isherwood, in Los Angeles. Isherwood took him to a 20th Century Fox studio, where a submarine movie was being filmed. Water was hosed onto the conning tower rising out of a pool and an actor, sticking his face out of it, was saying something. Mishima, who had often seen filmmaking, was not impressed. It was a hot midsummer day, and the scene was refreshing, but that was about all.

Isherwood at the time was working on a film script of *Jean-Christophe*[12]—or so Mishima understood. In fact, Isherwood was hoping to do "a possible rewrite" on his own film adaptation of Romain Rolland's novel for the producer Jerry Wald—a point worth noting if only because one of the things that would impress Mishima during his New York stay was the number of rewrites film and stage scripts casually go through in America.

On July 16, Isherwood wrote in his diary: "Nice Yukio Mishima, whom I met yesterday and took out to see John van Druten. But oh, the hopelessness of communication! Here's this guy, with all of his qualities, his ear for words, etc.—and nothing of it came across." Van Druten had made a play out of *Sally Bowles*, one of Isherwood's Berlin stories, calling it *I Am a Camera*, which was a great Broadway success.[13] The play would later become *Cabaret*.

"The well-to-do young novelist James Merrill," who invited him to stay in his house in Stonington, Connecticut—"an old seaside town with only nineteenth-century buildings"—was probably another writer Strauss arranged for Mishima to meet. This was on August 16, sometime after he arrived in New York. The following day Merrill's friend, "a very wealthy middle-aged man who has done absolutely nothing since he was born," took the two out yachting. Merrill and Mishima discussed the balance between description and conversation in a novel. Merrill quoted a European critic's metaphor, which Mishima thought beautiful. It was to the effect that a conversation in a novel should be like a splash that flies out of a wave when after slowly rising it topples. If Mishima indeed understood that much of what Merrill said, that was because, as is often the case when learning a foreign language, Mishima's hearing was far better than his ability to speak.

Back at Merrill's house around four, both took a nap on the rooftop. Then there was a cocktail party. It was an informal affair in a resort town. Merrill the host was barefoot. A "hysterical duchess" took apart a Japanese wooden egg-shaped mosaic and neither she nor anyone else could put it back together, turning everyone into a nervous wreck. A duchess? Perhaps she was one. Perhaps it was a nickname.[14] In any case, this would become a scene in Mishima's next novel, *Kyōko's House*.

## *Mishima's Play in New York*

During August the idea of staging some of his modern nō plays in New York came up and became definite. The Knopf edition of the Keene translations included a notice asking anyone interested in producing the plays to get in touch with the translator. From among the several who showed interest, Mishima selected two, Keith Botsford and Charles "Chiz" Schultz, both young, as producers. Their idea was to link two of the five plays, *The Lady Aoi* (*Aoi-no-ue*) and *Sotoba Komachi* (the original title retained in English), with a kyōgen in between, and produce them as one. Mishima agreed, told them the outlines of four kyōgen, and the three chose *Hanago*, a comic followup on *Hanjo*. He then asked Keene, who had left for Japan shortly after Mishima arrived in New York, to translate it. The contract said that the play would open in October. He was to receive an advance of sixty dollars ("a cute income!"), which he would split with Keene.[15] With that, on August 28, Mishima left for Puerto Rico.

This may be a good place to consider what Mishima did or tried to do in recasting the themes of classical nō plays in modern settings and thought. As Keene pointed out in the introduction to his translations, the practice is common—his examples are Cocteau's *Infernal Machine*, O'Neil's *Mourning Becomes Electra*, and Brecht's *Threepenny Opera*—and it may not be "necessary to be acquainted with the original play in order to appreciate the new one." Still, "a knowledge of the earlier work adds a dimension and permits us to measure the workings of a modern intelligence against a familiar background."[16] Here let us look at Mishima's 1951 play *The Damask Drum* (*Aya no tsuzumi*), if only because a Japanese classical scholar tried to analyze what Mishima was trying to do with it.

The original *Aya no tsuzumi*, attributed to Zeami Motokiyo (ca. 1364–1443), like all nō plays, is short and simple.[17] It tells of an old garden sweeper in a makeshift imperial palace who has a glimpse of a court lady and falls in love with her. The lady, hearing of this, avers, "Love knows no distinction between high and low," and tells him to strike a drum she has hung on a katsura tree by a pond, saying that if he strikes it and she hears the sound, she will give him another glimpse of herself. Overjoyed, the old man strikes the drum and continues to do so, but there is no sound. He doesn't know that the drum is made of twilled fabric. Driven to despair, he throws himself into the pond and kills himself.

The court lady, told of what happened to the old gardener, begins to be troubled by the lapping sound of waves in the pond that sounds like a drum. Wasn't the drum she gave the old man supposed to make any sound? Then the old man appears as a vengeful ghost and forces her to beat the drum on the katsura tree. Fatigued and weakened, she throws herself into the pond. Having seen this, the old man turns into "an evil snake" and disappears into "the abyss of love."

Mishima's play also consists of two distinct scenes but is fairly long (most plays have to be long in comparison with nō plays, although this does not apply to the time required for nō staging), and it has more characters. The story, set in a modern world, unfolds in two offices on the third floors of two buildings facing each other across a street. One, belonging to a none-too-fashionable lawyer, is old, "a room of good intent," "a room of truthfulness," while the other, belonging to a *haute couture* dressmaker is "a room of evil design," "a room of falsity." The two offices are set to the right and left on the same stage.

The protagonist is an old janitor who works in the old office. The office has just closed for the day. The conversation between the janitor, named Iwakichi, and a young spunky secretary, named Kayoko, reveals that he saw three months ago a beautiful woman in the dressmaker's room across the street—"in a golden fur coat," whose hair is "as dark as the night sky"—and has since been in love with her. Furthermore, he's been writing her a letter a day, with Kayoko as deliverer. Today's is the hundredth.

In the dressmaker's office, which opens for business just about the time the law office closes, appears a group of three: two young men, Toyama and Kaneko, and a teacher of Japanese dance, Fujima. Toyama is obviously a lover of the beautiful woman in question, for now identified as "the lady." Kayoko delivers Iwakichi's letter for the day. Kaneko accepts it. Soon the dressmaker, "Madame," joins the group and reveals that she has been entrusted with every one of Iwakichi's letters to "the lady," one of her best customers, but has never shown any of them to her, using them instead to clean the comb for her five "wirehaired fox terriers."

When "the lady," Hanako, shows up, Kaneko hands her Iwakichi's letter. When she opens and reads it, Toyama and Kaneko read aloud snatches from it and make fun of Iwakichi. Then Fujima thinks up a trick to play on him: throw a drum, one of his stage props, into Iwakichi's room with a note telling him to beat it; if Hanako hears the sound through the city noise, she will fulfill his dream of kissing her once.

Hanako—who remains silent throughout the first half of the play—gives a nod to the ruse. They open the window, call out to Iwakichi across the street, and the old man, who has been lurking in his darkened office in the hopes of having a glimpse of Hanako, opens his window and receives the thrown drum. Reading the note, he hangs the drum on the potted katsura tree in his office and beats it but it doesn't make any sound. Quickly finding out that the drum, made of cloth, is not meant to make any sound, he despairs and throws himself out of the window to his death. The group in the dressmaker's office, chatting and laughing among themselves, is unaware of what has happened, until a store clerk bursts in to tell them the news of Iwakichi's death.

The second part of the play consists of a conversation between Hanako and the Ghost of Iwakichi. It is midnight. Hanako comes in the dressmaker's office with the keys she snitched from the Madame. Having broken away from a dinner party midway, she is in a short coat over an evening dress. As she begins to talk in a low voice, the Ghost of Iwakichi emerges from the window out of which he threw himself and gradually moves toward the dressmaker's office. The window opens on its own. Hanako admits she has come drawn by him but tells him that death is "not proof enough of true love." When he tells her he has no proof to show her, she responds: "Proofs are all over me. Women are filled with proofs of love. Filled with proofs of the kind that, once you pull them out, cease to be love." The Ghost declares he will make "the drum of twilled woolen fabric" sound to demonstrate he's still in love with her. She says, "Please do."

The Ghost beats the drum and, surprise! it makes a sound "merrily." Exulting, he says, "It's made a sound! It has! You've heard it, the sound of the drum, haven't you?" But Hanako says, "with a shrewd smile," that she has not. Bewildered, he beats and beats, but she says she doesn't hear anything. Desperate, he decides to beat the drum as many times as the number of letters he wrote: one hundred. As the number grows, he grows weaker, even as she insists she can't hear anything. When he finishes one hundred times, he, the Ghost, fades away. Toyama bursts in and, grabbing and shaking Hanako, tells her everyone has been worried about her. The play ends as Hanako *dreamily* says, "I would have heard it, if only he had beaten it one more time."

Konishi Jin'ichi, who would go on to write a massive history of Japanese literature competitively with Keene—his in five volumes, Keene's in four—contemplated *The Damask Drum* as a means of understanding the Mishima literature as a whole. The production he saw was the second one, in 1955, which incorporated obvious nō elements: nō masks, special vocalization, the way of walking called *suriashi*, "foot sliding," and the fact that Hanako was played by the nō actor Kanze Shizuo, then twenty-four years old and later a living national treasure. But every character was dressed in modern dress—with Kanze in a bordeaux evening dress, shoulders bared. It had a string quartet in place of the traditional flute and drum accompaniment.

After explaining the western critical terms "theme," "motif," and "message," Konishi concluded that whereas Zeami and Mishima pursue the same "motif" in their plays, they are completely different in "theme" and "message." In sum, Mishima's references to classical nō—and they are not limited to his "modern nō plays" but some of the novels as well—are merely "casual hoops" or else "invisible hoops" around his works, so that it is good if you notice them, but doesn't do much harm if you don't. It all depends on how deeply you wish to understand his "themes."[18]

## *Caribbean Tour*

The tour of the Caribbean Islands, Mexico, and the American Southwest and South was part of his original plan, but the prospect of staging his own play in New York wasn't, and it gave him something to look forward to, although, writing about it later, he also professed that he didn't like the idea of having work to do while traveling.

In Puerto Rico after a flight of six hours, Mishima found the poverty "extreme" that nonetheless came with "something noble" about it. The island was also, he gathered, "the supplier of raw material for atrocious crimes in New York." On August 29 he visited the Castle of San Felipe del Morro with Alfred Knopf's introduction. The following day he was in Ciudad Trujillo, Santo Domingo, so renamed, in 1936, after "the dictator"—a word he was forewarned not to use. It was "a beautiful quiet town in the Dominican Republic." One evening he saw the bemedaled general himself: he was looking out to the sea with several of his aides and several highly polished cars and motorcycles parked nearby. It was part of his daily walk, Mishima was told. Four years after Mishima's visit, Santo Domingo would regain its old name as Trujillo was assassinated.

In Port-au-Prince, Haiti, where he arrived on Monday, September 2, he had a definite purpose: to see the "real" voodoo. But the real thing was not scheduled for the time being, he learned from the rich and voodoo-follower Frenchwoman to whom he brought a letter of introduction from New York. He saw a tourist version instead. It did not completely disappoint him and he wrote a detailed account of the rite. Poverty and the flies swarming on every bit of food—fruits and meats sold in the open market—impressed him. Eight years later he would recreate the image in his afterword to a book of poems by the avowedly homosexual poet Takahashi Mutsuo, *Sleeping Sinning Falling (Nemuri to okashi to rakka to)*: "the most fertile hilltop market enveloped in coal-black flies."[19]

Still, because of the food or something else, there he came down with horrible diarrhea. Three weeks later, in New Orleans, he read about Duvalier's *coup d'état* and declaration of martial law, the beginning of Papa Doc's infamous reign. In Havana, "always packed with American tourists," he heard about time bombs set up and exploded in the midst of "the pleasure city," even in what was claimed to be the world's largest nightclub, the Tropicana. Mishima was told these were the doings of antigovernment forces. "Still," he wrote, "the sky above Havana was infinitely blue and the dark eyes of Cubans seemed alive only in pursuit of sensuality." Less than a year after he wrote these words, Fidel Castro entered Havana.

On September 13, he was in Uxmal, Yucatán, where he came down with a high fever. The diarrhea in Port-au-Prince and the fever in Uxmal would make him associate the tropics with death for the rest of his life, though in the case of Uxmal and Chichén-Itzá, the Mayan death cult and the "death-oppressive" green of the landscape played a considerable part in it. Mishima, at any rate, was reeling as he took a taxi to Mérida to fly to his next stop, Mexico City, where he arrived on September 15, the eve of Independence Day. The next morning he opened the window of his hotel room and was enchanted to see a sea of brilliant colors: people out in parade dresses and costumes. "Here," Mishima noted, "red is a men's color as it was during Japan's Age of Warring States."

From Mexico City he flew to the border town facing El Paso, Ciudad Juárez. "El Paso," Mishima wrote, "is a town located in that part of the state of Texas where it wedges into the state of New Mexico. . . . It looks as if Texas has managed to push aside New Mexico, barely, to stick its lips out to kiss Mexico." He spent some time in the bright afternoon sun in Ciudad Juárez to say farewell to "the fascinating country possessing vast areas still not endowed with the benefits of culture, a country mixed with bullfights, monstrous Mayan ruins, sombreros, music, dance, ferocious tequila, poetry and cruelty."

Mishima bought the *New York Times* while traveling, wherever he could get it, and looked for a notice on the staging of his play in vain. In Santa Fe (as in Mexico, the *Times* came a week late), he finally bought the Sunday edition—"shockingly thick, as heavy as a telephone directory, of which I once joked, 'I can't do bodybuilding while traveling in America so I lift the Sunday edition of the *New York Times* in place of a barbell'"—and read the theater section from one corner to the other but again found nothing. He began to feel uneasy about the whole venture, and the unease increased as he headed back toward New York. And some of the cities he went through may not have been entirely encouraging.

Natchez, Mississippi, to which he may have had to fly because the city had decided much earlier to forego the railroad on the ground that it would be too noisy for its quietude, felt hushed by eight-thirty in the evening, if not altogether dead, and was faintly menacing, like "a large uninhabited insect-cage." Though Mishima did not note it, not far from there, in Little Rock, the racial turmoil that started earlier that month was escalating. He probably learned the word "antebellum" in relation to Natchez; he noted that "prewar" meant "before the Civil War" in the old city, which was reputed to have the largest number of "antebellum" houses intact.

New Orleans, especially the Vieux Carré, was "an enfeebled, emaciated, barely breathing, piteous remnant of Europe," even though he liked it as he had the deteriorating cities built by the Europeans in the Caribbean Islands and Mexico.

---

In early October he arrived back in New York, at midnight. He phoned Keene in the morning and the first thing he did was to ask about the play. "Well, I know nothing about it. I think there's been no progress," Keene said in Japanese. The answer "considerably angered me," Mishima wrote. Why this turn of events angered him is easy to guess. In Japan once a decision is made to produce a play, the date will be set, and the play will be staged according to schedule—especially if it is a play by someone as well-known as Mishima.

What Mishima learned several days later, when he invited Botsford and Schultz to dinner to discuss the matter, was that the two started looking for a director for the production as Mishima left for the Caribbean but did not find one during his month-long absence. He accepted the explanation proffered by Botsford, a man of "aristocratic" mien and bearing, "barely thirty years old." Botsford was born in Brussels, in 1928, a son of an Italian duchess and a wealthy descendant of an early immigrant who settled in Connecticut in the 1630s, Mishima was told. He was rich enough to do whatever he pleased; he was scornful when he heard Mishima had been in Mexico for just two weeks, saying he spent one whole year there. Still, at the time he was working for CBS TV to earn an independent income.

The meeting made Mishima decide to stay in New York until he saw his play produced, with a new plan to open the play in January. The decision in time would force him to move from a midtown luxury hotel to one in Greenwich Village. Though a celebrity author back in Japan, he was not a man with inexhaustible funds. His accounts tell us what a self-respecting sojourner with a good income could do but not indefinitely.

After arriving to New York, and also after his return from the

Caribbean, Mexico, and the American South, he stayed in the Gladstone Hotel, on 52nd Street, east of Park Avenue. With the Seagram Building just then under construction on its north side, it was in a luxury area. It was a regular haunt of Marilyn Monroe, Mishima learned, and in the hotel registration he spotted names preceded by "Sir," "Lord," "Count," and so forth. But the Gladstone was not in the class of the Waldorf Astoria Hotel a few blocks to the south, which was said to be for the *nouveau riche*, much less the Plaza Hotel, near Central Park, which Mishima heard was for the truly wealthy. (In one of his New York episodes, Mishima describes a man, obviously himself, unable to find a convenient toilet, forced to rush into the Plaza Hotel for a men's room, where he is startled to find an old attendant.)

Initially, Mishima expected to spend about thirty dollars a day: twelve to thirteen dollars for the three meals, just below ten for the hotel, and eight to ten for the theater. That, in his estimation, was what you needed to enjoy a "both modest and luxurious life" in New York. At the time thirty dollars was equivalent to half the monthly salary of a college graduate newly employed by a corporation in Japan, at least in exchange-rate terms. If you wanted to go to a nightclub you needed another thirty and, for a woman, twenty or more, Mishima added. (In another New York episode, he describes a man fresh from Japan who spends some time bar-hopping with a woman who tells him she was in Japan; back at the hotel, he discovers she, obviously a prostitute, had stolen all the cash he had on him.[20])

As his stay in the city lengthened, he became conscious about money and began jotting down his daily expenses: "$1 for taxi; $13 for taking someone to lunch; $2.50 for tea; $8 for dinner alone; $1.50 for cinema and taxi; total of $26," this, without counting the hotel charges. Deciding that twenty-six dollars a day was too much for "a puritan life" like his, he learned to use the subway, till then too scary a thing to do. In the end he switched hotels. After looking at a couple of candidates his friends found for him, he decided on the Van Rensselaer Hotel, on East 11th Street, and moved there in early December. It charged four dollars a day, and the old man at the front desk smiled at Mishima, something his counterparts at the Gladstone never did, except when Mishima checked out.

The first morning he called the front desk and asked for room service, as he had done at the Gladstone. "What room service?" was the response. The bellboy came to the phone. He said there was nothing like what Mishima asked for: eggs (sunny-side up) and bacon. But he would get coffee and toast for him. In forty minutes an extraordinarily tall (so thought Mishima, who was just about five feet and five inches) black man, dripping wet, appeared at the door with a paper bag. It contained toast, which still retained some warmth, and a paper cup with coffee. Obviously the man had gone out in the rain to get them at a nearby drugstore.

About a month earlier, on November 6, Mishima and Botsford met Mordecai ("Max") Gorelik, who put himself forward as a stage designer. Apparently at his wife's instigation, Gorelik, famous for his sets for *Golden Boy* and an old friend of Arthur Miller, invited them to supper at their cluttered, dingy apartment. But Botsford, who thought Gorelik's design represented "old realism," accepted the invitation just as a matter of courtesy. He had no intention of employing him. And the supper proved to be a dismal affair.

Purged during the McCarthy Red-hunt, Gorelik was by then a broken middle-aged man. He let his wife domineer throughout the supper, whose main feature was "a bowl of salad as big as a horse crib" placed at the center of the table. And though Mrs. Gorelik, a "small, slim, sharp-eyed" woman whose "smile does not form a smile," interested Mishima as "a type," her insistence, which was kindly but misguided, that Mishima use soy sauce on the salad did not help. The only saving grace was that Mishima had an excuse to leave early: a show at City Center at eight.

Mishima's impression of the Goreliks was so much the worse probably because of the time he had spent at the Harvard Club earlier that day. Mrs. Laughlin, vice president of New Directions, had read *Confessions of a Mask*, liked it, and invited him to a late lunch. At the time the Harvard Club maintained a strict segregation between male and female, and Mrs. Laughlin had to meet him in a room adjacent to the main lobby where women were allowed. She was a "tall, unpretentious woman" with a pair of somewhat small eyes which Mishima found endearing. She was "intelligent but tolerant," and, with the editor-in-chief Robert McGregor citing what Angus Wilson and Christopher Isherwood said in their letters recommending publication of *Confessions*, the session was altogether flattering.

From what Mishima chose to write, it is difficult to pinpoint what happened as regards the planned staging of his play, largely because he wasn't fully apprised of what was going on. But in time someone Mishima called Dan was chosen as manager, and James Avantos, who, Mishima was told, directed Shelley Winters and John Bennett, as director, Hugh as stage designer, and Keith Botsford's wife, Ann, as costume designer. Then, in mid-November, Dolores del Rio, who had agreed to play the lead role, canceled her agreement. The idea appears to have been to have a famous actress for that role, the rest to be recruited from unknown talents.

It was only when Dolores del Rio dropped out—or perhaps a few weeks earlier—that Botsford and Schultz took out an ad in *Show Business*. A hundred or so aspirants signed up. Mishima attended a couple of auditions and saw several at a time. Once there was a tall blond who introduced himself as a former GI stationed in Japan. He turned out to be an exact copy of James Dean, his "wraith," as far as acting went, if not his appearance; whether he looked up, smiled, or was simply fidgety, the youth was a resurrection of the late actor who remained as popular in Japan as in the rest of the world.

(Either Botsford or Schultz once took Mishima to Jerry's, a cheap restaurant at 54th Street and Sixth Avenue, and told him it used to be Dean's haunt. They sat in a corner which Dean used to occupy. On the shelf above it was a basket full of withered flowers, "from a fan." The waiter Louis was the same one who appeared in Robert Altman's *James Dean Story* that came out that year.)

They accepted Dean's "wraith" because he was so good, although both Botsford and Co. and Mishima agreed in their dislike of the method acting famously promoted by the Actors Studio—"a cradle of Marlon Brando and James Dean, the reform factory for Marilyn Monroe." Still, Mishima once visited the studio to see Lee Strasberg discuss acting with students.[21]

Botsford and Co. also professed to dislike having the playwright hanging around during the auditions, and Mishima had no choice but to stay away after a few sessions although he loved to discuss with Botsford and Co. the men and women who had just left. Once he began to do so, there was no more word from the men, not even about the progress on the negotiations they were supposed to be undertaking with well-known actresses to replace Dolores del Rio.

## *Broadway Diversions*

Meanwhile, Mishima saw as many musicals as he could. He knew "New York intellectuals" disdained musicals, as they did Cecil B. DeMille's movies, but regular plays were somewhat difficult for him because of his inadequate command of English—just as they had been during his first stay in New York five years earlier. Including *My Fair Lady*, he saw the following musicals and wrote comments on them, even while lamenting that the playbills did not give the outlines of the plays so he might make errors.

> *Happy Hunting*: book by Howard Lindsay and Russell Crouse. Ethel Merman, "Queen of Musicals," was satisfactory and her *Mutual Admiration Society* utterly enjoyable. But the book was beneath comment and the overall production disappointing. (Mishima, who took "admiration" to be "administration," had seen her in *Call Me Madam*, in 1952.)
>
> *The Most Happy Fella*: book, music, and lyrics by Frank Loesser. "Deeply moved," Mishima wrote. "New York intellectuals attack *The Most Happy Fella* as too sentimental but to an eye familiar with the Shinpa this isn't that sentimental and this is likely to be the musical that the Japanese would find most attractive." An Italian operetta superimposed on a vineyard in the American West in the 1920s, it represents well "the international aspect of the United States." Mishima noted that at the time the union rules required every Broadway show to begin at eight-thirty and end a little after eleven.
>
> *My Fair Lady*: music by Frederick Loewe; book and lyrics by Alan Jay Lerner. Mishima professed not to understand why the lead actor Rex Harrison was regarded as "the embodiment of sex appeal among English women," but

he nonetheless admired his "suave and austere" acting, saying Harrison was comparable to the kabuki actor Kikugorō VI in his "delicate and agile moves." (Onoe Kikugorō VI, who established a school for acting, was especially famed for his accomplished dancing.) Mishima concluded his lengthy comment with: "The beauty of the society ladies who line up in the final racetrack scene made me despair, reminding me of so many of the bit actresses who appear on the Japanese stage." He saw it at least twice—once, on the ticket that Strauss's secretary extracted from the Mark Hellinger Theater by "intimidating" them by saying, "A famous Japanese playwright is coming to write about American theater, so make sure to reserve the very best ticket for him," and another time, on a scalper's ticket that cost $30, on December 21. "For a while after I saw it the first time," he wrote, "I didn't understand why people were making such a big deal of it, but as I saw other musicals, I came to think it was after all an outstanding one."

*New Girl in Town*: book by George Abbott; music and lyrics by Bob Merrill. "This type of nostalgic musical in America loses some of its attraction with foreign viewers like us; we do not feel nostalgia for a particular era and particular customs and manners. For example, Westerners would simply feel odd to see the customs and manners in Japan's Rokumeikan era."

*South Pacific*: Mishima had seen this musical in 1952 and had been impressed by "Bali Ha'i." This time he saw an amateur summer-theater production in Lambert, New Jersey. He could hear multitudes of insects shirring outside the tent. (He also saw *Macbeth* in Central Park with an occasional airplane flying low, drowning the speeches on stage.)

*Li'l Abner*: book by Norman Panama and Melvin Frank; lyrics by Johnny Mercer; music by Gene de Paul. Mishima noted that the choreographer and director Michael Kidd, famous in Japan for choreographing *Guys and Dolls*, was also the greatest attraction of this show, and wrote he was particularly impressed by the bride-catching scene, in Act II. The setup of the comedy obviously did not bother Mishima: it has to do with what a peaceful village might do when the government chooses it for an atomic bomb test site because it has nothing to commend itself. His citing a well-known Japanese theater critic who saw the show and praised Kidd's choreography tells us that it was a great privilege for a Japanese to see a New York musical in the late 1950s.

*West Side Story*: book by Arthur Laurents; music by Leonard Bernstein; lyrics by Stephen Sondheim; choreography by Jerome Robbins. The only "fresh" musical Mishima was able to see that season, and he could do so only because his CBS TV friend, which is to say, Keith Botsford, acquired a ticket for him. He found Robbins' power over the production excessive and, though he thought the fight scenes impressive, the romantic scenes between the modern Romeo and Juliet were too conventional and sugary.

*Jamaica*: book and lyrics by E. Y. Harburg; music by Harold Arlen. The story line may be too trashy for words but a great success as a sheer entertainment, in Mishima's opinion. Also closest to Nichigeki shows in Japan, Mishima thought. The main attraction was the superb Lena Horne, who, despite her movie successes, had been expunged from Hollywood because she married a white director. "New York is the most advanced city in racial matters, and here there is practically no racial prejudice," Mishima noted. "Still Josephine Baker has bitter memories of having been rejected by first-class hotels and first-class restaurants." Ricardo Montalbán, who played the seamstress Horne's fisherman lover, played a kabuki actor in Marlon Brando's movie *Sayonara*, released not long before. Equally impressed by the black dancers who filled the stage, Mishima regretted he would not be able to use them on the Japanese stage.

*The Threepenny Opera*: music by Kurt Weill. One of the Off-Broadway shows Mishima saw, at Theatre de Lys (today's Lucille Lortel Theatre). "The actors here are not at all famous," Mishima wrote, "but they had a complete mastery in acting and I thoroughly enjoyed the play." This production had started two years earlier and would run another five years.[22]

One thing that unconditionally enthralled Mishima was the New York City Ballet. Its twentieth New York season opened on November 19, and Mishima saw all the performances he could. The ones he left notes on were: *The Cage* (music by Stravinsky; choreography by Jerome Robbins); *Apollo* (music by Stravinsky; choreography by George Balanchine); *L'Apre-midi d'un faune* (music by Debussy; choreography by Jerome Robbins); and *Western Symphony* (music by Hershy Kay; choreography by George Balanchine).

The worst off-Broadway show or the worst show of any kind was a production of Victor Hugo's *Ruy Blas*, which he saw on December 19, at the Royal Playhouse, on East 4th Street. The drafty, dingy, musty theater had only about twenty people in the audience, with Mishima apparently the only one who paid for the $1.70 ticket. The sets and costumes were all worn-out.

One actor "came onstage with a book in hand and frequently looked at it as he walked about the stage," Mishima wrote, "so I thought that was an odd prop. It turned out he was reading from a script. He was perhaps a last-minute understudy." Nine years later he would produce the play himself despite severe economic constraints of the small theatre troupe with which he was involved. The translation was one he "rhetorically adapted." By then he had seen the Comédie-Française production of the great "theatrical drama" that had much impressed him with its "somber, gorgeous sets and costumes as if Velasquez' paintings had started to move."[23]

---

In early November, Hiraizumi (née Kajima) Mieko invited Mishima to her apartment. Her husband, Wataru, was a son of the historian Hiraizumi Kiyoshi, best known as an ardent proponent of *kōkoku shikan*, which holds the Tennō to be the *raison d'être* of Japanese history. Hiraizumi Kiyoshi resigned his post as professor at the Imperial University of Tokyo on the day Hirohito announced Japan's surrender, but continued to proselytize his view. Wataru, unlike his two older brothers who became historians, entered the foreign service in 1952 and was assigned to New York as Japan was admitted to the United Nations, in December 1956. He went on to become a member of the Diet—conservative, as may be expected—and later served as chairman of the Kajima Peace Institute, which his father-in-law Morinosuke created, originally as a cultural institute, in 1957, to satisfy his bookish inclinations.

Wataru remained a good friend of Mishima's. Mieko well remembered Mishima's visit to their Manhattan apartment: he stayed in one room for some time, intently looking out the window and taking notes as dusk fell. She would see some of the descriptions incorporated into *Kyōko's House*. In the story her name is Sugimoto Fujiko, that of her husband, an elite employee of a large trading company, Seiichirō, and their apartment is on 56th Street, between Sixth and Seventh Avenues:

> Even though buildings of the same height stood shoulder to shoulder like the tines of a comb on the street side, the view of what formed the interior yard for the block presented something different: low roofs, roof gardens, and the balconies sticking widely out created highs and lows; and, beyond them, you could sometimes see the rear windows of old houses made of red bricks. As a matter of fact, right below the window of this third-floor apartment was a narrow, vacant roof garden stretching out. Oddly, though, there was no entry to or exit from it except the window. Seiichirō and Fujiko kept a stack of firewood for the fireplace right outside the window.
>
> On the roof garden, in the splashing rain, were a couple of pots in which the flowers were so completely dead you couldn't tell what they originally were, along with a broken, misshapen wicker chair. There was no earth you could see but several tall plane trees rose from among the eaves. November had just begun, but their broad, yellow leaves had mostly fallen, plastering the concrete floor of the roof garden and the wicker chair like advertising leaflets....

About the time he moved to the Van Rensselaer Hotel, Mishima still assumed that Botsford and Co.'s schedule was on track. In an interview published in the daily *Tokyo Shinbun*, on December 2, he stated that the play would start at the Actors Playhouse, in the West Village, in January and last for about a month. The theater has only about one hundred fifty seats and, though that will be good from the perspective of "a close merger between actors and audience," the income will naturally be small. He did not plan to move it to "a large Broadway theater," he said, obviously tongue-in-cheek, even if it proved to be a smash hit.

In a separate UP dispatch, asked when he planned to return to Japan, Mishima was quoted as saying he would pack up and flee if the *New York Times* gave a foul review.[24] Not long afterward, responding to a request for an essay by the daily *Yomiuri Shinbun*, he maintained the same outlook. He spoke of his expectations, as he had "never imagined in Tokyo," to "stay on in New York to welcome the New Year." Saying he could openly speak ill of them because his "merry, good" friends "couldn't possibly read a newspaper in Japanese," he wrote: ". . . the producer Keith is the leader of a boy gang, the other producer Chiz a lazybones, the manager Dan a shapeless Danny Kaye, the director Jimmy Greek-born and a Lotus-Sutra bonze, and the stage designer Hugh a carefree guy; add to these Keith's beautiful wife Ann (who is doing the costume design), and you might have a fine Italian operetta troupe."[25] By the time these words saw print, on January 3, 1958, he *had* fled New York.

The quick unraveling, from Mishima's perspective, started on December 14, when he went to a party at the Japan Society, then on 49th Street between Fifth and Madison, next to Saks Fifth Avenue, and had a surprise encounter. Among those gathered, mostly Japanese, someone said, introducing him to someone else: "This is the famous Mr. Mishima Yukio." Mishima turned to look; it was Kuniko. The two almost dropped their champagne glasses. Mishima said, in his baritone, "My name is Mishima." Kuniko, with her husband at her side, managed only, "How long are you going to stay here?" In the course of the evening she once heard him give his famous laugh. She had come, with her two children, to live in New York in the summer of the previous year to accompany her husband, an employee of Japan's only bank permitted to handle foreign currencies in those days: the Bank of Tokyo.

In those days, and until much later, it was a rare Japanese corporate or government employee who had the luxury of taking his wife, let alone his children, to an overseas post. Perfectly mindful of this, Mishima contrived to describe Fujiko, in his story, as a daughter of an enormously rich man—as Mieko actually was—who was able to send her to New York independently of her husband. Something similar probably was the case with Kuniko.

The Japan Society party was "a torture" to Mishima, and not just because of his encounter with Kuniko. Many of the Japanese gathered there had heard about his play that was going to be produced in New York and wanted to know when that was going to happen. Their curiosity was only to be expected; it was something that had never happened before. Two days later, on December 16, Mishima, no longer able to contain himself, telephoned the director, Jimmy. "Our negotiations with a couple of well-known actresses all fell through," the director said. He was in unusually low spirits. "Unless we can find one by the end of this week, we won't be able to do the play as planned." "December 16th was the worst day," Mishima wrote.

The next evening he called Schultz, easier of the two producers to talk to, and arranged to meet him the following day. The foundation from which additional funds were sought had also turned down the application, Schultz explained when they met. The reason was the explosion of the first US satellite, Vanguard. Already disheartened by the Soviet Union's spectacular success with Sputnik I, on October 4, followed by the equal success of Sputnik II, on November 3, all Americans turned "cautious" at the ridiculous American failure on December 6.

It isn't clear whether the money-giving foundations reacted that fast, for the chain of events occurred in just two months. But it certainly was a "blow to US prestige," as the *New York Times* put it. The fall of the stock of Martin Company, the manufacturer of Vanguard rockets, was so precipitous that the New York Stock Exchange had to halt its trading. Moreover, Schultz said, there was a string of contretemps with actresses.

That night Mishima could not sleep. The following day he made phone calls to change and make reservations—change the flight back to Japan via Europe to first class and make reservations with the very best hotels in Europe. "I could no longer stand breakfast in a paper bag," he wrote. On Christmas Day he wrote a long letter to Tennessee Williams expressing sadness at being unable to see his own play produced in New York. On New Year's Eve he flew out of New York to Spain, "welcoming the New Year" in Madrid. He left Rome on January 8, and arrived back in Tokyo on January 10, 1958.

CHAPTER FOURTEEN

# Marriage

*I am paying attention to my health so that I may live until I am 150 years old.*

—Self-portraits at eighteen and thirty-four

"Once, it was in America, you see, I tried to live for six months all alone," Mishima told Kojima Chikako nearly a dozen years after the fact. "From that experience, I know very well, I felt it painfully, a human being can't live all by himself." Kojima was an editor of *Shinchō* assigned to Mishima beginning with *The Temple of the Golden Pavilion* and thus fated to go to Mishima's house on the morning of the day of his death—to receive the last installment of the tetralogy, *The Sea of Fertility*.

Mishima told Kojima about his six-month stay in America on June 24, 1968, when she went to receive the last installment of Part II of the tetralogy, *Runaway Horse*. She remembered the remark because the seeming acceptance of a normal marriage it suggested contrasted markedly with his obvious excitement over the ending of the story he had just completed: the young terrorist's death by disembowelment.[1]

It is not clear when Mishima, who at one time or another had vowed not to marry until forty, changed his mind. The day his marriage became formal with an exchange of dowries, on May 9, 1958, he wrote in the diary-format criticism *The Nude and the Costume* he started in *Shinchō*, "I think it was three years ago that the idea of 'marriage' gradually began to ripen in my head."[2] Perhaps. As he said to Kojima, though,

/ 311

it may well have been during his stay in New York that he made a firm decision, for there was one person who heard him make the vow in that city: Yoshida Mitsuru, at the time stationed there as an official of the Bank of Japan.

Mishima had met Yoshida on December 21 that year and spent the entire day with him. One thing that surprised Yoshida during the daylong excursion—and there were several memorable things—was Mishima's eagerness to talk about his marriage plans. He appeared quite serious even as he "joked" that no young girl from a good solid family would marry a writer like himself. Still, he discussed two basic "conditions" for the woman willing to marry him.

First of all, she should not show any overt interest in what her husband writes. The ideal would be someone who had never read a single novel of his. The second one was the opposite: she nevertheless must always keep in mind that her husband is a writer. She should not fool around or snooze away thoughtlessly while he is struggling to write. After discussing these and other details, Mishima announced he'd be married next year.

Yoshida, well known for his epic *Requiem for Battleship Yamato* (*Senkan Yamato no saigo*), was an ensign who survived the sinking of Japan's largest battleship. He wrote its first draft in a single night after Japan's defeat. The Occupation censored it.[3] Mishima, who had been acquainted with Yoshida since about the time he was completing his law studies at the University of Tokyo, in 1947, became one of the first to read the manuscript. When it was published, in 1952, he composed a brief but heartfelt tribute.

Comparing the only large-scale naval suicide sortie in world history with the Battle of Thermopylae, Mishima wrote: "Be it blind faith or primitive religion, the battleship *Yamato* was a symbol of one old virtue, one great moral imperative, by which a man could die. Its destruction was the death of a religion. Confronted with its death, the warriors were placed under the equal condition of life and within the order of a perfect imperative, and their youth unexpectedly faced an 'absolute.' You cannot deny that beauty."[4]

Yoshida kept a close account of that December day in his diary. When he arrived at Mishima's hotel, Mishima asked him to wait while he took care of some business over the phone. Apparently learning that the production of his play was postponed, Mishima, without rancor, quickly arranged flights and such for leaving New York. It was a sparkling Saturday. So the two writers took the train up the Hudson to Tarrytown to visit Washington Irving's manor, Sunnyside. At one point Mishima said: "I'm going to build a house sooner or later, but I wonder if it's going to be open to the public like this after I die?"[5]

Other than the marriage plans, one other thing surprised Yoshida that day: Mishima's bitterness about the "ineradicable" superiority complex he said the Americans have over the Japanese. (In his published or public accounts of his associations with Americans, he gives nary a hint that he witnessed that complex.) Yoshida's own conclusion after his two-year stay in the United States was that "almost no social life was possible separate from racial differences in this country" but that, when it came to the Japanese, their mortal enemy till a dozen years earlier, the Americans were well-mannered enough "to accept them with a smile and tolerance lest vivid memories of the ferocious battles be reawakened."

By late in the evening Mishima was visibly tired, but then he said, "Let's go to a bar I save for special occasions." The moment he said so, he had a second wind. Somehow Yoshida guessed what kind of bar it would be, and he was right. It was one for homosexuals, a tiny hole-in-the-wall joint in the West Village. What Yoshida didn't know was that it was the same one to which Donald Richie had taken Mishima five years earlier. It was called Mary's.[6]

## *Arranged Marriage by Choice*

Once told of his son's desire to be married, Azusa moved quickly. He had nagged his son about his bachelorhood. Mishima, after all, was, by tradition, the one responsible for the Hiraoka household, and he couldn't stay unmarried forever. Besides, his younger brother, Chiyuki, had been married for three years now. Shizue, who looked tired out from taking care of her hospitalized husband—he was laid up in the University of Tokyo Hospital in November—was happy to hear the news, too. Azusa began looking for candidates as though he was given a thrilling assignment.

The first thing Azusa did was to make a "public announcement" through the alumni association of the Peers School, Ōyūkai, the Society of Cherry-Blossom Friends. A number of résumés with photographs soon began to arrive. Azusa, the picky type, made the first selection. Mishima then narrowed it.

At last, one photograph caught Mishima's attention. She was a graduate of the Peers School. Shizue probed the matter through her friends in the upper-class society and learned that Mayuzumi Toshirō knew her. The young woman had become acquainted with him as she visited him backstage with her musician friend. Both Azusa and Shizue asked him for help. Mayuzumi soon learned that the woman wasn't at all interested in meeting Mishima for a possible marriage. But Mishima insisted and Mayuzumi agreed to arrange for him an "accidental" meeting with her at Ketel, himself escorting her. Mishima was charmed, took her to a nightclub and danced, but she still wasn't interested.

Famous women's colleges and universities were also explored, among them the University of the Sacred Heart. Founded in 1914 as a higher school for Christian education for women, the Sacred Heart had become, in 1948, the first women's university during the postwar educational reform. It was a magnet for daughters of the higher echelon of Japanese society. As it happened, before the Hiraokas started making bridal inquiries, the university had routinely recommended Shōda Michiko "with confidence."

Michiko's father was president of Nisshin Seifun, a large wheat-powder manufacturer and for many years known overseas as the producer of "cup noodles." That was credential enough, but she was unusually good-looking and an outstanding student as well. She was the *president*—the title in English—of the student body, was studying English conversation, and was active in a variety of sports, especially ten-nis. (Tennis in those days was a sport only the well-to-do could afford. That's why the "tennis match" between the Crown Prince and a daughter of a very rich man became such a glamorous affair to the Japanese. Now, having tennis courts appears to be routine in high schools and such in Japan. Times change.)

Azusa laid out a careful plan: his son and Miss Shōda would *casually* meet at the Kabuki-za, then secretly repair to a small but prestigious Japanese restaurant on the Ginza that Azusa knew about through his bureaucratic connections. The meeting duly took place, but the matter did not go further. The Shōdas were in a delicate position. Just then the Imperial Household was making quiet inquiries. In fact, in November that year Crown Prince Akihito's engagement to Shōda Michiko would be announced, with the marriage scheduled for April of the following year. This outcome would spawn the speculation among some Mishima readers a decade later that the heroine of *Spring Snow* was modeled after Her Highness Princess Michiko.[7]

Yuasa Atsuko came to the rescue. At the time, her daughter was a student at the Elementary Division of the Peers School, and she was in the same class as a son of Komatsu Shizuko, a sister-in-law of the renowned Japanese-style painter Sugiyama Yasushi. Shizuko, when she learned that Atsuko's friend, Mishima Yukio, was looking for a bride, told her that her niece, Yōko, was a sophomore at another Christian institution, Japan Women's University. She soon brought a photo taken by Akiyama Shōtaro, then famous for his photographs of women that adorned the covers of weekly magazines.

That was on March 23, and Mishima liked what he saw: the photo showed a charming woman with a perfectly round, lovely face. That day, in the "diary" he had begun in the April issue of *Shinchō* Mishima noted that his long novel finally started moving forward.

Here some backtracking is needed.

---

Even while in New York, Mishima had kept up a considerable presence in Japanese theater and literature. A month after he arrived in New York his play *The Morning Azalea (Asa no tsutsuji)* was staged in Tokyo. Sending a program note for it, he wrote: "Coming to America, you are surprised to see among hotels and houses of the wealthy so many buildings that are in Victorian style, of nineteenth-century taste. Those who put themselves forward as modern do not simply call them Victorian style but *ugly* Victorian style. In the Japanese eye, though, it symbolizes old Europe and makes us feel most nostalgic about it, and it is not at all *ugly*. *The Morning Azalea* is that kind of Victorian-style drama. It is a drama overflowing with an old-fashioned, nineteenth-century taste."[8]

Indeed it is. A miniature of *The Rokumeikan*, the play describes an overnight dance party at a viscount's mansion in 1927, during which, instead of a fratricidal attempt, the news of the collapse of the bank catering to the peerage arrives. The kabuki actor Nakamura Utaemon played the lead role and the actress Nagaoka Teruko directed it.

September saw the publication of a limited edition of *Virtue Falters* and its film version was released in late October. October also saw the Bungaku-za revive *The Rokumeikan*; the troupe would tour the country with the play for more than a year, visiting a total of thirty-five cities. And in November Shinchōsha started the publication of "selected writings of Mishima Yukio" in nineteen volumes—only three years after it put out his "selected writings" in six volumes. Each volume came with a photo of the author and the author's own commentary, among other paraphernalia.

Back in Japan, in mid-February Mishima wrote another play for the Bungaku-za, *The Rose and the Pirate*, which he explained was inspired by a production of *The Sleeping Beauty* by the Royal Ballet he saw in New York, in particular its *grand divertissement*. He had this to say on the writing of the play in the "diary":

> Once you start writing a piece, you find all the plans you had laid out before doing so betrayed one after another irresistibly—this is something a writer experiences all the time, and I am not surprised by it in the least. But this time, this rule was brought home to me with unusual clarity. I say this because during my idle days and months in New York I was determined not to write a single manuscript, so I single-mindedly made plans for this drama in my head, giving thorough thought to its structure, fully working out the devices in the details, so that I was supposed to be able to write it according to plan, with great ease.
>
> Nonetheless, the moment I started writing it, I began to realize that the plan that had seemed so precise was ramshackle with many cracks, with the upshot that I had to redo everything except for the main theme....
>
> The day before yesterday I told Mr. Fukuda Tsuneari about this, and he responded, with his usual concision, "Unless you start writing it, the perspective doesn't open up." Perspective is a skillful choice of word.[9]

While in New York Mishima may have been determined not to write a single manuscript, but there was at least another piece of writing he had begun to plot: the "long novel" mentioned above. Yoshida

Mitsuru remembered Mishima telling him about a lengthy story he planned to write as soon as he went back to Japan, which would be about "five young people." Each time the two went into a restaurant or a coffee shop, he would pull a notebook out of his briefcase and take careful notes on the details of the place: "the darkness of the room, doors, walls, chairs, tableware, waiters, guests, everything." Asked why he was doing that, he said the story he had in mind would have scenes in New York.[10]

So, in the March 10 entry of *The Nude and the Costume* he noted: "Fine. Warmth in the afternoon honeylike. / Thinking every day of starting to write a full-length *kakioroshi* novel, *Kyōko's House*, I'm too afraid to pull myself together to do it. For a one thousand-page product, explorations in the brain alone serve no purpose." *Kakioroshi*, which simply means "just written," refers, when applied to novels and such, to a writing of substantial length that is not serialized but published upon completion. Mishima explained why he had chosen this approach when he finished the novel toward the end of June 1959: "It was my wish for some time to write a long *kakioroshi* novel, which comes from my Western addiction. If it is customary for Western writers to turn out one novel every two or three years, it can't be that Japanese writers, who are financially more blessed, cannot do the same. In fact, try it and you can do it."

As it turned out, *Kyōko's House* was fated not to be a model *kakioroshi*. When the Hachi no Ki group decided to publish their own members-only quarterly, *Koe*, in September 1958,[11] he placed the first two chapters in its inaugural issue. "One difficulty no novelists of the West expect is the mental burden under which Japanese writers must do such work while living in the midst of the incessant hurly-burly of Japanese journalism," he went on to say. "This spiritual burden made me exaggerate my hardship and unnecessarily stiffened my resolve. Any Western novelist may have done it as if it was just the work of making a small pond in his garden with his own hands, but I often had the impression that I was engaged in constructing a dam."

This observation was certainly true of Mishima. He was journalistically among the most provocative and prolific writers, and that was not just because of his ability to turn out, in quick succession, greatly different kinds of fiction and essays, long and short. It was also because of his ability to inhabit the disparate worlds of fiction, criticism, theater, film, and sports with equal ease and energy. One is even tempted to add another ability of his—to have his presence felt in Japan while staying overseas for months on end. No journalist worth his salt could ignore him for long.

---

Mishima's marriage proceeded in parallel to Shizue's illness.

Shizue, who with the onset of menopause had been complaining for some time about the discomfort she felt around her neck, finally went to see a surgeon through a relative's introduction. The doctor said it might be a malignant tumor and urged her to see a cancer specialist as soon as possible. Two days later Mishima took her to one by taxi. At first the oncologist had a pleasant smile on his face, as is customary, but upon examining her neck his expression changed, which Mishima did not miss. The doctor called in his intern and, as the two carefully reexamined her neck and throat, he said, "*Gefährlich.*" Shizue did not know German but Mishima did; the word meant "dangerous."

After the examination, the doctor asked Shizue to leave the room, telling Mishima to stay, and, as soon as she left, he came to the point at once: he thought she had advanced cancer and had only several months to live. In trying to convey the news to Azusa's niece by phone, Mishima could not stop sobbing, in the end crying loudly.

Shizue was taken to the University of Tokyo Hospital, where after further examinations it was decided she needed hospitalization. The day before the hospitalization, Mishima took her to a Chinese restaurant, then to the New York City Ballet, which was visiting Japan then. "I have never seen such a mysterious ballet," Mishima recollected half a year later. "There was neither sound nor color, only human beings leaping up and down like shadows."[12]

That was in early April. On April 13, Mishima met Sugiyama Yōko at Ketel, with Atsuko serving as the young woman's chaperon. The three then repaired to Hamasaku, one of the famous Japanese restaurants on the Ginza, and, after dinner, to a nightclub. As he danced with Yōko, he noticed, he told Atsuko later, she wasn't "fluid" in her movements, a sign that she hadn't "played around" much. Afterward he thanked Atsuko and offered to send Yōko home by taxi. Atsuko then knew the meeting was a success. The following morning Mishima telephoned her and said, "She is very good." After that the marriage process moved forward like clockwork.

On April 21 he met Yōko for the second time, again with Atsuko accompanying her. First, the three of them saw *Stage Struck*, Sydney Lumet's film with Susan Strasberg and Henry Fonda (which gave Mishima an opportunity to savor the still-fresh memories of New York, including staring at Fonda at FAO Schwarz and meeting Strasberg's father at the Actors Studio[13]), then went to the restaurant George's, before going to a nightclub in Aoyama. The following day he went to a barber and had a crewcut.

On April 30 Atsuko and Komatsu Shizuko came to visit the Hiraokas at their Midori-ga-Oka house and discussed the overall schedule. The following day Shizue underwent surgery. It was found that her tumor was not malignant. At the news Mishima burst out crying. On May 5 Mishima, along with his father, invited Mr. and Mrs. Sugiyama, their daughter Yōko, as well as Yuasa Atsuko and Komatsu Shizuko, to a Chinese restaurant, and set the wedding date. During the dinner Mishima announced, in a manner that struck Atsuko as a bit too businesslike: "I've just started a long novel of one thousand pages. Once this work gets on track, I'll have no time for marriage and such. I would hope to settle this matter before that occurs."

On May 9, dowries were exchanged between the Hiraoka and Sugiyama families, as noted earlier. In the entry in his "diary" that day, he indulged in a lengthy, overtly literary justification of his decision to marry.

"To align myself with the customs and morals of this society and live more or less in it while continuing a work that puts all customs and morals in doubt is an extremely obvious logical contradiction," he wrote. "I have perhaps spent many more years than anyone learning gradually the wisdom of life that you must first bind yourself up in order to be truly free. Just as the leisurely swimmer rids his entire body of tension and lets himself float in a most relaxed fashion, I ought to acquire the art of letting myself float in the sea of contradictions, or so I realized."

"The famous passage in Kierkegaard's *Either/Or* had charmed me for a long time," he went on: "'Marry and you will regret it. Do not marry and you will also regret it'"—the words perhaps from *Diasalmata*. "I also remembered well the episode that Flaubert, while taking a walk in a park late in his life, saw a family with a perambulator and said, 'I could have had a life like that.'"

After carrying on in similar vein awhile longer, Mishima stepped into a convoluted argument as he sometimes did:

> It isn't that a man cannot choose, but it is the free will that ultimately knows the impossibility of choice; it is for this reason that the free will that refuses to affirm the fact that there is only one life can resist fate.... And an action is a bastard child who is born between fate and the free will, and a man, in truth, can never know if his action is a result of an incitement of fate or an error committed by the free will. In the end it seems to me that to deal with yourself as you do in floating your body in the sea is a mark of the greatest respect you can pay your life. ... After thinking things like these I have decided to marry.

The question is: Were the Sugiyamas unaware of Mishima's homosexuality or at least his open or public association with it? The answer: They were of course aware of it. As the marital prospect quickly advanced, Sugiyama Yasushi at one point is said to have asked Azusa: "There's rumor that Mr. Mishima is homosexual. Is that true?" Azusa was upset and replied angrily: "There's no such fact. My son has described that world as his literary topic and that has spawned misunderstandings."

But then he committed a slip of the tongue. "You see, sir, it's to deny such rumor that my son wants to get married as soon as possible, and that's his intent." That almost wrecked the marriage; Sugiyama wanted to annul the proposal. But his daughter Yōko strongly objected to the annulment. Why? The guess may well be right: She, who was still in college, wanted to marry Mishima the famous man, if not the man himself.[14]

## *The Honeymooners*

On June 1, Hiraoka Kimitake and Sugiyama Yōko were wed at Meiji Memorial Hall, a detachment of Meiji Shrine. Mr. and Mrs. Kawabata Yasunari served as official matchmakers. The reception was held at International House, a Western-style hotel equipped with a Japanese garden intended for visiting foreigners. For the format Mishima chose a cocktail party, something few Japanese held in those days *personally*, especially for a wedding reception. The layout of International House allowed guests to freely saunter out of the reception area into the garden and come back in. After building his own house, Mishima would throw a cocktail party from time to time, with a professional bartender, himself formally attired in tuxedo.

For the master of ceremony, Mishima turned to Roy James, who had become Yuasa Atsuko's live-in companion toward the end of the preceding year. Roy, originally one of the regulars of her house salon, had begun to live in her house. When Atsuko met him and added him to her salon, he was a struggling gaijin serving as an emcee at Nichigeki Music Hall and doing other odd jobs. After she came to know him, she found he had an unusual background. Despite his English name and despite his—to the Japanese—unmistakably "Western" appearance of blond hair and blue eyes, he was Turkish. His father was a lieutenant of the Turkish Army that fought the Soviets in Siberia and was defeated, and who had come to Japan via Korea. Living as he did close to a Turkish school as a boy,[15] Mishima likely knew that the existence of Turks in his city was a result of Japan's pre-defeat foreign policy extending to the land of Mustafa Kemal Atatürk.[16]

Roy's father was a Muslim cleric and chose Ramadan, the name of the holiest of months in the Islamic calendar, for his son, Abdul Hannan Safa, who was born in Keiō University Hospital, in 1929. Nicknamed "Hannan Boy," he grew up as the darling of neighborhood mothers, in Shitamachi, an enclave for the poor, as opposed to Yamanote, an enclave for the upper class, where Atsuko grew up.

Toward the end of the Second World War, as Turkey severed its relations with Germany and declared war against it and Japan, Abdul Hannan became an enemy alien, was rounded up for hard labor, and almost died. In the confusion of the last phase of the war, not many Japanese knew, as Atsuko certainly did not, that Turkey had become an enemy country and, in consequence, one of the victorious nations with Japan's defeat. Atsuko's husband at the time, Shun, perhaps because he found himself in a not altogether comfortable position as an American Nisei working in a defeated Japan, was particularly kind and considerate to Roy. It was he who suggested that he live in the Yuasa household.

Initially with Mishima's help, Roy would start getting some real work and went on to become a highly successful emcee, ranked as the most popular TV emcee for sixteen consecutive years. With his wit and vast and exact memory, he was also popular among those holding corporate meetings.

The reception over, the newlyweds at once left on a two-week honeymoon. They went west. After staying in Odawara overnight, they went to Hakone, where Mishima saw woodblock prints from early Meiji at a shop in front of the hotel and sent them off to James Merrill and James McGregor as gifts. Their next stop was the hot-spring town of Atami. Then they traveled to Kyoto by dome car. On the train Mishima overheard a passenger say, "In Hakone yesterday I met the Prime Minister and had a long conversation with him about the cabinet he is forming." At that moment, indeed, Kishi Nobusuke was trying to work out his second cabinet, which he would announce on June 12, only to fall, two years later, following the greatest antigovernment movement in modern Japan.

In the ancient capital they visited the Daiei Studio to see the movie of *The Golden Pavilion* in the making. The scene they saw being filmed was where Ichikawa Raizō, playing the protagonist, was severely criticized by his friend, played by Nakadai Tatsuya. With the temple itself objecting, the title had been changed to *Conflagration* (*Enjō*). The film, which Ichikawa Kon directed, went on to win several prizes, including one at the Venice International Film Festival. The couple also went to see Utaemon perform at the Minami-za. In Osaka, Mishima bought two neckties made of Tatsumura fabric and sent them to Christopher Isherwood.

"In the evening, Roy James, who served as master of ceremony at our wedding reception and who happened to be in the area for work, came to visit," Mishima wrote in the June 10 entry of his "diary." "In order to launch myself as a jazz singer in the future, Roy, I'd say, is going to be an important friend." One of the things Mishima did during the trip was to take Yōko to nightclubs and cabarets. That night it was Arrow, a "new, *chic* club with a spacious garden." It was its opening night and Roy had served as emcee.

The next day the couple took a coastal liner to Beppu, the hot-spring town in Kyushu. Just before the ship reached Kobe, around six in the evening, Mishima took a bath—"out of the whimsical desire to take a bath aboard a ship," a motive which, Mishima wrote in his "diary" that day, was "absurd." Nonetheless it led him to a chain of thought:

... such absurd motives lurk everywhere in life, and you can't say none can form a trigger of historical events such as the assassination of Marat. If there were utterly motiveless acts, it would become easy to grasp the purity of desire, but modern life brims with multifarious motives; as a result, the actual presence of desire has become unclear. Motiveless crimes are no more than the products of fantasy in modern times, and the more motiveless the crime seems, the more irrational, the more nonsensical the motive that prompts it may be. As I wrote *The Temple of the Golden Pavilion*, which was an investigation of the motive of a crime, even a shallow, silly idea of "beauty" could be enough of a motive for a crime of arson on a national treasure. Meanwhile, if you take another viewpoint, to live through modern times, it is possible to believe in a single silly, shallow idea and amplify it until it becomes the fundamental motive of life itself. That's what Hitler did. But by setting up such a motive, directionality is lost, so that one mistake you make in steering, and you can turn it into a motive for death, a motive for suicide.

The following morning the couple arrived in Beppu and went directly from the port to Mt. Takasaki, a hill nearby famous as a refuge for monkeys. At the hotel, Mishima had no time for a nap; he was beset with requests for autographs and pithy writings on *shikishi*, blank decorative paper boards made for that purpose. In the evening, an NHK reporter came to interview him.

Mishima's marriage, in fact, was such a journalistic event that he was subjected to interviews and asked to contribute articles once it happened. In one of the interviews, he explained the reasons for one of his conditions: his preference for a "round face"—that is, the kind of face his brand-new wife had. "I prefer a round face because mine is elongated," he told the interviewer. "If both of us have elongated faces, like my parents do, it won't be good eugenically. That will produce a child like me. If someone with an elongated face comes to me as my wife on top of that, it will produce someone like a horse with a top hat."[17] As far as that sort of thing goes, he'd like someone shorter than he, he said, because, as his American biographer John Nathan put it, "Mishima was a small man, though he never gave that impression."[18]

After dinner the two went out to town and saw the movie *All About Marriage* (*Kekkon no subete*), which concluded by extolling arranged marriage. The fast-paced director Okamoto Kihachi's debut work, it featured the popular singer-actress Yukimura Izumi playing the lead and Nakadai Tatsuya "an ordinary man" she finally decides to marry. Mishima found it "very good." Close to midnight, the two went to a cabaret called Silver. There a striptease dancer recognized Mishima, so the whole house welcomed the newlyweds.

The next evening he heard that a local movie theater was showing *Virtue Falters*, so after dinner he and Yōko went to see it: "I was surprised that it was dumber than I'd ever imagined. I can't think of any film that could be stupider than this. Besides, I don't know who spread the rumor, but when the movie was over and we came out, there was a crowd at the entrance; we'd gone to see a movie but they had come to watch us."

The next day, on June 14, they took a "hot-spring" train to Hakata. A man who said he was a plainclothesman and a fan of Mishima's work asked him for an autograph and gave him a bottle of beer as a token of gratitude. But his expression of gratitude didn't stop there. At each station he would stick his head out of the window and loudly announce the identity of the man he was with. Crowds would gather and look in. Many offered comments. One of them said loudly enough so the Mishimas could hear: "With all of us watching them like this, they must be embarrassed."

In Hakata, they saw a US war film featuring Robert Mitchum and Curd Yürgens, *The Enemy Below*. On June 15 they took a flight from Fukuoka back to Tokyo, the first air flight for Yōko.

## *Young Friends*

The marriage brought some cheer to the Hiraoka household in Midori-ga-Oka. For one thing, Mishima started to go out more often with some of the young members of the neighborhood association. Remnants of the Tokugawa Period, when smallest administrative units were created and made responsible for the actions of the residents, neighborhood associations continue to play a role in matters such as fire and burglary prevention, upkeep of sanitary standards, neighborhood beautification, making festival arrangements, and even dispute resolution. Among the men Mishima often spent time with were Matsumura Motomi, heir of a sushi restaurant whom he came to know at the bodybuilding gym, and Tsukada Keiichirō, who ran a café.

One day, at Mishima's request, they took him to a ghost house set up in Tamagawa Park. In the entry of his "diary" for July 10, he wrote: "Night: With friends in Jiyū-ga-Oka as my guides, I went to the Ghost Festival in Tamagawa Park. It was a ghost festival that wasn't scary at all. I pulled the giant rubber snake afloat in midair, and the stagehand who was manipulating it near the ceiling barked at me, 'You, fucking bastard!' I wanted to use a scene from the festival in Chapter 3 of *Kyōko's House*, but the experience doesn't seem to provide good material."

Matsumura and Tsukada recalled the incident somewhat differently. The rubber snake, large mouth open, tried to swallow the three, fully expecting them to flee. But Mishima was clumsy and got entangled in the contraption, almost pulling the whole thing down. The stagehand became angry and subjected Mishima to considerable tongue-lashing. Finally freed, the three came outside. Mishima spotted a group of hoods idling. Apparently having heard that Matsumura was a good street fighter, he urged him to fight them. He didn't seem to know you couldn't just start fighting anyone without provocation. Matsumura and Tsukada fondly recalled how their friend loved to look like a hood, though—with a crewcut and in a black leather jacket.

In Chapter 3 of *Kyōko's House*, two of the four main male characters, Natsuo the painter and Shunsuke the boxer, with Shunsuke's mother, visit a spot near the park by the Tama River late one summer afternoon. But that they do after visiting Tama Cemetery to offer prayers to Shunsuke's brother who was killed in the Solomon Islands, in 1942. There is no mention of a ghost festival.

The two young friends remembered a few other things from that evening. After the ghost festival they decided to visit Mishima's house, which was not very far. On the way was a railway crossing. The signal was flashing and ringing but there was no train in sight just yet, so the two crossed. Mishima did not until the train came and went. The two asked him why. His reply: "I'm not that cheap." Arriving at his house, they found Yōko listening to a record. After a while Tsukada asked her to dance and she agreed. But no sooner had they started to dance than Mishima came between them and stopped them.

The "diary" entry for that day ends: "In his journals, Gide wrote on a piece he was working on, 'Today too I was immersed in moving this large lump just a little forward.' When you are involved in a long novel for a considerable length of time, you marvel how appropriate his expression was."

## *A Bad Guy's House*

That summer Yōko became pregnant. About the same time Mishima decided to build a house, but it wasn't until October 13 that he signed a contract. Satō Ryōichi, vice president of Mishima's principal publisher, Shinchōsha, knew Hokonohara Yasuo, an architect on the staff of the design section of Shimizu Corporation, one of Japan's largest construction companies, and he arranged to have the architect and the novelist meet in his office. Hokonohara was also an abstract painter—what the Japanese call a painter of "modern art"—who was young but already known as a prickly, sometimes irascible character. Legend had it that once he barked at the head of his section over a design he found unacceptable, "Resign, sir! Resign from this company right now!" Coming from a young subordinate who, besides, flaunted long hair like an out-of-date art student, was of "a thin type both in muscle and bone," and wore a jacket of his own design with "mysteriously wide lapels" and "a dated Bohemian tie," this impetuous outburst may have startled the section chief but won him popularity among his colleagues.

When Mishima explained in detail the kind of house he had in mind during their first encounter in Satō's office, Hokonohara was mightily put out. "Mr. Mishima was one client who imposed on you, the designer," he wrote, "his quirks or preferences, or shall I call them the *stink* you couldn't possibly stand, anyway strong quirks, and yet gave you no solutions. [He wanted the house to be] Victorian Colonial style. . . . So I asked him bluntly, 'You mean the sort of house you often see in Westerns that some *nouveau riche*, a bad guy with a Colman mustache, inhabits.' To this, what d'you know, his instant riposte was, 'Yes, I like a bad guy's house.' That defeated me completely, and I decided to take it on seriously." Mishima then added, "My ideal is to sit in an aloha shirt and jeans in the middle of Rococo furniture," which further exasperated the architect, as Mishima himself recalled.[19]

Hokonohara and Mishima wrote these things when Shinchōsha's art magazine asked both men to describe the building of the house after it was completed, in May 1959. By then they were good friends. Mishima wrote that in his household the architect was called Hoko-ten, an abbreviation of Hokonohara Tennō, akin to saying "Emp. Hoko," because there was no way of beating him in any argument. Mishima, who was shown Hoko-ten's article before it went to press, found it very funny, so did Yōko when he told her what it said, probably verbatim. She laughed so hard she pleaded with him to stop because it might damage her body. She had given birth to her first baby not long before, on June 2, 1959. They had named the girl Noriko.

In his article Mishima repeated the point he made in his program note for *The Morning Azalea* about his fondness for what the New Yorkers condemned as "*ugly* Victorian," and added, "The last blooming of Baroque taste that had lingered into the nineteenth century is ultimately my notion of Europe, and to me so-called Europe is nothing more than something that glitters, something luridly colored."

"My argument is," he went on, "that if you are to build something in accordance with *modern* architecture fashionable these days"—and here he may have been thinking of the Seagram Building—"you should go one step ahead of Japonica and build an exact copy of Katsura Detached Palace." By "Japonica," Mishima probably had in mind something akin to Japonisme. Katsura Detached Palace was famously singled out by the German architect Bruno Taut as the finest example of Japanese architecture. Though Taut's prewar stay in Japan was short, his praise touched many Japanese intellectuals—not just because it came from a European but also because it occurred when the international ostracism of Japan was growing. Ishikawa Jun's 1939 novel, *Line-Drawing* (*Hakubyō*), is in part a complex argument with Taut's view.

Mishima, in any case, wanted to take advantage of modern amenities in daily life, but buildings of Japanese-style simplicity were eminently unsuited to them. Hokonohara intimated that "instruments of convenience of civilization" wouldn't sit well with the kind of European-style house he envisioned, either, but Mishima was insistent. He wrote, "According to my stubborn theory, what *modern art* architecture aims for stands at the opposite end of the conveniences of living, and all modern mechanical instruments are philosophically in contradiction of such architecture." In short, he wanted "a most anti-Zen-temple house."

Seven years later, when a magazine for young readers offered to show his house and some of his favorite possessions with glossy photos, Mishima elaborated on his choice of architectural design and explained where some of the interior décor came from:

> I am innately fond of bright Mediterranean culture and love Latin colors. Further intoxicated by Latin American Colonial architecture, I decided to transplant its tropical beauty and melancholy to Japan, built a house in Spanish Colonial style, and decorated its interior with French antiques as well as Spanish antiques. The fan-shaped, inlaid Spanish frame at the very end of this photogravure is my first memorable purchase. As to the furniture, my wife and I visited as many antique shops in Madrid as we could, until our legs turned into wooden sticks, devoted as we were to the grand decorative beauty of Spanish Baroque.[20]

The two-story house, in its subdued elegance, was more Palladian, perhaps, than "Victorian Colonial," the term Mishima stuck to in explaining its design to inquiring journalists and editors, as he had in various writings. In the equally European garden, facing the main building where he lived with Yōko, stood a white statue of Apollo with a lyre. The statue was surrounded by mosaic pavement depicting the twelve zodiacal animals. Mishima imported it from Italy. In addition, he built a separate house, quite an ordinary, Japanese-style, one-story house, for Azusa and Shizue to live.

Whatever Mishima's ideas for it, Fukushima Jirō most likely gave an accurate appraisal of the elaborate European building he worked out. Fukushima, who, upon reading *Forbidden Colors*, had impulsively visited Mishima to find out where the gay bar called Redon was and ended up an old-fashioned student-help for the Mishima household, had gained the impression, from magazine photos and such, that the building was "grand and resplendent." But when he visited Azusa and Shizue following Mishima's death and actually saw it, he felt it was "a kind of fraud" perpetrated on "the congested Tokyo," Mishima's "dream maximally packed into a small plot of land." Yes, the garden railings, the pots with palms, outdoor tables and chairs with complex designs, and the nude statue erected at the center of the garden were all pure-white.

Instead of "the splendor unthinkable in Japan" attributed to the building by various commentators, however, Fukushima saw something "dwarfish" about the whole setup.[21] That sense of things dishearteningly diminished may be inevitable after the person closely associated with them disappears, especially when that person is an outsized personality like Mishima Yukio. But there must be a good deal of truth to what Fukushima found.

## *Deadly Serious about Learning Kendō*

Toward the end of the fall of 1958, Mishima took up kendō. He sought advice from Chūō Kōron president Shimanaka Hōji, who told him to talk to one of his editors, Kasahara Kinjirō, who held four dan in the sport. Mishima duly telephoned Kasahara—an occasion the editor remembered distinctly, except perhaps for the dates. Mishima sounded unusually stiff and formal. Asked why he wanted to learn kendō, he became even more awkward, only saying he just wanted to do it, asking for an introduction to an appropriate dōjō. From his tone Kasahara felt something deadly serious about the request.

The next evening Mishima came to the publisher's building as instructed. As Kasahara walked him to the dōjō, which was in the Dai-ichi Seimei Building that once housed the GHQ, he explained the kinds of gear he would need. When the two reached the dōjō, which was on the fourth basement, Mishima stiffened even more, "like a first grader about to go into his classroom for the first time," asking in low tones such things as when to take off his shoes and where to put them. They then sat on their knees in the hall outside the dōjō and offered prayers to the shrine built inside it. When Kasahara said, "This is all you need to do," Mishima for the first time looked relieved.

Actually, Shimanaka had asked Yano Ichirō, president of the insurance company, to give Mishima special permission to become a member of the dōjō. Also, Mishima had checked a couple of dōjō before he turned to Shimanaka.

Kasahara recalled he took Mishima to the dōjō one fine day in early September 1959, but Mishima had written he had visited the dōjō for the first time on November 28, 1958.[22] Kasahara, of course, was recalling the old event more than a few years after Mishima's death in which a sword played a crucial role, and that may explain why he remembered his "deadly serious" tone and such but not when that happened.

At any rate, it was in kendō that Mishima found his home, "the ideal of harmony between body and spirit." When he was at the Peers School he had had to do it, along with judo, archery, and horseback riding, but as a boy he had recoiled from "the shouts unique to kendō." Those "indescribably vulgar, barbarous, intimidating, shameless, nakedly physiological, anticivil and anticultural, antirational, animalistic shouts filled the boy's heart brimming with bashfulness." But now, twenty-five years later, he truly loved them. Why the change?

> I came to recognize on my own and tolerate for myself the shouts of "Japan" that lie at the base of my spirit. In these shouts is bluntly revealed that which modern Japan is ashamed of, tries desperately to hide. These are linked to the darkest memories, linked to the fresh blood that was shed, that originated in the most honest memories of Japan's past. These are the shouts of the depth consciousness of the race that lurks and flows underneath the superficial modernization. That kind of monstrous Japan has been chained, left unfed for a long time, enfeebled, and moaning, but he can shout out now, borrowing our mouths, in the dōjō for kendō.[23]

In April 1959 Mishima's new house was completed and the family started to move. On the 10th of that month, Crown Prince Akihito married Michiko, the union touted as one of "tennis mates." Mishima, getting up at one-thirty p.m., as was his wont, practiced kendō solo in the garden, and turned to TV to see the marriage procession. As the horse-drawn carriage with the prince and his bride moved through the Palace Plaza, a young man threw a stone at it, dashed to it, and tried to climb into it. He was immediately pulled off it by several policemen and wrestled down, but Mishima had seen not just the parabola the stone made but also Princess Michiko "arch backward in astonishment."

"My excitement when I saw it was extraordinary," Mishima wrote. "A [stage] drama never happens this way. This was in the territory of fact, without a foreshadowing, without a dialogue to be heard. But when this poor, unhappy nineteen-year-old youth, who called himself an opponent of the Tennō system, put his feet on the step of the carriage in glittering gold, and came face to face with His and Her Highnesses, there, unmistakably, human beings came face to face. That moment was far more glittering than the decorations of the carriage and the gold braiding of the outriders' uniforms."[24]

In the evening Mishima went to NHK Hall to hear the cantata he wrote in celebration of the newlyweds. It is indicative of his fame and prestige that the National Broadcasting Corporation commissioned him, rather than an established poet, to compose words for an epithalamium. Mishima came up with a duet in classical language, which he openly called a "parody" of the love songs exchanged between the mythological Prince Magari no Ohine and Princess Kasuga in the *History of Japan* (*Nihon shoki*).[25] Mayuzumi composed the music. Wilhelm Schüchter conducted. It was broadcast on NHK TV and Radio.

Just about the same time, Mishima wrote an essay titled "Portrait at Eighteen and Thirty-four" to contrast himself sixteen years apart. Saying he is now a *danna-sama*, a term blending endearment and certain respect from the perspective of a third party, he wrote: "I lord it over my wife appropriately, I behave in accordance with common sense within the family, I am building my own house, I am cheerful not to a small degree, I like to badmouth other people now just as I did in the past. I am delighted when someone says I look younger than I am, I follow fashions and dress frivolously, I pretend I have absolutely no interest in things unless they are vulgar. I try not to say anything serious, I have a lot of contempt for intellectual vanity, I seldom read books."

This last was of course an obvious pretense in the guise of self-deprecation. Reading on his own was impressive enough. For example, in the early part of the year he had read, with concentration, the works of the mycologist (especially slime fungus), folklorist, and naturalist who made his name in England through magazines such as *Nature*, Minakata Kumagusu, and the folkloric interpreter of Japanese literature and poet Orikuchi Shinobu, both prolific writers. Also, in a country that prizes taidan and group discussions among well-known writers, Mishima could not go many days without some magazine asking him to take part in one session or another to analyze a writer or writers, let alone write a blurb on a book or someone's "complete works," brand-new or reissued.

"I am paying attention to my health so that I may live until I am 150 years old. I go to kendō Mondays and Fridays, I go to bodybuilding Tuesdays, Thursdays, and Saturdays," he continued. "Comparing my body with other writers' flabby bodies or bodies like boiled chickens with the meat all stripped away, I pretend to think that no one has a body as excellent and taut as mine. Besides, this being the thirteenth year in my life as a novelist, I no longer have to live day to day so fearful of them."

To end this short "literary autobiography," he changed his subject rather abruptly: "Even so, I am sometimes tempted simply to join the Self-Defense Forces or something. I'd hate to die of a disease or under an atomic bomb, but I wouldn't mind getting killed with a gun."

Having written this, Mishima remembered again a question a friend of his asked back in 1943, using the German word for "die": "Are you prepared to *sterben*?"

Earlier in the essay, he had explained that the friend, on a baseball team, had just been diagnosed with pulmonary infiltration, and described his reaction this way: "I felt the world suddenly go dark before my eyes, I felt painfully that I couldn't possibly die when my life had barely begun." When his friend's question came back as an echo, he wrote: "If I'm so asked as straightforwardly, I'll have no choice but to reply, No, I'm not prepared. But the idea of death nonetheless remains the sweetest mother of my work."[26]

CHAPTER FIFTEEN

# Kyōko's House

> "You praise my work first and other critics stop praising it."
> —Mishima to Okuno Takeo

As he brought his first *kakioroshi* novel to a close, Mishima mused that he had long been troubled by the "eerie, ominous, incredible feelings at the prospect of completing it sooner or later."[1] The forebodings, if they had to do with the fate of the novel, came partly true. *Kyōko's House*, published in September 1959, did well commercially, if not well enough for someone as successful as Mishima by then was; it sold 150,000 copies in the first month. But it was a critical failure. Some of the more prominent reviewers dismissed it as too redolent of Mishima himself. Coming right after his marriage and all the great effort he put into the work, such reviews let Mishima down severely.

Not that opinions were unanimous. Among the initial reviewers, Okuno Takeo praised it highly. It is "a model of classical psychological fiction" and "Mishima's greatest masterpiece since *Confessions of a Mask*," he wrote in the review that appeared in the same month as the novel. "In depicting modern youth, it is, in artistic perfectibility, far above Ishihara Shintarō's *The Fissure* (*Kiretsu*) and Ōe Kenzaburō's *Our Era* (*Warera ga jidai*)." But the participants in the year-end group review of literary works that year in *Bungakukai* were at once dismissive and merciless, all five agreeing that *Kyōko's House* was a failure.

Hirano Ken said that he saw Mishima "used all the material he

/ 333

had on hand in full," but that the story has "no climax." Yamamoto Kenkichi was oddly backhanded. Mishima had never created a failure, be it *The Sound of Waves* or *Virtue Falters*, he said, but "this time he has made a big mistake for the first time." Usui Yoshimi offered an observation that carried the air of a personal *coup de grâce*: Compared with the worlds Mishima created in other works, the one here "seems broad if the question is whether it is broad or narrow, but in the end it is narrow. The setup of the characters is all filled with Mishima-style stereotypical paradoxes, isn't it? The whole thing is set up with paradoxes that come with the sense that they become shallow if repeated too often. Since he set up characters paradoxically as he pleased and did nothing but to line up samples of their paradoxical interpretations as he pleased, the story is truly monotonous."

The two other participants, Etō Jun and Saeki Shōichi, both agreed that *Kyōko's House* was a failure. Of the two, Etō was somewhat conciliatory, albeit cryptic. Mishima "may have had the idea of mirroring the outside [in his characters]," he said. "I think it is Mishima's *trick*: saying he'd mirror the outside while mirroring the inside." Etō went on to amplify his view later when he took up the novel to place it in the context of Mishima's oeuvre up to that time, and we will take a look at it in a moment. What irritated some of the initial respondents obviously was that *Kyōko's House* was too much about and of Mishima.

"All the [four] characters who appear in the novel merely represent the various aspects of Mishima Yukio," Saeki said. Or, as Okuno put it, albeit not to condemn, Mishima "poured all his multifarious experiences" into this novel, so that "one is tempted to wonder if he had deliberately designed his life so as to write it."[2] In other words, the four young men around whom the story moves are all Mishima's alter egos.

So Fukui Shunkichi, the student boxer, embodies the thought-erasing physicality of sports Mishima idealized. Funaki Osamu the aspiring actor is a narcissist who, while losing himself in women, becomes so acutely conscious of his scrawny body that he takes up bodybuilding. Yamagata Natsuo the Japanese-style painter is an aesthete who for a while becomes trapped by mysticism—an area that fascinated Mishima. And Sugimoto Seiichrō the salaryman and the most argumentative and articulate of the lot is also a cautious, calculating climber of the corporate ladder who acts responsibly even as he swears a paradox, "How can you live without the conviction that the world is bound to perish?"

Mishima was, financially and in other ways, a supremely responsible man.

As to this last point, Mishima made it plain, just before the marriage, for example, that he was not a writer in the Bohemian mold. "I by nature hate most upheavals and troubles," he wrote for the ladies' monthly *Fujin Kōron*. "Therein lies the difference between my way of life and the way of life of old-fashioned writers and, more recently, of self-destructive types such as Dazai Osamu and Sakaguchi Ango."[3] We have seen Dazai. Sakaguchi was also prone to alcohol (and drugs), and died of brain hemorrhage. One might even add that Seiichirō, though not allergic to alcohol, is no more than a social drinker, just as Mishima was.

There is a fifth character, the woman in the title of the novel, Kyōko, but her role is largely to be a "mirror," which is what the Chinese character for *kyō* of her name means—that is, to show to the reader the comings-and-goings of the four men who get to know one another in her house. (Her open house was modeled after Yuasa Atsuko's salon in real life. The novel did not sell better than it did, at least for the first few years, because Atsuko, upset that her house was described as "carrying the feeling of a brothel," told the publisher Shinchōsha not to advertise the book—an action she regretted later.[4] Kyōko herself is presented as exquisitely attractive and wholly liberated as Atsuko actually was.)

"Because I depicted 'an individual' in *The Golden Pavilion*, I decided to depict 'an era' in *Kyōko's House*," Mishima explained in the ad copy for his publisher that was not used because of Yuasa Atsuko's intervention. "The protagonist of *Kyōko's House* is not a person but an era. You might say that this novel is not part of the so-called postwar literature but part of 'the-postwar-era-is-over' literature"—that is, what may be called the "post-postwar" era today. "I tried to delineate some of the typical examples of emotion and psychology of an era that believed that 'the postwar era is over.'"[5]

What Mishima meant to suggest through the four male alter egos was the sense of being up against the wall that was the era. The period covered is from April 1954 to April 1956, and there was ample reason for those so inclined to feel they are in a dead end.

At the start of the story, for example, Natsuo refers to an incident of "just last month": "a Japanese fishing boat at the Bikini Atoll was hit by a nuclear test fallout, its crew suffered atomic bomb sickness, the people all over Tokyo feared atomic tuna, and the price of tuna crashed." The matter is brought up more or less as a passing thought to suggest external events do not touch the aesthete. In fact, it was an "extraordinary social disaster" that darkened the prospects of Japanese society.

On March 1, 1954, the fishing boat *Daigo Fukuryū Maru* and its twenty-three-man crew became the first direct victims of the series of nuclear tests the United States had been conducting since the second half of the 1940s. It was a result of American scientists' underestimation of the megatonnage of the hydrogen bomb they exploded that day and the shift in the direction of the wind after the explosion. The fishing boat was outside the designated radius of the test, to no avail. All the crewmen suffered from radiation and one died. The tuna they had caught had to be dumped; so were all the fish the other boats caught in the waters adjacent to the testing area. In November that year the movie *Godzilla* (*Gojira*) was released; in it a giant monster resembling a Tyrannosaurus Rex revived by nuclear tests brings destruction to Japan.[6] The Geiger counter, used not just to measure the radiation of fish brought back from the South Pacific but also to measure radiation in the rains brought by the typhoons, would become ubiquitous in the news programs, its sinister clicking sound a symbol of something ominous, for years to come.

Mishima contrasts the Japanese society so situated with the annihilated cityscape that was Japan less than a decade earlier, and calls it "a wall"—a wall the four young men all feel they face, "without saying it, without talking about it."

> They couldn't tell whether it was the wall of the age or the wall of society. Either way, a similar wall had utterly collapsed during their boyhood, revealing a boundless expanse of rubble in the bright outside light. The sun rose from the horizon beyond the rubble, and set on it. The daily sunrise that dazzled fragments of glass bottles gave beauty to the innumerable scattered pieces. The boundlessly cheerful, the boundlessly free boyhood in which it was possible to believe that the world consisted of rubble and fragments had disappeared. The one certain thing now was that there was this huge wall and that the four were standing before it, face to face with it.

However, the four men react to this situation differently. "I'll smash up this wall," Shunkichi the pugilist resolves. "I'll turn this wall into a mirror," Osamu the lazy actor thinks. "I'll paint on this wall, no matter what," Natsuo decides, to turn it into "a mural of landscape and flower." And Seiichirō the most worldly and ambitious tells himself. "I'll become this wall. The thing is for me to transform myself into the wall itself."

As it turns out, Shunkichi stumbles into a brawl with a bunch of hoods the very night he wins a championship belt, gets his right hand smashed, and joins an extreme rightwing group;[7] Osamu commits double-suicide with a female loan-shark who is ugly and older; and Natsuo gets sucked into Shinto mysticism until one morning he is amazed by a single daffodil left by his bedside, which reminds him of the Chinese Emperor Huizong's painting of daffodils and a quail, and decides to move to Mexico.

As to Seiichirō, he simply redoubles his eschatological sense of the world. Now working in an office in the midst of Wall Street, he one day sees the *Herald Tribune* blaring in its headline "the unprecedented prosperity" of the US economy. The United States has already gotten out of the 1953–54 recession, improving upon all the economic indicators of the past with unexpected speed. In fact, the national income will easily increase by $20 billion and reach $320 billion. The waves of this economic boom have reached the shores of Europe and Asia as well, dashing "the wishful thinking of Marxist economics" while proving that capitalism can resurrect itself like a phoenix.

Seiichirō knows there is "no falsity, no exaggeration whatsoever" to this account, though its triumphant tone reminds him of a college paper reporting a victory in a football game. As someone who works on Wall Street, where "worldwide prosperity originates," he witnesses the truth of it every day. "That threat known as historical inevitability, that ancient astrology, can frighten no one any longer." But to him, it was exactly "a clear omen of what he called 'the collapse of the world.'" New York, because it is the engine of worldwide prosperity, is the very place that will touch it off. And by the time the waves of "the monstrous prosperity of this country" fully reached the "Oriental island nation" Japan, each of the small group of four men would have chosen "a personal death, through a personal tragedy, of a design appropriate for each," even though, as Seiichirō saw it, they would have "merely added themselves to a ring of reincarnation. Beyond these physical or spiritual deaths surely waited a grotesque, disgusting *reincarnation*!"

## *Nihilism and Fascism*

When he completed *Kyōko's House*, Mishima had written in his "diary" for *Shinchō* that "the womb that gave birth to it" was his 1954 short story "The Room You Can Lock" (*Kagi no kakaru heya*) and that, in that sense, it was "a study of Nihilism."[8] "The Room You Can Lock" recreates Mishima as a fresh bureaucrat in the Finance Ministry remarkably well—he used the daily log he kept at the time to reproduce the protagonist's "totally unmoored" sentiments and the "dark, *pathetic*" environment of a country destroyed and occupied—though he termed its focal part "fiction": a weekly sexual visit with a married woman he happens to meet on a dance floor, Kiriko (her husband never comes home until very late). Kiriko, with cardiac beriberi, collapses on him during sex and dies soon. He then plays with her nine-year-old daughter until he discovers that the child, with an early onset of menstruation, begins to act like a seductress. Writing about this story nearly a dozen years later when his short stories were collected, he ventured it might have provided premonitions for "the advent of Mr. Ōe Kenzaburō," his "view of eroticism," adding it was "free for the reader to see premonitions for the political situation after 1954."[9]

Mishima had given a succinct assessment of the era in a short story a year earlier, in 1953, "A Memorandum on Eguchi Hatsu-jo" (*Eguchi Hatsujo oboegaki*): "The age of the Occupation is an age of humiliation. It is an age of falsity. It is an age of obedience face to face and disobedience when the back is turned, of physical and spiritual prostitution, and of machination and deception." The story's protagonist, Eguchi Hatsuko, is the antithetical reincarnation of the prostitute in medieval legend, Eguchi, described in *Eguchi*, a nō play attributed to Kan'ami (1333–84). The medieval predecessor is said to have turned into the Bodhisattva of Universal Virtue for her understanding of this world after exchanging tanka with the poet Saigyō (1118–90).

Mishima shared Seiichirō's conviction in "the collapse of the world." He made a historical examination of it in "On New Fascism," an essay he wrote a few months after "The Room You Can Lock" as his response—"a term paper"—to some leftists who decried him as a Fascist. Citing such thinkers as Bertrand Russell (*Power: A New Social Analysis*), the British Communist R. Palme Dutt (*Fascism and Social Revolution*), the "philosopher of Fascism," Giovanni Gentile, and the German theologian Helmut Thielicke, he begins with two propositions: that Communism and Fascism are common in that they aim for government based on a worldview, rather than government based on technicalities, such as parliamentarism, and that—this is secondary—whereas the Fascism of Europe appealed to the bourgeoisie and therefore to the intelligentsia, its Japanese imitation never did. Why? It was because "Fascism pandered to Nihilism."

"Europe at the start of the twentieth century brimmed with the tides of antirationalism deriving from Nihilism. By pandering to this [state of affairs] Freud and Fascism emerged. Their forerunner was Nietzsche," Mishima summed up. "According to Helmut Thielicke, the Nihilist, by holding nothingness as absolute, faced the collapse of the self and the collapse of the world and condemned himself to the *Funktionär* that is a cog in a piece of machinery, thereby creating ground for accommodating Fascism." But such a social functionary was in essence "a lamblike drug addict" and was useless. Fascism chose those who advocated "active Nihilism" and were "Nietzsche's epigones."

> The Nihilist faces the collapse of the world. The world loses its meaning for him. Here the psychology of despair comes to the fore, and the despairer hopes to preserve as best he could the meaninglessness he has grasped. The Nihilist becomes a thorough hypocrite. Because his whole premise is meaninglessness, he has the supreme freedom to act as if he had meaning, and becomes, as it were, a versatile man.

So analyzed, nothing is as remote from Fascism as the Japanese right-wing's "optimism."

Mishima concludes this tract with his "favorite theory": "'Beauty' always exists as a symbol of relativistic salvation lest the Nihilist fall into absolutist politics"—or try to work out absolutist government. "Beauty works to bring back the eyes of the Nihilist, who tends to make nothingness absolute, to contemplate on the abyss of relativism. And that is the urgent task of today's art."[10]

Without reference to Mishima's analysis of Fascism or the fictional antecedent as "a study of Nihilism," Etō Jun wrote, almost two years later, a full review of *Kyōko's House*. He first judges that *Kyōko's House* "fails as a full-length novel" and that "you rarely get a novel so *static*, so devoid of conflicts among the human beings" depicted.

But Etō has a second judgment to make. The novel is "nothing but a brilliant success," he asserts, if it is read not as an attempt to describe realistically a particular period of postwar Japan but as an effort to project Mishima's view that postwar Japan was just "a giant 'blank.'" Indeed, "What lives in 'Kyōko's house' is the spirit of the era called 'postwar,'" he goes on to note. "This spirit is entirely alien to what popular historians of thought call social reformism, democracy, new education, what the revolutionary intellectuals of the late 1930s called 'the second youth,' and all other fragments of Zeitgeist, and yet it is what lurks at the bottom of it all."

*Kyōko's House* ends with seeming abruptness. After the four young men have left Kyōko's salon in one way or another, her divorced husband returns with the very reason that prompted her divorce of him intact: the dogs. "The seven shepherds and the Great Dane, unchained almost at once, came dashing in through the door. The air resounded with their roars and the large guestroom in no time filled with the canine smell." In plotting the novel, Mishima meant to bring down the curtain on the "disorder" Kyōko brought on through her salon—she "feared" it—but does this man represent or symbolize anything? After all, he remains unnamed and hidden throughout the narrative only to reappear at the end, with an improbably large pack of dogs. Is he "a symbol of habit and dailiness," though designed to shatter Kyōko's poise instantly, as Etō suggests?[11]

Here let us suppose that the husband who comes back represents Kishi Nobusuke, whose postwar political comeback began with a mystery.

## *Reemergence of Kishi Nobusuke*

On December 24, 1948, the day after Tōjō Hideki and six others were hanged as a result of the decisions made by the International Military Tribunal for the Far East, a shabby-looking man shuffled out of the front gate of the Sugamo Prison: head closely cropped, forehead wide, eyes enormous, and front teeth protruding, he was in US-issue military fatigue, complete with field cap and laced boots, all too large for him. He was taken by US army jeep to the official residence of Yoshida Shigeru's cabinet secretary Satō Eisaku, in Nagata-chō. The guard did not recognize him and would not let him in for a while, even though he was Satō's older brother and until only a few years earlier one of the most powerful bureaucrat-politicians: Kishi Nobusuke.[12]

Three years earlier, on September 15, 1945, Kishi was arrested on charges of Class A war crimes by the victorious nations for the upcoming military tribunal, and on December 8, the fourth anniversary of Japan's attack on Pearl Harbor, sent to the Sugamo Prison. As noted earlier, following the Second World War, the victors categorized war crimes into three classes A, B, and C: Class A for "crimes against peace," Class B for "crimes against humanity," and Class C for "conventional war crimes." The seven men who were hanged were all from among Class A suspects.[13]

Most of those concerned, including Kishi's daughter, thought that the arrest spelled the end of his life. Yet, detained though he was for three years, no indictment came, and he was released instead—the day after the hanging of the seven. This outcome prompted a range of speculations. Was it because he brought down Tōjō in the midst of war or was it because the United States decided on the need for highly capable men as its policy toward Japan changed with the worsening of the Cold War? His return to political power, at any rate, was "rough and straight," one biographer put it.[14]

There were some detours on the way. Kishi was not indicted after he was taken in custody, but he was among those "purged" from public office, until Japan gained independence as the Peace Treaty took effect, in April 1952. A few days before that, however, he established the Association for Rebuilding Japan with three goals: writing Japan's own Constitution (to replace the one the Occupation had given), establishing Japan's own military (not a detachment of the US forces), and pursuing Japan's own diplomacy (rather than as an US subsidiary). In the general election that October, all the candidates from the association lost.

In March of the following year Kishi joined Yoshida's Liberal Party[15] and the next month ran for the House of Representatives and was elected. In December he became chairman of the party's committee to look into the possibility of rewriting the Constitution. Less than a year later, in November 1954, Kishi was expelled from the Liberal Party. A great schism had developed among the conservatives. Those gathered under Yoshida Shigeru, prime minister since May 1946 except for the period from May 1947 to October 1948, believed in light armament—some remilitarization couldn't be avoided because of the United States, but Japan's economy was too weak to support full armament—and favored a pursuit of international trade.

But there were also those who argued that Japan ought to seek a "true independence" and recover its glory days before the war. Kishi was at the forefront of the latter group; hence his ejection from the party.[16] They coalesced around Hatoyama Ichirō—who had established the Liberal Party following Japan's defeat but then was "purged"—and formed the Democratic Party, and Kishi became the new party's secretary-general. The following month the Yoshida cabinet fell.

However, the two parties merged in less than a year, in November 1955, to form the Liberal Democratic Party (LDP), and Kishi became its secretary-general. A year on, in December 1956, Kishi lost out to Ishibashi Tanzan to be the party head, namely, prime minister, getting the post of foreign minister instead. But Ishibashi, the farsighted journalist-turned-politician, promptly became ill, and in two months, Kishi succeeded him. This turn of events would lead at least one commentator half a century later to wonder how different a path Japan might have taken had Ishibashi run the nation for several years.[17] There was ample ground for the wonderment.

In 1912, when the Mayor of Tokyo—at the time, Tokyo was a city (*shi*), hence "mayor" (*shichō*)—made a "mob-like" effort to raise funds for a building to commemorate the Meiji Emperor, Ishibashi, a young journalist, had objected, arguing that such a large sum should not be wasted on "a shrine of wood and stone." Instead, a "Meiji Prize," akin to the Nobel Prize, ought to be set up to magnify the great democratization that had occurred during the emperor's reign. In 1922, when territorial expansion was fast becoming the *de rigueur* national goal, Ishibashi demonstrated statistically how international trade would help the nation far better than colonization through force and advised abandonment of Korea, Taiwan, and Sakhalin, not to mention "national interests" in Manchuria and elsewhere.

And, in 1970, a few months before Mishima killed himself, Ishibashi lamented that it was none other than the succession of conservative administrations that had turned into "dead law" the no-war "peace Constitution" that the conservative Prime Minister Shidehara Kijūrō had helped to write. The Constitution by then had become the model for the world, he pointed out.[18]

The formation of the LDP, in any event, would create what was later called "the 1955 Regime": the conservative party's hegemony of Japanese politics for the next forty years. Long-term, ironically, the LDP's policy was not too different from Yoshida's: to strengthen Japan's economy while relying on the US military under the US-Japanese Mutual Security Treaty. Still, Kishi pushed his policy for "a new era for US-Japanese relations" and his seeming stress on the military alliance had generated such an animosity that the first nationwide group for a "unified action" against the treaty had formed by the time Mishima started work on *Kyōko's House*. The opposition to Kishi would soon lead to the greatest political movement in postwar Japan. And Mishima would become more than a third-party observer of it.

---

The critical failure of *Kyōko's House* was a blow to Mishima. Okuno remembered Mishima telling him, "You praise my work first and other critics stop praising it. From now on I don't want you to be the first to praise me too much."[19] But the effect was far worse and far-reaching than the somewhat jocular remark suggested, Mishima said three years before his death.

In late 1967, as his seemingly rightwing political activities were becoming overt, he had a taidan with the leftist film director Ōshima Nagisa. Ogawa Tōru, the editor of *Eiga Geijutsu*, arranged it at Mishima's request. Ōshima, who was making a series of outlandish movies, would startle the moviegoers of the world a decade later with *In the Realm of Senses*.[20] As it turned out, the two men did not have much to disagree on. When Ōshima mentioned *Kyōko's House* was one of two Mishima novels he wanted to turn into a film, Mishima recalled critics' negative reactions to the novel and compared himself at that point to a despairing mother on a bridge ready to throw her baby into the river. But none of the people watching tried to stop her and, after she dumped her baby into the river, arrested her.

Mishima's metaphor, conjured eight years after the fact, is too obscure to make much of, and Ōshima did not ask him to clarify. It is notable nonetheless because Mishima ended by saying that critics' failure to understand what he was trying to do in *Kyōko's House* "must have put me out of whack, I'm sure." It may well be that, as Ogawa, the moderator of the taidan, observed, the reviewers are so concerned with the "technicalities" of the novel—the fact that Mishima broke himself up into four characters and made them act themselves out—that they failed or refused to see the whole personal struggle.[21]

Etō Jun ended his commentary with a prediction: "Mishima will never write about his generation, especially after the failure that is *Kyōko's House*." It would prove largely correct.

## *Translatese and The Constitution*

While working on his longest novel, Mishima managed to write, among other things, a weekly column for a period of sixteen months, from July 1958 to November 1959. Titled *Lectures on Unethical Education* (*Fudōtoku kyōiku kōza*), it was a series of lighthearted essays on how not to behave as society expects. The idea was provocative enough to be turned into a film even as he was continuing the column, in December 1958.

In the film Mishima was given the role of playing himself as author. His family had not opposed his writing the column, but to them appearing in a movie was a different matter; they objected. Mishima ignored them and played the prescribed role, to say a few words in "the prologue" and "the epilogue" of the film. The single night's filming experience taught him the difficulty of being natural on camera, he wrote in his "diary."[22] Tsukioka Yumeji, who had played the protagonist in the film version of *Virtue Falters*, was among the actresses who appeared in the film.

In September and October of that year, in four Saturday sessions, each lasting for two hours, Mishima dictated what amounted to a whole book. The act, which was done at the request of *Fujin Kōron*, would be a feat in itself, but he did it in a genre that requires much thinking and reading: an established author citing exemplary writings and commenting on them to impart to the reader an idea of what he thinks admirable writing ought to be like. The result, titled *Bunshō tokuhon*, which is the standard nomenclature for the genre,[23] begins with the French critic Albert Thibaudet's distinction between *lecteurs* and *liseurs* and ends with a list of neologisms in James Joyce's *Finnegans Wake*, with citations in between not just of prose, usually the focus in books of this genre, but also of poetry, drama, criticism, and translations, classical and modern, Japanese and European.

On translation, indeed, Mishima had some important points to make. *Hon'yaku-bun* or language resulting from the act of translation, though not necessarily *translatese*, has exerted "the most profound influence" on the language that modern Japanese writers employ, that is, *kōgo-bun*, writing in spoken language, he explained. The development of *kōgo-bun* has been an integral aspect of modern Japanese. It was, Mishima noted, "what linked Japanese history to the world history of the West, what attempted to reform Japanese language to keep in step with [advanced] materialistic civilization."

There have been several consequences of this. Some early translators felt it necessary to create belles-lettres. The most famous among them is Mori Ōgai, whose translation, from 1892 to 1901, of Hans Christian Andersen's *The Improvisatore* as *Sokkyō shijin* was done in such an elegant, classical language that it has since been accepted as a masterpiece on its own; whether Andersen's original was written in comparable language was scarcely an issue. Mishima cites two translations in similar vein—of the last two stanzas of what Poe incorporates into *The Fall of the House of Usher* as one of Roderick Usher's "rhymed verbal improvisations." One of the translations is by the English professor and poet Hinatsu Kōnosuke and the other by Tanizaki Seiji, Jun'ichirō's younger brother and a professor of English. Reading them one would be hard put to imagine the original as a simple, balladlike composition.

Yokomitsu Riichi, of the New Sensibility School, represents another extreme; he sometimes wrote in "a deliberate translation-style" in order to "stimulate and refresh our sensibility," Mishima observed. Some of his writings may strike the reader as *translatese* even today, though they were Yokomitsu's own writings, not translations at all. Similarly, "who would doubt when told that Mr. Ōe Kenzaburō's writing, as it is, is a translation of Sartre?" Nonetheless, "though in prewar days his writing would have been regarded as *translatese*, now, we don't feel it's that much of *translatese*."

Mishima knew fully the ever-shifting nature of Japanese language and gave illuminating, convincing examples. Nevertheless, he could not help taking a stab at the language of the Constitution then a dozen years old.

"I think you will remember that Constitution that was a mysterious literal translation of English after the war's ending, that literal translation of the MacArthur Constitution," he said. "It was composed, yes, with something resembling prose in spoken language in Japanese, but it was a truly monstrous, hideous prose, and not a few people must have felt the sorrow of the Occupied over the fact that it became the Japanese Constitution. If Japan had been occupied during the Meiji Era" and given a Constitution, he added, its "translation must have been composed in far more fluid belles-lettres."24

The Meiji Constitution, promulgated in 1889, is written in simple, Chinese-influenced *bungo*, "literary language."

Given Mishima's knowledge and understanding, it would be redundant to add words on the language of "the MacArthur Constitution," but by the time he gave his judgment, not many Japanese would have noticed the particular linguistic aspect of the document Mishima condemned, even though the team assembled to write the constitution, led by the Harvard-trained lawyer Lt. Col. Charles L. Kades, drafted it and took care to have it translated faithfully, without much addition or subtraction. (Shidehara Kijūrō, the prime minister mentioned earlier, denied in his memoirs that the Constitution was imposed upon Japan, pointing out that he agreed with the idea of abandoning the military altogether and that of calling the Tennō "a symbol.")25

The result was far ahead of the US Constitution in many ways. The leaders of the drafting team were New Dealers eager to lay down ideal legal principles for a backward, immature nation. And a backward, immature nation Japan was, at least in the eyes of the Occupiers. "Measured by the standards of modern civilization, [Japan] would be like a boy of twelve as compared with [the Anglo-Saxon] development of forty-five years," MacArthur summed up his assessment of the country he had ruled until President Truman fired him.26 The former SCAP's observation "delighted" Mishima very much. "Legally speaking, by criminal law no one under the age of fourteen is liable for criminal responsibility." That would mean, among others, Japan's "so-called war criminals should be free of responsibilities," Mishima wrote with sarcasm a year after MacArthur's testimony in the US Senate.27

In any event, the great majority of the Japanese have liked the document. All attempts to revise it since, including those by Kishi and Mishima, have gotten nowhere, although interpretations of certain articles, most notably the no-war clause, are a different matter.

---

October 24, 1958, was a busy day, even for Mishima. An editor of *Bungei Shunjū* came to visit and told him that he was assigned the role of Ikyū of the Beard in the classical kabuki *Sukeroku*—a contemptible figure in the glorious play—in the publisher's annual yearend *bunshigeki*, in which popular writers play all the figures in the drama. In the evening he went to the Kabuki-za to discuss the upcoming production of a one-act kabuki comedy he wrote, *Fond of Young Women: The Sash-Taking Pond* (*Musume-gonomi obitori-no-ike*). The stage contraption devised for the play "will astonish the audience," Mishima happily noted in his "diary." The kabuki was staged from the first to the twenty-sixth of November with Utaemon playing the lead role of Princess Kiku and Kubota Mantarō directing.

Past eight o'clock he went to the nightclub Manuela in tuxedo because the invitation to the performance of the chanson singer Koshiji Fubuki said "black tie." Spotting him, Kawaguchi Matsutarō cried, "Aha! Here comes the idiot, the idiot! I was told to come in tuxedo, too, but came in a regular suit, and the only guys who've come in tuxedo are Tōhō executives!" Kawaguchi, himself an executive of the company but also a popular writer-cum-film-director, then forced Mishima and those other executives to line up and dance the *cancan*. That "surprised me," Mishima wrote.

Koshiji's duet with Raymond Conde was "tasteful and very good indeed," but it was "wasted" because of all the noise the audience made. Conde, a Filipino who had come to Japan in 1932, married a Japanese, and settled down, was also a top clarinetist through much of Japan's long love affair with jazz during the postwar period. Around eleven Mishima went to the Meiji-za to attend the rehearsal of a dance drama he had written, *Crossing All the Bridges* (*Hashi-zukushi*). He came home at one-thirty in the morning.

More than half a year later, on May 12, 1959, Mishima met Koshiji to discuss the play he was going to write for her. But the two had known each other since August of 1953 when the ladies' magazine *Fujin Asahi* asked them to discuss "the Paris the two of us saw." Koshiji, who had started out with the Takarazuka Revue and, after leaving it, achieved stardom as a singer and actress, had just spent a few months in Paris "to study the real thing"; chanson, which was quickly gaining enormous popularity in Japan, was part of her repertoire, and it was thrilling for her to hear Édith Piaf actually sing.

It was telling of the reputation of Paris in those days: Koshiji could not see what was so great about Paris for some time, but the cultural supremacy of the city was such that she felt compelled to walk about any number of streets, always in high heels, even though that pained her feet horribly. Among the Japanese notables who were in the city at the time were Kobayashi Hideo and Kon Hidemi.[28] Mishima became good friends with Koshiji after the taidan—they appeared so close indeed that for some time Shizue was convinced her son would marry the famous singer-actress.

On August 18 Mishima completed the play promised for Koshiji: *Onna wa senryō-sarenai*—the title may be literally translated "A Woman Is Never Occupied," with the caveat that "occupied" here refers to the Occupation. It concerns a love affair between Karayama Izuko, a widow heiress to a coal-mine fortune, and James Evans, a lieutenant colonel attached to the GHQ as chief of political affairs who is supposed to have a direct line to the SCAP.

The plot hinges on Evans's ability to manipulate Japanese politics—including the power to remove names from the list of people to be "purged"—and a socialist trying to become prime minister, so the actual time is 1947, when Katayama Tetsu won the premiership. Written to bring out Koshiji's seemingly breezy attractiveness, the play may be slight. But it is notable for Mishima's complete refusal to allow any language barrier despite the setting, with everyone speaking natural Japanese, and for the following scene where Evans, after dancing with Izuko, compliments her beauty against the backdrop of the bombed-out city of Tokyo. Izuko wants to have some fresh air and has him open the window. It is January:

... By the window is your beautiful profile. Yours is a truly luxurious, gorgeous profile. Coming through a war of that magnitude, just as though it had been a brief shower, here's your truly Oriental noblewoman's profile transmitting Japan's ancient history, its expensive, lascivious blood. In the meantime, there under the starry midwinter sky spreads endlessly the burnt-out city, dotted with the lamps of bomb shelters, miserable, dark, unhygienic lives, the ugliest scars of war enveloped in the darkness. The night-wind blows in through tin doors, and inside, rolled in soiled futon a great many families are fighting starvation and cold. . . . What kind of contrast is this? What a cruel disparity! This is a truly Oriental contrast. . . .

The play was produced at the Geijutsu-za, from the second to the twenty-seventh of September. Koshiji played the lead role, of course, and Nagaoka Teruko directed it.

---

In mid-September Mishima met Tennessee Williams, who was visiting Tokyo, partly to see a Japanese production of *A Streetcar Named Desire*, for a taidan. Donald Richie and Williams' secretary, Frank Merlo, attended the session as "observers." Williams, who had seen the rehearsal of his play just before the conversation, begins by complimenting the Japanese actors and actresses, adding he wished they'd done the play in some Japanese style, say, kabuki-style. Mishima responded by saying that reproducing the original manner of staging is exactly the Japanese way, be it in kabuki or something else.

At one point Mishima says he prefers the original *Cat on a Hot Tin Roof* to Williams's rewrite for Elia Kazan, and Williams happily agrees though he says he always values the stage director's opinions and tries to incorporate them—an interesting response given Williams' well-known eagerness to accept Kazan's suggestions.[29] Throughout the session Mishima called Williams by his personal name while Williams called Mishima by his surname. The taidan was duly published in the monthly *Geijutsu Shinchō* under the title of "Nippon as Seen by a Playwright."[30]

For two days at the end of November, the 28th and 29th, Mishima played the role of Benten Kozō in the *bunshigeki*. Kawatake Mokuami's 1862 kabuki, *Aoto zōshi hana no nishiki-e*, features five robbers, Benten

Kozō among them. But when the scenes with Benten Kozō alone are pulled together and staged, as is often done with kabuki plays, the title changes to *Benten musume meo no shiranami*,[31] and it was in this telescoped version that Mishima got to play the female-impersonating extortionist who, when cornered by the police, disembowels himself. NHK televised the whole one hour of it.

About that time Daiei had the idea of turning *Kyōko's House* into a movie. Nothing came of it, but Nagata Masaichi, president of the movie studio, asked Mishima to come by to confer. Mishima did so, on November 30. Right off the bat, Nagata said he was interested in bringing in someone like Mishima to attract more moviegoers, to wit, to use Mishima as "Mishima Yukio."

Dressed smartly for the occasion, Mishima asked, What do I look like? If you were to play a role the way you look, Nagata answered, you should be "a bad guy opposite the handsome lead. The role of a fellow who has lost his way would be good. The more yakuzalike, the better." Mishima liked that and signed an exclusive contract with the company as a film star. He also liked Nagata's subsequent announcement: "Cocteau in the West, Mishima in the East. The East and the West happen to be in the same orbit."

The following month Mishima wrote an essay, "I Want to Be an *Objet*." (In art and related fields, the Japanese routinely use the French word *objet* for "object.") He packed it with aphoristic statements that at times verge on sophistry but essentially reveal the truth about himself.

Someone like the writer Ishihara Shintarō's brother, Yūjirō, may think that appearing in movies to "act" makes him "action-oriented," Mishima observed, but "expressing oneself through writing is far more action-oriented." This is because "action-oriented" means "to work according to one's free will, build whatever world he likes through words, and create what doesn't exist in reality or what resembles reality." In that sense, the only "action-oriented" person in filmdom is the director. To put it another way, all *actions* in film are *fake*, but "I am very much drawn to *fake* actions like that, as if my will has been taken away by someone else, and that's why I want to an actor."

"I am frequently fatigued hiding myself. I become exhausted hiding myself repeatedly. If I were to reveal myself, I could do only *fake* things." It is in movies, rather more than on stage, that *fake* actions look most *real*. The movie actor's acting is "the remotest from action while looking like action." In other words, "The movie actor is an *objet* in the extreme." And "I'll find it more interesting if I'm treated as much of an *objet* as possible."

By the time he wrote these things, the script for his first movie was being prepared, and its director picked, Masumura Yasuzō, as well as the actress to play the heroine, though he could not disclose her name yet, he said. He had asked for as intense a love scene as possible—his wife opposed it—and for scenes where he could show off his chest hair, the one part of his body in which he had "confidence." Masumura wondered about the "confidence" part, because he hadn't shown it to him yet.[32]

The role given Mishima was indeed that of the son of a yakuza, opposite one of the more handsome movie actors of the day, Funakoshi Eiji, who had played the Japanese architect in Alain Resnais' film that year, *Hiroshima mon amour*. The script had been originally written for Ishihara Yūjirō but had been shelved because of the fear that the last scene where the protagonist was to be gunned down would mar his image.[33]

## *Invasion of Privacy*

In January 1960 he started a ten-month serialization of a new novel, *After the Banquet* (*Utage no ato*). It would bring him the first lawsuit on "invasion of privacy" under the new Constitution.

For the Tokyo gubernatorial race in 1959, the Socialist Party put up Arita Hachirō as its candidate against the LDP candidate, Azuma Ryōtarō. If Azuma was a prominent physician, an authority on sports medicine, Arita, who was to be the model for Noguchi Yūken in *After the Banquet*, was a prominent diplomat whose political thinking and career reflected the difficult international maneuvering required of Japan before the country went to war and who, after its defeat, tried to help chart a new course for it.

After serving as minister or ambassador in Austria, Hungary, Belgium, and Luxemburg, Arita became ambassador to China in January 1936, just a month before the uprising on February 26, soon called the 2.26 Incident. But three months later, he was called back to become foreign minister in the cabinet of Hirota Kōki, who, himself a diplomat, was fated to become the only civilian to be sentenced to death during the Tokyo Trial and hanged.

Arita went on to serve as foreign minister in three more cabinets: the first Konoe cabinet, from October 1938 to January 1939; the Hiranuma cabinet, from January to August 1939; and the Yonai cabinet from January to July 1940. He was of the group that argued for "working out order in East Asia with East Asian countries," rather than with European countries and the United States. He was, for that reason, reluctant to ally Japan with Germany but went along with the Japanese-German anticommunism pact, signed in November 1936. He was opposed to strengthening the pact, but at the army's insistence, the government went on to include Italy in November 1937, and Hiranuma Kiichirō's cabinet sought to strengthen the pact further. That cabinet famously collapsed when the German-USSR Non-aggression Treaty was announced, in August 1939, with Hiranuma resigning with the bemused utterance, "The heaven and earth of Europe has produced a monstrously labyrinthine phenomenon."

Toward the end of the war, Arita submitted "an address to the Throne" to counsel surrender when such a stance, if publicly known, could have easily cost him his life. In fact, on August 15, the day of surrender, both Hiranuma, then president of the Privy Council, and Prime Minister Suzuki Kantarō were attacked by an army unit brandishing machine guns and their houses were burnt down. Hiranuma, though he headed a large rightwing group, was known to be a vocal critic of the military for its inability to defend Japan from the American onslaught. Suzuki had brought the surrender.

Under the Occupation, Arita was "purged." In 1953 he was elected to the House of Representatives as an advocate of non-remilitarization of Japan. Two years later the Socialist Party chose him as its candidate for governor of Tokyo, but he lost. For the 1959 race the party tried again, and this time Arita might have won. But Kishi Nobusuke, working on a revised US-Japanese Security Treaty, pulled out all the stops to destroy the "peace advocate," and Arita lost, again. One thing Kishi did was to immobilize Arita's wife, Azekami Terui, the model for Fukuzawa Kazu in *After the Banquet*.

Unlike Arita, who had education and a distinguished diplomatic career, Azekami, who married him, a widower, in 1953, had come up the ladder in the "water trade" the hard way. But in 1950, she, by then in her early forties, purchased the Hannya-en, a mansion so called because parts of the Hannya Temple in Nara, along with a nō stage once owned by a daimyo, had been moved to its spacious garden, turned it into a high-class Japanese-style restaurant, and in no time succeeded in making it a popular haunt of moneyed conservative politicians and business leaders. Arita and Azekami, in short, made an incongruous, fascinating couple.

During her husband's 1959 gubernatorial campaign, Azekami first mortgaged her restaurant to raise campaign funds without telling Arita. Then, with her prime customers quickly falling off, she tried to sell it. A large real estate company offered to buy it. Kishi stepped in and quashed the deal. His LDP distributed a "document with no source identified" purporting to chronicle Azekami's sexual liaisons in eyewitness detail, which weekly magazines happily picked up. One day before the vote, the LDP spread the rumor that Arita, then seventy-four, was on his deathbed. After the election, Arita divorced her.

All this was public knowledge. Further, in planning a fictionalized account of the election, Mishima read Azekami's own accounts and visited her at her restaurant with his editors and received her approval for the story that he wanted to write and, through her, Arita's as well. To show his approbation, Arita sent him his book just published, *They Call Me Hachi the Idiot* (*Baka-hachi to hito wa iu*), autographed.[34]

Yet as the serialization of Mishima's novel progressed, Arita grew agitated and started pressing the publisher of *Chūō Kōron* to suspend it. When Shinchōsha published the fiction in book form, in November, he sued Mishima for alleged invasion of privacy, the following March.

Arita's focus in his lawsuit was on the "Peeping-Tom" descriptions of his bedroom acts with his wife in *After the Banquet*. But because there are in fact only a few of them in the novel and they are as unavoidable as they are slight, Arita may well have been really upset by Mishima's not too positive a description of him as outwardly a knowledgeable, cultured European-style gentleman who in reality hasn't outgrown old-fashioned Confucian ideas and can act like someone uneducated and unrefined.

When Fukuzawa Kazu, in the novel, sees Noguchi Yūken for the first time during the reunion of a group of former diplomats at her restaurant, the Setsugo-an, she is most impressed by his dignity, refinement, and refusal to take part in small talk, in particular the kind of nostalgic recollections retired diplomats are wont to flaunt: a colorful, idyllic life in Dominica, Hermann Göring with his young lover glimpsed on the subway, this or that operatic performance in this or that city. The group makes a distinct contrast to the down-to-earth, even ostentatiously vulgar conservative politicians she knows so well. But even in this group of men who have managed to preserve their stylish European airs, Noguchi sets himself apart.

"His manly face had a rustic simplicity that he seemed never to lose and, unlike the others, his attire showed no pretentious or dandyish airs," Kazu observes. Arita was from Sado Island, in the Japan Sea, off the coast of Niigata, once a favored place for exile. "Above his sharp, clear eyes ran eyebrows like shapes drawn in brushstrokes with excess force. Such superb individual features conflicted with one another, emphasizing their disharmony with his skinny body. Besides, though he always maintained a smile on his face, he seldom nodded in agreement."

Kazu falls in love with him. With her trained eyes, she notices that the nape-side of his collar is slightly discolored, like "a faint shadow," but that only arouses her maternal instinct. The two start dating. Gradually, inevitably, though, Kazu begins to see that he is not what he appears to be—or at least that his dignity and studied superiority is not a born part of him.

Once she invites him to the Kabuki-za. At every sorrowful climax of the play she sheds tears—Mishima famously did the same—whereas Noguchi remains "cold, detached." During the intermission, he asks, obviously amused, "Why do you cry at such a silly, foolish play?" But then, when he realizes he's lost his cherished Dunhill lighter the "consternation" he displays is "astonishing." The authoritative, impassive composure he had maintained up to that moment vanishes. "The expression on his face as he groped into every pocket, half rising from his seat, muttering, 'No, not here, not here,' was totally different from what he normally showed." His loss of composure grows worse until, out in the hall, an usherette holds up a lighter and asks if it is what he's looking for. (This was self-caricature on Mishima's part: A woman friend remembered Mishima once behaving the same way.)

When Noguchi discovers that Kazu has mortgaged her restaurant to raise funds for his election campaign and has been campaigning for him besides, distributing posters, giving speeches, and so on, Noguchi, feeling his honor betrayed, beats her, kicks her as she collapses on the floor.

Arita may have been irked further because Mishima quoted some passages from the "mysterious document" verbatim as if to authenticate the slanderous concoction. In one scene, for instance, Yamazaki Motoichi, a disillusioned Communist-turned-election strategist, tells Kazu: "How big a campaign the election of Tokyo governor requires? Well, here's an example: suppose you want to put up two election bills on each of all the utility poles throughout Tokyo. There must be 150,000 to 160,000 poles, so you got to have 300,000 bills. If the bills cost ¥3 a piece, that makes it ¥900,000. Assume it costs ¥1 to put up a single bill, and the total will be ¥1,200,000. That's a sum that can take care of a small election campaign."

To this Kazu says: "Policy and such are secondary. All you need for an election is money and feeling. I am an uneducated woman. I mean to slug it out with only those two things on my side." It is these words of Kazu's that were put in the mouth of Azekami in "the document." The real Azekami had "encountered many difficulties since girlhood," in the complainant Arita's own words, before rising to the top of her world and who, having hobnobbed with old-style, often unprincipled politicians for some time now, was familiar with their words and actions, and so is Kazu portrayed in *After the Banquet*. In the event, Kazu's response sounds natural. But coming right after the campaign strategist's calculating tone, it may have made her, in Arita's eyes, particularly vulgar.

In its decision, the district court agreed with Arita on three of the four demands he made, turning down only the main one asking the defendants, Mishima and his publisher, to take out a full-size advertisement in each of the three major daily newspapers, *Asahi*, *Mainichi*, and *Yomiuri*, to apologize for "the great trouble" they'd given him with the publication of *After the Banquet*. Mishima and Shinchōsha were ordered to pay four-fifths of one million yen, the monetary damages Arita claimed, the remaining one-fifth deemed Arita's responsibility. The notion of punitive damages is alien to the Japanese judiciary and the amount of requested compensation is cut unless the lawsuit is judged wholly meritorious. (In 1961, the year Arita brought the suit, average monthly pay for a company employee was ¥24,000, but substantial bonuses were routine, so a million yen was equal to what such an employee made in just about two years.)

Mishima and Shinchōsha appealed, Arita died in March 1965, and in the spring of 1966 the Arita side made a reconciliation offer: not a single word of *After the Banquet* need be changed. At the end of November that year, the Tokyo Superior Court, an appeals court, accepted the agreement between the two parties. Because Arita "died, savoring the satisfaction that he had imported into Japan a new legal concept of privacy," whereas the defendants were able to maintain the principle of "no amendment of the original text," the matter "ended well for all," Mishima concluded.[35] But the suit was, he also noted, "an unfortunate event which led the so-called rights of privacy astray into various questions in diverse terrains such as social reputation and personal affairs, cultural values and critical aspects of artistic works."[36]

Several years later he added that he lost confidence in the Japanese court system after the trial and decision because the judge ignored Arita's lies. When asked by Mishima's lawyer if he had given his book to Mishima, Arita indignantly insisted he never had, that he might have given his book to such writers as Mori Ōgai and Natsume Sōseki but not to a disreputable one like Mishima. Mishima's lawyer then offered as evidence the autographed copy Arita had presented Mishima with, but that did not sway the judge's view. Apparently to the judge, Arita's reputation as a former foreign minister was more important.[37]

The lawsuit, in any case, at once made "invasion of privacy" part of the Japanese language, with the English word *privacy* intact because no exact counterpart was thought to exist in Japanese. The lawsuit became a landmark.

With his lawsuit Arita may have drawn unnecessary attention to himself, for the focus of the novel is not on the candidate so much as on his wife who makes an all-out effort to help him. When Mishima met Azekami before writing the story he told her the subject he had in mind, for it was "a conflict between politics and love," adding: "I have a beautiful image of the woman protagonist for this novel, and I am hoping to draw, through you, an ideal figure, a positive human being." At the outset of his story Mishima describes Kazu this way:

> Kazu evinced a streak of wild rusticity in her voluptuous, elegant figure and always brimmed with strength and passion. A man whose mind worked in an intricate manner felt ashamed of his own complexity in front of her, and a man whose mind had grown enfeebled felt greatly encouraged or else crushed just to see her. A woman who, by some blessing from heaven, is equipped, as she is, both with masculine

decisiveness and feminine headstrong passion in one body, can go much farther than a man.

Kazu was cheerful in every corner and niche of her character, and her indomitable self had a simple, beautiful form. Since her youth, she preferred loving to being loved. Her childlike rusticity hid some pushiness that she had, and the many kinds of malice of the tiny human beings that surrounded her nurtured her untrammeled, simple heart further.

Among the many women Mishima created, Fukuzawa Kazu is one of the most fully drawn and convincing. Her real-life counterpart, Azekami Terui, made substantial donations when a museum to commemorate Arita Hachirō was built on Sado Island where he was born. She outlived him by twenty-four years.

CHAPTER SIXTEEN

# The 2.26 Incident, *Yūkoku*

*The arrêt that leads to the summit separates two abysses: the pleasure-tinged death wish (not, perhaps, without an element of narcissistic masochism), and the animal fear arising from the physical instinct for survival.*

—Dag Hammarskjöld

*Eroticism, it may be said, is assenting to life up to the point of death.*

—Georges Bataille

In February 1960 the filming of *Windblown Dude* (*Karakkaze yarō*) started, with Mishima playing the lead role: young heir of a declining yakuza family. The director, Masumura Yasuzō, by happenstance, was Mishima's classmate at the Faculty of Law at the University of Tokyo, although he had gone back to study philosophy after joining the movie studio Daiei, in 1947. Other than the academic background, he had another similarity with Mishima: an abiding fascination with lowbrow life. Of the nearly sixty movies he made, a sizable number had to do with yakuza.

However, angry that the studio president chose a total amateur for the lead actor, Masumura was tough and relentless as he drove Mishima hard throughout the filming; and Mishima behaved like an obedient student. In one scene Masumura cried "NG!" more than a dozen times; each time Mishima, standing ramrod straight, responded with "Hai!"—"Yes, sir!"—and redid the scene.[1]

On March 1, in the scene where he was to be gunned down on an escalator in a department store, Mishima, believing he had to go for real, dropped flat on his back on the moving machine, the backside of his head striking it hard. There was little external injury, but a doctor feared the effects of a concussion and required him to remain in the hospital for ten days. The movie was completed in the meantime and it was released on March 23. Masumura was as famous for his fast-paced work as for his stern directing and often turned out four movies a year, as he did that year.

Mishima wrote several accounts of the acting experience, among them a monologue in the voice of a down-and-out yakuza talking about the proper way of handling mistresses. At one point, incongruously, the young man says, "And because women are stupid as you know . . . we don't teach our mistresses Kant's philosophy nor make them read Gide's novels."[2]

Another was a short story, "Star," which, in the voice of a popular twenty-three-year-old actor playing a down-and-out yakuza, gives in some fascinating details the process of filming, in contrarian fashion. Here, again, inadvertently perhaps, Mishima revealed himself. Early on in the story the young actor says: "I'm twenty-three, the age when you are supposed to be able to manage any tough work. But as a result of uninterrupted fatigue and sleepless nights for the last half year, I *know* my youth is rapidly approaching twilight." Mishima, then thirty-five, was a night owl who, though he slept until past noon, kept up a busy nightlife. But during the filming, he had to report to work early in the morning and often stay with the crew until late into the night. Even then he kept up his writing schedule.

Toward the end of the story, the fatigued protagonist is seized with a death wish. Kayo, his plain, thoughtful attendant who doubles as his lover, says she understands the sentiment:

> Being a star is in every respect a question of appearance. But appearance is the only stereotypical model, the only model that has taken shape, for "true recognition" for society at large, and this they are fully aware of. Society knows that the origins

of the recognition are ultimately in the fountain of falsity that we profess. The only thing is that the fountain can't do without a mask covering it so everyone may feel safe. The star is that mask. On the other hand, the real world is always hoping for the death of the star. That's because if the mask stays the same, they'll know the existence of the fountain. You constantly need a new mask.

Mishima wrote the title song of the movie and sang it.[3] Fukazawa Shichirō, the author of *On the Narayama Song*, composed the music. King Record, which had started out as a unit of the publishing house Kōdansha in 1931 and become independent in 1951, put out the record. Mishima, in any event, knew that he was "an alarming ham," as he told Donald Keene.[4]

On March 16, while he was required to be in the hospital because of the fear of a concussion, Mishima began rehearsing *Salome* under his direction, with Kishida Kyōko playing the lead role. In his brief statement on directing the play, Mishima wrote, "For more than twenty years now, it has been my dream to direct Oscar Wilde's *Salome*. If you allow me to exaggerate a bit, I joined the Bungaku-za only because of my wish to be allowed to direct *Salome* some day. Imagine my joy when I learned it would become a reality."

But his "is not Oscar Wilde's *Salome* so much as a joint work of us three, Hinatsu Kōnosuke, Aubrey Beardsley, and me," Mishima explained: Hinatsu, because Mishima used his "magnificently elegant and abstruse translation," rather than the other existing version, Mori Ōgai's (both Wilde's French original and Alfred Douglas' English translation are simple, and so is Ōgai's, which is from a German translation); Beardsley, because he put before Wilde's words Beardsley's illustrations that utterly ignore period authenticity, including those of books of Zola and Flaubert; and Mishima himself, because he regarded it as his interpretation.[5] Kishida remembered him shedding his usual easygoing self and turning deadly serious as director. The production opened on April 5 and moved on to Nagoya, Osaka, and Kyoto.

In May Mishima, along with Nagaoka Teruko and three others, became a planning advisor of the Bungaku-za.

On June 26 Mishima met a married couple—not identified—at the Prince Hotel, in Shinagawa, and swam in the pool there with them. With his vaunted body, he may have thought he presented a fine spectacle as he swam, but he swam poorly. Though not on the same occasion, Kita Morio once bathed with him. Mishima plunged in and swam a length with the breaststroke. Kita followed him after a while, quickly overtook him with the crawl, and waited for him at the other end of the pool. "I expected him to say at least 'You're faster than you look.' But he didn't say a word, he didn't even smile. He got out of the pool without looking at me and went into the bar."[6]

Kita, a psychiatrist by profession, won the Akutagawa Prize that year for his fictionalized account of one part of the Nazi Directive Night and Fog: the annihilation of the mentally ill. His father, the tanka poet Saitō Mokichi, was also a psychiatrist and ran a mental hospital.

Mishima and the couple then had dinner on the Ginza and went to Asakusa to have some fun at The New World, a large entertainment center built a year earlier. The visit gave him an idea for a short story: a young, serious, loving couple who, it turns out, perform sex for a small, secret gathering of rich women. Their job is merely hinted at in the words of a middle-aged female pimp whom they meet at The New World before the session that evening. The title of the story, "Million-yen Rice Crackers" (*Hyakuman-en senbei*), comes from the name of one of the food items Mishima saw sold in the garish building.

On August 2, he had a threesome discussion with Itō Sei and Saeki Shōichi on the two currents of modern Japanese literature, Shiga Naoya and Tanizaki Jun'ichirō, for *Gunzō*. That day he sent invitations for a party on the following Sunday. One to Okuno Takeo read:

> I haven't been in touch with you since *Othello*. Now, on August 7 (Sunday), past 6 in the afternoon, I will have a small dance party called an Aloha Meet in my garden. Please make sure to come with your wife. Men are required to wear an aloha shirt.[7]

The reference to *Othello* is obscure, but the aloha shirt had gained Japanese admiration for American tourists who flaunted their predilections for flashy colorfulness as they flooded Japan. The party was held around the statue of Apollo. Shibusawa Tatsuhiko remembered Mishima opening it with greetings in English and Japanese—there were a number of foreign guests—by saying, "I am happy that the most beautiful ladies and gentlemen under heaven have gathered this evening." Mishima loved to greet his guests at his parties in similar fashion. For the Aloha Meet he had engaged the popular singing trio, Three Graces, to provide songs for the dancers.

Following the dances Mishima screened Donald Richie's film as well as the photographer Hosoe Eikō's film, *The Navel and the Atomic Bomb* (*Heso to genbaku*). Hosoe would later take some of the more memorable photos of Mishima.[8]

---

In the middle of that month Mishima went on a trip to collect material for his next novel, *Beastly Entanglements* (*Kemono no tawamure*), a story of psychological self-entrapment, seduction, and murder. It deals with a dandyish scholar-dealer of expensive porcelains, his wife who avows no jealousy for his many affairs but secretly has a private eye follow him, and a college student employed to help him in his store who falls in love with her. It is a variation of *Thirst for Love*, although, unlike that other novel, any real-life source for the narrative line, if there was one, remains unknown. Mishima wrote that it was only when he heard *Leonore Overture* as conducted by Herbert von Karajan at La Scala in January 1961—five months after he collected basic descriptive material—that he was finally able to settle on the overall structure of the novel.[9]

Regardless, Mishima was assiduous in gathering information. He went to Hamamatsu to see the airbase, although in the story the character who is in the Air Self-Defense Force is a minor one, and also to see a manufacturer of musical instruments, although in the story the visit translates into a single paragraph worth of description of the assembly of a ukulele. He stayed for a week in the fishing port of Arari, on the west coast of the Izu Peninsula, to observe the milieu for a seaside nursery that supplies exotic plants to a Tokyo wholesaler. Mishima's assiduity in information gathering may be typically seen in a passage like this:

> The dendrobium's faintly red flowers allowing you to glimpse their dark purple far inside did not seem to suggest that they were hiding their bashfulness; rather, they seemed to have

ostentatiously locked it away. The Hawaiian anthurium's brilliant red is like synthetic resin with the cat-family's leathery tongue sticking out of it. The tiger tail's seaweed-resembling pliant form that belies the tough quality of its spotted, dark-green leaves fringed in light yellow. The improved Decora Elastica's large, oval leaves, the Ananas's ferocious green leaves with lateral black stripes. The Kwannon bamboo's glossy leaves profusely sprouting from its hairy, skinny stalks. . . .

It was while he was on this trip that Arita Hachirō telephoned him at his home to lodge his protest on "invasion of privacy" for the first time. That and Arita's subsequent insistence on privacy—but months before he actually brought the suit—led Mishima to write an essay, "Privacy." Recalling the weeklong stay at an old-fashioned inn in Arari port, where not just the inn but also the whole port totally ignored the idea of "privacy"—with a town loudspeaker blaring announcements, transistor radios (then new on the market and popular) "emitting monstrous noise," trucks crashing by on the road right next to the inn, people in the next room partitioned by paper doors carousing till late at night—he wrote: "In a city, you wouldn't tolerate the noisy radio of your neighbor, but here all the radios competed in noise. If you can't stand your neighbor's noise, all you have to do is to turn up your radio louder."

"There's no need to copycat Western-style privacy," he concluded, for "if everybody gets used to [all the noise] and feels no pain, that's all you need in life."[10]

## *The 2.26 Incident*

On August 28 he completed *After the Banquet*. He then set out to write, and finished writing in mid-October, what would become his most famous, and to himself the most important, story, "Yūkoku." (The title has been translated as "Patriotism" and the story is so known in English; but, as Mishima himself pointed out and as we will see, there is a problem with the choice of the English word, so we will stay with the original word.) The story begins:

On February 29, of the eleventh year of Shōwa (that is,

on the third day from the eruption of the 2.26 Incident), Lt. Takeyama Shinji, the 1st Infantry Regiment, the Imperial Guards Division, agonizing since the occurrence of the incident that his close friends were participating in the rebel army, became pained and furious at the situation in which fighting within the Imperial Army seemed inevitable, and carried out suicide by disembowelment with his military sword in the eight-mat room of his home at 6 Aoba-chō, Yotsuya Ward. His wife, Reiko, also carried out suicide by sword to follow him in death. The lieutenant's will had just a single phrase, "Long live the Imperial Army," while his wife's will apologized for lack of filial respect in dying before her parents, saying, "The day that has to come for a soldier's wife has come," and so forth. The last moments of a fiercely loyal man and his fiercely loyal wife were truly such as to make the demons and deities weep. The lieutenant was thirty years old, his wife twenty-three; it was less than half a year since their nuptials.

The "incident" is so called because it began in the predawn hours of February 26, 1936, with a series of assassinations of high-ranking government officials. Army units led by two dozen junior-grade officers—"young officers" in standard Japanese accounts[II]—assaulted and killed the Lord Keeper of the Privy Seal Saitō Makoto, Minister of Finance Takahashi Korekiyo, and Inspector-General of Military Education Watanabe Jōtarō. The three other targets—Prime Minister Okada Keisuke, Former Lord Privy Seal Makino Nobuaki, and Grand Chamberlain Suzuki Kantarō—managed to escape or survive. Of the three who survived, Suzuki, severely wounded, would serve as prime minister to end the Pacific War, whose origins may be found partly in what happened as a result of the 2.26 Incident.

What prompted the assassinations was the social unrest that had brought to the fore the notion that, if the Tennō were allowed to step forward and rule the land, all the problems would be straightened out. Since ancient times there was in China the belief that an enlightened ruler could be, and often was, blocked from manifesting his "shining mind" by his corrupt aides and councilors.

For the 2.26 Incident officers who held this idea, the immediate precedent was the Meiji Restoration, in 1868, which they believed ushered in a great age for Japan by restoring the Tennō system to replace the Tokugawa shogunate. But since the Meiji Emperor's death, in 1912, the nation had only declined because the parliamentary system and other European-style developments increasingly inhibited the free exercise of the Imperial Mind. As Capt. Andō Teruzō, one of the leaders of the insurrection, succinctly explained, "We believed that, if we felled the high councilors and cabinet officers who beclouded the Imperial Brightness, His Majesty would decisively carry out a Shōwa Restoration."[12] Or, as the "Statement of Purpose of the Uprising" detailed in a prose encrusted with classical Chinese words and concepts:

> Both internally and externally in a truly grave emergency, if we did not punish now His Majesty's unprincipled, deceiving councilors who have destroyed the National Polity (*kokutai*), and sweep away the evil elements that have long blocked the Divine Glory and prevented His Majesty's Renewal, the Imperial Rule would become empty.... It is our proper duty to slash off the evil councilors and military bandits by His Majesty's side and smash their core. If we, His Majesty's children and His arms and legs, did not fulfill our absolute duty, we would not be able to avert self-destruction and decline. Thus we men of like concern and like mind have risen simultaneously to annihilate the evil bandits in order to restore the Great Principle (*taigi*), rack our humble brains to preserve and bring it to light, so we the humblest of our Divine Nation may express our opinion however insignificant.[13]

The statement made clear that all those in power were to blame for running down the nation: the *genrō*, elder statesmen, those who made a special contribution to the formation of the Meiji government; the *jūshin*, high councilors or those who had served as prime minister or lord keeper of the privy seal; the *gunbatsu*, the military establishment;[14] the *zaibatsu*, the financial and corporate establishment; the *kanryō*, the bureaucrats; and the *seitō*, the political parties—every entity or group more interested in staking out its own turf than in what people really needed.

Directly behind the fermentation of this idea was the widespread poverty among the peasants, especially in the Tōhoku region that suffered from chronic crop failures, and the sufferings of struggling ordinary people. One consequence was rampant "human trade": selling young daughters to brothels. A large proportion of the military personnel, both officers and regular conscripts, were of peasant stock or else the sons of mom-and-pop store owners or poor workers who were as adversely affected. In fact, and ironically, among those assassinated in the Incident, Watanabe Jōtarō, who had risen to the rank of full general, was unable to finish grammar school because his adoptive father was a poor peasant.

With the government apparently doing nothing to cure the social ills, there inevitably arose among a number of military officers the strong sense that something had to be done. Indeed, remarkably in an age when "special higher police" and other apparatus were set up to eradicate anything remotely associated with communism and socialism, these officers openly told their men that *aikoku*, patriotism, which was to form the spiritual core of every soldier, meant destroying the capitalist system such as it was to build a new nation of peasants and workers strong on defense.[15]

Here the meanings of the two terms that appear to form the core of the insurgents' argument, *kokutai*, "National Polity," and *taigi*, "Great Principle," need some clarification because Mishima would start spouting them with seeming earnestness soon enough.

Simply put, *kokutai* means "polity." But the nationalists used the word with the pregnant sense that Japan is unique because it is a land ruled by the Tennō whose genealogical line has never been broken. This thesis started with Kitabatake Chikafusa (1293–1354) in his treatise *An Account of Our Divine Sovereigns and Their Orthodoxy* (*Jinnō shōtō ki*) written when the Tennō institution was in serious decline. It was taken up and pushed with great seriousness by scholars of National Learning toward the end of the Edo Period when the Tennō was in practical eclipse.

The argument of National Learning was fundamentalist to the core: it accepted and presented as incontrovertible truth certain descriptions in the early documents such as the *Record of Ancient Matters* (*Kojiki*), compiled in 712, and the *History of Japan* (*Nihon shoki*), in 720, both composed to justify the Tennō line. Fukuzawa Yukichi, the prominent leader of "civilization of enlightenment," i.e., Westernization, in the Meiji Era, deeply annoyed by the orotund arguments pushed toward the end of the

Edo Period, defined *kokutai* as nothing more than the general makeup and milieu of an independent country or society, applying the English word "nationality" to the word as early as 1875.[16] But to no avail.

With the rise of chauvinism following the Manchurian Incident, in 1931, a push to "clarify and manifest *kokutai*" intensified. That led the Ministry of Education, in 1937, to compile a catechism, *The True Import of Kokutai* (*Kokutai no hongi*), which begins with the assertion: "The Great Empire of Japan is eternally ruled by Tennō whose line is unbroken for thousands of generations and who uphold the Divine Edict of their original Imperial Ancestor. This is our *kokutai* that has remained unchanged since time immemorial."[17] That was one reason why in 1945 when confronted with the demand for an unconditional surrender, the Japanese leaders were obliged to insist on "the preservation of *kokutai*," unnecessarily prolonging the war.

Because of these developments in the recent past, the sense of incongruity and disbelief must have been uppermost when Mishima, the celebrity author with a wide-ranging cultural mastery, started spouting the term *kokutai* well into the 1960s. In the end Mishima did not go beyond defining *kokutai* as "the *identity* of Japanese folk and Japanese culture, with its essence lying in the perpetuity that is not affected by changes in political administrations,"[18] but it is not clear whether that helped.

*Taigi*, "Great Principle," is a Confucian term (*dayi* in Chinese) meaning an immutable principle or justice, although as with its lesser version *gi*, "principle" (*yi* in Chinese), it is so amorphous as to be practically meaningless. It is closely associated with *shisei* (*zhicheng*), which, as we shall see, Mishima used in the film version of "Yūkoku." It means sublime, supreme sincerity or unwavering dedication. Both terms apply to human conduct in general and to a man's service to his lord or to his state in particular.

The young officers' attempt for imperial restoration failed. Hirohito refused to entertain anything like the idea of taking over as ruler. A firm believer in the constitutional monarchy established during the Meiji Era—to him *kokutai* meant just that—he was outraged by the blatant attempt to trample upon the government by killing some of its members who had the constitutional duty to "assist" him, and demanded an immediate suppression of the uprising. He is known to have declared at one point, "I would lead the Imperial Guards Cavalry to put them down!" Although it was something that happened between His Majesty and his top aides within the Palace, his strong position somehow leaked out, creating a clear image of the Tennō, it is said, for the first time.[19]

Nonetheless it took fully three days to put down the uprising because his councilors did not take his word as absolute and act promptly, and because the idea of a Shōwa Restoration had many sympathizers in the top echelons of the government—and among college students and professors. Bōjō Toshitami, for one, recalled the excitement among his fellow students at the Peers School during the uprising, especially those whose older brothers were military officers, with one professor of philosophy setting aside his usual lectures and talking about the need for such a restoration "with a ferocious tone."[20] Members of the top echelons who were sympathetic started with Army Minister Kawashima Yoshiyuki and His Majesty's Chief Aide-de-Camp Honjō Shigeru. Lt. Gen. Kashii Kōhei, Commander of the Tokyo Garrison, was another; he hesitated to move against the insurgents, even after he was ordered to implement martial law.

Those sympathetic to the cause were also found among the members of imperial houses. One was Hirohito's distant but important relative, Prince Fushimi Hiroyasu, then Chief of the Naval Staff; he had taken part in the Russo-Japanese War and was admired by his men for his mettle and naval skills. Hirohito's uncle, Prince Higashikumi Naruhiko, then Chief of the Army Aviation Headquarters who, after Japan's defeat nine years later, was fated to serve as prime minister as the first and only member of imperial lineage to do so, was another. Closer home, Hirohito's own brother, Prince Chichibu Yasuhito, then a colonel, was the one man the young officers had counted on the most.[21] His association with them was such that Hirohito, along with some of his top aides, feared that Chichibu might usurp him.

The strong sympathy at the top was clear in the first official response to the insurgents that was issued in the name of the Minister of the Army—3:30 pm of the 26th or nearly half a day after the series of assassinations came to light. It consisted of five points: "1. As to the purpose of the uprising, it has been brought to the Imperial attention; 2. We recognize that your conduct was based on the earnest desire to manifest *kokutai*; 3. As to the present state in which *kokutai* manifests itself in reality (including corrupt customs), we can only think of it with trepidation [i.e., We think you are correct]; 4. All military councilors have agreed to do their best in accordance with the above points; 5. As for the rest, we simply await the Imperial decision."

Despite the military regulation of the day, "A rebellion starts the moment it leaves the barracks," the Army Ministry refused to call a spade a spade: "the military units that have been taking action since this morning" (3:00 pm, Feb. 26); "occupying military units" (10:30 am, Feb. 27; the term survived until 7:00 am, Feb. 28); "resisting military units" (4:00 pm, Feb. 28); "the Kofuji Unit" (between the last two because the order issued at 7:00 am, Feb. 27, told the insurgents to "act under the command of Col. Kofuji, Guards Commander, Kōjimachi District, the First Division"); and "enemy" (in Martial Law Operation No. 14, issued at 11:00 pm, Feb. 28). It was not until 5:30 pm of February 28 that the uprising was termed "a rebellion."[22] For their part, those who aimed for a Shōwa Restoration studiously avoided words such as "revolution," "*coup d'état*," and "*Putsch*"; they believed what they had in mind was nothing of the sort.[23]

Within the military there existed a great schism between those who, like the young officers, thought that having the Tennō as direct ruler would solve pressing social ills (Kōdō-ha, "Imperial Way Faction") and those who pushed for reform through a rational control or discipline of policy (Tōsei-ha, "Control Faction").[24] The process of deciding how to deal with the insurgents was also the process of resolving the conflict between the two factions, with the latter group winning.

Also, faced with a real action, not just the idea of one, and with Hirohito's adamant opposition—he may well have been the first to use the word *hanran*, "rebellion"—the sympathizers wilted, made an about-face, or later denied involvement. Among them, Gen. Mazaki Jinzaburō, the hero for the young officers, appeared on the morning of the assassinations at the Ministry of the Army the insurgents had occupied and encouraged them with words to the effect, "Well done. Leave the rest to me."[25]

But all Mazaki ended up doing was drag out the final decision. Later he would insist he had nothing to do with the insurgency. He was indicted but acquitted. Those concerned knew the officers killed Gen. Watanabe Jōtarō not just because he was chosen to replace Mazaki as inspector-general of military education but also because he upheld the view of the Tennō as a "state organ," whereas Mazaki denounced it.

More important, the young officers who hatched and carried out the idea of Shōwa Restoration had not thought of a contingency: What if the Tennō refused to go along? When they realized that an Imperial Edict for Restoration was not coming, they felt profoundly betrayed. Many were prepared to die if the Tennō publicly recognized they'd done it as "a just army to honor the Tennō" (*sonnō gigun*). That did not happen.

The army leadership that had behaved like a drunken schizophrenic midway through the uprising acted with vengeful speed once the uprising faltered and collapsed.

First, when the officers who had led the uprising assembled in the residence of the Minister of the Army following the collapse, they were told that their only honorable recourse was to kill themselves on the spot. The army leaders had gone as far as preparing three dozen coffins ready in the next room. Most officers took that as an affront. Even those who had avowed to take responsibility and kill themselves changed their minds and decided to clarify their intent through legal proceedings. Only one of them, Capt. Nonaka Shirō, persuaded that any attempt to do so during court martial would only bring him disgrace, shot himself. Because of the circumstances, however, the suspicion has persisted that he was killed.[26]

Failing in blatant coercion, the army set up a special military tribunal and tried those involved—but not those in higher echelons who aided and abetted them—in secrecy, without defense attorneys, and in a single trial with no appeals, and executed sixteen officers by a firing squad. It followed this action a year later by executing two more officers along with two civilians alleged to have provided the insurgents with philosophical underpinnings.

Isobe Asaichi, one of the two officers who were kept alive for more than a year for close questioning, left prison writings Mishima would especially value in his understanding of the failed uprising, especially the fact that Isobe went to death fulminating against the Tennō. Kita Ikki, one of the two civilians, was the advocate of "genuine socialism" who had served the Father of Modern China Sun Yat-sen as an aide during that country's revolution. Mishima would also take up Kita's theory head on, later.

The army, soon taken over by the Control Faction, cleaned out the principal sympathizers, that is, the leaders of the Imperial Way Faction, demoting or retiring them where they could. It also, fatefully, reintroduced the requirement that the ministers of the army and the navy be officers on active duty. That furthered the militarization of Japan.

---

Aside from the savage killings, the motive and aim of the insurgents had something genuinely appealing. Katō Shūichi, the towering intellect of modern Japan who was seventeen when the uprising occurred, avowed he was not "sympathetic with the rebellious officers," but still recognized their "sincerity." What the incident and its aftermath revealed in naked form, Katō wrote in his autobiography, was a political process "in which sincerity is met with betrayal, idealism met with exploitation, and yesterday's loyalty construed as today's conspiracy as soon as one has outlived his usefulness."27

Katō was reflecting on the past, but Mishima, when he was about the same age, seventeen, had written an essay praising the Buddhist treatise *Establishment of the Teaching for the Protection of the Country* (*Risshō ankoku-ron*) of Nichiren (1222–82) and in it noted that he saw in the young officers the same "burning desire" to rectify the situation as that the firebrand Buddhist of the thirteenth century had manifested.28 Years later he would define what the officers had tried to do as a "moral revolution." The *"tragisch Ironie"*—the phrase he used in the same analysis—was that it was not self-evident to the one being that most counted, the Tennō.29

## *The Seppuku: Disembowelment*

For now, in "Yūkoku," Mishima focused on one result of the old Japanese way of expressing sincerity by the sword: disembowelment. "Yūkoku," he wrote five years later, was "the only work which, from start to finish, was born only of my brain and which realized its world through words."30 In truth, it was not all his fantasy and imagination. He had a direct source of inspiration.

In "Disembowelment" (*Seppuku*), published in September 1943, Wada Katsunori had written: "Among those who committed suicide [during the 2.26 Incident] were Capt. Nonaka Shirō in the rebel army and Maj. Amano Takeo and others in the Imperial Army. Of these, the death of Lt. Aoshima Kenkichi and his wife vividly recalled the death by sword of Gen. and Mrs. Nogi." Nogi Maresuke, along with his wife Shizuko, killed themselves to follow Emperor Meiji in death on the day of the latter's funeral, September 12, 1912. Wada continued:

> The lieutenant, of the Transport Battalion of the Imperial Guards Division, was, upon the eruption of the Incident, made commander of the ——unit and assigned to guard duty: he was continuing his various activities without sleep or rest when, on the evening of the 28th, he was ordered by Battalion Commander Yuasa to take his turn to rest and came home around eleven o'clock.
>
> But the lieutenant, profoundly agonizing since the Incident began that his close friends were participating in the rebel army, thought he would not be able to bear it should the Imperial Army end up fighting within itself. He had been intently waiting for them to feel responsible for their actions and commit suicide swiftly. But they were in the end labeled with the stigma of rebels. Anxious for what situation might ensue come morning, he decided to settle it all by death. When he told these sentiments to his wife Kimiko, she said she'd gladly accompany him. The two put on formal attire as man and wife and wrote a will. The lieutenant calmly cut his stomach straight from left to right with his military sword and further stabbed his throat, thus killing himself excellently. His wife followed him. She wrapped a blanket around her waist and stabbed her throat with a Japanese sword, thus meeting her death as admirably.[31]

What Mishima decided to do in "Yūkoku" was to describe what is not at all mentioned in the original account: the reality of such "excellent" and "admirable" deaths. "Yūkoku" was an "attempt to thoroughly analyze ... and inspect with precision" what lies behind the florid clichés employed for those "brave in loyalty and fierce in morality," such as "scattered like a flower" and "as gallantly as cherry blossoms at the moment of scattering," he wrote when the story appeared as part of a selection. So, after plunging his sword—its blade with white cloth tightly wound around it for gripping except for the several inches toward the tip—into the left of his stomach with the intention, no doubt, of calmly pulling it straight to the right:

> Even though he had exerted the force himself, he felt as if someone had given the side of his stomach a painful blow with a thick iron rod. For a moment his head reeled, and he didn't know what had happened. The several inches of naked blade was already completely buried in the flesh, and the paper his fist gripped was in direct contact with his stomach.
>
> His consciousness returned. The blade surely pierced the peritoneum, the lieutenant thought. It was hard to breathe, his chest throbbed violently, and he could tell that in a depth so far, far from him he couldn't think it was his inside, a terrifying, ferocious pain was boiling up as if the earth tore apart and hot lava was flowing out. The ferocious pain immediately came close to him at a terrifying speed. The lieutenant was about to groan despite himself, but suppressed it by biting into his lower lip.
>
> So this is seppuku, the lieutenant was thinking....

To provide "clinical descriptions ... in such abundance," Mishima went on to observe, would "not in the least detract from the monumentally heroic character of the hero and the heroine."[32] Mishima knew well killing oneself by cutting one's stomach was far from easy. He knew that the attempt to die by Capt. Kōno Hisashi, who was wounded in leading the assault on Makino Nobuaki, hospitalized, and reduced to killing himself with a fruit-knife his brother Tsukasa smuggled in, was agonizing, messy, and prolonged, contrary to the brother's description of it in utterly clichéd phrasing, even though he, Mishima, almost replicated the phrasing in rendering Iinuma Isao's death at the end of *Runaway Horse*.[33]

Mishima knew, too, the equally prolonged agony of Minister of the Army Anami Korechika, who, after the Tennō sided with those of Prime Minister Suzuki Kantarō's maneuver who were for surrender, killed himself with a short sword, without a *kaishaku*, a second—although what's remarkable, in retrospect, about Mishima's reference to Anami's seppuku is the reason he found it admirable: the war minister carried it out without giving a hint of what he was going to do to anyone around him.³⁴ Mishima seems not to have mentioned Ōnishi Takijirō, but he must have heard about the way "the Father of the Kamikaze" killed himself. The day after Japan's defeat, Ōnishi wrote, with a brush, a testimonial to apologize for sending the men under his command to useless deaths and committed seppuku, as Anami did, without a second, refusing any kind of medical intervention. It took him more than fifteen hours to die.³⁵

There was something else: the sensuality of disembowelment with a blade. Mishima wrote: "The story of 'Yūkoku' itself is no more than an unofficial part of the 2.26 Incident, but the spectacle of love and death, the perfect melding and potentiation of Eros and *taigi* described here, is the only bliss I expect in this life." He stated this when yet another selection of his short stories including "Yūkoku" was published, in 1968.

"If some busy person asked to read just one story by Mishima which embodies his essence that condenses all the good things and bad things about him, he would do well by just reading 'Yūkoku,'" he added.³⁶ This was, he noted, a reminder. In 1965 he had written, at the end of his afterword to the last of the six-volume selection of his short stories: "I imagine that even a reader who never once has read my writings will be able to have an unerring idea of me as a novelist by just reading this short story titled 'Yūkoku.'"

There he had also said: "The 2.26 Incident is the one incident that has extended important influence to my spiritual history. The sensation I had when I was eleven years old was repeatedly ruminated on and became a yeast that formed my own ideas of 'breakdown,' 'tragedy,' and 'heroism.'"³⁷

Ruminate on the failed uprising he surely did. A year after the short story, he wrote a play, *The Tenth-Day Chrysanthemum* (*Tōka no kiku*), to describe the empty life of a target of assassination in an uprising who has survived, with the suggestion that the uprising was the 2.26, albeit with a twist: The time specified for the play is "within the 24 hours from the night of October 13 to the early evening of the following day, the 14th, in the Twenty-Seventh Year of Shōwa (1952), that is, the year the Japanese–United States Peace Treaty went into effect." The title of the play derives from the fact that September 9 (to be exact, the 9th of Ninth Month by the lunar calendar), following Chinese tradition, is Double-Yang Day, also known as Chrysanthemum Day. Because of this festival rite, the chrysanthemum was considered to be of little use on the following day, the 10th.

In 1965 Mishima turned the story "Yūkoku" into a film, of which we will see more later. The following year, he worked out a story purported to be a first-person eye-witness account, "Voices of the Heroic Souls" (*Eirei no koe*), to present the executed officers of the 2.26 Incident, along with the Kamikaze pilots, as spirits unable to rest because the Tennō betrayed them. And in the summer of 1970, a few months before his death, Mishima chose "Yūkoku" to represent his work when he had an opportunity to co-edit the Penguin anthology of modern Japanese literature *New Writing in Japan* with the English scholar Geoffrey Bownas.

Here, what Mishima said of the word *yūkoku* may be noted. In his introduction to the English anthology, he pointed out that the word, though translated as "patriotism" by Geoffrey W. Sargent, "conveys more than a hint of melancholy: the word *yū* is related to the verb 'to feel grief' and grief is the emotion sustaining this story."[38] It is an old Chinese word (*youguo*) meaning "worried about the state of the nation" and is different from a word of far more recent vintage that is the standard Japanese equivalent of "patriotism": *aikoku* or *aikokushin*, "loving one's country." Mishima suspected the latter word was coined as Christianity flooded into Japan after the country opened itself to international commerce and diplomacy in the mid-nineteenth century and with it a word corresponding to *agape* had to be devised because the concept of "love" as in "loving one's country" was alien to the Japanese.

The word *aikokushin* gave him "gooseflesh," he wrote in an essay on the word, in early 1968. "To tell the truth, I don't like the word *aikokushin* much. Somewhat like *aisaika* [the uxorious man], it gives my back gooseflesh. The meaning of this 'I don't like' is a bit different from the symptoms of political allergy certain sensitive people feel with the word. For some reason I just don't care for such words; if I could, I'd keep my face turned away from them. This word smells of something made by the government. Also, it doesn't have a pedigree or gentleness as a word. Somehow it has the air of something sneakily forced upon you. Something that understandably creates resentment lurks at its bottom."[39]

In fact, when he turned the short story into a film five years later, initially for foreign consumption, Mishima left the original title untranslated. "If '*yūkoku*' were translated as '*aikoku*,' the nuances of the sentiments of the young officers of the 2.26 Incident will disappear," wrote Isoda Kōichi, who, though born six years after Mishima, displayed a sense of deep affinity in understanding Mishima. "Nevertheless, the [sub]title '*ai to shi no saigi* [the rite of love and death]' suggests that the Japanese act of '*jijin* [killing oneself with a sword]' is linked to the universal human question of '*eroticism* and death.' One reason he is internationally appreciated is that his *national* sentiment is simultaneously equipped with universality as humanview."[40]

One question remains: What prompted Mishima to take up the 2.26 Incident in this particular fashion? Mishima, ever the self-analyst, wondered about that himself. In mid-1966, writing on the occasion of publishing "The 2.26 Incident Trilogy," he spoke of the once-in-a-lifetime bliss for Lt. Takeyama and his wife that he had described in "Yūkoku." The couple would have missed it, he wrote, had they waited until the following day because the very next day the lieutenant would have learned that the internecine battle in the Imperial Army had been averted. So where did he get "the conviction that such a bliss, once missed, even by just one night, would never come again in your life?" Mishima went on to respond to his own wonderment:

> Directly, in this very conviction lay the core of my experience of the war, also the experience of reading Nietzsche during the war, and also my sympathy with the philosopher Georges Bataille, who should be called "the Nietzsche of *Érotisme*." Bataille, who was a devout Catholic until his adolescence, one day experiencing "the death of God," plunged into research of *érotisme*.... Surely, with the breakdown of the 2.26 Incident some great god died. At the time an eleven-year-old boy, I merely felt it only vaguely, but when I encountered [Japan's] defeat in war at the hypersensitive age of twenty, I felt that the terrifyingly cruel sense of the death of god at the time might be closely related to what I had intuited as a boy of eleven.[41]

Several months before writing "Yūkoku," Mishima had reviewed the Japanese translation of Georges Bataille's *L'érotisme*. "Bataille's virtue" lies in sticking to "the banal notion," Mishima wrote unable to resist his fondness for paradoxes, that "one must begin by doubting all sorts of cultural taboos in order to rediscover ... the image of the world that has disintegrated into fragments and scattered away," and for that Bataille proposes "the unifying principle" of eroticism. "As a result," Mishima said, "it appears that the vestiges of eroticism you can see in those individual fragments are, on the contrary, incrassating in an age like ours; it also appears that against the humanism of the West, now 'death' is appearing on the stage as a major principle of civilization."[42]

Bataille, who begins his book with the thesis "Eroticism, it may be said, is assenting to life up to the point of death," describes orgasm this way: "On the one hand the convulsions of the flesh are more acute when they are near to a black-out, and on the other, a black-out, as long as there is enough time, makes physical pleasure more exquisite." Bataille is known to have called brothels his churches, hence perhaps the reference to time constraints. "Mortal anguish does not necessarily make for sensual pleasure, but that pleasure is more deeply felt during mortal anguish."[43] Mishima may have had such passages in mind in describing the death throes of Lt. Takeyama.

Another source of impetus for the writing of "Yūkoku" may have been *The Aristocrats' Staircase* (*Kizoku no kaidan*), a novel by Takeda Taijun for which Mishima had written a blurb a year earlier. A first-person narrative by a seventeen-year-old who serves her father, the prime minister, as a secret scribe, the fiction obliquely deals with the 2.26 Incident. The narrator Himiko's father, Nishinomaru Hidehiko, is modeled after the famously womanizing aristocrat Konoe Fumimaro, though, unlike the fictional character, Konoe at the time was not prime minister nor, for that matter, did his candidacy to succeed Okada Keisuke after the latter's narrow escape work because his sympathy for the rebels was known. Like the real prime minister, Hidehiko escapes harm—only to have an assignation with Himiko's same-age friend Setsuko who is in love with none other than Himiko herself.

Himiko's brother, Yoshihito, who in turn is in love with Setsuko, is a sensitive army officer who fails to be part of the uprising because Himiko, who adores him, drugs him while he is visiting his family to say a tacit farewell; she's learned what he's up to in advance. Waking up the next morning, Yoshihito dashes off to his assigned location, too late. Ashamed, he goes into the woods, tries to kill himself by disembowelment, but fails. Taken to a hospital, he dies after being in agony for nearly a day—in the manner of Capt. Kōno Hisashi in real life.

In "Yūkoku," Lt. Takeyama commits suicide because his officer friends, knowing he is newly married, do not tell him of the imminent event. In *The Tenth-Day Chrysanthemum*, Hidehiko escapes assassination with the help of his mistress. Mishima, beginning his blurb with the sentence, "The 2.26 Incident that I experienced in my boyhood, I might say, defined the idea of heroism throughout my life," called *The Aristocrats' Staircase* "a brilliant work."[44]

But it may well have been, above all, Donald Keene, the translator of his modern nō plays, who inspired Mishima to take up the 2.26 Incident the way he did. He once suggested that Mishima consider dealing with the incident as an embodiment of "the action of pure human beings, people who acted utterly unselfishly, people who acted 100 percent for an ideal," as he told the journalist Tokuoka Takao when the two traveled the western part of Japan together a year after Mishima's death. Keene, a first lieutenant of the US Navy during the war, had been profoundly moved when he, a language officer, read the captured diaries and letters of Japanese soldiers on Guadalcanal. What struck him was the unadorned idealism they expressed in sheer suffering and agony before their annihilation—something he hadn't detected in the letters of American soldiers he read as a censor.

Also, soon after the war, when sent to Qingdao, Keene came to know a courteous former officer of the Japanese Navy who told him of the idealism that had driven a group of young military officers, including himself, to carry out what was to be known as the 5.15 Incident. The man, Murayama Noriyuki, had been part of the assault groups that, on May 15, 1932, killed Prime Minister Inukai Tsuyoshi, the revered proponent of "preservation of the Constitution." Like all other participants Murayama had got off with a relatively light punishment—he was released with the sentence of ten years of imprisonment greatly reduced—a fact that gave the participants of the 2.26 Incident false expectations, it was said. They thought they'd be given an ample opportunity to air their views, as the participants in the 5.15 Incident had been, and never be condemned to anything like executions.

Indeed, great sympathy had been expressed for the perpetrators of the 5.15 Incident. With the unemployment rate sky high and the appalling destitution of peasantry continuing, the government seemed to take only wrong steps. The planners of the uprising said in their manifesto, "We weep for Japan's present state and, though barehanded, are about to light the bonfire of a Shōwa Restoration as a forerunner of society." Whether their action would succeed or fail was not the issue, the manifesto said. The important thing was that the citizenry as a whole would follow suit and rise.[45] Again, Kita Ikki's philosophy was behind it.

These things had led Keene to look into, among others, the philosophy of the politician Nakano Seigō.[46] When Keene had suggested the 2.26 Incident as a possible topic for him, Mishima said he wouldn't touch it, pleading ignorance of Manchuria. What Mishima meant is not clear, but the leaders of the uprising had acted at the time as they had because most of them, along with their units, had been scheduled to be shipped off to Manchuria where several years earlier the Japanese military had set up a puppet nation, Manchukuo. Once there, they'd have no way of directly appealing to the Tennō. Mishima did not refer to Manchuria in "Yūkoku." But he was careful to note that the 2.26 Incident embodied for him "the purity and innocence, the audacity, the youth, and the death" of the men who carried it out.

---

Two years after writing the blurb for *Aristocrats' Staircase*, Mishima read a critical analysis of Yasuda Yojūrō, the writer who had mesmerized him awhile in his youth, and was moved to write, "Linking the fulfilling sense of life with death has long been at the center of my aesthetics." The analysis, by the poet Ōoka Makoto in his *Criticism of Lyricism* (*Jojō no hihan*), said, and this is a part Mishima quotes, "Mr. Yasuda himself, who says 'action' is the sublime expression of the sense of beauty in the absolute sense (in other words, in the suicidal sense), *does not act*, and he affirms that *ironically*. What matters is not to act, he's saying, the only thing that matters being the sublime aesthetics expressed through action."

This "exquisite analysis" gave him a foreboding "sense of affinity," Mishima wrote, adding: "Mr. Ōoka cites one example after another of 'the degradation' of Mr. Yasuda' style, displaying a sharp hand in extracting its logical inevitability and consistency, thereby forcing the reader to slide down in a single swoop from the spiritual decadence to the self-aware aesthetic of defeat, to the self-denial of the word, to demagogy, to death, in the second decade of Shōwa [1935–45]. Come to think of it, I live in such halcyon, eventless days, and yet can't somehow separate myself from the attraction of death, maybe thanks to Mr. Yasuda (though this is rather a joke)."

Mishima wrote this on April 27, 1961 in an entry for a "diary" to be published in a small magazine.[47] That evening, after an hour's body-building exercise, he had dropped into a bookstore on the Ginza and happened upon *Criticism of Lyricism*. As soon as he went home, he read the book in one sitting and wrote a letter of thanks to its author, whom he hadn't met. Shortly afterward he rewrote the diary entry to turn it into a brief review for the *Tokyo Shinbun* and said, "The existence of Mr. Yasuda Yojūrō is an eerie myth, a dramatic life of a specialist on the paradox between beauty and death, his long postwar silence in itself a myth." Yasuda, an advocate of chauvinistic Romanticism who had been influenced by German Romantics such as Friedrich Hölderlin and Friedrich von Schlegel, fell silent on the heels of Japan's defeat and had yet to break the silence.

"Essays are rare," Mishima continued, "that have discussed as superbly as this one how terrifying, thrilling, and also attractive it is to live and die in a single era, turning one's life and philosophy into a drama." This essay "lays out an ominous prophetic insight and view of destiny on the fundamental structure of the Japanese sense of beauty and, after reading it, we are given the impression of facing a dark sea."[48]

As the Mishima editor and critic Tanaka Miyoko pointed out, however, such a reading may well have "bewildered Ōoka himself." What Ōoka had actually done in *Criticism of Lyricism* was to expose "the philosophical weakness" of the wartime generation by targeting Yasuda as representative of the amorphousness of their thinking in order to "say a last farewell to the roguish 'lyricism' that was a chronic disease for the Japanese." In the event, through "this brilliant sleight of hand," was Mishima simply announcing his readiness to turn himself into a myth?[49]

CHAPTER SEVENTEEN

# Assassinations

*Japan's leading postwar author.*
—*The New York Times*, November 1960

*The poet Benn and the philosopher Heidegger furnished quotes for the apocalyptic mood. The background to it all was the thoroughly researched and soon to be expected death by the atom.*
—Günter Grass

In November 1960 when Mishima and Yōko arrived in the United States on the first leg of their world tour, John F. Kennedy was about to defeat Richard Nixon for the presidency. As it turned out, the Ambassador Hotel in Los Angeles where they had made a reservation was Nixon's campaign headquarters, and on the day they arrived at the hotel, November 7, they were asked to stay that night at the Gaylord Hotel across the street; Nixon's entourage had taken up the place on the eve of Election Day.

"Travelers' feelings are simple," Mishima wrote. "Out of the fury that we'd been kicked out of our hotel one night, we came to hate Nixon completely and only hoped that Kennedy would win." This turn of events was all the more rankling because in Japan he had been repeatedly told Election Day would be November 4 and Mishima had stopped in Hawaii specifically to avoid the election-day brouhaha. Oddly, in Hawaii, too, no one seemed to know or care for Election Day, even though "Hawaii had just joined the Union and had acquired the right to vote for the first time." Still, when he watched on TV a smiling Nixon giving a concession speech as his wife stood by, "weeping with an indescribable expression," Mishima decided that the man was "quite a wily old fox."[1] He loved Disneyland, though—had "never thought such an exciting place could exist," he wrote Kawabata.

Arriving in New York on November 10, Mishima and Yōko put up at the Astor Hotel, then "right smack in Times Square." Five days later they saw his plays staged at the Theatre de Lys as part of the presentations of the American National Theatre and Academy (ANTA). They were two of his "modern nō plays," *Hanjo* and *Aoi no Ue*, the latter titled *The Lady Akane* for the occasion. Lucille Lortel, the "very wealthy" Connecticut backer of the theatre, had pointed out that *Aoi no Ue* was unpronounceable for the Americans (her own suggestion was "Lady Saito"—likely because Saitō was the name of the proprietress of the eponymous restaurant, one of the few that offered Japanese food in New York at the time). Before the staging, she invited Mishima and his wife to the Plaza Hotel where she lived while in the city. As a result, he had occasion to see its rooms, not just its men's room.

The ANTA Matinee Series in the Greater New York Chapter presented five playwrights every fall, one playwright each on a Tuesday, for five weeks. That year the five included Beckett and Ionesco. Mishima impressed the *New York Times* drama critic Louis Calta. *Hanjo* and *The Lady Akane* demonstrated why he was regarded as "Japan's leading postwar author," who was "versatile, subtle and effective," Calta reported.[2]

Anne Meacham played Yasuko Rokujō, the principal character of *The Lady Akane*. Calta noted she had "recently covered herself with glory as a last minute replacement for the leading player in 'Hedda Gabler,'" while Mishima wrote that she had "risen to stardom since appearing in Tennessee Williams's *Suddenly, Last Summer*," in January 1958, probably because the Japanese poster for the film version of the play featured Elizabeth Taylor in a swim suit. Mishima had a bouquet of "a dozen large white chrysanthemums" delivered to Meacham.

"At one o'clock that night, the morning edition of the *New York Times* came out," he wrote. "I bought a copy in the elevator of my hotel after midnight, read it in my room, and tasted some excitement. It was what you call 'a rave,' and, I would say, a review I hadn't expected." He added, however, that New York critics tended to be tough on Broadway but generous to Off-Broadway, to the "conscientious" shows in particular. Many in the audience, Mishima noted, were middle-aged and those in the know, and most women wore fur coats.[3] Two weeks later, Mishima was on a panel with Edward Albee and Jack Gelber at the same theater.

Although the possibility of seeing his plays staged in New York had been a source of excitement and disappointment three years earlier, Mishima had not planned his world trip or his third visit to New York on account of it. He learned of the production from Donald Keene after laying out a meticulous itinerary.[4] It was during this New York stay that he met Greta Garbo, a meeting that "deeply moved him." Faubion Bowers, "the savior of kabuki," invited Mishima and Yōko to his house and also Garbo.[5]

On December 2, the two left the United States and went to Portugal (of Lisbon, he exclaimed, "What a beautiful town!"[6]), Spain, then on to Paris. There, in the city where during his first visit eight years earlier he had lost all his cash, Mishima, now with his wife, went to see Jean Cocteau, the man he had admired since his youth, rehearse three of the short plays he'd written when young. In one of them, *The Shadow*, Kishi Keiko played the lead role. Kishi, the popular Japanese actress, three years earlier had married Yves Ciampi who directed the joint French-Japanese film *Typhon sur Nagasaki* in which she was paired with Danielle Darrieux, and had since lived in Paris. She won Mishima's admiration as much as Cocteau who "seemed to have a halo" when he appeared. His sickly body wrapped in a brown coat, he sat in the seat right in front of Mishima and Yōko to direct, gesturing with his long arms and his "famously beautiful fingers."

"Those who don't understand this never will," Mishima wrote, "but it is a difficult thing indeed for a Japanese to act using a foreign language in a foreign country, in a play by a foreigner, among foreign actors and actresses"—especially in Paris where the people are hypersensitive about their own language. Cocteau's attempt at stylization rendered the judging of Kishi's acting somewhat moot. Still, "the fighting spirit and passion" of the "delicate-bodied" actress, with "her beautiful voice," deeply moved him.

In London Mishima met and had a pleasant two-hour talk with

Arthur Waley, the famous (and at the time the only) translator of *The Tale of Genji* who would not visit Japan lest he be disappointed by the changes modern times had brought to the country. He also met the poet Stephen Spender who had visited Japan. On New Year's Day the couple were in Rome. Mishima visited Giovanni Aldini, a professor of marble sculpture, in his studio. Aldini was working on a replica of a statue of Apollo owned by the City of Rome, for the city. Mishima asked the sculptor to make another one for him, and Aldini agreed. The 1,500-pound replica was delivered half a year later and installed in the middle of Mishima's garden.

Mishima and Yōko then went to Athens, Cairo (where the Great Pyramid of Giza struck him as "an indecent monument," a marker of "an unimaginably dark civilization, an ontological civilization on whose strength the Europeans have never once depended"[7]), then—via Karachi, Calcutta, and Bangkok—on to the final destination of their trip, Hong Kong. There they stayed for five days. With or without Yōko, Mishima made the point of visiting bad places, opium dens and waterborne brothels among them.

The Tiger Balm Garden in particular impressed him.

Built in 1935 by the philanthropist Hu Wen-hu (the second *hu* meaning "tiger") who had amassed a fortune from the cough drop he invented, the eight-acre garden made only of garishly painted concrete and stone presented, the English pamphlet said, a "typical landscape of Oriental beauty." In his essay, "What Goes Against Beauty," which was prompted by the garden, Mishima meditated on what might constitute "beauty." The garden reminded him of Poe's tale "The Domain of Arnheim" and the landscape-gardening aesthetics of the story's unimaginably wealthy protagonist, Ellison, such as his assertion, "The original beauty [of the country] is never so great as that which may be introduced." Yet Ellison's aesthetics, rooted in idealized notions of "the glory that was Greece / And the grandeur that was Rome," paled in the face of "the ultimate collection of bad taste" that was the Tiger Balm Garden. The Chinese extravaganza in which "grotesqueries never elevate themselves to abstraction"[8] appalled and mesmerized Mishima.

## *Rightwing Killers*

The couple returned to Haneda Airport on January 20. Less than two weeks later a murder implicating Mishima occurred.

Late on the evening of February 1, a young man, loudly saying, "I'm a rightwinger!" barged into the residence of Shimanaka Hōji, president of the publishing house Chūō Kōron, and, brandishing a knife, killed Shimanaka's maid and seriously wounded his wife. The killer, who surrendered himself to the police early the following morning, said he had meant to kill Shimanaka for publishing Fukazawa Shichirō's short story "Tale of a Stylish Dream" (*Fūryū mutan*), in his monthly magazine *Chūō Kōron*, but Shimanaka wasn't home.

The story was an inconsequential, even jokey, account of a dream, real or made up, of a leftwing revolution in which the reigning Tennō and his spouse, along with the Crown Prince and Princess, are beheaded. If some of Fukazawa's earlier stories had described stark daily necessities that subsumed morality, "Tale of a Stylish Dream" had little to do with anything—or, if it did at all, made fun of the leftwing through a play on a Chinese character where *sayoku*, "leftwing," came out as "left-greed." But there they were: the heads of the Tennō *et al* rolling about on the street, with the author in his own dream cursing Empress Dowager Shōken, the Meiji Emperor's consort. To rightwing groups, the story was glaring *lèse majesté*. The seventeen-year-old perpetrator, Komori Kazutaka, had been, in fact, a member of the Patriotic Party until shortly before the act.

Actually, less than three months earlier, another member of the Patriotic Party had committed an assassination that reverberated throughout the world. A few weeks before Mishima and Yōko left Japan, on October 12, a young man dashed onto the stage in Hibiya Town Hall where Chairman of the Socialist Party Asanuma Inejirō was giving a speech, and stabbed the chairman to death—a spectacle caught and witnessed on TV and wired globally. The perpetrator, Yamaguchi Otoya, was, by coincidence, also seventeen. Not long after the December issue of *Chūō Kōron* with Fukazawa's story went on sale, members of rightwing groups started showing up at the publishing house to protest and threaten. The publisher hastily replaced the editor of the monthly, but the rightwing kept up the pressure, demanding dissolution of the company.

Then, in early January, the February issue of the monthly *Bungakukai* appeared with Ōe Kenzaburō's story "The Political Boy Dies" (*Seiji shōnen shisu*). What the author intended as the second half of the novella *Seventeen*, it had as its protagonist a youth modeled after the Asanuma assassin, "a seventeen-year-old who is fearful of death and others' eyes, exhausted from masturbation and delusion, and burning with the sense of impotence and self-loathing," that is, "a diddly *dickhead* masturbatory impotent crybaby brainless *dupe* like a dog with an excessive inferiority complex." These are the narrator's self-characterizations in a story written in the form of a letter addressed to himself. The confessor hangs himself in the penitentiary, where he is sent after lengthy questioning at the Metropolitan Police Department and the Tokyo District Prosecutors Office.

Yamaguchi killed himself in real life, as he does in the story. But Ōe, well known for maniacal descriptions of masturbation, did not stop there. After making the young man proclaim himself to be "the chosen boy with a true rightwing soul," he appends a note saying the suicide had a smell of ejaculation in his pants when his body was taken down. Rightwing groups could not contain themselves any longer. On January 30, just two days before Komori went to Shimanaka's residence with the plan of killing him, they assembled at Hibiya Town Hall—the same place where Asanuma had been assassinated—to "protect our citizens from a Red Revolution."

The murder at the Shimanaka household threw Mishima into turmoil. As soon as he heard the news on the radio, he rushed to Shimanaka's house and accompanied him to the hospital. Word was out that Mishima himself had recommended the publication of Fukazawa's story, and he was receiving life-threatening phone calls and letters, some threatening to set fire to his house. Suspicious men turned up in his neighborhood.

The murder also prompted the Metropolitan Police Department to provide "several hundred commentators" with protection, Mishima wrote to Donald Keene. A plainclothes officer, with gun in pocket, began to stay close to Mishima around the clock and in his house when he was home.

"Every day a police *body guard* is with me," he wrote his translator, "so I can't even go to a barber by myself; I don't know if I should call this state of affairs amusing or what, but going to a night club with a bodyguard, I feel like a *little king* [Mishima's English] and nice.... Is a Nazi era coming to Japan as well?" (In the same letter Mishima said the Japanese newspapers were reporting that the NY theater showing his plays was "full house every day," even though Robert McGregor had written that the attendance was scant, with "only thirty-five people showing up even on Saturday evenings."9 The Players Theater was showing three of his plays at the time, with Herbert Machiz directing. The Japanese media tended to exaggerate any United States and European reactions to things Japanese.)

In truth, the situation became so unsettling around the time Mishima wrote these words that he issued a statement denying his editorial involvement: "According to what I hear, about [*Chūō Kōron*] carrying that 'Tale of a Stylish Dream,' rumor's abroad that despite the fact that the president of the Chūō Kōron objected, I pressured him to print it. This is an outrageous misunderstanding, there isn't even the fact of my recommending it.... If my name was used, people in some quarters used it as an excuse out of desperation."10

This, according to Ide Magoroku, was not exactly true. Ide, then an assistant editor at the publisher Chūō Kōron, went to see Mishima to pick up a manuscript the magazine had requested. The manuscript turned out to be "Yūkoku." In handing it over to him, Mishima asked Ide to tell the editor-in-chief to consider publishing it in *Chūō Kōron* along with Fukazawa's work, which turned out to be "Tale of a Stylish Dream." Evidently, the editor-in-chief had previously asked Mishima for his opinion of the Fukazawa story. Ide had no idea what the story was like, but conveyed Mishima's message.

As it happened, "Yūkoku" shortly appeared in another magazine specializing in fiction with which Ide was involved, but "Tale" in *Chūō Kōron* a little later. Years afterward, reflecting on the rising rightwing clamor at the end of the 1950s and what happened as a result of the publication of Fukazawa's story, Ide wondered if Mishima did not mean to counterbalance it with his story—to kill the "poison" of Fukazawa's rambunctiously anti-Tennō-house tale with the "poison" of his seemingly super rightwing tale. Ide, in fact, even wondered if Mishima did not write "Yūkoku" for that particular purpose.11

The rightwing threats did not abate. Fukazawa Shichirō withdrew from the literary world altogether, resuming his guitar-strumming drifter's life, until he settled on what he called Love Me Ranch, in Saitama, where he refused to see anyone but his closest friends. He also permanently proscribed publication of "Tale of a Stylish Dream." Ōe followed suit, removing "The Political Boy Dies" from his own oeuvre. The two stories have since been available only in pirate editions.[12]

More deleterious was the self-censorship Chūō Kōron and other publishers began to practice. They toned down liberalism and progressivism. In one well-known case, Chūō Kōron cancelled the publication of the January 1962 issue of its monthly *Shisō no Kagaku* just before it went on sale. The issue was devoted to the Tennō system. For Mishima, the incident may have marked his turning away, some say, from the orthodox notion of rightwing toward something more esoteric or more personal.[13]

If the United States at the time was gearing up for serious confrontation with the Soviet Union, first to climax in the Cuban Missile Crisis, Japan had entered what was later dubbed "the political season"—a deceptively mild term for the violent confrontation between left and right, with its focus on the Tennō system, that would last for a dozen years. There were always possibilities for overt rightwing or anticommunist acts.

In December of that year, for example, thirteen men were arrested in a plot against the Diet, later called "the only attempted *coup d'état* in postwar Japan." One of the men was Miyake Taku, a leader of the 5.15 Incident who, after release from prison, had become a rightwing activist. In fact, the attempted coup in its naïveté had a striking resemblance to the plot three decades earlier, though there were some differences. It had, unlike the 5.15 Incident but like the 2.26 Incident, some supporters among the ranking officers of the military, the Ground Self-Defense Forces, though this time none of the officers were subjected to prosecutorial interrogation. The attempt was also international in nature. At least one Korean and one Chinese businessman as well as a major general in the Korean Army were to supply weapons if the uprising had actually occurred.

The plotters, led by a Japanese industrialist who had enriched himself in shipbuilding during the Pacific War, advocated *san'yū*, the three no's: No tax, no unemployment, and no war. No tax was to be achieved through drastic budget cuts and privatization of public corporations; no unemployment through massive public works programs; and no war through prevention of foreign invasions by developing missiles and space weapons. The Japanese have no monopoly on such glaringly contradictory policy ideas, to state the obvious. In any event, to achieve these aims, the plotters meant to assassinate some Cabinet officers and so turn the government rightwing in a single stroke.

One of the "victims" of the San'yū Incident was Yamamoto Kiyokatsu, who would later play an important role in Mishima's life. Then a colonel and an intelligence officer in the GSDF Staff Office, Yamamoto led the effort, with the Tokyo Metropolitan Police Department, to reveal the plot and succeeded in doing so. But Yamamoto's report did not reach Kaihara Osamu, director-general of defense who practically ran the Defense Agency (his nickname was Emperor Kaihara), enraging the man. Unlike some of his superiors, Yamamoto did not have to resign, but his next post, military attaché at the Japanese Embassy in Thailand, was cancelled.[14]

## *Japanese Myths*

On March 15, while the Shimanaka Incident was still hot, Mishima was hit by Arita's invasion-of-privacy lawsuit. His immediate concern was the English translation of *After the Banquet* that Donald Keene had agreed to undertake, a contract with Knopf already signed. He wrote Keene about uncertainties created by the lawsuit, asking him to find out about its effect on publication of the translation, and suggesting *Thirst for Love* or the novel he was writing just then, *Beastly Entanglement*, for Keene to consider should Knopf decide to drop *After the Banquet*. "I jumped for joy," he wrote three weeks later when he received a letter from Keene saying Knopf saw no problem.[15]

Mishima's trust in Keene and dependence on him was considerable by then. Earlier, *Holiday* magazine had asked him to contribute an essay and Mishima had agreed, evidently on condition that the magazine would ask Keene to translate it. The essay was about the "myths" that Americans were—and still are—prone to hold about the Japanese. It began:

> Japan first became famous for *samurai, harakiri, Fujiyama,* and *geisha*. She then became famous for low wages and shoddy export goods, then for her people's "inscrutable smile." Then

> she became famous for her warlike people, but once defeated, became famous for *kimono, ikebana,* girls with the quality to be the chastest wives in the world, quiet friendship, *cameras, transistor radios,* woodwork, porcelain, paper lanterns, *tempura, sukiyaki,* and the great philosophy of Zen....

The Japanese automobile, which had been laughed off the California highway a few years earlier, still had a long way to go before establishing a beachhead in the United States.

Some of these "myths" may be considered "scandalous" by the people themselves, Mishima went on to note. Take *Sayonara,* the 1957 Marlon Brando film, which won four Oscars. Based on James Michener's story in which an American military officer during the Korean War falls in love with a Japanese woman, it was a modern version of what had been for the Japanese the most scandalous myth of them all: *Madama Butterfly*. During the Second World War the Japanese government treated the opera as a national insult and banned its production. The question has to do with the foreign view of Japanese wives.

> We, the spoiled Japanese men, take it for granted that our wives wash our backs when we take a hot bath, but for Americans this simple service appears to be a cause for great excitement. When you think of it, though, don't American ladies happily wash the backs of their beloved dogs? In the event, it may well be that they don't want to wash their husbands' backs out of respect, because they make distinction between dog and husband.
>
> In Japan, too, there are wives and there are wives. I know a married woman nicknamed Tange Sazen, the name of a legendary samurai who lost an eye from a wound in combat. She got this nickname because she loves to sleep late. Every morning her husband gets up, washes his face, makes his breakfast, eats it, and, finally, when he is ready to go to work and says, "See you later," she opens an eye, barely, to signal her acknowledgment of his departure, before falling back to sleep.[16]

This essay, "Japan: The Cherished Myths," in Keene's translation, appeared in the October issue of *Holiday* that was entirely devoted to

Japan. (The translation above is not Keene's.) To mark the Japan special, Curtis Publishing invited Mishima to a symposium in San Francisco, in mid-September. Among the speakers who gathered were Faubion Bowers, from New York, and Laurens van der Post, the Afrikaner who was a Japanese POW in Indonesia during the war. Two decades later Ōshima Nagisa would make a film based on van der Post's experience in Japanese prison camps, *Merry Christmas Mr. Lawrence*, with David Bowie, Sakamoto Ryūichi, and Kitano Takeshi, aka Beat Takeshi. Ōshima, it is said, had Mishima in mind as the model of Capt. Yonoi, the young, intense, homosexual, sword-brandishing commandant of the prison camp.

At the symposium Mishima gave a speech in English, and it was titled "Japanese Youth." He had prepared and practiced it in Tokyo, with Burton Martin, a teacher at Waseda University. Martin's comment to the effect that Mishima's English was like someone who can follow dance steps but can't walk straight delighted Mishima as "exquisite."

Mishima's subject was the typical young man of the day, "a youth of twenty hanging out at a corner of the street ... quite tall ... his appearance is like an American, particularly when he lights a cigarette," to quote from his English. Tall because he had grown up with America's postwar nutritious largess, and looking like an American because doing so was the wish of every Japanese youth, as it still is. "Wearing blue-jeans, a gay-coloured summer-shirt, a straw hat with a colourful ribbon and a heavy suntanned skin proving his pleasant summer life on the seashore," Mishima went on. Was he poking fun at Ishihara Shintarō, the fellow writer and future governor of Tokyo, and those who came under his influence? Perhaps, though one must say Mishima himself also dressed like that when occasion required.

The question, Mishima posited, is what happens as the Japanese youth matures. A "synthesis of the occidental logic and the oriental intuition" is attempted, but for the Japanese it is a "tragic cultural task." For lo and behold: "99 percent of the Japanese play golf, or see KABUKI, or chant KOUTA with GEISHA girls, or see NOH plays and a Hollywood movie in a single day, or eat a beef-steak after a tea-ceremony without thinking about it."[17] Before the audience of 300, Mishima was happy that people laughed when he thought he joked,[18] although his English, which he spoke in a raised voice, was "almost incomprehensible," Bowers decided.[19]

On April 13 Mishima, jointly with Shinchōsha, sent the Japan Writers Association a petition for support of his position on Arita's lawsuit. Two days later he went to the association and presented his argument before its Speech and Expression Committee. The association agreed to support him. Afterward he visited the president of the Japan PEN Club, Kawabata Yasunari at the time, and asked for the club's support. On the 20th, the first court hearings were held on the lawsuit. On May 13 Mishima, together with the president of Shinchōsha, attended the regular meeting of the PEN Club. The club agreed that the lawsuit was unjust, though it did not issue a formal statement to that effect.

It was in his letter later that month suggesting that his club's issuing a formal statement at that juncture might not be a good idea that Kawabata asked Mishima to recommend him for the Nobel Prize. The idea of a Japanese writer receiving the international prize was gaining credence in Japan as the translation of Japanese literature into foreign languages quickly increased. Limiting the scope to Mishima's works of that year alone, English, Italian, and Yugoslavian translations of *The Sound of Waves* were published, and so were German, French, and Finnish translations of *The Temple of the Golden Pavilion*.

Mishima at once complied with Kawabata's request. The letter he wrote, translated into English by Saeki Shōichi for the club, began: "In Mr. Kawabata's works, delicacy joins with resilience, elegance with an awareness of the depths of human nature; their clarity conceals an unfathomable sadness, they are modern yet directly inspired by the solitary philosophy of the monks of medieval Japan."[20] Kawabata would not receive the prize until seven years later, in 1968, but by then Mishima himself was a serious contender.

During the same month of May, Mishima sought out a detective story that had left an indelible impression on him as a boy: *Black Lizard* (*Kuro-tokage*) by Edogawa Ranpo. Rare among Edogawa's many stories, it features a "bad woman" as protagonist: an extraordinary enchantress who loves nothing better than to dance in a packed house with only jewelry on her body, a robber-kidnapper, and a sadist to boot. The woman, who calls herself Black Lizard, battles Edogawa's famous creation, the private eye Akechi Kogorō.

Mishima wanted to reread the story to turn it into a play. He completed the play, by mid-July. In the play, he brought to the fore the love engendered between the two antagonists, kidnapper and private eye. First staged the following March with the doyenne of the Shinpa Mizutani Yaeko and Akutagawa Hiroshi in the lead roles, *Black Lizard* went on to create a boom for the Edogawa story, which hadn't enjoyed anything of the sort before, and Mishima's play with the same title would in time bring national fame to the extraordinarily beautiful transsexual singer-actor Maruyama Akihiro as creator of "modern *oyama*," female impersonators. He of course played Black Lizard. Mishima famously said to Maruyama once: "You have just one flaw: You don't fall in love with me."

As Mishima predicted, the Arita lawsuit dragged on for several years, but it had one side-effect before long: Mishima's withdrawal from the literati group Hachi no Ki Kai. One member, Yoshida Kenkichi, sided with the plaintiff. A former diplomat's son who had studied at Cambridge University, Yoshida knew Arita well and at first tried to play a reconciler's role, suggesting that Mishima visit Arita.[21] It did not work. Exasperated, he said to Mishima, at one Hachi no Ki Kai meeting, "You are a Philistine. Don't act big." He was known for his impeccable English-style gentlemanliness but also for straight talk of a flamboyant variety. Whether the face-to-face insult occurred during the November gathering in 1961 is not known, but that was the last session Mishima attended. Some time afterward the monthly fraternal group dissolved.

At the end of November the Bungaku-za began staging *The Tenth-Day Chrysanthemum*, with Sugimura Haruko, Kishida Kyōko, and others. After a month in Tokyo, the production moved to Nagoya, Kyoto, and Osaka. In January the play won the Yomiuri Bungaku Prize.

## *Nuclear Threat and UFO*

The January 1962 issues of four different monthly magazines carried four stories by Mishima, two short, the other two the first installments of full-length novels to be serialized. In addition, the *Mainichi Shin-*

*bun* carried his essay on January 14. Three of the five were thematically related.

To begin with the two thematically *un*related pieces, one of the novels, *Love Dashes* (*Ai no shissō*), that started in the ladies magazine *Fujin Club*, was meant as light reading but with a tricky setup: an author, himself a character within the novel, decides to write a love story about a young man and woman he knows and for that end takes steps to make them fall in love with each other, but the couple, realizing what's happening, resist; further, each of the characters, including the author-narrator, is given a chapter or chapters to provide a first-person narrative.

One of the short stories, "The Thermos Bottle" (*Mahōbin*), in *Bungei Shunjū*, tells of a one-night affair between a Japanese businessman visiting San Francisco and a woman who was his lover until several years ago but is now, like him, married. The title comes from the protagonist's unsettling discovery that his child and his former lover's child both react exactly the same way to the thermos, "the magic bottle" as the Japanese call it.

(The story shows how Mishima's reaction to the Golden City had changed. In his visit a decade earlier he had noted the horrible taste of the miso soup he ate at a Japanese restaurant, which, most likely, was run by someone of Japanese descent who had gone through the relocation experience. In "The Thermos Bottle," he describes, albeit in fiction, a Japanese woman who is prospecting to set up a Japanese restaurant "based on a totally new concept" in the city.)

The other story, "Flowers on a Hat" (*Bōshi no hana*), like "The Thermos Bottle," was obviously inspired by Mishima's visit to San Francisco, but it is different. It reads not so much like fiction as an account of what Mishima actually experienced. Indeed, it may well have been, considering the subject of the other novel he had started and the newspaper article he wrote for the *Mainichi*. The vignette, in *Gunzō*, describes a hallucinatory vision of mankind's annihilation that the first-person narrator has while sitting in San Francisco's Union Square.

So, sitting in Union Square one day in September, "a truly beautiful season when the sunlight from the clear sky, unique to California, is filled with an appetizing richness like bread baked golden," the narrator overhears a fat passerby, perhaps an Italian American, loudly say "Dag Hammarskjöld" to his companion. "The news of the UN Secretary-General's death in a mystifying plane accident was reported yesterday."

Perhaps in consequence, the utterly peaceful details of the scene the narrator observes in the park, the "absurdly solid, glittering, blessed things," begin to make him uneasy. Then everything freezes: a mother sitting on a bench knitting, her baby son in a walker near the bench, the young woman sitting next to the mother who appears to be a typist, a gentleman walking by with a cane—each captured in minute detail in the narrator's observing eyes. Behind this momentary hallucination was talk of a catastrophic war.

> When I left Japan my mind was filled with visions of war. I'd heard that even in America, in one part of California, there is an area believed to be safe even if a hydrogen bomb were dropped, and that a great many citizens of the East had actually moved there. Bomb shelters have spread in short order, and even large corporations like US Steel have begun manufacturing them. But to me, all these things were neither new nor fresh. Anyone who doesn't believe in the annihilation of the world today is either a romantic too *blessed* for words or too much of a realist to see a moment ahead—either way someone blind. The question is when it will come.

The Berlin Crisis had begun in mid-August, and on the day Mishima left for San Francisco, the United States had resumed nuclear testing, on which it had set a unilateral moratorium three years earlier after completing the largest series of such tests. The American and Soviet leaders were vying in grand posturing, as when Nikita Khrushchev boasted that the Soviets weren't afraid of hydrogen bombs because Russia was so vast it could absorb any number of them.

This last is what Mishima quoted in his essay for the *Mainichi Shinbun* titled "Eschatology and Literature." Starting the essay with "a conventional phrase in nō drama, 'the Former Buddha already gone, / the Latter Buddha yet to appear, / we're born in a dream in between,'" Mishima went on to observe that no one could be sure that "This year 1962 will end with this lament," an observation repeated since Japan's medieval ages. As he explained, the Former Buddha is Sakyamuni, the Latter Buddha Maitreya, "the future Buddha" who is said to appear to succor the world 5,670 million years after Sakyamuni attained nirvana.

"The end of the world may come" before the year is up, Mishima wrote. The reason was simple: "At least the end of the world has come to exist as a scientific possibility since the invention of the hydrogen bomb. Thus it is as if the advent of the Maitreya has been guaranteed by this scientific possibility."

"Literature is always on the side of the eschatological view of the world," Mishima asserted. But in the past, eschatology, which has existed in any age, was in the domain of religion or philosophy. In fact, "no thought was more encouraging for literary creation and for the recording function of literature than the thought that the world would soon end," for it enabled the writer to leave with the wish: "Beautiful one, stay awhile." But now it has entered the domain of science, which is "premised on the synoptic, conceptual, mechanistic view of the world." This being so, "the moment literature accepts it, it collapses." The dilemma for literature is that it cannot be on the side of hope, either. The question for novelists, then, is how to handle "the specificities of life that are fluttering in their hands" without being on the side of despair or on the side of hope.[22] The essay in effect described the approach he took in one of the two novels he had started about the same time, *The Beautiful Star* (*Utsukushii hoshi*).

*The Beautiful Star* is a science fiction of sorts in that "it melds the real and antireal" to an unusual degree, as the student of German literature Takahashi Yoshitaka put it.[23] The people who make up the two opposing forces in the story—a family of four whose head, Ōsugi Jūichirō, tries to save mankind through world peace, and a group of three men led by a "permanent assistant professor" of law, Haguro Masumi, who are determined to destroy it through "euthanasia of all mankind"—are all presented as entirely believable beings in their everyday specificities.

Yet they are also extraterrestrials—or, to be precise, humans whose "minds and bodies are completely governed by the souls of extraterrestrials"; the four Ōsugis each believe they came from Mercury, Venus, Mars, and Jupiter, while the three evil men know they are from the unknown planet 61-Cygni, in the constellation Cygnus which, Mishima in his fastidiousness took care to note, the German astronomer Friedrich Bessel discovered in 1838. In addition, all of them see flying saucers, vehicles from the extraterrestrial world. Indeed in his lecture series, Jūichirō argues that world peace can be achieved "according to the teachings of the flying saucers" and it is on one that the family, led by the cancer-ridden, dying Jūichirō, tries to escape Earth.

What lies behind all this is, of course, the nuclear contest between the two superpowers. "The Soviet Union has finally tested a nuclear bomb of 50 megatons," Jūichirō laments at the outset of the tale. That historic event occurred on October 30, 1961. "They are about to commit the horrible crime of disturbing the harmony of the universe. If America follows suit . . . the end of mankind on Earth will be sure to come. When rescuing humans from that fate is our family's mission, how powerless we still are, how nonchalant our society is!" In this setup, "the beautiful star" of the title wryly refers to Earth.

(In one passage describing the three evil men, Mishima couldn't help taking the authorial liberty of interjecting himself in a contemporaneous, though self-deprecatory, fashion. The three are invited to the Kabuki-za by a politician sympathetic to their cause, even though, uncouth and uncultured as they are, they are unlikely to be interested in kabuki. They watch Danjūrō's "exit six leaps" in *Kanjinchō*, with some interest. But when the last play on the program, "Mishima Yukio's *The Sardine Hawker & the Dragnet of Love*," opens, their leader Haguro offers that "a new kabuki play by such a novel-writer isn't worth seeing," his two companions agree, and the three decamp. How Haguro, a narrow-minded law teacher at a college far from Tokyo, is conversant with Mishima's various writings, isn't explained, but no matter. Beginning on April 1, 1962, the play in question was staged for the second time at the Kabuki-za, with Utaemon, Kanzaburō, Minosuke, and so forth.)

Did Mishima believe in flying saucers? "For several years before writing this novel," he wrote after the novel came out in book form following its serialization in *Shinchō*, "I was absorbed in 'flying saucers.' More than a few times did the two of us, Mr. Kitamura Komatsu and I, try to observe them from my roof during summer nights. But no matter what effort we made, flying saucers did not show up. At least in my eyes they didn't. And so I was suddenly enlightened to the belief that 'flying saucers' must be an artistic concept."[24]

Among the books Ōsugi Jūichirō reads in the novel is *The Flying Saucers Are Real* by Donald Keyhoe.

## Ghostwriting

That fall Mishima edited a "Kawabata reader" for Kawade Shobō. In the threesome talk he had with the author and Nakamura Mitsuo to be included in the project, he started by bringing up Kawabata's stories the writer himself was known to dislike, "Birds and Beasts" (*Kinjū*) and *Sleeping Beauties* (*Nemureru bijo*), expressing his special fondness for them.

"Birds and Beasts" deals with the protagonist's preference of pets—goldcrests, Nippon terrier, what have you—over humans and with his realization, which he comes to accept, that animal lovers, so called, necessarily perpetrate cruelties on animals.[25] In his 1955 essay Mishima had chosen it among Kawabata's "best three," asserting that with this 1933 story Kawabata became "a tragedian" who would "ceaselessly explore the blind life force in amorality like that of the behavior of birds and beasts."[26]

*Sleeping Beauties* describes a secret house of sexual entertainment where old men of means, mostly impotent, pay to lie by one or two young naked girls drugged to sleep all night, on the understanding that no touching is allowed. Mishima called the novella "the apex of *decadence*" and "the lowest depths of beauty" when he was asked for an essay for the *geppō* to go with a volume in the complete works of Kawabata. When Shinchōsha published the story along with two others in a paperback edition, just before Kawade asked him to edit the Kawabata reader, Mishima brought up Edward Seidensticker as the only person, aside from himself, who called it "an indisputable masterpiece," even though, he added, their views of literature were "as different as summer and winter."

"Where in ordinary novelistic techniques, dynamic differentiations of personalities are made through conversation and action, this work, on account of its essential nature, differentiates six young women by employing extremely difficult, extremely ironic techniques," Mishima was unstinting in his praise. "Because the six are asleep and remain mum, it leaves no physical depictions, other than those of various bodily movements and mumblings in sleep. Its persistent, detailed, *necrophilic* physical depictions, you may say, are at the apex of idealistic lechery. Yet the work as a whole is palpably oppressive, because revulsion is always woven into this sexual fantasy, and also, because the adoration of life is always mixed with a denial of life."[27]

In the threesome talk, Kawabata recognized that underlying some of his stories was "self-revulsion, self-denial," saying that he was "embarrassed" about *Sleeping Beauties*. Yes, he said, when he wrote "Birds and Beasts," he had many birds, such as a shrike and an owl—the reader may marvel at the lively, graphic description of an owl at feeding time—and several dogs. He also said he had meant *Sleeping Beauties* to be complete with what later became Part I, but his *Shinchō* editor asked him to continue so as to make it long enough to make a book, hence a novella of five parts. This revelation delighted Mishima.[28]

Yet all this could have entailed a dose of duplicity on the part of everyone involved. As Kawabata candidly admitted in his own afterword to *The Old Capital* (*Koto*), his long-term dependence on sleeping pills had gotten worse just before he started serializing the novel in the *Asahi Shinbun* in early October 1961. As a result, he barely knew what he was writing throughout the serialization, although he managed to finish it, at the end of January 1962. Shortly afterward, he stopped taking sleeping pills, but that precipitated such violent withdrawal symptoms that he was rushed to University of Tokyo Hospital and remained unconscious for ten days. Sure enough, when he finally mustered enough of his wits and sat down to revise the story for publication in book form, Kawabata found many "irregularities," a number of "places that do not make sense."[29]

Kawabata was truthful about the sleeping pills and hospitalization after the fact but not about the novel that concerns beautiful twin sisters in Kyoto. The daily installments as he wrote them, for a total of 107 installments, were mostly unusable, and someone else had to rewrite them. As Mishima tells it, this hospitalization was done in secrecy.[30]

Behind this was the common practice of famous or popular writers having ghostwriters, often magazine editors but also independent writers. Kawabata had had a couple of writers, including the redoubtable Itō Sei and the noted critic Senuma Shigeki, who had stood in for him since before the war. One *Shinchō* editor averred that among the leading postwar writers only Mishima Yukio and Ōe Kenzaburō did no such thing.

Mishima himself was not truthful, either; he had written much—how much remains unknown—of *Sleeping Beauties*, which was serialized in *Shinchō* from January 1960 to November 1961, with a good deal of interruption, with Kawabata's hospitalization at the end of 1960.[31] In other words, Kawabata had started the newspaper serialization of *The Old Capital* even as he finished the monthly serialization of *Sleeping Beauties*.

Yet *Sleeping Beauties* went on to win the Mainichi Publishing Culture Award.

---

In February Mishima had a taidan with the photographer Hosoe Eikō for the photo magazine *Camera Geijutsu*. Hosoe had been having photo sessions with Mishima since the previous fall for the cover of a collection of his critical essays, *Beauty's Assaults* (*Bi no shūgeki*). When Hosoe showed up at Mishima's house, the writer was sunbathing on his verandah with nothing on his upper body except for sunglasses. "Today I'm your subject. I won't mind whichever way you shoot me," Mishima said. Thereupon Hosoe picked up the garden hose nearby and wound it around Mishima's body and began shooting. This session lasted for two hours, with Mishima uttering nary a word of protest. Hosoe liked photographing Mishima and asked for, and had, other sessions, in other places—such as the dancer Hijikata Tatsumi's studio in Meguro, an abandoned factory in Kamedo, and a construction site where Aoyama Church once stood. The photo sessions lasted from September 1961 to the spring of 1962.

The result, published March 1963 as *Rose Punishments* (*Bara-kei*),[32] would win Hosoe the photo critics' award, the highest prize in the field, and enhance Mishima's reputation as an exhibitionist that was already great enough. Mishima bought a number of copies and sent them to his friends overseas.[33]

Hosoe created images in four categories, Mishima explained in his introduction to the book: "Everyday Life," which was meant to demonstrate Mauriac's observation, "All humans are madmen when alone"; "A Laughing Clock or a Lazy Witness," which turned Mishima into a derisive witness of human life as a whole; "Various Sacrileges," which enabled him to move freely in "the ancient aesthetic forms of holiness and sensuality" that "transcend time and space"; and "Rose Punishments," which brought to the fore "the cruel, thorny rose," the symbol of "torture and never-ending *slow death*" that ends in "an ascension to the dark sun."

The world to which Hosoe transported him, "through the jujutsu of his lens," Mishima wrote, was "bizarre, distorted, derisive, grotesque, barbaric, and sex-pervaded," which nonetheless had "in its invisible tunnel a lyrical, sparkling undercurrent flowing, purling." Or it was a city that was "naked, comical, grim, cruel, also excessively decorative and so monstrous as to force you to look away," that nonetheless had "in its underground path a lyrical, transparent river flowing inexhaustibly."[34]

In early April 1962 Kawabata Yasunari asked Mishima for a sentence from *Hagakure* written in his own hand—the sentence Mishima had selected and written as epigraph for his volume in a modern writers series: "As Lord Teika's word handed down to us has it, the ultimate in the way of poetry, it is said, lies in taking good care of yourself."[35] (Lord Teika is the poet Fujiwara no Teika, 1162–1241.) The volume was in Shūeisha's modern Japanese literature series that came out in March. It included six of Mishima's short stories and two essays in addition to *Kyōko's House*. This publication followed a volume devoted to the author in Kadokawa's Shōwa literature series in February that included four of his novels and one of his novellas. In March Shinchōsha had published Mishima's "complete plays."

*Hagakure*, which is only too famous for its opening assertion, "The way of the warrior, I've found, is to die," is a large compilation of observations of Yamamoto Tsunetomo (also Jōchō: 1659–1719) that Mishima had counted among his favorite books since the war years, and Fujiwara no Teika was one of the greatest poets of his time. Earlier that year, Kawabata had been hospitalized after "abusing" sleeping pills, then suddenly not taking them, as Mishima who went to see him described it, comparing the situation to the caisson disease.[36] That probably prompted Kawabata's request a few months later.

Shizue, who thought her son's calligraphy clumsy, told him not to take the senior author's request seriously. Mishima agreed but Kawabata insisted. So he went to a well-known stationer specializing in calligraphic supplies and bought quality paper and ink. He practiced hard, creating "mountains of waste paper," finally sending Kawabata the one his mother "approved as more or less acceptable." Kawabata wrote to thank him graciously, saying in his letter of April 17, "No matter what your mother may say, your calligraphy is admirable."

"But," Mishima wrote in an account of this affair, "I feel that these words of Teika's have behind them a subtly dark secret meaning."

> I, who was sickly and feeble in childhood and have recently become a *ridiculous* "health first" nut, understand the benefits of health, while I also understand the indescribable unsoundness of physical health unknown to those who are born healthy.
>
> The eeriness of being healthy, the sickly concern of paying attention to one's health all the time, the monstrous sensual charm lurking in various exercises, the horrible discrepancy between external and internal, the arrogance that gives the decadence of every mind and nerve the colors of the blue sky and the golden wheat . . . these are the monstrous symptoms that neither methamphetamine, heroin, marijuana, hashish, nor sleeping pills give.
>
> Mr. Kawabata, who asked for calligraphy in my terrible hand, may have seen through this secret quite early on.[37]

Mishima wrote these words that summer for a monthly newsletter accompanying one of the volumes of Kawabata's complete works then being published. In Japan, "complete works," either of individual authors or of select periods, are published in monthly installments, each volume with a pamphlet carrying short essays by various hands, an ad for the upcoming volume, and such. Later that year, Mishima edited a Kawabata reader for Kawade Shobō Shinsha and wrote the introduction. In it he characterized the author as "a mind with the least secrets" he'd known, asking: "What is a secret? Could a human being have a significant secret? So his mind asks us at once. This is a destructive question, but he never pursues it with logic," because "it is certain that just asking the question freezes us."[38]

On May 2, his second child, a son, was born, and he named him Iichirō.

A week later he worked out the framework for what would become his largest and last oeuvre, the tetralogy *The Sea of Fertility* (*Hōjō no umi*), even though it took him two more years to make its theme more or less public. That was when he wrote an essay on *The Tale of Middle Councilor Hamamatsu* (*Hamamatsu Chūnagon monogatari*) on the occasion of Iwanami Shoten's publication of the newly annotated text of the medieval tale for its famed series of Japanese classics. The annotator was Matsuo Satoshi, Mishima's teacher of Japanese grammar at Peers School.

The tale, attributed to Fujiwara no Takasue's Daughter (born 1108), is an international romance, as it were, as it encompasses Japan and China and, like her diary *Sarashina nikki*, emphasizes the importance of dreams; and in it transmigration plays a pivotal role. With its emphasis on dreams, the tale is like Gérard de Nelval's writings, Mishima wrote, and "it is difficult to determine which has greater weight, dream or life. In this regard, like the words in Shakespeare's *Tempest*, it leaves you truly feeling, 'We are such stuff / As dreams are made of.'" Running through *The Tale of Middle Councilor Hamamatsu* is the belief, Mishima continued, that "if dream precedes reality, what we call reality is more uncertain, and if an eternal, immutable reality does not exist, transmigration is more natural."

This suggests, "In the author's eyes, reality must have appeared that attenuated. And the experience that reality begins to appear attenuated is an existential one, as it were, so if we sympathize at all with this tale that at first blush seems ridiculous, it is precisely because we, too, have discovered ourselves that we live in an age in which we cannot be satisfied with a solid, immovable reality."

The essay, "Dream and Life," was printed in the newsletter accompanying Volume 77 of Iwanami's series of classical Japanese literature, to be completed in one hundred volumes.[39]

In December Mishima started a column for a women's magazine *Josei Myōjō*. Called *The First Sex* (*Daiichi no sei*), an obvious reference to Simone de Beauvoir's 1949 book, *The Second Sex*, but lighthearted, these monthly columns dealt with men in generalities in the first year and, in the second, with individuals.

The individuals Mishima chose were: the Duke of Edinburgh (Prince Phillip), Kaneda Shōichi (a baseball pitcher who was breaking a number of records), Ōishi Kuranosuke (the leader of the forty-seven samurai), Elvis Presley, Horie Ken'ichi (the young man who became the first to cross the Pacific solo, on a yacht), Fidel Castro, the actor Sonoi Keisuke, Prime Minister Nehru, Daimatsu Hirobumi (a survivor of the disastrous Battle of Imphal[40] who turned a women's volleyball team he managed into the world's No. 1, leading it to win the gold medal in the Tokyo Olympic Games and who, soon afterward, was invited by Chou Enlai to help establish a women's volleyball team in China), Alain Delon, Shinran (the religious leader famous for postulating, "Even a good person goes to the Pure Land; why couldn't an evil person?"), and, at his editor's insistence, "the novelist named Mishima Yukio."

In this third-person assessment of himself, Mishima quoted his own assertion, "A man's characteristics are brain and brawn," and described himself as a man who, "even with his vaunted literary brain and artificially nurtured brawn, was unable to win one of the biggest fights under heaven, a lawsuit," thereby making himself "a true laughingstock." By then it was late 1964. The lawsuit was the one about *After the Banquet*. The decision in September was against him and his publisher, and they had appealed.

## *Hayashi the Recanter*

Just about the time he started serializing *The First Sex*, Mishima finished an extended essay he had been working on for some time: an analysis of the Marxist turned nationalist writer Hayashi Fusao. The two-decade period from the 1920s to Japan's defeat, in 1945, that forced writers and intellectuals like Hayashi to abandon, renounce, or betray their beliefs is a difficult chapter in modern Japanese history. Equipped with the Public Safety Preservation Law of 1925 and other measures, police agencies ran amok.

The victims among writers ranged from Kobayashi Takiji, whom the police tortured to death, in 1933, with the most horrible methods imaginable, for writing stories depicting wretched labor conditions, to Tanizaki Jun'ichirō, whom the Army Ministry's Press Section proscribed from continuing to serialize his novel *Makioka Sisters* (*Sasameyuki*) in *Chūō Kōron* on the grounds that the novel was inappropriate for wartime, in 1943. Tanizaki, for that matter, felt it incumbent to delete, voluntarily, one chapter from his translation into modern Japanese of *The Tale of Genji* for fear of *lèse majesté*. In between were people like Hayashi Fusao who, as a result of interrogation, imprisonment, or torture, recanted. That this harsh, repressive regime ended in a war that devastated the country prompts some critics to blame the victims.

So, for the towering conservative scholar of Japanese literature Konishi Jin'ichi, the people targeted for persecution were simply wrongheaded. Marxism is "a philosophy of hatred," besides the fact that such political thought can hardly translate into "literary arts." The Japanese intellectual milieu in the 1930s also left a great deal to be desired for having "no scholars able to criticize Marx-Leninism"; the United States, in contrast, had such scholars, Konishi asserts, as witness the development, in the latter half of the 1930s, of the New Criticism that proposed to separate literary products from the circumstances that spawned them. Konishi barely contains his disgust with the Proletariat Movement and such. He refers to Hayashi just once in his massive history of "Japanese literary arts," for criticizing the movement he had early been a part of.[41]

For Katō Shūichi, the question was integrity. He recognized that "Marxism helped open the eyes of a generation of writers to political and social phenomena," but concluded that, precisely because of that, "after 'recanting,' many writers could become active supporters of [Japan's] war and militarism. Erstwhile Socialist theoreticians also worked to turn [the expansionist slogan] 'The Greater East Asian Coprosperity Sphere' into a theory." There was another dimension to the problem, in Katō's view: the "unexpected offspring produced by the fad of Marxism." Either in reaction to the socio-economic theory or through the process of recanting it, or even completely apart from it, they developed and "focused on an ideology that was the opposite of Marxism"—namely, "particularism as opposed to universalism, nationalism as opposed to internationalism, irrationalism as opposed to rationalism."[42] Yasuda Yojūrō, who founded the Japan Romantic School, was of this group. Kamei Katsuichirō, who had recanted before becoming a charter member of the magazine, was one of the more prominent among them. Katō doesn't mention Hayashi even in passing.

Neither Konishi nor Katō tackles the question of what recanting under the threat of torture entailed—not at least in the literary histories where they offer these arguments. Mishima did, in focusing on Hayashi.

Hayashi, while a student at the Imperial University of Tokyo, became, in early 1926, one of the thirty-three students arrested in the government's first attempt to eradicate Marxism under the Public Safety Preservation Law. That time he was imprisoned for ten months. In 1935, in prison again, he reflected on what had ensued in the ten years since the Kyoto Gakuren Incident, and realized he had spent four of them in detention pens, detention houses, or prisons, the remaining six years on parole; he had been taken to fifteen or sixteen police stations and had been tried about the same number of times. The prisons that had incarcerated him were in Kyoto, Tokyo, Chiba, and Shizuoka.

(*Gakuren* stood for Gakusei Shakai Kagaku Rengōkai, Students Federation of Social Science. In the 1910s, groups for studying social science were set up in higher schools, professional schools, and universities. "Social science" here meant Marxism. Their popularity quickly spread and the government became nervous. The result was the Public Safety Preservation Law. The federation's second meeting was held in July 1925 at the Imperial University of Kyoto, hence Kyoto Gakuren. Among the thirty-three arrested, at least two were tortured to death.)

Reading Hayashi's writings from the earliest and including those in prison written in diary or epistolary form, Mishima saw the writer develop a distinction between "sentiments" (*shinjō*) and theory or "thought" (*shisō*). A typical example of "sentiments" is Hayashi's disappointment, despite himself, when his mother came to see him in prison in a different hairstyle. The new hairstyle destroyed his image of the mother who had nurtured him for three decades, he felt, musing: "This is one of the conservative emotions, but I'd like to think such conservatism should be allowed." Examples of "thought" or, to be exact, the emotions that led him to Marxism were legion: pity for "one bullied by poverty," reflections on "people who became victims of social expediencies," and so forth. What happened in the course of thinking in his long incarceration was, first, the desire to unify those "sentiments" and "thought," and, then, "the cold realization" that there was no difference between the two.

Mishima's analysis may not persuade those who view Hayashi as someone who "switched sides from the extreme left to the extreme right." For them, the first evidence of his betrayal is found in the historical novel Hayashi had begun even before his formal recanting, *The Youth*. The novel deals with Inoue Kaoru and Itō Hirofumi, who played vital roles during the revolutionary period that led to the Meiji Restoration but went on to play even more vital roles in government and industry after the new regime came into being. The two initial ideas for those who dedicated themselves to "regime change," from the shogunate to the imperial or monarchial system, were "upholding the Tennō" and "repelling the aliens" or keeping the country from colonization by Western powers.

But during the crucial period of a decade or so in which the movement split the country, the second idea transformed itself into that of "opening the country." Inoue and Itō, two of the many bright men sent to Europe and the United States to study how to devise ways of "repelling the aliens" were among those who underwent the complete transformation. And, in *The Youth*, Hayashi makes them exclaim after returning from overseas study: "We could become radical advocates for opening the country only because we were radical advocates for repelling the aliens! Therein lies a likeable human secret." This can be taken as a blatant attempt of self-justification and it was.

Not that Hayashi did not agonize over recanting. He thought over "the spiritual inferno" that someone in his position faced, "with despair on the right, quagmire on the left." But Mishima found him "unique" and "logical" in the recanting process and decided that "a recanting such as his could not become a question of conscience." He added:

> The question that many intellectuals agonized over when faced with recanting must have been whether in adhering to Marxism alone lay a complete expression of spiritual freedom. Some of them, even as they sniffed out, with mind's transcendental ability, that outside Marxism there also was territory for spiritual freedom, couldn't help being concerned that, for the time being, all the territory outside Marxism was in the hands of government authorities, under their approval. Indeed, any *approved* form of spiritual freedom is the most heinous form of spiritual freedom.

Mishima began this close literary analysis, the longest he would ever write of any writer, by recalling his first visit with Hayashi. The publisher of the newspaper for which Hayashi wrote reviews was in a ramshackle building that still retained the devastations of the war, with its corners burnt, crumbling. In the immediate postwar chaos, the people who started the paper evidently hadn't given much thought to its name for it was simply, generically, called *Shin-yūkan*, "a new evening edition." As Mishima left, Hayashi, already tipsy in the afternoon, pissed from the third or fourth floor where his editorial room was, which had few windows intact.

Mishima at the time had hardly read Hayashi; he'd known only of his notoriety as an *opportunist* or worse, the word being part of the lingo popular among leftists at the time. But the older writer treated him, a young writer, with "a youthful straightforwardness that was unique to him," and Mishima was impressed. He decided to read his writings by putting himself "under the same, equal destiny" Hayashi had met. By so doing, he discovered "the beauty and gentleness of sentiments he normally hid from others' eyes, as well as the other side of those qualities, the sense of despair, revealed here and there in his writings, like the small wildflowers blooming in the cracks of a stone fence."

Mishima's essay, which saw print in the February 1963 issue of *Shinchō*, was not all adulatory. He was perceptive as a literary critic and pointed out weaknesses where he saw them. As he explained in his afterword when the long essay came out in book form the following year, his motive for examining Hayashi was twofold: "one was my righteous anger at the prejudice against Mr. Hayashi of the world at large, and one was [a need to] straighten out my own youth that I had to think about variously in relation to the problems [he presented]."

The year 1963 also saw Hayashi start serializing in *Chūō Kōron* an argument that would earn him even more opprobrium: *Affirming the Greater East-Asian War (Dai-Tōa Sensō kōtei-ron)*. That year the *Asahi Shinbun* chose him to write its monthly literary review—a point worth noting in view of the liberal stance for which the national daily would become famous, if it still had not.

CHAPTER EIGHTEEN

# Contretemps

> *At age thirteen Noboru was convinced he was a genius . . . and that the world is made up of some simple symbols and decisions.*
>
> —*The Sailor Who Fell from Grace with the Sea*

In January 1963 Mishima learned of a revolt at the Bungaku-za. Fukuda Tsuneari the Shakespearean translator stole a total of 29 members out of the company of 118 to form his own troupe, Kumo (Cloud). Fukuda had joined the Bungaku-za in 1952, provided it with his original plays and translations such as *Hamlet*, and directed some, then had withdrawn from it in 1956 over disagreement with Sugimura Haruko. Early on as a member of the Hachi no Ki Kai, Mishima had observed, "When it comes to writers, however close you may be to them, you never know when you may get stabbed in the back."[1] That casual observation he had made at the gathering of friends proved true first when Yoshida Kenkichi insulted him to his face. Fukuda's action was the second: Fukuda pulled off the coup by keeping Mishima—and everyone not involved—"outside the mosquito net."

One person who deeply regretted joining the exodus was Mishima's close friend, Kishida Kyōko. When Fukuda broached his plan to her, she said she'd come along if Mishima joined the deserters. Fukuda said he'd tell him himself but asked her to keep the matter secret in the meantime. When Kishida asked Mishima about it later, he replied glumly: "He told me he was leaving just a day before the news appeared in the newspapers. How can you make an appropriate move in just one day?" The breakup of the Bungaku-za hit the headlines on January 14, 1963.

Yoshida Chieko, the manager of the troupe who reluctantly went along with Fukuda because those departing entreated her that the new troupe needed a professional manager, recalled that Fukuda, whose only motive was to become "the boss," was wary of her joining him: "Intrigue and suspicion are the two sides of the coin. In the end, I quit eight months after I switched," she said.

In his memoirs on the Bungaku-za, Kitami Harukazu, the actor who was also assigned by the company to chronicle its official history, wrote: "As may be known from the fact that he passionately directed *Macbeth* and wrote and directed *Akechi Mitsuhide* that was based on it, Fukuda's persistent dramatic interest lay in betrayal and rebellion. And just like those figures, he may well have been someone who could not trust not just others, but himself as well. Or, perhaps like Hamlet, he was at once a dreamer and an intriguer, who tried to live aggressively, sincere and considerate while also cruel." As a result, the moment the intrigue "was realized, you could see he'd inevitably hurt those surrounding him."[2] Akechi Mitsuhide (1528?–82) rebelled against his overlord, Oda Nobunaga, and killed him. Within thirteen days he was attacked and killed by Toyotomi Hideyoshi (1537–98), another warlord with allegiance to Oda.

With Fukuda, dissension surfaced on his approach soon enough. The first major complaint was that he staged only the plays he translated. The Kumo troupe opened with the production of his translation of *A Midsummer Night's Dream* and carried on in the same vein. In 1967 Fukuda would be forced to move away to set up another company.

What disquieted Mishima was not so much Fukuda's action as the fact that he had been kept in the dark about the move. If told of it in advance, he might have been sympathetic. After all, even as he set about helping rebuild and reorient the Bungaku-za, he wrote a congratulatory message for the Kumo when Fukuda issued a manifesto on the official formation of his company. One reason for the revolt was the size of the Bungaku-za. It had grown too large for a group that was supposed to be tight-knit and communal. Early on, when a different troupe joined the company, two currents or factions had formed within the company and Iwata Toyo'o, for one, had foreseen an eventual breakup. More recently, conflicts between the founding members, along with those who joined a few years later, and younger ones had been coming to the fore.

Another reason, which was not evident for a while but would blow up in less than a year, was political. Like many progressively minded groups in literature and art, the Bungaku-za was becoming increasingly left-leaning. Not just that the Soviet Union was riding high as the adversary of the United States, but Communist China was eminently, ostensibly, succeeding in its "smile diplomacy." Japanese intellectuals invited to China on friendship tours were regaled with enticing spectacles. Murayama Tomoyoshi, who had turned *The Temple of the Golden Pavilion* into a play, was one of them. Meeting a number of "ordinary folks" on one of those tours, he was "taken aback," he had written following a 1957 tour of China. It was only a dozen years since Japan had been forced to abandon its prolonged, ravaging military presence in China and two dozen years before the Chinese government started protesting the way certain incidents were treated in Japanese textbooks.

"The people have utterly changed from what they were before the Revolution. They are mildly disposed, full of smiles, kind, self-sacrificial, abounding with love, brimming with joy, full of hope, plain-spoken, and artless." The transformative powers of "scientific socialism" were obvious, wrote the man who should have known better.[3] During a friendship tour in 1965, Murayama would be further impressed by a highly organized, disciplined display of humanism accorded a member of the visiting Japanese group who fell into a coma.[4]

Similar experiences enchanted many members of the Bungaku-za, the company's actress-leader, Sugimura Haruko, on down. Mishima had seen only the anomalous tip of China, Hong Kong, on his world tour, but he had doubts. After the Bungaku-za toured China in the fall of 1960 along with two other troupes, Kubota Mantarō invited the leading participants to his house for a party. There much of the talk was, apparently, how wonderful China was, but Kubota seemed none too happy about it. When the Bungaku-za discussed what to stage in China before the tour, the host country's advisor had turned down *The Rokumeikan*, flatly saying anything by Mishima would be unacceptable. The other candidate, *A Woman's Life* (*Onna no isshō*), Morimoto Kaoru's play directed by Kubota, was accepted but only with revisions for the Chinese production. China offered only simplistic "revolutionary" plays to the visitors (as well as their own people).

Kubota could not take it any longer when an actress during his party blurted out, "Political ideas have priority over theater." He kept drinking cup after cup for a while, until suddenly he sat upright and announced, "Well, then, I'll part company with all of you tonight," and wept—as Iwata who was there recalled three years after the defection.[5] Both Kubota and Iwata must have bitterly recalled that nearly a quarter of a century earlier they had founded the Bungaku-za to counter the "politicalism" of the day.

For now, however, Mishima energetically set out to help rebuild the shrunken company. Calling the defection "a happy revolution" as he would the Meiji Restoration only in that one could claim external forces prompted it,[6] he joined its board of directors and worked out its future direction, proposing a three-prong approach, as the *Asahi Shinbun* reported on February 23: first, newly written plays and translated plays; second, plays such as *Tosca* stressing theatricality and drama that made the theater attractive in the first place and kept it that way before modern realism took over; and third, plays that bring out the best of Japan's classical drama.[7]

Mishima had already provided plays for the three categories for the Bungaku-za, although the company had yet to formally stage any of his modern nō plays that fall in the third category. This may have frustrated Mishima; some of them had already been produced in foreign countries—the United States, Brazil, Germany, and Sweden. Also, in Japan, it was not the Bungaku-za but a Shinpa troupe that fully staged one of them, *The Damask Drum*, for the first time, and that did not happen until the previous May.

What may have been a surprise to many was the mention of *Tosca* in the second category. In March, when Victorien Sardou's drama, *La Tosca*, on which of course Puccini's opera was based, appeared on the Bungaku-za's short list of plays scheduled for production in the immediate future, Mishima wrote that the idea of staging *La Tosca* was to show "what was once considered the most *theatrical* in Europe." Kabuki during the Meiji Era absorbed foreign theater far better. "There could be works of art that may be second-rate as literature but first-rate as theater. Now that the Bungaku-za has years of experience, it should be able to do something like this. Our wish is for the audience to savor the joy of a play full of breathtaking romance and suspense."[8]

Mishima had given a good deal of thought to the matter. He had long been troubled by the watering down of theater and drama brought about by the Shingeki that was born in mid-Meiji to move against the theatricality embodied in kabuki and had maintained its stance ever since. He could not stand "the wakelike feeling" engendered at modern Japanese theaters, "in particular the death-ash feeling during a Shingeki production," he wrote in one of his several essays explaining or, to be exact, defending his choice of *La Tosca*. The recognition of the problem was nothing new. Kishida, Kubota, and Iwata had proclaimed in 1937, in their manifesto for setting up the Bungaku-za, that their aim was to get out of both "the atmosphere of the traditional, convention-bound 'theater' and the awkwardness of the unnecessarily radical 'Shingeki'" so that the new company might "offer the intelligent masses 'entertainment for the spirit' through the stage."[9]

Mishima recalled how profoundly moved he had been by the Comedie Française production of Victor Hugo's *Ruy Blas* he saw during his visit to Paris in December 1960; the stage-set for the opening was "as solemn as one of Velásquez's court paintings," with the rest equally elaborate and well done. The Parisians in the know counseled against his wasting his time on such a play, echoing Sainte-Beuve's condemnation of the play, such as "Typical Hugo, nothing left out, powerful and sublime some would say, more gross and violent than ever: a certified incurable, magnificently historical, and with huge red capital letters."[10] So the schism existed in France as well.

To remedy the situation in Japan, staging a French Romantic play might work as good medicine, Mishima thought, but *Ruy Blas* and another of Hugo's plays, *Hernani*, would be too difficult for the Japanese stage. In the end, Mishima hit upon *La Tosca*, which brought Sarah Bernhardt such extravagant fame. Mishima even quoted Oscar Wilde who, according to Bernhardt's memoirs, was in a throng of several thousands welcoming her when she landed in Folkestone, England, and shouted, "Hip, hip, hurrah! A cheer for Sarah Bernhardt!" and strewed an armful of lilies in front of her.

> I have a wishful prospect that a repeated staging of French Romantic plays might, just might, fill the gap between Shin-

geki and tradition in modern Japan. This is because, regardless of the literary value of the scripts and the differences in languages, the plays of the Romantic School are linked to Japan's traditional plays through the commonality in the idea of theater. In that respect, common points are more easily found in lowbrow scripts which focus on staging and acting.[11]

In June the Bungaku-za, according to plan, produced Sardou's play in Andō Shin'ya's translation adapted by Mishima. It then toured Nagoya, Kobe, Osaka, and elsewhere.

## The Joyful Koto

Even as he was doing all this, in March when the Kumo announced it was open for business, Mishima penned for it a message, "Resurrection of 'The Joy of Theater,'" to say that what Fukuda stated in his manifesto accorded with what he had in mind. He agreed with Fukuda on three main arguments: that the new Japanese theater created in the latter part of the nineteenth century had confused the attraction of the West and the attraction of Western theater, committing the error of employing theater as an instrument of Japan's modernization; that it had mistaken what was just the *modern* West for the West itself; and that it had shut itself up in a closed world and narrow professionalism.

The same thing could be said not just of theater but literature and art as well and, in this respect, Fukuda's was criticism of modern Japan as a whole, Mishima wrote. Yet, precisely because of that, he thought Fukuda was going too far in blaming everything on the Tsukiji Shōgekijō, the "little theater" established in 1924 on ideas extracted from Stanislavski's methods, German Expressionism, Meyerhold's biomechanics, and so on. What was important was not "to question anew what the 'theater' Shingeki should aim for," as Fukuda put it, Mishima said, but to acquire the ability to say simply, "This is or isn't theater."[12]

If losing a sizable number of its members was the first blow to the Bungaku-za, in May Kubota suddenly died—of food poisoning. Invited to a "gourmet party" thrown by the painter Umehara Ryūzaburō, he reacted badly to the clam in sushi and suffocated. Not long afterward, Iwata, the last of the three founders of the theater company, resigned his post as special advisor. Then, in November, the month John F. Kennedy was assassinated, the Bungaku-za faced a situation that led to Mishima's decision to break with it, prompting an additional fourteen of its members to defect. This occurred over the play the company had commissioned him to write.

The play, *The Joyful Koto* (*Yorokobi no koto*), has to do with Matsumura, a senior officer of the public safety section of a police precinct, and Katagiri, a rookie cop who looks up to him as his model, his father figure. Katagiri uncovers what appears to be a secret code, which Matsumura learns points to the schedule of a train carrying the prime minister. A plot against the train suspected, Katagiri is assigned to the case. The train is derailed anyway, resulting in a large number of casualties. Katagiri finds out that it was the work of the radical right, or so he thinks.

It turns out, however, that Matsumura was all along a secret agent of the radical left, and the train derailment was an elaborate ploy to smear the rightwing, a revelation that severely tests Katagiri's trust in human beings in general, Matsumura in particular. The title refers to a melody on the Japanese musical instrument the rookie begins to hear in his head after this betrayal, just as a traffic cop says he does when all the noise subsides while controlling traffic.

In the initial discussion of *The Joyful Koto*, the Bungaku-za leadership, with Mishima participating, agreed that the play was neither "political" nor "ideological" but that it dealt with "social phenomena." The case can surely be made that Mishima's point was to raise the simple question: When you admire someone, are you admiring his personality or his ideology? What happens when one's simpleminded trust in someone is betrayed? In explaining his intent, Mishima himself suggested that through such betrayal alone can one, a simpleminded one, become "a self-aware human being," and that the melody on the koto Katagiri begins to hear may be a means of that salvation.[13]

But he went on to say he would purposefully avoid "annotating" what that melody was meant to be, leaving its interpretation to the director of the play and the audience. Muramatsu Takeshi puzzled this out in his Mishima biography. He noticed that Mishima had just been to Kansai to gather material for his next novel, *Silk and Insight* (*Kinu to meisatsu*), and would begin to write it just two days after he finished *The Joyful Koto*. In the novel, Okano, the would-be bystander who plays the pivotal role in the drama and clearly Mishima's alter-ego, is presented as a lover of Heidegger and, through him, Hölderlin's poetry, in particular "Homecoming" (*Heimkunft*). Indeed, Heidegger's book, *Elucidations of Hölderlin's Poetry* (*Erläuterungen zu Hölderlins Dichtung*), provides a "philosophical annotation" to the novel.

Muramatsu also noted that Mishima, in pointing out the similarities between the betrayed rookie cop and the female protagonist of the play he wrote next, *A Hint of Love* (*Koi no hokage*), used the German word *Sorge* in his program note indicating that it was the original of what was translated as *urei*, "melancholy," in a Japanese translation of Heidegger's book that Mishima apparently used. Through these he deduces that Mishima had in mind the last part of the poem that ends with these lines: "Yet a lyre to each hour lends the right mode, the right music, / And, it may be, delights heavenly ones who draw near.... / Whether he likes it or not, and often, a singer must harbour / Cares like these in his soul; not, though, the wrong sort of cares."[14]

In any event, after the rehearsal started, with the production set for January, some in the company suddenly began arguing for cancellation on the grounds that it was too obviously anti-left, anti-labor. In September the Supreme Court had handed down its decision on the Matsukawa Incident dismissing the prosecution's fourteen-year-old argument that it was all a Communist conspiracy, but here was Mishima's play that pivoted on the radical left's contrivance and betrayal. Besides, all the characters except for an old maid who works in the precinct office are policemen, and they naturally mouth a fair amount of anti-left vituperations. Some actors assigned to it, visibly upset, said they couldn't possibly say their lines. After heated arguments, the company decided to cancel the play, the decision contingent on the consent of Sugimura Haruko upon her return from China. She opted for putting it "on hold," an indefinite postponement.

Kitami Harukazu, who would leave the company soon after this turmoil and set up his own troupe, NLT (an acronym of "new literature theater"), suspected foul play: the Communist Party worked on some members to agitate against *The Joyful Koto*. Whether that was the case or not, the Rōen—Kinrōsha Engeki Kyōgikai (Workers Theater Congress)—an arm of the national labor union, told the Bungaku-za that it would never again buy Bungaku-za tickets for its members if the troupe produced this play. That would be a huge blow because at the time, the organization had enormous clout in lining up audiences.

An even greater blow was the announcement of NHK, Japan's national broadcasting corporation, that it would not broadcast the play live.

A delegation went to Mishima on November 21 and offered three reasons for the company's decision to put the play on hold: artistic, commercial, and ideological. Mishima countered with his cancellation, stipulating in a written agreement that the Bungaku-za's decision was based solely on ideological reasons. On the 25th, he informed the Bungaku-za of his resignation. Then, in an open letter that the *Asahi Shinbun* carried on November 27, he mounted a blistering attack on the theater troupe. "Art always has a sting in it. It has poison in it. You cannot *not* swallow poison, merely sucking in honey," he wrote. "I wanted to make you stronger by pulling you out into a north wind," but as long as the Bungaku-za wanted to stay "in a greenhouse," he had "no choice but to part company with all of you."[15]

The Bungaku-za pointed out in its response, which the *Asahi* duly carried on December 7, that it was "prejudice and distortion" on Mishima's part to point to the ideological aspect as the sole reason for the breakup because they had proposed three.[16] But Mishima, who most likely wanted to test the troupe politically, could only regard the two other reasons as superfluous. Artistically, *The Joyful Koto* may not be among Mishima's best, but the Bungaku-za had produced much inferior plays, as Kitami argued during the discussion at the troupe. Commercially, the Rōen's threat precisely pointed to the ideology or political aspect of it.

Had the fracas not occurred, Mishima might have argued that he intended *The Joyful Koto* partly as a counterweight to *The Tenth-Day Chrysanthemum*, which has to do with a rightwing assassination attempt. Later, when he wrote the play *My Friend Hitler* (*Waga tomo Hitler*), he explained that he had written the all-male play as a counterweight to the all-female *Madame de Sade* (*Sado Kōshaku Fujin*).[17]

Luckily, Asari Keita, manager of the brand-new Nissay Theatre—just completed the previous September, with the Berlin Philharmonic playing on the grand opening night—promptly bought the production rights to *The Joyful Koto* and announced its staging in short order. He had commissioned Mishima to write an opera in the summer of 1963. He might have thought that a play mostly with policemen was none too sexy, but he wanted to add Mishima to his staff, which he did as he bought the play, and assumed that the play would be all right if coupled with the opera, titled *Minoko*.[18] Mishima was relieved and happy and "*hustled*"—his English; it had become a fad word—for its success. One thing he did was to revise the play, which had already seen print in *Bungei* magazine (February 1964), to clarify the point of each act and scene, so as to emphasize "anticommunism in Act 1, its *Antithese* (antithesis) in Act 2, nihilism as its *Synthese* (synthesis) in Act 3, Scene 1, and salvation in Act 3, Scene 2," as he explained, deliberately using Marxists' favorite terminology, *Antithese* and *Synthese*. He seldom, if ever, revised his plays.[19]

But *Minoko* would create another contretemps. The plan was for Mishima to write the libretto, for Mayuzumi Toshirō to compose the music, and for Asari to direct. Mayuzumi—who had composed music not just for Mishima's epithalamium for the Crown Prince and Princess but also for the film versions of several of his works, including *Lectures on Immoral Education*—wanted a "grand opera." Mishima, excited by the prospect of writing one, this time for real, chose to go through three careful steps: prepare an outline of the play in three acts and show it to Mayuzumi and Asari for comments; write the script and do the same; finally, after incorporating his collaborators' opinions and comments, go over the script, word by word with them. He did the last step in a single all-night session at the Imperial Hotel, on July 4. He managed to work out only the first two acts with the two men, but finished Act 3 on July 17.

But in February, when an orchestra to be conducted by Ozawa Seiji, a chorus, and singers were lined up for rehearsal in April, a month before the scheduled production, Mayuzumi, who had pleaded for postponement, delaying the production by three months, wanted one more month: he had composed midway through Act 2, but he wouldn't be able to finish the rest in time. Mishima refused. He would not speak to him thereafter until Mayuzumi got in touch with him at the end of April 1970 to get permission for his opera *Kinkakuji*, based on *The Temple of the Golden Pavilion*, when the Berlin Opera asked to produce it. In his testimony during the "Mishima Incident" trial, Mayuzumi recalled Mishima telling him: "I listen to you talk on TV, and your thinking resembles mine, but be careful *never* to allow the rightwing to take advantage of you."[20]

"It took me time because it was my first opera," Mayuzumi said ruefully. "Susano'o no Mikoto"—the wild brother of Amaterasu Ō-mikami, the Sun Goddess—"appears on a motorcycle, and the one he falls in love with is a vestal." *Minoko* is set in a modern-day autumn festival. Mayuzumi was able to find a source of inspiration for Act 1 in a festival on Oki Island, but had no such luck with the rest.[21] "It may have been influenced by *West Side Story*, but it was radically new. One of these days I'd like to finish the composition for Act 3 and see the opera staged. At the time I desperately tried to keep the promise in my own way, but couldn't. I was to blame."

## *How He Wrote*

"My methodological effort is to make my subconscious activity more alert and quick," Mishima wrote in an essay that *Bungaku* solicited on how he wrote his novels and stories. It was shortly before the fracas about *The Joyful Koto* erupted. "My subconscious does not start moving vividly in an unlimited, formless situation. There are writers whose subconscious starts acting better in a rubbery chaos. I am not a writer of that type. My mind does not become free unless I bind it up with something, determine exactly the direction and purpose for it, and determine precisely the route to it." In sum, he was "in methodology obviously a classicist."

Specifically, he took four steps in writing a story: discover a subject, study its *milieu* (his French), plot the structure, then write. Defining the second step of studying the milieu as "the work of immersing [the subject] in as precise specificities as possible," he explained: "If it's a story based on a news item and such, I go as far as checking court records and police files. Even when it's a totally imaginary story, I carefully check the details of the professions the principal characters are supposed to hold, the details of the lives they're supposed to lead, so I may give them specificity." He paid special attention to the landscape and environment in which his characters are supposed to do things.[22]

A good example may be the short story "The Sword" *(Ken)* that appeared a month earlier, in the October 1963 issue of *Shinchō*. The story reads like a straight narrative based on a sport whose environment Mishima loved and knew well: kendō. Yet he visited places and prepared extensive notes: on college campuses and their surroundings, what men on college kendō teams do and say, how they train during their summer camp, their daily schedules and expenditures, how many pushups they do. Also, for the background of the summer training camp for the team he described in the story, he consulted some of the notes he had on the Izu Peninsula port where he had spent time collecting material for *Animal Entanglement*.

He did not use most of the details he had gathered. Among the discarded was a story about the supervisor of a students' kendō team. In his notes Mishima had written of an instructor who was superb at kendō and accomplished in shakuhachi, ikebana, and tea ceremony besides, but who also loved nothing better than to engage in sex with pretty, young boys on the team. Senior students told juniors to sleep with him, and so on.[23] In the story, the man is presented as a stern but gentle, upright man dedicated to kendō. No sexual peccadillos with boys.

"The Sword" was turned into a movie the next April. Ichikawa Raizō, who had played the protagonist in the film *The Temple of the Golden Pavilion*, played the captain of the kendō team who, determined to excel at the sport of his choice and to be correct in every respect and at all times or else to kill himself, kills himself after the members of his team break one of the rules he lays down during their summer training camp. The story was also turned into a TV drama not long afterward and broadcast in May.

An equally good but fuller example to illustrate Mishima's approach to story-writing may be the novel he wrote in the first five months of that year. A year earlier, Kōdansha had asked him to be the first to write for their new series, Novels of Today, and he had agreed. He thought up a story with a sailor as protagonist and told his editor, Kawashima Masaru, that he'd like to visit Yokohama, one of Japan's largest ports. So, one morning in March 1962, Kawashima, along with fellow editor Matsumoto Michiko, met Mishima at his house, drove to the port town, and spent the day exploring it. They made a second trip in September.

From the two trips Mishima made at least three notebooks. One of them, apparently with a section missing, is devoted to details on the crew on a freighter. Through the introduction of Matsumoto's younger brother, Mishima with his two companions was allowed aboard a 7,340DW freighter during the second trip and was able to elicit a great deal of facts on the crew: ranks, duties, roles, how each person is addressed. In addition, Matsumoto prepared a report at Mishima's request after the first trip—on what the business of retailing clothes entails, how the Customs House examines the crew's possessions, and how a private-eye company operates, including the format of the report its employees prepare. Japanese publishers provide well-known authors with such assistance.

What may be the first of Mishima's notebooks begins, with his words in English italicized. Triangles and circles are Mishima's:

△Child scolded, his *Peeping* found out by his mother. Ryūji assumes a hypocritical attitude of a compassionate generous father. Father-mother-child's dramatic scene.
◯Load (1) depends on weather (2) also, [leaving port] can be delayed for reasons such as when [the load] increases from three thousand tons to five thousand tons; accordingly, sailing also delayed.
Even while loading, *Watch* should be on for appearance. Not officially but you can have third officer stand in for you with chief officer's permission.
◯Uniform only at reception on board.
Summer—short-sleeve shirt with epaulets. White trousers (there's also a special jacket) and a crew hat.

△March 18 afternoon, clear.
△*Center Pier's* landscape
We enter though the Customs House, and right up front, on the sidetrack passes a freight train pulled by an old-fashioned engine belching black smoke.
Withered plane trees. A mysterious town whose only aim is the sea. An abstract mysterious town whose heart is drawn only to one side. Warehouse companies' buildings. Warehouses made of red beautiful bricks. A lot of ships.

△*Center Pier*
  *Imerina* Otaru-bound
  *Korean Bear* (Pier 8)
△*South Pier*
  *Eastern Galaxy* Nagoya-bound
△*T. Pier*
  Hatsushima *Pier*

From this opening section, Mishima would use almost all the description in "*Center Pier*'s landscape," in Part II, Chapter 1 of the story, though much refined. The notes go on in similar fashion, page after page, interspersed with drawings, with occasional hints of someone providing technical terms, such as "king post," "derrick booms" (at times Mishima thought the term was "derrick beams"), and "heavy cranes." There is a great deal of what he observed, in the kinds of detail that add the sense of immediacy: waves, dirty water with wood fragments, seagulls, flags, tugboats, the names of destinations such as Singapore, Lagos, Ababa. "A gull flies. The evening sun shines yellow on its belly. Its belly and the undersides of its wings faintly yellow and bright. Egg color."

Then come plans and ideas for the story: "In this novel, in Part I, man and woman, ~~each character~~, play 'obvious' roles perfectly." Then this: "What stops life's supreme moment, it can only be death." And then: "*gogo no eikō no catastrophe.*" *Gogo no eikō*, "afternoon tug," would become the title of the story for which he was preparing these notes, though at one point the title was *umi no eiyū*, "the hero of the sea." After a while Mishima starts listing particulars on clothes retailing, which he interrupts—or so it appears although that may be true only if the notebook is taken as a consecutive whole—with a clinical description of the physical effects of poisoning (by sleeping pills, German-made *paramin*) and a deep abdominal cut or cuts. This notebook ends with a cry, "Cold! Cold!"

On the group's second trip to Yokohama, Mishima was stylishly dressed, in slacks and shoes, both white, a dark or black half-sleeve shirt, and large dark glasses. Kawashima took his old Loreiflex and left a number of photos. The fruit of the trip was the second notebook, which combines more of the details of the story Mishima planned with what he learned during the port visit, and the partial notebook mentioned earlier.

Yet assiduous note-taking was not the only order of the day. Mishima, who wanted to become, among other things, a *madorosu* (from the Dutch word *matroos*, "sailor," "seaman"), after exploring the port and the town and visiting a ship, took his two editors barhopping. He downed the cocktail Angel's Kiss at every stop, sang, autographed the panties of barmaids when asked, and danced with a shy Matsumoto well into the night—"just like a *madorosu*," Kawashima reported.

The story, Mishima's notes suggest, was to focus on the sailor Ryūji's "suicide wish," a result of "the discrepancy between the inner and outer" lives of the man, his bleak spiritual life for all the romantic image that the *madorosu* conjures in popular songs and such (or did, in those days). "A lady entertaining a suicide wish, while touring a ship, exchanges dark looks with a low-ranking crewman with a suicide wish." "Wants to die in the trembling of caresses. Wants to die while being caressed. Wish for a luxurious death." "The proprietress of a Western *haut-couture* goods store ... happens to get acquainted, in a bar, with a low-ranking crewman. Albeit a muscular young man, he entertains a suicide wish. 'Kill me! Kill me!'" "The widow takes interest in him, and the two [begin to] love each other."[24]

There is a fanciful story behind the English title the novel *Gogo no eikō* came to have: *The Sailor Who Fell from Grace with the Sea*. The original title can be vague or mysterious with the word *eikō*, which, with the Chinese characters Mishima gave it, means "tugging" or "towing" but as a homophone means "glory." And, indeed, the story emphasizes Ryūji's youthful wish for "glory" that has come to naught.

"When I was unable to come up with anything in English better than *Glory Is a Drag*," wrote John Nathan, who translated the story and went on to write a biography of Mishima, "I went to Mishima for help." Nathan was a student at the University of Tokyo at the time. "Mishima remarked that it would be nice to have a long title in the manner of *À la Recherche*..., paused, then rattled off a dozen titles which I jotted down in English. When I read them back, Mishima chose *The Sailor*."[25]

*The Sailor* has yet to be turned into a movie in Japan, but six years after Mishima's death, Lewis John Carlino did so in the United States, with Sarah Miles and Kris Kristofferson playing the lead roles.

For that matter, another story of Mishima's became a foreign film, though much later: *The School of the Flesh* (*Nikutai no gakkō*), which he serialized throughout the year of 1963 in *Mademoiselle* as he wrote *The Sailor*. In 1998, Benoît Jacquot turned it into *L'école de la chair*, with Isabelle Huppert and Vincent Martinez in the lead roles. The main character of the story, a thirty-nine-year-old woman who, like the widow in *The Sailor*, runs a *haut-couture* store, chases a twenty-one-year-old gigolo who works in a gay bar. On the face of it, this story may appear very different from *Le Diable au corps* in which a teenager indulges in sex with a just-married woman. But Mishima clearly meant *The School of the Flesh* to echo the French novel. Not just that Radiguet's title comes out as *Nikutai no akuma* in Japanese, but in both stories there are a good deal of decision, indecision, and second-guessing.

## *Orgasm as Music*

The year 1964 opened with Mishima beginning to serialize two novels: *Music* (*Ongaku*) in *Fujin Kōron* and the aforementioned novel *Silk and Insight* in *Gunzō*. Of the two, *Music* takes the form of a psychoanalyst's report on the progress of a young beauty who confesses frigidity—"music" is her metaphor for orgasm—and on his growing nonprofessional interest in her. Written when, as the narrator says at the outset, "the profession of psychoanalysis is gradually beginning to attract attention [in Japan] though its popularity in no way compares with that in America," the story sets out to track down, in the manner of a detective story, a woman's sexual experience in clinical details that ends with a revelation of her incest with her brother.

That particular form of incest is a subject that fascinated Mishima since boyhood. "For a long time I have felt something most sweet in a brother-sister love heightened to lust," he had written when his play four years earlier, *Tropical Trees* (*Nettaiju*), was staged. The sentiment dates from his reading as a boy, he said, of the Eleventh and Twelfth Nights of *One Thousand and One Nights* where the forbidden love is consummated in a grave.[26] In *Tropical Trees*, too, the consummation ends in death, presumably, though in it the incest is triangular: sister-brother-mother.

In *Music* Mishima makes incest forced and sordid, perhaps because of the need to give the psychoanalytical thriller some credibility. At the end of the story, he appends a "bibliography" listing six sources in foreign languages, three in German and three in English, obviously to endow the analyst-narrator with the air of a specialist.

Though he had pursued Freud and Jung for a while, following his interest in Hirschfeld and Ellis, in the end he did not develop high regard for psychoanalysis. In the essay he wrote at the request of *Life* for its special issue on Japan, which the weekly prepared ahead of the Tokyo Olympic Games that fall ("the first time this Western event has ever been held in the Orient"), Mishima twitted American intellectuals for their fascination with psychoanalysis.

Citing Terentius's words "I am a human being, so nothing human is strange to me," Mishima said, in an obvious nod to Oscar Wilde: "The ordinary man may become enraged to see Caliban's face in a glass, but the intellectual isn't the least bit afraid. Even if coming face to face with oneself may at times be the same as peering into hell."²⁷ This is because "in any country the intellectual is his country's 'consciousness' itself, someone who represents under the light of consciousness the depth consciousness and the unconsciousness of instinct buried in the history, traditions, and culture of his folk." Or that is what one expects from an intellectual of any country.

"And yet in America it appears that, just as a sailor's disease once infected even royalty, the ordinary man's disease of fearing coming face to face with himself has infected the intellectual. I was amazed to see many intellectuals and artists frequent psychoanalysts. Shouldn't it be rather that the psychoanalysts come to the artists to ask questions? In our country, a man comes around to the kitchen every morning to pick up the day's laundry"—at least that was how dirty clothes were taken care of in bourgeois neighborhoods in those days—"but in America you must collect days' worth of dirty clothes and such and take them to the cleaners yourself."

Mishima ended the essay this way: "One thing I can't understand is America's dishonorable image, which the country has disseminated to the world, of a man helping his wife do dishes, but it is possible that Americans will be rescued even from this evil and restore their prestige in the near future: for one, through the promotion of new ethics that a man doing such a thing is worse than committing robbery or killing someone; for the other, thanks to none other than automation."²⁸ This paragraph was dropped when the essay appeared in Donald Keene's translation in the September 11, 1964 issue of *Life* with the title "A Famous Japanese Judges the U.S. Giant."

## Silk and Insight

If *Music* was designed to some extent to titillate the readers of the highbrow women's magazine with what was purported to be frank, clinical discussions of female sex, *Silk and Insight* was altogether a different affair, an attempt to describe "Japan's father," as the working title of the novel had it. To do so, Mishima posits the Japanese-style owner of a textile company against a European-infatuated intellectual who is deployed to destroy him.

The protagonist of the novel, Komazawa Zenjirō, is an idealistic albeit self-serving businessman. President of a textile mill by Lake Biwa, Komazawa says his employees are his sons and daughters. He makes them obey him but also protects them, he believes, with fatherly benevolence. He puts all of them in dormitories where no privacy is allowed. All personal effects, including letters, are subject to inspection by "dorm mothers." Marriages among employees aren't allowed. *Silk and Insight* was, in fact, based on an actual labor strike—called Japan's first human rights strike—ten years earlier, in 1954, and among the demands the employees of the actual company involved, Ōmi Kenshi, made during the strike under the guidance of a number of outside labor unions were freedom of marriage and respect for privacy.[29]

Komazawa's absolutist paternalism works well for him, and his business thrives, until a meddler comes in. Murakawa, president of a rival company who proudly keeps abreast with the latest American management theories and machinery, sees weaknesses in Komazawa's pre-modern management style, most obviously the pent-up employee frustrations in a slave-labor environment, and decides to destroy him. He sends his friend Okano to incite Komazawa's young employees to revolt. Educated in Germany before the war, Okano has managed himself well in straddling prewar and postwar Japan as a suave, sophisticated man of the world who upholds Heidegger's philosophy and loves nothing better than Hölderlin's poetry. He joins the fraternal gathering of chief executives of textile companies Komazawa hosts.

"Business is tears, Mr. Okano," Komazawa explains. They are aboard a ship Komazawa has chartered for the occasion to cruise the lake. "I truly think that I am the father and those who work in my factory are my daughters and sons. They guessed that this was the day their father finally made it big, and sang our company song so intently, with all their hearts, and sent our guests on their way, that sentiment, that's what's valuable. Precisely the same sentiment has borne Komazawa Textiles along."

Komazawa is aware of the contempt of his fellow presidents but he knows he is right. Things Japanese are the very best. "The Japanese still aren't aware of good things that are uniquely Japanese, they still haven't shed the habit of letting Westerners tell them, only then telling themselves, 'Well, I see. In that case, I'll try that,'" he tells a president unlucky enough to have to listen to him. "It wouldn't do, wouldn't you say, unless the Japanese themselves awake to the good things about Japan. Why is it? We have the best landscapes in the world, the best girls in the world, we have such beautiful sentiments."

But it is during this cruise, which Komazawa intended as a celebration of his own accomplishment to impress his rivals, that a disaster strikes: a fire touched off by an overturned movie projector in a dorm kills two dozen employees and hurts more than 300, a result of Komazawa's restriction on his employees' free time outside the company premises. In short order Okano picks a young, bright employee named Ōtsuki to lead a strike against the company. Komazawa never understands the reasons for such an act of unfilial insubordination.

"I am speaking the same Japanese language you speak, am I not?" Komazawa asks the young man when Okano arranges a meeting between the two. Told that more than 80 percent of the employees working for him are women and they are forced to do so in pitiful conditions, he is genuinely puzzled. "Well then, what do you want me to give those girls? Clothes? Pretty clothes? Is that what you call liberty, equality, and peace? . . . I gave them money. I provided lodging. I fed them. Now they wanted pretty clothes, so you said, Oh sure, sure, and followed whatever those girls said, did you? I had made a distinction between what I should give them and what I should not, but you can't make that distinction."

In this construct, Komazawa versus Okano is Japan versus the West or traditional Japan versus Western-infatuated Japan, and Komazawa versus Ōtsuki is father versus son, Mishima explained in an interview with the *Asahi Shinbun*. The daily evidently thought clarification was called for because, although the novel dealt with a socio-historically important event that advanced modern values, the author's position on the leading characters he created and the issues involved was not immediately clear. The story one might expect to be schematic is not.

So, Komazawa, "the enemy of the people," is defeated; Ōtsuki, the embodiment of youth and progress, is triumphant. But Okano, "the man who thinks he has created a philosophy of destruction" and thus represents "the imported thought of intellectuals that has not taken root in Japanese soil," is made to succeed Komazawa as president of Komazawa Textiles, the very thing he successfully destroyed.

At the same time, there is Komazawa's wife, Fusae. Long disabled by tuberculosis, the very disease that felled so many young women in the textile industry during Japan's industrial and military expansion that largely depended on it, Fusae, the symbol of the dark side of Japan's modernization, haunts Komazawa's existence as a curse.

One must also consider the title Mishima chose for the fictionalized account of an actual labor dispute and its outcome: *kinu to meisatsu*, "silk and insight." It echoed *kinu to gunkan*, "silk and warships," the pithy proverb dating from the Russo-Japanese War that said the production and export of silk fabric and thread enabled Japan to buy and build warships. Work at textile factories was one of both pain and pride, as a chronicler of the sufferings of young women who worked in harsh textile factories has pointed out. The greatest warship Japan ever built, the battleship bearing the country's ancient name, *Yamato*, led, in the last phase of the Pacific War, a Kamikaze sortie without air cover, only to be sunk by American carrier-based bombers. The destruction of the *Yamato*, in that regard, was a sad end to that chapter of Japanese history.[30]

So what is the "insight"? His employees triumphant, Komazawa is struck down by a stroke. And yet, he is given the last word. Dying and forgiving all, he is made to muse: "The truth that only he knows and the heart that only he values" have remained incomprehensible to those who have defeated him, but the happiness they've won "will in time prove to be a counterfeit jewel." That, Mishima said, is the insight. He also said, "I wanted to depict a drama of this mysterious figure encrusted with old moral ideas." The man represented the Tennō, he told a friend.[31]

## *The Olympian Reporter*

For the Tokyo Olympics, in the fall of 1964, all the major dailies seem to have asked Mishima to cover the event. After all, he was not just the most glamorous writer of the day, but also one deeply engaged in sports. He did not betray their expectations. For the *Mainichi*, *Asahi*, and *Hōchi*, for each of which he became a special correspondent, he wrote articles on boxing, weightlifting, swimming (women's 100-meter backstroke, men's 1,500 meter), track and field (800-meter, 20,000-meter race walk, and 100-meter dash), gymnastics, and women's volleyball (newly added to the Games along with judo), as well as the opening and closing ceremonies. In these articles, he produced some of his most lyrical prose. Here's how he described the US sprinter Robert Hayes. As the athletes get down at the starting line—

What happened next, I no longer know. Hayes, his coal-black body in a dark blue shirt, was surely at the starting line, but is now way beyond, having broken the tape. A record of ten seconds flat. In that duration there surely was something that rushed before my eyes, like a black flame. Besides, the figure that burnt into my eyes in that instant was neither flying, nor tumbling, but correctly took "the shape of a human being running" as it moved its four limbs precisely as the spokes of a wheel stretched in the four directions from the center of a human physique. How could such a complicated, hard-to-deal-with form dash through a 100-meter space with such divine speed? He accomplished the feat of switching from this to the other side of a space wall.[32]

Ichikawa Kon, who made a film version of *The Golden Pavilion*, captured Robert Hayes and other sprinters in this race in unforgettable slow-motion close-ups in his documentary of the Games, *Tokyo Olympiad*.

Mishima took the main meaning of Japan hosting the Olympic Games in 1964 to be this: the country finally joining the ranks of the advanced nations of the West by, yes, regaining their good graces. A quarter of a century earlier, in 1940, Tokyo was scheduled to host the Olympics—following Berlin—but had to give up the honor because, aside from its own war in China, a war had started in Europe. Then came the war with the United States and other European countries and the devastation, followed by food aid, among other things, from the main adversary. It was to demonstrate recovery, and that it has attained some technological prowess on the way, that the Shinkansen, the Bullet Train, among other things, was built, with its launch timed to run, inaugurally, and it did, on October 1, exactly ten days before the opening ceremony of the international athletic feast.

There were of course lopsided aspects to Japan's economic, technological, and cultural state, as Arthur Koestler, sent to Japan by *Life* for its Japan special, readily noticed: Tokyo is "the first city in the world with a monorail system linking airport to urban center—but it has no citywide sewage system." A man famous for all sorts of his own inferiority complexes, Koestler also did not overlook "Olympicitis"—the fear among some quarters that Japanese women might divorce their husbands in droves for tall, good-looking Caucasian athletes who would descend upon them with the Games.³³

Mishima was uncharacteristically wistful when he wrote for a small magazine about the post-event funk that prevailed in Japan, "All the Pleasures Are Now Over":

> The Olympics over, there are so many people who have collapsed into a state of funk.
>
> When you think of it, in the almost one hundred years since Japan sailed out into the modern history of the world, we've frequently had "lantern marches" [to celebrate military victories] and savored the so-called national excitement many times, but there had never been such a single-mindedly peaceful festival on which so much money was expended with abandon and which lasted for two weeks besides. Furthermore, it had the elements of "a safe war," "a war with no bloodshed," "a clean war," and everyone was able to enjoy this "war" without worry and enjoy "Japan's victory."
>
> In this Olympics, come to think of it, we went the opposite of what we said during the war, "Luxury is foe," and put into practice Mr. Hayashi Fusao's amusing dictum, "Luxury is friend." All the citizens learned the joy of profligacy. Instead of receiving alms from someone else, we learned the joy of squandering money, inviting people, playing the host's role, indulging in happy concerns for others, and succeeding in all this.

Mishima couldn't resist a yakuza-style analogy. "It was as though someone who in his youth was poor, hot-blooded, spread his name with each brawl, but who gradually became less hot-blooded, paid more attention to his business, made some money, and joined the ranks of gentlemen ... who, then, decided to gather together a host of friends to an extravagant banquet and made a success of it." Mishima also could not help contrasting Japan following the defeat of the war with the West and Japan nineteen years since through two images of the Tennō. "When during the opening ceremony I saw His Imperial Majesty in so obviously an excellent mood and his dignified figure as he accepted IOC President Brundage's request and declared the opening of the Games,

I recalled his sad photograph with Marshal MacArthur nineteen years ago and was overwhelmed by the contrast."³⁴

By the "sad photograph" he meant the one carried on the front pages of all Japanese newspapers toward the end of September 1945. A photo taken during Hirohito's first visit to Supreme Commander for the Allied Powers Douglas MacArthur, it had, to the left, the tall, conquering general in his service uniform and at ease, arms akimbo, and, to the right, the Tennō rigid in tuxedo and at attention, arms straight down on his sides. MacArthur was a master of theater, as his aide-de-camp Faubion Bowers once observed, and it casually, indelibly, showed who was the boss. Among the Japanese who saw it first there were cries of *lèse majesté*, and newspapers initially did not carry it, but the Occupation Headquarters quashed the demurral.

For the *Yomiuri*, Mishima wrote a series of five separate articles to discuss various sports as he actually experienced them. He began: "If I act like a regular sportsman in any way, my friends who knew me as a pale-faced young aspiring writer in bygone days won't be able to help a contemptuous sneer just as someone might as he sees a *nouveau riche* trying to hide his poverty-stricken days of the past." Admitting his "intense physical inferiority complex" until he reached his thirties, Mishima went on to describe his sudden decision to try bodybuilding— "a gospel" as it turned out, but which nonetheless would make him "a laughingstock, the material for many a cartoon for years to come." Still, "if there's anything truly exciting in the world, nothing beats the knowledge that your strength is increasing from day to day. It is one of the most essential joys for a human being."

## *Aiming for the Nobel Prize through a Translator*

*Silk and Insight*, which Mishima had written as "a summing-up" of his literary endeavors for the several years up to that time, was, despite the Mainichi Art Prize it won a month after its publication, a commercial disappointment. It sold only 15,000 copies, with an additional 3,000 copies printed after the prize. For comparison, *Kyōko's House*, albeit a critical failure, sold 150,000 copies initially and much more later. *The Sailor Who Fell from Grace with the Sea*, a well-told tale with a faint echo of the popular Western in the early 1950s, *Shane*, sold 50,000.

Perhaps its subject lacked immediacy. Among the literary works of the day, Ōe Kenzaburō's *A Personal Matter* (*Kojinteki-na taiken*) was a barely disguised account of the author having a brain-damaged child and, although its ending was counterintuitive and criticized by many,[35] won the Shinchō Literary Prize that year. Kojima Nobuo's *The Hugging Family* (*Hōyō kazoku*), the winner of the newly created Tanizaki Jun'ichirō Prize the following year, dealt with the perturbations of a college-instructor-translator of English literature whose wife commits adultery with a young American soldier staying with them—a timely subject when the presence of GIs was growing in Japan with the expansion of the Vietnam War.[36]

Of the two writers, Kojima, who was ten years older than Mishima, was among the writers then being touted as "third new faces," while Ōe, who was his junior by ten years, had accomplished a swift rise to fame as remarkable as Mishima's a decade earlier. At any rate, it was over Ōe's *Personal Matter* as much as *Silk and Insight* that Mishima and John Nathan broke their writer-translator relationship.

Nathan, a linguistically gifted youth who became the first American to enter the University of Tokyo as "a regular student," in 1963, translated *The Sailor* for Knopf. In February 1965 the editor Harold Strauss wrote Mishima that Nathan had done "an outstanding job" of it when he read the translation. To celebrate, Mishima invited Nathan to a Japanese restaurant. In the euphoria in which sake flowed, he asked the young scholar to become his "official translator" with the Nobel Prize in mind and Nathan happily agreed.

But when he went home and read *Silk and Insight*, which he knew Mishima wanted him to take on next, Nathan "found it empty of genuine feeling. Furthermore, the writing was jugular, a gorgeous example of what Japanese critics were calling 'Mishima-beauty.'" In the meantime he had been drawn to *A Personal Matter*. He started translating it with Strauss's agreement but did nothing with *Silk and Insight*. By late that year, especially after receiving in mid-October Mishima's gossipy letter quoting, among other things, "the famous woman critic Dominique Aury at Gallimard" extravagantly praising his translation, *The Sailor*, he felt guilty enough to seek a meeting with Mishima "to tell him the entire truth."[37]

In mid-November Mishima invited him to his house. After some hesitation, Nathan divulged his change of heart, saying the style of *Silk and Insight* was such that he didn't think he "could make it work in English." Belatedly told of what he might have guessed, Mishima responded by saying, "You're wise not to try something you're not confident about. I'm glad you told me."

What is remarkable about Nathan's description of this turn of events is the courtesy Mishima maintained throughout the meeting. Still, not long afterward Nathan heard that Mishima spoke of him as "a hoodlum seduced by the Left." Mishima in fact never got in touch with him again. It is easy to see why, although Nathan professed not to "understand very fully what was behind Mishima's adamant repudiation" even as he sat down to write his biography several years later.[38] After all, it was not just that Ōe was Mishima's rival—in a *Gunzō* poll of readers on the writers they wanted to read most, Ōe came first, he second, in 1963, though Mishima was first, Ōe third, in 1964[39]—but it was at Mishima's parties that Nathan and Ōe had met.

Ōe, born in 1935 and now "the standard bearer of the postwar generation," was gaining popularity, especially among leftist students, with a series of essays expressing postwar angst that was compounded by the failure of the mass opposition to the revised US-Japanese Mutual Security Treaty. Among other things, he helped to popularize the notion of "victim versus victimizer" in reference to the atomic bombs America dropped on Hiroshima and Nagasaki versus Japan's war against China.

In the summer of 1966, Nathan, still in his mid-twenties, felt compelled to vent himself when *Life* asked him to write on Mishima. The portrait he provided was lively in a manner possible only for someone who had spent a good deal of time with the man, but it came with a killer sting.

"Mishima has a rare capacity for enjoying himself, and he loves nothing better than a party. He has only to walk into a room full of people and it belongs to him," Nathan began describing Mishima at parties.

> Mishima weighs into a party with gusto, delighting over the food, mixing experimental drinks, neighing hoarsely at all the jokes, including his own. Talking Japanese or his ungrammatical but fluid, arresting English, Mishima is clever, amusing, astute, catty. He will amuse himself by shocking. "You know, I can't write about something unless I've seen it happen," he will say too loudly. "I'm a little too worried now because I want

to do a novel about a homicide." Then he is off again, hee-hawing, singing in English, drinking tequila with lemon and salt in imitation of Marlon Brando.

Mishima threw these parties himself more often than not. "He is a lavish entertainer; his parties bring together well-known writers and critics, diplomats, movies stars, US embassy people, visiting publishers from New York," Nathan continued. "Invitations are in English, engraved on Tiffany stationery. Drinks are served upstairs, waiters in black tie and white gloves serving caviar from silver trays. Dinner, at eight, is always good, impeccably *de rigueur*: when the menu calls for shellfish, guests are provided with gleaming precision tools designed to get the most out of the mollusks."

These descriptions were ensconced in the pictorial spread worthy of the famous photo magazine and sure to have delighted Mishima: pictures of him in casual wear sitting at the center of his round couch, in a sailor's costume and singing, arm-wrestling with his muscle-bound torso bared, doing kendō in a white costume with what appears to be a real sword (rather than the usual bamboo *shinai*), sitting in a white suit in front of a blowup of a still from the seppuku scene in the film *Patriotism* with the sword poised to stab his bared left abdomen, and sitting on a Western chair in formal Japanese attire.

Yet Nathan took care to show flashes of a dagger. After noting Mishima's "creative energy" was such that "it would be difficult to find a Western writer of his caliber who could equal his output," and assuring the reader that "No other Japanese commands a verbal range so vast or manipulates the language with such absolute precision," he concluded his assessment of Mishima's work this way: "In several of his more recent novels, spindly, schematized characters are crushed under the weight of lush description. The elegance of his style is unequaled in Japanese literature, but he has had increasing trouble making people come alive on paper."[40]

Again, it is easy to imagine how deeply this offended and hurt Mishima. Their relationship completely severed, Nathan would return to Mishima again only after his death, to write a biography of the man. *Mishima* came out in 1974.[41]

CHAPTER NINETEEN

# The Nobel Prize

*"The more deeply you wound me,*
*the more deeply you love me."*

—Gabriele d'Annunzio, *Le Martyre de Saint Sébastien*

John Nathan opened his *Life* essay thus: "Yukio Mishima is Japan's likeliest candidate for the Nobel Prize in Literature, and there can be no doubt that he will someday be capable of deserving it. Certainly, Mishima desires the prize: he makes no secret of his avidity for international recognition."

When did Mishima begin to entertain the notion of receiving a Nobel Prize? It could have been early—for example, in May 1961, when Kawabata asked him to write a letter recommending him for it. But the Swedish newspaper *Dagens Nyheter* in December 1963 carrying an article on the world's leading authors ("*Världen ledande författare*") and including him among the nineteen selected for it may well have been the decisive moment.

The accompanying list was a glamorous one that included some living, some dead. Four of the six Americans on it had received the prize: Pearl Buck (1938), William Faulkner (1949), Ernest Hemingway (1954), and John Steinbeck (1962). Also on the list was Albert Camus, the 1957 recipient, who was perhaps at the height of his fame in Japan then. And Mishima had one key ally willing to push him toward the prize: Donald Keene.

/ 435

In May 1964 Keene, at the request of his publisher, the Grove Press, became a member of the American delegation for the fourth Formentor Literary Prize, which was, in his estimation, "second only to the Nobel Prize in its influence."[1] Unlike the Nobel Prize, it had been established only three years earlier, in 1961, by a consortium of publishers. But Samuel Beckett and Jorge Luis Borges were its first recipients, and just before the jury for the fourth award convened in the Schloss Mirabelle, in Salzburg, the award money of ten thousand dollars had been announced. There were no other international prizes of comparable prestige. One consequence, of course, was that "there were titanic conflicts and dark intrigues more characteristic of Wagner to the German north and Verdi to the Italian south than of this quiet Mozartean museum," reported Melvin J. Lasky in his short, wry account of the proceedings.[2]

"Oratory flared" among the forty critics and writers who came from thirteen countries, though the seven delegations, even as each carried the name of a country, were not represented by their nationals alone. The British delegation, for example, was composed of a Dutch, Canadians, Americans (among them Mary McCarthy), and even an Austrian. The "clear front-runner," which became the final winner, was the Russian-born French writer Natalie Sarraute's latest book, *Les Fruits d'Or*, "a novel about a novel," Lasky wrote, "which is competing for a prize and is widely praised and meanly destroyed by a ruthless band of literary critics."

In fact, that was almost exactly what happened to the novel itself. "Miss McCarthy thought the book to be already 'a Classic,' but Mr. Herbert Gold saltily doubted whether it could ever be 'read for a second time.'" Other pronouncements were equally divergent. Roberto Moravia called it "a masterpiece," John Weightman "a joke," "a disaster," and "a bore," while "the Indian vice president of the meeting, the red-turbanned Sikh Kushwant Singh, protested that he could not even read the book 'the first time' and threatened to turn his back on 'the whole of decadent European literature.'"

Amidst all this, Keene left a distinct impression making a case for Mishima—as distinct as McCarthy did, making a case for Sarraute. "The Americans, under the influence as they often are of an 'old Orient hand' (in this case, Prof. Donald Keene from Tokyo), argued for the Japanese candidate, Mishima," Lasky reported. The book Keene pushed was *After the Banquet* that he had translated himself. His speech, delivered in French—the lingua franca in those days, though Lasky couldn't help twitting it: "Some called it 'franglais,' others 'frenglish'")—and it had measurable effect, for "on the penultimate ballot the Japanese led all the rest."

As "the laws of literary politics" have it, Keene's backing in the end did not work, but he was unfazed. Serving as a member of the American delegation for the Formentor prize at least three more years, he kept pushing Mishima and, after each session, told Mishima, we assume, of where he stood, as he had, in a taidan with him, a month after the Salzburg meeting. In it he stressed that Mishima's reputation was so great he was known "even in small European countries such as Finland, Denmark, and Norway." Moreover, he pointed out that his literature could be internationally appreciated because of its lack of "exoticism," without reference to "geisha and seppuku." Two days after the taidan, on June 18, Mishima left for New York to discuss future publishing plans with Knopf. When the taidan was published early the next year, it was titled "Mishima Literature and Internationality."[3] Little wonder Mishima was expansive about the Nobel Prize when he drank with John Nathan in February 1965.

Mishima's "internationality," indeed, only seemed to grow. And the aristocratic setting for prize-giving he soon witnessed must have inflamed his desire for the Nobel Prize.

In March 1965 he spent two weeks in England at the invitation of the British Council. The two short accounts of the sojourn he wrote for the *Mainichi Shinbun*[4] showed him to be a unique man of the world. He found time to go to a local gym for bodybuilding while attending a round of literary, cultural functions. But the first event he was invited to may have given him the most favorable impression. On March 11, the day he put up at the Kingsley Hotel (now Thistle Bloomsbury), he was among the two hundred guests for the ceremony at "Lady Johns' beautiful mansion"[5] to honor Ivan Morris, the translator of *The Temple of the Golden Pavilion*, with the Duff Cooper Prize for his account of aristocratic life during Murasaki Shikubu's days, *The World of the Shining Prince*. The former prime minister Harold Macmillan was the prize giver and he reminisced suavely about the days when Duff Cooper, the dashing politician, and he were both young. Those "happy days," especially for the upper class, were "forever gone," he said.

Noting that Morris's book had been preceded by Arthur Waley's translation of *The Tale of Genji*, Mishima brought up his long-standing view of Japanese culture as consisting of two contrasting aspects. He observed that Japan's *tawayameburi*, "muliebrity," first introduced to Britain's intellectual class by Waley, was being further explicated by Morris's book, even as Japan's *masuraoburi*, "virility," was making itself felt through the films of Mifune Toshirō as an "action hero." Kurosawa Akira's movies featuring Mifune had appeared successively: *Throne of Blood*, in which Mifune played Macbeth transplanted to Japan's Age of Warring States, in 1957; *The Hidden Fortress*, in which he played a warrior-commander, in 1958; *Yojimbo* and *Sanjuro*, in which he played a scruffy swashbuckler, in 1961 and 1962.

On the evening of March 12, Mishima had a reunion with Keith Botsford. The would-be drama producer seven years earlier, now married, Botsford invited him to dinner at the Café Royal. Two days later, Sunday, Mishima, along with Mr. and Mrs. Ivan Morris, was a lunch guest of Margot Fonteyn at her villa outside London.

The British ballerina, who had received the title "dame," that day was "completely wrapped in dark brown"—blouse, tights, and boots—and "vivacious, talking happily, entertaining people, enjoying herself," even as "she fussed over her disabled husband," Mishima wrote. Fonteyn's husband, the reckless Dr. Alberto ("Tito") Arias, had been shot nine months earlier, in June 1964, and was now a paraplegic. The shooting was done in retaliation: in 1959, Arias, with seven other men, had perpetrated what *Time* called "a low-comedy invasion" of his own country, Panama, to overturn the government and miserably failed.[6] Mishima couldn't help exclaiming to the boyish Fonteyn, "Today you are just like Fidelio!"

Among the writers Mishima met were Edna O'Brien, of *The Country Girls*, and Angus Wilson, who had strongly recommended publication of *Confessions*. O'Brien, meeting with him for dinner after the cocktail party Secker & Warburg threw for him at the Arts Theatre Club, told him she'd been rather scandalized during the cocktails. A total stranger in a leather jacket had grabbed hold of her as soon as she stepped in and said, "When this is over, let's go out." Mishima found her to be "typically Irish, full of gentle sensitivity, and with a homey feel."

The time with Wilson, who invited him to his "isolated mountain hut" in Sussex, was "the most profitable during this stay in England," Mishima wrote. Wilson regaled him with a number of stories. He said, for example, that during the summer, nightingales kept warbling throughout the night so that he had to close all the windows. When he was growing up, the middle class was so poor it was part of the table manners to leave some food on the plate—to show, perhaps, that they were not totally starved. In England, actors gained respectability only in the latter half of the nineteenth century and went on to acquire aristocratic airs. John Gielgud was, Wilson told Mishima, the last of that generation who could no longer find his place among the new actors. In that respect, they were just like kabuki actors in Japan, Mishima said. Wilson, who had remained a fan of Japanese literature, highly praised the Abe Kōbō novel, *The Woman in the Dunes*, which had come out the previous year, in Dale Saunders's translation.

Mishima was interviewed for the *Sunday Times*, the *Guardian*, and the BBC. After the *Times* interview appeared, on March 21, he was surprised by the swift effect it had. The hotel attendants became visibly courteous. In a restaurant a gentleman came up to him and asked, "Is it true you work until midnight and eat breakfast at two in the morning?" Obviously part of the interview was garbled. A woman writer accusingly said to him, "The British newspapers fuss about you foreign writers. They completely ignore us, their own."

The *Guardian* interview did not appear until he left England and arrived in Paris, on March 26, and the BBC interview until April 19. By then Mishima had finished the filming of *Yūkoku*.

## *Filming* Yūkoku

In his detailed account of the preparations and making of the film, as well as its outcome, Mishima wrote that, once he thought of turning the story into a film, his mind never strayed from it. He looked for small animal figurines the lieutenant's wife is supposed to have collected, from one shop window to another, until he found what he liked. Before he left Japan, he decided that the background music for the film would be the *Liebestod* aria from Wagner's *Tristan und Isolde*, so he searched for "a new edition of an old recording of it," but he could not find one even at the largest record store in London.[7] Donald Richie, the greatest observer of the Japanese film industry in the preceding fifteen years, said he "suggested the *Liebestod* as suitable music" for the film and "found the right recording": "Stokowski's 1939 version on 78s."[8]

Mishima did practically everything for the movie *Yūkoku*: he wrote the scenario for it, directed and produced it, and played the role of the protagonist, Lt. Takeyama. It was a silent movie, and he handwrote the four intertitles in four languages to be made part of it, for from the outset he planned it for Japanese, English, German, and French audiences—but especially the non-Japanese viewers.

Mishima financed the entire cost that in the end came to ¥1,259,570. For a few things he turned to his friends. Fujii Hiroaki serving as production manager assembled the crew, and Dōmoto Masaki, who had directed some of Mishima's "modern nō plays," stage-managed it. One of the difficulties was finding an actress to play the lieutenant's wife, Reiko. The woman Mishima had in mind had to be "homespun, feminine, but quietly passionate," someone of whom "an ordinary army lieutenant during the 1930s would think, My wife is the most beautiful woman in the world." After meeting the women his eminent friends recommended, he found, via Fujii, such a figure in Yamamoto Noriko, a nineteen-year old who had given up becoming a film actress after playing a couple of small roles. In *Yūkoku*, she appeared with the stage name of Tsuruoka Yoshiko.

The movie was filmed in utter secrecy, in just two days, April 15 and 16, and submitted to the Tours Festival for Short Movies the next year. In the message he prepared for the festival, Mishima called the film *Les Rites de l'Amour et de le Mort* and began by speaking of the spectacle of seppuku or death "through drawing out the intestines" as described by the terrified members of the foreign embassy who demanded punishment for those who attacked and killed foreigners in the mid-nineteenth century—a spectacle which you can no longer see except in theater. His reference was to the Sakai Incident. On the 15th of Second Month 1868, a band of Tosa samurai killed and wounded eleven French sailors. In response, the French consul-general demanded punishment of the samurai and in the end twenty of them were chosen to disembowel themselves. The French officers made to witness the procedure grew so aghast they are said to have stopped the proceedings when the eleventh man finished his turn.[9]

> The meaning of the calligraphy written in the scroll [hung in the alcove in the film] is *shisei* (sublime sincerity). Never once in Japanese history did the essence of an age reveal itself in the

rite of *death* as starkly as it did during the period of just about ten years after 1936.

Neither had there been young men who wanted to be sublime beings in the rite of death as much as the officers of the *Imperial Guards Division* at the time did. For them there was no point in living except to heighten the samurai tradition to a purer form.

But the young men of that age group at the time also had a desire for *love*, that is, sexual desire. In that respect, too, they wanted to be sublime, tried to be ritualistic.

Mishima then spoke of the nō-stage setting he used for the film, for in nō "concretism lies in the expression of essential things." The officer's hat for the Imperial Guards Division he wore in the film was a nō mask, and the white kimono the woman wore was "a wedding dress, its color signifying a pure death." He added that the music he used was the 1936 recording of Wagner's *Tristan und Isolde*.

*Les Rites de l'Amour et de le Mort* became one of the two finalists but lost out to the other candidate because the jury fiercely split. The critic for *Variety*, Gene Moskowitz, was for it and indignant about the outcome. Under the heading, "Tours 11th Shorts Fest Bestows Prize First Time But Nothing For Brilliant Japanese Gore," he asked, "But what can be said about a fest that gives absolutely nothing to the most audacious, brilliant and personal film shown in competition?"[10] In other words, it was a great success.

Among the prominent Americans who wanted to see *Yūkoku* while visiting Tokyo later were Edgar Snow, of *Red Star Over China* fame, and Leonard Bernstein. Mishima was busy on both occasions, and asked the film's production manager Fujii to arrange a private viewing. Bernstein watched the film intently, with a stern look on his face, Fujii recalled. "*The Rite of Love and Death* is wonderful and I was terribly moved," the composer-conductor said afterward. "But I have one question for you: Why did Mishima use Wagner's music, not traditional Japanese music?" Fujii could only manage, "Because Mr. Mishima likes Wagner." Bernstein cracked a smile and left, with "Best regards to Mishima."[11]

It was perhaps while he "wandered around the cold towns of Tokyo toward the end of January searching for a military uniform from the time of the 2.26 Incident"—or after the filming was over—that Mishima had a couple of "dates" in a sadomasochists' club in "Tokyo's gay ghetto in Shinjuku."

"Mishima liked to pretend he was committing seppuku," a man called Ryūtarō recalled for a visiting writer from England forty years later. "I had to watch, and eventually he brought along a sword and showed me how to stand behind him as his *kaishaku*. He also had other props. He would write out a death poem"—a poem, usually in tanka form, that a samurai or a soldier would write before killing himself. "And oddest of all, he pulled a huge length of red cloth from his briefcase. What's that? I asked him before we started. 'Blood,' he said. 'Blood and guts.'" For the filming of *Yūkoku*, pig guts and "buckets of blood" were secured.

"I was impressed the first time we did this. Mishima got hard at once and as he died he came. Without touching himself at all. I had never seen anyone do that before. I didn't find the role-playing at all arousing and wanted him to fuck me, but he didn't want to—I think I was just a witness to something he wanted to do in front of an audience."[12]

Ryūtarō, then twenty years old, was requested to wear a high-school uniform for these sessions. About the same time he wrote *Yūkoku*, Mishima had also penned a short story for the gay magazine *ADONIS* describing a man carrying out seppuku with a high-school student. In the story, "Execution of Love" *(Ai no shokei)*, published in *APOLLO*, a special issue of *ADONIS*, in October 1960, a junior high-school gym teacher carries out the act urged by a "beautiful boy," a student he loves but apparently has never touched, who has brought a knife for that purpose. The teacher, with features resembling Mishima, including his age, is named Ōtomo Shinji. The story was published under the pseudonym of Sakakiyama Tamotsu.[13]

---

Following Mishima's death, Yōko, who had been scandalized by the film *Yūkoku*, demanded to have all of it destroyed. Fujii Hiroaki was given the unenviable task of doing so, and he did it all by himself. He collected forty-three prints in all and burnt them in an incinerator one by one. But he begged Yōko to preserve at least an entire set of the negatives. She agreed. So he packed it in a wooden "tea box," part of Yōko's trousseau, that she offered. Then the matter was forgotten. Some years after Yōko's own death, in 1995, Fujii mustered the courage to ask to see the set again. After a search, he found not just the "tea box," neatly tucked away in a corner of the storeroom of the Mishima house, containing all the negatives with Japanese, English, French, and German intertitles, but all the material related to the filmmaking carefully packed in several cases—the evidence of Yōko's respect for her husband's work. That was how *Yūkoku* was turned into a DVD and made part of the complete works that was being published.[14]

## *The Vietnam War*

The student movement that would capture so much of Mishima's attention in the last part of his life took a vigorous turn in January 1965 when Keiō University students rallied to protest the doubling of tuition. Student activism of the 1960s was worldwide, and in most countries, it shared some common elements: the influx of baby boomers into colleges and universities and the students' growing impatience with unchanging academic institutionalism.

But the largest common denominator was the opposition to America's escalating violence in Vietnam, and that, too, took a palpable turn in the first months of the same year. In March, the United States started bombing North Vietnam under the code name of "Rolling Thunder," and landed two battalions in Da Nang. There were already twenty-three thousand marines active in South Vietnam.

In April, the writer Kaikō Takeshi, with several others, founded a citizens' movement against the war calling itself "Peace for Vietnam! Federation of Citizens and Cultural Organizations," soon known by its Japanese acronym Beheiren. It was at Kaikō's proposal that the Beheiren raised ¥2.4 million—or $6,700 at the exchange rate of the day—to take out a full-page antiwar ad in the *New York Times*. The ad appeared in November that year.

Kaikō had a direct motive to lead such a movement. In February, as the *Asahi Shinbun*'s "emergency correspondent," he had joined a military operation around Ben Cat, to the northwest of Saigon, with the Asahi photojournalist Akimoto Keiichi, that ended in a disaster. A five-hundred-man strong South Vietnamese combat unit, with nine US "advisers"—despite their direct intervention in the war, American soldiers were technically not regarded as co-equal to the South Vietnamese forces—was trounced by "invisible snipers" as soon as they sallied forth into a jungle. In Kaikō's own group of two hundred, only seventeen managed to regroup. By observing the daily comings and goings in Saigon and United States and Vietnamese soldiers in Fort Ben Cat, Kaikō had concluded, as proved prescient, that only the National Liberation Front (Vietcong) and Buddhist monks had any kind of unifying power.

Kaikō, who had won the Akutagawa Prize just before Ōe did, would write three novels based on his experience of the Vietnam War, the third one unfinished. The first one, *Into a Black Sun* (*Kagayakeru yami*), in 1968, won the Mainichi Shuppan Bunka Prize. When he learned the Ministry of Education was giving him its literary prize for the second, *Darkness in Summer* (*Natsu no yami*), in 1972, he declined on the grounds that a novelist had no reason to receive a literary award from the government. The real reason was the war that still raged. In his reports from Saigon, back in 1965, he had conveyed Vietnamese intellectuals' hope that Japan would intervene to end the war and had started a peace movement. But the Japanese government had gone on to consistently, powerfully, endorse the US intent to annihilate "the Vietcongs."[15]

## *Translating d'Annunzio*

That spring, Saeki Shōichi and Muramatsu Takeshi revived *Hihyō*, "Criticism." Mishima joined the members-only quarterly magazine and began his share of contribution with the first part of his translation of Gabriele d'Annunzio's drama, *Le Martyre de Saint Sébastien*. To do the translation of the work on the legendary martyr who had enchanted him since he was a boy, Mishima did something not many writers at his age and in the midst of an extraordinarily busy life would do: learn another language for one specific purpose of translating a play.

Mishima had long looked for d'Annunzio's play translated into German or English, the two languages he could read, until he concluded that there was none and that if he wanted to read it he had to do so in the language in which the Italian poet and dramatist wrote it: French. If no one had translated it into English or German, that was because, a scholar had concluded a few years earlier, "the French writings of Gabriele d'Annunzio are of peripheral significance in his literary career" and because "except for occasional references in general studies of the author, they were completely forgotten." This is not to say that the critical reaction to *Le Martyre de Saint Sébastien* was all negative when it was first staged. Although there were "many disparagers," Léon Blum, among others, "expressed astonishment at the fact that a foreigner had been able to compose a dramatic poem with such mastery of the resources and vocabulary and rhythm."[16]

Mishima set out to translate with Ikeda Kōtarō, a young French student Muramatsu recommended. It turned out to be "the awesome work of collaborative translation," he wrote—"awesome" because he knew nothing of French. "First I studied the grammar and proceeded to do the translation work, like a crawling ant, ascertaining with Mr. Ikeda the case and the person of each letter and phrase, inquiring on the meanings of each word in great detail. We did all-night work once every week. And even in the midst of this painstaking labor, I enjoyed mining bit by bit the voluptuous images rich with sensuality unique to d'Annunzio. At times we debated a single word for several hours. I was moved à la 'beginning Dutch learning.'"

This last refers to *Beginning Dutch Learning* (*Rangaku koto-hajime*), an account of the difficulties Sugita Genpaku (1733–1817) and other physicians met when they tried to decipher Dutch medical books for the first time in the early nineteenth century.

During the Edo Period, when Holland was the only European country with which Japan maintained trade relations, some physicians who came into possession of illustrated medical books brought from that country[17] realized that Dutch medicine was far more advanced than theirs, which was basically Chinese medicine. A small group of them decided to crack Dutch to learn what the books said but at once faced monumental difficulties. There were no Dutch-Japanese dictionaries at the time and none of the official Japanese interpreters stationed in Nagasaki, the only port that allowed foreigners to come and stay, were of any help because their grasp of the language was primitive. Sugita's book, published in 1815, described the time-consuming, nerve-racking process the physicians had to go through.

In working on d'Annunzio's drama, Mishima of course had plenty of French-Japanese dictionaries and he had in Ikeda immediate help on hand. Yet he set himself a task that those Dutch learners might not have thought of. "I would translate several lines," he wrote, "consulting Mr. Ikeda's word-for-word translation, trying as best I could to turn them into sentences that sounded right as Japanese but that would also keep any Japanese odor at a distance." "Japanese odor" or *washū* referred to any Japanese turn of phrase that might slip in when the Japanese wrote in classical Chinese; because classical Chinese was assumed to work under rigid rules, any such infraction was considered a defect or an error. Put differently, Mishima tried to achieve in this translation something grammatically *and* culturally natural. No wonder Mishima concluded his description of the exercise by saying, "For the first time I touched the *Dämon* of the work called translation."[18]

The work took over a year, ending at 5:30 on the morning of July 14. Mishima was exact in recording such matters. That evening he threw a party for a small group of his artist friends, though not to mark the completion of the work but to celebrate the expansion of his house.

The translation was serialized in *Hihyō* in three installments. When an imprint specializing in art books, Bijutsu Shuppansha, agreed to publish a deluxe edition of the translation the following year, Mishima wrote a concise, scholarly essay tracing the shifting legend of Saint Sebastian whose "existence is extremely doubtful," noting that, as far as artistic presentations of the figure are concerned, the saint did not shed all his clothes to become naked until twelve hundred years after his presumed death.[19]

For this edition he selected fifty out of the great many pictures of martyrdom he had collected, including the sixty he had purchased in a print shop in the piazza di Spagna, in Rome. This he did, he wrote, following the example of d'Annunzio who wrote he had collected two hundred pictures of Saint Sebastian's martyrdom to write the play. Mishima had two of the pictures, one by Reni and one by Sodoma, reproduced in color for his book.

In his essay on Saint Sebastian, Mishima cited the following lines as his favorites—the words of the archer Sanaé in Act IV, just before Sebastian orders his men to shoot him:

> They are far off, already far off!
> You can no longer see the horses

of the squadron. A white croup
disappears in the bend of the road, behind
the Tombs: the decurion.
He has never looked back.
Lord, now we are going
to untie you.[20]

Yet one imagines that Mishima was happy to read at long last—and translate—d'Annunzio's loving description of the martyr tied naked to the trunk of a laurel tree "like a beautiful Diadumene"—d'Annunzio makes the emperor call him Adonis.

> They have stripped the Martyr in order to tie him to the trunk of a great laurel-tree with cords of Spanish grass. Standing, his naked feet on the knotted roots, he rests on the svelte column of his right leg the weight of his body smooth as ivory; his wrists bound above his head, he resembles the beautiful Diadumenos fastening the band about his forehead.
>
> It is the Archers of Emesa that Augustus has ordered to revenge with their arrows the Empire's Sun-King. They are overcome with love and fear. Sanaé, the archer with eyes of different colors, is among them. He watches the plain.[21]

And Mishima surely envisioned what he was to bring to himself when he came upon Sebastian's *cri de cœur* in the course of the exchange of love between Sebastian, the leader of the First Cohort,[22] and his men who adore him but have been ordered to kill him, Sebastian, the seeker of pain and suffering,

> I tell you, I tell you:
> he who most deeply
> wounds me most deeply
> loves me.[23]
>
> (Tr. Michael O'Brien)

This, Mishima judged, is where "the conflict between Eros and agape is driven up against the wall."[24]

## *The Boom and Fatigue*

The Japanese later characterized the decade of the 1960s in their country as "golden," a period of double-digit economic growth. The nation's gross domestic product increased fivefold in nominal terms (2.6 times in real terms) over the span of ten years. The per capita income quadrupled, even as the actual prices of daily items, such as eggs, beer, and electric bulbs, remained steady. By the time the Japanese economy was judged to be the second largest in the world, in January 1968, the days of underfed, snotty-nosed kids running around in dirty, shabby clothes were gradually fading.[25] Instead, obesity among children was becoming a matter of social concern. Some children were unable to complete some events in an athletic meet because they ran out of breath too easily.

The titles of the government's annual economic white papers from the mid-1960s onward tell the happy prospects Japanese policy makers faced. The report for 1965, the year Satō Eisaku, Kishi Nobusuke's brother, became prime minister, was called "the tasks for stable growth." This was followed by "the road to continuous growth" (1966); "improving efficiency and social welfare" (1967); "the Japanese economy in the midst of internationalization" (1968); "confronting abundance" (1969); and "the new dimensions of the Japanese economy" (1970). The economy of the second half of the decade was called "the Izanagi boom" in reference to the deity in Japanese mythology who, with his spouse, Izanami, is said to have populated the Japanese archipelago with a myriad of deities, thereby creating the country.

One cannot refer to this dizzying economic growth, later termed a "miracle," without reference to its enormous cost. Some of the results of unchecked pollution came to the fore during the same decade. Among them were "the four great pollution diseases": the Minamata Disease, in Kumamoto (neurological syndrome caused by methyl mercury dumped into the coastal waters); the Second Minamata, in Niigata; the Yokkaichi Asthma (caused by sulfurous acid gas spewed into the air); and the Itai-itai (It-hurts!-it-hurts!) Disease, in Toyama (caused by cadmium dumped into a river).

At just the midpoint of this "golden decade," even as the publication of Kōdansha's six-volume selection of Mishima's short stories was under way, in the usual monthly installment-payment fashion of a volume a month, Shinchōsha offered to put out a single-volume selection. Mishima chose four stories for it and wrote an afterword in which he said: "I put together these four pieces this time because they were written about the same time and have a common theme. This selection must be the most degenerate of all my works. My sense of fatigue, powerlessness, and the decadence of the sentiment that soured and rotted—I put all that in these four pieces."

"I feel something unspeakably ominous in these works," he continued. "But what subtle part of the Zeitgeist was it that made me write such pieces? The medium"—that is, he the writer—"often does not know the face of the deity that has possessed her."[26]

What are the four stories and what are they like?

"The Strange Tale of the Pale-Moon Villa" (*Gettan-sō kitan*), published in the January 1965 issue of *Bungei Shunjū*, is a horror story subtly, cleverly narrated in the manner of an old-fashioned tale—say, à la Edgar Allan Poe. A young handsome marquis, while in his villa on a cape, compels his young companion servant to rape an idiot girl so he may see human beings copulate. He is only interested in watching things, observing things. This happens during the summer before he marries a beautiful woman. Not long after the marriage, he is found dead, on the beach, apparently having fallen off the cliff. Foul play is suspected but no perpetrator is found.

The main narrator, the marquis's young servant, knows, however, who did it. The marquis's eyes were gouged out and stuffing the eye sockets were oleaster berries—the same berries the idiot girl was picking when raped. The beautiful marquise, when told of the rape from the servant, tells him her own secret: during her marriage there was no sex, with her husband only interested in "looking at every nook and corner of my body, earnestly."

"Pilgrimage to the Three Kumano Shrines" (*Mi-Kumano mōde*), published in the January issue of *Shinchō*, depicts a folklorist-poet who clumsily, in a palpably amateurish fashion, attempts to turn himself into a myth as he visits the three holy places of Kumano with an admiring female tanka-disciple-cum-caretaker, Tsuneko.

The scholar—"the dean of Japanese literature at Seimei University, a doctor of literature, who is also known as a tanka poet"—was modeled after the charismatic folkloric interpreter of Japanese literature Orikuchi Shinobu who sought to ascertain the origins of old Japanese words and customs such as the Tennō's original role. Orikuchi noted, for example, that the word *Shintō* itself is a formulation under the influences of the alien religion Buddhism that regarded the combination of folkloric beliefs and practices as "heretical" and that what is often assumed to be indigenous about it is hard to establish.[27] He wrote poems in tanka and other forms under the penname of Shaku Chōkū. Like Mishima a devotee of kabuki, Orikuchi was a noted homosexual who was known, at least among some of his students and colleagues, for his pronounced aversion to women.

Mishima, when young, was familiar with Orikuchi's books of poems that revealed a complicated upbringing—not too dissimilar to his own—and went on to read much of his other work. Although it was during the period from 1958 to 1959 that he read his many volumes with a great focus typical of him—he read in tandem the works of Minakata Kumagusu—Mishima showed his sure grasp of the man's accomplishment when he wrote an essay following Orikuchi's death, in 1953. The essay was for *Mita Bungaku*, the literary magazine of Keiō University where the scholar-poet taught.

"Just as Pater depicted in *Marius the Epicurean* the appearance, rituals, and customs of deities of the heretical ancient world who were gradually forgotten and betrayed, if you read Mr. Orikuchi's *Introduction to the Origins of Japanese Literature*, you can clearly observe the fates of the deities of ancient Japan in the infant deities who retain their influences in the tales of wandering nobles and in the themes of Mother's Land which reemerge in the biographical novels after the Heian Court," he observed with a sweeping sentence in a short but sweeping essay.

"Tales of wandering nobles," *kishu ryūri tan*, is a literary genre strongly associated with Orikuchi. In such tales, an aristocrat is typically "exiled" or forced to wander far from Kyoto, in outlying regions, to atone for his sins in one way or another. Orikuchi also stressed the importance, in ancient Japan, of the concept of "Mother's Land," *haha no kuni*, which he proposed was the same as the netherworld. By the time he wrote *Pilgrimage*, in any event, Mishima was turning against the kind of literary or folkloric speculation that earned Orikuchi fame.

"Because Japan had none of that ugly, vulgar violence of Christian culture, the greatest misfortune that overturned ancient culture," Mishima continued:

Mr. Orikuchi managed to end his life of living in the ancient world even as he lived in modern times possessed as he was by the remnants of deities that still remain in the Japanese race, without falling into scholastic positivism as Frazer did in *The Golden Bough* or without aligning himself with the convention of discovering a new Christianity as Pater made Marius do. Western Grecianists and Heathenists are dogged by a trace of the edginess or the sense of guilt that they are heretics to Christianity, with only people such as Goethe, Winckelmann, and Pater coming close to achieving the rounded airs of a classicist. If and when Mr. Orikuchi's achievement is widely introduced to the West, people will be surprised that such a healthy "ancient" lived in the twentieth century.[28]

"Peacocks" (*Kujaku*), published in the February issue of *Bungakukai*, was meant to be "the reverse of Dorian Gray," Mishima explained, adding that he "loved it the most" among the four. A man named Tomioka, who inherited considerable assets from his landowner father, is suspected of slaughtering a large number of peacocks in a nearby children's park because he was seen watching the birds in total absorption. A detective who visits him to inquire, while being kept waiting in the guest room, notices, among the carelessly scattered exotic bric-a-brac including a graphic, painted peacock made in metal on a mantelpiece, a photo portrait of an "incomparably beautiful boy" who appears to be sixteen or seventeen.

When the man he has come to question shows up, the first thing the detective notices in the tall, lean man with scholarly bearing of about forty-five is his face that "reveals terrible ravage": "His hair had a sprinkling of gray strands, and his skin was enfeebled and flaccid. His facial features were well proportioned, but that proportionality had too pronounced an air of something made to order, the feeling of a miniature landscape garden left alone for a long time and covered with dust: a pond thick with dust, a tilting red bridge, a small stone lantern, a rustic porcelain house where dust has collected even in its interiors."

In time, the detective is told that the "boy of celestial beauty" in the photo is Tomioka in his youth. The story surely has a good deal of self-projection. Photos of Mishima as a child and well into his teens show him to be an oval-faced embodiment of innocence, whereas those at about the time he wrote these stories show him to be a man with a haggard, ravaged face albeit with large alert eyes. (Saeki Shōichi, Mishima's associate and professor of English, characterized Mishima as "a person of eyes, a writer obsessed with lucidly seeing through things."[29]) As a purposeful reversal of *The Picture of Dorian Gray*, the story reminds the reader of what Basil Hallward says of the portrait he did of Dorian Gray: "I have put too much of myself into it."[30] In Oscar Wilde's novel, of course, Dorian remains beautiful and youthful while the figure painted in his portrait grows uglier and uglier as he continues to commit immoral acts.

The fourth story, "The Morning of Innocent Love" (*Jun'ai no asa*), was published in the June 1965 issue of *Nihon*, just before it was included in the selection. A well-to-do married couple, both "inordinately youthful-looking," are found murdered on the terrace of their house. A college student is soon arrested and readily confesses—the second half of the story consists entirely of the questions and answers between a detective and the young man—that he and his girlfriend were separately, unknowingly, lured into the couple's house to have sex with them, he with the wife, she with the husband, in separate rooms. When he wakes up early next morning, the student realizes what has happened. Then, when he sees the married couple passionately kissing each other on the terrace just outside the room, he kills them with the knife he happened to have—out of "an admixture of admiration and anger," "an anger blended with joy and yearning."

The husband, Ryōsuke, and the wife, Reiko, had fallen in love when he was twenty-three, she eighteen, and married seven years later, with the war in between. Since then, "they had lived in memories of love only the two of them knew. . . . They had bet each moment on their first encounter, that beautiful first astonishment. In her fifty-year-old husband Reiko repeatedly saw the vestiges of the twenty-three year old, and in his forty-five-year-old wife Ryōsuke constantly discovered the freshness of the eighteen-year-old."

"What the two tried to evoke was a simple thing," the story tells us. "One morning in May, a virginal girl's eyes intently look at the youth she loves, the field is full of dew, the horizon is hugely blocked by the anxieties of war and life, a separation is scheduled, a kiss brushes by their lips like the first flush of dawn. . . . Such an unforgettable form of bliss of love" was what they wanted to relive from moment to moment. But "the husband was always there, and the wife was always there.... From the moment being there becomes certain, corruption advances. Unlike an ordinary couple of this world, [Ryōsuke and Reiko] tried to resist this corruption and disintegration effect." When they realized they had run out of "poetry, imagination, and acting, they thought up the most unnatural method"—entrapping a young couple for sex for one night so they might have "that kiss that ripened on a girl's lips one morning in May."

So, in these four stories Mishima depicted a young aristocrat who is only interested in observing things and is killed as a result, a scholar who ineptly tries to turn himself into a myth of his own making, a man who is "the reverse of Dorian Gray," and a couple who try to relive "the first astonishment" of love forever, fail in the end, and are murdered. Decadent and degenerate these stories may or may not be, but Mishima may well have thought, "I have put too much of myself into these stories."

## *The Sade Case*

Toward the end of June, Mishima started the play *Madame de Sade* and completed it two months later. As the source material, he credited the book on Sade by Shibusawa Tatsuhiko, a student of French literature and sexual perversion he had known since the mid-1950s when he had happily responded to Shibusawa's request for a foreword to a selection of Sade's writings in his translation, then urged him to write an extensive essay on Sade for the magazine he was editing. Ever since, he had been "thrilled" to read each of the younger author's new books, once even buying a book, unable to wait for a complimentary copy he had expected. (It soon turned out to have been sent to Mishima's previous address).[31]

The title Mishima chose for the play, though, was the same as that of the psychiatrist Shikiba Ryūzaburō's book that had come out twenty years earlier, and his characters were all women, with the focus on Sade's wife, Renée, rather than on the man who inspired the word "sadism." Also, Mishima had used some of Shikiba's other books for his other writings. As a result some conjectured that Mishima's primary idea came from Shikiba's book. But, when Shibusawa's life of Sade came out, in September 1964, Mishima found his approach "intense."

"I was not quite satisfied with Mr. Shikiba Ryūzaburō's dilettantish biography of Sade," Mishima had written Shibusawa, "so I felt my thirst was slaked [by your book], and at the same time I was surprised that he did only such sinless things in his real life."[32] In the afterword to the play, he also explained that his aim was to "attempt a logical elucidation of the mystery" that remained in Shibusawa's book: Renée's unflagging devotion to her husband while he was in prison, followed by her abrupt renunciation of the man the moment he was set free.[33]

From a different perspective, Mishima gave a different explanation. Since his early days as a writer, he had insisted that, of the three genres of fiction, poetry, and drama, the last one was the second best means of the author "making a confession"—that is, revealing himself—poetry being the very best, and fiction the least fit for that purpose. In *Madame de Sade*, he put himself in the position of the Marquis de Sade as assessed by others in his absence: his wife Renée saying he is *not* a monster, his mother-in-law Mme. de Montreuil saying he *is* a monster, and so on. He was "not as great as de Sade," he took care to note, but he wanted to show how diversely assessed he was among diverse people.[34]

In any event, in crediting Shibusawa's work prominently—he cited its title on the title page of his play as if it were the subtitle—Mishima inserted himself into the so-called Sade Incident. Back in 1960, when the sale of the second half of Shibusawa's translation of *L'Histoire de Juliette, ou les Prospérités du vice* was banned, Mishima had written Shibusawa: "If you become an ex-convict as a result of this incident, I'll have an ex-convict among my friends, and there'll be no greater honor for me."[35]

The following year, Shibusawa, along with his publisher, was indicted on possession of pornographic material. Some of the leading writers of the day, such as Endō Shūsaku and Ōe Kenzaburō, lined up as "special defense counsel"—by Japanese law, those with no legal credentials but with expertise on the relevant field can offer themselves as such with a status equal to that of a lawyer, rather like "expert witnesses" in the United States—and defense witnesses. The Sade Case, nevertheless, would drag on for nine years, until 1969. So, Mishima with *Madame de Sade*, in which he took care to include descriptions of some salacious sexual acts, was openly ridiculing the legal proceedings, which Shibusawa himself constantly subverted with his decision to have "a festal time" with it.

When finally the Supreme Court handed down its verdict, finding the defendants guilty as charged, the penalty it imposed was seventy thousand yen—a puny sum, which Shibusawa did not let go without publicly pouting, suggesting that it was in itself a travesty of justice.

As always, Mishima had some acute, at times self-mocking things to say about the play on hand: in this instance, the "oddity" of "a Japanese playwright writing a play about the customs of France, and that of the eighteenth century." "In Japan, there is the infamous 'translated-drama acting.' In the West, there is no such thing," he observed. "In the West, there was no such need; for a long time, if the role of an Oriental was called for, the actor had only to make slant eyes, open his arms like a baby, and toddle about on tiptoe to satisfy the audience adequately." In contrast,

> Japan's Shingeki, as is universally known, started out with redhead [i.e., European] plays to rebel against traditional theater, and that inevitably brought about the development of "acting by mimicking redheads," which, having the tradition of mimic-acting in medieval kyōgen unconsciously in its background, while at the same time completely wiping away its elements of parody and criticism, was engrossed in mimicking Westerners' language and behavior single-mindedly, with fool's honesty, carefully, in deadly seriousness. (What a Japanesey effort!) It was a truly clumsy, makeshift bridge, but it was, in any case, the only bridge that linked our theater to the West.

"Whatever you might say," Mishima continued, "that acting, after a history of several decades, has shown some worthy results as it has reached the stage of being able to produce Western plays that Westerners do not find too ridiculous. The only stylized acting that Shingeki actresses and actors who, though they are Japanese, can't even play a geisha or can't look right with sword on hip (these are verily the symbols of the modern Japanese) have nurtured and inherited is what is called 'translated-drama acting.'"

The expression Mishima chose for "play a geisha" is *kimono o kite tsuma o toru*, "wear a kimono and hold up the front hem," which is what a geisha is expected to do when she stands up and walks—something any kabuki actor who plays a woman's role executes naturally, gracefully.

Mishima went on to add, tongue-in-cheek: "Japan's so-called translated-drama acting has become a rare cultural asset that ought to be the crown of the world, realizing world theater one step ahead of everyone else."[36] Here, "the crown of the world" is the commonly accepted Japanese translation of *über alles in der Welt*.

## *Self-appointed Japanese Expert*

On September 5, Mishima left, with Yōko, for another world tour, which would last until October 31. The two traveled to New York, Stockholm, Paris, Hamburg, and Bangkok before returning to Tokyo. The Vietnam War was worsening, but he included Bangkok in his itinerary because of the Phra Phang, the Temple of Dawn, there. He planned to use it in his tetralogy, *The Sea of Fertility*, the first installment of which he had submitted to *Shinchō* for its September issue.

Mishima also crossed over to Cambodia to visit Angkor Thom, in Siem Reap. There, when he saw the stone statue of "the Leper King," he had an idea for a new play on the assumption that the Leper King was Jayavarman VII, the conqueror and unifier of Cambodia who out of his deep religiosity built the ruinously extravagant Angkor Thom. In truth, the statue in question may represent not the king, but "a god of death." Also, though much of the king's life is shrouded in mystery and legend, what is known suggests he lived to ninety or so. Yet because the partially lichen-covered statue, in the traditional Buddhist posture of "sitting in meditation," shows a youthful-looking full-bodied man,[37] Mishima, that night, in his room of the Auberge de Temple, in front of the walled city, worked out the outline of a play about a king who dies of leprosy in his youth that was to embody the notion, "The body is eternal, youth immortal."[38] The play in the end would be titled *The Terrace of the Leper King (Raiō no terasu)*.

It was while Mishima and Yōko were in Stockholm, from September 22 to 27, that the Associated Press in two dispatches from that city mentioned Mishima as a candidate for the Nobel Prize, and it was while the two were in Bangkok, where they stayed the longest, from October 12 to 30, that the wire service, again from Stockholm, reported, on October 14, that Mishima was among the finalists.

These dispatches inflamed the Japanese mass media. The only

Japanese winner of a Nobel Prize till then was the physicist Yukawa Hideki, who had received it, in 1949, for his prediction in the mid-1930s of the existence of the meson. The timing of the award and the nature of the field—the international prize came when Japan was still struggling with the aftermath of the war, including the nuclear devastations—had left the greatest impression on the Japanese. But since then there had been no Japanese recipient of the prize.

Among others, the *Yomiuri Shinbun* carried a long article with a zealous title, "The Nobel Prize and Japanese Literature," in its evening edition of October 15th. To the daily's embarrassment and the disappointment of all Japanese, the news from Stockholm the very next day was that the prize went to the Russian writer Mikhail Sholokhov whose masterwork, *And Quiet Flows the Don*, had won great acclaim. Less than a week later, however, the Japanese media became worked up again: a Nobel Prize was awarded to a Japanese after all! The field was in physics once more: Tomonaga Shin'ichirō shared the prize with Harvard's Julian Schwinger and Caltech's Richard Feynman. Japan's international celebrity author had lost out in literature, but no matter: the media immediately turned its massive attention to Tomonaga.

Mishima remained a strong contender for the literary prize for the next few years, until Kawabata Yasunari received it, in 1968. Keene would later write that, in May 1970, when he was in Copenhagen, he learned that Mishima had failed to get the prize because a self-appointed Japanese expert "on the basis of the few weeks he spent in Japan," who had "extremely conservative views," denounced Mishima as "a radical." As a result, the Swedish Academy that may have already decided on Mishima chose Kawabata, whom the "expert" strongly pushed.[39]

When the prize went to Kawabata, Mishima remarked to the poet Takahashi Mutsuo, "If I, not Kawabata, had gotten it, Japan's seniority system would have collapsed with great clatter," adding, "If another Japanese gets it, it will not be me, but Ōe [Kenzaburō]."[40] His prediction came true, albeit over a quarter of a century later. Ōe won the prize, in 1994.

Mishima had gotten in touch with Takahashi, back in 1964. Intrigued by *The Rose Tree: Fake Lovers (Bara no ki: Nise no koibito-tachi)*, the book of poems he received from its author, Mishima telephoned the unknown young man for dinner at an expensive Chinese restaurant on the Ginza, and chatted with him. He then wrote a laudatory afterword for Takahashi's next book, *Sleeping, Sinning, Falling*. "Mr. Takahashi was exempted from the human rule that every boy grows up to be a young man," his being a world "where he did not have to go down to the bottom of the sea, down to the bottom of the vagina which many a young man mistakes for a philosophy, mistakes for profundity," Mishima said, rather graphically. He also cited John Rechy's *City of Night* to exalt Takahashi as one of the "ethereal angels" in the third of the categories made in the novel.[41]

Not long after he was honored with the afterword, Takahashi realized he had said, in a newspaper interview about to be published, something that Mishima might consider rude. He urgently sought a meeting with him. Mishima met him in a hotel bar in Akasaka that evening. Upon learning what the young man's agitation was all about, he laughed. Mishima said he had assumed that Takahashi had been blackmailed by punks and needed money, showing him a bundle of cash he had brought in his bag. Mishima then urged Takahashi to agree to any interview, not to miss any chance to become better known.[42]

CHAPTER TWENTY

# Shinpūren, Men of the Divine Wind

*"Are you not 'turning perilously rightist'"?*
—Tokuoka Takao

In the spring of 1966, when he wrote "Voices of the Heroic Souls" (*Eirei no koe*)—*eirei*, "heroic souls," is a term of respect for the war dead—and handed the manuscript to Shizue to read, as he routinely did with his writings, Mishima said: "I finished writing it in one stretch last night. It completed itself." He also told her, according to her recollections six years after his death: "My hand started to move on its own and the pen slid over the paper of its own will. It wouldn't have stopped even if I had tried to stop it. At midnight I heard low voices mumble in every corner of my room. It appeared to be the voices of many people. I listened, and understood they were the words of the soldiers who died in the 2.26 Incident."

A few nights earlier, he had told her, with tears in his eyes, about the miserable backgrounds of those soldiers. When she read the manuscript, she felt "the blood throughout my body chill." She also feared that something had "possessed" her son.[1]

Whatever Mishima may have told Shizue, "The Heroic Souls" is far from a piece of automatic writing. Yes, in it, he describes what are purported to be the delirious utterances of a medium in a Shinto session called *kamugakari*, "deity-possessed," that the narrator says he has attended. In the variety of *kamugakari* described here, a medium, possessed by a deity or deities, gives voice to a person or a group of persons, apparently unprompted save by an accompanying instrument.

But at the end of what he presented as a recreation of one such session, Mishima was careful to list eight books as material on which it "greatly relied." Four of them had to do with the 2.26 Incident; two about the Occupation, including a biographical account based on documents of the diplomat Shidehara Kijūrō, who became the second prime minister after Japan's defeat; one about the Kamikaze forces;[2] and one about *reigaku*, a study on the use of the medium in Shinto. Mishima could have easily added *Hagakure*; he makes the medium quote a couple of passages from it.

Further, when "The Heroic Souls" was made part of "the 2.26 Incident trilogy" shortly after its publication in the June issue of *Bungei*, Mishima explained that his narrative was structured like a nō drama—to be exact, the structure of its *shuramono* category in which the ghost of a warrior appears to retell his defeat in battle and his inability to rest in peace in death.[3]

At any rate, when interviewed by the daily *Fukui Shinbun*, Mishima explained that "The Heroic Souls"—or "the 2.26 Incident trilogy"—was an expression of his frustrations or irritations. Closely analyzing his own aesthetics, he found an admixture of a belief in "classical beauty and eroticism," as well as his "experience of the war," he said. Ultimately, the whole thing would have to come to the Tennō system.

The danger in Japan, Mishima added, was the fact that "the gap between classical rationalism such as *American democracy* and what is *emotional* that exists in the Japanese is gradually widening."[4] By thus bringing in the Tennō system, he knew he was taking a plunge—it would be "a fiction," he told Fukushima Jirō, that would show "the origins of [my] rightwing thinking."[5] And in "The Heroic Souls," the Tennō, though not so clearly identified, is made to die at the hands of the aggrieved, resentful souls of the officers of the 2.26 Incident who were executed, as well as the Kamikaze pilots.

This *kamugakari* session is conducted by just two persons: a *saniwa*, "the divine judge," who in this instance doubles as the player of a musical instrument—usually a six-string koto but here a flute, a natural stone the size of two fists put side by side with a hole through it—and a *kannushi*, the shrine priest who is the chief officiator but in this instance serves as medium. The age of the *saniwa*, Kimura Sensei, is not given, except to hint that he is middle-aged or older. The *kannushi*, Kawasaki Shigeo, is a twenty-three year-old male who "may be called a beautiful boy, with pale, clear features, thin eyebrows, a nervous, narrow, shapely nose, and small, gentle lips which may be mistaken for a lady's." He became blind in an accident when he was eighteen but has "since opened his spiritual eyes under Kimura Sensei's guidance." The medium's role is to give voice to "our present concern."

Prompted by the stone flute Kimura plays, Kawasaki begins to sing, "with a barely discernible smile on his face, suddenly clapping his hands rhythmically." What startles and thrills the narrator is Kawasaki's voice. It is usually a husky whisper, but this time it apparently represents a chorus coming from somewhere in the distance. And what the chorus does is to describe Japan at this very moment, in the middle of high economic growth, with sarcasm—in a combination of modern and classical or literary languages.

As the narrator self-consciously explains, the medium, "even after a divine soul leans on him and occupies him, does not necessarily speak the words of the deity in the ancient language of the *Kojiki* and *Nihon Shoki* if it is a new soul. He freely speaks the modern language, at times using modern words and phrases that may strike some as discordant." This out-of-place explanation brings to mind a scene in *Silk and Insight* where Okano goes to see Masaki—a member of the prewar Holy War Philosophy Institute turned Shinto medium. Even as he is fascinated by his friend's transformation, Okano cannot help making sharp-edged observations on the man. "Heroic Souls" begins:

> Too ineffably awe-inspiring to speak of,
> Your Majesty—before you we prostrate ourselves and say:
> Now, the four oceans are not necessarily calm
> but in Yamato Nation under the sun
> a belly-slapping, dancing world has emerged;
> under your virtuous rule, peace fills the world,
> people look at one another with smiles loosened by peace;
> benefit and loss crisscrossing, friend and foe allied,
> foreign monies make people run about;
> those who no longer want to fight love even cowardice,
> only nefarious battles prevail in the dark;
> husband and wife, good friends, can't trust each other,

false humanism turned into means of food,
hypocritical amity covers the world....

The litany continues, in a rising chorus "imbued with inexplicable anger and lamentation," the narrator reports, but it ends with an abruptly accusatory question: "Why did Your Majesty become a human being?" And with that the medium collapses with exhaustion, panting.

In the second part of the *kamugakari*, the medium, prompted by the *saniwa*'s inquiry, "Which deities are you? Kindly respond," states: "We are the souls of the betrayed." The medium goes on: "We are the ones who thirty years ago raised a just army, were given the infamous label of rebels, and were killed." Thirty years before 1966 is 1936, so these are the souls of the officers who were executed, the narrator reminds us, in consequence of the 2.26 Incident.

The narrator's stress in his account of the incident, which, albeit put in the mouth of a medium, is based on various documents, including exact quotations, is on "the supreme purity" of the "love (*koi*)" that the officers felt for the Tennō—"His Majesty the Grand Marshal astride a white horse, distant and small, as the figure of Living Deity for whom we are to die"—and the Tennō's utter failure to grasp that sentiment, compounded by his declared willingness to suppress them as rebels himself. The officers' sentiment is embodied in the words of a captain who shouted as the men were led to the execution ground: "After we die, all of us will go to His Majesty, with blood on us. And, even if we die, we will exert ourselves for the sake of our Great Lord. Long Live the Emperor! Long Live the Great Japanese Empire!"

The medium's song, a grief-stricken cry that the Tennō reacted to the officers' uprising as a human being, not as a deity as he should have, thereby "abandoning" them, ends, again, with the question: "Why did Your Majesty become a human being?" Toward the end, the medium is "grieving like a demon." He collapses, writhes on the floor, and faints.

The third part of the *kamugakari* introduces the souls of the Kamikaze pilots, the "younger brothers" of the 2.26 Incident officers—"We who offered our lives to His Majesty's State in an attempt to stir up the last Divine Wind for the Divine State at the very moment when we were about to be defeated in war." But the Divine Wind did not come. The reason was this: "Ever since you ascended the High Honored Seat, Your Majesty has always been a human being." That is understandable.

His Majesty is a sincere human being. Nevertheless, "just twice in the history of Shōwa, Your Majesty should have been a deity. . . . [You] should have been a deity in your duty as a human being"—"Once, when our older deities rose up; once, after our deaths, after our country was defeated."

As the voices of lamentation and remonstration continue, the medium begins to be pushed around by unseen hands, violently—"a horrifying spectacle." He then begins his last "song." The souls of the Kamikaze pilots say everything was all right: Japan's defeat, farmland reforms and socialist measures under the Occupation, and so forth, except one thing: "Your Majesty should not have said you were a human being."

> Had Your Majesty wrapped your holy body in ritual garb,
> night and day blurred, in the innermost part of the Court,
> prostrate before the souls of your Imperial Ancestors,
> performing rites for the souls of those who died for you, The
>     Deity,
> simply purifying yourself, praying,
> how venerable you might have been.
> Why did Your Majesty become a human being?
>   Why did Your Majesty become a human being?
>     Why did Your Majesty become a human being?[6]

As the medium repeats the refrain, clapping his hands, his clapping grows irregular and his voice trails off, becoming almost inaudible, until he falls backward, lies supine, motionless. The blind young man is found dead, his face no longer his, but one "transformed into the amorphous face of someone, someone you cannot tell who."

Mishima wrote he began seriously looking into the 2.26 Incident, along with Kamikaze pilots, as his preparations for *The Runaway Horse* (*Honba*),[7] the second of the tetralogy *The Sea of Fertility*, got under way. The story was to deal with the nationalistic movement preceding the uprising, but he found the Tennō system intractably "lying at the rock bottom of it all."

The reaction to "The Heroic Souls" was considerable. The refrain conjured up, in a journalist, the bizarre image of "a blood-dripping knife pressed onto the Tennō's chest."[8] When *Sunday Mainichi* interviewed him on the work, Mishima insisted that the motive of the young officers who rose up on February 26, 1936, was "pure" as they believed they were "saving the country." The Tennō was to blame for branding them as "rebels," even though it may have been the result of "the scheming of the old counselors who surrounded him, who were cowardly, timid, and shrewd," he said, adding, "So as to remove the stigma from the surviving families at least, His Majesty should send them an Imperial Messenger" to apologize "as soon as possible."

As agrarianism inevitably moves to capitalism, feudalism to modern industrialism, "love" (*ai*) between two parties, without a third party or "medium," becomes more and more unattainable, leading to D. H. Lawrence's "agnosticism of love," Mishima argued. In Japan, that third party forming the apex in that triangular relationship was the Tennō or deity born of agrarianism. He was, yes, definitely for the Tennō system.[9]

## *Screams of Heroic Souls*

With "The Heroic Souls" soon to appear in *Bungei* (in its June issue), Mishima was surprised to be asked, after kendō practice one day, to read a manuscript titled *Screams of Heroic Souls* (*Eirei no zekkyō*). Funasaka Hiroshi, who asked him to read it, was one of his "seniors" in the dōjō, whom Mishima had known for twenty years. He owned Taiseidō Shoten, a bookstore he had frequented since junior high school when Funasaka's father ran it.

Mishima knew Funasaka was passionate about kendō and encouraged his employees to take it up. But he had not thought that the man—a burly kendōka with "a physique like a heavy tank," who was "extremely polite and deferential," yet highly competitive, a man of "straightforward seriousness coupled with perseverance"—would also write. The coincidental title prompted Mishima to start reading the manuscript on the spot even though it was bulky with twelve hundred pages. Some moments later, he asked if he could keep it for a while. Funasaka, who had brought it with much hesitation and trepidation—he had seen enough people approach the celebrity author with the same purpose, only to be spurned out of hand—could not believe his luck.

Mishima brought the manuscript back a week later with many notations. He told Funasaka it would make a great book, and asked him to show him the first galley. Funasaka, who had never written a book, eagerly incorporated Mishima's suggestions, which included deletion of a great many paragraphs that reduced the size of the manuscript to one third of the original. Bungei Shunjū accepted the result. When Funasaka showed him the galley, Mishima brought it back to the dōjō a week later, again. To Funasaka's consternation and gratitude, the galley came back with a heartfelt, revelatory preface.[10]

Funasaka was an improbable survivor of the Battle of Angaur (Ngeaur), which took place from September to October 1944. The battle on the tiny island—its area is three square miles—tends to be overshadowed by that on Peleliu (Beliliou), a larger coral island six miles to the north, though its area is still a mere five square miles. Angaur and Peleliu are just two of the more than two hundred islands that make up the Palau Archipelago. Both battles were what Mishima called in his German concoction *Vernichteter Kampf*,[11] though many others in the Pacific could be so characterized, including the last and largest, the Battle of Okinawa.

Some American historians have questioned whether the Battle of Iwo Jima, another battle of annihilation, was necessary. The Palau part of the US Mariana and Palau Campaign was definitely not.

"Many believed after the battle—and still believe today—that the United States didn't need to fight it as a prerequisite to General MacArthur's return to the Philippines," E. B. Sledge, who took part in the Peleliu Battle as a twenty-one-year-old US marine, noted in his account of his experience years later.[12] Or, as a chronicler of the Pacific War wrote, it was "the one operation [the Joint Chiefs] had failed to cancel," because Adm. Chester W. Nimitz, commander of the Pacific Ocean Areas, insisted on it.[13] In any event, it turned into "the toughest battle of the entire Pacific war," according to Maj. Gen. (and later Gen.) Roy S. Geiger, who commanded the III Amphibious Corps, "the most vicious and stubbornly contested battle of the war," according to Gen. Clifton B. Cates, who also commanded the Marine Corps.

"Most of the enemy garrison on Peleliu died," Sledge wrote. "Only a few were captured. Estimates as to the exact losses by the Japanese vary somewhat, but conservatively, 10,900 Japanese soldiers died and 302 became prisoners. Of the prisoners only seven were soldiers and twelve sailors. The remainder were laborers of other oriental extractions."[14]

The Angaur battle was smaller in scale, but no less annihilative. All the 1,286 men of the Japanese garrison (1,100 soldiers plus 186 islanders) were killed except for 36, who were taken prisoner, Funasaka among them. And how Funasaka fought! Part of the elite regiment of the Kwangtung Army uprooted from Manchuria and moved to Angaur earlier that year, Funasaka, a twenty-four-year-old sergeant, kept fighting even after the wound on his left thigh nearly put him out of action, on "a battlefield without water or food." With several more serious wounds, and with most of his comrades dead or dying, he managed to crawl close to the enemy camp, with the intent of destroying the command post with hand grenades. Only then was he spotted and shot down. When he came to, three days later, it was in the enemy field hospital on Peleliu. (By coincidence, Sledge's primary weapon was a 60mm mortar; Funasaka's was a simplified or primitive mortar.)

Altogether he had suffered twenty-three wounds all over his body. To name only the more serious, in addition to the "laceration on his left femoral region," his first wound, and "the bullet wound on the cul-de-sac on the left side of his neck" that finally felled him, he had "two penetrating bullet wounds on his left upper arm, head concussion, sprained left shoulder, bullet wound in the cul-de-sac of the left side of his abdomen." Years later, Robert E. Taylor, a US marine who took part in the battle, but by then a professor at the University of Massachusetts, wrote Funasaka a letter: "We cannot forget your brave actions at the time. All Japanese will forever be proud of you."[15]

*Screams of Heroic Souls* was "neither a novel nor a literary work nor a so-called document, but simply something that has given flesh to a scream"—a scream of someone who felt, "Those heroic souls have allowed me to live as their rapporteur," Mishima wrote in his preface. To him Funasaka, who may have killed or wounded as many as two hundred American soldiers, including three he felled with a sword, was the very embodiment of "the truth of bravery and decisiveness."[16]

In an important way, indeed, Mishima's advice that Funasaka shorten his manuscript to one third of the original may have gone against Funasaka's original intent even as it turned it into a highly readable account of a diehard's bravery and fortitude. Funasaka's purpose of writing a twelve-hundred-page narrative—extracted from three thousand pages of notes he had made from interviews with thirty survivors and surviving families, not just battle documents—was to convey the "screams" of all those soldiers who were vanquished in the face of an enemy force twenty times as large with unimaginable firepower.

Funasaka went on to write several books on Palau battles, giving one of them, published in 1977, the title *There Was No Great Principle on the Island of a 'Shattering-Like-a-Jewel' Battle*.[17] It was a strong negation of the rightwing militarists' insistence during the war that fighting and dying for the Tennō entailed the *taigi*, and that for an entire fighting unit, the larger the better, "shattering like a jewel" was the most glorious manifestation of it. The account, which was renamed *Secret: A Record of a Palau Battle* (*Hiwa Palau senki*) when it was reprinted in 2000, with the original title shunted into a subtitle, concerns 2nd Lt. Takagaki Kanji who led a sword-wielding commando unit to Garagon (Ngarchelong) Island, at the northern tip of Babeldaob, and was killed, but whose death was erased from the war records because his action was judged not to have occurred in an officially commendable fashion.

---

In June, the film *He, The Complicated One* (*Fukuzatsuna kare*) opened. It was based on Mishima's novel of the same title serialized in the women's weekly *Josei Seven*, which was, in turn, based on the life of Abe Jōji. Mishima had become acquainted with Abe around 1953 when Abe, a member of the yakuza group Andō Gumi, was working as a bouncer at a gay bar. It was largely because he was impressed by Abe's handling of a drunken gaijin that Mishima took up boxing when he thought he was ready. He decided he was unfit for the sport and gave it up after about a year, but he kept in touch with Abe. When Abe had the opportunity to write an afterword to Mishima's novel, the erstwhile bouncer wrote he was surprised to see himself accurately described, up to the age of twenty-seven, though some details were Mishima's concoctions. For example, the protagonist of the novel, Miyagi Jōji, is an airline steward popular among his female coworkers, and his uniform hides fabulous tattoos on his body. He was indeed an airline steward and, yes, he was popular among women, but he did not have tattoos.

Mishima adored yakuza. And the Andō Gumi, during its existence, had attracted a good deal of attention because its members were all stylishly dressed in gray suits and many in its top ranks were college graduates. Andō Noboru, who founded it in 1952, was not one, but he was a good-looking man and a surviving Kamikaze pilot to boot. After disbanding his group twelve years after founding it, he went on to become a popular actor and singer. In that regard, he may have benefited from a film which was based on his erstwhile henchman's life. Abe Jōji himself established his own career as a popular author.

One thing Abe recalled after Mishima's death was Mishima's phone call the night before, asking him to finish his bottle of liquor reserved at Club Misty, in Roppongi. Mishima had followed the custom known as "bottle keep." A customer has the bar he frequents keep a bottle of liquor, preferably of an expensive brand, with his name tag, for a certain period of time. The bar in Roppongi was one of the places where Mishima had kept such a bottle. As Abe recalled, the brief conversation ended like this.

"It must be brandy or whisky, sir. It won't go bad if left alone. Are you going on a long trip?"

"Yeah, I am."[18]

On the last day of that month, Mishima went to see The Beatles perform at the Budōkan, a large building for "martial arts" as the name says, and was flabbergasted to witness the reality of "Beatle mania." A large contingent of policemen had been readied for the event, including those positioned to line the inner walls of the ground floor of the building where no one was allowed to enter. The stage atop the triple-story platform was so far from where he was seated, in the third row on the second floor, that it would have required the kind of rocket that 007 carried on his back to get near the singers, Mishima mused. It was "the worst stage construction imaginable."

The frenzied screams that started as soon as The Beatles began to sing were such that they drowned out most everything. The only snatch of song he could hear was the word "yesterday." Watching young women screaming and blubbering, he thought: "These girls, unlike me, came here after going through the dormant period and the early symptoms of Beatle mania in order to have the final, severe paroxysms, so their mental preparedness is different."

"I apologize for bringing in the devout Buddhists in Vietnam for comparison," he went on with deliberate irreverence, "but these girls have come here, as it were, to have a party to set themselves on fire to commit suicide: before coming here, they pour oil on themselves, soak their bodies in it adequately, and the moment they see the time is right, strike a match themselves, so they get a quick result."

Mishima recalled his excitement during the boxing match between Harada Masahiko and Éder Jofre, the Brazilian fighter who would attain championships in two weight classes, that he had watched just a month earlier, in the same place, and had to conclude he did not feel even one-hundredth of the excitement with The Beatles. The only thing he admired was the efficient, unobtrusive ability of the police to control crowds.[19]

On July 9 and 10, he appeared as a guest in Maruyama Akihiro's charity recital and sang a song he wrote, "The Sailor Killed by Hong Kong Flowers." The song tells the story of a second mate who, falling in love with a pretty girl in Yokohama, botches his navigation task as a result of that infatuation. While he is suspended, a storm hits. Chagrined, he readies himself to stab the bouquet the girl gave him during a storm. The next day finds he had stabbed himself to death instead.[20]

## *Men of the Divine Wind*

On August 28, two months after the "2.26 Incident trilogy" appeared, Mishima went to Kumamoto to "grasp the spirit of the Shinpūren"[21] whose revolt occurred there, in October 1876. In *The Runaway Horse*, he planned to give the pivotal role to the revolt. It was to provide the spiritual backbone to the eighteen-year-old terrorist Iinuma Isao, the protagonist of the second volume in the tetralogy and the reincarnation of the aristocrat Matsugae Kiyoaki, the protagonist of *Spring Snow*. As part of his preparations for the novel, Mishima went to see the Saegusa Festival, at Isagawa Shrine, in Nara, in mid-June, and returned to the ancient city, this time with Donald Keene, to visit the Ōmiwa Shrine and stayed in the mythical compound for three nights.[22] It is during the dedicatory kendō contest at the Ōmiwa Shrine that Honda Shigekuni, through whom the four novels unfold, becomes acquainted with Iinuma.

The Shinpūren Revolt was perhaps the most singular among the samurai uprisings that occurred as the Meiji government set out to do its work.

The movement to replace the Tokugawa shogunate with a Tennō-led government came into being as a result of the convergence of two basic factors. One was the sense, which was historically always present, that the Tennō was the legitimate ruler of Japan; after all, *shōgun*, "general," was the title the Tennō bestowed upon his or her top military commander, and the military houses that established government from the twelfth century onward coveted the title. The other was the anxiety over the Tokugawa shogunate's inability to deal with the growing foreign menace as expansionist England, France, Russia, and United States reached the Japanese Archipelago.

After Commodore Matthew Perry forced Japan to open itself, in 1854, these two political ideals, expressed as "Revere the Tennō" and "Expel the Barbarians," came to the fore. Naturally, two counter ideals also emerged: *sabaku*, "Help the Tokugawa Government," and *kaikoku*, "Open the Country." These four ideals made shifting combinations to create "a derby" among them, as Mishima jokingly put it,[23] producing some ironic results. In the end, those who advocated restoring the Tennō as ruler and opening the country won.

But the new, Meiji regime born as a result took some missteps. One that would lead to the Shinpūren Revolt was a double policy reversal. On the day it issued the Charter Oath, with the last of its five articles urging the people to seek knowledge throughout the world, the new regime reinstituted the strict ban on Christianity, the one international policy, as it were, that the isolationist Tokugawa shogunate had rigorously enforced until it abolished it in 1857, three years after the agreement with the American emissary, Matthew Perry.

At about the same time, it put Shinto at the top of governance; like Christianity it was a heresy to the Confucian Tokugawa shogunate that had officially regarded Shintoism as no more than a mumbo-jumbo concocted by Urabe (Yoshida) Kanetomo (1435–1511).[24]

These developments were glad tidings to those who yearned to return to the classical era when pristine Shinto was imagined to have prevailed. But the government soon abandoned the two measures, the one on Christianity because of foreign pressure, the one on Shinto because of its incompatibility with the urgent need to import and adopt modern technologies. The reversal was naturally a crushing blow to fervent believers in classicism, many of them samurai.[25]

Samurai suffered another—this one, fatal because economic—blow. The new government sharply downgraded their status first by cutting back on their entitlements, such as guaranteed income. Then, in the name of Westernization, it forbade them to carry the sword, the soul of the samurai, and ordered them to shed their traditional hairdo. Many of the samurai revolts that followed reflected outrage on their radically changed status. The Satsuma Rebellion, from February to September 1877, led by Saigō Takamori, one of the prime creators of the Meiji government, was the largest.[26] The Shinpūren Revolt, in October 1876, was among the smallest but was, as noted, singular.

"The people in the important positions in the present government destroyed the Tokugawa Dynasty by advocating isolationism and expulsion of aliens," one nationalist writer born a few years before the start of the Meiji regime summed up. "It was for that reason that the heroic men of Shinpūren sacrificed themselves, accomplishing whatever little they could."

Yet, once those advocates took over the governance, "they in no time forgot their former words and followed the policy of opening the country far more servile than the Tokugawa government." Even more intolerably, they were "adopting the aliens' sartorial rules and imitating the aliens' foods." If such men were allowed to continue like this, "the aliens would take over the Divine Nation within ten years."[27]

The 170 men who formed the group were absolute believers in the Shinto divinity of the Tennō and dedicated followers of the method of divination called *ukei*. Indeed, the real name of the group was Keishintō, "respect-[Shinto]-deity-faction." Shinpūren, "men of the divine wind," was the label they received because of the members' excessive belief in Shinto. The label has since stuck.

These men rebelled against Westernization in no ordinary fashion. Some refused to touch the paper money the government issued as a European way of doing things; when they *had* to handle banknotes, they used chopsticks—as people would cremated bones. Some refused to walk under the telegraph lines as equally despicable; when they could not avoid doing so, they held up a white fan over their heads.[28] The telegraph, along with the railroad and lighthouses, was one of the modern technological advances the government began to promote, in 1870, as among its top priorities in Japan's industrialization. Some sprinkled salt, for purification, when they came across someone in Western clothes.

The divination method *ukei* that Ōtaguro Tomoo, the leader of the Shinpūren, followed had ancient origins. In standard Shinto rites, the officiator sways back and forth a *mitegura*, a wooden stick adorned with several pieces of white paper, to call forth a deity. *Ukei*, in addition to the *mitegura*, required the use of four pieces of paper crumpled into balls and placed on a ceremonial tray: written on one of them is "yes" on the matter on which you are asking for divine judgment; on the three others, "no." The diviner, after swaying the *mitegura*, lightly drags it across the tray. If the crumpled paper that sticks to the paper pieces of the *mitegura* says "yes," you take the action you have in mind; if "no," you don't. Thus the chance of your getting "yes" is one out of four.[29]

Ōtaguro, the officiator at the Shingai Shrine, and his comrades, many of them the officiators of other shrines themselves, had not completely ignored rational elements. Ever since they hatched the idea of a revolt, he had conducted *ukei* from time to time. Once he had done so when he saw an opportunity he could not overlook. Two years earlier, in February 1874, a group of samurai in Saga had revolted and a large contingent of soldiers was dispatched from the Kumamoto Castle—the forbidding fort of the Hosokawa fiefdom that had been turned into one of the government's outlying "pacification bases"—to suppress them, leaving only about two hundred men behind. Saga is just about forty-four miles north of Kumamoto as the crow flies. When he heard about it, Ōtaguro took ablutions, clapped his hands, and conducted *ukei*. His comrades watched him closely, with bated breath. But he drew "no." The revolt was cancelled.

When they did revolt, and mounted a night raid on the Kumamoto Castle, the men stuck to what they believed to be ancient ways. They employed only traditional weapons, such as swords, spears, and halberds. (One member suggested the use of guns but was overruled.) The two thousand soldiers guarding the fort equipped with modern weapons were taken by surprise but in no time regrouped and smashed the rebels. The ancient armor made of cloth and wood pieces that some donned, which provided little protection against arrows, was of no use. In the end 123 of them were killed or, wounded, committed suicide. Among them were teenagers.

The leader of the Saga Revolt, incidentally, was Etō Shinpei, another enabler of the Meiji Restoration who helped to establish Japan's modern judiciary system. The central government, uneasy about the mounting discontent in Kyūshū, of which Saga is a part, reacted swiftly with an overwhelming force and quashed the revolt in no time. Etō was captured in March while fleeing, hastily tried in April, and beheaded. He was posthumously pardoned in 1919, on the occasion of the engagement of a Korean prince to a Japanese princess.

---

In Kumamoto lived the greatest local authority on the Shinpūren: Araki Seishi. Araki had also known Hasuda Zenmei in his youth. To meet him, Mishima asked Shimizu Fumio to write a letter of introduction.[30]

Araki had tried to carry out, two days after Japan surrendered, something similar to what the Shinpūren had seventy years earlier. He formed a group of about three hundred diehards that counted among them military officers, junior high school students, and housewives, named it *sonnō giyūgun*, "a volunteer army upholding the Tennō," and barricaded himself with them in the Fujisaki Hachiman, Kumamoto's main shrine. They raised a banner saying "I alone will remain unsullied in heaven and earth," a resolve attributed to Wake no Kiyomaro, of the eighth century, when he managed to thwart a Buddhist monk's attempt to usurp the throne. Their vow was to fight with the expected occupation forces to the last man, Deity willing.

On that occasion, Araki and Iwashita, the chief officiator of the Fujisaki Hachiman, took on the role of ascertaining the divine will. The judgment, which Araki announced with great excitement as he jumped down from the altar with foam in his mouth, turned out to be that the resistance of the kind they wanted to pursue would go against the divine will and "trouble His Majesty's mind." So they called it off, with only Araki and Iwashita to disembowel themselves. But the two did not carry out their own pledge, either—a turn of events that in retrospect appears more comic than tragic. (Mishima recognized it as what it was. In a letter thanking Araki later for sending him his own account of the event, he wrote he had not asked him about it earlier because he thought it would be "rude."[31])

Still, Araki had gone on to become a weighty local cultural asset whose presence was deemed indispensable to any important event, with the sobriquet "Lord Higo"—Higo being the old name of the region. He edited and published a magazine, *Nihon Dangi*.[32] As it happened, Fukushima Jirō, fifteen years earlier a naïve university student who visited

Mishima on impulse to learn the whereabouts of a gay bar described in *Forbidden Colors*, was now Araki's close literary associate and a prize-winning writer. In fact, he had renewed his friendship with Mishima when he won a prize for his novel, in 1961. So it was he, with Araki, who met Mishima at Kumamoto Station, past five on the afternoon of August 27, 1966.

Mishima emerged from the train in a white half-sleeve shirt and white slacks, his head close-cropped. He looked like "a member of a high-school gymnastic team on a summer training camp." He carried two enormous trunks. On their way to the parking lot, Fukushima offered to carry one of them, but Mishima declined, saying carrying them was good for his arms.

The three went to the hotel, named Castle, in English. Mishima chatted with Araki in the lounge, and, after Araki left, invited Fukushima to his room. He stripped down, leaving only the white *fundoshi*, the traditional loincloth made of a sash six feet or longer, proudly revealing a well-tanned, muscular body.[33] "There was no longer a smidgen of that bodily fragility of fifteen years ago, like a bird trembling right after its feathers to protect its entire body have all been plucked off." He turned his back and urged Fukushima to grab his haunch. He then told him that you had to work really hard to make your buttock muscles so firm. The two made love, but again the younger man found the result unsatisfactory.[34]

Fukushima remained Mishima's companion and guide during his stay in Kumamoto, to the last day of August. If he was embarrassed to find Mishima more knowledgeable about certain specifics of his own city than he was, he was amazed that Mishima, the great celebrity who had told him that he intended to carry out this trip incognito, had some media people planted at some strategic points. He also dressed in such flashy fashion he could only attract attention in the generally staid neighborhoods of Kumamoto.[35]

On the evening of the second day in Kumamoto, Mishima invited Araki, along with Hasuda Zenmei's widow, Toshiko, to an old-style restaurant. The two others he invited were Fukushima and, apparently at Araki's suggestion, a professor who had served as one of the directors of a powerful "patriotic" speech-censorship organization in the last phase of the war.

The next day, when Araki offered to take him to the Shingai Shrine,

Mishima courteously declined, saying he would like to savor quietly the nature of Kumamoto with which the Shinpūren men were familiar. This impressed Araki as much as Mishima's erudition on the Shinpūren. During the talk at the restaurant the previous night, Araki had found that Mishima evidently had read all the books on the subject he knew, despite the self-deprecation before the meeting that he "hadn't studied the matter well enough."[36]

Ōtaguro Yasukuni, the officiator of the Shingai Shrine, remembered Mishima's visit on August 29 very well. It was very hot, with cicadas shrilling away. Mishima, who came alone, stayed for about an hour. The shrine is a secluded island in the middle of a farmland crisscrossed by asphalt roads, with houses dotting the landscape. A number of large camphor trees five hundred years or so old block the sky, overshadowing whatever is underneath their foliage. Both the main shrine and the prayer shrine are modest. Most things appear to remain the same as they must have been when they were built in the early Edo Period.

"Mr. Mishima kept saying that the Shinpūren men were great people," Araki later wrote. "Their way of thinking was the most Japanese in all Japan, so was their action, he said. He was drawn to the Shinpūren, he explained, because he came upon it while thinking about what in Japan might correspond to the spirit of resistance symbolized by Gandhi's spinning wheel. He said he *had* to take up the group as a way of contemplating Japan."[37] Mahatma Gandhi turned to the primitive spinning wheel as a symbolic act of fighting the machine-woven clothing flooding India.

Mishima went to Kumamoto to feel what the area was like. He had formed the idea of what the Shinpūren meant to him a few months before making the trip. In a book-length, seven-part taidan with Hayashi Fusao on "the true nature of the Japanese"—the subject that perennially fascinates the Japanese—he had boiled down the question to: What can the Japanese do to fight the West without using Western weapons? His own answer: the Shinpūren. Why?

It was "the thoroughness of thought," he explained. "When thought emerges as an action, something impure is sure to come in. Tactics are bound to come in, and with it human betrayal....With the Shinpūren, it wasn't that you could choose any means to an end, but the means was equal to the end, the end was equal to the means," he went on.

"Everything was left to the divine will, so there could not have been any schism between the end and the means as there is in every political movement. It's the same as form and content in art, I'd say. I think therein lay the most original, in a way, the most *fanatic* experiment in purity of the Japanese spirit." In another taidan with Hayashi three years later, while discussing the differences between the modern rightwing and leftwing, Mishima asserted that what mattered was not "theory" but "sincerity."[38]

Before leaving Kumamoto, Mishima purchased an old sword at an antique shop. He did not imagine he would soon receive a sword of a distinguished pedigree. He also bought twenty sword guards—apparently for his friends in kendō. He was a generous gift-giver. (For Araki, he had brought a German-made, battery-powered timepiece of ultra-modern design. Shorn of decorative elements, it was about five inches in diameter and very thin and had only long and short gold-coated hands against the dark gray dial.) Back in his hotel room with Fukushima, he stripped naked, except for the white fundoshi, put on a headband, and brandished the sword intensely.[39]

In his letter to Araki thanking him, Mishima wrote that the "unexpected effect" of visiting Kumamoto was the discovery that the region was his "hometown as a Japanese," even though he had no one in his family from there; he felt he had been "*heimatlos* for a long time." He used the word "hometown" (*furusato*) in the Japanese sense of where all the sentiments and feelings that make up one's being originate. He also wrote: "It seems to me that the Shinpūren has brought about one transformation in my intellectual history." In his letter to him three years later, he enclosed a copy of the article he wrote on the Shinpūren at the request of the *London Times*.[40]

Out of what he learned from Araki's writings and others on the subject, including the petition on the sword ban that Kaya Harukata wrote, which he found at a dealer of old books, Mishima wrote up a nonfiction account of the Shinpūren and inserted it into *The Runaway Horse* as a drama within a drama. That is the booklet entitled "The Historical Account of the Shinpūren" that Iinuma Isao recommends to the men he truly trusts. He wants to "create the Shinpūren of Shōwa."

Not that Iinuma as a terrorist follows anything like *ukei* in pursuing and killing the *éminence grise* or "the pope" of the financial world Kurahara Busuke. When he learns from a special notice in a newspaper, "How Political and Financial Leaders Spend Their Year-End and New Year," that Kurahara is in his villa in Atami, Iinuma decides to seize the opportunity. By then he also knows Kurahara is not the kind of man who guards his life. His action is impulsive only in so far as he heads to the financier's villa after learning the man committed a sacrilegious act: during a Shinto rite he inadvertently sat on a *mitegura*.

In Kurahara Busuke, Mishima drew the essence of the bureaucratic mind, at least as it has manifested itself in Japan. In the novel he is not a bureaucrat, but when a young, feisty viscount asks him during a dinner party, "What is the people's ultimate happiness?" Kurahara answers, "It's the stability of the currency." He goes on to point out: "The economy is not an eleemosynary enterprise, so we can't help sacrificing about 10 percent of the populace. That way we can be sure to save the remaining 90 percent. If you leave them alone, 100 percent of them will happily destroy themselves."

Ikeda Hayato, the then Prime Minister Satō Eisaku's immediate predecessor in that position, had won notoriety for his "misstatements" not long after Japan's defeat. In one, he suggested that the poor should be content to eat wheat—in a country where wheat is considered much inferior to rice. He was then serving both as minister of international trade and industry and as minister of finance, and the statement created an uproar. In another, he stated that in an economic readjustment you couldn't avoid some small businesses going bankrupt and some of their owners committing suicide. For this statement, he received a vote of no confidence that forced him to resign.[41]

Kurahara is by no means a coldhearted man, as Mishima takes care to depict. He is merely insightful and influential in economic matters. It is for that very reason, however, that the simpleminded, hot-blooded Iinuma regards him as the source of all social ills. Still, Iinuma's aim lies elsewhere. A university student accomplished in kendō, Iinuma insists that the Shinpūren revolt was not a failure when Lt. Hori, the army officer he admires, suggests it was. When Hori asks, "Well, then, what is your faith?" Iinuma does not hesitate but says simply: "The sword." Hori asks, "All right. Let me ask you, then. What do you desire the most?" Iinuma hesitates somewhat, but says: "The sun... at sunup, at the top of a cliff, looking at the rising sun ... looking down at the brilliant sea, by the trunk of a noble pine tree ... to kill myself with a sword."

That is what he does as soon as he assassinates Kurahara, though he does so in the darkness of the moonless night, not at sunup as he had hoped it would be.

---

Late that fall Mishima received a letter from a man identifying himself as a former officer in the army medical corps who examined the corpses of Lt. Aoshima Kenkichi and his wife after they killed themselves, during the 2.26 Incident. The letter-writer, Kawaguchi Ryōhei, said he decided to write because he had just read "Yūkoku." "Having little medical knowledge," Mishima promptly wrote back, "I had a hard time describing the lieutenant's death in my story "Yūkoku." To prepare for revision in the future, I would greatly profit should you be kind enough to write down for me the detailed clinical process to death after the seppuku you inspected, as well as the manifestations of pain."[42] Kawaguchi gave a detailed response; soon after Mishima's death, he published an article in a magazine, "I Taught Mishima How to Do Seppuku."

Mishima wrote Kawaguchi on November 1. On November 11, the Tennō and his spouse held a garden party. Mishima and Yōko were among the guests. If he had an opportunity to speak to the Tennō, Mishima does not seem to have left any writing on it.

---

For a month starting on November 19, Mishima's stage extravaganza *The Arabian Nights* was produced at the Nissay Theatre. Kitaōji Kin'ya, who had just debuted as a film actor and the second son of the good-looking kabuki-actor-turned film actor Ichikawa Utaemon, played the lead role of Sindbad. Mishima appeared on the stage as "the poet's slave" a couple of times. Mishima would write *The Terrace of the Leper King*, based on the Cambodian king Jayavarman VII, with Kitaōji in mind. His youth and beauty impressed him.

That fall, when *Screams of Heroic Souls* came out, Funasaka Hiroshi told Mishima he'd like to give him a sword as a token of gratitude. He collected swords. Mishima declined a number of times but Funasaka persisted, and finally managed to invite him to his house. When he took out two swords of Seki no Magoroku make, Mishima examined them according to form. He became mesmerized.

Seki no Magoroku refers to the generations of swordsmiths of Seki, in Mino (today's Gifu), from the early sixteenth century onward. The swords made by the first generation, Kaneko Magoroku Kanemoto, and the second are highly prized. The two Funasaka showed Mishima— one, 2.34 feet long, the other a littler shorter—were of later generations, but both were certified as "very valuable." In the end Mishima accepted the longer one. Its cutting edge was chipped a little near the sword-guard, suggesting its use in actual combat.[43] He later turned it into a *guntō*, "military sword," to be carried à la saber. It was this sword that he took to the Eastern Ground Self-Defense Force Headquarters, on November 25, 1970.

Nakamura Taisaburō, who owned the sword before selling it to Funasaka, was the "supreme master" of the Toyama School of iaidō that was developed by the Japanese Army in the 1920s by combining the expertise of several schools for modern hand-to-hand combat. The school almost died out with the demise of the army. After the Self-Defense Forces came into being, however, some took it up, thereby reviving it.

Nakamura taught Mishima kendō a few times, but it was with Funasaka's son, Yoshio, of the Ōmori School, that Mishima studied iaidō—which, Funasaka stressed, entails the move for *kaishaku*, seconding someone disemboweling himself to behead him, an act "indispensable to the last moment of a samurai." Of the twelve forms that make up the Ōmori School iaidō, the seventh was *kaishaku*, and Mishima was particularly intent on mastering it, Yoshio recalled. In the spring of 1967, when he took a demonstration test after a year's training and was accorded one dan, Mishima, ever a man of perfect manners, sent Yoshio a present of expensive fabric from Eikoku-ya, "the English Shop," of the Ginza.

Funasaka would later be chagrined to reflect that he, the father, gave Mishima a sword and, Yoshio, the son, taught him how to use it to have himself beheaded.[44]

## *Mishima and Kendō*

This may be a good place to see how well Mishima did in the sports he took up.

In kendō he was initially regarded as too clumsy, and he never seems to have attained agility. His wrists were too stiff, either innately, from writing constantly, weightlifting, or for some other reason, and he was unable to correct the problem.[45] As a result, he never learned to move quickly enough to hit the opponent's wrist. But he made steady progress in acquiring dan. He was awarded one dan in April 1961, two in 1963, four in May 1966, and five in August 1968. When the International Kendō Championship was held in April 1969, he took part in it. He had a draw with a kendōka from Taiwan.

Mishima started training in iaidō, the art of drawing the sword in a sitting position, in November 1966, and was awarded one dan in February 1967, two in December 1969. He began karate in February 1967 and was awarded one dan in June 1970. In these sports the greater the number of dan, the higher the rank. The ranks range from one to ten, eight to ten being honorary.

Still, awarding dan in these sports, unlike measuring the time required to run a certain distance or the amount of weight lifted, is subjective. As a result, the suspicion persisted that Mishima got all the dan as "honorary" or celebrity privilege. Shiine Yamato, the brash twenty-six-year-old when assigned to the irreverant weekly *Heibon Punch* in the spring of 1968, decided to find out. He interviewed the kendōka who actually had faced Mishima in practice and training sessions, starting with Yoshikawa Masami, the seven-dan police instructor whom Mishima admired and followed wherever he could. But no one seemed willing to give a straight answer, until an instructor at the Tokyo Metropolitan Police Department who also held seven dan, said, "It's not whether Mr. Mishima is good at it or not; his is a spiritually strong 'sword style.' He grasps the essence of the matter. He will be real five-dan in three years. Spiritually, he's more than five-dan, though."

As soon as the issue of the weekly came out with his article with the heading, "A Real Five-dan in Three Years," Shiine had a phone call from Mishima. He expected fully to receive a tongue-lashing. Instead, Mishima, without saying a word on the article, suggested he train in kendō with him. So Shiine ended up doing just that, buying all the necessary kendō gear and training with him.[46]

Some years later and in a different setting, one blunt answer came from Mishima's former upperclassman at Peers School, then director of New Year's Tanka Recitation at the Imperial Palace: Akita Kazusue. A natural at kendō while a student who later headed his alma mater's Kendō Club, he was also an important figure in the publishing field and a friend of Mishima's. After Mishima's death, Bōjō Toshitami had occasion to ask him, "Wasn't Mishima clumsy at kendō?" Akita was tall, skinny, and dark, yet was apparently the model for the kendō instructor in Mishima's short story, "The Sword," who looks exactly the opposite. He answered: "That's an understatement. I wouldn't give him one dan, let alone three, I told him."

At that, Bōjō had an epiphany: Mishima chose certain sports to pursue, knowing full well he was clumsy at them. That was his way of facing the world.[47]

CHAPTER TWENTY-ONE

# "The Way of the Warrior is to die"

> *Death can become an object of blind ardor, of a hunger like that of love . . . this unsung battle against emptiness, barrenness, fatigue, and the disgust for existing which brings on a craving for death.*
>
> —Marguerite Yourcenar, *Memoirs of Hadrian*

On the "dark, rainy, wintry afternoon," of December 19, 1966, just after he finished writing the first installment of *The Runaway Horse*, Mishima had what would prove to be a fateful visit—"an incident that caused a revolutionary change" in him or, as he put it to Kojima Chikako, the Shinchō editor assigned to him: "It's, like, scary. What you've written as fiction emerges as fact. Or, the other way round: fact sometimes precedes fiction."[1]

The visitor was a young man who came to see him through Hayashi Fusao's introduction: Bandai Kiyoshi. Bandai was on the editorial staff of the new *Ronsō Journal*, "controversy journal." He, along with the magazine's editor-in-chief, Nakatsuji Kazuhiko, had found employment after graduating from Meiji Gakuin University, but both had soon quit, hoping to start a magazine for the Minzoku-ha. This school of thought had newly emerged out of *minzokushugi*, "nationalism,"[2] but had a strong dose of antimodern sentiments, with an affinity to *kōkoku shikan*, which interprets Japanese history with the Tennō as its center.

Nakatsuji and Bandai, who wanted their magazine to be a vehicle for views that, while based on Hiraizumi's stance, went beyond it—views conveying "sound conservatism," as they put it—sought and found a sponsor for their publishing venture. But all the contributors they had been able to recruit till then were minor writers who were known for their patently "hawkish" views but little else. They wanted a contributor of considerable repute who would appeal to the general reader. By then the American terms "hawks" and "doves" had become part of Japanese political jargon.

At the time, students movements were dominated by leftists. Many who took part in them or were sympathetic to them included the bright, articulate, and well read. They could sprinkle their arguments not just with quotations from Marx and Lenin, but also with references to modern European writers such as Sartre and Camus, even Radiguet. The students of rightist inclinations, in contrast, tended to be less articulate, unable as they were to cite a range of thinkers freely, let alone foreign ones, and they were afraid that, even if they tried to do so, they would lose in debate with those of leftist leanings.

But it was Bandai's very inarticulateness that stirred Mishima as no other young man ever had. As he heard the laconic young man explain, haltingly, how he found some likeminded young men who agreed to do something about the need to "rectify the distortions in Japan" but were struggling, Mishima found himself "moved"—was surprised at himself reacting in such fashion, far more than by what Bandai had to say, as he wrote for the *Ronsō Journal* ten months after their encounter.[3] He saw in Bandai a phantom of the Shinpūren. He promised the visitor he would do whatever he could for the journal. And he did, beginning with the magazine's inaugural January 1967 issue.

Still, it was not Bandai but another young man who, encouraged by Bandai, came to see him, that would play a crucial role in helping Mishima create his own version of the Shinpūren, Tate no Kai, "the Shield Society":[4] Mochimaru Hiroshi. A student at Waseda University, Mochimaru was executive director of the Japanese Students Alliance—Nihon Gakusei Dōmei or Nichigakudō, for short—only recently formed out of frustration with the leftist domination of student bodies or, as its founders put it, for "the normalization of Waseda."

The formation of Nichigakudō had strong backing from Waseda's Oratorical Society, some of whose members would go on to occupy prominent positions in the Liberal Democratic Party. Among them were three prime ministers: Kaifu Toshiki, 1989–1990; Obuchi Keizō, 1998–2000; and Mori Yoshirō, April to July 2000. One might add to the list Tamazawa Tokuichirō, director-general of the Defense Agency, 1994–95. This indicates the existence of a strong conservative current despite the outward dominance of radical students in those years.

Mochimaru, at any rate, was planning to launch a student paper for the Minzoku-ha. Unlike Bandai, he had leadership qualities, an ability to express himself logically, articulately, and an ability to organize things and execute plans effectively. He would go on to become Mishima's informal aide-de-camp.

Mishima contributed a congratulatory article, "For the True Voice of Youth," to the inaugural issue of Mochimaru's *Nihon Gakusei Shinbun* that came out in February 1967. In it, though, he had to add a writerly point: "The abstruseness of the prose of student newspapers utterly confounds me. Their prose is difficult to understand not because it is profound. Its difficulty results from people writing things they don't understand, feigning they do. I want you to talk only about the thought you have firmly grasped with your hands, in lucid words, in clear language. Prose so written is the true 'voice of youth.'"[5]

In April 1967 Mishima had yet another occasion to deal with "heroic souls." For a new recording company's venture called Poemusica, he recited a poem accompanied by music.[6] The poem, *Heaven and the Sea: Seventy-Two Chapters Dedicated to the Heroic Souls*, was by Asano Akira, and the music by Yamamoto Naozumi. Asano, a survivor of the Battle of Sunda Strait, in 1942,[7] wrote the elegy, a sequence in simple words and images, for all the Japanese soldiers killed in subsequent battles in the South Seas. Mishima called it, with more than a touch of hyperbole, "a lyric that is at the same time an epic, a single poet's work that is at the same time a national work, a modern poem that is a classic poem that immediately leads to the *Man'yōshū*," which, with "its immense ability to move you and in the depth of its lamentation, matches Greek tragedies, for example, Aeschylus's *The Persians*."[8]

Three years earlier, Mishima had taken up Asano's 1963 book of poetry *Cold Color* (*Kanshoku*), the winner of the Yomiuri Bungaku Prize, while serializing his observations on various arts in *Geijutsu Seikatsu*, and praised its beauty as lying in expressing "fury cleansed of all political character."⁹ Like many bright young men in the 1920s and 1930s, Asano had shifted his political stance. He had studied French law and public finance at the Imperial University of Tokyo and, in 1926, joined the Japan Communist Party. He almost made it as a member of its Central Committee but in 1928 was arrested and jailed, for two years. While on parole, he read Schopenhauer's book *The World as Will and Representation* and decided to part company with Marxism. He became a follower of the Japan Romantic School and turned himself into a prolific critic advocating radical nationalism until Japan's defeat. It was in fact while he was part of the army's propaganda unit attached to its Expeditionary Force that his ship was sunk.

A week after the recording, Mishima began training with the Ground Self-Defense Force (GSDF) or what would normally be called the army.

## *Experiencing the Military*

The Self-Defense Forces (SDF) are an anomalous military. The United States famously made Japan declare, in Article 9 of the Constitution, that the country shall never maintain any "war potential." It was a chunk of idealism dreamed up following the furies of war and imposed on a country regarded as a historical aberration, a particularly belligerent nation. Helen Mears, a member of the US labor advisory committee for Japan soon after the country's defeat, penned a polemic against that view, *Mirror for Americans: Japan*, "as a full-scale critic of American policy in Asia." The Occupation's response was to ban the publication of its Japanese translation.[10]

Sure enough, the United States had to reverse its "no-war" stance in a few years and forced Japan to build armed forces, as we have seen. The result, the SDF, was not to be a military because of the Constitution. This pretense was accomplished partly by turning the Japanese word *gun*, meaning "military" or "armed," into "a taboo," as Mishima pointed out.[11] Overt or covert linguistic tricks were deployed to deny the existence of anything military.

None of the terms *rikugun*, "army," *kaigun*, "navy," and *kūgun*, "air force" was employed. Instead, the three service branches were separated by the words *rikujō*, "ground," *kaijō*, "maritime," and *kōkū*, "air," with no suggestion of "military." The word *hei*, "soldier," was shunned, too, in favor of *taiin*, "unit member." The word *hohei*, "foot soldier," was replaced by *futsū*, "regular." Likewise, a whole new nomenclature was devised for the military ranks. These linguistic sleights-of-hand have been successful; there is an amorphous sense among the Japanese that the SDF or any of its three "defense forces" is *not* "military." The SDF calls the act of any non-SDF person, such as Mishima, who join it to have a taste of it for a limited period *taiken nyūtai*, "joining the unit for actual experience," not *guntai taiken*, "military experience."¹²

Mishima had started plotting for training with the GSDF soon after his return from Kumamoto. He knew the GSDF would not easily accept his request, and pulled strings. He discussed it with an executive at *Sunday Mainichi*, a retired lieutenant general, and the second in command at the Defense Agency, among others.¹³ Itō Keiichi, then director of public affairs at the agency, recalled how Mishima's request confounded his higher-ups.

"Almost all such requests came from companies that wanted to have their new employees experience life with us for a couple of days," Itō said. "So we were surprised to receive a request for half a year. Those in the upper echelon said that would be too much even if they were to make an exception. In the end, the compromise was struck that we'd accept him at several bases, for the maximum of two weeks at each." The SDF did not want to be accused of providing a training ground for revolutionists and terrorists—or rightwingers.¹⁴

So, starting on April 12, and ending on May 27, 1967, Mishima was attached to three different units: the Officer Candidate School, in Kurume, Fukuoka; the Regular Division of the Fuji School at Camp Takigahara, Shizuoka, on the outskirts of Mt. Fuji, where he took the Advanced Officer Course and trained as a *ranger* (the term directly adopted from the US Army); and the Parachute Division, in Narashino, Chiba.

His participation was kept secret, because, Mishima explained in his account "Actually Experiencing the SDF,"¹⁵ the Defense Agency wanted it that way while Mishima himself wanted to be exposed to military life just as it was, with no special treatment. Luckily, many of those he mingled with did not recognize him—or those who did treated him as a regular fellow. He was given no rank, so a couple of officers, apparently unaware of the arrangement, barked at him, "Where in hell is your insignia!"

In the Officer Candidate School, which combines the practices of Japan's old Military Academy and West Point in devising tight, detailed schedules for each day, Mishima had a taste of standard clothes inspection. "Without advance notice, they conduct uniform inspections at morning roll call," he wrote. "If they find something amiss, you must do ten pushups to reexamine your conduct. That's their custom. They found one button on my chest unhooked, too, and I had to do ten pushups."

One thing he noticed was the use of the Japanese language. The school accepts both graduates of the National Defense Academy and graduates of regular colleges. Those from regular colleges were evidently finding it hard to use the imperative mood in telling a fellow candidate to do something as required. As he heard a student inspector correct some students who had used polite language, Mishima realized how narrow the range of usage for command forms in Japanese was.

At the Fuji School, where he stayed the longest, he learned to drive a tank (though he refused to learn to drive the car he owned; his wife drove it), marched and bivouacked with soldiers of the artillery unit, took a class on tactics, and trained as a ranger.

"Tactics is the one *esoteric*"—his English—"field of study that has been regarded since [Japan's] former military as that which sharply distinguishes between officer and ordinary soldier," he wrote. "The only fields of study that have ever interested me are criminal lawsuits and tactics." As to the training as a ranger, he was honest. "At the 'sailor crossing' in which you cross a valley on a single rope put up between two cliffs, with a mountain stream down below, I failed a number of times, until finally I managed to do it more or less. As these things continued, my fatigue accumulated day by day, and I began to quail, though I hate to concede defeat." At the Parachute Division, he had permission not to do parachuting for fear of head concussion, though he jumped twice from the thirty-three-foot tower.

At the "mammoth school," he found that, "by some strange fate," the barracks were exactly the ones where he had stayed during the school field maneuvers more than two dozen years earlier. But there were differences. "Since the US Army used them, the walls were all painted green, and flush toilets were installed, so there was none of the toilet smell that had once pervaded the place all day. There was also no hint of bedbugs, several of which used to sprinkle down from your pillow when you shook it."

Out on the maneuvering grounds one day, he thought he recognized a friend. "In the field that developed a Renaissance-style landscape as the evening settled in . . . I saw a farmer sowing seeds from time to time, indifferently. I felt he was Mr. Fukazawa Shichirō. He works as a peasant, I'm walking nearby in steel helmet. Though both are in temporary costumes, now a thousand miles separate us!"

Even for someone who follows a more or less standard daily routine, it would be hard to go through the kind of physical training to which Mishima was subjected. But Mishima was a writer with a socially and artistically dizzying schedule, who, in addition, followed the daily regimen of writing and reading from around midnight to the crack of dawn, sleeping until past noon, then going out to fulfill social, literary, athletic, and other engagements—or just to enjoy himself. Reversing this upside-down day-and-night routine alone could have brought on debilitating fatigue to a young healthy man. He was forty-two years old.

For all that, Mishima managed, without much difficulty, though with occasional permission not to do certain things and to take occasional breaks ("celebrity privileges"), to complete a well-organized program apparently made to show "all about the SDF"—or at least the GSDF part of it. The choice of that branch was his own. If Japan were attacked, it would be the one to play the most important role, he reasoned.

## *The Soldier Who Has Come Home*

While Mishima was "actually experiencing" the GSDF, the weekly *Heibon Punch* conducted a six-week-long popularity contest, "All Japan Mr. Dandy," among its readers, estimated to reach eight hundred thousand. In its May 8 issue the weekly published the result: Mishima was Number One, followed by the actor Mifune Toshirō, the film director Itami Jūzō, Ishihara Shintarō, the actor Kayama Yūzō, and so forth. Commenting on the result, Mushiake Aromu said: "Yukio Mishima has said, 'I don't want to be a dandy, and I don't think I am one, either.' But he got the highest vote. . . . This is ironic. This is exciting."[16]

Mishima's "secret" participation in military training was treated as a sensation when it came to light. The weekly *Sunday Mainichi*, an executive of whose publisher had an important hand in arranging it, naturally allocated an exceptional spread of eight pages to Mishima's own account, in its June 11 issue, and a series of questions and answers between its top-of-the-line journalist Tokuoka Takao and Mishima. The industrial daily *Nihon Sangyō Shinbun* and the weekly *Shinchō* each got some crumbs, the former a short one in which Mishima voiced his objection to companies taking advantage of the SDF by sending their employees for a brief stint, and the latter a set of several photos of Mishima in the military with the captions he provided.

Mishima's account was lyrical; he had expected certain things from military life and got them. He was elated as he answered Tokuoka's questions, "like a schoolboy who is telling how wonderful the school excursion was to a boy who couldn't make it."[17] But many of "the twenty-six questions" Tokuoka put to Mishima, "the soldier who has come home," were political, and timely.[18] The journalist did not hesitate to ask touchy questions and Mishima did not hesitate to answer them.

Above all, the question of Constitutional legitimacy that came with the birth of the SDF had not abated. Just two weeks before Mishima started training at the Officer Candidates School, a district court had handed down a decision on the Eniwa Case. In 1962 a dairy farmer in Chitose, Hokkaidō, destroyed some equipment of the GSDF, saying that the unit stationed there had engaged in artillery training without advance notification as promised. In its decision on March 29, the court avoided the Constitutional question but found the farmer not guilty on the basis of the SDF Law. In a debate in the Diet in July that year, a member of the Socialist Party referred to the Eniwa Case and cited a 1964 survey that found 88 percent of law professors considered the SDF unconstitutional or its existence questionable.

At the same time, there was growing unease about Mishima, Japan's greatest celebrity author of the day, "turning perilously rightist in recent years," as Tokuoka put it. Sugawara Kunitaka, the editor at Shinchōsha in charge of *The Runaway Horse* then being serialized and one of the few to whom Mishima had disclosed his plan in advance, was unable to hide his distress when told of it. Sensing the matter was going too far, he had pleaded with Mishima: "People who defend this country will always appear. This has been a tradition since *sakimori*"—the border guards created in the second half of the seventh century after Japan lost a war on the Korean Peninsula, in 663.

"You are an incomparable writer we cannot do without. There are many works no one else can write. Rather than have you defend this country, I would do it. Please simply write. You may not know it, but you are a genius. You are an invaluable person."[19]

In the background were the escalating Vietnam War and the rising antiwar movement. In June 1966 the United States started bombing Hanoi, declaring there were no longer "sanctuaries" in North Vietnam. In August there were huge antiwar demonstrations in San Francisco and New York. In September the American troop strength in South Vietnam reached 320,000, topping the size of that country's military forces. In April 1967 another wave of antiwar demonstrations were held in San Francisco and New York, half a million people taking part. In Japan, student movements were gathering steam, partly in anticipation of the renewal of the US-Japanese Mutual Security Treaty in three years.

Tokuoka's question on the Constitutional legitimacy of the SDF had to do with whether Mishima sensed the armed forces suffered from something akin to "the guilty conscience of someone with a shady past." The question had come to the fore as early as 1960, a mere six years after the creation of the SDF, in 1954. That year the literary critic and editor Usui Yoshimi interviewed a range of SDF personnel, from the chief of the Defense Agency to regular troops, and concluded his findings with an ominous suggestion that the sense of humiliation the 230,000 armed men suffered—that they were constitutionally invalid—might explode someday.

Usui had a particular precedent in mind: During the disarmament period following the First World War, military men were treated as social outcasts so that many refused to wear uniforms in public. One result, in his view, was the rise of the fanatical nationalism in the military in the years that followed. The 5.15 and 2.26 Incidents were partly manifestations of that nationalism.[20]

In reply, Mishima said he recognized the existence of such a sentiment in the GSDF, but added, referring to common epithets thrown at him: "I believe that in my thinking I am neither militarist nor fascist. What I hope for is simply to place a national army in its proper position as a national military." *Kokugun*, "national army," was the proper term for the Japanese military before it was abolished, in 1945.

In truth, the Japanese were not black and white on that issue. On the "renunciation of war" clause that is Article 9, Tokuoka pointed out: "There are many Japanese who think that the SDF as it is now came into being as a result of the linguistic contortion of 'the military without war potential.' On the other hand, there are also many who insist on the view, based on the idea that 'every nation has its own right for self-defense,' that the SDF is Constitutional." His question was whether Mishima's thoughts on the matter changed after he "experienced" the GSDF.

Mishima said no, his thoughts did not change. His position was that there was "no need to amend the Constitution." At the time there was the argument, as there still is, that the Constitution should be amended if the SDF were to continue to exist. Mishima said "the enormous amount of political and social energy" that such a move would require might as well be used elsewhere—a view he would reverse by late 1969. As to the Eniwa Case, Mishima spoke of the view of some within the SDF that the court should have treated the case as a Constitutional question and found the SDF unconstitutional, just to clarify the matter.

Tokuoka asked if the SDF had any independent "hypothetical enemy," which is one *raison d'être* of any military, and, if not, whether it existed to "suppress domestic riots." There surely was suspicion to that effect at the time. Not just that the US-Japanese Mutual Security Treaty subordinated Japan to the United States, or that the SDF was just a detachment of the US military, but also that, in the rising antiwar sentiment worldwide, the SDF with no "war potential" could only exist for domestic use.

"I had the impression that they are doing their best to avoid keeping any particular country in mind as a hypothetical enemy," Mishima replied. But the erstwhile law student that he was, he had to add: "When Article 3 of the SDF Law says that the SDF exists for 'self-defense in case of direct or indirect invasion,' I think 'indirect invasion' assumes nothing other than a civil war. But I felt that within the SDF there is something that prevents them from coming right out and saying that it assumes a civil war, so I told them, 'You should clearly assume a civil war.' That's because it's the only battle you can think of that the SDF is tasked to fight in the immediate future."

How about the SDF men's "view of life and death"? Tokuoka

asked. In the prewar military, "preparedness to die" (*shi no kakugo*), as Mishima put it in his response, was what every soldier was expected to have. Aside from the samurai tradition, there was the stern injunction in the 1882 Imperial Rescript to the Soldiers and Sailors (*Gunjin chokuyu*): "Be resolved that duty (*gi*) is heavier than high mountains, death lighter than a goose feather." There was also the 1941 Code of Conduct in the Battlefield (*Senjinkun*) with the fateful article that was taken to mean: "When faced with surrender, kill yourself."[21]

Mishima replied that he was generally dissatisfied with the SDF's spiritual education. "Either fearful of the reaction of the troops or fearful of the reaction of society at large," the SDF attempted "no education that might lead to a view of death and life," he explained. Still, there ought to be a clear distinction between education for regular recruits and education for officers—the former on "the pursuit of happiness, the latter on preparedness to die," he said. The famous phrase in the US Declaration of Independence was made part of Article 13 of the Japanese Constitution.

Tokuoka brought up "Voice of the Heroic Souls" and the disillusionment with "the Human Declaration" Mishima spelled out in it, and asked what was the opinion of the Tennō among the SDF people.

"There was no interest, to a surprising degree. It truly surprised me," Mishima replied. But he found even more disconcerting what he had heard: the Tennō wanted "to avoid standing by the honor guard from the SDF in welcoming a foreign emissary at Haneda"—at the time the only international airport in Japan. Mishima knew that Article 13 of the SDF Law places the Tennō at the top of those to receive the honor guard.

Wasn't his joining the SDF to "actually experience it" just another sign of Mishima's proclivity to flaunt his "eccentricity"? After all, not just boxing and bodybuilding, he had acted in his own film *Yūkoku*, and sung chansons onstage. "Tell us your apologia in advance," Tokuoka urged.

"I won't mind it at all if some say I've done it 'to show off my eccentricity,'" Mishima responded. "I always ask myself, 'Why do you want to do so many things?'"

"Are you not 'turning perilously rightist'"?

"The rightwing and the SDF are totally different matters," Mishima answered. "For example, what the rightwing is mainly concerned about is 'the Tennō,' but as I told you a moment ago, there is absolutely no 'Tennō question' in the SDF today. Those on the left call everything 'rightist-oriented,' but I'd like them to think more strictly."

## Supporting the Vietnam War

By then the United States was a "nation divided by a bloody jungle war whose beginnings are lost in controversy and whose final outcome is unpredictable," as *Newsweek* put it in issuing a Vietnam War special, timing it with the celebration of Independence Day. The magazine set aside a section for the opinions of foreign intellectuals, among them the Australian novelist Morris West, the French diplomat André François-Poncet, Kingsley Amis ("one of a tiny band of British literary figures supporting United States Vietnam policy"), C. P. Snow (recently knighted), Golo Mann (Thomas Mann's son). Mishima, "perhaps Japan's most popular novelist," was one of the three Japanese whose views were sought.

"It was America," he was quoted as saying in "A Tarnished Image Abroad," "which taught Japan the concept of democracy and freedom, but it was a very primitive, naïve concept—a feeling something like peace. And the Japanese believed this concept very honestly and simply and were shocked that America's concept of freedom and democracy could include American involvement in a distant war in Vietnam." In other words, Mishima thought the United States was "doing the right thing in Vietnam."[22]

When *Heibon Punch* got hold of this *Newsweek* special, its editors decided to make a sensation out of it, but before doing so, they talked to Mishima to confirm he said what he had. "You can take it as they put it," Mishima responded. "I'm someone who still affirms the Great East Asian War"—the Pacific War—"and I support America's Vietnam policy, too. Don't you agree? What would happen if America was defeated and withdrew?" He then added, "In this heat, I have no intention of dealing with the idiots of Beheiren."

A controversy monger by design, the weekly directly took Mishima's remarks to the anti–Vietnam War group. Kaikō Takeshi refused to respond head-on: "I'm busy; ask others, please." Konaka Yōtarō, the writer whose role was to work for international collaboration for the cause, visiting Paris, Hanoi, and Stockholm, was diplomatic: "I personally respect Mishima and am one of his admiring readers. But I'd like to think we started this anti–Vietnam War movement as idiots." Only Oda Makoto retorted sharply: "If that's what Mishima is saying, I have no time to get involved in such idiotic remarks as his." The actress Hiiro Tomoe recalled seeing Mishima in GSDF uniform on TV and said, "When I saw him like that, I questioned Mr. Mishima's existence itself," adding, "Something like that is physiologically repulsive."[23]

---

Did Mishima decide to "actually experience" military life as one concrete step on his road to death? If he did, exactly what did he have in mind? He did not do so simply to provide realism to the military life he might describe in *The Runaway Horse*, as Matsumoto Seichō suggested,[24] or did he? Mishima had fully anticipated such questions to be raised, so he dealt with them at the outset of his account of the GSDF experience—giving no real answers.

He did not mind whether other people interpreted his action "seriously or nonseriously, politically or apolitically," he wrote. The only thing he wanted to make clear was that he was "opposed to the conscription system, opposed to turning into an obligation the matter of national defense, which, by its nature, is an individual's right in any democratic country." He clearly conveyed this view within the SDF, where he was able to talk to "men in all ranks, from generals to corporals," he wrote.[25]

In fact, he had, although he had been more interested in the technical aspects of the use of the GSDF. In a lengthy interview he had conducted with Capt. Kikuchi Katsuo, his caretaker at the Fuji School, Mishima had begun by saying, "As a Japanese male, I have the honorable right to take part in national defense," and closely questioned him on "*coup d'état*, the Constitution, the deployment of the GSDF for domestic security, conscription, civilian control," and such. To Kikuchi, recalling the interview nearly four decades later, it was clear that Mishima's "true purpose of training with the GSDF" was to find out what the officer class of the army was planning to do to deal with the rising turmoil at the extension of the US-Japanese Mutual Security Treaty in 1970.[26]

Still, we may pause to ask what Mishima's "true purpose" was.

He had already begun to write what some would later call his "suicide project," and the work he took up next was to make excerpts from and comment on *Hagakure*, the large compilation of the samurai Yamamoto Tsunetomo's observations, which, as noted earlier, is famous for its opening dictum, "The way of the warrior, I've found, is to die."

But before we retrace Mishima's thoughts on death, we must look at one question that lingered: how the GSDF would continue to accept someone like Mishima in the future. It was resolved in his favor, without fanfare, in August that year, by the Office of the Chief of Staff of the GSDF (its official English name: "the Ground Staff Office"), Mishima happily reported to Capt. Kikuchi. He learned this when he went to the Defense Agency where he was also told of the elaborate procedure the GSDF had set up to prevent members of rightwing or other similar extremist organizations from getting into it.

As fate would have it, the man who met Mishima and explained the special program to him—one of the five people that made up the Ground Staff Office—was Gen. Mashita Kanetoshi.[27]

## *Thinking of Death*

In considering the trajectory of Mishima's life, many have pointed to the poem he wrote the day after he turned fifteen, "The Disaster" (*Magagoto*), as something that clearly adumbrated what would come. It begins:

> Every evening, come evening,
> I stood by the window and waited for the unexpected,
> for a ferocious sand swirl of calamity
> like a night rainbow to surge toward me
> from beyond the city streets.

And it ends:

> I wait for the disaster.
> Good news was bad news.
> Today again the forehead of the runover dead was black
> and my blood froze clotty red....[28]

This poem attracted the attention of commentators because it opened the section "Poems at Age Fifteen" when the first of nineteen volumes of Mishima's "complete works" was published, in 1957—the first time his poems saw print in that manner. In it some have detected Mishima's projection of his own "*narcissistic* death." In truth, *Bad Poems* (Mishima's English), his sixth original compilation where it was placed, has other poems that spell out a fascination with death.

In "Report of Death" (*Fuin*), for example, the barely fifteen-year-old poet compares himself waking in "a corner of a room of dusty night darkness" to "a dead person awakening in the abyss of blackened gold dust," and says, "I am not afraid of death; what I fear is eternity." It ends: "Hearing a report of a death, my heart rejoices / more than it does hearing news of a birth."[29] In another poem he imagines a suicide.

> Thanks to the antique dealer's sun
> the floral patterns on the curtain had withered,
> the furniture faded, the air
> festering yellow.
> In the old mirror wet with the air
> my face wavered flat, yellow.
> ... Soon death flew up like flies
> noisily, faintly, here and there in the room.[30]

Of course, the "calamity" in "The Disaster" may well have been "'the Holy War' in whose faith wartime boys found an opportunity for self-destruction," as Mishima put it—the war with China, before it avalanched into the larger one with the United States and others.[31] For years before the prolonged, then expanded war ended, many young men did not expect to live to twenty-five.[32] It was "with the phantom, in my head, of a nighttime air raid that was bound to come" that Mishima wrote, in February 1945, the short story that sweetly described double suicide, "Circus."[33]

By then death was everywhere. "Profuse deaths surrounded me: deaths in war disasters, deaths in the line of duty, deaths from wounds and illnesses at the front, deaths in battle, deaths from being run over by the train, deaths from illnesses," as Mishima enumerated them in describing, in *Confessions of a Mask*, how he seriously thought of committing suicide one night and decided against it because it would look "ridiculous" in the midst of deaths "like an abundant autumn harvest." Still, when he heard the news that Hiroshima was wiped out and the government said that white clothes would be effective against the "new-type bomb," he deliberately walked about wearing white clothes.[34]

"I learned it was an atomic bomb several days later, from a professor, definitely," Mishima wrote. "This is the end of the world, I thought. This eschatological view of the world has been the only foundation of my literature ever since, although it probably was not something that suddenly came into being as a result of the atomic bomb so much as something that had existed unseen in me from the outset."[35]

In his testament to "commemorate August 1945," he cited in full Lt. Wakabayashi Tōichi's homiletic poem, which we have seen, because, in arguing that life is "holy" and therefore suicide must be rejected as "a kind of spasm" and yet one must train oneself spiritually for the inevitable death, the "military deity" of Guadalcanal embodied the eschatological sense that prevailed in the period of civil disturbance of Japan's Middle Ages.[36]

The idea of suicide, double suicide, took an intense literary twist in *The Bandit*, the novel Mishima started a month or so after he learned of Mitani Kuniko's betrothal. After what he takes to be betrayal by the woman he loves, Yoshiko, the protagonist Akihide chooses another woman with whom to commit suicide. Still, initially it is suicide that he wants. "Defeated in his [quest for the] last assignation [with Yoshiko], did not Akihide single-mindedly hope for death just as a man trudging on a desert with a fierce thirst yearns for water? He must have noticed that at that instant his yearning for Yoshiko had been marvelously switched to that for death." The second chapter was originally titled "The Suicide Planner."

In the spring of 1948, Mishima wrote an essay for *Ningen*, "The Murderous Weapon of the Seriously Ill," in which he posited:

> Does suffering kill a human being?—Nay.
> Does an ideological torment kill a human being?—Nay.
> Does grief kill a human being?—Nay.
> There is only one that kills a human being in the East or the West, in ancient or modern times: "Death."

Here "the seriously ill" was his generation: those who survived the war.[37]

That June, Dazai Osamu and his mistress Yamazaki Tomie committed double suicide. When a women's magazine asked him for an essay on their deaths, Mishima responded with alacrity. But he focused on the act of double suicide itself, rather than address what the popular writer's choice of that manner of death might mean, the subject the editor had in mind. Calling his "an oddball's" view, he argued that double suicide—he used the two common words for it, "dying for love" (*jōshi*) and "proving one's heart" (*shinjū*) alternately—is a matter of form, not of spirit, that it is "an artificial form," and that, in the sense that "simultaneity" in the natural death of two persons loving each other is highly unlikely, it is "an artistic act, a creative act." In making his case, he would treat double suicide of those of different sexes as the same as that of those of the same sex "in the manner of [Otto] Weininger."

He went on: "man's darkness at its base derives from 'the unknowability of simultaneity'" and double suicide is a way of cracking that unknowability. He cited Edgar Allan Poe's story "The Assignation" as an example. In describing "double suicide that does not lose simultaneity, [with the two deaths occurring] merely in different places," the story "heightens it to the joy of holy elucidation of that unknowable mystery." Idealization, then, is inevitable to "'the simultaneous death' artificially brought on."

Yet, in the end, "double suicide has not once been understood *from inside*." In his play *Shinjū yaiba wa kōri no tsuitachi*, the master depicter of double suicide, Chikamatsu Monzaemon, could only allow Heibē to utter, "Lovely oh lovely," as he cuts his lover Kokan's throat with a razor before he cuts his own. It is because of this unknowability that people since mythological times have sought salvation in "decorating" the people who commit double suicide—as in the case of Prince Karu and Princess Sotōri.[38]

With this idea much on his mind, he went to a gathering of Matinée Poétique just about that time and posited, "If it's between a young couple, double suicide can be beautiful and should be all right, shouldn't it?," only to win round condemnation, Mishima recalled some years later.

Matinée Poétique was a group formed in 1942 by a dozen poets—mostly young, most of them readers of Western poets such as Baudelaire and Mallarmé—who wanted to remedy "the anarchic situation of hopelessly easy modern [poetry writing] in Japan"[39]—an exasperation that had arisen because outside *traditional* tanka and haiku and lyrics, free verse had long come to be equated with "modern" poems. So they wrote poems in set forms and with rhyme schemes. Some of the group, such as Nakamura Shin'ichirō and Katō Shūichi, were tough-minded men of letters, but the poems they produced were promptly laughed out of existence. As Katō noted in his memoir, the fault was with the group's idea itself: "employing contemporary Japanese as the raw material to approximate symbolist poetry, premised as it was on fin-de-siècle French."[40]

Mishima went to the gathering because he was drawn to the group's very endeavor that looked utterly "out of season" in the chaos following Japan's defeat. But he was soon put off by the group's "French odor," he wrote, if not by the criticism of his advocacy of double suicide.[41]

"I dislike human beings who commit suicide," Mishima announced in late 1954. An Akutagawa Ryūnosuke reader was planned, and he was asked to contribute an essay.

Akutagawa had killed himself at age thirty-five. Mishima explained he disliked weaklings, perhaps because he himself was "as gentle, as easily hurt, as a lamb, as a dove, lachrymose, lyrical, and sentimental." The dislike might, in that sense, be a warning against himself. He didn't like suicide in any event, because it was a manifestation of weakness. "Suicide requires a kind of courage," he admitted. "I thought of committing suicide, and I think it was simply because of my cowardice that I did not carry it out. But I can in no way respect a man of letters who commits suicide."

One such writer he cited, other than the subject of his essay, was the French advocate of Fascism and collaborator Drieu La Rochelle whose suicide following the German retreat was thought to be "political," but was, Mishima judged, something "commanded by a most *decadent* artistic conscience." To explain, he brought in the samurai and seppuku. "For the samurai there were virtues they set for themselves. For them, seppuku and other forms of self-killing were, within their own moral code, no more than actions on the same plane as that of devising a strategy, carrying out an attack, and engaging in a duel. For this reason, I accept a samurai's suicide. But I do not accept the suicide of a man of letters."

"Akutagawa committed suicide because he liked suicide," Mishima concluded. "I dislike that way of living, but I have no right to say accusatory things about someone else's way of living." He made clear what he was objecting to: the tendency to regard as important the confessional mode of writings Akutagawa adopted in the last phase of his life.

Mishima was conscientious about the task given him, of course, that of assessing Akutagawa's writings. Akutagawa was comparable to Ueda Akinari as a writer of short stories, Mishima said. Ueda "intensely disliked not just man's five greeds but mankind itself," whereas Akutagawa was a "feeble-minded genius who tried to live sincerely, truthfully, against his dispositions." Still, Ueda's *Tales of Rain and Moon (Ugetsu monogatari)*—Mizoguchi Kenji's film *Ugetsu*, which had won the Silver Lion Award of the Venice Film Festival in the previous year, was based on some of his stories—and an able collection of Akutagawa's stories "will make an interesting contrast in the history of literature," Mishima wrote.[42]

---

It wasn't as if the thought of death was constant or continual. One day in the summer of 1955, Mishima wondered why the thought of death that had never left him from boyhood until his twenties had "receded into the distance so suddenly," he wrote in his diary-format criticism, *A Novelist's Holiday*. The wonderment was occasioned by the death on the previous night of the seventy-eight-year-old doctor who ran the hospital across the street. Mishima had once believed he'd die at age twenty, and the belief stayed with him well after he had passed that age.

He knew there was nothing special about the change. "The despair and disillusionment I felt when I finally decided I had to live was something every twenty-four-year-old youth tastes. Many of young people's suicides are the afterimages of the fierce vanity concerning death during boyhood. People do not easily die out of despair." Yes, during some idle moments he still thought of "a desirable death": death by a stray bullet, for example. "This death by a stray bullet, this *situation* of a genuine murder, is something I have thought through, death as a total approval of the indolence of a happy spirit," he mused. "In my boyhood, I, too, dreamed of my own heroic death!"[43] The realization may have partly reflected the fact that he was enjoying "his golden period when his creative powers were at their fullest."[44]

But the thoughts on death never left him. The United Kingdom announced a plan to seek production of hydrogen bombs and France that of atomic bombs in March. The heads of the Big Four—Dwight Eisenhower, Nikolai Bulganin, Anthony Eden, and Edgar Faure—gathered in Geneva in July to discuss ways of reducing tensions between the Eastern and Western blocs. And the summit only reminded Mishima of the US agreement earlier that year to pay "compensation" to the victims of a hydrogen bomb test in the Bikini Atoll aboard a Japanese fishing boat, and of the staggering "imbalance" that had come to exist between the bomber and the bombed in Hiroshima and on the "invasion into every corner of our daily life" of the bomber's ability to "crush his sensitivity under the intellectually conceptualized image of the world."[45] Two years earlier, he had stressed the importance of death as "a strictly individual matter" in his comment on the "eschatological" sense that was the result of stupendous mass killings that the Atomic Age had rendered thinkable.[46]

And, as he concluded *A Novelist's Holiday*, Mishima brought up *Hagakure*, the most famous compilation of "lessons on death" that a samurai had left, or, as Mishima put it, "an incomparably mysterious moral tract in which not Diogenestic paradoxes but wisdom on action and decision keep producing paradoxes."[47]

"In a couple of years I'll be forty; it's about time I made a plan for the rest of my life. I feel good to think I've lived longer than Akutagawa Ryūnosuke, but now that I've reached this point, I must try to live as long as I can at any cost," Mishima mused in a filler-like essay for a small magazine in the summer of 1962. "When it comes to the average life span in ancient times, it was eighteen years during the Bronze Age, twenty during the Roman Empire, it is said. Heaven in those days must have been brimming with beautiful youths, but the spectacle of Heaven these days must be ugly indeed." He decided to live at any cost, because "when a human turns forty, you can't hope to dream of dying beautifully."[48]

"Already I'm beginning to think being young or youthful is something absurd," he wrote a year later in concluding the account of his literary pilgrimage days. "Well then, do I look forward to 'being old'? I ask, but I can't take that either. So is born the idea of death that is *now*, momentary, second-by-second. This, for me, may be the only idea that is truly vivid, truly erotic. In that sense, I may be innately diseased with an incurable romantic disease. It may be that the I at twenty-six, the I the classicist, the I who felt closest to life was, by chance, *counterfeit*."[49]

The novel he published a few months after he wrote these words, *The Sailor Who Fell from Grace with the Sea*, drew, from a fellow writer, a strong reaction. The focus of the story, from the narrative viewpoint, is on Noboru, the thirteen-year-old son of a widow who runs an expensive imported apparel store. He is a member of a group of six teenagers, everyone "sensitive, awfully intelligent, beautiful boys who are cruelty itself, and kill a cat to test their courage." Not just kill but dissect the animal. The boys then kill the sailor Ryūji because he does not just sleep with Noboru's mother but marries her—and dissect him, though the dissection is merely hinted.

Dōmoto Masaki, Mishima's "playmate" in the theater who, among others, served as associate director for the film *Yūkoku*, recalled the omitted section Mishima showed him: "The description of the cruel dissection was full of metaphors of glittering oceans and exotic foreign sights, as intoxicating as the stories of *Arabian Nights*. The pubic hair is seaweed that enwraps a pearl shell, the manroot and glans turn into the minaret and roof of an Islamic mosque and are torn and peeled even as they glitter blindingly in a golden sunset. A perfection by a solemn collapse."⁵⁰

Still, the motif of the novel, the adult Ryūji's death wish and its fulfillment—though not by the wisher's own hand—is obvious. It is while recalling his dream of death, "a wish for a luxurious death," that Ryūji drinks a poisoned tea offered him, without knowing it:

> Boiling with scorching melancholy and ennui, overflowing with vulture and parrot, and palm trees everywhere! Royal palms. Peacock palms. Death had come out of the glitter of the sea, spreading, pushing toward him like a thunder cloud. He blissfully dreamed of a solemn, incomparably spectacular death before the eyes of thousands of people, the opportunity that had been lost to him forever. If the world, in the first place, had been prepared for a death overflowing with such glittering light, there'd be no wonder if it went to ruin because of it.

Among the reviewers of the story, who were mostly favorable though indifferent, Hinuma Rintarō stood out. Writing for the *Yomiuri Shinbun* in October, Hinuma noted the "anguish" Mishima evinced in it and spoke of the difficulty the writer had to expect as he "set out on a new journey" that "inevitably accompanied the end of his spiritual drama that visited him with the perfect death of his youth."[51] Or, as he put it bluntly when he asked Mishima: "When are you going to die?" It was because of this question, which Hinuma asked on more than one occasion, that, when told of his death, in 1968, Mishima blurted out, "Did he commit suicide?" Hinuma hadn't, but he was Mishima's age and his death was sudden.

"I feel as though Mr. Hinuma and I talked only about death," Mishima reflected when he wrote about him for the literary magazine *Hihyō* through which the two had come to know each other. "When I think of it now, he had known, with an insight unique to someone near death, the dangers of the direction my literature is aiming toward, as if it were the palm of his hand. Whenever we met, he recommended that I commit suicide on the spot.... He insisted, he urged, that my committing suicide right now would be like Kirillov's logical death and my literature would be perfected by that alone."

Kirillov is Alexei Nilych Kirillov in Dostoevsky's *Demons*, the man who is resolved to take his own life and does, arguing, "If there is God, then the will is all his, and I cannot get out of his will. If not, the will is all mine, and it is my duty to proclaim self-will [by killing myself]." At the end of a document he is asked to sign declaring he had committed the murders that he hadn't, Kirillov writes, in French: *Liberté, égalité, fraternité ou la mort!*[52]

Hinuma had "misunderstood" him, Mishima went on to say, that he, Mishima, had "publicly stated" that he "would never commit suicide as a man of letters." The reason was simple: "Because literature has no ultimate responsibility, a man of letters cannot find a truly *moralisch* [moral] trigger for suicide. I do not recognize anything other than a *moralisch* suicide. That is to say, I do not recognize anything other than a samurai's killing himself with his own sword."[53] The term Mishima used for killing oneself in the last sentence translated here is *jijin*, "self-blade."[54]

In mid-1966, when a women's weekly asked Mishima for an homage to bullfighting to go with a series of photographs, he gladly complied. "Among the roughest, life-risking jobs men do, there are few whose essence so depends on elegance and beauty," he began the article, "The Matador's Beauty." "Unlike America's dust-smelly, dingy cowboy, the matador wears a courtier-like gorgeous silk costume." What makes the matador what he is? It's the fact that he wears nothing "under that showy costume"—no protector, no underwear. And, of course, "a man can rightfully don a colorful, resplendent suit only when he involves himself with death, courage, and a spurt of blood.... The matador is beautiful because of the danger and even more beautiful because of death."

Of the bullfight, Alphonso Lingis would write what would have delighted Mishima, though more than a dozen years after his death. "No woman spread-eagled in a strip show is as brazenly exhibited as the matador in the corrida," the American philosopher observed. "His body and his blood are exalted in a monstrance of scarlet velvets, spun-silver lace, and jewels over against the black fury of the bull. Insolence flaunts his torso, contempt splays his thighs, flash-fires of foolhardy intelligence crackle across his tensed and cynical posturing, his testicles and penis jeweled in the codpiece and provocatively exposed to the lusts of the crowds."[55]

Mishima ends his homage with the penultimate stanza of García Lorca's poem on the writer-matador who was gored in August 1934, "Llanto por Ignacio Sánchez Mejías":[56]

> No one knows you. No one. But I sing you.
> I sing for the sake of the figure you cut and your grace.
> The signal ripeness of what you came to know.
> Your appetite for death and the savor of its taste.
> The sadness beneath the valor you show.
>
> (Tr. Forrest Gander.)

In September, the monthly *Gunzō* published Mishima's story that seemed to honestly describe an actual incident that directly involved him and his family, along with his meditation on it. It's titled "From the Wilderness" (*Kōya yori*).

Early one morning during the rainy season, an about forty-day period from June to July, Mishima is awakened by a commotion outside. He has just gone to bed, at six o'clock, and fallen asleep. Evidently, someone is trying to break into the house. Mishima finally gets up and, with wooden sword in hand, goes downstairs. After a good deal of excitement in the household, he goes back up to his study because of the noise of a windowpane shattering upstairs, and finds there a skinny, tall young man standing in the semi-darkness—trembling, with a large volume of the encyclopedia plucked from the bookshelves open before him.

Mishima has never before seen a face "as horribly pale as that of the young man." Still, he feels relieved, figuring that this must be one of "the standard-issue literary, ideational madmen." He asks the intruder, "What have you come here for?" The young man tenses up, but says, "Please tell me the truth." He repeats it a couple of times.

> "Please tell me the truth."
> I did not understand what he meant, but I said as mildly as I was able to manage.
> "All right. I'll tell you the truth whatever it is." By doing this, I thought I'd bide my time.
> At that moment my shoulder was pushed from behind.
> A policeman came in. Two more policemen came in.
> "Please tell me the truth," the youth said once again, as if fevered.
> "Well, then, let's go to a quiet place and talk, relaxed," said one of the policemen in uniform.
> The youth obediently walked out of the study, guarded by two policemen. One of them took the green encyclopedia from the youth's hands and went out, carrying it with him. I recognized a small stain of blood on the fore-edge of the volume.
> Strange enough, I was thinking that the policemen would lead the youth into a quiet room so I might talk with him. But the moment they approached the entrance to the kitchen, they suddenly pushed the young man from behind, trying to thrust him outside. The young man began to struggle. . . .

The young man is taken away, Mishima and his father, Azusa, are later summoned to the police station for questioning; after two hours of that, the man is brought in for identification, and it's over. But Mishima can't get rid of the youth's image, can't help thinking about him, until he begins to recognize himself in him—that "the fellow is my shadow, my echo." So he decides to do what the young man asked him to do: to tell the truth.

The truth is, Mishima explains, that, even though his mind, as that of a novelist, is vast and contains many things, such as an airport and a central terminal, tree-lined streets, shopping areas and residential areas, and he is thoroughly familiar with all the details, this map of his mind doesn't record "the vast territory" that he normally neglects—the territory whose existence he can't deny.

> It is a vast wilderness that surrounds the metropolis that is my mind. It must be a part of my mind, but it is an undeveloped, barren, bleak region that is not recorded in my map. It is wild and barren as far as the eye can see, with neither leafy trees nor sprouting wildflowers. Here and there rocks stick out, the wind blows over them, sprinkles sand on them, and carries it away. I know the existence of this wilderness but haven't walked toward it, though I know I once visited it and must visit it some day, once again.
>
> Evidently, that fellow has come from that wilderness....

After "From the Wilderness," Mishima would publish just two more short stories before his death.

In an interview conducted by the *Mainichi Shinbun* in March 1966 to mark his "first appearance on French TV," there was the following exchange between the interviewer and Mishima.

> Q: Are you serious [i.e., Do you think you are a serious-minded person]? Do you think you are akin to Salvador Dali?
> A: It is my flaw that I am serious about everything, and it is also the root cause of my comicality. Dali is not at all comical. He is sublime.
> Q: Do you think suicide is a form of apologia?
> A: There are two kinds of suicide. One is suicide from weakness and defeat. One is suicide from strength and courage. I despise the former and praise the latter.
> Q: What do you think of human life?
> A: I do not necessarily think it's supreme.
> Q: Aren't you afraid of dying?
> A: I'm sure I'll be scared when I die, but at least I'd like to die

pretending it's nothing. That's a courtesy to the humans who are alive.⁵⁷

At the end of the year, Mishima was solicited for an essay by the *Yomiuri Shinbun* on "the first thoughts for the New Year"—to appear on January 1, 1967. Titling it "Hesitancy at the Start of the Year," he opened the essay as if the heading were part of the sentence that followed: "In fact, there has been something special about the way I've felt welcoming the New Year for the last couple of years." He will turn forty-two in the middle of the month, he'll write about that special feeling to see if it is only his or something common to people his age. Following the custom, the daily had asked a group of prominent figures to record their sentiments for the New Year.

Two years earlier he had started a tetralogy "in the hopes of at least leaving some scratch marks on the surface of the earth," and on every New Year's Day he had hoped he'd live until he finished it, that he'd finish it as soon as possible. Since it must be natural for anyone who has taken on a big enterprise past the midpoint in life to hope to live until the work is done, he assumes he is no different from most people in that regard. What might make him different from others was this: "At the start of every year, a mysterious, sorrowful hesitation assaults me. Shall I call it a hesitation or shall I call it an inability to give up? Thing is, I wouldn't be able to complete this big novel until five years from now at the earliest, but by then I will be forty-seven."

That will mean that, as long as he waits until the completion, he'll have to "forsake a spectacular heroic end forever. It's this unsettling foreboding that the extremely difficult decision might come this year on whether to give up becoming a hero or to give up completing the lifework."

Mishima then imagines someone telling him: You must give up the dream of becoming the kind of "action hero" you have in mind by age thirty; to talk about such things twelve years beyond that is as silly as "an old spinster putting on thick makeup." He imagines his riposte: "But I still have physical strength not inferior to that of young men"—adding parenthetically, "Such thinking may be 'an old man taking a cold bath'"—"and I think that age forty-two is still not too late an age demarcation point, though barely, to become a hero." Mishima then brings up, in a forum where one is supposed to talk about one's plans and such, two figures who weren't that young when they died.

"Saigō Takamori died at age fifty as a hero; the other day when I went to Kumamoto to research the Shinpūren, I was moved to discover that Kaya Harukata, one of the leaders of that revolt—which tends to be regarded as a foolish action of young men—who pulled off a spectacular end to his life, died when he was my age. If I did [something similar] now, I, too, would be able to do it before reaching the final age to be a hero."

Saigō Takamori, who led the Satsuma Rebellion, in 1877, had himself beheaded by his aide when wounded with gunshots in the middle of what was to be the final battle. The last forty-odd men who had survived with him were killed or killed themselves in the ensuing *mêlée*. In thinking of Saigō and Kaya, Mishima also thought of Ernest Hemingway who had shot himself six years earlier. The American writer had yearned for "an adventuresome heroic death," but every such opportunity "ran away from him, until finally he committed suicide in a manner most contrary to his wishes." Mishima concluded: "I don't want to end up like that."[58]

A year later Mishima would write an homage to Saigō, in the form of a silent address to his famously chunky statue in Ueno Park. In the manner of Ezra Pound offering to reconcile himself with Walt Whitman, saying, "I have detested you long enough.... I am old enough now to make friends," Mishima offered to make friends with the leader of the rebellion whose outcome was never in doubt. He'd been put off by him for a long time, not just because of his "grotesque" physique à la a sumo wrestler but also because of the "vulgarity" he sensed in his compatriots' adulation for him: the Japanese assume one condition for being admired as a great man is "amorphously antirational."

But now, not so much because of the times, as because of his own age, "The time has come for the beauty of your heart to clarify itself like the dawn light," Mishima told the statue. "You knew tears, knew strength, you knew the vanity of strength, you knew the fragility of an ideal. And you knew what responsibility was, what it was to respond to people's trust. You knew, and you acted."[59]

CHAPTER TWENTY-TWO

# Death in India

> *A religion is discarded by the fundamental force of the "nature" of the locality as it becomes refined, systematized philosophically, and acquires universality.*
>
> —Mishima, *Indo tsūshin*

Shortly after "actually experiencing the SDF," Mishima sat down to write an extended commentary on *Hagakure*. He did so for a publisher that had just started a series of books on "the wisdom of the Japanese," and his was to be the second. He took to the work with relish because he had extolled its virtues twelve years earlier; now, he could detail the whys and wherefores of his admiration in the larger context of his achievements and conduct.

*Hagakure*—it means "hidden in foliage," but here the title will stay untranslated[1]—was one of the three books he had admired and always kept handy during the war, the two others being Radiguet's *La bal du Compte d'Orgel* and the collected works of Ueda Akinari, Mishima explained. Of the latter two, Radiguet's attraction faded over time because he, Mishima, survived the war and did not die before turning twenty; so did Akinari's, although, with Akinari, Mishima did not clearly remember why he had once been so taken with the Edo writer, except perhaps that Akinari represented for him an anti-Zeitgeist stance and his skill as a writer of short fiction. Akinari studied with scholars of National Learning, but was dismissive, for example, of the idea of exalting things that are supposed to be purely, genuinely Japanese, such as the "Yamato spirit."

Only *Hagakure*, which was promoted, and popular, during the war, "the season of death," when young men vied to read Paul Bourget's *Le Sens de la mort*, for example, but which, along with most other things so treated during the war, was, as soon as Japan was defeated, trashed "as repulsive and to be forgotten," remained with him—no, it began to "radiate more light" in him after the war. "That may be because," Mishima mused, "*Hagakure* is by its nature a paradoxical book like that. During the war, it was a luminous body placed in the light; but it was in the darkness that it truly began to radiate its light."[2]

The compendium, put together by a young samurai named Tashiro Tsuramoto who visited Yamamoto to hear him talk and recorded his words, in the manner of Eckermann's conversations with Goethe, over a period of seven years, is indeed a paradoxical book. For starters, it seems to advocate death over life, asserting that, when you have a choice to live or die, you must choose to die, but Yamamoto himself died peacefully, "on the tatami," neither in a sword fight nor by seppuku. He was leading an eremitic life after taking Buddhist tonsure, when Tashiro decided to elicit his opinions on various matters and jot them down. This is a little hard to take, given the famous dictum, given also his advocacy of a "frenzied death"—a readiness to plunge into a fight, be it military or personal, in a state of frenzy, regardless of the consequences, even if, that is, you knew you would be immediately overwhelmed and killed.

So, in the celebrated passage, which is in the opening of the compilation, Yamamoto says: "The way of the warrior, I've found, is to die. In a situation with a choice, you can only choose at once to die. There's nothing complicated about it. With calmness you just go right ahead. Talk such as, 'You're missing the mark' or 'It's a dog's death,' may be good for a sophisticated warrior's way, urbane style. But, for us, in a situation with a choice it isn't necessary to hit the mark."

It was chiefly because of these statements that during Japan's war with Western countries, *Hagakure* was "strongly recommended for the young men heading to the battlefields to resolve" to face death. It was also because of the book's inextricable linkage to the war that those who knew the famous dictum but did not read the book evoked "a reprehensibly fanatic image" of it. But, as what follows the quoted passage shows, Yamamoto was not exactly urging you to seek death.

"We all want to live. There's always a better reason for what you want. If you miss the mark and live, you'll be a coward. That's the tricky line. If you miss the mark and die, you may be crazy but it won't be shameful. That's the solid way of the warrior." At any rate, "If you relive your death every morning and evening and remain in a constant state of death, you will achieve freedom in the warrior's way and complete your duty without making a mistake during your life."

In other words, you achieve freedom by acting as if you were already dead, Yamamoto says, and that is the philosophy of *Hagakure*, Mishima avers. Yamamoto also advocates opting to die when you face a decision to live or die. Not that you are bound to face such a decision in your life. You may never have such an occasion. It is simply that "death = choice = freedom" is the ideal schema for the samurai.

> The way of the warrior is something you must contemplate in every detail, day and night, on the assumption that you may not be able to live through the day. You may win or lose, depending on the circumstances. But you can't shame yourself. You must die. If you have shamed yourself, you must revenge yourself on the spot. No wisdom is required for this. An accomplished warrior doesn't think whether he's going to win or lose, but dashes into the place of death with single-minded determination. In so doing he rids himself of all "illusions."

Yet, as Mishima makes sure to note, Yamamoto also posits what can be the antithesis of the famous or infamous dictum underpinning *Hagakure* philosophy: "A man's life is truly brief. You should live doing whatever you like to. In this world, which lasts for a duration of a dream, it is foolish to live doing only what you don't like to, suffering.... Appropriate to my present circumstances, I think I'll go out less and mainly sleep while alive."

Yamamoto studied Zen, which was important to the samurai, and is said to have achieved enlightenment. So there may be little contradiction between his insistence on the samurai's willingness to die at any moment and the carefree state he calls for at the same time. Yet the contrast is stark and may surprise those who approach the book with preconceptions.

Yamamoto has a range of homely advice, not necessarily for the samurai class. In addition, there are general social observations, among them what Mishima calls the *Hagakure*-style "political ideal (*rinen*) of democracy," to wit: "It is hard to achieve what you desire by insisting on the Principle (*gi*) because you hate the unprincipled (*fugi*). If you nonetheless adamantly insist on the Principle, believing that it is the supreme thing, you tend to make more mistakes than not. Above the Principle there is the Way. It is hard to find it easily. That would require highest wisdom and intelligence. When you see it, [you will realize that] things like the Principle are small."

In any event, while working on the commentary on *Hagakure* or soon after finishing it, Mishima wrote a short essay, "Beautiful Death."[3] There, he again brought up ancient Greece where "the ideal was to live beautifully and die beautifully," adding, "The ideal of our way of the warrior must have been the same." The difficulty in modern Japan was simple: if it is "difficult to live beautifully," it was "even more difficult to die beautifully." There are two conditions for living and dying beautifully: you have work to which you can devote yourself sincerely and your country or people (*minzoku*) are worth dying for gracefully, without hesitation. If the country or the people are in an unsound state where whatever you do doesn't matter one way or the other, you must first rectify the situation.

The samurai were respected, Mishima continued, because it was thought that at least they were able to die without hesitation. He had asked the SDF to accept him for training for he likewise had respect and love for the soldiers. SDF troops were no longer regarded as or perceived to be the same as prewar "soldiers," but no matter. To enable himself to act without hesitation, he thought he had to learn "the martial way."

"In the absence of martial training, a man can regard himself as a weakling in whatever way he wants to, can justify himself for any cowardly, excusable act, can surrender himself to any demand. That way, his ultimate safety will be guaranteed."

"Once a man decides to follow the martial way," in contrast, "his safety will no longer be guaranteed. That is because then no cowardly, excusable act will be permitted any longer and, where the odds are overwhelmingly against him, there is no other way than for him to either die fighting or kill himself. But only then will he be able to die beautifully and perfect his life honorably."

Here, again, Mishima used the word *jijin* for "killing oneself." That samurai tradition was carried forward to the Second World War, and he wrote "Beautiful Death" by way of thanking the GSDF. But whether the intended readership understood what he was talking about in the way he meant it is altogether another matter.

## *The Young Man Called Morita Masakatsu*

It may well have been on June 19, 1967, in Café Victoria, in Roppongi, that Mishima for the first time met Morita Masakatsu, the young man fated to commit double suicide with him, as it were.

The previous November Morita, a freshman at Waseda University finally after flunking entrance exams for two years in a row, had, when approached, readily joined the just-formed student body Nichigakudō and, the following February, had become a founding member of the National Defense Society, a study group. Mishima's meeting on June 19 was with the Society's representatives. When the news broke of Mishima's "actual experience with the GSDF," its members begged him to find an appropriate place for them to do the same, and he had worked out just such a place with the Defense Agency: Camp Kita-Eniwa, in Hokkaidō. Subsequently, thirteen members of the society trained there for a week, starting on July 2.

It is assumed that Morita was among the students gathered at the café that day. But, even assuming that he was there, Mishima may not have seen in the young man anything other than a regular student except for his unusually round baby face—the kind of face to which he was partial. Still, in ten months Morita jotted down in his diary that, in his opinion, he and Mishima liked each other. Morita's excitement over Mishima in time would become intense enough to lead some later commentators to suggest that, absent him, Mishima might not have taken the path he took.

Morita was born the last child of an elementary school principal, on July 25, 1945, in Yokkaichi, Mie, barely a month before Japan's surrender. Yokkaichi, an industrial city, had begun to be bombed in June, turning a large part of it into wasteland. It was in a bomb shelter, in fact, that he was born. His father wondered if he should name his fifth child Hirakazu ("peace") or Masakatsu ("sure victory"). He opted for the latter—the vain hope that the Japanese military would win.

In high school Masakatsu was an ordinary, even an indifferent, student with no strong views one way or another. His diary entries show him, for example, vacillating between admiration for the student federation Zengakuren's ready resort to violence and condemnation of it.

Zengakuren is the acronym of Zen Nihon Gakusei Jichikai Rengōkai, a federation of the student bodies of 145 colleges and universities that was formed in September 1948 in revolt against the militarism and patriotism imposed on institutions of higher education until Japan's defeat, in 1945, as well as the institutions' own heavy-handed bureaucratic governance. The Communist Party that gained freedom under the Occupation held sway over it from the outset. Led by Takei Teruo, a student at the University of Tokyo and a Communist, the Zengakuren fought a succession of noncampus political issues that arose as the Cold War worsened: MacArthur's Red Purge, the Korean War, and the Peace Treaty. Following the Denunciation of Stalin and the Hungarian Upheaval, however, the federation, in 1958, began to split with the Communist Party and the split led to further splits, as we will see later. Takei himself was expunged from the party during 1960 when he criticized it.

Morita Masakatsu was a young man without any intellectual training, susceptible, and, if anything, romantic, who also, like most youths, entertained the thought of death from time to time. He could easily fall for strong notions. If Waseda was not in an upheaval when he became a student there and if no one had asked him to join a new student group to be formed, he might as well have joined the Zengakuren.

In August 1967, he saw the film *Japan's Longest Day* that deals with the Palace Incident. Learning that a divided cabinet had decided to surrender, with the Shōwa Tennō siding with those who argued for it, some of the staff officers at the Ministry of the Army tried to overturn the decision. In the turmoil, Lt. Gen. Mori Takeshi, Commander of the 1st Imperial Guards Division, and Lt. Col. Shiraishi Michinori, of the 2nd General Army, were killed. When they learned the coup failed, two of the principal schemers, Maj. Hatanaka Kenji and Lt. Col. Shiizaki Jirō, shot themselves. What he came away with from the film, Morita noted in his diary, was "protection and preservation of *kokutai*," Japan's reason for being as a nation. Minister of the Army Gen. Anami Korechika disemboweled himself on account of that slogan, leaving a blood-splattered testament simply stating, "With death I apologize for my great crime." Okamoto Kihachi directed the film. Mifune Toshirō played the general. It is reputed to have the longest scene of seppuku ever.⁴

Morita knew Mishima to be an internationally famous author. The month he matriculated at Waseda, Mishima's *Yūkoku* opened as "a film for adults only" and attracted a great deal of attention. Later, when he heard about Mishima's proposal for a "homeland defense corps," and that was after he became a founding member of the National Defense Society, Morita jotted down in his diary that it was "incongruous" for the "foppish" Mishima to entertain such an idea—not imagining he would in time tightly knit himself into the inexorable scheme "the fop" was devising. What attracted him most about Mishima in the end may well have been the older man's insistence that you must be willing to die for any idea you think important.

In turn, the eagerness of the National Defense Society, which included those involved in the *Ronsō Journal*, may well have led Mishima to the idea of forming a militia later that year.⁵

---

Mishima's argument on the 2.26 Incident as "a moral revolution" that had appeared in the March issue of *Bungei* that year⁶ had elicited a cordial but strong endorsement, as it were, from Kawabata Yasunari. It came in his reply to Mishima's letter, requesting an article for *Hihyō* upon resumption of its issuance. "I marveled to read your great writing in *Bungei*," Kawabata wrote. "It might be rude for me to say this as if it were something new, but it is indeed a splendid, great writing; for a long time [after reading it] I found myself admiring it, almost stunned. I had no thoughts of my own on the 2.26 Incident, but your excitement came through to me sentence by sentence, the rhythm ever heightening." He then added, "I thought your letter to Miss Mori Mari was also incomparable."⁷

Not long after this exchange of letters, Mishima and Kawabata, along with two other writers, Ishikawa Jun and Abe Kōbō, took action about another revolution—the one that had started just a few years earlier: the Cultural Revolution. On February 28, the four writers issued "an appeal" objecting to China's attempt to "suffocate academic and artistic freedom." Addressed to the world, it stated that the four were "transcending right-left ideological positions." They were mindful that Mishima was gaining notoriety as a rightwing monstrosity while Abe and Ishikawa were known for their left-leaning views. They were also mindful of Japan's recent past. They brought up the notion of "patriotism through literature"—their government's wholesale attempt to impose "thought control" on all activities during the war just two decades earlier.[8]

In addition, Kawabata remarked, each of its four signers had a different view of the Cultural Revolution. It is not immediately clear what those views were, but Mishima in the end may have been wrong in his understanding of that stupendous political upheaval. A week or so earlier, he had been shown some photos of the Red Guards savaging the people they decided to label the enemies of the Revolution—political leaders, prominent writers, and others, with placards with their "crimes" written on them hung from their necks—and he had said that, if forced into such a position, he'd put up a fight and die. He had also recalled a young actor who, four years earlier, had refused to play a role in his play, *The Joyful Koto*, exclaiming, "I can't say such anticommunist lines!" On both counts, he may have been right in his indignation.

But he was wrong in his wish that Mao Zedong and Lin Biao win the battle. "It would be terrifying if those Mao and Lin were criticizing won and joined hands with the Soviet Union," he observed. As it would turn out, the Mao-instigated revolution was far darker in nature. Mao and Lin apparently split, with a quarrel, if it was, leading to Lin's death, and the eventual defeat of Mao's agitation led to a gradual relaxation of the Communist ideology. Mishima was correct only in observing that China's future was "outside prediction."[9] By early that year, 1967, even Japan's Communist Party was revolting against the Chinese Communist Party's attempt to control it.

At the same time, opposition to the US war against Communism was quickly growing. Even as Mishima began his military training, huge anti–Vietnam War rallies were staged in New York and San Francisco, on April 15, with half a million participating. In May, the International War Crimes Tribunal convened in Stockholm by Bertrand Russell and Jean Paul Sartre judged the United States guilty in its conduct in Vietnam. On July 23, a race riot erupted in Detroit, which would turn out to be the largest of its kind in US history; it was touched off by wholesale arrests of blacks welcoming back Vietnam veterans. (That happened a few days after the Wuhan Incident that had exposed the schisms among the Chinese communists to be violent enough at popular levels to force Mao, who was in Wuhan for mediation, to flee.) Anti–Vietnam War rallies and movements kept spreading throughout the world. Regardless, the United States continued expanding its forces in Vietnam, until, at the end of the year, Gen. William Westmoreland announced the number of US soldiers under his command totaled 478,000.

## *Resplendent Epistolary Exchange*

In his letter to Mishima expressing his admiration for his writing on the 2.26 Incident, Kawabata mentioned Mishima's "letter" to Mori Mari. He was referring to Mishima's response to Mori's letter to him that had just appeared in "Resplendent Epistolary Exchange," a publication gimmick of the ladies' monthly *Fujin Kōron*.

Mori, Ōgai's eldest daughter and a regular guest at Mishima's Christmas parties—with professional bartenders and catered food—had begun her epistle by asserting that some of the words Shibusawa Tatsuhiko chose to characterize the Marquis de Sade in his book on the marquise—*innocence*, *monstruosité*, and *senteté*—were perfectly suited to Mishima. She detailed the de Sade that Shibusawa described, then turned to Mishima's puzzling behavior—as typified by his unseemly eagerness to try everything and his alarming choice of attire such as "loud aloha shirts." Why, she wanted to know, for example, did he have to appear in "a ceremonial dress of the tropics" in order to explain how it differed from a waiter's garb? She did all this before concluding nonetheless that all that type of behavior was "natural" because he was like "a child who demanded a new toy every day."

Along the way, Mori, casually yet obviously to flatter Mishima, brought up her father, Ōgai—the one writer she knew Mishima esteemed. "Although Mr. Mishima has a dark side," she wrote, "he, meanwhile, also has a side as bright as a pellucid blue; he has brightness in his intellect—intellect to me is a dark place—and has a sober brain like Ōgai, *and* like me, and his common sense is well developed."

All the odd things he does, at any rate, are "compelled by curiosity and an inquisitive mind that derive from your innate, *innocent* nature," wrote Mori, sometimes using the third person, sometimes the second person, in referring to him, and ended her epistle: "Having understood this, I will give up on the fact, as something I can't do anything about, that you don't dress in a manner that would emphasize your face—the mystifying, my favorite, face, the one I like next to that of Nureyev, that of [Jean-Claude] Brialy—with extraordinary eyes you cannot forget once you see them. Since I have badmouthed you so much," she concluded. "I shall simply add that the photograph of you costumed like a slave (is that what you were?) in *The Arabian Nights* that I saw the other day was wonderful."[10]

In his response Mishima followed the indirect approach Mori had taken. Instead of addressing Mori's sartorial and other complaints about him first, he began by noting "the literary paradise" Mori created for herself, going on to praise *The Joy of Sweet Honey (Amai mitsu no yorokobi)*, a story just published in *Shinchō*. He said that it was, "as it were, a Japanese Colette's work, a work that should be called a Colette permeated with Fauvism, a sensual masterpiece." The story described in dreamy, sensitive detail a pubescent girl's lambent sexual stirrings that are at once narcissistic and incestuous. Mori had established her reputation ten years earlier with a prize-winning collection of essays, *My Father's Hat (Chichi no bōshi)*, which spelled out her adoration for her father. "Sweet honey," obviously redundant, was, in fact, how she had characterized the feeling with which her father had enveloped her.[11]

In praising Mori as a Japanese Colette, Mishima cited André Gide's observation in *Prétextes* to the effect that the most important quality for an artist is sensuality. That must have made Mori doubly happy. She had lived in Paris for a little over a year not long after marrying, in her teens, a student of French literature, Yamada Tamaki. There she had experienced what would later be called culture shock, and the sojourn may have been too short for a proper understanding of the city and its culture; but, as often happens in such cases, she remained enamored of things French.

Mishima then analyzed Mori's exact understanding of lust, not just the amorphous desire of a pubescent girl (named Moira or Moïla in the story at hand) but also the more direct desire of a grown male (named Peter Orlov), marveling at her "accurate knowledge of male lust." Indeed, Mori had written several stories about homosexual, bisexual lovers—featuring characters named Guido, Paulo, Hans, and such, acting out their assigned roles, one should add, in totally Japanese settings.[12]

In using such names Mori followed the examples of her father and some of his contemporaries. Ōgai named his first son Oto (Otto), the other sons Furitsu (Fritz) and Rui (Louis), his first daughter Mari (Marie), the second Annu (Anne). He also named Mari's first son Jakku (Jacque).

Such naming was popular for a while. What set Ōgai apart was that he also often drew on Chinese classics for those names. So, in the case of his first son, he chose a set of two Chinese characters that read "oto" in Japanese but meant "tiger" in classical Chinese, because the son was born in the Year of the Tiger. In addition, he had a good reason for choosing European names. While studying military medicine in Germany, from 1884 to 1888, he had noticed German and other European friends had trouble correctly pronouncing his personal name, Rintarō. [13]

Finally getting to the heart of the matter, as it were, Mishima adopted a mock-serious tone to reject, indignantly, Mori's comparison of him to "a fatso like the Marquis de Sade." Her epistle was itself "a wonderful literary piece, yes," Mishima wrote, but she was wrong in everything she said about him. How could he, an adult, be "*innocent*," to give the most obvious example? The most appalling of all was "the horrible sartorial taste" she intended to foist on him. He didn't want her to be his "sartorial advisor" in any way whatsoever because,

> "A black silk muffler with two stripes in white or gray"—what foppish taste is that? That you should want such a foppish muffler to snake around me, a simple, spartan guy who, may I tell you this, even in this extreme cold, the severest in decades, goes about naked under a shirt, wearing no overcoat, let alone a muffler! A striped kimono (*tōzan*) with a black collar, a Hakata obi, with a woolen inverness—you better have your favorite, Yoshiyuki Junnosuke, be decked out like that.

Yoshiyuki Junnosuke was a popular novelist who, though prone to illnesses, flaunted being a womanizer with various affairs under his belt, even as he showed off his frivolity. Born in 1924 and thus a bit older than Mishima, Yoshiyuki was grouped with Endō Shūsaku and several other writers as "the third new faces." He, like Dazai Osamu, was the kind of writer Mishima despised. Mishima, who prided himself in dressing correctly as occasion required, goes on:

I look far better in a kendō uniform made of white cotton fabric layered and roughly sewn together. Aside from that, while I respect your preferences for things French in every way, I am one who feels nauseated by the male fashion of that country in every way. A men's coat with raglan sleeves—how revolting that is! When it comes to men's fashion in Europe, Italy (north) is first, next comes England, then Germany, that's all. Please, in the future as well, I beg you to drop the thought completely of what I ought to wear.[14]

Mori Mari, born in 1903, was a relatively late comer to the literary scene. She began publishing her translations of French writers—Musset *(On ne badine pas avec l'amour)*, Maupassant *(Le Horla* and others), Loti, Alphonse Daudet, Florent Fels, Gyp or Sibylle Gabrielle Marie Antoinette Riqueti de Mirabeau *(Mademoiselle Loulou)*—in the second half of her twenties and her own essays in her thirties. Deprived of her income as the copyrights to her father's works expired, shortly after Japan's defeat, in 1945, she was plunged into poverty, the state that would be with her for the years that followed. She had been divorced from her second husband, Satō Akira, a professor of medicine, back in 1931, and never married again.

It was in her mid-fifties that she won her first literary recognition; in 1957, her essays on her father was awarded the Japan Essayists Club prize. This was followed by the Tamura Toshiko prize, in 1961, for her stories about homosexual, bisexual lovers, *The Lovers' Forest (Koibito-tachi no mori)*. In 1975, her full-length novel *The Room of Sweet Honey (Amai mitsu no heya)* won the Izumi Kyōka prize. This last, which she finished five years after Mishima's death, won the prestigious prize partly because of his extravagant praise of *The Joy of Sweet Honey*, which formed the middle section of the completed novel. She died in 1987, at age 84.

## Death in India

On September 26, Mishima, with Yōko, left for India at that country's invitation. In Mishima's estimation, the Indian government invited one "oddball" character a year. Two years earlier it was the playwright and stage-director Iizawa Tadasu who, as editor of *Asahi Graph*, had devoted an entire issue to the photos of the victims of atomic bombs as the San Francisco Peace Treaty took effect, in 1952, and the US ban on such photos became moot. A year before, it was the social anthropologist Nakane Chie who was known for her studies of villages in India. Her book published that year (1967) judging Japanese society is "vertical" would become an unprecedented bestseller.[15]

The couple arrived in Bombay (now Mumbai) on the same day, went to Aurangabad on the 29th, Jaipur on October 1, Agra on the 2nd, and New Delhi on the 3rd, where Yōko took a flight back to Japan the day after. Mishima went on to Benares (Varanasi) on the 7th and to Calcutta (Kolkata) where he stayed from the 8th to the 11th. He then flew to Bangkok where he stayed, with an excursion to Laos, until he returned to Japan on October 23. He visited Thailand partly to avoid Japanese journalists' obsession with the Nobel Prize, partly to gather more information for *The Temple of Dawn* (*Akatsuki no tera*), the third in his tetralogy, *The Sea of Fertility*.

In Aurangabad, Mishima visited the Ajanta and Ellora Caves—the latter, a temple partially built in a cave, "somewhat resembles the Mayan Chichen Itza and Angkor Wat," but "Ellora is the most refined" of the three, Mishima noted; in Jaipur, the Pink City—"the pink town built by Maharaja Jai Singh in the eighteenth century"—and Amber Fort (Amber Palace); in Agra, the Taj Mahal; and in Benares, Sarnath outside the city, and the ghats—"the stone-paved [steps] along the Ganges River where people at once bathe, rest, and cremate," as Mishima put it. What he observed at the ghats so profoundly affected him that he went there twice, in the manner Honda Shigekuni does in *The Temple of Dawn*. Honda holds together the narrative thread of the four novels.

Mishima, a state guest, made courtesy calls to President Zakir Hussain and Prime Minister Indira Gandhi, in New Delhi. He found President Hussain to be "a truly great man." "A national industrialization is something we must do, and we can't avoid modernization, but what do you think about the harm that comes with it?" Mishima asked the President who received him in his official residence, the Rashtrapati Bhavan. In asking the question, Mishima probably had in mind not so much the pollution that was engulfing Japan at the time as the cultural distortions. "I believe there are absolute limits to such harm," Hussain replied. Mishima took it to reflect his confidence in Indian culture and marveled if there was any Japanese willing or ready to say that much about Japan.

With Prime Minister Gandhi, Mishima caught a whiff of what India had just begun to undertake. She was "extremely tired, looking sad" when he walked into her office, he reported. Yet, as they talked, "she began to unwind, showing truly beautiful smiles, and when the talk turned to the food question, her eyes grew intense." Amid continued reports of starvation deaths, the plan for what was later to be known as India's Green Revolution had just been put into motion that year.

One day in New Delhi, Mishima invited a colonel (infantry) of the Indian Army to his hotel room and talked for one and a half hours. The Indian-Chinese relations were tense, and the two armies had just had two consecutive border clashes, in September and in early October. The colonel expressed frustrations over the Chinese Army's "human wave tactics" that treated casualties as nothing to be bothered about. As to his own army, so many were unemployed in his country that they never had any trouble in getting new recruits, but they did suffer from shortages of technical officers. When Mishima asked him about the kind of militia he was apparently thinking of forming, the colonel dismissed the idea out of hand. "Militias are just rich men's hobbies; they are no use in war."[16]

Mishima also talked with a round of "writers and professors in Marathi, Gujarati, Hindi, and Bengali," but what impressed him the most was India's "stubborn" perseverance in the outmoded ways, he told the journalist Tokuoka Takao in Bangkok. Tokuoka, who was in the Thai capital "in reserve" for the Vietnam War in case the two special correspondents the *Mainichi Shinbun* maintained in Saigon were found inadequate for the escalating war, was ordered to find and interview Mishima on the Nobel Prize to prepare an "in case he wins it" article. But when he, not knowing that Mishima was in Bangkok to avoid that particular topic, went to look for him in a hotel—and found him, as he expected, at the Erawan Hotel—he was told not to touch the subject. Tokuoka complied, and the two talked about other matters, among them India.[17]

For Tokuoka, this was his second meeting with Mishima. Less than half a year earlier, he had interviewed him on "actually experiencing" the GSDF. Still, he was disconcerted by the writer's "loony sincerity" when he found him in the crowded "steak room" of the prestigious hotel, earnestly explaining the need for Japan to revise its Constitution so the country might have a proper army—to an aloha-clad, ruddy-faced American tourist with a baseball cap, sitting across the table. The American must have recognized Mishima from an article in *Life* and said hello to him.[18]

Before his visit, his preconceptions of India were no different from those of most people, Mishima was honest to tell Tokuoka; it was "a country you couldn't do anything about, burdened as it was with all sorts of difficult problems, beginning with food crises, droughts, and population." But he found the actual country "extremely attractive." "As many as six hundred million human beings resist Europeanization and protect the outmoded ways, be it a religion or everyday customs, one way or another." There had to be *something* about such a country.

Tokuoka could not disagree more, but in a different sense. Three years earlier, he had headed a small group of journalists accompanying the torch bearers for the Tokyo Olympic Games, from Olympia to Calcutta, in a small made-in-Japan car and, perhaps because of the rough terrain the group had had to ride through of Iraq, Iran, and Afghanistan, he found India, the destination of that leg of the torch-bearing, intolerable.

It was not just that Tokuoka, as a member of the Japanese populace fetishistic about cleanliness, couldn't take the squalor in India. Why, for example, wouldn't, couldn't, those who seemed to seize every chance to find time to beg for money, for food, work, instead, on the bridge they were supposed to be working on? Why didn't Jawaharlal Nehru do something about such things, instead of giving noble sermons on the international stage? In citing an example of work, Tokuoka may have had in mind the work ethos that had earned a considerable reputation for Japan with the Olympic Games: every construction project completed on time. But Mishima simply laughed, telling Tokuoka that it was wrong to expect India to "be like Japan."[19]

"In India everything is out in the open. Everything is presented, everything forces you to 'confront' it. Life and death, and the famous poverty as well," he wrote in an article for the *Asahi Shinbun* that saw print upon his return to Japan. "Bombay, the first city I visited, was a beautiful town. Including its dirtiness, it is beautiful in a way that's hard to describe." In front of his hotel stood "the resplendent Seagate where once upon a time the Queen of England and Viceroys landed and entered India. In the sea wind of the Arabian Sea coarsened mud color, around the gate styled like an arch of triumph the color of burnt sienna, women in saris of various colors, women carrying a load on their heads, lacquer-black beggars, sailors in white clothes make up a colorful tableau."

The last viceroy of India was Lord Mountbatten whose role in its Independence and the Partition, in 1947, has since been criticized. His previous title was the Earl of Burma. In that capacity, he, who was so proud of his good looks and loved to appear in his resplendent naval uniform, had become the last member of the British royalty to look after British—or rather, European—interests in Southeast Asia when Britain, Holland, and France tried to take back their colonies after Japan was beaten, in 1945. The Dutch attempt to retake their former colony, Indonesia, with their colonial military's "pathological abhorrence of reason and moderation toward Indonesians,"[20] wrote Laurens van der Post, Mountbatten's aide during the transition, led to tens of thousands of deaths, whereas the French attempt to regain control of Vietnam led to the disastrous, horrendous American intervention.

"The people in the streets of New York are simply walking on their feet. But here, people are not simply walking on their feet," Mishima observed. "Some are walking, some stop walking, some are squatting, some lying down, some eating banana, children are jumping around, old people are sitting atop a tall platform—then, white holy cows join in, dogs join in, caged parrots join in, flies join in, trees thick with green join in, red turbans join in, beautiful saris join in. They join in, move, merge, working together to paint a picture of 'life' that completes itself moment by moment and then again moves on."

Then there is "death," willy-nilly. On "the superbly crescent-shaped west bank" of the Ganges, right next to the devout Hindus earnestly performing ablutions that get rid of every possible sin, cremations go on day and night, "out in the open." This is done in accordance with the Hindu belief, Mishima noted, that death immediately turns you into the five elements of air, earth, water, fire, and ether before samsara or transmigration, which, as we have noted, is the grand theme he chose for the tetralogy he was writing.

And, speaking of death, "Hinduism is a religion of sacrifice."

Instead of a great many human beings once offered up for sacrifice in Jaipur, today goats are offered. Especially in the State of Bengal, where,

> because the object of worship is Great Mother Goddess Kālī who is starved for blood, in the famous Kalighat Kalika, in Calcutta, thirty to forty goats every day, four hundred of them on special festival days, are sacrificed, right before people's eyes. This may be the only place in the world where a sacrificial rite is performed so openly.
>
> The kid, neck placed in the collar of the sacrificial platform, raises screams of grief, before his head is lopped off with a single stroke.... Here is a glimpse into the bloody-red truth of humanity that humans should properly confront but modern life has hidden away under its thick mask of hygiene.

"Whenever I thought of the decline and disappearance of Buddhism in this country," Mishima mused, "I could not help thinking of the rule that a religion is discarded by the fundamental force of the 'nature' of the locality as it becomes refined, systematized philosophically, and acquires universality."

Mishima called open cremation, open goat beheading, and some other things he saw in India "horrors of the real world,"[21] but it was there that he had an epiphany: Where there is a problem, "for the problem itself, solution is not everything." As a matter of fact, "if solving a problem is to make it disappear, India as a whole, does not, in truth, wish such a solution." Indeed, in India's stubborn adherence to the outmoded ways, he saw the possibility that India might be preparing to give the world "a new spiritual value at the end of its blind, advanced technologization."[22]

That, at least, was what he felt when he saw an American youth performing ablutions at a ghat in Benares, "praying in earnest." It was during that decade that many Westerners went to India in search of truth or enlightenment. So, early in the decade, Allen Ginsberg and Gary Snyder went there, as did the Beatles, though, in their case, after Mishima's visit.

The descriptions of the spectacles near the Seagate and in the Kalighat cited above may well have been tamed for the consumption of newspaper readers. When he recreated some of what he had observed in *The Temple of Dawn*, which was serialized in *Shinchō*, from September 1968 to April 1970, he was far more graphic, far more exact.

In the novel, Honda finds himself in Bangkok, in the fall of 1941, to look after a lawsuit for a large trading company; it had sold a large quantity of antifebrile pills that was largely found spoiled upon arrival in Thailand, and the Thai buyer sued. When the suit is resolved in its favor, the company offers him a free trip to any country as a token of gratitude. There is a stiff wind of war in the air, and this may be the last chance for any Japanese to travel in that part of the world with impunity, it is explained. Honda takes India, and selects a couple of places to visit with "a compass of intuition."

Arriving in his hotel in Benares after a long train ride, Honda quickly bathes in cold water. He is agitated with "mysterious youthful expectations," Mishima wrote. "Outside hotel windows, the air was filled with the suffocating westerly sun. He felt as if he'd be able to grasp the mystery with his hands just by plunging himself" into it.

> For all that, Benares was a town at once extreme in sacredness and extreme in squalor. On both sides of the alley where the sun filtered in over the eaves were rows of shops selling fried foods and sweets, an astrologer's house, shops selling starch by measure, everything heavy with foul smell, humidity, and disease. He passed through it and was out on a cobbled plaza facing the river, where he saw, squatting in rows on both sides of it, swarms of lepers who had come on pilgrimage from all over the country, now begging while awaiting their deaths. Many pigeons. The scorching 5 pm sky. Only several copper coins stuck to the bottoms of the tin cans in front of the beggars. Lepers, some with one of their eyes crushed in red, were holding up their fingerless hands in the evening sky, like mulberry trees after pruning.
>
> There were cripples in all shapes; dwarfs jumped about. These were rows of bodies like undeciphered ancient letters lacking in common signs....

Benares is "a carpet so ugly as to be resplendent," Honda muses. But it is there, at the Manikalnika Ghat, "the apogee of purification," that Honda, as he watches the crematory fires from a boat on the Ganges, undergoes a kind of spiritual epiphany.

> Corpses were committed to the fire one after another. As the ropes binding them burned and disintegrated, as red and white corpse sheets scorched and disappeared, he saw a black arm suddenly lift itself, a corpse arch its body in the fire like someone turning and tossing while asleep. With those set afire earlier, the color of black ashy charcoal was exposed. The sounds of something boiling over reached him over the water. Hard to burn were the skulls. A caretaker of cadavers carrying a bamboo pole constantly went back and forth, stabbing and smashing the skulls; even after the bodies had turned to ash, the heads smoldered. The black muscles of his arms stabbing and smashing the skulls glowed in the flames, its clonk-clonk sounds bouncing against the walls of the temple.
> The languidness of the purification to return to the four elements, the useless fragrance that remains even after the human flesh that resists it dies....

It is this cremation scene that Honda vividly remembers in the denouement of *The Temple of Dawn* when his villa burns down and two of his guests, a couple with a death wish, turn to ashes.

---

Tokuoka the journalist was surprised when Mishima casually told him the amount of "manuscript fee" he was paid by literary magazines for his "serious" novels and other things. It was, in Tokuoka's estimation, less than one third the weekly *Sunday Mainichi* for which he worked would pay. That, in turn, would mean that a single installment in the monthly *Shinchō* for which Mishima was serializing *The Runaway Horse* just then would earn him an amount he could "blow just by going out one night." In fact, for Mishima "who loved kitsch but also loved first-class things, it may not have been enough for a single meal with drinks," Tokuoka thought.[23] No wonder he had to write so assiduously for popular, entertainment weeklies and such, and do other things that paid him well, to make real money.

One mystery in Tokuoka's recollections of Mishima in Bangkok had to do with the Rose Palace. That was one thing he wanted to see, Mishima told Tokuoka, because it would appear in one of his novels. Tokuoka, who had seen the palace several times—"a smallish two-storied palace surrounded by a hedge of bougainvilleas"—thought it would be a cinch to arrange such a visit, although the palace was then being used as the Thai Army's command post for hunting down communists. At the time Thailand still hadn't sent its troops to Vietnam to fight with US forces, so the units assigned to fight communists on Thai borders to the northeast and the west were the only ones that were in combat operations.

Tokuoka got in touch with his acquaintance in the Thai government, director-general of information and culture at the foreign ministry. What he learned was off-putting: Mishima had already tried to secure a visit through a number of channels. That persistence had turned off those involved, besides the fear, it was explained, that intelligence on communists might leak through Mishima. The bit about intelligence greatly amused Mishima, but Tokuoka's effort came to naught and the visit didn't work out. Or so he believed.

So he was surprised, a few years later, to open *The Temple of Dawn* that Mishima gave him and read in it a detailed, precise description of the Rose Palace! The mystery was solved, though only partly, several years after Mishima's death. When he happened to meet Yōko in New York, she told him that she had helped her husband peek into the palace by parting one section of the bougainvillea hedge surrounding it. Mishima's descriptions included those of the interiors, so most likely Mishima had visited the palace during his stay in Bangkok two years earlier and this time he had merely wanted to refresh his memory. Even so, if Yōko's story was true in any way, as it must be, the couple had put themselves in a dangerous situation indeed, Tokuoka was horrified to reflect. If the guards had seen them, they could have shot them dead on the spot.

There was one thing Tokuoka remembered about his interview with Mishima in Bangkok. When he wrote it up, he showed it to Mishima for corrections. He later wondered if he was one of the lucky few whose manuscripts Mishima proofread. Mishima, in any case, made necessary corrections and approved it. It was only when Tokuoka was about to send it to Tokyo that he had a call from Mishima, who asked him to delete one sentence, which he did. The sentence, as he recalled, went like this: "The Japanese can live in peace and quiet because America is fighting communism for them."[24]

While in Bangkok, Mishima paid a brief visit to Laos because his brother Chiyuki was stationed at the Japanese embassy in Vientiane. Chiyuki arranged for the two to have an audience with King Savang Vatthana, who lived in Luang Prabang as a modest gentleman-farmer. The meeting lasted for almost an hour because Mishima and the "husky, dignified, and obviously wise" king discovered they shared a great interest in Proust. Mishima found a country without "elevators or means of making international phone calls." It is "so laid back and peaceful you can't imagine it is in fact a war-torn country that's about to be divided up," he wrote to Araki Seishi. Still, it was by a US military cargo plane that the two brothers were flown back to Vientiane, with its aft ramp left open; that scared Chiyuki but delighted Mishima.[25]

Savang Vatthana would turn out to be the last king of Laos. In 1975 the communist Pathet Lao brought down the royalist military junta, in the aftermath of the Vietnam War. The deposed king died in captivity.

---

Before leaving for India, Mishima had rehearsed his latest play, *The Decline and Fall of the Suzaku*, which the theater troupe NLT began to stage while he was away, on October 13, and continued until the 29th. It was to mark another literary step in the course Mishima would follow toward his final act.

The four-act play deals with the blue-blood aristocrat Grand Chamberlain Suzaku Tsunetaka's determination to remain "loyal" to the Imperial wishes in the face of his country's impending catastrophe. He refuses to do anything, except his help in bringing down the cabinet responsible for the war. As a result, not just the country and the Tennō, but also his own son, a freshly commissioned naval ensign, is destroyed.

But Mishima was apparently afraid that the reader and audience might think that the play has to do with the familial turmoil of someone exalted enough in lineage to be close to the country's highest decision-makers yet irresolute and philanderous in his private affairs. He took care to explain his design in the note attached to the play when it appeared in the October 1967 issue of *Bungei*. "The theme of this play is an existential analysis of the spirit of *shōshō hikkin*. That is, the axis of the drama lies in the way perfectly passive loyalty evolves, unbeknownst to the person, into fealty as a kind of identification. What corresponds to Heracles' madness is *kochū* as madness or else fidelity as destruction."[26] We have seen the term *shōshō hikkin* (Chapter 5); *kochū*, "solitary loyalty," is the ability or willingness to remain loyal to a cause, in isolation, when all others have given up such an effort. By "Heracles' madness," Mishima refers, he explained, to that described in the Euripides drama, *The Madness of Heracles*.

Mishima made the same point in his program note, except for *shōshō hikkin* and *kochū*, but must still have been uncertain of the adequacy of his explanations. When a newspaper asked for an interview on the play, he took another tack. "When I wrote earlier about the 2.26 Incident," he told the *Nagoya Times*, "I depicted a loyalty that pushed itself to the very end. It is the kind of loyalty that, in its attempt to follow the Imperial Mind, went as far as killing His Majesty's closest aides." On the face of it, what takes place in the play may appear "the opposite" of what happened in the 2.26 Incident, Mishima said. The protagonist, Marquis Suzaku Tsunetaka, "surmises His Majesty's Mind"—that is, an unspoken command, "Do nothing about the situation"—"and goes on to destroy himself."[27]

Here, the word Mishima uses for "destroy himself" is *horobiru*—"die down," "perish," "fade away." In the play, Tsunetaka goes on to live, even after his nation is destroyed, but only as an empty shell. So, when Ritsuko, who would have become his daughter-in-law had he taken the simple step, which was perfectly in his power, of blocking his son from going to a doomed battlefield, demands, at the close of the play, that he *horobiru*, Tsunetaka is startled and blurts out: "How could I possibly destroy myself? I destroyed myself long, long ago."

But what the young officers of the 2.26 Incident did and what the nobleman of the play does are no different: both follow the subjectively understood loyalty, Mishima explained. This is because loyalty can only be subjective; it is something "more metaphysical and complex" than, for example, the willingness to respond to a simple request such as "Bring me a cup of tea, will you?" In one's relationship to the Tennō, "all you can do is to surmise [the Imperial Mind] and remain steadfastly loyal to it."[28] In the notes he had prepared to write *The Suzaku*, Mishima had put the matter in clearer terms, for there he had defined the two contrasting aspects of such loyalty as "terrorism" and "inaction."[29]

Mishima's intent aside, Ōoka Shōhei took up *The Suzaku* in his monthly literary review for the *Asahi Shinbun* to discuss it with two other works because, he explained, all three dealt with the question of loyalty: Abe Kōbō's play *Enomoto Takeaki*, which appeared in *Chūō Kōron*, and Shiba Ryōtarō's novella "To Cut His Stomach" (*Hara o kiru koto*), in *Bungei Shunjū*. Noting that loyalty is "an ethical question on which a human being bets his life," Ōoka rejected the three writers' attitudes toward it as either too "romantic" (Mishima), too "caricaturistic" (Abe), or too "dramatic" (Shiba) to his liking.[30]

Of the three characters they depicted, Mishima's is a concoction albeit with strong historical references that were, the author admitted, rearranged with "sleight of hand." The two others are historical figures. Shiba's subject, Gen. Nogi Maresuke, became well known worldwide because he committed *junshi* on the day of the Meiji Emperor's funeral to follow him in death. In fact, "To Cut His Stomach" was the second half of Shiba's two-part biography of Nogi, the first part being "Fort" *(Yōsai)*, and, as soon as it came out, the two were put in one book and published under the title of *Junshi*.[31]

Abe's subject, Enomoto Takeaki, was less known. As one character in the play puts it, he has been "ignored" in recent years[32] because, Ōoka noted, he has been "a problematic figure in various ways." Appointed commander of the shogunate naval fleet just before the Tokugawa government collapsed, he took his fleet to Hokkaidō and established what he claimed to be "the legitimate government," but he surrendered when he lost in the climactic battle, instead of fighting to death or committing suicide.

What makes Enomoto "problematic" historically is that after some imprisonment he served the Meiji government with distinction, in a round of high posts. In that regard, he was like Katsu Kaishū. Katsu played a crucial role in persuading his government, the Tokugawa, to surrender, but then he allowed the new government to appoint him to high posts. While they were alive, some thought the two men's conduct dishonorable. Among the most prominent who did so, Fukuzawa Yukichi, the foremost leader of "civilization enlightenment" during Meiji, argued that samurai ethic—as a matter of fact, a rule applicable to any society—would have required them to live in obscurity, declining to serve the new government in any way.[33]

Ōoka did not entirely condemn Mishima. He praised him for his "dramatic manipulation" to clarify his "rejection" of a "downward-moving" loyalty. But he was harsh on the other two. He faulted Abe's interpretation of Enomoto's "betrayal" as based on his "ignorance." (Abe casts Enomoto as a man who sought "a third way" that was neither pro-Tennō nor pro-Tokugawa.[34]) As to Shiba's Gen. Nogi, Ōoka suggested that Shiba did not really comprehend "the ethical question such as *junshi*"—a daring indictment of an extremely popular author famed for turning out one bestselling historical fiction after another. Regardless, if Mishima was unaffected one way or another by Abe's play about the samurai with whom Mishima's great- and great-great-grandfathers fought, Enomoto Takeaki, he may well have been affected by Shiba's account of the Russo-Japanese War hero, who was the tenth President of the Peers School, Nogi Maresuke, as we will see later.

Five years after writing this review, Ōoka would turn down his election to the Japan Art Academy on "loyalty" grounds—that he had allowed himself to be taken prisoner during the Pacific War and survived.

CHAPTER TWENTY-THREE

# The Anti–Vietnam War Movement

*Culture includes . . . the action of a naval officer who jumped out of his human torpedo, brandishing his Japanese sword, the moment it surfaced in the New Guinea Sea on a moonlit night and was killed.*

—Mishima

While Mishima was away visiting India and Thailand, the anti–Vietnam War movement had taken a radical turn in Japan. On October 8, 1967, three thousand college students gathered at Haneda Airport to block Prime Minister Satō from visiting South Vietnam. With all the main accesses to the airport sealed by riot police, their attempt failed. Satō left Japan, toured East Asia, and, in Australia, made explicit his government's support for the continued US bombing of North Vietnam. But during the protestors' clash with the police, a student from Kyoto University named Yamazaki Hiroaki was killed. His death revived the memories of 1960 when another such death ocurred. The clash, dubbed the 10.8 Haneda Struggle (or the First Haneda Incident, in reference to the second such clash a month later), also revived the student movement in a major way.

The incident also marked an escalation of violence. Declaring theirs was a "*Gewalt* struggle," students wore helmets, masked their faces with towels, and carried long square lumber for weapons. They called their primitive weapons *gebabō*, a concoction from the German

/ 533

*Gewalt*, "force," "right," and the Japanese *bō*, "pole" or "stick." Armed with *gebabō*, they at times threatened to overwhelm the riot police. The use of lumber, in fact, would become routine in subsequent clashes, not just between protestors and police, but between student factions. The Zengakuren, in 1958, had split into pro– and anti–Communist Party factions—called Yoyogi and anti-Yoyogi Factions because the Japanese Communist Party is headquartered in Yoyogi, Shibuya, Tokyo—and the anti-Yoyogi Faction later split further into factions.[1] The internecine clashes among the factions would begin to be called *uchi-geba*, short for "internal *Gewalt*."

The escalating violence mesmerized Mishima, but he was contemptuous of collective action for certain aims. "At the time of the Haneda incidents I truly thought," he would publicly say a year later, perhaps with the insouciance deriving from the creation of the assassin Iinuma Isao: "If you don't want Prime Minister Satō to go to America, why not kill him? It would be so simple. Terrorism is a one-man act, and that might go against their theory of organizing the people, but I'd say they just don't have the guts. They have no guts to do it alone."[2]

The idea of assassination was not, of course, something favored by the majority, aside from the fact that most would not dare make such a bald statement. Also, they were sympathetic, as Mishima was not, to Communism in general and, in particular, to the small Communist country, North Vietnam, that was putting up a fight against the giant capitalist country, the United States. On the day of the first airport clash, a group of forty-six writers and others issued a statement announcing the formation of a "10.8 Rescue Society." Among its signers were the writers Ōe Kenzaburō, Sata Ineko, and Sugiura Minpei, as well as the historian Hani Gorō, the sociologist Hidaka Rokurō, and the philosopher Mutai Risaku. Six days later, Ōe, along with several others from the same group, formed a new group of twenty-one to issue a statement condemning "state power."

"The violence of the police armed by state power and the protest by students through physical action, when compared calmly," their statement said, "are not the same in degree of the nature of violence. We wish not only to criticize the students for the excesses of their action but to protest the Japanese government with a hundred times greater force."[3]

The nationwide rally against the war held on October 21—part of the global rally called for by American students—drew an estimated 1.4

million participants. The government grew ever more wary and stubborn in reaction. At the end of that month, for example, when TBS broadcast Japan's first news documentary showing life in North Vietnam, Satō's Liberal Democratic Party demanded that the TV station oust the journalist who made the documentary, Den Hideo. The demand was reminiscent of Tōjō Hideki's sacking of a journalist during the Pacific War for writing that Japan was losing.

On November 11, the day before Satō was scheduled to leave for the United States, the seventy-three-year-old patent attorney Yui Chūnoshin poured kerosene over himself and lit it near the Prime Minister's Official Residence (he died two days later). This was in protest of Satō's support of the bombing of North Vietnam. In his act, Yui followed not just the examples of the Vietnamese monks who were immolating themselves in protest, but also those of two Americans two years earlier: the Quaker Norman Morrison, who burned himself to death outside the Pentagon, and the Catholic Robert Allen LaPorte, who did the same outside the United Nations building in New York City.

On the day of Satō's departure for the United States, another three thousand students tried to block him and clashed with the riot police near Haneda Airport. Satō's stated aim in visiting President Lyndon Johnson on that occasion was to negotiate the reversion of Okinawa, over which the United States held administrative rights since the 1952 San Francisco Peace Treaty. But the protestors were opposed not to the official aim itself but to the likely coupling of the Okinawa reversion with the upcoming renewal of the Mutual Security Treaty. It was also obvious that Satō would reiterate his support for America's conduct in Vietnam, one pressing thing Johnson asked him to do.

That, indeed, was what actually happened. The joint communiqué, signed by Johnson and Satō in Washington, on November 15, emphasized the prime minister's "view that reciprocal action should be expected of Hanoi for a cessation of the bombing of North Vietnam"—that is, he would support the bombing until North Vietnam acquiesced to US demands. As to returning Okinawa to Japan, the document merely noted that "the two governments should keep under joint and continuous review the status of the Ryukyu Islands, guided by the aim of returning administrative rights over these islands to Japan."[4] The United States did not return Okinawa to Japan until 1972; even then, it did not change its military arrangements except to promise not to bring in nuclear weapons.

## *Fatherland Defense Corps*

The radicalized leftist movement—now called the New Left, following the example abroad—alarmed those on the right. Bandai Kiyoshi and Nakatsuji Kazuhiko, of the *Ronsō Journal*, and Mochimaru Hiroshi started to visit Mishima with tense expressions. During the few months remaining of the year 1967, Mishima prepared with them two articles, one short, one long, on the need to create a "fatherland defense corps" (*sokoku bōeitai*), which he chose to call, in English, "Japan National Guard"—JNG, for short.

The short one, titled "Temporary Proposal for JNG" and issued in the name of "JNG Headquarters" but with no mention of Mishima's name, was a pamphlet addressed to corporations, for fundraising purposes. It opened with a statement that must have either startled or amused those who actually read it, to wit: "The most important issue for Japan under present circumstances is the establishment of a national ideal and to make young men understand with their own bodies 'What is the Great Principle?'" By then, it was twenty-two years since Japan's vanquishment and it is hard to imagine many corporate executives taking naturally to the exhumed word *taigi*, "the Great Principle," although some may have felt nostalgic about it.

"Many young men," the proposal went on, "do mouth a resolve to take up a gun and fight when Japan is violated, but the fact of the matter is that they have no clear grasp of how to do it or the locale of the true enemy." It then quickly proceeded to the need to protect corporations as it was "an important part of fatherland defense." Yet the knowledge alone would not do because, "without a strong philosophical *backbone*," it would "collapse right underneath their feet at a moment's notice."

The pamphlet did not explain the philosophy that was supposed to form the *backbone* or how the *taigi* was to be inculcated. It did mention, however, the importance of group life and physical training. What exactly did the JNG Headquarters propose to do? To become a conduit to the GSDF. It would look after company employees who were graduates of junior high school or high school—in Japan compulsory education is up to junior high school—for ten days to a month so they could experience the armed forces, perhaps once a year, or twice, in spring and fall, if necessary, then return them to the company as JNG members. For this, the JNG HQ would only ask for per diem expenses for meals and travel and the cost of a uniform.[5]

The longer version, "Why a Fatherland Defense Corps Is Necessary," was far more detailed, spelling out the careful thought Mishima evidently had given to the question.[6] Whether or not he believed in the Domino Theory that was the official *raison d'être* of America's destruction of Vietnam, he focused on "indirect invasion"—citing passages from Lenin's *Leftwing Communism: An Infantile Disorder*—and on the need for the kind of paramilitary force he had in mind. For the latter, he summarized the military and paramilitary arrangements of England, Sweden, Norway, Switzerland, France, and Communist China, then listed the pros and cons of the militia systems as analyzed by a Swiss soldier. At one point he explained that he rejected the Japanese word *minpei*, the usual word for the English word *militia*, in favor of "fatherland defense corps," because *minpei*, "people soldiers," sounds "shabby and unattractive."

The argument such as Mishima developed with his remarkable knowledge of relevant laws and regulations—he referred to, among other things, the Hague Convention Respecting the Laws and Customs of War on Land to explain a need for a uniform, and Japan's Labor Standards Law to clarify what a company was allowed to do with its employees—was that the SDF could play only limited roles in national defense under the US-Japanese Security Treaty. Still, even with the detailed agreement that the document stated had already been worked out with the GSDF, the professed aim was surprisingly modest: eventually to form a hundred-man "private officer corps," with the first twenty to "experience" the SDF beginning in the upcoming spring. The document ended with a three-stanza song for the proposed corps. The second stanza included the word *tate*, "shield."

Although JNG officers were to be unpaid and practically all the expenses were to be taken care of by participating companies, Mishima decided that some funds were needed for the planned organization. Mochimaru knew Sakurada Takeshi, founder and executive director of the Japan Economic Federation (Nikkeiren); Hayashi Fusao, who advised him on fundraising, had put him in touch with the man. Once called, in reference to Buddhist cosmology, "one of the Four Guardian Kings of the corporate world," and a heavyweight in government circles, Sakurada at the time was also chairman of the Federation of Tokyo Societies for Cooperation with the SDF that was founded in 1966. Even as anti-American sentiments rose with heightening antiwar feelings, many who were concerned about the low status in which the overall society held the SDF created support organizations for it.

So, with Mochimaru, Mishima went to see Sakurada. Sakurada was just one of several he met for fundraising, his first experience in the field, but it did not take him any time to recoil from the pecuniary effort. He was too proud to seek money from people who necessarily tried to assess the worth of his enterprise, if not his own worth, on the spot.[7]

These meetings also provided Mishima with a reminder that Mochimaru had been receiving money from those in the corporate world for the Nichigakudō he headed. In addition, he learned that Tanaka Seigen (also Kiyoharu) played a sizable role as a sponsor of the *Ronsō Journal*. Tanaka, a prominent rightwing corporate fixer who had come to national attention in late 1963 when he was shot and badly wounded in front of a public building, in a yakuza infighting, was one fascinating character in modern Japan.

While a student at the Imperial University of Tokyo, Tanaka joined the Communist Party and became the advocate-leader of "an armed CP." Arrested and jailed in 1930, he married another Communist also in jail. He eventually recanted, though he was not let out for ten years after his change of heart. During the first movements against the US-Japanese Mutual Security Treaty, Tanaka, by then a rightwing leader, nonetheless became famous for his sympathy for the Zengakuren. Among his associates was Friedrich August von Hayek, the Austrian-born professor of economics at the University of Chicago.

Mishima, in any event, soon decided not to get involved with the corporate world in any way.

On January 19, 1968, the nuclear aircraft carrier USS *Enterprise*, which, in December 1965, had become the first such carrier to take part in the Vietnam War, steamed into Sasebo, Nagasaki. The United States had asked for permission for the port call the previous September, and the Satō cabinet had given it. The news galvanized those opposed to the war. Not just that Japan was the first country to be attacked with nuclear bombs. *Enterprise* was regarded as "the core of the unilateral violence in the Vietnam War" that the United States indulged in—its use was a "cowardly" act for it enabled America to bomb Vietnam at will from a spot far out of reach for the Vietnamese, as a participant in the movement against the port call put it. Also, for the Japanese government to admit the carrier into a Japanese port was to openly recognize Japan's status as a base for America's war.[8]

Three days before the carrier arrived, the main opposition parties: Socialist, Clean (Kōmei), and Communist, issued a statement condemning the carrier's visit. Large numbers of students gathered at the University of Kyūshū, in Fukuoka, not far, by train, from the naval port. Their demonstrations continued until January 23, when the carrier weighed anchor to return to Vietnam, only to reverse course toward the Japan Sea on the news of North Korea's capture of the intelligence ship USS *Pueblo* that day.

Most of the mass media and citizens of Sasebo City were sympathetic to the demonstrators. They may not have been particularly ideological, but they did yearn for peace. The expanding war nearby also provoked a sense of nationalism; America was bullying a small country, Vietnam, and taking advantage of another, a country it had defeated, Japan. Worse, the riot police used excessive violence including unrestrained use of tear gas, which, creating terrible burn blisters on the skin, was suspected at once of containing toxic chemicals used in Vietnam. The police even hurtled tear gas canisters into the hospitals the wounded students were carried into. The police chief in charge in the end admitted the excess and apologized.[9]

The New Left quickly gained momentum. In February students joined the local opposition to the US attempt to build a new field hospital for American soldiers wounded in Vietnam, in Ōji, in northern Tokyo. The US Army had once maintained its Far East cartographical bureau on thirty acres of land but had moved the office to Hawaii, in 1966. Subsequently, the ward had requested a return of the vacated lot in the densely populated residential area, in vain. Now the news was that the unused buildings were to be turned into a hospital. By then the number of American wounded who were brought to Japan was said to reach four thousand every month. About four hundred students clashed with the police guarding the buildings on January 20.

Then, on the 26th, another thousand students joined the local opposition to the building of an airport in Sanrizuka, outside Narita City, Chiba, and clashed with riot police. This protest had little to do with the war in Southeast Asia, but with the Japanese government's forcible attempt to bury under concrete some of the most fertile land to accommodate Japan's increasing role in international commerce. It would become the longest-running antigovernment movement in Japan's modern history.

It was on that day, the 32nd anniversary of the 2.26 Incident, that Mishima signed a blood oath with Bandai, Nakatsuji, Mochimaru, and several others, pledging a willingness to die to prevent "a leftist revolution." This he did in the editorial office of the *Ronsō Journal*, which was in a building on the Ginza. All those present in the room, including Mishima, were soon to become part of the first group of JNG men to join the GSDF to "experience" it. The other students came from Waseda, Kanagawa, and Meiji universities, as well as the Tokyo University of Foreign Studies. Mochimaru had recruited them. There was considerable excitement and tension in the room.

"All of us who were there, only about ten really, made an incision on our small fingers with a knife," Mochimaru explained. "If the blood congealed, we wouldn't be able to use it with a brush [that is, as ink], so we had a plate ready with salt in it. We wrote 'We hereby pledge to become the cornerstones of our Imperial Nation' on rolled paper and signed it by turns. Of course, Mr. Mishima signed it first, eagerly. He used his real name, Hiraoka Kimitake."[10]

One aspect of the blood oath, however, evidently became a sticking point for Mishima later. Just about a month before his suicide, Mishima got in touch with Mochimaru, who had grown alienated from him by then. They met in Café Almond, in Roppongi. Mishima quickly came to the point. He said he'd been concerned with the blood oath, adding that he'd remembered Mochimaru had kept the signed paper. Mochimaru had. He took it to the Roman Gekijō, in Kanda, the following day, as asked. Mishima burnt it right before his eyes. The oath, which had been made before Mishima formally launched the Shield Society, clearly indicated a close linkage to the *Ronsō Journal*. Mishima wanted to erase any suggestion of that linkage because of Tanaka Seigen. The

Shield Society was entirely created and maintained with Mishima's own money.

## *Col. Yamamoto Kiyokatsu*

Col. Yamamoto Kiyokatsu's imagination was stirred when shown the pamphlet "Why a Fatherland Defense Corps Is Necessary." Fujiwara Iwaichi, then in retirement after serving as commander of the First Division of the GSDF, saw it and asked Col. Hirahara Kazuo to pass it on to Yamamoto, director of information education at the GSDF Research School. "Information" here was yet another linguistic camouflage for the new military and actually meant "intelligence." Fujiwara was the second to head the school, which Yamamoto had helped to found, in 1954. During the Second World War, Fujiwara's intelligence and propaganda unit in India and elsewhere in Southeast Asia was known as the F-Kikan that helped establish the Indian National Army.[11]

As he handed the pamphlet to Yamamoto and conveyed Fujiwara's suggestion that he meet its author, Hirahara, director of research at the school, said simply that he couldn't follow Mishima's argument. Perhaps Yamamoto should have taken that observation to heart. After all, as a professional soldier, Yamamoto also had some reservations about Mishima's idea when he read the pamphlet. But not long afterward he met Mishima, as arranged by Fujiwara, and, impressed by Mishima's apparent resolve, went on to spend some crucial moments with Mishima in developing his "fatherland defense corps."

Yamamoto was a graduate of the prewar Military Academy and the Military Staff College.[12] At the time of Japan's defeat he was a major and an instructor at the army's Nakano School that trained spies, and, like many with similar backgrounds, later joined the ranks of the military created despite Article 9 of the Constitution: the National Police Reserve Force, in 1950, which became the Security Force, in 1952, then the SDF, in 1954. He was sent to the United States, to the Special Warfare School, in 1958, including two months at Fort Bragg to study special operations.[13] At the time he met Mishima, he was in charge of nurturing intelligence officers in case the GSDF had to do "special" domestic security work.

During the First Haneda Incident and thereafter, the police at times faced the danger of being overwhelmed by demonstrators and by the people who were sympathetic to the demonstrators. Students happily resorted to violence, and regular citizens often sided with them, throwing stones at the police. But that alone would not put the matter within the parameters of the GSDF's domestic security concerns. What Yamamoto and others feared was the outcome of the Cultural Revolution. Should the pro-Soviet forces win in that power struggle, and should the war in Vietnam turn out badly for the United States, then China's or Chinese-USSR's indirect or even direct invasion of Japan could become a distinct possibility. And were that to occur and were Japan's New Left to work with Chinese infiltrators, the police would be inadequate.[14]

By law, the GSDF was allowed to get itself involved in domestic security matters only under strict conditions. Equally important, the position of the SDF at the time was precarious, with the Japanese populace on the whole indifferent or hostile to it. The core of the force that the GSDF might deploy for domestic security would be infantry, but if a tank or an armored vehicle were to crush and kill a female college student in a turmoil of the kind some expected and if that were to be caught by a TV camera and broadcast, public sentiment would instantly turn against the SDF. On the other hand, if a citizens' group were crushed and bloodied while opposing student demonstrators who were obviously backed up by foreign infiltrators, then demand for the SDF to send out its domestic security force would quickly rise.

What Yamamoto was doing at the GSDF Research School was to develop intelligence personnel just for such a contingency. And for such intelligence work, civilian collaboration would be indispensable, particularly in urban warfare. But civilian collaboration could not be arranged overtly. Mishima's idea of having a militia as spelled out in his blueprint for a "fatherland defense corps" could fill the void. It was, for Yamamoto, a dream come true.

"Truly, I thought a duck came to me carrying scallions on its back," Yamamoto said, using the metaphor for someone unexpectedly showing up with exactly what you wanted. By the time he made the remark, in the mid-1990s, he was living in leisurely comfort. In 1972, after serving as vice commandant of the Research School, he had retired from the SDF with the rank of major general. He then worked for a construction company as an executive, in a typical "descent-from-heaven" arrangement.

However, the revelations after Mishima's death of his relationship to the famous man had created some controversy. As a result, Yamamoto was compelled to write his own account of it, and one of the things he felt he had to clarify was that the promotion to the rank of major general was a matter of formality: he held it just half a day. He had to do this, he wrote, because he was disconcerted to find that Mishima's father, Azusa, had written in *his* account that a SDF *general* who had "betrayed" his son was "still in good health and skillfully keeping up his popularity."[15]

In any event, Yamamoto had some reservations about Mishima's idea for a fatherland defense corps. For one, such a corps, Mishima argued, would require the GSDF's "guidance and assistance." It would also require "funding assistance by *minzoku* capital"—an amorphous term that could mean a patriotic entity or a group of capitalists. As Yamamoto saw it, such an entity or group would necessarily be political. Suppose Mishima was trying to avoid any political involvement and therefore proposing dependence on the GSDF, the force already had the SDF Reserve, as well as the Taiyūkai, a veterans association, government-certified but with no overt political affiliation.

Second, Yamamoto suspected that a "free, voluntary warrior corps" of the kind Mishima envisioned would assume, however tacitly, the people's right to bear arms. Historically, Toyotomi Hideyoshi, after unifying Japan, took that right away from the peasants through the "sword hunting" order, in 1588, and the Meiji government took it away from the samurai through "the sword-abolishment order," in 1876. To insist on the right to bear arms now would not just erode the political foundation of the ruling Liberal Democratic Party, Yamamoto thought, but also render moot the *raison d'être* of the SDF. Without arms, however, any private "warrior corps" would collapse from within.

Despite such concerns, Yamamoto, who agreed with Mishima in his view of the Tennō as the central factor of the identity of Japanese culture, admired, even more importantly, Mishima's grasp of global power relations and domestic laws. So he was eager to meet the man when the occasion arose, toward the end of 1967, at a Japanese restaurant in Akasaka.

As often happens in such meetings, however, neither Fujiwara, let alone Hirahara, nor Mishima would bring up the subject that Yamamoto thought was the purpose of the meeting as they drank and idly chatted. Exasperated, Yamamoto, who had arrived somewhat late because he wasn't familiar with the fashionable part of Akasaka, blurted out, a little ironically, as he recalled: "I assume, sir, that writing about something and acting it out are very different. You are a man of letters. You should concentrate on writing, shouldn't you, sir, because you can certainly achieve your purpose through your writing?"

Mishima looked Yamamoto in the eye and said in the loud voice that would soon become familiar to him: "I've already given up on writing. I don't have a smidgen of interest in things like the Nobel Prize." With that Yamamoto decided to do whatever he could for Mishima.[16]

If Yamamoto felt lucky to meet Mishima, Mishima was impressed to meet him. Here was a man who was neither a callow university student nor an officer produced by the SDF, a postwar outfit, but one of the elite from the prewar Imperial Army, and on active duty. So, when Yamamoto raised probing issues, Mishima was quick to admit his lack of knowledge in military matters. Theirs, then, was a happy encounter. Following Mishima's death, nonetheless, Yamamoto would often wonder if Mishima would have killed himself the way he did had he not sought Mishima out and worked with him. In the end he wrote five books on Mishima before his own death, in 2001.

## *What Is Fiction?*

Giving up on writing was, on the face of it, simply false. Mishima was still serializing *The Runaway Horse*, with two more novels to go to complete the tetralogy. Further, he, if anything, would go on to write many more polemical essays as well as entertainment pieces—the latter, a sizable source of income, which would become indispensable for financing the activities of his JDG, soon to be renamed the Shield Society. Even if he had not thought of the extra expenses to come just at the moment Yamamoto asked him about his writing, what did he mean by that statement, assuming that he meant something by it?

For now, just one extended essay of his may be mentioned: "What Is Fiction?" Mishima began serializing it in *Nami* in the spring of 1968 and would end it in the issue that came out in the month of his death. It dealt with the nature of what lay at the core of his writing profession.[17] And in the closing installment of the series that lasted for three years, he chose to discuss two things—one broad, the other something close at hand.

Mishima compared "the ideal fiction" to "the bizarre, giant marine beast" he had recently seen in a zoo: the Southern elephant seal. His description of the animal—with its "bodily smell, its beastliness, its solitude, the naturalness it stubbornly maintains in a place utterly quarantined from nature, its spindle-shape morphological necessity to ride the ocean currents, its absolute absence of conversation and its boundless ability to depict ordinariness, its humorous monotony that never bores you, its obstreperous refrain of a theme, and its shit"—is a tour de force of keen observation and information digested on the spot.

He also brought his central concern to the fore. He took up a short story of Murakami Ichirō, "Cdr. Hirose" *(Hirose kaigun chūsa)*, "a fiction boundlessly remote from the Southern elephant seal," a Balzac. He decided to read it, he explained, because he had admired Murakami's book on Kita Ikki, published that year, and began his brief commentary by noting that it was an "extremely clumsy story," which, all the more for it, "emitted a fragrant scent."

The Hirose of the story's title is Hirose Takeo, the naval officer whose head was blown away by a direct shell hit at the outset of the Russo-Japanese War; he was searching for a subordinate lost aboard a ship being sunk to blockade Port Luxu (Port Arthur). Murakami's first-person narrative concerns the writer himself. A naval officer during the Greater East Asian War, the narrator "I" was deeply moved by a ceremonial tribute to Cdr. Hirose in its midst. Having survived the war, though, even as he managed to marry the woman he had yearned for while death was close by, he cannot drive away the melancholy that recurs in his happy though destitute life.

In his essay of 1960, as a matter of fact, Murakami had simply written: "My life ended on August 15 [of 1945], I should have died [that day]. The fifteen years [since then] have been an unnecessary addition."[18] Mishima was echoing a similar sentiment when he said, "My Shōwa is neatly cut off in its twentieth year," namely, 1945. That was his response to a question the *Asahi Shinbun* asked a group of people when Shōwa turned into the longest era in history, in July 1970.[19]

Mishima observed that only a few other stories he had read "presented, as lucidly as this short story, the contrast between the happiness of dying beautifully and the happiness of living social ordinariness as the unbearable cruelty of choosing one or the other," concluding that "the overwhelming idea of 'the happiness of death' never ceases to press on this earthly happiness."

Murakami was a follower of the Japan Romantic School, which believed that "lyricism must necessarily be accompanied by fury." He was therefore repelled by the kind of "easygoingness" that Yasuda Yojūrō displayed, as he pointedly noted in his taidan with Mishima in late 1969.

It was during the same taidan that Mishima had dismissed out of hand any possibility either for him or for his Shield Society to incite a revolution. There was "a difference between revolution and counterrevolution," he said, adding "the only thing you have to do in a counterrevolution is to die." He said, "Once you say, 'I'll die in November'" as a man of letters, "you must absolutely die" in that month.

Five years after Mishima's death, Murakami, who had told Mishima during the same taidan, "I'm not sure I can cut my stomach well enough," killed himself by slashing his carotid artery with a sword. [20]

## *A Community of Warriors*

Mishima led the first JNP group to train with the GSDF, from the 1st to the 30th of March 1968, though he had to be absent for ten of the thirty days for his own work. The group was assigned to Camp Takigahara, on the south side of Mt. Fuji. It was an exhausting but exhilarating experience, he wrote Capt. Kikuchi, his friend since Kurume. The 30th was a drizzly day, but as Mishima's group left the camp ground a little past noon, the regimental commander and all the instructors came to the gate to see them off and shook hands with each, tears streaming down the cheeks of everyone, both on the staying and departing sides. One student cried for an hour after the group got on a bus home. "A community of warriors" he had been dreaming about for many years had finally materialized, Mishima wrote.

Some of the training wasn't easy for the forty-three-year-old writer. He had to skip completing at least one arduous course: a march that required the troops to slog 22 miles knocked him out at its last leg of 1.25 miles where they had to dash, guns ported, for an attack, forcing him to be carried by a jeep, to his chagrin. In fact, the whole exercise fatigued him so, he felt his brain had become too fuzzy for work, he admitted.

Still, on April 3, he went to pay a courtesy call to the new chief of staff of the GSDF, and on April 4, the day he wrote Kikuchi, he had gone to see the commandant of the Fuji School to express gratitude and secure an agreement to accept another group in the summer.[21]

His own physical inadequacy aside, his glowing report to his GSDF friend belied a considerable disappointment and worry. The later estimate of the actual number of participants in the first group varies from twenty to thirty, all in their early twenties, but only about ten of them were fit enough to keep up with the required regimens, and barely. Part of the reason was that five of those who had signed up canceled at the last minute because the student strike at their university, Chūō, ended and they had to go back to class. That had forced Mochimaru, chief of students, to quickly find replacements in the Nichigakudō. Among the replacements was Morita, who had been laid up with a broken leg in a ski accident. He joined the group one week late.

This turn of events forced Mishima and Mochimaru to reassess their plans. First of all, they would try to recruit the more physically fit for the next group. Second, they would abandon the idea Mishima had suggested, however unthinkingly, of training ten thousand JNG men. The greater their goal, the greater the number of dropouts and failures to deal with would be. There was also, Mishima pointed out, what he called "group egoism"—something like an amorphous sense of tyranny a large body of people engenders. He had seen its worst manifestation during the war, a point he would repeat. Instead, they would focus on creating a hundred-man officer corps, as had been publicly announced.[22]

It was following this training session that Morita wrote, in the group journal the Nichigakudō kept: "Mishima Sensei expressed admiration for my fighting spirit when he saw my leg that had been broken, the day I arrived, late. Besides, we are both close-cropped and we at once liked each other (am I overstating?)."[23]

―――

Soon after the first training session, Shiine Yamato, of *Heibon Punch*, telephoned the famous man for the first time. He was surprised when Mishima himself picked up the phone, not a secretary or assistant, not even a maid. Famous writers, especially prolific ones, are known to have an assistant who sometimes writes for them. After listening to the young man explain the plan he had in mind for his weekly magazine, Mishima proposed a meeting, naming a place and time—"clearly, simply, ... without any hint of hesitation or calculation."

The designated place was the Coffee House, in the Imperial Hotel. When the luxury hotel designed by Frank Lloyd Wright decided to add a restaurant for light dining within its premises, it chose an American-style diner and gave it a generic name. American visitors were quickly increasing because of the Vietnam War. Mishima showed up five minutes before the appointed time. When he walked in the door, about one hundred customers, mostly women, that filled the restaurant, turned to look. He was dressed in an Italian-made white half-sleeve polo shirt, deeply cut to the stomach—the early spring weather was chilly—and black pants and black shoes. He looked like "a dandy Adriatic seaman." Shiine almost saw an "aura" emanating from the man.

As he explained his plan to do an article, "Mishima Yukio's elegant personal life at home," Shiine felt better and happier. Mishima's responses were "not too polite, not too general, not too cold, not too meddlesome," his voice bubbling up "like a honeydew spring." When Mishima set his attaché case on the table—exactly the same model the James Bond films had made familiar—and opened it, he expected him to pull out some esoteric gadgets, but all Mishima pulled out was a few sheets of paper.[24]

About the same time he met Shiine, Mishima ordered a uniform for the JNG. The designer was Igarashi Tsukumo, who made suits for Charles de Gaulle. He, perhaps via Mishima, may well have been inspired by the US Air Force Academy uniform; *Heibon Punch* had given it a three-page photo display three years earlier, and the design Igarashi came up with closely resembled it.[25] Tsutsumi Seiji, president of the Seibu Department Store, put Mishima in touch with Igarashi. Mishima himself designed the hat, with an overt suggestion of what Nazi officers used to wear, with a distinct curve on the top. His initial order was for twenty-five sets.

Tsutsumi, whom Mishima had known since around 1955 when he became president of Seibu and published a book of poems, was an unusual man. Born in 1927 to a businessman-politician and one of his mistresses, he joined the Communist Party while studying economics at the University of Tokyo and became a leader of the Zengakuren in its early years. But he was so successful and innovative in his business, he became, during the 1970s and 1980s, a superstar in the business world, even as he continued to publish books of poetry and novels. He was accorded a doctorate in economics for his book criticizing consumer society, in 1996. In 2007 he was elected to the Japan Art Academy. A few months before ordering the JNG uniform, Mishima had written Tsutsumi to thank him for the new book of poems he had sent him. A poem-by-poem commentary, the letter is a marvel of conscientiousness and insight.[26]

On April 29, the Shōwa Emperor's Birthday and a national holiday, Mishima invited Muramatsu Takeshi to lunch at the Takanawa Prince Hotel.

"In the banquet room was a large partition screen set up," Muramatsu recalled. "From behind it appeared the [JNG] members who had switched into a uniform, one after another. I was startled, my eyes opened wide. Mr. Mishima watched the change of my expression with amusement." Then they lined up in front of the screen, which was gold, and sang a song. "Be strong, righteous, and be tough. / We pursue both literary and martial ways...." Mishima had written the lyrics. The young men followed this with a song satirical of Mishima, sung to the tune of *The Sound of Music*. "I know no other moment when Mr. Mishima looked as happy as he did while the young men in the newly made uniforms solemnly sang a song making fun of him."[27]

## Spy Training

Yamamoto Kiyokatsu, who visited Mishima's first JNG group while they were training at Camp Takigahara, started training the same men in mid-May in the basics of indirect invasion and urban guerilla warfare. For his lectures and other gatherings, Mishima arranged a variety of places—inns, his acquaintance's house, and theaters, in the middle of Tokyo or its suburbs—all at his own expense. Yamamoto was impressed, even moved, by Mishima's eagerness to learn. In his memoir focusing on his association with Mishima, he detailed some of the things he did with him.[28]

For his lecture on espionage, on May 27, for example, he cited the Noshiro Incident—the discovery in the early morning of April 1, 1963, of two bodies cast up on the shore of Noshiro City, Akita, a prefecture on the Japan Sea side of northern Honshū. The two—one Korean, one Japanese, both male—were apparently spies North Korea had sent. Their possessions—Soviet-made pistols, maps, code, a list of random numbers, wireless, and sizable amounts of dollars and yen—and other items found nearby did not suggest otherwise. But perhaps some authority wanted it hushed up: the case was quickly disposed of as a botched attempt by illegal immigrants.

Yamamoto described the case to explain certain things spies were expected to carry and, also, that spies could meet unceremonious deaths. Mishima was engrossed by the topic but especially by the photo of the two dead men Yamamoto handed out. When Yamamoto suggested that the case could have been hushed up, he cried out, with a touch of anger: "Why did they leave such a grave matter unexplored?" When recess came, he urged Yamamoto to forgo it and continue the lecture.

The following day, Yamamoto had the pleasure of surprising Mishima. Just before taking up the topic of the day, he casually played a tape recorder and saw Mishima's large eyes widen when he heard his own voice: It was a recording of himself and his men at the café where he had taken them after Yamamoto's lecture the previous day. Yamamoto then showed a film of Mishima and his men walking—as inconspicuously as possible, as instructed—into the inn where the gathering of the previous day had been held. He had placed some of his men to do the secret recording and filming.

Yamamoto's subject of May 28 was intelligence and counterintelligence. The lecture over in the morning, he gave the afternoon to practical training. By then he had observed what a celebrity Mishima was. The mass media paid close attention to every move he made, every step he took. Of course, Yamamoto had known all that to some extent from the outset, so one basic understanding between the two had been that Mishima would take extra caution not to reveal what he was doing with Yamamoto—that Yamamoto would cease his "cooperation" with Mishima the moment any of their work was known to anyone outside. If a journalist got wind of the secret undertaking, Yamamoto taking sole responsibility and resigning would not have worked. Given the legal and political position of the SDF and its standing among the general populace, the director-general of the Defense Agency, even the prime minister, could be forced to resign.

That day, as a matter of fact, Mishima had shown up at the designated place in disguise—with a Coleman moustache. One topic Yamamoto had dealt with the previous day surely was the importance of disguise for spies, but even so! That moustache was what made the popular vaudevillian Tony Tani, for one, appear so comical. Unable to suppress his smile, Yamamoto asked if the disguise worked. Mishima was crestfallen. "On the streetcar on the Sōbu Line coming here, a student-like fellow asked me, 'Aren't you Mr. Mishima?' I tried to fib, but...."

The training that afternoon had to do with intelligence delivery. The task was collecting information in Roppongi and passing it to a certain man in a bookstore in Yotsuya. The Defense Agency, along with a number of foreign consulates, was located in Roppongi, and a large number of Chinese agents were known to be using mahjong houses and restaurants as their operational bases. Mishima, with a Coleman moustache and in sunglasses, became impatient that he wasn't given any task.

Yamamoto raised the level. One day it had to do with delivering a secret document as might happen when an agent decides to become a double agent for money. In the setup Yamamoto created, three people were involved: A, B, and C. A and C are known to each other, but they do not know B nor are they known to him. A is told to make certain signals at a designated place (e.g., the entrance of a department store), within a given timeframe (12:55 a.m. to 1:05 p.m.), and deliver a document to someone who recognizes his signals (B); he must do this in such a covert way that no one will not notice. C, who is in surveillance of A at one remove (a café across the street), approaches B as soon as he receives a document from A and finds out his name and company without creating any suspicion. Yamamoto says he enlisted the help of his friend who had made a great reputation in intelligence before Japan started its invasion of China, in 1937, but does not say whether Mishima took part in this particular exercise.

The place Yamamoto chose for the training of terrain surveillance would turn out to be fateful: the Eastern Headquarters of the GSDF, in Ichigaya. He chose it just in case Mishima's group might have to work with the GSDF, but also to introduce Mishima to one of his colleagues, a colonel.

The task for Mishima's group was to study the layout of the HQ buildings. The "operation" was a great success; the GSDF welcomed the public and the young men acted like any other curious citizens. One student even asked for and got a cup of coffee at the adjutant's office.

Yamamoto had no way of imagining what would happen there, in the same place, in two and a half years.

Yamamoto designed the last training as a summing-up of all the elements of espionage he had taught. It was a daylong exercise, beginning in early morning and ending near midnight. The place where the trainees were told to gather, as the day progressed, was San'ya, the slum area in Arakawa Ward, in Tokyo, that had been known for several large-scale riots since 1960 (officially the name San'ya had ceased to exist in the renaming of places in 1966, as frequently happens in Japan).

When Mishima turned up at Benkei Bridge, in Akasaka, at six in the evening, before moving on to San'ya, Yamamoto marveled at his skillful disguise as a day-laborer: in a dirty alpine hat, a worn-out jacket, and in wooden clogs, and his face, hands, and feet dusty. No wonder: The moment he learned that the next and last destination was San'ya, Mishima, a man of theater, had a makeup specialist go to a house not far—the residence of a translator of his works into English, as it turned out—and wait for him.

The only problem with his disguise, as far as Yamamoto was concerned, had to do with the way he carried a towel. Almost all laborers carry such a towel to wipe off their sweat and for other purposes. But they do so around their neck; Mishima came with his tucked into his belt, rather in the manner of the students of prewar higher schools when they wanted to look rough, tough, non-elite. Upon further thought, though, Yamamoto guessed that Mishima did so in defiance of the violent student demonstrators who masked their faces with towels. Mishima openly disliked them for that.

Yamamoto likely was unaware of it, but Mishima had used San'ya in his novel three years earlier, *Music*. That is where the psychoanalyst-narrator, his assistant Akemi, his beautiful young patient Reiko, and her boyfriend Ryūichi go to the slums—in disguise. They do so to look for Reiko's brother whose long-term sexual relationship with her is assumed to be the cause of her frigidity. "I was in shabby trousers and a wrinkly open-neck shirt that I had pulled out of a drawer, and Akemi, having removed all her makeup, in slacks made of mangy black serge and a gray blouse, the two of us looking like a down-and-out stylish artist couple," and so on.

When the day's exercise was over past ten that night, the group repaired to a restaurant for review and dinner. The restaurant, Yōrō no

Taki, was not far, as it was next to the Ekōin, in Asakusa, the old Buddhist temple for the nameless dead. "This is the first time I had an experience like this. We are truly grateful to you, sir!" Mishima exclaimed, repeatedly, as he drank, until he got quite tipsy, and teary, as he seldom did. Yamamoto prudently took him home himself, alarming the Mishima household with its master in strange guise and drunk.

## *The Teach-in*

On June 16, Mishima took part in his first "teach-in." The teach-in that day was not for a gaggle of people gathered to voice divergent, opposing opinions for argument and debate, if mainly to persuade the persuaded. It was done as part of the campus festival of Hitotsubashi University, originally set up as a private school to study commercial law, in 1875, by Mori Arinori, Japan's first consul in the United States and later its first minister of education. Mori believed that commerce would be the backbone of Japan in its dealings with foreign countries. Had Japan followed his vision, it might have had a different fate, but he was assassinated, in 1889, at age forty-two, for advocating the adoption of English as national language and other "unpatriotic" views.

Mishima spoke at a symposium held at the university's Institute for Japanese Culture. There were two other speakers: Nakatsuji Kazuhiko, of the *Ronsō Journal*, and Fukuda Nobuyuki, a physicist at the Tokyo University of Education known for his infatuation with Rev. Sun Myung Moon, the founder of the Unification Church. Nakatsuji discussed "Popular Culture and Revolution," and Fukuda, "Energy Revolution."

Mishima started his topic, "Principles of National Reformation," by citing Carl von Clausewitz's words, "War is a political act by other means; policy is war by peaceful means," and Mao Zedong's statement: "Politics is war without bloodshed while war is politics with bloodshed."[29] He then went on to discuss "the May Revolution," in Paris, and the assassination of Robert F. Kennedy, in Los Angeles, earlier that month.

Mishima referred to the RFK assassination to contrast democracy, in which, he said, assassinations are unavoidable, with Communism, in which purges accompanied by executions are. There is no reason for condemning assassinations in a democracy, he said, for there are good and bad assassinations. Was he by any chance thinking of his grandfather Sadatarō warning "the commoner Prime Minister" Hara Takashi of the assassination plot that was in fact carried out? (Hara wrote in his diary, on February 20, 1921, that Hiraoka Sadatarō and another man separately came to tell him that a plan to assassinate him was afoot. He was killed by a switchman at Tokyo Station, on November 4 that year.)

Was he a devil's advocate? Probably not. Some students naturally asked obvious questions. Even conceding that assassinations are "unavoidable in a democracy," a student asked, is it not "going too far" to kill someone like RFK, who had a large number of supporters, just because one doesn't like one aspect of the man?

As to the May Revolution, Mishima confessed he had "a classical notion of a revolution," as a "basic force for overturning power." A revolution has two components, rational and emotional, and for it to succeed, the two must work together but also must have the military's support. The May Revolution failed not just because the rational forces (workers) and the emotional forces (students) sometimes came close, sometimes went separate ways but also because they failed to elicit any support from the military.

By the time he spoke, de Gaulle, who had dissolved the National Assembly, was coming down hard with repressive measures, but his policy had the danger, Mishima predicted, of pulling the rational and emotional elements solidly together.[30] That did not happen. De Gaulle handily won the election, on June 23.

In separate remarks—before the election and for the *Ronsō Journal*—Mishima assessed the French student movement differently, calling it a new mode of revolutionary method that "escalated" from a demand for "simple educational reform" to economic struggle to political struggle. Noting that there were moments when some expected it to succeed as "the first revolution in an advanced industrialized country," he said that in the process, R. Palme Dutt's formula for a fascist takeover, through the "betrayal" of elements of the left, almost worked.[31]

In the event, strikers went back to work and students went on vacation, but there evidently was considerable anxiety among some French observers. The anti-Marxist philosopher-journalist Raymond Aron, while sympathetic to the students' criticisms of their educational system, was concerned that the fragile social fabric would come apart if the workers and students succeeded in their demands, even as he dismissed the turmoil they created as "a psychodrama acted out on the stage where once the genuine item had been performed in repertoire." The historian Tony Judt, who, then a student at the University of Cambridge, joined "the revolution," took it seriously, and had "fun," was later inclined to share Aron's "skeptical words."³² Mishima might have agreed to Aron's assessment had he known it—at least later.

In the Hitotsubashi teach-in, Mishima inserted into his talk an image strikingly similar to the one he had conjured in a substantive article that had just appeared in *Chūō Kōron*. To illustrate the importance of taking responsibility for one's pronouncements in the context of freedom of speech, he cited the story of an army lieutenant who suddenly dashed, with his sword drawn, and shouting, into throngs of Russian soldiers and was clobbered to death on the spot. He heard about it from someone who was on the scene. That happened, he said, when the Japanese army was disarming itself in front of the Russian army in Manchuria, in 1945. Mishima's point: "speech is the same as the Japanese sword." No matter how many thousands your opponents, you are on your own, a single Japanese sword.³³

---

One evening in March, Mishima conducted an orchestra at a pop concert under Dan Ikuma's directorship, a role he was given because he was a celebrity willing to take on anything. On the last day of the same month, he went with his family to the banks of the Tama River on a leisurely "grass picking" excursion, an old custom of collecting edible wild plants such as horsetail sprouts and watercress. Yōko drove, stopping the car here and there as they went. The cherry trees had just begun to bloom and willow trees were burgeoning.

The beauty of the latter reminded Mishima of a phrase from Ueda Akinari: "Blue, blue are the spring willows, but do not plant them in your garden." It is the opening sentence of one of Akinari's short stories, "Pledge by Chrysanthemum Flower" *(Kikka no chigiri)*, and is followed by a warning: "In intercourse, do not associate yourself with someone frivolous. A willow may easily flourish, but it can hardly withstand the first autumn wind. It may be easy to make friends with someone frivolous, but he can quickly go away." The story has to do with two men who adopt each other as brothers. Before parting, they pledge to meet again on Chrysanthemum Day, the 9th of Ninth Month, of the following year. But one of them, unexpectedly finding himself under a form of house arrest in a distant place, kills himself to turn into a ghost to carry out the pledge.

Later, when solicited by *Shōsetsu Shinchō* for one of those ephemeral filler-like essays for which most Japanese monthlies set aside space for writers, politicians, and such, Mishima wrote about that spring day, ending the essay, "Old Spring," with a note that it was on the following day, April 1, that Japanese dailies issued extras—something that "had been forgotten in daily life since TV stations opened," as he pointed out in a different essay[34]—on the news that President Lyndon Johnson announced his decision not to run for reelection and that he was suspending the bombing of North Vietnam for peace talks.[35]

CHAPTER TWENTY-FOUR

# *Sun and Steel*

*The hallowing of Pain*
*Like hallowing of Heaven,*
*Obtains at a corporeal cost—*
*The Summit is not given*

—Emily Dickinson

In mid-April, 1968, Mishima, with Matsuura Takeo and Nakamura Nobuo, pulled out of the theater troupe N.L.T. to set up a new one, Rōman Gekijō, "Romantic Theater," and became its supervising director. At that moment Matsuura was directing *Black Lizard* at the Tōyoko Gekijō, with the transvestite Maruyama Akihiro playing the sexy, evil heroine. From the 3rd to the 5th of May, Mishima, with Hayashi Fusao and Muramatsu Takeshi, took part in a seminar held by the Japanese Students Alliance.

In June, he wrote the introduction to Yatō Tamotsu's selection of photos of "naked festivals" *(hadaka matsuri)*, in which men take part naked save for loincloths. In speaking of these festivals, Mishima gave a wry but succinct history of how the Japanese, perceiving themselves to be uncivilized or uncultured in comparison with Westerners, had acted perversely since the mid-nineteenth century, unaware that the Westerners themselves came laden with cultural hypocrisies. The Japanese failed to notice, for example, that something like which part of the body is to be hidden in public is not a matter of civilized or uncivilized. As a result, such routine things as men and women mingling naked in a hot spring and mothers suckling their babies exposing their breasts were quickly suppressed as "barbaric."

So were the ancient festivals of men naked except for loincloths jostling to achieve a goal—such as carrying a set of yin-yang balls from one place to another, as happens in the Tamaseseri, at Hakozaki Shrine, in Hakata. But now that Japan had become *advanced* enough to export transistor radios, people felt confident enough to pull some "feudal customs" out into the open—when, alas, these, suppressed and forgotten too long, were about to disappear forever.[1]

About the same time, Mishima had a taidan with Genda Minoru on national defense. Genda, a skilled pilot who had taken part in Pearl Harbor and other battles as a staff officer of the naval airborne division and two and a half years on become one of the devisors of the Kamikaze tactic at the General Staff, was among the many who made a smooth transition to the SDF, where he achieved the rank equivalent to the US four-star general in the Air Self-Defense Force.

At the time of the taidan with Mishima, Genda was running for reelection for the House of Councilors. Mishima's brief, laudatory essay on him for the *Asahi Shinbun*[2] could have only enhanced his reputation as leader of the "Genda Circus" and as "the hero of the sky" in prewar years. Mishima began his report this way: "As soon as I met Mr. Genda, I asked, 'Do you still pilot airplanes, sir?' [He replied,] 'Yes, sometimes. It's easier than walking.'" Given his fame, however dubious in some ways, Genda's reelection was a cinch. In the end he served in the Upper House for twenty-four years.

Also in June, Mishima joined sixty-two other experts from various fields to found the Japan Cultural Congress, and was duly elected one of its directors. The roster of charter members included such notables as Kobayashi Hideo, Fukuda Tsuneari, the historian Hayashi Kentarō, the painter Hayashi Takeshi, and the architect Taniguchi Yoshio, who years later would be commissioned to design the new building of the Museum of Modern Art, in New York.

The initial idea for the creation of the JCC may well have come from the CIA or one of its tentacles, but among Japanese intellectuals there was enough unease about the milieu generated by the anti-Security Treaty movement, which had seen its earlier peak in 1960, to agree on setting up a forum for those advocating "responsible freedom" that would reject extreme leftist and rightist positions.³ But the forum, when it was created, stressed that Japan as a mass society was facing a crisis as it had cut itself off from tradition and that individual thinking was being neglected by mass thinking.

Such sentiments are always amorphous, as those expressed by the JCC certainly were, but its goal was even more so: to make Japan "a philosophical bridge between the East and the West amid increasing complications and rising tensions in international relations."⁴ Here the East-West dichotomy is that between Soviet-style Communism and American-style capitalism, not the Kiplingesque one between Europe and Asia. Before the Second World War, some Japanese intellectuals advocated that Japan become a bridge to enable the two different cultural spheres such as seen by Kipling to "meet." The Christian leader Uchimura Kanzō was one of them; toward the end of the nineteenth century he argued that Japan's geopolitical role would be to play just such an intermediary, and his book, *On the Earthman (Chijin-ron)*, was reissued at the start of the Pacific War. The committee in effect intended to resurrect that role in a completely different setting.

Mishima stated his reason for joining the group in a *Yomiuri Shinbun* article. He was irritated that "the minority" had to be put on the defensive vis-à-vis "the majority." The majority insisted that they were for "peace" and therefore "antiestablishment," which automatically made those who did not accept their positions and views "antipeace" or else the drum-beaters for the establishment. He felt that the prevailing black-and-white discrepancy was wrong.⁵

He remained a JCC director until the spring of 1970. The JCC disbanded in 1994, but *Shokun!*, the magazine created for it and published by Bungei Shunjū, lasted until 2009.

In July Mishima had a taidan with Fukuda Takeo, briefly his superior at the Ministry of Finance two decades earlier and now the secretary-general of the Liberal Democratic Party. In it he proposed the idea of splitting the SDF into two groups, one for the United Nations, the other for national defense only. He put the idea forward in reference to a recent survey by the weekly *Yomiuri* of sixty-odd people in a range of fields that found "an overwhelming majority was for leaving the Constitution as it is"—that is, keeping Article 9 intact—"while not recognizing the SDF as a military force."⁶

Later that year he elaborated on the idea, first for the bulletin of the Japan Federation of Employers' Association,[7] then in a "free talk" (*hōdan*) for the monthly *Bungei Shunjū*.[8] In the final form he envisioned, the sticking point was the US-Japanese Mutual Security Treaty, but his idea remained the same: 90 percent of the land force, 10 percent of the air force, and 40 percent of the maritime force would be reorganized purely for national defense, unrelated to the treaty, "not for America," while 10 percent of the land force, 90 percent of the air force, and 60 percent of the maritime force would be reorganized as a genuine detachment of the UN police reserve, which Mishima thought would come into being sooner or later. The problem was the puny size of the SDF as it was. There was no way for a force of 160,000 to defend the country, because at least a million-man force would be needed. Another problem was the nation's infrastructure, with the highways not built to bear tanks, and so forth.[9]

## *Decadence and National Defense*

From that spring to summer, Mishima took on several disparate literary ventures, not counting *The Runaway Horse*, which he was about to complete, or the series of essays mentioned earlier, "What Is Fiction?" To name just three, they were: serving as sole editor of a special issue of *Hihyō* that focused on decadence; starting a series titled *Spiritual Lectures for Young Samurai* for a new magazine; and writing an essay, "On Defending Culture."

As editor of the decadence special, Mishima selected, for illustrations, four paintings by four painters: Taiso Yoshitoshi, Takehisa Yumeji, Desiderio da Settignano (1428?–64), and Aubrey Beardsley. He did so because "they have in common a certain debility, a certain paranoia." Throughout his painterly career, Yoshitoshi displayed "tireless taste for blood and gore," Mishima explained, an understandable propensity of a man who "survived the turmoil of the last phase of the Tokugawa government" when assassinations and other killings were rampant, that culminated in the series *28 Folks with Heroic Names*. But he chose one with "a concentrated expression of *grotta*"—what Mishima meant by "grotta" is obscure—that "reveals a soul trembling with a happy conjunction of his own physiology and the excitement of the peripheral nerves of the age."

Yumeji, "the most moderate of the four" selected for the special issue, nonetheless "was not lacking in a certain amoral eye common with Beardsley," Mishima wrote. In fact, he speculated, the Japanese painter-illustrator, chiefly known for what might be called "lyrical ennui"—of which, like wearing "a flannel kimono in late spring, you can't tell whether it derives from a slight fever, or from the weather"—must have been influenced by "Beardsley's sharp, nonresisting decadence." Simple kimono made of flannel (*neru* in Japanese) were prized as early summer wear during Yumeji's era. Mishima chose his painting depicting an opium den, even as he noted that Yumeji had "compromised with the moderating sensibility of Taishō culture and his works could never have demonic depth or lurid satire."

"About Beardsley, I needn't add any superfluous words," Mishima wrote, even as he could not help choosing *Priest* to observe that "with its pale arrogance and what may be called an enfeebled kingly power," it must be the illustrator's self-portrait.[10]

He learned about Desiderio, as well as the painting he chose, from Shibusawa Tatsuhiko, Mishima wrote. "This sense of collapse is the most symbolic and most concrete expression of the sense of European decadence, of the collapse of the world. Continually, vividly reflected in the eyes of this unique painter obsessed all his life with a dream of a great collapse of a great building must have been the image of the destruction, which was to be, of Europe. And that great building," Mishima closed his introduction to the special issue, *Decadent Art*, "never has had any resident in it. He, I venture, may have had premonitions of the disappearance of human beings in advance of the collapse of culture."[11]

By chance or by design, the decadence special of *Hihyō* carried the last installment of Mishima's most remarkable contemplation on body and death, *Taiyō to tetsu* (*Sun and Steel*). But we will look at it a little later.

---

*Spiritual Lectures for Young Samurai* was a series of twelve essays for the rather comically named monthly magazine *Pocket Punch Oh!*—the naming inspired, it was said, by Marshall McLuhan's "the medium is the message" and because it was pocket-sized, though a more "intense" version of the weekly *Heibon Punch* for the young, with more photos of naked girls and such.[12] Mishima's series was suggested by the literary critic Mushiake Aromu who had read Mishima's review of Jean-Pierre Melville's *Le Samouraï* in the film arts magazine *Eiga Geijutsu* the previous year.[13] In the review, Mishima had expressed admiration for the French film, with Alain Delon playing a perfectionist hit man, even as he condemned John Huston's *Reflections in a Golden Eye*. Melville depicts a world, Mishima wrote, where "there are no social and political issues, where only the beauty of self-directing etiquette starts to glow as ethical, where there is only life and death, where, besides, the borderline between life and death is none other than the thin rim of an elegant fedora."

In the movie, the contract killer, before going out of his bachelor flat (*garçonnier*) to carry out a killing, checks his getup in the mirror, and touches the rim of his hat at the end of his narcissistic, preening ritual. Mishima then cited words from the swordsman Miyamoto Musashi's *Book of Five Elements (Gorin no sho)* to characterize the rule of action that Delon the Hitman follows: "Your mind shouldn't follow your body, nor should your body follow your mind. Your mind must be cautious while your body is not."

*Spiritual Lectures*, at any rate, is not exactly what one might expect from its title. Like some of his other writings of a similar nature, it turns out *not* to be a bunch of pep talks, however outlandish the opinions expressed may be Mishima-style, despite the headlined topics such as "the courageous man," "manners," "trust," "dress," and "the order for the old and young." Rather, it mainly concerns the complications that modern youth has to cope with as a result of changing times and influences.

The section, "On the literary feeble bodies," is a case in point. "Literary feeble fellows" (*bunjaku no to*), in Mishima's youth, meant those who were physically weak on account of their pursuit of learning in general and literature in particular. Mishima begins by mentioning his days in higher school when the tough students who advocated the notion, "military might decides all—*budan-ha*, and they were all members of sports clubs such as baseball and rugby—took it upon themselves to openly upbraid and intimidate 'literary feeble bodies.'" In fact, there was a case of severe bullying in the fall of 1936, the year of the 2.26 Incident, that was serious enough to grab the headlines: one night a group of *budan* students called out *bunjaku* students one by one and beat them up, necessitating hospitalization of some.[14]

So one might expect Mishima, who showed off his bodily development even as he kept up his literary prowess, to advise would-be writers among the readers to pay equal attention to body and mind. But, no. The last thing he wants to do is to act like any of those *bundan* bullies, Mishima said. Instead, now that Japan is brimming with "a *bunjaku* spirit," he wants the reader to know fully "what a deceitful spiritual structure *bunjaku* adherents have."

"I have always felt the danger," he wrote, "that literature itself makes you lose sight of morality." This is because false or "second-class" literature is that which is written to exhort each man to work toward an ever higher spirit," whereas "true literature" shows you "with what horrible destinies human beings are filled" and tells you that "there is nothing in our life, that at the bottom of humanity lurks an unsalvageable evil."[15]

From July 25 to August 23, Mishima led the second JNG group to train with the GSDF, at the same camp, Takigahara. This time there were thirty-three students.

## *Defending Culture*

Mishima probably meant "On Defending Culture," published in the July issue of *Chūō Kōron*, to make a theoretical case for establishing the Shield Society, a justification of "the Tennō system as a cultural concept." However, his argument provoked a strong putdown from the one critic who counted: Hashikawa Bunzō. A professor at Meiji University who taught history of Japanese political thought and a literary critic, Hashikawa was one of the few close readers of Mishima's works who had consistently shown a positive appreciation, though he avowed his interest lay in matters historical rather than literary.

For example, in an essay, "The Young Generation and the Postwar Spirit"[16]—here *seishin*, of which "spirit" is a translation, is a Japanese word chosen for the German *Geist*, just as *seishinshi*, "spiritual history," later in this paragraph, is a term chosen for *Geistesgeschichte*—Hashikawa expressed the kind of empathy for *Kyōko's House* that only a contemporary with kindred sensibility could have felt. He characterized the novel as "a requiem" for what Mishima called "a brutally lyrical era" when Japan was in utter ruins.

"Someone like Mishima who worshipped the image of 'ruins,'"

Hashikawa had argued, had to be "driven into a life of 'isolation and asceticism'" as the "metahistoric, eternal elements" receded along with the ruins and "the *reactionary* process called dailiness" set in. Mishima's works interested him because they enabled him to sense something akin to a spirit turning variously luminous as "the image of that sanguinary 'war'" transmuted itself. In short, they created for him "a document of wartime and postwar spiritual history."

In contrast, Ishihara Shintarō was merely atavistic—shamelessly so, even, in his historical ignorance, Hashikawa judged. His novella, *The Season of the Sun*, won the Akutagawa Prize in 1955 and mesmerized the Japanese mass media throughout the ensuing year—the very period that Mishima defined as the ending of the postwar era in *Kyōko's House*. What made Hashikawa indignant was the young writer's striking resemblance to Haga Mayumi, a scholar of German literature who, along with Yasuda Yojūrō and Kamei Katsuichirō, was a member of the Japan Romantic School.[17]

"The similarities between the two in spiritual history are such as to make one sense almost a certain kind of historical scandal," Hashikawa wrote. Though one emerged a decade after Japan's defeat, the other a decade before it, they are "two Don Quixote's, each clothed in a banal Romanticism"—not just "in their worship of the senses and mystification of the body" that have been standard since Friedrich Schlegel, "in their crudity and frippery in logic and rhetoric, in their naïveté in relation to 'good upbringing' but also in their lack of irony that is common to orthodox Romantics." The Ishiharas were well-to-do enough to own a sailing boat, a luxury at the time and an important prop in his novel, and Haga was a son of a prominent scholar.

Ishihara's "ignorance of the historical inefficacy of his own ideas is astonishing," Hashikawa went on. Just as Haga's exaltation of the body developed into a justification of Japan's invasion of China via xenophobic nationalism, so did Ishihara's "emotive activism" lead to worship of dictatorship via a sense of political crisis. Some decades later Ishihara would win international notoriety by spouting "flamboyant nationalism" as governor of Tokyo.[18]

As we have seen, *Kyōko's House*, with four male characters pursuing different goals, had drawn largely poor reviews, so Hashikawa's comments, though not a literary accolade, intrigued Mishima. He saw his oeuvre in the context of "spiritual history," even while disparaging his younger rival, Ishihara. As a result, Mishima turned to Hashikawa for an afterword, in 1964, when Shūeisha offered to publish a fairly large volume of Mishima's works "in the author's own selection": four novels, two short stories, a play, and an essay. Hashikawa consented, and wrote "Asceticism of Someone Who Died Young."[19]

In it, he noted that Mishima was "one of the most admirable narrators" of his own spiritual history, though his approach to self-introspection set him apart from other Japanese in that his compared with that of "the Calvinist's self-examination filled with pessimism and awe." The determinant was the war—*Orgia* or *Todesgemeinschaft* in Max Weber's terminology. "Dying young was self-evident." Accordingly, "the artificial resplendence of Mishima's style, in truth, embodies an ascetic effort to construct a precise alibi for the absence of life." Older than Mishima by just three years, Hashikawa was affected by the war's destruction, physical and human, that he witnessed, as much as Mishima was. He had escaped the atomic bomb in Hiroshima by sheer chance.

Again, in 1966, when the publisher Bungei Shunjū planned a total of forty-three volumes of "modern Japanese literature," beginning with Mori Ōgai, and decided to give a single volume to Mishima, one of only several living authors chosen for the series, Mishima asked Hashikawa to write his literary biography. Hashikawa again agreed, and came up with an account of substantial length. It was the first one, as a matter of fact, that began with Mishima's grandfather, Sadatarō, in describing Mishima's life.

"I am grateful to you from the bottom of my heart for writing such a fine biography," Mishima wrote when he saw the manuscript. "Long ago, when you kindly wrote about *Kyōko's House*, I remember your saying you are not interested in Mishima's literature itself, your main interest being in spiritual history. Indeed, I feel that, with such an approach, you see accurately what lies at the base of my attitude, that is, what I am betting on literature, or what I am *making use* of literature for. . . . With this writing of yours, I am filled with joy that I have gained a true acquaintance."[20]

Mishima added that he learned a great deal—things like the exoteric and esoteric aspects of the Tennō system and the question of orthodoxy in Shinpūren thinking—by rereading Hashikawa's books, such as the one on the Japan Romantic School. Indeed, Hashikawa as scholar probably knew more than Mishima did, not just about the Tennō system, but also about the Shinpūren and *Hagakure*.

All the more because these things had led Mishima to trust Hashikawa as an astute judge of what he was doing, the university professor's putdown of "On Defending Culture," printed in the September issue of *Chūō Kōron*, came as a great surprise to him. He was "crushed" by the manner in which Hashikawa "skillfully pointed to my deception and logical defect," Mishima wrote in his "Open Letter to Mr. Hashikawa Bunzō," which the same monthly printed the following month. He called Hashikawa "a most faithful double agent," whose "clarity of style and sharpness of brain" suggests not so much someone "demonic" as someone who sold himself to the demon."[21]

How did Mishima advance his argument in defense of culture? If he were to argue for "the Tennō system as a cultural concept" as part and parcel of "culture," he had to define "culture" and the role of "the Tennō system" in it. He did, but did so limply. "On Defending Culture" is at once convoluted and discursive; it is loaded with lumps of assertions hard to understand unless you are familiar with certain strands of historical ideas, and it touches on too many complex issues in a limited space.

Shed all the abstract terms and notions liberally studding it, Mishima's argument may be summed up as follows: "Culture" is all inclusive, in the case of Japan covering both "the chrysanthemum" and "the sword"; but the postwar bureaucrats in foreign and cultural affairs did their utmost to sunder the chain linking the two, focusing only on all those things that are "gentle and unthreatening," that is, things that "the chrysanthemum" represents. What is needed is for the Tennō to link the two back together to restore the cultural "totality."

By the two metaphors, one a flower, the other a weapon, Mishima was referring to what the American cultural anthropologist Ruth Benedict had famously put forward as the two opposing characteristics of Japanese culture in a tract commissioned by the US War Department during the war, *The Chrysanthemum and the Sword*. Indeed, some may be surprised that Mishima brought up Benedict's famous though simplistic metaphorical taxonomy of Japanese culture to explain his position. Mishima was aware of this. In a taidan with Tsutsumi Seiji toward the end of 1969, he explained: "There is Ruth Benedict's book called *The Chrysanthemum and the Sword*; no book makes fun of Japan as much as this one. But I find interesting her way of division of culture as 'the chrysanthemum' and the martial way as 'the sword.'"[22]

So, what is Japanese culture in its comprehensive totality like? Culture is "neither something material (*mono*) nor a formless national spirit" that is sometimes assumed to exist before anything like culture takes shape in the formation of a nation, Mishima writes. Rather, it is "something transparent and crystalline through which you can see the national spirit." It "includes not only the so-called artistic works but actions and action patterns."

"Culture includes," Mishima explains, things ranging "from a pattern in nō [acting] to even the action of a naval officer who jumped out of his human torpedo, brandishing his Japanese sword, the moment it surfaced in the New Guinea Sea on a moonlit night and was killed, as well as the innumerable wills left by the special attack forces."

The "human torpedo" is a torpedo turned into a mini-submarine whose crew of one or two was expected to die upon his vessel's contact with his target, an enemy warship. Most of these suicide vessels failed to come in contact with their targets and, forced to drift, were lost at sea. Mishima's man drifted to the shore instead, so he could jump out of his vessel, wielding his sword or otherwise. Like the lieutenant he described in the teach-in at Hitotsubashi University, it was the image Mishima was projecting for himself.

Culture includes, Mishima goes on, "both 'the chrysanthemum and the sword,' from *The Tale of Genji* to modern fiction, from the *Man'yōshū* to avant-garde tanka,[23] from the Buddhist statues at the Chūsonji to modern sculptures, from flower arrangement and tea ceremony, to kendō and jūdō—not just these, but from kabuki to yakuza sword-fight films, from Zen to military etiquette."

## *The Tennō System as a Cultural Concept*

This definition of culture, Japanese culture, which Mishima makes in one of the clearer passages in "On Defending Culture," is certainly comprehensive and "total"—perhaps too much so. Mishima tries to cover so many developments, political, cultural, and social, it even appears that he at times loses his train of thought, as he seldom did in this kind of argument. This seems to be especially the case where he tries to define "the Tennō system as a cultural concept."

In arguing for such a Tennō system, Mishima leaves one vital point unclarified: exactly when, if ever, in Japanese history the Tennō embodied both chrysanthemum and the sword. One might think the Tennō did in the Meiji government, for in the Imperial Rescript to the Soldiers and Sailors, in 1882, the Meiji Emperor asserted he held "ultimate authority in both literary and martial fields."[24] But, no, the Japanese nation under the Meiji Constitution was made possible, Mishima argued, "on the corrosion of cultural totality."

He begins by citing the scholarly or philosophical attempts to define the Tennō and his role by such stalwarts as Sasaki Sōichi, Watsuji Tetsurō, Tsuda Sōkichi, and Maruyama Masao—attempts made mainly in the years following Japan's defeat and as a result of the US Occupation's introduction and imposition of the notion of the Tennō as "the symbol of the state."

As a matter of fact, Mishima's reference to "exoteric" and "esoteric" aspects of the imperial system in his letter to Hashikawa mentioned earlier reflected a theory that emerged during the process.

The philosopher Kuno Osamu, for example, posited that Meiji oligarchs endowed the constitutional monarch they created in the person of the Tennō with those dual attributes. The Tennō in that new guise was, on one hand, an "absolute monarch with boundless authority and power," while, on the other, he was "a limited monarch whose authority and power were circumscribed by the constitution and other things." The "absolute monarch" or exoteric aspect was for the government to control the populace, whereas the "limited monarch" or esoteric aspect was for the government to control the Tennō.

This duality may not be as farfetched as it appears. The American political scientist Robert Dahl, for one, has noted something similar as regards the US presidency.[25]

Likewise, Mishima's good friend Nakamura Mitsuo had argued, as early as 1956—a mere eleven years after Japan's defeat—that "the great weakness of the governing system of modern Japan" lay in the fact that "the Tennō, even as he was situated at the pinnacle of government, was regarded as a being that transcended government, was not responsible for the actuality of governance, and was powerless."

Yes, in modern Japan, governing was carried out "in the name of the Tennō," Nakamura conceded, and, yes, "those in the position to make use of [the name of the Tennō] pushed irrational acts in the name of the taboo [i.e., the Tennō]," but the Japanese people "understood, as a matter of common sense, that the Tennō was not involved in the actuality of governance and had no power to do so." This argument holds true, Nakamura added, only on the premise that "the Tennō system was to be blamed as an institution but not the Tennō as an individual," that "the Tennō was absolutely powerless as a politician." That premise was true, Nakamura concluded.[26]

But Mishima quotes Sasaki, Watsuji, et al., only to assert that Japanese culture centers on the aesthetic notion of *miyabi*, elegance, urbanity, in court poetry, whose "wellspring is the Tennō." This is because, Mishima says, all the other important aesthetic principles later developed, such as *yūgen*, *hana*, *wabi*, and *sabi*, were *miyabi no manebi*, imitations or derivatives of that "supreme aesthetic value." *Hana*, "flower," in this listing is what Zeami Motokiyo in his dramaturgy of nō put forward as the symbol of all that is beautiful and elegant.

That indeed may be the case, but does it follow that "the Tennō is the very source to which the honors of the chrysanthemum and the sword ultimately return"? Does it further follow that "military honors must also be given by the Tennō as a cultural concept," that "the substance of the Imperial authority to confer honors"—the Meiji Constitution states, "The Tennō confers titles of nobility, rank, orders and other marks of honor" (Article 15)—"must be restored to the Emperor," and that the Emperor "must of course accept the honor guards and must directly confer regimental flags with his own hands"?

Since the Shōwa Constitution cites "awarding honors" as one of the "acts" the Tennō performs (Article 7, Section 8), Mishima clearly meant the authority to confer military honors. It was a sore point to him that the Shōwa Emperor did not review the honor guards. Still, here is indeed a logical defect, a leap in logic. Mishima was probably aware of this even as he made the argument, for in the concluding paragraph that follows, he tried to explain why he made this kind of argument. But the concluding paragraph itself seems to contain a leap in logic.

When he traveled in Southeast Asia, Mishima wrote, he heard about or witnessed the Communist-linked patriotic front singing a song in praise of the king for troop unity (Thailand) and the leading Communist force, Pathet Lao, that occupied two-thirds of the country, still expressing respect and admiration for the king (Laos). In the circumstances, there is a distinct possibility for "a Communist government under the Tennō system" that might come about peacefully, because Japan is a representative democracy. But "Communist government or Communist-accommodating government is the opposite concept of freedom of speech."

Yes, again, that may well be the case. But does it follow that "the urgent task is to link the Tennō and the military with a bond of honor," even with Mishima's own caveat that the restoration of that authority to confer honors must be accomplished "not with the Tennō as a political concept, but with the Tennō as a cultural concept"?

In his criticism of "On Defending Culture,"[27] Hashikawa did not fail to point to the illogicality of this concluding paragraph. There are some basic problems in Mishima's premises.

First, if Mishima is putting forward "the Tennō system as a cultural concept" because of his fear of Communism, and doing so on the premise that the Tennō alone has the ability to preside over the "cultural totality," that imperial ability was lost under the Meiji Constitution, as Mishima himself points out, was it not? Even more to the point, the theory of a modern nation state, Communist or otherwise, is incompatible with the notion of the Tennō as supreme reviewer of all aesthetics (*bi no sōransha*), is it not?

Second, a direct linkage between the Tennō and the military may be effective as a simple means of preventing a Communist revolution, but the moment the linkage occurs, the Tennō loses his position as embodiment of a cultural concept and assumes his position as embodiment of a political concept, does he not? We already learned that under the Meiji Constitution, did we not?

Mishima, only too aware of these defects, is forced to summarize Hashikawa's criticisms in his open letter—this time clearly, unencumbered with convoluted logic.[28]

As far as such arguments go, the saving grace may be that Mishima's belief in the importance of the freedom of speech was absolute. In another essay on the same subject he wrote not long after "On Defending Culture," he made it clear that no one in authority should be allowed to discriminate among cultural manifestations.

"We are willing to protect kabuki and bunraku, but we must suppress such decadent [cultural manifestations as] psychedelics and 'I've ended up dying'—that's what politicians think," he wrote. "I don't accept that kind of thinking." Japanese culture, any culture, is all-inclusive, period. "Be it good or bad, old or new, what is manifest is the Japanese spirit."[29] The essay was somewhat incongruously titled "Link the Chrysanthemum and the Sword with a Bond of Honor." "I've ended up dying" was a phrase in the new vocal trio The Folk Crusaders' novelty song that had become a hit, "The Drunkard Has Come Back."

---

Whether politicians knew Mishima's contempt for them or not, Hoshina Shigeru, the cabinet secretary of the Satō administration, asked Mishima, at the end of the year, if he would consider running for political office—as a candidate for the Liberal Democratic Party, of course. The idea was far from off the wall. In July that year, in the national elections for the House of Councilors, among the top vote getters were five non-politicians, led by Ishihara Shintarō. The four others were Aoshima Yukio, the writer and film director who later served as governor of Tokyo, 1995–99; Kon Tōkō, the Buddhist bishop who was also an exceedingly popular writer of often rambunctious characters; Daimatsu Hirobumi, who, as we have seen, managed the Japanese women's volleyball team that won the gold medal in the Tokyo Olympic Games; and Yokoyama Knock (real name: Yamada Isamu), the comedian who later served as governor of Osaka, 1995–2000, only to be accused of sexual harassment and convicted.

Elections for the House of Councilors are divided into national and local, and these five were all elected on the national ticket, which is rather like a celebrity contest. The five were unsurprisingly dubbed "talent [celebrity] candidates."

There was one surprise: the seemingly apolitical Kawabata Yasunari managed Kon Tōkō's campaign. The two had known each other since their New Sensibility School days in the 1920s. Kawabata's lively discussion of the campaign afterward may also have come as a surprise to many, as it showed his grasp of world affairs or his happiness in talking about them.

"It would be best without something like that, that's self-evident," Kawabata said of the US-Japanese Mutual Security Treaty, for example. But when you think of Japan's domestic and international politics, not to mention Japan's foreign trade in which the United States is the largest partner, you can't think of the treaty as something "isolated and alone," he pointed out. The "leftwing and progressives" talk about the treaty "as if you can cut it off as you might one of your arms," he said—perhaps in a wry reference to a fetching story he had published a few year earlier, "One Arm" (*Kataude*). The story opens with a young woman taking off her right arm with her left arm to "lend it one night" to her lover, and goes on to describe in sensual detail what happens in consequence.[30]

## *The Suicide Project*

*Sun and Steel*, which Mishima serialized in *Hihyō* from November 1965 to June 1968, was, simply put, his "suicide project"—"a detailed proposal" based on "a calculation for its execution"—even as some readers ridiculed it as "a solipsistic game of an idea" when it appeared, Tanaka Miyoko wrote.[31] Mishima himself observed, toward the end of a series of taidan with Nakamura Mitsuo, that it was "difficult for a living writer to prove his writing act and some other act come from the same root," even though *Sun and Steel*, which he was writing just then, was a sincere attempt to do so. He said this just after telling Nakamura that he was "a seppuku specialist."[32]

At the outset of the essay, Mishima stated that he opted for "an intermediate form between confession and criticism" in order to describe something he found hard to express through "the objective art genre of the novel." The result was an extended meditation on how he reached the decision to kill himself.

Mishima was an unusually precocious child but grew up a physical weakling. So, in the manner of "In the beginning was the Word," he starts by noting that with him there was first the word and only then, much later, the body. And the body, by the time it emerged, had already been worm-eaten by the word. Employing the image of a Shinto shrine that uses trees simply stripped of their bark (*shiraki*, in Japanese, or "white trees"), Mishima says it was as if termites (*shiroari*, "white ants") appeared first, followed by a gradual emergence of a white tree already infested by them. Hence the boy's assumption of the existence of "the body that should be" with no involvement of the word, the language. It was in the end thanks to the sun and steel that he learned the language of the body as he might "a second language." The essay, then, will be a history of learning that language, which will be "incomparable" and "most abstruse," Mishima predicts at the start.

So, there had to be the sun. He encountered it twice. The first time was in the summer of Japan's defeat, in 1945. "The brutal sun that was shining on the overabundant summer grass on the borderline between wartime and postwar. (The borderline was no more than a series of wire fence half buried in the summer grass, leaning whichever way, collapsing.)" It was, he recalls, "a very close, even summer sunlight, as it intently poured onto all phenomena. The grass and trees thick with green that remained there wholly unchanged, though the war was over, illuminated by the ruthless midday sun, were soughing in a breeze like a clear illusion. It would not disappear even when my fingers touched the tips of those grasses; I was surprised."

The sun's relentlessness made an indelible impression on someone who, "already at age fifteen," had written these lines: "Even then the light comes to shine. / People praise the sun. / I, in a dark hollow, / avoid the brightness, throw out my soul." As he goes on to explain, he had been enamored with the Novalis-style night and the Yeats-style "Irish twilight" since boyhood. Surely, the entire poem, "In Praise of the Sun" (*Nichirin raisan*), retains marks of "Hymns to the Night," a series of paragraphs expressing a yearning for death by the forerunner of German Romanticism, and *The Celtic Twilight*, a collection of folktales whose title became synonymous with the literary movement the Irish poet led.[33]

> Out in the sun,
> I become a tender maiden.
> Without looking at his face clearly even once,
> I cast out myself before my lord.
>
> Though remorse is also a form of rest,
> brightness does not easily permit it.
> Before the regret, repeatedly,
> I cast out a new cliff.
>
> This is none of your business,
> I've always thought.

And I cast out my imbecile labor
as if it were a corpse.

Even then the light comes to shine.
People praise the sun.
I, in a dark hollow,
avoid the brightness, cast out my soul.[34]

The only way for the boy to be anti-Zeitgeist was to regard the sun as the enemy. As the war ended, however, he began to perceive that doing so would be to "fawn on the Zeitgeist."

The sun struck him the second time six years later, at the end of 1951, on his way to Hawaii aboard the SS *President Wilson*. Thereafter it became impossible for him to sever his relationship with the sun, even as he kept doing his work during the night. But "the sun incited me to pull my thinking out of the depths of the night with its intestinal sensibility to the bulges of muscles wrapped in a bright skin." So it was a matter of time before he faced iron, before, as he put it, "a dark, heavy, cold lump of iron, something that seems to have further condensed the essence of the night, was placed in front of me."

When he felt he had built enough muscle through bodybuilding, Mishima finally experienced the physical side of the summer festival of his area, Jiyū-ga-Oka, in 1956, by joining the bearers of a portable shrine, something he had dreamed of doing since a boy. The shrine weighed two thousand pounds, and a team of forty men in spiffy festival uniform carried it out of Kumano Shrine into the streets and, after making the rounds, finally back to the shrine, as it "swayed, moved, leapt up, and enthusiastically teetered out of control,"[35] sometimes crashing into someone's hedge.

It was while sharing the physical pain and intoxication with a group of men, while staring at "the eerily blue sky, as it was squeezed up high one moment and collapsed upon me in the form of an abyss the next," like "a ferocious giant bird with his wings spread wide," that he had an epiphany: "a glimpse of *collective visual sense*," a realization that the blue sky he was staring at and the blue sky his fellow shrine bearers, "the ordinary young men of the street," were staring at were identical. It was a moment he had long been waiting for. It was also what he had called "tragic." It was a moment when "the use of the muscle easily clarified what the word had mystified," comparable to the moment you know "the meaning of eroticism."

"In my definition of tragedy," Mishima explains, "the tragic *Pathos*"—here the word is German—"is born where the most average sensibility acquires a prestigious, exclusive sublimity at a certain moment; it is never born where a unique sensibility flaunts its prestige. Accordingly, those involved with the word may be able to produce tragedy but cannot participate in it. Furthermore, the prestigious sublimity had to be based strictly on a kind of physical courage."

"Heroism, intoxication, clarity," and other such factors that make up what is tragic are born when "an average sensibility equipped with a certain amount of physical strength happens to encounter just such a prestigious moment that's been prepared for you." This is because "tragedy requires antitragic vitality and ignorance, and, above all, a certain 'incongruity.' For someone to become divine at a certain moment, he cannot possibly be a deity or anything close to a deity in normal times."

Physical strength or the muscle alone is often inadequate, of course. A muscle-bound man often "stores a feeble mind" within his muscles, Mishima has witnessed. In his own case, however, the word came first, so "virtues the word evokes, such as calm and fortitude, had to emerge through physical symbols." And there was another vital factor. Possession of a perfect physique was not in itself the ultimate aim, for "at the end of such classical formation lurked a romantic intent."

> The romantic impulse that had been an undercurrent in me since boyhood had meaning only as the destruction of a classical perfection; readied in me like a prelude containing all the various themes of the entire music, it had drawn a deterministic structure before I acquired a single thing. That is, even as I deeply held a romantic impulse for death, I had demanded a strictly classical physique as its vessel; my romantic impulse for death had not had an opportunity to realize itself, from a strange view of destiny, for the simple reason, I had believed, that I was ill-equipped with good physical conditions. A romantic, heroic death required strong, sculpturesque muscles; if feeble, flabby flesh faced death, there would only be a comical incongruity, I thought. Even as I yearned to die young, at age eighteen, I felt I was not suited for dying young. That was

because I lacked the muscle suited for a *dramatic* death. That what had had me survive until after the war lay in that incongruity deeply wounded my romantic pride.

We need not ask how much of this is retroactive reasoning, justification as an afterthought. The process of muscle building, the straining of the muscle necessarily leads to moments of "the pure sense of incomparably transparent strength," which, Mishima found, is "the exact opposite of the word." And the word—that which gives form to the so-called imagination—is duplicitous. For imagination has allowed human beings to avoid physical pain by, for example, projecting amorphous things like "spiritual pain," when, as he has come to perceive it, pain is the only "physical guarantee of consciousness" with which to reach "the essence of being," that is, "the essence of action, the essence of strength." Furthermore, "behind the pain there is a certain light, which has a deep relationship with the light that lurks behind strength."

As he trained his muscles, he thus began to have a glimpse of "another sun that was different from the sun that had endowed me with blessings for a long time, another sun full of dark flames of fervor, the sun of death that, even as it never burns your skin, has an even more unusual brilliance."

So, for the "romantic, heroic death" he had in mind to occur, neither alcohol nor drugs would do. It would require another form of iron, steel: the sword.

It is in this meditation that Mishima described his style of writing. A man with a chameleon-like ability to mimic other styles in his youth, he had long acquired "a style that befits my muscles"—with "ornaments comparable to fat stripped off," even as it "deliberately maintained muscular ornaments," those that, like the "manliness condensed in kendō," "may be useless in modern civilization, but are still necessary for dignity and aestheticism." It was not a style, Mishima explained, that "accommodates, but a style that single-mindedly refuses." Because he valued "class formalism above all else," he preferred "a style like the step-up platform at the entrance of a samurai house on a winter day."

What about his pursuit of "both literary and martial arts"? He begins with an assertion: If "the martial logic" lies where "a burning desire for death does not lead to misanthropy or apathy but on the contrary links to fulfilled power, the glory of the apex of life, or a will to fight," there will be nothing that goes further against "the literary logic." This is because the latter means to expend one's life on "making artworks that preserve an eerily long life." There, "death is suppressed even as it is secretly used as momentum, power is single-mindedly devoted to the building of an illusion," and so forth. To put it another way, the martial art represents life "scattering away as a cherry flower," whereas the literary art means "nurturing an everlasting cherry flower," when "the everlasting cherry flower is an imitation flower."

Accordingly, "to be accomplished in both literary and martial arts is to be at once a cherry flower that scatters and a cherry flower that doesn't." It means to be equipped "in one body with the two most contradictory desires of humanity and the two dreams of realizing those desires." It is a dichotomous world where, if one is substance, the other must necessarily be illusion, and where either substance faces death. "It is a terrifying death that visits a human being that has never lived in the end, but he can ultimately dream that a death that is not such a death exists in the 'martial' world that is illusion."

That is, to be accomplished in both literary and martial arts means to be able to "remain unperturbed" in the secret knowledge that death, be it brought by the ultimate collapse of the logic of death or that of the logic of life, is "not especially providential." It has nothing that leads to "salvation by a dream."

---

Toward the end of the summer of 1968, *Heibon Punch* published the result of its readers poll, "Mr. International." Top vote-getter: President Charles de Gaulle; second, Mishima Yukio; third, Ho Chi Minh; fourth, Matsushita Kōnosuke, the founder and chairman of Matsushita Electric Industrial; fifth, Dr. Christiaan Barnard, the first physician to succeed in heart transplant; sixth, John Lennon; seventh, Ishihara Shintarō; eighth, Mao Zedong; ninth, Stokely Carmichael; and tenth, Fidel Castro. Robert Kennedy was the top runner in the survey until he was assassinated on June 5 and was dropped from the list.[36]

## *Supersonic Flight as Ejaculation*

When *Sun and Steel* was published in book form, in October 1968, Mishima added his account of riding a two-seat F-104, on December 5, of the previous year, as epilogue. The supersonic interceptor, with a lieutenant colonel steering it, flew out of the Hyakuri Air Base, located on the Pacific coast side of Ibaraki, headed out to the ocean, bore down south, flew inland around Mt. Fuji, and returned. The experience provoked thoughts of ejaculation and death in Mishima.

"The F-104, this silvery sharp phallus, tears apart the big sky at an erection angle," Mishima muses as the fighter takes off with him ensconced in the backseat. "I'm tucked into it like a single spermatozoon. I will learn how a spermatozoon feels at the moment of ejaculation."

The jet fighter climbs ten thousand feet, twenty thousand feet, and reaches Mach 0.9, then G comes. "But because it was a gentle G, it was not pain but a pleasure," he recalled. His chest "was momentarily empty," and that was that. "My field of vision was occupied by a slightly gray blue sky. It was the sensation of taking a bite off a corner of the blue sky and swallowing this clump down. My rationality was cleanly preserved. All was quiet, vast, and on the surface of the blue sky spurted dots of semen, the white clouds."

Mishima also reflected on death. "I am someone who's taken interest only in the edge of the body and the edge of the spirit, the border of the body and the border of the spirit," he declared. "I've never had interest in the abyss. Let's leave it to the others. Because the abyss is shallow. Because it is banal." The question is what lies beyond "the edge of the edge." Is all you will find "a purfle dangling toward the void"?

The contrasting entities of body and spirit had, for Mishima, something similar at their extremes. When he pushed his body to "a blinding fatigue," he at times witnessed what he called "the daybreak of the body." Likewise, when he pushed his spirit to the brink, "at the risk of falling into the void," he at times glimpsed "a glimmer of the dawn of the spirit." Yet the two had never "harmonized themselves." He had "never discovered in a physical action the cold, terrifying satisfaction resembling an intellectual adventure," even as he had "never tasted in an intellectual adventure that selfless heat, that hot darkness of a physical action."

Where do they link themselves? "There has to be somewhere a domain where the ultimate of action is stillness and where the ultimate of stillness is action." And if there is "a higher principle" that unifies the two, it has to be death, Mishima had thought. But at a high altitude in a supersonic fighter jet, he realized that he had considered death as something "too mysterious." The physical aspect of death was "simple and clear." The simple fact of the matter was this: "The earth is wrapped in death."

Mishima ends his account of the F-104 flight with a poem, "Icarus." In it, the speaker, Icarus, crashes onto the earth, "the iron plate," rather than into the sea, and he, presumably dead, asks if the whole thing was something "the earth where I belonged" schemed in order to punish him:

> Was everything what the earth where I belonged schemed,
> the blue of the sky a hypothesis,
> for the intoxication of the wax on my wings
> to be scorched for a fleeting moment,
> a plan heaven secretly aided besides,
> to hand down a punishment on me?
> Was the punishment for the crime
> that I did not believe in myself,
> or that I believed too much in myself,
> was too impatient to know where I belonged,
> or was boastful that I had known all,
> tried to fly toward the unknown,
> or to the already known,
> either way a single dot, a blue symbol?

CHAPTER TWENTY-FIVE

# The Shield Society, Counterrevolution

*The perfect type of the man of action is the suicide.*
—William Carlos Williams, *The Descent of Winter*

Soon after Hashikawa Bunzō tore apart his argument on the Tennō system, Mishima conceived a play with the provocative title of *My Friend Hitler* (*Waga tomo Hitler*) and finished writing it on October 30, 1968.

The drama has four historical figures: Ernst Röhm, chief of staff of the *Sturmabteilung* (Storm Detachment, SA); Gregor Strasser, the socialist theoretician; Gustav Krupp, the industrialist; and Adolf Hitler. It has to do with the Night of the Long Knives, in 1934, when Hitler had Röhm and Strasser assassinated. Mishima said he was inspired to write it when he read Alan Bullock's *Hitler: A Study in Tyranny*, originally published in 1952, but he made it plain that his play includes things unlikely to have happened or contrary to known fact. For example, Strasser, whom he depicts as a mousy intellectual schemer to provide a contrast to the plainspoken, simpleminded Röhm, in reality seems to have been a big, hard-drinking, boisterous man.

Why Hitler? Did you write the play because you like Hitler? many asked him, Mishima wrote in one program note. No, the fact that he wrote a play about someone doesn't mean he has "an obligation" to like the person. "To be honest, I feel a terrifying interest in Hitler, but if the question is whether I like or dislike him, I can only answer, I don't like him," Mishima said. "Hitler was a political genius but was not a hero.

He thoroughly lacked the refreshing, sunny quality indispensable to becoming a hero. Hitler is as gloomy as the twentieth century."

Politically, he was extremely interested in the Röhm assassination. If it's the iron law of politics that to prepare a nation for mobilization requires elimination of both the extreme left and the extreme right so as to create a semblance of the middle road, that's what Hitler accomplished overnight, Mishima proposed. Japan, on the other hand, lacking any such political will, and doing everything *ad hoc*, had needed a whole decade to get rid of the left—the suppression of Communism in the 1920s—and the right—the execution of those involved in the 2.26 Incident, in 1936.

He also had a literary motive to write *My Friend Hitler*, Mishima explained: to create a male twin of *Madame de Sade*. He wrote the play with four male characters, in a German Rococo setting, to go with the earlier play with six female characters, in a French Rococo setting. The figures of four and six themselves derive from his love of the old Chinese *belle-lettres* style known as *siliu-pianli-ti*, in which four-six-character phrases form parallelisms, bringing up an unexpected analogy. In other words, there was "no deep meaning" in the choice of Hitler itself, he said.

When it comes to contrasting *My Friend Hitler* with *Madame de Sade*, though, another explanation he provided may be more pertinent. "The female elegance, boredom, the reality of sex, and the chastity in *Madame de Sade* corresponds to the male robustness, passion, the idealism of sex, and the friendship in *My Friend Hitler*," wrote Mishima. He filled the character of Röhm with "Japanese sentimentality" and through dramatic exaggeration turned the man into someone akin to Saigō Takamori. In that scheme, Hitler is akin to Ōkubo Toshimichi, who successfully drove Saigō out of government.

"Both Marquise de Sade and Capt. Röhm are unconsciously thrust toward George Bataille's so-called 'impossibility of Eros,' struggle, break down right in front of it, and are defeated," the playwright explained. "Just before their stretched fingers almost touch man's deepest secret, the door to the ultimate temple, Marquise Sade denies tragedy on her own, and Röhm buries himself in tragic death. That is man's fate."[1] This description recalls the scene in *The Temple of the Golden Pavilion* where the protagonist Mizoguchi struggles to open the door to the Kyūkyokuchō and fails.

The last time Mishima brought up Bataille in writing, it may be noted here, was in the summer of 1969, in "What Is Fiction?" Naming him along with Pierre Klossowski and Witold Gombrowicz as among the modern writers of the West he paid greatest attention to, Mishima explained he did so because they share the characteristics of evincing "a raw, also rough, rude linkage between metaphysics and the human body that appears to connect directly the eighteenth and twentieth centuries," as well as "antipsychologism, antirealism, *erotic* abstractism, direct symbolic techniques, and the view of the universe lurking behind them."

He discussed *Madame Edwarda*, in which a prostitute reveals herself to be God ("well and truly a mystical as much as an obscene book, at least if one understands its mysticism as *absolutely* obscene"), with the contrasting *My Mother*, in which the narrator's mother reveals herself to be a bitch, far worse than his father, a debauchee ("not a novel about incest or, if it is, this only incidental, a plus"[2]).

These two stories show, Mishima wrote, that Bataille manages to "express through language the holiness lurking in the experience of *eroticism* even as he realizes it is impossible to attain it through language (though this has also to do with the impossibility of re-experiencing through language)." Mishima ends his close analysis of the stories with a pointed remark: "It was Bataille that cut open for us the abyss of *eroticism* the vulgar psychoanalyst of Vienna could not possibly reach."[3]

*My Friend Hitler* was published in the December 1968 issue of *Bungakukai*.

## *The Military Uniform*

On October 3, 1968, Mishima spoke at a teach-in at Waseda University. It was arranged by the Shōshi-kai, "Respect History Club," a rightist-leaning entity that was a recruiting conduit for the JNG. It was a big draw. Two years earlier, Robert Kennedy had drawn a large crowd, but Mishima's was larger.

Two days later, Mishima formally launched the JNG, now officially named the Shield Society, at the Japan Education Center, in Tokyo. More than forty members of the society gathered in uniform. *Heibon Punch* gave a ten-page spread to the event, five in color, five in black and white photographs by Izumi Shigeru, who was known for "drawing eroticism out of actresses."[4] Mishima was asked to write an essay to go with it, and did: "Conditions for a Man to Wear a Military Uniform."

The uniform, which, along with the Shield Society, would become a butt of ridicule and wonderment, was partly his reaction to the *military look* in clothing that had become popular in the preceding few years, Mishima explained. But he was also partial to color and style. "Loud colors such as red, gold, and green were originally for sartorial decorations for men." However, "there must be certain conditions and determination for a man to wear loud colors."

The matador's brilliant costume would look intolerably "foppish" on someone "without the backbone of the manly profession of death.... A man without such conditions and determination puts on a *gray flannel suit* to prove he is a sheep of the society," Mishima went on. Sloan Wilson's 1956 novel *The Man in the Gray Flannel Suit* was translated into Japanese years before seemingly every single American journalist writing about Japan, no matter what the subject, decided it was de rigueur to characterize Japan as a society of "conformists." Arthur Koestler had noted the other side of the coin four years earlier when *Life* asked him to write an essay on Japan for the 1964 Tokyo Olympics: in the United States "the organization man still sees himself as a rugged individualist."[5] Mishima explained that, whereas the *gray flannel* suit is meant to blend its wearer into his surroundings, the military uniform is meant to render its wearer "conspicuous," to warn off those who see it.

Mishima was proud of the uniform he had worked out and asked the readers of the weekly magazine to give it a close look if they saw someone in it on the street. Still, even as he stated that "the military uniform is the supreme means for a man to bedeck himself," he maintained it wasn't all that serious. In listing the distinctive features of the uniform, he noted that what was inside the scabbard of the dagger to go with the uniform was "no different from a toy," not a real thing, "in accordance with the regulations of the Metropolitan Police Department," and that the uniform was trademarked so "no outsider would be able to make exactly the same thing." He ended the essay with: "For inquiries on becoming a member [of the Society, call] 572-5744."

Calls came, at once. About two hundred people phoned within three days after the weekly magazine hit the newsstand, Mochimaru Hiroshi recalled. Some were naturally threats. One man shouted, "Let the Zengakuren kill you all!" Nonetheless, there were many applicants, compelling Mishima to work out the bylaws.⁶

Years later, Muramatsu Takeshi, reflecting that Mishima finished writing *My Friend Hitler* eight days after launching the Shield Society, on October 13, guessed that Mishima was projecting himself in Röhm who had isolated himself by insisting on leading *his* militia, the SA.⁷

## *The Nobel Prize Recipient*

On October 17, Kawabata Yasunari received the Nobel Prize. Upon hearing the news at the Japan Publishers Club, Mishima stood by at the Mainichi Shinbun Company, with the NHK reporter Date Munekatsu and the Shinchōsha editor Nitta Hiroshi, to confirm it, wrote an article congratulating Kawabata on the spot for the daily, went home to change clothes, and, with Yōko, visited him in his house in Kamakura to offer him congratulations.

"That Mr. Kawabata Yasunari has received the Nobel Prize is a proud moment for Japan, an honor for Japanese literature. Nothing is more felicitous than this," Mishima began his accolade. "Mr. Kawabata, having inherited the most brittle, the most ineffable traditions of Japanese literature, has kept walking in front of the very tip of the crisis of this country that has always hurried in its modernization. . . . Under his classical, elegant style," Mishima continued, "lurks the most pointed theme of modern literature, the question: 'In the first place can one human being love another?' 'The impossibility of love' at times drifts lyrically, melts mythically, but always floats above his works like an ominous cloud.

"And 'beauty,' as if to deride that impossibility, quietly emerges out of the snow in *Snow Country*, out of the scenic old temple of *The Old Capital*, or in the form of a beautiful woman carrying a wrapping cloth in *Thousand Cranes*, only to mysteriously walk past us."⁸

Yet Mishima could have been displaying considerable duplicity—greater, perhaps, than he had six years earlier when he had edited the Kawabata reader. As the scuttlebutt at the time had it, Mishima fired off letters to some in the publishing world condemning Kawabata receiving the prize, calling *Snow Country* "trashy patchwork," and those in the know perfectly understood what he was talking about.⁹ Today that rumor may be well nigh impossible to prove, but Mishima had expressed his antipathy to Kawabata's literature publicly a year earlier. In the first part of a series of four taidan with Nakamura Mitsuo, Mishima stated that he had never once been "*charmed* by Mr. Kawabata's literature," he had never been "influenced by Mr. Kawabata in literary techniques," and that he had never been his "*sympathizer*." In fact, he could "not stand the *yin*" nature of Kawabata.[10]

As Donald Keene tells it, Kawabata, not Mishima, getting the Nobel Prize may well have been "an accident." UN Secretary-General Dag Hammarskjöld, deeply impressed by *The Temple of the Gold Pavilion*, had recommend Mishima for the prize before he died in 1961. The Swedish Academy took the recommendation seriously. In 1967 a reliable source had told Keene that the prize winner next year would be Mishima. But, as noted earlier, a know-nothing intervened at the last minute, arguing Mishima was too much of a radical to deserve the prize.

Keene evidently told Mishima this turn of events, which he learned in May 1970. A *Shinchō* editor who met Mishima that summer remembered him saying with bitterness that Hammarskjöld's premature death had prevented him receiving the prize.[11]

Kawabata receiving the Nobel Prize was such a big event that the *Asahi Shinbun*, for one, carried the full text of his speech, which is fairly long, on December 16, 1968.

## *International Antiwar Day*

October 21 was International Antiwar Day when demonstrations against the Vietnam War took place worldwide. In Japan it turned into a series of violent clashes that in the end prompted the Metropolitan Police Department to apply Article 106 of the Criminal Code, the law against the "crime of disturbance." In consequence, the police arrested 912 people, the largest mass arrest in postwar Japan.

The principal mover of the mass protests was the Zenkyōtō, the acronym of Zengaku Kyōtō Kaigi, the All-Campus Joint-Struggle Conference. The coalition had started out just a half a year earlier to focus on campus democratization and had quickly become a powerful force. By then campus democratization was practically inseparable from the anti–Vietnam War movement that, in turn, was equated with blocking of the renewal of the US-Japanese Mutual Security Treaty coming up in two years, in 1970.

That day anywhere from three to five thousand coalition followers massed on the University of Tokyo campus alone. Large numbers of demonstrators gathered elsewhere as well, despite the Public Safety Commission's prohibition of all public assemblies and demonstrations that day. Various groups broke into the premises of the Defense Agency, the Diet, and Shinjuku Station. They also clashed with riot police in Ochanomizu and the Ginza. They threw broken-up flagstones and Molotov cocktails and brandished square lumber poles. The riot police, armored with duralumin shields, responded with truncheons and tear gas.[12]

What prompted the application of Article 106 late that evening was the rampage on Shinjuku Station, the main railroad junction in Japan for American matériel for the Vietnam War. More than a thousand students took part, with a crowd of ten thousand cheering on.[13] Although the police force mobilized for the day totaled twelve thousand, it at times gave the impression of being pushed around, with clashes taking place throughout the metropolis all at once.

The day turned into a memorable one for Mishima and the members of the Shield Society that Yamamoto Kiyokatsu trained. Yamamoto mobilized not just the Shield Society but also his Research School. About forty Shield Society cadets, as Mishima might have called them in English, were dispersed throughout the metropolis to "collect intelligence" or "grasp the actual situation." Mishima, appointed "special correspondent" by the *Sunday Mainichi*,[14] spent the day with a journalist the weekly provided and an intelligence officer Yamamoto provided.

Mishima started the day on "the campus of Japan [Tokyo] Medical and Dental University in front of Ochanomizu Station," Yamamoto recalled. "The student units engaged in close combat with the riot police kept up their fierce resistance by putting up barricades near there and in front of Meiji University," which was close by. "His eyes bloodshot with Molotov cocktails flying and spurting out black smoke and the tear gas from gas canisters, Mr. Mishima stood in its midst without even twitching a muscle."

After a while, Mishima moved to the Ginza. It was "a horrendous disaster area as [student] fighting units involving crowds and the riot police continued advancing and retreating, fiercely clashing," Yamamoto wrote. "Mr. Mishima suddenly climbed up to the roof of the police booth on Ginza 4th Street. He kept staring at the street battles, for all the crisscrossing stone missiles. For some reason his body kept trembling slightly. Perhaps it was the excitement of someone facing his first battle." According to other accounts, it was from the roof of a parking garage that Mishima watched the clashes for three hours.

It was when Mishima and Yamamoto retreated to a room in a building in Akasaka for a lunch break, well past noon, that he sensed Mishima was looking for "a place to die"—part of a samurai idea of dying in a suitable battle. To calm him down, Yamamoto offered him the whiskey he had ready. Mishima instantly became furious and cried: "What! A drink in a situation like this?!" He violently stood up and left.

Past eleven that evening, they gathered again, at the same place in Akasaka. Mishima asked Yamamoto to review the day's action. Sensing Mishima was thinking of something big, which could only be a more overt action, Yamamoto declined, and suggested the group "fall out" at once. All they were doing that day was to put what they had learned so far to practical use. The situation was still far from serious enough for the JSDF to mobilize its domestic security force. Mishima's group must exercise utmost caution not to act rashly. They should not make any move that might provoke either security authorities or the mass media.

Mishima's expression stiffened. In a moment, he told a young man to tell the members of the Shield Society gathered downstairs to move to the National Theater, then left the room without saying anything further. Again, Yamamoto felt that Mishima was looking for "a place to die." Mishima's contempt, Yamamoto guessed in retrospect, lay in the thought that "a soldier may shed blood when ordered, but not out of an inner order or demand."[15] The two men had approached the matter differently. The incident would mark the beginning of the eventual split between Mishima the military or security amateur and Yamamoto the professional soldier.

Actually, Yamamoto, writing with remorse after Mishima's death, may have read too much into Mishima's mind or at least tried to present a particular image of him. Mishima may have been "excited" or "exhilarated" that day, but not quite somber, except perhaps in Yamamoto's presence.

Chiyuki, whom Mishima visited at the Ministry of Foreign Affairs to eat the lunchbox he brought with him, remembered his brother's palpable excitement; so did Shibusawa Tatsuhiko who that evening met him, along with a few others, to discuss his new magazine at a restaurant in Roppongi. Mishima showed up in a helmet, khaki battle fatigues, and boots, and kept making phone calls, apparently to keep up-to-date on where the demonstrators were heading.[16] (Yamamoto neglected to mention Mishima's conspicuous getup that day. As commander of the day's intelligence-gathering activity he should have prohibited any such thing.) Similarly, a woman who saw Mishima that day on Ginza 4th Street, recalled a man very different from the one Yamamoto presented.

"Someone who was with me said, 'Look, that's Mishima Yukio,' and pointed at him," the woman, a student and a member of the Beheiren at the time, recalled with clarity. "So I looked and sure it was him. It was, like, he'd come to enjoy a fireworks festival. He watched, with a smile on his face, the clashes between the demonstrators and the police, and when stone-throwing got fierce and the police broke ranks, he looked ready to jump up and clap his hands" to applaud the students.[17]

The woman's observation, in fact, hit the bull's eye. Excited as he was about the turmoil of the day, Mishima was not necessarily aligning himself with the police. Later that year, he made clear that his main complaint was that those running around calling for "a revolution" weren't risking their lives. They threw stones at the riot police from a safe distance or smashed the windows of streetcars—"Even I could do such things." The students in helmets color-coded by faction were like "swarms of ladybirds," he snorted. The talk, when published in *Bungei Shunjū*, was titled "Turn Tōdai into a Zoo," a twist on the students' call for "turning Tōdai into the bastion of antiestablishment."[18] Tōdai is the acronym for the University of Tokyo.

Worse, with their faces masked with towels, they looked as ludicrous as if they were about to do "major house cleaning" or something, as he put it in a taidan with Iida Momo. "The trouble is I have a sentimental sympathy" for them, he said. Iida was the top graduate of the Tōdai Faculty of Law in Mishima's class. He was employed by the Bank of Japan upon graduation, just as Mishima was by the Finance Ministry, but tuberculosis forced him to quit. Recovering, he joined the Communist Party but was later expelled. Still, his sympathy was solidly with the antiestablishment side.

Mishima insisted that if he unsheathed a sword he'd wound or kill people, prepared to die himself. In many internecine clashes during the student movement, athletic clubs and such were rightist-leaning, and rightwing organizations sent thugs to help them. In one instance a man had appeared with a sword and wounded several.[19]

Probably about the time Yamamoto and Mishima had the last exchange of the day, an overturned armored vehicle was set afire in front of Shinjuku Station and demonstrators ran amok on the platforms and tracks. Close to midnight, the decision to apply the law against disturbances was made. All that while, the GSDF's domestic security arm had been placed on alert in secret. But there was no need to put it into operation.

The following day, the top dailies blared such headlines as "Shinjuku Turned into Lawless Zone" (*Mainichi*) and "Law against Disturbances Applied to Student Demonstrators" (*Asahi*). Disturbances the demonstrators created had indeed made a serious impression. The New Left announced the creation of "liberated zones" in various parts of Tokyo.

But there is a difference between "disturbance" (*sōran*) and "civil war" (*nairan*) as Japanese criminal law defines them. The former refers to "the group act of violence or threat" in a specific area of society, whereas the latter refers to an overt act of "destroying the nation's administrative structure or eliminating the nation's power in its territory to exercise power in its stead." And the latter could only, in limited circumstances, lead to the JSDF activating its domestic security unit.

That was Yamamoto's assessment and he was right. Yes, the New Left's actions "greatly shook the capital," he wrote:

> But it was not a battle in the living space of those involved in it, but a battle in a certain assumed situation; accordingly, there could not have been anything like a total destruction of the living space. As long as there is no total destruction, tomorrow is sure to come. As long as there is a tomorrow, social order has not been destroyed. The ordinary citizens who have joined the demonstrators will return to their daily lives as commuting workers overnight. The Zenkyōtō's battles that cannot gain a regional sympathy may appear for a moment as

if they involve ordinary citizens, but as long as their battles are not rooted in their own living space, they will soon become isolated, unable to continue and expand the battles.

"A large city is like a large vessel with water in it. The water may be disturbed by something, but unless the vessel is destroyed, it regains its quiet state in no time," Yamamoto observed.[20]

In fact, not far from the "liberated zones," salarymen who had little interest in International Antiwar Day except as a spectator sport or as an exciting piece of news had the usual cocktails under the red lanterns on their way home that very day and the pachinko halls were as raucous as ever, with "The Warship March," the all-time favorite among the Japanese military songs, blaring away. The Shield Society's "intelligence gathering" activities did not even look into those routine aspects of daily life; if its members became excited, as they certainly did, they did so in the same way that Zenkyōtō students did.

Regardless of it all, his experiences that day may well have become a vital turning point for Mishima, at least as his mother saw it. That evening, he returned to his quaint house in a quiet residential district, unhurt. But his "excitement was such that it was almost uncontrollable," Shizue recalled, in 1977. "As I look back, wondering when Kimitake clearly began to be driven to action, it was from the Shinjuku Station demonstration incident. . . . I was fascinated to hear him talk in great detail [about what he had seen and done that day], gesticulating, but I was also spooked. I felt what had lain hidden deep in his heart spurted out all at once, with a great force."[21]

## *Joy of Death*

On the 26th and 27th of that month, Mishima's two-act ballet *Miranda* was staged at Nissay Theatre. In July Ozawa Kinshirō's ballet based on the film *Yūkoku* had been staged, but *Miranda* was Mishima's own—and his only—ballet. The Ministry of Education had commissioned him to write "a Japanese ballet" to commemorate the hundredth anniversary of the first year of the Meiji Era. It was "a tough assignment indeed," Mishima wrote. The question was how to blend Japanese elements into an essentially foreign form. He did not want to create something like the ballet version of the *Mikado* that he had seen abroad. The dresses for the samurai were "exactly right," but he was disheartened when a ballerina showed up onstage in white tights but with her upper body in a long-sleeved kimono that reached only to her waist.

So he decided to base his ballet on the Italian circus troupe Chiarini's that had toured Japan in the nineteenth year of Meiji (1886). He constructed his story backward, first imagining a *grand pas de deux* between a young female Italian equestrian acrobat/tightrope walker and a young Japanese fishmonger. Because the men working in the fish markets in Japan in those days, like most other workers, wore tights-like pants reaching the knees and jackets open in front but tied at the waist, and because there was nothing strange about an Italian female acrobat appearing in a tutu, that would solve the problem of the dancers' freedom of movement without straining the imagination of the audience.[22]

In his notes for the ballet, Mishima, appropriately for the assignment, had, as the ballet's theme, "the joy of civilization and enlightenment"—"civilization and enlightenment" being the Japanese government's slogan for Europeanization during the early part of Meiji.[23] By "joy," he meant that of the reconciliation between Japanese chauvinists and Japanese proponents of Europeanization. In the notes he also cautioned himself not to make *Miranda* look like *West Side Story*. That musical by Leonard Bernstein had won such popularity in Japan that some of those who could afford it flew to New York to see it.

The acrobat/tightrope walker Miranda, trapped in her love for the fishmonger Seikichi and a Japanese politician who, even as he spouts Europeanization, demands she become his mistress, pleads to be allowed to be with Seikichi if she succeeds in her last tightrope act. She wins assent but fails in the act, and dies in Seikichi's arms. Mishima could not resist repeating the fate that he had given the tightrope walker in his story, "Circus."

Tachibana Akiko directed the ballet. Tani Momoko, then Japan's best ballerina, played Miranda.

In November the inaugural issue of *Le Sang et la Rose* (*Chi to bara*[24]) appeared. Subtitled "A Comprehensive Study in Eroticism and Cruelty," the "highbrow" magazine was topped by a series of nine photos, starting with two of Mishima as model—one showing him as a naked man except for an ample white loincloth against a large, dark tree, hands held up with a rope and three arrows shot into his torso, titled "The

Martyrdom of Saint Sebastian" (with the subtitle "*Les morts masculines*") and the other showing him as a naked man washed up on a rock, titled "Death by Drowning." Shinoyama Kishin was the photographer. These were two in a series to be called *A Man's Death* (*Otoko no shi*), with Shinoyama photographing Mishima in various postures, and the sessions would last until just before Mishima's death, with Mishima assuming that the collection would come out after his immolation; the photos were to be "images of his greatest and ultimate joy."

In these and other photo sessions, Mishima was an eager and compliant participant, naturally, although in the session for "Death by Drowning," which took place on the Kamakura beach, he was uncharacteristically reluctant to take off his small white loincloth, until the artistic director Horiuchi Seiichi told him it wouldn't work unless he did. Curious onlookers were milling around.[25]

The idea of modeling as Saint Sebastian no doubt delighted Mishima, but that year there was an immediate predecessor: George Lois' photo, "The Passion of Muhammad Ali," that had adorned the cover of the April issue of *Esquire*. It showed Ali "as a martyr refusing to fight in a bad war."[26]

The inaugural issue of *Le Sang et la Rose* also carried a series of essays by some of the more prominent writers of the day—among them, Inagaki Taruho, Haniya Yutaka, Nonaka Yuri, Yoshiyuki Jun'nosuke—but Mishima's essay titled in English, "All Japanese Are Perverse," topped them.[27]

## *The Tōdai Turmoil*

The unrest at the University of Tokyo, known as the Tōdai Turmoil or Struggle, depending on whether you took the administrators' or the students' viewpoint, started in January 1968 when the students at its Graduate School of Medicine went on strike "indefinitely." They were opposed to unpaid internship as well as to the new registration system that the government, recognizing the inequity of the internship, had proposed in the Diet. In the internship system, graduates of medical schools were required to serve as unpaid interns for a year before taking national examinations. In the new registration system, they would take the exams at once and those who passed them would be registered as physicians but then would be required to go through "clinical training" for two years. During that period they were to be paid but the pay was too low to make much difference.[28]

Before the students at Tōdai Medical School struck, those at other universities had gone on strike for a variety of reasons, but the action at Tōdai and what happened there subsequently would go on to symbolize the student movement of the 1960s. Kawashima Hiroshi, a leader of the Tōdai Zenkyōtō who took part in the barricading or "blockading," on July 2, 1968, of the university's Yasuda Auditorium, the nine-story clock tower where its president had his office and where its entrance and graduation ceremonies are held, wrote in the monthly *Bungei Shunjū* that for the protesting students the auditorium in the end became "the bastion of Japan's student movement, no, the bastion of Japan's class struggle."[29] It had come to symbolize "Japan's modernization and imperialism lasting a century." By then the call was for "dismantling the Imperial University." The students were using two slogans of the Cultural Revolution, "Rebellion has reason" and "Revolution is no crime"—the slogans Mao Zedong had come up with back in 1939.[30]

Mishima threw himself into the Tōdai Turmoil on November 10, when he, along with Agawa Hiroyuki, went to the university to see if they could win release of the dean of the Faculty of Literature and historian Hayashi Kentarō from the hands of the students who put him "under house arrest" at the Yasuda Auditorium. Agawa, a naval first lieutenant who after the war started out writing for the purpose of pacifying the war dead, had won two years earlier the Shinchōsha Literary Prize for his biography of Adm. Yamamoto Isoroku, who devised the Pearl Harbor attack. He would write biographies of two more admirals, Yonai Mitsumasa, who helped to end the war as the last Minister of the Navy, and Inoue Seibi, Japan's last full admiral.

The rescue mission failed. Hayashi, mindful of the delicate, however lopsided, negotiations with the students continuing, asked them to leave him alone. His "house arrest" would last 173 hours, until he was carried out on a stretcher to be hospitalized.[31]

—

For four days from December 21, Mishima and the Shield Society had intense study sessions with Yamamoto. The sessions took the form called "lodging together": all the participants stay in one place night and day for a given period. Yōko's aunt Komatsu Shizuko provided space for the gathering. Komatsu ran Tokiwa-ken, a restaurant specializing in lunch boxes sold at train stations. Tokiwa-ken had acquired the concession rights to sell lunch boxes at Shinagawa Station back in 1923, and it had a seven-story factory near it. Mishima was allowed to use, free of charge, the relatively large room on the first floor of the building set aside for the employees' rest and relaxation; he also had all the meals free. That was a great help to Mishima who took care of all the expenses related to the Shield Society. The room also had a blackboard. That, too, helped.

The four-day session consisted of four eight-hour lectures, one each day, all about guerrilla warfare: introduction, management, and engagement. Yamamoto took the lectures seriously; so did Mishima, who took meticulous notes, just as he did in preparing to write novels and plays. During a question-and-answer session, a member of the Shield Society asked Yamamoto, with deadly seriousness, whose assassination would help Japan the most. It was Morita Masakatsu. That is the very question Iinuma Isao, the protagonist of *The Runaway Horse*, asks (in Chapter 13) while visiting Lt. Gen. Kitō's house with two of his plotters and being entertained by his daughter, Makiko. The question suggested that Morita had closely read the novel and was imagining himself to be the incarnation of Isao who equated loyalty to the Tennō with death.

---

On January 19, the University of Tokyo "fell."

Early on the morning of January 18, 1969, the Metropolitan Police Department dispatched an eighty-five-hundred-man riot police force to dismantle the students' occupation and "blockading" of the Yasuda Auditorium and other buildings on the Tōdai campus. The police had gathered a total of ten thousand tear gas grenades from all over Japan and an array of water canons for the occasion. They were also able to secure, albeit long after opening their assault because of jurisdictional disputes, the help of fire engines capable of blasting water powerful enough to smash through the boarded-up windows of the auditorium.

The barricading students put up a fierce resistance to counter the assault, throwing down broken-up flagstones and Molotov cocktails, not to mention chairs and desks. (In his *Bungei Shunjū* article, Kawashima Hiroshi insisted that the Molotov cocktails were meant not to explode.³² He was clearly mindful of Mishima's talk of escalation of weapons in an earlier issue of the monthly.) By the end of the day the police succeeded in dislodging the occupiers of two dozen classrooms and others, including those of the faculties of law and engineering, though not the Yasuda Auditorium.

The one weapon neither side used was the gun. Sassa Atsuyuki, chief of staff of the riot police and the younger brother of Teiko, the woman Mishima dated after the war, reminds us of this in his detailed account of the battle titled *The Fall of Tōdai* (*Tōdai rakujō*). In the midst of the confrontation, an American journalist he knew, named Fisher, ran up to him, red-faced, and shouted, "Why don't you shoot them? Kill them! Shoot them!"³³ The Japanese riot police does not carry guns, except for a few high-ranking officers.

As night fell, the police left a twenty-three-hundred-man force on the campus. The next day the police used four thousand tear gas grenades and succeeded late that afternoon in dismantling the occupation. "Yasuda Castle fell."

Casualties were high. A total of 710 police officers were injured, 31 seriously, although these figures included those deployed outside the Tōdai campus. More than two-thirds of the riot police were sent for support and to deal with the large numbers of students and citizens who demonstrated around Ochanomizu Station, Meiji University, and Chūō University, snarling up traffic.³⁴ The proportion of student casualties was much higher: 270 of the 400 students arrested on the Tōdai campus alone were found to be wounded, many seriously. One became blind. The police inevitably kicked and beat up the students when they cornered or arrested them, as Shima Taizō has detailed in his account of the Tōdai Struggle from a student's viewpoint. He was in a position to know. Then a student at the School of Science, Shima had taken on the job of "commander of the Yasuda defense unit."³⁵ Luckily, he went on to become an authority on primates and was decorated by the government of Madagascar for his study of the aye-aye. Many weren't that lucky.

Why did the students' resistance and violence escalate to that point? Kawashima summed up the answer: the students' mounting anger at "the teachers, the school authorities, the riot police, the Minsei, and the rightwing students."³⁶ Sassa was sympathetic, at least as regards the first part of Kawashima's statement. Himself a graduate of Tōdai's Law Faculty, he pointed to the academic ills that drove the students to "the struggle": "the feudalistic authoritarianism that remained old and unchanged, the empty content of lectures that did not deserve the name of 'the highest academic institution,' the inefficient bureaucratic management far removed from modern reality, the extremely impotent customs of professorial conferences."[37]

The Minsei, the acronym of Minshu Seinen Dōmei, the Democratic Youth League, was the Yoyogi (Communist) Faction of the Zengakuren (it still is). In the power struggles within the leftwing groups, the Minsei directed its disciplined violence against the Zenkyōtō, which itself was splintered into factions and frequently resorted to internal violence. At times, the Communist faction strongly supported the students on strike, and at other times it seemed to withhold its support, in the end creating a situation where, "as long as it maintained its dubious attitude, the Tōdai Struggle could not end without the government's strong-arm tactics"—the police force.[38] As Mishima saw it, the Minsei was a scheming, hypocritical organization that took advantage of the students' call for autonomy without believing in it even as the Zenkyōtō pursued its "phantom." He detested it.[39]

As it happened, January 18 was the day Mishima's theater troupe, Rōman Gekijō, had its inaugural production at Kinokuniya Hall. The drama he selected for it was *My Friend Hitler*. That evening Mishima went to his alma mater to observe the clash between the police and students but came away disappointed, again, that no students fought with the police by risking their lives.

Still, that day and the next, he feared that a student or two might jump off the roof of the Yasuda Auditorium in suicide. Some of those who watched the police-student clashes on TV wondered about that possibility.[40] Aside from a law professor who, obviously angered by the destruction of his research chamber, suggested that four or five students jump to death from the clock tower,[41] the thought may have echoed the experience two decades earlier: soldiers opting for suicide over surrender.

On the second day, Mishima telephoned Sassa urging him to devise some way of preventing the students from jumping off the clock tower; he also called the National Police Agency to suggest spraying hypnogenic gas over the tower from a helicopter to put the students there to sleep—a tactic that had already failed with tear gas; the helicopter blades dispersed the gas into thin air. Mishima's concern, however, was peculiar to himself: he reasoned that just one student jumping off the roof and killing himself would instantly immobilize the riot police because of the uproar it would create. Furthermore, the appearance of a daring suicide among the protesting students would put the leftwing on equal footing with the kind of "Japanism" he had in mind: readiness to die for a cause.[42]

The government's use of force in ending the students' protests at Tōdai led to an ironic result, at least for the time being. It prompted students at other universities to go on strike or barricade themselves in important buildings of their campuses. In the end, students at sixty-eight out of seventy-five national universities, eighteen out of thirty-four other public universities, and seventy-nine out of two hundred seventy private universities went on strike. That in turn prompted the police to apply similar tactics, beginning with the Department of Literature at Nihon University, Japan's largest university, on February 18. Nihon University was where the Zenkyōtō movement had started.

Nonetheless, "the Fall of Tōdai" took something vital out of the student movement, as Mishima would be disappointed to learn in time. It would also create a number of casualties in the nonphysical sense. Kawashima was one of them. A graduate student at the Faculty of Urban Engineering who dreamed of becoming "a freelance architect," he would later be arrested as a result of his involvement with the Red Army that committed murders. His part in the Tōdai Struggle might not have entirely ruined his future, but his arrest in connection with that group did.

There was one thing about the outcome of the Tōdai Struggle that might have led Mishima to change his view of the Shōwa Emperor had he known it. When Commissioner of the Metropolitan Police Department Hatano Akira went to His Majesty to report on the latest security situation, he had fully expected him to commend the police for a job well done. Instead, the question he received was: "Did anyone die on either side?"—that is, either on the side of the students or that of the police. When told no one had, His Majesty looked happy. Sassa was as disappointed to learn of this as Hatano had been surprised, but he had to recognize that from the Tennō's perspective that was the way it must be: members of the *Gemeinschaft* that is Japan should not hurt each other. After all, the Shōwa Emperor, widely known to be a great fan of sumō, never once disclosed which wrestlers he favored. Taking sides was not his role.[43]

The Tennō's concern could have reminded Mishima of the agony of the soldiers during the 2.26 Incident: a possible inability to avoid internecine fighting.

---

On January 31, the last day of the *My Friend Hitler* production at Kinokuniya Hall, when the curtain came down and went up again, Muramatsu Takeshi was startled to see Mishima walk in from stage left in the Shield Society uniform and smartly salute the audience. Mishima briefly explained what the Shield Society was all about. "Nevertheless," Muramatsu heard Mishima say, "I, the author of this play, love playing soldiers better than the three meals of the day, I hear people say, or that I'm always dreaming of the past, they dare say. I can't tolerate that!" At this, the audience erupted with laughter, clapping.

During the end-of-the-run party that followed, Muramatsu commended Mishima for pulling off such an entertaining bit, which made Mishima happy. But Nakamura Nobuo, who played the role of Krupp, was none too pleased. He was put off that Mishima had shunted the actors aside at the curtain call.[44]

*My Friend Hitler* went on to Nagoya and Osaka, then Akita, Niigata, before coming back to Tokyo.

## *The Thai Princess*

Shinchōsha published *Spring Snow* in January 1969 and *The Runaway Horse* the following month. Mishima used the opportunity to tell an anecdote of the kind only storytellers can. For background research for *Spring Snow*, he had visited a round of imperial convents in Kyoto and Nara. At one of them, the abbess asked the purpose of his research. He told her: In his story a young blueblood aristocratic woman betrothed to an imperial prince falls in love with a marquis's son, becomes pregnant, aborts the baby, and takes Buddhist vows at a convent. Thereupon, the nun suspiciously looked at him and asked: "Where did you hear the story?"[45]

Mishima's critic friend Okuno Takeo, for one, gave unstinting praise to *Spring Snow*, saying in his review that, after overcoming the initial difficulties he had with the novel, he "felt a real intoxication as never before," finding in it "extraordinarily serious art that has abandoned all calculations and ostentations and that transcends all ages," although he added the novel that followed, *The Runaway Horse*, was simply not to his taste.[46]

There was one thing that had made Okuno apprehensive about *Spring Snow*, however. It was the dark, foreboding image with which Mishima opens the story: a sepia photograph from the Russo-Japanese War that mesmerizes the novel's protagonist, Matsugae Kiyoaki. It shows thousands of soldiers in a memorial service for those killed in the Battle of Delisi, on Liaotung Peninsula, in June 1904. At the center of the photograph, distant, tiny, but evidently tall, is a cenotaph in plain white wood.

On the afternoon of February 16, Sunday, the *Shinchō* editor Kojima Chikako brought two young Thai women to Mishima's house. Kojima would occasionally dig up factual information for Mishima for the novels he serialized in her monthly. In the case of *The Temple of Dawn* that had started the previous September, she had already found out things like the Tokyo taxi fare and how people dressed the year the Occupation ended. This time it was to find someone he could use as the model for Jin Jan,[47] the Thai princess in the novel. Jin Jan had already appeared in it, but as an infant girl whom Honda Shigekuni has an opportunity to meet just before Japan goes to war, simultaneously with the United States (Pearl Harbor) and Britain (Malay Peninsula). Now, Mishima wanted to envision her as an adult.

The young woman Kojima found, with some difficulty—there were not many Thai women in Tokyo—had a strikingly white face, "wondrously glossy" thick hair, and a pair of "heavy, moist black eyes that almost made you forget the existence of her eyebrows." She was a student of economics at the University of Tokyo and was named Suwanchit. As Kojima suggested, as instructed by Mishima, she came with a friend. Mishima did not want a young woman who agreed to meet him—someone she didn't know—to feel uncomfortable during the meeting.

For two hours, Mishima took care, as he always did with every guest, not to bore the two young visitors. There was not much to talk about, however, for all the months of unprecedented campus turmoil at Tōdai where the two young women studied. Perhaps, as foreign students, they stayed on "extraterritorial" terrain, Kojima wondered. Still, as they chatted, Mishima showed visible enchantment with Suwanchit, at times looking, Kojima thought, like an adolescent boy flustered to find himself close to a sensuous woman. The friend she brought, named Ditamat, apparently had "overseas Chinese" blood in her. She looked more Chinese than Thai.

When the meeting came to a close, Kojima realized that Mishima's aim was to spend some more time with the young women, in a different setting. The women agreed to meet him again, this time on the Ginza. The date finally chosen, again with Kojima as conduit, would turn out to be more than six weeks later, the last day of March. First, Ditamat dropped out, so Suwanchit insisted on bringing a chaperone, the "mama" of her dormitory. Then, when the date approached, she canceled the meeting, which was to be in the Coffee House, of the Imperial Hotel.

When Kojima told this turn of events to Mishima on the phone, he sounded truly disappointed. But after a while he told her he had decided to change the storyline. As initially planned, Honda, meeting the Thai princess as a grown person in Tokyo seven years after Japan's defeat, was to gradually fall in love with her.[48] But in the novel actually written, Honda, learning that Jin Jan is in Tokyo as a student, sends his wife, Rie, to pick her up for their housewarming party, but Rie fails to find the princess where she is supposed to be despite the firm promise made on the phone. The reason given when she called the dormitory for foreign students was that the Japanese family with whom a new Thai student was staying had invited her to dinner.

## *For Counterrevolution with No Efficacy*

Mishima's "Counterrevolution Manifesto" appeared in the February issue of the *Ronsō Journal*. In some ways, his reasoning in this piece may be as hard to grasp as that in "On Defending Culture," but he makes one thing clear: By counterrevolution he meant total opposition to Communism, an ideology that is contemptible because of its advocacy for "a better future society." Rejection of a belief in the future was "the action principle of the Kamikaze Special Attack Forces"[49]—a dubious proposition at best, even as most on those suicide missions sincerely believed that their deaths would do some good for their country. Mishima was, in any case, arguing for rejection of the efficacy or usefulness of any action. And he knew, perhaps with wry amusement, that some had understood his line of thinking with alarm or disgust.

When the weekly *Asahi Journal* interviewed him in March, Mishima put that "principle" in a starker light, as if that were necessary. "Everything is *counterfeit*," he declared. "Both governance and art, as long as they cling to efficacy in any form, are *fiction*," he said, using English for the last word. "Only death is fact. What is the ultimate as proof of existence is death." The matter, of course, had to do with himself, rather than a general principle: "When an artist tries to resist this dailiness=fiction, there is only death. Death as fact. Something like *ideology* is not the issue." That artist was himself. "Unless I feel death somewhere, I cannot engage in artistic work."

But he would "hate to die of anything like cancer, *worse than death itself*," he insisted. Also, he despised "a man-of-letters' suicide," he said, of the kind his literary nemesis in his youth, Dazai Osamu, perpetrated: one "that piles on the self-collapse from art, life." At least "Hemingway's suicide with a hunting gun is closer to 'manly death.'" Conclusion: "Because I at present am friendly with death, I am happy. And so, my life is worth living."[50]

Naturally, some of Yamamoto's colleagues were perplexed. Even those who agreed with Mishima on his anticommunist stance could not take his "action principle." Yamamoto particularly remembered to write about a fiery-tempered man he identified as "M"—a classmate of his from the prewar army days. M insisted that Yamamoto introduce him to Mishima so he might point out "a big error" in Mishima's scheme. So, the night before the anniversary of the 2.26 Incident, when Mishima had told him he'd come to visit, Yamamoto also invited M to come. As soon as the three sat down, M "concentrated his gunfire attack" on a single point. The argument between M and Mishima, which was violent, went like this, as Yamamoto recollected:

> M: What on earth would a movement that doesn't take efficacy into account be like? What would you do if someone

told you that you are just playing with words, no, you are just playing with "thought"?

Mishima: That's not it. This is not a matter of playing with words or a matter of thought. Fact is, it's to bet your own life on it and get killed while cutting down enemies (*kirijini*). That action will create people who follow you!

M: If you truly aim to change Japan, if yours is an action for that, don't you think it's meaningless unless you win once you act? If that's the case, you necessarily have to have weapons that are superior to your enemy's, be they tanks or missiles. The kind of spiritualism you talk about would of course be needed, but I'd say spiritualism that isn't backed up with instruments is just a whiff of fantasy!

Mishima: No, you don't understand. Your approach to this question is all wrong. As long as it is our goal to defend our culture with our own bodies, the only weapon we need is the Japanese sword!

The judgment that the excessive stress on the efficacy of the *Yamato damashii*, the spirit supposed to be unique to the Japanese, had lured the country into an unwinnable, disastrous war was inculcated into not just the officers of the SDF but all Japanese.[51] But Mishima was not amused. Yamamoto later received his complaint, indirectly, that he was asking him to meet "strange people."

Yamamoto felt, in retrospect, that Mishima was trying to lead the Shield Society in the *kirijini* ideal of the Shinpūren, which was totally incompatible with the need for material superiority in weaponry in the modern thinking of warfare. In that regard, he regretted that he had brought in M to raise such a basic issue with Mishima without Mishima's prior agreement. Late that night Mishima left in a ceaseless snow, just like the night of the 2.26 Incident.[52]

The same "principle" also created a schism within the Shield Society, prompting its "mainstream" faction to move to expel the others.[53]

---

Mishima had to ask the young Thai women to meet him again so many days later because of his extraordinary schedule. Three days after spending two and a half hours with them, he started another "lodging together" with the Shield Society. This time they rented the temple Shōgetsu-in, near the GSDF Camp Asagasumi.

The temple was no Tokiwa-ken. It provided no meals so the participants mainly relied on the canned foods they brought. There was no heating, either; the men slept in their sleeping bags. Neither smoking nor drinking was allowed, and communication with the outside world was banned, though the temple was in Itabashi Ward, not far from the center of Tokyo. After calisthenics at eight every morning Yamamoto started his lecture of the day. He also trained his students in secret surveillance of the area surrounding Asagasumi Camp as well as an infiltration of the camp, though the latter did not go beyond a plan discussed and analyzed.

Following the five-day session, Mishima led the third group of Shield Society members to train with the GSDF. Among the ten new recruits who took part in the military training that month was one who had spent ten years—half of his life—in France because of his father's assignment. Asked by a fellow recruit if the French were as "revolutionary" as they were reported to be, putting up barricades and clashing with police, he said, no, they were "conservative, class-conscious, and racist." France is "a country that regards itself as the center of the world." The social influence of leftist students and intellectuals such as Sartre and Beauvoir was "extremely limited." He joined the Shield Society because he heard it would enable him to take part in military training. In France he had thought of joining the Foreign Legion.54

The GSDF training took up almost all of March, from the first to the 29th, although he took some nine days off to work on pressing matters. By then he had been sitting on a couple of literary-award committees, such as the one for the Akutagawa Award, but had also agreed to be a member of a brand-new one Shinchōsha had set up. As he had written a few months earlier, one such award-committee required him to read seven or eight full-length novels into which, he stated, "each author had put his heart and soul," and the work was "a great spiritual burden." Characteristically, however, Mishima mentioned the work not to complain, but to make fun of the subject on which the weekly *Asahi* solicited a brief essay on his "reading technique," saying someone who approaches reading as a "technique" can only be "vulgar, plebeian, and pompous."55

Another thing he did during the break from military training was to go to an area called Nino'oka, in Gotenba, Shizuoka, a spacious open land with a view of Mt. Fuji favored by the well-to-do for their villas. The visit was, of course, to acquire knowledge of the milieu of the locality where he planned to set Honda's villa in *The Temple of Dawn*.

CHAPTER TWENTY-SIX

# The Yakuza

*"Such decent Japanese as he will gradually disappear."*
—Tsuruta Kōji on Mishima

Around the time the Tōdai Struggle peaked, Mishima saw two yakuza movies in a row, both featuring Tsuruta Kōji, and the cool, knowledgeable accolade he gave the second of the two, *Gamble in Don's Honor (Sōchō tobaku)*, would change the appreciation of a popular genre that artistic-minded critics had treated as lowbrow. Kasahara Kazuo, who wrote the screenplay, said Mishima's article gave the genre "citizenship, however small."[1]

Like cowboys and gunfighters in America, yakuza and samurai were popular film subjects from early on in Japan. Yakuza films attracted great directors in the second half of the 1920s: Itō Daisuke, who made a trilogy on the historical yakuza Kunisada Chūji, in 1927, and Tsuji Kichirō, who made a film on Kutsukake Tokijirō, the fictional yakuza created by the playwright and novelist Hasegawa Shin, in 1929.[2] After Japan's defeat, the subject regained popularity, but each decade came with a different treatment of yakuza. The yakuza depicted in the 1950s were mainly those from the end of the Edo Period and often included historical figures topped by the most popular film subject, Yamamoto Jirochō, of Shimizu Port,[3] and his men. In these films everyone was stylishly dressed, à la grand kabuki.

Kurosawa Akira abruptly put an end to it. With his *Yōjimbō* (1961),

/ 605

he brought down-to-earth realism to the genre, beginning with the protagonist, played by Mifune Toshirō. The man, as befits a masterless samurai, was presented as scruffy and grungy, and the yakuza as what the word means: useless, trashy. Kurosawa enhanced the effect by the black and white medium he still favored. There may have been nothing "realistic" about the ronin's prowess as swordsman, but the sword-fight scenes showed arms severed, blood splattering, people cut up screaming. Clean, kabuki-style yakuza films quickly lost ground.

The great Zatōichi series followed. The 1962 film about a blind masseur as a preternatural swordsman, played by Katsu Shintarō, was such a hit that two dozen more were made within the next dozen years. The series, too, stressed the down-to-earth quality of yakuza life, though, again, there was nothing realistic about the masseur's swordsmanship.

Along with the series came films dealing with "modern yakuza," those mainly of the years preceding the Second World War. Where earlier ones had often depicted rival yakuza houses coming into conflict and ending in spectacular scenes of two groups of men fighting, the new yakuza films put their narrative focus on the schisms in human relations unavoidable in a world of violence bound by a simple code of honor, loyalty, and a senior-junior bond that, as things start going wrong, cannot be sustained in the end.

*Gamble in Don's Honor*, the film that captivated Mishima, however, reversed the prevailing narrative pattern of the yakuza films of the decade. Instead of conflicts between rival groups, it deals with one that arises within a single yakuza group, the Tenryū Family. After the family head, *sōchō*, is struck down by a stroke, a top henchman tries to hold it together. He doesn't just fail; in pursuing his aim, he brings down the whole house.

The unraveling begins when the *sōchō*'s "brethren" and "group leaders" gather to pick his successor and settle on the most respected group leader, Nakai. However, Nakai declines the honor in deference to Matsuda, his simple-minded, hot-tempered, violence-prone coequal, on the grounds that he, Nakai, is from a different house and thus an "outsider," whereas Matsuda, albeit in jail now, is more rightfully heir in that regard. Senba, one of the "brethren," who had anticipated Nakai's reaction and worked out a "consensus" behind the scenes, at once moves to name the *sōchō*'s son-in-law as successor, and his motion is accepted on the spot. The rest of the film follows the consequences of Nakai's choice that, however admirable by yakuza code, ends in his killing Matsuda, the blood-brother he tries to help, not to mention Senba.

"What thread of natural inevitability is extended to each sequence so meticulously!" marveled Mishima after noting that he saw the film in an "ideal environment," a small rundown joint where the ticket seller wasn't even in her booth when he showed up and where the toilet odor amply wafted into the auditorium as the door to it opened and closed. The place was crowded, and he had to sit in the front row where the seats were so low he inadvertently stepped on the one he chose.

"What sophistication rules, without a bit of showiness, what absolute indifference to the world outside the story is maintained!" *Gamble* makes it clear that the story begins in the spring of 1934, a year as turbulent as any other in modern Japanese history, but it does not allow anything suggestive of outside events—such as the ascent to the throne of Japan's puppet emperor, Puyi, in its puppet state, Manchukuo, and the great fire in Hakodate that killed two thousand people—to intrude into the story.

"How every character preserves a set pattern faithfully, even in breaking a code, in rebelling, how dedicated each character is to the stylistic perfection of a closed society!"

As Mishima does not fail to note, there is one episode that "might collapse this small world." That's where Senba's conspiracy surfaces; his plan from the outset has been to take over the Tenryū Family for funding a patriotic group by paying for the heroin imported to Japan—a slight suggestion of Japan's opium use in Manchukuo and China. But it comes out at the very end, and there's "no ideology" introduced, "no hint of criticism." The film constitutes "a tragedy set up at the extreme edge of absolute affirmation," a tragedy that "in every detail, just like a classical drama, accords with human truth."[4]

This assessment by Mishima would win *Gamble* the status of a "masterpiece," but, self-revealing as it was, it would have some ironic consequences. It led the architect-cum-poet-cum-film-critic Watanabe Takenobu to call *Gamble* a "super yakuza film" and predict yakuza films would not survive unless they "change[d] key." He had in mind the French film critic André Bazin who characterized *Shane* as a "super western," a western "that would be ashamed to be just itself, and looks for some additional interest to justify its existence."

Yakuza films did, indeed, change key after *Gamble*. In the 1970s they would turn "documentary"-like, presenting themselves as based on actual incidents. But Watanabe's characterization would be invoked to condemn Mishima's manner of death as nothing more than to live "a super yakuza film." Meanwhile, his death would compel Kasahara, who had been moved by Mishima's praise of the movie of which he wrote the script, to give up writing yakuza films altogether.[5]

Just as Mishima liked yakuza films, so did many college students, those in the student movement included. Mishima in his essay noted that the one fellow who was waiting at the ticket booth when he got to the rundown theater to see *Gamble* somewhat late looked "like a student." Many in the audience were, we may assume, members of the New Left. Shima Taizō, who had barricaded himself in the Yasuda Auditorium, reports he was "embarrassed" by his fellow students' infatuation with *ninkyō*, the most important yakuza code, a readiness to sacrifice oneself for someone in an impossible situation—à la Sydney Carton. The previous fall, it was an important theme of Tōdai's annual student festival. At least one large poster with a painting of a tattooed yakuza was up on a wall in the Komaba campus.[6] A later critic would point out all of that represented "an intense yearning for a homosocial worldview."[7]

## *In Praise of the* Shinbō Tachiyaku

Aside from yakuza infatuation, it would be misleading to assume in any way that the student movement in Japan at the time was all seriousness. Like similar movements elsewhere, it had many festive elements, a large dose of the desire to enjoy the moment. In fact, "festive" and "festival" were the two words often used by the participants. Shiine Yamato, Mishima's editor at *Heibon Punch*, took part, with his girlfriend, in International Antiwar Day demonstrations on October 21 as if joining a festival. When running away from the riot police in a group of several students, he surely felt "only the sense of terror sprout" in his mind, but when running around with several thousands of them, it was as if "having fun in Disneyland"—though, as he took care to note, the theme park did not exist in Japan yet.

When he learned the Zenkyōtō of the University of Kyoto planned a "Pharisees-Barricade Festival" in April, he called the organizers to ask if he could bring a nude model to shoot her as part of the campus event. The fellow who picked up the phone said, Sure, mouthing what sounded pseudo-philosophical: "I think a festival is something like a struggle, whereas a struggle is something like a festival."

A Zenkyōtō leader at the university was more up front about the *raison d'être* of the movement: "We'd like to enjoy ourselves doing whatever we want to even as we crush the establishment. We want to destroy everything that has the breath of government power on it: our university's clock tower, the riot police, *Punch*, all of them. We'd like to engage in truly provocative actions in every field. We are, you know, reformers of academic pursuits, arts, and sex life."

The two-week-long programs for the event included go-go dance parties, movies, celebrity lectures, performances by rock'n'roll bands and avant-garde theater troupes, ending with a happening for which campus walls would be "liberated" for mural painting with quantities of paint and thinner provided. Among the films to be shown were *A Hard Day's Night* (Japanese title: *The Beatles Are Coming, Yah, Yah, Yah!*), *Violated White Uniform (Okasareta Byakui*—a young man's attempt to murder lesbian nurses), and *The Dutch Wife in the Wilderness (Kōya no Dutch Wife*—a horror film inspired by A. Bierce's "Occurrence at Owl Creek Bridge").[8]

Mishima, in any event, was as emphatic in determining *Gamble in Don's Honor* to be a masterpiece as in stressing his "empathy" for the lead actor who played the protagonist Nakai, Tsuruta Kōji. Not because Tsuruta was one of the top yakuza stars, nor because he had been ranked, albeit when a little younger, "the most handsome movie star" for a number of years. It was because in his recent yakuza movies, Mishima said, Tsuruta was superb in the role of *shinbō tachiyaku*, in kabuki a lead character who is required to remain passive, often till near the end.

Above all, the reason for his strong feeling for Tsuruta may lie in the fact, Mishima mused, that Tsuruta's "intra-war emotions, his switch to the *shinbō tachiyaku* role, and the bags developing under his eyes have all become my own problems." Tsuruta, who was Mishima's age, was in the naval air reserve during the final phase of the war and regarded himself as an undeserving survivor of a Kamikaze unit. The yakuza Tsuruta's final act is "an outburst of what may be called the heroism of indecisiveness." Using the word *shigarami*, a set of relational considerations that constrain one from taking certain steps, Mishima concludes with a passage that may almost sound parodic:

Whether liberating oneself from *shigarami* is something manly is highly doubtful. Whether freedom makes someone manly is extremely doubtful. Tsuruta's actions on the screen are caused not as a solution by the cutting apart of the entanglements of *shigarami* that press down on him in mutually contradicting layers, but always in accordance with "the pure *shigarami*" that he has found in a variety of *shigarami*, "the *shigarami*" that is the fundamental principle common to a variety of *shigarami* that he has extracted.

What that is, is hard to say. But murder is always a sadness, and necessity and inevitability always go against a "readily understandable justice."

A few months after the essay appeared in *Eiga Geijutsu*, *Playboy* arranged a taidan between Mishima and Tsuruta. The give-and-take between writer and actor, as may be expected, centered on yakuza and being Japanese. When Tsuruta toward the end said now was the time for a Shōwa Restoration and Mishima said he'd throw himself into it if necessary, Tsuruta said: "Mr. Mishima, when that happens, please give me a call. I'll grab my military sword and rush to your side." Mishima's response to this was his usual raucous laughter.

The two middle-aged men liked each other so much, Mishima invited Tsuruta and his wife to his house to continue the conversation. When the time finally came for the Tsurutas to go home, Mishima, ever a stickler for manners and etiquette, came out, with Yōko, to see them off and, despite the rain, kept standing at the gate, until the Tsurutas' car went out of sight, moving Tsuruta to say to his wife, "Such decent Japanese as he will gradually disappear," the *Playboy* editor reported.[9]

---

In early April Mishima finished writing *The Terrace of the Leper King*, the play inspired by a stone statue he saw in Angkor Thom, in the fall of 1965. Partially covered with lichen and said to be that of Jayavarman VII, the statue came with the legend that the Cambodian ruler who built the Bayon was a leper. The combination of two opposites, "extreme gloom and extreme splendor," was a subject favored by the Late Romantics as typified, Mishima noted, in Villiers de l'Isle-Adam's masterpiece, *Duke of Portland*, for example. In the *conte*, the young, adventurous, fabulously wealthy English nobleman who excels in boxing and fox-hunting is brought down by leprosy.

(The *fin de siècle* tale has a single footnote appended to it that must have struck a chord in Mishima. It says, in part: "The author has been obliged to modify slightly the actual character of the Duke of Portland—since he writes this tale *as it ought to have occurred*."[10] As pointed out earlier, the historical Jayavarman VII did not die young and his leprosy is no more than conjecture provoked by the lichen covering the stone statue.)

"With [the king's] body collapsing, his giant cathedral goes on to complete itself," Mishima wrote. "That terrifying contrast, it seemed to me, is a metaphor for an artist's life in which the artist is destroyed even as he transfers all his being into his artwork."[11] The resplendent Bayon that rises is "eternal youth," even as the one who instigated the building can no longer see it, blinded as he is by leprosy. The play ends with a paean to the youthful physique that survives the death of the spirit.

It was a similar combination of two opposites in the Late Romantic vein that Mishima stressed in Kawabata Yasunari when the *Mainichi Shinbun* asked him for a short essay on him that same month of April. Kawabata attained *yūgen*, the aesthetic ideal the medieval poet Fujiwara no Teika strove for, which Zeami two centuries later placed at the core of his dramaturgy: "In nō drama, *yūgen* and the flower are almost synonymous," Mishima posited. *Hana*, "flower," being what Zeami called "the life of nō," this statement may be unsurprising. What is not is the next sentence: "That is, what is most gloomy and what is most resplendent are synonymous." And: "There, a girl's truly happy, clear smile and the cold beauty of her corpse come out of the same fountain."

Mishima summed up the beauty of Kawabata literature as *reien*, "cold sensuosity." Though probably "unplanned," his representative work is called *Snow Country*, Mishima judged. Mishima was evidently mindful that Teika's thirty-one-syllable poem Zeami singled out as embodying *yūgen* was "No shelter for halting the horse to brush off my sleeves, here at Sano Ferry this snowy evening." Zeami's metaphor for the ultimate of *yūgen* was "snow in a silver bowl."[12]

## *Japanese* Odysseus

That April Mishima took on two jobs: one to write a kabuki play, the other to play a role in a feature film.

On the 18th, Mishima had a young visitor from the National Theatre, Orita Kōji. Orita brought the request that Mishima write a kabuki to be staged that fall to mark the theater's third anniversary. Mishima, a member of its board of directors, did not just agree to do so; in short order, he decided to direct it himself. And, beginning with a phone call a week later to tell Orita, "I'd like to make a Japanese *Odysseus*; the Japanese Odysseus is Tametomo," he threw himself into the task with the intensity of someone who had absolutely nothing else to do.

Minamoto Tametomo (1139–70?) is a warrior who briefly shows up in a contemporary account of the half-day internecine battle known as the Hōgen Disturbance, in 1156. Many legends were born out of the few facts known about him. Toward the end of the Edo Period Takizawa Bakin wove together a number of those legends, adding new stories of his own making along the way, to write *A Wonder Tale: The Moonbow (Chinsetsu Yumiharizuki)*, a fantastic, highly entertaining romance. Mishima based his kabuki on Bakin's narrative, using the same title. In his play, however, he focused on two themes, largely of his own concoction: Tametomo's unswerving loyalty to Emperor Sutoku (1119–64), who was trapped into the Hōgen Disturbance, defeated, and exiled, as well as the warrior's wish—perennially thwarted—to commit disembowelment to follow him in death. Tametomo was also exiled.

"That every drama contains in it a confession is my pet theory," Mishima wrote of those two themes, but especially the latter, in the program note to the play when it was staged in November. "Speaking of myself the author, Tametomo's frustrations, his exclusion from a resplendent fate, his image as 'an unfinished hero,' and his clear, lofty character are what I consider my ideals, so I made an effort" to bring out those qualities, he explained. But he also made clear his "predilections for decadence and evil," pointing to the scene where a group of beautiful maidens, led by Princess Shiranui, torture a traitorous man to death even as the snow falls incessantly. And the princess in the scene wears a fur, Mishima added, because she is meant to be a Japanese *Venus im Pelz*.[13]

Mishima decided to direct the kabuki, probably because he knew it was to be his last full-length play, except the jōruri version he made of it. Also, it was to embody his own ideals in the classical form that had initiated him into the world of theater. Publicly, though, he explained that he decided to direct it because of the unique method of kabuki production that had come to prevail.

Classical kabuki did not have a "director" such as found in modern theater or, for that matter, the kind of "playwright" taken for granted today. In each kabuki troupe, the lead actor was in essence the director. As to the scripts, each troupe had a chief writer (*tate-sakusha*) who had at least three colleagues to work with. They would work out a script after picking a subject or theme from the repertoire or a group of known stories, then revise it to accommodate the actors' wishes. In this arrangement, scripts were often prepared with specific actors in mind. As individual actors' popularity and income grew, the role of playwrights, such as it was, became even less important.[14] The kabuki theater, then, had much in common with the theater in Shakespeare's time, where "the play was fitted to the performers," and also with the eighteenth- to nineteenth-century opera theater, where the "composer had to fit his music to the voices available to him in a particular opera house."[15]

In Mishima's view, the kind of playwright-actor collaboration just described ended with Uno Nobuo, whose kabuki for Onoe Kikugorō VI, in 1935, became a smash hit. Uno continued to write and work for Kikugorō and other actors well into the 1950s. But after that, the old ways returned, principal actors making do with traditional techniques they learned, occasionally devising their own. The so-called director's role became increasingly limited to explaining to the actors "the writer's intent, characters, and psychological descriptions."[16]

"Not that I am so vain as to think I can do more than that," Mishima added. One real difficulty for Mishima with a new kabuki lay in producing it independent of troupes of which there were two production companies, Shōchiku and Tōhō. (This excludes the leftist and highly popular Zenshin-za, established in 1931, that brought real women into kabuki to play women's roles.)

The newly created National Theatre did not have its own troupe. When it staged a kabuki, the actors had to be recruited from either of the two troupes, the groups made in admiration of Kikugorō VI and Kichiemon I, both dead by then. Mishima, because of his fame and the respect he had won among kabuki actors, was able to draw from both troupes, but their schedules permitted them only about a week to get together to rehearse *after* the runs of their own troupes' engagements were over.

Luckily, the opening night of the fall production at the National Theatre begins late in the season. In the case of *The Moonbow* that year it was set to be the fifth of November. But because it was a new play and he wanted to turn it into an extravaganza, Mishima decided to have the stage sets, some of which would require innovative technical ingenuity, and everything else ready by the time the actors met for the first time.

In addition, kabuki is a "music drama" that "demands musicality in the accompanying music of course, but also in the speeches"[17]—written, basically, in seven-five syllabic patterns—and Mishima wanted to incorporate into his play a good deal of gidayū chanting (narrative) and nagauta singing. Both had to be composed. Especially with gidayū, the timing between narration and action must be worked out in detail, which sometimes requires revision of the script—work between chanter and author. "I cannot forget the artistic excitement," Mishima recalled, "of devising directorial schemes while listening to Enza's narration as he played it late at night in a hotel in Osaka enveloped in the rainy season, on July 1." The great gidayū narrator Tsurusawa Enza, here the fifth generation, spent four days just on the scene where "crow-tengu" (crow-faced flying humans) show up, Mishima said.

All this, not to mention the making of stage sets and mechanisms, meant a tight working schedule. The first staff conference was held on May 12, before Mishima sat down to write the play. He finished Act I of the three-act play by the end of June, Act II by the end of July, and Act III on September 1. Little wonder that, soon after he agreed to take on the work, he started summoning Orita, "be it during the day, the evening, or past midnight," to discuss complex details, often "scolding" him—most likely for the young man's inability to carry out his instructions exactly.

## Kill!

The other job Mishima took on in April was the role of a samurai assassin in Gosha Hideo's movie to be called *Kill!* (*Hitokiri*). Based on Shiba

Ryōtarō's story, "The Killer Izō" (*Hitokiri Izō*), it would deal with historical figures, with Mishima playing Tanaka Shinbē, one of the Tennō-loyalist assassins of men on the side of the Tokugawa regime in its final phase. His co-actors were all popular movie stars: Nakadai Tatsuya (in the role of Takechi Hanpeita, the leader of the Tennō loyalist group of the Tosa Fiefdom), Katsu Shintarō (Okada Izō), who was also the producer of the film, and Ishihara Yūjirō (Sakamoto Ryōma)—Shintarō's brother who was equally popular as a singer. Mishima did not accept the offer Gosha came to make himself on the spot but that evening he phoned him to say yes. *Kill!* was the first feature film Gosha was going to make. Till then he had directed popular TV dramas notable for scenes of fast samurai action.

Once he got into it, Mishima was delighted to surmise the reasons why Gosha came to him, and he *loved* all of them. He was doing kendō, however "poorly," and, by brandishing a sword (albeit made of bamboo), selling "the samurai image." Society at large regarded him as a fellow "exalting terrorism." Casting him in the film, the film company's "calculation" went, would cut the publicity cost that much; after all (and this is *not* something he said; there was no need for it), he was one of the biggest celebrities of the day. All such considerations were obviously discussed behind his back, completely ignoring his "intellectual part," and he liked that a great deal. In truth, Hashimoto Shinobu, the scriptwriter who had worked with Kurosawa Akira beginning with *Rashōmon*, is known to have exclaimed, "A masterstroke!" when told of casting Mishima in the role of Tanaka.

Once the filming started, Mishima noticed shooting sword-fight scenes excited everyone involved, including himself. "Fiction it may be, but that the intent to kill takes everyone present to seventh heaven, is, come to think of it, an odd human fact."[18]

Indeed, the two solid days that were needed to film the scene where two groups of men clash in the confines of an inn "passed 'like a dream,' to exaggerate a bit." What made Mishima happy was that all the samurai who attacked him "were slashed up and fell for me. When the filming of the great riotous scene where blood splashed and fumed was over, I felt no fatigue at all, but was brisk both in mind and body, wanting to cut up several dozen more men." Mishima asked Yōko to come from Tokyo to watch the filming.

He also delighted in pretending each man he was killing was an actual person he did not like. "Even after I returned to Tokyo"—the film was made in a studio in Kyoto—"my work on a novel made great progress. I hear that Saint-Saëns was more famous as a cultivator of roses than as a composer. I wish I would become more famous as a killer than as a novelist."[19]

The film *Kill!* would later attract attention because of the scene where Mishima enacts realistically, intensely, Tanaka grabbing the sword shown him as evidence of assassination and killing himself with it—as if to say, as Mishima put it, "Darn, why bother?" He acted out the stabbing of his stomach with the sword (made of bamboo) and cutting it sidewise with such passion and intensity that the skin of his abdomen tore and bled.

But playing that role also entailed a delicious twist for him. As he wrote to Hayashi Fusao, the man who was suspected of lack of oversight that prompted Tanaka to commit suicide and was temporarily placed under house arrest was none other than his ancestor, Nagai Naomune, at the time magistrate of Kyoto.[20]

## *The Debate*

April 28 was Okinawa Day. The previous November the Okinawans' desire to end US military rule had seen its first-step fulfillment when the US had finally allowed them to directly vote for the head of the Ryūkyū Administration and Yara Chōbyō, who called for an immediate, unconditional return of Okinawa, had won the election. It was quickly followed by the election, in December, of Taira Ryōshō, with the same demand, as mayor of Naha.

The day turned into yet another one of large-scale demonstrations and violence. The Socialist Party, the Communist Party, and the National Federation of Workers Unions for the first time had agreed to hold rallies throughout the nation together. But there was a catch. The anti-Yoyogi Faction of the Zengakuren was denied participation, so its members engaged in what they called guerilla warfare in Tokyo, clashing with riot police in Shinbashi Station, and attacked police booths in Shinbashi, Ginza, and Sukiyabashi, setting some on fire. The government applied the Subversive Activities Prevention Law. The law, which the ruling party had rammed through the Diet in 1952 as the perceived threat of the Soviet Union mounted, was anticommunist legislation, pure and simple. The police arrested a total of 967.

Yamamoto Kiyokatsu remembered how Mishima practically barged into his house that day, demanding to know why he was doing nothing. After taking him out into a black limousine, Mishima made his driver run parallel to large groups of demonstrators, at one point allowing the car to be isolated in a swirling mass of people who, if they recognized Mishima, could have turned violent and overturned the limousine.

Mishima then took Yamamoto to the National Theatre where he guided him down to the mechanisms below the stage, in the cellar, that allowed people and props to spring out onto the stage, then to the roof where he told Yamamoto he planned to hold a parade of the Shield Society. The Japanese name of the cellar, *naraku*, which, like its other name, "hell," means "abyss," and the theater's proximity to the Imperial Palace were too suggestive to Yamamoto to resist conjecturing Mishima's "true intent."[21]

Mishima gave a characteristic assessment of the turmoil of Okinawa Day when he responded, on May 13, to the invitation of his alma mater's Zenkyōtō to engage in debate with the students. He began by telling them that, on the morning of April 28, he met "someone on the so-called establishment side"—perhaps Yamamoto. The man said the students creating turmoil were all "deranged," but Mishima did not agree with him. He was not saying that to "fawn" on them. What concerned him was that there was not a bit of distress or anxiety in the government official's eyes. He admired him for that, but that raised a question: Suppose he, Mishima, were on the side of the Zengakuren?

He then brought up François Mauriac's novel *Thérèse Desqueyroux* to illustrate his point. In his 1927 story, Mauriac makes his protagonist Thérèse attempt to poison her husband, Bernard. Some time after surviving the poisoning and testifying in court, to keep his social status intact, that his wife had never done anything like trying to take his life, Bernard asks her: "What *was* your motive?" Thérèse, who had given much thought to the likely question, answers, as Mishima explained: "I'm not sure that it wasn't simply to see that look of uncertainty, of curiosity—of unease which, a moment ago, I caught in your eyes!"[22]

Wouldn't you Zengakuren people want to see some anxiety "in the eyes of Japan's powers that be, its establishment?" *He* would, though "from a different direction," he said. His failure to detect any distress in the establishment figure's eyes discouraged him, as a matter of fact, and he's been "dispirited ever since April 28." This provoked laughter from the students, like some of his paradoxical remarks. But he was, as usual, truthful; he was beginning to sense the prospects for a serious clash between establishment and antiestablishment were diminishing.

As far as the Mauriac story goes, one suspects what Thérèse struggles to say later may have come close to Mishima's state of mind at the time: "What I wanted? It would be a great deal easier to tell you what I didn't want. I didn't want to be for ever playing a part, to go through a series of movements, to continue speaking words, that were not my own; in short, to deny at every moment of the day a Thérèse who. . . ."[23]

In any event, reminding the students that they had invited him to debate on the understanding that both sides agreed on the necessity for violence, however politically opposed they may be, Mishima volunteered that only recently a member of the ruling Liberal Democratic Party had asked him to add his name to the party's parliamentary resolution opposing violence but he had declined, because he had "never once opposed violence since I was born."

"What terrified me the most," he said, was the kind of move toward compromise that had become clear just about a week before the fall of the Yasuda Auditorium. On January 10, as many as eight thousand students had massed to a meeting in the Chichibu Rugby Stadium intended to resolve the autonomy question between students and faculty. Among the nonpolitical students, called *nonpori*, antipathy to violent confrontations, between students and police, and among student factions, had grown. The meeting did not produce any tangible result, but it was evidence nonetheless of the growing yearning for "order"— not just growing, it "was permeating Japan."

Mishima did not like it. The Chichibu meeting did not "concern itself a bit with ideology, sense, or logic." Besides, it was led by the Minsei, clearly showing that the Liberal Democratic Party was in cahoots with the Communist Party. Referring to the depiction of him as a "modern gorilla"—his nickname for himself—on a poster announcing his visit placed outside the auditorium, he declared he'd happily remain as "primitive" as a gorilla to maintain integrity. He wanted "the Liberal Democratic Party to be more reactionary, the Communist Party to be more violent."

"A human being must do what he must when the time comes,"

Mishima said. The large hall-like classroom was full, and Mishima, who had won fame for making outrageous statements in public, did not disappoint his audience for he went on to say, "I think I must do it, so I'll do it when the time comes, though I still don't know when it will be. The reason I don't know is that you, too, are sloppy"—"you," of course, meaning the students he was addressing. One possibility of "doing it" he had in mind, he made it clear, was a violent confrontation with students.

"When I take action, I have no other way than doing it illegally like you," he continued, reminding the students that their violent actions were illegal. "If I kill someone illegally, with the thought of a duel, I'll be a homicide, so when that happens, I think I'll want to die by killing myself or by some other means before a *patrolman* gets hold of me. I don't know when that moment will come, but I'd like to become a good gorilla as a 'modern gorilla,' by strengthening my body to meet that moment."

Indeed, what Mishima was hoping to occur was for a "disturbance" to turn into a "civil war," he told Muramatsu Takeshi. If that happened, the JSDF would field its domestic security force. But between the declaration of civil war and the actual fielding of the security force, there would be "a crack," and it would be during that short space of time that he would lead his Shield Society into battle with the students so he might be able to die.[24]

When told he accepted the Tōdai Zenkyōtō's invitation to debate and was walking into a crowd of violence-prone students all by himself, some of his friends became concerned, so did the Shield Society (and, unbeknownst to him, even the National Police Agency). Mishima dismissed the concern with a laugh, turning down the idea of some of his friends accompanying him, as well as the police offer to provide him with a security guard, and went to Tōdai in a short-sleeved polo shirt and slacks to face a far larger crowd than the organizers had expected, about one thousand young men and women.

Nevertheless, he had responded to the invitation with "a considerable resolve," he told the students frankly, humorously; after all, as the adage has it, "A man faces seven enemies once he steps out of his gate." Despite the easygoing air he maintained, he was concerned enough in fact, the rightwing education commentator and friend Izawa Kinemaro revealed after Mishima's death, to carry a dagger with him. If true, photographs of that occasion do not show it. Perhaps he was wearing a *haramaki* and holding the weapon underneath it. A *haramaki*, a long sash wound several times around the stomach, is a yakuza accouterment. The idea is to prevent the guts from spilling when you are slashed in the stomach. As far as such things go, Mishima was no doubt wearing a fundoshi.

Izawa added that a couple of students had vowed beforehand that they would "defeat Mishima in debate, so he won't be able to talk himself out of it and will be forced to disembowel himself on the stage." Sensing the peril, ten members of the Shield Society quietly placed themselves in the second row of the classroom.[25] In the end, nothing remotely resembling violence occurred.

The debate that day was informal and, without any topics agreed upon beforehand, meandered. Mishima had thought of five topics for debate and declared, at the outset, that he would face whatever issues they might raise "on the premise that [the two sides] would not understand each other." But the Zenkyōtō had not lined up a proper number of students to engage him on any specific questions.

Still, some students had read Mishima well and pondered on his "philosophy of life," and Mishima announced he recognized the value of what the students had done—"smashing the nose of self-conceit" that pervaded the "intellectualism" of Tōdai. Among the icons of such intellectualism the students had abused was, Mishima noted approvingly, Maruyama Masao, the much admired Tōdai scholar of modern Japanese history and advocate of "postwar democracy." There was, further, the sense that, as student "A," who played the role of moderator, was honest to say amid laughter, Mishima, for the students, deserved the honorific address *sensei* far better than "the Tōdai teachers loitering around there." So, contrary to the usual assessments, the two sides were not without points of agreement.

For one thing, Mishima explained he had come to regard Communism as his "enemy." He was initially interested in eroticism—like Ōe Kenzaburō, he said, eliciting laughter—but eroticism necessarily requires "the other," albeit in reference to Sartre whom he detests, he said. And as he became wearied of eroticism, he had to create some kind of *illusion* (his English) that was "the other." The result was Communism.

For another, Mishima's concept of the Tennō became clearer. A student identified as "H"—who obviously could not decide whether he should be rude or respectful to Mishima—proposed that the kind of Tennō that Mishima had written about in "Voices of the Heroic Souls" and elsewhere can "exist as beauty that is at once supreme and most forbidding," as Mishima may put it, only because it does *not* exist or else is utterly "unrealistic." If Mishima is "a writer who pursues beauty," as he must be, he shouldn't join the SDF for a couple of days or "playact a weird rightwinger," but "confine himself in the beauty" he is pursuing. Once he steps out of that confine, "H" suggested, his action degrades the Tennō as embodiment of "beauty, the community fantasy, the community model."

That was the spirit of the mid-nineteenth-century slogan, "devotion to the Tennō," Mishima responded, saying he was glad to find someone with that spirit. When another student promptly accused him of being facetious, Mishima pointed out what he professed he had always maintained: that "as a political concept there is almost no distinction between the direct rule by the Tennō in the first year of Shōwa and the kind of direct democracy talked about at present," the "one common factor" between the two being "the dream that the people's will directly links to the nation's will without going through the intermediary medium of a power structure." He went on to add: "Because this dream was not once fulfilled, all the prewar *coups d'état* failed."

There is a difference, Mishima continued. The earlier form carried the name Tennō, whereas what the students are trying to achieve now doesn't. They think "sticking the Tennō to it will do no good." They, in other words, have never thought about "the people at the bottom of Japanese society" or "the people's *mentality*" (English his). But if they did, "what may not succeed might," he said. The point, in short, was a matter of naming, a matter of semiotics.

Mishima was consistent. The debate would be remembered mainly by one point he made: that, had the students barricading themselves in the Yasuda Auditorium uttered the word Tennō, he would have gladly joined them, or, as he put it toward the end, "If you simply called the *Tennō* a *Tennō* for me, I'd gladly join hands with you." This, however, led Mishima to tell the students "a personal impression" that would confound even some of the Shield Society. Mochimaru Hiroshi, for one, had never heard Mishima reveal that emotive aspect in any of the many conversations he had with him.[26]

"I am born during the war, you see," he said—meaning that his youth coincided with the time when Japan was at war. "His Majesty was sitting in a place like this, and I saw him remain absolutely still for three hours. Whatever you may say about it, for three hours, he, like a wooden statue, remained absolutely still, during my graduation ceremony. I received a watch from a Tennō like that. I have a personal debt like that."

Among the teachings on imperial conduct handed down since the tenth century was one dictating that the Tennō remain imperturbable and impassive in all circumstances. Also, the special education Hirohito received as constitutional monarch, from several prominent tutors, combined British and samurai traditions. Among the tutors while he was in the Peers School's elementary division, Gen. Nogi Maresuke, then president of the school, taught him to be always mindful that he was to be the Grand Marshal, that is, supreme commander of all armed forces. That included being spartan with himself to the point of frugality. Hirohito evidently followed these lessons to the end of his life. The austere image of Hirohito astride a white horse stock-still during a grand military review lasting for hours, for example, was a familiar one to all prewar Japanese, if not finding themselves in the presence of the Tennō maintaining the same posture, as Mishima did.[27]

Mishima's personal revelation, as it were, inevitably elicited laughter among the students, but he finished what he had started to say. "Such things happen in a man's personal history. And I cannot deny it within me no matter how I try. He was truly admirable, the Tennō at that time."

"In May this year," Mishima wrote six months later, on the occasion of the first official parade of the Shield Society, "I happened to be summoned by students of the Radical Left and had a *thrilling* debate with them. It became a book, and a bestseller. The students who were my opponents in the debate and I agreed to split the royalties fifty-fifty. So probably they bought helmets and Molotov cocktails, and I purchased summer uniforms for The Shield Society. Everybody says this wasn't too bad a deal."[28]

For the debate, Mishima took a cameraman and a stenographer from Shinchōsha with the idea of turning it into a book. But, as he told Tsutsumi Seiji later, without irony, when he arrived at the designated hall, he found the students had summoned mass media—TV stations, weeklies, newspapers. They were ahead of the game![29] As a result, TBS devoted a thirteen-minute segment to it in its primetime news hour that day. The transcript of the entire proceedings, which lasted for two and a half hours, with supplementary essays by Mishima and three students representing the Zenkyōtō, came out the following month under the title of *Beauty, the Community, and the Tōdai Struggle (Bi to kyōdotai to Tōdai Tōsō)*.[30]

---

The Shield Society's "surveillance-investigative training" under Yamamoto was growing more rigorous. One day in early June, the month *Kill!* was filmed, Mishima invited Yamamoto, along with his fellow officers, to dinner at the restaurant of the Yamanoue Hotel, in Ochanomizu, when one such training session was over. As soon as everyone was ushered into a private room, Mishima asked the waiters to leave, telling them that he'd order dinner after a discussion was over, and locked the door. This startled Yamamoto. He saw that Mishima had invited only those he trusted the most. Despite himself, his legs shook at the thought of Mishima finally announcing his "decision."

He was right. Mishima pulled out a piece of paper from his inner jacket pocket and read it aloud. It was his action plan, and it consisted of three items. But the first was so "shocking" and farfetched that Yamamoto did not remember the second and the third, or so he averred in his memoir. That first item said Mishima would storm into the Imperial Palace with the Shield Society and defend it to the last man. Such an idea indeed would have unnerved anybody in their right mind. Still, it is too bad that Yamamoto did not remember when and under what condition Mishima explained he would do it. He did remember more or less, however, Mishima announcing he had already formed a suicide squad and given swords to its nine members.

Yamamoto could think of forming a special unit to defend the Imperial Palace, but only for preventing riotous people from breaking in, which, if that were to be assumed, would require hand-to-hand-combat training that was radically different from the kind of "surveillance-investigative" training Yamamoto was putting the Shield Society through.

After some awkward moments, Mishima struck a match and burned in an ashtray the piece of paper he had read from. A Western-style dinner, with knife and fork, followed, though when a waiter asked him if he would prefer bread or rice, he barked, "I hate bread!"

At one point during dinner Mishima suggested that they do their next training on the premises of the Prime Minister's Official Residence. Yamamoto promptly objected. Some in the mass media were already referring to what Mishima and his group were doing as "the rightwing's armed training." Yamamoto felt he had to forestall any action that might give any such idea. Since they had come to know each other, Yamamoto had come to agree with Mishima that the ultimate act for the Shield Society might involve the Tennō. But he had also come to realize that they had two separate scripts leading to it, whatever *it* might be.

One of the officers, bewildered by what appeared to be Mishima's thinking, sarcastically offered: "Shall we then go to your house, set up straw figures, and practice" cutting them up with swords? Setting up a straw figure and cutting it up, in lieu of a corpse, was what samurai used to do for sword practice. Mishima looked glum but unfazed.[31]

About a month before his death, Mishima told Isoda Kōichi, a student of English literature who had debuted in 1960 as a literary critic with his essay on Mishima, that what he truly wanted to do was to kill the Tennō in the Imperial Palace. Was that also what he had in mind when he broached to Yamamoto and others the idea of storming into the Imperial Palace and defending it with a suicide squad? Perhaps. But Isoda was recollecting his last conversation with Mishima with a somewhat convoluted explanation and an interpretation of what happened subsequently. As he saw it, Mishima chose to do what he did in the GSDF compounds because he knew he wouldn't be able to get into the Imperial Palace. According to Isoda, Mishima thought his act of killing "the human Tennō" would paradoxically prove that he was the transcendental being as depicted in "Voices of the Heroic Souls," even as he established his own identity as a loyal subject by that act.[32]

Be that as it may, the idea necessarily brings to mind at least two earlier military involvements with the Imperial Palace. The leaders of the 2.26 Incident did not try to occupy it; for them such a move would have constituted the worst case of *lèse majesté*. During the Palace Incident—an attempt, from the afternoon of August 14 to the morning of August 15, 1945—to prevent Japan's surrender, part of the Imperial Guards Division did, but to no avail.

The palace, in any event, is not something you can "storm into" with a force of less than a hundred men. Built where Edo Castle once rose, with some of the donjons and other buildings retained, it is a sprawling area of 350 acres. Was Mishima just testing Yamamoto as to his seriousness in joining him when the time came, on the upcoming International Antiwar Day, October 21?

In July Yamamoto was promoted to vice commandant of the GSDF Research School. His assignment to develop intelligence personnel was over, though that did not mean his association with Mishima was.

Mishima planned to hold the first parade of the Shield Society to mark the first anniversary of its formation to go with International Antiwar Day. As noted before, Mishima was responsible for all the costs involving the Shield Society. Here, let us take a brief look at the pecuniary aspect of maintaining a group such as the one Mishima created.

There were first the uniforms. Though the society's membership still had not reached Mishima's aim of one hundred, he ordered one hundred and one sets of summer and winter uniforms—that "one" being himself. Estimates vary, but Shiine Yamato thought each set cost ¥120,000 and each hat ¥20,000. So that alone came to more than ¥14 million. Then there were boots, fatigues, and such, not to mention the costs for various activities: impromptu gatherings at cafés, lodging for intensive lectures and such for several days, sending members to the GSDF for training.[33] "There is no way the national budget could be used for students planning to join a private organization," a new Shield Society recruit thought when handed the military gear at the society's office, and he was right.[34] What did all such expenditures mean to Mishima?

One way of assessing it is to go back to the payments for his writings. Popular weeklies and such paid him a good deal more, but the staid monthly *Shinchō* paid ¥1,500 a manuscript page for his tetralogy *The Sea of Fertility*, serialized from September 1965 to January 1971. With his customary precision, he planned to allocate 750 pages for each of the four linked but separate novels, and he followed the plan for the first three, more or less. That means he earned just about ¥1,125,000 for each, somewhat more than what Mochimaru Hiroshi, chief of students, drew for his salary as editor of the *Ronsō Journal* for a year.

There were of course royalties for the four novels published in book form, in addition to those for all the other books. But we can see why Mishima hinted at the financial burden of maintaining the Shield Society when he and Yamamoto repaired to a restaurant following the latter's lecture to the members of the society, on May 23, 1969. Mishima had handed an envelope containing one thousand yen to each of the approximately one hundred participants in the lecture.[35] As he told Yuasa Atsuko, who years earlier had run a salon that inspired *Kyōko's House*, the cost was "not negligible."

Or, as he candidly admitted, he learned that "the morality of any movement" is determined by money. For that reason, he had "never received a single penny of assistance from anyone," he wrote. "All the funds come from my royalties." That was the "economic reason" he was unable to increase the number of Shield Society members beyond one hundred.[36]

He may even have changed his mind on the publication schedule of the tetralogy because of the need for money. When he set to work on it, Mishima had planned to publish it all at once when the entire serialization was over. But sometime after he completed the first two novels, *Spring Snow* and *The Runaway Horse*, he had the strong urge to publish them in book form. The explanation he provided for this change of plan had nothing to do with money, of course. "The work of continuing to write such a long narrative as this without having any reaction"—from critics, for literary critics rarely, if ever, took up something under serialization for comment—"is work like that of a subway operator who doesn't see outside scenery all day long, someone mocked me," he explained. He agreed, and decided to go outside to enjoy fresh air and scenery, so he might take up the remaining work with a refreshed mind. "Otherwise, the first half [of the narrative] would remain knotty in my head, become accumulating dregs in my heart, and unnecessarily hamper [further] work."[37]

CHAPTER TWENTY-SEVEN

# Wang Yangming: "To know is to act"

*What do you think of people calling you brazen?*
"I absolutely agree with them. It's as if the word were made for me."

—Mishima in an interview

It was because of money that Mochimaru Hiroshi and half a dozen others connected to the *Ronsō Journal* had to part company with Mishima in the summer of 1969.

The periodical did not win many subscribers or buyers, the total number of copies sold of each issue falling far short of the goal of ten thousand at the best of times. Out of desperation, Nakatsuji Kazuhiko, editor-in-chief, and Bandai Kiyoshi once again turned to Tanaka Seigen for funding. They knew it would bring ire from Mishima. It certainly did, but through an unintended route.

In a meeting Tanaka bragged he was the "patron" of Mishima and the Shield Society. A friend of Mishima's happened to be at the meeting and duly conveyed Tanaka's words to him. Mishima lost his temper. The upshot: at the end of August, seven *Ronsō Journal* people quit the Shield Society. What hurt Mishima was that they were also among the original ten who made the blood-oath. Muramatsu Takeshi witnessed part of the process, as well as the result.

After a Japan Cultural Council conference, Mishima took him to a café in the Akasaka Prince Hotel nearby. Nakatsuji was already there.

As soon as they sat down, Mishima told Nakatsuji to "quit magazine editing and pack up and go home." He did not explain why, and the young man did not ask the reason, either. Muramatsu thought his role was simply to witness something already agreed upon.

Mishima tried to persuade Mochimaru to cut his relationship with the journal but not with the Shield Society. In fact, he wanted him to focus on the militia. Till then the society was conducting its business in the journal's editorial office, but now it would have its own "command post." As always, Mishima would take care of all the expenses, including Mochimaru's salary. But Mochimaru would not agree to the proposition. He planned to marry his fiancée in the fall, and did not want to wholly subordinate himself to Mishima. He needed a job of his own, a life of his own, while nurturing his own political thought. He did not want to be the kind of man often found among rightwingers—spouting vainglorious ideas without their feet on the ground, he explained to Mishima.

Mishima saw his point, saying he had regarded him as his right-hand man because of such rectitude and independence. Yet he was not persuaded why Mochimaru was reluctant to accept an independent job he offered. He did not see why the young man was unwilling to take total control of the Shield Society, which he had practically run from the outset.

In fact, a schism had been developing between the two for some time. Mochimaru was the man Mishima trusted the most, but he had different ideas on some critical points. He often warned Mishima against his reliance on Yamamoto in military matters, reminding him how during the 2.26 Incident the senior officers had all turned against "the young officers" once the planned uprising became reality. A few years after Mishima's death, he would even go to see Yamamoto to tell him that he, Yamamoto, had incited and betrayed Mishima.

But he agreed with Yamamoto on what the Zenkyōtō and others were doing: it would *not* lead to a "revolution." "We would rise against a leftwing revolution as a counterrevolutionary force, that was self-evident," he said of the Shield Society. Citing "Counterrevolutionary Manifesto," he pointed out that for a counterrevolutionary force, there ought to be "just one battle," and it would have to be "a life-or-death battle." In the event, the Shield Society was a force to *react*. The Shōwa Restoration that the young officers of the 2.26 Incident advocated was a revolution, and that was to *act*, Mochimaru reasoned, using the English words *action* and *reaction*. But the leftwing students were unlikely to start a revolution. He did not see why Mishima seemed so *pressed* about International Antiwar Day. In the end he told Mishima that he would quit both the *Ronsō Journal* and the Shield Society but would help the society's activities from outside. Mishima had no choice but to agree, but it was a serious blow.

"His sorrow was not ordinary," wrote Muramatsu who received a phone call from the dismayed Mishima on the matter. "It was not a lament over the loss of an important right-hand man so much as the grief of a father betrayed by his son." As it happened, a few months earlier Mishima had written: "You don't have to bring up a faraway figure, Che Guevara; a revolutionary has to be betrayed by the subordinates he trusts just as Kita Ikki was betrayed by the young officers."

Whether it was all a betrayal or not, Mochimaru, Nakatsuji, Bandai, and others leaving Mishima reminded Muramatsu more of Mishima's own creation, Iinuma Isao, the protagonist of *The Runaway Horse*. Half of those who had agreed to Iinuma's plan for a Shōwa Restoration drop out when they learn that the army has refused to work with them.[1]

Yamamoto Kiyokatsu, however, guessed, in retrospect and as an outsider, that what happened was all Mishima's doing. "The true reason" for Mishima's action, he wrote, lay in his decision to replace "the chief of students" in order to "completely sever the [*Ronsō Journal*'s] relationship to rightwing forces." By doing so, he would be able to shed more of "the political nature" from his "private defense movement," Yamamoto thought.[2]

The essay in which Mishima invoked Che was on Kita Ikki and in it he said: "Neither have I been influenced by Kita Ikki's thought nor have I been awakened to something by him." The denial would later prompt some to challenge Mishima on his veracity. But Mishima went on to say: "Yet, behind the various phenomena of Shōwa history that interest me has always stood the lanky figure of Kita Ikki in Chinese garb, like a weirdly towering peak. It was an ominous image, but it was also the idealized image of a Japanese revolutionary that is tragic in a certain way."

Iinuma Isao, the fictional character Mishima created to represent the quintessence of those who agitated for a Shōwa Restoration in actual history, closely reflects the ideas Kita propounded. Isao's initial plan is to blow up several power substations in Tokyo, assassinate a few weighty financiers, and occupy and set the Bank of Japan on fire to touch off enough turmoil to prompt the institution of martial law. That would enable the placement of the financial industry "under the direct control of the Tennō," a vital step toward sweeping national reform to save the people suffering from dire poverty. Their deeds done, all would gather in front of the Imperial Palace and disembowel themselves.

Death by disembowelment aside, martial law as impetus of national reform and the belief in the Tennō's power to carry it out if the matter were left to his sole decision were central to Kita's 1919 treatise *Outline of a Legislative Draft for Reform of Japan* (*Nihon kaizō hōan taikō*), as Mishima explained. The Tennō's right to do so derived from *tōsuiken*, the prerogative of supreme command. (The argument resembles that for "unitary presidency" in the United States). In truth, the Tennō's powers under the Meiji Constitution were severely hemmed in, but no matter.

Mishima's essay was lucid and sober. Mishima characterized Tennō worship as "illogical," citing Kita's comparison, in a much earlier treatise, of the imperial system that had taken shape by the early twentieth century to "the worship of clay idols practiced by indigenous people in Oriental villages." Though he disavowed any influence from the man who held such sway over the young leaders of the 2.26 Incident, Mishima took special pleasure in discussing Kita. His genius, he wrote, could only be compared with that of Otto Weininger—in "fierceness," in both "chaos and insight in the youthful thought process," in "impetuosity in developing logic," and in "the delicacy of the intuition that supports it all." Also, both thinkers did not want to be less than brilliant.[3]

Mishima was equally honest in his self-analysis even in lighter, casual circumstances, as in a short interview the fiction magazine *Shōsetsu Seven* did with him just about the same time, for its July issue. Among "the ten blunt questions" the interviewer asked was: Tell us just one "episode" you remember from the periods of "experiencing the SDF." Mishima's answer: "At the officers' club, they were talking among themselves. 'There he is, Mishima.' 'The guy looks like a playboy mixed into a peasant, doesn't he?' Sharp, don't you think?"

Another "blunt" question: What do you think of people calling you *brazen*? Mishima's answer: "I absolutely agree with them. It's as if the word were made for me."[4]

## *No Art Superior to Death*

From July 26 to August 23, Mishima led the fourth group of Shield Society members for training at GSDF Camp Takigahara. As in the past, he slipped away from time to time to do other things, but during this stay at the camp he kept a sporadic diary.[5] Among the things he described were Mt. Fuji at various times of day and in shifting weather; some of the training he went through, such as helicopter rappelling; pinks, daylilies, thistles, and other wildflowers in bloom covering the training grounds; Typhoon No. 9 hitting the area directly from Okinawa, which he had visited in July for background information for *The Moonbow* because the play contains scenes on the islands albeit in imagined ancient times. Mishima also noted how the GSDF tried to cut costs by simplifying some equipment in comparison with the US military, the SDF's overseer. As he told the bureaucrats at the Ministry of Finance when he was invited to give a talk there two months later, the budget for the SDF was so stringent that the troops had to buy toilet paper themselves.[6]

One military observation he quotes comes from a Capt. Gotō: "Sportsmen and military men closely resemble each other, but sportsmen fight in *top condition*, whereas military men fight in lowest *condition*. So drink and degrade your *condition*." Perhaps the captain was a holdover from the Imperial Army, though he used English for "top condition" and "condition."

The entry for August 19, Tuesday, opens with a curt note: "practice parade; all afternoon." That day the Shield Society had its regular monthly meeting, and the practice was for the first public full-dress parade scheduled for November 3. In a letter two weeks earlier, Mishima had asked Kawabata to attend it by way of expressing his appreciation of the two books the senior writer had sent him, his Nobel Prize acceptance speech turned into a book, *Japan the Beautiful and Myself* (*Utsukushii Nihon no watakushi*),[7] and his two talks at the University of Hawaii earlier that year, also turned into a book, *The Existence and Discovery of Beauty* (*Bi no sonzai to hakken*).[8]

In his letter Mishima had said that, in the Nobel Prize speech, Kawabata explained "the bright, lifelike essence of nothingness for the first time so Westerners might readily understand it," and, in the Hawaii talks, that "the several pages on cups at the outset" reminded him of "Proust's description of the kitchen"—the way the French writer depicted a knife, the tip of an asparagus, and such, "in colossal detail." The first of the two talks Kawabata gave in Hawaii opens with a reference to "the beauty of the assortment of glasses gleaming in the morning sunshine on a long table on a corner of the terrace restaurant which extends onto the beach." Kawabata at the time was staying at the Kahala Hilton Hotel.

The letter of August 4, however, had ended on a startling note, a result perhaps of the subject of the two books. In both—in the case of the Hawaii talks, the second one, which he gave on May 16, 1969—Kawabata had referred to suicide in Japan.

In the Stockholm speech Kawabata cited his own 1933 essay whose title was taken from Akutagawa Ryūnosuke's will in which the man contemplating suicide spoke of nature looking ever more beautiful in consequence. Kawabata mentioned Dazai Osamu, along with his avant-garde painter friend who used to say, "There is no art superior to death" and "To die is to live," and Zen master Ikkyū who had attempted suicide twice. "I neither extol nor sympathize with" those who commit suicide, but his painter friend, who was born in a Buddhist temple and graduated from a Buddhist school, "must have had a different view of death from that of the West."[9]

His reference to suicide in the Hawaii talk was literary, rather than factual, but he was far from condemnatory of the act if not explicitly sympathetic. He had, after all, started out by closely describing his life with a dying grandfather (*Jūrokusai no nikki*, 1925), once described himself as "a master of funerals" (*Sōshiki no meijin*, 1923), and was for a while fascinated by the Egyptian *Book of the Dead* (*Shisha no sho*, 1928) and séance (*Jojōka*, 1933). So, in his talk, he cited poems in the *Man'yōshū* lamenting legendary youths, both male and female, who killed themselves because of complications of love, as well as the passages about Ukifune in *The Tale of Genji* after she has tried to kill herself for a similar reason.

"Be it a fish that swims in a pond or a deer that calls in the mountains, it would be sad indeed not to help it after it is captured by a human and about to die," says a Buddhist monk who happens by Ukifune who has failed to drown herself. "Human life does not last forever, but it would not do *not* to extend the life of someone dying if only by one or two days."

Kawabata then quoted an interpretation of this story by Umehara

Takeshi, who had switched his field of scholarly investigation from German philosophy focused on Nietzsche to classical Japanese literature not long after the war, that Murasaki Shikibu here is arguing that succoring even "a human being who must end her life, a human being as hopeless as that . . . lies at the core of Mahayana Buddhism."[10]

These passages may well have led Mishima to unburden himself in uncharacteristic fashion. "For four years now, while being laughed at, I have been single-mindedly making preparations little by little toward the year 1970," he wrote. He did not come right out and say what the preparations were for, only that he did not want to be taken to be "tragic," though he would not mind if it provided "an idea for a cartoon." "What I fear is not death, but my family's honor after my death. Were something to happen to me, society at large would at once bare its teeth, start finding fault with me, and turn [family honor] into, I think, something dishonorable and trashy.

"I do not mind myself getting laughed at while alive, but I cannot bear my children getting laughed at after my death. You are, Mr. Kawabata, the only person who could protect them from that happening and I am single-mindedly dependent on you from now on."[11]

---

The latter half of the diary he kept at Camp Takigahara is devoted to a close description of the music for the gagaku *Ranryō'ō* and the instrument used to play it, the flute called *ryūteki*, with Mishima's own drawings of the instrument. Gagaku is a ceremonial dance that reached Japan from the Asian Continent in the seventh century and was adopted by the court.

The story *Ranryō'ō* is based on a legendary Chinese general Lanling Wang who was so glamorously handsome, it was said, that he had to wear a demonic mask when leading his troops into battle lest they become too enamored of his beauty to neglect to fight. Mishima's description of the music—to be exact, what goes through his mind as he listens to the *ryūteki*—is appropriately lyrical, until he comes to the realization, "The sound *flows without any development*. This is what's important!" Anyone who has listened to the gagaku flute for a proper duration will agree with Mishima on the "no-development" part, though some may question whether that's what makes the music important.

Mishima in no time turned this fragmentary diary into what was to be the last short story he would write, *Ranryōō*. There the realization just referred to is somewhat elaborated: "I knew that the music of the flute flows without any development whatsoever. You make no development, that is important. If music is to be truly faithful to the continuation of life (just as the flute is so faithful to human breathing!), what can be purer than that it makes no development."

"And when I came to, the sound of the flute was about to explore into a certain depth of no return," the narrator reports. "I recognized the pale, smooth back of the sound of the flute. I do not know the depth of what sort of feeling it is, but it will pierce through the feeling, enter an even deeper, transparent, tenebrous border, which will suddenly grab our world and crush it, just as a child unthinkingly squishes the fruit of a Chinese lantern plant in her palm."

The story ends with the flutist abruptly telling the narrator: If the enemy you are thinking of is different from the enemy I am thinking of, well then, I will not fight.

Although Mishima does not mention it in his diary, on the evening of August 23 one of the Shield Society members came to his room to play the gagaku flute. The young man was Sekikawa Masakatsu, a Doshisha University student. Sekikawa, identified as "S" in the story, went on to become an authority on gagaku.

## *The Most Terrifying* Lèse Majesté

On September 4, Kikuta Kazuo's stage adaptation of *Spring Snow* opened at Hibiya Geijutsu-za. Kikuta, the founder of the theater, was a popular playwright and songwriter. Other than his original works, he had turned *Gone With the Wind* into a play. With Ichikawa Somegorō and Sakuma Yoshiko in the lead roles, *Spring Snow* proved so successful that the planned closing date of September 28 was extended by three months, to December 27.

In the program note for the dramatization, Mishima observed that in writing the novel he was not too different from Proust, who wrote about aristocratic life in great detail even though he had "not come from an aristocratic family," or from Stendhal, who wrote about high society even though he "did not know much about it." The difference was, he went on, that Bōjō Toshitami, "the blue-blood aristocrat," had given his story "a big stamp of approval."

Earlier that year Bōjō had written Mishima a long letter to tell him how moved he was by *Spring Snow* that had just come out in book form. He felt as if it described his own family, he said, but in the same letter he had noted a single error in the use of a term in the New Year's Tanka Recitation. Mishima at once wrote to thank him, assuring Bōjō that, coming from the *"Arbiter Elegantiarum,"* his commendation gave him "the most definite joy," thereby reviving a friendship that had practically been dead for two decades. When Fuji TV proposed to turn the novel into a drama series, Mishima agreed on condition that Bōjō supervise period authenticity.

In that work, Bōjō found another error: In the novel, the New Year's Tanka Recitation ceremony is supposed to take place in the second year of Taishō Era (1913), but that was not possible: that year the nation was in mourning for the Meiji Emperor. At any rate, the drama, in six parts, was aired from the end of February to early April in 1970.[12]

As to the novel's central concern, Mishima spoke of the difficulty of constructing a love story in modern times. The reason is simple: "absolute obstacles" to love that two young people have to surmount have ceased to exist. As he had clearly spelled out fourteen years earlier when he had given a series of "lectures on love" to the readers of the monthly *Myōjō*, most of the traditional inhibitions and understandings, real or imagined, had vanished or were vanishing fast with the "freedom" Japan's defeat and the US Occupation had brought. Though taking the form of suggestions and advice by a know-all writer on a meteoric rise, the "lectures" were in truth a candid, liberal description of the sexual mores of Japan around 1955, homosexual and heterosexual, premarital and marital.[13]

In the early part of the Taishō Era when *Spring Snow* is set, however, some obstacles still existed, Mishima said. "The biggest, highest taboo imaginable" or "the most terrifying *lèse majesté*" an imperial subject could commit was to "violate" an imperial princess. A daughter of a ranking aristocrat betrothed, with "imperial approval," to an imperial prince, as Ayakura Satoko is in the novel, was in effect an imperial princess. Perhaps, Mishima suggested, though he was talking about his own novel, Matsugae Kiyoaki, the fiction's "Hamlet-type protagonist of indecisiveness, violated the taboo so he might savor 'true love.'"[14]

## *The Ultimate Action Is Death*

Mochimaru spoke for the last time on October 12, the day the Shield Society rehearsed its parade on the roof of the National Theatre. They then moved to Ichigaya Hall, where the mutual aid association of the Defense Agency was headquartered. Mochimaru recommended Kuramochi Kiyoshi, a Waseda student, to succeed him as "chief of students" on the ground that Kuramochi's ability to take care of practical matters was good. Mishima evidently agreed with him, but he chose Morita Masakatsu instead. He may have seen in him a resemblance to his own creation, Iinuma Isao. The Shield Society's business office was moved to Morita's apartment.

Regardless of the differences in the assessment of what the Zengakuren might actually accomplish, International Antiwar Day, on October 21, that year was expected to create the biggest demonstrations in the battle against the renewal of the US-Japanese Mutual Security Treaty next June. Mishima himself foresaw "fierce clashes" between students and police, even as he expected the treaty would be "automatically extended" in the middle of next year, as he observed on October 15, in a speech at his former employer, the Ministry of Finance. His classmate Nagaoka Minoru, then director of the secretariat at the most powerful bureaucracy, had invited Mishima as part of the activities to mark the ministry's hundredth anniversary. For the title of his talk, Mishima had suggested "something big like 'Issues facing Japan now,'" as he put it. His talk, discursive and entertaining, ended on a personal note. When it was transcribed and published in the December 1970 issue of *Bungei Shunjū*, it was titled "What Is Japan?" That indeed was Mishima's peroration.

The question is not, Mishima said, whether you are for or against the security treaty. Some may simply say that those for the treaty are for the United States and those against it are for the USSR but putting the matter in that fashion would be like "dividing Americans into whites and blacks." The former would leave the question "What is Japan?" unanswered, just as the latter would not tell you what America is all about.

When the question of for or against the security treaty blows over, another dichotomy is likely to arise, between those who regard themselves as Japanese and those who do not, Mishima said, citing a brief conversation he had with a hippie at the time of his debate with Tōdai students. His dandruff-covered hair reaching his shoulders, the young man dismissed Mishima face to face as "a caged animal" and, when asked, said he had no nationality, despite his unmistakable "Mongolian-Japanese" appearance. With the sense of growing authoritarian oppression starting to pall over Japan even as traveling overseas became easier by the day because the Japanese were growing richer by leaps and bounds, such sentiments were gaining popularity. *I'm Going to See Everything (Nandemo miteyarō)*, Oda Makoto's account of global wandering on practically no money, had become a perennial bestseller since its publication at the start of the decade.

Mishima ended his talk by telling the financial bureaucrats that it was with that eventuality in mind that "I am readying my literature, readying my thought, or readying my action."[15]

Here, if "action" sounds a little out of place, that is because the Japanese word Mishima chose for it, *kōdō*, had a special, even esoteric, meaning to him. Back in 1955, he had made a concise assessment of Yamamoto Tsunetomo of *Hagakure*, calling the samurai a *kōdōka*, "a man of action," and characterizing as "Epicurean" Yamamoto's statement: "There is nothing other than the immediate thought (*nen*) of the moment. I go on putting one thought on top of another and my life takes shape. Having realized this, I have nothing that keeps me busy, have nothing I seek. I simply live by keeping this one thought in mind."

Mishima took *nen* in Yamamoto's statement to mean the same as "decision" and "decision" the same as "action." As we have seen, Yamamoto is famous for the dictum, "The way of the warrior, I've found, is to die. In a situation with a choice, you can only choose at once to die." The ultimate action is death, be it natural death or some other death, such as one by disembowelment, Mishima argued. That being the case, "The judgment of the situation that spawns the judgment on death drags behind it a long chain of judgments, and honing oneself in endless judgments suggests a long time of tension and concentration that a man of action must put up with."

A man of action thus inhabits a world in which he is "always drawing before his eyes a circle that can be perfected only by adding the last single dot." But, unable to add the dot, "he, from second to second, discards the circle that can't be linked without that dot to face another circle, yet still another." An artist or a philosopher, in comparison, inhabits a world in which he "keeps adding layers of gradually spreading concentric circles around him." The question is: "When death arrives, which one will have a more intense sense of perfection, the man of action or the artist?"[16]

This was fourteen years earlier. Now, not long before his speech at the Finance Ministry, Mishima had begun a series of essays on "action" for the monthly *Pocket Punch Oh!*, beginning with its September issue. Titled *Introduction to a Study of Action (Kōdō-gaku nyūmon)*, the series was clearly meant to clarify the meaning of "action" through handy examples.

"Action has its own unique logic," he had begun the opening essay. "Therefore, once it starts, it does not cease until its logic ends." He then quickly brought in his favorite weapon: "The Japanese sword, once you draw it, begins a unique movement," for, "as long as it is drawn, it cannot rest in the scabbard without [achieving] the aim of cutting something, or someone."

"Action is swift," while "life in one sense can take a long time." Consider the men on the Kamikaze forces who flew themselves into death. People remember their action, but pay little thought to "the time of their life and their training that may have extended to several hundred hours." Thus: "Action, exploding for a second like a firework, has the mysterious power to summarize a long life."[17]

In the second essay, Mishima takes up "military action" to point to the contradiction between action and power in most military organizations: the greater the responsibility, the further from "action." Only a guerrilla unit can escape this inevitability, for in it each member must be a true man of action even as he is required to display "an inhuman loyalty" to the whole. Still, it is only in "the beauty of an individual action" that we can try to find "the beauty of a human action."[18]

In discussing "psychology of action" in the third, he admits that the human mind often prevents an action from taking place, even though "the action itself usually occurs with a speed that leaves no room for psychology." This is because "to think of the future and think of the past is man's unique nature, and the hard-to-deal-with ability called imagination, which animals lack, constrains man. How easy it would have been for [the men on] the Kamikaze forces had they not been tormented by imagination!"[19]

## *"'Student Militia,' Charge!"*

The demonstrations on International Antiwar Day were indeed large. The Socialist Party, the Communist Party, and the Federation of Labor Unions made a unified front in organizing nationwide rallies to demand not just the ending of the war in Vietnam and the abandonment of the US-Japanese Mutual Security Treaty, but also the immediate, unconditional reversion of Okinawa and the immediate dissolution of the Diet. In addition, the Zenkyōtō and other student groups were expected to make their own moves.

It was the *Yomiuri Shinbun* that raised the stakes for Mishima. On October 19, the right-leaning national daily carried an article with a sensational headline, "'Student Militia,' Charge!," with as sensational a subheading suggesting that a group was undertaking fierce training with guns "for *yūkoku*" and that its unusually long stay with the GSDF had raised some eyebrows. One of those quoted for the article was the influential journalist Ōya Sōichi whose comment in this instance carried a good deal of weight because he was known to be a friend of Mishima's. Ōya suggested that the Defense Agency had gone a little too far in accommodating Mishima.

"Instead of being pleased about acquiring fifty or eighty militia-like friends, they should think of the reaction of the great majority of the Japanese people. As I see it, most people do not support it," Ōya said. "I understand well why Mr. Mishima can't help feeling agitated about Japan's present situation, but if you create an organization such as his and act [as he does], you will provoke those of the antiestablishment groups and worsen the confrontation." He then warned: he sensed "the budding of Nazism" in what Mishima was doing.

Two days later, on International Antiwar Day, the morning edition of the *Yomiuri* carried another article on Mishima—this time a taidan between Mishima and Ōya's "student" and friend Murakami Hyōe. The taidan itself may have been intended to convey Mishima's "true intent," but the accompanying article pointed out that an increasing number of people were expressing alarm that Mishima, a contender for the Nobel Prize only recently, had created something like the Shield Society.[20]

On the anticipated day, the rallies organized by political parties and labor unions drew more than eight hundred sixty thousand people nationwide, the largest number since the peak of the 1960 antisecurity treaty movement. The government deployed thirty-two thousand police men assembled from all over Japan, its core force the four thousand five hundred riot police, in Tokyo. In anticipation, Mishima had set up a command post in his house, secretly equipped with a wireless, apparently to tap police communications. Placed in the middle of the guestroom, it was a cumbersome affair, five feet wide and three feet high. Shiine Yamato, who had requested Mishima's article on the day for his weekly and was to accompany him, thought of Che Guevara when he saw the machine and smelled cigar smoke in the room. Mishima liked to smoke Romeo y Julieta on special days.[21]

But the day turned out to be a dud, to Mishima's disappointment—or was it? The main, obvious reason was the police. Also, partly as a result of the police campaign, the majority of people were quickly turning against the student movement and the violence that came with it.

The aggressive use of police force had become routine since the siege of the Yasuda Auditorium in January. The first big day following that was supposed to be April 28 Okinawa Day, but that did not happen. The police were relentless, even resorting to "preemptive arrests" which, as Mishima later suggested, would have provoked cries of illegality a few years earlier.[22] They even disrupted "the antiwar folksong fest" that the Beheiren had organized in the plaza on the west side of Shinjuku Station on June 29; they used tear gas and arrested sixty-nine people. The after-the-fact explanation the police proffered was that the gathering created a traffic jam. Such strong-arm tactics led to the radicalization of one Communist faction of the Zengakuren. Toward the end of August the Communist Alliance announced the formation of the Red Army.

Also, some vigilante groups had sprung up. On International Antiwar Day there were even scenes reminiscent of wartime Japan: in various parts of Tokyo, women's groups voluntarily went to police precincts and prepared food for the policemen.[23]

The result was far less violence in Tokyo than many had anticipated. During the day small bands of student demonstrators simply dashed through various parts of the metropolis like gusts sweeping through an empty house, prompting the *Asahi Shinbun* reporter to call them "sweep-through guerrillas." In the evening, a sizable number of students finally managed to pour onto the railway track at Shinjuku Station, their strategic focus, and forced the National Railway to halt the operation of the line. But they were arrested in no time. The area around the station saw an estimated ten thousand people gather at its peak, but no violent clashes. Otherwise, with more than two-thirds of the "normally blinding neon signs" switched off early in the evening, the areas like the Ginza and Shinjuku that would otherwise be dazzlingly bright and noisy were bleak and quiet.[24]

The bleak and quiet scene was what Mishima saw when he arrived in Shinjuku late in the afternoon—dressed in a black leather jacket over a white see-through shirt, jeans, and leather laced-up shoes, topped by dark glasses and a racecar helmet—with some members of the Shield Society. The police hold on the east entrance to the station was far tighter than a year earlier, he noticed, as he described the scene for *Pocket Punch Oh!*. Though he did not tell the readers, he had asked the Metropolitan Police to put the Shield Society under its command but had been rebuffed.[25]

"There was nary a suggestion or a hint of the masses that had formed a terrifying *mob* around the east entrance" a year earlier, Mishima wrote, summing up the day in "Effects of Action." "Terrifying" was the word Mishima used in several other places when referring to the nature of the mass of people that year. With all the stores and shops closed and all the surrounding buildings shuttered, the area had turned into "an ominous *no-man's land*."

It was "an ominous, nihilistic space" the riot police had created behind them, where no demonstrators would dare get in. The "iron rule of guerrillas" requires that they maintain an escape route through the masses who protect them. The students had greatly improved their resilience as well as the ability to quickly gather and disperse. But there were no masses they could count on. To that extent, they were now "calculating" their moves in response to the strategies worked out by the police, Mishima observed.

In fact, a great part of the masses had largely deserted the students. At one point in the windy evening mixed with rain, Mishima watched the owner of a mom-and-pop store pour a bucketful of water over a student. When fellow students quickly gathered around him to protest, the man's wife came out and barked at them. The students beat a dispirited retreat, a spectacle so memorable that Mishima would mention it in several of his subsequent articles. It was Tuesday, and people were exasperated and angry with violent demonstrators that they had to close their stores.

Clearly, overwhelming government power had dramatically cut the effectiveness of the demonstrators. It was such that watching them unable to put up a good fight was "frustrating," Mishima wrote. He walked about in Shinjuku muttering furiously, "This is no good. Absolutely no good." As he complained to Morita later in the evening as they drank in Roppongi, it was as if Tokyo was "under martial law."[26] It was a supreme irony.

So what's next? If "the so-called guerrilla warfare" without any plan to achieve "a decisive effect" from the outset, save to "engender a certain anxiety" in society at large, also fails to attract the serious attention of the mass media, as the demonstrators that day obviously did, then anyone who plans such warfare will "be driven into rethinking his tactic." When that happens, "the only truly effective action will be for him to sacrifice himself for a terrorism aimed at the most extreme effect." But "because we cannot think of our personal effect or personal gain on the other side of death, the political effect must be sought in some suprapersonal place."[27]

October 21 would become a decisive point for Mishima—or so he would declare in his manifesto prepared for November 25, 1970. Yet Mishima surely had known the day would be a disappointment, Yamamoto Kiyokatsu wrote: Sassa Atsuyuki, chief of the riot police, had told him, as he had Yamamoto, that the police security measures this time around would preclude the day from becoming anything like a repeat of the October 21 of 1968.[28]

---

Regardless, eye-catching political events continued to unfold. In "Action and Waiting," Mishima took up the Daibosatsu Pass Incident—an arrest, on November 5, 1969, of fifty-three members of the Red Army in a mountain house west of Tokyo. The radical group planned to attack both the prime minister's official residence and the Metropolitan Police HQ to take hostages so they might demand or force release of its imprisoned members. To do so, several dozen members gathered near Daibosatsu Pass—made famous by the title of Nakazato Kaizan's unending narrative, much of which has to do with a samurai on a rampage[29]—to train with weapons, mostly swords and Molotov cocktails. But the police gathered enough intelligence on their scheme and raided the house where they had gathered. Among those arrested was the founder-chairman of the Red Army, Shiomi Takaya.

Citing this incident, Mishima mocked the leaders of the Red Army: they had freely spouted military terms but failed to observe the basic requirement of infantry training, that is, putting a few men on guard duty. Mishima's focus, however, was on the radical students' inability to "wait," of which the police took advantage by giving enormous pressure to put the situation under control in the shortest time possible. Any "action" requires the ability to wait for "the right opportunity," Mishima suggested, and the ability to do so is "the courage most essential to action."[30]

A month later, Mishima himself had a close call: he barely missed finding himself on a Korean airliner hijacked to North Korea. He had gone to South Korea as part of a group to look into the North's guerrilla activities in the South, in particular the operations of Unit 124 that the North set up for guerrilla operations in the South. Nearly two years earlier, on January 21, 1968, a commando unit of thirty-one had crossed the DMZ and managed to get close to the Blue House, South Korea's presidential residence. Its purpose was to assassinate the president and liberate South Korea. They ran into the police and in the ensuing two-week battle, most of them were killed. It was two days after the infiltration, on January 23, that the North captured the US intelligence-gathering ship, the *Pueblo*.

The group Mishima joined included his translator-scholar friend Ivan Morris who, with some others, had founded Amnesty International USA. After inspecting an area in question, on the east coast of the peninsula, the group flew back to Seoul, on the afternoon of December 10. The following afternoon, the same flight was diverted to North Korea. For all the strict airport security checks South Korea performed, the deception was easy: the only thing the hijacker did was put himself in the uniform of a brigadier general of the South Korean Army.

The essay dealing with this experience, "Planning an Action," concerns the unplannability of most "actions," and his point here may be forced but is revealing. Taking the example of a battlefield charge, he posits that only irrational mental power can bridge the gap between the rational plan and the unknowable dead-end it may run up against and that the Japanese sword can best represent that mental power.[31]

## The Officer with His Sword Drawn

In "The Beauty of Action," he again brings up the image of a naval officer leaping out of his "special submarine" on a moonlit night, his sword drawn, only to be shot dead. Here, he is a little more specific and says it happened in Australia. There indeed was a submarine attack in Sydney Harbor, on May 31, 1942, but the image he put forward was likely to be no more than "a story handed down."[32] Or he mixed it up with what may have happened on the same day in Diego Suarez, Madagascar.

That day in Sydney Harbor, one of the three midget ("special") submarines launched from three submarines to attack the Allied ships anchored in the harbor became entangled in the antisubmarine net and its crew of two scuttled their own vessel and killed themselves. One midget submarine was spotted; after repeated attacks, it was damaged, and its crew killed themselves. Just one succeeded in sinking a ship, escaped, but was then lost. (Sixty-four years later, in November 2006, a group of scuba divers found the submarine sitting on the bottom of the sea a few miles off the harbor.) The operation in Madagascar went better. The two midget submarines seriously damaged the battleship HMS *Ramillies* and sank a tanker.

Following the Madagascar attack, the crew of one submarine were sighted on land. They were shot dead. However, the Royal Navy's investigations of the Diego Suarez attack appear to have been far less thorough and not much detail is known, let alone whether one of the Japanese had time to draw his sword.

The two attacks, at any rate, were reported in Japan, evidently with patriotic emphasis. "Just now at 7:30 pm, having finished hearing the news on the special-submarine attacks in Madagascar and Australia, I am writing this card to you, sir," Mishima scribbled to his teacher Shimizu Fumio. "I feel as if I have a lump in my throat and do not think I can talk with any kind of ordinary words. So grateful am I for the Imperial Glory that tears are on the verge of overflowing my eyes and running down my cheeks," the seventeen-year-old used a vocabulary and style reserved for matters related to the Tennō.

"At the same time I cannot restrain myself from feeling bright and clear, and I feel as if hearing the laughter of the eighty-thousand deities filling the azure skies in the South."[33] That many deities are imagined to fill the Japanese land and romp.

As far as such things go, we would love to know how Mishima reacted to Rear Admiral Gerard Charles Muirhead-Gould's honorable action. The Royal Navy's Officer in Command of Sydney Harbor at the time of the attack, the admiral had the bodies of the crew of the two midget submarines raised from the harbor and, despite strong protests, gave them a naval funeral, and returned their ashes to Japan. Mishima's remaining or collected essays or letters from that period have no reference to the gallant deed.

---

The two items he chose to go with the twelve-installment series on "action" when a publisher offered to turn it into a book were *The Aesthetic of Ending (Owari no bigaku)*,[34] a series he did three years earlier for a women's weekly *Josei Jishin*, and an extended essay, "Yangming School as a Philosophy for Revolution" (*Kakumei tetsugaku to shite no Yōmeigaku*),[35] that he did for the monthly *Shokun!* Mishima said he did these for the readers of particular magazines, noting, in the case of *The Aesthetic of Ending*, that he did the series "half frivolously." The essays for young women, in truth, are lighthearted as they deal with the "endings" of such things as marriage, phone conversation, male virginity, the beautiful face, quarrels, manners, and jealousy, each illustrated with common daily examples, but they inevitably include some telling observations.

The news that Kasai Masae, captain of the Japanese women's volleyball team that won the gold medal in the 1964 Tokyo Olympic Games, has become a housewife, for instance, prompted Mishima to reflect that Kasai may have ceased to be a hero but that she, being a woman, has the privilege of beginning anew as a woman. A man has no such luck. A man's heroic act lasts as heroic for only about five minutes. The rest of his life is, well, "the rest of his life." In the event, is it not best to die with the act?

This reasoning may be non sequitur, as Mishima obviously knew, but it did not prevent him from succumbing to fondly recollecting the state funeral he watched of the greatest hero of the Russo-Japanese War, Adm. Tōgō Heihachirō, even though the victor of the Battle of Tsushima was, he suggested, someone who lived too long after his heroic act.

He passed away in a good era, so the ending of this hero was a truly grand ending of a hero. In my life I am unlikely to see again the ending of a hero so resplendent, so like a sunset. For the great opportunity to watch the state funeral of the Admiral of the Fleet, we grammar-school children were made to stand solemnly erect, in a row, for hours on end, by Chidorigafuchi Park. The procession of the state funeral slowly began to approach from the direction of Kudan. When a cortège of foreign military attachés in military uniform of various colors came into view, walking with that unique way of walking, moving one foot forward, pulling the other foot to the same level, then moving one foot forward again, the white plumes on their helmets were like a column of wonderful tropical birds approaching.

Chidorigafuchi Park is on the bank of the west moat of the Imperial Palace. Kudan is where the Yasukuni Shrine is located. When Mishima wrote this, the national shrine for the war dead was far from becoming a subject of international protest and condemnation it would be a few decades later. China, in a civil-war turmoil that Japan aggravated, had its own delegation participate in the funeral. It was June 5, 1934. The cortège was "interminable, the casket being quietly pulled ... until finally, without seeing the procession to the end, I suffered from cerebral anemia and fainted."

Mishima's description is a reminder, if any is needed, that he grew up in an era when military accomplishments were duly honored and exalted. For Tōgō's funeral, the Great Powers of the day, as well as countries such as China and Holland, dispatched warships to send honor guards to take part in it. Mishima was a typical *aikoku shōnen*, "boy patriot," as he put it just before his death, when asked in an *enquête* about his reaction to the news of Japan's assault on Pearl Harbor. He was a good respondent to all sorts of questionnaires Japanese publishers love to send to writers and such, although he avowed that he tore up all of them when he received them.[36]

This *enquête*, by the *Sunday Mainichi*, had to do with the then contentious question of what to call the Japanese part of the Second World War: the Greater East Asian War, as the Japanese conservatives insisted, or the Pacific War, as the US Occupation insisted on calling it. Mishima was for the former because, he explained, a country should be able to name a war in which it is involved on its own.[37] (Gore Vidal, who believed that the Pearl Harbor attack was merely FDR's success in provoking Japan, called it "the American-Japanese War of 1941–1945.")[38] The responses to the query appeared in the November 29, 1970, issue of the weekly.

## *"To know is to act"*

The other item, the one about the Chinese Confucian thinker Wang Yangming (1472–1529), was a knowledgeable but easy-to-understand attempt to provide a philosophical underpinning to Mishima's "action." Wang, who was also an able military commander, advocated the unity of knowledge and action, "To know is to act," or, as he put it in one of his explications, "Those who are supposed to know but do not act simply do not yet know." In China his "dynamic idealism" influenced, among others, the founder of modern China Sun Yatsen and the philosopher Xiong Shili. In Japan it became one great backbone of the Meiji Restoration.[39] In fact, Wang's philosophy, called Yōmeigaku in Japan, may have had more varied or historically conspicuous influence in Japan than in China.

Aside from those who were mainly dedicated to philosophizing, the followers of Yōmeigaku included Yamaga Sokō, the military strategist for the Akō fiefdom that produced the famous forty-seven samurai; Ōshio Heihachirō, the police inspector who revolted out of anger at the government's refusal to succor the poor and starving in the continuing famines; Yoshida Shōin, the firebrand advocate of expelling barbarians who pleaded with Cmdr. Matthew Perry to take him to the United States just so he might acquire the technological wherewithal to repel foreign interferers like Perry himself; Saigō Takamori, who rebelled to alleviate the plight of his samurai followers brought on by a government he helped to create that nevertheless put an end to the samurai class; and Nogi Maresuke, who disemboweled himself to express remorse for his failure to carry out his military duties properly for the Tennō.

Indeed, "the intellectual milieu engendered by Yōmeigaku ended with Gen. Nogi," Mishima said. Thereafter, rejected by "Taishō culturalism and Taishō humanism," Yōmeigaku "went underground only to become a hotbed for radical rightwing thought" and "a special instrument of a segment of the military." He might have added that, among the writers representative of what Mishima called "Taishō culturalism," Akutagawa Ryūnosuke wrote a story titled "The General" (*Shōgun*) to twit Nogi Maresuke. Still, he did not forget to add that underlying the New Left was "the ethos of the unity of knowledge and action."

Ōshio Heihachirō (1793–1837) was one of the men Mishima chose to describe at some length in his extended essay. He initiated "a riot almost hopeless for the relief of the poor" and ended up burning down a quarter of Osaka, bringing greater suffering to the people. "Yōmeigaku has *dämonisch* elements that those who possess the Apollonian rational mind find it hard to comprehend." It is imbued with "mysterious anti-intellectualism and actionism," and Ōshio's was a "Dionysian action." It was natural, then, the Apollonian Mori Ōgai, in writing his document-based account, *Ōshio Heihachirō*, should have failed to develop any "empathy" for the man.

"The philosophy that prepares a revolution and the sentiment that underpins the philosophy have, in every case," Mishima observed, "the two pillars of nihilism and mysticism." Take the French Revolution: It "hid the Marquis de Sade's deep nihilism behind Rousseau's optimistic philosophy." As well, "some of the Jacobins went to the Grand Lodge of Scotland to hear its oracles," as Gérard de Nerval pointed out, Mishima said. Likewise, the Nazi Revolution had its mysticism formed by Alfred Rosenberg in *The Myth of the Twentieth Century*, "against the background of the active nihilism Nietzsche and Heidegger had prepared."

What is notable about Mishima's argument is that it appears to have been inspired by Shiba Ryōtarō's account of Gen. Nogi Maresuke, *Junshi*, especially by Shiba's description in Part II, "To Cut His Stomach," of how Yōmeigaku influenced a series of Japanese thinkers. In particular, Mishima must have been struck, even shaken, by the way Shiba opened the section: "The mysterious declivity that his death must not be a natural death began quite early in Nogi Maresuke." Then, before starting his précis of Yōmeigaku in Japan, Shiba wrote: "The idea that one must make oneself the actor of one's spirit and must not act in any other way was one of the very unique thoughts handed down until Meiji."[40] The two were exactly what he was about, Mishima must have felt. This explains why death became central to his accounting of Yōmeigaku.

Thus, looking into Ōshio Heihachirō, Mishima draws attention to the thinker's observation in his most important treatise on Wang Yangming, *Senshindō sakki*, the book Saigō Takamori, the leader of Japan's "last *national* rebellion," loved to read to the end of his life: The sage "does not resent his body dying but resents his mind dying."[41] As to Saigō, Mishima paraphrases a passage from one of his writings: The fear of death is a sentiment you develop after you are born. You do not fear death before your birth. You can see the nature of death only when you detach yourself from your body. You must discover the truth of not fearing death within your fear of death. That is to return to your true nature before your birth.

From Yoshida Shōin he quotes what he finds to be "the most terrifying, unforgettable phrase" in one of his letters to a young man: "Compared with the everlastingness of heaven and earth, even pines and oaks are like gnats." The letter says at the outset:

> That you have not yet reached enlightenment on death and life is too silly for words. Let me say: If you regret death at sixteen, seventeen, eighteen, you will regret death at thirty, and even if you become eighty, ninety, you will never feel it is enough. There are things who live only half a year, like insects in grass and insects in water, but they don't think they are too short; there are things that live several hundred years, like pines and oaks, but they don't think they are too long. Compared with the everlastingness of heaven and earth, even pines and oaks are like gnats.

When he wrote this Shōin himself was in his late twenties. He would be beheaded before he turned thirty.

That Shiba's story must have prompted Mishima to inquire into Yōmeigaku is suggested by the letter he wrote half a year after the story appeared: It was to Yasuoka Masahiro, reputed to be not just the greatest Yōmeigaku scholar in modern times but also the greatest political *éminence grise* who counted among those who respected him Chiang Kaishek.

In his letter thanking Yasuoka for giving him, through Izawa Kinemaro, one of his books hard to come by, Mishima denigrated Etō Jun for making a big fuss about Zhu Xi philosophy—the mainline Confucian school of thought the Tokugawa shogunate adopted for governance—

only since returning from teaching at Princeton University. Mishima also dismissed as "unscientific" Maruyama Masao for giving just half a page to Yōmeigaku in his famous tome on Japanese political thought in recent centuries. In contrast, Mishima praised "the popular writer" Shiba Ryōtarō for "seriously studying" Yōmeigaku.[42]

Mishima dictated the Yōmeigaku article in a series of nine sessions, as he had the series on "action." Tanaka Kengo, the editor of the essay, was deeply impressed by Mishima's "astonishing brain." He met Mishima nine times at a restaurant where the writer would come with several books to quote from. After the meal, Mishima would start his dictation, only occasionally dipping into a book. The result when transcribed required scarcely any editing, and each dictation came to the more or less specified length of nine pages.[43]

The last installment of the seamless essay was published two months before his death, in the September 1970 issue of *Shokun!* As he included it in the aforementioned book, Mishima wrote an afterword and said he hoped some readers, when the time came, would realize "So this is what he meant to say." These essays, unlike his novels and such, are full of his own "experience, sighs, and frustrated feelings."

CHAPTER TWENTY-EIGHT

# The Constitution

*"The Self-Defense Forces are unconstitutional!"*

—Mishima in his final speech

On October 27, Mishima attended Nippon Columbia's announcement at the Akasaka Prince Hotel to issue a record of Ichikawa Ebizō declaiming *Kanjinchō* and Mishima reading "the upper volume" (Act One) of *The Wonder Tale*. The following day his kabuki play was rehearsed for the first time. Four days later, he summoned all the "group leaders" of the Shield Society—each leader heading a company of eight or nine men—to his house to review the International Antiwar Day ten days earlier and work out the details of the parade three days later.

As to what happened on October 21, 1969, he noted that matters had developed in such a way that prospects for the GSDF deploying its domestic security force had disappeared. The possibility of the deployment was not Mishima's fantasy. At the start of the same month, the GSDF had carried out a large-scale exercise for that purpose at the Fuji School with journalists invited—in other words, openly. No deployment of the security force meant no involvement of the Shield Society, Mishima said, and asked how the society should respond, though they would have the parade as planned. The letter of invitation had already been sent.[1]

Morita, the new chief of students, proposed to surround the Diet with the GSDF and the Shield Society to force the legislators to work

/ *651*

out a draft for Constitutional revision. Mishima demurred. He mentioned the difficulty of acquiring necessary weapons and the difficulty of doing anything of the sort while the Diet was in session.[2] The idea, if anything, was as unrealistic as the one Mishima himself had suggested to Yamamoto of sending a commando to defend the Imperial Palace. Still, Mishima would soon take up the idea of Constitutional revision seriously, an idea he had rejected earlier. He broached his decision to members of the Shield Society on December 22, when they had a one-day training with the GSDF at Camp Narashino, in the northwest corner of Chiba Prefecture.

## *The Rooftop Parade*

The Shield Society held its first public parade, as planned, on November 3, Culture Day, on the roof of the National Theatre that has an up-close view of the Imperial Palace. November 3 is the Meiji Emperor's birthday and was celebrated as such before Japan's defeat; after the war the reason for keeping it as a national holiday was changed from a Tennō's birthday to "culture."

At three in the afternoon, eighty-four members of the society turned toward the Imperial Palace, stood at attention, and sang *Kimigayo*—the national anthem though it did not legally become that until 1999. It goes, in Basil H. Chamberlain's inimitable 1890 English translation:

> Thousands of years of happy reign be thine;
> Rule on, my lord, till what are pebbles now
> By age united to mighty rocks shall grow
> Whose venerable sides the moss doth line.

The young men represented a total of seventeen universities, including the University of Tokyo, Nihon University, Waseda University, and Gakushūin University—this last the division for higher education set up after Mishima's alma mater, the Gakushūin (Peers School), ceased to be private and became public during postwar educational reform, along with the abolishment of peerage.

Then, with Gen. Ikarii Junzō (Ret.), commander of the Fuji School until eight months earlier, at the review stand, with Mishima tensely standing somewhat behind him to the left, the society did a march-past for fifteen minutes with the Fuji School's military band playing. Among the other SDF officials attending were Gen. Fujiwara Iwaichi (Ret.) and former Administrative Vice Minister of the Defense Agency Miwa Yoshio.

Mishima was lucky to have these men. As the day of the parade approached, the mass media got hold of the news and started looking at the politicians and SDF men on the invitation list, creating considerable unease among them. Many cancelled their participation, including Kawabata Yasunari, who called Mishima the day before the parade to tell him firmly that he would not attend, deeply disappointing Mishima. Of the total of 107 writers, actors, and such who were invited, only 50 attended.

Following the parade, a reception was held in the grand dining room on the second floor of the National Theatre. Fujiwara and others gave congratulatory speeches. Mishima gave his, in English, his garb changed into a white military uniform. He summed up what he said in the pamphlet prepared and distributed on the occasion, "On the Shield Society."[3]

What did some of the participants think of the whole affair?

Henry Scott-Stokes, the Tokyo bureau chief of the *Times* and by then Mishima's friend, was "embarrassed": "Parade was most embarrassing; students marched back and forth in their silly uniforms while Mishima stood at one side. Felt embarrassed for Mishima. Prayed all the time that students would not bungle their marching and tumble off the roof or something; just wanted parade to end. (Why should it matter to me?)" The end of the day's entry on Mishima: "Not inappropriate that these activities staged within (and on top of) a theater."[4]

At least one guest had an impression not too dissimilar. Muramatsu Takeshi told a reporter for the right-leaning daily *Sankei Shinbun* that the Shield Society was a "'theater troupe' the Romanticist Mishima created. It's interesting that he is creating a new form at a time when forms are collapsing." In his literary biography of his friend, Muramatsu practically skipped describing the parade, observing merely that Mishima had planned it on November 3 obviously because he had not expected anything of finality to occur on October 21, International Antiwar Day.

Another guest, Tsutsumi Seiji, observed, in a taidan with Mishima not long afterward, that Mishima's was "not a political movement but a romantic one." Those who regarded it as "a rightwing political movement" completely missed Mishima's "spirit and aesthetic."

It was during this taidan with Tsutsumi that Mishima stressed again the importance of freedom of speech—by praising the United States for allowing the report on the My Lai Massacre to be published while the war was still raging, adding that you could not imagine the Japanese Army or government would have done anything like that while at war. The example he cited was the Nanjing Massacre.[5] It was about the time Mishima had the parade that the journalist Seymour Hersh exposed the mass murder that had occurred in a Vietnamese village in March 1968.

As to the uniform, the *Sankei* reporter described it as in "a loud style that at first glance made you think of the doormen of a first-class hotel."[6] Some Shield Society members were even more mocking. It is appropriate only for *chindon'ya*, they said—clownish ad men in outlandish costumes who walk about the streets playing the several instruments they carry on them.[7]

"Among the guests were," Scott-Stokes wrote, "Kazuko Aso [daughter of Japan's best-known postwar Prime Minister, Shigeru Yoshida] and the young Konoe [adopted grandson of the wartime Prime Minister]; also actresses—particularly liked Mitsuko Baisho, hefty girl, should be more of them."

The *glamorous*—i.e., buxom—Baishō Mitsuko had appeared with Mishima in *Kill!*. Muramatsu Eiko, the actress Mishima was "nurturing" was there, and so was Atsumi Mari, who, still in her late teens, had appeared in soft porn films. All to Mishima's taste! Asked why she decided to attend the parade, Atsumi replied, "I felt *somber and solemn*. The Shield Society don't give people trouble, so they're better than the Zengakuren, I think."[8]

One thing to be noted about the day is the weather. Henry Scott-Stokes jotted down: "Not good weather. A light drizzle most of the time. Gray Tokyo." Yamamoto Kiyokatsu, who was naturally on hand, recalled: "It was a dazzlingly clear day from morning on" and the parade was executed "in the autumn sun that poured down."[9] Who is more trustworthy, the *Times* reporter or the ranking Japanese military intelligence officer?

## *A Wonder Tale*

Two days after the parade, *A Wonder Tale: The Moonbow* opened at the National Theatre. Scott-Stokes, who was invited by Mishima and took his Japanese girlfriend, judged: "The production was curiously amateur." It had "lots of technical hitches; heavy objects crashed to the earth backstage; cast not knowing where to stand. Worthy of a high school."

Stage glitches that night no doubt chagrined Mishima and the technical staff who spent so much time and thought on devising traditional and new props and effects on grander, "modern" scale. But Scott-Stokes, who wasn't used to kabuki, may have been mainly bemused by the "monumental staging." For one thing, he found the title *Chinsetsu: Yumiharizuki* "as long as" the play.[10] The play was long, yes, it lasted for five hours, but the title certainly was not, as far as kabuki titles go.

The theater critic for the *Asahi Shinbun* got the *spectacle* part right. He saw that Mishima's was an attempt to "restore *theatricality*" lacking in Japan's modern plays, and thought the Stage Arts Study Group of the National Theatre deserved a "distinguished service" prize for what they accomplished. "All the characters are like those from fairy tales and monstrous legends or else from animations," so that "the protagonist" of the play was none other than "the visuality and protean-transformation delights of the scenes." He was so captivated by the series of spectacles lined up one after another that he found one scene—nefarious, funny, and crucial to the narrative—"longwinded" and "tacked on," because it lacked spectacles.[11]

Muramatsu Takeshi attended the production on closing night, on November 27, and went to a sushi restaurant with Mishima and Yōko by the car she drove. He was surprised to hear Mishima say what he wanted to depict in the play was the Shinpūren, he reported.[12]

Mishima did not get some of the things he wanted for the kabuki production. When he had decided on the subject of the play, for example, he had proposed the actor to play Tametomo: Ichikawa Somegorō VI. He did not get him, and he appears to have regretted it to the end.[13] But there were also serendipities.

Whether or not he suggested the actor to play Princess Shiranui is not known, but Bandō Tamasaburō V who got the role "thrilled" him, prompting him to call his advent "a miracle." A handsome, willowy youth then nineteen, Tamasaburō was not from a kabuki family but had entered the classical theater while taking dance lessons from a kabuki actor to reduce the aftereffects of the polio he suffered in infancy. His demeanor while rehearsing and acting in *The Moonbow* impressed Mishima so much that, when he took part in the Third Young Kabuki Actors' Festival at the National Theatre the next August, he wrote a heartfelt paean to the *waka-oyama*, young female impersonator, who is "delicate, elegant, and sensuous, like a figurine made of ivory."

"When his body like a green lacewing sways pliantly on the stage," Mishima rhapsodized in the program note for the festival, "a lyrical beauty accompanied by a certain precarious sense overflows. And what is important above all else is his old-fashioned, nobly beautiful face." For "if kabuki loses the power of a beautiful face to seize people's hearts as if it is a matter of privilege, the artistic power of old actors' profound training alone will not suffice to maintain it. Since Zeami, the Japanese Way of Art has been supported by a boy's 'timely flower' and an old man's 'true flower,' the two in tandem."[14]

Tamasaburō would go on to become one of the most celebrated Japanese actors in the decades following Mishima's death.

## *Madama Butterfly's Offspring*

The year's last big demonstrations were mounted on November 16 in an attempt to prevent Prime Minister Satō from visiting the United States. The rally organized by the Socialist Party to call, mainly, for an unconditional, immediate return of Okinawa drew seventy thousand people to Yoyogi Park. But the riot police stopped the seven thousand protestors heading toward Haneda in the Kamata area, some distance west of the airport. The arrests that day exceeded nineteen hundred, a far larger number than the previous record, the fifteen hundred apprehended on International Antiwar Day. That same day (November 15, US time) there was the largest anti–Vietnam War rally in Washington, D.C., with a quarter million people taking part.

In his meeting with Satō, President Richard Nixon agreed to the Okinawa reversion, not immediately but in 1972, and with the proviso that it would not affect the functions of its military bases in Okinawa in any way. Nixon was reducing the US troops in Vietnam but had no intention of cutting back on the US military presence in the Far East.

Apparently with the Satō-Nixon meeting in mind, the *New York Times* asked Mishima to contribute an article, which appeared on November 29, 1969: "Okinawa and Madama Butterfly's Offspring." Mishima's suggested title, in English, was "Stage Left Is Right from Audience,"[15] and he made a brilliant exposition of the perverse ideological confusion among the leftists and rightists that had come to prevail in Japan over the preceding decade, although Mishima's sarcastic details were skimped necessarily in the *Times* version.

"Those who insist on the independence of the Japanese *minzoku*, oppose American military bases, oppose the security treaty, and shout, 'Return Okinawa at once,' would be nationalist and rightwing, in a standard understanding abroad," Mishima wrote in his original article. "But in Japan, they are leftwing and Communist." He knew that the definitions of leftwing and rightwing are different from one country to another, as he made clear in a taidan with Hayashi Fusao a little earlier. In Western Europe, for example, rightwing means anti-Semitic, but the split is generally between internationalism and chauvinism.

Take a recent case in France, Mishima suggested. In a survey during the May Revolution, the French were asked to choose de Gaulle *ouï* or de Gaulle *non*. The choice, in short, was between France or Communism. But if a similar survey were to be taken in Japan, the question would have to be the approval or disapproval of the US-Japanese Mutual Security Treaty, and that would mean a choice between pro-America or pro-Soviet/China, with no considerations of Japan.[16]

"A certain section of the traditional rightwing, completely deprived of their stock-in-trade nationalism by the leftwing," Mishima wrote, "countered the leftwing demonstration against the port call of the American nuclear aircraft carrier *Enterprise* by sallying forth with the American flag in the left hand and the Japanese flag in the right. In that, they were just like Madama Butterfly's child on the operatic stage."

The leftists' behavior is no less strange. Referring to "the radical leftists" with whom he had debated earlier that year, he argued: "In their exaggerated linguistic expression, they are in the traditional Chinese mode, and in their love of the people's court system, they are in the modern Communist Chinese mode, even as they are internationalist in their rejection of Japanese tradition." They are also, Mishima added, obviously to poke fun at himself, "in the samurai-style rightwing mode in their affirmation of terrorism."

In a similar vein, he went on to observe: Yakuza movies "depict the world of traditional outlaws, press on you the old Japanese *mentality*, and, in their sentimentalism and *heroism*, their affirmation of violence and illogicality, appeal most to the rightwing Japanese heartstringism, or so leftwing 'cultured people' have reasoned as they condemned them outright." The genre of films he brought up would begin to be known widely in the United States only some years after he wrote this, perhaps with Sydney Pollack's 1975 film, *The Yakuza*.

Here, too, a reversal of sorts occurred, Mishima pointed out. "The Japanese-style John Waynes have become the students' *idols*, and the leftist students always go to see these movies the night before their violent demonstrations to recharge their hearts with passion."

Mishima, "author and playwright, heads a small nationalistic student group," the *Times* caption to his article noted.

## *Prospects for the 1970s*

The December general election showed a clear shift in popular sentiments that had occurred. The ruling Liberal Democratic Party won a fewer number of votes than in the previous election but still increased its seats to three hundred, whereas the Socialist Party reduced the number of its seats by a dramatic 35 percent, from one hundred and forty to ninety. The idea of blocking the extension of the US-Japanese Mutual Security Treaty in 1970 had become a fantasy, as Mishima had predicted.

"When the domestic market becomes completely saturated and no more consumption becomes possible," Mishima predicted in a taidan with Nosaka Akiyuki, the author of *Pornographers*, at the end of 1969, "there's nothing more left to make than weapons, don't you think?" Then, nationalism, hitherto camouflaged in the "fakery" of US military protection, will reveal itself.

The issue at hand was the prospects for the 1970s, and Mishima was referring to the talk of *jishu bōei*, "autonomous defense"—Japan's national security not entirely dependent on the United States—and the ambitious Fourth Defense Plan that was gaining ground within the ruling Liberal Democratic Party. (Like many such terms created under duress, political or otherwise, *jishu bōei* was dubious, *jishu* suggesting volunteerism. Years later, the term would change to *dokuritsu bōei*, "independent defense.") As Mishima would state in his manifesto a year later, since it was "self-evident that the United States [would] not be happy with Japan's autonomous military protecting its own homeland," if Japan did "not restore its autonomy within the next two years, the SDF would "end up as America's mercenaries in perpetuity." That, Mishima pointed out, was what the leftists argued.

In the meantime, the Japanese manufacturing industry, the driving force of the double-digit economic growth throughout the 1960s, was flooding not just the domestic but foreign markets as well with consumer goods. Overseas, it had led to heightened calls for trade restrictions on Japan, which, Mishima was suggesting, would inevitably compel the industry to turn seriously to weapons manufacture to survive, reducing the need to buy practically all weapons from the United States. That would bring the talk of nationalism to the fore.

As it turned out, the growing trade deficit the United States accumulated with much of the rest of the world, created, most contentiously, by Japan's textile exports as Mishima mentioned in the taidan,[17] would force Richard Nixon to terminate the fixed exchange rate regime—the core of the Bretton Woods System—in the summer of 1971, throwing Japanese industry into the biggest quandary since the war, and the idea of "autonomous defense," along with the Fourth Defense Plan, would quickly fade. This Mishima presciently foresaw—though not in the form it took and he certainly did not foresee its effects on Japanese industry.

But Nixon's action was still one and a half years away. For now, the Japanese economy continued to expand, and the Expo '70, the world fair held in Osaka that year—with the "comically self-congratulatory" theme of "Progress and Harmony for Mankind," as a later writer noted[18]—would draw, during the six months of its operation, from mid-March to mid-September, more than sixty-five million attendants or half the Japanese population. But, as Mishima did *not* foresee, the year would become the last one with double-digit economic growth, thereby making the extraordinarily successful world fair the fitting last chapter of "the leisure boom" that had started a decade earlier and so perturbed Mishima—or so he said.

Mishima, for that matter, *had* foreseen a sudden rapprochement between China and the United States that would totally bypass Japan, as actually happened in February 1972, when Richard Nixon flew to Beijing and met Mao Zedong. Such a turn of events would plunge Japan to the bottom of a valley, able only to "eavesdrop" on the two countries high above, Mishima had predicted as early as the spring of 1968, when Lyndon B. Johnson was US president. Japan would be left "an orphan in the Orient," abandoned even by Taiwan.[19]

All that would occur after his death. As the year 1969 turned into 1970, one paradox for those observing Mishima was his pursuit of Constitutional revision in earnest just when, as he assessed publicly, and accurately, any chance for it had receded at least "by a decade." The revision had become only a remote possibility because, he explained—in *Ushio*, the magazine of the religiopolitical organization Sōka Gakkai—the ruling LDP gained the conviction from its experience on International Antiwar Day that it could maintain the status quo. That day it used the police in the manner of martial law, but the LDP won "popular support," instead of provoking protests.[20]

Or, as he put it in a speech at a January gathering of the Kokumin Kyōkai, People's Association—the LDP's powerful fundraising arm—the LDP must have come away from October 21 with "the judgment that *not* changing the Constitution [had] two extreme merits, international and domestic." Domestically, by not tampering with the Constitution, the ruling party could continue to appease the leftists who clung to "the Peace Constitution"; internationally, it could evade the US pressure on Japan to send its troops overseas—to Vietnam—by citing "the no-war clause" that is Article 9, which none other than the United States had imposed on Japan. That meant, Mishima said, the Japanese did "not live in an era for fundamental reform" of the Constitution.

Mishima's purpose in this speech was to call for serious considerations of "true nationalism." In his view, such nationalism at its core would have to be based on what most appealed to the Japanese heart, namely the Tennō—"the only thing with which [Japan] could squarely counter every foreign interference by force," the only thing "with thousands of years of history and tradition."

Mishima was talking to a conservative group, but he readily

conceded: "any mention of the Tennō immediately brings to mind the harm" that "the prewar Tennō system, under the Meiji Constitution," had brought about. "Harm" was too benign a word. Not just the Tennō system as set forth in the Meiji Constitution, but the abuses of power perpetrated by militarists and chauvinists who took advantage of it were the very reason for a strong, persistent demand since the International Military Tribunal for the Far East that Hirohito be called to account for his "war responsibility."

But the Tennō was something the Japanese in each age have "created and recovered with all their might," Mishima went on. In that sense, "there is always a new Tennō system, always the present Tennō system, and there is the eternal Tennō system based on the continuation of these present Tennō systems." The Tennō he had in mind was one who is "not glued vainly to political power, but a selfless entity that is perennially accommodating," he proposed.[21]

This view was true to history to a great extent but radical in a way, and it must have elicited some noteworthy reactions from the audience. But the Q&A session, if there was one, appears not to have been recorded in a readily accessible form. There was a strong sense, not limited to the conservatives, that Article 9 had to be rewritten just so as to recognize the SDF for what it was: a military. But even many of those in the audience that day who thought Constitutional revision was needed were likely bemused by Mishima's assertion of the malleability of the Tennō institution.

## *The Unity of Rite and Governance*

That same month, January 1970, Mishima had another occasion to argue for Constitutional revision, this time in a national daily. The *Yomiuri Shinbun* did a miniseries on the subject of "reification of a principle," and asked the novelist Ishikawa Tatsuzō, the historian Inoue Kiyoshi, and Mishima, in that order, to discuss the question. Ishikawa, of "the societal school," the brand for writers who take up contemporary social issues in their fiction, titled his essay "the student movement as rejection response"; Inoue, the Marxist known for his strong condemnation of Japan's prewar militarism and postwar conservatism, called his "an aftershock of the fierce upheaval of all the people."

Mishima found both arguments lacking. Ishikawa was sharp in his analysis, such as when he recognized in the student movement "a kind of self-disintegration wish like that Dazai Osamu had," Mishima wrote. But the writer erred in taking a neutral stance trying to understand the Zenkyōtō that began by rejecting such an understanding in the first place. He was off the mark, too, Mishima said, in asking the students to "nurture a toughness that doesn't weaken under heavy cultural pressure," because their "rejection response" naturally included rejection of any attempt for salvation. Such talk reminded him of "the Kingdom of God and dubious salvation" in Thomas Mann's *Magic Mountain*, Mishima said. Ishikawa's positing "an advanced cultural state" was also questionable at best.

Mishima faulted Inoue by noting that the historian committed a "logical contradiction" in asserting, "in his eagerness to defend the students," that they showed courage in invoking "the right to silence." Refusal to self-incriminate is something that must be maintained by staking one's life, Mishima argued. But by adding it to basic human rights, the legal system has become "the very culprit that has allowed a soft-structure society to form by relativizing thought." In the circumstances, exercising the right is "no proof of courage."

"Soft-structure society" is the term coined by the political scientist Nagai Yōnosuke, to whose views Mishima often agreed. A professor at the Tokyo Institute of Technology struggling daily to understand the protesting students, Nagai came up with the idea of distinguishing societies engulfed by student protests into two types: "hard-structure societies" and "soft-structure societies." The former included East European countries and developing countries, where student protests were barely tolerated because they could lead to the overthrow of the establishment. Among the latter were Germany, France, Japan, the United States, and such, where "antiestablishment" movements were treated as manageable.

Nagai explained that he hit upon these terms in reference to the *jū-kōzō*, "soft- or resilient-structure," then used to describe the high-rise buildings being permitted in earthquake-prone Tokyo with the rationale that architects and builders could now construct tall structures resilient enough to absorb most earthquakes.[22]

If Mishima's linkage of the soft-structure society to the right not to self-incriminate raised some eyebrows, as it must have, there was more.

For a real "transformation" to occur, Mishima went on, one must begin by recognizing that modern Japan had nearly lost "the unity of rite and governance"—the coexistence at the top of the polity of the Tennō who conducts rites and the entity that governs.

The nation-state as conceived and analyzed in modern political science is the latter, Mishima said, and it is "centrifugal"; it gives an increasing portion of its power to local communities while doing the same externally as it moves toward international cooperation, the world federation, and such. In contrast, the ritual part of the polity is "centripetal"; though "normally invisible," it is the source of a nation's history, tradition, and culture—its *Ethos, Pathos,* and *eroticism.*" If the former is oriented toward humanism and rationality, the latter is oriented toward irrationality and sentimentalism. The problem of modern Japan, created by the Occupation, is that the governing entity was brought to the fore while leaving the ritual side of the state "lingering like a shadow behind it," without really vanquishing it.

Mishima argued that the Satō-Nixon communiqué of the previous November[23] rendered the Japanese Constitution more meaningless than ever, even as it enabled the document to gain a "more mysterious, demonic power" as a result. Now the only possibility for Constitutional revision would be through a *coup d'état* by the right or a violent revolution by the left, but chances for either's occurring were practically nil, "as everyone knows," he wrote. (More than two decades later, in 1992, Maj. Yanai Shinsaku, an instructor at the GSDF Research School, would be fired for suggesting that there ought to be a military coup to end endless political corruptions.[24])

Nonetheless, he had to talk about the Constitution because it is where the idea of "state" appears most clearly and the state is where the question of "loyalty" comes in, which necessarily has to do with homeland defense, Mishima said. Absent Constitutional revision, then, one thing that can be done is to split the SDF into two entities: one, the Japanese contingent of "the UN Police Reserve"[25] ("centrifugal" as it is for international cooperation, the world federation, and such), and the other, a force dedicated to homeland defense, to fight indirect invasion, without any military alliance or treaty with the United States or any other country ("centripetal" as it is for true nationalism). The SDF thus split, it would at least clear away the "suspicion" that, though the law says the Japanese prime minister is ultimately responsible for the armed forces, the SDF in truth is under the command of the US president.

As before, he had in mind an exact proportion for each armed service to be divided into: for the UN, 90 percent of the air force, 70 percent of the maritime force, and 10 percent of the ground force; for homeland defense, the rest. The basic idea for the homeland defense force, to be "absolutely independent," would be "loyalty to the Tennō as chief of the ritual state." This force would include "a sizable number of militias." His Shield Society was "a pioneer" in that regard.

Mishima, ever clear-eyed, did not forget to add: When he explained the idea of splitting the armed forces to "an English friend"—most likely Henry Scott-Stokes, of the *Times*—the friend said, "It's too logical to be realistic." He knew himself it was a "dream tale." He ends his tract, "Transformative Thought," by insisting that he does not believe in "political efficacy," that his aim is to "create a reality that can never be phenomenized or relativized," and that the action for that can only be "an ultimate action with death in mind."[26]

## *Constitutional Oddities*

Mishima's conception of the Tennō system aside, the Constitution that took effect in May 1947, the second year of the US Occupation, has some readily recognizable oddities. As Mishima pointed out when he wrote out the "issues to be examined" in May, July, and September 1970 for the thirteen-member group of the Shield Society assigned to consider the matter, some of them law students, there is "an obvious logical contradiction" between the first two articles of Chapter I, The Emperor. In what appears to be an official English translation it reads:

> Article 1. The Emperor shall be the symbol of the State and of the unity of the People, deriving his position from the will of the people with whom resides sovereign power.
>
> Article 2. The Imperial Throne shall be dynastic and succeeded to in accordance with the Imperial House Law passed by the Diet.[27]

The statement that the position of the Emperor comes from "the will of the people" surely contradicts the statement that follows, that the Imperial position is "dynastic." What if the people changed their collective mind, assuming that their "will" was such when the Constitution was written? The Japanese text makes the gap even more acute: Article 1 says that the Tennō's position shall be "based on the total will of the Japanese people" (*Nihon kokumin no sōi ni motozuku*), even as Article 2 follows it up by saying that "the Tennō's position shall be hereditary" (*kōi wa seshū no mono*). As Mishima noted, wouldn't it be "funny" to say that something based on the people's will is "hereditary"?

This oddity was something those concerned became aware of early on. Among the early proposed revisions of the Constitution, one by Nakasone Yasuhiro, in 1961, restated the first two articles this way:

> Article 1: Japan, with the Tennō as the center of the unity of the Japanese people, shall be a democratic state with sovereign power residing with them.
>
> Article 2: The Tennō shall be Japan's head of state and shall represent Japan.
>
> Article 3: The Tennō's position shall be inherited by a person in the Imperial line in accordance with the Imperial House Law.[28]

Nakasone, a lieutenant commander when Japan was defeated and a member of the Diet when he wrote the draft, was director-general of the Defense Agency when Mishima was pushing his argument, and would go on to serve as Prime Minister for five years beginning in 1982.

The difficulty with Article 9, which is Chapter II, Renunciation of War, is something else. The problem here lies in the stark discrepancy between what it says—"land, sea, and air forces, as well as other war potential, will never be maintained"—and the very existence of the SDF. It has compelled one administration after another to come up with "one forced interpretation after another, merely adding to its abstruseness," as Hatoyama Yukio, who became Prime Minister in September 2009, stated in his "An interim report on a tentative idea for Constitutional reform."[29]

In his draft for revision, Nakasone simply assumed Japan's right to maintain a military, though only for international cooperation and self-defense. As to the "use of force as means of settling international disputes," he kept what Article 9 of the existing Constitution says.[30]

The majority of Constitutional scholars regarded the SDF as unconstitutional, stated Satō Isao, dean of the Faculty of Law at Sophia University and himself a Constitutional authority, when called to provide testimony during the "Mishima Incident" trial, held from March 1971 to April 1972. Satō was counselor at the Cabinet's Legislative Bureau—comparable to the Office of Legal Counsel, of the US Department of Justice—when the Constitution was drafted under the SCAP, Gen. MacArthur. It would be a matter of "evaluation of facts" whether or not the document as a whole was imposed on Japan, he stated, but the Emperor and Renunciation of War Clauses certainly were.[31]

"To put it plainly," Mishima wrote, "Article 9 is a letter of apology of the defeated nation Japan to the victorious nations." Whether Japan voluntarily wrote "the letter" or the United States forced it on Japan was "no longer a big issue." The issue was simply that the article is like "a pledge tied down with two or three layers of oath" and, "if interpreted logically," Japan is made to abandon "its right to self-defense"[32]—although MacArthur forced Japan to violate both the article and the oath when he ordered the creation of a military. In his harangue on the day of his death, Mishima shouted, "The Self-Defense Forces are unconstitutional! You men are unconstitutional!"

The draft for a revised or altogether rewritten Constitution that the Shield Society finally worked out, three months after Mishima's death, was sprinkled with words Mishima liked to flaunt, such as *kokutai* ("The Tennō shall be the *kokutai*"), *shinchoku*, "divine edict" ("The Tennō shall conduct rite and ceremony by divine edict"), and Kokugun, "the National Army" ("The Tennō shall be the source of honor for the National Army"). So, as Mishima had insisted, the Tennō's role was to be limited to rite and ceremony even as the National Army was to seek its honor in its service to the Tennō.

Given this context, one surprise may be this article: "The Tennō's position shall be hereditary and not limited to the male line." Limiting the Tennō's position to males was something the Meiji oligarchs decreed by law, and it began creating problems a few decades after Mishima's death when the Shōwa Emperor's oldest grandson had difficulty siring a son. Mishima simply wanted to rescind the rule.

Mishima's idea for Constitutional reform was radically different from all the other ideas as regards the Tennō. "Mr. Mishima takes up the Tennō as a cultural concept. He cuts it off from the concept of nation-state, the concept of government, holding that the Tennō is the source of the value of Japanese culture that transcends government," explained Satō Isao on the witness stand. "The Tennō represents, should represent, Japan's historical tradition, culture, and the Tennō's position as holder of culture should be made clear. That was his opinion." Sato continued:

> In contrast almost all the opinions on reform as regards the Tennō hold that the powers [of the Tennō] as an organ of the nation-state should be expanded and strengthened, or that, because [the term] "symbol" is unclear, it should be made "head of state" as his powers are strengthened. Mr. Mishima holds that doing so would go against the essence of the Tennō. His argument for reform holds that the Tennō is the center of culture. No one else holds the same argument for reform as Mr. Mishima.33

What irked Mishima with the Tennō as presented in the Constitution written after Japan's defeat was that "the Westerners who know nothing but [Judeo-]Christian culture could judge other religions only with the preconceptions of the monotheists' religious intolerance." They "fantasized the religious source of every aggressivism in National Shinto and ignored Shinto's non-religious uniqueness with its function to purify secular customs, refusing to understand Japan's *syncretism* centering on extremely non-religious Shinto."34

Muramatsu Takeshi would have gone a step further. Familiar with some of the constitutional monarchies of the West, he knew that "sacred" and "inviolable," the terms used to define the status of the Tennō in the Meiji Constitution, were common—as in Article 13 of France's Constitutional Charter of 1814, he could have added.35 What Mishima sought was *enracinement*, Muramatsu pointed out to explain what his friend had in mind. It was Muramatsu, indeed, who noted that the idea that the Tennō should be completely separated from matters of politics and governance did not begin with Mishima.

Prime Minister Hara Takashi, for example, wrote in his diary, on September 2, 1920: "If the Imperial Household cuts any direct relationship to political affairs and becomes an agency for charities and awards, it will become stable."[36] The Occupation's judgment Mishima was fuming against was represented best in the flat statement in the manual on Japanese religions that its Civilian Information and Education Section prepared: "Tennōism, or Kokutai Shinto, is belief in the emperor (*tennō*) as the living incarnation of the Sun Goddess, and thus as a manifestation of the Absolute." Thus Japan was a "theocratic state."[37]

As to the possession of armed forces or "the National Army," as Mishima preferred to call it, the first of the proposed articles worked out under his guidance stated: "The Japanese people shall have the sublime right of homeland defense." Yet the military service would be a voluntary duty: "The [Japanese] people shall not have conscription imposed upon them."[38] Homeland defense must be carried out by those who believe in its importance. Whether Mishima, in rejecting conscription, recalled the searing conflict he had experienced in the induction tests a quarter of a century earlier is moot. At any rate, reintroducing conscription would have been even more difficult than Constitutional revision itself.

## *"Shall We Do It?"*

On New Year's Day 1970 Mishima had a family photo taken at the entrance of his house; Shizue sensed it would be the last such photo. That evening there was a party Mishima threw for members of the Roman Gekijō as well as the Shield Society, and invited some other friends. One of the guests, Maruyama Akihiro, at one point saw standing at attention near Mishima's left shoulder a dark green shadow of a figure with a military hat with a chinstrap and a military sword. Khaki was the color of the prewar army uniform. When he said he thought it resembled someone related to the 2.26 Incident, Mishima rattled off more than a dozen names and, the moment he named Capt. Isobe Asaichi and Maruyama exclaimed, "That's him!," Mishima turned pale.[39]

If that was foreboding, either before or after the apparition, Mishima told Yamamoto Kiyokatsu, another guest, what would turn out to be a glimpse into the plan, however vague, that Mishima was laying out in his mind. The Shield Society "might turn against the SDF," he said.[40]

By the time Yamamoto decided to write an account of his relationship with Mishima, ten years after the latter's death,[41] a mass of information on what had happened, particularly in the last years of Mishima's life, was out and that must have colored much of his recollections. Among other things, Kuramochi Kiyoshi clearly stated, when called to testify during the "Mishima Incident" trial, that Mishima, along with Morita, chief of students, had decided in the fall of 1969 to die a year later,[42] and the NHK journalist Date Munekatsu, one of the two men Mishima told in advance to be at the scene of his final act, had published a detailed report on the trial two and a half years after the event. Still, it is worth tracking what Yamamoto remembered from his association with Mishima following the New Year party.

In mid-January, he had a phone call from Mishima. It was simply to tell him that Nakasone Yasuhiro had phoned him to "explain himself"—that is, to apologize. During a New Year news conference, Nakasone, who became director-general of the Defense Agency on January 14, by coincidence Mishima's birthday, had dismissed the Shield Society as "Takarazuka soldiers"—comparable to the toy soldiers played by the Radio City Music Hall Rockettes—and Mishima had expressed his anger. Yamamoto thought that Mishima called him to indicate that Nakasone's private apologies cancelled out his derisive comment. Mishima had feared that the GSDF would stop working with the Shield Society. He was wrong, he later decided. Mishima was beginning to give up on getting any "cooperation" from it.

Muramatsu also thought that at that juncture Mishima had counted on the SDF. As it happened, Mishima had his forty-fifth birthday in Muramatsu's new house, bringing as a gift a small table he had bought in Granada. While there Mishima heard the news that Nakasone had become director-general of the Defense Agency and at once telephoned his acquaintance at the Agency. Whether Mishima talked to Nakasone at the time or Nakasone returned his call Muramatsu does not say. But he was certain that Mishima was concerned about Nakasone's intentions.

Nakasone, who would go on to have a taidan with Mishima and invite him to talk to his groups, was not alone among conservative politicians who had to be careful about Mishima. Even if they privately approved what Mishima was doing, they were unable to show in public that they did. Muramatsu recalled how Mishima telephoned him, on February 22, that none other than Prime Minister Satō had called him, albeit through his deputy cabinet secretary, to offer to defray the costs of the Shield Society to the tune of one million yen a month.[43] As we have seen, Satō's party had tried to persuade Mishima to run for the Diet, but this offer was a different animal altogether. Had it become public knowledge, it would surely have brought down the Satō administration.

Late in January, past seven in the evening, Yamamoto had another call from Mishima, this time asking him to come to his house at once. He had an unusual guest from Korea and he wanted him to meet him. Upon arrival, Yamamoto found Mishima having dinner with a man. He turned out to be a former general of the Korean Army who had made arrangements for Mishima and his group's visit in Korea the previous month. Now director of an institute to study domestic and foreign affairs, he was on his way to the United States. The main topic of conversation Yamamoto recalled was *bushidō*, the way of the samurai. After returning from Korea, Mishima had lamented how South Korean military officers had twitted the Japanese visitors, to which he had no proper way to respond.

"We Korean soldiers have taken away the *Yamato damashii*, the Japanese spirit, from Japanese soldiers, so there cannot possibly be anything like a 'spirit' left in Japan" except perhaps "'promotion spirit,'" the desire to get promoted, they had mocked, Mishima told Azusa after his return from Korea. Many of those who had risen to the top ranks of the Korean military since that country's independence following Japan's defeat were former officers of the Japanese Army and Navy. They included President Park Chung-hee, who had graduated as a top student from Japan's Military Academy and was a lieutenant in the Manchukuo Army when Japan surrendered.

As a matter of fact, Azusa heard, after his son's death, that President Park told a Japanese visitor, "So I see *bushidō* was still alive in Japan." Korea had sent troops to Vietnam and their soldiers had gained fame for their ferocity. Japan, of course, had not fought in the war. In the meantime, Japanese businessmen in Asia were being called "ugly Japanese."[44]

Regardless, Yamamoto, an investigator of the San'yū (Three No's) Incident who had heard rumors about other "incendiary" joint schemes between Korea and Japan, was wary and steered clear from any specific talk. By then he had felt that the aim of Mishima's Shield Society had grown to be far more "untransparent" than he had taken it to be. He was a little annoyed, too, by the discrepancy between the urgency in Mishima's phone call summoning him and the pleasant atmosphere of dinner conversation he found when he arrived.

But, past nine, as soon as the Korean guest left with Yōko, who, at Mishima's request, was to drive him to a station nearby, Mishima turned a serious face to Yamamoto and asked, "Shall we do it?" This sudden, unexpected query elicited a sudden, unexpected response from Yamamoto, according to his own admission: "If we're going to do it, please cut me down first and do it!"

Luckily, no further words were exchanged. Mishima poured some more drink for Yamamoto, Yōko returned, and Yamamoto left. On his way home, Yamamoto was inexplicably touched by what had happened that night.

Two months later, he had another unforgettable encounter with Mishima. Mishima came to visit, unannounced. He was dressed in Japanese attire, as he seldom was in those days, and carried a sword, though wrapped in a brocade scabbard protector. Yamamoto became tense, recalling his own words, "Cut me down," in the previous meeting. Invited in, Mishima put his sword against the wall behind the couch where he sat, as if to hide it. Yamamoto was a little relieved, but it was his wife who saved the moment. Noticing where Mishima had put his sword, she suggested she put it in a more appropriate place. Mishima obediently handed it over to her, and she placed it horizontally on the piano behind where Yamamoto was sitting, though in doing so she unnecessarily—in Yamamoto's view—revealed that he, too, had a sword.

The conversation turned less awkward, with Mishima bringing up the subject, among other things, of Fujiwara Iwaichi running for office, but it never flowed. When he stood up to leave and walked toward the entrance, Mishima turned to Yamamoto briefly and said, "Col. Yamamoto, you are cold." This, too, was unexpected, but so was Yamamoto's own response that quickly came out of his mouth: "If you are going to do it, I beg you do it while I'm in uniform."

Yamamoto recalls how deeply agitated he became by his own response, but not *why* he was—nor why he adamantly refused when Fujiwara asked him not long afterward to take off his uniform to direct his election campaign, except that he told his superior officer, in unmistakable terms, that he wanted to stay with Mishima. Fujiwara planned to run on defense issues just when the SDF's ability to attract recruits had fallen far short of the target and that was creating scandals, among them the lowering of standards and the cheating by recruiting officers. Fujiwara would lose in an election a year later.[45]

CHAPTER TWENTY-NINE

# Hailstones, Ghouls, Golden Death

"*Sensual* quiétisme"
—Mishima on Tanaka Mitsuko's poetry

Among the spate of essays that Mishima wrote in the brief period from the end of 1969 to the start of 1970 was a preface to the book by Michael Gallagher, *Bombs and Ginkgo* (*Bakudan to ichō*). Gallagher, the translator of Nosaka Akiyuki's *Pornographers*, had won, on the strength of the work, a contract with Knopf to translate the first two volumes of Mishima's tetralogy, *The Sea of Fertility*. So the book had a preface by Nosaka as well, but it had another, by the devout Christian Endō Shūsaku.

Gallagher had offered to translate Endō's 1958 novel, *The Sea and Poison* (*Umi to dokuyaku*), a fictionalized account of the vivisection of one of the captured B-29 crew at the Imperial University of Kyūshū toward the end of the war. Endō's suggestion in the novel that the Japanese doctors may have acted as they had because they were devoid of the "conscience" they could have derived from faith in a Christian God—that, in other words, the "godless" Japanese lack any independent ethical sense as they are only concerned about "social punishment" or an assessment of their deeds only relative to what other people may think—had touched off strong controversy, and that may well have hindered him from working on his planned sequel.[1]

Endō's subject was particularly apt for Gallagher. A paratrooper during the Korean War who studied Japanese while training to be a

/ 673

Jesuit priest, Gallagher had worked as a day laborer in Kamagasaki, the ghetto in Osaka that attracted the debris of human society "like the scum caught by the net at the end of a drainage pipe," in Nosaka's arresting image, and had also taught English at the University of Tokyo. But he had decided to give up on pursuing theology. His book *Bombs and Ginkgo* described his experiences in Kamagasaki and Tōdai, with the odd combination in the title deriving from the author imagining the bombs raining down from B-29s and turning Osaka into ashes and the ginkgo leaves used for the Tōdai badge.[2]

Mishima praised Gallagher for "the monstrosity of his spirit that watched both Kamagasaki and Tōdai from the same perspective," adding that he could do so because "he was a believer of absolute freedom that may be called active apathy, that hates to belong to anything in the end," where "love and despair almost converge."[3]

Aside from the value of Gallagher's book, which is detailed, vivid, and seldom judgmental, Mishima wrote his preface, as the two other writers did theirs, obviously out of a sense of obligation, but he was an obliging man in that regard. A year earlier, for example, he had written an appreciation of the haiku poet Hatano Sōha for *Haiku* magazine for the simple reason Hatano was his upperclassman when he wrote haiku at the Peers School, even though, unlike Hatano, he had left the genre soon afterward. Writing the appreciation enabled him to relive his haiku days. Sōha, the haiku name of Yoshihide, was a grandson of a former Minister of the Imperial Household.

"A junior-high-school student, I tagged along with him, taking part in haiku sessions and going on haiku excursions," Mishima wrote. "Mr. Kyōgoku Kiyō, a Peers School alumnus and a haiku poet of the Hototogisu School, greatly loved him for his talent, which may have been one reason he approached the Hototogisu group. The haiku sessions in Viscount Kyōgoku's residence were elegant and classical, as they were held in the guestroom with its floor covered with a ceremonial scarlet cloth, even in wartime. Finding myself seated at the end of the honored guests, cowed by the atmosphere, I made myself small."[4]

## *Sensual* Quiétisme

Another preface he wrote was for Tanaka Mitsuko's book of poems, *Hailstones That Faded on My Palms* (*Waga te ni kieshi arare*). Tanaka was a poet Itō Shizuo admired, and Mishima's preface exquisitely captures the pure femininity of the poet and her poetry.

"Miss Tanaka Mitsuko during wartime lived in Tsukiji Akashi-chō, and I, still a high-school student, once visited her there," Mishima wrote, recalling, again, what had happened three decades earlier. "The place name Tsukiji Akashi-chō was an area that I, at the time familiar with Kaburaki Kiyokata's essays, yearned for along with the images of his beautiful women, and Miss Tanaka who lived there was a beautiful person." Kaburaki was famed for his paintings in Ukiyoe-influenced style of imagined Meiji women. "It was summer, and in the guestroom on the second floor were reed screens put up, each thin space between reeds filled with the sea light of the sky of Tsukiji. And Miss Tanaka was such a muliebrile person she was barely able to cope with the strong briny winds that rushed around the guestroom."

Mishima then cites two poems. One of them has the first line for its title.

> Sorrow
> has become a beautiful ague
> and entered
> my flesh.
> Your lips
> fragrant
> have left a mark.
> Sorrow
> resembles an acquired garden
> that is quiet,
> in quietude.

"Placed in front of such a sensual *quiétisme*, how noisy would even Comtesse de Noailles appear!"[5] Mishima knew that Itō, enraptured by Tanaka's first book of poetry, *Highlands (Kōgen)*, that had come out at the end of 1942, had written her, "If you keep up this tone and succeed with long pieces, it will be like reading Lady Noailles in *Collection of Corals* (although, because I do not know French, I cannot say much about it)." Anna de Noailles, the poet reputed to have been of striking beauty and elegance, counted among her admirers many French writers and artists such as Proust, Colette, Cocteau, and Rodin. *Collection of Corals* or *Sango-shū* is a small anthology of French poems and prose pieces Nagai Kafū published in 1912, in his translation, including three poems of the countess: *Soir romantique, Le Fruitier de Septembre,* and *En face de l'Espagne*.

Did Mishima wonder if Itō's pedagogic eagerness to correct Tanaka's grammar and help revise her poems might have ruined her poetry to some extent and discouraged her from publishing her second book until long after Itō's death? Most likely.[6]

---

Mishima was probably more than eager to write a preface to a biography of the man whose manner of death had become an increasingly pressing matter to him when it came along: Hasuda Zenmei.

"There is a dizzying disconnect, a *contrast*, between Mr. Hasuda's literary work and his spectacular death," and that may have led to a ready-made misunderstanding, he wrote. "When, right after the war's termination, Lt. Hasuda carried out his own dramatic end by shooting his regimental commander on account of his enemy-coddling act and killing himself at once, Mr. Hasuda's enemies who heard about it must have thought it was a natural corollary of the *fanaticism* of a wartime rightwing *ideologue*."

The truth lay elsewhere, Mishima stressed. "Such a fierce anger as his, such a defiant act as his, was a genuine corollary of the gentleness of a certain noncompromise, and the origins of everything were in that 'gentleness.'" It was something "his enemies did not try to know, did not want to know." Mishima then quoted a few sentences from Hasuda's essay on Prince Ōtsu (663–86), the legendary youth accomplished in both literary and martial arts who was trapped into committing suicide: "I think people of such an era must die young," Hasuda had written, and then added: "I know dying in such a way is my culture today."

Japanese intellectuals were the same during wartime as they are today, to an "astonishing" degree, Mishima asserted, in "their cowardice, their cynicism, their objectivism, their common sentimentality like that of a rootless plant, their insincerity, their toadyism, their gestures of resistance, their self-righteousness, their inaction, their talkativeness, their readiness to change their words." In fact, the situation was even worse when these characteristics were "adorned with wartime hypocrisy." When Hasuda smelled the "stench they emitted" and observed firsthand "how they poisoned the essence of culture," he could only be "driven to fury for the sake of the culture as he understood it with his boyish noncompromise."

Writing these words for Odakane Jirō's *Hasuda Zenmei and His Death* (*Hasuda Zenmei to sono shi*), Mishima was to some extent superimposing his oft-stated view on a man whose knowledge, save for that of experience on actual battlefields, was far less and whose thinking process was far simpler or entirely different. Yet he was clearly telling the truth when he wrote: "As my age has approached his at his death"—Hasuda killed himself when he was forty-one—"what his death, what the form of his death, meant, suddenly illuminated my illusion like a revelation."[7]

Yamamoto recalled Mishima coming to visit, again unannounced, toward the end of April. Mishima handed him a thick book. "This book has determined what I am today," he said, and left. The book was the Hasuda biography.[8] Hasuda Zenmei became a handy way for Mishima to hint at his plans, to those who knew, however vaguely, of the wartime writer and the fate he chose. Kojima Chikako, for example, remembered Mishima saying to her when she was visiting him in October to receive an installment of the last of his tetralogy—that is, about a month before bringing about his own death: "I'm finally beginning to understand how Hasuda Zenmei felt. That is what Zenmei was trying to say."

They were waiting for the other guests of the day to come out of the house. Mishima had summoned a taxi to take gifts to two hospitalized friends of his, the writer Funahashi Seiichi and the artist Yoko'o Tadanori. Kojima recollected these words more acutely perhaps because, earlier in his guestroom, Mishima had turned, with a suddenly serious face, to one of his visitors, a senior alumnus of the Peers School, and, seemingly out of nowhere, said: "Mr. Akita, recently there's a tendency to regard swords as artworks, ornaments, but what do you think? I object to that. Swords are ... practical tools."[9]

## *A Paean to Manga*

During the same period Mishima penned a paean to manga. Manga had come to the forefront of postwar Japan's popular culture largely, he pointed out, as a result of the explosive successes of manga magazines for adolescent boys that were then fueled by college students' enthrallment with them.

In fact, behind the "revolutionary" student movement in the 1960s were, some suggested, the college students deeply affected by Shirato Sanpei's two extravagant series, *Book of Ninja's Martial Arts* (*Ninja bugei chō*) and *Kamui Legend* (*Kamui den*). Unlike his predecessors, Shirato presented ninja as people from the underclass up against the oppressors, and his realism was striking, especially in the way he detailed the rigors of peasants' daily life. As befits a son of a painter in the Proletariat Movement in the 1930s, Shirato put forward a Marxist interpretation of history in his graphic narratives. Inevitably, his ninja, along with the peasants they tried to help, were beaten and crushed in the end.[10]

Mishima insisted, however, that he did not care for Shirato or any other manga artist with a political or educational agenda. Instead, he loved manga such as Hirata Hiroshi's savage samurai tales and Akatsuka Fujio's wild slapstick placed in modern-day Tokyo. Akamatsu's *Mōretsu A-Tarō*, then at the peak of its popularity, was his favorite. The title character is a fierce (*mōretsu*) but gentle-hearted Edo-ite boy whose name, "A-Tarō," comparable to "A-John," comes from the fact that his father, obsessed with I-Ching divination, planned to have lots of boys and name them A-Tarō, B-Tarō, C-Tarō, and so on, as they came, but his wife died as soon as she gave birth to the first one. So A-Tarō is the only son he got. The good son runs a grocery store for his father, surrounded by a rambunctious gang of neighbors. The stories have to do with all the outlandish fracases they create.

Mishima was a fan of manga since his adolescence in the 1930s, when Tagawa Suihō's extraordinarily popular and endless series on a stray black dog—hence his name Norakuro—turned soldier ruled the day and Mishima developed his preference for "awfully vulgar, awfully intelligent manga" as something "indispensable for [his] physiological health."[11] Now, he vied with his children for the latest issues of manga magazines, some of them weeklies, as they were delivered. He naturally could not help but reflect on the generational differences: When he was in higher school and university, he and his fellow students could not "give up the vanity, in the presence of others, that you read highbrow books." But now even the members of his Shield Society openly read nothing but manga as they lay in the bunks of GSDF barracks!

Still, it was not in Mishima to do anything like telling the youth to stay away from graphic narratives. His essay, after all, was originally titled: "I'd Like You to Develop Off-the-wall Cultivation."

What he was afraid of, he explained, was what might happen when the young people became bored with manga. They might seek "cultivation"—in the sense of *Bildung*—of the kind that characterized the Taishō Era, seeking ideas such as "humanism" and "cosmopolitanism." His fear was not unfounded, he suggested. Look at the manga artist Mizuki Shigeru. Mizuki had exhibited such "magnificent talent" when he had started out with ghouls and ghosts, but once he turned to Miyamoto Musashi, he, alas, regressed to what Akutagawa Ryūnosuke and his era strove to achieve!

Mishima frowned upon the kind of swordsman Musashi had become after the wildly popular, drawn-out account of the man that Yoshikawa Eiji had written in the latter half of the 1930s: the epitome of the seeker of the Way, in his case the unity of the sword and Zen. Postwar movies about Musashi mostly stressed that aspect of the swordsman, beginning with the three-part series Inagaki Hiroshi directed in the mid-1950s, with Mifune Toshirō in the role of Musashi.

Mizuki, who was drafted and sent to Rabaul, on New Britain Island, during the war and lost his left arm—and that was some years before he established himself as a manga artist[12]—was particularly good at recreating the ghoulish tales he heard when a child, and Mishima was drawn to them. He was an admirer of Ueda Akinari, as we have seen. Just about a year before his paean to manga, he had devoted some of his ruminations on the art of fiction that he was continuing in the magazine *Nami* to explain how such tales can be "masterpieces."

One of the two stories he had recently read was Inagaki Taruho's latest, titled "I, Sanmoto Gorōzaemon, Dismiss Myself with Your Permission, Sir,"[13] he explained. As Mishima reveals quickly, the story is basically a translation into modern Japanese, albeit with some clever twists, of the well-known graphic narrative from the 1780s *Tōtei bukkai-roku*—also known as *Inō mononoke roku*—in which a phantasmagoric monster with a host of ghouls under his command tries to scare a boy named Heitarō night after night, but fails. And when he realizes he has, he shows up in human form, more or less, and courteously dismisses himself, leaving a mallet with the boy. Mishima cited this story as an example of how in "language art," the same quality can be attained between "dream and reality, fantasy and fact."

The other tale he chose to describe was Kunieda Shirō's 1925 story recently reprinted, *Divine State's Tie-Dye Castle (Shinshū Kōketsu-jō)*. Written with a touch of German Romanticism, with some scenes suggestive, Mishima noted, of Poe's "The Domain of Arnheim" and "Landor's Cottage," as well as Izumi Kyōka's story about a magically alluring woman living alone with a crippled idiot for a husband in the depths of mountains, "An Itinerant Priest of Mt. Kōya" (*Kōya hijiri*), the unfinished tale has to do with a fog-shrouded castle in the middle of a lake which, in truth, manufactures red tie-dyed cloth (dyed with human blood!) in its basement factory.

As Kunieda makes clear in the story, the idea of a castle where human blood is used as dye stuff comes from the thirteenth-century collection *Tales Gleaned in Uji (Uji shūi monogatari)*. But he makes the story far more ghoulish by presenting the lord-president of the castle, always wrapped in white cloth, as a man suffering from "galloping leprosy"—yes, Villiers de l'Isle-Adam's "Duke of Portland"—who turns anyone he touches instantly into an incurable, horrifying leper. When the fief lord finally sallies forth from his castle, he dons a bright red blood-dyed jacket that makes him look like a flame as he moves about in the town in the darkness of night.

"It becomes self-evident that the aim [of Kunieda's story] lies not in mystery-solving but in turning terror itself into beauty and fascination," Mishima wrote. Characteristically, in discussing this novel, which was ignored as no more than "an odd specimen of pulp fiction" when it appeared, Mishima cited the distinction between story and plot E. M. Forster made in *Aspects of the Novel*, to wit: "'The king died and then the queen died,' is a story. 'The king died, and then the queen died of grief,' is a plot."[14]

To go back to manga, Mishima pointed to what likely had touched off the extraordinary popularity of manga in postwar Japan.

"The tendency among the youth not to read difficult books but to avidly read graphic novels," he wrote, "makes no exception to the rule that the phenomenon that occurs in America occurs necessarily in Japan, too, *and* in a somewhat Japanized form. When I went to America for the first time, in 1952, I was surprised by the flood of *comics*, and was surprised again to learn that those crude manga without a smidgen of the sophistication of the 'Blondie' of the past were more the reading material for adults." Mishima had arrived in the United States when the Golden Age of Comic Books, so called, was entering new territory.

In fact, even though the Occupation banned samurai movies with "feudalistic" content, it freely allowed Hollywood movies that included Westerns with revenge and other "feudalistic" themes, as well as Disney's animated films, and, with them, inadvertently or otherwise, encouraged the culture of comic books.

What did Mishima mean by Japanization? "Compared with American *comics*, Japanese graphic tales are a shade more grim and dark both in eroticism and cruelty. To make up for it, though, they are *avant-garde* in nonsense. You will see how I, in search of *comics* that never exist in America, have entered this way (!)"—as in the *way* of the warrior, he meant, hence the exclamation mark—"through graphic samurai tales. The upshot of all this is that I have become friends with Gosha Hideo, bad-mouthed as he is as a cartoonish director, and we talk about everything, agree on everything."[15]

As we have seen, Gosha directed the film *Kill!*

## "*The Oval Portrait*"

On February 20, Mishima completed the third novel of his tetralogy, *The Temple of Dawn*. It ends with Honda Shigekuni—the reserved, dignified lawyer who holds together the narrative thread through the four stories but also a Peeping Tom—getting caught by his own wife while spying on his prized guest, the Thai princess Jin Jan, making love to another woman through a hole in the wall, then watching his newly built villa burn down in a spectacle that reminds him of what he had seen in Benares.

Several days after finishing the novel, Mishima wrote what he called "my gloomy monologue, which will be of no interest to others." It turned out to be of great interest to others, naturally, though, at least to one commentator, it read like "an extremely obfuscating, truly bizarre confession."

People might imagine him enjoying a respite before taking on the next volume, the final one of the tetralogy, as might a soldier on a march taking a short rest, Mishima wrote, but, in truth, he was feeling "extremely unpleasant." Why? Whenever he starts to write, two "realities come into being: that of the fictional world and that of the real world. Some writers may confuse the two, as when Balzac, on his sickbed, famously asked for the doctor he created in one of his novels. But his own methodology requires that the two never be confused, Mishima asserted.

In fact, for him "the most fundamental impulse for writing is always born of the conflict and tension between these two realities." Nor do "the temporal future of the fictional world and the temporal future of the real world" merge in the manner of "parallels in non-Euclidian mathematics," as happens in Poe's story, "The Oval Portrait," in which the moment a painter completes the portrait of his beloved wife "of rarest beauty" by giving it the final tint, she dies.

For him, "to write is not to continue to be captivated by the inspiration of the nonreal world," but to confirm his freedom moment by moment—"not the so-called writer's freedom, but the freedom to decisively choose either of the two realities, at any point in time." The choice, in short, is between giving up literature or the real world. The "unspeakable unpleasantness" that he felt when he completed *The Temple of Dawn* came from that "psychology," Mishima said. What happened? "The moment one fictional world was completed and closed, all reality outside fiction turned into wastepaper." And this happened neither as a result of his freedom nor as his choice, leaving him as puzzled "as if duped by a fox."[16]

This "monologue"—and the above is just one way of paraphrasing what Mishima wrote—is "obfuscating," because, for one thing, as he appears to generalize the matter, *The Temple of Dawn* was certainly not the first fiction he completed, and, for another, he left unexplained why he chose to make this confession at that juncture. So, Morikawa Tatsuya, a Buddhist priest, sought what might have prompted the "monologue" in *The Temple of Dawn* itself.

Mishima made it clear that he intended the tetralogy to embody the Buddhist philosophy of transmigration-reincarnation in general and, in the third novel, *ālaya-vijñāna* (the eighth or seed consciousness) in particular. Indeed, Mishima, through Honda, devotes a good part of *The Temple of Dawn* to an exposition of *ālaya-vijñāna* that forms the core of the *vijñapti-mātratā* (consciousness- or mind-only) theory of Mahayana Buddhism. *Ālaya-vijñāna* is at times called the eighth consciousness, because it comes after the eye-, ear-, nose-, tongue, body-, mind-, and thought-consciousness (*manas-vijñāna*). In some ways it may be comparable to depth psychology, but it is said to be exceedingly difficult to comprehend. Morikawa proposed that Mishima engaged in the "monologue" because in the course of writing *The Temple of Dawn*, he "firmly glimpsed, if for a second, how the dizzying world that this gigantic thought"—*ālaya-vijñāna*—"opens up actually exists." At that moment, "the entire reality and life that Mishima had lived was turned into void and nothingness."[17]

But you can take a less religiophilosophical view and say that with the "monologue" Mishima was simply telling those who might care about such things that he was ready to pursue death as single-mindedly as *Hagakure* prescribed, and as the Shinpūren did. All the talk of "two realities," "freedom," "choice," and, above all, "the real world turning to waste paper," was merely to confuse. So was his announcement five months later, as he reflected on his twenty-five years as a writer, that all he had done was nothing more than an accumulation of "excrement."[18]

His worldly ambition—his attachment to this world, to put it in Buddhist terms—remained strong, nonetheless. It was in fact in the letter to Donald Keene dated one day after his death, November 26, 1970, that he pleaded with the American scholar to see to it that the tetralogy in English translation be published properly because he believed that, if that is done, "readers will be sure to appear from somewhere in the world who understand me."[19] The letter began: "I have finally become what my name says, the Death-Enchanted Ghostly Demon with a Tail."

The dead giveaway in the "monologue," if we may call it that, was this statement: "But there still remains one volume. There remains the final volume. The words, 'Once this volume is finished,' are the greatest taboo for me now. That is because I cannot think of the world after this [tetralogy] ends, and also because to imagine that world is at once loathsome and terrifying."

Worldly concerns Mishima carried to the end, but he did start to cut worldly ties. He "frantically concentrated on work from the year-end to February," finishing *The Temple of Dawn*, he told Keene just about the time he wrote the "monologue," in a letter dated February 27. Now, he began taking care of the various "commitments one by one" that had "hooked" him—that is, the essays and such he had agreed to write.

He was feeling dispirited, Mishima explained. Until the preceding year, he had hopes for his "own small *Götterdämmerung*," but following the general elections in December, "everything suddenly quieted down, just as it had after the 1960 upheaval" against the US-Japanese Mutual Security Treaty, and all "the sense of danger disappeared..., and accordingly I, too, lost all perkiness."[20]

## *"Golden Death"*

The disappearance of a personal *Götterdämmerung* meant the need to change the narrative direction of "the final volume," Mishima indicated to Muramatsu in March.[21] At a very early stage of plotting and planning for *The Sea of Fertility*, when he had not decided whether the drawn-out story of metempsychosis encompassing the first three quarters of the twentieth century was to be told in four or five volumes, he had envisioned the following for the fourth volume:

> The fourth volume—the forty-eighth year of Shōwa [1973]. Honda already in old state. Various figures that appear to be the protagonists in the first, second, and third volume come and go around him, but they are the ones that had already completed their missions, and are fakes. Throughout the four volumes, he searches for a protagonist but cannot find one. Finally when about to die at age eighty seventy-eight, an eighteen-year-old boy appears, and, just like an angel, radiates with eternal youth. (It cannot be thought that the protagonists till then have disappeared and escape transmigration when they

have reached nirvana. The female protagonist in the third volume has ended in a miserable death)
Seeing a sign on the boy, Honda becomes exhilarated and grabs the impetus for his own nirvana.
When you think of it, this boy, the boy from the first volume, is an embodiment of *ālaya-vijñāna, ālaya-vijñāna* itself, *ālaya-vijñāna* that is Honda's seed.
When Honda is about to die and enter nirvana, he sees beyond the window the boy setting sail toward the sky of light. (Death of Baldassare)[22]

In the actual story he wrote, "the boy" is handsome and brilliant yet a monster. Although his nefarious schemes, and his spirit, are quashed by a wilier character, Honda ends up facing nothingness instead of nirvana or deliverance from worldly bondage. The title of the story, which Mishima apparently settled on after he started location research in May, was *The Decay of the Angel* (*Tennin gosui*). The original phrase means "five-stage decay of the heavenly being" and embodies the Buddhist belief, with details varying somewhat from one sutra to another, that a heavenly being loses his divine faculties in the following fashion as he approaches his death: he starts batting his eyes; the flowers of his tiara begin to wither; his clothes begin to collect dust and bodily grime; he begins to sweat in his armpits; he begins not to return to his own seat but to sit in any place. Ōe no Asatsuna (886–958) wrote:

> Whatever is alive is bound to die.
> Lord Shakya was unable to escape the smoke of sandalwood.
> When pleasure is exhausted sadness comes.
> Even the heavenly being meets the day of five-stage decay.[23]

The one commitment Mishima disposed of that he cited for Keene shows what was expected of someone of Mishima's stature. An afterword to an anthology of three writers, Uchida Hyakken, Makino Shin'ichi, and Inagaki Taruho, Volume 34 in the Japanese literature series by Chūō Kōron, the work required him to make a selection for each of the three and present it with a knowledgeable, insightful, and enticing analytical commentary.[24] Although Mishima regarded Uchida as the greatest prose stylist in "Shōwa literature" and admired Inagaki for his "philosophical bigness" and was thoroughly familiar with their writings,[25] a writer with a far smaller range of activity than Mishima would surely have found such an assignment time-consuming and daunting.

Another essay Mishima wrote in similar vein was on Tanizaki—this one for Volume 6 in the Japanese literature series by Shinchōsha dedicated to the other Japanese author who had been rumored to receive the Nobel Prize but died, in 1964, without doing so. Mishima began by noting that he had already discussed Tanizaki's entire œuvre, as he indeed had, and since he did not like to repeat himself, he would take up "Golden Death" (*Konjiki no shi*), one of the works Tanizaki disliked and shunned after writing them—he deleted it from his "complete works"—because such pieces often contain "a certain important impetus." Unlike Kawabata's "Birds and Beasts" (*Kinjū*), which the author also disliked and shunned, but which is a masterpiece in Mishima's opinion, "Golden Death" is "an obvious failure." Nevertheless, "in disgust and indulgence, a writer can sometimes go over the boundary despite himself. His sensibility can go over the limits of reason, destroy the form, and there allow a glimpse into an unexpectedly vast wilderness."

What Mishima did with "Golden Death" was to schematically analyze the story's protagonist Okamura's criticism of the German enlightenment philosopher Lessing's aesthetics (*Laocoon*) and link it to Tanizaki's principal stories. Okamura's thought and life, as described by the narrator, Tanizaki's proxy, follows his argument for the unity of life and art that ends in his own "golden death" in a paradise he creates for himself. Okamura is so wealthy—if not as fabulously wealthy as the Ellison in Poe's story, "The Domain of Arnheim"—that he can create an opulent setting in which to carry out his conclusion: "Art is an embodiment of sexual desire. Artistic pleasure is a kind of physiological or sensual pleasure. Therefore, art is not something spiritual but something wholly sensual." So his "final proposition" may be summed up: "The ultimate of sensual creation can only lie in one's aesthetic death."

Tanizaki wrote this story when the first tide of European psychology, psychoanalysis, and psychopathology was swamping Japan,[26] but he saw danger, Mishima concludes, in this line of thinking and turned back and away from it.

Mishima, greatly more knowledgeable about art than Tanizaki was when he wrote "Golden Death," in 1914, made sure to deride the "poverty" of the great master's grasp of art as represented by Okamura's favorite artists: the ukiyo-e painter Utagawa Toyokuni in Japan and Henri de Toulouse-Lautrec in the West. The combination was typical of the Taishō Era, Mishima insisted. Yet there is more than a grain of self-caricature when he condemns "the utopia of beauty" Okamura has created where the following things are proudly on display: copies of sculptures of Michelangelo and Rodin, Giorgione's *Sleeping Venus*, the tableaus of nymphs by Lucas Cranach and other Western masters, "a mixture of Rome and China that doesn't make any distinction between the *fin de siècle* and esoteric Buddhism." All this "exposes the ugliness of Japanese culture that has lost a unifying style." It is reminiscent of the Tiger Balm Garden in Hong Kong, Mishima added.

He went on: "Compared with the disastrous situation where the slaves of pitiful Taishō Era culturalism have ended up as today's opinion leaders, Okamura's gallant self-sacrifice is something that should have been regarded as a model."[27]

Mishima's commentary on "Golden Death" helped to reignite interest in Tanizaki's long neglected Taishō stories.[28]

Mishima also found time to "supervise" the translation by Yōko and her friend Matsubara Fumiko of *Les petites filles modèles* of the Countess of Ségur and write a foreword to it. Noting in his foreword that no elements of the "beautiful" world the Russian-born aristocratic French writer described—"the period, daily environment, religion, and customs"—are "relevant to Japan now," Mishima stressed that was "the very reason the book should be read in Japan now." That was why, he said, he advised his wife to choose "old-fashioned, grandly antiquated, elegant expressions" for conversations among the characters in the book, even though they may sound too "roundabout, even ridiculous to the ear used to crude modern conversations."[29]

---

Among Mishima's friends who later realized he had begun cutting off ties to the world that spring was Muramatsu. He had a call from Mishima on April 18 to ask if he could come to a get-together at the restaurant Kitchō a week later. Asked what the occasion was, Mishima replied it was to welcome back Saeki Shōichi, professor of American literature, from Toronto.

Up to around 1960, going abroad was a considerable undertaking for most Japanese, and it was common for friends and relatives to send off the chosen and welcome them back at the airport (by then far less often at a seaport). But as the decade progressed, overseas travel became common enough for people to dispense with such rituals, let alone holding a welcome-back party at a high-class restaurant.

The party, in truth, turned out to be "strangely somber, without Mishima's loud laughter or jokes." Some of the things Muramatsu recalled Mishima bringing up were none too positive, either, and that did not help. For example, he lamented that Michael Gallagher, translating *Spring Snow*, asked him what *tōgū* ("eastern palace," the metaphor for "crown prince") meant. How could anyone who did not know a word like that dare to translate such a novel? He asked Saeki to look for better translators for the third and fourth novels.

Also, by way of announcing that he was going to quit the Japan Cultural Council, Mishima proposed discontinuing *Hihyō*. Muramatsu was thinking something similar, and Saeki did not object, so they agreed to suspend their magazine. It was months afterward that it struck Muramatsu that Mishima had meant the Kitchō gathering to be "a farewell banquet."[30]

It was toward the end of July that Muramatsu was alarmed and sensed something was going awry. He belatedly read the "excrement" article mentioned earlier: it had appeared in the *Sankei Shinbun* on July 7. Titled "Promises I Haven't Kept: 25 Years Inside Me"—the subtitle was the name of a series the daily started to mark the twenty-fifth anniversary of Japan's defeat—Mishima's essay, which topped the series, sounded like "his divorce letter to Japanese society." Overshadowed by a "nothing-has-worked, I-don't-give-a-damn" tone, it ended with a prediction for Japan: "I am deepening my sense every day that, if things continue as is, 'Japan' may cease to exist. If it does, there may remain in its place, in one corner of the Far East, a great economic power that is inorganic, empty, *neutral*, intermediate-color, wealthy, and shrewd."[31]

CHAPTER THIRTY

# Toward Ichigaya

*What I was looking for was some spontaneous natural suicide.*

—*Confessions of a Mask*

According to the Tokyo District Public Prosecutor's opening statement at "the Mishima Incident" trial, Mishima began to take a series of concrete steps to execute his plan in early April 1970.[1]

Four members of the Shield Society eventually took part in Mishima's plan: Morita Masakatsu, twenty-four, a senior, Department of Education, Waseda University; Koga Masayoshi, twenty-two, a senior, Department of Engineering, Kanagawa University; Ogawa Masahiro, twenty-two, a senior, Faculty of Law, Meiji Gakuin University; and Koga Hiroyasu, twenty-three, a graduate, Faculty of Law, Kanagawa University.

Of the four, the two Kogas had different Chinese characters for the *ko* of their surnames: "small" for Koga Masayoshi and "old" for Koga Hiroyasu; henceforth, the former may be sometimes identified as the younger Koga, the latter as the older Koga. The older Koga, who joined the Shield Society in August 1969, was at the time studying for the state judicial examination, reputedly one of the toughest exams in Japan.

Both Koga's were members of the Seichō no Ie, "The House of Growth," a religiopolitical organization based on an amalgamation of

/ 689

Shinto, Buddhism, and Christianity, according to its founder Taniguchi Masaharu. Mishima's grandmother Natsuko became its fervent follower and chanted its catechisms every day, so that Mishima found himself chanting them as his sister Mitsuko's death approached.[2] One of its teachings, the older Koga testified at the trial, was that to live as a Japanese is to live the history of Japan, that to keep the Japanese nation alive is to keep oneself alive. In that sense, the philosophy of the Seichō no Ie, which still has a sizable number of followers today, represents the fundamentalist variety of patriotism—or did, at the time.

On April 3 or 5, 1970, Mishima asked the younger Koga, in the Coffee House, of the Imperial Hotel, if he was willing to "stay with him to the very end." On April 10, Mishima asked Ogawa Masahiro the same question, while the young man was visiting him. Both Koga and Ogawa agreed, guessing the consent would entail death. In mid-May, while talking with Morita, Koga, and Ogawa when they were with him in his house, Mishima suggested that the best way to accomplish their aim would be for the GSDF and the Shield Society to go to the Diet as an armed rebel force and demand Constitutional revision.

Some members of the Shield Society often went to Mishima's to discuss things. They did so mostly when he was free of any other engagements—that is, during the hour he sunbathed on the verandah on the second floor, from the time he got up until about one o'clock. One day it was cloudy, so someone asked him: What's the point of being out on the verandah with his clothes off in weather like that? Mishima's answer left an indelible impression on the young men: I am weak-willed by nature, so if I don't do something I'm supposed to do just once, on any excuse, I'll stop doing it altogether by finding one excuse after another. That's why I do this even when it's drizzly.[3]

---

On May 8, Mishima had a taidan with Shibusawa Tatsuhiko and there hinted at "a foolish act" he was likely to commit, adding that he was saying so "as a matter of probability" and he could not tell whether the act would be "political or personal." The topic of the taidan was Inagaki Taruho, with its transcript to go with a volume devoted to him in Chūō Kōron's Japanese literature series.

A year earlier, Mishima had caused Inagaki to become the first winner of the Japan Bungaku Taishō, "grand prix for Japanese literature," for *The Aesthetics of the Love of Boys* (*Shōnen-ai no bigaku*) or, as Inagaki himself called it in Latin at one stage of rewriting it, *Principia Pædophilia*. It is an erudite, discursive, at times humorous, exaltation of and speculation on the ass and anus from the viewpoint of loving boys in their early teens. Inagaki's argument, by then familiar among his fans, was that, of the trinity of erogenous zones, in his nomenclature the "V(agina) sensitivity," "P(enis) sensitivity," and "A(nus) sensitivity," the third and last was "*the* ace." In October Mishima had also penned a succinct accolade when Inagaki's book *The Aeroplane Dudes (Hikōki yarō-tachi)* came out.[4]

Still, the more he praised Inagaki, the more Inagaki, "being extremely shy," badmouthed him, Mishima told Shibusawa. Among the things Inagaki said was this: "Mishima Yukio's face is as repellent as a gibbeted head with its popped eyes."[5] In any case Mishima was resolved *not* to meet the writer he admired "for two reasons" that had nothing to with Inagaki's reaction. For one, he did not want to destroy the image of a smartly dressed boy he had formed of Inagaki since he began reading him a long time ago. Inagaki, Mishima's senior by a quarter of a century, was nearly seventy by then.

The other reason is "extremely private." It has to do with a "foolish act." People all over Japan will laugh at him for it, damn him for it, but there will be just one person who will not: Inagaki. He may be "flattering himself" by assuming that, but he is "convinced" of it, Mishima said. This is because Inagaki is "the only writer who knows man's secret," the only person who "understands man's feelings *metaphysically*, ready to catch with a hook, anywhere it may be, what emits from man's secret as it dashes through heaven and hell."[6]

In fact, in *The Aesthetics*, Inagaki made one reference to Mishima when he attributed the following remark to him: "The cherry blossoms and maple leaves seen in [Japanese] classics mean 'blood' while the moon, geese, white clouds, eight-fold haze, dew, and so forth are [parts of] our body. However, the Way of Shikishima"—love of boys in Inagaki's understanding—"is such an *abstraction* in the first place. Only those with no ability to enchase VPA in 'the framework of a different time and space' end up being called a sexual molester or a philistine."

Most important perhaps, in the same book, Inagaki had said this: "One completes his dandyism by 'death.' No matter what the manner of death, there is no one who does not gain some sensuality and elegance by death."[7]

---

On June 13, Mishima got together with the same three—Morita, Koga, and Ogawa—in Room 821 of the Hotel Okura, in Akasaka, and proposed the following: Because it became clear that they could not count on the GSDF, they would carry out the plan on their own, with these components: Take over a GSDF munitions depot to secure weapons, threaten to blow it up, while capturing the commander-in-chief of the Eastern Army, in Camp Ichigaya, as hostage, so they may demand an assemblage of troops, appeal to them, and, with the troops willing to go along with the Shield Society, occupy the Diet, and force it to adopt a resolution for Constitutional revision.

The idea, Mishima surely knew, was impractical and unrealistic. Willing or not, none of the GSDF troops were under his command, unlike, say, the troops during the 2.26 Incident who were under their officers' command. The distance from Camp Ichigaya to the Diet is 2.8 kilometers or 1.7 miles on foot; that meant, as Mishima's group marched to the Diet, GSDF or police intervention would be inevitable. The Diet's resolution itself would be only the first step for revising the Constitution; and so forth.

Luckily, the three young men questioned Mishima's proposal, though from a different angle. It would be hard to find the location of any GSDF munitions depot. But, even if one were found, the Shield Society would have to be split into two units, one for seizing the depot and the other for seizing the commander of the Eastern Army. (Whether the point was raised or not, Mishima no doubt knew the troops had to follow elaborate procedures to get their weapons loaded.)

The plan to seize a GSDF munitions depot dropped, Mishima proposed, and the three others agreed, that the Shield Society have a parade on the drill ground in front of the Eastern Army's HQ building to mark its second anniversary and take the commander hostage while he is reviewing the parade.

The "Eastern Army," it may be noted, is the English name for what may be given literally as "Eastern Theater Unit," which, of course, hides, however clumsily, any *military* suggestion. In reality, it corresponds to the Imperial Guards Division in the prewar army. It is, in other words, an elite force. Also, Camp Ichigaya is where Japan's Military Academy was initially set up, back in 1874, and where, after the country started war with the United States and others, the General Staff Headquarters were. Following Japan's defeat, the Occupation used its main buildings for the International Military Tribunal for the Far East to try Japan's wartime leaders, sentencing Tōjō Hideki and six others to death by hanging. (In 1994, the Eastern Army HQ moved to Asagasumi. Ichigaya Hall, where Mishima started having the Shield Society's monthly meetings in January 1969, later became the Hotel Grand Hill Ichigaya.)

Gen. Mashita Kanetoshi, who would end up being taken hostage on November 25 and watch Mishima disembowel himself and then decapitated, had a history as laden with Japan's recent military past.

The top graduate of the War College, class of 1941, and a major at the time of Japan's surrender, Mashita served as *kaishaku*, i.e., decapitator, when his classmate at the War College, Maj. Haruki Makoto, disemboweled himself, two days after Japan's surrender, on August 17, 1945. Haruki was a staff officer on Saipan with the task of building the island's defenses. He was transferred to a different post some time before the US assault but had felt he hadn't done a good job ever since the island's fall. Mashita agreed to serve as second because he did not want his friend to die "an unsightly death as a soldier," he testified at the Mishima Incident trial.

---

Mishima and the three youths kept under tight wraps what they were planning and plotting. But Mishima continued to drop hints as to what at least *he* was after, directly or indirectly. In an open letter published in the *Mainichi Shinbun*, on June 11, for example, he criticized Ishihara Shintarō, a member of the House of Councilors, for openly complaining about his own Liberal Democratic Party. What he was angry about, he wrote, was the general "anything-goes" atmosphere of the day, including "insider criticism." A true samurai or a true man would either put up with the body he serves in silence or commit a *kanshi*, killing yourself to warn someone else of his improper behavior. That is *shidō*, the samurai's moral or ethical principle, Mishima wrote.[8] Some of the postmortem explainers, as it were, of Mishima's act would resort to the idea of *kanshi*, Kawabata among them. Mishima was not discouraging it.

Mishima's talk of *shidō* attracted attention, not least because his target was a fellow-writer-turned-politician, and Tokuoka Takao, of the *Mainichi*, interviewed Mishima about the principle. Question: You say, Once you join an organization, don't criticize it. Isn't that suppressing resistance, demanding mindless obedience? Answer: Resist if you must, but do so with a do-or-die resolve. Question: Isn't *shidō* an anachronism? Is there any use in being a samurai when no one is practicing *shidō*? Answer: Yes, it may be anachronistic, but one person practicing it will be fine. It is a spiritual *dandyism* a man should flaunt.

The interview was published in the July 12 issue of the *Sunday Mainichi*.[9]

## *"Madness" and Death*

On the same day that his open letter to Ishihara appeared, Mishima gave a talk at Waseda University students' history club, Shōshikai. His topic, in seven segments, ranged from social ("do not expect human beings to understand each other"), to historical ("Japan's postwar Constitution and the US-Japanese Mutual Security Treaty are 'Siamese twins'"), to political ("the Liberal Democratic Party and the Communist Party are the same in that they *know* they are liars").

But the focus of his talk, urging individual "isolation," was to quote the words of the posthumously most famous Japanese patriot à la Patrick Henry, of the United States, Yoshida Shōin: "You seek power, I seek loyalty." At the time, Shōin's group aiming to defeat the Tokugawa shogunate was split into two camps, one for an immediate action, regardless of obstacle and outcome, the other arguing that the timing was not yet ripe. Shōin belonged to the former, a negligible minority.

In referring to the famous firebrand, Mishima stressed that "loyalty" in this case meant a road to death, all alone and discarded in a barren field. It was the road he had chosen. In an era when killings and deaths were common and frequent, Shōin often equated dedication to a cause with death, at times clearly stating his death wish, as when he wrote to the then teenager and the later powerful bureaucrat-politician Shinagawa Yajirō in the spring of 1859: "My age is 30"—by traditional counting—"and it has not been just two or three times that I decided to die. Nevertheless I ended up not dying. Hearing me say this, you will say Shōin is lying, but people do not kill me no matter what."

In his talk, Mishima also pointed out that Shōin spoke about *kyō*, "madness," late in his life of 29 years, aware that he was at variance with the populace who were all content and "cynical." Shōin had indeed spoken of "madness," as in "Madman's Testament" he composed in early 1858, while under house arrest. It opens: "The great illness under heaven lies in people not knowing the wherefores of the illness. Unless people know the wherefores of the illness, how is it possible to make a plan for it?" It was his "plan" for equalizing the rigid, ossified class system within the samurai class, and people, he said, dismissed his ideas as "violent" and "mad"—too out of step, too out of kilter.[10]

---

On June 21, when they assembled in Room 206 of the Yamanoue Hotel, Mishima told his three comrades that he had secured permission to use the heliport in Camp Ichigaya for the Shield Society's calisthenic exercises, but the heliport was way too far from the office of the commander of the Eastern Army. That meant they had no choice but to switch the hostage target to the commander of the 32nd Regiment, whose office was much closer. The weapon would be a Japanese sword and he, Mishima, would be responsible for it. The one responsible for taking the group into the camp would be Koga, the only one among them with a driver's license. Koga would also acquire an appropriate car for the action. Mishima had a car but no driver's license. Yōko drove the car.

On June 22, the Satō government announced that the US-Japanese Mutual Security Treaty would be automatically extended the following day by another ten years. The next day an estimated 770,000 people rallied nationwide to protest the government's action but with no effect. Mishima and his group simply ignored it.

On June 30, Mishima met Saitō Naoichi to prepare a will. He had first visited the lawyer, Azusa's classmate at the First Higher School and the Imperial University of Tokyo, around 1955, to learn about trials and court decisions. On that occasion, Saitō told him about the Shinpeitai Incident of 1933, a large-scale plan for a *coup d'état* that was uncovered, with conspirators arrested, before anything happened. Mishima told him it was the kind of subject he'd like to take up some day. After Mishima and his publisher lost in the *After the Banquet* case, in 1964, Saitō had led the appeal.[11]

Mishima's will said that his estate would be divided in accordance with the law, but with one exception: the copyrights to *Confessions of a Mask* and *Thirst for Love* would be bequeathed to his mother Shizue. Saitō, who served the Osaka High Court as chief justice, would be the one Mishima was to direct Koga to consult after the execution of their plan.

The meeting of the four on July 5, in the same hotel, this time in Room 207, was to elaborate on the plan. Mishima said that, while the Shield Society is exercising or training in the heliport, he would walk over to the office of the regimental commander and take him hostage. The date would be that of the society's monthly meeting in November. On July 11 Koga bought a 1966-model white Toyota Corona with the ¥200,000 Mishima provided.

---

Meanwhile, the Liberal Democratic Party decided to push the idea of having Mishima run for governor of Tokyo the following year, and its leadership arranged a meeting with him. As Muramatsu Takeshi recalled, on July 13, Chief Cabinet Secretary Hori Shigeru, who had spoken to Mishima several times, invited him to the restaurant Kitchō. Muramatsu was also invited partly because he was urging Hori to set up an agency to deal with the worsening pollution problems, by then a pressing national concern. Also present were Deputy Cabinet Secretary Kimura Toshio and the Yōmeigaku scholar and political *éminence grise* Yasuoka Masahiro.

Mishima, however, was irritable on anything *political* from the outset of the meeting, at one point even accusing Muramatsu, indirectly, of getting involved in environmental issues. The only outcome of the meeting was Mishima's offer to put his thoughts on defense in "literary terms," so Hori and others might turn them into "political terms." Soon afterward Mishima dictated two articles and sent the tapes to Hori.[12] His understanding was that his ideas would be taken up in a cabinet conference, but, he told Yamamoto Kiyokatsu in sending the transcripts to him by express mail on August 10, he gathered that Director-General of Defense Nakasone had written a long letter to block any discussion of Mishima's ideas, and that was that.[13]

At the time, the government was deliberating on "the basic direction of national defense." But Mishima thought that the LDP's position was, on one hand, to "curry favor with the United States with an open stress on the US-Japanese Mutual Security Treaty and, on the other, to treat the Three Non-nuclear Principles"—that Japan shall not possess, manufacture, or allow nuclear weapons onto its land—"as nothing more than the Satō cabinet's public pledges," a lie, that is. It was, in short, "a cross between international cooperationism and nationalism." As it would turn out nearly forty years later, in 2009, the non-nuclear principles were a lie.

In any case, Mishima said a position such as his, that Constitutional revision must come first, will "plunge into something less than that of a minority."[14]

When Mishima wrote this to Yamamoto, he was in Shimoda where he was conducting location research for the last volume of the tetralogy. Donald Keene happened to be in Shimoda, and Mishima showed the ending of the story he had already written. Keene, out of courtesy, declined to read it.

In truth, there was little or nothing that policymakers could use in the two lines of argument Mishima submitted to Hori. In the main one, "Bushidō and Militarism," his basic assessment of the global military situation may have been as correct as it was standard—that nuclear weapons have nullified total wars, limited wars inevitably create sizable domestic opposition, and so forth—but his conclusion that therefore Japanese culture, centering on the Tennō and *bushidō*, must be restored had little political relevance or practicality.

In the subsidiary argument, "The Regular and Irregular Armies," Mishima lamented that the GSDF was utterly deficient in its preparations for guerrilla warfare and, as it stood, the Japanese troops were no more than mercenaries for the US military.[15] That assessment, however correct, also had little applicability, at least for LDP politicians, given the power relations between Japan and the United States.

At the end of July, and again at the end of August, Mishima and three young men met in the Hotel New Otani, at its swimming pool, and, after some discussion, agreed on the need to add another member to the group. On September 1, on their way home after a meeting to work on Constitutional reform, Morita and Koga took Koga Hiroyasu to Café Parkside, in Nishi-Shinjuku, and explained their plan to him. It was close to midnight. The older Koga recalled in his testimony during the trial how he agreed to go along:

> At the time [the younger] Koga asked me, "Can you die with Mishima Sensei?" I did not ask for details, but I thought, They are going to do the do-or-die uprising. I was not surprised because since I had joined the Shield Society, I was determined to give my life to the cause of awakening Japan.
> When told, "We'll do it in Camp Ichigaya," I said to Morita, "Please count me in."

On September 9, over dinner at a French restaurant on the Ginza, Mishima explained the team's latest plan to the new member: While the Shield Society is exercising at Camp Ichigaya, he will bring in a Japanese sword, the five of them will go to the office of the regimental commander on the pretext of showing an *iai* pattern, the drawing out of the sword, and take him prisoner for two hours to compel him to assemble troops so they may "appeal" to them. But then Mishima gave away the catch, the truth: It will not be possible to persuade any of the troops to join them. No matter: he, Mishima, must die. The date will be November 25. The older Koga reaffirmed his decision to join the team.

On September 15, the group, now of five men, went to see Togakure School Ninpō Demonstration Performances in Chiba, Tokyo's neighboring prefecture to the east. The Togakure School stressed the ninja art that Mishima thought highly of and wished to study if he had the time.[16]

On their way back, they stopped at an eatery in Sumida, Tokyo, that served boar meat. They then went to the sauna in the posh Isetan Kaikan, adjacent to the Shinjuku pleasure quarters. There Mishima narrowed the scope of the overall participants in the plan for November 25. He will pick the members of the monthly meeting of the Shield Society to be called forth that day. He will exclude anyone who has a relative in the Self-Defense Forces.

On September 19, Mishima asked Takahashi Mutsuo to come to a meeting of three—the other two being Mishima and Morita—specifying the Daini Hamasaku, a Japanese restaurant on the Ginza. When Takahashi arrived at the restaurant a little late, he found the two men drinking over fugu sashimi in a private room on the second floor. No sooner had he entered the room than Mishima took a formal posture and said to him:

> Allow me to say a word. The man named Morita Masakatsu here with us today may die in the near future or he may survive to become a worthless old man. But, whatever may happen, Morita Masakatsu who is here now is a being with a certain value. For some time now I wanted someone to remember him just as he is now, and decided there is no one but you, Takahashi, who would do that. So today I'll have him tell us about himself since his birth, the stories even I haven't heard.

Takahashi later realized that Mishima had meant it as an announcement of what would happen soon, a kind of will. That evening, though, he thought Mishima had started another jokey act and simply enjoyed fugu and drinks, barely listening to Morita as he mumbled his life story, scarcely touching the food. After the restaurant, the two men took Takahashi to a sauna in Roppongi. He guessed Mishima frequented it with the members of his Shield Society.[17]

On October 2, the five men assembled in Daiichirō, a Chinese restaurant on the Ginza. The plan Mishima laid out then was detailed: The Shield Society's meeting on November 25 will start at 11 in the morning. The members will begin their exercise at 1:30 p.m. at the heliport of Camp Ichigaya. Mishima will take part in the meeting in regular clothes, not in Shield Society uniform, excuse himself at 12:30 on the pretext of a funeral he has to attend, and the younger Koga, also in regular clothes, will drive him back to his house to pick up his sword, which will be put in the trunk. The two then will collect the two journalists Mishima trusts who will be waiting at the Palace Hotel. The purpose of having two journalists will be to have the entire action reported exactly as it unfolds. They will then enter Camp Ichigaya from its left inner gate, stop at the office of the commander of the 32nd Regiment, and, with the journalists in the car, take the commander hostage. The four young men agreed to the plan.

---

Muramatsu Takeshi met Mishima, at the restaurant Tsutaya, in Yotsuya, on October 7. Alarmed by the *Sankei Shinbun* article, "25 Years Inside Me," he had asked for a meeting, via Izawa Kinemaro, and Mishima had picked the date and place. Muramatsu had felt that he had been "in a state of severed relationship" with Mishima, though he did not explain the reason in his biography of Mishima. He knew, however, that Izawa, the "patriotic" historian, was "the one person Mishima still kept close to."

Mishima showed up in a half-sleeve shirt. One of the first things he said was, "I hear you gave a talk in Seoul, in French." Muramatsu indeed had, at the conference of the International PEN held in Seoul, in July. He spoke in French, at the urging of one of the directors, Agawa Hiroyuki, who wanted the world to know that English was not the only foreign language Japanese could handle. Mishima said he had heard about it from Donald Keene. The American scholar had attended the conference.

"More important," Muramatsu said, to change the subject, "I gather that you finished writing the last chapter of *The Decay of the Angel*."

Mishima blanched. He wanted to know who told him that. Instead of giving the answer, Muramatsu explained why he had requested the meeting: The *Sankei* article worried him.

"I see," Mishima responded. "So you understand Japanese. I thought you understood only French." The remark prompted Izawa, who was with them, to mutter, "How rude!" Muramatsu asked Mishima to rescind his remark, but Mishima's response was, if anything, even ruder: "The first thing you've got to do is to expel the barbarians in your head." The word he used was *jōi*. His deadly serious face at that moment made Muramatsu think of Iinuma Isao, the protagonist of *The Runaway Horse*.

Mishima took Muramatsu home by taxi. In the taxi he kept saying, "I can't wait any longer," "I don't like it"—apparently the way Japanese society had turned out to be. Muramatsu, who till the end of the previous year had heard Mishima repeat the word *kirijini*—dying while fighting with a sword—guessed that, if Mishima were to act in a drastic way, he would do so the coming year. Among other things, in the latest installment of *The Decay of the Angel*, Honda Shigekuni had just adopted Yasunaga Tōru, the beginning of a turn of events in the slowly unfolding drama.[18]

On October 19, Mishima and the four young men got together at the photo studio Tōjō Kaikan, in Chiyoda, to have a commemorative photo taken, everyone in Shield Society uniform.

---

October 21, International Antiwar Day, Mishima had a taidan with the screenwriter Ishidō Toshirō for *Eiga Geijutsu*. He had loved the film monthly for its outlandish approach to "film art." The topic for the taidan was war and yakuza movies. Before the session started, Ogawa Tōru, the magazine's editor-publisher who served as moderator, arriving late, mentioned the demonstrators he had seen on his way. That prompted Mishima to say he too had come across students on his way, but they would not do anything to him even as they clearly recognized him. He looked extremely displeased when he said this. Later reports put the number of those who rallied to protest that day at 370,000 nationwide, with 219 arrested.

Of the recent movies brought up in the taidan, *Gunbatsu*, an account of Shōwa up to Japan's defeat as an upheaval within the military, was one both Ishidō and Mishima roundly condemned for its utter lack of a sense of drama. No one did anything, according to the movie, but the horrendous war was the result. Just like the LDP today, Mishima said in disgust. What about Fascism? There was no such thing in Japan; if there had been, Japan would have produced some attractive personalities. The makers of the film could have at least brought in Nakano Seigō, for example, he said.

Mishima praised *Tora! Tora! Tora!*, along with *Airport*, for the parallelism employed. *Tora! Tora! Tora!* was the first Hollywood movie on Japan's assault on Pearl Harbor that took into account the Japanese viewpoint. To present both Japanese and American viewpoints, two directors, one American and one Japanese, were assigned. The 20th

Century Fox producer Darryl Zanuck's first choice for the Japanese side was Kurosawa Akira. Agawa Hiroyuki, a former naval officer, cried at the scene in the former where Adm. Yamamoto Isoroku reviews his troops, Mishima mentioned. Do you not have some *illusion* about the war because you did not go to war? Ogawa asked. I might have some *nostalgia*, though I was "relieved like everyone else" when the war was over, Mishima replied.

When *Shindemoraimasu*, the yakuza film featuring Takakura Ken and Ikebe Ryō, both as good-looking as the actor Tsuruta Kōji, was brought up, Mishima quickly said he had enjoyed Sudō Hisashi's recent article in *Eiga Geijutsu* arguing that "Tsuruta must be taken back from Mishima." Sudō would go on to direct his own films though none would have anything to do with yakuza.

When Ishidō, himself a graduate of the University of Tokyo, said what he liked the most about *Shindemoraimasu*—"Kindly die for me," a courteous, lethal expression Takakura had first used in an earlier yakuza film just before killing his baleful enemy, had become a fad word since— was the setup in which Takakura's mother is blind, Mishima responded to indicate it wasn't such *giri*, obligations, and *ninjō*, emotional complications, between mother and son that moved him:

> Hmm. I wonder if I have some homosexual elements in me, though I do not think I am a homosexual . . . At the end [of the movie], where Ikebe and Takakura eye each other and, without saying a word, go [to battle], when I see a scene like that, my heart is wrenched, I get a lump in my throat. Now yakuza films are the only thing that carries forward the traditions of Japanese culture.

*Shindemoraimasu* has a scene, toward the end, where Takakura, playing a taciturn loner as usual, declines the offer of a man on his side, who feels obliged to join him in the final fight, and walks into the enemy camp all alone—although the character played by Ikebe, whose obligations are subtler, joins him. A yakuza forced to go through humiliations so acting in the denouement was routine in such films, and this particular film probably had nothing to do with what Mishima did. Yet, less than two weeks later, on November 2, he told Morita Masakatsu not to die with him. But there was no way for Morita, fired up for several months whose nerves were dangerously on edge by then, to accept Mishima's word at that late date. By September or October, Morita's friends remember him saying, "If Mishima doesn't do anything at this late date, I'll kill him."[19]

The taidan took place at a cheap students' diner in Yūraku-chō at Mishima's request. Watching him eat a dish of omelet with rice busily as a student would, as if it were the best food he ever savored, Ishidō imagined the way he might eat with the troops at GSDF.

With the taidan over, Mishima pulled out an envelope from his pocket and showed it to Ishidō and Ogawa. The letter was from a man identifying himself as a group chief of a yakuza gang in Osaka, a former navy Pilot Trainee, who said he was a close reader of Mishima's rightwing writings and pledged that if something happened to him, he would immediately bring fifty men to his side.

"You see, you can't attack me too much," Mishima said. "Remember there's someone like this to back me up." Thereupon he laughed his famous laugh and quickly disappeared into the night.[20]

## *Glass Cover*

On October 25, exactly a month before the date of his planned death, Mishima sat down and wrote a heartfelt tribute to Azuma Fumihiko, his writer friend at the Peers School who had died twenty-seven years earlier. Azuma's father had proposed to collect his son's writings, and Mishima at once had arranged to have Kōdansha publish them. The tribute was his foreword.

*Akae*, the wartime "group magazine" of the three friends "gathered under the hypothesis of youthful death," nonetheless "did not have a fragment of the shadow of war lying on it," Mishima wrote. "Young people today must find it difficult to imagine such a nonpolitical season." Yet there was at the time "the self-evident premise that literature is something to be axenically cultured; there was no resistance, no loud cries, nay, not even escapism. . . . We lived in another, different hour. And death constantly flickered above our heads like the sunshine falling deeply among the trees."

The great many books written about the war may impress young readers "only with unique experiences," making them "captives of a dark *idée fixe* about the wartime life. It tends to be forgotten that there too was ordinary life, there were ordinary grief, joy, sadness, and happiness, there was dailiness, there was quietness, there were even dreams. For example, it was at a musical performance during the war that I heard the *clavecin*, its sounds so beautiful I had never heard anything like it before or since."

And those sounds of the *clavecin* were "Mr. Azuma's stories," Mishima continued. "They were, as it were, the acts of an extremely pure youth who, blessed as an incurable patient, was able to keep the fierce actions of the age outside the door."

> In an age when quietness itself was anti-age, just depicting subtle psychology, sentiments that were "not urgently needed," was anti-age. The consolations for fighting men were considered useful momentarily, but they, too, became "not urgently needed." In that age only those ill and children were free. But it was a freedom with no one to play with, full of pain, solitary, barren. So the sounds of a *clavecin* began to flow beautifully.[21]

Toward the end of that month, Mishima, at his home, discussed a limited luxury edition of *Confessions of a Mask* with Kōdansha editors, Matsumoto Michiko among them. He proposed a cover made of glass because, he explained, even though the story that had earned him his fame was supposed to be a narrative told with a mask, it was in fact plainly autobiographical. He then had his wife Yōko bring the two issues of *Akae*—the magazine had ended with Azuma's death. When Matsumoto read his editorial commentaries and said, "You were saying in those days exactly what you are saying today," he agreed with her with a laugh.

On November 3, Mishima discussed a plan to prepare a "definitive" bibliography of his works with his wife Yōko and Shimazaki Hiroshi, the Taiwanese-born editor of a mystery magazine known also as a distinguished bibliographer.

That was around noon. In the evening he met his young comrades at Café Almond, in Roppongi. The men then repaired to the lounge of

Sauna Misty, where he told them, as the prosecutor's summary put it: "I am grateful that you have worked with me with the resolve to die until now. But someone must see to it that the regimental commander not commit suicide. I ask the three of you to undertake the task: [the younger] Koga, [the older] Koga, and Ogawa. I ask Morita to do the *kaishaku* neatly. Don't make me suffer too much."

The three who were told to live agreed, more or less. During the trial, the older Koga, who had ended up decapitating both Mishima—with a final stroke after Morita botched it—and Morita, and who therefore had been vital to police questioning, added some more detail: At Sauna Misty, Mishima showed the young men the draft of the manifesto to be displayed on the day of the action and the demands he would make after taking the regimental commander hostage. Mishima also said, after stressing the importance of protecting the life of the hostage: "It is easy to die; it is difficult to live. You must put up with that difficulty." These were exactly the words he wrote in his "order" to the younger Koga to go to the lawyer Saitō Naoichi after the event.

November 4: Mishima received karate lessons from Nakayama Masatoshi—the last session with the famous head of the Japan Karate Association.

From later that day to November 6, Mishima and the Shield Society trained in Camp Takigahara. After the training was over, Mishima threw a party at Gotenba Inn for the participating members of the Shield Society and some of the GSDF men. He meant it as an occasion to convey a tacit farewell to the members of the Shield Society not asked to take part in the final act. Toasting with everyone, he became pretty drunk.

Around this time, Azusa happened to show his son Sadatarō's framed calligraphy. Mishima expressed admiration for his grandfather's calligraphy and asked to keep it. The phrase Sadatarō had chosen was the well-known words of the Chinese Confucian scholar Hu Yin (1098–1156): "Do everything humanly possible and await heaven's judgment" (or "Having done everything humanly possible, I await heaven's judgment").[22]

November 10: Morita, the two Kogas, and Ogawa went to Camp Ichigaya, entered its compound on the pretext of meeting Capt. Kikuchi Katsuo, made certain that there was space to park a car near the barracks of the 32nd Regiment, and reported the findings back to Mishima. Kikuchi was stationed in Ichigaya then. He received more than thirty letters and cards from Mishima, from August 1967 onward, but he kept only about half of them, burning the rest, mostly the more recent ones, after Mishima's death. The last one he kept is dated May 23, 1970. In it Mishima congratulated him on completing the GSDF's command and general staff course (CGS).

The December issue of *Chūō Kōron* went on sale carrying Mishima's taidan with Ishikawa Jun with the title, "Concentrating in Order to Burst." Following Mishima's death, many likely found it uncannily, immediately, prophetic. It was, in truth, an expression Ishikawa used in praise of writers such as Sakaguchi Ango who presumably did their work with no thoughts of leaving it for posterity. The general drift of the conversation was condemning the idea of "preserving culture," as evinced in building the Museum of Modern Japanese Literature.[23]

## *Four Rivers of Action*

On the evening of November 11, Mishima had a small gathering of people, Yōko included, at Tōbu Department Store, for the Mishima Yukio Exhibition set to open the following day. It was a show Mishima had decided to have back in May when he saw an exhibition of his collaborator–graphic designer Yoko'o Tadanori's "complete works," held in Matsuya Ginza. Ever a perfectionist, he had consulted Kuzui Kinshirō, the founder of the Art Theater Guild, on it.

That evening, when the Shinchōsha editor Nitta Hiroshi brought up his plan to publish his "complete works," Mishima expressed his wish that it cover not just his novels, stories, and other writings, as is usually done, but also the recordings of his readings, photos, and his film *Yūkoku*. Photos aside, the inclusion of voice and moving images became easy only with the advent of CD and DVD technologies. As a result, realizing his wish had to wait until Shinchōsha's second attempt at zenshū to commemorate the thirtieth anniversary of Mishima's death. The first zenshū, in thirty-five volumes plus a supplement, published from 1973 to 1976, had no recordings, either of voice or image.

For the exhibition, Mishima wrote an introduction to go with the catalogue. In it he posited that four "rivers" flowed through his life: the book, the stage, the body, and action. Or, as he put it in the *Tokyo Shinbun* interview a week earlier, his life was "a four-horse carriage," which could not run with any one horse missing. On each of the four components of his life, he wrote a mini-essay, concluding the one on "the river of action" thus: "This river of action and the river of the book frontally collide. However you may be for 'both literary and martial arts,' the coexistence of the two may occur only at the moment of death."[24]

"Living is *Satyricon*, all sorts of things mixed together," Mishima said in the *Tokyo Shinbun* interview. Fellini's film *Satyricon* was shown the previous year, but eighteen years earlier Mishima had written a brief review of *Satyricon* in Iwasaki Ryōzō's translation where he characterized the work as depicting "degeneration itself, powerfully, healthily, accurately," in such a way as to remind him of "an Italian fish market that still nakedly exposes under the sun [the work's] raw smell, flies, fierce colors, sickening fertility of life and consumption lust."[25]

November 12: Mishima, along with Morita, the younger Koga, and Ogawa, saw his exhibition. As the interviewer intimated by saying Mishima's having an exhibition like that was akin to making his own grave, people must have sensed something. The show, which lasted for six days, until the 17th, drew an astonishing average of ten thousand people a day. The department store had expected a daily draw of one thousand at most. The large attendance made Mishima happy but not the store management because most of the viewers were not interested in shopping.[26]

That evening Mishima had dinner with Henry Scott-Stokes, at the Fontainebleau, a restaurant in the Imperial Hotel. The journalist, who had received a short note from Mishima in early October saying, "Finishing the long novel"—*The Sea of Fertility*—"makes me feel sometimes as if it will be the end of the world," found him "in a most aggressive mood" that night. "Charming as usual but flashes of great aggression. Implied that I might as well pack my bags and go home, as 'no foreigner can ever understand Japan.' Think he went a little far. In a sense, no Japanese can ever 'understand' the West. So what?"

Mishima was "also strangely critical of the Western scholars in the field of Japanese studies; insisted, looking me straight in the eyes, that the scholars ignore the 'dark' side of the Japanese tradition and concentrate upon the 'soft' aspects of Japanese culture. Why is he being rude these days? And where has his sense of humor gone to?"

His behavior after dinner was, if anything, even more jarring. He shot out of the restaurant when normally he would have accompanied his guests down in the elevator. Worse, he "crushed a note into the hands of the elevator man." In Japan tipping is not done, not to mention in such crude fashion.[27]

To Scott-Stokes it was clear he was rushing to the next appointment. If he in fact was, it may well have been to the one with the four young men at Café Parkside. It was there that, close to midnight, Morita asked Ogawa to serve as his *kaishaku* and Ogawa agreed.

For the Mishima family, November 13, Friday, was the parent visitation day at their son's grammar school. Mishima went with Yōko, watched Iichirō in class, and then chatted with the principal for three hours.

---

November 14: Mishima and his comrades again assembled at Sauna Misty. Mishima told them that on the day of action he would hand copies of the manifesto and the commemorative photos they had taken together to NHK reporter Date Munekatsu and the *Sunday Mainichi* reporter Tokuoka Takao. Then the five men went over the draft of the manifesto Mishima had prepared.

Mishima had known Date more than two years if we take what he said as fact, though he may well have known him since the latter covered the *After the Banquet* lawsuit for NHK. His letters to Date and Tokuoka, both dated November 25 and both exactly the same except for the last part where he thanked each for his friendship and named the other recipient of the same letter, show how precisely Mishima had expected the planned action might or might not turn out.

The letters began: "Allow me to omit the preliminaries. I will begin with the matter at hand." He was preparing the letter for fear, Mishima said, that the SDF might cover up the whole thing because it would take place in its own compound. He asked each recipient of the letter to understand that, if everything worked out according to plan, "it would be no more than a minor incident," that "it would be no more than our personal *play*"—his English, meaning action—"no matter how you might look at it." He knew what he was going to do would strike most as an act of derangement. "No matter how deranged an act it may seem, I would like you to understand that to us it derives from our sense of *yūkoku*." The handwriting was as neat and fluid as that in the manuscripts he had received, with no sign of mental stress of any kind, Tokuoka noted as he read the letter.

In making this arrangement with two reliable reporters, Mishima, a student of terrorists in modern Japan, may well have had in mind the case of Nanba Daisuke, who, at age twenty-four, attempted assassination of Crown Prince and Regent Hirohito, on December 27, 1923 when the Taishō Emperor was ill. A son of a member of the Diet and from a distinguished family, Nanba was first taught to worship the Tennō but, as he observed rampant social injustices and the killings of Socialists and Koreans following the Great Kantō Earthquake, he decided to be a terrorist. When he worked out the assassination plan, he sent letters of intent to newspapers and labor unions lest his act be regarded as a result of derangement after the fact. He also sent "severing relationship" letters to some of his closest friends lest they be harshly interrogated on suspicion of conspiracy.

His attempt failed, and Nanba was arrested. The government and prosecution, unable to condemn his act on the ground of insanity, tried to force him to admit remorse. But Nanba refused to express any such sentiment, insisting to the very end that he was right in doing what he had tried to do. Nearly a year later, he was sentenced to death and executed shortly afterward.[28]

The event was scheduled to take about two hours to play out, Mishima told the two journalists. Still, something might go wrong.

"In the extraordinarily unlikely event that I have to call off the whole thing because of an unexpected prior contretemps"—here, what was meant by "prior" (*jizen no*) would become clear only after the event—"and return to Ichigaya Hall, it should happen by 11:40. If that were to happen, I would like you to return to me this letter, manifesto, and the photos, and forget about the whole thing. This may be asking too much, but I hope you will be understanding."[29]

Mishima would arrange the delivery of the letters by hand in such a way that the two reporters would receive them separately—at Ichigaya Hall where select members of the Shield Society would be having its monthly meeting—just about the time his action would start.

November 15: The weekly *Yomiuri* called for its phone survey on the outlandishly coincidental topic, "Great People's Manner of Death." Mishima responded: "Not a writer's but a warrior's decisive death!" His Japanese played on the words *bunshi*, "litterateur," and *bushi*, "warrior."[30]

---

Mishima wrote a short afterword to what was to be a volume of Mori Mari's writings in her own selection and mailed it to the editor. The publication plan was later cancelled and his accolade was not used as intended. In it he eulogized Ōgai's daughter as "a brilliant female writer most stern with words. A painter-composer who furthermore uses those words like colors and music. The supreme postwar sanity that has feigned derangement. A child born of a canary, a parrot, an armadillo, and a hedgehog." She is, he concluded, "Something that in any event is indescribable. Something before which you can only take your chapeau off."[31]

Sometime that day he telephoned Ōwada Mitsuaki (Kōmyō), the famous tattooist in Yokohama, and asked if he would tattoo him, but was told a mere seven or ten days, obviously the span of time he had in mind, would not be enough for any respectable job. Mishima must have known that. Perhaps he wished that Ōwada might do to him as Seikichi does to a young, beautiful, (latently) sadomasochistic female in Tanizaki's short story "Tattoo" (*Shisei*), carrying out the excruciatingly painful work that normally takes one to two months in a single day, from one morning to the next. As Tanizaki said in his story, tattooing was practiced rather widely during the period he described, but by the mid-twentieth century, it was favored only by the narrow stratum of society that Mishima liked: the yakuza.

November 16: Mishima wrote a heartfelt introduction to his

horseback-riding instructor Innami Kiyoshi's book, *The Equestrian Reader (Bajutsu tokuhon)*. When with the Imperial Guard Regiment (cavalry), Innami had the honor of being one of the riders in the wedding procession of Crown Prince Hirohito, in 1924; was a cavalry instructor of Baron Lt. Nishi Takeichi who would win a gold medal as an equestrian during the Los Angeles Olympic Games of 1932 and perish on Iwo Jima; was a colonel on the staff of the Kwantung Army when Japan surrendered; then, captured by the Russian army, was detained in Siberian concentration camps. Released and returned to his homeland, in 1949, he found horses and horseback riding disappearing fast with the abolishment of the military and the aristocratic class even as horse races grew ever more popular. In the end, Innami became an instructor for hobbyists and was still active at age seventy-four when his book went into print. Mishima, one of his students though never "one of the best," helped him with the writing of the book and its cover design.

"I loathe women who do kendō, but from the start I have loved women who ride horses," Mishima wrote. "I cannot bear women invading kendō which is purely Japanese and forms a purely male world." In truth, women had existed in kendō since prewar years and their number had started to increase from about the time Mishima took it up.

In contrast, "because horsemanship initially developed in European high society and was an elegant social instrument, the picture will not be complete without female figures in it." Lt. Gen. Kuribayashi Tadamichi, commander-in-chief of Iwo Jima, had noticed this while studying in the United States, reporting to his infant son, with pictures, how, in the US Army, officers' wives rode along with their husbands. He was in the cavalry himself.[32]

"Women's dignified air was once seen in the geisha of the Meiji Era," Mishima wrote, "but today it is a characteristic that can be seen only in the women members of a horseback-riding club. In the way such a powerful, giant beast is ruled under a woman's delicate hands, there remains a particular sort of *romanticism* and, if I may say so, a kind of poeticism."[33]

The following day, November 17, Mishima used a woman's image in another way. In a letter to Shimizu Fumio, he compared Japan following its defeat to a young widow. "This is a vulgar metaphor, but, because she was still young, if just one Japanese man had stood up for her, he could have turned her into a real woman." In reality, all the men who showed up for her had despicable motives, in the end forcing her simply to "grow old, full of wrinkles."

"*The Sea of Fertility* is coming to an end, but I tell my family and publisher that it's taboo for them to say, 'When this ends. . . .' This is because, to me, for this to end is nothing less than for the world to end. I once wrote the great temple Bayon into a play, *The Terrace of the Leper King*; this novel has been my Bayon."[34]

CHAPTER THIRTY-ONE

# The Seppuku

*Mishima had a strong idea of being a "samurai."*
—Ishikawa Jun

*I like very much the* Hagakure *idea that one must die a dog's death.*
—Mishima to Nakamura Mitsuo

The day he wrote his last letter to his erstwhile Peers School teacher Shimizu Fumio, Shinoyama Kishin finished photographing Mishima for the photo series *A Man's Death*. Among the photos Shinoyama had taken were those of "Mishima drowning in mud, Mishima with a hatchet in his brain, Mishima beneath the wheels of a cement mixer truck, and of course Mishima as Saint Sebastian, arms roped above his head to a tree branch and arrows burning deliciously into his armpit and flank." There was also a photo of Mishima sitting "naked on the floor with a dagger buried in his abdomen, and, standing behind him, with a long sword raised waiting to behead him on his signal, is Shinoyama."[1]

Later that afternoon, Mishima attended a party at the Imperial Hotel to celebrate the publication of the one thousandth issue of *Chūō Kōron* where the winners of the Tanizaki Jun'ichirō Prize, given by the same publisher, were also honored. Mishima, one of the judges of the prize, spotted Mrs. Tanizaki and apologized to her for having recently taken up for discussion the work her husband had not liked after writing it, "Golden Death," and quickly left the party with the young poet Takahashi Mutsuo, saying he could not stand the company of old people.

Nosaka Akiyuki, who attended the party, saw Mishima come out of it surrounded by painters and such and walk straight to the elevator to leave. He kept looking down, chin drawn, forehead prominent. Nosaka and a couple of writers of detective stories sitting in the couches in the lobby agreed: Mishima carried a "pretty eerie atmosphere."[2]

## *The Last Taidan*

November 18: Mishima invited the photographer Saitō Kōichi to the Kōrakuen gym to shoot members of the Shield Society, himself included, practicing karate. Saitō had been taking photos of Mishima for several days for his series, "portraits of Shōwa writers." In the dimly lit gym, Mishima pointed out Morita, the older Koga, and others for him, saying, "They are all good fellows." Like most who observed Mishima's body with some care, Saitō noted it "unbalanced"—the upper part "excellent" but the lower part "poor and weak." Still, Mishima looked perfect in karate garb, he thought. The two-hour karate session over, Saitō came out of the gym with him. It was a fine day. When he told him he had taken enough photos, Mishima sounded a bit disappointed but walked away with the usual "See you again."[3]

That evening Mishima had what was to be his last taidan. The Marxist literary critic Furubayashi Takashi had started a series of talks with writers of "the postwar school," and he chose Mishima for the seventh person in the series. The result turned out to be less a regular taidan in which two people say whatever comes to mind on a loosely set topic than a standard interview where a well-prepared person asks probing questions. Furubayashi was not just probing but frequently antagonistic. Mishima in fact had turned down his earlier requests for a taidan.

Thus Furubayashi began the taidan by announcing, "Whereas I have made my arguments from the standpoint of defending 'postwar,' it seems to me that you, Mr. Mishima, go out of your way to call postwar principles your enemies, praise the Tennō system, and fan militaristic sentiments as you do with 'the Shield Society.' As I think you know, until now I have written only Mishima criticisms—or have written only your accusations and attacks."

Yet the transcript of the two-hour-long questions and answers shows Mishima never lost patience or became irascible or dismissive even when Furubayashi became overbearing. Perhaps, having read the preceding six interviews Furubayashi had done, as he said he had, Mishima decided to use the occasion to clarify himself on certain points.

So, when asked, bluntly, about his "cynical" statement that his sister's death, which occurred soon after Japan's defeat, was a more serious blow to him than "the shock of the defeat" itself, Mishima responded: "I'd be lying if I said I wasn't unsettled by Japan's defeat or that I didn't feel a sense of liberation as the postwar era arrived." He was "completely muddled" for a few years after Japan's surrender.

When questioned on the "purity-orientation" in his writings—such as the focus on physicality over intellectuality as in the heroes of the novel *The Sound of Waves* and the short story "The Sword," or the focus on tidiness over messiness as when he presents the Tennō in "The Voices of Heroic Souls" as a figure astride a white horse who gallops over the fresh snow—Mishima brought up Georges Bataille as the European thinker to whom he felt the greatest affinity, and explained: Just as Bataille argued that a taboo must exist for you to have a chance for a sense of liberation, so in Japanese culture there once were the contrasting notions of *hare*, "public or formal," and *ke*, "private or informal." In today's world of relativism where taboos or the idea of *hare* has ceased to exist, one must seek something transcendental or absolute to experience eroticism.

Furubayashi did not miss a beat and said, somewhat derisively: So, in your case, Mr. Mishima, that goes directly to your idea of the Tennō. Mishima agreed, unperturbed, then added: As far as that goes, a feudal lord would do just as well.

At the same time, Mishima admitted to his ineradicable fascination with "muddy, dark spiritualism"—"things that are very *fanatic*, obscuranticismic." "That's Dionysus in me," he added. "My Dionysus leads to the Shinpūren, leads to the Southwest War, leads to the Saga Revolt and others, to those destructive impulses that ought to be called dark obscuranticism"—the insistence on remaining unenlightened.

What may surprise in this taidan is that Furubayashi ends up completely surrendering to Mishima. Once, in a keynote speech at a literary symposium, he focused on attacking him, Furubayashi tells Mishima. But when he was finished, Hirano Ken, the novelist known for raising contentious issues, spoke up and said, "If you like Mishima so much, come right out and say it. That would make your argument more logical." When he thought about it, Hirano was correct, Furubayashi admits. He also tells Mishima that he has bought all of his great many books, except for a couple of titles, so one book dealer offered to buy the whole thing for a whopping sum. He had even gone to see *The Moonbow*, he confesses.

Younger than Mishima by just two years, Furubayashi, following Japan's devastation and defeat, had turned to Marxism in a state of utter despondency—"*kyodatsu*, that eerie psychological blankness."[4] But he had felt the years since had been for him nothing more than a *yosei*, life lived just for the sake of living after the meaningful part of one's life is over, he confided. As a draftee, he was sent to naval air bases in Kyūshū where, he later discovered while looking at the lists of Kamikaze pilots, he had known a number of men who flew off to their deaths. Whenever he thought of them, he said, everything about his postwar life turned "blank."

Nakamura Kenji, the editor of the book-review weekly *Tosho Shinbun* that was carrying Furubayashi's series, remembered the evening session distinctly. Arriving at Mishima's house with the interviewer and a stenographer at eight in the evening as told, he saw the man walk into his guestroom with an attaché case, in a half-sleeve shirt. Already flush with alcohol, he took out a cigar case as soon as he settled down on a sofa, picked one cigar for himself and, as he offered one to Furubayashi, said, "I am totally immoderate in drinking and smoking." Nonetheless, he was "clear and full of confidence throughout the interview."

Nakamura also did not forget to note that, the interview over, Mishima asked the stenographer when the transcript might be ready. When told that it would be in a week and he would have plenty of time to correct and amend the script, he "simply nodded, wordlessly."

What sticks in the mind of the reader of the taidan is Mishima's response when Furubayashi expressed the fear, common among liberals, that Mishima's activity with the Shield Society was paving the way for Japan's remilitarization and reintroduction of conscription or at least allowing the rightwing and conservatives to take advantage of him.

Mishima said if some were taking advantage of him, let them. He was different from them. "You will find out soon enough."⁵

Reading the taidan to write a memoir of his association with Mishima a quarter of a century later, the journalist Tokuoka Takao noticed Mishima say, toward the end, "I think I'm already like Petronius. And, to exaggerate, I think the human being who knows the Japanese language will come to an end in my *generation*." Here Tokuoka thought Furubayashi's interlinear note, "Roman Emperor Nero's aide and author of *Satyricon*," might mislead. What Mishima had in mind surely was the Petronius at his death as described by Henryk Sienkiewicz in *Quo Vadis*. There the Arbiter Elegantiæ has a Greek physician cut the vein at the bend of his arm and slowly dies. Having come out in Kimura Ki's translation in 1928 as part of Shichōsha's world literature series, *Quo Vadis* was a book most students of his generation read.⁶

---

November 19: Mishima and the four young men got together in the lounge of the sauna of Isetan Kaikan. He told them the exact apportionment of time to each step of the planned action: twenty minutes for the assemblage of troops after taking the regimental commander hostage, for the sole purpose of taking him hostage was to force him to order the troop assemblage; thirty minutes for Mishima's speech; and five minutes each for the speech of each young man. For the "speech" of each youth, Mishima evidently used the ancient term *nanori*, declamation to introduce oneself on an ancient battlefield. Then they will declare the disbandment of the Shield Society, and shout, "Long Live the Emperor!" three times. Morita asked whether he can kill the hostage if the demands are not met. Mishima said, No, he must be left unharmed.

That day he wrote Bōjō Toshitami to thank him for writing him to say he had seen his exhibition. "Looking back upon the path I have followed, it is all vague and bleak, and I feel no special sensation about it. I think my Golden Age was when I was fourteen, fifteen years old. As a matter of fact, in those days, the moment I came home, I'd ask, 'Haven't I received a letter from Bōjō-san?,' then open your envelope the color somewhere between birch and apricot—such literary manna dew I have not come across since."

He does "not feel like reading recent novels," he told the man who had been his literary co-aspirant more than three decades earlier. So he read Georges Rodenbach's *Bruges-la-Morte* and was "intoxicated by its fin-de-siècle fragrance, even though the story is a trifling one of sexual love." Also, he found Julien Gracq's novel *Un beau ténébreux* "highly readable, because it has the feel of fin-de-siècle literature modernized, although the translation is no good." Earlier that day he faced "fifteen, sixteen opponents in a quick succession" in kendō. He does that sort of thing perhaps because he is "so straightforward as to be dumb even with newcomers," but he feels "greatest while in the thick of kendō" because then he "can forget everything."[7]

Writing to Murakami Ichirō the same day, Mishima said that among the books he read of late were Plato's *Phaedo* and Kusaka Genzui's writings.[8] *Phaedo* describes Socrates' discourse on why he is willingly taking poison. The main point is stated toward the beginning: The true disciple of philosophy "is ever pursuing death and dying; and if this is true, why, having had the desire of death all his life long, should he repine at the arrival of that which he has been always pursuing and desiring?"[9] Kusaka, Yoshida Shōin's brother-in-law, was wounded in the battle at the Hamaguri Gate on the 19th of Seventh Month (August 20), 1864, and killed himself the next day while being cared for in the nobleman Takatsukasa's house. He was twenty-four.

November 20: Mishima visited Shinoyama's studio with Morita Masakazu and made the final selection of photos. But the book never saw the light of day. Following what happened five days later, on November 25, both Shinoyama and Bara Jūji Sha that had sponsored the project decided against its publication. There was Yōko's strong objection to consider as well. As a result, the exact line-up of twenty to forty photos taken for this project remains unknown.[10]

November 21: Morita went to Camp Ichigaya, got in on the pretext of delivering one of Mishima's books, *Introduction to Action*, to the regimental commander, Col. Miyata Akiyuki, and learned that he would be away on the date of the planned action. Later that day, when the five men assembled at the Chinese restaurant Daiichirō, Morita told Mishima about it. After their discussion, they decided to switch the hostage target to the commander of the Eastern Army, Gen. Mashita Kanetoshi. Mishima telephoned the general and made an appointment to meet him at 11 o'clock.

That day and the next, at Mishima's instructions, the four youths went to Shinjuku Station Building with the ¥4,000 he gave them and bought cords with which to tie up the camp commander, wire and other things that might be needed to barricade his office, the calico large enough to write the demands on and be displayed before the gathered troops, a bottle of brandy for an analeptic purpose, a canteen, and whatnot.

November 22, Sunday: Mishima took Yōko and the two children to the sculptor Wakebe Junji's studio to see the life-size clay model of himself. He had been posing for Wakebe on Sundays since early fall. That evening he took his family, along with his brother Chiyuki and his family, to Suegen, an old Japanese restaurant in Shinbashi. He was dressed in a polo shirt and jeans.

While driving in Yokohama that night, Morita asked the younger Koga to take over the role of *kaishaku* if he were unable do it. Koga agreed.

November 23: The five men gathered in Room 519 of the Palace Hotel, in Marunouchi. They cut the cords to appropriate lengths and rehearsed the exact steps of their planned action several times. When he played the role of Gen. Mashita being gagged and tied up, Mishima put up serious resistance. He practiced his speech, with the TV turned up. At one point Morita asked him what the absorbent cotton was for. "To plug our assholes," Mishima replied. In disembowelment one sometimes loses control and defecates. As he wrote the manifesto on the white cloth with brush and ink, he laughed and said, "This isn't going to be worth a penny"—either self-mockery of a man who was strict on payment for what he wrote or a prediction of a man who knew exactly what would *not* happen.

They prepared headbands, with *shichishō hōkoku*, "to be born seven times to serve the country," written on them, the red sun at center. *Shichishō hōkoku* was one of the militarist-rightwing slogans during the war, and it was commonly attributed to the genius of guerilla warfare Kusunoki Masashige (1294–1336), although in the fourteenth-century *Chronicle of Great Peace (Taiheiki)* it was Masashige's brother Masasue who said something similar but not exactly in the phrasing later accepted and flaunted.[11] Mishima of course knew all that.

Around eight-thirty that evening Mishima met Morita at the high-class restaurant Shiki, in Sukiyabashi, then the two moved to join the others at the restaurant specializing in shrimp, Tsurumaru. He urged the young men each to compose a *jisei*, a farewell-to-the-world poem, in this instance in the 5-7-5-7-7-syllable tanka form. He told them not to try to be clever but say whatever they wanted to say. Some would later dismiss Mishima's own compositions—he wrote two—as conventional and flat, but that would be missing the point. Being conventional was the very point of such compositions.

In this regard, the Chikuma editor Azuma Hiroshi had it right. Even as he condemned the first as straight out of any of the samurai fighting for the Imperial causes at the end of the Tokugawa Period and the second as belonging to someone like Lord Asano, of the forty-seven samurai incident, he said, "their old-fashioned cookie-cutter quality eerily moves you."[12]

> *Masurao ga tabasamu tachi no sayanari ni ikutose taete kyō no hatsushimo*
> The sword a man grips clatters in its scabbard, the years I've endured it, today the first frost

> *Chiru o itou yo ni mo hito ni mo sakigakete chiru koso hana to fuku sayoarashi*
> Ahead of both world and men loath to scatter a flower scatters as midnight gale blows

The first tanka may allude to a *Man'yōshū* poem: *Masurao no satsuya tabasami tachimukai iru Matokata wa miru ni sayakeshi*, even as it may also echo a famous one of the shogun Minamoto no Sanetomo (1192–1219): *Mononofu no yanami tsukurou kote no ue ni arare tabashiru Nasu no shinohara*, "As a warrior lines up arrows in Nasu field of bamboo grass hailstones spatter on his handguards." The second poem may allude to a tanka by Fujiwara (Nijō) Sadatame: *Kazu naraba yo ni mo hito ni mo shiraremashi wagami no ue ni amaru ure'e o*: "Were I worthy both world and men would know: all this melancholy that bears down on me."[13]

November 24, morning: The five rehearsed again in Room 519 of the Palace Hotel. Each took turns in playing Gen. Mashita. At one point Morita asked, "Where is the carotid artery?" "Silly, you don't even know that? Here," Mishima said. "Be careful. Don't skewer me." At eleven he called Gen. Mashita to confirm the appointment the next morning.[14]

About two in the afternoon Mishima called Date Munekatsu, of NHK, to confirm the time he could call again the next morning. He also called Tokuoka Takao, of the *Mainichi*, to do the same, saying it's "a purely personal matter," nothing that would "excite a scandal sheet for women."

About three he called Kojima Chikako, his editor at *Shinchō*. He told her he'd like to hand her a manuscript the following morning, but he would have to go out in the morning for a regular meeting of the Shield Society. Are you an early riser? She replied she was up by seven or seven-thirty every morning so there should be no problem. He said, "Well . . . in that case . . . would you be able to come here around 10:30?"

Kojima, who was used to going to his place to pick up a manuscript in the afternoon, at an exact time he would specify, felt it odd, felt even a bit anxious, but she decided Mishima perhaps wanted to "casually" show her members of the Shield Society in uniform, something she actually hadn't seen yet. She had heard him boast how "cool" his men looked.[15]

Around six in the evening, the five men showed up at Suegen. Toyo-san (real name: Akama Yuriko), the maid assigned to the private room Mishima had reserved, remembered the occasion well. Obviously—in retrospect, perhaps—to boost the gathering's mood, Mishima gossiped about the actresses he admired: Fuji Junko, who had gained sudden, great popularity among the lovers of yakuza films, especially those in the student movement; Wakao Ayako, who had played his opposite in the film *Windblown Dude*, in addition to appearing in two films based on his novels; and Sakuma Yoshiko, who had played Ayakura Satoko in the stage production of *Spring Snow* in the previous year—all with, one may note, roundish faces like his wife Yōko. Mishima talked about Katsu Shintarō, who starred in the film *Kill!* with him (and helped him act in certain scenes), observing that he was a fascinating man who played his real self in films and such.

When she returned to the room after a while, Toyo-san found Mishima lying on his side as if meditating and the four young men in stolid silence. "I had thought I'd become more sentimental when the final moments came," he said, "but I feel nothing. In the end, it may be some third-party who has seen us that becomes sentimental."

Around eight, the men left Suegen. The younger Koga drove. On the way home, Mishima said: "Gen. Mashita is a great man, and I feel terrible doing something like this to him, but he'll understand if I kill myself before his eyes." He added, "If troops suddenly came at us before we entered the commandant's room, we'd have no choice but to bite our tongues and die."

He handed the older Koga his green pocket notebook with his schedules closely written in it and asked him to burn it.

As Azusa recalled, Mishima came home around ten, and he stepped into the dining room directly from the terrace. It was his wont to come to his parents' place after evenings out and tell funny stories, punctuating them by his usual laughter, before repairing to his room to work. That night, however, he asked, "Where's Mother?" Told she went to a wedding ceremony but would be back soon, he sat around chitchatting distractedly until Shizue came back. She said, "My, you rarely come to us at this time." Mishima apparently paid his evening courtesy visit to his parents, when he was in Tokyo, closer to midnight. "Are you done with your work?"

"Yes. I am completely tired out tonight. Mother, I'd like to go to bed early."

"Please do. You sure look tired. You work too hard. The best thing is to lie down."

"Yes, I'll do that. Good night."

The parents' Japanese-style house and Mishima's Western-style one were linked by something like a corridor. Shizue walked Mishima to the end of the room and said, "Take good care of yourself." She watched him walk away.

"For a month or two till then Kimitake had been looking more exhausted by the day, but he looked particularly bad that night," she would recall. "It's only about ten yards to his entrance but he trudged toward it, head down, shoulders sagging. Worried by his beaten appearance, I watched him intently until he disappeared, as I seldom did."[16] The accumulating toll on Mishima of the course he had been pursuing was apparent to those who paid attention, as well as in some of the photos during that period.

---

The younger Koga dropped Morita at his apartment, in Nishi-Shinjuku, and he and the two others, Ogawa and the older Koga, returned to his apartment, also in Shinjuku, to spend the night. The three discussed the matter of *kaishaku* further. Ogawa asked the younger Koga to take over if he could not do it for Morita, and Koga agreed. But the three had agreed that each would do whatever any of the other two might not be able to do.

In the meantime, Morita went out, had a simple meal ("rice with tea poured over it") at a diner, went back to his apartment around one thirty in the morning, and entrusted his roommate and Shield Society member Tanaka Ken'ichi with Mishima's letters to Date and Tokuoka with the instruction that they be handed to the two reporters when they show up at Ichigaya Hall. He then went out, telephoned a friend who worked as a cashier at a "midnight bar," and took a walk with her. He returned to the apartment around three.

## *The Day of His Death Was a Brilliant Autumn Day*

On November 25, Wednesday, Mishima got up at eight. It was a brilliant autumn day. While he was shaving, a phone rang and the maid picked it up. It was from Yōko. As always, she had taken the children to their schools—Noriko, then eleven, to the Primary School Division of Mishima's alma mater, in Shinjuku, and Iichirō, then eight, to the Ochanomizu University Elementary School, in Bunkyō. Then, on her way to the Equestrian Club, in Setagaya, for morning horseback-riding, she remembered something, hence the call. Before the maid hung up, Mishima snatched the phone from her, as he had never done in the past. Yōko repeated what she had told the maid. Mishima said, "Oh, I see," and hung up. Shizue was also out for work on the mediation committee of a local family court.

Around ten, Mishima telephoned Gen. Mashita to confirm the appointment. He did the same with Date and Tokuoka. A few minutes later, the younger Koga walked in the gate. He had parked the car with Morita, Ogawa, and the older Koga in it about ten yards away from Mishima's house. The four young men all had the Shield Society uniform on, but wore a coat or a cardigan over it lest they attract attention, their hats tucked away in shopping bags. They had washed the white Corona at a gas station on the way.

Mishima handed a large envelope to the maid, telling her to give it to Kojima, of *Shinchō*, who would soon show up. He then handed Koga three envelopes and told him to go back to the car and read them. The envelopes, for the two Kogas and Ogawa, each contained three ¥10,000 bills and a "directive." The directive confirmed the role of each of the three young men who were to survive—in the case of the younger Koga, to protect the hostage, Gen. Mashita, with the older Koga. As "the list of demands" issued during the act also showed, Mishima seriously feared the possibility of a soldier taken hostage in such circumstances attempting suicide. The three were ordered to surrender themselves as soon as the act was over, so they might "explain the spirit of the Shield Society in court." The directive gave the name of the lawyer to turn to, Saitō Naoichi, and his address. The money was for initial legal costs. It made it clear that Mishima alone was responsible for the entire action. In that regard, his killing himself with a sword was "natural," he wrote, but Morita was to be admired for his "gallantry" in volunteering to kill himself as "a model" for the young people concerned about the present state of Japan.[17]

Mishima came out in Shield Society uniform, complete with the hat. He had the Seki no Magoroku refashioned into a military sword on his left hip and his brown leather attaché case in his right hand. The case contained, among other things, two daggers, one of them an "armor-piercer," originally used for cutting the enemy's head off after hand-to-hand combat. The young men saluted. Mishima returned it, and asked if the three men accepted his orders. When he received an affirmative, he got into the front passenger seat, and the car left. It was around 10:15.

When their car came out on the south side of the Meiji Shrine's Outer Park, which lies southwest of Ichigaya, they found it a little early, so they drove around the park twice. At one point, Mishima said, "If this were a yakuza film, something like the *giri* and *ninjō* song of "A Lion Amid Peonies" (*Karajishibotan*) should start just about now, but we are more cheerful than we'd expected, aren't we?" He began singing the song. The four young men followed. *Karajishibotan* is a 1966 film featuring Takakura Ken and Ikebe Ryō. The title referred to the fanciful tattoo the lead actor Takakura flaunts on his body. Takakura also sang the title song.

---

Because she had always visited Mishima from her office, not from her own residence as she did that morning, Kojima Chikako miscalculated the time needed for the route and arrived at his house at 10:40, late by ten minutes. The maid she knew well told her Mishima was already gone, as she handed her an envelope. Kojima knew Mishima was strict on time and she had never been late, but she couldn't help but wonder: Was the time he had specified "that exact"? Could he not wait for a few minutes? Does he get impatient when the matter has to do with the Shield Society?

Then she remembered his "somewhat clouded voice" the previous day, and had a momentary doubt. She put that away, yet felt "tripped up." Then there was the envelope. Mishima's envelopes in the past were always unsealed so she might check the contents on the spot if she wanted to, but this one was "sternly sealed." Vaguely troubled and bothered, she went to her office. She was in for a surprise when she opened the envelope and checked the manuscript. The top page read, "*The Decay of the Angel* (Final Installment)," while on the last page were the words, in Mishima's neat handwriting,

*The Sea of Fertility*: Finis
November 25, the Forty-fifth Year of Shōwa

Kojima was perturbed. She had sensed that the completion of the tetralogy would not be far in the future, but had not expected it to occur with the installment for this month. With other manuscripts, Mishima had never failed to tell her when the serialization was going to end. She was confused and kept wondering as she sat at her desk. Then she noticed a commotion in the office. Something was wrong with Mishima. All the editors and others were rushing to the third floor where there was a TV set. Soon the news came: Mishima has attempted to kill himself with a sword. Shortly after twelve-thirty his death was confirmed.

Confounded, with memories of Mishima in the past several months rushing through her head "like a kaleidoscope," Kojima went back to her desk, on the fourth floor. She started examining the manuscript. At 140 pages it was double, triple the usual size. It contained chapters twenty-six to thirty. She started to read. Reading, she heard Mishima's voice as if each character he had written raised itself from the manuscript to speak to her.

"His decline deliberately proceeded, and his end was quietly being foretold," read a passage in Chapter 28. Honda Shigekuni is now eighty-one. "Like the hair that pricks the nape of your neck on your way back from a barber, death pricked the nape of Honda's neck each time he remembered it, though he was oblivious of it when he did not. As he contemplated on how all conditions for welcoming death had ripened by some force, he was mystified that death had not yet visited him."

"A sign saying '27 km to Nara' caught his eye," read a passage in Chapter 29. "Time flowed. Every time he saw such a sign, he thought of the phrase, 'the milestone on the journey to the Netherworld.'" Honda is now on his way to Nara by taxi to visit the Imperial convent Gesshōji where Ayakura Satoko, Matsugae Kiyoaki's lover six decades ago, is the presiding nun. "It seemed unreasonable for him to take the same road back again. One sign after another loomed on the road, clearly showing him the way to go. . . . 23 km to Nara. Death was pressing on him one kilometer at a time."[18]

In the last chapter Honda leaves his taxi and starts to walk the approach to the temple gate, which is of considerable distance. Mishima's description of his protagonist's struggle to reach his destination seems to begin to run even more parallel to his own.

---

Mishima, with the help of four young men, carried out his goal according to plan—almost. The first hitch came with Maj. Sawamoto Taiji, who was serving as Gen. Mashita's aide to look after his guests, when he checked to see, through a special small transom on one of the double doors to the general's office, if the guests were ready for tea. He could not see clearly, but something was awry. So he walked over to the operations office across the hall.

Col. Hara Yūichi, director of the office, came out and looked in the transom. He could not see clearly, either, but thought that the general, seated on the sofa opposite the doors, against the balcony, moved oddly. He tried to get in and found the doors locked. He threw his body against them and managed to make a crack. Someone shouted, "Don't try to come in!" Hara noticed a folded paper on the floor. He took it back to his office and read it. It was a list of demands. Unless all the demands were met, they would kill the general and Mishima would kill himself, it read.

The whole notion was preposterous. Instead of following the demands, the first and foremost of which was assemblage of all troops on the base in front of the main building by 11:30 so Mishima might give a speech, the men on hand decided to rescue the general. That day, in one of the conference rooms on the same floor, a group led by Vice Chief of Staff, Maj. Gen. Yamazaki Akira, was deliberating on administrative plans for the next fiscal year, and in another room, a group led by Lt. Col. Nakamura Nobumasa was working on year-end exercise plans.

Lt. Col. Kawabe Haruo led the first group to break in, from the chief of staff's office, which, facing the general's, was to the left. He pushed the door with his back and tumbled in. Mishima swung up his sword and wounded him on the right side of his head and the right cheek. Kawabe shouted, "Stop that!" Mishima shouted back, "Don't get in my way!" and struck at him. Kawabe raised his arm to block the blow and received a deep cut on it. Sgt. 2nd Class Kasama Juichi sustained three wounds on his right arm, including a broken ulna. Lt. Col. Nakamura jumped in and met Mishima eye-to-eye. He tried to wrest the sword with his left hand as Mishima swung it down, cutting deeply. Nakamura never completely recovered the hand's function.

After this group was successfully repelled at the door, seven more men broke in from the vice chief of staff's office, which was to the right of the general's. Maj. Gen. Yamazaki first grappled with Morita who had a dagger. Lt. Col. Takahashi Kiyoshi, who had a wooden sword, struck Morita on the right wrist, and Morita dropped his weapon. Mishima saw this and struck at Takahashi who, in blocking the blow with his wooden sword, almost lost his right thumb and received a deep cut on his right forearm. Maj. Terao Katsumi received a long slashing wound on his back and a cut on his right forearm. Col. Kiyono Fujio threw an ashtray with legs at the younger Koga who was guarding Gen. Mashita. Mishima attacked him. Stepping back, Kiyono threw a large globe at him but stumbled and fell. His right upper and lower thighs had a slash and his right shinbone was broken. As the men retreated under Mishima's menacing sword, Yamazaki received a cut on his back close to his hips.

For all the wounds he inflicted, in the end on eight men, Mishima used his sword in such a way as to minimize the damage, or so Gen. Mashita, who watched what unfolded while gagged and tied, and one of the victims, later testified. Still, Mishima's Seki no Magoroku was sharp. One stroke down an officer's back sliced his uniform about twenty inches as with a razor.

It was only after the second group failed that the officers decided to accept Mishima's demand and told Mishima that. Mishima told them to summon the troops by twelve. It was already 11.35. At 11:40, the assembly order was given through the PA system. At 11:44, Ogawa and Morita came out on the balcony, hung the cloth with the manifesto written on it, and scattered copies of its printed version to the crowd of about eight hundred people who had gathered below. Among them were Date and Tokuoka and other journalists. By then helicopters of the news media were clattering in the sky.

At twelve o'clock Mishima emerged on the balcony with Morita. Both wore a *shichishō hōkoku* headband. Mishima held a drawn sword, but he handed it to Morita before climbing the parapet to give a speech. Loud jeering and heckling started soon from among about one thousand troops assembled on the double. The noise of the helicopters was deafening as they circled back to the place. Yet Tokuoka, taking notes on the ground not far from the parapet, was surprised how loud, clear, and rhythmical Mishima's voice was. He at once sensed that Mishima had trained not just his body but his throat through kendō and body-building just for this purpose. He was also impressed by the ferocity of the hecklers. The troops' anger at Mishima having wounded their officers was real.[19]

In his speech Mishima tried to cover the main points of the manifesto: that unless the SDF effects Constitutional reform, there will be no Constitutional reform, and the SDF will forever remain part of the US military; and that, as it stands now, the SDF is unconstitutional—"all of you are unconstitutional!" Mishima thundered.

Even as he harangued the troops, shouting, pleading, Mishima was obviously concerned about the time; he occasionally checked his wristwatch. Finally, he asked: "Isn't there anyone among you fellows who will follow me?" The jeering grew ferocious. He then remained silent for a while. Then he said, the last sentence slowly: "All right, I can tell you are not rising up for Constitutional reform. I have lost my dream for the Self-Defense Forces. Well then, I will shout 'Long Live the Emperor.'" He turned toward the Imperial Palace, to the east-southeast, took a "correct sitting position," lower legs tucked under the thighs, shouted

"Long Live the Emperor" three times, and disappeared from the balcony. It was 12:10.

Mishima ducked back in the general's office through the window. As he unbuttoned his jacket and stripped naked (he had nothing underneath), he removed his wristwatch and gave it to Ogawa, saying something like "I couldn't help it" (or "I had no other way to do it"), according to Gen. Mashita. He also said, "I have nothing against you, sir. I did this to return the Self-Defense Forces to the Tennō," according to the older Koga.

Mishima quickly stepped to the opposite side of the room, turned toward the balcony, sat down correctly, and held the armor-piercer with both hands. When Morita stood behind him to his left, sword poised, Mishima shouted "Yah!" which rang out through the halls. He stabbed his left abdomen and pulled the short sword to the right. Morita swung his Seki no Magoroku down. His first stroke cut into Mishima's shoulder, his second cut his neck by half. Gen. Mashita saw Mishima's body fall forward. Morita tried two more strokes, but could not sever Mishima's head.

Koga Hiroyasu finished the job.

Morita took off his uniform and sat down. Ogawa, who was supposed to do the *kaishaku*, was guarding the front doors. The older Koga did the work. He beheaded Morita with a single stroke.

The wound Mishima made by disembowelment started 1.6 inches below his navel, 5.5 inches long from left to right, and 1.6 to 2 inches deep. Twenty inches of his intestines came out.

It was a magnificent seppuku.

# Epilogue

*Here completed is a life of arduous labor and diligence with no breathing space.*

—Takeda Taijun

*"I have yet to know what life is; how can I know what death is?"*

—Kawabata Yasunari quoting Confucius

At seven on the evening of Mishima's death, the Defense Agency had a large farewell party for Obata Hisao, who had retired five days earlier as the agency's administrative vice minister. Every one of any notable rank, Chairman of the Joint Chiefs of Staff Itaya Ryūichi on down, took part. Over the five hundred bottles of beer, of large Japanese size, readied with buffet-style food, the participants mostly gossiped about, one supposes, what had occurred at the Eastern Army Headquarters earlier that day, at the expense of the retired vice minister. Asked why the party was not postponed, the agency's director of public affairs replied: "This farewell party had been planned days before, and there's absolutely no reason something like this is affected by a *happening* like the Mishima Incident."

American-style happenings had become popular among Japanese artists.

Nagaoka Minoru, director of the Finance Ministry's secretariat, also attended a party that evening. His position was comparable to that of corporate senior vice president for personnel, and by then all the twenty-five other people who had entered the ministry with him back in late 1947 had dropped away or "descended from heaven." Nagaoka went home near midnight, slightly tipsy. Mrs. Nagaoka greeted him and told him that their two sons were still up. They wanted to know "why what happened to Mr. Mishima happened the way it did," she said.

"Mr. Mishima must have had his own thoughts," Nagaoka told his sons, ages thirteen and sixteen. "For the moment, I do not have the confidence to explain why this, why that."

Mishima's body was autopsied at the Keio University Hospital before it was returned to the Mishimas, past three on the afternoon of November 26. In accordance with his will, it was dressed in a Shield Society uniform. A sword, some of his writing paper, and his fountain pen were placed in his coffin. A private funeral was held in some haste because his body had to be taken to a crematorium before it closed. The body was incinerated a little after six.

The Seki no Magoroku Mishima used, with which Morita Masakatsu tried to behead Mishima but failed and with which Koga Hiroyasu completed the beheading and then beheaded Morita, was surrendered to the police. Later it was lost.

Mishima had specified his funeral be done in Shinto style, even as he had allowed the Hiraoka family to conduct *their* funeral for him in Buddhist style. He had also asked that the Chinese character *bu* 武, "martial," be incorporated in his posthumous Buddhist name but not *bun* 文, "literature" or "writing," because he had given up on it, he had said. But after some thought, Azusa and Shizue decided to include both. So the Buddhist priest worked out *Shōbu-in bunkan Kōi koji* 彰武院文鑑公威居士, "Martial Illuminator and Literary Mirror Layman Kimitake."[1]

The memorial service for Mishima was held at Tsukiji Honganji, on January 24, 1971. The Honganji is an old Buddhist temple that had been transformed into an Indian-style building when it was rebuilt in 1934. The flower artist Adachi Tōko designed the altar for the occasion and the "clean simplicity" she effected won wide admiration. One hundred relatives and one hundred and eighty guests attended the ceremonies. Kawabata Yasunari officiated. In his remarks, he noted that the memorial service had been delayed by two months because the Mishima family, "to put it in an old-fashioned way, confined themselves at home, by closing their gate, to keep themselves in humility." As to Mishima's death, he cited Confucian words: "I have yet to know what life is; how can I know what death is?"[2]

Hiraoka Azusa was moved and impressed, not so much by the formally attired relatives and guests that had gathered, as by the ordinary people in everyday dress who made up most of the estimated eighty-two hundred people who came to offer prayers.[3]

---

Mishima had planned to declare disbandment of the Shield Society on November 25, 1970, on the balcony, but he lost the chance to do so as a result of the *mêlée* he had not exactly expected. Kuramochi Kiyoshi learned of Mishima's decision in his letter to him—and another to the members of the Shield Society—that Yōko handed him by summoning him that night. Debate ensued within the society, but in the end the members accepted Mishima's statement in his letters that their organization cease to exist "with the uprising." On February 28, 1971, they gathered at Shintō Misogi Daikyōkai, in Nishi-Nippori, Tokyo, and Kuramochi read a "declaration" that the society had ceased to exist on the day of Mishima's death. Yōko attended the ceremony. The Shield Society is known to have held no service or ceremony related to itself or Mishima thereafter.[4]

---

The trial on "the Mishima Incident" was held in seventeen separate sessions, from March 23, 1971 to March 23, 1972. The day it opened, at the Tokyo District Court, it snowed; the day it ended, it was windy. The NHK reporter Date Munekatsu, who attended every session and chronicled the proceedings, called the first session "spring snow," the last "spring storm," in his account.

The trial was for Koga Masayoshi, Ogawa Masahiro, and Koga Hiroyasu who were indicted on "confinement leading to injury, violence, injuries, compelling performance of public duty"—this last would be "obstruction of justice by violence or threat" in US law—and "murder by agreement." But the trial necessarily focused on Mishima Yukio and his thought.

Mishima might have approved the chief judge, Kushibuchi Osamu, and the chief of the defense team his lawyer Saitō Naoichi lined up, Kusaka Asanosuke, as appropriate for "the samurai Mishima Yukio," as Date put it. Both came from families with strong samurai traditions.

Kushibuchi, who had grown up under the tutelage of his father who was a senior staff officer of the Imperial Japanese Army, was the eighteenth-generation descendant of the warrior-commander Fukushima Masanori (1561–1624) and counted among his forebears the founder of the sword–fighting school Shintō Ichiryū. Among the Kushibuchi heirlooms was a sword of Seki no Magoroku make. Kushibuchi himself practiced *suburi*, solo sword movement. He was also an amateur violinist who played a 1710 Stradivarius.

Kusaka had as much samurai blood as Kushibuchi. His great-grandfather was the founder of one branch of the sword-fighting school Munen-ryū, and his oldest brother, Ryūnosuke, the fourth-generation master of the school, became a vice admiral in the Imperial Japanese Navy, as did his paternal cousin, Jin'ichi.

The two admirals received different postwar assessments, however. Kusaka Ryūnosuke was criticized for his tactical decision not to pursue the US fleet after the initial success at Pearl Harbor. It was, critics said, based on the thinking of Munen-ryū fighting. He also won dubious fame for his action as the last chief of staff of the Combined Fleet; he ordered Vice Adm. Itō Seiichi, the commander-in-chief of the navy's "last sortie" a few months before Japan's surrender, to "die gallantly as forerunner of the one hundred million Japanese shattering themselves." The sortie ended in a destruction of three thousand lives. Yoshida Mitsuru, who survived the sortie aboard the flagship *Yamato* that sank, called it "an operation that will live in the naval annals for its recklessness and stupidity."[5]

In contrast, Kusaka Jin'ichi's reputation grew after Japan's defeat.

He insisted, for example, that all the "war crimes" his subordinates were accused of were actions derived from his orders.

Kusaka Asanosuke, at any rate, was one of the top lawyers of the day. He was a Supreme Court justice until the year before, from 1962 to 1970. For the trial of the Mishima Incident, he served as defense counsel for the first time. He foresaw the focus of the trial and lined up witnesses who could explain Mishima's actions and philosophy best. Among the evidence submitted and accepted was Emmanuel Looten's poem titled *Les Rites de l'Amour et de le Mort*. In submitting it, Mayuzumi Toshirō explained that Looten read it at a memorial service for Mishima held in Paris on June 26. The poem was reminiscent of one Harriet Monroe, founder-editor of *Poetry*, wrote upon learning of the death of Gen. Nogi Maresuke six decades earlier.[6]

In his closing argument, Kusaka cited the 1941 Supreme Court decision on the Shinpeitai Incident of 1933 in making his case for leniency. The 1941 decision had let all the defendants go free on the ground that their scheme of inciting a civil war "could not possibly be recognized as intending to illegally change the Constitution and other institutions." Interestingly, just a year earlier, in 1940, Kusaka himself had served as chief judge at the trial of the Second Shinpeitai Incident, a similar though smaller-scale rightwing plan to assassinate the then prime minister, Adm. Yonai Mitsumasa. In his decision, he found all ten conspirators guilty as charged.

---

Chief Judge Kushibuchi handed down his decision on April 27, 1972, sentencing Koga Masayoshi, Ogawa Masahiro, and Koga Hiroyasu to four years in prison minus the one hundred eighty days of detention; they had been held until July 7, 1971, when they were released because they were unlikely to jump bail or destroy evidence. The prosecution had asked for a five-year imprisonment.

Judge Kushibuchi explained he recognized that the Constitution in general and the status of the Tennō and the military in particular are subject to debate, but the "unexceptionable principle of democracy" requires that "the bases of governance be managed through discussion." The court, in any event, operates under the Constitution as it exists and is in no position to assess the right or wrong of the views of the accused.

Also, when Mishima decided to kill himself, the defendants should have done their best to stop him. Instead, "despite the fact that they are studying at the highest institutions of learning," they assisted him in that act, thereby "driving a man of great talent to death." The defendants may say that was *bushidō*, but "it is extremely doubtful if that has anything to do with true *bushidō*."

Still, "ultimately Mishima was the leader of the entire affair, and the defendants simply carried out the followers' roles." The relatives of Mishima and Morita have compensated for the harm done to the SDF officers as best they could. Furthermore, "the defendants maintained gentlemanly manners and a clear, honest attitude showing willingness to accept any judgment of law throughout the trial," which, except for their conduct in this incident, would be "a model in daily life." These were the ameliorating factors considered, the judge said.

In the news conference following the court's decision, Yōko said, "As he stated in his will to his lawyer, Mr. Saitō Naoichi, my husband had hoped we would help the three people to have a new beginning as soon as possible, and that is also what I had hoped. I have not changed my mind in that regard."

The three young men were released, in the fall of 1974; they had served two and a half years of their four-year sentences.

---

The day the decision was handed down, ten mass transit labor unions struck, immobilizing 2.5 million commuters. It was also, Date Munekatsu noted, the day five SDF soldiers tried to submit to the Director-General of the Defense Agency a letter saying they would refuse to be sent to the Okinawa Base. Okinawa was to be formally "reverted" to Japan on May 15, but at the end of March a secret agreement between the United States and Japan was exposed in the Diet that the Japanese government would take over the entire "rental" costs of all the land needed for US military facilities as a condition for reversion. In his "manifesto," Mishima had asked, "What does the Okinawa reversion mean?"

The five soldiers were subjected to disciplinary dismissal on May 4. They appealed. On July 6, 1995, that is, nearly a quarter century later, the Supreme Court handed down its decision on what had become "the 4.27

Antiwar Defense Forces Personnel Incident." The verdict: the dismissals were constitutional.[7]

---

On March 3, 1977, four armed men, including two former members of the Shield Society, barged into the head office of the powerful Japan Business Federation and took twelve employees hostage, demanding annulment of "the Yalta-Potsdam Regime." Told all four were admirers of Mishima, Yōko rushed to the JBF and helped persuade the men to release the hostages and surrender themselves.

---

Reflecting on Mishima and his death a dozen years later as he looked at the photos of the day, and marveling how "beautifully dressed he was as he stood erect on the balcony," Yashiro Seiichi could not help hearing, he wrote, the voice of his deceased actor-friend Akutagawa Hiroshi playing Macbeth, reciting the lines, in Japanese translation—

> To-morrow, and to-morrow, and to-morrow
> Creep in this petty pace from day to day
> To the last syllable of recorded time,
> And all our yesterdays have lighted fools
> The way to dusty death....[8]

In November 1985, a cenotaph made of rock ten feet high was erected for Mishima Yukio at the top of a hill west of the house where Hiraoka Sadatarō was born. Mishima may have forgotten his paternal grandfather's birthplace, but the birthplace of one of the most illustrious men the town produced did not forget his illustrious grandson.[9]

**Notes**
**Bibliography**
**Index**

# Notes

For important remarks on sources, see the headnote to the Bibliography, particularly with regard to the "complete works" published as *Mishima Yukio zenshū* (Shinchōsha, 2000–2006), which contain the principal texts of Mishima's writings used for this book. In these Notes, these volumes are identified as Zenshū, Hokan, or Bekkan, followed by volume and page numbers (e.g., Zenshū 38, 68). Source and page citations from these *zenshū* volumes are given only to Mishima's essays and such, but not to his novels, stories, and plays, with a few exceptions.

## Prologue

1  "Kagi no kakaru heya," Zenshū 19, 209–12. The short story, based on the diary-like notes Mishima had taken in those days, *may* recreate the environ best.

## Chapter One: Peasant Ancestors and Grandfather

1  Imai Seiichi, *Taishō democracy*, Nihon no rekishi series, vol. 23 (Chūō Kōron Sha, 1966), 408–9.
2  Shiba Ryōtarō, *Banshū-Nada monogatari*, vol. 1 (Kōdansha, 2004), 55.
3  "Sadatarō" can also be read "Jōtarō" and "Teitarō." Nosaka Akiyuki, *Kakuyakutaru gyakkō* (Bungei Shunjū, 1991), 241.
4  "Enshigan no tabibito," Zenshū 27, 647.
5  Terasaki Hidenari and Mariko Terasaki Miller, eds., *Shōwa Tennō dokuhakuroku* (Bungei Shunjū, 1991), 69.
6  Letter to Mitani, February 6, 1945, Zenshū 38, 909. The hours needed by train from Tokyo to Kakogawa cited earlier come from Mishima's letter to Mitani, February 11, 1945, on the same page.
7  "Watashi no isho," Zenshū 34, 153–56.
8  "Ajisai no hana," Zenshū 34, 553–57. Hiraoka Azusa, *Segare: Mishima Yukio* (Bungei Shunjū, 1996), 69.

9   Letter to Mitani, January 1, 1945, Zenshū 38, 902.
10  Andō Takeshi, *Mishima Yukio no shōgai* (Natsume Shobō, 1998), 87–88. For the call for the entire nation to die, see Hiroaki Sato's online *Japan Focus* essay, "*Gyokusai* or 'Shattering like a Jewel': Reflection on the Pacific War" (accessed July 11, 2012).
11  Letter to Mitani, February 11, 1945, Zenshū 38, 909.
12  Hiraoka, *Segare*, 70–73.
13  Ibid., 71.
14  Fukushima Jurō, *Saitei shiryō: Mishima Yukio* (Chōbunsha, 2005), 73–74.
15  The eleventh Tokugawa shogun, Ienari, is reputed to have had forty concubines and sired fifty-three or fifty-five children with them. His twenty-first daughter, Yō, was married to Maeda Nariyasu, in 1827. The extravagant gate Nariyasu built on that occasion was painted scarlet, hence the name. During the Meiji Era the Maeda mansion was placed under the jurisdiction of the Imperial University. Since then, the Akamon has been the nickname of the University of Tokyo. Kitajima Masamoto, *Bappan-sei no kumon* (Chūō Kōron Sha, 1974), 296. Hiraoka, *Segare*, 184. As to the lack of any record at the temple on the donated "red gate" and the possibility that the Akamon story was made up, see Etsugu Tomoko, *Mishima Yukio bungaku no kiseki* (Kōronsha, 1983), 77–79.
16  Fukushima, *Saitei shiryō*, 77–78. One of the oft-quoted condemnations appears to have come from Nakano Shūshūshi in the February 1971 issue of *Nōmin Bungaku*. Nakano Shūshūshi was the penname of a former reporter for the *Sankei Shinbun* who was originally from Hyōgo and had visited Mishima's domicile to write his article. Itasaka Gō, *Kyokusetsu: Mishima Yukio: Seppuku to Flamenco* (Natsume Shobō, 1997), 80–81. See also the Japanese Wikipedia entry on Hiraoka Takichi, which quotes paragraphs from the article in the August 1972 issue of the monthly *Uwasa*: http://ja.wikipedia.org/wiki/平岡太吉 (accessed July 11, 2012).
17  Etsugu, *Mishima Yukio bungaku no kiseki*, 76–80.
18  Nosaka, *Kakuyaku-taru gyakkō*, 121–25.
19  Some have cast doubt on the credibility of this line of research. The death registers or *kakochō* before the untouchable class was officially abolished contained information on class distinctions, and they are shown only to scholars with special credentials. See Itasaka, *Kyokusetsu: Mishima Yukio*, 85–94.
20  The Tokugawa government set up the Kaisei-jo, the Institute for Discovery and Fulfillment, in 1863, for foreign studies. It changed its name to Kaisei Gakkō (Kaisei School) when the regime changed to Meiji in 1868.
21  Frank Gibney, *Five Gentlemen of Japan: The Portrait of a Nation's Character* (Avon, CT: EastBridge, 2003; originally 1953), 100.
22  Fukushima, *Saitei shiryō*, 74–75.
23  *Gendai Hyōgo-ken jinbutsu-shi* (Ken'yūsha, 1911), 67. Available online from the National Diet Library http://kindai.da.ndl.go.jp/info:ndljp/pid/777760/72 (accessed July 11, 2012).
24  Nosaka, *Kakuyaku-taru gyakkō*, 167–70. Nosaka's summary account may be among the best.
25  "Takahara Kaidō cho *Kyokuhoku Nippon* jo," *Natsume Sōseki zenshū* 11

(Iwanami Shoten, 1966), 598. In *Mishima Yukio no shōgai*, 17–18, Andō Takeshi says he is tempted to speculate that Sadatarō may have been the model for Hiraoka Tsunetarō in Sōseki's 1909 fiction *Sorekara* and Yasui (with no personal name) in his 1910 fiction *Mon*. But, even if Sōseki was untruthful in saying he did not know much about Sadatarō, Sadatarō's meteoric rise in the bureaucracy and his conduct in his personal life make Andō's speculation no more than an idle fantasy. In *Sorekara*, Hiraoka Tsunetarō is the protagonist Daisuke's friend and a failed bank employee whose wife, Michiyo, becomes the object of Daisuke's passionate love. In *Mon*, Yasui is the protagonist Sōsuke's student friend who leaves Japan for Manchuria when his wife O-yone and Sōsuke fall in love with each other. This is noted here only because Andō's unthinking suggestion is cited in some references.

26   Fukushima, *Saitei shiryō*, 81–94. Fukushima quotes the July 7, 1914 editorial of the *Karafuto Nichinichi Shinbun* defending Sadatarō in its entirety.

27   Nosaka, *Kakuyaku-taru gyakkō*, 83.

## Chapter Two: Samurai Ancestors and Grandmother

1   The characters for Nagai Naomune are also read Naotada, Naotoshi, and Naoyuki.

2   George Sansom, *A History of Japan 1615–1867* (Stanford, CA: Stanford University Press, 1963), 21.

3   Tanabe Taichi (1831–1915), Naomune's contemporary diplomat, named the three vassals in his talks on Japan's diplomatic history of the period, *Bakumatsu gaikō-dan*, in 1898.

4   Naomune's grandson, Dr. Nagai Tōru's memoir. Etsugu, *Mishima Yukio bungaku no kiseki*, 103.

5   Masao Miyoshi, *As We Saw Them: The First Japanese Embassy to the United States* (Philadelphia: Paul Dry Books, 2005), 19–20.

6   Katsube Mitake, ed., *Hikawa seiwa* (Kadokawa Shoten, 1972), 380.

7   Konishi Shirō, *Kaikoku to jōi*, *Nihon no rekishi* series, vol. 19 (Chūō Kōron Sha, 1974), 130–60.

8   Ibid., 443.

9   Tsunabuchi Kenjō, *Kō: Enomoto Takeaki to gunkan Kaiyōmaru no shōgai* (Shinchōsha, 1986), 126.

10  Katsube, *Hikawa seiwa*, 173.

11  It was only five years after the Japanese had started to learn from the Dutch how to sail the oceans, and the Japanese ocean-going skills and discipline were inadequate for what proved to be the thirty-seven-day crossing of the Pacific Ocean, more than thirty days of it in stormy weather. As it happened, the USS *Fennimore Cooper* had been shipwrecked while surveying Japanese harbors and ports, and its captain, John M. Brooke, and his ten-man crew were aboard the *Kanrin Maru* to return to the US, and that helped. There was also Japan's strict class system not based on talent, knowledge, and skill that rendered the work of the Japanese crew less than ideal. In modern naval parlance, Kimura Yoshitake (Kaishū) was commander-in-chief of the ship, Katsu Rintarō (Kaishū, in different Chinese characters) captain. Brooke

regarded Kimura as embodying the worst aspects of the class system even as he thought well of Katsu, but the system so rankled Katsu that he once announced, in the midst of the Pacific, his decision to abandon the *Karin Maru* to return to Japan by one of the small boats that the ship carried, as Kimura recalled later. Katsube, *Hikawa seiwa*, 306–10. Iwamoto Yoshiharu, ed., *Kaishū zadan* (Iwanami Shoten, 1983), 244–49. Matsuzaki Kin'ichi, ed., *Fukuō jiden* (Keiō Gijuku Daigaku Shuppankai, 2009), 129–39. Miyoshi, *As We Saw Them*, 25–26.

12  Ōya Atsushi's section in the *Watashi no rirekisho* series, vol. 22 (Nihon Keizai Shinbun Sha, 1964), 417–18. Muramatsu Takeshi, *Mishima Yukio no sekai* (Shinchōsha, 1996), 23–24.

13  Sansom, *A History of Japan*, 18–21.

14  Takahashi Tomio, *Seii tai-shōgun* (Chūō Kōron Sha, 1987), 216.

15  Sansom, *A History of Japan*, 235–39.

16  The requirement that a samurai be accomplished in both literary and martial arts was codified in Article One of the first *Regulations for the Military Houses* laid down by the Tokugawa government in 1615. Ishii Shirō, ed., *Kinsei buke shisō* (Iwanami Shoten, 1974), 454. For an interpretation of *bunbu ryōdō* by an early follower of the Wang Yangming ideals, Nakae Tōju, see Hiroaki Sato, trans. and comp., *Legends of the Samurai* (New York: Overlook Press, 1995), xxii–xxiii.

17  Yamakawa Kikue, *Bakumatsu no Mito-han* (Iwanami Shoten, 1991), 324–46. Yamakawa Kikue, *Buke no josei* (Iwanami Shoten, 1990), 147–61.

18  For Nagai Naomune, see the entry for the winter recess of 1937, Zenshū 42, 45. For Matsudaira Yoriyasu, "'Matsudaira Yoriyasu den' sōsaku note," Hokan, 414–21. There Mishima gives the two Chinese characters for Naomune the reading "Naotoshi" and refers to him by his court title, *genbanokami*, "chief of temples, shrines, and diplomacy."

19  "Shinkan," Hokan, 28–33. The incomplete story is *Ryōshu* (Fief Lord), Zenshū 20, 654–56.

20  "Olympia," Zenshū 26, 76–79.

21  Actually, Taka had fourteen children but two of them died soon after birth.

22  Muramatsu, *Mishima Yukio no sekai*, 25.

23  Sadatarō's brother, Manjirō, was also married to a descendant of a high-ranking samurai. His wife, Hisa(ko), was a daughter of Sakurai Keizō, whose father was the house administrator (*karō*) of the Akashi Matsudaira fiefdom. Etsugu, *Mishima Yukio bungaku no kiseki*, 228.

24  Hiraoka, *Segare*, 34.

25  Nosaka, *Kakuyaku-taru gyakkō*, 81.

26  Ibid., 82. In US terms today, Sadatarō's debt would be $23 million relative to the US President's annual pay of $400,000. Among the products in which Sadatarō involved himself were "Japanese paper," black lead, coal in Taiwan, sugar in the South Pacific, pulp in Karafuto (successful), colonial real estate, and furs (pp. 170–71). On New Year's eve of 1919, he was arrested in Dairen (today's Dalian) on suspicion of heroin smuggling—evidently for political funds. He was released apparently because he was a former high government official. In *Mishima Yukio no shōgai*, 18, Andō Takeshi quotes fully the Tokyo

        *Nichinichi Shinbun* article reporting the arrest.
27    Hiraoka, *Segare*, 33.
28    Etsugu, *Mishima Yukio bungaku no kiseki,* 86–91.
29    Nosaka, *Kakuyaku-taru gyakkō,*, 80.
30    Andō, *Mishima Yukio no shōgai*, 31. Quoted from Kafū's *Danchō-tei nichijō*.
31    "Shinkan," Hokan, 30.
32    "Hiraoka Kimitake jiden," Zenshū 26, 420–21.
33    Hiraoka, *Segare*, 36–39.
34    Ibid., 37–38.
35    Nosaka, *Kakuyaku-taru gyakkō*, 130–31, 178–79, and elsewhere. Nosaka's speculation is worth mentioning because it created a good deal of controversy. See also Itasaka, *Kyokusetsu: Mishima Yukio*, 142–48.
36    Hiraoka, *Segare* 42. Hiraoka Shizue, "Boru no gotoku," *Gunzō* special *Nihon no sakka 18: Mishima Yukio* (Shōgakukan, 1990), 198, 204.
37    "Meiji to kanryō," Zenshū 32, 32–33.
38    Nosaka, *Kakuyaku-taru gyakkō*, 109–11, 180, and elsewhere.
39    Hiraoka, *Segare*, 33–34, 252–53.
40    Kishi Nobusuke, *Waga seishun: oitachi no ki, omoide no ki* (Kōzaidō, 1983), 190–93.
41    Kitaoka Shin'ichi, "Kishi Nobusuke," in Watanabe Akio, ed., *Sengo Nihon no saishō-tachi* (Chūō Kōron Sha, 2001), 144–49. Chalmers Johnson, *MITI and the Japanese Miracle: The Growth of Industrial Policy, 1925–1975* (Stanford, CA: Stanford University Press, 1982), 113–14.
42    Iwami Takao, *Kishi Nobusuke: Shōwa no kakumeika* (Gakuyō Shobō, 1999), 21, 53–85, and elsewhere.
43    Kōno Ichirō, *Kōno Ichirō jiden*, ed. Denki Kankō Iinkai (Tokuma Shoin, 1965), 72–74.
44    Hiraoka, "Boru no gotoku," 202.
45    John Nathan, *Mishima: A Biography* (Boston and Toronto: Little, Brown and Company, 1974), xiv–xv.
46    Hiraoka, *Segare*, 45–46.
47    Hiraoka, "Bōru no gotoku," 197.
48    Muramatsu, *Mishima Yukio no sekai*, 15–17.
49    Mitani Makoto, *Kyūyū: Mishima Yukio* (Chūō Kōron Shinsha, 1999). 167. Muramatsu, *Mishima Yukio no sekai*, 53–56.
50    "Homerareta koto," Zenshū 36, 416.
51    Hiraoka, *Segare*, 40.
52    "Waga manga," Zenshū 29, 166.
53    Nathan, *Mishima*, 30–31.
54    Hiraoka, *Segare*, 53–54.
55    "Kaidai," Zenshū 15, 696.

## Chaper Three: "The Boy Who Writes Poems"

1    Hayashi Shigeru, *Taiheiyō sensō, Nihon no rekishi* series, vol. 25 (Chūō Kōron Sha, 1967), 54. Handō Kazutoshi, ed., *Shōwa-shi tansaku 1926–1945*, vol. 4 (Chikuma Shobō, 2007), 153–54.

2     Radhabinod Pal, *Dissentient Judgment of Justice Pal* (Kokusho-Kankokai. 1999), 581. Pal was one of the eleven justices on the International Military Tribunal for the Far East but the only one versed in international law.
3     "Shina ni okeru waga guntai," Zenshū 26, 24–25.
4     Elizabeth Gray Vining, *Windows for the Crown Prince Akihito of Japan* (Japan and Rutland, VT: Charles E. Tuttle, 1989; originally 1952), 164. Then the interest in the mass killings quickly faded. Joshua A. Fogel, *The Nanjing Massacre in History and Historiography* (Berkeley: University of California Press, 2000), 12. In their 1959 history of Shōwa, *Shōwa-shi* (Iwanami Shoten), 152, Tōyama Shigeki et al. cited the figures the US journalist Edgar Snow gave in his 1941 book, *The Battle for Asia*: more than 42,000 killed during the Japanese occupation of Nanjing but more than 300,000 killed during the Japanese army's advance from Shanghai to Nanjing. Hayashi Shigeru followed suit in his *Taiheiyō sensō*, 64, without citing the source. Since the early 1970s, when the massacre again came to the fore because of the *Asahi Shinbun* journalist Honda Katsuichi's reportage from China, the assessments by historians and commentators on the numbers of Chinese soldiers and civilians killed during the rampage, which lasted four months, have varied widely, from 20,000 to 300,000. Suzuki Akira's *"Nanking dai-gyakusatsu" no maboroshi*, which was published in 1973 and won a prize, created a sensation suggesting that the massacre was a *maboroshi*, "phantom." The expanded edition of the book, *Shin "Nanking dai-gyakusatsu" no maboroshi* (Asuka Shinsha, 1999), is a strenuous attempt to ascribe to Edgar Snow the responsibility of creating the *maboroshi*—regardless, the author explains, of "whether [the massacre] occurred or not"; see p. 31. Ten years before Suzuki came out with the expanded edition of his book, however, the Kaikōsha, the association of former army officers, had compiled a documentary history of the Nanjing Battle that took into account China's official documents and concluded that the Japanese army killed 16,000 Chinese POWs and another 16,000 civilians, a total of 32,000, the number—excluding Chinese soldiers—killed in battles. See Handō Kazutoshi, *Shōwa-shi: 1926–1945* (Heibonsha, 2009), 198. As to Japanese textbooks' varying estimates of casualties in the face of Chinese and Korean protests, see Hiroaki Sato, "No Easy Answer to Textbook Controversy," *Japan Times*, Oct. 29, 2001 (online; accessed July 11, 2012).
5     Kikuchi Nobuhei, ed., *Shōwa 12 nen no Shūkan Bunshun* (Bungei Shunjū, 2007), 362–63. The title of this anthology misleads. The magazine from which the articles are drawn is not the weekly *Bunshun*, but the monthly *Hanashi*. The editor chose the title on grounds that the monthly in effect was the predecessor of the weekly.
6     "Aki ni-dai." The poem was later revised, separated into two poems, and included in two of more than a dozen books of poems Mishima compiled, each with a different title. The first part, titled "Aki," is in *HEKIGA*, Zenshū 37, 110–11; the second part, "Jakushū," in *Kodama*, Zenshū 37, 169–70.
7     Bōjō Toshitami, *Hono'o no gen'ei* (Kadokawa Shoten, 1971), 9–13.
8     After Mishima's death, there was naturally an outpouring of reminiscences published. Sakai Hiroshi's "nonliterary" recollections, published in March

1971, were among them. Andō Takeshi, *Mishima Yukio "Nichiroku"* (Michitani, 1996), 35–36. Sakai also gave a talk on the same subject at the second memorial service for Mishima, http://mishima.xii.jp/kaiso/yukokuki/2th/index.html (accessed September 1, 2012).

9   "Fuseji," Zenshū 27, 302–4. Also "*Shitei*," Zenshū 27, 41.
10  "Yokokōji," Zenshū 37, 401–2.
11  *Isshūkan shishū*, Zenshū 37, 521–39.
12  "Uchi no koneko," Zenshū 23, 37.
13  "A Certain Country" and "Aru kokudo," Zenshū 37, 319–22.
14  Mishima has left an unfinished story titled "Bōjō-haku no yaen." He obviously meant to recreate the baroque atmosphere of the grand Bōjō mansion. Zenshū 20, 652–53.
15  "Kaidai," Zenshū 19, 788–90.
16  Bōjō, *Honō no gen'ei*, 61.
17  *Shōsetsu no kamisama*—*shōsetsu*, "fiction," in this instance means not "novels" so much as "short stories." The reason Shiga won that admirable appellation, it is said, was his short story published in 1920, "The Boy's Deity" *(Kozō no kamisama)*. In the story, a shy member of the House of Peers happens to glimpse a boy unable to pay for a piece of sushi he is dying to eat. Later he goes to a dealer of scales, finds the same boy working as an apprentice, takes him out on the pretext of having him carry the scale he bought, and, after asking a sushi restaurant proprietress to allow the boy to eat as much sushi as he wants, disappears. At the end of the story, the author wonders whether or not he should end the story by turning the generous stranger into a deity for the boy but, deciding that would be "a little cruel" to him, leaves the matter open-ended.
18  Bōjō, *Honō no gen'ei*, 47. The Japanese word for "sentimental" here is *amai*. Azuma Fumihiko details his reaction to Shiga's rejection in his story "First Frost" *(Hatsushimo)*, included in *Azuma Fumihiko sakuhinshū* (Kōdansha, 2007).
19  *Fujidana no sugaru*, etc., Zenshū 37, 808.
20  "Haha o kataru," Zenshū 30, 651–52. Originally a talk. Transcript published in the October 1958 issue of *Fujin Seikatsu*.
21  "Aku no hana—kabuki," Zenshū 36, 216–17. The recording of this talk was not discovered until years after Mishima's death. When it was, it was transcribed and published under the title given here.
22  "Watashi no henreki jidai," Zenshū 32, 306.
23  Yuasa Atsuko, *Roy to Kyōko* (Chūō Kōron Sha, 1984), 114. Yuasa wrote essays on some parts of her life in *Fujin Kōron*. When they were gathered in a book, she deleted the reference to "incest" in her essay on Mishima. The original description is quoted by Yashiro Seiichi in his *Kishu-tachi no seishun: ano koro no Katō Michio, Mishima Yukio, Akutagawa Hiroshi* (Shinchōsha, 1985), 68.
24  Katō Shūichi, *Nihon bungaku-shi josetsu*, ge (Chikuma Shobō, 1991), 341. Yoshida Seiichi, "Kaisetsu," Izumi Kyōka, *Uta andon, Kōya hijiri* (Shinchōsha, 2003), 279.
25  "Ajisai," Zenshū 26, 44–50.
26  "Ajisai no haha," Zenshū 34, 553.

27  Hiraoka, *Segare*, 56–57, 62, 84. "Haha o kataru," Zenshū 30, 653–54.
28  Nosaka, *Kakuyaku-taru gyakkō*, 111–15. Nosaka does not directly name Mume's sons, Yoshiaki and Shigeru, only saying they were Mume's second and third sons.
29  Hiraoka, *Segare*, 110.
30  Ōuchi Tsutomu, *Fascism e no michi*, Nihon no rekishi series, vol. 24 (Chūō Kōron Sha, 1967), 226–28.
31  Hiromatsu Wataru, *"Kindai no chōkoku" ron* (Kōdansha, 1989), 126–39, Hiromatsu quotes extensively from Sano and Nabeyama's joint statement in discussing the phenomenon of *tenkō*, "recanting." Oketani Hideaki also discusses it in *Shōwa seishin-shi* (Bungei Shunjū, 1996), 119–24. See also Rikki Kersten, "The Emperor and the Left in Interwar Japan," *The Emperors of Modern Japan*, ed. Ben-Ami Shillony (Leiden, Netherlands, and Boston, Brill: 2008), 107–36. After recanting, many ended up supporting Japan's imperialist causes. For an interpretation of why they did so, see Katō, *Nihon bungaku-shi josetsu*, 458–59.
32  "Haji," Zenshū 28, 198.
33  Mitani, *Kyūyū*, 36.
34  Ibid., 164–65.
35  *Akikaze ya* and *Akikaze ni*, Zenshū 37, 804–5. The editors of this "collected poems" volume unaccountably extracted all the haiku and tanka from Mishima's books of poems where they exist with poems in other forms and placed them in a single section. Hokan gathers together a good many other haiku and tanka, 193–96.
36  "Nagai Einosuke-shi cho *Uguisu* o yomite" and "Tanizaki Jun'ichirō-shi cho *Yoshino kuzu* dokugokan," Zenshū 26, 57–69, 639–40. Nagai's story, like many others of his, dealt with the lives of the downtrodden in the Tōhoku (Northeast) region. Mishima wrote these papers probably soon after he advanced to his fourth year at the Middle Division, in April 1940.
37  "Fushin," Zenshū 37, 449. The poem is dated January 26, 1940.
38  Bōjō, *Honoʾo no gen'ei*, 70–71, 81.
39  "*Waga shishunki*," Zenshū 29, 342–46.

## Chapter Four: Literary Correspondents

1  Matsumoto Tōru, ed., *Nenpyō Sakka Tokuhon: Mishima Yukio* (Kawade Shobō Shinsha, 1998), end of 1940. This chronology is unpaged. Hereafter referred to as *Tokuhon*.
2  Kane, one of Natsuko's five sisters, was married to Isozaki Seikichi, who attained that title as an engineer. Born in 1877, he was sixty-three in 1940 when Mishima wrote the story. One of Natsuko's brothers, Sōkichi, was a commander in the navy.
3  "Kaidai," Zenshū 15, 702.
4  "Azuma Takashi kei o kokusu" and "Azuma Takashi chōshi," Zenshū 26, 406–13.
5  Tomioka Kōichirō, ed., *Mishima Yukio: jūdai shokanshū*, (Shinchōsha, 1999). Twenty-one of these letters had appeared in the July 1988 issue of *Shinchō*, as

Tomioka points out in his afterword. Yamaoka Yorihiro, "Azuma Fumihiko to iu bōken," in *Azuma Fumihiko sakuhinshū* (Kōdansha, 2007), 393–94.
6   Letter to Shimizu, March 5, 1942, Zenshū 38, 547–48.
7   "Dōwa zanmai," Zenshū 26, 53.
8   Satō Sōnosuke, "Jūsannendo no shishū," *Kōhon: Miyazawa Kenji zenshū*, vol. 14 (Chikuma Shobō, 1982), 1082.
9   Letter to Azuma, February 24, 1941, Zenshū 38, 59.
10  *Sept mystères du destin de l'Europeis*, by Jules Romains and translated into English as *Seven Mysteries of Europe* and briefly reviewed in *Foreign Affairs* in 1941, and *Tragédie en France*, by André Maurois and translated into English as *Tragedy in France*, were both published in 1940. The Japanese translation of the title of the latter is *France yaburetari*, "France Defeated." A commentator on a 2005 reissue of the Japanese translation notes that the original Japanese edition appeared in October 1940, just a month after Maurois's book was published. Germany's occupation of Paris occurred on June 14 that year.
11  "Kaidai," Zenshū 15, 705–6. A decade later Mishima rewrote the story by changing the narrator, though not the title.
12  Letter to Azuma, January 21, 1941, Zenshū 38, 49–50.
13  "Radiguet," Zenshū 26, 80–87. About the same time perhaps, Mishima wrote two unfinished essays: "Radiguet to sono sakuhin," of which "Radiguet" evidently is a rewrite, and "*Le Diable au corps* ni tsuite," Zenshū 36, 511–18.
14  *Hagakure nyūmon*, Zenshū 34, 475.
15  "Issatsu no hon," Zenshū 32, 624. "Waga seishun no sho," Zenshū 33, 596.
16  Okuno Takeo, *Mishima Yukio densetsu* (Shinchōsha, 1993), 103.
17  Shigeta Mariko, *Tahuho/Miraiha* (Kawada Shobō Shinsha, 1997), 25, 63. Hatori Tetsuya's "Sakka annai," Kawabata Yasunari, *Suishō gensō, Kinjū* (Kōdansha, 1992), 307.
18  "Kaisetsu," Zenshū 36, 170.
19  "Sanpūko ga happyō sareru made," in *Inagaki Taruho zenshū*, vol. 8 (Chikuma Shobō, 2001), 231. An inveterate rewriter, Inagaki later changed the title to "Utsukushiki itokenaki fujin ni hajimaru" (included in *Inagaki Taruho zenshū*, vol. 7, Chikuma Shobō, 2001), a phrase that appears in Mori Ōgai's translation of *Faust*. The eight stories in the original selection were dispersed into three volumes of the twelve-volume zenshū: 1, 3, and 7.
20  Letter to Azuma, November 16, 1941, Zenshū 38, 101–2.
21  "Favorite," *Inagaki Taruho zenshū*, vol. 3 (Chikuma Shobō, 2000), 177–78.
22  Letter to Azuma, December 29, 1941, Zenshū 38, 109.
23  *Azuma Fumihiko sakuhinshū*, 55.
24  There is a chronological discrepancy between Mishima and Azuma on this story. Azuma noted that he completed *Winterscape* in November 1942, a year after Mishima's letter. The chronology attached to a collection of his writings, with Mishima's foreword, more or less follows Azuma's dating and notes that Azuma wrote the story "from November to December" 1942. It adds that, with Muro'o Saisei's compliments, the story was published in the February 1943 issue of *Mita Bungaku*. *Azuma Fumihiko sakuhinshū*, 55, 413. In the letter discussed here Mishima congratulates Azuma on the news that his story has been accepted by *Mita Bungaku* with Saisei's high praise. Zenshū 38, 109–10.

25   Shimizu Fumio, "*Hanazakari no mori* o megutte," geppō, *Mishima Yukio zenshū* (first series), vol. 1 (Shinchōsha, 1975).
26   See Chapter Sixteen: "The 2.26 Incident, *Yūkoku*."
27   Odakane Jirō, *Hasuda Zenmei to sono shi* (Chikuma Shobō, 1970), 148 (statement of purpose), 140 (Hasuda's diary of February 17, 1938), and 476–83 (Moto'ori Norinaga).
28   Uiyamabumi.
29   Simon Winchester, *The Meaning of Everything: The Story of the Oxford English Dictionary* (Oxford: Oxford University Press, 2003), 29.
30   Handō, *Shōwa-shi tansaku 1926–1945*, vol. 6 (Chikuma Shobō, 2007), 384.
31   Nakamura Yukihiko, ed. and annot., *Ueda Akinari shū* (Iwanami Shoten, 1959), 312.
32   Odakane, *Hasuda Zenmei*, 508–19. For Mishima's thoughts on the Niwa incident, "Taidan: Ningen to Bungaku," Zenshū 40, 151–53.
33   Odakane, *Hasuda Zenmei*, 5–7, 578–87. Odakane, after interviewing those who were involved with Hasuda, emphasized that Hasuda's action was partly because of the suspicion that Nakajō was Korean. A later writer ascertained that Nakajō was not, but even if he was, there were a number of Korean officers in the Japanese Army, including a lieutenant general.
34   Shimizu Fumio, "Mishima Yukio no koto," *Gunzō* special *Nihon no sakka 18: Mishima Yukio* (Shōgakukan, 1990), 76. Odakane, *Hasuda Zenmei*, 593–94.
35   Odakane, *Hasuda Zenmei*, 464.
36   Letter to Azuma, July 24, 1941, Zenshū 38, 81. Also, Zenshū 15, 707. For some reason, Horiguchi translated the title of the poem not as *rufuran*, "refrains," but as *shanson*, "chanson."
37   Horiguchi Daigaku, *Gekka no ichigun* (Shinchōsha, 1955), 125–26. In his translation, Horiguchi changed the title from "Refrains" to "Chanson." Mishima used the second stanza as the epigraph to his story.
38   "*Hanazakari no mori, Yūkoku* kaisetsu," Zenshū 35, 173.
39   Odakane, *Hasuda Zenmei*, 9–20.
40   This is more or less Shimizu's recollection. Mishima himself has left different accounts, saying in one that it was largely his own devising and in another that he worked out the Yukio part with Shimizu. He liked *Man'yōshū*-style tanka and admired the tanka poet Itō Sachio (1864–1913), so they suggested Yukio as sounding alike, etc. "Man'yō-chō ga sukide—watashi no pen-name," Hokan, 156–57. In that brief essay, written for the weekly *Mainichi*, he suggests that the name sounded "sissy" and he was "embarrassed" by it. See also "Atogaki" to the 6-volume *Mishima Yukio sakuhinshū*, Zenshū 28, 114–15. His father Azusa's account is very different. Hiraoka, *Segare*, 94–96. Azuma's father, Suehiko, a noted scholar of law and a publisher, thought that Mishima was inspired by the name Yukiko, a character in one of his son's stories. *Azuma Fumihiko sakuhinshū*, 396.
41   Shimizu, "*Hanazakari no mori* o megutte."
42   "Kamunagara no michi" and "Radiguet," Zenshū 26, 88–90 and 80–87.
43   Letter to Azuma, November 10, 1941, Zenshū 38, 100.
44   Hiroaki Sato, "Repercussions of War Gone Bad," *Japan Times*, January 25, 2009.

45 Hayashi, *Taiheiyō sensō*, 122–24, 234–36.
46 Letter to Azuma, January 7, 1942, Zenshū 38, 111.
47 *Kaisen no shōsho* can be found at http://homepage1.nifty.com/sira/war/index.html (accessed July 11, 2012).
48 "Taishō," Zenshū 37, 708–9. The two Chinese characters for the word are also read *Ō-mikotonori*.
49 Odakane, *Hasuda Zenmei*, 470 (Itō's *Taishō*), 486–87 (*Haru no yuki*), and 504–5.
50 Letter to Azuma, February 16, 1942, Zenshū 38, 116.
51 *Karafuto Nichinichi Shinbun*, August 22, 1930, 2.
52 Letter to Azuma, February 3, 1943, Zenshū 38, 141.
53 "Shōwa 19-nen Shōgatsu," Zenshū 26, 418–19.
54 "Batsu (Bōjō Toshitami cho *Matsuei*)," Zenshū 27, 149–50.
55 Letter to Tokugawa, September 25, 1943, Zenshū 38, 704–5.
56 "*Kiken*," Zenshū 19, 619–20.

## Chapter Five: First Love

1 "Gakushūin no sotsugyōshiki," Zenshū 29, 499.
2 "Jūhassai to sanjūyonsai no shōzōga," Zenshū 31, 224.
3 Yamamoto Shichihei, *Ichi-kakyū shōkō no mita Teikoku Rikugun* (Bungei Shunjū, 1987), 29.
4 Matsumoto, *Tokuhon*, 1944 section.
5 Letter to Azusa and Shizue, January 14, 1945, Zenshū 38, 814.
6 Mitani, *Kyūyū*, 14 and 50.
7 Fuji Masaharu, *Fuji Masaharu sakuhinshū*, vol.1 (Iwanami Shoten, 1988), 404–7.
8 Letter to Azuma, September 4, 1943, Zenshū 38, 962–63.
9 Letter to Shimizu, November 14, 1943, Zenshū 38, 581.
10 The Hosei University online series: "Genron, shuppan, gakumon kenkyū ni taisuru dan'atsu," http://oohara.mt.tama.hosei.ac.jp/rn/senji2/rnsenji2-176.html (accessed July 11, 2012). Noda Untarō, *Hai no kisetsu* (Shūdōsha, 1958), 3–4.
11 Letter to Fuji, March 25, 1944, Zenshū 38, 855.
12 "*Hanazakari no mori* shuppan no koro," Zenshū 30, 285.
13 "Watashi no henreki jidai," Zenshū 32, 278.
14 Okuno, *Mishima Yukio densetsu*, 131–32.
15 *Karafuto Nichinichi Shinbun*, August 22, 1930.
16 "Kaidai," Zenshū 15, 708–9.
17 Shōno Junzō et al., eds., *Itō Shizuo, Tachihara Michizō, Maruyama Kaoru* (Shinchōsha, 1968), 23, 112.
18 Letter to Shimizu, November 4, 1943, Zenshū 38, 581–82.
19 Odakane, *Hasuda Zenmei*, 506–7.
20 Odakane Jirō, *Shijin, sono shōgai to unmei: shokan to sakuhin kara mita Itō Shizuo* (Shinchōsha, 1965), 725–26.
21 Itō Shizuo, *Itō Shizuo zenshū*, 312–314. Mishima's foreword to *Hasuda Zenmei to sono shi*, Zenshū 36, 60–63.

22  "Itō Shizuo-shi o itamu." Zenshū 28, 138–39.
23  "Batsu ni kaete." Zenshū 26, 441. "Itō Shizuo-shi o itamu." Zenshū 28, 138–39.
24  "Waga aishōgin," Zenshū 36, 649.
25  Letter to Shimizu, August 25, 1944, Zenshū 38, 594.
26  Hayashi, *Taiheiyō sensō*, 354.
27  Ibid., 327–35, 417–24. Iwami, *Kishi Nobusuke*, 84–85. 156–57. This made Kishi suspect that he might be assassinated. The commander of the Tokyo Kenpeitai indeed came to threaten him, but Kishi managed to repel him.
28  Mitani Takanobu, *Kaisōroku* (Chūō Kōron Sha, 1999), 37, 75–79.
29  Liza Dalby, *Kimono: Fashioning Culture* (New Haven, CT: Yale University Press, 1993), 131 and elsewhere. The collection of descriptions of daily life during the war by ordinary people, *Sensō-chū no kurashi no kiroku* (Kurashi no Techō Sha, 1979), has photos and descriptions of *monpe*, 20–21.
30  *Waga shishunki*, Zenshū 29, 370.
31  "Musuko no bunsai," etc., Zenshū 39, 131. It is a threesome discussion between Mishima, Shizue, and Tamura Akiko, an actress-director of the Bungaku-za.
32  Mitani, *Kyūyū*, 162.
33  Hiraoka, *Segare*, 87.
34  "Hanazakari no mori no koro," Zenshū 34, 616–17.
35  Letter to Azuma, March 15, 1942. Zenshū 38, 959.
36  Both letter and article are included in F. D. Dickins's biography, *The Life of Sir Harry Parkes, Sometime Her Majesty's Minister to China and Japan* (London: Macmillan, 1894). See the translation by Takanashi Kenkichi, *Parkes den* (Heibonsha, 1984), 84–92.
37  Mishima spelled it in his notes for the story, *Zirkus*.
38  Letter to Azuma, July 29, 1943, Zenshū 38, 169–70.
39  Paul Kahn, adapt., *The Secret History of the Mongols: The Origin of Chingis Khan* (Cheng and Tsui Company, 1998), 11–12.
40  Mishima reading "Circus" and other works on cassette tape (Shinchōsha, 1988).
41  Noda Utarō, *Hai no kisetsu* (Shūdōsha, 1958), 117, 136–38, 227–31. As to when Noda initially conveyed Mishima's wishes to Kawabata, see Kawabata Yasunari, Mishima Yukio, *Ōfuku shokan* (Shinchōsha, 2000; originally 1977), 211–12.
42  The letters between Kawabata and Mishima are assembled in Kawabata Yasunari, Mishima Yukio, *Ōfuku shokan*. Mishima's letters to Kawabata are also included in Zenshū 38. Some of Mishima's early letters to Kawabata and all of Kawabata's letters to Mishima are included in *Kawabata Yasunari zenshū hokan 2: Shokan raikan shō, nikki, techō, note* (Shinchōsha, 1984).
43  "Kūshū no ki," Zenshū 26, 515–18.
44  Hiraoka, *Segare*, 111. Also, Mishima's letter to parents on January 29, 1945, Zenshū 38, 827–28.
45  Muramatsu, *Mishima Yukio no sekai*, 63.
46  Mitani, *Kyūyū*, 15–16.
47  "Baldassare no shi," Zenshū 26, 578–79.
48  Marcel Proust, *Pleasures and Days,* trans. Andrew Brown (Hesperus Press, 2004), 14.

49  Letter to Mitani and letter to Azusa and Shizue, January 20, 1945, Zenshū 38, 905 and 818–19.
50  Okuno, *Mishima Yukio densetsu*, 137.
51  The Brothers Čapek, *R.U.R. and The Insect Play* (Oxford: Oxford University Press, 1961). The description of the brothers comes from the back cover of this edition.
52  "Shōwa 19-nen Shōgatsu," Zenshū 26, 618–19.
53  Letter to Mitani, January 6, 1945, Zenshū 38, 903.
54  Alan Tansman, "Bridges to Nowhere: Yasuda Yojūrō's Language of Violence and Desire," *Harvard Journal of Asiatic Studies*, vol. 56, no.1., June 1996, 69.
55  Konishi Jin'ichi, *Nihon bungei-shi*, vol. 5, (Kōdansha, 1985–1992), 841.
56  Robert Wargo, *The Logic of Nothingness: A Study of Nishida Kitarō* (Honolulu: University of Hawaii Press, 2005), 1–7.
57  Quoted in Oketani Hideaki, *Shōwa seishin-shi: sengo-hen* (Bungei Shunjū, 2003), 344. For Tansman's partial translation, see "Bridges to Nowhere," 38.
58  Konishi, *Nihon bungei-shi*, 840.
59  Hiromatsu, *"Kindai no chōkoku" ron*, 181.
60  Oketani, *Shōwa seishin-shi*, 150–52.
61  "Kakekotoba," Zenshū 26, 380–83. The essay was published in the November 1943 issue of *Bungei Bunka*.
62  "Watashi no henreki jidai," Zenshū 32, 274–75.
63  The quoted words are of Gen. Curtis LeMay, who, with Robert McNamara, planned and executed the incineration of Japan; these words are cited in many places. The figures are from the Tokyo air raid survivor Saotome Katsumoto's reconstruction of the raid in *Tokyo dai-kūshū* (Iwanami Shoten, 1971),183–90. For a brief account of the raid, see Ronald H. Spector, *Eagle against the Sun: The American War with Japan* (New York: Free Press, 1985), 504–5. For Mary McCarthy, see Kai Bird and Lawrence Lifschultz, *Hiroshima's Shadow* (Branford, CT: Pamphleteer's Press, 1998), 303. It took fifty-seven years for Saotome and others to create a museum to commemorate the disaster, The Center of the Tokyo Raids and War Damage. See also Hiroaki Sato, "Great Tokyo Air Raid Was a War Crime," *Japan Times*, September 30, 2002 (online; accessed July 11, 2012).
64  Mitani, *Kyūyū*, 63. The account here blends what Mitani says in his book and what Mishima says in *Confessions* and *My Puberty*.
65  Saotome, *Tokyo Dai-kūshū*, 191–212.

## Chapter Six: The War and Its Aftermath

1  Inose Naoki, *Shōwa 16-nen natsu no haisen* (Chūō Kōron Sha, 2010; originally 1983). The title of the book, which is devoted to the Total War Research Institute (Sōryokusen Kenkyūsho), says that the war had been lost even before it started. Terasaki and Miller, *Shōwa Tennō dokuhakuroku*, 246–48.
2  Hayashi, *Taiheiyō sensō*, 378–79.
3  Ishihara Kanji, *Sensō-shi taikan*, (Chūō Kōron Shinsha, 2002), 30. Tsunoda Fusako, *Amakasu tai'i* (Chikuma Shobō, 2005), 302–6. Aoe Shunjirō, *Ishihara Kanji* (Chūō Kōron Shinsha, 1992), 440–41.

4   Nakano's "*Senji saishō-ron*" can be found (with Japanese encoding) at http://www.sal.tohoku.ac.jp/~kirihara/senji.html (accessed July 11, 2012).
5   Kihira Teiko, *Chichi to ko no Shōwa hishi* (Kawade Shobō Shinsha, 2004), 144–54.
6   *Nichibei shōtotsu no hisshi to kokumin no kakugo* (Keibunkan, 1921). The 128-page book probably was an extended version of one of Uesugi's speeches. Three years earlier, Uesugi had published a much larger book titled *Nihonjin no dai-shimei to shin-kiun*, "The great mission for the Japanese and a new opportunity." He was a demigod among rightwingers.
7   Ōmori Yoshitarō, "Hito to shite no Minobe Tatsukichi hakushi," Handō Kazutoshi, ed.,*"Bungei Shunjū" ni miru shōwa-shi*, vol. 1 (Bungei Shunjū, 1995), 297. The Marxist scholar-journalist Ōmori's article was originally published in 1935.
8   Parabellum was the penname of the German author Ferdinand Heinrich Grautoff. The book published in the US was a translation. The July 12, 1908 review in the *New York Times* was titled "Banzai—How Japan Fought the U.S.—and Lost."
9   The General Staff devised this measure, which Ōnishi himself called *gedō*, "something outside the command structure, heretical," Ōnishi was opposed to the idea of going to war with the United States." Handō, *Shōwa-shi tansaku 1926–1945*, vol. 6 385, 398, 412. In *Nobility of Failure* (New York: Holt, Rinehart and Winston, 1975), Ivan Morris devotes a whole chapter to the subject, in "The Kamikaze Fighters." He dedicated the book to Mishima Yukio.
10  The five-syllable phrase *kamikaze no (kamukaze no)* was originally an epithet that modified Ise, the region typhoons frequently visit. Ise is where the most important shrine was built.
11  Handō, *Shōwa-shi tansaku 1926–1945*, vol. 6, 405. Ugaki Matome, *Sensōroku* (Hara Shobō, 1968), 126–36.
12  Hiromatsu, *"Kindai no chōkoku" ron*, 17–19. Nakamura Mitsuo, *Nihon no kindai* (Bungei Shunjū, 1968), 9.
13  The short essay is partially quoted in Noda, *Hai no kisetsu*, 114–15. Yokomitsu wrote it at the request of the all-powerful Information Bureau (Jōhō-kyoku) that planned to publish a propaganda magazine for the Chinese.
14  Letter of Mitani, April 21, 1945. Zenshū 38, 917–18. Mitani, *Kyūyū*, 92–93.
15  "Shōwa 20-nen 8-gatsu no kinen ni," Zenshū 26, 551–59.
16  Letter to Shimizu, June 18, 1943, Zenshū 38, 574.
17  By private correspondence.
18  "Watashi no henreki jidai," Zenshū 32, 279.
19  Yamamoto Shichihei,*Aru ijō taikensha no henken* (Bungei Shunjū,1988),79–80. This story is worth citing if only because Yamamoto, who served the war as a lieutenant in an artillery unit, was among the most skeptical writers on the war.
20  There is a problem with this poem. It may well have been a concoction. Wakabayashi Tōichi wrote poems, one of them even set to music, but his writings assembled for a memorial volume by a group of survivors half a century after his death do not include it or make any reference to it. So who wrote the

poem? Probably the makers of the film on the soldier. But, whether it was in fact written for the film is well nigh impossible to ascertain today. The script, by Yasumi Toshio, was apparently lost. The movie itself was confiscated by the Occupation, and by the time it was returned to Japan by agreement between the Library of Congress and the National Museum of Modern Art, Tokyo, in 1967, only 8 minutes of the original 92 remained. The remaining portion does not have anything like a poem like this. Private correspondence from Nagasaka Toshihisa, who saw the movie at the National Film Center.

21  Letter to Noda, September 2, 1945, Zenshū 38, 756.
22  Letter to Mitani, August 22, 1945, Zenshū 38, 921.
23  Mitani, *Kyūyū*, 112–14. The word Mishima used for "universalization" is *sekaika*, not the English-Japanese hybrid *gurōbaru-ka* that came to dominate the discussions of the world economy in the last part of the twentieth-century. Nor was it "internationalization" or *kokusaika* that became Japan's national slogan not long after his death.
24  Letter to Shimizu, May 2, 1944, Zenshū 38, 588–89. "Genjū-an no ki," Miyamoto Saburō et al., eds., *Bashō bunshū* (Iwanami Shoten, 1959), 189.
25  Sakamoto Tarō et al., eds. *Nihon shoki*, ge (Iwanami Shoten, 1965), 181.
26  *Nagoya Times* interview with Mishima on *Suzaku*, Zenshū 24, 725–26.
27  "Sengo goroku," Zenshū 26, 560.
28  "8 gatsu 15 nichi zengo," Zenshū 28, 526.
29  Shiga Naoya, "Kokugo mondai," published in the April 1946 issue of *Kaizō*. The short essay begins by recalling Japan's first consul to the US Mori Arinori's famous advocacy of abandoning Japanese in favor of English: *Shiga Naoya no Nihongo haishi-ron*. It may be read online.
30  Letter to Mitani, October 5, 1945, Zenshū 38, 922–23. Mitani, *Kyūyū*, 124–27.
31  Among recent books, John Dower's *Embracing Defeat: Japan in the Wake of World War II* (New York: W. W. Norton, 1999), 123–32, gives the most detailed account of what the Japanese government did. See also Handō Kazutoshi's *Shōwa-shi: sengo-hen, 1945–1980* (Heibonsha, 2009), 19–21. Unaccountably, Rōyama Masamichi practically skips the subject in *Yomigaeru Nihon*, 40–41. Rōyama's treatment sharply contrasts with Konishi in *Kaikoku to jōi, Nihon no rekishi*, vol. 19, 93–96, where he gives a detailed account of the women provided to some of the first Americans, including Consul Townsend Harris.
32  "Shūmatsu-kan kara no shuppatsu—Shōwa 20-nen no jigazō," Zenshū 28, 516. "Hachigatu jūgonichi zengo," Zenshū 28, 527. Letter to Shimizu, August 16, 1945, Zenshū 38, 604.
33  "Shūmatsu-kan," 517. Hiraoka, *Segare*, 79–80. Kihira, *Chichi to ko no Shōwa hishi*, 214.
34  Muramatsu, *Mishima Yukio no sekai*, 134. "Shūmatsu-kan," 516.
35  *Shibai nikki*, Zenshū 26, 94–264.
36  The renaming had occurred on September 22. James R. Brandon, "Myth and Reality: A Story of Kabuki during American Censorship, 1945–1949," *Asian Theatre Journal* 23.1 (2006), 1–110, footnote 37 (online). Shirō Okamoto, *The Man Who Saved Kabuki: Faubion Bowers and Theatre Censorship in Occupied Japan*, trans. and adapt. Samuel L. Leiter (Honolulu: University of Hawaii, 2001), 66.

37  October 4, *Shibai nikki*, 180–81.
38  Okamoto, *The Man Who Saved Kabuki*, 52–54, 149.
39  Ibid., 72. The translation is based on the original interview.
40  *Shibai nikki*, Zenshū 26, 211.
41  Mitani, *Kyūyū*, 151.
42  "Gūkan," Zenshū 36, 548.
43  The official and legal "titles" of the rescript are both long. The text is online, in the National Diet Library website, where the page of the *Kanpō* (government register) that prints it is shown. It can also be read in such books as Kanda Fuhito and Kobayashi Hideo, eds., *Sengo-shi nenpyō: 1945–2005* (Shōgakukan, 2005), 172–73, and Tsurumi Shunsuke and Nakagawa Roppei, eds., *Tennō hyakuwa*, ge (Chikuma Shobō, 1989), 192–94.
44  George Sansom in *The Western World and Japan* (New York: Knopf, 1949), 318. "For an important charter of this character the oath is remarkably vague," Sansom observed, and went on to provide two entirely different translations to discuss it.
45  Ben-Ami Shillony, *Enigma of the Emperors: Sacred Subservience in Japanese History* (Folkestone, Kent: Global Oriental, 2005), 205. Henderson, who taught at Columbia University before and after the war, evidently told Wilhelmus Creemers about his role when Creemers was doing research to write his doctoral thesis at Columbia, "State Shinto After World War II: 1945–1965" (1966). Theodore McNelly, "The Role of Monarchy in the Political Modernization of Japan," *Comparative Politics*, vol. 1, no. 3. (April 1969), 373–74. Also, Dower, *Embracing Defeat*, 308–14. Judging from other accounts, such as the one by the then Minister of Education Maeda Tamon, R. H. Blyth played the pivotal conduit's role. Tsurumi and Nakagawa, *Tennō hyakuwa, ge no bu*, 192–224. Both Henderson and Blyth would go on to play seminal roles in the understanding of haiku in the United States and elsewhere.
46  George Sansom, *A History of Japan to 1334* (London: Cresset Press, 1958), 25–26.
47  Orikuchi Shinobu, "Ōmubematsuri no hongi," included in *Kodai kenkyū*, vol. 2 (Chūō Kōron Sha, 2003), 128. The lecture was originally given in 1928. See also "Shintō ni arawareta minzoku ishiki" in the same volume. It was given in the same year.
48  Tsurumi and Nakagawa, *Tennō hyakuwa, ge no bu*, 644–46.
49  Ōuchi, *Fascism e no michi*, 378–83. For Ohara and Minobe, see Frank O. Miller, *Mitobe Tatsukichi: Interpreter of Constitutionalism in Japan* (Berkeley: University of California Press, 1965), 220–44. For the Shōwa Emperor's view and knowledge of the theory of the Tennō as a state organ, see the journalist Takamiya Tahei's detailed account of the matter, "Tennō kikan-setsu to Heika no senken," in Handō, *Shōwa-shi tansaku: 1926–45*, vol. 3, 134–60.
50  Terasaki and Miller, *Shōwa Tennō dokuhakuroku*, 30–31.

## Chapter Seven: To Be a Bureaucrat or a Writer

1  The Japanese word *taidan* will be retained throughout this book. One of Mishima's early editors explained why taidan (dialogues) and *zadankai*

(group discussions) are popular in Japan: they elicit multifaceted opinions on a single topic; elicit honest opinions coming out unexpectedly; produce unexpected results from a combination of participants and topics; are easy for the reader; and impose less burden on the writer's time and energy and less financial burden on the publisher than the solicited manuscript. Kimura Tokuzō, *Bungei henshūsha: sono kyō'on* (TBS Britannica, 1982), 212–13.

2  "Taidan: Ningen to bungaku," Zenshū 40, 73–74. This taidan was conducted in July 1967. Here the minus figure given is "120."

3  Yoshida Nagahiro, "Mishima Yukio shoki sakuhin no mondai," Toshokan Forum, No. 5, 2000. Can be found online (with Japanese encoding) at http://web.lib.kansai-u.ac.jp/library/about/lib_pub/forum/2000_vol5/2000_5_3.pdf (accessed on July 11, 2012).

4  "Watashi no henreki jidai," 283.

5  Kojima Chikako, *Mishima Yukio to Dan Kazuo* (Kōsōsha, 1989), 49–50. Letter of January 9, 1946, also quoted in Andō, *"Nichiroku,"* 86–87. Not in Zenshū 38.

6  "Watashi no henreki jidai," Zenshū 32, 283–84.

7  Kawabata wrote the fictionalized account twice, first in five installments, from August 1942 to April 1947, and second, in four installments, from August 1951 to May 1954. Seidensticker translated the book as *The Master of Go*.

8  "Kawabata Yasunari inshōki," Zenshū 26, 563–66. Letter to Noda Utarō, Zenshū 38, 761.

9  Kawabata Hideko, *Kawabata Yasunari to tomo ni* (Shinchōsha, 1983), 187–89.

10  For "Yokohama jiken" and attendant torture, see Hōsei University's website, Chapter 6 of "Taiheiyō sensō-ka no rōdō undō."

11  Kon Hidemi later included the essay in *Sanchū hōrō* (Chūō Kōron Sha, 1979; originally 1954). See "Satomura-kun no koto," 109–25. Kon was lucky enough to escape Luzon, through Taiwan, back to Japan, but up to 80 percent of the Japanese soldiers and others were killed or died during the Battle of Luzon which, on the Japanese side, largely consisted of escaping enemy pursuers who relied on bombardments, bombings, and strafing. Unless Kon revised the piece later, the word that irked the American censors was not *tekigun*, "enemy military," as Kimura wrote, but *tekki*, "enemy aircraft."

12  During the London Conference to determine the legal rules for the tribunals, the Soviet delegate I. T. Nikitchenko put it most bluntly: "a person who had not acted on the part of the European Axis powers would not have committed a crime." Richard Minear, *Victors' Justice: The Tokyo War Crimes Trial* (Princeton: Princeton University Press, 1971), 93. As a result, the war crimes of the victorious nations were not considered. As US Supreme Court Justice William O. Douglas wrote, agreeing with Justice Radhabinod Pal, one of the eleven judges of the Tokyo Military Tribunal, the Tokyo Trial "did not . . . sit as a judicial tribunal. It was solely an instrument of political power" (ibid., 66). Or as the layperson Elizabeth Gray Vining, the English tutor to the then Crown Prince Akihito, put it simply, the whole setup was a legal sham. She asked: "Could a court be impartial and justice be served, when the judges were also the prosecution and the outcome of the trial was known from the beginning? Under ordinary circumstances would we consider a trial fair in

which the judge and jury were friends and relatives of the murdered man?" Vining, *Windows for the Crown Prince*, 169.
13   Kimura, *Bungei henshūsha*, 203, 217–18, 238–42.
14   "Watashi no henreki jidai," Zenshū 32, 284–87.
15   Letter to Kimura, May 4, 1946, Zenshū 38, 486.
16   Kimura, *Bungei henshūsha*, 136–61.
17   The legendary Sassa Narimasa (d. 1616 or 1639). Kihira, *Chichi to ko no Shōwa hishi*, 10–11.
18   "Dance jidai," Zenshū 27, 205–7.
19   In his autobiography, *Peeling the Onion*, Günter Grass says the same thing happened in Germany.
20   Itasaka, *Kyokusetsu: Mishima Yukio*, 25–31.
21   Sassa Teiko, "Mishima Yukio no tegami," an eighteen-part serialization in the weekly *Asahi*, from December 13, 1974, to April 11, 1975. The description of "an incident" appears in the January 31, 1975 installment; letter on Mitani Kuniko quoted in the December 27, 1974 installment.
22   Sassa Teiko, "Mishima Yukio no tegami," February 28, 1975 installment.
23   Kihira, *Chichi to ko no Shōwa hishi*, 245. Sassa Teiko became Kihira Teiko on marriage.
24   Ibid., 164.
25   "Kaidai," Zenshū 1, 680–81. The passage in *Confessions* occurs on 346–47.
26   Meredith Weatherby, trans., *Confessions of a Mask* (New York: New Directions, 1958), 233–35.
27   *Kaikei nikki*, Hokan, 522–23.
28   Minear, *Victors' Justice*, 6.
29   "Waga aisuru hitobito e no hatashijō," Zenshū 26, 631–33.
30   Inose Naoki, *Picaresque: Dazai Osamu* (Shōgakukan, 2002), 16, 376–67. Dan Kazuo thought that the word *shayō* came from the last line of the kanshi Gen. Nogi Maresuke wrote during the Russo-Japanese War: *Kinshū jōgai shayō ni tatsu*, "Outside the Jinzhou Castle I stand in the setting sun." Dan Kazuo, *Shōsetsu: Dazai Osamu* (Iwanami Shoten, 2000), 219–20. Because the word *shayō* also means (as a homophone) "at the company expense," it became a fad word as part of *shayō-zoku*, meaning those employees who made payments on the pretext that what they did was for the company.
31   *Watashi no henreki jidai*, Zenshū 32, 286–90.
32   *Shōsetuka no kyūka*, Zenshū 28, 562.
33   *Kaikei nikki*, Hokan, 538. As for the serialization of *Shayō*, see the chronology in Dazai Osamu, *Ningen shikkaku*, *Ōtō* (Kadokawa Shoten, 1989), 163.
34   Yashiro, *Kishu-tachi no seishun*, 39–44.
35   Etsugu, *Mishima Yukio bungaku no kiseki*, 151–72. Etsugu's review includes some of the comments on Mishima's assault on Dazai in the "diary" as well as a list of the participants and an interview with some of them.
36   Phyllis Lyons, *The Saga of Dazai Osamu: A Critical Study with Translations* (Stanford: Stanford University Press, 1985), 1.
37   "Kaidai," Zenshū 16, 757, 760–61.
38   "Hayashi Fusao ron," Zenshū 32, 338.
39   Letter to Hayashi, November 6, 1947, Zenshū 38, 780.

40   *Kaikei nikki*, Hokan, 623, 630.
41   "Musuko no bunsai," etc., Zenshū 39, 132.
42   Kimura, *Bungei henshūsha*, 148–50.
43   Letter to Kimura, July 24, 1946, Zenshū 38, 487–88.
44   Henry Scott-Stokes, *The Life and Death of Yukio Mishima* (New York: Farrar, Straus and Giroux, 1974), 18–19.
45   Hiraoka, *Segare*, 83, 97. Zenshū 39, 133.

## Chapter Eight: Confessions

1   Kawabata's letter of October 30, 1948, *Ōfuku shokan*, 58.
2   Letter to Sakamoto, November 2, 1943, Zenshū 38, 507.
3   "Je suis la plaie et le couteau! / Je suis le soufflet et la joue! / Je suis les membres et la roue, /Et la victime et le bourreau!" The English translation is by Michael O'Brien.
4   Letter to Kawabata, March 3, 1946, Zenshū 38, 242–46. Also, Zenshū 1, 664–65.
5   "Watashi no henreki jidai," Zenshū 32, 286–91.
6   Aeba Takao's appraisal quoted in Etsugu, *Mishima Yukio bungaku no kiseki*, 143–44.
7   Some have suggested that the day Yoshida Shōin was beheaded, 27th of Tenth Month, of the 6th year of Ansei, falls on November 25, 1859, by the solar calendar. See Hiraoka, *Segare*, 11–12. In truth, that day seems to fall on November 21. Another speculation has it that November 25 is 49 days before Mishima's birthday, January 14, and that, therefore, he intended to be reborn on his birthday according to the Buddhist idea of transmigration and rebirth that was the theme of his tetralogy, *The Sea of Fertility*. Forty-nine days is what is needed for rebirth. Nakamura Akihiko, *Resshi to yobareru otoko: Morita Masakatsu* (Bungei Shunjū, 2003), 261.
8   The German words mean: "the curious sexual life of a man" / "the curious" / "high-strung/ curious/ strange / the eccentric / unusual sexual life of a man." Courtesy of Doris Bargen.
9   "Kaidai," Zenshū 1, 677.
10  "Kaidai," Zenshū 1, 673.
11  Inose Naoki, *Magazine seishun-fu: Kawabata Yasunari to Ōya Sōichi* (Shōgakukan, 2002), 113.
12  Kawabata Yasunari, *Kawabata Yasunari zenshū hokan 1: Nikki, techō, note* (Shinchōsha, 1984), 445, 458. Sasakawa Takahira, *Kawabata Yasunari: Ōsaka Ibaraki jidai to seishun shukan-shū* (Izumi Shoin, 1991), 111–12.
13  Hatori Tetsuya, *Sakka no jiden 15: Kawabata Yasunari* (Nihon Tosho Center, 2002), 57–76, 311–12. *Shōnen* included in this volume consists of excerpts.
14  Jinzai Kiyoshi, "*Kamen no kokuhaku* hyō," *Mishima Yukio senshū*, vol. 4 (Shinchōsha, 1958), 203–6.
15  Maeda Akira's "Kaidai," Tayama Katai, *Futon, Ippeisotsu* (Iwanami Shoten, 2002; originally 1930), 140.
16  Hanada Kiyoteru, "Sei-Sebastian no kao," *Gunzō* special *Nihon no sakka 18: Mishima Yukio*, 110–17.

17 Shindō Ryōko, *Shindō Ryōko shishū* (Shichōsha, 1989), 124.
18 Kimura, *Bungei henshūsha*, 150.
19 Letter to Shikiba, July 19, 1949. Zenshū 38, 513–14. Also, Zenshū 1, 678–79. Ellis has *Sexual Inversion* and *Love and Marriage*.
20 Mochizuki Mamoru, *Sei to seikatsu* (Shisōsha, 1949), 177–79.
21 Lionel Trilling, *Liberal Imagination* (New York: Doubleday Anchor Books, 1950), 232.
22 Magnus Hirschfeld, *Sexual Anomalies: The Origins, Nature, and Treatment of Sexual Disorders* (White Plains, NY: Emerson Books, 1956), 199–200, and the Publishers' Note. This summary in English does not give the editor's name.
23 Norman Davies, *Europe* (Oxford: Oxford University Press, 1996), 876–77.
24 Muramatsu, *Mishima Yukio no sekai*, 12 and 162–64.
25 Scott-Stokes, *Life and Death of Yukio Mishima*, 6–7.
26 Muramatsu, *Mishima Yukio no sekai*, 96.
27 "Tōzoku sōsaku note," Zenshū 1, 611. "Kaidai," 661–64.
28 Letter to Ninagawa quoted in Andō, *"Nichiroku,"* 120. The letter is not included in Zenshū 38.
29 The Mishima editor Tanaka Miyoko noted that the name Matsugae Kiyoaki and the title of the novel of which he is the protagonist come from a twelfth-century song Mishima cited at age eighteen in an essay on the celebratory aspect of classical Japanese poetry. The second half of the song, as Mishima copied it, reads: *Matsugae kazashi ni sashitsureba / haru no yuki koso furikakare*, "When I dress my hair with a pine twig / it is the spring snow that flutters down on me." Tanaka Miyoko, *Mishima Yukio: Kami no kagebōshi* (Shinchōsha, 2006), 29–30. Mishima, "Kotohogi," Zenshū 26, 362. However, Mishima is likely to have made an error in copying the song; in the original, *matsugae*, "pine twig," appears as *umegae*, "plum twig." Kawaguchi Hisao and Shida Nobuyoshi, eds., *Wakan rōei shū, Ryōjin hishō* (Iwanami Shoten, 1976), 464, 472. The possibility that Mishima used a text with a variant cannot be ruled out, but the context suggests *umegae* is correct. Courtesy of Kyoko Selden.
30 Muramatsu, *Mishima Yukio no sekai*, 109–11.
31 Hiraoka, *Segare*, 227–28.
32 Muramatsu Eiko, "Saigo no enshutsu," geppō to Zenshū 26, 1–2.
33 Shindō Ryōko recalls being unsettled watching Mishima looking at the staging of another play of his. When she expressed puzzlement after the curtain, he had a perfectly legitimate reason for his reactions. *Shishū*, 123–24.
34 Romano Vulpitta's afterword is to the 1996 paperback edition of Muramatsu Takeshi's *Mishima Yukio no sekai*, 593.
35 Muramatsu's own afterword, ibid., 581.
36 Muramatsu Takeshi, *Shi no Nihon bungaku-shi* (Kadokawa Shoten, 1981), 335 and the afterword.
37 Haniya Yutaka, "Mishima Yukio," *Gunzō* special *Nihon no sakka 18: Mishima Yukio*, 75. Mishima's letter to Haniya in October 1949, Hokan, 230–31.
38 The *Yomiuri* interview, on December 9, 1949, "Nichibei gassaku no shinzen opera," Hokan, 140–41.
39 Herbert Passin, *Encounter with Japan* (Kodansha International, 1982), 183.
40 Letter to Kimura, December 16, 1949, Zenshū 38, 490–91.

41  "Dan Kazuo *Hanagatami*," *Zenshū* 26, 433–36.
42  Letter to Dan, December 16, 1949, *Zenshū* 38, 689–91.
43  Dan Kazuo, *Shōsetsu: Dazai Osamu*, 2–4. Dan's "novel" is a description of the author's association with Dazai Osamu, but Dan categorized it as a novel, rather than a biography, because it was one person's account and did not contain much objective, third-party material.

## Chapter Nine: Boyfriends, Girlfriends

1   Fukuda Tsuneari, "*Kamen no kokuhaku* ni tsuite," Mishima Yukio, *Kamen no kokuhaku* (Shinchōsha, originally 1950), 210–20.
2   Matsumoto, *Tokuhon*, entry of May 1949.
3   Yashiro, *Kishu tachi no seishun*, 94–95.
4   Ibid., 66. "Kataku ni tsuite," *Zenshū* 27, 178–80.
5   Yashiro, *Kishu tachi no seishun*, 99–108 (Chapter 7) and Chapter 11. Kimura, *Bungei henshūsha*, 160.
6   Gene Reeves, trans., *The Lotus Sutra* (Somerville, MA: Wisdom Publications, 2008), 113. Burton Watson, trans., *The Lotus Sutra* (New York: Columbia University Press, 1993), 56–57.
7   All included in *Zenshū* 21. *The Wise Men from the East* was printed in the March 1939 issue of *Hojinkai Zasshi*.
8   Letter to Azuma, January 26, 1941, *Zenshū* 38, 51.
9   "Gikyoku o kakitagaru shōsetsugaki no nōto," *Zenshū* 27, 222–29. Hofmannsthal's words are translated from the Japanese Mishima quotes.
10  Jon Livingston, Joe Moore, and Felicia Oldfather, eds., *Postwar Japan: 1945 to the Present* (New York: Pantheon, 1973), 133–38. Miyazawa Kiichi, then Ikeda's aide and later minister of finance (five times) and prime minister, described the conditions of the Japanese economy at the time Dodge came to impose his plans following his death, in 1964. "Mr. Dodge's ban'yū," Handō, *"Bungei Shunjū" ni miru Shōwa-shi*, vol. 2, 293–310. Michael Schaller, *The American Occupation of Japan: The Origins of the Cold War in Asia* (Oxford: Oxford University Press, 1985), 145.
11  The account left by Takeuchi Keisuke, one of the ten arrested, and jailed, and interrogated, shows how rampant the police and prosecutorial brutalities were at the time, besides the disheartening fact that "the defense lawyer" was in cahoots with the authorities. Even as the nine of them were acquitted, Takeuchi, evidently innocent, was sentenced to death but died in prison in 1967 before the execution.. "Oishii mono kara tabenasai," *"Bungei Shunjū" ni miru Shōwa-shi*, vol. 2, 320–40.
12  Yamazaki's testament and such are included in *Zenshū* 2, 695–99.
13  Kimura, *Bungei henshūsha*, 155–56.
14  Andō, *"Nichiroku,"* 132–33.
15  "Mukashi to ima no kakaku," *Keizai Yōran* (Keizai Kikakuchō Chōsakyoku, 1999), 8–9.
16  Nosaka, *Kakuyaku-taru gyakkō*, 18. As Nosaka notes, *kakuyaku*, "brilliant," "glittering," was one word Mishima used at the moment of his characters' death.

17 Letter to Kawabata, September 10, 1956, Zenshū 38, 271.
18 Yuasa, *Roy to Kyōko*, 106. The word for "pompom girl" is *pan-pan*, the etymology of which is debated to this day, one candidate being the Indonesian word for woman, *perempuan*. Okuyama Masurō, comp., *Kieta Nihongo jiten* (Tokyōdō Shuppan, 1993), 224 and the Wikipedia entry on the word.
19 Hashikawa Bunzō, "Mishima Yukio den," *Hashikawa Bunzō chosakushū*, vol. 1 (Chikuma Shobō, 1985), 276.
20 "Kōgen hotel," Zenshū 27, 423–27. The essay has a passage that may scandalize an American or European reader; Mishima takes a bath with the 4-year-old daughter of Mr. and Mrs. Watanabe and plays with her.
21 "Bōgetsu bōjitsu," Zenshū 27, 147–48. Characteristically, in this lighthearted, self-deprecating essay, Mishima cites Delacroix's description of Théodore Géricault in his *Journals* and refers to the Book of Revelations.
22 Shibusawa Tatsuhiko, *Mishima Yukio: Oboegaki* (Chūō Kōron Sha, 1986), 15.
23 For a complete list, see Yashiro, *Kishu-tachi no seishun*, 131.
24 For the *Asahi Shinbun* article and Mishima's essay, "Kumo no Kai hōkoku," Zenshū 27, 350–52, 714–16. See also Yashiro, *Kishu-tachi no seishun*, 132–33.
25 Yomota Inuhiko, ed., *Ōoka Shōhei: Bungaku no unmei* (Kōdansha, 1990), 57–68. Nakamura's haiku went: *Hachi no ki no moenokoritaru yosamu kana*, "With just the embers of the potted tree left, the night is cold."
26 Yuasa, *Roy to Kyōko*, 86–89.
27 *Kinjiki* refers to seven specific colors whose use was restricted to the Tennō and his immediate relatives but it appears not to be part of gay lingo. Ishii Tatsuhiko, by private correspondence.
28 Letter to Kawabata, September 10, 1956. Zenshū 38, 269–71.
29 Full sentence: "La mort, nous l'avons déjà remarqué, je crois, dans l'analyse des Confessions, nous affecte plus profondément sous le règne pompeux de l'été." Here Baudelaire is discussing Thomas De Quincey's *Confessions of an English Opium-Eater.*
30 Fukushima Jirō, *Mishima Yukio: Tsurugi to kanbeni* (Bungei Shunjū, 1998), 61–82, 103–36.
31 Letter to Kawabata cited above (note 17).
32 Helmuth Ketel (1893–1961) in *Chintao Doitsu-hei furyo kenkyūkai*, no. 0395 www.melma.com/backnumber_150772_4743420/ (accessed July 11, 2012).
33 Nosaka, *Kakuyakutaru gyakkō*, 20.
34 Ibid., 21–22.
35 Andō, *"Nichiroku,"* 134. See also Inagaki Taruho's taidan, "An Evening with Mr. E(dogawa)," which was originally published in the May 1951 issue of *Sakka*, and is included in Taruho's *Zenshū*, vol. 3 (Chikuma Shobō, 2000), 346–66.
36 Yuasa, *Roy to Kyōko*, 117–20. "Gorgeous" and "graceful" are the English words Yuasa chose. Kajima Mieko made public only one letter she received from Mishima. That was the one she had from him when she married, in 1957, and she made it public when *he* married, in 1958. Zenshū 38, 964.
37 Handō, *Shōwa-shi: 1926–1945*, 317. During the grand ceremony to celebrate the 2,600th anniversary of Japan's foundation (in A.D. 1940), Handō, then fifteen, was surprised to hear, on the radio, Prince Takamatsu offering formal

felicitations to the Tennō, ending his words with "*Shin* Nobuhito." He did not know even the Tennō's own brothers were his "subjects."

38    Kojima Tsuyoshi, *Kindai Nihon no Yōmeigaku* (Kōdansha, 2006), 173–74. Yoshida's grandson and Prime Minister Asō Tarō's book, *Yoshida Shigeru no ryūgi* (PHP Kenkyūsho, 2000). For *kokutai*, see Chapter Sixteen: "The 2.26 Incident, *Yūkoku*."

## Chapter Ten: Going Overseas

1    Letter to Kawabata, September 10, 1951. Zenshū 38, 269–71. Stanford University's online archive, "Guide to the Wallace Earle Stegner papers: concerning the Asian-American Literary Exchange, 1949–1954" (accessed July 11, 2012).

2    Hino Ashihei's "soldier trilogy" consists of *The Wheat and the Soldier (Mugi to heitai)*, which, published in August 1938, sold 1.2 million copies; *The Soil and the Soldier (Tsuchi to heitai)*, September 1938; and *The Flower and the Soldier (Hana to heitai)*, August 1939. All three were published by Kaizōsha. In 1940, Hino received the Asahi Shinbun Culture Award for the trilogy.

3    Hino Ashihei, "Yobitai ichinichi nyūtai ki," Handō, *"Bungei Shunjū" ni miru Shōwa-shi*, vol. 2, 404–22.

4    Nakano Yoshio, "Jieitai ni kansuru shikōteki teian." Nakano Yoshio, *Akunin Raisan*, ed. Anno Mitsumasa (Chikuma, 1990), 298–99.

5    Yomota, *Ōoka Shōhei*, 66.

6    *Apollo no sakazuki*, Zenshū 27, 507–641. Unless otherwise noted, episodes in this section come from this book.

7    "Enshigan no tabibito," Zenshū 27, 651–52.

8    "Radiguet ni tsukarete—watashi no dokusho henreki," Zenshū 29, 147.

9    *Apollo no sakazuki*. Zenshū 27, 529–30. The group discussion "*Salome* to sono butai." Zenshū 39, 242.

10   Letter to Kawabata, September 10, 1951, Zenshū 38, 279. Gore Vidal's own 1995 introduction to *The City and the Pillar* (New York: Vintage, 2003), xiii–xiv. Christopher Bram, *Eminent Outlaws* (New York: Twelve, 2012), 8–9. Gore Vidal, *Point to Point Navigation* (New York: Doubleday, 2006), 147.

11   Donald Richie, *The Japan Journals: 1947–2004* (Berkeley, CA: Stone Bridge Press, 2004), 46–47.

12   Donald Richie's private letter, 9 June 2004.

13   Letter to Kawabata, February 13, 1952, Zenshū 38, 272–73.

14   "Minami no hate no miyako e," Zenshū 28, 70.

15   *Apollo no sakazuki*, Zenshū 27, 567–68. The English name, "market gardening ants," is Huxley's. The description Mishima quotes, in Japanese, is likely to come from Huxley's book simply titled *Ants*, published in 1930.

16   Saeki Shōichi, *Hyōden: Mishima Yukio* (Chūō Kōron Sha, 1988; originally Shinchōsha, 1978), 183–224. Nathan, *Mishima*, 112.

17   Andō, *"Nichiroku,"* 145–46. This letter to Kamogawa is one of those that appeared in print somewhere but then were prevented from becoming more "public." It is not included in Zenshū 38.

18   "Paris ni horezu," Zenshū 27, 645–46.

19  Rand Castile, *The Way of Tea* (Tokyo and New York: John Weatherhill, 1971), 177.
20  The English quotation here is from Sir Richard Jebb's translation of *Oedipus at Colonus*. In the nietzsche.holtof.com translation, Silenus says: "What would be best for you is quite beyond your reach: not to have been born, not to be, to be *nothing*. But the second best is to die soon."
21  Joshua Foa Dienstag, "Nietzsche's Dionysian Pessimism," *American Political Science Review*, vol. 95, no. 4, December 2001, 929.
22  "*Hanjo* haiken," Zenshū 27, 659–64.
23  "Eiga *Rondo* no koto," Zenshū 27, 670–73.
24  "Jean Rossi-saku, Aoyagi Mizuho-yaku *Fukō na shuppatsu*," Zenshū 27, 676–78.
25  "Eiga *Shōjo Olivia*," Zenshū 27, 679–81.
26  "Nikutai no akuma," Zenshū 27, 697, and "Shiseru wakaki tensai Radiguet to eiga *Nikutai no akuma* ni taisuru watashi no kansatsu," Zenshū 28, 25–28.
27  Shōno Junzō, one of Itō's students at junior high school, respected his teacher's wishes and excluded the four poems Mishima named from the Shinchōsha edition he edited in 1968: *Itō Shizuo, Tachihara Michizō, Maruyama Kaoru*.
28  July 29, 1955, *Shōsetsuka no kyūka*, Zenshū 28, 637–38.
29  "Itō Shizuo," Zenshū 28, 126–29.
30  "Gendai seinen no mujun o han'ei—Hoan Daigaku," Zenshū 28, 149–53.
31  Yashiro, *Kishu-tachi no seishun*, 187–89, 193–94; also 19–23, 71–81. Akutagawa quoted, ibid., 148. Mishima, *Watashi no henreki jidai*, Zenshū 32, 309.
32  "Katō Michio-shi no koto," Zenshū 28, 535–37. See also Yashiro, *Kinshu-tachi no seishun*, 20–23.
33  Letter to Keene, July 29, 1962, Zenshū 38, 380. Yashiro's accounts vary. When he wrote about it for the first time, he appears to have specified the date (December 31, 1953) and the place (a bar on the Ginza)—see the section on the last part of 1953 in Matsumoto Tōru's *Tokuhon*—but when he assembled his recollections in a book, he was not quite certain. Yashiro, *Kishu-tachi no seishun*, 211–12. Mishima also played with Keene's name, unless of course Keene himself did. The set of characters he came up with for him in the same letter was 怒鳴門鬼韻, "Roaring Naruto's demonic trope"—Naruto being the strait between Awaji Island and Shikoku famed for its giant tidal whirlpools.

## Chapter Eleven: The Girlfriend

1  "Kamijima no omoide," Zenshū 28, 455–57. Originally written for a local publication, hence the polite language. The proper pronunciation of what Mishima called "Kamijima" may be Kamishima, though it may be depend on who is doing the pronunciation.
2  Hiraoka, *Segare*, 97–99.
3  "Jūhassai to sanjūyonsai no shōzōga," Zenshū 31, 216, 220–22. The original title for *Gunzō* was *Bungaku jiden*, "literary autobiography."
4  For the comments on *The Sound of Waves*, see Matsumoto, *Tokuhon*.
5  Yomota Inuhiko, *Nihon eiga-shi 100 nen* (Shūeisha, 2000), 132–33.
6  Mishima wrote at least a dozen articles on Kamishima and *The Sound of*

*Waves*. Most of the information in the preceding paragraphs related to Mishima is extracted from "*Shiosai* roke zuikōki," Zenshū 28, 377–83, and "Kamijima no omoide" (note 1, above).

7   Yomota, *Nihon eiga-shi 100 nen*, 134.
8   Sometimes translated as *Hell Screen*.
9   "Nakamura Shikan ron," Zenshū 27, 151–52.
10  Another name of jōruri. This came about because in the 1910s the Bunraku became the sole troupe to perform jōruri, the others having closed shop.
11  "Boku no *Jigokuhen*," Zenshū 28, 338. One of the sources of the play is "Saru-Genji sōshi," as Mishima makes clear in "*Iwashi-uri koi no hikiami* ni tsuite," Zenshū 28, 385–86. The story is included in Ichiko Teiji, ed. and annot., *Otogi sōshi* (Iwanami Shoten, 1958).
12  Liza Dalby and Nagasaka Junko by private communications.
13  "Eiga, kekkon o kataru," in Yamauchi Yukihito, ed., *Mishima Yukio eiga-ron shūsei* (Wise Shuppan, 1999) 386–95.
14  Andō, *Mishima Yukio no shōgai*, 170.
15  Minakami Tsutomu, *Kinkaku enjō* (Shichōsha, 1986; originally 1979), 243–44.
16  Nakamura Mitsuo, "*Kinkakuji* ni tsuite," Mishima Yukio, *Kinkakuji* (Shinchōsha, 1960), 306.
17  "Muromachi no bigaku—Kinkakuji," Zenshū 33, 401–2.
18  Okuno Takeo, "Kaisetsu," Ishihara Shintarō, *Taiyō no kisetsu* (Shinchōsha, 1957), 318–20.
19  July 6, *Shōsetuka no kyūka*, Zenshū 28, 576.
20  "Shinjin no kisetsu," Zenshū 39, 263.
21  "Ishihara Shintarō-shi," Zenshū 29, 201–2.
22  *Shōsetsuka no kyūka*, Zenshū 28, 578–79.
23  Letters to Gotō Sadako remain uncollected.
24  "Muromachi no bigaku—Kinkakuji," Zenshū 33, 400–402.
25  Ibid., 401–2.
26  Letter to Tamari, November 9, 1955, Zenshū 38, 686.
27  Tamari Hitoshi, geppō to Zenshū 28.
28  "Bodybiru tetsugaku," Zenshū 29, 285.
29  Yuasa, *Roy to Kyōko*, 123.
30  Okuno, *Mishima Yukio densetsu*, 337–39.
31  "Jikkanteki sports-ron," Zenshū 33, 162–65.
32  Okuno, *Mishima Yukio densetsu*, 364.
33  Yuasa, *Roy to Kyōko*, 121–27.

## Chapter Twelve: The Kinkakuji

1   "Bi no katachi," Zenshū 39, 277–97.
2   Nakamura Mitsuo, "*Kinkakuji* ni tsuite," Mishima Yukio, *Kinkakuji* (Shinchōsha, 1960), 306–7.
3   Saeki Shōichi's afterword, Mishima Yukio, *Kinkakuji* (Shinchōsha, 1960), 298–99.
4   "Atogaki," Zenshū 28, 387–89. For his program note, see Zenshū 22, 687–89.
5   Andō, *"Nichiroku,"* 167.

6 "Kaisetsu," Mishima Yukio, *Hanazakari no mori, Yūkoku* (Shinchōsha, 1967), 285.
7 Letter to Mishima, October 23, 1956, Kawabata Yasunari, Mishima Yukio, *Ōfuku shokan*, 98–99. Letter to Kawabata, November 1, 1956, Zenshū 38, 278–80. The sales figure is from Andō, *"Nichiroku,"* 198.
8 April 12, 1959. *Ratai to ishō*, Zenshū 30, 225.
9 Letter to Harold Strauss, July 30, 1955. *Kawabata Zenshū hokan*, vol. 2 (Shinchōsha, 1984), 371. The main part of Kawabata's letter had to do with the "extremely shy" William Faulkner's visit to Japan.
10 Keene's letter quoted by Mishima, March 19, 1959, *Ratai to ishō*, Zenshū 30, 215.
11 The New York dispatch quoted in full, Zenshū 29, 777–78.
12 Richie, *Japan Journals*, 148 and elsewhere. Also, Peter Grilli, e-mail of October 24, 2004.
13 Donald Keene, comp. and ed., *Modern Japanese Literature: From 1868 to Present Day* (New York: Grove Press, 1956), 429–38.
14 *Ratai to ishō*, Zenshū 30, 149–51.
15 Yamamoto's comment quoted in *Tokuhon*. Ishii Tatsuhiko, "Rokumeikan," *Kokubungaku*, July 1986 (Mishima special), 94.
16 James Legge, trans., *The She King; The Book of Ancient Poetry* (Trübner and Co., 1876), 190.
17 "Kaidai," Zenshū 22, 656–57, 659–61.
18 Tomita Hitoshi, *Rokumeikan—gi-Seiyōka no sekai* (Hakusuisha, 1984), 224–27.
19 "Rokumeikan no koto domo," Zenshū 37, 807–8.
20 Kuno Akiko, *Rokumeikan no kifujin: Ōyama Sutematsu* (Chūō Kōron Sha, 1993), 204. Ōyama Sutematsu, the author Kuno's great grandmother, spent ten years in the US, from 1871 to 1881, and attended Vassar. She was unusually long-legged for a Japanese woman of the day, Kuno writes.
21 Claude Schumacher, ed., *Victor Hugo: Four Plays* (Methuen, 2004), xxxii. Lucretia's cry in Richard J. Hand's translation., ibid., 286.
22 Muramatsu, *Mishima Yukio no sekai*, 362.
23 Comments on *The Rokumeikan* are in "'Rokumeikan' ni tsuite" (three essays with the same title) and "Gakuya de kakareta engekiron," Zenshū 29, 288, 326–27, 334–45, 419–31.
24 "Hidari no hiza no chiisana kizuato," Zenshū 29, 423–24.
25 "Kame wa usagi ni oitsuku ka—iwayuru kōshinkoku no sho-mondai," Zenshū 29, 278.
26 Letter to Kawabata, November 1, 1956, Zenshū 38, 279–80.
27 "Shōsetsu to wa nani ka," Zenshū 34, 735.
28 NHK morning interview on January 26, 1958. Zenshū 30, 9.
29 "*Britannicus* shūji no ben," Zenshū 29, 500–501.
30 "Shūjisha atogaki," Zenshū 29, 510–15.
31 "Chōhen shōsetsu no gekika—*Kinkakuji* ni tsuite," Zenshū 29, 537–38. Speilhagen's observation is translated from the Japanese Mishima quotes.
32 "*Hanjo* ni tsuite," Zenshū 29, 593–94. The English translation is from Rainer Maria Rilke, *The Notebooks of Malte Laurids Brigge*, trans. M. D. Herter Norton (New York: W. W. Norton, 1949), 202. Or, as William Needham has

it in his translation (online): "at her prime she lamented not one who had left her embrace empty but the one who was no longer possible, the one who had grown by their love," http://archive.org/stream/TheNotebooksOfM alteLauridsBrigge/TheNotebooksOfMalteLauridsBrigge_djvu.txt (accessed July 11, 2012). An English translation of the original *Hanjo*, by Royall Tyler, is included in Donald Keene, ed., *Twenty Plays of the Nō Theatre* (New York: Columbia University Press, 1970), 129–45. In the translation, it is called *Lady Han*.

33   Andō, *"Nichiroku,"* 213. "New York buratsuki," *Zenshū* 30, 265–68.

## Chapter Thirteen: Overseas Again

1   "Mukashi to ima no kakaku," *Keizai Yōran*, 270, 5 (for statistics). For Nakano's words, Handō, *Shōwa-shi: sengo-hen: 1945–1989*, 413. For a general description, Rōyama Masamichi, *Yomigaeru Nihon*, Nihon no rekishi series, vol. 26 (Chūō Kōron Sha, 1967), 36.
2   Rōyama, *Yomigaeru Nihon*, 210–20.
3   "Denki sentakuki no mondai," *Zenshū* 29, 125.
4   "Gaiyū nikki," *Zenshū* 30, 49–50. One of his "diaries" he wrote for publication.
5   Klieger, Christiaan, *The Images of America: The Fleischmann Yeast Family* (Mount Pleasant, SC: Arcadia Publishing, 2004), 74–77.
6   Hiroaki Sato, "Tracking Mishima's Footsteps in Florida," *The Japan Times*, February 28, 2005 (online; accessed July 11, 2012).
7   "Kōkaku no awa," *Zenshū* 31, 519–20. The conversational tone of the original essay is a result of the fact that he wrote it in the form of a letter to Nakamura Mitsuo, then the editor of *Koe*.
8   "New York no kanemochi," in *Tabi no ehon*, *Zenshū* 30, 689–92. *Apollo no sakazuki*, *Zenshū* 27, 538–41.
9   "Nihon bundan no genjō to Seiyō bungaku to no kankei," *Zenshū* 29, 630–47.
10   "Influences in Modern Japanese Literature," *Zenshū* 30, 16–31. This one remains as printed in two installments in the February 7 and 9, 1958, editions of the *Yomiuri Japan News*. As with his American speech, there seems to be no record of the date of the speech.
11   "Shuppatsu no ben," *Zenshū* 29, 615.
12   "New York buratsuki," *Zenshū* 30, 265.
13   Christopher Isherwood, *Diaries: 1939–1960* (New York: HarperCollins, 1996), 710. "I am a camera" is a phrase that appears at the outset of Isherwood's Berlin stories.
14   August 17, 1957, *Gaiyū nikki*, *Zenshū* 30, 50–52. *Gaiyū*, "overseas excursion," is a word for foreign travels that was becoming old-fashioned by then. The "diary" was originally published in several issues of *Shinchō*. For the rest, unless otherwise noted, most of the accounts from what proved to be six-month-long travels derive from *Gaiyū nikki*, *Zenshū* 30, 49–69, and *Tabi no ehon*, *Zenshū* 29, 651–764. Most of his travel accounts—excluding those of 1951–52—are collected in a single paperback volume, *Gaiyū nikki* (Chikuma Shobō, 1995).
15   Letter to Keene, August 23, 1957, *Zenshū* 38, 333–37. Mishima spelled the

16  name *Shults* and different spellings are given elsewhere. The New York Public Library has a Charles "Chiz" Schultz collection.
16  Keene, Donald, trans., *Five Modern Nō Plays by Yukio Mishima* (Tokyo and Rutledge, VT: Charles E. Tuttle, 1967; originally New York: Knopf, 1957), xv.
17  The text available online at the Japanese Text Initiative of the Universities of Virginia and Pittsburgh, with Arthur Waley's translation. The nō play *Koi no omoni* is a variation on the story.
18  Konishi Jin'ichi, "Shinjitsu to kyogi no higan," *Gunzō* special *Nihon no sakka 18: Mishima Yukio*, 32–47. To conclude his five-volume history of Japanese literature, Konishi returns to Mishima and nō to observe that in his academic opinion Mishima's understanding of nō was a little short of complete. *Nihon bungei-shi*, 983. See also the list of Mishima plays produced, Zenshū 42, 744.
19  "Batsu," Zenshū 33, 459–62. The book is Takahashi Mutsuo's *Nemuri to okashi to rakka to* (Sōgetsu Art Center, 1965). A complete translation is included in Hiroaki Sato, trans., *Mutsuo Takahashi: Sleeping Sinning Falling* (San Francisco: City Lights, 1992).
20  "New York no tameiki," Zenshū 30, 250–64. It consists of three episodes. These are Episodes 3 and 1.
21  Descriptions of James Dean's "wraith," the restaurant Dean used to haunt, and the Actors Studio appear in Zenshū 29, 701–2 and 725–29, and in "Dean to Broadway," Zenshū 30, 270–71.
22  "America no musicals," *Tabi no ehon*, Zenshū 29, 735–62. See also "New York de musicals o mite," Zenshū 29, 617–23.
23  "*Ruy Blas* no jōen ni tsuite," Zenshū 34, 135–36. The translation, Hokan, 55–128.
24  "Haikei o New York ni kaeru," Zenshū 29, 765–66, 779.
25  "New York no hono'o," *Tabi no ehon*, Zenshū 29, 713–15.

## Chapter Fourteen: Marriage

1  Kojima, *Mishima Yukio to Dan Kazuo*, 69–71. For her initial assignment to Mishima, see 91–92. Sometimes Kojima is identified by her real name Kojima Kikue, as in Hiraoka, *Segare*, 156.
2  *Ratai to ishō*, Zenshū 30, 107. Descriptions and quotations with dates in this chapter come from this "diary," unless otherwise noted.
3  Richard Minear, trans., *Yoshida Mitsuru: Requiem for Battleship Yamato* (Seattle: University of Washington Press, 1985), xxix–xxxii.
4  "Ichi-dokusha to shite," Zenshū 27, 669. Mishima's letter to Hayashi, February 21, 1948, Zenshū 38, 785.
5  At the time of writing of this book, the house is not open to the public.
6  Yoshida Mitsuru, "Ikoku nite" and "New York no Mishima Yukio," *Senchūha no shisei-kan* (Bungei Shunjū, 1980), 169–87, 251–58. The date for Mishima learning the postponement of the play and scheduling his decamping of New York seems at odds with the date suggested in Mishima's own account. See Zenshū 29, 705–7.
7  In 1967, when the journalist Tokuoka Takao spent some time with Mishima,

Mishima told him he had met Shōda Michiko. Tokuoka Takao, *Gosui no hito* (Bungei Shunjū, 1999), 136–40. In 1969, when a Shield Society member and an unusually well-read Mishima fan asked Mishima the same question, Mishima, losing his usual cheer and composure, admitted that such a meeting for marriage did take place. Murakami Tateo, *Kimitachi ni wa wakaranai: Tate no Kai de mita Mishima Yukio* (Shinchōsha, 2010), 109–10.

8   "*Asa no tsutsuji* ni tsuite," Zenshū 29, 616.
9   Entry of February 19, 1958, Zenshū 30, 79. For Mishima's comments on *The Rose and the Pirate*, "Bara to kaizoku ni tsuite" and "Atogaki," Zenshū 30, 246–49.
10  Yoshida, *Senchūha no shisei-kan*, 256.
11  The statement of purpose, Zenshū 36, 500.
12  "Haha o kataru," Zenshū 30, 657–660. Originally in the October 1958 issue of the women's monthly *Fujin seikatsu*.
13  "*Joyū shigan* o megutte," Zenshū 30, 291–94.
14  Itasaka, *Kyokusetsu: Mishima Yukio*, 57–59.
15  "Torukojin no gakkō," Zenshū 26, 26–27.
16  Selcuk Esenbel, "Japan's Global Claim to Asia and the World of Islam: Transnational Nationalism and World Power, 1900–1945," *The American Historical Review*, vol. 109, no. 4, October 2004. Esenbel, professor of history at Bogazici University, Istanbul, points out: "Muslim Tartars, former Young Turk officers and intelligence men, even Ottoman loyalists [who] joined the diaspora of Pan-Islamists and Pan-Turkists under Japanese protection" as Japan engaged in empire-building in the 1920s and 1930s. "Some had been involved in the Basmaci uprising of the Turkic populations in Central Asia in 1922." Abdul Hannan's father may have been part of the uprising.
17  "Boku no risō no josei," Zenshū 30, 302–3.
18  Nathan, *Mishima*, 151. Nathan himself is a tall, big man.
19  "Owner no ben," Zenshū 31, 234–37, 694–95.
20  "Otoko no bigaku," Zenshū 34, 383–85.
21  Fukushima, *Mishima Yukio: Tsurugi to kanbeni*, 31.
22  The entry toward the end of 1958, Matsumoto, *Tokuhon*, and *Ratai to Ishō*, Zenshū 30, 174.
23  "Jikkanteki sports-ron," Zenshū 33, 157–66.
24  April 10, 1959, *Ratai to ishō*, Zenshū 30, 223–25.
25  "Shukukonka: cantata," Zenshū 37, 772–73.
26  "Jūhassai to sanjūyonsai no shōzōga," Zenshū 31, 225–27.

## Chapter Fifteen: *Kyōko's House*

1   June 29, 1959, *Ratai to ishō*, Zenshū 30, 236.
2   Okuno, *Mishima Yukio densetsu*, 367–69. In this book Okuno reproduces his review that appeared in the September 1959 issue of the weekly *Dokushojin*. Muramatsu, *Mishima Yukio no sekai*, 320–21.
3   "Sakka to kekkon," Zenshū 30, 308–9.
4   Yuasa, *Roy to Kyōko*, 120–21.
5   "*Kyōko no ie*—soko de watashi ga kaita mono," Zenshū 31, 242.

6     For a proper appreciation of this film, see Steven James Snyder, "The Original *Godzilla*: New Criterion Release Celebrates the Greatest Monster Movie," *Time*, January 25, 2012.

7     The rightwing part aside, the idea of Shunkichi getting his right hand smashed may well have been inspired by the greatest-moneymaking movie of 1957 from the Nikkatsu Studio, *Arashi o yobu otoko*, written and directed by Inoue Umeji and starring Ishihara Shintarō's brother, Yūjirō, in which something to the same effect happens. Tanaka, *Mishima Yukio: Kami no kageboshi*, 158.

8     June 29, 1959, *Ratai to ishō*, Zenshū 30, 238–39.

9     "Kaidai," Zenshū 19, 787. Mishima's afterword to his collected short stories in six volumes published in 1965, Zenshū 33, 412.

10     "Shin-Fascism-ron," Zenshū 28, 350–59. For Marguerite Yourcenar's comment on Fascism and Mishima, see *Mishima: A Vision of the Void* (New York: Farrar, Straus and Giroux, 1986), 111–18.

11     Etō Jun, "Mishima Yukio no ie," Fukuda Kazuya, ed., *Etō Jun Collection*, vol. 3 (Chikuma Shobō, 2001), 352–72. The essay, originally printed in the June 1961 issue of *Gunzō*, is included in the *Gunzō* special *Nihon no sakka 18: Mishima Yukio*, 118–30. For Mishima's plot design, see Tanaka, *Mishima Yukio: Kami no kageboshi*, 159.

12     As was routine in prewar Japan, Kishi Nobusuke was adopted when young. In his case, the adoption meant doubling back to his "real" family, for his father, Satō Hidesuke, himself had been adopted from the Kishis. One account says he was in work clothes when let out of prison. A maidservant also did not recognize him and thought he was a vagabond—a *homeless* man in today's lingo. Iwami, *Kishi Nobusuke*, 162. At the time Japan was full of people without homes.

13     Crimes against peace and humanity were newly created categories; as the British government's memorandum stated at the time, they "are not war crimes in the ordinary sense, nor is it at all clear that they can be properly described as crimes under international law." Minear, *Victors' Justice*, 8.

14     Iwami, *Kishi Nobusuke*, 151–64. See also Minear, *Victors' Justice*, 106–7.

15     In November and December 1945 five political parties came into being, three conservative, the other two Socialist and Communist. For the next several years, these, along with some new ones, continued to break up and merge, until most of the conservative wing coalesced into the Liberal Democratic Party, in November 1955. "Liberal" in this context does not mean what it is usually supposed to mean. Rōyama, *Yomigaeru Nihon*, the foldout at the end of the volume.

16     Handō Kazutoshi, *Shōwa-shi: 1945–1989* (Heibonsha, 2009), 421.

17     Ibid., 420.

18     "Orokanaru jingū kensetsu no gi" and "Dai-Nippon-shugi no gensō," Matsuo Takayoshi, ed., *Ishibashi Tanzan hyōron-shū* (Iwanami Shoten, 1984), 29–32 and 101–21. Chō Sachio, "Kaisetsu," Ishibashi Tanzan, *Tanzan kaisō* (Iwanami Shoten, 1985), 417–18. Hiroaki Sato, "Ishibashi's 'Alternative Reality' for Japan," *Japan Times*, March 27, 2006 (online; accessed July 11, 2012).

19     Okuno, *Mishima Yukio densetsu*, 369.

20   A graphic reconstruction of the life of Abe Sada, a woman who killed her lover, cut off his penis, and carried it around until she was apprehended. Because filming graphic sex was not possible in Japan then, Ōshima made the film in France. His script closely follows Abe's statements during the preliminary hearings. See Nanakita Kazuto, ed., *Abe Sada densetsu* (Chikuma Shobō, 1998), 19–86.
21   "Fascist ka kakumeika ka," Zenshū 39, 755–56.
22   December 17, 1959, *Ratai to isshō*, Zenshū 30, 182–88.
23   The genre may largely be derived from French literary tradition. In English, H. W. Fowler's *Modern English Usage* and such, as well as *The Elements of Style*, by William Strunk, Jr. and E. B. White, are too prescriptive to fall in this genre, whereas *Understanding Poetry* and others by Cleanth Brooks and Robert Penn Warren seem intended not for "the general reader" but for college students.
24   *Bunshō tokuhon*, Zenshū 31, 32–39, 94–96.
25   Shidehara Kijūrō, *Gaikō 50 nen* (Chūō Kōron Shinsha, 1987; originally 1951), 220–24.
26   "Transcript of Testimony by MacArthur: Senators Question General for the Third Day," *New York Times*, May 5, 1951. Dower, *Embracing Defeat*, 550–52.
27   "Nihonjin wa yahari 12-sai ka?" ("Are the Japanese Twelve Years Old After All?"), Hokan, 143. Hiroaki Sato, "Irony of Being in the Company of '12-year-olds,'" *Japan Times*, June 25, 2012.
28   Iwatani Tokiko and Koshiji Fubuki, *Yume no naka ni kimi ga iru—Koshiji Fubuki memorial* (Kōdansha, 1999), 41–42, 48, and the last page of the first photo section. The book includes Koshiji's writings about Paris, including her diary.
29   "Kazan managed to do quite a damage to Tennessee's plays while, simultaneously, making them into sexy melododramatic commercial hits," and Williams, "who loved glory almost as much as his inventions, made no fuss then or later." Gore Vidal, *Point to Point Navigation* (New York: Doubleday, 2006), 69. In the case of *Cat on a Hot Tin Roof*, Kazan changed Williams's metaphor "a summer storm" into a real storm, Vidal reports.
30   "Gekisakka no mita *Nippon*," Zenshū 39, 328–41. By some odd affectation, Japan is called "Nippon" and written in *katakata* syllabary when it is presented, as here, as a country in a Westerner's eye.
31   Some kabuki titles are too fancifully convoluted to make much sense, but the title of the shortened version means something like "the young woman Benten the male-female robber." *Shiranami*, "white wave," harkening back to old Chinese stories, means "robber."
32   "Boku wa *objet* ni naritai," Zenshū 31, 294–300.
33   The producer Fujii Hiroaki's 2010 interview on Masumura Yasuzō and *Karakkaze yarō*, http://ja.wikipedia.org/wiki/からっ風野郎.
34   The Tokyo District Court's decision on September 28, 1964: *Utage no ato jiken*: Wa: No. 1882. It contains the arguments of both complainant and defendant. Online. Keyword search: "*Utage no ato jiken*." (Accessed July 11, 2012.)
35   "*Privacy* saiban no wakai zengo," Zenshū 34, 276.
36   "*Utage no* ato jiken no shūmatsu," Zenshū 34, 269.

37  "Mishima Yukio: Saigo no kotoba," a taidan with Furubayashi Takashi, Zenshū 40, 764.

## Chapter Sixteen: The 2.26 Incident, *Yūkoku*

1  Shiine Yamato, *Heibon Punch no Mishima Yukio* (Shinchōsha, 2009), 133. Itasaka, *Kyokusetsu: Mishima Yukio*, 28–29.
2  "*Karakkaze Yarō* no jōfu-ron," Zenshū 31, 409.
3  *Karakkaze yarō*, Zenshū 37, 773–74.
4  Letter to Keene, April 21, 1960, Zenshū 38, 357.
5  "*Salome* no enshutsu ni tsuite," Zenshū, 31, 389–90. "Waga yume no *Salome*," Zenshū 31, 419–20. Also the English scholar Yano Hōjin's comment during the zadankai, "*Salome* to sono butai," Zenshū 39, 348.
6  Charles Sprawson, *Haunts of the Black Masseur: The Swimmer as Hero* (New York: Pantheon Books, 1992), 296. Sprawson doesn't cite sources for his mellifluous book, unfortunately.
7  Letter to Okuno, August 2, 1960. Zenshū 38, 217.
8  Shibusawa, *Mishima Yukio: Oboegaki*, 17–18. Shibusawa's recollections may be a little confused; Donald Richie's first film officially mentioned appears to be *Wargames*, which he made in 1962.
9  "Waga shōsetsu," Zenshū 31, 675–76.
10  "Privacy," Zenshū 31, 500–503.
11  The description derives from the national reform movement started by a group of young officers in the army and navy in the 1920s. Ben-Ami Shillony, *Revolt in Japan: The Young Officers and the February 26, 1936 Incident* (Princeton University Press, 1971), 13–24. By the time the 2.26 Incident occurred, four of the five leaders were in their thirties, only one in his twenties. Ibid., 128.
12  Matsumoto Seichō, *Shōwa-shi hakkutsu*, vol. 8 (Bungei Shunjū, 2005), 178. Volumes 5 to 9 chronicle the 2.26 Incident with ample citations of documents.
13  The full text is quoted in a number of accounts: among others, Takahashi Masae, *2.26 Jiken* (Chūō Kōron Sha, 2007; originally 1965), 25–26; Handō, *Shōwa-shi tansaku 1926–1945*, vol. 3, 253–54; and Taneno Nobuyuki's fictionalized account of the Incident, *Hanran* (Gakken Bunko, 2004), 442–44.
14  *Gunbatsu* is an amorphous term. Here, paradoxically, it may refer to those in the military who pushed the importance of the military in national affairs from the 1920s onward. Takahashi Masae, *2.26 Jiken*, 143–46.
15  Matsumoto, *Shōwa-shi hakkutsu*, vol. 6, 257–58. Many officials and opinion-makers equated the ideas of "the young officers" with Communism and its equivalents. See Shillony, *Revolt in Japan*, 67–68.
16  Fukuzawa Yukichi, *Bunmei-ron no gairyaku* (Keiō Gijuku Daigaku Shuppankai, 2009), 38–39.
17  The original is online. It became one of the documents translated into English following Japan's defeat. Herbert Passin, *Society and Education in Japan* (Kodansha International, 1965), 257–59, and footnote.
18  Matsufuji Takejirō, *Chitagiru Mishima Yukio "kenpō kaisei"* (Mainichi Ones, 2003), 100.

19  Hayashi Kentarō, *Shōwa-shi to watashi* (Bungei Shunjū, 2002), 99.
20  Bōjō, *Honō no gen'ei*, 17–19.
21  Shillony, *Revolt in Japan*, 101–2 and elsewhere.
22  Matsumoto, *Shōwa-shi hakkutsu*, vol. 8, 101–4.
23  Takahashi, *2.26 Jiken*, 163–64.
24  Ōuchi, *Fascism e no michi*, 399–403.
25  Isobe Asaichi's testimony. See Takahashi Masae, *2.26 Jiken*, 63.
26  Matsumoto, *Shōwa-shi hakkutsu*, vol. 8, 196–204.
27  Katō Shūichi, *A Sheep's Song: A Writer's Reminiscences of Japan and the World*, trans. and annot. Chia-ning Chang (Berkeley, CA: The University of California Press, 1999), 102. Katō's original words in *Hitsuji no uta* quoted in Takahashi Masae, *2.26 Jiken*, 250.
28  "Nichiren no koto *Risshō ankoku-ron* no koto nado," *Zenshū* 26, 369–73. For an English translation of Nichiren's treatise, see Philip B. Yampolsky, ed., *Selected Writings of Nichiren* (New York: Columbia University Press, 1990), 11–41.
29  "'Dōgi kakumei' no ronri," *Zenshū* 34, 357, 366. Shillony, *Revolt in Japan*, 172.
30  "Atogaki," *Zenshū* 33, 415–16.
31  "Kaidai," *Zenshū* 20, 791–93.
32  "Atogaki," *Zenshū* 31, 515–16.
33  Details of Kōno's death in Matsumoto, *Shōwa-shi hakkutsu*, vol. 8, 235–44.
34  Mitani, *Kyūyū*, 161. As various accounts tell it, people around Anami expected him to kill himself. In that regard, Mishima's supposition wasn't quite right.
35  Kōdachi Noaki, *Tokkō no Shin'i: Ōnishi Takijirō wahei e no message* (Bungei Shunjū, 2011), 296–98.
36  "Kaidai," *Zenshū* 20, 793.
37  "Atogaki," *Zenshū* 33, 415–16.
38  Yukio Mishima and Geoffrey Bownas, eds., *New Writing in Japan* (London: Penguin, 1972), 22.
39  "Aikokushin," *Zenshū* 34, 648.
40  Isoda Kōichi, *Junkyō no bigaku* (Tōjusha, 1969), 152.
41  "2.26 Jiken to watashi," *Zenshū* 34, 111–12.
42  "Eroticism," *Zenshū* 31, 414.
43  Georges Bataille, *Erotism: Death and Sensuality*, trans. Mary Dalwood (San Francisco: City Lights, 1987), 11, 105. The English title is that of the 1987 City Lights edition of 1962 translation, *Death and Sensuality: A Study of Eroticism and the Taboo*.
44  "Brilliant na sakuhin," *Zenshū* 31, 229.
45  Matsumoto, *Shōwa-shi hakkutsu*, vol. 3, 200–202.
46  Tokuoka Takao, with Donald Keene, *Tōyū kikō* (Chūō Kōron Sha, 1973), 147–53.
47  "Nikki," *Zenshū* 31, 585–86.
48  "Ōoka Makoto cho *Jojō no hihan*," *Zenshū* 31, 567–68.
49  Tanaka, *Mishima Yukio: Kamo no kagebōshi*, 197–202.

## Chapter Seventeen: Assassinations

1. "Daitōryō senkyo," Zenshū 31, 507–9.
2. "Theatre: Two Noh Plays by Mishima; Both on the Theme of Shattered Romance Presented by ANTA Matinee Series," *New York Times*, November 16, 1960.
3. "Kōkaku no awa," Zenshū 31, 517–22. The production was big enough a deal for the Japanese media and the *Mainichi Shinbun* carried a sizable dispatch from New York on it. The article is reproduced in Zenshū 31, 706–7.
4. Letter to Keene, October 15, 1960, Zenshū 38, 361.
5. Letter to Kawabata, November 24, 1960, Zenshū 38, 293.
6. "Porutogaru no Omoide," Zenshū 31, 559.
7. "Pyramid to mayaku," Zenshū 31, 524–27.
8. "Bi ni sakarau mono," Zenshū 31, 546–58.
9. Letter to Keene, February 23, 1961, Zenshū 38, 365–66.
10. "*Fūryū mutan* no suisensha de wa nai," Zenshū 31, 534–35. The statement was published in Mishima's main publisher Shinchōsha's weekly magazine.
11. Muramatsu, *Mishima Yukio no sekai*, 349–52.
12. Such as the second issue of *Scandal Dai-sensō* (Rokusaisha, 2002). This issue reprints both "sealed" stories, *Fūryū mutan* and *Seiji shōnen shisu*. The literary critic Watanabe Hiroshi says Ōe's story *Seventeen*, which continues to be published, is "crippled" without *Seiji shōnen shisu*. Watanabe Hiroshi, "Kaisetsu," Ōe Kenzaburō, *Seiteki ningen* (Shinchōsha, 1989), 233.
13. Muramatsu, *Mishima Yukio no sekai*, 358. He quotes Mishima's brother Chiyuki denying ever telling Nathan that the Shimanaka Incident and other rightwing actions led to "Mishima's 'swing to the right' to his determination to overcome the 'profound fear of the Right.'" See Nathan, *Mishima*, 187.
14. Yamamoto Kiyokatsu, *Yūmon no sokoku bōei fu* (Nihon Bungei Sha, 1980), 89–90.
15. Letters to Keene, March 16 and April 4, 1961. Zenshū 38, 366–72.
16. "America-jin no Nihon shinwa," Zenshū 31, 631–32.
17. "Japanese Youth," Zenshū 31, 641–49. The text is in English.
18. "*Holiday* shi ni manekarete," Zenshū 31, 650–53.
19. Faubion Bowers, "A Memory of Mishima," *Village Voice*, December 3, 1970 (online; accessed July 11, 2012).
20. "Recommending Mr. Yasunari Kawabata for the 1961 Nobel Prize for Literature," Zenshū 31, 572–73, and Kawabata Yasunari, Mishima Yukio, *Ōfuku shokan*, 149–51, 238–39. Zenshū 31 says Mishima's original Japanese does not remain. That suggests the Japanese version in *Ōfuku shokan* is a translation of Saeki's translation.
21. Muramatsu, *Mishima Yukio no sekai*, 370.
22. "Shūmatsukan to bungaku," Zenshū 32, 19–22.
23. Okuno Takeo, "Kaisetsu," *Utsukushii Hoshi* (Shinchōsha, 1967), 365.
24. "'Soratobu enban' no kansoku ni shippai shite," Zenshū 32, 649.
25. Kawabata Yasunari, *Suishō gensō, Kinjū* (Kōdansha, 2005), 201–2.
26. "Kawabata Yasunari best three," Zenshū 28, 459.
27. "Kaisetsu," Zenshū 34, 601–2.

28  "Kawabata Yasunari-shi ni kiku," Zenshū 39, 379–80 and 389–90.
29  Kawabata Yasunari, "Atogaki," Koto (Shinchōsha, 2008), 242–43.
30  "Saikin no Kawabata-san," Zenshū 32, 108.
31  Itasaka, Kyokusetsu: Mishima Yukio, 254–60. The practice of ghostwriting (daisaku) among literary writers since Meiji had to do with the apprenticeship system and "the literary guild" but the matter appears largely unexplored. See Sone Hiroyoshi, "Daisaku no kowasa" (Kaien, September 1968), 166–67. A glimpse of Itō Sei ghostwriting for Kawabata may be gained in Itō's letters to Kawabata, Kawabata Yasunari zenshū hokan 2, 121–36. Prof. Ōta Reiko, of Shōwa Joshi Daigaku, helped corroborate this information through private correspondence.
32  About this title Marguerite Yourcenar wondered if it may come from D'Annunzio's play about Saint Sebastian where "the Emperor suggests smothering Sebastian under a mound of roses." *Mishima: A Vision of the Void*, 129.
33  Hosoe Eikō, "Shashinshū Bara-kei ni matsuwaru ni san no episodes," geppō to Zenshū 38.
34  "Hosoe Eikō josetsu," Zenshū 32, 417–23.
35  Kawabata's letter to Mishima, April 7, 1961, Ōfuku shokan, 152.
36  When Kawabata was hospitalized in the fall of 1958 and asked Mishima what he might take to the hospital, Mishima provided an astonishingly detailed list of nearly eighty items. Letter to Kawabata, October 31, 1958, Zenshū 38, 283–87.
37  "Saikin no Kawabata-san," Zenshū 32, 108–10.
38  "Kawabata Yasunari tokuhon josetsu," Zenshū 32, 144.
39  "Yume to jinsei," Zenshū 33, 46--48.
40  In this battle, from March to June 1944, 78,000 of the 90,000 Japanese soldiers became casualties. Mutaguchi Ren'ya, who planned the operation and forced its execution despite fierce opposition, is counted among the worst generals Japan produced during the Second World War.
41  Konishi, Nihon bungei-shi, 770–76.
42  Katō, Nihon bungakushi josetsu, 458–59.

## Chapter Eighteen: Contretemps

1  Yomota, Ōoka Shōhei, 68.
2  Kitami Harukazu, Kaisō no Bungaku-za (Chūō Kōron, 1987), 210.
3  Murayama Tomoyoshi, Shinobi no mono, vol. 2 (Iwanami Shoten, 2003), 541.
4  Murayama, Shinobi no mono, vol. 3, 398–99. Hiroaki Sato, "China Wasn't Always So Critical of Japan," *Japan Times*, May 30, 2005 (online; accessed July 11, 2012).
5  Kitami, Kaisō no Bungaku-za, 190, 214.
6  "Shiawasena kakumei," Zenshū 32, 414.
7  "Kaidai," Zenshū 32, 705–6.
8  "*Tosca* ni tsuite," Zenshū 32, 435.
9  Kitami, Kaisō no Bungaku-za, 11.
10  "C'est le genre Hugo au complet, du fort et du sublime selon certains, plus de

grossier et de violent que jamais; un certificat d'incurable, magnifiquement historié, et avec de grosses majuscules rouges." The English translation is by Michael O'Brien.

11  "Romantic engeki no fukkō," Zenshū 32, 466. Hiroaki Sato, "Same Hot Buttons a Hundred Years Later," *Japan Times*, January 29, 2007 (online; accessed July 11, 2012).

12  "'Engeki no yorokobi' no fukkatsu," Zenshū 32, 428–30.

13  "Kaidai," Zenshū 24, 714–15.

14  "Aber rein Saitenspiel leiht jeder Stunde die Töne, / Und erfreuet vielleicht Himmlische, welche sich nahn. . . . / Sorgen, wie diese, muß, gern oder nicht, in der Seele / Tragen ein Sänger und oft, aber die anderen nicht." Michael Hamburger, trans., *Friedrich Hölderlin: Poems and Fragments* (a bilingual edition; Cambridge, England: Cambridge University Press, 1980), 261. A literal translation Guido Keller prepared for this book: "But a string play lends every hour the notes / and delights perhaps Heavenlies which approach. . . . / Sorrows like such must, gladly or not, in the soul / carry a singer and often, but the others not."

15  "Bungaku-za shokun e no 'Kōkaijō,'" Zenshū 32, 618–20.

16  Kitami, *Kaisō no Bungaku-za*, 228.

17  To be exact, the translation should be "Marquise de Sade." But when Donald Keene translated the play into English, he called it *Madame de Sade*, explaining, Mishima noted in the play's deluxe edition, that the difference between the male and female forms of the peerage title in English, "marquis" and "marquise," would be too slight and confusing to English readers, besides the fact that Grove Press, which published his translation, was known at the time for issuing Marquis de Sade's writings in translation, which might have compounded the problem. "Gōkaban no tame no hobatsu," Zenshū 34, 437–38.

18  Muramatsu, *Mishima Yukio no sekai*, 419.

19  "Kaidai," Zenshū 24, 714–15.

20  Date Munekatsu, *Saiban kiroku: "Mishima Yukio jiken"* (Kōdansha, 1972), 211.

21  Muramatsu, *Mishima Yukio no sekai*, 420.

22  "Waga sōsaku hōhō," Zenshū 32, 607–14.

23  "*Ken* sōsaku notes," Zenshū 20, 765.

24  Mishima's notes, along with Kawasaki's essay and Matsumoto's report, are in Zenshū 9, 621–85, 680–95.

25  Nathan, *Mishima*, 190.

26  Zenshū 23, 678. The literary critic Matsumoto Tōru found the book Mishima read: an expensive volume published in 1934, with Mishima's inscription in Roman alphabet: "Allabian /night / May 20th 1935 /K. Hiraoka." It is a Japanese translation of Edward Lane's translation, *Stories from Thousand and One Nights*, revised by Stanley Lane-Poole, edited by Charles W. Eliot for The Harvard Classics. Geppō to Zenshū 36, 2. Only the episode of the 11th Night, "The Story of the First Royal Mendicant," has to do with brother-sister love. The episode of the 12th Night also occurs in an underground setting.

27  In his preface to *The Picture of Dorian Gray* (London: Penguin Classics, 2000), which is a collection of aphorisms, Oscar Wilde says: "The nineteenth century dislike of Realism is the rage of Caliban seeing his own face in a

28  Hokan, 160. Mishima's original title for the essay was "Waga America no kage," with the English *reflection* given the reading of *kage*, "shadow."
29  Onna-tachi no Genzai o Tou Kai, ed., *55-nen taisei seiritsu to onna-tachi* (Impact Shuppankai, 1987), 94–104.
30  Yamamoto Shigemi, *Aa Nomugi Tōge: aru seishikōjo aishi* (Kadokawa Shoten, 1987), 360–65.
31  "Chosha to ichijikan." Zenshū 33, 213–14. As to the lack of clarity of the novel, see Tanaka, *Mishima Yukio: Kami no kagebōshi*, 189. "Jushōsha no aisatsu." Zenshū 33, 251. Okuno, *Mishima Yukio densetsu*, 398.
32  "Kūkan no kabe-nuke otoko," Zenshū 33, 184–85.
33  Arthur Koestler, "For Better or Worse: Her Course Is Set," *Life*, September 11, 1964. The article is largely unpaged. Michael Scammell's biography, *Koestler: The Literary and Political Odyssey of a Twentieth-Century Skeptic* (New York: Random House, 2009), does not mention Koestler's visit to Japan that year.
34  "Kanraku hatete...." in "Shūtō zuihitsu," Zenshū 33, 134–35.
35  As Ōe himself noted. Ōe Kenzaburō, *Kojinteki-na taiken* (Shinchōsha, 1995), 256–57. Ōe also noted that Grove Press, the publisher of its English translation, suggested the ending be dropped, but he refused.
36  Ōhashi Kenzaburō's afterword to Kojima Nobuo, *Hōyō kazoku* (Kōdansha, 1988), 273–74.
37  John Nathan's translation in *Mishima*, 206–7. Mishima's original letter, October 18, 1965, Zenshū, Hokan, 227–29.
38  Nathan, *Mishima*, 203–9.
39  The polls are cited in the 1964 section of *Tokuhon*.
40  "Japan's Dynamo of Letters," *Life*, September 2, 1966, 25–31. Nathan's essay, 28–31, comes with the title or caption, "I am a garish man with garish tastes" (online; accessed July 11, 2012).
41  In his biography Nathan quotes from his *Life* essay as saying that reading Mishima's novels was like "attending an exhibition of the world's most ornate picture frames," but no such words appear in the essay.

## Chapter Nineteen: The Nobel Prize

1  In "Serving on Literary Prize Jury," the 38th installment in his "Chronicles of My Life in the 20th Century" for the *Yomiuri Shinbun*, Donald Keene gives the year as 1965. The chronicle has been translated into Japanese by Kakuchi Yukio as *Watashi to 20-seiki no chronicle* (Chūō Kōron Sha, 2007).
2  Melvin J. Lasky, "A Letter from Salzburg: Baroque and Roll," *Transition: A Journal of the Arts, Culture and Society*, vol. 4, nos. 14–19. 21–22.
3  "Mishima bungaku to kokusaisei," Zenshū 39, 478–86.
4  "London tsūshin," published March 25, 1965, and "London kikō," published April 9 and 10, 1965. Zenshū 33, 435–38, 449–55.
5  Mishima kept a diary while in London. Hokan, 631–41. In it Mishima gave the name of the hostess of the occasion as "Lady Johns."

6   "The Hemisphere: Another Payoff," *Time,* June 19, 1964.
7   "Seisaku ito oyobi keika," Zenshū 34, 35–64. The booklet accompanying the DVD of the film, Zenshū 41, 44–45.
8   Christopher Ross, *Mishima's Sword: Travels in Search of a Samurai Legend* (Cambridge, MA: Da Capo Press, 2006), 200.
9   Doris G. Bargen, *Suicidal Honor: General Nogi and the Writings of Mori Ōgai and Natsume Sōseki* (Honolulu: University of Hawai'i Press, 2006), 146–47.
10  The February 2, 1966 *Variety* article, with Mishima's translation of it, is reproduced in the booklet that is part of Zenshū 41, 46.
11  Fujii Hiroaki, "Eiga *Yūkoku* no ayunda michi," Bekkan, 10–11.
12  Ross, *Mishima's Sword,* 193, 200.
13  Hokan, 41–54.
14  Fujii, "Eiga *Yūkoku* no ayunda michi," 11–13.
15  The *Asahi Shinbun* published Kaikō's dispatches in its weekly and (in the case of the disastrous operation) on the front page of its daily newspaper. The publisher then put them out in book form, in March 1965, under the title *Betonamu senki* and abundantly illustrated with Akimoto Keiichi's photographs. For Vietnamese intellectuals' hope, see *Betonamu senki* (Asahi Shinbunsha, 1990), 288–89. The book is included in the twelve-volume collection *Kaikō Takeshi zen-sakuhin, Essays 2* (Shinchōsha, 1974). The Fort Ben Cat operation is described, 194–212. For Kaikō raising 2.4 million yen to take an ad in the *New York Times* and declining to accept the Ministry of Education literary prize, see his chronology in *Zen-sakuhin, Essays 3,* 262–63.
16  Giovanni Gullace, "The French Writings of Gabriele d'Annunzio, *Comparative Literature,* vol. 12, no. 3 (Summer 1960), 207, 213–14.
17  Kurosawa Akira's film *Akahige* (Red Beard; 1970) has a scene where the girl rescued from a house of prostitution flips through one of these Dutch books as she dozes and becomes startled as she comes to a page showing the human anatomy.
18  "Honzukuri no tanoshimi," Zenshū 34, 238–39.
19  Here Mishima refers to George Kaftal's monograph, *Iconography of the Saints in Tuscan Painting.*
20  "Ils sont loin, ils sont déjà loin! / On n'aperçoit plus les chevaux / de la turme. Une croupe blanche / disparaît au détour, derrière / les Tombeaux: le décurion. / Il n'a jamais tourné la tête. / Seigneur, nous allons maintenant / te délier." Mishima quotes this in the original.
21  "On a dépouillé le Martyr pour l'attacher au tronc d'un grand laurier avec des cordes de sparte. Debout, les pieds nus sur les racines noueuses, il repose sur la tige svelte de sa jambe doite le poids de son corps lisse comme l'ivoire; et, les poignets liés au-dessus de sa tête, il ressemble au beau diadumène qui se ceint du bandeau./ C'est aux Sagittaires d'Emèse que l'Auguste a ordonné de venger par les flèches le Soleil seigneur de l'Empire. Ils son éperdus d'amour et de crainte. Sanaé, l'archer aux yeux vairons, et parmi eux. Il épie la plaine."
22  So called in *The Golden Legend,* translated and adapted from the Latin by Granger Ryan and Helmut Ripperger (Arno Press, 1969; originally 1941), 104–10.
23  "Je vous le dis, je vous le dis: / celui qui plus profondément / me blesse, plus

24  profondément / m'aime."
24  "Atogaki (Sei Sebastian no junkyō)," Zenshū 34, 187–94.
25  Araki Nobuyoshi's *Satchin* (Shinchōsha, 1994) vividly captures how children appeared in the early 1960s. He took the photos assembled in the album while a student at Chiba University.
26  "Atogaki," Zenshū 33, 472–73. Also Zenshū 20, 803–4.
27  Orikuchi Shinobu, "Shintō ni arawareta minzoku ronri," *Kodai Kenkyū II: Norito no hassei* (Chūō Kōron Sha, 2003), 96.
28  "Orikuchi Shinobu," Zenshū 28, 208–9.
29  Saeki, *Hyōden*, 14.
30  Oscar Wilde, *Picture of Dorian Gray*, 6.
31  Letters to Shibusawa, June 5 and September 10, 1956; December 26, 1959; January 1, 1960. Zenshū 38, 515–16, 522–23.
32  Letter to Shibusawa, September 22, 1964, Zenshū 38, 530.
33  "Batsu," Zenshū 33, 585.
34  "Taidan: Ningen to bungaku," Zenshū 40, 87, 94.
35  Letter to Shibusawa, May 16, 1960, Zenshū 38, 524.
36  "'Sado Kōshaku Fujin' ni tsuite," Zenshū 33, 587–89.
37  George Cœdès, *Angkor: An Introduction* (Oxford: Oxford University Press, 1963), fn. 93: "The so-called 'Leper King' was probably a god of death, who once held a staff in his right hand. This popular appellation is due solely to his lichen-covered body which gives the appearance of leprosy. Jayavarman VII may have suffered from leprosy, but his statue is not a representation of him."
38  "*Raiō no terasu* kōgai," Zenshū 35, 466.
39  Donald Keene, *5 Modern Japanese Novelists* (New York: Columbia University Press, 2003), 25.
40  Takahashi Mutsuo, *Tomodachi no tsukurikata* (Magazine House, 1993), 142.
41  "Batsu," Zenshū 33, 459–62.
42  Takahashi, *Tomodachi no tsukurikata*, 11.

## Chapter Twenty: *Shinpūren*, Men of the Divine Wind

1  Hiraoka, "Boru no gotoku."
2  Inoguchi Rikihei and Nakajima Tadashi, *Shinpū tokubetsu kōgekitai* (Nihon Shuppan, 1951). The most famous of the books on the subject when it appeared probably because it glorified the "Kamikaze spirit," it was translated into English as *The Divine Wind* (Annapolis, MD: US Naval Institute, 1958). The authors, Capt. Inoguchi and Cdr. Nakajima, were involved in the formation of special attack forces, but they were later accused of having beautified the forces. Takagi Toshirō, *Rikugun tokubetsu kōgekitai, jōkan* (Bungei Shunjū, 1983), 481.
3  "2.26 Jiken to watashi," Zenshū 34, 117–18.
4  The *Fukui Shinbun* article of June 6, 1966, is reprinted in Zenshū 34, 767–68.
5  Fukushima, *Mishima Yukio: Tsurugi to kanbeni*, 167.
6  Mishima wrote a different, longer version, titling it "The Evil Counselors' Song." Zenshū 20, 714–20.

7   The title *Honba* is translated *Runaway Horses* (in plural) by Michael Gallagher. But since the horse in the title obviously refers only to the story's protagonist Iinuma Isao, the English should be in the singular.
8   Tokuoka, *Gosui no hito*, 38.
9   "Mishima Yukio-shi no 'ningen Tennō' hihan—shōsetsu 'Eirei no koe' ga nageta hamon," Zenshū 34, 126–29.
10  Funasaka Hiroshi, *Seki no Magoroku: Mishima Yukio, sono shi no himitsu* (Kōbunsha, 1973), 87–91, 89.
11  It includes a misspelling. "The common term in German would be *Totale Vernichtung* (Hitler meant the annihilation of Jews, of course) or, grammatically correct, *Vernichtender Kampf* (which I never heard)." Guido Keller by private communication.
12  E. B. Sledge, *With the Old Breed: At Peleliu and Okinawa* (Oxford: Oxford University Press, 1981), 52.
13  Spector, *Eagle against the Sun*, 420.
14  Sledge, *With the Old Breed*, 53, 155–56.
15  Funasaka Hiroshi, *Eirei no zekkyō* (Bungei Shunjū, 1966), 29, 194, 156–59. Taylor's words are translated from Funasaka's Japanese translation. Funasaka's book was translated into English by Jeffrey D. Rubin as *Falling Blossoms* and published by Times Books International in 1986.
16  "Jo (Funasaka Hiroshi cho *Eirei no zekkyō*)," Zenshū 34, 263–67.
17  Translation: *Gyokusai-sen no kotō ni taigi wa nakatta*.
18  Abe Jōji, "Kaisetsu," Mishima Yukio, *Fukuzatsuna Kare* (Shūeisha, 1987), 332–37.
19  "Beatles kenbutsuki," Zenshū 34, 168–72.
20  "Zōka ni korosareta funanori no uta," Zenshū 37, 784–88.
21  Mishima's letter to Fukushima Jirō in mid-July 1966. Fukushima, *Mishima Yukio: Tsurugi to kanbeni*, 171.
22  It was during their time together in Nara that Keene appears to have created a "famous anecdote" suggesting that Mishima showed little knowledge of ordinary things, such as the names of plants. It had to do with the variety of pine known as *mematsu*, "female pine" (*Pinus densiflora*). Mishima did not even know *mematsu* is another name of *akamatsu*, the most common species of pine in Japan—that the name was not meant to sexually distinguish the species from the other one called *omatsu*, "male pine" (*Pinus thunbergiana*)!

  One interesting aspect of this anecdote is the involvement of the journalist Tokuoka Takao. Tokuoka cited Keene's story—which appeared in the *Mainichi Shinbun* the day after Mishima's death—in his 1973 account of his travels with Keene without comment (*Takuyū kikō* [Chūō Kōron Sha, 1981], 46–47), but later, in his 1996 book on Mishima, argued that Keene probably got something wrong or came to a hasty conclusion (*Gosui no hito*, 118–19). In his second reference to the story, Tokuoka cited a botanist who closely examined the way Mishima described various plants to marvel at his accurate observations of details.
23  "Shikyaku to kumichō," Zenshū 40, 514.
24  Ogyū Sorai, *Taiheisaku*. Maruyama Masao et al., eds., *Ogyū Sorai shū*

(Iwanami Shoten, 1973), 451. Sorai (1666–1728) was a political and philosophical counselor to the eighth Tokugawa shogun, Yoshimune (1684–1751).

25  Muramatsu, *Shi no bungakushi*, 418–25.

26  Satsuma is an old name of Kagoshima. The Japanese name of the civil war is *Seinan sensō*, "Southwest War," or *seinan no eki*, "War of the Southwest," southwest being the direction of Satsuma from the viewpoint of the government in Tokyo.

27  Sugiyama Shigemaru, *Kodama Taishō-den* (Chūō Kōron Sha, 1989; originally 1918), 115. With Saeki Shōichi's afterword.

28  By the time Hasuda Zenmei went to junior high school, in the late 1910s, such stories would provoke great mirth as well as a sense of awe. Odakane, *Hasuda Zenmei*, 18–19.

29  In the *Chronicles of the Age of Deities* (*jindai-ki*), the word *ukei* or its variant appears where Susano'o (Storm Deity) goes to see Amaterasu (Sun Goddess). Sakamoto Tarō et al., eds., *Nihon Shoki*, jō (Iwanami Shoten, 1977), 104. According to the editors' explanation of *ukei*, 559, the diviner sets out with the premise that if A happens, it proves AA, whereas if B happens, it proves BB, then asks for "the *shin'i*," the divine will.

30  Letter to Shimizu, July 31, 1946, Zenshū 38, 619.

31  Letter to Araki, June 26, 1967. Zenshū 38, 187.

32  Fukushima, *Mishima Yukio: Tsurugi to kanbeni*, 173.

33  For an illustration of how to wear a fundoshi, see Ross, *Mishima's Sword*, 196.

34  When Fukushima's book came out in the spring of 1998 and became a runaway bestseller, Mishima's daughter and son, Noriko and Iichirō, brought a lawsuit ("cease-and-desist") against Fukushima and his publisher Bungei Shunjū on the ground that his use of Mishima's letters without permission infringed on the copyright law and Mishima's *jinkaku-ken*, "personality rights," a form of libel (*Asahi Shinbun*, March 25, 1998).

On March 30, the Tokyo District Court issued a preliminary injunction accepting the petitioners' argument and ordered Bungei Shunjū to recall all the copies within seven days. Bungei Shunjū said that the decision was based on prejudice against homosexuals and that the cease-and-desist order was an abuse of Constitutional rights. The critic Kawamura Minato was against the recall from the standpoint of freedom of speech but said the matter should have been argued from the standpoint of violation of privacy. The critic Matsumoto Ken'ichi, who had written about Mishima, recalled that a book touching on Mishima's homosexuality had been suppressed two decades earlier, and stated that the surviving members of the Mishima family should be more "relaxed" about such things (*Asahi Shinbun*, March 31, 1998). Matsumoto's reference was to a Japanese translation of John Nathan's biography of Mishima.

On October 18, 1999, the Tokyo District Court handed down a decision stating that letters were subject to copyright protection, the first such judgment in Japan. The court also ordered a payment of 5 million yen and publication of an ad of apology. The judge recognized that letters were different from literary works, but argued that those published in Fukushima's book went beyond "seasonal greetings and simple replies." Bungei Shunjū said they would appeal the decision as a constitutional issue (*Asahi Shinbun*, October 19, 1999).

On May 23, 2000, the Tokyo Supreme Court affirmed the lower court's decision. The judge explained that the letters in question included "sentences creatively expressing Mishima's thought and feelings," which placed them within copyright protection. Bungei Shunjū found the reasoning "lacking in persuasiveness" and said it would appeal (*Asahi Shinbun*, May 23, 2000). On November 9, 2000, the Supreme Court turned down the appeal as without merit (*Asahi Shinbun*, November 10, 2000).

35 Fukushima, *Mishima Yukio: Tsurugi to kanbeni*, 176–83 and elsewhere.
36 Mishima's letter to Araki, August 15, 1966. Zenshū 38, 181. Fukushima, 185–86.
37 Fukushima, *Mishima Yukio: Tsurugi to kanbeni*, 185–86.
38 "Taiwa: Nihonjin ron," Zenshū 39, 634. This taidan includes a succinct account of Shinpūren's behavior, 632–33. "Gendai ni okeru uyoku to sayoku," Zenshū 40, 576.
39 Fukushima, *Mishima Yukio: Tsurugi to kanbeni*, 222–24.
40 Letters to Araki, September 3, 1966 and October 10, 1969. Zenshū 38, 183, 190.
41 The first occurred during a Diet session in December 1950 and the second in November 1952. The second one was a "clarification" of the remarks he had made in March 1950. At the time Japan had plunged into recession following America's economic emissary Joseph Dodge's imposition on the Japanese government of a strict balanced budget and other stringent belt-tightening measures. See Chapter Nine. In the March 1950 statement, Ikeda had said: "We can't help some people going bankrupt because of the recession in the process of economic readjustment. For some time to come we must follow a thorny path." Watanabe, *Sengo Nihon no saishō-tachi*, 179–81.
42 Letter to Kawaguchi, November 1, 1966, Hokan, 203–4.
43 Funasaka, *Seki no Magoroku*, 72–82. The length is given in Japanese as 2 *shaku* 3 *sun* 5 *rin*. It comes to 71.2 cm.
44 Ibid., 178–83. In his account of the search for the sword Funasaka gave Mishima after Mishima's death, *Mishima's Sword*, Christopher Ross describes how Funasaka gave the sword to Mishima, 1–14; Magoroku XXVII's assessment of the sword, which he examined at the police after the incident, that "it was a Kodai Kanemoto, perhaps the fourth or fifth generation. There was evidence of the sword having been shortened at some time. The signature may have been removed then—all genuine Kanemoto swords are signed," 162; a famous Sword Polisher (*togishi* and *mukansha*) who chose to remain unnamed, cited his student's opinion: "He told me the sword was not Seki no Magoroku, not Kanemoto I or Kanemoto II, but was a later-generation Kanemoto sword. The later-generation Kanemoto swords represented a decline in quality and are not so valuable or collectible," 182; Nakamura Taisaburō, not so identified by name but as the Swordmaster who sold the sword to Funasaka, who said: "It was not Seki no Magoroku. It looked like

the second Kanemoto, but was not by him. If it had been I would never have sold it," 220. For Funasaka's own detailed description, see *Seki no Magoroku*, especially 106.

45   Hiraoka, *Segare*, 221.
46   Shiine, *Heibon Punch no Mishima Yukio*, 56–58.
47   Bōjō, *Honō no gen'ei*, 145–46, 164–65.

## Chapter Twenty-One: "The Way of the Warrior is to die"

1   Kojima, *Mishima Yukio to Dan Kazuo*, 65.
2   *Minzokushugi* is often translated as "nationalism," or vice versa. Depending on the Chinese characters used, *minzoku* can mean customs, mores, folklore, etc., of a particular group of people or a larger, distinct ethnic group itself; but the distinction between 民族 and 民俗 as used in *minzoku-gaku* can become a matter of emphasis. Japan's *minzoku-gaku*, meaning "folkloristics" or "ethnography," is a field of study that came into being in the 1920s and 1930s under the influences of European and American thought, with the word *minzoku* carrying the strong sense of German *Volk*. As a result, the word *minzoku* tended to have nationalistic overtones, especially in prewar Japan. This is clear in Japan's prewar slogan characterizing the Japanese as the "leading" *minzoku*, even amid a call for "a pan-East Asian *minzoku*"; it was a notion put forward to counter the Caucasian view of themselves as racially superior to every other race. The difficulty of finding the single-word English equivalent of *minzoku* may be seen in Kevin M. Doak's article, "Building National Identity through Ethnicity: Ethnology in Wartime Japan and After" (*Journal of Japanese Studies*, vol. 27, no. 1, Winter 2001).
3   "Seinen ni tsuite," Zenshū 34, 562–63.
4   One of the students who joined Mishima in "experiencing the GSDF" suggested Mitate-kai, and the name was accepted for the group they had formed. It was based on a tanka by Tachibana Akemi (1812–68), who for a while studied with a follower of National Learning: *Ōgimi no shiko no mitate to iu mono wa koko ni naru mono zo to susume masaki ni*, "Saying, 'The Great Lord's so-called ugly Imperial shield is right here,' advance before everyone else." Mishima later proposed to change it to Tate no Kai, saying that *tate no* sounds better than *mitate*. Hosaka Masayasu, *Mishima Yukio to Tate no Kai jiken* (Kadokawa Shoten, 2001), 149. The poem alludes to No. 4373 of the *Man'yōshū*, one of the poems offered by a border guard named Okinaga no Mahito Kunishima: *Kyō yori wa kaeriminakute Ōkimi no shiko no mitate to idetatsu ware wa*, "Starting this day, without regrets, I set out as an ugly Imperial shield." *Shiko no*, here given as "ugly," is self-deprecation, but it is also interpreted to mean, "tough." *Mi* of *mitate* is an honorific, and *tate*, "shield," is a metaphor for "soldier." The soldier as a shield also appears in the section of the twenty-first Tennō, Sushun, in *Nihon Shoki* in the passage on Yorozu. See Sato, *Legends of the Samurai*, 13–15.
5   "Hontō no seinen no koe o," Zenshū 34, 330.
6   Kawase Kenzō, "*Ten to umi* record-ka no koro," geppō to Zenshū 34.
7   The naval battle on the night of February 28, 1942, in which a Japanese task

force with a large troop convoy sank the USS cruiser *Houston* and the Australian HMAS cruiser *Perth*. But two Japanese transport ships were also sunk—accidentally, by a Japanese warship. Asano was aboard one of them.

8   "*Ten to umi* ni tsuite," Zenshū 34, 397.
9   "Geijutsu dansō," Zenshū 32, 558.
10  Richard Minear, "Helen Mears, Asia, and American Asianists," International Area Studies Program, University of Massachusetts at Amherst, Asian Studies Committee Occasional Papers Series, 1981, No. 7, 5–7. Also, Richard H. Minear, "Cross-Cultural Perception and World War II: American Japanists of the 1940s and Their Images of Japan," *International Studies Quarterly*, vol. 24, no. 4, December 1980, 571–78.
11  "Kōdōgaku nyūmon," Zenshū 35. 610.
12  Inose Naoki, *Kūki to sensō* (Bungei Shunjū, 2007), 40–44. Hiroaki Sato, trans., *Japanese Women Poets* (Armonk, NY: M.E. Sharpe, 2007), 475–76.
13  Tokuoka, *Gosui no hito*, 37–41.
14  Muramatsu, *Mishima Yukio no sekai*, 481.
15  "Jieitai o taiken suru," Zenshū 34, 404–13.
16  Shiine, *Heibon Punch no Mishima Yukio*, 28–29.
17  Tokuoka, *Gosui no hito*, 53.
18  "Mishima kikyōhei ni 26 no shitsumon," Zenshū 34, 414–22.
19  Muramatsu, *Mishima Yukio no sekai*, 482–83.
20  Nakano, *Akunin raisan*, 293–94.
21  The *Senjinkun* (Code of Conduct in the Battlefield) was prepared in an attempt to deal with the loss of military discipline on the battlefields in China of the kind "not seen in the Sino-Japanese and Russo-Japanese Wars"—"violence against officers, desertions, rape, arson, and pillage." Issued in the name of Army Minister Gen. Tōjō Hideki, in January 1941, the code, in its main part, told the soldiers not to get drunk, not to be carried away by lust, to treat noncombatants with kindness, and so on. After Japan's defeat, the code won notoriety, "from the standpoint of humanism," as Shirane Takayuki explained, because of that infamous article. Shirane, who had studied philosophy at the Imperial University of Kyūshū and written books, was pulled from a Chinese front to join a small group to prepare the document at the Department of Military Education. The *Senjinkun* was intended to supersede the *Gunjin chokuyu*.

The article in question, however, when scrutinized, may have said something far less dire. Kyoko Selden who parsed the "no surrender" article says that the two-part sentence in parallelism says something like: "Thou shall not suffer the shame of being taken prisoner while alive; thou shall not leave the ill repute of crime and penalty when you die"—that is, "Do your best not to be taken prisoner." So interpreted, it may be close to a standard admonishment in any military code of conduct.

Shirane Takayuki, "'Senjinkun' wa kōshite tsukurareta," in Handō, *Shōwa-shi tansaku 1926–1945*, vol. 5, 143–46. Sato, "*Gyokusai.*" Another explanation for "no surrender" was that treatment of POWs was savage.

22  "The Vietnam War and American Life," *Newsweek,* July 10, 1967, 5 and 60.
23  Shiine, *Heibon Punch no Mishima Yukio,* 12–13.
24  Kubota Hiroko, "Mishima Yukio to Matsumoto Seichō no Tōnan Asia," *Mishima Yukio kenkyū* 10: *Ekkyō suru Mishima Yukio* (Kanae Shobō, 2010), 115.
25  "Jieitai o taiken suru," Zenshū 34, 404.
26  Kikuchi Katsuo, "Mishima-shi no kangeki to zasetsu," geppō to Zenshū 38.
27  Letter to Kikuchi, August 25, 1967. Zenshū 38, 455.
28  "Magagoto," Zenshū 37, 400–401.
29  "Fuin," Zenshū 37, 377–78.
30  "Mishiranu heya de no jisatsusha," Zenshū 37, 384.
31  "Kasugai Ken-shi no uta," Zenshū 31, 207. Yamauchi Yukito, "Mishima Yukio to tanka," *Mishima Yukio kenkyū* 10: *Ekkyō suru Mishima Yukio* (Kanae Shobō, 2010), 135–36. Yamauchi's purpose in his essay is to discuss the tanka poet Kasugai Ken's fateful encounter with Mishima.
32  Muramatsu, *Mishima Yukio no sekai,* 76–77.
33  "Kaidai," Zenshū 16, 758. The ending dots are part of the poem.
34  *Kamen no kokuhaku,* Zenshū 1, 328, 335. Mishima repeated the story about wearing white clothes in 1967 when the *Asahi Shinbun* asked for his comment on the Hiroshima bombing on its anniversary ("Watashi no naka no Hiroshima—genbaku no hi ni yosete," Zenshū 34, 447–48; the original title of the article was: "Minzokuteki fungeki o omoiokose" or "Remember the Fury as a People"). But Mishima was wrong about "white clothes." As Muramatsu Takeshi correctly recalled, what the government did—an appallingly delusionary act, no doubt—was to advise wearing white clothes to *reduce* the burns from the bomb. Muramatsu, *Mishima Yukio no sekai,* 102–3. Muramatsu notes that the fear of an atomic bomb being dropped on Tokyo became palpable on the night of August 12. The crew of a B-19 that was shot down had predicted it.
35  "Watashi no naka no Hiroshima," Zenshū 34, 447–48.
36  "Shōwa 20-nen 8-gatsu no kinen ni," Zenshū 26, 551–52.
37  "Jūshōsha no kyōki," Zenshū 27, 29.
38  "Jōshi ni tsuite—yaya kyōgeki na giron," Zenshū 27, 108–13.
39  Nakamura Shin'ichirō, *Nakamura Shin'ichirō shishū* (Shichōsha, 1989), 120.
40  Katō, *Sheep's Song,* 180.
41  "Watashi no henreki jidai," Zenshū 32, 296–97.
42  "Akutagawa Ryūnosuke ni tsuite," Zenshū 28, 404–6.
43  *Shōsetsuka no kyūka,* Zenshū 28, 565–67.
44  Tanaka Miyoko, "Kaisetsu," Mishima Yukio, *Shōsetsuka no kyūka* (Shinchōsha, 1982), 300.
45  *Shōsetsuka no kyūka,* Zenshū 28, 610–11.
46  "Shi no bunryō," Zenshū 28, 186–89.
47  *Shōsetsuka no kyūka,* Zenshū 28, 646.
48  "'Junbungaku to wa?' sonota," Zenshū 32, 81.
49  "Watashi no henreki jidai." Zenshū 32, 323.
50  Dōmoto Masaki, *Kaisō: kaitentobira no Mishima Yukio* (Bungei Shunjū, 2005), 70–71.
51  Muramatsu, *Mishima Yukio no sekai,* 386.

52   Richard Pevear and Larissa Volokhonsky, trans., *Demons* (New York: Vintage, 1995), 617, 621.
53   "Hinuma-shi to shi," *Zenshū* 35, 184–85.
54   *Jijin* is traditionally applied to the act of killing oneself with a sword. But Mishima used the same word when the marathon runner Tsuburaya Kōkichi (1940–68), second lieutenant of the GSDF, committed suicide because of his inability to participate in the Mexican Olympic Games. Tsuburaya used a razor blade. "Tsuburaya nii no jijin," *Zenshū* 34, 652–54.
55   Quoted in Allen Guttmann, *The Erotic in Sports* (New York: Columbia University Press, 1996), 70. Lingis's article, "Orchids and Muscles," originally appeared in *Journal of the Philosophy of Sport*, 1986. It was later collected in *Foreign Bodies* (London: Routledge, 1994).
56   "Tōgyūshi no bi," *Zenshū* 34, 130–31.
57   "France no terebi ni Hatsu-shutsuen," *Zenshū* 34, 31–32.
58   "Nentō no mayoi," *Zenshū* 34, 284–87. A. E. Hotchner has pointed out the possibility that Hemingway might have killed himself exasperated by the FBI's hounding. A. E. Hotchner, "Hemingway, Hounded by the Feds," *New York Times*, July 1, 2011.
59   "Dōzō to no taiwa—Saigō Takamori," *Zenshū* 34, 665–66. "A Pact" in Richard Sieburth, ed., *Ezra Pound: Poems and Translations* (New York: Library of America, 2003), 269.

## Chapter Twenty-Two: Death in India

1   Mishima noted that there are four conjectures on where the suggestive title came from: an allusion to Saigyō's tanka (*Hagakure ni chiritodomareru hana nomi zo shinobishi hito ni au kokochi suru*); the suggestion that Yamamoto provided service to his lord in seclusion as his abode was hidden in foliage; a reference to the persimmon tree near Yamamoto's abode that was called *Hagakushi* (leaves hiding the fruit); and the fact that Saga Castle, of the Nabeshima fiefdom that Yamamoto served, was famous for its many trees with glorious foliage. *Hagakure nyūmon*, *Zenshū* 34, 491–92. Saigyō, despite his reputation as an ascetic seeker of enlightenment, left a great many tanka on *koi*, "love." This one is in the cluster of "love" poems in the middle volume of his collection *Sankashū* (no. 599). It comes with the heading, "Love in the metaphor of a remaining flower," and says, "This flower that has stayed, without scattering, behind the leaves—I feel as if I've met the person I long for." *Shinobu koi*, love one simply "endures" without disclosing it to the person one yearns for, is an important theme in classical verse. It was the kind of "love" that Yamamoto argued was at the heart of a samurai's loyalty and devotion to his lord. Mishima agreed wholeheartedly.
2   *Hagakure nyūmon*, *Zenshū* 34, 474–540. When it was published in 1967, Mishima's commentary was accompanied by a body of excerpts with translations into modern Japanese by Kasahara Nobuo which formed Part 2. The zenshū omits that part.
3   "Utsukushii shi," *Zenshū* 34, 440–41.
4   The film was based on the account of the same name, compiled by the Pacific

War Research Society led by Handō Kazutoshi and published by Bungei Shunjū, in 1965. Kodansha International published its English translation in 1968. For an account of Anami's seppuku, see Tsunoda Fusako's biography, *Isshi, daizai o shasu: rikugun daijin Anami Korechika* (Shinchōsha, 1983), 442–56. Tsunoda is an unusual biographer of military leaders. Finding herself with her emaciated baby when Japan surrendered, she decided, a few decades later, to look into some of the military leaders who might have been responsible for the fate of Japan. Other than Anami, she wrote about Gen. Honma Masaharu, who was executed for what happened in Bataan, and Gen. Imamura Hitoshi, who dedicated his life after defeat to the welfare of his former soldiers.

5   Nakamura, *Resshi to yobareru otoko*, 1–69.
6   "'Dōgiteki kakumei' no ronri," Zenshū 34, 348–71.
7   Mishima's letter to Kawabata, February 13, 1967, and Kawabata's letter to Mishima, February 26, 1967, Kawabata Yasunari and Mishima Yukio, *Ōfuku shokan*, 182–84.
8   "'Gakumon geijutsu ni jiritsusei o': Kawabata-shi ra Bunka Kakumei ni appeal," *Asahi Shinbun*, March 1, 1967. "Bunka Dai-Kakumei ni kansuru seimei," Zenshū 36, 505.
9   "Kono 'ichimai no shashin' o dō miru ka," Zenshū 34, 331. Mishima's remarks quoted in the weekly *Asahi*, February 24, 1967.
10  Mori Mari, *Watashi no bi no sekai* (Shinchōsha, 1984), 152–60.
11  The Mori Mari special of the monthly *Eureka: Poetry and Criticism*, December 2007, 192.
12  The name Peter may be out of place, for the character is supposed to be Russian and it should be "Pyotr." In any case, we can assume that the story contains a good deal of autobiographical material. Japan had a sizable number of Russian immigrants during the period Mori describes, from the end of the Russo-Japanese War well into the 1920s.
13  Mori Oto, *Chichioya to shite no Mori Ōgai* (Chikuma Shobō, 1993), 124–28.
14  "Anata no rakuen, anata no gin no saji," Zenshū 34, 372–78.
15  "Taidan: Ningen to bungaku," Zenshū 40, 145.
16  Letter to Kikuchi, October 20, 1967. Zenshū 38, 460.
17  Most of what he did and observed is detailed by Mishima himself in the interview Tokuoka conducted for the *Mainichi Shinbun*. "Indo no inshō," Zenshū 34, 585–94.
18  Tokuoka, *Gosui no hito*, 90–96.
19  Ibid., 99–100.
20  Laurens van der Post, *The Admiral's Baby* (New York: William Morrow, 1996), 236.
21  Letter to Shibusawa, October 23, 1967, Zenshū 38, 535.
22  "Indo tsūshin," Zenshū 34, 595–600.
23  Tokuoka, *Gosui no hito*, 110–11.
24  Ibid., 101–5, 130–31.
25  Hiraoka, *Segare*, 210–12 (Chiyuki's recollections). Letter to Araki, October 23, 1967, Zenshū 38, 188.
26  "*Suzaku-ke no metsubō* ni tsuite," Zenshū 34, 566–67.

27  Ibid., 568–70.
28  "Kaidai," Zenshū 24, 725–26.
29  Ibid., 688.
30  "Chūsei o tēma no sansaku," *Asahi Shinbun* (evening edition), 29 September 1967.
31  *Junshi*, to kill oneself to follow one's lord's death, was forbidden early in the Tokugawa regime, as in the *buke sho-hotto*, Various Regulations for the Military Houses, in 1663. Ishii, *Kinsei buke shisō*, 458. Nogi's *junshi* prompted Harriet Monroe to pen an ode, published in the second issue of *Poetry*, the magazine she had just started. Among others, the American journalist Stanley Washburn wrote an admiring biography, *Nogi*.
32  Abe Kōbō, *Tomodachi, Enomoto Takeaki* (Kawade Shobō Shinsha, 1967), 126.
33  Fukuzawa Yukichi, *Yasegaman no setsu*, *Meiji jūnen: Teichū kōron* (Kōdansha, 1985). His argument was originally published in 1901.
34  Abe, *Tomodachi, Enomoto Takeaki*, 127. As Abe noted in his afterword, 221–22, the play was based on his novel with the same title that elicited diametrically opposing views of the Enomoto as presented by Abe.

## Chapter Twenty-Three: The Anti-Vietnam War Movement

1  After 1961, the anti-Yoyogi Faction was run by the Revolutionary Marxist Faction (known by its acronym Kakumaru-ha), but in 1963 it spawned a faction within it, the National Committee of the Alliance of Revolutionary Communists (Chūkaku-ha). In 1966, the Chūkaku-ha and two other subfactions of the anti-Yoyogi Faction—the Alliance of Socialist Students (Shagakudō; also called by the German *Bund*) and the Liberation Faction of the Alliance of Socialist Youths (Shaseidō Kaihōha)—formed a united front, creating "the Three Factions," Sanpa Zengakuren. In 1968, their unity crumbled, but the three groups continued to be called by their group name. See chart in Sassa Atsuyuki, *Tōdai rakujō* (Bungei Shunjū, 1993), 43. Also the entry on *gakusei undō* in Heibonsha's encyclopedia *Sekai dai-hyakka jiten*.
2  "Tōdai o dōbutsuen ni shiro," Zenshū 35, 361.
3  Quoted in the October 14, 1967 online entry "Sengo gakusei undō kōsatsu." www.marino.ne.jp/~rendaico/sengogakuseiundo.htm (accessed July 11, 2012).
4  "Joint Statement of Japanese Prime Minister Sato and US President Johnson," dated November 15, 1967, "The World and Japan" Database Project: Database of Postwar Japanese Politics and International Relations, Institute of Oriental Culture, University of Tokyo. Online. The Japanese text uses the word Okinawa as well as Ryūkyū but the English sticks to the word Ryukyu. www.ioc.u-tokyo.ac.jp/~worldjpn/documents/texts/JPUS/19671115.D1E.html (accessed July 11, 2012).
5  "JNG ka'an," Zenshū 34, 623–25.
6  "Sokoku bōeitai wa naze hitsuyō ka," Zenshū 34, 626–43.
7  Hosaka, *Mishima Yukio to Tate no Kai jiken*, 125–26.
8  Shima Taizō, *Yasuda Kōdō: 1968–1969* (Chūō Kōron Sha, 2005), 2–4.
9  Ibid., 7–10.
10  Hosaka, *Mishima Yukio to Tate no Kai jiken*, 130–31.

11  F-Kikan, "F" standing for Fujiwara and *kikan* meaning "service," has a number of Internet references. Fujiwara's greatest success was his help in forming the Indian National Army. Joyce Chapman Lebra's book, *The Indian National Army and Japan* (Institute of Southeast Asian Studies, 2008; originally published as *Jungle Alliance: Japan and the Indian National Army*, by Asia/Pacific Press, 1971), is a full account of Fujiwara's effort to create the Indian National Army. Lebra was most likely the only foreign woman on the Ichigaya compound the day Mishima pulled his final act; she was doing her research on her book. Joyce Lebra, "Eyewitness: Mishima," *New York Times*, November 28, 1970.

Lebra's book is based on Japanese documents and Indian views and describes the complicated wartime ventures dispassionately. Louis Allen is dismissive of Japanese wartime intelligence efforts in general and of the Indian National Army in particular: the latter was, he wrote, "dissolved in 1942 by its chief, Captain (later General) Mohan Singh, and was resurrected under the aegis of Subhas Chandra Bose in 1943. It took part, almost entirely ineffectively, in the campaign against the British in Arakan and Manipur in 1944, but played a small part in the achieving of Indian independence in 1947, as a result of public opinion roused by the court-martial of three of its leaders in the Red Fort, Delhi, in 1945." Louis Allen, "Japanese Intelligence Systems," *Journal of Contemporary History*, vol. 22, no. 4, 1987, 559.

12  Rikugun Daigakkō, which existed from 1883 to 1945. It was modeled after the German Kriegsakademie and was comparable to the US War Army College. Bōei Daigakkō that came into being in 1954 sounds similar to the prewar institution by name, but as its English name, The National Defense Academy, suggests, it is the equivalent of the US Military Academy. By the time Yamamoto went there, the staff college's study period was reduced from three years to one.

13  Yamamoto, *Mishima Yukio: Yūmon no sokoku bōei fu*, 82–88.
14  Ibid., 48–49.
15  Ibid., 27–29.
16  Ibid., 62–68.
17  "Shōsetsu to wa nani ka," Zenshū 34, 683–758.
18  Isoda, *Junkyō no bigaku*, 395. Murakami's book was titled *Senchūha no jōri to fujōri* (The Wartime Generation's Rationality and Irrationality).
19  "20 nen de puttsuri kireteiru—saichō no gengō Shōwa." Zenshū 36, 242.
20  "Shōbu no kokoro to funnu no jojō," Zenshū 34, 608–21. Also, *Shōbu no kokoro: Mishima Yukio taidan-shū* (Nihon Kyōbun Sha, 1970), 172–89.
21  Letter to Kikuchi, April 4, 1968, Zenshū 38, 461–62.
22  Hosaka, *Mishima Yukio to Tate no Kai*, 133–35.
23  Nakamura, *Resshi to yobareru otoko*, 93.
24  Shiine, *Heibon Punch no Mishima Yukio*, 18–23.
25  Ibid., 95.
26  Letter to Tsutsumi, December 29, 1967, Zenshū 38, 693–98.
27  Quoted in Matsumoto, *Tokuhon*, in its April–May 1968 section (the book

28 Yamamoto, *Mishima Yukio: Yūmon no sokoku bōei fu*, 96–116.
29 Carl von Clausewitz, *On War*, trans. Anatol Rapoport (London: Penguin, 1968; original trans. 1908). Clausewitz says: "War is not merely a political act, but also a real political instrument, a continuation of political commerce, a carrying out of the same by other means" (119). In his famous tract Clausewitz insists that "War is an instrument of policy" (411). Mao's words come from *On Protracted War*. See online "Quotations from Mao Tsetung." www.marxists.org/reference/archive/mao/selected-works/volume-2/mswv2_09.htm(accessed July 11, 2012).
30 "Kokka kakushin no genri," Zenshū 40, 209.
31 "Gogatsu kakumei," Zenshū 35, 137–38.
32 Tony Judt, "Three More Memoirs," *New York Review of Books*, February 25, 2010, 19. Also by Judt see *Postwar: A History of Europe Since 1945* (London: Penguin Books, 2006), 411–12, and *The Burden of Responsibility: Blum, Camus, Aron, and the French Twentieth Century* (Chicago: University of Chicago Press, 1998), 151.
33 "Kokka kakushin no genri," Zenshū 40, 207.
34 "*Kurotokage* ni tsuite," Zenshū 35,119. The government-sponsored broadcasting corporation (NHK) started experimental TV broadcasting in June 1956, and the private broadcasting company TBS started TV broadcasting in April 1955.
35 "Furui haru," Zenshū 35, 114. The essay appeared in the June issue of the monthly devoted to fiction.

## Chapter Twenty-Four: *Sun and Steel*

1 "Jo (Yatō Tamotsu shashin-shū *Hadaka matsuri*)," Zenshū 35, 121–28.
2 "Genda Minoru—konna kōho konna hitogara," Zenshū 35, 129.
3 Hayashi, *Shōwa-shi to watashi*, 329.
4 "Kaidai," Zenshū 35, 769. The quotation is from a summary of the council's statement.
5 "Filter no susuharai," Zenshū 35, 131.
6 "Makeru ga kachi," in Mishima Yukio, *Wakaki samurai no tame ni* (Bungei Shunjū Sha, 1966), 201–3.
7 "Watashi no jishu bōei ron," Zenshū 35, 233.
8 Hayashi, *Shōwa-shi to watashi*, 291.
9 "Tōdai o dōbutsuen ni shiro," Zenshū 35, 364–65.
10 According to Shibusawa Tatsuhiko, who said he helped Mishima in Western "decadent art," the Beardsley picture Mishima chose, *Sōjō*, "priest," was an illustration of Beardsley's erotic writing, *Under the Hill*, that appeared in the first issue of the magazine, *The Savoy*. Shibusawa, *Mishima Yukio: Oboegaki*, 63. A great deal of Beardsley material is online, including what appears to be the complete edition of *Under the Hill*, but it is difficult to identify Mishima's choice without recourse to the summer 1968 issue of *Hihyō* where his article and the artworks he chose appeared.

11   "Decadence bijutsu," Zenshū 35, 115–16.
12   Shiine, *Heibon Punch no Mishima Yukio*, 69, and Fukuda Kazuya, "Kaisetsu," *Mishima Yukio: Wakaki samurai no tame ni* (Bungei Shunjū Sha, 1996), 273–74.
13   "*Samurai* ni tsuite," Zenshū 34, 676–79.
14   Bōjō, *Honō no gen'ei*, 29–33.
15   "Bunjaku no to ni tsuite," Zenshū 35, 100–102.
16   Hashikawa Bunzō, "Wakai sedai to sengo seishin," *Hashikawa Bunzō chosakushū*, vol. 4, 298–301.
17   Haga Mayumi is the "M. H." in Mishima's open exchange of letters in the February 1947 issue of *Gozen* on "the future of mankind and the fate of the poet." "M. H.-shi e no tegami: jinrui no shōrai to shijin no unmei," Zenshū 26, 596–603.
18   John Nathan, "Tokyo Story," *New Yorker*, April 9, 2001, 108.
19   Hashikawa Bunzō, "Yōsetsusha no kin'yoku," *Hashikawa Bunzō chosakushū*, vol. 1, 266–72. Included in the *Gunzō* special *Nihon no sakka 18: Mishima Yukio*, 26–31.
20   Letter to Hashikawa, May 29, 1966, Zenshū 38, 766–67.
21   "Hashikawa Bunzō-shi e no kōkaijō," Zenshū 35, 205–6.
22   "2.26 shōkō to Zengakuren gakusei to no danzetsu," Zenshū 40, 587.
23   Mishima was not feigning knowledge of avant-garde tanka. In 1956, when Tsukamoto Kunio dedicated to him his first book of tanka *Tale of Burial at Sea (Suisō monogatari)* and sent him a copy, Mishima, evidently taken by Tsukamoto's pieces that rejected tradition except for the form, at once recommended him to *Bungakukai*, which duly reprinted a group of ten tanka from it. Tsukamoto, who put himself at the forefront of the avant-garde movement in tanka soon after the war, retained that status till his death, in 2005, effortlessly combining his knowledge of "old European things" with that of "Japan's medieval vocabulary," as Mishima characterized his tanka, although, in the same letter noting that, in 1965, Mishima told him that he, along with Fukuda Tsuneari, did not believe in the characterization of "avant-garde." Letter to Tsukamoto, February 12, 1965, Zenshū 38, 692.
24   *Gunjin chokuyu* may be read online. www.asahi-net.or.jp/~uu3s-situ/oo/Gunzin.tyokuyu.html (accessed July 11, 2012).
25   Quoted by Takeuchi Yoshimi, "Kenryoku to geijutsu," *Nihon gendai bungaku zenshū* 93 (Kōdansha, 1968), 351. Robert Dahl, *How Democratic Is the American Constitution?* (2001), 111–15. Dahl calls US presidency "a hybrid."
26   Nakamura, *Nihon no kindai*, 357–58.
27   Hashikawa Bunzō, "Bi no ronri to seiji no ronri," *Hashikawa Bunzō chosakushū*, vol. 1, 239–58. Hashikawa traces the origins of Mishima's view of culture as a "comprehensive totality" as well as "the Tennō as a cultural concept" to the ideas of National Learning proponents such as Motoori Norinaga (1730–1801). He characterizes as "an astonishing idea in the history of human thought" the worldview such as propounded by Moto'ori Norinaga in *Tamakushige* that both good and bad things occur by divine decree so that attempts to eliminate bad things are vain (250–52).
28   "Hashimoto Bunzō-shi e no kōkaijō," Zenshū 35, 206.
29   "Eiyo no kizuna de tsunage kiku to katana," Zenshū 35, 192–93.

30 Kawabata Yasunari, "Senkyo jimuchō funsen no ki." *"Bungei Shunjū" ni miru Shōwa-shi*, vol. 3, 310–26. Kawabata's view on the security treaty, 319–20.
31 Tanaka, *Mishima Yukio: Kami no kagebōshi*, 240–43.
32 "Taidan: Ningen to bungaku," Zenshū 40, 169–70. The four taidan were conducted on July 10, August 17, September 13, and November 10, 1967.
33 Stephen Coote, *W. B. Yeats: A Life* (London: Hodder and Stoughton, 1997), 114.
34 "Nichirin raisan," Zenshū 37, 473–74. The poem is dated 15.3.20, i.e., March 20, 1940.
35 "Tōsui ni tsuite," Zenshū 29, 306.
36 Shiine, *Heibon Punch no Mishima Yukio*, 30–31.

## Chapter Twenty-Five: The Shield Society, Counterrevolution

1 "Sakuhin no haikei—*Waga tomo Hitler*," "*Waga tomo Hitler* oboegaki," and "Ittsui no sakuhin—*Sado kōshaku fujin* to *Waga tomo Hitler*," Zenshū 35, 319–20, 386–88, 472–73.
2 Michel Surya, *Georges Bataille: An Intellectual Biography*, trans. Kizysztof Fijalkowski and Michael Richardson (London and New York: Verso, 2002), 309, 442. Mishima observed that the Japanese readers of Bataille had been tormented by foul translations until Ikuta Kōsaku's that he took up for discussing the French writer. In this regard, it is amusing to note that Ikuta translated as "octopus" what the translators of Surya's book gave as "squid" in the following passage: "She was seated, she held one leg stuck up in the air, to open her crack yet wider she used fingers to draw the folds of skin apart. And so Madame Edwarda's 'old tatters' looked at me, hairy and pink, just as full of life as some loathsome squid. 'Why,' I stammered in a subdued tone, 'why are you doing that?' 'You can see for yourself,' she said, 'I'm god.'" Michel Surya, *Georges Bataille*, 305. Mishima, indeed began his review of Muro Junsuke's translation of *Eroticism* by saying: "The books I want to read, books that draw my interest, often come, strangely, in bad translation. The translation of this book, too, is terrible." "*Eroticism*—Georges Bataille cho, Muro Junsuke yaku," Zenshū 31, 411–15.
3 "Shōsetsu to wa nani ka," Zenshū 34, 710–21.
4 Shiine, *Heibon Punch no Mishima Yukio*, 95–96.
5 Koestler, "For Better or Worse."
6 "Gunpuku o kiru otoko no jōken," Zenshū 35, 298–99, 772–73. Shiine, *Heibon Punch no Mishima Yukio*, 95–97.
7 Muramatsu, *Mishima Yukio no sekai* (Shinchōsha, 1996), 526.
8 "Chōju no geijutsu no hana o," Zenshū 35, 220–22.
9 Itasaka Gō, *Shinsetsu: Mishima Yukio* (Natsume Shobō, 1998), 46–52.
10 "Taidan: Ningen to bungaku," Zenshū 40, 64–65.
11 Keene, *5 Modern Japanese Novelists*, 24–25. Fujita Mitsuo, "Atogaki," Mishima Yōko and Fujita Mitsuo, eds., *Shashinshū: Mishima Yukio: '25–'70* (Shinchō, 2000). The book is unpaginated.
12 Shima, *Yasuda Kōdō*, 110.
13 Some of the details from the front-page articles on October 22, 1968 of the

*Asahi Shinbun.*

14 Or a "special correspondent for Shinchōsha," according to Yamamoto, *Mishima Yukio: Yūmon no sokoku bōei fu*, 133.
15 Ibid., 135–37.
16 Shibusawa, *Mishima Yukio: Oboegaki*, 9.
17 Itasaka, *Kyokusetsu: Mishima Yukio*, 176–79.
18 "Tōdai o dōbutsuen ni shiro," Zenshū 35, 360–61.
19 "Seiji kōi no shōchōsei ni tsuite," Zenshū 40, 432, 437.
20 Yamamoto, *Mishima Yukio: Yūmon no sokoku bōei fu*, 135–36.
21 Hiraoka, "Bōru no gotoku," quoted in *Tokuhon*, end of 1968.
22 "Ballet *Miranda* ni tsuite," Zenshū 35, 243.
23 "Kaidai," Zenshū 24, 699.
24 *Le Sang et la Rose* is the French name given by the editor Shibusawa Tatsuhiko.
25 Shiine, *Heibon Punch no Mishima Yukio*, 260–62.
26 The 1968 *Esquire* cover of Muhammad Ali and comments are online (accessed July 11, 2012).
27 The four issues of *Chi to bara* are partially online. http://homepage2.nifty.com/weird~/titobara.htm (accessed July 11, 2012).
28 In fact, the medical students had gone on strike a year earlier, on March 23, and it had lasted until March 27; but it had not created the kind of chain reactions within Tōdai that the one in January 1968 did. Toyokawa Kōhei, "*Genkyō* ni mo iwasete hoshii," "*Bungei Shunjū*" ni miru Shōwa-shi, vol. 3, 359–76. Toyokawa was dean of the school and was accused of being responsible for the turmoil, hence the title of his article. Hayashi, *Shōwa-shi to watashi*, 295–96.
29 Kawashima Hiroshi, "Yasuda Kōdō sai-senkyo sengen." "*Bungei Shunjū*" ni miru Shōwa-shi, vol. 3, 346, 350.
30 Yomota Inuhiko, *High School 1968* (Shinchōsha, 2004), 71.
31 Hayashi, *Shōwa-shi to watashi*, 315–16.
32 Kawashima, "Yasuda Kōdō sai-senkyo sengen," 348.
33 Sassa, *Tōdai rakujō* (Bungei Shunjū, 1996), 123.
34 Ibid., 279–80.
35 Shima, *Yasuda Kōdō*, 178–80, 271–73.
36 Kawashima, "Yasuda Kōdō sai-senkyo sengen," 350.
37 Sassa, *Tōdai rakujō*, 129.
38 Shima, *Yasuda Kōdō*, 158–76, especially 176.
39 "Minsei no chikara koso osorubeki mono da," Zenshū 35, 383–84. Also his taidan with Iida Momo, "Seiji kōi no shōchōsei ni tsuite," Zenshū 40, 422–41.
40 Yomota, *High School 1968*, 71.
41 Kawashima, "Yasuda Kōdō sai-senkyo sengen," 348.
42 Andō, *"Nichiroku,"* 366; also Zenshū 42, 304, and Sassa, *Tōdai rakujō*, 16. But Sassa, in his book, does not mention the kind of gas Mishima recommended. He may have done so when his account was initially serialized in *Bungei Shunjū*.
43 Sassa, *Tōdai rakujō*, 313–15.
44 Muramatsu, *Mishima Yukio no sekai*, 527–28.

45  "'Haru no yuki' ni tsuite," *Zenshū* 35, 515.
46  Okuno, *Mishima Yukio densetsu*, 432–35.
47  *Jin Jan* as transliterated from the name given in the novel; Jao Jan is one Thai reading from the Chinese characters given for "princess" (*jao*, "royal") and "moonlight" (*jan* or *chan*, "moon"). A Thai says "Jan Jao" is probably correct.
48  Kojima, *Mishima Yukio to Dan Kazuo*, 52–61.
49  "Hankakumei sengen," *Zenshū* 35, 389–90. The manifesto is followed by *hochū*, "supplementary notes." These are the result of the discussions between Mishima and the members of the Shield Society, which he orally summarized. Hosaka, *Mishima Yukio to Tate no Kai jiken*, 164.
50  "Sōrei naru 'kyokō' no tenkai," *Zenshū* 35, 426–27.
51  *Yamato damashii* meaning an iron resolve unique to the Japanese is of relatively recent vintage. When the expression appears in Genji's words in the *Otome* chapter of the *Tale of Genji*, it is used in the sense of "commonsensical judgment": *zae o moto to shite koso, Yamato damashii no yo ni mochiiraruru kata mo tsuyō haberame*, "Only when you have Chinese learning as foundation, your ability will be stronger to exercise your commonsensical judgment in daily life." By the time Takizawa Bakin used the phrase in the late Edo Period, it came to mean a resoluteness unique to the Japanese but not necessarily in the positive sense. In Volume 4 of Part 2 (Chapter 24) of *Chinsetsu Yumiharizuki*, the deceased Emperor Shutoku (Sutoku), appearing as a ghost, admonishes Minamoto no Tametomo not to hasten to follow him in death, saying, *Koto ni semarite shi o karonzuru ha, Yamato damashii naredo ōku wa omoibakari no asaki ni nite, manabazaru no ayamari nari*, "Driven up against the wall, it may be the Japanese spirit to make light of death [i.e., to choose to die], but in many cases it resembles shallowness in thinking, an error of the unlearned."
52  Yamamoto, *Mishima Yukio: Yūmon no sokoku bōei fu*, 160–63.
53  Hosaka, *Mishima Yukio to Tate no Kai jiken*, 164–65.
54  Murakami, *Kimitachi ni wa wakaranai*, 23–25.
55  "Watashi no dokusho-jutsu," *Zenshū* 35, 374–75.

## Chapter Twenty-Six: The Yakuza

1  "Tsuruta Kōji ron," *Zenshū* 35, 413–17. Tsuneishi Fumiko, "Sandome no jijin," *Eureka* (November 2000), 238.
2  Yomota, *Nihon eiga-shi 100 nen*, 72–73.
3  Yamamoto Jirochō, usually known as Shimizu no Jirochō because of the port where he did his business, counted among his associates some of the prominent officials of the day and was accorded a biography while alive. Amada Guan (1854–1904), of samurai stock, who survived the Boshin War as a young man and became one of Jirochō's henchmen and was then adopted, published *Tōkai yūkyō den*, in 1884, as a farewell gift as he annulled the adoption. The hagiographic narrative went on to become the greatest source of countless tales about the man in the years that followed. In *Shimizu no Jirochō* (PHP Kenkyūsho, 2006; originally Bungei Shunjū, 2002), Kurogane Hiroshi

did a two-volume manga recounting of the man's life and times largely to remedy the hagiography.
4  "Tsuruta Kōji-ron," Zenshū 35, 413–17.
5  Tsuneishi Fumiko, "Sandome no jijin," 240–41. Bazin's words are quoted from Gary Johnson's online article, "In Focus: The Western, an Overview" (accessed July 11, 2012).
6  Shima, *Yasuda Kōdō*, 146–47.
7  Yomota, *High School 1968*, 65.
8  Shiine, *Heibon Punch no Mishima Yukio*, 45–49.
9  "Shikyaku to kumichō," Zenshū 40, 515, 791.
10  Hamish Miles, trans., *Sardonic Tales* (New York: Alfred A. Knopf, 1927), 69. The original title is in English.
11  "*Raiō no terasu* ni tsuite," Zenshū 35, 511.
12  "Kawabata bungaku no bi—reien," Zenshū 35, 448–49. For Zeami's citation of Teika's poem, see J. Thomas Rimer and Yamazaki Masaharu, *On the Art of the Nō Drama: The Major Treaties of Zeami* (Princeton: Princeton University Press, 1984), 117. For the original paragraph in Zeami's treatise *Yūgaku shūdō fūken* where Teika's poem is cited, Hisamatsu Sen'ichi and Nishio Minoru, eds., *Karon-shū, nōgakuron-shū* (Iwanami Shoten, 1965), 444–45. For "snow in a silver bowl" in Zeami's treatise *Kyūi*, ibid., 448.
13  "*Yumiharizuki* no gekika to enshutsu," Zenshū 35, 730.
14  Urayama Masao and Matsuzaki Hitoshi, eds., *Kabuki kyakuhon shū, jō* (Iwanami Shoten, 1960), 9–11. The theater critic and tanka poet Ishii Tatsuhiko has provided some of the details here.
15  Gary Wills, *Verdi's Shakespeare: Men of the Theater* (New York: Viking, 2011), 8–13.
16  "*Chinsetsu yumiharizuki* no enshutsu," Zenshū 35, 732.
17  "*Yumiharizuki* no gekika to enshutsu," Zenshū 35, 728.
18  "*Hitokiri* Tanaka Shinbē ni funshite," Zenshū 35, 508–10.
19  "*Hitokiri* shutsuen no ki," Zenshū 35, 518–19. See also *Tokuhon*.
20  Letter to Hayashi, June 13, 1969, Zenshū 38, 798–99.
21  Yamamoto, *Mishima Yukio: Yūmon no sokoku bōei fu*, 168–72. Yamamoto also remembered Mishima going up onto the stage where Matsumoto Kōshirō was rehearsing his role in *A Wonder Tale* and giving him acting instructions, with Mishima's wife Yōko alone watching in the audience. But there obviously was confusion in Yamamoto's memory: It was too early for any rehearsal of the play.
22  "Il se pourrait que ce fût pour voir dans vos yeux une inquiétude, une curiosité du trouble enfin: tout ce que depuis une seconde j'y découvre." François Mauriac, *Thérèse*, trans. Gerard Hopkins (London: Penguin, 2002; originally 1928), 109–10. As Mauriac made it clear, the story was based on an actual case in his youth. See Raymond MacKenzie's translation, *Thérèse Desqueyroux* (Lanham, MD: Rowman and Littlefield, 2005), 3–4. Thérèse's motive is at least dual, lesbianism and freedom in daily living, which must both be suppressed in a rural Catholic milieu.
23  "Ce que je voulais? Sans doute serait-il plus aisé de dire ce que je ne voulais pas; je ne voulais pas jouer un personnage, faire des gestes, prononcer des

formules, renier enfin à chaque instant une Thérèse qui...." François Mauriac, *Thérèse* 111–12; MacKenzie, *Thérèse Desqueyroux*, 121.

24 Muramatsu, *Mishima Yukio no sekai* (Shinchōsha, 1996), 524.
25 Hosaka, *Mishima Yukio to Tate no Kai jiken*, 199–200.
26 Ibid., 210.
27 See recollections of Suzuki Taka (1883–1971) who served as Hirohito's nanny for eleven years, before marrying Kantarō, later an admiral, grand chamberlain, and prime minister—Tsurumi and Nakagawa, *Tennō hyakuwa*, jō, 23–43—as well as recollections of Kanroji Osanaga (1880–1977), an aristocrat who spent a great deal of time at the Imperial Palace (53–57). Suzuki tells how Hirohito, then Prince Michi, loved to wrestle but insisted on having the pants that developed holes at the knees mended, rather than asking for a new pair. That was part of the teachings of Gen. Nogi Maresuke, whom he insisted on calling "His Excellency, the President." Both Suzuki and Kanroji describe Gen. Nogi's final visit with Prince Michi, two days before he disemboweled himself to follow Emperor Meiji in death.

The postwar Japanese rightwing and conservatives became increasingly disenchanted with the Tennō institution as the martial (*bu*) aspect of the Shōwa Emperor before Japan's defeat was deemphasized and the stress on austerity in imperial life was relegated to lower status as his son became Tennō. Ben-Ami Shillony, "Conservative Dissatisfaction with the Modern Emperors," in Shillony, *Emperors of Modern Japan*, 147–54.

28 "'Tate no Kai' no koto," *Zenshū* 35, 722.
29 "2.25 shōkō to Zengakuren gakusei to no danzetsu," *Zenshū* 40, 588.
30 *Mishima Yukio vs Tōdai Zenkyōtō: Bi to kyōdōtai to Tōda tōsō* (Kadokawa Shoten, 2000; originally 1969). *Zenshū* 40, 442–506.
31 Yamamoto, *Mishima Yukio: Yūmon no sokoku bōei fu*, 185–88.
32 Andō, *"Nichiroku,"* 403–4.
33 Shiine, *Heibon Punch no Mishima Yukio*, 95.
34 Murakami, *Kimitachi ni wa wakaranai*, 20.
35 Yamamoto, *Mishima Yukio: yūmon no sokoku bōei-fu*, 183–84.
36 "'Tate no Kai' no koto," *Zenshū* 35, 722.
37 "Watashi no kinkyō—*Haru no yuki* to *Honba*," *Zenshū* 35, 295–96.

## Chapter Twenty-Seven: Wang Yangming: "To know is to act"

1 Muramatsu, *Mishima Yukio no sekai*, 530–32. Hosaka, *Mishima Yukio to Tate no Kai jiken*, 216–17, 219–20.
2 Yamamoto, *Mishima Yukio: Yūmon no sokoku bōei fu*, 193.
3 "Kita Ikki ron," *Zenshū* 35, 497–504.
4 "Mishima-shi ni zubari 10 shitsumon," *Zenshū* 35, 506.
5 Notes for *Ran'ryō'ō*, *Zenshū* 20, 777–82.
6 "Nihon to wa nani ka," *Zenshū* 35, 693.
7 Kawabata Yasunari, *Utsukushii Nihon no watakushi: sono josetsu*, with E. G. Seidensticker's translation (Kodansha, 1969).
8 Yasunari Kawabata, *Bi no sonzai to hakken* or *The Existence and Discovery of*

9   *Beauty*, trans. V. H. Viglielmo (Mainichi Newspaper, 1969).
9   Kawabata, *Utsukushii Nihon no watakushi*, 16–20; Seidensticker,'s translation 61–63.
10  Kawabata, *Bi no sonzai to hakken* (Mainichi Shinbun Sha, 1969), 63–64. Yamagishi Tokuhei, ed., *Genji monogatari*, vol. 5 (Iwanami Shoten, 1963), 345.
11  Letter to Kawabata, August 4, 1969. Zenshū 38, 308. *Ōfuku shokan*, 199.
12  Letter to Bōjō, March 12, 1969, Zenshū 38, 872–73. Bōjō, *Honō no gen'ei*, 91, 129–36.
13  *Shin ren'ai kōza*, Zenshū 29, 15–123. The series of twelve "lectures" begins with an overview of Greek (Platonic) love, Christian love, and "Japanese love."
14  "*Haru no yuki* ni tsuite," Zenshū 35, 661.
15  "Nihon to wa nani ka," Zenshū 35, 699–701.
16  August 3, 1955, *Shōsetsuka no kyūka*, Zenshū 28, 646–50.
17  *Kōdōgaku nyūmon*, Zenshū 35, 606–10. *Kōdōgaku* today means "ethology," but Mishima did not use it in that sense. One is tempted to apply "actionism," except that "actionism" is likely to mislead because of the art movement so designated.
18  *Kōdōgaku nyūmon*, Zenshū 35, 612–14
19  Ibid., 614–15.
20  Hosaka, *Mishima Yukio to Tate no Kai jiken*, 229–30. The taidan is not included in Zenshū 39 and 40 or in *Shōbu no kokoro*.
21  Shiine, *Heibon Punch no Mishima Yukio*, 73–75.
22  "'Henkaku no shisō' to wa," Zenshū 36, 32
23  Muramatsu, *Mishima Yukio no sekai*, 532. Quoting the report of the Metropolitan Police Department.
24  Hosaka, *Mishima Yukio to Tate no Kai jiken*, 233–34. Quoting from the *Asahi Shinbun* of October 22, 1969.
25  Muramatsu, *Mishima Yukio no sekai*, 540.
26  Hosaka, *Mishima Yukio to Tate no Kai jiken*, 234–35. Andō, "*Nichiroku*," 379.
27  *Kōdōgaku nyūmon*, Zenshū 35, 623–27.
28  Yamamoto, *Mishima Yukio: Yūmon no sokoku bōei fu*, 204.
29  Okamoto Kihachi's 1966 film *Sword of Doom* (English title), with Nakadai Tatsuya in the lead role of the blinded swordsman Tsukue Ryūnosuke, is based on this story.
30  *Kōdōgaku nyūmon*, Zenshū 35, 631–32.
31  Ibid., 635.
32  Ibid., 640.
33  Letter to Shimizu, June 5, 1942, Zenshū 38, 554–55.
34  *Owari no bigaku*, Zenshū 33, 711–14.
35  "Kakumei tetsugaku to shite no Yōmeigaku," Zenshū 36, 658–59.
36  "2.26 shōkō to Zengakuren gakusei to no danzetsu," Zenshū 40, 585.
37  "Dai-Tōa Sensō ka Taiheiyō Sensō ka," Zenshū 36, 658–659.
38  Gore Vidal, "Japanese Intentions in the Second World War," *Dreaming War: Blood for Oil and the Cheney-Bush Junta* (New York: Thunder's Mouth Press, 2002), 72–74, 85–98. Also Vidal's novel *The Golden Age* (New York: Doubleday, 2000).
39  Wing-tsit Chan, trans. and comp., *A Source Book in Chinese Philosophy*

(Princeton University Press, 1963), 654–58, 668–69. "Dynamic idealism" is the translator-compiler Chan's characterization.

40  Shiba Ryōtarō, *Junshi* (Bungei Shunjū, 1978), 99, 110–11.
41  Paragraph 162, *Seishindō sakki*, Sagara Tōru et al., eds., *Satō Issai, Ōshio Chūsai* (Iwanami Shoten, 1980), 430–31. The origin of this observation is traced to that of Confucius in *Zhuangzi*: "No sadness is greater than that of the mind dying; next comes someone dying." Mori Mikisaburō, trans. and annot., *Sōji: Gaihen* (Chūō Kōron Sha, 1974), 318–19.
42  Letter to Yasuoka Masahiro, May 26, 1968, Hokan, 238–39.
43  "Kaidai," Zenshū 36, 691–92.

## Chapter Twenty-Eight: The Constitution

1   The invitation, Zenshū 36, 671.
2   Date, *Saiban kiroku*, 237. Koga Masayoshi's testimony during the Mishima trial.
3   "'Tate no Kai' no koto," Zenshū 35, 720–27. It appeared in the British magazine *Queen*, in its January 7–20, 1970, issue in an English translation by Ivan and Nobuko Morris as "The Shield Society."
4   Scott-Stokes, *Life and Death of Yukio Mishima*, 16–17.
5   "2.26 shōkō to Zengakuren gakusei no danzetsu," Zenshū 40, 586, 591, 593.
6   The *Sankei* article is printed in full in Zenshū 35, 785–86. Muramatsu, *Mishima Yukio no sekai*, 534.
7   The Tokyo Metropolitan Police Department's report. Included in Date, *Saiban kiroku*, 58. Most of the court proceedings on the "Mishima Incident" are collected in the Date book. Unless noted, details on some of the actions and words of those involved in the following account come from it.
8   Shiine, *Heibon Punch no Mishima Yukio*, 98.
9   Yamamoto, *Mishima Yukio: Yūmon no sokoku bōei fu*, 209–12. Matsufuji Takejirō, the *Mainichi* reporter who describes himself as having frequently written about Mishima and the SDF, followed Yamamoto in saying it was a clear day when "the autumn sun poured down" in his mindlessly zealous book, *Chitagiru Mishima Yukio "kenpō kaisei,"* 202–3. Then twenty, he was not there.
10  Scott-Stokes, *Life and Death of Yukio Mishima*, 17.
11  Takemura Toshio, "Hengen jizai no omoshirosa," *Asahi Shinbun*, November 22, 1969.
12  Muramatsu, *Mishima Yukio no sekai*, 536–37.
13  Andō, *"Nichiroku,"* 370. The quote comes from Orita Kōji, *Mishima Yukio "Shibai nikki"* (Chūō Kōron Sha, 1991).
14  "Tamasaburō-kun no koto," Zenshū 36, 271–72.
15  "Stage-Left Is Right from Audience," Zenshū 35, 740–43.
16  "Gendai ni okeru uyoku to sayoku," Zenshū 40, 568.
17  "Ken ka hana ka," Zenshū 40, 599–600. The Sato-Nixon talk on Japan's textile exports to the US during the meeting that year produced a famous episode in the annals of translation/interpretation: the discrepancy between what Satō said—probably, *Zensho shimasu*—or, rather, his interpreter's translation of it—probably, "I'll do my best"—and what Nixon later claimed he

had understood from what was conveyed by the interpreter—that Satō said something like "I'll take care of it."
18  Kojima, *Kindai Nihon no Yōmeigaku*, 190.
19  Hiraoka, *Segare*, 107–8.
20  "Dōshi no shinjō to hijō," *Zenshū* 36, 22.
21  "70 nendai shinshun no yobikake," *Zenshū* 36, 25–27.
22  Nagai Yōnosuke, *Jū-kōzō shakai to bōryoku* (Chūō Kōron Sha, 1971), 233–35.
23  "Joint Statement by President Richard Nixon and Prime Minister Eisaku Sato, Washington, D.C., 21st November, 1969." Online. www.presidency.ucsb.edu/ws/index.php?pid=2334 (accessed July 11, 2012).
24  David Sanger, "Japanese Major Suggests a Cure for Scandals," *New York Times*, October 16, 1992. Sanger, then Tokyo bureau chief of the *Times*, naturally called the SDF "the military," the GSDF "the army."
25  Later the name agreed upon was UN Department of Peacekeeping Operations.
26  "'Henkaku no shisō' to wa," *Zenshū* 36, 30–38.
27  From the Hanover Historical Texts Project, scanned by Jonathan Dresner, Harvard University. The translation must be official—most likely the one Occupation lawyers wrote—for all the English texts available online, including the one put out by the Japanese government, show little variance save orthographic.
28  *Seiron*, ed., *Kenpō no ronten* (Sankei Shinbun News Service, 2004), 69–70.
29  *Kenpō kaisei shian no chūkan hōkoku*. www.hatoyama.gr.jp/tentative_plan/1-1.html (accessed July 11, 2012).
30  *Kenpō no ronten*, 95.
31  Date, *Saiban kiroku*, 223–25.
32  "Mondai teiki," *Zenshū* 36, 118–36.
33  Date, *Saiban kiroku*, 225.
34  "Mondai teiki," *Zenshū* 36, 127.
35  The Meiji Constitution (1889) was written by considering a number of constitutions of Europe and the United States. Prewar Japanese interpreters of the Constitution differed on whether the Tennō's sanctity and inviolability referred to his legal, political, or ethical status or whether it derived from his status equal to state (e.g., Hozumi Yatsuka). Regardless, not long after Hirohito's declaration on January 1, 1946, that he was not a deity but a human being, the philosopher Tanabe Hajime voiced regrets, from the viewpoint of political philosophy, that Hirohito did not express his "moral" responsibility more explicitly, whereas Nanbara Shigeru, president of the Imperial University of Tokyo, suggested, on Hirohito's birthday, that Hirohito must be feeling "most deeply" his "moral and spiritual responsibility" to his ancestors. Ienaga Saburō, *Nion kindai kenpō shisōshi kenkyū* (Iwanami Shoten, 1967), 204. A statement expressing his "profound regrets under heaven" for having allowed "unprecedented calamities" to occur because of his "lack of virtue" was prepared sometime in late 1948, but it was not made public because of dissension among his top aides. It was discovered and published only in the summer of 2003. Katō Kyōko, "Chin no futoku naru," etc., *Bungei Shunjū* (July 2003), 96–113.

36 Muramatsu, *Mishima Yukio no sekai*, 543, 547–48.
37 William K. Bunce, *Religions in Japan: Buddhism, Shinto, Christianity* (Tokyo and Rutland, VT: Charles E. Tuttle Company, 1955), 108.
38 Matsufuji, *Chitagiru: Mishima Yukio "kenpō kaisei,"* 127–29. The draft by Mishima and the Shield Society surfaced more than three decades after the trial, in November 2003.
39 Hiraoka, *Segare*, 199–200.
40 Yamamoto, *Mishima Yukio: Yūmon no sokoku bōei fu*, 223.
41 Actually, Yamamoto published his first essay explaining his relationship to Mishima in the weekly *Playboy* five years after Mishima's death, but Yōko stopped him for copyright infringement. Yamamoto, *Mishima Yukio: Yūmon no sokoku bōei fu*, 33, 290.
42 Date, *Saiban kiroku*, 162.
43 Muramatsu, *Mishima Yukio no sekai*, 548–49, 550–51.
44 Hiraoka, *Segare*, 107.
45 Yamamoto, *Mishima Yukio: Yūmon no sokoku bōei fu*, 223–38.

## Chapter Twenty-Nine: Hailstones, Ghouls, Golden Death

1 Saeki Shōichi, "Kaisetsu," Endō Shūsaku, *Umi to dokuyaku* (Shinchōsha, 2010), 204–8.
2 Michael Gallagher, *Bakudan to ichō*, trans. Ōta Hiroshi (Kōdansha, 1970). The three prefaces are unpaginated. Kamagasaki was renamed, for appearance's sake, Airin Chiku "Love-pity District." The original English version appears not to have seen print.
3 "*Bakudan to ichō* jobun," *Zenshū* 36, 11–12.
4 "Hatano Sōha: hito to sakuhin," *Zenshū* 35, 269–76. See also Hiroaki Sato, "Hatano Sōha: 1923–1991," *Roadrunner*, November 2009, vol. 9, 4.
5 "*Shishū Waga te ni kieshi arare* jobun," *Zenshū* 36, 44–48.
6 Odakane Jirō includes Itō's letters to Tanaka in *Shijin, sono shōgai to unmei*, 670–73, 706–21. One commentator has suggested that in taking up Tanaka as his "disciple" or "student," Itō may have felt as Rilke did in writing to Franz Kappus. One sees in any event that the "refracted, elegant, sensual, profoundly intimate refinement" of her poetry—Itō's words in his letter to her of May 29, 1943—was the opposite of what he attempted to do in his poems.
7 "*Hasuda Zenmei to sono shi* jobun," *Zenshū* 36, 60–63.
8 Yamamoto, *Mishima Yukio: Yūmon no sokoku bōei fu*, 238–39.
9 Kojima, *Mishima Yukio to Dan Kazuo*, 31–32.
10 *Ninja bugei chō*, from 1959 to 1962, with its subsidiary sequel, as it were, *Sasuke*, from 1961 to 1966. Shirato started *Kamui den* in 1965 and ended it in 1971.
11 "Waga manga," *Zenshū* 29, 166–69.
12 Mizuki Shigeru, *Musume ni kataru otōsan no senki* (Kawade Shobō Shinsha, 1995).
13 Translation of *Sanmoto Gorōzaemon tadaima taisan tsukamatsuru*.
14 "Shōsetsu to wa nani ka," *Zenshū* 34, 693–704, 727–31. It is Mishima's commentary here (the latter part of Part 4) that was used as an afterword in a recent edition of *Shinshū Kōketsu-jō* (Kawade Shobō Shinsha, 2007), 449–54.

For the original tale about the "tie-dye castle," see Watanabe Tsunaya and Nishio Kōichi, eds., *Uji Shūi Monogatari* (Iwanami Shoten, 1980), 376–79. The tale is supposed to describe what Jikaku the Great Teacher (Ennin, 794–864) experienced in China, in 845, when Emperor Wu tried to destroy Buddhism. Jikaku was in China to study Buddhism, from 838 to 847. In the text Kunieda quotes (59–61), the tale number was 167; in the Iwanami edition, it is numbered 170.

15  "Gekiga ni miru wakamono-ron," Zenshū 36, 53–56.
16  "Shōsetsu to wa nani ka." Zenshū 34, 737–42.
17  Morikawa Tatsuya, "Kaisetsu," *Akatsuki no tera* (Shinchōsha, 1977), 375–77.
18  "Hatashieteinai yakusoku—watashi no naka no 25 nen." Zenshū 36, 213.
19  Letter to Keene, Zenshū 38, 453.
20  Ibid., 448.
21  Muramatsu, *Mishima Yukio no sekai*, 558–59. As far as is known, Keene was the only person who received the postmortem letter, as it were. Dated November 26, 1970, it was, like all his other letters to Keene, in Japanese. One of Mishima's last letters was also to a foreign scholar-translator, Ivan Morris, but it was dated November 25. The letter to Morris, which was in English, was partially quoted and discussed in the December 12, 1970, issue of the *New Yorker*. Morris went on to write *The Nobility of Failure: Tragic Heroes in the History of Japan*, 1975, and dedicated the book to Mishima. Readers of the kind Mishima wanted to have surely appeared. For example, the *New York Times* on May 12, 1974, carried an article, "The Decay of the Angel," Alan Friedman's great appreciation of the tetralogy. Friedman took the occasion of reviewing the fourth volume, translated by Edward G. Seidensticker, to discuss the entire cycle, *The Sea of Fertility*.
22  "*Tennin gosui* sōsaku note," Zenshū 14, 652.
23  Kawaguchi Hisao, ed. and annot., *Wakan rōei shū* (Iwanami Shoten, 1976), 254–55. Also, the first episode in the *Konjaku monogatari* (Tales Ancient and Modern), compiled in the early twelfth century. Mishima said Seidensticker suggested the title *Tennin gosui*. Scott-Stokes, *Life and Death of Yukio Mishima*, 21. Tokuoka Takao thought that the same Iwanami *Wakan rōei shū* he lent Mishima while in Bangkok in the fall of 1967 may have had something to do with the choice of the title, although he also did not fail to note of course that Mishima was thoroughly familiar with Japanese classics. Tokuoka, *Gosui no hito*, 143–47. For the first edition of *Tennin gosui*, Yōko designed the cover.
24  "Kaisetsu," Zenshū 36, 164–78.
25  Shibusawa, *Mishima Yukio: Oboegaki*, 183.
26  Shimizu Yoshinori, "Tanizaki bungaku no jikken-bo," Tanizaki Jun'ichirō, *Konjiki no shi* (Kōdansha, 2005), 242–43.
27  "Kaisetsu." Zenshū 36, 80–96.
28  Shimizu Yoshinori, "Tanizaki bungaku no jikken-bo," 245–48.
29  "Jo," Zenshū 36, 208–10.
30  Muramatsu, *Mishima Yukio no sekai*, 559–60.
31  Ibid., 563–64. "Hatashieteinai yakusoku—watashi no naka no 25nen," Zenshū 36, 214–15.

## Chapter Thirty: Toward Ichigaya

1. As noted elsewhere, most of the court proceedings are collected in Date, *Saiban kiroku*.
2. Nosaka, *Kakuyaku-taru gyakkō*, 93–94, 108.
3. Hosaka, *Mishima Yukio to Tate no Kai jiken*, 277.
4. "Inagaki Taruho shō," *Zenshū* 35, 667.
5. Blog: *Jack no danwashitsu*, http://jack4afric.exblog.jp/7244855 (accessed July 11, 2012). When Inagaki said it is not clear.
6. "Taruho no sekai," Shibusawa, *Mishima Yukio: Oboegaki*, 184–85.
7. *Inagaki Taruho zenshū*, vol. 4 (Chikuma Shobō, 2000), 139, 169. Whether these passages were in the edition Mishima recommended for "the grand prize" cannot be readily ascertained. The version in *Inagaki Taruho zenshū*, vol. 4, is the one "expanded and corrected" twice after receiving the prize.
8. "Shidō ni tsuite—Ishihara Shintarō e no kōkaijō." *Zenshū* 36, 179–82.
9. "'Seishinteki dandyism desu yo'—gendaijin no rule." *Zenshū* 36, 187–201.
10. "'Koritsu' no susume." *Zenshū* 36, 183–91. "You seek power, I seek loyalty" is likely a brief restatement of a passage in Shōin's letter dated 16th of First Month, 6th year of Ansei (1859), addressee unknown. Yoshida Tsunekichi et al., eds., *Yoshida Shōin*, vol. 61 of *Nihon Shisō Taikei* (Iwanami Shoten, 1978), 285. For Shōin and death, 315. The age thirty here is by lunar counting. It was also to Yajirō that he talked about the importance of transcending death. Tokutomi Sohō, *Yoshida Shōin* (Iwanami Shoten, 1981; originally 1883), 168. The relevant part of Shōin's letter to Yajirō quoted reads: "The various friends of mine resident in Edo, such as Kusaka [Genzui: 1840–64], Nakatami [Shōsuke: 1828–62], and Takasugi [Shinsaku: 1839–67] all differ from me in our views. Where we differ, I intend to seek loyalty; my various friends intend to seek power. However, each person has a good point, and I am not saying my friends are no good. Practically all the people under heaven intend to seek power. Only I and several comrades intend to seek loyalty. We are deficient in power, while in excess of loyalty." *Yoshida Shōin*, 285, 636, and (for *Kyōfu no sho*) 581–86.
11. Date, *Saiban kiroku*, 216–17.
12. Muramatsu, *Mishima Yukio no sekai*, 562–63.
13. Eight years later, Hori denied that the tapes, though he duly delivered them to Satō, were to be considered in a cabinet conference, or that Nakasone wrote a letter to block its considerations. *Zenshū* 36, 691.
14. Letter to Yamamoto, August 10, 1970, *Zenshū* 38, 946–47.
15. "Bushidō to gunkokushugi" and "Seikigun to fuseikigun," *Zenshū* 36, 247–70.
16. Itasaka, *Kyokusetsu: Mishima Yukio*, 266–67.
17. Takahashi, *Tomodachi no tsukurikata*, 143–44.
18. Muramatsu, *Mishima Yukio no sekai*, 565–69.
19. Nakamura, *Resshi to yobareru otoko*, 187. Andō, *"Nichiroku,"* 404.
20. "Sensō eiga to yakuza eiga," with Ishidō's afterword, in Yamauchi., *Mishima Yukio eiga-ron shūsei*, 584–95.
21. "Jo," *Zenshū* 36, 363–65.
22. Hiraoka, *Segare*, 26.

23  "Haretsu no tame ni shūchū suru," Zenshū 40, 723.
24  "Mudai," Zenshū 36, 371–72. For the *Tokyo Shimnbun* interview, 693–94.
25  "Petronius-saku 'Satyricon,'" Zenshū 27, 668.
26  Hiraoka, *Segare*, 188.
27  Scott-Stokes, *Life and Death of Yukio Mishima*, 23–25. Mishima's letter to Scott-Stokes, Zenshū 38, 650.
28  Imai, *Taishō Democracy*, 413–17.
29  Letter to Date, Zenshū 38, 674–75, and Date, *Saiban kiroku*, 13–15; letter to Tokuoka, in Tokuoka, *Gosui no hito*, 245–47.
30  Andō, *"Nichiroku,"* 406.
31  "Mudai," Zenshū 36, 401.
32  Yoshida Tsuyuko, ed., *"Gyokusai sōshireikan" no e-tegami* (Shōgakukan, 2002), 158.
33  "Jo (Innami Kiyoshi cho *Bajutsu tokuhon*)," Zenshū 36, 381–87.
34  Letter to Shimizu, Zenshū 38, 628–29.

## Chapter Thirty-One: The Seppuku

1   Nathan, *Mishima*, 267.
2   Nosaka, *Kakuyaku-taru gyakkō*, 58–59.
3   Saitō Kōichi, "Finder of naka no Mishima-san," geppō, Zenshū 24, 4.
4   Dower, *Embracing Defeat*, 88–89 and elsewhere.
5   "Mishima Yukio: Saigo no kotoba," Zenshū 40, 739–82. Nakajima Kenji's recollections, 797.
6   Tokuoka, *Gosui no hito*, 271–76.
7   Letter to Bōjō, Zenshū 38, 875–76.
8   Quoted by Andō Takeshi in *"Nichiroku."* Letters to Murakami are not included in Zenshū 38.
9   MIT Classics. http://classics.mit.edu/Plato/phaedo.html (accessed July 11, 2012).
10  Shiine, *Heibon Punch no Mishima Yukio*, 260–62.
11  Gotō Tanji and Kamada Kisaburō, eds., *Taiheiki*, vol. 2 (Iwanami Shoten, 1961), 159. Sato, *Legends of the Samurai*, 187.
12  Hiraoka, *Segare*, 250. For Lord Asano's *jisei*, see Sato, *Legends of the Samurai*, 319.
13  The *Man'yōshū* poem is No. 61; it is attributed to a "servant's daughter." All that which precedes the place name Matokata, "Target Shape," modifies it: "Target Shape (that a man gripping his arrows faces and shoots) is brilliant to behold." The second poem is *Shoku Senzai Wakashū*, no. 1884.
14  Hiraoka, *Segare*, 242–43. Throughout his descriptions of these men's actions and deeds, Azusa does not indicate the sources.
15  Kojima, *Mishima Yukio to Dan Kazuo*, 8–9.
16  Hiraoka, *Segare*, 12–13.
17  "Meireisho" and "Yōkyūsho," Zenshū 36, 678–81.
18  Kojima, *Mishima Yukio to Dan Kazuo*, 9–12.
19  Tokuoka, *Gosui no hito*, 257–60.

## Epilogue

1. Hiraoka, *Segare*, 22.
2. "Mishima Yukio sōgi aisatsu," *Kawabata Yasunari zenshū*, vol. 34 (Shinchōsha, 1982), 76.
3. Hiraoka, *Segare*, 23.
4. Letters to Kuramochi and the Shield Society, Zenshū 38, 495–96, 672–73. Hosaka, *Mishima Yukio to Tate no Kai jiken*, 50–55, 304–5.
5. Yoshida Mitsuru, *Chinkon senkan Yamato* (Kōdansha, 1974), 325, 426. Yoshida Mitsuru, *Teitoku Itō Seiichi no shōgai* (Bungei Shunjū, 1977), 160–61. Sato, *"Gyokusai."*
6. Looten's poem quoted in full Japanese translation in Date, *Saiban kiroku*, 211–14. The original has not been ascertained. For Harriet Monroe's poem "Nogi," see Sato, *Legends of the Samurai*, 341–42.
7. For Ide Kentarō's legal analysis of the case: http://blogs.yahoo.co.jp/cosmopolitanlife/29839181.html (accessed July 11, 2012).
8. Yashiro, *Kishu-tachi no seishun*, 213. The Shakespearean text: Alfred Harbage, ed., *William Shakespeare: The Complete Works* (New York: Viking), 1969, 1133. Kenneth Muir, ed., *Macbeth* (London: Routledge, 1992), 153.
9. Nosaka, *Kakuyaku-taru gyakkō*, 254.

# Bibliography

Mishima was a prolific writer with wide-ranging references to Japanese and foreign literature and arts. In his life of forty-six years, he penned thirty-four novels, more than one hundred and seventy short stories, nearly seventy plays (most of them staged during his lifetime), six hundred sixty poems, and a great many essays, reviews, and blurbs. He had more than three hundred thirty taidan, "dialogues," which, along with *zadankai*, "group discussions," are popular among Japanese magazine editors. His writings, including more than eight hundred letters—a great many more were lost or withheld from publication—and sixty-five taidan and zadankai transcripts, required forty-five volumes to cover in the second (and the latest) attempt for "complete works," *Mishima Yukio zenshū* (Shinchōsha, 2000–2006). Of these forty-four volumes, volume 41 is dedicated to his readings, talks, and such reproduced on seven CDs; volume 42, of nine hundred pages, to chronology and various bibliographies; a *hokan* (supplementary volume), of another nine hundred pages, to a collection of writings missed in earlier volumes plus an index; and a *bekkan* (extra volume) to the film *Yūkoku* on DVD.

The Mishima chronology in volume 42 begins with Mishima's paternal grandfather Hiraoka Sadatarō's birth, on June 4, 1863, and ends with an exhibition to mark the eightieth anniversary of Mishima's birth and thirty-fifth anniversary of his death, on April 23, 2005.

Mishima's works are also published in a large number of paperback and other editions. From those editions, only those cited in the notes because of some other writers' afterwords and those notable for some other reasons may be found on the list below. As is usually the case with similar compilations by Japanese publishers, most do not give the names of editors. Unless noted, Japanese books on the list are all published in Tokyo.

A great many of Mishima's writings exist in English translation and, no doubt, many more are being translated. But in principle they are not listed here.

Agawa Hiroyuki. *Inoue Seibi*. Shinchōsha, 1986. A biography of Japan's last admiral.
———. *The Reluctant Admiral: Yamamoto and the Imperial Navy*. Translated by John

Bester. Tokyo, New York, San Francisco: Kodansha International, 1979. A biography of Yamamoto Isoroku, who planned the Pearl Harbor attack
———. *Yonai Mitsumasa.* Shinchōsha, 1982. A biography of Japan's last minister of the navy. He served as prime minister, in 1940.
Akita, George. *Evaluating Evidence: A Positivist Approach to Reading Sources on Modern Japan.* Honolulu: University of Hawai'i Press, 2008.
———. *Foundations of Constitutional Government in Modern Japan: 1868–1900.* Cambridge, MA: Harvard University Press, 1967.
Akitsu Takeshi, ed. *Mishima Yukio goroku.* Taka Shobō, 1993.
Akiyama Shun et al. *Mishima Yukio.* Shōgakukan, 1990. *Gunzō* special *Nihon no sakka,* vol. 18.
Andō Takeshi. *Mishima Yukio "Nichiroku."* Michitani, 1996. Day-to-day chronicles of Mishima's life, beginning with Nagai Naomune and ending with an entry on the staging of two plays of Mishima in June 1996. Interspersed with quotations from various sources not clearly identified. Identified as *Nichiroku* in the Notes.
———. *Mishima Yukio no shōgai.* Natsume Shobō, 1998.
Aoe Shunjirō. *Ishihara Kanji.* Chūō Kōron Sha, 1992.
Araki Nobuyoshi. *Satchin.* Shinchōsha, 1994. A photo album of children in the early 1960s.
Azuma Fumihiko. *Azuma Fumihiko sakuhinshū.* Kōdansha, 2007. With Mishima's foreword (originally published in March 1971 when the collection came out) and Yamaoka Yorihiro's commentary.
Bargen, Doris. *Suicidal Honor: General Nogi and the Writings of Mori Ōgai and Natsume Sōseki.* Honolulu: University of Hawai'i Press, 2006.
Barnett, Erin, and Philomena Mariani. *Hiroshima: Ground Zero 1945.* International Center of Photography, 2011.
Barr, Pat. *The Deer Cry Pavilion.* London, Melbourne, Toronto: Macmillan, 1968. An at times jaundiced account of Japan's Westernization, from 1868 to 1905. The title refers to the Rokumeikan as a symbol of that process.
Bataille, Georges. *Erotism: Death and Sensuality.* Translated by Mary Dalwood. San Francisco: City Lights Books, 1957.
Bird, Kai, and Lawrence Lifschultz, eds. *Hiroshima's Shadow: Writings on the Denial of History and the Smithsonian Controversy.* Branford, CT: The Pamphleteer's Press, 1998.
Bram, Christopher. *Eminent Outlaws: The Gay Writers Who Changed America.* New York: Twelve, 2012.
Brothers Ćapek, The. *R. U. R. and The Insect Play.* Translated by P. Selver and adapted for the English stage by Nigel Playfair. Oxford: Oxford University Press, 1961.
Bunce, Willliam K. *Religions in Japan: Buddhism, Shinto, Christianity.* Rutland and Tokyo: Charles E. Tuttle, 1955. A report of the Occupation's Civilian Information and Education Section prepared in 1948.
Bōjō Toshitami. *Honō no gen'ei.* Kadokawa Shoten, 1971. The author's association with Mishima.
Bywater, Hector C. *The Great Pacific War.* New York: St. Martin's Press, 1991; originally 1925. The book predicted the US-Japanese war with strategic details. A new edition was published to mark the 50th anniversary of Pearl Harbor.

Castile, Rand. *The Way of Tea*. Tokyo and New York: John Weatherhill, 1971.
Chandler, David P. *A History of Cambodia*. Boulder, CO: Westview Press, 1986.
Clausewitz, Carl von. *On War*. Translated by Anatol Rapoport. London: Penguin Books, 1968; originally 1908.
Cœdès, George. *Angkor: An Introduction*. Translated and edited by Emily Floyd Gardiner. Oxford: Oxford University Press, 1986; originally 1963. Has a photo of what is supposed to be a stone statue of Jayavarman VII, the "Leper King."
Cohen, Theodore., *Remaking Japan: The American Occupation as New Deal*. Edited by Herbert Passin. New York: The Free Press, 1987
Coote, Stephen. *W. B. Yeats: A Life*. London: Hodder and Stoughton, 1997.
Dalby, Liza. *Kimono: Fashioning Culture*. New Haven, CT: Yale University Press, 1993.
Dan Kazuo. *Shōsetsu: Dazai Osamu*. Iwanami Shoten, 2000; originally 1949.
Date Munekatsu. *Saiban kiroku: "Mishima Yukio jiken."* Kōdansha, 1972. A close account of the Mishima Yukio Incident trial, with abundant citations of reports, court statements, and decisions.
Dazai Osamu. *Ningen shikkaku, Ōtō*. Kadokawa Shoten, 2001.
———. *Shayō*. Shinchōsha, 1993.
Dickins, F. D. *Parkes den*. Part 2 of *The Life of Sir Harry Parkes, Sometime Her Majesty's Minister to China and Japan*. Translated by Takanashi Kenkichi. Heibonsha, 1984.
Dienstag, Joshua Foa. "Nietzsche's Dionysian Pessimism." *The American Political Science Review*, vol. 95, no. 4 (December 2001), 923–37.
Doak, Kevin M. "Building National Identity through Ethnicity: Ethnology in Wartime Japan and After." *Journal of Japanese Studies*, vol. 27, no. 1 (Winter 2001), 1–39.
Dōmoto Masaki. *Kaisō: Kaiten-tobira no Mishima Yukio*. Bungei Shunjū, 2005. A stage director's recollections of his association with Mishima.
Donleavy, J. P. *The Ginger Man*. New York: Grove Press, 1988. This sex-saturated 1955 novel is worth mentioning here because of US publishers' indecisions on publishing *Confessions of a Mask*.
Dostoevsky, Fyodor. *The Brothers Karamazov*. Translated by Constance Garnett. New York: Random House, 1996.
———. *Demons*. Translated by Richard Peaver and Larissa Volokhonsky. New York: Vintage Books, 1995.
Dower, John. W. *Cultures of War: Pearl Harbor, Hiroshima, 9-11, Iraq*. New York: W. W. Norton, 2010.
———. *Embracing Defeat: Japan in the Wake of Word War II*. New York: W. W. Norton, 1999.
Edogawa Ranpo. *Kurotokage. Edogawa Ranpo shū*. Vol. 9. Kōbunsha, 2002.
Ellis, Havelock Ellis. *Studies in the Psychology of Sex*. Vol. 2: *Sexual Inversion*. Minneapolis, MN: Filiquarian Publishing. Undated.
Endō Shūsaku. *Umi to dokuyaku*. Shinchōsha, 1960.
Esenbel, Selçuk. "Japan's Global Claim to Asia and the World of Islam: Transnational Nationalism and World Power, 1900–1945." *The American Historical Review*, vol. 109, no. 4, October 2004, 1140–70.
Etsugu Tomoko. *Mishima Yukio bungaku no kiseki*. Kōronsha, 1983. A stress on the

Mishima genealogy, tracing one branch to the warrior clan, the Taira, hence to Emperor Heijō (also Heizei: 774–824).
Fogel, Joshua A. *The Nanjing Massacre in History and Historiography*. Berkeley: University of California Press, 2000.
Fuji Masaharu. *Fuji Masaharu sakuhinshū*. Vol. 1. Iwanami Shoten, 1988.
Fukazawa Ichirō, *Narayama-bushi kō*. Shinchōsha, 1964.
Fukuda Kazuya, ed. *Etō Jun collection*. Vol. 3. Chikuma Shobō, 2001.
Fukushima Jirō. *Mishima Yukio: tsurugi to kanbeni*. Bungei Shunjū, 1998. An account of the author's time with Mishima. Mishima's children sued, and won, on the grounds that the book included, without permission, Mishima's letters. (See note 34, Chapter Twenty.)
Fukushima Jurō. *Saitei shiryō: Mishima Yukio*. Chōbunsha, 2005. Includes accounts of Mishima's birthplace and quotations from records related to Hiraoka Sadatarō.
Fukuzawa Yukichi. *Bunmei-ron no gairyaku*. Edited by Tozawa Yukio. Keiō Gijuku Daigaku Shuppankai, 2009.
———. *Fukuō jiden*. Edited by Matsuzaki Kin'ichi. Keiō Gijuku Daigaku Shuppankai, 2009.
Funasaka Hiroshi. *Eirei no zekkyō: Gyokusai-tō Angaur*. Bungei Shunjū, 1966. Mishima edited it, wrote an introduction, and arranged its publication.
———. *Hiwa: Palau senki*. Kōjinsha 2000; originally 1977.
———. *Peleliu-tō gyokusai-sen*. Kōjinsha, 2000; originally 1981. Describes the Battle of Peleliu.
———. *Seki no Magoroku: Mishima Yukio, sono shi no himitsu*. Kōbunsha, 1973. The author gave Mishima the sword he used at Ichigaya.
Gallagher, Michael. *Bakudan to ichō*. Translated by Ōta Hiroshi. Kōdansha, 1970.
Gayn, Mark. *Japan Diary*. Tokyo and Rutland: Charles E. Tuttle, 1981; originally 1948.
Gibney, Frank. *Five Gentlemen of Japan: The Portrait of a Nation's Character*. Avon, CT: EastBridge, 2003; originally 1953.
Gluck, Carol. *Japan's Modern Myth: Ideology in the Late Meiji Period*. Princeton: Princeton University Press, 1985.
Grass, Günter. *Peeling the Onion*. Translated by Michael Henry Heim, San Diego: Harcourt, 2007.
Gullace, Giovanni. "The French Writings of Gabrielle d'Annunzio." *Comparative Literature*, vol. 12, no. 3. (Summer 1960), 207–28.
Guttmann, Allen. *The Erotic in Sports*. New York: Columbia University Press, 1996.
Handō Kazutoshi. *"Bungei Shunjū" ni miru Shōwa-shi*. 4 vols. Bungei Shunjū, 1995.
———. *Shōwa-shi: 1926–1945* and *Shōwa-shi: Sengo-hen, 1945–1989*. Heibonsha, 2009.
———, ed. *Shōwa-shi tansaku 1926–1945*. 6 vols. Chikuma Shobō, 2007.
Harootunian, Harry. *Overcome by Modernity: History, Culture, and Community in Interwar Japan*. Princeton: Princeton University Press, 2000.
Hashikawa Bunzō. *Hashikawa Bunzō chosakushū*. Vol. 1. Chikuma Shobō, 1985.
Hata Ikuhiko. *Nankin Jiken*, Chūō Kōron Sha, 1986.
Hatori Tetsuya, ed. *Kawabata Yasunari. Sakka no jiden* series, vol. 15. Nihon Tosho Center, 2002.
Hayashi Kentarō. *Shōwa-shi to watashi*. Bungei Shunjū, 2002.

Hayashi Shigeru. *Taiheiyō Sensō. Nihon no rekishi* series, vol. 25. Chūō Kōron Sha, 1967.
Hino Ashihei. *Tsuchi to heitai, Mugi to heitai*. Shinchōsha, 1953.
Hiraoka Azusa. *Segare: Mishima Yukio*. Bungei Shunjū, 1996; originally 1972. Mishima's father Azusa's quirky but valuable comments and reminiscences on his son, interwoven with his wife Shizue's.
Hiraoka Shizue. "Boru no gotoku." Originally in the December 1976 issue of *Shinchō*. Partly included in the *Gunzō* special, *Nihon no sakka* series, vol. 18, *Mishima Yukio* (which see); with excerpts in the chronology, Zenshū 42. Mishima's mother Shizue's recollections of her life with her son that include excerpts from her diary.
Hiromatsu Wataru. *"Kindai no chōkoku" ron*. Kōdansha, 1989.
Hirschfeld, Magnus. *Sexual Anomalies: The Origins, Nature, and Treatment of Sexual Disorders*. White Plains, NY: Emerson Books, 1956.
Horiguchi Daigaku. *Gekka no ichigun*. Shinchōsha, 1955; originally 1925. A famous anthology of Horiguchi's translations of French poetry.
Hosaka Masayasu. *Mishima Yukio to Tate no Kai jiken*. Kadokawa Shoten, 2001.
Hosoe Eikō. *Shashinka: Hosoe Eikō no sekai (A World of Eikoh Hosoe)*. Seigensha, 2006. A gallery publication. It includes a selection of photos of Mishima Yukio in *Barakei*.
Hugo, Victor. *Four Plays: Marion de Lorme, Hernami, Lucretia Borgia, Ruy Blas*. Edited and with an introduction by Claude Schumacher. London: Methuen, 2004.
Ienaga Saburō. *Nihon kindai kenpō shisō-shi kenkyū*. Iwanami Shoten, 1967.
———. *The Pacific War: 1931–1945*. New York: Pantheon Books, 1978. A translation by Frank Baldwin of Ienaga's *Taiheiyō sensō*, 1968.
Imai Seiichi. *Taishō democracy. Nihon no rekishi* series, vol. 23. Chūō Kōron Sha, 1966.
Inagaki Taruho. *Inagaki Taruho*. Chikuma Shobō, 2008. Includes 15 stories.
———. *Inagaki Taruho (Inaguaqui Taroupho) zenshū*. 13 vols. Chikuma Shobō, 2000–2001. Among them: vol. 1, *Issen ichibyō monogatari*; vol. 3, *Vanilla and Manila*; vol. 4, *Shōnen-ai no bigaku*; vol. 7, *Miroku*; vol. 8, *Akaki seiza o megurite*.
Inoguchi, Rikihei, Tadashi Nakajima, and Roger Pineau. *The Divine Wind*. Annapolis, MD: US Naval Institute, 1958. A translation of an early, idealized Japanese account of the special attack force.
Inose Naoki. *Chosakushū*. 12 vols. Shōgakukan, 2001–2. Among these selected works are: vol. 3, *Magazine seishun-fu: Kawabata Yasunari to Ōya Sōichi*; vol. 4, *Picaresque: Dazai Osamu den*; vol. 5, *Mikado no shōzō*; vol. 8, *Nihonjin wa naze sensō o shitaka: Shōwa 16-nen natsu no haisen*; vol. 12, *Kurofune no seiki: gaiatsu no Nichi-bei miraisen-ki*. This last describes how both sides on the Pacific predicted and sometimes inflamed the inevitability of the war between Japan and the United States, beginning with books such as *Banzai!* by Parabellum, the penname of the German author Ferdinand Heinrich Grautoff, and *The Valor of Ignorance* by Homer Lea, both of which appeared in 1909.
———. *Kokoro no ōkoku: Kikuchi Kan to Bungei Shunjū*. Bungei Shunjū, 2008.
———. *Kūki to sensō*. Bungei Shunjū, 2007. Touches on the duplicitous terms used for the Self-Defense Forces as a military.
———. *Persona: Mishima Yukio den*. Bungei Shunjū, 1995. Originally serialized in the weekly *Post*, from January 6 to October 13, 1995.

Inoue Kiyoshi. *Meiji Ishin. Nihon no rekishi* series, vol. 20. Chūō Kōron Sha, 1966.
Iriye, Akira. *Pearl Harbor and the Coming of the Pacific War: A Brief History with Documents and Essays.* Boston: Bedford/St. Martin's, 1999.
Irokawa Daikichi. *Kindai kokka no shuppatsu. Nihon no rekishi* series, vol. 21. Chūō Kōron Sha, 1966.
Isherwood, Christopher. *The Berlin Stories.* New York: New Directions, 1963.
———. *Diaries: Volume One, 1939–1960.* Edited and with an introduction by Katherine Bucknell. New York: HarperCollins, 1997.
Ishibashi Tanzan. *Ishibashi Tanzan hyōron-shū.* Edited by Matsuo Takayoshi. Iwanami Shoten, 1984.
———. *Tanzan kaisō.* Iwanami Shoten, 1985.
Ishihara Kanji. *Sensō-shi taiken.* Chūō Kōron Shinsha, 2002.
Ishihara Shintarō, *Taiyō no kisetsu.* Shinchōsha, 1957. With Okuno Takeo's commentary.
Ishii Shirō, ed. *Kinsei buke shisō.* Iwanami Shoten, 1974.
Ishii Tatsuhiko. "Rokumeikan." *Kokubungaku,* July 1986 (Mishima special), 94–99.
Ishikawa Jun. *Bunrin tsūshin.* Kōdansha, 2010.
———. *Edo bungaku shōki.* Kōdansha, 1990.
———. *Hakubyō.* Shūeisha, 1979.
———. *Kankanroku.* Mainichi Shinbun Sha, 1973.
Isoda Kōichi. *Junkyō no bigaku.* Tōjusha, 1969.
Itasaka Gō. *Kyokusetsu Mishima Yukio: Seppuku to Flamenco.* Natsume Shoten, 1997. An attempt to understand Mishima on the conjecture that he tried to hide the humble origins of his paternal grandfather's ancestors.
———. *Shinsetsu: Mishima Yukio.* Natsume Shobō, 1998.
Itō Shizuo. *Itō Shizuo zenshū.* Jinbun Shoin, 1971.
*Itō Shizuo, Tachihara Michizō, Maruyama Kaoru. Nihon shijin zenshū,* vol. 28. Shinchōsha, 1968.
Iwami Takao. *Kishi Nobusuke: Shōwa no kakumeika.* Gakuyō Shobō, 1999. A notable journalist's assessment of Kishi as a "revolutionary."
Iwamoto Yoshiharu, ed. *Kaishū zadan.* With annotations by Katsube Mitake. Iwanami Shoten, 1983. A collection of Katsu Kaishū's talks, with remembrances of the man by those who knew him.
Iwatani Tokiko and Koshiji Fubuki. *Yume no naka ni kimi ga iru.* Kōdansha, 1999.
Izumi Kyōka. *Kōya hijiri.* Shūeisha, 1992. With Yamada Yūsaku's "Kaisetsu," Okuda Eiji's "kanshō" (and a fabulous illustration), and a chronology.
———. *Nihonbashi.* Iwanami Shoten, 1953. With Satō Haruo's "kaisetsu."
———. *Shunchū, Shunchū gokoku.* Iwanami Shoten, 1987. With Kawamura Jirō's "kaisetsu."
———. *Uta'andon, Kōya hijiri.* Shinchōsha, 2003. With Yoshida Sei'ichi's 1950 "kaisetsu."
———. *Yashagaike.* Kōdansha, 1979. With Nakai Hideo's "kaisetsu" stressing Mishima Yuko's admiration of Izumi Kyōka.
Johnson, Chalmers. *MITI and the Japanese Miracle: The Growth of Industrial Policy, 1925–1975.* Palo Alto: Stanford University Press, 1982.
Judt, Tony. *The Burden of Responsibility: Blum, Camus, Aron, and the French Twentieth Century.* Chicago: University of Chicago Press, 1998.

———. *Reappraisals: Reflections on the Forgotten Twentieth Century.* London: Penguin Books, 2009.
Jūzenkai, comp. and pub. *Gunshin Wakabayashi chūtaichō tsuitōroku: Ato ni tsuzuku mono o shinzu.* Private edition. The title is based on Lt. Wakabayashi's famous last words for the title, *I Trust Others Will Follow Me (Ato ni tsuzuku mono o shinzu).*
Kahn, Paul, adapt. *The Secret History of the Mongols: The Origin of Chingis Khan.* Boston: Cheng and Tsui, 1998.
Kaikō Takeshi. *Betonamu senki.* Asahi Shinbunsha, 1970.
———. *Kaikō Takeshi zen-sakuhin.* 12 vols. Shinchōsha, 1974. Among these volumes are *Essays 3*, which includes *Betonamu senki*; *Shōsetsu 8* and *9*, which include *Kagayakeru yami* and *Natsu no yami.*
Kanagawa Bungaku Shinkōkai and Takahashi Mutsuo, eds. *Shibusawa Tatsuhiko seitan 80 nen kaikoten.* Yokohama: Kanagawa Bungaku Shinkōkai, 2008.
Kanda Fuhito and Kobayashi Hideo, ed. *Sengoshi nenpyō: 1945–2005.* Shōgakukan, 2005.
Kanemoto Masataka. *Katakuna ni miyabitaru hito: Hasuda Zenmei to Shimizu Fumio.* Hiroshima: Keisuisha, 2001.
Karatani Kōjin. *Nihon kindai bungaku no kigen.* Kōdansha, 2009.
Kasahara Tokushi. *Nankin Jiken.* Iwanami Shoten, 1997.
Katō Shūichi. *Nihon bungaku-shi josetsu.* 2 vols. Chikuma Shobō, 1980.
———. *A Sheep's Song: A Writer's Reminiscences of Japan and the World.* Translated and annotated by Chia-ning Chang. Berkeley: University of California Press, 1999.
Katsube Mitake, ed. *Hikawa seiwa.* Kadokawa Shoten, 1972. A collection of Katsu Kaishū's casual talks with Katsube's life of Katsu.
Kawabata Hideko. *Kawabata Yasunari to tomo ni.* Shinchōsha, 1983.
Kawabata Yasunari. *Bi no sonzai to hakken: The Existence and Discovery of Beauty.* With a translation by V. H. Viglielmo. Mainichi Shinbun Sha, 1969.
———. *Izu no odoriko, Onsen'yado.* Iwanami Shoten, 1952.
———. *Jūroku-sai no nikki, Shōne,* etc. *Sakka no jiden* series, vol. 15. Nihon Tosho Center, 1994.
———. *Kawabata Yasunari zenshū.* Vol. 34: *Zassan 1.* Shinchōsha, 1984.
———. *Kawabata Yasunari zenshū hokan 1: Nikki, techō, note.* Shinchōsha, 1984.
———. *Kawabata Yasunari zenshū, hokan, 2: Shokan raikan shō, nikki, techō, note.* Shinchōsha, 1984.
———. *Koto.* Shinchōsha, 2008.
———. *Meijin.* Shinchōsha, 1970. With Yamamoto Kenkichi's commentary.
———. *Nemureru bijo.* Shinchōsha, 1967. With Mishima Yukio's commentary.
———. *Suishō gensō, Kinjū.* Kōdansha, 1992. With commentaries of Takahashi Hideo and Hatori Tetsuya.
———. *Utsukushii nihon no watashi: sono josetsu.* Kōdansha, 1969. With E. G. Seidensticker's translation.
———. *Yukiguni.* Shinchōsha, 1987. With commentaries of Takenishi Hiroko and Itō Sei.
——— and Mishima Yukio. *Ōfuku shokan.* Shinchōsha, 2000.; originally 1997.
Keene, Donald. *Dawn to the West.* 2 vols. Boston: Holt, Rinehart and Winston, 1984.

———. *5 Modern Japanese Novelists*. New York: Columbia University Press, 2003.
———. *World Within Walls: Japanese Literature of the Pre-modern Ear: 1600–1867*. Boston: Holt, Rinehart and Winston, 1976.
———, trans. *Five Modern Nō Plays by Yukio Mishima*. Tokyo and Rutland, VT: Charles E. Tuttle, 1967.; originally New York: Knopf, 1957.
Kihira Teiko. *Chichi to ko no Shōwa hishi*. Kawade Shobō Shinsha, 2004.
———. "Mishima Yukio no tegami," in 18 installments in the weekly *Asahi*, from December 13, 1974 to April 11, 1975. Kihira's recollections of her association with Mishima in the early postwar years.
Kikuchi Nobuhei, ed. *Shōwa 12 nen no "Shūkan Bunshun."* Bungei Shunjū, 2007.
Kimura Tokuzō. *Bungei henshūsha: sono kyō'on*. TBS Britannica, 1982.
Kishi Nobusuke. *Waga seishun: oitachi no ki, omoide no ki*. Kōzaidō, 1983.
Kita Morio. *Yoru to kiri no sumi de*. Shinchōsha, 1960.
Kitajima Masamoto. *Bappan-sei no kumon*. Nihon no rekishi series, vol. 18. Chūō Kōron Sha, 1974.
Kitami Harukzau. *Kaisō no Bungaku-za*. Chūō Kōron Sha, 1987.
Klieger, P. Christiaan. *The Images of America: The Fleischmann Yeast Family*. Mount Pleasant, SC: Arcadia Publishing, 2004.
Kōdachi Naoki. *Tokkō no shin'i: Ōnishi Takijirō wahei e no message*. Bungei Shunjū, 2011.
Kodama Kōta, ed. *Nenpyō, chizu*. Nihon no rekishi series, bekkan, vol. 5. Chūō Kōron Sha, 1967.
Kojima Chikako. *Mishima Yukio to Dan Kazuo*. Kōsōsha, 1989. A Mishima editor's account of her association with Mishima (and Dan Kazuo). Kojima famously went to Mishima's house to receive the last installment of the fourth volume of the tetralogy, *Hōjō no Umi*, on the day of his death.
Kojima Nobuo. *Hōyō kazoku*. Kōdansha, 2009.
Kojima Tsuyoshi. *Kindai Nihon no Yōmeigaku*. Kōdansha, 2006. An account of the influence of Wang Yangming thought from Ōshio Heihachirō to Mishima Yukio.
Kon Hidemi. *Higeki no shōgun: Yamashita Tomoyuki, Honma Masaharu*. Chūō Kōron Sha, 1988.
———. *Sanchū hōrō*. Chūō Kōron Sha, 1978. Includes an account US Occupation censors did not want to see in print.
Konishi Jin'ichi. *Nihon bungei-shi*. 5 vols. Kōdansha, 1985–92.
Konishi Shirō. *Kaikoku to jōi*. Nihon no rekishi series, vol. 19. Chūō Kōron Sha, 1974.
Kōno Ichirō. *Kōno Ichirō-den*. Tokuma Shoten, 1965.
———. *Kōno Ichirō jiden*. Edited by Denki Kankō Iinkai. Tokuma Shoin, 1965.
Kunieda Shirō. *Shinshū Kōketsu-jō*. Kawade Shobō Shinsha, 2007. With Mishima's commentary.
Kuno Akiko. *Rokumeikan no kifujin: Ōyama Sutematsu*. Chūō Kōron Sha, 1993; originally 1988.
Kurashi no Techō, ed. *Sensō-chū no kuashi no kiroku*. Kurashi no Techō Sha, 1979; originally 1968.
Kuribayashi Tadamichi. *"Gyokusai shikikan" no e-tegami*. Edited by Yoshida Tsuyuko. Shōgakukan, 2002. A collection of letters the commander of Iwo Jima wrote, with his own drawings, to his son Tarō while stationed in the United States.

Includes some letters to his daughter and his wife from Iwo Jima.

———. *Iōtō kara no tegami*. Bungei Shunjū, 2006. Kuribayashi's letters from Iwo Jima to his wife Yoshii. With Handō Kazutoshi's commentary.

Kurogane Hiroshi. *Shimizu no Jirochō*. 2 vols. PHP Kenkyūsho, 2006.

Kuroha Kiyotaka. *Taiheiyō Sensō no rekishi*. 2 vols. Kōdansha, 1985.

Lea, Homer. *The Valor of Ignorance*. New York: Harper and Brothers, 1909. It predicted, wrongly, that Japan would attack and defeat the United States.

Lebra, Joyce Chapman. *The Indian National Army and Japan*. Singapore: Institute of Southeast Asian Studies, 2008. Originally published in 1971 as *Jungle Alliance: Japan and the Indian National Army*. Fujiwara Iwaichi and the formation of the Indian National Army.

Lifton, Robert Jay, et al. *Six Lives, Six Deaths: Portraits from Modern Japan*. New Haven, CT: Yale University Press, 1979. Includes assessments of Nogi Maresuke and Mishima Yukio.

Livingston, Jon; Joe Moore; and Felicia Oldfather. *Imperial Japan: 1800–1945*. New York: Random House, 1973. A collection of papers and articles.

———. *Postwar Japan: 1945 to the Present*. New York: Random House, 1973. A collection of papers and articles.

McNelly, Theodore. "The Role of Monarchy in the Political Modernization of Japan." *Comparative Politics*, vol. 1. no. 3 (April 1969), 366–81.

Maesaka Toshiyuki. *Taiheiyō Sensō to shinbun*. Kōdansha, 2007. A history of censorship in modern Japan, with an emphasis on censorship during the Pacific War.

Matsufuji Takejirō. *Chitagiru Mishima Yukio "kenpō kaisei."* Mainichi Ones, 2003.

Matsumoto Ken'ichi. *Mishima Yukio no 2.26 jiken*. Bungei Shunjū, 2005.

Matsumoto Tōru, *Mishima Yukio no saigo*. Bungei Shunjū, 2000.

———, ed. *Nenpyō sakka tokuhon: Mishima Yukio*. Kawade Shobō Shinsha, 1990. A chronology with quotations and commentaries illustrated with photos.

Mears, Helen. *Mirror for Americans: Japan*. Boston: Houghton, Mifflin, 1948. A blunt judgment that the US Occupation was based on a distortion of Japanese history.

Mikuriya Takashi and Oshio Kazuto. *Wasurerareta Nichibei kankei—Helen Mears no toi*. Chikuma Shobō, 1996.

Minakami Tsutomu. *Kinkaku enjō*. Shichōsha, 1986; originally 1979. A biography of Hayashi Yōken, who burned down the Kinkakuji. Though fictionalized, the account reproduces a number of documents related to Hayashi.

Minear, Richard. *Victors' Justice: The Tokyo War Crimes Trial*. Ann Arbor, MI: Center for Japanese Studies, University of Michigan, 2001; originally Princeton: Princeton University Press, 1971.

Mishima Yukio. *Circus, Tabi no ehon, Daijin*, with *Sakusha danwa*. 2 cassettes. Shinchōsha, 1988. Mishima reading three of his stories.

———. *Fukuzatsu na kare*. Shūeisha, 1987. With an afterword by Abe Jōji, the model of the novel.

———. *Gakusei to no taiwa*. 2 cassettes. Shinchōsha, 1988. The recording of the teach-in at Waseda University on October 3, 1968. The transcript included in "Kokka kakumei no genri," *Zenshū* 40, 204–307.

———. *Gikyokushū*. 2 vols. Shinchōsha, 1990. All Mishima plays except for the early ones.

———. *Hagakure nyūmon*. Shinchōsha, 1983. With Kasahara Nobuo's translations into modern Japanese of passages Mishima quoted.
———. *Jūdai shokanshū*. Shinchōsha, 1999.
———. *Kamen no kokuhaku*. Shinchōsha, 1984. With Fukuda Tsuneari's commentary.
———. *Kinkakuji*. Shinchōsha, 1993. With Nakamura Mitsuo's commentary.
———. *Mihappyō shokan*. Chūō Kōron Sha, 1998. A total of 97 letters to Donald Keene. All collected in Zenshū 38.
———. *Shishū*. Yamanakako, Yamanashi: Mishima Yukio Bungakukan, 2000.
———. *Shōbu no kokoro: Mishima Yukio taidan-shū*. Nihon Kyōbun Sha, 1970.
———. *Wakaki samurai no tame ni*. Bungei Shunjū Sha, 1966.
——— and Fujita Mitsuo. *Shashinshū: Mishima Yukio, '25~'75*. Shinchōsha, 2000; originally 1990. A small selection of photos of Mishima with his wife as one of the editors.
——— and Geoffrey Bownas, eds. *New Writing in Japan*. London: Penguin, 1972.
*Mishima Yukio botsugo 30 nen*. The monthly *Shinchō* special, November 2000. Includes two short stories, five essays, and poems not published till then.
*Mishima Yukio: 30-nengo no aratana chihei*. The monthly *Eureka* special, November 2000.
Mitani Makoto. *Kyūyū Mishima Yukio*. Chūō Kōron Shinsha, 1999; originally 1985. Mishima and Mitani, his classmate at Peers School, had regular correspondence the two called "Saturday communications" from late 1944 to the fall of 1945. Following Mishima's death, Mitani assembled what he had kept and published them with comments, along with essays remembering his friend. The letters are collected in Zenshū 38.
Mitani Takanobu. *Kaikoroku: Jijūchō no Shōwa-shi*. Chūō Kōron Shinsha, 1999; originally 1980.
Miyoshi, Masao. *As We Saw Them: The First Japanese Embassy to the United States*. Philadelphia: Paul Dry Books, 2005; originally 1979.
Mizuki Shigeru. *Musume ni kataru o-tōsan no senki*. Kawade Shobō Shinsha, 1995.
Morris, Ivan. *The Nobility of Failure*. New York: Holt, Rinehart and Winston, 1975. Morris dedicated the book to Mishima.
Murakami Tateo. *Kimi-tachi ni wa wakaranai: Tate no Kai de mita Mishima Yukio*. Shinchōsha, 2010. A Shield Society member's recollections of a month-long military experience with Mishima.
Muramatsu Takeshi (also Gō). *Mishima Yukio no sekai*. Shinchōsha, 1996; originally 1990. An excellent literary biography by a scholar of French literature, though as a friend close to the Mishima family he apparently felt obliged to downplay if not deny Mishima's homosexuality (bisexuality) and rightwing tilt. With Romano Vulpitta's afterword.
———. *Shi no Nihon bungaku-shi*. Kadokawa Shoten, 1981.
Murayama Tomoyoshi. *Shinobi no mono*. 5 vols. Iwanami Shoten, 2003.
Nagai Kafū, trans. *Sango-shū*. Iwanami Shoten, 1991. Nagai's small anthology of French poetry in his translation, originally in 1912.
Nagai Yōnosuke. *Jūkōzō shakai to bōryoku*. Chūō Kōron Sha, 1971.
Nakamura Akihiko. *Resshi to yobareru otoko: Morita Masakatsu no monogatari*. Bungei Shunjū, 2003. A biography of the man who disemboweled himself along with Mishima.

Nakamura Mitsuo. *Jidai no kanshoku*. Bungei Shunjū, 1970.
———. *Nihon no kindai*. Bungei Shunjū, 1968.
——— and Mishima Yuko. *Taidan: Ningen to bungaku*. Kōdansha, 2002. A series of taidan between the two writers originally published in book form in 1968. Included in Zenshū 40, 43–173.
Nakano Yoshio. *Akunin raisan*. Edited by Anno Mitsumasa. Chikuma Shobō, 1990.
Nanakita Kazuto, ed. *Abe Sada densetsu*. Chikuma Shobō, 1998.
Nathan, John. *Mishima: A Biography*. Boston and Toronto: Little, Brown and Company, 1974. An account by a scholar Mishima once regarded as his official English translator.
Natsume Sōseki. *Sōseki zenshū*, vol. 11. Iwanami Shoten, 1966. Includes a reference to Hiraoka Sadatarō.
Nelms, Henning. *Scene Design: A Guide to the Stage*. New York: Dover Publications, 1970.
Noda Utarō. *Hai no kisetsu*. Shūdōsha, 1958.
Nosaka Akiyuki. *Kakuyaku-taru gyakkō*. Bungei Shunjū, 1991. A biography by a writer who found certain parallels in his life and Mishima's.
Odakane Jirō. *Hasuda Zenmei to sono shi*. Chikuma Shobō, 1970.
———. *Shijin, sono shōgai to unmei: shokan to sakuhin kara mita Itō Shizuo*. Shinchōsha, 1965.
Ōe Kenzaburō. *Hiroshima note*. Iwanami Shoten, 2005.
———. *Kojinteki-na taiken*. Shinchōsha, 1995.
———. *Seiteki ningen*. Shinchōsha, 1989.
Okamoto Shirō. *Kabuki o sukutta otoko*. Shūeisha, 1998. Translated and adapted by Samuel L. Leiter as *The Man Who Saved Kabuki: Faubion Bowers and Theatre Censorship in Occupied Japan* (Honolulu: University of Hawai'i Press, 2001).
Oketani Hideaki. *Shōwa seishinshi*. Bungei Shunjū, 1996.
———. *Shōwa seishinshi: sengo-hen*. Bungei Shunjū, 2003.
Okuno Takeo. *Mishima Yukio densetsu*. Shinchōsha, 1993. Largely a collection of Okuno's reviews of Mishima's works.
Onna-tachi no Genzai o Tou Kai, ed. *55-nen taisei seiritsu to onna-tachi*. Impact Shuppankai, 1987.
Ōoka Shōhei. *Leyte senki*. 3 vols. Chūō Kōron Sha, 1974.
———. *Nakahara Chūya*. Kōdansha, 1989. A biography of the poet Nakahara Chūya based on Ōoka's association with him.
———. *Sensō*. Iwanami Shoten, 2007; originally 1970.
Ōsugi Kazuo. *Nitchū 15-nen sensō-shi*. Chūō Kōron Sha, 1996. An exploration of whether China and Japan could not have prevented the expansion of the conflict before Japan's occupation of Nanjing at the end of 1937.
Ōtani Kenshirō, trans. *Nihon no Tennō seiji*. Simul Shuppankai, 1979. Translation of David Titus, *Palace and Politics in Prewar Japan* (New York: Columbia University Press, 1974).
Ōuchi Tsutomu. *Fascism e no michi. Nihon no rekishi* series, vol. 24. Chūō Kōron Sha, 1967.
Pacific War Research Society, comp. and trans. *Japan's Longest Day*. Tokyo and Palo Alto: Kodansha International, 1968.
Pal, Radhabinod. *Dissentient Judgment of Justice Pal*. Kokusho-Kankokai, 1999.

Passin, Herbert. *Encounter with Japan.* Kodansha International, 1982.

———. *Society and Education in Japan.* Kodansha International, 1985; originally 1965.

Poe, Edgar Allan. *Complete Tales and Poems.* New York: Vintage Books, 1975.

Proust, Marcel. *Pleasures and Days.* Translated by Andres Brown. London: Hesperus Classics, 2004.

Richie, Donald. *Different People: Pictures of Some Japanese.* Kodansha International, 1987. Contains thumbnail sketches of a wide variety of people, including Mishima and Kawabata. *Japanese Portraits: Pictures of Different People* (Clarendon, VT: Tuttle, 2006), is a somewhat expanded edition.

———. *The Japan Journals: 1947–2004.* Edited by Leza Lowitz. Berkeley, CA: Stone Bridge Press, 2004.

Rilke, Rainer Maria. *The Notebook of Malte Laurids Brigge.* Translated by M. D. Herter Norton. New York: W. W. Norton, 1949.

Rimer, J. Thomas, ed. *Not a Song Like Any Other: An Anthology of Writings by Mori Ōgai.* Honolulu: University of Hawai'i Press, 2004. Includes Hiroaki Sato's translation of *Ōshio Heihachirō.*

———. *Toward a Modern Japanese Theatre: Kishida Kunio.* Princeton: Princeton University Press, 1974.

———, trans., and Yamazaki Masakazu, ed. *On the Art of Nō Drama: The Major Treaties of Zeami.* Princeton: Princeton University Press, 1984.

Ross, Christopher. *Mishima's Sword: Travels in Search of a Samurai Legend.* Cambridge, MA: Da Capo Press, 2006.

Rōyama Masamichi. *Yomigaeru Nihon. Nihon no rekishi* series, vol. 26. Chūō Kōron Sha, 1967.

Saeki Shōichi. *Hyōden: Mishima Yukio.* Chūō Kōron Sha, 1988. A collection of critical essays by Mishima Yukio's friend and professor of American literature.

*St. Andrews Review,* vol. 1, no. 4, 1972. Includes one of the earliest assessments in English of Mishima's death based on his work: Irina Kirk's "Death—Life—Work of Yukio Mishima." There was only a handful of translations of Mishima's work at the time, with Kirk assuming that *Sun and Steel* was Mishima's "last book." But her appraisal was unerring.

Sakurai Chūichi and Lindley Williams Hubbell et al., trans. *Ze-Ami Kadensho.* Kyoto: Sumiya-Shinobe Publishing Institute, 1968.

Sansom, George. *A History of Japan 1615–1867.* Palo Alto: Stanford University Press, 1963.

———. *A History of Japan to 1334.* London: Cresset Press, 1958.

———. *The Western World and Japan.* New York: Knopf, 1949.

Saotome Katsumoto. *Tōkyō dai-kūshū.* Iwanami Shoten, 1971. A survivor's reconstruction of the air raid on the night of March 9 (early March 10), 1945.

Sassa Atsuyuki. *Tōdai rakujō: Yasuda Kōdō kōbō 72 jikan.* Bungei Shunjū, 1996.

Sato, Hiroaki, trans. and ed. *Legends of the Samurai.* New York: Overlook Press, 1995. Translations from *Hagakure* in Chapter Twenty-two are from this book.

———, trans. *Mishima Yukio: Silk and Insight: A Novel.* Armonk, NY: M. E. Sharpe, 1998.

———, trans. and ed. *My Friend Hitler and Other Plays of Yukio Mishima.* New York: Columbia University Press, 2002.

Scammell, Michael. *Koestler: The Literary and Political Odyssey of a Twentieth-Century Skeptic.* New York: Random House, 2009.
Schaller, Michael. *The American Occupation of Japan: The Origins of the Cold War in Asia.* Oxford: Oxford University Press, 1985.
Schrader, Paul, director. *Mishima: A Life in Four Chapters.* DVD of the 1985 film. New York: Criterion Collection. Date not given.
Scott-Stokes, Henry. *The Life and Death of Yukio Mishima.* New York: Farrar, Straus and Giroux, 1974. A biography by a journalist who knew Mishima in his last several years.
*Seiron* editorial board, ed. *Kempō no ronten.* Sankei Shinbun Sha, 2004.
Sekai Heiwa Kenkyūjo (Institute for International Policy Studies), comp. *Kenpō Kaisei shian* (2005). A semi-governmental institute's proposal for Constitutional reform. In print and online.
Shiba Ryōtarō. *Harimanada monogatari, 1.* Kōdansha, 2004.
———. *Hitokiri Izō.* Shinchōsha, 1969.
———. *Junshi.* Bungei Shunjū, 1978.
Shibusawa Tatsuhiko. *Mishima Yukio: Oboegaki.* Chūō Kōron Sha, 1986.
Shidehara Kijūrō. *Gaikō 50-nen.* Chūō Kōron Shinsha, 1987; originally 1951.
Shiga Naoya. *Kozō no kamisama, Kinosaki nite.* Shinchōsha, 1985.
Shigeta Mariko. *Taruho / Miraiha.* Kawade Shobō Shinsha, 1997.
Shiine Yamato. *Heibon Punch no Mishima Yukio.* Shinchōsha, 2007. Shiine, an editor at Heibonsha who covered Mishima for the last three years of his life, recalls his association with "the superstar," with his own analysis of various ideas of Mishima.
Shillony, Ben-Ami. *Enigma of the Emperors: Sacred Subservience in Japanese History.* Folkestone, Kent: Global Oriental, 2005.
———. "Myth and Reality in Japan of the 1930s." In *Modern Japan: Aspects of History, Literature and Society.* Edited by W. G. Beasley. Berkeley: University of California Press, 1975, 81–88.
———. *Politics and Culture in Wartime Japan.* Oxford: Oxford University Press, 1981.
———. *Revolt in Japan: The Young Officers and the February 26, 1936 Incident.* Princeton: Princeton University Press, 1971. Translated into Japanese by Kōno Tsukasa as *Nihon no hanran* (Kawade Shobō, 1975). The translator is the older brother of Capt. Kōno Hisashi, who was forced to disembowel himself with the fruit knife Tsukasa snuggled into the hospital in the aftermath of the 2.26 Incident.
———, ed. *The Emperors of Modern Japan.* Leiden, Netherlands, and Boston, Brill, 2008.
Shima Taizō. *Yasuda Kōdō: 1968–1969.* Chūō Kōron Shinsha, 2005.
Shimomura Kainan. *Shūsen hishi.* Kōdansha, 1985; originally 1950.
Shinoyama Kishin. *Mishima Yukio no ie.* Bijutsu Shuppansha, 2000; originally 1995. A collection of Shinoyama's photos of Mishima's house.
Silva, Arturo, comp., ed., and intro. *The Donald Richie Reader: 50 Years of Writing on Japan.* Berkeley, CA: Stone Bridge Press, 2001.
Sledge, E. B. *With the Old Breed: At Peleliu and Okinawa.* Oxford: Oxford University Press, 1990; originally 1981.

Sone Hiroyoshi. "Daisaku no kowasa." *Kaien*, September 1968, 166–67. This brief essay gives a glimpse into the practice of ghostwriting among some of the prominent writers. As the title of the essay suggests, there is danger in discussing modern Japanese writers without knowing ghostwriting.

Spector, Ronald H. *Eagle against the Sun: The American War with Japan*. New York: Free Press, 1985.

Sprawson, Charles. *Haunts of the Black Masseur: The Swimmer as Hero*. New York: Pantheon Books, 1992.

Sugiyama Shigemaru. *Kodama Taishō den*. Chūō Kōron Sha, 1989; originally 1918.

Sumiya Mikio. *Dai-Nippon Teikoku no shiren*. Nihon no rekishi series, vol. 22. Chūō Kōron Sha, 1966.

Surya, Michel. *Georges Bataille: An Intellectual Biography*. Translated by Krzysztof Fijalkowski and Michael Richardson. New York: Verso, 2002.

Suzuki Akira. *Shin "Nankin dai-gyakusatsu" no maboroshi*. Asuka Shinsha, 1999.

Suzuki Tadashi. *Enshutsuka no shisō*. Ōta Shuppan, 1994.

Suzuki Yūko, ed. *Yamakawa Kikue hyōronshū*. Iwanami Shoten, 1990.

Takahashi Masae. *2.26 jiken*. Chūō Kōron Sha, 2007; originally 1965.

Takahashi Mutsuo. *Jūni no enkei*. Chūō Kōron Sha, 1970. With Mishima's blurb.

———. *Nemuri to okashi to rakka to*. Sōgetsu Art Center, 1965. With Mishima's afterword and Yoko'o Tadanori's wicked cover design.

———. *Tomodachi no tsukurikata*. Magazine House, 1993.

Takahashi Satoshi. *Shimizu Jirochō to bakumatsu ishin*. Iwanami Shoten, 2003.

Takahashi Tomio. *Seii-taishōgun: Mō hitotsu no kokka shuken*. Chūō Kōron Sha, 1987.

Takaya, Ted. T., trans. *Modern Japanese Drama: An Anthology*. New York: Columbia University Press, 1979. Includes plays by Abe Kōbō, Mishima Yukio, Yashiro Seiichi, Yamazaki Masakazu, and Betsuyaku Minoru.

Takeda Taijun. *Kizoku no kaidan*. Iwanami Shoten, 2000. With Sawachi Hisae's explanation of the historical background of the novel.

Takeuchi Yoshimi. "Kenryoku to geijutsu." In Nakajima Kenzō et al, *Nihon gendai bungaku zenshū*. Vol. 93. Kōdansha, 1968, 346–59.

Tanaka Miyoko. *Mishima Yukio: Kami no kageboshi*. Shinchōsha, 2006. A collection of insightful essays Tanaka wrote for each of the Zenshū volumes.

Tanaka Mitsuko. *Waga te ni kieshi arare*. Bokuyōsha, 1970. With Mishima's exquisite preface.

Tanizaki Jun'ichirō. *Konjiki no shi*. Kōdansha, 2005. With Shimizu Yoshinori's commentary.

———. *Tade kū mushi*. Shinchōsha, 1995. With Yamamoto Kenkichi's 1956 commentary.

Tansman, Alan. "Bridges to Nowhere: Yasuda Yojūrō's Language of Violence and Desire." *Harvard Journal of Asiatic Studies*, vol. 56, no. 1 (June 1996), 35–75.

Tayama Katai. *Futon, Ippeisotsu*. Iwanami Shoten, 2002. With Maeda Akira's 1930 commentary and Sōma Tsuneo's 1972 commentary.

Terasaki Hidenari and Mariko Terasaki Miller, eds. *Shōwa Tennō dokuhakuroku*. Bungei Shunjū, 1991. The Shōwa Tennō's "monologues" prepared soon after Japan's defeat with annotations and commentary.

Tokuoka Takao. *Gosui no hito*. Bungei Shunjū. 1999. A series of essays on Mishima by a journalist who did some of the most important interviews with him.

———. *Takuyū kikō*. Chūō Kōron Sha, 1981; originally 1973. Recalling Mishima with Donald Keene.
Toland, John. *The Rising Sun: The Decline and Fall of the Japanese Empire*. New York: Random House, 1970. Toland begins this famous account of the "decline and fall" with an account of the 2.26 Incident.
Tomita Hitoshi. *Rokumeikan: gi-Seiyōka no sekai*. Hakusuisha, 1984.
Tōyama Shigeki et al. *Shōwa-shi*. Iwanami Shoten, 1959.
Trilling, Lionel. *Liberal Imagination*. New York: Doubleday Anchor Books, 1950.
Tsunabuchi Kenjō. *Kō: Enomoto Takeaki to gunkan Kaiyōmaru no shōgai*. Shinchōsha, 1986. Document-based fictionalized account of Enomoto Takeaki and his Dutch-built warship.
Tsunoda Fusako. *Issai yume ni goza sōrō: Homma Masaharu Chūjō den*. Shinchōsha, 1975. A biography of a general who was tried and shot in Manila for the Bataan Death March. His American defense team appealed the case to the United States Supreme Court, to no avail.
———. *Isshi, taizai o shasu: Rikugun Daijin Anami Korechika*. Shinchōsha, 1983. A biography of a general who disemboweled himself upon Japan's surrender, in 1945.
———. *Sekinin, Rabaul no shōgun Imamura Hitoshi*. Shinchōsha, 1987. A biography of a general who, after release from prison as a war criminal, spent the rest of his life for the welfare of his former soldiers.
Tsurumi Kazuko. *Minakata Kumagusu*. Kōdansha, 2008.
Tsurumi Shunsuke and Nakagawa Roppei, eds. *Tennō hyakuwa: ge no kan*. Chikuma Shobō, 1989.
Ugaki Matome. *Sensōroku*. Hara Shobō, 1968. Vice Adm. Ugaki's diary during the Pacific War.
Vidal, Gore. *The City and the Pillar: A Novel*. New York: Vintage International, 2003. This 1948 novel describing a homosexual as protagonist is noted here for American publishers' hesitation to publish *Confessions of a Mask*.
———. *Point to Point Navigation: A Memoir 1964–2006*. New York: Doubleday, 2006.
———. *United States: Essays 1952–1992*. New York: Random House, 1993. Includes a perceptive essay on Mishima, "The Death of Mishima."
Vining, Elizabeth Gray. *Windows for the Crown Prince Akihito of Japan*. Tokyo and Rutland, VT: Charles E. Tuttle, 1989; originally 1952.
Waldron, Arthur, ed. with an introduction and note. *How the Peace Was Lost: The 1935 Memorandum: Developments Affecting American Policy in the Far East: Prepared for the State Department by Ambassador John Van Antwerp MacMurray*. Stanford, CA: Hoover Institution Press, 1992.
Washburn, Stanley. *Nogi: A Great Man against a Background of War*. London: Andrew Melrose, 1913.
Watanabe Akio, ed. *Sengo Nihon no saishō-tachi*. Chūō Kōron Sha, 2001. Seventeen essays on seventeen prime ministers in postwar Japan, from Higashikuni Naruhiko to Takeshita Noboru.
Wilde, Oscar. *The Picture of Dorian Gray*. Edited and with an introduction and notes by Robert Mighall. London: Penguin, 2000.
———. *Salome: A Tragedy in One Act*. Translated by Lord Alfred Douglas. Drawings by Aubrey Beardsley. Mineola, NY: Dover Publications, 1967.

Wills, Gary. *Verdi's Shakespeare: Men of the Theater.* New York: Viking, 2011.
Wilson, George Macklin. "A New Look at the Problem of 'Japanese Fascism.'" *Comparative Studies in Society and History*, vol. 10, no. 4. (July 1968), 401–12.
Winchester, Simon. *The Meaning of Everything: The Story of the Oxford English Dictionary.* Oxford: Oxford University Press, 2003.
Yamakawa Kikue, *Bakumatsu no josei.* Iwanami Shoten, 1983.
———. *Oboegaki: Bakumatsu no Mito-han.* Iwanami Shoten, 1991.
———. *Onna nidai no ki.* Heibonsha, 1972.
Yamamoto Hirofumi. *Seppuku: Nihonjin no sekinin no tori kata.* Kōbunsha, 2003.
Yamamoto Kiyokatsu. *Mishima shisō "Tennō shinkō."* Genshū Shuppan Sha, 1994.
———. *Mishima Yukio: Yūmon no sokoku bōei fu.* Nihon Bungei Sha, 1980. Recollections of the days Yamamoto spent with Mishima and the Shield Society.
Yamamoto Shichihei. *Aru ijō taikensha no henken.* Bungei Shunjū, 1988.
———. *Ichi-kakyū shōkō no mita Teikoku Rikugun.* Bungei Shunjū, 1987.
Yamashita Kōsaku, director. *Sōchō Tobaku.* DVD of the 1968 film. Toei Video. Date not given.
Yamauchi Yukihito, ed. *Mishima Yukio eiga-ron shūsei.* Wise Shuppan, 1999. A compendium of everything Mishima said and wrote about movies.
Yanagita Kunio. *Mariko.* Shinchōsha, 1980. A biography of the daughter of Terasaki Hidenari and Gwen.
Yashiro Seiichi. *Kishu-tachi no seishun: ano koro no Katō Michio, Mishima Yukio, Akutagawa Hiroshi.* Shinchōsha, 1985. A playwright/stage director's recollections of three associates: Akutagawa Hiroshi, Katō Michio, and Mishima Yukio.
Yasuda Yojūrō. *Yasuda Yojūrō bunko* series. Vol 1: *Nihon no hashi* (2001); vol. 10: *Mōkyō* (2000); vol. 29: *Sokoku seiron I* (2002). Kyoto: Shingakusha.
Yomota Inuhiko. *High School 1968.* Shinchōsha, 2004.
———. *Nihon eiga-shi 100 nen.* Shūeisha, 2000.
———, ed. *Ōoka Shōhei: Bungaku no unmei.* Kōdansha, 1990.
Yoshida Mitsuru. *Chinkon senkan Yamato.* Kōdansha, 1974.
———. *Senchūha no seishi-kan.* Bungei Shnjū, 1980.
———. *Teitoku Itō Seiichi no shōgai.* Bungei Shunjū, 1977.
Yoshida Shigeru. *Nihon o ketteishita hyakunen*, with *Omoidasu mama.* Chūō Kōron Sha, 1999.
Yoshimoto Takaaki. *Kaitei shimpan: Kyōdō gensō-ron.* Kadokawa Shoten, 1982.
Yoshimura Akira. *Tengu sōran.* Asahi Shimbun Sha, 1994.
Yoshizawa Kenkichi. *Gaikō 60-nen.* Chūō Kōron Sha, 1990; originally 1958.
Yourcenar, Marguerite. *Memoirs of Hadrian.* New York: Farrar, Straus and Giroux, 1963. Translated with Grace Frick. Yourcenar knew that Mishima admired *Memoirs of Hadrian.* See also *Mishima: A Vision of the Void*, p. 102.
———. *Mishima: A Vision of the Void.* Translated by Alberto Manguel with the author. New York: Farrar, Straus and Giroux, 1986. A short, sympathetic biographical assessment.
Yuasa Atsuko. *Roy to Kyōko.* Chūō Kōron Sha, 1984. Yuasa was the model for Kyōko in Mishima's novel, *Kyōko's ie.*

# Index

Abbott, George (1887–1995), American man of theater, 305
Abe Jōji (b. 1937), writer, 467–68
Abe Kōbō (1924–93), novelist, playwright, 211, 439, 515, 516, 531
ACCF. *See* American Committee for Cultural Freedom
*Account of Our Divine Sovereigns and Their Orthodoxy, An (Jinnō shōtō ki)*, 366
"Action and Waiting," 642–43
"action-oriented" movies, 350–51
"Actors Theater," 193
Adachi Tōko (1939–2006), flower artist, 732
*ADONIS*, 442
Aeba Takao (b. 1930), critic, 171
*Aeroplane Dudes, The (Hikōki yartachi)*, 691
*Aesthetic of Ending, The (Owari no bigaku)*, 645
*Aesthetics of the Love of Boys, The (Shōnen-ai no bigaku)*, 691
*Affirming the Greater East-Asian War (Dai-Tōa Sensō kōtei-ron)*, 408
*After the Banquet (Utage no ato)*, 351, 352, 363, 404, 436, 696, 708; English translation of, 389; story of, 353–55
Agawa Hiroyuki (b. 1920), novelist, 593, 700, 702
agrarianism, 464
*Ai no fuan*. *See Anxiety of Love, The*
*Ai no kawaki*. *See Thirst for Love*
*Ai no shissō*. *See Love Dashes*
air raids, 9, 18, 751; B-29, of Tokyo, 122–23, 783; B-29, of Yamanote, 124; casualties, in Tokyo, 116; essay depicting, 117–18; threat to Ōta-chō, Gunma, 116
*Airport* (movie), 701
*Ajisai*. *See* "Hydrangea."
AJP. *See* Association of Japanese Publishing
*Akae*, 78, 703–4; first issue of, 97
Akama Yuriko (n.d., aka Toyo-san), restaurant maid, 721
Akamon (University of Tokyo nickname), 740
Akatsuka Fujio (1935–2008), manga artist, 678
"Akamon [Red Gate] Incident," 21–22

Akechi Mitsuhide (1528?–82), warrior–commander, 410
Akihito (b. 1933), 125th Tennō, 58, 217, 315, 755; engagement announcement, 315; marriage with Michiko, 330
Akimoto Keiichi (1930–79), photojournalist, 443
Akita Kazusue (1915–97), kendōka, 481, 677
Akiyama Shōtaro (1920–2003), photographer, 314
Akutagawa Hiroshi (1920–81), actor, stage director, 194, 239, 258, 285, 393, 736
Akutagawa Ryūnosuke (1892–1927), writer of short stories, 193, 247, 261, 280, 499, 501, 632, 648, 679
Alain-Fournier (Henri Alban-Fournier, 1886–1914), French author, 240
*ālaya-vijñāna*, 683
Albee, Edward (b. 1928), American dramatist, 383
Alcock, Rutherford (1809–97), British consul, 33
Aldini, Giovanni (n.d.), Italian sculptor, 383
Alfred A. Knopf, 70, 277, 287, 293, 294, 389, 432, 437, 673; Keene translations, 294; translations of Japanese novels, 272, 273
Ali, Muhammad (b. 1942), American boxer, 592
*All About Marriage (Kekkon no subete)*, 324
All-Campus Joint-Struggle Conference, 585
Allied Powers' bombings of Germany, 107
Altman, Robert (1925–2006), American film director, 303
*Amai mitsu no heya*. *See Room of Sweet Honey, The*
*Amai mitsu no yorokobi*. *See Joy of Sweet Honey, The*
Amano Takeo (n.d.), army major, 371
American Committee for Cultural Freedom, 225, 290; as advocate of anticommunist socialism, 224; correspondents of, 224
American critics, reviews of Japanese novels, 272–74
American National Theatre and Academy, 382
American-style capitalism, 559
Amis, Kingsley (1922–95), English novelist, 493
Anami Korechika (1887–1945), minister of the army, 128, 129, 374, 514, 771, 785; seppuku of, 373
Andersen, Hans Christian (1805–75), Danish author, 345

/ 819

Andō Gumi, yakuza group, 467
Andō Noboru (b. 1926), yakuza, actor, writer, 467–68
Andō Shin'ya (1927–2000), translator of French literature, 285
Andō Teruzō (1905–36), army officer, 365
*androphiles*, 181
Angaur, Battle of, 465–66
*Animal Entanglement*, 420
Anna de Noailles, Comtesse (1876–1933), Romanian-French writer, 675–76
ANTA Matinee Series, 382
ANTA. *See* American National Theatre and Academy
anticommunism, 165, 198–99, 224, 352, 418, 516, 529, 534, 581, 600–601, 617. *See also* communism; Communist Party
anti-Security Treaty movement, 558. *See also* US-Japanese Mutual Security Treaty
anti-Tōjō sentiments, 108
anti-Vietnam War movement, 533–56; community of warriors, 546–49; documentary on North Vietnam, 535; Fatherland Defense Corps, 536–41; "*Gewalt* struggle," 533; intellectual's support to, 534; killing of Yamazaki, 533; opposed construction of airport, 540; protest against Satō, 535–36; rally against war, 534–35; splitting of Zengakuren, 534; violence during, 533–34
anti-Yoyogi Factions, 534, 616
*Anxiety of Love, The (Ai no fuan)*, 196
*Ao no Jidai*. See *The Blue Age*
*Aoi no Ue*, 294, 382
*Aoi sanmyaku*. See *Blue Mountain Range, The*
Aoshima Kenkichi (d. 1936), army officer, 371
Aoshima Yukio (b. 1932–2006), governor of Tokyo, 571
*Aoto zōshi hana no nishiki-e*, 349
*Apollo*, 307
APOLLO (issue of *ADONIS*), 442
*Apollo no sakazuki*. See *Apollo's Cup*
*Apollo's Cup (Apollo no sakazuki)*, 222
*Arabian Nights, The*, 478, 502, 518
Araki Seishi (1907–81), historian, 473, 475, 529; Fukushima association with, 474; met Mishima at Kumamoto Station, 474; Mishima's letter to, 473, 476
Arias, Roberto ("Tito") (1918–89), Panamanian diplomat, 438
*Aristocrats' Staircase, The (Kizoku no kaidan)*, 377, 378, 379
Arisugawa Takehito (1862–1913), Taruhito's adopted son, fleet admiral, 45
Arisugawa Taruhito (1835–95), imperial prince, army general, 38
Arita Hachirō, (1884–1965), diplomat, minister for foreign affairs, 351, 357, 363; as ambassador to China, 351; candidate of, against Azuma Ryōtarō, 351; divorced Azekami, 353; elected to House of Representatives, 352; as foreign minister, 351–52; lawsuit against Mishima for invasion of privacy, 353, 355–56, 393; Mishima and publisher apology to, 355; opposition of, to Japanese-German anticommunism pact, 352; suspension of Chūō Kōron, 353

Arlen, Harold (1905–86), American songwriter, 306
*Armance*, 172, 233
Aron, Raymond (1905–83), French philosopher, journalist, 554
*Asa no tsutsuji*. See *Morning Azalea, The*
*Asahi Graph*, 521
*Asahi Journal* interview of Mishima, 601
*Asahi Shinbun*, 46, 49, 127, 145, 152, 155, 157, 166, 205, 221, 232, 273, 399, 408, 412, 417, 427, 443, 523, 545, 585, 640; articles rejected by, 152; essay on Genda in, 558; filed with the CIE, 152; "On Wartime Premiership" article in, 127; review of *A Wonder Tale: The Moonbow*, 655; review of *The Suzaku*, 531
Asano Akira (1901–90), poet, 484
Asanuma Inejirō (1898–1960), Socialist leader, 385
Asari Keita (b. 1933), stage director, businessman, 417–18
Ashikaga Yoshihisa (1465–89), 9th Ashikaga shogun, 147
Ashikaga Yoshimasa (1436–90), 8th Ashikaga shogun, 133
Ashikaga Yoshimitsu (1358–1408), 3rd Ashikaga shogun, 254, 255
Asō Kazuko (1915–96), essayist, 654
*Aspects of the Novel*, 680
assassination, 108, 323, 381–408, 417, 534, 553–54, 560, 581, 594, 616, 709; of Asanuma Inejirō, 385; of high-ranking government officials, 364, 368, 369, 374, 378; by Patriotic Party member, 385; by rightwing killers, 385–89; of Shimanaka, 386
Association for Rebuilding Japan, goals of, 341
Association of Japanese Publishing, 102; objectives of, 101–2; "project application" requirement of, 102
Association of Tokyo Stock Exchange Regular Members, 3; advisorship to, 4
Atlas, Charles (1892–1972), bodybuilder, 261
atomic bombings of Hiroshima and Nagasaki, 108, 122, 269, 433, 497, 501, 565, 783
Atsumi Mari (b. 1950), actress, 654
Aury, Dominique (Anne Desclos: 1907–98), French journalist, novelist, 432
*Autumn at the Shūgakuin, The (Shūgakuin no aki)*, 119
*Autumn: Two Pieces*, 60–61, 74
Avantos, James (n.d.), stage director (?), 303
*Aya no tsuzumi*. See *Damask Drum, The*
Ayukawa Gisuke (Yoshisuke: 1880–1967), corporate executive, politician, 49
Azekami Terui (1906–89), restaurant proprietress, 355, 357; campaign fundraising efforts of, 352–53; Mishima's visit to, 353; purchasing of Hannya-en (mansion), 352–53; "water trade" and, 352
Azuma Fumihiko (penname of Takashi, 1920–43), friend of Mishima, 66, 78, 101, 747–48; criticism of "Tinted Glass" by, 77–78; literary correspondence with Mishima, 77, 78–79; Mishima's tribute to, 703–4; as writer, 78, 101, 747–48
Azuma Hiroshi (n.d.), editor, 720
Azuma Ryōtarō (1893–1983), governor of Tokyo, 351

*Bad Poems*, 63, 496
Baishō Mitsuko (b. 1946), actress, 654
*Bajutsu tokuhon*. See *Equestrian Reader, The*
*Baka-hachi to hito wa iu*. See *They Call Me Hachi the*

*Idiot*
Baker, Josephine (1906–75), American-born French dancer, 306
Balanchine, George (1904–83), Russian-born choreographer, 307
ballets in New York: *Apollo*, 307; *Cage, The*, 307; *L'Apre-midi d'un faune*, 307; *Western Symphony*, 307
Balzac, Honoré de (1799–1850), French novelist, 545, 682
Ban Junzaburō (1908–81), comedian, 260
Bandai Kiyoshi (n.d.), editor, 482, 483, 484, 536, 627
*Bandit, The (Tōzoku)*, 140, 244, 497; depiction of Yoshiko in, 184–85; Kawabata's preface to, 168, 169
Bandō Minosuke VI (1906–75), kabuki actor, 397
Bandō Tamasaburō V (b. 1950), kabuki actor, 655–56
Bangkok, Mishima's trip to, 384, 456, 521, 522, 528–29, 799
*Bara to kaizoku*. See *Rose and the Pirate, The*
*Bara-kei*. See *Rose Punishments*
Barnard, Christiaan (1922–2001), South African cardiac surgeon, 577
Bashō. See Matsuo Bashō.
Bataille, Georges (1897–1962), French thinker, 376, 581, 715, 790
Baudelaire, Charles (1821–67), French poet, 498
Bazin, André (1918–58), French film theorist, 607
Beardsley, Aubrey (1872–97), British illustrator, 179, 360, 560–61, 788
*Beastly Entanglements (Kemono no tawamure)*, 362
Beatles, The: mania, 468–69; performance at Budōkan, 468
"Beautiful Death," 512, 513
*Beautiful Star, The (Utsukushii hoshi)*, 396, 397
"Beauty of Action, The," 644
*Beauty's Assaults (Bi no shūgeki)*, 400
Beauvoir, Simone de (1908–86), French writer, 403
Beckett, Samuel (1906–89), Irish writer, 436
*Beginning Dutch Learning (Rangaku koto-hajime)*, 445
Benares: Kalighat, 525–26; Mishima's description of, 521, 525–27; Manikalnika Ghat, 526–27
Benedict, Ruth (1887–1948), American anthropologist, 566–67
Bennett, John (1928–2005), English actor, 303
*Benten musume meo no shiranami*, 350
Berlin Crisis, 395
Bernhardt, Sarah (1844–1923), French actress, 413
Bernstein, Leonard (1918–1990), American composer, 306, 441, 591
Bessel, Friedrich (1784–1846), German astronomer, 396
*Bi no shūgeki*. See *Beauty's Assaults*
*bi no sōransha*, 570
Bierce, Ambrose (1842–1913), American writer, 609
Bigot, Georges (1860–1927), French cartoonist, 279
Bikini Atoll, 335, 501
"Birds and Beasts," *(Kinjū)*, 398–99
*Birth of Tragedy, The*, 235
*Bitoku no yoromeki*. See *Virtue Falters*
*Black Lizard (Kuro-tokage)*, 215, 216, 392–93, 557
*Blind's Tale, The*, 79–80
blood oath, on 32nd anniversary of 2.26 Incident, 540–41

*Blue Age, The (Ao no jidai)*, 193, 197, 201, 244
*Blue Mountain Range, The (Aoi sanmyaku)*, 245
Blum, Léon (1872–1950), French prime minster, 445
Blyth, R. H. (1898–1964), English teacher, authority on haiku, 754
"Boats for Feeding Hungry Ghosts" *(Segaki-bune)*, 263–64
bodybuilding, 260–62, 299, 325, 334, 380, 431, 437, 492, 574, 728
Bōjō Toshitami (1917–90), writer, 61, 62, 77, 78, 96–97, 368, 481, 635; daily letter-writing to Mishima, 65–66, 717–18; "Dance" *(Mai)* story of, 74–75; meeting Mishima in school, 61–62; relationship with Mishima, 96–97; *Spring Snow*'s influence on, 635
*Bom Dia Señora*, 229
*Bombs and Ginkgo (Bakudan to ichō)*, 673, 674
*Book of Changes, The*, 41
*Book of Documents, The*, 41
*Book of Five Elements (Gorin no sho)*, 562
Borges Jorge, Luis (1899–1986), Argentine writer, 436
*Bōshi no hana*. See "Flowers on a Hat"
Botsford, Ann (n.d.), Keith Botsford's wife, 303
Botsford, Keith (b. 1928), American/European writer, 294, 300, 302, 303, 306, 308, 310; on Gorelik's design, 302; Mishima's reunion with, 438
"bottle keep" custom, 468
Bourget, Paul (1852–1935), French novelist, 510
Bowers, Faubion (1917–99), "savior of kabuki," 141–42, 383, 391, 431
Bowie, David (b. 1947), English musician, 391
Bownas, Geoffrey (1923–2011), 375
boxing, 262, 467, 469, 492
"Boy, The" *(Shōnen)*, 66, 75, 174–75
"Boy Who Writes Poems, The," 64, 74
Brando, Marlon (1924–2004), American actor, 303, 306, 390
Brazil, Mishima's trip to, 228–29; Carnival, 230; gay life, 231; Japanese immigrants, 229; at Lins, 229; at Sao Paulo, 229
Brialy, Jean-Claude (1933–2007), French actor, director, 518
*Brilliant Backlight, The*, 70–71
*Britannicus*, 285, 292
British Council, 437
Britten, Benjamin (1913–76), British composer, 233
Broadway plays, Mishima's critiques of, 304–7
*Brothers Karamazov, The*, 172
Brown, Holloway (n.d.), friend of Donald Richie, 228
Brundage, Avery (1887–1975), American IOC president, 430
Brunswick (gay bar), 181, 189, 209; bartender trainees at, 214; Mishima's companions at, 214, 216
Buck, Pearl (1892–1973), American Nobel Prize–winning writer, 435
Buddhist postmortem limbo, 42
Bulganin, Nikolai (1895–1975), Soviet prime minister, 501
Bullock, Alan (1914–2004), British historian, 580
*bunbu ryōdō* (both literary and martial arts), 35, 741
*Bungakukai*, 256, 333, 386, 451, 582, 789; *My Friend Hitler* published in, 582; symposium on "overcoming modernity," 130

Bungaku-za, 193, 239, 262, 278, 285, 316, 360, 393; Chinese opposed Mishima's creation of, 411; founding managers of, 193–94; left-leaning of, 411; members lost by, 414–15; Mishima as planning advisor of, 360; play (*The Joyful Koto*) on hold, 417; production of Sardou's play, 414; rebuilding by Mishima, 412; resignation of Iwata from, 414–15; revolt in, 409–11; shortlisting of *La Tosca*, 412–13; size of, 410; tour of China, 411–12
*Bungei*, 418, 515
*Bungei Bunka*, 100, 131; "Imperial Declaration" in, 94; objectives of, 85; penname proposed during editorial meeting of, 91–92; poems contributed by Itō to, 105; "Spring Snow" in, 95
*Bungei Shunjū*, 17, 288, 347, 394, 449, 465, 531, 559, 560, 565, 588, 593, 595; lawsuit against, 779–80; plan for "modern Japanese literature," 565; "What Is Japan?," 636
*bunjaku no to*. See "Literary feeble fellows"
bunraku. See jōruri
*Bunshō tokuhon*, 344
Burckhardt, Jacob (1818–97), Swiss cultural historian, 235
*Bush Warbler, The (Uguisu)*, 73
"Bushidō and Militarism," 697
Byron, Lord (1788–1924), English poet, 233
Bywater, Hector (1884–1940), British journalist and writer

*Cage, The*, 307
Calta, Louis (1913–90), American theater critic, 382
*Camera Geijutsu*, 400
Camp Ichigaya, 692, 693, 695, 698, 700, 706, 718
Camp Takigahara, 486, 546, 631, 705; Mishima's diary-keeping at, 633–34; spy training at, 549–53
Camus, Albert (1913–60), French Nobel Prize–winning writer, 239
Čapek, Karel (1890–1938), Czech playwright, writer, 117, 118
Caribbean tour, 297–98
Carmichael, Stokely (1941–89), American political leader, 577
Carracci, Ludovico (1555–1619), Italian painter, 225
Castro, Fidel (b. 1926), Cuban revolutionary, 403, 577
*Cat on a Hot Tin Roof*, 349
Cates, Clifton B. (1893–1970), US Marine Corps general, 465
"Cdr. Hirose" *(Hirose kaigun chūsa)*, 545
*Celtic Twilight, The*, 573
censorship, 63, 127, 138, 152; of kabuki and other plays, 140–41; of Kamakura Bunko, 151; of open sexual expression, 173; "project application" and, 102
Chamberlain, Basil H. (1850–1935), British Japanologist, 652
Charter Oath, 143, 144, 145, 470
*Chi to bara*. See *Le Sang et la Rose*
Chiang Kaishek (1887–1975), Chinese military and political leader, 649
*Chichi no bōshi*. See *My Father's Hat*
Chichibu Yasuhito (1902–53), prince, major general, 368
*Chijin-ron*. See *On the Earthman*
Chikamatsu Monzaemon (1653–1725), jōruri and kabuki writer, 117, 188, 498
*Chinsetsu Yumiharizuki*. See *Wonder Tale, A: The Moonbow*
Chopin, Frédéric François (1810–49), Polish composer and pianist
Chou Enlai (1898–1976), Chinese political leader, 404
Christianity, Shinpūren Revolt and, 470
*Chronicle of Great Peace (Taiheiki)*, 719
*Chrysanthemum and the Sword, The*, 566–67, 568, 569, 571
Chrysanthemum Day, 374, 556
*Chūō Kōron* (company and magazine), 353, 408, 555, 563, 566; Mishima afterword to Japanese literature series by, 685–86; *Enomoto Takeaki* in, 531; Mishima's taidan with Ishikawa Jun in, 706; *"On Defending Culture"* in, 563, 566; rightwing pressure on, 385; self-censorship by, 388; Shichirō's short story published in, 385
*Chūsei*. See "The Medieval Period"
Ciampi, Yves (1921–82), French director, 383
CIE. See Civil Information and Education Service
"Cigarette, A" *(Tabako)*, 153, 154
"Circus" *(Sākasu)*, 114–16, 496, 591
*City and the Pillar, The*, 227, 277
*City of Night*, 699
Civil Information and Education Service, 152, 189, 199, 219, 246; censorship of kabuki and other plays, 140–41
class composition, 37
class system, 695; after collapse of Tokugawa rule, 24
Claudel, Paul (1868–1955), French diplomat, writer, 204
Clausewitz Carl, von (1780–1831), Prussian military theorist, 553, 788
Cocteau, Jean (1889–1963), French poet, artist, 180, 281, 350, 383
Colette (1873–1954), French novelist, 518
*Collection of Corals*, 676
*Collection of Poems for a Week*, 64
Comedie Française, 213, 413
comic books. See manga
communism, 161, 165–66, 198, 339, 366, 529, 581, 657, 768; Mishima's opposition to, 534, 553, 570, 600–601, 620; opposition to US war against, 516; rise of, in China, 223; suppression of, 581. See also anticommunism
Communist Party, China, 223
Communist Party, Japan, 72, 198, 485, 516, 538, 548, 616, 618–19, 694, 768; agitation against *The Joyful Koto*, 416–17; nationwide rallies organized by, 616, 639; revolt against Chinese Communist Party by, 516; Zengakuren split with, 514, 534
Conde, David (1906–?), US Occupation officer, 247
Conde, Raymond (1916–2003), Filipino-Japanese musician, 347
Conder, Josiah (1852–1920), British architect, 279
*Confessions of a Mask (Kamen no kokuhaku)*, 7, 12, 16, 19, 41, 99, 108, 109, 124, 157, 158, 159, 244, 333, 438; demotic title of, 172–73; depiction of love for Kuniko in, 185–86; depiction of Maizuru in, 260; English translation of, by Weatherby, 227, 275; epigraph in, 171–72; Fukuda's afterword to, 192; glass cover for, 704; Hanada Kiyoteru's review of,

177–78; Hirschfeld's reference in, 181–82; homosexual yearnings in, 174–78; initial response to, 175; I-novel format selection for, 169–70; Jinzai's review of, 176–77; limited luxury edition of, 704; manuscript submission for, 171; narrative gap in, 179; notes on kissing Kuniko in, 183–84; opinions of writers and critics on, 177; pricing of, 202; reality and fiction in, discrepancies between, 183–88; self-advertisement for, 172; sexual confession in, 172–74
*Conflagration (Enjō)*, 322
*Confusion of Feelings*, 190
*Constant Nymph, The*, 239
Constitution of Japan. *See* Japanese Constitution; Constitutional revision; MacArthur Constitution; Shōwa Constitution
Control Faction, 369, 370
Cooper, Duff (1890–1954), British politician, 437
*Corpse and Treasure, The (Shibito to takara)*, 195
Counterrevolution Manifesto, 600–604
Countess of Ségur, Sophie (1799–1874), French writer, 687
*Country Girls, The*, 438
Cranach, Lucas (1472–1553), German painter, 687
Creemers, Wilhelmus (n.d.), historian, 754
*Criticism of Lyricism (Jojō no hihan)*, 379, 380
Cros, Guy-Charles (1879–1919), French poet, 90
*Crossing All the Bridges (Hashi-zukushi)*, 347
Crouse, Russell (1893–1966), American playwright, librettist, 304
Cuban Missile Crisis, 388
Cultural Revolution, 515; *Joyful Koto, The* and, 516; slogans of, 593; Yamamoto Kiyokatsu's fear from, 542

Dahl, Robert (b. 1915), American political scientist, 568
Daibosatsu Pass Incident, 641–42
Daiei Studio, 322
*Daigo Fukuryū Maru*, 336
*Daiichi no sei. See First Sex, The*
Daiichi Seimei Building, 140, 329
Daimatsu Hirobumi (1921–78), volleyball coach, 403–4, 571
*Dai-Tōa Sensō kōtei-ron. See Affirming the Greater East-Asian War*
Dali, Salvador (1904–89), Spanish painter, 506
*Damask Drum, The (Aya no tsuzumi)*, 285, 294–97, 412
*Damie garasu. See* "Tinted Glass"
Dan Ikuma (1924–2001), composer, 555
Dan Kazuo (1912–76), novelist, 190–91
"Dance" *(Mai)*, 74, 75
dandyism, 16–18, 691, 694
d'Annunzio, Gabriele (1863–1938), Italian writer, soldier, 435, 444–47
Daolong. *See* Dōryū
*Darkness in Summer (Natsu no yami)*, 444
Darrieux, Danielle (b. 1917), French actress, 383
Date Munekatsu (1928–88), journalist, 584, 669, 721, 732, 735; Mishima's letter to, 708–9
Daudet, Alphonse (1840–97), French novelist, 520
Dazai Osamu (1909–48), novelist, 261, 273, 275, 335, 498, 519, 601, 632, 662, 759; background of, 160–61; literary encounter with Mishima, 161–64; reputation and image of, 164; "self-caricaturization" in works of, 160; suicide of, 170
de Gaulle, Charles (1890–1970), French president, 548, 554
de Noailles, Anna (1876–1933), French poet, 675, 676
de Paul, Gene (1919–88), American composer, 305
Dean, James (1931–55), American actor, 303, 766
death, thoughts on, 495–508, 590–92
death and eroticism, 358, 376, 377, 591–92
"Death by Drowning," 592
"Death in Midsummer" *(Manatsu no shi)*, 210
"Death of Baldassare Silvande, The," 117, 118
Debussy, Claude-Achille (1862–1918), French composer, 307
decadence: and national defense, 560–63; special issue of *Hihyō* on, 560–61
*Decadent Art*, 561
*Decay of the Angel, The (Tennin gosui)*, 685, 700, 701
*Decline and Fall of the Suzaku, The (Suzaku-ke no metsubō)*, 136, 529–32
Deer Cry Hall. *See* Rokumeikan, The
Deer Garden Temple. *See* Kinkakuji
del Río, Dolores (1905–83), Mexican actress, 303, 304
Delon, Alain (b. 1935), French actor, 404, 562
DeMille, Cecil B. (1881–1959), American film director, 304
Democratic Youth League, 596
*Demons*, 503
Den Hideo (1923–2009), journalist, politician, 535, 580
*Descent of Winter, The*, 580
Desiderio da Settignano (1428?–64), Italian sculptor and painter, 560
Dewey, John (1859–1952), American philosopher, educator, 169
*Diable au corps, Le*, 80, 236, 237, 423
*Diasalmata*, 319
Dickinson, Emily (1830–86), American poet, 557
Diego Suarez attack, 644
disembowelment. *See* seppuku
"Distance-Riding Club" *(Tōnorikai)*, 204, 219
*Divine State's Tie-Dye Castle (Shinshū Kōketsu-jō)*, 680
Dodge, Joseph (1890–1964), American banker, 198, 202, 780
"Dodge Line," 198, 202
dōjō, 329–30, 464, 465
Dōmoto Masaki (b. 1933), playwright, director, 440, 502
Dōryū (Daolong: 1213–78), Chinese monk who emigrated to Japan, 271
Dostoevsky, Fyodor, 172, 503
double suicide, 170, 185, 188, 208, 496–99, 513
Double-Yang Day, 374
Douglas, Lord Alfred (1870–1945), British author, 360
Douglas, William O. (1898–1980), US Supreme Court justice, 755
draft card, 14; induction notice, 16; private second class, 15
draft physicals, 100; conscription age for, in 1944, 10; Hiraoka Kimitake's turn for weight lifting, 11–12; at Kakogawa Town Hall, 11; orientation for, 10; passing grades, 12; rice-bag-lifting test of strength, 11, 13; at Shikata, 9–10; written test and

vision test, 12
"Dream and Life," 403
"Drunkard Has Come Back, The," 571
*Duke of Portland,* 611, 680
Durbin, Deanna (b. 1921), American singer and actress, 75
Dutch learning, 33, 445–46, 776
Dutt, R. Palme (1896–1974), British Communist theoretician, 339, 554

East Maizuru, 260
"Eastern Army," 692, 693, 695, 718, 730
East-West dichotomy, 559
Economic Planning Agency, annual "white paper" on economy, 288
Eden, Anthony (1897–1977), British prime minister, 501
Edo Period, 22, 23, 201, 366, 367, 475, 605, 612; *chigo* game popularity during, 62; Dutch-Japanese trade relations during, 445; National Learning toward end of, 366; surnames of commoners during, 22–23
Edogawa Ranpo (Hirai Tarō; 1894–1965), writer of detective stories, 216, 392
*Eguchi Hatsujo oboegaki.* See "*Memorandum on Eguchi Hatsu-jo, A*"
*Eiga Geijutsu,* 343, 562, 610, 701, 702
*Eirei no koe.* See "Voices of the Heroic Souls"
*Eirei no zekkyō.* See Screams of Heroic Souls
Eisenhower, Dwight (1890–1996), US president, 501
Ellis, Havelock (1859–1939), British psychologist, 180
Endō Shūsaku (1923–96), novelist, 519, 673
*Enemy Below, The,* 324
*Enjō.* See *Conflagration*
Enomoto Takeaki (1836–1908), admiral, 33, 34, 531–32
ephebophiles, 181
*Equestrian Reader, The (Bajutsu tokuhon),* 711
eroticism, 338, 460, 575, 582, 620, 663, 681, 715–16; and death, 358, 376, 377, 576–77, 591–92
espionage, lecture on, 549–50
*Esquire,* 592
Esquire, The (dance hall), 5, 6
*Establishment of the Teaching for the Protection of the Country (Risshō ankoku-ron),* 371
*Esugai no kari.* See "Yisugei's Hunt"
Etō Jun (1932–99), literary critic, 334, 340, 649
Etō Shinpei (1834–74), politician, 472
Euripides (c. 480–406 B.C.), Greek tragedian, 530
Europe, Mishima's trip to, 383–84
Europeanization, 523, 591
"Expel the Barbarians," 35, 470, 647, 700
extraterrestrials, 396

F-104 flight, 578–79
"*Fall of the House of Usher, The,*" 84, 345
*Fall of Tōdai, The (Tōdai rakujō),* 595, 597
farm bill, 49–50
Fascism, 338–40, 701
*Fascism and Social Revolution,* 339
Fatherland Defense Corps: fundraising for, 537–38; JNG and, 536–37; longer version of, 537; Mishima's blueprint for, 542; pamphlet on importance of, 536–37, 541; reservations of, about Mishima's idea, 543; Yamamoto Kiyokatsu and, 541–44

Faulkner, William (1897–1961), American Nobel Prize–winning writer, 287, 435
Faure, Edgar (1908–88), French prime minister, 501
"Favorite," 83
Fellini, Federico (1920–93), Italian film director, 707
Fels, Florent (1893–1977), French Dadaist, 520
*Femmes Damnées,* 237
Feuillère, Edwige (1907–98), French actress, 237
Feynman, Richard (1918–88), American physicist, 457
*Finnegans Wake,* 345
First Haneda Incident, 533, 541–42
*First Sex, The (Daiichi no sei),* 403, 404
*Fissure, The (Kiretsu),* 333
5.15 Incident, 388
Flaubert, Gustave (1821–80), French novelist, 319
Fleischmann, Julius (1900–1968), American philanthropist, 290–91
"Flowers on a Hat" *(Bōshi no hana),* 394
flying saucers, 396
*Fond of Young Women: The Sash-Taking Pond (Musume-gonomi obitori-no-ike),* 347
Fonda, Henry (1905–82), American actor
Fontaine, Joan (b. 1917), American actress, 239
Fonteyn, Margot (1919–91), English ballerina, 438
*Forbidden Colors (Kinjiki),* 210, 211, 213, 227, 243, 244, 328, 474; homosexual theme of, 209; Part II of, 207; serialization of, 207, 208
*Forest in Full Bloom, The (Hanazakari no mori*; story and collection) 31, 45, 52, 96, 100, 102, 116, 147, 148, 243; challenges faced in publication of, 102–3; decadence and aestheticism of stories in, 118; depiction of marriages between samurai and aristocratic families in, 45; depiction of Natsuko's illness in, 42–43; five stories in, 112; Fuji's interest in, 101; as gift to Makoto, 111; half-a-year waiting period during, 107; lauding Itō in afterword of, 106; name typo in, 111; publication in *Bungei Bunka,* 84–85; publication permission for, 104; Rilke-esque story of, 89–91; request for Itō's laudatory preface to, 104, 105–6
Formentor Literary Prize, 436–37
Forster, E. M. (1879–1970), English novelist, 680
Fourth Defense Plan, 658, 659
Francois-Poncet, André (1887–1968), French politician, diplomat, 498
Frank, Melvin (1913–88), American screenwriter, 305
Frazer, James George (1854–1941), Scottish social anthropologist, 451
Frechtman, Bernard (n.d.), American translator, 273
French Romantic plays, staging of, 413
French student movement, Mishima's assessment of, 554
Freud, Sigmund (1856–1939), Austrian psychoanalyst, 180
"From the Wilderness" *(Kōya yori),* 504–6
*Fudōtoku kyōiku kōza.* See *Lectures on Unethical Education*
Fuji Junko (b. 1945), actress, 721
Fuji Masaharu (1913–87), poet, novelist, 31; on Hayashi Fujima's poetry, 100–101; letter to Hasuda, 101
Fujii Hiroaki (n.d.), film producer, 440, 442–43
*Fujin Asahi,* 348

Fujin Club, 394
*Fujin Kōron*, 197, 335, 344, 424, 517
Fujiwara (Nijō) Sadatame (n.d.), poet, 720
Fujiwara Ginjirō (1869–1960), businessman, politician: as "administrative inspector," 103; as Minister of Commerce and Industry, 104; sense of indebtedness to Sadatarō of, 95–96
Fujiwara Iwaichi (1908–86), army general, 541, 653, 671, 787
Fujiwara no Takasue's daughter (b. 1108), poet, 403
Fujiwara no Teika (Sadaie, 1162–1241), poet, 401
Fukazawa Shichirō (1914–87), musician, writer 281, 385; as author of *On the Narayama Song*, 360; withdrawal from literary world by, 387–88
Fukuda Nobuyuki (1921–94), physicist, 553
Fukuda Takeo (1905–95), prime minister, 559
Fukuda Tsuneari (1912–94), Shakespearean translator, playwright, stage director, 177, 192, 205, 316, 410, 558; arguments of, with Mishima, 414; betrayal of Bungaku-za, 409–11; complaint against, 410; as JCC charter member, 558; manifesto of, 414
Fukuhara Ryōjirō (1868–1932), politician, 26
Fukunaga Takehiko (1918–79), student of French literature, novelist, 258
Fukushima Jirō (1930–2006), writer, 208, 328–29, 460, 473, 476; association with Araki by, 474; lawsuit against, 779–80; making love with Mishima, 209–10, 474; as Mishima's factotum, 209–10; on model for Yūichi, 211; stay at Imai Beach with Mishima, 210
Fukushima Masanori (1561–1624), warrior-commander, 733
*Fukuzatsuna kare*. See *He, The Complicated One*
Fukuzawa Yukichi (1835–1901), educator, 366, 531
Funae Fujio (n.d.), 8, 10; Hiraoka Kimitake and, 10–11, 13–14; induction order and physical education of, 15; on induction chances of Hiraoka, 15
Funahashi Seiichi (1904–76), novelist, 677
Funakoshi Eiji (1923–2007), actor, 351
Funasaka Hiroshi (1920–2006), bookseller, writer, 464; books on Palau battles, 467; gift of sword to Mishima by, 478–79, 780; part of Kwangtung Army, 466; survivor of Battle of Angaur, 465
Funasaka Yoshio (n.d.), Hiroshi's son, 479
fund raising, 342, 353
*fundoshi*, 474, 476, 620
*Funktionär*, 339
Furubayashi Takashi (1927–98), literary critic, 717; background of, 716; series of talks with writers of "the postwar school" by, 714; taidan with Mishima, 714–17
Furuichi Kimitake (1854–1934), civil engineer, professor, 24–25
*Fūryū mutan*. See *"Tale of a Stylish Dream"*
*fuseji* censorship, 63, 151
Fushimi Hiroyasu (1875–1946), prince, 368
Futabatei Shimei (1864–1909), translator of Russian literature, novelist, 273–74
*Futon*, 177, 178
*Fuyugeshiki*. See *"Winterscape"*

gagaku, 633, 634
Gakusei Shakai Kagaku Rengōkai (Gakuren; Students Federation of Social Science), 406
Gakushūin. See Peers School
Galbraith, John Kenneth (1908–2006), American economist, 224–25
Gallagher, Michael (b. 1930), American translator of Japanese literature: background of, 673–74; experiences with Kamagasaki and Tōdai, 674; translation of *Spring Snow* by, Mishima's reaction to, 688; translation of *The Sea and Poison* by, 673
*Gamble in Don's Honor (Sōchō tobaku)*, 605, 609; influence on yakuza films of, 606–7; Mishima's assessment of, 607
Gandhi, Indira (1917–84), Indian prime minister, 521–22
Gandhi, Mahatma (1869–1948), Indian political leader, 475
Garbo, Greta (1905–90), Swedish actress, 383
gay bars, 213, 217–18, 227, 230–31, 423, 442, 467, 473–74; Brunswick, 181, 209, 214–15; Redon, 209, 328; in Saint Germain, 231; by Shinjuku Station, 215–16
"Gefährlich," 318
Geiger, Roy S. (1885–1947), US Marine Corps general, 465
*Geijutsu Shinchō*, 349
*Geistesgeschichte*, 121, 563
Gelber, Jack (1932–2003), American playwright, 383
Gélin, Daniel (1921–2002), French actor, 236
Genda Minoru (1904–89), general, politician, 558
"General, The" *(Shōgun)*, 648
Genghis Khan (1162?–1227), Mongolian conqueror, 115
*Genjū-an no ki*. See *Record of a Phantom Hut*
Genroku Era (1688–1704), 22–23, 117
Gentile, Giovanni (1874–1944), Italian philosopher, 339
German Expressionism, 414
German-USSR Non-aggression Treaty, 352
*Gettan-sō kitan*. See *"Strange Tale of the Pale-Moon Villa, The"*
"*Gewalt* struggle," 533
ghostwriting, 398–404, 773
*Gianni Schicchi* (opera), 225–26
Gide, André (1869–1951), French author, 180, 518
Gielgud, John (1904–2000), English actor, 439
Ginsberg, Allen (1926–97), American poet, 525
Gionji, 259
Giorgione (1477/8–1510), Venetian painter, 689
Giovanni Aldini, 384
Giraudoux, Jean (1882–1944), French novelist, diplomat: influence on Katō Michio, 239
*Godzilla (Gojira)*, 336
Goethe, Johann Wolfgang von (1749–1832), German writer, politician, 451
*Gogo no eikō*. See *Sailor Who Fell from Grace with the Sea, The*
Gold, Herbert (b. 1924), American novelist, 436
"Golden Death" *(Konjiki no shi)*, Mishima's commentary on, 686–87, 714
*Golden Pavilion, The (Kinkakuji)*, 247, 254, 264, 322, 335, 429; English translation of, 272; information gathering efforts for, 259–60, 262–63; Kobayashi Hideo's review of, 265; movie based on, 322, 429; Murayama's version of, 286; protagonist of, motive

of, 266–68; sales of, 272, 282; serialization of, initial reaction to, 263; Yomiuri Literary Prize for, 283
Gombrowicz, Witold (1904–69), Polish novelist, 582
Gorelik, Mordecai (1899–1990), theater designer, 302
*Gorin no sho.* See *Book of Five Elements*
Gosha Hideo (1929–92), film director, 681; *Kill! (Hitokiri)* movie of, 614–16
Gotō (née Toyoda) Sadako (b. 1935), 283, 286; dating Mishima, 248–49, 263; depiction of, in *The Sunken Waterfall,* 250; ends affair with Mishima, 262–64; last meeting with Mishima, 286; Mishima's letter to, 259, 262–63; Yuasa Atsuko's assessment of affair of, 263
Gotō Shōjirō (1838–97), politician, 113
*Götterdämmerung,* disappearance of, 684
Gracq, Julien (1910–2007), French writer, 718
Grass, Günter (b. 1927), German novelist, 381
Great Ansei Persecution, 33
"Great East Asia War and Japanese Literature, The," 120–21
*Great History of Male Love (Nanshoku ōkagami),* 188
Great Kantō Earthquake, 8, 41, 709
*Great Mirror, The,* 79, 80
"Great People's Manner of Death," 710
Greece, Mishima's trip to, 233–35
Greek tragedy: asymmetrical beauty of, 234; verse drama starting with, 235–36
Ground Self-Defense Forces (GSDF), 489, 495, 536, 537, 669, 690, 703; cost-cutting measures of, 631; domestic security matters and, 542, 589; Eastern headquarters of, 551; JNG Headquarters as conduit to the, 536–37; large-scale exercise of, at the Fuji School, 651; Mishima joining, 540; Mishima's thoughts on, 490–91, 494, 513, 522, 697; munitions depot of, plan to seize, 692; training at, 485, 486, 488, 546–47, 551, 563, 603, 625; Yamamoto retired from, 542
GSDF Research School, 541, 542
Guadalcanal, Battle of, 127, 133, 378, 497
guerrilla warfare, 642, 697; lecture session on, 594; training at Camp Takigahara, 594
Guevara, Ernesto "Che" (1928–67), Argentine revolutionary, 629
*Gunzō,* 361, 394; Mishima's works published in, 164
*gyokusai,* 98
Gyp (Sibylle Gabrielle Marie Antoinette Riqueti de Mirabeau; 1849–1932), French writer, 520

Hachi no Ki Kai, 317; members of, 205; origin of name of, 205–6
*Hachi no ki.* See *Potted Tree, The*
Haga Mayumi (1903–91), student of German literature, 564
*Hagakure,* 401, 460, 495, 501, 511, 512, 566, 637, 683; during war, 510; meaning of, 509, 784;
Hagiwara Sakutarō (1887–1942), poet, 104
Hague Convention Respecting the Laws and Customs of War on Land, 537
Haguro Masumi, 396, 397
*Hai no kisetsu.* See *Season of Ashes, The*
haiku, 152, 194, 206, 277, 499, 674; by Mishima, 64, 73, 279
*Haiku,* 674

*Hailstones That Faded on My Palms (Waga te ni kieshi arare),* 675
Hakozaki Shrine, 558
*Hakubyō.* See *Line-Drawing*
*Hamamatsu Chūnagon monogatari.* See *Tale of Middle Councilor Hamamatsu, The*
*Hamlet,* 409, 410
Hammarskjöld, Dag (1905–61), UN Secretary General, 394, 585
Hanada Kiyoteru (1909–74), journalist, novelist, 177
Hanai Takuzō (n.d.), lawyer, 30
*Hanazakari no mori.* See "Forest in Full Bloom, The"
Hani Gorō (1901–83), Marxist historian, 150, 534
Haniya Yutaka (1909–97), novelist, 189, 592
*Hanjo,* 235, 286, 294, 382
*Happy Hunting,* 304
*Hara o kiru koto.* See "To Cut His Stomach"
Hara Setsuko (b. 1920), actress, 245
Hara Takashi (1856–1921), prime minister, 554, 668
Hara Yūichi (n.d.), army colonel, 726
Harada Masahiko (b. 1943), boxer, 469
Harada Ryūki (n.d.), poet, 160
Harburg, E. Y. (1896–1981), American songwriter, 306
Harris, Townsend (1804–78), first US Consul General in Japan, 45
Harrison, Rex (1908–90), English actor, 304–5
*Haru no isogi.* See *Spring Hurries*
*Haru no yuki.* See *Spring Snow*
*Haru to shura.* See *Spring and Asura*
Haruki Makoto (1912–45), army major, 693
"Haruko," 164, 165
Hasegawa Kazuo (1908–84), actor, 133
Hasegawa Shin (1884–1963), novelist, playwright, 605
Hashi Ippa (n.d.), Mishima's maternal great-great-grandfather, 40
Hashi Kendō (1823–81), Mishima's maternal great-grandfather, 40
Hashi Kenzō (1861–1944), Mishima's maternal grandfather, 40
Hashi Tomiko (b. 1875), Mishima's maternal grandmother, 20, 68
Hashikawa Bunzō (1922–83), political scientist, 580; criticism of "On Defending Culture," 570; influence on Mishima of, 565–66, 789; Mishima's biography by, 565–66; Mishima's interest in works of, 564, 568; reviews of *Kyōko's House* by, 564–65
Hashimoto Shinobu (b. 1918), film scriptwriter, director, 615
*Hashi-zukushi.* See *Crossing All the Bridges*
Hasuda Toshiko (n.d.), Zenmei's wife,
Hasuda Zenmei (1904–45), student of Japanese literature, critic, 84, 85, 95, 101, 473, 474; essay on Prince Ōtsu by, 676; fracas over *Naval Battle,* 87; influence of, on Mishima, 91, 676–77; letter to Mishima for book publishing, 101; literary work and his death, disconnect between, 676–77; National Learning and, 86–89; salvo against Niwa by, 87–88; service in the army of, 88; violent action and death of, 88; on writer of "The Forest in Full Bloom," 89
*Hasuda Zenmei and His Death (Hasuda Zenmei to sono shi),* 677
Hata family, 9

Hatanaka Kenji (1912–45), army major, 514
Hatano Akira (1911–2002), commissioner of Metropolitan Police, 597
Hatano Sōha (1923–91), haiku poet, 674
Hatoyama Ichirō (1883–1959), prime minister, 342
Hatoyama Yukio (b. 1947), prime minister, 665
Hayashi Fujima (1914–2001), poet, physician, 100
Hayashi Fusao (1903–75), novelist, 100, 168, 178, 407, 408, 430, 475, 482, 537, 557, 616, 657; after Japan's defeat, 404; arrest of, 405; fame and popularity of, 165; and Marxism, 405–6; meeting with Mishima by, 165–66; Mishima's views on, 407–8; stories written by, 166; views of, on "sentiments" and "thought," 406
Hayashi Kentarō (1913–2004), historian, 593; house arrest of, 593; as JCC charter member, 558
Hayashi Shōken (Yōken, 1929–56), arsonist of Kinkakuji, 265, 268; confession of, 254; death of, 266; failed suicide attempt of, 266; hometown of, 260
Hayashi Takeshi (1896–1975), painter, 558
Hayek, Friedrich August von (1899–1992), Austrian economist, 538
Hayes, Robert (1942–2002), Olympic sprinter, football player, 428–29
*He, The Complicated One (Fukuzatsuna kare)*, 467
*Heibon Punch*, 480, 488, 493, 547, 548, 561, 577, 582, 608
Heidegger, Martin (1889–1976), German philosopher, 381, 416, 426, 648
Heifetz, Jascha (1901–87), American violinist, 248–49
Hemingway, Ernest (1899–1961), American Nobel-Prize-winning author, 287, 508
Henderson, Harold G. (1889–1974), American haiku writer, 144, 754
Henry, Patrick (1736–99), American politician, 694
*Herald Tribune*, 337
Hersh, Seymour (b. 1937), American journalist, 654
*Heso to genbaku*. See *Navel and the Atomic Bomb, The*
Hibiya Town Hall, 385, 386
Hidaka Rokurō (b. 1917), sociologist, 534
*Hidden Fortress, The*, 438
Higashikumi Naruhiko (1887–1990), prince, prime minister, 368; imperial emissaries of, 14; as prime minister following Japan's defeat, 13–14
Higashikuni Toshihiko, 229
*Highlands (Kōgen)*, 675
Higuchi Ichiyō (1872–96), novelist, 236
*Higyō*. See *Secret Drug, The*
*Hihyō*, 444, 446, 503, 515, 560, 561, 572, 688
Hiiro Tomoe (b. 1941), actress, 494
Hijikata Tatsumi (1928–86), dancer, 400
Hikari (Light) Club, 197
*Hikōki yarōtachi*. See *Aeroplane Dudes, The*
Hinatsu Kōnosuke (1890–1971), student of English literature, poet, 345, 360
Hino Ashihei (1907–60), novelist: as a "soldier writer," 220; visit to "Police Reserve Force," 220
Hinuma Rintarō (1925–68), literary critic, 502–3
Hirahara Kazuo (n.d.), army general, 541, 543
Hiraizumi (née Kajima) Mieko (n.d.), 217, 307, 308, 310; at Brunswick with Mishima, 214, 216; at Kanetaka's party, 213–14
Hiraizumi Kiyoshi (1895–1984), historian, 307–8, 483

Hiraizumi Wataru (b. 1929), Mieko's husband, diplomat, politician; bureaucratic career of, 307–8
Hirano Ken (1907–1978), novelist, 177, 256, 333–34, 716
Hiranuma Kiichirō (1867–1952), prime minister, 352
Hiraoka (née Hashi) Shizue (1905–87), Mishima's mother, 2, 41, 102, 183, 202, 328, 348, 401, 459, 590, 668, 696, 722; candidate selection of, for Mishima's marriage, 313–14; desire of, to divorce from Azusa, 183, 202; "disjointed remembrances" with Azusa, 50–56, 111, 167, 210; illness of, and Mishima's marriage, 318, 319; interview of, for biography of Mishima, 50–51; marriage to Azusa, 40; Mishima's love for, 68–69; on Natsuko's tyrannic behavior, 43–44, 45, 51, 59; reaction on reading "Sorrels," 55–56; reaction to Kimitake's induction order, 18, 20; reaction to Natsuko's death, 68; as secret conspirator of Mishima's writings, 69
Hiraoka (née Nagai) Natsuko (1876–1939), Mishima's paternal grandmother, 2, 27, 34, 38, 39, 58–59, 201, 690, 746; death of, 67; feudalistic sentiments of, 67; as follower of Seichō no Ie, 690; forebears of, 21; illness of, 42–43, 54; influence of, on Hiraoka Kimitake, 45–46, 67–69; marriage to Hiraoka Sadatarō, 27, 38; personality and character of, 39–40, 42, 44–45, 51; stay in Tokyo of, 28
Hiraoka (née Sugiyama) Yōko (1937–95), Mishima's wife, 2, 315, 704, 723; meeting with Mishima, 318–19; movie and cabaret with Mishima, 319; pregnancy of, 326; *Stage Struck* with Mishima and Atsuko, 319; statement after "Mishima Incident" trial, 735; wedding with Mishima, 320–24
Hiraoka Azusa (1894–1976), Mishima's father, director-general of Ministry of Agriculture and Fisheries, 2, 18, 21, 25, 38, 39, 60, 139, 183, 187, 210, 241, 263, 320, 328, 505, 543, 670, 705, 722; arrangement by, for Kimitake's visit to Sadatarō's hometown, 21, 23, 31; candidate selection for Mishima's marriage by, 313–14; concerns of, on Mishima's literary "successes," 148, 166–67; discussion with Kimura, of, 166; "disjointed remembrances" with Shizue of, 50–56, 111, 167, 210; efforts of, to select as isolated island, 241–42; at funeral of Mishima, 732; hatred for literature by, 110–11; Hiraoka Yoshiaki as regular companion of, 70–71; Japanese-style crew-cut of, 202; on Kimitake's rejection chances, 12–13; letter to Mishima during his Osaka days, 71–72; marriage to Hashi Shizue, 40; as Mishima's business manager, 203; Nosaka writings on, 70–71; personality and character of, 71; reaction of, to army's rejection of Mishima, 19–20; return of, from Osaka to Tokyo, 84; role of, in wrecking epochal farm bill, 49; Shizue's desire to divorce, 183, 202; taking care of family expenses of, 70, 71; urging Mishima to become a novelist, 137
—bureaucratic career of: 6, 47–50, 93; as director-general of forestry management in Osaka, 59–60, 69–70; as director of rice, 70; lifestyle in Osaka of, 70–71
—paternal genealogical search of: 22; motive in, 23; peasant family of, 23–24
Hiraoka Chiyuki (1930–96), Mishima's brother, diplomat, 2, 6, 17, 18, 31, 53, 58, 59, 202, 719; meeting with Mishima by, 587–88; and Mishima visit to

Laos, 529
Hiraoka family: "domicile" or legal permanent residence of, 10; Fujiwara Ginjirō's "funeral gift" to, 95; new residence of, in Midori-ga-Oka, 201–4; store name of, 22–23
Hiraoka Hisatarō (b. 1865), Mishima's paternal granduncle, 30
Hiraoka Iichirō (b. 1962), Mishima's son, 402, 708, 723, 779
Hiraoka Kimitake (Mishima Yukio's real name; 1925–70): appointment to Ministry of Finance, 5; birth of, 40–41; composition titled "The Owl," 53; daily letterwriting to Bōjō, 65–66, 717–18; disregard of Sadatarō, 46; description of Natsuko's disease, 42–43; domicile, 10, 13; in Elementary Division of Peers School, 53–54; essay "Our Military in China," 58; family tree, 2, 6–7; as fan of manga, 678–81; father of (see Hiraoka Azusa); Funae Fujio conversation with, 13–14; induction order, 16–21; in junior high school, 58–59, 61–62; kabuki and nō plays, exposure to, 67–68; Natsuko's illness and, 42–43; playing with female children, 45; poetry writings, 60–66 of; proposal for penname of, 91–92; reluctance to talk about non-samurai ancestors, 21; school and college education, 15–16; sex talk among school friends, 75–76; and student labor mobilization program, 16; taking draft physicals (see draft physicals); terrified of Azusa, 59–60; will of, 16–17. See also Mishima Yukio
—personality and character of: arrogance, 74, 105; expressionless face of, 51–52; formal and courteous, 45; impassiveness, 51–52; Natsuko's influence on, 44–46, 748; as prankster, 72; "pride," 105
Hiraoka Kōtarō (1851–1906), nationalist leader, 23
Hiraoka Magozaemon (n.d.), Mishima's paternal ancestor, 2, 22, 23
Hiraoka Manjirō (1860–1923), Mishima's paternal granduncle, lawyer, 2, 23, 30; career of, 25, 30; education of, 24
Hiraoka Mitsuko (1928–1945), Mishima's sister, 2, 6, 17; death of, 139; fifth death anniversary of, 206
Hiraoka Mume (b. 1872), Mishima's paternal grandaunt, 22, 30, 70, 746
Hiraoka Sadatarō (1863–1942), Mishima's paternal grandfather, administrator of Karafuto (Sakhalin) Agency, 2, 58–59, 554, 565, 705, 736, 741; arrest of, 742–43; character and temperament of, 28; commercial interests of, 742; death and funeral of, 95; education of, 24, 25; book on international private law of, 26–27; Hyōgo Prefecture, views on, 28; marriage of, to Natsuko, 32, 38; Mishima's overt disregard of, 44–46; statue of, in Karafuto Shrine, 96
—ancestors of: discussed, 21–28; peasant family, 23–24; Takichi (Azusa's grandfather), 23–24, 30–31; Tazaemon (Azusa's great grandfather), 21–22
—bureaucratic career of: accomplishments during, 27; as administrator of Karafuto, 27, 28, 29; described, 6–7, 11, 31; family conditions following collapse of, 39, 70; local postings of, 27; political conflicts of, 29–30
Hiraoka Takichi (1833–96), Mishima's paternal great-grandfather, 2, 22, 30; sons and daughter of, 23–24; urban and elitist descendants of, 31; wife of, 2, 23, 24
Hiraoka Tazaemon (n.d.), Mishima's paternal great–great-grandfather, 2, 24; and "Akamon (Red Gate) Incident," 21–22
Hiraoka Tsuru (1836–1916), Mishima's paternal great-grandmother, 23, 24
Hiraoka Yoshikazu, Mishima's paternal granduncle's son, 30, 31, 70–71
Hiraoka Yoshio, Mishima's paternal granduncle's son, 30, 31
Hirata Hiroshi (b. 1937), manga artist, 678
Hirohito (1901–89), 124th Tennō, 13, 41, 51, 73, 88, 307, 367, 754; absolutism in constitutional interpretation of, 128; announcement of Japan's surrender by, 144, 307; failed assassination attempt of, 367–68, 709; "renunciation of divinity" rescript issued by, 142–45, 797
Hirohito, Crown Prince, 41, 794; austere image of, 622; special education of, as constitutional monarch, 622; wedding procession of, 711
Hirose kaigun chūsa. See "Cdr. Hirose"
Hirose Takeo (1868–1904), naval commander, 545
Hiroshima mon amour, 351
Hirota Kōki (1878–1948), prime minister, 351
Hirschfeld, Magnus (1868–1935), German sexologist, 180, 424; reference to, in Confessions of a Mask, 181–82
Hisano Toyohiko (1896–1971), novelist, economist, "anti–Marxist modernist," 82
History of Japan (Nihon Shoki), 150, 188, 331, 366, 461, 779, 781
Hitler, Adolf (1889–1945), German politician, 322
Hitler: A Study in Tyranny, 580
Hitokiri Izō. See "Killer Izō, The"
Hitokiri. See Kill!
Hiwa Palau senki. See Secret: A Record of a Palau Battle
Ho Chi Minh (1890–1969), Vietnamese president, 577
Hoan Daigaku (security academy), Mishima's visit to, 238–39
Hōden, 9, 13
Hofmannsthal, Hugo August Hofmann von (1874–1929), Austrian dramatist, 196, 236
Hōgen Disturbance, 612
Hōjinkai Zasshi, 77–78; Autumn: Two Pieces, 60–61; contributions of Bōjō in, 74; haiku in, 73; "Mansion" novella, 80; Mishima's poems accepted by, 60–61; "Tinted Glass" (Damie garasu), 77
Hōjō no umi. See Sea of Fertility, The
Hōjō Tokiyori (1227–63), shogunate regent, 271
Hokonohara Yasuo (n.d.), architect, 326–27
Hölderlin, Friedrich (1770–1843), German poet, 104, 233, 380, 416, 426
"Holy Life," 134
homosexuality, 174–75, 179, 277, 298, 391, 450, 457, 518; depiction of, in Confessions of a Mask, 183; depiction of, in Forbidden Colors, 209; elements of, in Mishima, 62, 75, 83, 188, 207, 209, 230–31, 313, 320, 474, 635, 701, 702 779; Kinsey's treatment of, 181; Mochizuki's works on, 180–81, 182; play based on, 216; "true" and "pseudo," 180

INDEX / 829

Honba. See Runaway Horse, The
Hon'inbō Shūsai (1874–1940), go master, 150
Honjō Shigeru (1876–1945), chief aide-de-camp, 146
Hon'yaku-bun, 345
Hori Shigeru (1920–79), chairman of the House of Representatives: meeting with Mishima, 697; Mishima's argument submitted to, 696–97
Horie Ken'ichi (b. 1938), adventurer, 403
Horiguchi Daigaku (1892–1981), poet and translator, 79
Horiuchi Seiichi (1932–87), graphic designer, editor, 592
Horne, Lena (1917–2010), American singer, actress, 306
Horwitz, Brewster (n.d.), American translator, 274
Hoshina Shigeru (n.d.), minister of construction, 571
Hoshino Naoki (1892–1978), politician, corporate executive, 49
Hosoe Eikō (b. 1933), photographer, 362, 400
House of Councilors, elections for, 558, 571
House of Growth, The. See Seichō no Ie
House on Fire, The (Kataku), 194, 195, 196
Hōyō kazoku. See Hugging Family, The
Hu Wen-hu (aka Aw Boon Haw; 1882–1954), Burmese-Chinese entrepreneur, 384
Hu Yin (1098–1156), Chinese philosopher, 705
Hugging Family, The (Hōyō kazoku), 432
Hugo, Victor (1802–85), French novelist, dramatist, 280
Huizong (1082–1135), Chinese emperor, 337
"human torpedo," 567
humanism and decadence, 132
Huppert, Isabelle (b. 1953?), French actress, 423
Hussain, Zakir (1897–1969), Indian president, 521–22
Huston, John (1906–87), American film director, 562
Hyakuman-en senbei. See "Million-yen Rice Crackers"
"Hydrangea," 69
hydrogen bomb, 246, 336, 395–96, 500. See also atomic bombings of Hiroshima and Nagasaki,

"I, Sanmoto Gorōzaemon, Dismiss Myself with Your Permission, Sir," 679–80
"I Want to Be an Objet," 350
iai, 262, 479–80, 698
Ichigaya, 551, 689, 724, 787;
Ichigaya, Camp, 692–93, 695, 698, 699, 706, 718
Ichigaya Hall, 636, 693, 709–10, 723
Ichigaya Prison, 42, 55
Ichikawa Ebizō X (b. 1946), kabuki actor, 651
Ichikawa Fuae (1893–1981), feminist leader, politician, 157
Ichikawa Kon (1915–2008), film director, 322, 429
Ichikawa Raizō (1931–69), actor, 322, 420
Ichikawa Somegorō VI (b. 1942), kabuki actor, 634, 655
Ichikawa Utaemon (1907–99), kabuki and film actor, 478
Ichimura Uzaemon XV (1874–1945), kabuki actor, 142–43
Ide Magoroku (b. 1931), novelist, 387
Igarashi Tsukumo (n.d.), designer, 548

Ihara Saikaku (1642–93), novelist, haiku writer, 188
Ii Naosuke (1815–60), grand administrator, 33
Iida Momo (1926–2011), writer, 588
Iizawa Tadasu (1909–94), dramatist, director, 521
Ikarii Junzō (n.d.), army general, 652–53
Ikebe Ryō (1918–2010), film actor, 702
Ikeda Hayato (1899–1965), prime minister, 198, 477
Ikeda Kōtarō (n.d.), student of French literature, 445
Ikeda Tsutomu (1908–2002), student of Japanese literature, 85
Ikkyū (1394–1481), Zen master, 632
Ikuta Kōsaku (1924–94), translator, 790
I'm Going to See Everything (Nandemo miteyarō), 637
Imai Tadashi (1912–91), film director, 245
Imamura Hitoshi (1886–1968), army general, 8
"Imperial Declaration" (Taishō), 94–95
Imperial declaration of humanity, 142–46
Imperial Palace, 113, 137, 139, 481, 617, 623, 624, 630, 652, 728
Imperial University of Tokyo, 14, 15, 16, 17, 24, 47, 97, 104, 111, 120, 405, 485, 538, 695; Law Faculty of, 6, 110, 157; protest of, to Nakajima aircraft factory, 123
Imphal, Battle of, 107, 403
Improvisatore, The (Sokkyō shijin), 345
"In Praise of the Sun" (Nichirin raisan), 573
In the Realm of Senses, 343
Inagaki Hiroshi (1905–80), film director, 679
Inagaki Taruho (1900–77), author, 592, 685, 690; debut as writer, 81; debut work of, 81–82; as first winner of the Japan Bungaku Taishō, 691; manga works of, 679–80; Mishima's comment on Sanpūko of, 81, 82–83; reaction to Mishima's praise of, 691
India, Mishima's trip to, 520–32, 541; in Benares, 525–27; in Bombay, 521; discussion with Indian Army during, 522; discussion with Tokuoka about, 522–23; meeting with President Zakir Hussain during, 521–22; meeting with Prime Minister Gandhi during, 522; in New Delhi, 521–22; talked to writers and professors, 522; views on Hinduism, 524–25; views on India, 523–24
Indian National Army, 541, 787
Industrial rationalization movement, 48
"Infernal Transformation" (Jigokuhen), 247
Innami Kiyoshi (b. 1896), riding instructor, 711
Inō mononoke roku. See Tōtei bukkai-roku
Inoue Kaoru (1835–1915), foreign minister, 278, 406
Inoue Kiyoshi (1913–2001), Marxist historian, 661–62
I-novel, 82, 169–70, 177
Inpumon'in no Taifu (1130?–1200?), tanka poet, 237
Insect Play, The, 117, 118
International Antiwar Day, demonstrations on, 585–90, 608, 629, 636, 640–41; over Article 106, 585, 586; clash with police, 586; demands of unified front, 639; mass rejection of protests, 641; members of Shield Society, 586–87; Mishima in Shinjuku, 641–42; Mishima in Ginza, 586–87, 588; Mishima's expectations of, 636; nationwide rally, 639–40, 701; participation of Shiine Yama in, 608–9; police campaign and, 640; rampage at Shinjuku Station, 586; reaction of Ōya Sōichi to, 639; two-week-long programs for, 609; at University of Tokyo, 586; vigilante groups and,

640; Zenkyōtō and, 585
International Conference of Young Artists, 219
International House, 320–21
International Military Tribunal, 104–5, 159, 340–41, 66, 693
*International Private Law (Kokusai shihō)*, 26–27
*Into a Black Sun (Kagayakeru yami)*, 444
*Introduction to a Study of Action (Kōdō-gaku nyūmon)*, 638
*Introduction to the Origins of Japanese Literature*, 450
Inukai Tsuyoshi (1855–1932), prime minister, 378
*Irogotoshi*. See *Pornographers, The*
Irving, Washington (1783–1859), American author, 313
Isherwood, Christopher (1906–86), English-American novelist, 276, 293
Ishibashi Tanzan (1884–1973), prime minster, 342–43
Ishidō Toshirō (1932–2011), scriptwriter, critic, 701–3
Ishihara Kanji (1889–1949), army general, 128; on Japanese defeat in World War II, 126–27; under Tōjō regime, 127
Ishihara Shintarō (b. 1932), novelist, governor of Tokyo, 255–56, 261, 262, 333, 350, 391, 488, 564, 571, 577, 693
Ishihara Yūjirō (1934–87), actor, 350, 615, 768
Ishii Tatsuhiko (b. 1952), tanka poet; *The Rokumeikan* review by, 277
Ishikawa Jun (1899–1987), novelist, 327, 515–16, 706, 713
Ishikawa Tatsuzō (1905–85), novelist, 661–62
Ishizaka Yōjirō (1900–86), novelist, 245
Ishizuka Tomoji (1906–86), haiku writer, novelist, editor, 149
Isobe Asaichi (1905–37), captain, 370, 668
Isoda Kōichi (1931–87), critic, 376, 624
*Issen ichibyō monogatari*. See *One Thousand and One-Second Stories*
Itami Jūzō (1933–97), film director, 488
Itasaka Gō (b. 1948), Flamenco dancer, 156
Itaya Kōkichi (n.d.), businessman, 206–7
Itaya Ryūichi (1911–91), admiral, 730
*Itinerant Priest of Mt. Kōya, An*, 680
Itō Daisuke (1898–1981), film director, 605
Itō Einosuke (1903–59), novelist, 73
Itō Hirofumi (1841–1909), prime minister, 406
Itō Keiichi (n.d.), Defense Agency official, 486
Itō Sei (1905–69), writer, critic, 177, 281, 399; discussion with Mishima on Japanese literature, 361
Itō Seiichi (1890–1945), admiral, 733
Itō Shizuo (1906–73), poet, 101, 297, 675, 798; death of, 237; enraptured by Tanaka's book of poetry, 675–76; Mishima's attempt to imitate and learn from, 94–95; poems contributed to *Bunka Bungei* by, 105; preface by, Mishima's request for, 104–6; response of, to Mishima's request, 105; social and professional life of, 105; and war poems, 237–38
Iwasaki Ryōzō (1908–76), student of Western literature, 707
Iwase Tadanari (1818–61), diplomat, 33
*Iwashiuri koi no hikiami*. See *Sardine Hawker & the Dragnet of Love, The*
Iwata Kurō (1891–1969), authority on Edo haikai, 73
Iwata Toyo'o, (aka Shishi Bunroku, 1893–1969), playwright and writer, 193, 285, 411
Iwo Jima, Battle of, 465

Izawa Kinemaro (b. 1925), commentator, 619–20, 700, 701
Izumi Kyōka, 3, 69; prize, 520
Izumi Shigeru (n.d.), photographer, 583

Jacquot, Benoît (b. 1947), French film director, 423
*Jamaica*, 306
James, Roy (Abdul Hannan Safa; 1929–89), emcee, 321–22; "Hannan Boy," 321
Japan Art Academy, 549
Japan Cultural Congress, 225, 558; disbanded in 1994, 559; goal of, 559; initial idea for creation of, 558–59
Japan Economic Federation, 537
Japan Federation of Employers' Association, 560
Japan National Guard (JNG), 548; expenses and funds of, 537–38; formal launch of, 582–83; the Great Principle and, 536; training with SDF at Camp Takigahara, 549, 563; uniform for, 548
Japan Romantic School, 104, 115, 119–22, 161, 119, 190, 405, 414, 485, 546, 564, 565
Japan Women's University (Christian institution), 315
Japanese Constitution, 26, 174, 343, 378; Article 9 of, 220, 485, 541; Article 13 of, 492; drafting of, 346; translation of, Mishima's comment on, 346
Japanese Constitution, oddities of: position of the Emperor, 664–65; Renunciation of War, 665–66; status of SDF, 666
Japanese Constitutional revision, 485, 491, 652, 660; of Article 9, 661, 665; proposed by Nakasone Yasuhiro, 665, 666; splitting of SDF, 663; "sublime right of homeland defense," 668; Tennō as a cultural concept in, 667; "unity of rite and governance," 663
Japanese culture, 102, 569, 571, 667, 687, 697, 715; Benedict's interpretation of, 566–67; comprehensive totality of, 567; contrasting aspects of, 438, 708; identity of, 367, 543; Mishima's resolve to rebuild, 132–33
Japanese defeat in World War II, basic reason for, 126–27
Japanese Diet, 28, 86, 127, 592, 616, 652, 665, 670, 692; Eniwa Case, 489; ratification of peace and security treaty, 232
Japanese economy, 198–99, 659; annual "white paper" on, 288; growth of, throughout the 1960s, 448; post-Korean War, 219
Japanese film, international attention to, 221, 226, 253
Japanese immigrants: in Brazil, 229; differences between, 229
Japanese language, 56, 62, 86, 258, 487; ever-shifting nature of, 345–46; lawsuit for "invasion of privacy" part of, 356
Japanese manufacturing industry: following termination of fixed exchange rate regime, 659–60; growth of, throughout the 1960s, 659
Japanese military, 14–15, 98, 152, 379, 490, 514; clash with Chinese Army, 57–58; Code of Conduct of, 782; operation to take Imphal by, 107; rampage in Nanjing of, 58; situations in combat zones, 18; strategic and logistical blunder by, 133; war slogans adopted by, 107
Japanese National Railways, incidents involving, 198
"Japanese spirit" *(Yamato damashii)*. See "Yamato

spirit"
Japanese tourists and visitors, economic status of, 231
Japanese writers vs. Western writers, 317
Japanese-German anticommunism pact, 352
Japanese-United States Peace Treaty, 374
*Japan's Longest Day*, 514
Japan: and America, wealth discrepancy between, 290–91; ban on domestic aircraft manufacture in, 259; debate on "overcoming modernity" in, 130; industrial output of, in postwar era, 288; peace and security treaties signed by, 220–21; surrender of, to Allies, 126, 137
"Japan: The Cherished Myths," 390–91
Jayavarman VII (1125–1200), Cambodian king, 456, 478, 611, 777
JCC. *See* Japan Cultural Congress
Jellinek, Georg (1851–1911), Austrian legal philosopher, 145
*Jigokuhen*. *See* "Infernal Transformation"
*Jinnō shōtō ki*. *See Account of Our Divine Sovereigns and Their Orthodoxy, An*
Jinzai Kiyoshi (1903–57), Russian translator, writer, critic, 178, 205; review of *Confessions of a Mask* by, 176–77, 179
JNG. *See* Japan National Guard
Jofre, Éder (b. 1936), Brazilian boxer, 469
Johnson, Lyndon (1908–73), US president, 535
*Jojō no hihan*. *See Criticism of Lyricism*
Jordan, David Starr (1851–1931), American ichthyologist, 119
jōruri, 28, 67, 68, 141, 236, 237, 247, 248, 570, 613, 763
*Josei Myōjō*, 403
*Josei Seven*, 467
"Journal for *A Forest in Full Bloom*," 102–3
*Joy of Sweet Honey, The (Amai mitsu no yorokobi)*, 518, 520, 520
Joyce, James (1882–1941), Irish novelist, 345
*Joyful Koto, The (Yorokoshi no koto)*, 414–19, 516; Communist Party against, 416–17; initial discussion of, 415; Mishima's efforts in writing, 419–23; NHK refusal to broadcast, 417; Nissay Theatre's production rights to, 417; plans and ideas for, 422; story creation of, 422–23; story-writing approach in, 420
Judt, Tony (1948–2010), British historian, 555
*Jun'ai no asa*. *See* "Morning of Innocent Love, The"
Jung, Carl (1875–1961), Swiss psychologist, 424
*Junpaku no Yoru*. *See Snow-White Night, The*
*Junshi* (book), 531, 648
*junshi* (following one's lord in death), 531, 648, 786

kabuki, 67–68, 213, 226, 237, 655, 769; *Aoto zōshi hana no nishiki-e*, 349; based on Bakin's narrative, 612–13; *Benten musume meo no shiranami*, 350; director's role in, 613; "Infernal Transformation," 247, 248; Occupation censorship of, 140–42; *Sardine Hawker & the Dragnet of Love, The*, 248, 397; *Sukeroku*, 347; *A Wonder Tale: The Moonbow*, 614, 655–56, 793
Kabuki-za, 137, 215, 247, 248, 314, 354, 397; *Fond of Young Women: The Sash-Taking Pond* produced by, 347; *Phèdre* produced by, 285; *Yuya* produced by, 285
Kaburaki Kiyokata (1878–1972), painter, 675

*Kagayakeru yami*. *See Into a Black Sun*
*Kagi no kakaru heya*. *See* "Room You Can Lock, The"
Kaifu Toshiki (b. 1931), prime minister, 484
Kaihara Osamu (1917–2007), defense official, 389
Kaikō Takeshi (1930–89), author, 443–44, 776
*kaikoku* ("Open the Country"), 470
Kaisei Gakkō, 24, 40, 183, 740
*Kaisen*. *See Naval Battle*
Kaizōsha, censorship action against, 151–52
Kaji Ryūichi (1896–1978), journalist, 157, 221
Kajima Mieko. *See* Hiraizumi Mieko
Kajima Morinosuke (1896–1975), businessman, diplomat, 213
*kakekotoba*, 20, 121–22
*kakioroshi*, 243, 317, 333
*Kakumei tetsugaku to shite no Yōmeigaku*. *See* "Yangming School as a Philosophy for Revolution"
*Kakuyaku-taru gyakkō*. *See Brilliant Backlight, The*
Kamakura Bunko, 153, 166, 185, 201; censorship action against, 151
Kamei Katsuichirō (1907–66), writer, 161–62, 405, 564
*Kamen no kokuhaku*. *See Confessions of a Mask*
*kamikaze*, 129–31, 374, 428, 558, 716, 752, 777; Mishima's views on, 375, 460, 463, 600–601, 609, 638. *See also* "special attack force"
Kamishima, 241; filming of *The Sound of Waves* on, 246; Mishima's visit to, 241–42, 246
Kamogawa Tadashi (n.d.), Mishima's friend, 231
*kamugakari*, 459–60, 460–62; second part of, 462; third part of, 462–63
*Kanadehon chūshingura*, 66
Kan'ami (1333–84), dramatist, 338
Kanbara Ariake (1876–1952), poet, 149
Kanbori Shinobu (b. 1928), *Man'yōshū* scholar, 105
Kaneda Shōichi (b. 1933), baseball pitcher, 403
Kaneko Magoroku Kanemoto (active early 16th century), swordsmith, 479, 780
Kanetaka Kaoru (Rose; b. 1928), journalist, 211
Kan'in, Prince (Haruhito, 1902–88), prince and general, 88
*Kanjinchō*, 142, 397, 651
*kannushi*, 460–61
*Kanrin Maru*, 35, 741
*Kantan*, 193, 194
Kanzaburō. *See* Nakamura Kanzaburō XVIII.
Kanze Shizuo (1931–2000), nō actor, 297
Karafuto (Sakhalin) Agency: political problem in, 29–30; Sadatarō as administrator of, 7, 11, 13, 28–29, 39, 96
Karajan, Herbert von (1908–89), German conductor, 362
*Karajishibotan*. *See* "Lion Amid Peonies, A"
*Karakkaze yarō*. *See Windblown Dude*
karate, 262, 480, 705, 714
Kasahara Kazuo (1927–2002), movie script writer, 605
Kasahara Kinjirō (n.d.), editor, 329–30
Kasai Masae (b. 1933), captain of a volleyball team, 645
Kasama Juichi (n.d.), army sergeant, 727
Kashii Kōhei (1881–1954), army general, 368
Kästner, Erich (1899–1974), German poet, 104
*Kataku*. *See House on Fire, The*
*Kataude*. *See* "One Arm"

Katayama Tetsu (1887–1978), prime minister, 348
Katō Michio (1918–53), playwright: Jean Giraudoux's influence on, 239; Mishima's view on death of, 239
Katō Shūichi (1919–2008), physician, critic, 371; and Marxism, 405
Katō Yoshihide (n.d.), army colonel, 107, 247
Katori Kiyoko (1918–2008), Flamenco dancer, 156
Katsu Kaishū (1823–99), politician, 35, 531
Katsu Shintarō (1931–97), film actor, director, 606, 615, 721
Katsura Detached Palace, 327
Kawabata Masako (n.d.), Kawabata's adopted daughter (1943), 217
"Kawabata reader," 398, 402, 584
Kawabata Yasunari (1899–1972), novelist, 58, 82, 116, 185, 217, 320, 392, 401, 457, 611, 653, 750; Cultural Revolution and, 515–16; dependence on sleeping pills of, 399; embarrassed about *Sleeping Beauties*, 399; invited to attend parade, 631; Kon Tōkō's campaign managed by, 571; letters to Mishima, 750; as managing director of Kamakura Bunko, 151; meeting with Mishima, 149–50; at Mishima's funeral, 732; Mishima's request for article by, 515; Nobel Prize speech of, 631–32; Nobel Prize to, 584–85; postwar literary figures visiting, 149; as president of Japan PEN Club, 392; on sexual expression, 173; view on English translation of Japanese novels, 272–74; youthful homosexual yearnings of, 174–75
Kawabe Haruo (n.d.), army colonel, 727
Kawabe Torashirō (1890–1960), army general, 136
Kawade Shobō, 167, 168, 175, 398, 402
Kawaguchi Matsutarō (1899–1985), novelist, playwright, 347
Kawakami Kikuko (1904–85), novelist, 150
Kawakami Yasuko (n.d.), movie actress, 149
Kawasaki Chōtarō (1901–85), novelist, 149
Kawashima Hiroshi (n.d.), leader of a student movement, 593
Kawashima Masaru (b. 1923), editor, 420
Kawashima Yoshiyuki (1878–1945), minister of the army, 368
Kawatake Mokuami (1816–93), kabuki writer, 240, 349
Kay, Hershy (1919–81), American composer, 307
Kaya Harukata (1836–76), Shinpūren member, 476
Kayama Yūzō (b. 1937), actor, 488
Kaye, Danny (1913–87), American actor, dancer, 309
Keene, Donald (b. 1922), American scholar of Japanese literature, 273, 276, 378, 383, 697, 762, 774, 775, 778; on Kawabata winning Noble Prize, 585; Mishima's trust in, 389, 799; on philosophy of politician, 379; translation of *"Japan: The Cherished Myths,"* 390–91
Keiō University Hospital, 53, 321
Keisatsu Yobitai ("Police Reserve Force"), 220, 238, 541
Keishintō, 471
*Kekkon no subete.* See *All About Marriage*
*Kemono no tawamure.* See *Beastly Entanglements*
*Ken.* See "Sword, The"
kendō, 40, 150, 262, 329–32, 419–20, 464, 476, 477, 480–81
Kennedy, John F. (1917–63), US president, 381, 415

Kennedy, Margaret (1896–1967), English novelist, playwright, 239
Kennedy, Robert F. (1925–68), US attorney general, 553–54
Kenpeitai, 108, 121, 127
Kenreimon'in Ukyō no Daibu (b. 1157?), poet, 112
Ketel, Hellmuth (1893–1961), German restaurateur in Tokyo, 214
Keyhoe, Donald (1897–1988), American aviator, author, 397
Khrushchev, Nikita (1894–1971), USSR First Secretary, 395
Kidd, Michael (1915–2007), American choreographer, 305
Kierkegaard, Søren (1813–55), Danish philosopher, 319
Kihira Teiko. See Sassa Teiko
*Kikka no chigiri.* See "Pledge by Chrysanthemum Flower"
Kikuchi Akiko, 250–52
Kikuchi Katsuo (b. 1936), army general, 494, 706
Kikuchi Takeo (1875–1955), politician, 145
Kikuta Kazuo (1908–73), playwright, 634; adaptation into a play of *Spring Snow*, 634
*Kill! (Hitokiri)*, 614, 623; Mishima's acting work in, 615–16, 654, 681, 721
"Killer Izō, The" (*Hitokiri Izō*), 615
*Kimigayo*, English translation of, 652
Kimura Ki (1894–1979), writer, 717
Kimura Tokuzō (1911–2005), 176, 189, 195; censorship experienced by, 151–52; editorial collaboration with Mishima, 153–55, 179; Julien Sorel–inspired story idea based on Yamazaki, 200
Kimura Toshio (1909–83), chief cabinet secretary, 696
*Kinjiki*. See *Forbidden Colors*
*Kinkakuji* (novel). See *Temple of the Golden Pavilion, The*
Kinkakuji (temple), 247, 253, 259, 265–87, 418; burning of, 254, 255; history of, 254
Kinoshita Keisuke (1912–98), film director, 231, 252, 282
*Kinu to meisatsu.* See *Silk and Insight*
Kipling, Rudyard (1865–1936), English poet, novelist, 559
*Kiretsu.* See *Fissure, The*
Kirpal, Prem (n.d.), Indian educator, 272
Kishi Keiko (b. 1932), actress, 383
Kishi Nobusuke (1896–1987), prime minister, 101, 322, 341, 352, 448, 750, 768; academic performance of, 47; arrest of, 341; decision of, to join Ministry of Agriculture and Commerce, 47–48; demotion of, 104; expelling of, from Liberal Party, 342; as leader of "reform bureaucrats," 49; opposition to, 343; personality and character of, 47; as Prime Minister of Japan, 289–90; reemergence of, 340–44; as secretary-general of Democratic Party, 342; superiors of, 104; vision of, for "total war" system, 92; yearlong overseas tour of, 48; Yoshida's Liberal Party, joining, 341
Kishida Kunio (1890–1954), playwright, 193, 205, 211
Kishida Kyōko (1930–2006), actress, 211
Kita Ikki (1883–1937), political theorist, 104–5, 370, 379, 545, 629
Kita Morio (1927–2011), author, 361

Kitabatake Chikafusa (1293–1354), thinker, 366
Kitahara Hakushū (1885–1942), poet, 79
Kitahara Takeo (1907–73), novelist, 178
Kitami Harukazu (1920–95), actor, 410, 416
Kitamura Komatsu (1901–64), novelist, 397
Kitani Minoru (1909–75), go master, 150
Kitano Takeshi (Beat Takeshi; b. 1947), actor, director, 391
Kitaōji Kin'ya (b. 1943), actor, 478
Kiyono Fujio (n.d.), army colonel, 727
*Kizoku no kaidan.* See *Aristocrats' Staircase, The*
Klossowski, Pierre (1905–2001), French writer, 582
Kluger, Pearl (n.d.), Mishima's guide in New York, 224–25, 228
Knopf, Sr., Alfred A. (1892–1982), American publisher, 290, 293, 298
Kobayashi Hidemi (n.d.), Diet member's daughter, 217
Kobayashi Hideo (1902–83), critic, 205, 348, 358; on confession of arsonist, 254–55; on Hayashi's "madness," 268; as JCC charter member, 558; review of *The Golden Pavilion,* 265; on unhinged behavior, 255
Kobayashi Takiji (1903–33), novelist, 72, 404
Kobori (née Mori) Annu (1909–98), essayist, 519
*Kōdō-gaku nyūmon.* See *Introduction to a Study of Action*
Koestler, Arthur (1905–83), Hungarian-British author, 429, 583
Koga Hiroyuki (b. 1946), member of Shield Society, "older Koga," 689–99, 698, 714, 722–24, 729, 731, 733, 734; testimony on Seichō no Ie of, 699; police testimony of, 705–6
Koga Masayoshi (b. 1947), member of Shield Society, "younger Koga," 689, 699, 705–6, 707, 719, 721, 722–24, 733, 734
*Kogarashi.* See "Tree-searing Wind"
*kōgo-bun,* 345
*Koibitotachi no mori.* See *Lovers' Forest, The*
*Kojiki.* See *Record of Ancient Matters*
Kojima Chikako (Kikue: b. 1928), editor, critic, poet, 311, 482, 677, 721, 724, 725; next installment of last of tetralogy to, 721, 724, 725; with Thai women at Mishima's house, 599–600
Kojima Tomo'o (n.d.), boxing trainer, 262
*Kojinteki-na taiken.* See *Personal Matter, A*
*Kōjirin,* 56
*kokugaku,* 86. See *National Learning*
*kokumin,* 74
*kokumin* ceremonials, 74, 75, 97
Kokumin Kyōkai, People's Association, 660
*Kokusai shihō.* See *International Private Law*
*kokutai* ("national polity"), 86, 217, 365–68, 514, 666, 668
*Kokutai no hongi.* See *True Import of Kokutai, The*
Komatsu Shizuko (n.d.), 315; provided space for study sessions, 594; visit Hiraokas at Midori-ga-Oka house, 319
Komiya Toyotaka (1884–1966), student of German literature, 152
Komori Kazutaka (b. 1943), assassin, 385–86
Kon Hidemi (1903–84), director-general of Agency of Cultural Affairs, 152, 348, 755

Kon Tōkō (1898–1977), Buddhist abbot, politician, 571
Konaka Yōtarō (b. 1934), writer, critic, 493–94
Kondō Isami (1834–68), samurai, 33
Konishi Jin'ichi (1915–2007), student of Japanese literature, 119, 297, 405; interpretation of Mishima's *Aya no tsuzumi,* 297
Kōno Hisashi (1907–36), army captain, 373
Kōno Ichirō (1898–1965), minister of agriculture and fisheries, 49–50
Kōno Tsukasa (1905–90), writer, 393
Konoe Fumimaro (1891–1945), prince, prime minister, 37, 57
Koshiji Fubuki (1924–80), singer, actress, 349, 769; duet with Raymond Conde, 347; meeting with Mishima over play, 348
*Kōshoku.* See "The Lecher"
Kōta, Mrs. (n.d.), Hiraoka Sadatarō's friend, 20
*Koto.* See *Old Capital, The*
*Kōya hijiri.* See *Itinerant Priest of Mt. Kōya, An*
*Kōya no uta.* See "A Song of the Wilderness"
*Kōya yori.* See "From the Wilderness"
Krafft-Ebing, Richard von (1840–1902), Austro-German psychiatrist, 81–82
Kristofferson, Kris (b. 1936), American musician, actor, 423
Kristol, Irving (1920–2000), American journalist, 224
Krupp, Gustav (1870–1950), German industrialist, 580
Kubota Mantarō (1889–1963), haiku writer, playwright, 194, 347, 411; sudden death of, 414; unhappiness of, with China tour, 411–12
*Kujaku.* See "Peacocks"
Kumamoto Castle, 472
Kumano Shrine, summer festival at, 449, 574
Kumo, 410
*Kumo no Kai,* 205
Kunieda Shirō (1887–1943), writer, 156, 680
Kunisada Chūji (1810–51), yakuza, 605
Kuno Osamu (1910–99), philosopher, 568
Kuramochi Kiyoshi (n.d.), member of Shield Society, 636, 669, 732
Kuribayashi Tadamichi (1891–1945), army general, 711
Kuriyagawa Hakuson (1880–1923), student of English literature, critic, 273–74
Kuriyama Riichi (1909–89), student of Japanese literature, 85, 114
Kuroda Kanbē (also, Yoshitaka; 1546–1604), warrior-commander, 9
Kurosawa Akira (1910–93), film director, 246, 253, 438, 702; movies featuring Mifune, 438; *Rashōmon,* 221; worldwide fame of, 221; *Yōjimbō,* 605–6
*Kuro-tokage.* See *Black Lizard*
Kusaka Asanosuke (b. 1900?), Supreme Court justice, 733, 734
Kusaka Genzui (1840–64), samurai, 718
Kusaka Jin'ichi (1888–1972), admiral, 733
Kusaka Ryūnosuke (1892–1971), admiral, 773
Kusano Shinpei (1903–88), poet, 79
Kushibuchi Osamu (1923–2004), judge, 733–35, 773
Kusunoki Masashige (1294–1336), warrior, nationalist hero, 719
Kusunoki Masasue (d.1336), warrior, 719
Kuwabara Takeo (1904–88), student of French literature, 169

Kuzui Kinshirō (b. 1925), film theater manager, 706
Kyōgoku Kiyō (1908–81), haiku poet, 674
*Kyōko's House (Kyōko no ie),* 217, 294, 308, 317, 325, 333–57, 401, 431, 626; abrupt end of, 340; characters of, 334–35; critical failure of, 343–44; criticism of, 333–34; Hashikawa's reviews of, 563–65; Hirano Ken's criticism of, 333–34; initial reviews of, 333; Okuno Takeo's praise for, 333; protagonist of, 335; publication of, 333; story characters of, 308; story of, 335–38; study of Nihilsm and Fascism in, 338–40
Kyoto Gakuren Incident, 406
Kyoto School, 119–20
*Kyōko no ie.* See *Kyoko's House*

*La bal du Compte d'Orgel,* 509
*La Chèvre de M. Seguin,* 195
La Rochelle, Drieu (1893–1945), French writer, 499
*La Ronde,* 235–36
*La Tosca:* defending choice of, 413; Mishima's thought on shortlisting of, 413; staging of, 412–13
Labor Standards Law, 537
*Lady Akane, The,* 382. See also *Lady Aoi, The*
*Lady Aoi, The (Aoi-no-ue),* 294, 382
Laos, Mishima's trip to, 521, 529
LaPorte, Robert Allen (1943–65), American war protester, 535
*L'Apre-midi d'un faune,* 307
Lasky, Melvin J. (1920–2004), American journalist, 436
Laughlin, Ann Clark Resor (1925?–89), American publisher, 277, 302
Laughlin, James (1914–97), American publisher, editor, 277, 302
Laurents, Arthur (1917–2011), American playwright, director, 306
Lawrence, D. H. (1885–1930), English novelist, 173
LDP. See Liberal Democratic Party
*Le Diable au corps,* 80, 236, 237, 423
Le Gendre, Joseph Émile (1830–99), American army general, diplomat, 142
*Le Martyre de Saint Sébastien,* 435, 444, 445
*Le Rouge et le Noir,* 200
*Le Samourai,* 562
*Le Sang et la Rose (Chi to bara),* 591, 592
*Le Sens de la mort,* 510
Lea, Homer (1876–1912), American author, 128
"Lecher, The" *(Kōshoku),* 37, 40
*L'école de la chair,* 423
*Lectures on Unethical Education (Fudōtoku kyōiku kōza),* 344, 418
*Leftwing Communism: An Infantile Disorder,* 537
Legge, James (1815–97), Scottish sinologist, 278
Lenin, Vladimir (1870–1924), Russian revolutionary, 483, 537
Lennon, John (1940–80), English musician, 577
*Leonore Overture,* 362
Lerner, Alan Jay (1918–86), American lyricist, 304
*L'érotisme,* 376
*Les Fruits d'Or,* 436
*Les mal parties,* 235, 236
*Les morts masculines,* 592
*Les petites filles modèles,* 687

*Les Plaisirs et les Jours,* 118
*Les Rites de l'Amour et de le Mort,* 440, 441
Lessing, Gotthold Ephraim (1729–1781), German philosopher, 686
"Letter of Challenge to Those I Love, A," 160
Leyte Gulf, Battle of, 129
*L'Histoire de Juliette, ou les Prospérités du vice,* 454
Liberal Democratic Party, 342, 483, 543, 559, 618, 694, 696, 768; Hoshina Shigeru candidate for, 571; insider criticism of, 693; "1955 Regime" and, 343; policy of, 343; protest against documentary on life in North Vietnam, 535; success in December general election, 658
*Life,* 424, 425, 429, 433, 435, 523, 583
*Lighthouse, The (Tōdai),* 193, 207
*Li'l Abner,* 305–6
Lin Biao (1907–71), Chinese leader, 516
Lindsay, Howard (1889–1963), American stage producer, 304
*Line-Drawing (Hakubyō),* 327
Lingis, Alphonso (b. 1933), American philosopher, 504
Lins (Brazil), 228–30
"Lion Amid Peonies, A" *(Karajishibotan),* 724
"Literary feeble fellows" *(bunjaku no to),* 562
Loesser, Frank (1920–69), American songwriter, 304
Loewe, Frederick (1901–88), Austrian-American composer, 304
Lois, George (b. 1931), American art director, 592
Looten, Emmanuel (1908–74), French poet, 734
Lorca, García, 504
Lortel, Lucille (1900–99), American dancer, producer, 382
Loti, Pierre (Julien Viaud, 1850–1923), French writer, 280, 520
*Love Dashes (Ai no shissō),* 394
*Lovers' Forest, The (Koibitotachi no mori),* 520
*Lucrèce Borgia,* 280
Lumet, Sydney (1924–2011), American film director, 319
Luzon, Battle of, 755

MacArthur, Douglas (1880–1964), supreme commander of the US Occupation of Japan, 137, 141, 220, 431, 666; "supermanism" of, Americans and, 225
MacArthur Constitution, 346. See also Constitution of Japan
Machiz, Herbert (1923–76), American stage director, 387
Macmillan, Harold (1894–1986), UK prime minister, 437
*Madama Butterfly,* Japanese government's ban on, 390
*Madame de Sade (Sado Kōshaku Fujin),* 417, 453–54, 581, 774
*Madame Edwarda,* 582
*Made-in-Japan (Nippon-sei),* 244–45, 523
*Mademoiselle Loulou,* 423, 520
*Madness of Heracles, The,* 530
Maeterlinck, Maurice (1862–1949), Belgian playwright, 236
*Mahōbin.* See *"Thermos Bottle, The"*

Mailer, Norman (1923–2007), American writer, 173
*Mainichi Shinbun*, 140, 393–94, 395, 437, 498, 522; "Eschatology and Literature" in, 395; *Les mal parties* review of, 236; Mishima's essay on Kawabata in, 611; Mishima's interview conducted by, 506–7, 693–94; Mishima's open letter in, 693; on reopening of the Teikoku Theater, 140
Mainichi Shinbun Company, 684
Makino Nobuaki (1861–1949), politician, 364
Makino Shin'ichi (1896–1936), lord privy seal, 81, 685
*Makioka Sisters* (*Sasameyuki*), 404
Mallarmé, Stéphane (1842–98), French poet, 498
*Mamie*, 195
*Man in the Gray Flannel Suit, The*, 583
*Manatsu no shi. See* "Death in Midsummer"
Manchukuo, 49, 57
Manchurian Incident, 127, 367
manga: influence of, on student movement, 678; vs. American comics, 681; of Mizuki Shigeru, 679; *Mōretsu A-Tarō*, 678; on ninja, 678; Norakuro, 678; popularity of, in postwar Japan, 678, 681; *Tōtei bukkai-roku*, 679–80
Mann, Golo (1909–94), international historian, 493
Mann, Thomas (1875–1955), German novelist, 190, 201, 226
*Man's Death, A* (*Otoko no shi*), 592, 713
"Mansion" (*Yakata*), 79–80
*Man'yōshū*, 97, 120, 484, 567, 632, 720, 781
Mao Zedong (1893–1976), Chinese leader, 223, 281, 516–17, 553, 577, 593, 660
Marat, Jean-Paul (1743–93), French political theorist, 323
Marcel Proust, 117, 118, 190
*Marius the Epicurean*, 450
martial arts, 35, 131, 468, 568, 676, 678, 707, 731; and desire for death, 576–77
Martin, Burton (n.d.), English teacher, 391
Martinez, Vincent (n.d.), French actor, 423
*Martyrdom of St. Sebastian, The*, 591–92
Maruyama (later Miwa) Akihiro (b. 1935), 214, 393, 469, 557, 668
Maruyama Kaoru (1899–1974), poet, 79
Maruyama Masao (1914–96), political scientist, 568, 620, 650
Marx, Karl (1818–83), German philosopher, 483
Marxism, 165, 405, 407, 485, 786; Hayashi Fusao and, 405–6; as "social science," 406
Masamune Hakuchō (1879–1962), novelist, playwright, critic, 148, 273, 282
Mashita Kanetoshi (1913–73), army general, 495, 693, 718–21, 723–24, 726–27, 729
Masumura Yasuzō (1924–84), film director, 351; director of Mishima, 358–59; director of *Windblown Dude*, 358
*masuraoburi*, 133, 438
Matsubara Fumiko (b. 1938), translator, 687
Matsudaira Takako (Taka, 1857–1923), Mishima's paternal great-grandmother, 2, 34–35, 36, 37–38
Matsudaira Yorinori (1831–64), daimyo, disembowelment of, 35–36; rehabilitation of house of, 36
Matsudaira Yoritaka (1810–86), daimyo, Mishima's paternal great–great-grandfather, 2, 34, 35–36
Matsudaira Yoriyasu (1856–1940), Yoritaka's second son, 2, 36, 37, 39, 53
Matsukawa Incident, 416
Matsumoto Michiko (b. 1922), editor, 420, 704
Matsumoto Mitsuaki (n.d.), 31
Matsumoto Seichō (1909–92), writer, historian, 494
Matsumura Motomi (n.d.), sushi restaurant owner, 325
Matsuo Bashō (1644–94), poet, 135
Matsuo Satoshi (1907–97), student of Japanese literature, 403
Matsuoka Yōsuke (1880–1946), minister for foreign affairs, 49
Matsushita Kōnosuke (1894–1989), businessman, 577
Matsuura Takeo (1926–98), stage director, 558
Maupassant, Guy de (1850–93), French writer, 236
Mauriac, François (1885–1970), French novelist, 196, 400, 617–18, 793
Maurois, André (1885–1967), French writer, 747
May Revolution, 553, 554, 657
Mayuzumi Toshirō (1929–97), composer, 231–32, 246, 314, 418
Mazaki Jinzaburō (1876–1956), army general, 145, 369
McAlpine, Helen (n. d.), English reteller of Japanese tales, 286
McCarthy, Mary (1912–89), American writer, 12, 436
McCarthyism, 199, 302
McGregor, Robert (1911–74), American editor, 302, 387; visit to Japan, 275–76
McLuhan, Marshall (1911–80), Canadian philosopher, 561
Meacham, Anne (1926–2006), American actress, 382
"Medieval Period, The" (*Chūsei*), 133, 147, 153, 164, 165, 188
Megata Tanetarō (1853–1926), founder of Senshū School, 25
Meiji Constitution, 145, 346, 568, 797; "cultural totality" lost under, 570; Tennō system under, 569, 630, 661, 667
Meiji Emperor (Mutsuhito, 1852–1912), 229, 342, 365, 372, 385, 531, 635, 652; Meiji the Great, 145
Meiji Era (1868–1912), 25, 28, 46, 164, 166, 209, 223, 275, 279; class system, 109
Meiji government, 34, 35, 38, 120, 365, 367, 568; Charter Oath issued by, 143; concerns of unequal treaties, 26; inadequate legal system during, 26; Shinpūren Revolt and, 469, 471; slogan of, 48–49; "sword-abolishment order" of, 543
Meiji Memorial Hall, 320
Meiji Restoration, 25, 36, 364–65, 406, 412, 470–71, 472, 647
Melville, Jean-Pierre (1917–73), French filmmaker, 562
"Memorandum on Eguchi Hatsu-jo, A" (*Eguchi Hatsujo oboegaki*), 338
Mercer, Johnny (1906–76), American lyricist, 305
Merlo, Frank (n.d.), Tennessee Williams's secretary, 349
Merman, Ethel (1908–84), American actress, singer, 304
Merrill, Bob (1921–98), American songwriter, 305
Merrill, James (1926–95), American poet, 275, 276, 293–94, 322
*Merry Christmas Mr. Lawrence*, 391
Meyerhold, Vsevolod Emilevich (1874–1940), Russian

stage director, 414
Michelangelo (1475–1564), Italian artist, 687
Michener, James (1907–97), American author, 390
*Midsummer Night's Dream, A,* 410
Midway, Battle of, 130
Mifune Toshirō (1920–97), film actor, 247, 438, 488, 515, 606, 679
Mikawa Gun'ichi (1888–1981), admiral, 87
*Mi-Kumano mōde.* See *Pilgrimage to the Three Kumano Shrines*
Miles, Sarah (b. 1941), English actress, 429
military uniform, 582–84; Mishima in, 588; Mishima's essay on, 583; of Shield Society, 583
Miller, Arthur (1915–2005), American playwright, 224, 302
"Million-yen Rice Crackers" *(Hyakuman-en senbei),* 361
Minakata Kumagusu (1867–1941), naturalist, biologist, folklorist, 331, 450
Minamoto no Sanetomo (1192–1219), shogun, 720
Minamoto no Tametomo (1139–1170?), warrior, 612
Ministry of Agriculture and Commerce, 47–48
Ministry of Finance, 4, 5, 47, 137, 164, 167, 559, 631, 636
*Mino, My Bull (Mino, atashino oushi),* 699
Minobe Tatsukichi (1873–1948), Constitutional scholar, 128; Tennō as a "state organ" theory of, controversy over, 145, 146
*Minoko,* 418, 419
*Minomo no tsuki.* See "Moon on the Surface of the Water, A"
Minosuke. See Bandō Minosuke VI
Minsei, 595, 596; and Chichibu meeting, 618; disciplined violence against the Zenkyōtō, 596
Minshu Seinen Dōmei. See Minsei
*minzokushugi,* 482, 781
Mirabelle, Schloss, 436
*Miranda,* 590, 591
"Mishima Incident" trial, 418, 669, 732–36; police questioning of Koga Hiroyasu, 705; Satō Isao's testimony during, 666; Tokyo District Public Prosecutor's opening statement at, 689; Yōko's statement following, 735
"Mishima Literature and Internationality," 437
Mishima Yukio (1925–70): Hiraoka Kimitake's penname); action plan to defend Imperial Palace, 623, 624; admiration for grandfather's calligraphy, 705; admiration for Inagaki's works, 690–91; affinity of, with theatrical genres, 67–68; afterword written by, for Mori Mari's writings, 710; afterword written by, to Chūō Kōron Japanese literature series, 685–86; apology to Arita, 355; apology to Mrs. Tanizaki, 714; argument on Constitutional oddities, 664–65; attended party at Kanetaka, 211–13; birth of second child, 402; blunt self-analysis, 630; as "boy patriot," 646; calligraphy of, 401–2; Chichibu meeting, 618; cenotaph erected to, 736; close call in air, 643; co-editing of *New Writing in Japan,* 375; confessional habits of, 189–90; conversation with emigrant woman, 223–24; critical review of "Dance," 75; criticism of Ishihara Shintarō by, 693; cultural arguments of, 142–43; cutting off ties to the world, 687–88; on Daibosatsu Pass Incident, 643; debate with students of Radical Left, 622; debate with Tōdai students, 617–23; depicted as "modern gorilla," 618–19; description of US sprinter by, 428–29; desire for goodbye kiss with Teiko, 156–57; directorial debut of, 193; discussion on Japanese literature, 361; essay of, in praise of Ueno, 112; exhibition of works of, 706–7, 709–10; family photo at home, 668; as fan of manga, 678–81; as fan of yakuza, 35; fear of "humanism" and "cosmopolitanism" in, 679; on financial burden of maintaining Shield Society, 625–26; on Gallagher, 674, 688; at Green Hotel in Karuizawa, 203; grief over death of sister, 139, 715; grief over lost love, 139–40; growing confidence toward Bōjō, 74; as guest in charity recital, 469; haiku of, 73, 279; in Hakata with Yōko, 324; Hasuda's influence on, 88–89, 91; *Holiday* magazine and, 389; Imperial Hotel, 283, 418, 548, 600, 690, 707, 713–14; influence of Kita Ikki's thought on, 629–30; influence of Yōmeigaku on, 647–48; interviews of, by British media, 439; interview of, on anachronism, 694; interview of, on TBS, 68–69; interview of, by *Tokyo Shinbun,* 707; introduction written by, for *Equestrian Reader,* 710–11; involvement with CIE, 189; Ishihara Shintarō as competition for, 255–57; Itō Shizuo's influence on, 94–95, 106; Japanese court system and, 356; and Julien Sorel–inspired story idea based on Yamazaki, 200; on Japan's autonomous military, 658–59; "Journal for *A Forest in Full Bloom,*" 102–3; karate lessons from Nakayama Masatoshi, 705; on Katō Michio's literary works, 239–40; Kawaguchi and, 475; at Kumamoto to study Shinpūren, 475–76; on *La Ronde* (French film), 236; last night at home before death, 722; on *Le diable au corps,* 237; on *Les mal parties,* 236; letter from Kawabata to, 116; letter to Dan Kazuo, 190; letter to Murakami Ichirō, 718; life-size clay model of, at Wakebe Junji's studio, 719; love of, for Shizue, 68–69; love with Fukushima, 475; on "loyalty" and death, 694–95; meeting with Araki, 474–75; meeting with Arthur Waley, 383–84; meeting with Edna O'Brien, 438; meeting with Kawabata Yasunari, 149–50; meeting with Morita, Koga, and Ogawa, 690, 692; meeting with Saito, 188–89; meeting with Sassa Teiko, 155–56; as member of dōjō, 329; membership of literature groups, 205–6; and Michiko's marriage on TV, 330–31; on Nakasone's private apologies, 669; at Nichigeki Music Hall, 282; notebooks of, 420–22; vs. Ōe, 433; offer of, to elope with Itaya Ryōko, 206–7; on Okinawa Day turmoil, 617–18; one-night stay at Rinzai Zen temple, 259–60; outlandish dream of, 190; penname of, 91–92, 748; persuaded Mochimaru, 628; photographing of, for *A Man's Death,* 713; plan to prepare bibliography of works, 704; on playwright and actor collaboration, 613; police security of, 386–87; postwar entries to theater, 140–42, 193; at Prince Hotel, Shinagawa, 361; publishing his first book, 101–4; purchasing old sword, 476; reaction to censorship of plays, 141; reaction to Japan's assault on Pearl Harbor, 646–47; reaction to Tanaka Seigen's funding of *Ronsō Journal,* 627–28; rejecting officer-candidate course, 99–100; rejection

of Yasuda-style classicism, 121; resignation from Ministry of Finance, 167; resolution for postwar literary revival, 134–35; review of *Satyricon*, 707; royalty income of, 166, 202, 625–26; Roy James and, 321–22; "Saturday communication" to Mitani Makoto, 116, 121, 122, 128; self-explications of his novels, 244; severed relationship with Nathan, 434; severing relationship with *Ronsō Journal*, 627–29; signing contract with film company, 350; as special correspondent for Olympics, 428; speech in English, 391; started column for women's magazine, 403; stories of, turned into films, 244–45; strong feelings for Tsuruta Kōji, 609–10; study sessions with Yamamoto, 593–94; switch from *Ningen* to *Shinchō*, 200; taidan with Ishidō Toshirō for *Eiga Geijutsu*, 701–3; taidan with Ishihara, 257–58; taidan with Shibusawa Tatsuhiko, 690–91; taidan with Takamine Hideko, 252–53; talk at Waseda University students' history club, 694; talk of *shidō*, 694; Tamari Hitoshi as private coach of, 261; tanka of, 67, 720; thank-you letter to Araki, 476; thoughts on Murayama's version of *The Golden Pavilion*, 286; tribute to Azuma Fumihiko, 703–4; turmoil after Shimanaka murder, 386; turned short story into film, 375–76; Uesugi invoked by, 128–29; views on Americans, 313; views on kendō practices by women, 711; views on Kita Ikki and Tennō worship, 629–30; views on necessity for violence, 618; views on *nen* in Yamamoto's statement, 637; visit to ghost festival, 325; visit to Hiraizumi Mieko's Manhattan apartment, 308; visit to Hoan Daigaku, 238–39; visit to Kamishima, 241–43, 246; visit to Kishida Kunio, 211; visit to Makoto at his school, 122–23; visit to Shinoyama's studio with Morita Masakazu, 718; visit to Washington Irving's manor, 313; wartime assignment of, at Nakajima aircraft factory, 16, 116; wartime assignment of, at naval factory, 123–24; on wealth discrepancy between Japan and America, 290–91; will of, 695–96; words on "special attack force," 129; Yasuda's influence on, 119; Yokohama and, 420, 422; young friends of, 324–26. *See also* Hiraoka Kimitake
—acting and modeling of: acting experience, 359; *Black Lizard*, 393; direction of *Salome*, 360; direction of Matsumoto Kōshirō, 793; got role in movie, 344; lead role in *Windblown Dude*, 592; for *A Man's Death (Otoko no shi)*, 592; with Masumura Yasuzō, 351; photo session, 400; as samurai assassin in *Kill!*, 614–16; Yatō Tamotsu's photoshoots, 274
—coup attempt and seppuku of: apportionment of time for planned action, 717; assemblage of all troops, 727; commander of the Eastern Army as hostage target, 692, 718; for Constitutional revision, 689, 692; crowd gathering for, 728; directives to two Kogas and Ogawa, 724; draft of manifesto, 705, 708; entry into Camp Ichigaya, 699–700; farewell-to-the-world poem composed for, 720; Gen. Mashita hostage, 726; Japanese sword and, 698, 780, 784; letters to Date and Tokuoka, 708–9; list of demands, 726; meeting at Daini Hamasaku, 699; members of Shield Society involved in, 689, 698; Mishima's seppuku, 729; Mishima's speech, 728–29; Morita's death by seppuku, 729; reconnaissance of Camp Ichigaya, 706, 718; regimental commander as hostage target, 695, 696, 698, 700; rehearsal of planned action, 719, 720; Shield Society's meeting, 700; tacit farewell party at Gotenba Inn, 705; talk with reporters, 721; trial following, 732–36
—dating and romances of: Itaya Ryōko, 206, 212; Kajima (later Hiraizumi) Mieko, 213–14; Toyoda (later Gotō) Sadako, 249–50, 262–63
—death of: autopsy, 731; funeral of, 730; letter after, 683, 799; martial arts and desire for, 576–77; "romantic, heroic death" and, 576; reminiscences after, 744–45
—debate with Tōdai Zenkyōtō: on Communism, 620; description, 617–23; on "devotion to the Tennō," 621–22; friends and Shield Society concerns for, 619; his "philosophy of life," 620; mass media coverage of, 622–23; personal revelation, 621–22
—diary-keeping at Camp Takigahara: description of music for *Ranryō'ō*, 633–34; Mt. Fuji and shifting weather, 631
—first love (Mitani Kuniko) of: attraction toward Kuniko, 108, 109–10; declining engagement to, 125; depiction of first kiss, 124–25; exchange of letters and photographs, 124; grief over lost, 139–40; love for Kuniko, 185–86; meeting at Karuizawa Station, 124; reunion with, 157–60, 204, 309–10; stories based on, 165, 184, 283, 497; talk about, 156, 185–86, 197
—health of: autointoxication and asphyxia, 44; hospitalized due to concussion, 360; stomach pain, 249
—hobbies of: dancing, 156; horseback riding, 203–4. *See also* bodybuilding
—homosexuality of: in America, 227–28; discussed, 62, 75, 83, 188, 207, 209, 230–31, 313, 320, 474, 635, 701, 702 779; at gay bar in Saint Germain, 231–32; in Rio de Janeiro, 230–31
—house of: architectural design of, 327–28; decision to build, 326–29; move to new, 330
—kabuki play directed by: *Moonbow, The*, 614; problems faced in, 613
—literary correspondence with Azuma: 77, 78–79; comment on *Sanpūko*, 81–83; on fall of Singapore, 95; influence of Raymond Radiguet, 80–81; before Japan's assault on Pearl Harbor, 93; and relationship with Bōjō, 96–97; on sexual perversion, 81–84; summing up "literary life," 78–79; translation works, 80
—as literary figure: 147, 164, 577; appreciation of manga, 678–81; commentary on "Golden Death," 686–87; commentary on *Les petites filles modèles*, 687; on conflict and tension between realities, 682–83; editorial collaboration with Kimura, 153–55, 179; essay on Japan, 92; fascination with "muddy, dark spiritualism," 715; fundamental impulse for writing, 682; homosexual magnum opus, 207–11; influence of Georges Bataille on, 715; initial reaction to Ishihara's story, 256–57; as judge of annual new writers contest, 281; on Kawabata

literature, 611; Kuwabara's statement and, 169–70; literary encounter with Dazai, 160–64; meeting with Hayashi Fusao, 165–66; movie reviews, 236–37; on *On the Narayama Song*, 281–82; novels published, in December 1950, 196–97; orthographic dimension to writing, 56; as playwright, 284–87; preface written by, for Michael Gallagher's book, 673; preface written by, for Odakane Jirō's book, 676–77; preface written by, for Tanaka Mitsuko's book, 675; preference for paradoxes, 115; pressure to establish himself as, 148; "purity-orientation" in writings, 715; reaction to Etō Jun's views, 649; reaction to Gallagher's translation of *Spring Snow*, 688; rejection of Yasuda-style classicism, 121; "rhetorical rewrite" of Racine's *Britannicus*, 285; rise of Communism in China, 223; source of literary inspiration, 253–55; threnody for grandfather' death, 95; writerly versatility, 112–14
—marriage of: argument on marriage, 320; candidate selection assignment, 313; choice of arranged marriage, 313–20; conditions for marriage, 312; discussion with Kojima Chikako, 311–12; dowries exchanged, 319; finalizing wedding date, 319; and homosexuality, 320; and honeymoon, 322–24; as journalistic event, 323; meeting with Miss Shōda, 314–15; meeting with Yōko, 318–19; meeting with Yoshida Mitsuru, 312–13; Mishima's young friends, 324–26; movie and cabaret with Yōko, 324; public announcement of, 313–14; and Shizue's illness, 318, 319; wedding, 320–21; Yuasa Atsuko and, 315
—nationalist writings of: "Action and Waiting," 642–43; aphoristic statements, 135–36; "The Beauty of Action," 644; on Constitutional oddities, 664–68; "Counterrevolution Manifesto," 600–604; cultural chauvinism and, 119; on Daibosatsu Pass Incident, 643; description of state funeral of Tōgō Heihachirō, 645–46; essay on Kita Ikki, 629–30; essay on "Planning an Action," 643; essays for young women, 645; Iinuma Isao (fictional character), 629–30; *Introduction to a Study of Action (Kōdō-gaku nyūmon)*, 638; "The Medieval Period," 133; in Middle Division, 73; Occupation's judgment of Shinto's non-religious uniqueness, 667, 668; on perverse ideological confusion, 657–58; *Ranryō'ō*, 633–34; *Senshindō sakki*, 649; *Spring Snow*, 634–35; "Nawate Incident" *(Nawate jiken)*, 112–14; at time of graduation, 72–73; *Turn Tōdai into a Zoo*, 588; on voluntary self-sacrifice, 129, 130–32; vulgar metaphor, 711–12; "What Is Japan?," 636
—opinions and preferences of: homosexual tendencies, 178–82, 195, 210, 320, 702; "true nationalism," 660–61
—plays by: *The Anxiety of Love*, 196; *The Corpse and Treasure*, 195; *The Damask Drum*, 412; *Hanjo*, 286, 294; *The House on Fire*, 195, 196; *The Lighthouse*, 193; *The Route*, 195; *A Saintly Woman*, 196; *The Terrace of the Leper King*, 611; *Tosca*, 412; *The Wise Men from the East*, 195. See also kabuki; modern nō plays; nō plays
—publishing establishment and: Alfred A. Knopf, 272–73, 294, 389; *Heibon Punch*, 547, 548, 561, 577, 582; *Hihyō*, 444, 446, 503, 515, 560, 561, 572, 688; *Holiday* magazine, 389; *Life*, 425, 435, 523, 583; *Mainichi Shinbun*, 236, 393–95, 506–7, 522, 693, 694; New Directions, 276–77, 302; Nissay Theatre, 417–18; Sakurai Shoten, 165; Shinchōsha, 706–7; Shinpa, 285–86
—pursuit of women by: Itaya Ryōko (*see* Moriwaki Ryōko); Kawabata Masako, 217–18; Kajima Mieko (*see* Hiraizumi Mieko); Kobayashi Hidemi, 217; Seki Hiroko, 193; Toyoda Sadako (*see* Gotō Sadako). *See also* Yuasa Atsuko
—trips abroad of: Bangkok, 528–29, 799; Benares, India, 525–27; Caribbean tour, 297–300; Ciudad Trujillo, Santo Domingo, 298; Dominican Republic, 298; El Paso, Ciudad Juárez, 299; Greece, 233–35; Havana, 298; India, 520–32; Laos, 529; Lins, Brazil, 229–30; London, 233; Mexico City, 299; Natchez, Mississippi, 299; New Orleans, 298, 300; New York, 221–28, 294–97; Paris, 231–33; Port-au-Prince, Haiti, 298; Puerto Rico, 298; Rio de Janeiro, 228–29, 230–31; on SS *President Wilson*, 221–24; Uxmal, Yucatán, 299
—on World War II and its aftermath: aphoristic statements, 135–36; decline of Japan's literary arts, 131; "democracy" and "war responsi-bility," 136; on Hiroshima and Nagasaki, 108, 122, 269, 497, 501, 565; as onset of Medieval Period, 133; popularity of Occupation troops, 137–38; resolution for postwar literary revival, 134–35; special attack force and humanism, 129–32; testament on war and surrender, 131–34
*Mita Bungaku*, 84, 450
Mitaka Incident, 198
Mitani Kuniko. *See* Nagai Kuniko.
Mitani Makoto (1925–2000), Mishima's classmate, bank executive, 16, 18, 111, 137, 158; father of, 108–9; home of, 108; on Mishima' rejection of officer candidate course, 100; on Mishima's response to declaration of humanity, 142; Mishima's "Saturday communication" to, 116, 125; sisters of, 109–10
Mitani Takanobu (1892–1985), diplomat, grand chamberlain, 108–9
*Mitate-kai*, 781. *See also* Shield Society
Mitchum, Robert (1917–97), American film actor, 324
*mitegura*, 472, 477
Mitford, A. M., Lord Redesdale (1836–1917), British diplomat, 114
Mito Matsudaira. *See* Matsudaira Yoritaka
Miwa Yoshio (n.d.), politician, 653
Miyake Taku (1905–71), army lieutenant, 388
Miyamoto Musashi (1584?–1645), swordsman: *Book of Five Elements* of, 562; postwar movies about, 679
Miyata Akiyuki (n.d.), army colonel, 718
Miyazawa Kenji (1896–1933), poet, 79, 81
Miyazawa Kiichi (1919–2007), prime minister, 759
Mizoguchi Kenji (1898–1956), film director, 500
Mizuki Shigeru (b. 1922), manga artist, 679
Mizutani Yaeko (1905–79), actress, 393
Mochimaru Hiroshi (b. 1943), nationalist, 483, 536, 537, 547, 583, 621, 625, 627; blood oath with, to prevent "a leftist revolution," 540; decision by, to quit *Ronsō Journal* and Shield Society, 629; as executive director of Nichigakudō, 483; fundraising efforts of, 537–38; ideological differences of,

with Mishima, 628–29; Kuramochi Kiyoshi and, 636; leadership qualities of, 484; on Mishima's reliance on Yamamoto, 628; reluctance of, to accept Mishima's job offer, 628
Mochizuki Mamoru (1910–93), psychologist, 180
modern nō plays, 412, 440; *Aoi no Ue*, 382; *The Damask Drum*, 285; *Hanjo*, 286, 382; *Kantan*, 194; staging of, in New York, 294–97
modernity, 223; questioning validity of, 130; and Westernization, difference between, 130
Mogi Masa (n.d), journalist, 231
*Mokusei* (Fragrant Olive), 73
*Moltke v. Harden*, 182
*Mōmoku monogatari*. See *Blind's Tale, The*
Monroe, Harriet (1860–1936), American editor, poet, 734
Monroe, Marilyn (1926–62), American actress, 301
"Monster, The" *(Kaibutsu)*, 37
Montalbán, Ricardo (1920–2009), Mexican actor, 306
"Moon on the Surface of the Water, A" *(Minomo no tsuki)*, 112
*Moonbow, The*, 614, 656, 714
Morand, Paul (1888–1976), French diplomat, 81
Moravia, Alberto (1907–90), Italian novelist, 436
*Mōretsu A-Tarō*, 678
Mori Arinori (1847–89), minister of education, 553
Mori Mari (1903–87), writer, 515, 710; early life of, 520; first literary recognition of, 520; as Mishima's guest, 517; *My Father's Hat* by, 518; praised by Mishima, 518–19; understanding of lust by, 518; writings about Mishima by, 517–19
Mori Ōgai (1862–1922), surgeon general, writer, 172, 356, 565, 648; Dazai's opinion of, 164; translation works of, 345, 360
Mori Oto (1890–1967), physician, 519
Mori Takeshi (1894–1945), army general, 514
Mori Yoshirō (b. 1937), prime minister, 484
Morikawa Tatsuya (1922–2006), critic, 683
Mörike, Eduard Friedrich (1804–75), German novelist, 190
Morimoto Kaoru (1912–46), playwright, director, 411
Morita Masakatsu (1945–70), member of Shield Society and Mishima's companion to death, 547, 594, 636, 689, 698, 699, 702–3, 723, 724, 728; birth of, 513–14; as chief of students, 636, 651, 669; death of, by disembowelment, 729; decapitation of Mishima by, 729; desire of, to kill himself, 703; at exhibition of Mishima's works, 707; and *Japan's Longest Day*, 514; meeting with Mishima by, 513; Mishima's influence on, 515; participation by, in coup attempt and seppuku plan, 689, 690, 692, 698, 699, 703, 705–7, 708, 714, 718–20, 722–24, 727, 728, 729; and proposal to surround Diet, 651–52; reconnaissance of Camp Ichigaya by, 706, 718; rehearsal of planned action by, 719, 720; resistance movement and, 727; student life of, 514
Moriwaki (née Itaya) Ryōko (b. 1928?), 206–7, 211–13; Mishima's offer to elope with, 207
*Morning Azalea, The (Asa no tsutsuji)*, 315, 327
"Morning of Innocent Love, The" *(Jun'ai no asa)*, 452
Moroi Saburō (1903–77), composer
Morris, Ivan (1925–96), British translator, author, 227, 272, 273, 286, 437–38, 643, 799

Morrison, Norman (1933–65), American war protester, 535
Moskowitz, Gene (1921–1982), American theater and film critic, 442
*Most Happy Fella, The*, 304
Moto'ori Norinaga (1730–1801), advocate of *kokugaku*, 86, 789
Mountbatten, Louis, Lord (1900–79), British governor-general of India, 524
Muirhead-Gould, Gerard Charles (1889–1945), British admiral, 645
Munen-ryū sword-fighting school, 733
Murakami Hyōe (1923–2003), writer, 539
Murakami Ichirō (1920–75), poet, writer, 545, 546
Murakami Tomoyoshi (1901–77), playwright, 411
Muramatsu Eiko (b. 1938), actress, 187, 654
Muramatsu Takeshi (1929–94), critic, student of French literature, 53, 116, 140, 415, 549, 584, 619, 627; meeting of, with Mishima over *Sankei* article, 700–701; on Mishima's attempt to "restore theatricality," 655; and Mishima's family, 183; on Mishima's homosexual tendencies, 182–84, 186–88; on Mishima's idea for Constitutional reform, 667; on pollution problems, 696; on "theater troupe" of Shield Society, 653
Murayama Noriyuki (b. 1907?), naval ensign, 378
Murayama Tomoyoshi (1901–77), writer, 286 adapted *Golden Pavilion* into a play; impessed by China, 411
Mushiake Aromu (1923–91), writer, translator, 270, 488, 562
*Music (Ongaku)*, 424, 552
musicals in New York: *Happy Hunting*, 304; *Jamaica*, 306; *Li'l Abner*, 305–6; *The Most Happy Fella*, 304; *My Fair Lady*, 304–5; *New Girl in Town*, 305; *South Pacific*, 305; *The Threepenny Opera*, 306–7; *West Side Story*, 306
Musset, Alfred de (1810–57), French novelist, 520
Mustafa Kemal Atatürk (1881–1938, Turkish statesman, 321
*Musume-gonomi obitori-no-ike*. See *Fond of Young Women: The Sash-Taking Pond*
Mutaguchi Ren'ya (1888–1966), army general, 773
Mutai Risaku (1890–1974), philosopher, 534
*My Fair Lady*, 293, 304–5
*My Father's Hat (Chichi no bōshi)*, 518
*My Friend Hitler (Waga tomo Hitler)*, 417, 580, 598; finished writing, 584; historical figures in, 580; inspired to write, 580; literary motive to write, 581; vs. *Madame de Sade*, 581; production of, 598; published in *Bungakukai*, 582; reasons for, 580–81; selected for inaugural of Rōman Gekijō, 596
*My Mother*, 582
*My Pilgrimage Days (Watashi no henreki jidai)*, 149, 160, 171
*My Puberty (Waga shishunki)*: depiction of first kiss in, 124–25; depiction of yearning for love affair in, 110
Myōshinji, 259

Nabeyama Sadachika (1901–79), Communist leader, 72
Nagai (née Matsudaira) Taka (1854–1923), Mishima's

paternal great-grandmother, 34
Nagai (née Mitani) Kuniko (b. 1927), 111, 122, 155, 156, 171, 179; breakup with Mishima, 186, 188; depiction of kissing, in *Confessions of a Mask*, 183–84; depiction of love for, in *Confessions of a Mask*, 185–86; encounter with Mishima at New York, 309; evacuated to Karuizawa, 124; literary encounter with Mishima, 157–60; married life of, 156; Mishima's attraction toward, 108, 109–10, 124; on Mishima's homosexual tendencies, 182; Mishima's novel as revenge fantasy about, 197, 283; playing the piano, 109, 110; relationship with Mishima, 124–25; visiting Makoto at school, 122–23
Nagai Iwanojō (1846–1907), Mishima's paternal great-grandfather career in law, 34; marriage to Taka, 34–35
Nagai Kafū (1879–1959), novelist, 84, 148; French poems and prose published by, 676; writings on former residence, 41–42; in Yochō-machi, 41
Nagai Kunio (b. 1915), bank employee, 159
Nagai Naomune (1816–91), Mishima's paternal great-great-grandfather, 2, 32, 34, 37, 616, 742; as Japan's first navy minister, 33; as magistrate for foreign affairs, 33; in Meiji government, 34
Nagai Naonori (n.d.), Tokugawa *hatamoto*, 32
Nagai Natsuko. See Hiraoka Natsuko
Nagai Yōnosuke (1924–2008), political scientist, 662
Nagaoka Minoru (b. 1924), vice-minister of finance, 3, 5, 7, 15, 242, 636, 731; background and Hiraoka Kimitake, 6; bureaucratic career of, 3–6; father of, 6; meetings of, with Hiraoka Kimitake, 5, 6; personality and character of, 3; school and college education of, 15–16
Nagaoka Teruko (1908–2010), actress, stage director, 205, 315, 349; as planning advisor of Bungaku-za, 360
*Nagasugita haru*. See *Spring That Lasted Too Long, The*
Nagata Masaichi (1906–85), movie studio head, 350
*Nagoya Times*, 530
Naitō Arau (Arō, 1883–1977), translator of French literature, 285
Nakadai Tatsuya (b. 1932), actor, 322, 324, 615, 795
Nakagawa Kojūrō (1866–1944), founder of Ritsumeikan University, 29
Nakahara Chūya (1907–37), poet, 254
Nakai Kōzō (1834–94), politician, 113
Nakajima Aircraft Manufacturing Company, 16, 116
Nakajō Toyoma (d. 1945), army colonel, 88
Nakamura Ganjirō I (1860–1935), kabuki actor, 247
Nakamura Kanzaburō XVIII (1909–88), kabuki actor, 397
Nakamura Kenji (n.d.), editor, 716
Nakamura Kichiemon I (1886–1954), kabuki actor, 613
Nakamura Mitsuo (1911–88), student of French literature, 130, 205, 221, 254, 398, 572, 585, 713; afterword to *The Golden Pavilion*, 268; argument of, on Tennō system, 568–69; rejection of Mishima's literary works by, 147–48
Nakamura Nobumasa (n.d.), army general, 727
Nakamura Nobuo (1908–91), actor, 281, 557, 598
Nakamura Shin'ichirō (1918–97), poet, playwright, 245, 499
Nakamura Utaemon VI (1917–2001), kabuki actor,

241, 247, 248, 249, 315, 347, 397; as Nakamura Shikan VI, 247
Nakane Chie (b. 1926), social anthropologist, 521
Nakano Seigō (1886–1943), journalist, politician, 127, 379, 702; arrest and interrogation of, 127; as outspoken critic of Tōjō, 127; suicide and funeral of, 127
Nakano Yoshio (1903–85), student of English literature, 178, 220, 288
Nakasone Yasuhiro (b. 1919), prime minister, 697; apology to Mishima by, 669–70; as director-general of Defense Agency, 669; Japanese Constitutional revision proposed by, 665–66; on Shield Society, 669
Nakatani Noboru (1929–2006), actor, 281
Nakatsuji Kazuhiko (n.d.), editor, 482, 536, 553, 627, 628
Nakayama Gishū (1900–69), novelist, 193
Nakayama Masatoshi (1913–87), karate master, 705
Nakayama Taisaburō (1912–2003), iaidō master, 479
Nakazato Kaizan (1885–1944), novelist, 642
"naked festivals" *(hadaka matsuri)*, 557–58
*Nami*, 544; *What Is a Novel?* written for, 281–82
Nanba Daisuke (1899–1924), terrorist, 709
Nanbara Shigeru (1889–1974), university president, 797
*Nandemo miteyarō*. See *I'm Going to See Everything*
Nanjing Massacre, 58, 654, 744
*Nanshoku ōkagami*. See *Great History of Male Love*
*Narayama-bushi kō*. See *On the Narayama Song*
Nathan, John (b. 1940), translator, author, 323, 767, 772, 775, 779; depiction of Mishima at parties by, 433–34; interviews of, for Mishima biography, 50–51; judgment of, on "Sorrels," 55; severed relationship of, with Mishima, 434; on *Silk and Insight*, 432–33; translation works of, 432
National Defense Society, 513, 515
National Learning (*kokugaku*), 120, 366–67, 509, 781, 789; resemblance of, to Anglo-Saxon revival, 86; "Yamato spirit" popularity and, 86; Yasuda Yojūrō-style optimistic theory of, 117
National Mobilization Law (1938), 102
National Public Safety Commission, 4
*Natsu no yami*. See *Darkness in Summer*
*Natsuko's Adventures (Natsuko no bōken)*, 212–13, 244
Natsume Sōseki (1867–1916), novelist, 29, 258, 356, 741
*Nature*, 331
*Naval Battle (Kaisen)*, 87
*Navel and the Atomic Bomb, The (Heso to genbaku)*, 362
Navy Accounting School, Tsukiji branch of, 15–16
"Nawate Incident, The" *(Nawate jiken)*, 112–14
*Nayotake*, 239, 240
Nehru, Jawaharlal (1889–1964), Indian political leader, 403, 523
*Nemureru bijo*. See *Sleeping Beauties*
*Nemuri to okashi to rakka to*. See *Sleeping, Sinning, Falling*
Nerval, Gérard de (1808–55), French writer and poet, 117, 648
*Nettaiju*. See *Tropical Trees*
New Directions, 275–77, 302
*New Girl in Town*, 305
New Sensibility School, 82, 345, 571

*New Writing in Japan,* 375
New York, Mishima's trip to: American wealth and, 290–94; at bar in Harlem, 228; daily expenses of, 301; impression of the Goreliks, 302; at Japan Society party, 309–10; meeting with ACCF correspondents, 224–25; meeting with Julius Fleischmann, 290–91; meeting with Weatherby, 227; and Metropolitan Opera House, 225–26; and modern nō play production crew, 303–4, 309; musicals in, 304–7; at Radio City Music Hall, 291; on SS *President Wilson,* 221–24; and staging of modern nō plays, 294–97, 300–303, 308–9; surprise encounter with Kuniko, 309; at Van Rensselaer Hotel, 301–2
New York City Ballet, 307, 318
*New York Times,* 143, 299, 309, 310, 382, 657; full-page antiwar ad in, 443; review of Futabatei Shimei's story in, 273
NHK Hall, Mishima's visit to, 331–32
Nichigakudō (Nihon Gakusei Dōmei), 483, 513, 538, 547
Nichiren (1222–82), Buddhist proselytizer
*Nichirin raisan.* See "In Praise of the Sun"
Nietzsche, Friedrich Wilhelm (1844–1900), German philosopher, 226, 235, 339, 376, 633, 648
nihilism, 338–40; active, 339; antirationalism deriving from, 339
Nihon Bunka Kaigi, 225
*Nihon Dangi,* 473
*Nihon Dokusho Shinbun,* 13, 14
*Nihon Rōman-ha,* 115, 161
*Nihon Shoki.* See *History of Japan*
*Nijūshi no hitomi.* See *Twenty-four Eyes*
Nikkeiren. See Japan Economic Federation
*Nikutai no akuma,* Japanese translatioin of *Le Diable au corps,* 423
*Nikutai no gakkō.* See *School of the Flesh, The*
Ninagawa Chikayoshi (n.d.), student of French literature, 185–86
"1955 Regime," 343
*Ningen,* 158, 162, 165, 169, 174, 176, 200; filed with the CIE, 151; Jinzai's review published in, 176–77; Mishima's works published in, 153–54, 164, 497; royalty payment of, 166; shabby treatment of authors by, 201
Nino'oka, Mishima's visit to, 604
*Nippon-sei.* See *Made-in-Japan*
Nishi Takeichi (1902–45), army colonel, 711
Nishida Kitarō (1870–1945), philosopher, 120
Nishinomaru Hidehiko (character in *The Aristocrats' Staircase*), 377
Nissay Theatre, 417; *Arabian Nights, The* staged at, 478; *Miranda* staged at, 590; production rights of *The Joyful Koto,* 417
Nisshin Seifun, 314
Nitta Hiroshi (1928–2003), editor, 584; desire of, to publish Mishima's complete works, 706–7
Niwa Fumio (1904–2005), novelist, 87, 177
Nixon, Richard (1913–94), US president, 381–82, 656–57, 796
NLT, 416
*No Longer Human (Ningen shikkaku),* 164, 170
nō plays, 68; *The Damask Drum (Aya no tsuzumi),* 294–97; *Eguchi,* 338; *Hanjo,* 235, 286; *Kantan,* 194; *The Lady Aoi (Aoi-no-ue),* 294; *The Potted Tree (Hachi no ki),* 205–6; rhetorical style of, 121–22; *Sotoba Komachi,* 294; staging of, in New York, 294–97, 300–304, 308–10, 382; *yūgen* and flower in, 611
Nobel Prize, 392, 435–58, 521, 522, 544, 631, 639, 686; Americans receiving, 435; to Kawabata Yasunari, 584–85; Mishima aiming for, 431–34; Nathan mentions Mishima as candidate for, 435
Nobutoki Kiyoshi (1887–1965), composer, 98
Noda Utarō (1909–84), editor, critic, poet, 135, 150; dislike of Mishima by, 114–15; invitation of, to Mishima for fiction work, 114, 115; note to Kawabata for Mishima, 116
Nogi Maresuke (1849–1912), army general, 372, 531, 532, 622, 648, 756, 794; as follower of Yōmeigaku, 647
Noma Hiroshi (1915–91), novelist, 273
Nonaka Shirō (1905–36), army captain, 370
Nonaka Yuri (n.d.), collagist, 592
non-military military academy, 238–39
North Korea, 539, 643; guerrilla activities in the South, 643; spies sent by, 549–50
Nosaka Akiyuki (b. 1930), author, 45, 57, 69, 202, 658, 714; as bartender trainee, 214; job search by, 214; meeting with Mishima of, 215, 658; works of, on Mishima and his family, 70–71
Noshiro Incident, 549–50
"Not Falling in Love with Paris," 232
*Nothing Is More Expensive Than Something Free (Tada yori takai mono wa nai),* 221
Novalis (Georg Philipp Friedrich Freiherr von Hardenberg, 1772–1801), German philosopher, 573
*Novelist's Holiday, A (Shōsetsuka no kyūka),* 256, 258, 500, 501
nuclear testing by United States, 395
nuclear threat, 393–97; Berlin Crisis and, 395; hydrogen bomb, 396; nuclear contest between superpowers, 397
*Nude and the Costume, The (Ratai to ishō),* 272, 275, 311, 317
Nureyev, Rudolf (1938–93), ballet dancer, 518

Obata Hisao (n.d.), vice minister of defense, 730
O'Brien, Edna (b. 1930), Irish novelist, 438
Obuchi Keizō (1937–2000), prime minister, 484
Occupation censors, 173; Bowers's first salvo to counter, 142; of open sexual expression, 173–74; of *Sound of Waves,* 245–46; of Yoshida's works, 312
Oda Makoto (1932–2007), writer, 494, 637
Oda Nobunaga (1534–84), warlord, 410
Odakane Jirō (1911–90), biographer, 87, 94, 748; *Hasuda Zenmei and His Death* of, 677; on philistinism of Itō, 105
Ōe Kenzaburō (b. 1935), novelist, 204, 333, 338, 386, 339, 432, 454, 534, 620; as Mishima's predicted Nobel Prize winner, 457; translatese of, 345
Ōe no Asatsuna (886–958), scholar-poet, 685
officer-candidate course, 14, 16; Mishima's reasons for not choosing, 99, 100, 108; Mitani released from, 137
Ogasawara Yoshito (n.d.), Kawabata Yasunari's

friend, 174
Ogawa Bimei (1882–1961), novelist, writer of children's stories, 78–79
Ogawa Gorō (aka Takasugi Ichirō; 1908–2008), translator, novelist, 201
Ogawa Masahiro (b. 1947?), member of Shield Society, 733, 734
Ogawa Tōru (1914–89), publisher-editor, 343, 701, 703, 708
Ohara Naoshi (1877–1967), politician, 145
O-Ichi-no-kata (1547?–83), Oda Nobunaga's sister, 80
Ōishi Kuranosuke (1659–1703), leader of 47 samurai, 403
Ōji Paper, 95, 96, 102, 103
Okada Izō (1838–65), swordsman, 615
Okada Keisuke (1868–1952), prime minister, 364, 377
Okamoto Kihachi (1924–2005), film director, 324, 515
Ōkawa Shūmei (1886–1957), Asianist, 104–5
Okazaki Kazuichi (n.d.), businessman, 103
Oketani Hideaki (b. 1932), critic, 121
Okinawa, Battle of, 465; special attack force deployment in, 129
"Okinawa and Madama Butterfly's Offspring," 657
Okinawa Day turmoil, 640; Mishima's assessment of, 617; and parade of Shield Society, 617; rallies and guerilla warfare, 616
Okinawa reversion, 535, 656, 735
Ōkubo Toshimichi (1830–78), minister of home affairs, 581
Ōkuma Shigenobu (1838–1922), prime minister, 25, 26
Okuno Takeo (1926–97), critic, 256; on *Kyōko's House*, 333; on Mishima's physical fitness, 261–62; on *Spring Snow*, 599
*Old Capital, The (Koto)*, 399, 584; serialization of, 400
"Old Spring," 556
Olivia, Marie-Claire (b. 1931), French actress, 237
*Olympia*, 37
Ōmiwa Shrine, visit to, 469
*"On Defending Culture,"* 560, 567; Hashikawa's criticism of, 570; Mishima's argument in defense of, 566; published in *Chūō Kōron*, 563
*On the Earthman (Chijin-ron)*, 559
*On the Narayama Song (Narayama-bushi kō)*, 281, 282, 360
"One Arm" *(Kataude)*, 572
*One Thousand and One Nights*, 424
*One Thousand and One-Second Stories*, 82
Ongaku. See *Music*
Ōnishi Takijirō (1891–1945), admiral, 129; seppuku of, 374
*Onna wa senryō-sarenai*, 348
Ono Azusa (1852–86), legal scholar, 25
Ono Shigeru (n.d.), Hiraoka Mume's son, 22–23, 70
Onoe Kikugorō VI (1885–1949), kabuki actor, 119, 140, 305, 613
Ōoka Makoto (b. 1931), poet, 379
Ōoka Shōhei (1909–88), student of French literature, novelist, 205, 273, 531–32
Oppenheimer, Robert (1904–67), American physicist, 224
orgasm, 377; as music, 424–25
Oriental mysticism, 142–43
Orikuchi Shinobu (also Shaku Chōkū, 1887–1953),
poet, folklorist, 144, 331, 449–51
Orita Kōji (b. 1945), theater executive, 612
*Orphée* (dance drama), 282
Osaragi Jirō (1897–1973), novelist, 274
Ōshiko Shrine, 9
Ōshima Masamitsu (1884–1965), biologist, 119
Ōshima Nagisa (b. 1932), film director, 343, 391
Ōshio Heihachirō (1793–1837), philosopher, 647, 648
Ōsugi Jūichirō, 396
Ōtaguro Tomoo (1834–76), Shinpūren leader, 471, 472
Ōtaguro Yasukuni (n.d.), officiator of Shingai Shrine, 475
*Othello*, 361
*Otoko no shi*. See *Man's Death, A*
Ōtomo no Yakamochi (718?–85), poet, 97–98, 120–21
Ōtsu (663–86), imperial prince, 676
"Otto and Maya" *(Ottō to Maya)*, 112
*Our Era (Warera ga jidai)*, 333
"Oval Portrait, The," 682
Ōwada Mitsuaki (n.d.), tattooist, 710
*Owari no bigaku*. See *Aesthetic of Ending, The*
"Owl, The," 53
Ōya Atsushi (1885–1970), Mishima's maternal granduncle, 34, 35
Ōya Sōichi (1900–70), journalist, 639
Ozawa Kinshirō (n.d.), choreographer, 590
Ozawa Seiji (Seiji Ozawa; b. 1935), conductor, 418

Pacific War, 173, 364, 388, 428, 465, 493, 532, 535, 559, 646. See also World War II; World War II and its aftermath
Pal, Radhabinod (1896–1967), military tribunal jurist, 744, 755
Panama, Norman (1914–2003), American screenwriter, 305
Parabellum, German author Ferdinand Heinrich Grautoff's penname, 128, 752
Paris, 413; Japanese notables in, 348; Mishima's portrait of, 232–33; Mishima's trip to, 222, 233, 413, 456
Park Chung-hee (1917–79), Korean president, 670
Parkes, Harry (1828–85), British diplomat, 113–14
Passin, Herbert (1916–2003), American sociologist, 189, 224, 228
Pater, Walter (1839–94), English writer, 98, 450
"Patriotism." See "Yūkoku"
"Peacocks" *(Kujaku)*, 451
Peers School, 6; Higher Division of, 61, 99, 100, 111; Middle Division of, 59, 61, 63, 73; types of students at, 75
Percival, Arthur (1887–1966), British army general, 87
Perry, Matthew C. (1794–1858), Cmdr. of US Navy, 21, 35, 36, 470, 647
*Personal Matter, A (Kojinteki-na taiken)*, 432
perverts, divisions among, 181
petition, to Japan Writers Association, 392
*Phaedo*, 718
Philip, Prince, Duke of Edinburgh (b. 1921), Queen Elizabeth II's husband, 403
Piaf, Édith (1915–63), French singer, 348
*Picture of Dorian Gray, The*, 452
*Pilgrimage to the Three Kumano Shrines (Mi-Kumano mōde)*, 449
"Pledge by Chrysanthemum Flower" *(Kikka no*

*chigiri)*, 555
*Pocket Punch Oh!*, 561, 641; *Introduction to a Study of Action* for, 638; *Spiritual Lectures for Young Samurai* for, 561
Poe, Edgar Allan (1809–49), American writer and poet, 216, 345, 449, 498, 680, 682, 686
Police Reserve Force. *See* Keisatsu Yobitai
*Political Boy Dies, The (Seiji shōnen shisu)*, 386, 388
Pollack, Sydney (b. 1934), American film director of *The Yakuza*, 658
*Pornographers, The*, 70, 658, 673
Porto-Riche, Georges de (1849–1930), French dramatist, 197
"Portrait at Eighteen and Thirty-four," 331
*Postwar Analects*, 135
Potsdam Declaration, 136, 141
*Potted Tree, The (Hachi no ki)*, 205–6
Pound, Ezra (1885–1972), American poet, 508
poverty, 36, 37, 431, 520, 523, 630, 686; in Puerto Rico, 298; in Tōhoku region, 365–66
"Prayer Diary" *(Inori no nikki)*, 112
"Preparations for the Night" *(Yoru no shitaku)*, 164–65, 283
Presley, Elvis (1935–77), American singer, 403
*Prétextes*, 518
*Principia Pædophilia*, 691
"Principles of National Reformation," 553
prisoners of war, 159, 214, 391, 465, 466, 532, 782
privacy: invasion of, 351–57, 779–80; Mishima's essay on, 363
"Promises I Haven't Kept: 25 Years Inside Me," 688, 700
Proust, Marcel (1871–1922), French writer, 117–18, 190, 529, 632, 634, 676
pseudo-homosexual love, 180
Public Safety Preservation Law, 165, 404, 405, 406
Publishing Enterprise Ordinance, 102
publishing industry: government control of, 102, 175; restructuring of, 101
Puccini, Giacomo (1858–1924), Italian composer, 225, 412
"Puppy Waltz," 100
Putsch, 369

Qu Yuan (3rd–4th centuries B.C.), Chinese poet, 118

Racine, Jean-Baptiste (1639–99), French dramatist, 196, 285
Radiguet, Raymond (1903–23), French novelist, 92, 124, 178, 185, 239, 283, 423, 483, 509; place in Mishima's mind, 80–81
*Raiō no terasu*. *See Terrace of the Leper King, The*
*Rangaku koto-hajime*. *See Beginning Dutch Learning*
*Ranryō'ō*, description of music for, 633–34
*Ratai to ishō*. *See Nude and the Costume, The*
"rebellion," 369, 410
recanting political beliefs, 72, 165, 166, 286, 404–8, 538, 746
*Record of a Phantom Hut (Genjū-an no ki)*, 135
*Record of Ancient Matters (Kojiki)*, 107, 366, 461
Red Army, 597; failed plan of, to attack prime minister's residence, 642–43; formation of, 640
Red Purge, 199, 514

*Red Star Over China*, 441
Redon (gay bar), 208, 209, 328
*Reflections in a Golden Eye*, 562
"Regular and Irregular Armies, The," 697
Reinhardt, Max (1873–1943), American stage actor and director, 141
Reisman, David (1909–2002), American sociologist, 224–25
religion, early interest in, 195–96
Reni, Guido (1575–1642), Italian painter, 235
*Requiem for Battleship Yamato (Senkan Yamato no saigo)*, 312
Resnais, Alain (b. 1922), French film director, 351
"Resplendent Epistolary Exchange," 517–20
Rest and Amusement Association, 138
"Retired Emperor Kazan" *(Kazan-in)*, 80
"Revere the Tennō," 470
RFK (Robert F. Kennedy) assassination, 553–54
"Rich in New York, The," 291
Richie, Donald (b. 1924), American authority on Japanese film, 227–28, 274, 313, 349, 362, 439, 770
Ridgway, Matthew (1895–1993), US general, 220
Riefenstahl, Leni (1902–2003), German film director, 37
rightwing killers, 385–89; rising of, 387; threats of, to Fukazawa, 387–88. *See also* assassination
Rikugun Daigakkō, 787
Rilke Rainer, Maria (1875–1926), German poet, 104
*Risshō ankoku-ron*. *See Establishment of the Teaching for the Protection of the Country*
*Rite of Love and Death, The*, 441
Robbins, Jerome (1918–98), American choreographer, 306
Rockefeller, John D., III (1906–78), American philanthropist, 291
Rodenbach, Georges (1855–98), Belgian novelist, 718
Rodin, Auguste (1840–1917), French sculptor, 676
Röhm, Ernst (1887–1934), Nazi leader, 580
Röhm assassination, 581
Rokumeikan (Deer Cry Hall): 278, 279, 280
*Rokumeikan, The*, 315, 316; Countess Asako's role in, 278; literary layer of, 280; as reinterpretation of grand ball description, 280; reviews of, 277
Rokuonji. *See* Kinkakuji
Rolland, Romain (1866–1944), French writer, 293
Romains, Jules (1885–1972), French poet, 747
*Rōman Gekijō*, 187, 557, 596
*Ronsō Journal*, 482, 483, 515, 536, 538, 540, 553, 554, 600; Counterrevolution Manifesto in, 600–601; severing relationship with Mishima, 627; sponsored by Tanaka, 538
*Room of Sweet Honey, The (Amai mitsu no heya)*, 520
"Room You Can Lock, The" *(Kagi no kakaru heya)*, 338
Roosevelt, Franklin Delano (1882–1945), US president, 128, 647
Roosevelt, Theodore (1858–1919), US president, 28
*Rose and the Pirate, The (Bara to kaizoku)*, 187, 316
Rose Palace, mystery of, 528
*Rose Punishments (Bara-kei)*, 400
*Rose Tree: Fake Lovers, The (Bara no ki: Nise no koibito-tachi)*, 699
Rosenberg, Alfred (1893–1946), German theorist, 648

Rossi, Jean Baptiste (Sébastien Japrisot,1931–2003), French author, film director, 236
*Route, The (Rotei)*, 195
*Runaway Horse, The (Honba)*, 311, 373, 463, 476, 482, 489, 494, 527, 544, 560, 594, 626, 629, 700; Okuno review of, 599; pivotal role of revolt in, 469; published by Shinchōsha, 598; Shinpūren inserted into, 476
Russell, Bertrand (1872–1970), British philosopher, 339, 516
Russo-Japanese War, 28, 368, 428, 532, 545, 599, 645
*Ruy Blas*, 307, 413

*sabaku*, "help the Tokugawa Government," 470
Sade, Marquis de (1740–1814), French writer, 179
*Sado Kōshaku Fujin*. See *Madame de Sade*
Saegusa Festival, 469
Saeki Shōichi (b. 1922), student of American literature, 334, 687–88; discussion with Mishima on Japanese literature, 361; on Mishima's stay in Brazil, 230; on protagonist of *The Golden Pavilion*, 268; translation works of, 392
Saga Revolt, 472–73, 715
Saigō Takamori (1828–77), rebel leader, 471, 508, 581, 649; as follower of Yōmeigaku, 647
Saigyō (1118–90), tanka poet, 338
"Sailor Killed by Hong Kong Flowers, The," 469
*Sailor Who Fell from Grace with the Sea, The (Gogo no eiko)*, 423, 431, 502
Sainte-Beuve, Charles (1804–69), French critic, 413
Saint-Saëns, Charles-Camille (1835–1921), French composer, 616
Saipan, 693; fall of, 107–8, 267; first fleet of B-29s based in, 111
Saito, George (b. 1917), student of Japanese literature, 188–89
Saitō Kōichi (b. 1935), photographer, 714
Saitō Makoto (1858–1936), prime minister, 364
Saitō Mokichi (1882–1953), tanka poet, 361
Saitō Naoichi (n.d.), judge, 695, 733
Saitō Yoshirō (n.d.), Mishima's classmate at Peers School, 148
Sakaguchi Ango (1906–55), writer, 335, 706
Sakai Hiroshi (n.d.), Bank of Japan officer, 62
Sakakiyama Tamotsu, Mishima's pseudonym, 442
Sakamoto Kazuki (1921–2002), editor, 168
Sakamoto Ryōma (1835–67), samurai, 239, 615
Sakamoto Ryūichi (b. 1952), musician, 391
*Sākasu*. See "Circus"
Sakuma Yoshiko (b. 1939), actress, 634, 721
Sakurada Takeshi (1904–85), businessman, 537, 538
Sakurai Shoten, Mishima's fiction published by, 165
*Salome* (opera), 187, 225–26, 227, 360
San Francisco Peace Treaty, 521, 535
*saniwa*, 460–61
*Sanjuro*, 438
*Sankei Shinbun*, 653; "Promises I Haven't Kept: 25 Years Inside Me" article in, 688, 700
Sano Manabu (1892–1953), Japan Communist Party chairman, 72
Sanpa Zengakuren ("Three Factions"), 786
Sansom, G. B. (1883–1965), British historian of Japan, 143–44

San'ya, 552
San'yū Incident, 388; investigator of, 670; victim of, 389
Sappho (7th–6th century B.C.), Greek poet, 286
*Sarashina nikki*, 403
*Sardine Hawker & the Dragnet of Love, The (Iwashiuri koi no hikiami)*, 248, 397
Sardou, Victorien (1831–1908), French dramatist, 412
Saroyan, William (1908–81), American dramatist, author, 239
Sarraute, Natalie (1900–99), French writer, 436
Sartre, Jean-Paul (1905–80), French philosopher, 248, 345
Sasaki Sōichi (1878–1965), constitutional scholar, 568
*Sasameyuki*. See *Makioka Sisters*
Sassa Atsuyuki (b. 1930), security bureaucrat, 156, 595, 642
Sassa Hiro'o (1897–1948), journalist, 155
Sassa Katsuaki (1926–86), journalist, author, 155
Sassa Teiko (b. 1928), politician, 128, 155, 160; career, 157; family background, 157; meeting with Mishima, 155–56; refusal to kiss Mishima, 156–57
Sata Ineko (1904–98), novelist, 534
Satō Akira (1886–1965), pediatrician, 520
Satō Eisaku (1901–75), prime minister, 341, 448; demonstrations against visit to US, 535–36, 656; meeting with Nixon, 656–57, 796–97
Satō Haruo (1892–1964), writer, poet, 81, 131, 149
Satō Isao (1915–2006), constitutional scholar, 666, 667
Satō Ryōichi (1924–2001), publisher, 326
Satō Saku (1905–96), student of French literature, 258
Satō Yoshio (d. 1967), publisher, 245
Satomura Kinzō (1902–45), novelist
Satow, Ernest (1843–1929), British diplomat, 113
Satsuma Rebellion, 471, 508
*Satyricon*, 707, 717
Saunders, Dale (1919–95), student of Romance language literature, 439
Savang Vatthana (1907–78), Laotian King, 529
Sawada Junjirō (1863–?), sexologist, 173
*Sayonara*, 306, 390
Schlegel, Friedrich von (1772–1829), German poet, 380, 564
Schnitzler, Arthur (1862–1931), Austrian author, 236
*School of the Flesh, The (Nikutai no gakkō)*, 423
Schopenhauer, Arthur (1788–1860), German philosopher, 235, 485
Schüchter, Wilhelm (1911–74), German conductor, 331
Schwinger, Julian (1918–94), Nobel Prize–winning American physicist, 457
scientific socialism, 411
Scott-Stokes, Henry (b. 1938), British journalist, 167, 653, 707–8
*Screams of Heroic Souls (Eirei no zekkyō)*, 464–69, 478; manuscript for, 464–65; Mishima's advice on, 466; purpose of writing, 466
SDF. See Self-Defense Forces
*Sea and Poison, The (Umi to dokuyaku)*, 673
"Sea and the Evening Glow, The" *(Umi to yūyake)*, 270–71
*Sea of Fertility, The (Hōjō no umi)*, 186, 311, 402–3, 456, 463, 507, 521, 524, 544, 638, 673, 707–8, 712, 725, 757; plotting and planning for fourth volume of,

684–85; protagonist Honda Shigekuni of, 469, 521, 599, 681, 701, 726
*Season of Ashes, The (Hai no kisetsu)*, 115
"Season of the Sun, The" *(Taiyō no kisetsu)*, 255, 564; film based on, 258; Mishima's initial reaction to, 256–57; as winner of New Face Prize (1955), 256
Sebastian (d. circa 288), Christian saint and martyr, 176, 181, 227, 234–35, 266, 446–47, 591–92, 713
*Second Sex, The*, 403
*Secret Drug, The (Higyō)*, 207
*Secret: A Record of a Palau Battle (Hiwa Palau senki)*, 467
Seibu Department Store, 548
Seichō no Ie, 689–90
Seidensticker, Edward (1921–2007), translator of Japanese literature, 272
*Seiji shōnen shisu.* See *Political Boy Dies, The*
*Seinen.* See *Youth, The*
Seki Hiroko (1929–2008), actress, 193
Sekikawa Masakatsu (n.d.), gagaku authority, 634
self-centered sexual desire, 180
Self-Defense Forces, 332, 479, 485, 494, 602, 621, 630, 653, 659, 666, 698, 709, 728, 729; budget for, 631; Constitutional legitimacy of, 489–91, 550, 661, 665–66, 728; Kamikaze tactics and, 558; Mishima's idea of splitting, 559–60, 663; Mishima's plan for training with, 486, 488, 512; roles in national defense, 537, 542; size of, 560; spiritual education of, 491–92
Senda Koreya (1904–94), actor and stage director, 194, 205, 270
*Senjinkun* (Code of Conduct in the Battlefield), 782
*Senkan Yamato no saigo.* See *Requiem for Battleship Yamato*
*Senshindō sakki*, 649
Senuma Shigeki (1904–88), critic, 399
seppuku (disembowelment), 22, 35–36, 371–80, 434, 437, 440, 442, 478, 499, 510, 515; of Mishima, 572–77, 713–29
*setsuwa* narrative mode, 79–80
*Setting Sun, The (Shayō)*, 160, 161, 163, 164, 170, 273
*Sex and Life (Sei to seikatsu)*, 180
*Sexualpathologie*, 181, 182
*Shadow, The*, 383
*shayō*, 756. See also *Setting Sun, The*
*Shi o kaku shōnen.* See "Boy Who Writes Poems, The"
Shiba Ryōtarō (1923–96), novelist, 9, 531; account of Gen. Nogi Maresuke, 648; Mishima's appreciation for, 650
Shibusawa Tatsuhiko (1928–87), student of French literature, 361, 453, 517, 561, 588, 690
Shibuya, 6, 59, 201, 249, 534
Shichijō Shoin, 102, 103, 111, 147
*Shichishō hōkoku* (militarist-rightwing slogan), 719, 728
Shidehara Kijūrō (1872–1951), prime minister, 343, 346, 460
Shield Society (Tate no Kai), 187, 483, 546, 617, 619, 620, 639, 641, 651, 668, 671, 781; concerns for Mishima's debate with Tōdai Zenkyōtō, 619, 620; disbandment, 732; draft for revised Constitution, 664, 666; financial burden of maintaining, 625–26, 670; first public parade of, 622, 625, 636, 652–54; hostage target of, 692, 695; "intelligence gathering" activities, 586, 590; International Antiwar Day and, 586–87; JNG officially named as, 582; launch of, 540–41; led third group, Mishima, 603; members' gathering, 587; members involved in seppuku plan, 689, 690, 692, 693, 695, 698–701, 705, 710, 714, 716, 717, 721, 723, 724, 725; military uniform for, 582–84, 625; Mishima's physical inadequacy during GSDF training of, 546–47; Nakasone's derisive comment on, 669; photographing of members of, 714; rented temple for, 603; *Ronsō Journal* people's decision to quit, 627–29; schism within, 602; study sessions with Yamamoto, 593–94; "surveillance-investigative training" of, 623; theoretical case for establishing, 563; training at GSDF Camp Narashino, 652; training at GSDF Camp Takigahara, 603–4, 631–32
Shiga Naoya (1883–1971), novelist called "deity of fiction," 66, 77, 745; proposal of, to abandon the Japanese language, 137; views of, on Mishima's fiction work, 115
Shiina Rinzō (1911–73), novelist, 168
Shiine Yamato (b. 1942), editor, writer, 480, 547–48, 625, 640; at International Antiwar Day demonstrations, 608–9
Shiizaki Jirō (1911–45), army colonel, 415
Shikata, Hyōgo, 9–10, 15, 18, 19, 22, 23, 24, 31, 105
Shikiba Ryūzaburō (1898–1965), psychiatrist, 186, 453–54; Mishima's correspondence with, 179–80
Shillony, Ben-Ami, 132, 144
Shima Taizō (b. 1946), primatologist, 595, 608
Shimanaka Hōji (1923–97), publisher, 329, 385, 386
Shimazaki Hiroshi (b. 1933), editor, bibliographer, 704
Shimizu Corporation, 326
Shimizu Fumio (1894–1965), admiral (engineering), 25–26
Shimizu Fumio (1903–98), student of Japanese literature, 73, 104, 111, 131, 139, 473, 644, 711, 713; penname proposal for Hiraoka Kimitake, 91–92, 748; "teacher-disciple" relationship of, with Mishima, 85
Shimoyama Incident, 198
Shimoyama Sadanori (1901–49), president of Japan Railway, 198
Shinagawa Yajirō (1843–1900), minister of home affairs, 694, 800
*Shinchō*, 163, 188, 200, 201, 253, 254, 263, 286, 292, 311, 315, 338, 397, 399, 449, 456, 482, 489, 518, 526, 527, 585, 599, 625, 721, 723; Mishima's essay in February 1963 issue of, 408; "The Sword" in October 1963 issue of, 419
Shinchōsha, 200, 245, 247, 326, 327, 335, 353, 392, 398, 401, 449, 584, 598, 603, 622, 686; blurb for *Thirst for Love*, 192; lawsuit against, for invasion of privacy, 353, 355–56, 393; publication of "selected writings of Mishima Yukio," 316
*Shindemoraimasu*, 702–3
Shindō Ryōko (b. 1932), poet, 179, 758
Shingai Shrine, 472; Ōtaguro Yasukuni, officiator of, 475
Shingeki, 281, 413–14, 455
*shin'i* (divine will), 779
Shinjuku Station, 215, 589, 640, 719; demonstration at, 591; rampage on, 586

846 / INDEX

Shinmon Tatsugorō (1800?–75), leader of a firefighting group, 35
Shinoyama Kishin (b. 1940), photographer, 592, 713
Shinpa troupe: production of *The Damask Drum*, 412; production of *The Golden Pavilion*, 285–86
Shinpeitai Incident (1933), 695–96, 734
Shinpūren (Men of the Divine Wind), 91, 469, 473, 475, 476, 481, 483, 508, 655, 683, 715; as believers of Shinto divinity, 471; inspired by Gandhi, 475; *kirijini* ideal of, 602; Mishima's erudition on, 475; *mitegura* and, 472; Ōtaguro Tomo'o as leader of, 471–72; rebelled against Westernization, 471; *ukei* and, 471, 472
Shinpūren Revolt, 469; double policy reversal leading to, 470; and impact on samurai, 470–71; success of, 477; against Westernization, 471
Shinran (1173–1262), Buddhist leader, 404
*Shinshū Kōketsu-jō*. See *Divine State's Tie-Dye Castle*
Shinto, 175, 337, 450, 459–61, 470–71, 477, 572, 667, 690, 731, 732; and Kokutai Shintō, 668
Shintō Ichiryū sword-fighting school, 733
*Shin-yūkan*, 407
Shiomi Takaya (b. 1941), "supreme leader" of the Red Army, 642
Shiraishi Michinori (1910–45), army colonel, 514
Shirane Takayuki (n.d.), philosopher, 782
Shirato Sanpei (b. 1932), manga artist, 678
*Shiroari no su*. See *Termite Mound, The*
Shishi Bunroku. *See* Iwata Toyo'o
Shishido fiefdom, 34–36
*Shisō no Kagaku*, 388
Shitamachi, Tokyo, 321; B-29 bombing of, 122–23
*Shizumeru taki*. See *Sunken Waterfall, The*
Shōchiku, 141; films based on Mishima's stories produced by, 244–45
Shōda Michiko (b. 1934), Empress Michiko, 314, 315, 330, 767
Shōken, Empress Dowager (1849–1914), 385
*Shokun!*, 650
Sholokhov, Mikhail (1905–84), Russian writer, 467
*Shōnen*. See "Boy, The"
*Shōnen-ai no bigaku*. See *Aesthetics of the Love of Boys, The*
Short-term Active Duty Program, 14
*Shōsetsu Shinchō*, 556
*Shōsetsuka no kyūka*. See *Novelist's Holiday, A*
*shōshō hikkin*, 135–36, 529
Shōtoku Taishi (574–622), prince, 136
Shōwa Constitution, 569. *See also* Constitution of Japan
Shōwa Emperor, 41, 94, 569, 667, 794; birthday of, 549; "declaration of humanity" by, 142–46; Declaration of War, poem on, 94; Mishima's changed view on, 597. *See also* Hirohito
Shōwa Era, 41
Shōwa Restoration, 365, 379, 610, 628; contingency and, 370; government sympathizers of, 368–69; Iinuma's plan to drop out, 629–30
Shōwa Tennō. *See* Hirohito; Shōwa Emperor
"Shrine Officiator, The" (*Shinkan*) 37, 42
*Shufu no Tomo*, 107
*Shūgakuin no aki*. See *Autumn at the Shūgakuin, The*
Schultz, Charles (aka "Chiz"; n.d.), Mishima's theater associate in New York, 294, 300, 303, 309, 310
Shun, Yuasa (b. 1922?), American business consultant, 216
*shuramono*, 460
*Side Alley*, 63
Sienkiewicz, Henryk (1846–1916), Polish novelist, 717
*Silk and Insight (Kinu to meisatsu)*, 415, 424, 425–28, 461; commercial disappointment of, 431; comparison with other novels, 431–32; depiction of "Japan's father" in, 425; Komazawa Zenjirō (protagonist) of, 425–26; lack of immediacy in, 432; plot of, 425–28; title selection for, 428
"silk and warships" *(kinu to gunkan)*, 428
Singh K(h)ushwant (b. 1915), Indo-Anglican novelist, 436
Sledge, E. B. (1923–2001), American academic, 465
*Sleeping, Sinning, Falling (Nemuri to okashi to rakka to)*, 298, 458, 699
*Sleeping Beauties (Nemureru bijo)*, 316, 398; Kawabata's reaction to, 399; Mainichi Publishing Culture Award to, 400; monthly serialization of, 400; secret house of sexual entertainment depicted in, 398
*Sleeping Venus*, 687
Snow, C. P. (1905–80), English novelist, 493
Snow, Edgar (1905–72), American journalist, 441
*Snow Country (Yukiguni)*, 58, 273, 584, 611; Edward Seidensticker's translation of, 272; Kawabata's reaction to, 274; Mishima's view on, 584–85
*Snow-White Night, The (Junpaku no yoru)*, 193, 221, 244, 272
Snyder, Gary (b. 1930), American poet, 525
*Sōchō tobaku*. See *Gamble in Don's Honor*
social upheavals: against government-announced layoff, 198. *See also* International Antiwar Day, demonstrations on
socialism, 118, 150, 224–25, 366, 370, 411
Socialist Party, 351, 352, 385, 489, 616, 639, 656, 658
Society of Cherry-Blossom Friends, 313–14
soft-structure society, 662
*Sokkyō shijin*. See *Improvisatore, The*
Sondheim, Stephen (b. 1930), American composer, lyricist, 306
"Song of the Wilderness, A" *(Kōya no uta)*, 106
*sonnō gigun*, 370
*sonnō giyūgun*, 473
Sonoi Keisuke (b. 1934), actor, 304
Sorge, 416
"Sorrels" *(Sukanpō)*, 85; fantasy story, 54–55; Hashi Shizue's reactions on reading, 55–56
*Sotoba Komachi*, 294
*Sound of Music, The*, 549
*Sound of Waves, The (Shiosai)*, 227, 237–38, 245, 277, 334, 715; Daphnis and Chloë story behind, 243; film based on, 245–47; finding the right place for, 241–43; first literary prize to, 247; literary establishment reaction to, 244; in non-serialization format, 243; popularity of, 273–74; studios competing for film rights to, 245; translation of, 273, 392
*South Pacific*, 205, 305
Southeast Asia, 541; Communist force in, 569–70; European interests in, 524

Soviet-style Communism, 559
"special attack force" *(tokkōtai)*, 86, 567, 601; as annihilation of modernity, 129, 130; debate on, 130; deployment in Battle of Okinawa, 129; "moral laxity" associated with, 132; in Philippines, predilections for, 132; as ultimate form of *"decadence,"* 131
Speech and Expression Committee, 392
Spender, Stephen (1909–95), English poet, 383
Spielhagen, Friedrich von (1829–1911), German literary theorist, novelist, 286
*Spiritual Lectures for Young Samurai*, 560, 561, 562
*Spring and Asura (Haru to shura)*, 79
*Spring Hurries (Haru no isogi)*, 105
*Spring Snow (Haru no yuki)*, 186, 315, 626, 688, 721; background story of, 598; central concern of, 635; Fuji TV's proposal for, 635; Kikuta Kazuo's stage adaptation of, 634; New Year's Tanka Recitation ceremony in, 635; Okuno's praise for, 599; protagonist of, 469; published in January 1969, 598
*Spring That Lasted Too Long, The (Nagasugita haru)*, 215, 282, 286
spy training, 552, 553; at Camp Takigahara, 549
SS *President Wilson*, 221, 574; movies shown aboard, 222; third-class passengers of, 222–23
St. Sebastian painting, 176, 181, 266
"St. Sebastian's Face," 177
*Stage Struck*, 319
Stalin, Joseph (1878–1954), Soviet premier, 514
Stanislavski, Constantin (1863–1938), Russian stage director, 414
"Star," 359–60
Stegner, Wallace Earle (1909–93), American historian, writer, 219
Steinbeck, John (1902–68), American Nobel-Prize-winning writer, 435
Stendhal (1783–1842), French writer, 233
*"Strange Tale of the Pale-Moon Villa, The" (Gettan-sō kitan)*, 449
Strasberg, Lee (1901–82), American actor, acting teacher, 303
Strasberg, Susan (1938–99), American actress, 319
Strasser, Gregor (1892–1934), Nazi leader, 580
Strauss, Harold (1907–75), American editor, 272
Strauss, Richard (1864–1949), German composer, 225
Stravinsky, Igor (1882–1971), Russian-born composer, 307
*Streetcar Named Desire, A*, 26, 349
Strindberg, Johan (1849–1912), Swedish playwright, novelist, 78–79, 205
student labor mobilization program, 16
"'Student Militia,' Charge!," 639
student mobilization, 14
student movement in Japan: festive elements of, 608–9; influence of Shirato Sanpei's manga on, 678; move toward compromise in, 618; yakuza infatuation and, 608
Subversive Activities Prevention Law, 616
Suda Kunitarō (1891–1961), painter, 152
*Suddenly, Last Summer*, 382
Sudō Hisashi (b. 1933), film director, 702
Sugai Takao (n.d.), physician, 203–4, 216, 221
Sugamo Prison, 341
Sugawara Kunitaka (1926–92), editor, 210, 489–90

Sugimura Haruko (1906–97), actress, 205, 278, 409, 411, 416
Sugita Genpaku (1733–1817), physician, 445
Sugiura Minpei (1913–2001), novelist, critic, 534
Sugiyama Yasushi (1909–93), Japanese-style painter, 315
suicide, 164, 170, 194, 197, 199, 264, 364, 372, 378, 422–23, 498–99, 508, 580, 616, 632, 676, 724; and Mishima, 22, 67, 130–31, 134, 140, 188, 495, 496–97, 503, 506, 572–77, 689. *See also* seppuku
"suicide project," 572–77; Mishima's decision to kill himself, 572; *Sun and Steel* and, 572; views of Tanaka Miyoko on, 572
*Sukanpō*. *See* "Sorrels"
*Sukeroku*, 347
*Sun and Steel (Taiyō to tetsu)*, 572–79; German Romanticism and, 573; physical strength and, 575; published in October 1968, 578; sun's relentlessness depiction in, 573–76; tragedy, definition of, 575
Sun Myung Moon (1920–2012), religious leader, 553
Sun Yatsen (1866–1925), Chinese revolutionary, 647
*Sunday Mainichi*, 463–64, 486, 489, 527, 586; *enquête* by, 646, 694, 708
*Sunken Waterfall, The (Shizumeru taki)*, 250–54; kimono description in, 250–51
supersonic flight as ejaculation, 578–79
surrender of Japan, 88, 126–46, 184, 307, 352, 367, 624
Sutoku (1119–64), 75th Tennō, 612
Suwanchit (n.d.), Thai student, 600
*Suzaku-ke no metsubō*. *See Decline and Fall of the Suzaku, The*
Suzuki Kantarō (1868–1948), prime minister, 129, 364, 373; army attack on, 352
Suzuki Taka (1883–1971), Hirohito's nanny, 794
"Sword, The" *(Ken)*, 419, 420, 715
sword, unsheathed, 588–89
sword-abolition order, 543
Sydney Harbor, submarine attack in, 644
Symonds, John Addington (1840–93), English poet, critic, 252

*Tabako*. *See* "Cigarette, A"
Tachibana Akemi (1812–68), poet, 781
Tachibana Akiko (1907–71), dancer, 591
*Tada yori takai mono wa nai*. *See Nothing Is More Expensive Than Something Free*
Tagawa Suihō (1899–1989), manga artist, 678
*taigi* ("Great Principle"), 367, 467, 536
*Taiheiki*. *See Chronicle of Great Peace*
Taira no Sukemori (1158?–85), warrior, 112
Taira Ryōshō (1907–90), politician, 616
"Taishō culturalism," 648
Taishō Era, 12, 40–41, 49, 635, 721; culture, 173, 209, 561, 647–48, 679, 687,
*Taishō*. *See* "Imperial Declaration"
Taiso Yoshitoshi (1839–92), painter, 560
*Taiyō to tetsu*. *See Sun and Steel*
Takagaki Kanji (d. 1944), soldier, 467
Takahara Kiichi (b. 1927?), editor, 163–64
Takahara Misao (1875–1946), journalist, 29
Takahashi Kiyoshi (n.d.), army colonel, 727
Takahashi Korekiyo (1854–1936), prime minister, 364
Takahashi Mutsuo (b. 1937), poet, 298, 457, 699, 714

Takahashi Yoshitaka (1913–95), student of German literature, 396
Takakura Ken (b. 1931), film actor, 702
Takamine Hideko (1924–2010), actress, 252–53
Takarazuka Revue, 348
Takechi Hanpeita (Zuizan, 1829–65), samurai, 615
Takeda Taijun (1912–76), novelist, 256, 281, 377, 730
Takehisa Yumeji (1884–1934), painter, 560, 561
Takei Teruo (1927–2010), Zengakuren leader, 514
Takeuchi Yoshimi (1910–77), student of Chinese literature, 119–20
Takizawa Bakin (1767–1848), novelist, 612, 792
"Tale at the Cape, A" *(Misaki nite no monogatari)*, 147, 153, 154, 165, 184, 204
"Tale of a Stylish Dream" *(Fūryū mutan)*, 385, 387, 388
*Tale of Genji, The*, 74, 93, 96, 136, 384, 404, 792; culture and, 567; foundation of, 136; passages about Ukifune in, 632; translation of, 384, 404, 437–38
*Tale of Middle Councilor Hamamatsu, The (Hamamatsu Chūnagon monogatari)*, 403
*Tales from Yamato (Yamato monogatari)*, 281
*Tales Gleaned in Uji (Uji shūi monogatari)*, 680
Talking about Mother (TV program), 18
Tamagawa Aqueduct, 170
Tamari Hitoshi (b. 1933), bodybuilder, 261
Tamazawa Tokuichirō (b. 1937), minister of agriculture and fisheries, 484
Tamura Toshiko (1884–1945), novelist, 520
Tanabe Hajime (1885–1962), philosopher, 797
Tanabe Seiko (b. 1928), novelist, 58
Tanaka Kengo (b. 1928), editor, 650
Tanaka Ken'ichi (n.d.), member of Shield Society, 723
Tanaka Mitsuko (n.d.), poet, 675–76, 798
Tanaka Miyoko (b. 1936), critic, 380, 758; views of, on "suicide project," 572
Tanaka Seigen (Kiyoharu, 1906–93), businessman, 538, 540, 627
Tanaka Shinbē (1832–1863), swordsman, 615–16
Tanaka Toyozō (n.d.), Hiraoka Mume's husband, 30
Tani, Tony (1917–87), vaudevillian, 551
Tani Momoko (b. 1921), ballerina, 591
Taniguchi Masaharu (1893–1985), founder of Seichō no Ie, 690
Taniguchi Senkichi (1912–2007), film director, 246
Taniguchi Yoshio (b. 1937), architect, 558
Tanizaki Jun'ichirō (1886–1965), novelist, 73, 79, 282, 361, 404; "Golden Death" *(Konjiki no shi)* of, 686; *Some Prefer Nettles (Tade kū mushi)* of, 157–58, 274; "Tattoo" *(Shisei)* of, 710; *Yoshino Kudzu* of, 73
Tanizaki Jun'ichirō Prize, 432, 713
Tanizaki Matsuko (1903–91), Jun'ichirō's wife, essayist, 714
Tanizaki Seiji (1890–1971), student of English literature, 345
tanka, 64. 73, 87, 237, 338, 442, 450, 481, 499, 567, 635; by Mishima for farewell-to-the-world, 720; by Mishima's maternal grandmother Tomiko, 20; by Mishima on Natsuko's death, 67; by Moto'ori Norinaga, 86; by Yamazaki Akitsugu upon his death, 200
Tansman, Alan (n.d.), American scholar, 119
Tarama Toshihiko (b. 1929), Meiji Emperor's grandson, 229–30

Tashiro Tsuramoto (1678–1748), samurai scribe, 510
Tate no Kai. *See* Shield Society
Taut, Bruno (1880–1938), German architect, 327
*tawayameburi*, 133
Tayama Katai (1872–1930), novelist, 177
Taylor, Elizabeth (1932–2011), American actress, 382, 466
Taylor, Robert E. (n.d.), US marine, 466
"teach-in," 553–56; Hitotsubashi, 555; Mishima participation in, 553, 582; and "Principles of National Reformation," 553
Teika, Lord. *See* Fujiwara no Teika
*Tempest*, 403
*Temple of Dawn, The (Akatsuki no tera)*, 456, 521, 526, 527, 528, 599, 604; as an exposition of *ālaya-vijnāna*, 683; end of, 681–82; Mishima's experience during writing, 682–83; "monologue" in, 683–84
*Temple of the Golden Pavilion, The (Kinkakuji)*, 99, 247, 253, 311, 323, 418, 437, 581, 585; Dag Hammarskjöld impressed by, 585; information gathering efforts for, 259–60; protagonist in play based on, 411, 420; reviews of, 265; translations of, 392
"Temporary Proposal for JNG," 536
"10.8 Rescue Society," 534
*Tenbō* (literary magazine), 147, 170
Tench, Charles (n.d.), US army colonel, 141
*Tendenz*, 179, 186
*Tennin gosui. See Decay of the Angel, The*
Tennō system, 388, 460, 661, 754, 794; attempts to define, 568; Communist government under, 570; as cultural concept, 567–72; Hashikawa and, 580; interpretation of "renunciation of divinity" by, 142–45, 797; journalistic assault on, 142; linked with military, 570; Meiji Constitution and, 569, 797; Mishima's arguments on, 142, 330, 463–64, 563, 565–66, 568–69, 580, 661, 714; Nakamura's argument on, 568–69; National Learning, 86; "Oriental" cultures and, 142–43; Orikuchi's argument on, 144; restoration of, 364–65; Tennō-as-legitimate-sovereign argument, 35–36
*Tenth-Day Chrysanthemum, The (Tōka no kiku)*, 374, 378; *The Joyful Koto* as counterweight to, 417; staging of, 393; Yomiuri Bungaku Prize to, 393
"*Terakoya* Incident, the," 141
Terao Katsumi, Maj. (n.d.), military officer, 727
Terentius, Publius (195/185–159 B.C.), Roman playwright, 424
*Termite Mound, The (Shiroari no su)*, 230
*Terrace of the Leper King, The (Raiō no terasu)*, 456, 457, 712; source of inspiration for, 610
terrain surveillance, training of, 551
Teru, Princess (1925–61), daughter of Hirohito, 13; marriage to Morihiro, 13
*Tessa, la nymphe au coeur fidèle*, 239
Thai Princess, 598–600
Theognis of Megara (6th century B.C.), Greek poet, 235
There Was No Great Principle on the Island of a 'Shattering-Like-a-Jewel' Battle, 467
*Thérèse Desqueyroux*, 617
*Thermos Bottle, The (Mahōbin)*, 394
*They Call Me Hachi the Idiot (Baka-hachi to hito wa iu)*, 353

Thibaudet, Albert (1874–1936), French critic, 345
Thielicke, Helmut (1908–86), German theologian, 339
*Thirst for Love (Ai no kawaki)*, 193, 201, 244, 362, 389, 696; background of, 196; publisher's blurb for, 192; sales of, 202
*Thousand Cranes*, 272, 584
*Threepenny Opera, The*, 294, 306–7
*Throne of Blood*, 438
Tiger Balm Garden, 384, 687
Tinian Island, 108
"Tinted Glass" *(Damie garasu)*, 77–78, 81
Tison, Alexander (b. 1857), American lawyer, 26
Titian (1490–1576), Italian painter, 224
"To Be Left for the Generations to Come" *(Yoyo ni nokosan)*, 112
"To Cut His Stomach" *(Hara o kiru koto)*, 531, 648
Tōdai Medical School, 593
*Tōdai rakujō.* See *Fall of Tōdai, The*
*Tōdai.* See *Lighthouse, The*
Tōdai. See University of Tokyo
Tōdai Struggle. *See* Tōdai Turmoil
Tōdai students, Mishima's debate with, 637
Tōdai Turmoil, 592–98, 791
Tōdai Zenkyōtō, 593, 619
*Todesgemeinschaft*, 565
Togakure School Ninpō Demonstration Performances, 698
Tōgō Heihachirō (1848–1934), admiral of the fleet, 645–46
*Tōhō no hakase tachi.* See *Wise Men from the East, The*
Tōhoku region, poverty in, 365–66
Tōjō cabinet, 103, 104, 108
Tōjō Hideki (1884–1948), prime minister, 49, 107, 127, 340, 535, 693, 782; outspoken critics of, 127; as prime minister of Japan, 126
*Tōka no kiku.* See *Tenth-Day Chrysanthemum, The*
Tokiwa-ken restaurant, 594
*tokkōtai.* See "special attack force"
*Tokkōtai* (essay), 130
Tokugawa Ienari (1773–1841), 11th Tokugawa shogun, 740
Tokugawa Ieyasu (1543–1616), founder of the Tokugawa shogunate, 2, 32, 37, 97
Tokugawa Mitsukuni (1628–1701), second head of the Mito fiefdom, 35
Tokugawa Nariaki (1800–60), ninth head of the Mito fiefdom, 35
Tokugawa Period, remnants of, 324, 720
Tokugawa shogunate, 35, 38, 365, 649; administrative machinery of, 32–33; Christianity and, 470; class system during, and after collapse of, 24; and foreign menace, 470; isolationist policy of, 32–33; movement to replace, 469–70; reform group against, 36; split of, into two camps, 694
Tokugawa Yoshinobu (1837–1913), last Tokugawa shogun, 34
Tokugawa Yoshiyasu (1921–49), artist, 78, 97; depiction in "The Nobility," 98
Tokuoka Takao (b. 1930), journalist, 378, 489, 522–23, 708, 717, 721, 778, 799; interviewed Mishima, 694; Mishima's letter to, 708–9, 717; recollections of, of Mishima in Bangkok, 528–29, 799
*Tokyo Nichinichi Shinbun*, 278

Tokyo Olympics: hosting, 429; Mishima as reporter for, 428–31
*Tokyo Shinbun*, 141, 149, 204, 257, 308; interview of Bowers, 142; interview of Mishima, 380, 707
Tokyo: B-29 bombing of, 122–23; indefensibility in case of war, 8, 9; talk of moving capital from, 8
Tomonaga Shin'ichirō (1906–79), Nobel Prize–winning physicist, 457
*Tōnorikai.* See "Distance-Riding Club"
*Tora! Tora! Tora!*, 701–2
Total War Research Institute, 126
*Tōtei bukkai-roku*, 680
Tottori Yōichirō, 263–64
Toulouse-Lautrec, Henri de (1864–1901), French painter, 687
Toynbee, Arnold (1889–1975), British historian, 289
Toyokawa Noboru (b. 1905), student of Western philosophy, 62; views on Mishima's poems, 63
Toyotomi Hideyoshi (1537–98), warlord who unified Japan, 410, 543
*Tōzoku.* See *Bandit, The*
tragedy, definition of, 575
*tragisch Ironie*, 371
"Tree-searing Wind" *(Kogarashi)*, 84
*Tristan und Isolde*, 439, 441
*Tropical Trees (Nettaiju)*, 424
*True Import of Kokutai, The (Kokutai no hongi)*, 367
Truman, Harry (1884–1972), US president, 220
Tsuboi Sakae (1899–1967), novelist, 252
Tsubouchi Shōyō (1859–1935), Shakespearean translator, 41
Tsuda Sōkichi (1873–1961), historian, 568
Tsuji Kichirō (1892–1946), film director, 605
Tsukada Keiichirō (n.d.), café owner, 325
Tsukamoto Kunio (1922–2005), poet, 789
Tsukiji Honganji, 731–32
Tsukiji Shōgekijō, 414
Tsukioka Yumeji (b. 1922), actress, 344
Tsurusawa Enza V (1914–2001), gidayū narrator, 614
Tsuruta Kōji (1924–87), film actor, 605, 702; as lead in *Gamble in Don's Honor*, 606–7; Mishima's strong feeling for, 609–10
Tsutsumi Seiji (b. 1927), businessman, poet, writer, 622, 653; background of, 548–49; elected to Japan Art Academy, 549; as president of Seibu, 548
"Turn Tōdai into a Zoo," 588
*Twenty-four Eyes (Nijūshi no hitomi)*, 252, 253
*28 Folks with Heroic Names*, 560
2.26 Incident, 351, 363–71, 562, 581, 602, 624, 628, 630; assassinations of high-ranking government officials, 364; blood oath on 32nd anniversary of, 540; impact on Mishima of, 374; loyalty and, 530–31; and Meiji Restoration, 364–65; Mishima's argument on, 515, 530–31, 598; National Learning and, 366–67; poverty and, 365–66; protagonist of, 530; 32nd anniversary of, blood oath on, 540–41; "Voices of the Heroic Souls" based on, 375–76, 460; young officers and senior officers in, 628
"2.26 Incident Trilogy, The," 376–79, 460
*Typhon sur Nagasaki* (French-Japanese film), 383

Uchida Hyakken (1889–1971), novelist, 685
Uchida Ryōhei (1874–1937), rightwing leader, 23

Uchimura Kanzō (1861–1930), Christian thinker, 559
*uchiteshi yamamu*, wartime slogan, 107
Ueda Akinari (1734–1809), writer, 87, 500, 509–10, 555, 752
Uesugi Shinkichi (1878–1929), constitutional scholar, 128–29
UFO: extraterrestrials and, 396; Mishima's belief in, 397
Ugetsu-sō (Rain and Moon Mansion): essay in praise of, 112; party at, 111
*Uguisu*. See *Bush Warbler, The*
*Uji shūi monogatari*. See *Tales Gleaned in Uji*
*ukei* (divination method), 471, 472, 477, 779
Umehara Ryūzaburō (1888–1986), painter, 414
Umehara Takeshi (b. 1925), philosopher, 632–33
Umewaka Manzaburō II (1908–91), nō actor, 235
*Umi to dokuyaku*. See *Sea and Poison, The*
*Umi to yūyake*. See "Sea and the Evening Glow, The"
*Umi yukaba*. See "When Seagoing"
*Un beau ténébreux*, 718
Union Square, San Francisco, 394
University of the Sacred Heart, 314
University of Tokyo: barricading students at, 594–95; blockading of Yasuda Auditorium, 594; Hospital, 318; International Antiwar Day followers massed on, 586; opposition to unpaid internship at, 592–93
Uno Nobuo (1904–91), kabuki writer, 613
untouchable class, 740
Urabe (Yoshida) Kanetomo (1435–1511), Shintoist, 470
US Occupation forces, 5, 216; declared aim of, 151; popularity of, 137–38
Usami Okiie (1883–1970), chief aide-de-camp, 146
US-Japanese Mutual Security Treaty, 343, 352, 433, 535; blocking of, 535–86; idea of blocking extension of, 658–59; Kawabata's views on, 571–72; LDP's position on, 697; Mishima's views on, 506; nationwide protest against extension of, 695; question of for or against, 636; Tanaka and movement against, 538
USS *Enterprise*, 538–39
USS *Fenimore Cooper*, 741
USS *Pueblo*, 539
Usui Yoshimi (1905–87), editor, novelist: interview of SDF personnel by, 490; on Mishima's literary works, 147, 334
Utagawa Toyokuni (1769–1825), ukiyo-e painter, 687
*Utage no ato*. See *After the Banquet*
*Utsukushii hoshi*. See *Beautiful Star, The*

Van der Post, Laurens (1906–96), Afrikaner author, 391, 524
Van Druten, John (1901–57), English playwright, director, 293
Vanderbilt, Edith Stuyvesant Dresser (1873–1958), American socialite, 393
Velásquez, Diego (1599–1660), Spanish painter, 412
Venice International Film Festival, 322
Verlaine, Paul (1844–96), French poet, 179
*Vernichteter Kampf*, 465
Veronese, Paolo (1528–88), Italian painter, 234
Victorian style, Mishima's views on, 315
Vidal, Gore (1925–2012), American author, 227, 647
Vietnam War, 432, 443–44, 490, 539; Mishima's opposition to, 516–17; supporting, 493–94; US judged guilty for, 516–17; USS *Enterprise* role in, 538–39. See also anti–Vietnam War movement
Viglielmo, V. H. (b. 1926), American translator, 258
Villiers de l'Isle-Adam (1838–89), French Symbolist writer, 96
Vining, Elizabeth Gray (1902–99), tutor to Crown Prince Akihito, 58, 755
*Virtue Falters (Bitoku no yoromeki)*, 283–84, 324, 334; publication of limited edition of, 316; Tsukioka Yumeji and, 344
"Vita Sexualis," 172, 176, 177, 179
"Voices of the Heroic Souls" *(Eirei no koe)*, 375, 459–64, 621, 624
von Schlegel, Friedrich (1772–1829), German poet, 380

Wada Katsunori (n.d.), writer, 371
*Waga te ni kieshi arare*. See *Hailstones That Faded on My Palms*
*Waga tomo Hitler*. See *My Friend Hitler*
Wagatsuma Sakae (1897–1973), civil law scholar, 47
Wagner, Richard (1813–83), German composer, 142, 226, 436, 439, 441
Wakabayashi Tōichi (1912–43), army lientanant, 497, 752–53; charisma and reputation of, 133; movie based on last words of, 133–34
Wakao Ayako (b. 1933), actress, 721
Wake no Kiyomaro (733–99), Heian aristocrat, 473
Wakebe Junji (1911–95), sculptor, 719
*Wakōdo yo yomigaere!* See *Youths, Resurrect Yourselves!*
Walbrook, Anton (Adolf Wohlbrück, 1896–1967), Austrian actor, 236
Wald, Jerry (1911–92), American producer, 293
Waley, Arthur (1886–1996), English Orientalist, 384, 437–38; meeting with Mishima, 383–84
Wang Yangming (1472–1529), Chinese philosopher, 35, 627–50; Mishima's treatise on, 649
war crimes, 104–5, 152, 237, 516, 734, 755–56; classes of, 159, 341
*Warera ga jidai*. See *Our Era*
wartime assignment, 16, 116, 123–24
Washington Naval Treaty (1922), 14
Watanabe Jōtarō (1874–1936), inspector-general of military education, 364, 366, 369
Watanabe Kazuo (1901–75), student of French literature, 203–4
Watanabe Takenobu (b. 1938), poet, architect, 607
"water trade," 249, 352
Watsuji Tetsurō (1889–1960), philosopher, 568
Wayne, John (1907–79), American film actor, 658
"Weakness of Modern Japanese Fiction, The," 169
Weatherby, Meredith (1914?–97?), translator, publisher, 158, 227, 274–76
Weber, Max (1864–1920), German thinker, 565
Weightman, John (1915–2004), English student of French literature, 436
Weill, Kurt (1900–50), German composer, 306
Weininger, Otto (1880–1903), Austrian philosopher, 83–84
Welitsch, Ljuba (1913–96), Bulgarian operatic soprano, 226
West, Morris (1916–99), Australian novelist, play-

wright, 493
*West Side Story*, 306, 419, 591
*Western Symphony*, 307
Westernization, 471; in Meiji Era, 366; vs. modernization, 130; revolt against, 471
Westmoreland, William (1914–2005), US army chief-of-staff, 517
"What Is Fiction?," 544–46, 560; Bataille in writing, 582; comparison of, with "bizarre, giant marine beast," 545; Hirose Takeo and, 545; serializing in *Nami*, 544–45
"What Is Japan?," 636
"When Seagoing" (*Umi yukaba*), 97–98, 121
Whitman, Walt (1819–92), American poet, 508
Wilde, Oscar (1854–1900), Irish writer, poet, 79
Wilhelm, Kaiser II (1859–1941), German emperor, 182
Williams, Tennessee (1911–83), American playwright, 226, 310, 349, 382
Williams, William Carlos (1883–1963), American poet, 580
Wilson, Angus (1913–91), English novelist, 276, 438–39
Wilson, Sloan (1920–2003), American author, 583
Winckelmann, Johann Joachim (1717–68), German historian, 451
*Windblown Dude* (*Karakkaze yarō*), 358–59, 721
Winters, Shelley (1920–2006), American actress, 303
"Winterscape" (*Fuyugeshiki*), 84, 747
*Wise Men from the East, The* (*Tōhō no hakase tachi*), 195
*Woman in the Dunes, The*, 439
*Wonder Tale, A: The Moonbow* (*Chinsetsu Yumiharizuki*), 612, 655–56, 793
Workers Theater Congress, 416
*World of the Shining Prince, The*, 437
World War II, 238, 290, 321, 341, 390, 513, 541, 559, 606, 782; difference of officer and soldier during, 14–15; impact of, on Japanese college and higher school term, 15, 99; Japan's surrender, 126; Mishima's assessment of, 93
World War II and its aftermath: aphoristic statements, 135–36; decline of Japan's literary arts, 131; "democracy" and "war responsibility," 136; as onset of Medieval Period, 133; popularity of Occupation troops, 137–38; postwar literary revival, 134–35; special attack force and humanism, 129–32; testament on war and surrender, 134
Wright, Frank Lloyd (1867–1959), American architect, 203, 548
writing styles, 576

Xiong Shili (1885–1968), Chinese philosopher, 647

*Yakata. See* "Mansion"
yakuza, 34–35, 350–51, 358–59, 430, 467, 538, 567, 605–616, 658, 701–3, 710, 721, 724
yakuza movies: "A Lion Amid Peonies," 724; *Arashi o yobu otoko*, 768; "documentary"-like, 608; featuring Tsuruta Kōji, 605; *Gamble in Don's Honor*, 605, 606–7; *Gunbatsu*, 701; narrative pattern of, 606; popularity of, after Japan's defeat, 605; *Shindemoraimasu*, 702–3; themes of, 658; *Yōjimbō*, 605–6; Zatōichi series of, 606
Yamada Tamaki (1893–1943), student of French literature, 518
Yamaga Sokō (1622–85), military thinker, 647
Yamaguchi Otoya (1943–60), assassin, 385–86
Yamamoto Fujiko (b. 1931), movie actress, 245
Yamamoto Isoroku (1884–1943), admiral, 93, 593, 702
Yamamoto Jirochō (1820–93), yakuza leader, 605, 792–93
Yamamoto Kenkichi (1907–88), haiku explicator, 277, 334
Yamamoto Kiyokatsu (1919–2001), army general, 389, 541–44, 587, 602, 617, 642; on action plan to defend the Imperial Palace, 623, 624; agreement of, with Mishima on Tennō, 543; background of, 541; at construction company, 542; Cultural Revolution and, 542; *Hagakure* philosophy and, 510–12; invitation to Mishima, 601–2; lecture on espionage, 549–53; Mishima's intense study sessions with, 593–94; Mishima's reliance on, 628; objection to "the rightwing's armed training," 624; reaction to Fujiwara Iwaichi running for office, 671; Shield Society and, 586–87; spy training by, 549–53; studies in Zen, 512; Tashiro visit to, 510; training sessions by, 603; unforgettable encounter with Mishima, 670–71; as vice commandant of GSDF Research School, 625
Yamamoto Naozumi (1932–2002), composer, conductor, 484
Yamamoto Noriko (Tsuruoka Yoshiko; b. 1945?), actress, 440
Yamamoto Tsunetomo (also Jōchō; 1659–1719), author of *Hagakure*, 401, 495, 637, 784
Yamanashi Katsunoshin (1877–67), admiral, president of the Peers School, 99
Yamanote, 153, 251, 321; B-29 bombing of, 124
Yamashita Tomoyuki (1885–1946), army general, 88
*Yamato* (battleship), 25, 312; destruction of, 428
*Yamato monogatari. See Tales from Yamato*
"Yamato spirit" (*Yamato damashii*), 602, 670, 792; condemned by Akinari, 87; popularity and nationalist purity, 86
Yamazaki Akira (n.d.), army general, 727
Yamazaki Akitsugu (1922–49), businessman: as *après-guerre* youth, 200; family background of, 199; financing business of, 197; meteoric rise and fall of, 197–98; suicide of, 197, 199
Yamazaki Hiroaki (1949–67), student, 533
Yamazaki Tomie (1919–48), Dazai Osamu's mistress, 170, 498
Yanai Shinsaku (b. 1947), writer, 663
"Yangming School as a Philosophy for Revolution" (*Kakumei tetsugaku to shite no Yōmeigaku*), 645
Yano Ichirō (1899–1965), businessman, 329
Yara Chōbyō (1902–97), Okinawa governor, 616
Yasaka Shrine. *See* Gionji
Yashiro Seiichi (1927–98), playwright, stage-director, 160, 161, 163, 193–94, 258, 285, 736; in *Confessions of a Mask*, 194; on Katō Michio's literary works, 239–40; on literary encounter between Mishima and Dazai, 161, 163; on Mishima's homosexual tendencies, 195
Yasuda Yojūrō (1910–81), literary critic, 115, 117, 161, 379, 405, 564; aestheticism of, 120; atavistic thought of, 121; influence of, on Mishima, 119, 120,

379–80, 546; philosophical role of, 119
Yasuoka Masahiro (1898–1983), Yōmeigaku thinker, 649, 696
Yatō Tamotsu (1925?–73), photographer, 274, 557
Yeats, William Butler (1865–1939), Irish poet, 571
"Yisugei's Hunt" *(Esugai no kari)*, 115
*Yojimbo*, 438, 605–6
Yokohama Incident, 151
Yokomitsu Riichi (1898–1946), novelist, haiku poet, 82, 130, 345
Yoko'o Tadanori (b. 1936), graphic artist, 677, 706
Yokoyama Knock (aka Yamada Isamu; 1932–2007), governor of Osaka, 571
Yōmeigaku, 649, 650; *dämonisch* elements of, 648; followers of, 647; influence in China and Japan, 647
*Yomiuri Shinbun*, 177, 309, 457, 507, 559, 661; Hinuma Rintarō's writing for, 502; interview of Mishima, 189; phone survey conducted by, 710; "'Student Militia,' Charge!" article published by, 639; on taidan between Mishima and Murakami Hyōe, 639
Yonai Mitsumasa (1880–1948), prime minister, 103, 593, 734
*Yorokobi no koto*. See *Joyful Koto, The*
Yoshida Chieko (n.d.), actress, manager, 410
Yoshida Ken'ichi (1912–77), student of English literature, 205, 256, 393
Yoshida Mitsuru (1923–79), writer: on Americans acceptance to Japanese, 313; meeting with Mishima Yukio, 312–13; visit to Washington Irving's manor, 313
Yoshida Shigeru (1878–1967), prime minister, 342; congratulatory speech to Crown Prince, 217; peace and security treaties signed by, 220–21; on Shimoyama and Mitaka incidents, 198
Yoshida Shōin (1830–59), thinker, 341, 342, 647, 718 757, 800; commentary on "loyalty," 694; commentary on "madness," 695; as follower of Yōmeigaku, 647; letter of, 649
Yoshikawa Eiji (1892–1962), novelist, 679
Yoshikawa Itsuji (1908–2002), art historian, 205
Yoshikawa Masami (n.d.), kendōka, 480
*Yoshino Kudzu (Yoshino kuzu)*, 73
Yoshiyuki Junnosuke (1924–94), novelist, 519
Yotsuya, Tokyo, 5, 41, 53, 54, 364, 551, 700
"Young Generation and the Postwar Spirit, The," 563
Yourcenar, Marguerite (1903–67), Belgian-born essayist, 482, 773
*Youth, The (Seinen)*, 166, 406, 407

*Youths, Resurrect Yourselves! (Wakōdo yo yomigaere!)*: afterword to, 269–70; three acts of, 268–69
*Yoyo ni nokosan*. See "To Be Left for the Generations to Come"
Yoyogi (Communist) Faction, 534, 596, 786
Yuasa (née Itaya) Atsuko (n.d.), essayist, 68, 221, 261, 263, 289, 335, 626, 745; runs salon, 216–17, 335, 626; helps find a bride for Mishima, 315, 318–19; Roy James live-in companion of, 321
Yui Chūnoshin (1894–1967), attorney, 535
Yukawa Hideki (1907–81), Nobel Prize–winning physicist, 457
*Yukiguni*. See *Snow Country*
Yukimura Izumi (b. 1937), singer, actress, 324
*yūkoku*, 96, 375, 709
"Yūkoku," 363–71, 375, 515, 590; Americans desire to see, 441; appearance of, in fiction magazine, 387; background music for, 439; English translation of, 363; film based on, 375, 492, 502, 706; filming of, 439–43; financing of film of, 440; Fujii Hiroaki (production manager), 440; 2.26 Incident and, 374; Mishima decided to work on, 372–73; Ozawa's ballet based on, 590; source of impetus for writing on, 377; story, 363–64, 376; Takeyama committing suicide in, 378; Yamamoto Noriko as actress in, 440; Yōko scandalized by, 442
Yūryaku (419–79), 21st Tennō, 150
Yürgens, Curd (1915–82), German actor, 324
Yves Ciampi (1921–82), French director, 383

Zanuck, Darryl (1902–79), American producer, 702
*Zatōichi* series of films, 606
Zeami Motokiyo (c1364–1443), dramatist, 295, 569
Zen Nihon Gakusei Jichikai Rengōkai, 514
Zen temples, 22, 234, 254, 259–60, 289
Zengaku Kyōtō Kaigi, 585
Zengakuren, 514, 538, 617, 636, 654; anti-Yoyogi Faction of, 616; desire to end US military rule, 617–18; objectives of, 514; response to strong-arm tactics, 640; splitting of, 534; Tsutsumi as leader of, 548; Yoyogi (Communist) Faction of, 596, 640
Zenkyōtō, 585, 589, 593, 617, 623, 628; demonstrations on International Antiwar Day, 639; invitation to Mishima for debate, 617, 619–20; Minsei-directed violence against, 596; movement, 597, 609; "Pharisees-Barricade Festival," 608
Zhu Xi (1130–1200), Chinese philosopher, 649
Zola, Èmile (1840–1902), French writer, 260

www.ingramcontent.com/pod-product-compliance
Lightning Source LLC
Chambersburg PA
CBHW032125010526
44111CB00033B/78